PHRASES
&
SAYINGS

Nigel Rees

BLOOMSBURY

First published 1995 by
Bloomsbury Publishing Plc,
2 Soho Square, London, W1V 6HB

Copyright © 1995 Nigel Rees

The moral right of the author has been asserted

A copy of the CIP entry for this book is available
from the British Library

ISBN 0 7475 2168 9

10 9 8 7 6 5 4 3 2 1

Designed by Hugh Adams, AB3
Typeset by Hewer Text Composition Services, Edinburgh
Printed in Britain by Clays Ltd, St Ives plc

'Thou art a retailer of phrases, and dost deal in remnants of remnants'

William Congreve,
The Way of the World (1700)

'False English, bad pronunciation, old sayings and common proverbs; which are so many proofs of having kept bad and low company'

4th Earl of Chesterfield,
Advice to his Son on Men and Manners (1775)

Introduction

❦

This book is a selective examination of more than 5,000 phrases and sayings, detailing their origins, dates, meanings and use. But what is a 'phrase'? Although it is technically possible for a phrase to consist of one word, I have *mostly* limited myself to clusters of two or more words and left analysis of single words to the etymologists and lexicographers. Within this definition of a phrase, however, fall idiomatic expressions, proverbial sayings, stock and format phrases, nicknames, catchphrases, clichés, journalese, headline fodder, slogans, advertising lines, as well as titles of books and entertainments which either quote a specific source or themselves create a form of words. As to my choice of phrases and sayings for inclusion, I have simply concentrated on those about which there is something interesting to say with regard to their origins and use. I have not always restricted myself to phrases which have caught on in an enduring fashion – which might be the criterion for inclusion in a more formal dictionary – but have also incorporated phrases which may only have had a brief flowering. This is because to record them here may help to explain an allusion. In addition, even a briefly popular phrase can help to evoke a period and thus should be examined as part of the social history of the language. I use the term 'stock phrase' to describe a phrase that can't be said to have 'caught on' like a full-blooded catchphrase even though it may be used fairly frequently. By 'format phrase' I mean a basic phrase or sentence structure capable of infinite variation by the insertion of new words. A word about dating: when I say that a phrase was '*Current* in 1975', I mean that I simply have a record of its use then, *not* that I think it was first used in that year. It may also have been current long after that date. When I say that a phrase was '*Quoted* in 1981', I mean precisely that, not that it was originated in that year. It might have been coined long before. On the whole I have not indulged in speculation about when a phrase might have entered the language, but have simply recorded hard and fast examples of its use.

Cross references to other entries are made in SMALL CAPITALS. Because it saves repetition of basic information, I have grouped some radio and TV phrases under the name of the show they came from (e.g. *MONTY PYTHON'S FLYING CIRCUS*). The swung dash symbol ~ is used in cross references to indicate the headword.

In case you find my interpretation of alphabetical order puzzling, the phrases are listed in what is known as 'letter by letter' order – in other words, in alphabetical order of letters within the whole phrase exactly as it is written. Thus, for example, **nicely** appears before **nice one, Cyril** and **moving before Mr**.

Acknowledgements

❧

I am hugely indebted to the authors and publishers of books quoted in the text and to the editors and journalists of the many newspapers and magazines who have unwittingly provided citations.

In addition, as this book builds upon two predecessors – my *Dictionary of Popular Phrases* (1990) and *Dictionary of Phrase & Allusion* (1991) – I am most grateful to the many people who helped me with the entries in those two works, as well as to the considerable number who have suggested revisions and corrections. Then there are those who have urged me to include – or helped me with the writing of – the more than 1,500 *new* entries in this book. Many are mentioned in the individual entries alongside the information with which they have supplied me, but there are some who have been so generally supportive (sometimes without really knowing it) that an expression of my especial thanks is necessary here. They include: Roy Alexander; Dr J.K. Aronson; Jim Bennet; W.P. Brown; Brendan Bruce; Nicholas Comfort; David Cottis; Peter Curran; P. Daniel; R.K. Dann; Leslie Dunkling; T.A. Dyer; David Elias; Jack Forrest; W. Eric Gustafson; William Hartston; Sir David Hunt; Antony Jay; Miss M.L. King; Michael R. Lewis; R.P.W. Lewis; Frank Loxley; Malcolm Macdonald; Henry B. McNulty; Tony Miller; Ronald Monroe; Michael and Valerie Grosvenor Myer; Lyn Nuttall; Sally Farrell Odgers; Ian Porter; Steve Race; David E.T. Read; Betty Reid; Colin Richardson; Derek Robinson; Adrian Room; Judith Smith; Kevin Thurlow; Horst Vey; Martin Walker; Bill Watts; Marc Wilson.

I am also especially indebted, for their phrase detection skills, to readers of my 'Quote . . . Unquote' Newsletter, a subscription quarterly that is now published in the UK and the US. Then I must thank Armando Iannucci, Jon Naismith and Kathy Smith, recent successive producers of my BBC Radio programme *Quote . . . Unquote*, plus its many listeners; John B. Meade, producer, the production staff and many viewers of the Yorkshire Television/Channel 4 programme *Countdown*; the BBC Radio Research Library, London; the British Library Newspaper Library, Colindale; and the London Library.

In particular, I should like to remember with gratitude my collaboration with the late Vernon Noble, with whom I wrote *A Who's Who of Nicknames* (1987). I should especially like to thank Paul Beale, reviser of Eric Partridge's *Dictionary of Slang and Unconventional English* and *Dictionary of Catch Phrases* for his selfless encouragement and for his willingness to share his materials with me. And, once again, I must salute Donald Hickling who, for many years now, has aided me as fact-digger and general roving intelligence. Any mistakes are, however, entirely my own responsibility and I gratefully anticipate their being pointed out to me.

NIGEL REES

Abbreviations

Ӿ

Bartlett: *Bartlett's Familiar Quotations* (15th ed.), 1980, (16th ed.), 1992
Benham: *Benham's Book of Quotations*, 1907, 1948, 1960
Bible: The Authorized Version, 1611 (except where stated otherwise)
Brewer: *Brewer's Dictionary of Phrase and Fable*, (13th ed.), 1975, (14th ed.), 1989
Burnam: Tom Burnam, *The Dictionary of Misinformation*, 1975; *More Misinformation*, 1980
CODP: *The Concise Oxford Dictionary of Proverbs*, 1982
DOAS: Wentworth & Flexner, *Dictionary of American Slang*, 1960 (1975 revision)
DNB: *The Dictionary of National Biography*
Flexner: Stuart Berg Flexner, *I Hear America Talking*, 1976; *Listening to America*, 1982
Mencken: *H.L. Mencken's Dictionary of Quotations*, 1942
Morris: William and Mary Morris, *Morris Dictionary of Word and Phrase Origins*, 1977
ODCIE: *The Oxford Dictionary of Current Idiomatic English* (2 vols.), 1985
ODP: *The Oxford Dictionary of Proverbs* (3rd ed.), 1970
ODQ: *The Oxford Dictionary of Quotations* (2nd ed.), 1953, (3rd ed.), 1979, (4th ed.), 1992
OED2: *The Oxford English Dictionary* (2nd ed,) 1989, (CD-ROM version), 1992
Partridge/Catch Phrases: Eric Partridge, *A Dictionary of Catch Phrases* (2nd ed., edited by Paul Beale), 1985
Partridge/Slang: Eric Partridge, *A Dictionary of Slang and Unconventional English* (8th ed., edited by Paul Beale), 1984
Safire: William Safire, *Safire's Political Dictionary*, 1978
Shakespeare: The Arden Shakespeare (2nd series)

· A ·

à Becket. See BECKET.

abominable snowman, an/the. Phrase now used to describe anyone or anything indescribable and unpleasant. Originally, an unidentified creature of the Himalayas, which derives its name from the Tibetan *meetoh kangmi* [abominable snowmen] or *yeti*. It is said to raid mountain villages and to be tall, powerful and bearlike, with a near-human face. The name became known to European mountaineers attempting to climb Mount Everest in the 1920s and was popularized by climbing expeditions in the 1950s. In 1960 Sir Edmund Hillary found footprints which seemed to be those of an animal such as a bear. The mystery surrounding this creature gave rise to the detective novel *The Case of the Abominable Snowman* (1941) by Nicholas Blake. There was also a separate film on the subject, *The Abominable Snowman* (UK, 1957).

In 1953, David Eccles, Minister of Works responsible for the Coronation decorations in London, became known as 'the Abominable Showman'. General de Gaulle, having obstructed British entry to the European Common Market in the 1960s by saying '*Non!*', was dubbed 'the Abominable No-man'.

about. See THAT'S WHAT — IS ALL ∼.

Abraham's bosom. The place where the dead sleep contentedly. From Luke 16:23: 'And it came to pass, that the beggar died, and was carried by the angels into Abraham's bosom.' It alludes to Abraham, the first of the Hebrew patriarchs. Compare ARTHUR'S BOSOM.

Absent Without Leave. See AWOL.

absit omen. See *GESUNDHEIT!*

absolutely, Mister Gallagher!/ positively, Mister Shean! Phrases of agreement, or roundabout ways of saying 'yes', taken from the American vaudevillians (Ed) Gallagher and (Al) Shean whose act flourished in the early part of the twentieth century. The phrases were included in a popular song 'Mr Gallagher and Mister Shean' (1922) though there the order of words is 'positively, Mister Gallagher/absolutely, Mr Shean'. Each syllable of the adverbs is emphasized – e.g. 'pos-it-ive-ly' . . .

— abuse. This phrase-making format is used when describing (1) misuse of any substance, and (2) maltreatment of another person. Hence such phrases as: 'alcohol abuse', 'child abuse', 'drug abuse', 'heroin abuse', 'ritual abuse', 'satanic abuse', 'solvent abuse', 'substance abuse'. The format has been used in the first sense since the 1960s and in the second since the 1970s, but both constructions were especially prevalent in the 1980s. When applied to drugs and other 'substances', it seems an inappropriate construction, as though any blame for misuse could be placed on the substance rather than the user. It also rather begs the question of whether drugs and alcohol can ever be used 'properly'. In the US, the phrase 'substance abuser' has now largely replaced 'drug addict' and 'drunk'.

Academe. See GROVES OF ∼.

accident waiting to happen, an. A cliché frequently uttered in the wake of a disaster is that it was 'an accident waiting to happen'. This is the survivors' and experts' way of pointing to what, to them, seems the foreseeable and inevitable result of lax safety standards which will now probably only be corrected as a result of the tragedy. Much used in relation to the late 1980s spate of UK disasters (Bradford City football ground fire, Zeebrugge ferry overturning, Piper Alpha oil-rig explosion, Kings Cross Tube fire, Hillsborough football stadium crowd deaths). Used as the title of a 1989 book on the subject by Judith Cook.

acclamation. See DESPERATION . . .

according to Cocker. See COCKER.

according to Hoyle. See HOYLE.

accountancy/accounting. See CREATIVE ∼.

ace in the hole. A hidden advantage or secret source of power. An American phrase used as the title of a Cole Porter song in the show *Let's Face It* (1941), and of a Billy Wilder film (US, 1951), it came originally from the game of stud poker. A 'hole' card is one that is not revealed until the betting has taken place. If it is an ace, so much the better.

DOAS dates the use of the expression, in a poker context, to the 1920s, OED2 to 1915. In British English the nearest equivalent would be to talk of having an 'ace up one's sleeve'.

action. See INDUSTRIAL ∼.

action man. A person who is given more to action than to thought, named after a boy's doll which could be dressed in various military-type costumes with appropriate accoutrements. Prior to his marriage in 1981, Charles, Prince of Wales, was noted for his enthusiastic sporting activities in many fields. Coupled with his active service in the Royal Navy, such expenditure of energy caused him to be given the nickname.

A report of a General Medical Council disciplinary inquiry in the *Independent* (29 March 1990) stated: 'He told the hearing: "Mr Bewick is an Action Man, not a philosopher. Action Man's advantage is that at the drop of a hat, he can go anywhere and do anything."'

action this day. Subtitled 'Working with Churchill', the book *Action This Day* (1968)

is a collection of the reminiscences of those who had been closely associated with Winston Churchill during the Second World War. 'ACTION THIS DAY', 'REPORT IN THREE DAYS' and 'REPORT PROGRESS IN ONE WEEK' were printed tags Churchill started using in February 1940 to glue on to memos at the Admiralty.

actor laddie. Often used to describe the booming voice or manner of Victorian and Edwardian actors, this expression presumably derived from their habit of adding the somewhat patronizing endearment 'laddie' when talking to the junior members of their companies. The playwright Ronald Harwood singled out Frank G. Carillo as an example of the breed in the early 1900s: '[He] intoned rather than talked, in a deep, trembling voice ideally suited to melodrama and he used it with equal fortissimo both on and off the stage.' Sir Donald Wolfit, himself somewhat prone to this manner, described Carillo as one of the few actors he had actually heard use the word 'laddie' in this way.

actress. See AS THE BISHOP . . . under AS THE ART MISTRESS SAID . . .

actual. See YOUR ACTUAL under ROUND THE HORNE.

Adams, Fanny. See SWEET ∼.

Adam's rib. The film *Adam's Rib* (US, 1949) is about husband and wife lawyers opposing each other in court (it is also the title of a 1923 Cecil B. de Mille film about marriage with biblical flashbacks). The phrase alludes to Genesis 2:21–2 which states that God made woman from one of Adam's ribs. Compare SPARE RIB.

adjust. See DO NOT ∼ YOUR SET; PLEASE ∼ YOUR DRESS . . .

admirable Crichton, an. A resourceful servant. *The Admirable Crichton* is the title of J.M. Barrie's play (1902; films UK, 1918, 1957) about a butler who succours his shipwrecked aristocratic employer on a desert island. The term had earlier been applied to James Crichton (d 1585), the

Scottish traveller, and – broadly – to anyone of intellectual accomplishment.

advance Australia (fair). The song 'Advance Australia Fair' by Peter Dodds McCormick was first performed in Sydney in 1878, but the alliterative slogan 'Advance Australia' had apparently already existed when Michael Massey Robinson wrote in the *Sydney Gazette* (1 February 1826): ' "ADVANCE THEN, AUSTRALIA",/Be this thy proud gala/ . . . And thy watch-word be "FREEDOM FOR EVER!" '

As simply 'Advance Australia', the phrase became the motto of the Commonwealth of Australia when the states united in 1901. In the 1970s and 1980s, as republicanism grew, it acquired the force of a slogan and was used in various campaigns to promote national pride (sometimes as 'Let's Advance Australia'). In 1984, the song 'Advance Australia Fair', slightly adapted, superseded 'God Save the Queen' as the national anthem.

advertise. See IT PAYS TO ∼.

advertisement. See THIS ∼ DEGRADES WOMEN.

advise and consent. The title of Allen Drury's novel about Washington politics *Advise and Consent* (1959; film US, 1962) is taken from US Senate Rule 38: 'The final question on every nomination shall be, "Will the Senate advise and consent to this nomination?" ' In the US Constitution (Art. II, Sect. 2), dealing with the Senate's powers as a check on the President's appointive and treaty-making powers, the phrase is rather '*Advice* and consent'. Originally, George Washington as President went in person to the Senate Chamber (22 August 1789) to receive 'advice and consent' about treaty provisions with the Creek Indians. Vice-President Adams used the words, 'Do you advise and consent?' Subsequent administrations have sent written requests.

affairs. See DISCUSS UGANDAN ∼.

affluent society, the. The book *The Affluent Society* (1958) by the Canadian-born economist John Kenneth Galbraith is about the effects of high living standards on economic theories which had been created to deal with scarcity and poverty. The resulting 'private affluence and public squalor' stemmed from an imbalance between private and public sector output. For example, there might be more cars and TV sets but not enough police to prevent them from being stolen. Rev. Dr Martin Luther King Jnr, in a 1963 letter from gaol, used the phrase thus: 'When you see the vast majority of your twenty million Negro brothers smouldering in an airtight cage of poverty in the midst of an affluent society . . . then you will understand why we find it difficult to wait.' The notion was not new to the mid-twentieth century, however. Tacitus, in his *Annals* (c AD 115) noted that 'many, amid great affluence, are utterly miserable' and Cato the Younger (95–46 BC), when denouncing the contemporary state of Rome said: '*Habemus publice egestatem, privatim opulentiam*' [public want, private wealth].

The punning tag of **effluent society**, a commonplace by the 1980s, had appeared in Stan Gooch's poem 'Never So Good' in 1964, and before that.

afford. See IF YOU HAVE TO ASK THE PRICE . . .

Africa. See DARK CONTINENT; OUT OF ∼.

African-American/Afro-American. The enforcement of POLITICALLY CORRECT terms in the US during the 1980s meant that 'African-American' became an almost mandatory replacement for 'black' or 'Black' – though not necessarily among Blacks themselves. It is not totally clear why 'African-American' emerged in preference to '*Afro*-American'. Both terms had been in use in North America (and elsewhere) since the mid-nineteenth century (there is even an 1835 example of the term '*Africo*-American'.)

Although there is still apparently an Afro-American Studies Department at the City University, New York, the 'Afro-' version is definitely less common that it once was. Could this possibly be because the word 'Afro' is still associated with the bushy hairstyle popular in the 1960s?

after you, Claude!/no, after you, Cecil!
One of the most enduring phrases from the
BBC radio show *ITMA*, this exchange was
spoken originally by Horace Percival and
Jack Train playing two over-polite
handymen, Cecil and Claude. It still
survives in pockets as an admirable way of
overcoming social awkwardness in such
matters as deciding who should go first
through a door.

In the early 1900s, the American
cartoonist Fred Opper created a pair of
excessively polite Frenchmen called
Alphonse and Gaston who had the similar
exchange: 'You first, my dear Alphonse' –
'No, no, you first, my dear Gaston.'

again. See NEVER ~!; PLAY IT ~, SAM.

against. See HE WHO IS NOT WITH US . . .

age. See DANGEROUS ~; GOLDEN ~.

age before beauty! A phrase used (like
AFTER YOU . . .) when inviting another
person to go through a door before you. In
the famous story, Clare Boothe Luce said it
to Dorothy Parker, ushering her ahead.
Parker assented, saying, 'Pearls before
swine.' (Mrs Luce described this account as
completely apocryphal in answer to a
question from John Keats, Parker's
biographer, quoted in *You Might as Well
Live*, 1970).

The saying presumably originated when
people first started worrying about the
etiquette of going through doorways. It
does not occur in Jonathan Swift's *Polite
Conversation* (1738), as one might have
expected.

A variant reported from New Zealand
(1987) is **dirt before the broom**, though
Partridge/*Catch Phrases* has this as the
response to 'Age before beauty' (which it
describes as a 'mock courtesy'). Yet other
versions are **dust before the broom**
(recorded in Dublin, 1948) and **the dog
follows its master**.

ageist, to be. To discriminate and be
prejudiced against people on the grounds of
their age – especially if they are middle-aged
or the elderly, but also (technically) if they
are young. Most commonly, ageism is the
oppression of the young and of the old by

the age-group in the middle. The term was
coined by Dr Robert Butler, a specialist in
geriatric medicine, of Washington DC,
quoted in the *Washington Post* (7 March
1969) as saying: 'We shall soon have to
consider a form of bigotry we now tend to
overlook: age discrimination or age-ism,
prejudice by one age group toward other
age groups.'

agenda. See HIDDEN ~.

Age of Aquarius, the. 'This is the
dawning of the Age of Aquarius,' sang the
cast of the 'American tribal love-rock
musical' *Hair* (1968) in what was to become
something of a hippy anthem. Fellow
denizens of the 1960s also looked forward to
the astrological period with this name,
lasting two thousand years, that was said to
be beginning at that time (following the
Piscean Age). This new period held forth
the promise of more liberal values, world
freedom and brotherhood, as well as
promoting a general optimism.

age of miracles is past, the. As with the
similar **age of chivalry is past**, this
proverb is probably used more often now in
the slightly ironic *negative*, i.e. when saying
'the age of miracles is *not* past' or 'the age of
chivalry is *not* dead' out of feigned gratitude
for a stroke of good fortune or an
unexpected courtesy. In its original form,
'miracles' was current by 1602. In Edmund
Burke's *Reflections on the Revolution in France*
(1790), is 'the age of chivalry is gone'. In
about 1900, Oscar Wilde wrote in a letter:
'[Frank Harris] keeps BOSIE in order: clearly
the age of miracles is not over.'

age of the train. See under WE'RE GETTING
THERE.

agnus dei. See MASS PHRASES.

agonizing reappraisal, an. Political term
for a process of reconsideration, possibly
before a decision to make a U-TURN. The
modern use stems from a speech that John
Foster Dulles, US Secretary of State, made
to the National Press Club, Washington, in
December 1953: 'When I was in Paris last
week, I said that . . . the United States
would have to undertake an agonizing

reappraisal of basic foreign policy in relation to Europe.'

agony, Ivy. See under RAY'S A LAUGH.

agony and the ecstasy, the. A colourful coinage, now only used in mockery. *The Agony and the Ecstasy* is the title of a novel (1961; film US, 1965) by Irving Stone, about Michelangelo and the painting of the Sistine Chapel.

Compare what US novelist William Faulkner said in his speech accepting the Nobel Prize for Literature (10 December 1950): whatever was 'worth the agony and the sweat' was worth writing about.

agony aunt, an. One who answers questions about personal problems from readers of a newspaper or magazine (mostly British use). Hence the term **agony column**, originally a 'personal column' in newspapers containing messages for missing relatives (by the 1860s), but from the 1930s the name given to the space in which 'advice' journalism appears. Neither phrase was in wide use until the 1970s and neither is much used outside Britain.

Sob sister is a similar term for one who allows readers to weep on his or her shoulder. Although the name may be of American invention, such an adviser has long been known in British women's magazines, the subjects formerly being household management, etiquette and bringing up the family. Such columnists proliferated after the Second World War and some achieved eminence for their expert and sympathetic advice and information. See also MISS LONELYHEARTS.

agreement. See GENTLEMAN'S ~.

ahead. See GO ~, MAKE MY DAY; IF YOU WANT TO GET ~ . . .

ahh, Bisto! Bisto gravy browning has been promoted with this cry in the UK since 1919. The name is a hidden slogan, too. When the Cerebos company first put Bisto on the market in 1910, the product did not have a name. According to legend, the initial letters of the proposed slogan 'Browns, Seasons, Thickens In One' were rearranged to produce 'BISTO'.

The Bisto Kids, drawn by Will Owen, first appeared in 1919, sniffing a wisp of gravy aroma and murmuring, 'Ahh Bisto!' This is a phrase much played with in cartoon captions over the years – 'Ah, Blitzo!'; 'Ah, Bizerta!'; 'Ah, Crippso!'; 'Ah! Winston!'; 'Ah! Coupon free!'

ah, there's good news tonight! Even if there wasn't – the salutation of Gabriel Heatter (*b c* 1890), the American radio newscaster of the 1930s and 40s.

ah, Woodbine – a *great* **little cigarette!** A slogan current in 1957. Norman Hackforth – the Mystery Voice from BBC radio's *Twenty Questions* – spoke the line memorably in TV ads.

— Aid. In the mid-1980s, it became fashionable to give charitable fund-raising events names with the suffix '– aid'. This stemmed from the first such event – the recording of 'Do They Know It's Christmas', performed in 1984 by an ad hoc group of pop singers and musicians called **Band Aid**, in punning allusion to the Band-Aid brand of medical dressing. This record, successfully drawing attention to those suffering in the Ethiopian civil war and famine, laid the foundation of the **Live Aid** rock concert in July 1985. Similar, though in some cases much smaller-scale, events followed including Sport Aid (sponsored athletes), Mandarin Aid (civil servants), School Aid (children), Fashion Aid, Academy Aid (painters), Sheep Aid (agricultural events in Yorkshire) and Deaf Aid (no, only joking).

ain't. See AND THAT ~ HAY; ~ IT A SHAME? (under *ITMA*); IF IT ~ BROKE . . .; THINGS ~ WHAT THEY USED TO BE.

air. See BIRDS OF THE ~; TIME TO SPARE?, GO BY ~.

aisle, to go up the. To be married (in church) – an erroneous usage. Sir Thomas Bazley fired off a letter to *The Times* in July 1986: 'Sir, You report that Miss Sarah Fergusson will go up the aisle to the strains of Elgar's "Imperial March". Hitherto, brides have always gone up the nave. Yours faithfully . . . ' Indeed, the nave is the main route from the west door of a church to the chancel and altar; the aisles are the parallel routes at the side of the building, usually separated from the nave by pillars.

Aladdin. See IT WAS LIKE AN ∼'S CAVE.

alarm. See SET ∼ BELLS RINGING; SPREAD ∼ AND DESPONDENCY.

Alcoholics Anonymous. The name of a self-help organization for alcoholics, founded by Bill W(ilson) and Dr Bob S(mith) in the US in 1935. Now a worldwide organization, A.A. was founded on the principle of small groups of addicts giving each other mutual support. Members do not use their full surnames. When they are 'cured', they not only have to proclaim it, they know that they must keep in touch with the organization to prevent backsliding.

Alfie. See WHAT'S IT ALL ABOUT?

Alice. See PASS THE SICK-BAG, ∼ under I THINK WE SHOULD BE TOLD.

Alice-blue gown, an. Celebrated in song, the colour of this garment, a light-greenish blue, takes its name from a particular Alice – the daughter of President Theodore Roosevelt. The song 'Alice-blue Gown' was written for her by Joseph McCarthy and Harry Tierney in 1900, when she was sixteen, though apparently not published until 1919. In the late 1930s, there was another (British) song, called 'The Girl in the Alice-blue Gown'.

Alice in Wonderland. Quoted almost as extensively as Shakespeare and the Bible, *Alice's Adventures in Wonderland* (1865) and *Through the Looking Glass and What Alice Found There* (1872) by Lewis Carroll are alluded to for their particular characters and incidents and as a whole, to denote a mad, fantastic world.

See also ANGLO-SAXON ATTITUDES; CABBAGES AND KINGS; DECISIONS DECISIONS!; MAD AS A HATTER; MALICE IN WONDERLAND; WE ARE THE MASTERS NOW; WHITE RABBIT.

alienation effect. Bertolt Brecht's name for his theory of drama (in German '*Verfremdungseffekt*') – first promoted in 1937 – in which the audience has to be reminded that the play it is watching *is* a play and not real. The effect is to distance the watchers from the players, to prevent too much emotional involvement.

alive. See COME ∼ . . .; MAN ∼.

alive and well and living in — This format phrase probably began in a perfectly natural way – 'What's happened to old so-and-so?' 'Oh, he's alive and well and living in Godalming' etc. In the preface to *His Last Bow* (1917) Conan Doyle wrote: 'The Friends of Mr Sherlock Holmes will be glad to learn that he is still alive and well . . .'

The extended form was given a tremendous fillip when the Belgian-born songwriter and singer Jacques Brel (1929–78) became the subject of an off-Broadway musical show entitled *Jacques Brel is Alive and Well and Living in Paris* (1968–72). Quite why M. Brel should have merited the WHERE ARE THEY NOW? treatment is not too apparent, but the format caught on. The *Listener* (3 October 1968), quoting the *Daily Mail*, stated: 'The *Goon Show* is not dead. It is alive and well, living in Yorkshire and operating under the name of BBC Radio Leeds.' The format had earlier probably been used in religious sloganeering, possibly prompted by *Time* Magazine's famous cover (*c* 1966), 'IS GOD DEAD?': the *New Statesman* (26 August 1966) quoted a graffito, 'God is alive and living in Argentina'. This suggests that the formula might have been used originally in connection with Nazi war criminals who escaped prosecution and lived unharmed in South America. Other graffiti have included: 'God is not dead – but alive and well and working on a much less ambitious project' (quoted in 1979); 'Jesus Christ is alive and well and signing copies of the Bible at Foyles' (quoted in 1980). A headline from the *Independent* (25 June 1990): 'Socialism is alive and well and living in Moscow'.

In a letter to the *Independent* Magazine (13 March 1993), M.H.I. Wright wrote: 'When I was a medical student and young house physician 50 years ago, we had to write very detailed case-sheets on every patient admitted. Under the heading "Family History", we detailed each member of his family – for example, "Father, died of heart diseases in 1935; Mother, alive and well and living in London." One pedantic consultant insisted we drop the word "alive" because, as he said, how could the relative be "dead and well"?'

On the other hand, a US film in 1975 was burdened with the title *Sheila Devine Is Dead and Living in New York.*

all animals are equal, but some are more equal than others. A fictional slogan from George Orwell's *Animal Farm* (1945), his commentary on the totalitarian excesses of Communism. It had been anticipated: Hesketh Pearson recalled in his biography of the actor/manager Sir Herbert Beerbohm Tree that Tree wished to insert one of his own epigrams in a play by Stephen Phillips called *Nero*, produced in 1906. It was: 'All men are equal – except myself.'

The saying alludes, of course, to Thomas Jefferson's 'All men are created equal and independent', from the Preamble to the American Declaration of Independence (1776). It has, perhaps, the makings of a format phrase in that it is more likely to be used to refer to humans than to animals. Only the second half of the phrase need actually be spoken, the first half being understood: 'You-Know-Who [Mrs Thatcher] is against the idea [televising parliament]. There aren't card votes at Westminster, but some votes are more equal than others' (*Guardian*, 15 February 1989).

all done with mirrors, it's. Originally, a way of explaining how conjuring tricks and stage illusions were performed – when some, indeed, were done using mirrors – but without actually understanding how. Now used as a way of describing how anything has been accomplished when the method is not obvious. Admiration, but also a suspicion of trickery, is implicit in the phrase. Noël Coward uses it in *Private Lives* (1933); *They Do It With Mirrors* is the title of an Agatha Christie thriller (1952).

all dressed up and nowhere to go. A phrase used to describe forlorn indecision comes (slightly altered) from a song popularized by the American comedian Raymond Hitchcock in *The Beauty Shop* (New York, 1914) and *Mr Manhattan* (London, 1915):

> When you're all dressed up and no place to go,
> Life seems dreary, weary and slow.

The words gained further emphasis when they were used by William Allen White to describe the Progressive Party following Theodore Roosevelt's decision to retire from presidential competition in 1916. He said it was: 'All dressed up with nowhere to go.' The *OED2* has this phrase starting life in a song by 'G. Whiting' (1912), 'When You're All Dressed Up and Have No Place to Go'. But Lowe's *Directory of Popular Music* ascribes the song to Silvio Hein and Benjamin Burt.

allergy. See DREADED LERGY under *GOON SHOW.*

all for one and one for all [French: '*tous pour un, un pour tous*']. The motto of the Three Musketeers in the novel (1844–45) by Alexandre Dumas. As 'one for all, or all for one', it had appeared earlier in Shakespeare's *Lucrece*, ll. 141–4 (1594).

all gas and gaiters. To do with the church, especially the higher clergy. *All Gas and Gaiters* was the title of a BBC TV comedy series about the clergy (1966–70), taken from Charles Dickens, *Nicholas Nickleby*, Chap. 49 (1838–39): 'All is gas and gaiters' – gaiters (leg coverings below the knee) being traditionally associated with bishops.

all gong and no dinner. What you would say of a loud-mouthed person somewhat short on achievement. Partridge/*Slang* has a citation from *The Archers* in 1981. It may be a fairly recent coinage, though presumably dinner gongs are not as prevalent as they once were.

all good things must come to an end. A proverbial expression meaning 'pleasure cannot go on for ever'. There are versions going back to 1440 and as 'Everything has an end', the idea appears in Chaucer's *Troilus and Criseyde* (1385). The Prayer Book version of Psalm 119:96 is: 'I see that all things come to an end.'

all hell broke loose. This popular descriptive phrase comes from Milton's *Paradise Lost*, Bk.4, line 917 (1667), when the Archangel Gabriel speaks to Satan:

> Wherefore with thee
> Came not all hell broke loose.

As an idiomatic phrase it was already established by 1738 when Jonathan Swift compiled his *Polite Conversation*. There is 'A great Noise below' and Lady Smart exclaims: 'Hey, what a clattering is there; one would think Hell was broke loose'.

all human life is there. The only reference to this phrase in the *ODQ* appears under Henry James, 'Madonna of the Future' (1879): 'Cats and monkeys, monkeys and cats – all human life is there.' What is the connection, if any, with the *News of the World* which used the line to promote itself *c* 1958?

In 1981, Maurice Smelt, the advertising copywriter, told me: ' "All human life is there" was my idea, but I don't, of course, pretend that they were my words. I simply lifted them from *The Oxford Dictionary of Quotations*. I didn't bother to tell the client that they were from Henry James, suspecting that, after the "Henry James – WHO HE?" stage, he would come up with tiresome arguments about being too high-hat for his readership. I did check whether we were clear on copyright, which we were by a year or two . . . I do recall its use as baseline in a tiny little campaign trailing a series that earned the *News of the World* a much-publicized but toothless rebuke from the Press Council. The headline of that campaign was: " 'I've been a naughty girl,' says Diana Dors". The meiosis worked, as the *News of the World* knew it would. They ran an extra million copies of the first issue of the series.'

alligator. See SEE YOU LATER, ~ .

all in the mind. See under *GOON SHOW*.

all jam and Jerusalem. A popular misconception of the local Women's Institute groups in the UK is that their members are solely concerned with making jam, with flower arranging, and with singing the Blake/Parry anthem 'Jerusalem'. This encapsulation is said to date from the 1920s. Simon Goodenough's history of the movement is called *Jam and Jerusalem* (1977).

all kid gloves and no drawers. Describing a certain kind of woman, this is given as an example of colourful cockney bubble-pricking by Kenneth Williams in *Just Williams* (1985). He said it was used in his youth (1930s) to denote the meretricious.

Another version encountered in a Welsh context (1988) was, **(all) fur coat and no knickers** (which was also the title of play that toured the UK in the same year). A further one (1993), said to come from Lancashire, is: 'Red hat, no knickers.'

all my eye and Betty Martin. Meaning 'nonsense', *OED2* finds a letter written in 1781 by one S.Crispe stating: 'Physic, to old, crazy Frames like ours, is all my eye and Betty Martin – (a sea phrase that Admiral Jemm frequently makes use of).' The shorter expressions 'all my eye' or 'my eye' predate this. As to how it originated, Edwin Radford, *To Coin a Phrase* (edited and revised by Alan Smith, 1974) repeats the suggestion that it was a British sailor's garbled version of words heard in an Italian church: 'O, mihi, beate Martine' [Oh, grant me, blessed St Martin], but this sounds too ingenious. Probably there *was* a Betty Martin of renown in the eighteenth century (Partridge/*Catch Phrases* finds mention of an actress with the name whose favourite expression is supposed to have been 'My eye!') and her name was co-opted for popular use.

Compare GORDON BENNETT.

all that jazz. See AND ~ .

all our yesterdays. Almost every phrase from Macbeth's speech in Shakespeare's *Macbeth*, V.v.22 (1606) seems to have been used as phrase-making material:

To-morrow, and to-morrow, and to-
morrow,
Creeps in this petty pace from day to day,
To the last syllable of recorded time; And
all our yesterdays have lighted fools
The way to dusty death. Out, out, brief
candle!
Life's but a walking shadow; a poor
player,
That struts and frets his hour upon the
stage,
And then is heard no more: it is a tale
Told by an idiot, full of sound and fury,
Signifying nothing.

A slight exaggeration, but *All Our Yesterdays* is the title of Granada TV's 1960–73 programme devoted to old newsreels; *All My Yesterdays* is the title of Edward G. Robinson's autobiography (1973); 'full of sound and fury' is echoed in the title of William Faulkner's novel *The SOUND AND THE FURY* (1929); *Told By an Idiot* is a novel by Rose Macaulay (1923); *Tomorrow and Tomorrow* is the title of a film released in 1932; *The Way to Dusty Death* is a novel by Alastair Maclean (1973); and 'strutting and fretting' and the other phrases are frequently alluded to.

all over the place like a mad woman's underclothes. The writer Germaine Greer recalls that, when she was growing up in Australia in the 1940s, this was her mother's phrase to describe, say, an untidy room. In consequence, Greer used *The Madwoman's Underclothes* as the title of a collection of her assorted writings (1986).
Partridge/*Slang* does not find this precise expression but in discussing the phrase 'all over the place like a mad woman's shit' points to the euphemistic variants cited by G.A. Wilkes in *A Dictionary of Australian Colloquialisms* (1978): '. . . like a mad woman's knitting . . . custard . . . lunch box.' So, Australian it very much seems to be.

allowed. See IT IS DISGRACEFUL . . .

all publicity is good publicity. A modern proverb dating from at least the 1960s but probably it is as old as the public relations industry. Alternative forms include: **There's no such thing as bad**
publicity, **There's no such thing as over-exposure – only bad exposure, Don't read it – measure it** and **I don't care what the papers say about me as long as they spell my name right.** The latter saying has been attributed to the American Tammany leader 'Big Tim' Sullivan.
CODP includes it in the form 'Any publicity is good publicity' but finds no example before 1974, but in Dominic Behan's *My Brother Brendan* (1965), the Irish playwright is quoted as saying, 'There is no such thing as bad publicity except your own obituary.' James Agate in *Ego 7* (for 19 February 1944) quotes Arnold Bennett, 'All praise is good,' and adds: 'I suppose the same could be said about publicity.'

all quiet on the Western Front. A familiar phrase of the Allies in the First World War, used in military communiqués and newspaper reports, and also taken up jocularly by men in the trenches to describe peaceful inactivity. It was taken as the title of the English translation of the novel *Im Westen Nichts Neues* [Nothing new in the West] (1929, film US, 1930) by the German writer, Erich Maria Remarque.
Partridge/*Catch Phrases* hears in it echoes of 'All quiet on the Shipka Pass' – cartoons of the 1877–8 Russo-Turkish War which Partridge says had a vogue in 1915–6, though he never heard the allusion made himself. For no very good reason, Partridge rules out any connection with the US song 'All Quiet Along the Potomac'. This, in turn, came from a poem called 'The Picket Guard' (1861) by Ethel Lynn Beers, a sarcastic commentary on General Brinton McClellan's policy of delay at the start of the Civil War. The phrase (alluding to the Potomac River which runs through Washington DC) had been used in reports from McLellan's Union headquarters and put in Northern newspaper headlines.

all right. See ARE YOU ∼?; BUT I'M ALL RIGHT NOW under *ITMA*; I'M ∼, JACK; IT'LL BE ALL RIGHT ON THE NIGHT.

all right? – right! – stay bright! Verbal tic of Australian-born Alan 'Fluff' Freeman (*b* 1927), who became a DJ in Britain. The phrase was incorporated in the closing sequence of BBC radio's *Pick of the Pops*, which he introduced for many years. In 1982, Fluff told me that he got the procedure from a phone conversation with the actress Ann Todd. Signing off, he said (making an arrangement), 'All right ' right!' She rang him straight back and asked, 'What was that you said?' He had already forgotten but gradually recalled it. Ann Todd told him he ought to use it in his patter.

all's fair in love, war and —. The basic proverb here is 'All's fair in love and war' which *CODP* finds in the form 'Love and war are all one' by 1620 and well established by the nineteenth century. But nowadays I would say that the extended form – to include almost anything that the speaker might wish, most frequently politics – is more common.

'The Shadow Chancellor, Mr John Smith . . . said he did not expect to receive any special favours from his political opponents. "All is fair in love, war and parliamentary politics," he added' – *Guardian*, 23 January 1989. (Michael Foot MP had been quoted in 1986 as having said, 'I had better recall before someone else does, that I said on one occasion that all was fair in love, war and parliamentary procedure.') In 1982, Leonard Miall concluded a BBC Radio talk ('Byways in a Broadcasting Career') with: 'I suppose that all's fair in love, war and party politicals [i.e. broadcasts].'

all-singing, all-dancing. The worlds of computing and finance have both taken to using a phrase whose origins are pure Hollywood. For once, it is possible to be very precise about the source of a piece of popular phraseology. First, the computing use. From a report in the *Guardian* (3 October 1984) about a new police computer called 'Holmes': 'Sir Lawrence Byford is proud that Britain got there first. Holmes, he claims, is unique. "It should provide our detectives with unrivalled facilities when dealing with crimes such as homicides and serious sexual offences . . . it's the all-singing all-dancing act." The only thing it can't do, it seems, is play the violin.' And from a special report on computers in the same paper (24 June 1985): 'I'm knocking these

present notes together on the word-processor incorporated into Jazz, the all-singing, all-dancing "integrated" package from the Lotus Development Corporation.' Partridge/*Catch Phrases* dates the start of the computing use to about 1970.

The phrase is used every bit as much when writing about financial 'packages'. From a special report in *The Times* (8 November 1985): 'The City's financial institutions have been busily preparing themselves for the changes [i.e. BIG BANG the following year]. Many of the large stockbroking firms have forged links with banks: conceding their independence but benefiting from the massive capital injection which many believe will be necessary to cope with the new look all-singing-and-dancing exchange.' From 'Family Money' in the same newspaper (31 May 1986): 'There are a number of all-singing, all-dancing and rather moderately performing plans on the savings and insurance market. They offer just about every financial service under the sun without necessarily distinguishing themselves in any one particular field.'

The meaning is reasonably clear. What you should anticipate getting in each sphere is a multipurpose something or other, with every possible feature, which may or may not 'perform' well. A dictionary of jargon (1984) goes so far as to give the general business meaning as 'super-glamorised, gimmicky, flashy', when referring to a version of any stock product.

As such, the phrase has been used in many other fields as well – not least in show business. The source? In 1929, when sound came to the movies, the very first Hollywood musical, MGM's *Broadway Melody*, was promoted with posters bearing the slogan:

> *The New Wonder of the Screen!*
> ALL TALKING
> ALL SINGING
> ALL DANCING
> *Dramatic Sensation*

Oddly enough, in that same year, two rival studios both hit on the same selling pitch. Alice White in *Broadway Babes* (using Warners' Vitaphone system) was '100% TALKING, SINGING, DANCING'. And Radio's *Rio Rita* (with Bebe Daniels) was billed as 'ZIEGFELD'S FABULOUS ALL-TALKING, ALL-SINGING SUPER SCREEN SPECTACLE'. It was natural that the studios should wish to promote the most obvious aspect of the new sound cinema but it is curious that they should all have made use of much the same phrase.

all Sir Garnet. Meaning 'all correct', the phrase alludes to Sir Garnet Wolseley (1833–1913), a soldier noted for his organizational powers, who led several successful military expeditions from 1852–85, and who helped improve the lot of the Other Ranks. The expression was known by 1894. Wolseley is also celebrated as 'The Modern Major-General' in Gilbert and Sullivan's *Pirates of Penzance* (1879).

From the same source, *Sir Garnet* is the name of a boat in *Coot Club*, the novel (1934) by Arthur Ransome.

all's well that ends well. The Rev. Francis Kilvert's diary entry for 1 January 1878 has: 'The hind axle broke and they thought they would have to spend the night on the road . . . All's well that ends well and they arrived safe and sound.' Is the allusion to the title of Shakespeare's play *All's Well That Ends Well* (c 1603) or to something else? In fact, it was a proverbial expression before Shakespeare. *CODP* finds 'If the ende be wele, than is alle wele' in 1381, and points to the earlier form 'Wel is him that wel ende mai'. See also under WAR AND PEACE.

all the news that's fit to print. This slogan was devised by Adolph S. Ochs when he bought the *New York Times* and it has been used in every edition since – at first on the editorial page, on 25 October 1896, and from the following February on the front page near the masthead. It became the paper's war cry in its 1890s' battle against formidable competition from the *World*, the *Herald* and the *Journal*. At worst, it sounds like a slogan for the suppression of news. However, no newspaper prints everything. It has been parodied by Howard Dietz as 'All the news *that fits* we print'.

all the President's men. Carl Bernstein and Bob Woodward gave the title *All the President's Men* to their first WATERGATE book (1974, film US, 1976). It might seem to allude to the lines from the nursery rhyme 'Humpty Dumpty' (first recorded in 1803):

All the king's horses
And all the king's men,
Couldn't put Humpty together again.

There is also a Robert Penn Warren novel (and film, US 1949) based on the life of southern demagogue Huey 'Kingfish' Long called *All the King's Men*. More directly, the Watergate book took its title from a saying of Henry Kissinger's at the time of the 1970 Cambodia invasion: 'We are all the President's men and we must behave accordingly' (quoted in Kalb and Kalb, *Kissinger*, 1974).

all the world and his wife. Meaning 'everybody' – though the phrase is in decline now after the feminism of the 1970s. Christopher Anstey in *The New Bath Guide* (1766) has:

How he welcomes at once all the world
and his wife,
And how civil to folk he ne'er saw in his
life.

Jonathan Swift included it in *Polite Conversation* (1738): 'Who were the Company? Why; there was all the World and his Wife.' There is an equivalent French expression: 'All the world and his father.' From F. Scott Fitzgerald, *The Great Gatsby*, Chap. 4 (1926): 'On Sunday morning while church bells rang in the villages alongshore, the world and its mistress returned to Gatsby's house and twinkled hilariously on his lawn.'

all the world loves a lover. This modernish proverbial saying was used by James Agate in a speech on 17 December 1941 (reported in *Ego 5*, 1942). It would appear to be an adaptation of the established expression, 'Everybody/all the world loves a lord' (current by 1869). This had previously been built upon – for example – by Stephen Leacock in *Essays and Literary Studies* (1916): 'All the world loves a grafter – at least a genial and ingenious grafter – a Robin Hood who plunders an abbot to feed a beggar.'

all things bright and beautiful. The popular hymn (1848) by Mrs Cecil Frances Alexander, of which this is the first line, is still notorious for the other line about the 'rich man in his castle'. It also provided the author James Herriot with new titles for his volumes about life as a vet – books originally called *It Shouldn't Happen To a Vet*, *Let Sleeping Vets Lie*, *Vets Might Fly*, etc. When these titles were coupled together in three omnibus editions especially for the US market (from 1972), Mrs Alexander's hymn was plundered for titles and they became *All Things Bright and Beautiful*, *All Creatures Great and Small*, and *All Things Wise and Wonderful*. *The Lord God Made Them All* was given to a further original volume.

all this and Heaven too. As acknowledged in Rachel Fields's novel with the title *All This and Heaven Too* (1939, film US, 1940), Matthew Henry, the English Bible commentator (*d* 1714), ascribed this saying to his minister father in his own *Life of Mr Philip Henry* (1698). Compare the film title *All This and World War II* (US, 1976) and the classic *Daily Express* newspaper headline on Queen Elizabeth II's Coronation day (2 June 1953): 'ALL THIS – AND EVEREST TOO', announcing the conquest of the world's highest mountain by a British-led expedition.

all we want is the facts, ma'am. See under *DRAGNET*.

all women look the same in the dark. The least POLITICALLY CORRECT entry in this book. Contemptuous male view of women as sexual objects – sometimes, 'they all the look the same in the dark'. An established view by the mid-twentieth century at least. Compare the similar expression, 'You don't look at the mantelpiece when you poke the fire' (an old joke revived by John Osborne in *The Entertainer*, 1957), Ovid's more felicitous and diplomatic version in his *Ars Amatoria* (*c* 2 BC), 'The dark makes every woman beautiful', and the English proverb (known by 1546) 'All cats are grey in the dark'. Robert Herrick appeared to say much the same in 'No Difference i' th' Dark' (1648): 'Night makes no difference 'twixt

the Priest and the Clerk;/Joan as my Lady is as good i' th' dark.'

all your own. See under WHATEVER ELSE IT WILL BE . . .

almost a gentleman. The bill matter (i.e. the descriptive line that appeared on posters) of the music-hall comedian Billy Bennett (who died in 1942) was 'Almost a Gentleman'. John Osborne took it as the title of his second volume of memoirs (1991). Compare Daisy Ashford, *The Young Visiters*, Chap. 1 (1919): 'I am not quite a gentleman but you would hardly notice it but can't be helped anyhow.'

alone. See I WANT TO BE ∼; YOU'RE NEVER ∼ WITH A STRAND.

altered states. Where drugs take you. *Altered States* is the title of a novel (1979, film US, 1980) by Paddy Chayevsky (screen credit as 'Sidney Aaron'), a sci-fi thriller about genetic experimentation or, as one of the film guides puts it, about a 'psychophysiologist who hallucinates himself back into primitive states of human evolution, in which guise he emerges to kill'.

  This might have something to do with what Dr Albert Hofmann observed of his discovery, the psychedelic drug LSD. He noted in his diary for 1943: 'An intense stimulation of the imagination and *an altered state of awareness of the world*.'

alternative. See THERE IS NO ∼.

Alvar Liddell. See HERE IS THE NEWS AND THIS IS . . .

always. See ONCE A —, ∼ A —.

always a bridesmaid. See OFTEN A BRIDESMAID.

always merry and bright. The comedian Alfred Lester (1872–1925) – who was always lugubrious – was associated with this phrase, although it crops up in all sorts of other places. As 'Peter Doody', a lugubrious jockey in the Lionel Monckton/Howard Talbot/Arthur Wimperis musical comedy *The Arcadians* (1909), he had it as his motto in a song, 'My Motter'. *Punch* quotes the phrase on 26 October 1910. Somerset Maugham in a letter to a friend (1915) writes: 'I am back on a fortnight's leave, very merry and bright, but frantically busy – I wish it were all over.' An edition of *The Magnet* from 1920 carries an ad for *Merry and Bright* – a comic paper. P.G. Wodehouse uses the phrase in *The Indiscretions of Archie* (1921). Larry Grayson suggested that it was used as the billing for Billy Danvers (d 1964), the British variety entertainer, but I think his was, rather, 'Cheeky, Cheery and Chubby'.

always true to you in my fashion. The song with this title by Cole Porter from *Kiss Me Kate* (1948) echoes, consciously or unconsciously, the line 'I have been faithful to thee, Cynara! in my fashion' from the poem '*Non Sum Qualis Eram*' (1896) by Ernest Dowson.

Amami. See FRIDAY NIGHT IS ~ NIGHT.

amazing. See PRETTY ~.

amazing grace. Most people are familiar with the hymn 'Amazing Grace' from the great popular success it had when sung and recorded by Judy Collins in the early 1970s, but it is quite wrong for record companies to label the song 'Trad.'. The words of the hymn were written in the seventeenth century by John Newton (1725–1807), a reformed slave-trafficker. He (together with the poet William Cowper), wrote the *Olney Hymnbook* of 1779, and this is but one example from that work. The slightly complicated thing is that the *tune* to which 'Amazing Grace' now gets sung *is* a traditional tune – it is an old American one, though some say that it was an anonymous *Scottish* tune before this.

amber nectar. Nectar was the (sweet) drink of the gods, in classical mythology. 'Amber fluid' and 'amber liquid' are both Australianisms (acknowledged by the *Macquarie Dictionary*, 1981) for beer (particularly amber-coloured lager). Put all this together and you have the term 'amber nectar' used by Paul Hogan in 1980s TV commercials in Britain for Foster's. 'Amber-coloured fluid' was, however, a term for

cocktails used in the novels of the British-born writer, E. Phillips Oppenheim (1866–1946). In 1713, the *London and Country Brewer* was referring to 'the amber-coloured Malt'.

ambition. See SAVAGE STORY OF LUST AND ~.

Amen Corner. (1) A place near St Paul's Cathedral, London, where monks would conclude saying the Pater Noster as they processed on Corpus Christi Day. Hence the other place names: Paternoster Row, Ave Maria Lane, Creed Lane. (2) (in US use by 1860) the name given to the part of a church or meeting-house where people sat who used to assist the preacher by calling out the responses, especially 'Amen'. (3) The name of a British pop group of the late 1960s.

America. See LET'S GET ~ MOVING AGAIN; MIDDLE ~; ONLY IN ~ . . . ; SEE ~ FIRST.

America cannot stand pat. 'To stand pat', meaning 'to keep a fixed position or belief, to stand fast' may come originally from poker, in which you can decline to exchange the cards you are dealt. A 'pat hand' is one that is exactly suited to your purpose. In the 1960 US presidential election, John F. Kennedy pointed to the old slogan 'Stand pat with McKinley' as an example of Republican reaction. Richard Nixon countered with 'America can't stand pat' – until it was politely pointed out to him that he was married to a woman with that name. 'America can't stand still' was rapidly substituted.

America, Mr and Mrs North. See GOOD EVENING . . .

American. See AFRICAN- ~.

American as apple pie. The *OED2* does not find this expression before 1977. However, Flexner (1976) comments that 'the apple itself is even more American than apple pie and Americans have used the word often'. Confirming the position of the apple as central to American life, he also writes: 'Until the 20th century citrus boom, apples – raw, in cider, and cooked in many dishes – were the most popular and talked about fruit in America.'

American Caesar. Nickname of (1) Ulysses S. Grant – see BUTCHER (2) Douglas MacArthur (1880–1964), grandiose American general in the Pacific during the Second World War and then in Korea. Dismissed for insubordination by President Truman.

American dream, the. An expression used to describe the ideals of democracy and standards of living that inspired the founding of the United States, and which was probably coined by J.T. Adams in *The Epic of America* (1931). Before that, in 'America the Beautiful' (1893), Katharine Lee Bates had written of a 'patriot dream that sees beyond the years'. *The American Dream* is the title of a play (1961) by Edward Albee, and *An American Dream* (1965) is a novel by Norman Mailer.

American Gothic. Title of the painting (1930) by Grant Wood (1892–1942) which shows an American farm couple posing in a stiff fashion in front of their Gothic house. The man in overalls carries a pitchfork. His equally dour wife wears an apron. The artist's treatment of them has been described as 'half epic, half ironic'.

American way. See TRUTH, JUSTICE AND THE ~ under SUPERMAN.

am I right, or am I right? An expression brooking no debate. From American show biz, one suspects. It is in the script of the film *Shampoo* (US, 1975). Compare what Mae West asks in *I'm No Angel* (1933): 'Is that elegant, or is that elegant?'

ammunition. See PRAISE THE LORD AND PASS THE ~.

Amplex. See SOMEONE ISN'T USING ~ under EVEN YOUR BEST FRIENDS . . .

amused. See WE ARE NOT ~.

anatomically correct. A forerunner of the phrase POLITICALLY CORRECT and occurring in various medical contexts. For example, 'The Lippes loop [an intra-uterine contraceptive device] is the next most anatomically correct, commercially available device' – H.J. Davis, *Intrauterine Devices for Contraception* (1971). But the term became more widely known when 'anatomically-correct dolls' (i.e. dolls with genitalia) were used to enable children who might have been sexually abused to recount their experiences. They were much talked about in the UK during the 'Cleveland' affair of 1987, when social workers claimed to have found child abuse in a large number of cases but were subsequently judged to have made incorrect diagnoses.

anatomy of —, the. A title format, of which the first notable use was *The Anatomy of Melancholy* (1621) by Robert Burton. That book used the word 'anatomy' in an appropriate manner, its subject being a medical condition (*anatome* is the Greek word for dissection).

The modern vogue for 'anatomies' of this and that began with the film *Anatomy of a Murder* (US, 1959) and was followed by Anthony Sampson's *Anatomy of Britain*, first published in 1962 and revised a number of times thereafter.

ancestral vices/voices. *Ancestral Vices* is the title of a novel (1980) by Tom Sharpe; *Ancestral Voices* is the title of the first volume of diaries (1975) of the architectural historian, James Lees-Milne. Both derive from the poem 'Kubla Khan' (1798) by Samuel Taylor Coleridge, which contains the lines:

> And 'mid this tumult Kubla heard from far
> Ancestral voices prophesying war!

Lees-Milne went to the same source for his three subsequent diary volumes, *Prophesying Peace* (1977), *Caves of Ice* (1983) and *Midway on the Waves* (1985), viz:

> The shadow of the dome of pleasure
> Floated midway on the waves . . .
> It was a miracle of rare device,
> A sunny pleasure-dome with caves of ice!

and a good evening to you. See GLAD WE COULD GET TOGETHER.

and all because the lady loves Milk Tray. Cadbury's Milk Tray chocolates have been promoted with this line since 1968. On British TV, the line was the pay-off to action adverts showing feats of James Bond-style daring which led up to the presentation of a box of the chocolates to a suitably alluring female.

and all that jazz. 'And all that stuff, the rest, etcetera' – often with the dismissive suggestion 'and all that nonsense, rubbish'. American in origin, popular by 1959. From Gore Vidal, *Myra Breckinridge*, Chap. 6 (1968): 'He [was] so pleased to have me "on the team" and me so happy to be able to do work in Hollywood, California, a life's dream come true and – as they used to say in the early Sixties – all that jazz.'

All That Jazz was the title of a film (US, 1979) about the life and death of a choreographer.

and a special goodnight to *you*. Before becoming a DJ on British radio, David Hamilton (*b* 1939) was an announcer with a number of independent television companies, including Tyne Tees, ABC and Thames. In the days when TV programmes ended round about midnight, his romantic sign-off became so distinctive that he even made a record with the title – 'A Special Goodnight to You' (*c* 1967). At about the same time, the sign-off was also used by Barry Aldiss ('B.A.') on Radio Luxembourg and subsequently by several other broadcasters.

and awa-a-aay we go! On the *Jackie Gleason Show* on US television (1952–70), the rotund comic hosted variety acts, and used this phrase to lead into the first sketch. He had a special pose to accompany it – head turned to face left, one leg raised ready to shoot off in the same direction. Gleason's other stock (perhaps catch) phrases were **how sweet it is!, baby, you're the greatest!, one of these days . . . one of these days . . .** , and **pow! right in the kisser!** He also popularized the word **labonza** for posterior, as in 'a kick in the labonza'. In *The Life of Riley* (1949–50), Gleason's phrase in the light of any stroke of fate was **what a revoltin' development this is!** though this appears to have been taken over by William Bendix, who followed him in the part.

and Death shall have no dominion. The title of the notable poem (1936) on immortality by Dylan Thomas is a straightforward allusion to Romans 6:9: 'Christ being raised from the dead dieth no more: death hath no more dominion over him.'

and even your best friends won't tell you. See EVEN YOUR BEST . . .

and I don't mean maybe! An intensifier, to show that the speaker has just issued a command, not simply expressed a wish. Mencken lists it as an 'American saying *c* 1920'. The second line of the song 'Yes, Sir, That's My Baby' (*c* 1922) is: '. . . No, sir, don't mean maybe'. OED2 has it by 1926 (and in James Joyce, *Anna Livia Plurabelle*, 1928).

and in a packed programme tonight . . . A worn-out TV presentation phrase gently mocked by Ronnie Barker at the start of the BBC TV comedy show *The Two Ronnies* (1971–88). Compare his similar mocking of the dual presenters' IT'S GOODNIGHT FROM ME . . .

and I wish I was dead! See NOW THERE'S A BEAUT . . .

and justice for all. Phrase comes from the Pledge of Allegiance to the Flag (put into its final form by Francis Bellamy in 1892): 'I pledge allegiance to the flag of the United States of America and to the republic for which it stands, one nation under God, indivisible, with liberty and justice for all.' The idea of 'justice for all' is, however, one that goes back to the Greeks. It also gave rise to the remark by Lord Justice Sir James Mathew (*d* 1908): 'In England, justice is open to all, like the Ritz Hotel.' *And Justice for All* was the title of a film (1979) about the US legal system.

and now a word from our sponsor. One of the various ways of getting into a commercial break, taken from American radio and television and much employed in British parodies of same in the 1950s/60s – though never used in earnest in the UK (for the simple reason that sponsored TV of this type has not yet been allowed).

and now for something completely different . . . Catchphrase from MONTY PYTHON'S FLYING CIRCUS and used as the title of the comedy team's first cinema feature in 1971. Usually delivered by John Cleese as a dinner-jacketed BBC announcer, seated before a microphone on a desk in some unlikely setting, the phrase was taken from a slightly arch 'link' much loved by magazine programme presenters. These people were thus deprived of a very useful phrase. When introducing BBC Radio 4's breakfast-time *Today* programme in the mid-1970s, I sorely regretted this. After all, if you are introducing a magazine programme there is not much else you can say to get from an interview with the Prime Minister to an item about beer-drinking budgerigars. The children's BBC TV series *Blue Peter* is sometimes said to have provoked the *Python* use of the phrase.

It was first delivered by Eric Idle in the second edition of *Python* (on 12 October 1969), though it had also featured in some of the same team's earlier series *At Last the 1948 Show* (ITV, 1967).

and now, her nibs, Miss Georgia Gibbs! The standard introduction to the singer of that name on the US radio show *The Camel Caravan* (1943–7).

and so to bed. Samuel Pepys's famous signing-off line for his diary entries appears first on 15 January 1660. However, on that particular occasion, they are not quite his last words. He writes: 'I went to supper, and after that to make an end of this week's notes in this book, and so to bed.' Then he adds: 'It being a cold day and a great snow, my physic did not work so well as it should have done'. *And So To Bed* was the title of a play (1926) by J.B. Fagan, which was then turned into a musical (by Vivian Ellis, 1951).

and so we say farewell . . . The travelogues made by James A. Fitzpatrick (*b* 1902) were a supporting feature of cinema programmes from 1925 onwards. With the advent of sound, the commentaries to 'Fitzpatrick Traveltalks' became noted for their closing words:

And it's from this paradise of the Canadian Rockies that we reluctantly say farewell to Beautiful Banff . . .

And as the midnight sun lingers on the skyline of the city, we most reluctantly say farewell to Stockholm, Venice of the North . . .

With its picturesque impressions indelibly fixed in our memory, it is time to conclude our visit and reluctantly say farewell to Hong Kong, the hub of the Orient . . .

Frank Muir and Denis Norden's notable parody of the genre – 'Bal-ham – Gateway to the South' – first written for radio *c* 1948 and later performed on record by Peter Sellers (1958) accordingly contained the words, 'And so we say farewell to this historic borough . . .'

Compare SO, FAREWELL THEN.

and that ain't hay! Meaning, 'And that's not to be sniffed at/that isn't negligible,' usually with reference to money. The title of the 1943 Abbott and Costello film which is said to have popularized this (almost exclusively US) exclamation was *It Ain't Hay*. But in the same year, Mickey Rooney exclaimed 'And that ain't hay!' as he went into the big 'I Got Rhythm' number (choreographed by Busby Berkeley) in the film *Girl Crazy* (the scene being set, appropriately, in an agricultural college).

and that, my dears, is how I came to marry your grandfather. As though at the end of a long and rambling reminiscence by an old woman. Also used by the American humorist Robert Benchley (1889–1945) – possibly in capsule criticism of the play *Abie's Irish Rose* – and so quoted by Diana Rigg in *No Turn Unstoned* (1982).

and that's the top of the news as it looks from here! Sign-off of Fulton Lewis Jnr (1903–66), the American radio newscaster of the 1930s and 40s.

and that's the way it is. The authoritative but avuncular TV anchorman, Walter Cronkite (*b* 1916), retired from anchoring the CBS TV *Evening News* after 19 years – for most of which he had concluded with these words.

On the final occasion, he said: 'And that's the way it is, Friday March 6, 1981. Goodnight.'

and the best of luck! Ironic encouragement. Frankie Howerd, the comedian (?1917–92), claimed in his autobiography, *On the Way I Lost It* (1976), to have given this phrase to the language: 'It came about when I introduced into radio *Variety Bandbox* [late 1940s] those appallingly badly sung mock operas starring . . . Madame Vera Roper (soprano) . . . Vera would pause for breath before a high C and as she mustered herself for this musical Everest I would mutter, "And the best of luck!" Later it became, **"And the best of British luck**!" The phrase is so common now that I frequently surprise people when I tell them it was my catchphrase on *Variety Bandbox*.'

Partridge/*Catch Phrases* suggests, however, that the 'British' version had already been a Second World War army phrase meaning the exact opposite of what it appeared to say, and compares it with a line from a First World War song: 'Over the top with the best of luck/Parley-voo' (though that was not ironic).

and the next object is —. In the radio quiz *Twenty Questions*, broadcast by the BBC from 1947 to 1976, a mystery voice – most memorably Norman Hackforth's – would inform listeners in advance about the object the panellists would then try to identify by asking no more than twenty questions. Hackforth would intone in his deep, fruity voice: 'And the next object is "The odour in the larder" [or some such poser].'

The game appears to have been based on a popular nineteenth-century parlour game. See ANIMAL, VEGETABLE OR MINERAL.

and the next *Tonight* will be tomorrow night . . . The stock concluding phrase of the original BBC TV early evening magazine *Tonight* (1957–65). Cliff Michelmore, who used to say 'And the next *Tonight* will be tomorrow night . . . good night!', told me in 1979: 'The combined brains of Alasdair Milne, Donald Baverstock, myself and three others were employed to come up with the phrase.

There were at least ten others tried and permed. At least we cared . . . !'

and thereby hangs a tale. As a story-telling device, this is still very much in use to indicate that some tasty titbit is about to be revealed. It occurs a number of times in Shakespeare. In *As You Like It*, II.vii.28 (1598) Jaques, reporting the words of a motley fool (Touchstone), says:

> And so from hour to hour, we ripe and ripe,
> And then, from hour to hour, we rot and rot:
> And thereby hangs a tale.

Other examples occur in *The Merry Wives of Windsor* (I.iv.143) and *The Taming of the Shrew* (IV.i.50). In *Othello* (III.i.8), the Clown says, 'O, thereby hangs a tail,' emphasizing the innuendo that may or may not be present in the other examples.

and there's more (where that came from). In the GOON SHOW, this was sometimes said by Major Denis Bloodnok (Peter Sellers) and occasionally by Wallace Greenslade (a BBC staff announcer who, like his colleague, John Snagge, was allowed to let his hair down on the show). Possibly it was also said by Moriarty and others, too?

The origins of the phrase probably lie in some music-hall comedian's patter, uttered after a particular joke had gone well. Charles Dickens in Chapter 11 of *Martin Chuzzlewit* (1843–44) shows that the phrase was established in other contexts first: 'Mr Jonas filled the young ladies' glasses, calling on them not to spare it, as they might be certain there was plenty more where that came from.'

Jimmy Cricket, a British comedian, was exclaiming simply, 'And there's *more*!', by 1986.

and they all lived happily ever after. The traditional ending to 'fairy' tales is not quite so frequently used as ONCE UPON A TIME, but it is (more or less) present in five of *The Classic Fairy Tales* gathered in their earliest known English forms by Iona and Peter Opie (1974). 'Jack and the Giants' (c 1760) ends: 'He and his Lady lived the Residue of their Days in great Joy and Happiness.' 'Jack and the Bean-Stalk' (1807) ends: 'His mother and he lived together a great many years, and continued always to be very happy.'

A translation of 'Snow White and the Seven Dwarfs' by the brothers Grimm (1823) ends: 'Snow-drop and the prince lived and reigned happily over that land many many years.' From the same year, a translation of 'The Frog-Prince' ends: 'They arrived safely, and lived happily a great many years.' A Scottish version of 'Cinderella' (collected 1878) has: 'They lived happily all their days.'

The concluding words of Winston Churchill's *My Early Life* (1930) are: '. . . September 1908, when I married and lived happily ever afterwards.'

and this is what you do! See under MORNING ALL!

and this is where the story *really* begins. See under GOON SHOW.

and this too shall pass away. As Abraham Lincoln explained in an address to the Wisconsin State Agricultural Society (1859): 'An Eastern monarch once charged his wise men to invent him a sentence to be ever in view, and which should be true and appropriate in all times and situations. They presented him with the words, "And this, too, shall pass away." How much it expresses! How chastening in the hour of pride! How consoling in the depths of affliction!'

But who was the oriental monarch? Benham (1948) says the phrase was an inscription on a ring (according to an oriental tale) and the phrase was given by Solomon to a Sultan who 'desired that the words should be appropriate at all time'. The next year, 1860, Nathaniel Hawthorne wrote in *The Marble Faun* of the 'greatest mortal consolation, which we derive from the transitoriness of all things – from the right of saying, in every conjuncture, "This, too, will pass away."'

and when did you last see your father? There can be few paintings where the title is as important as (and as well known as) the actual picture. This one was even turned into a tableau at Madame Tussaud's where it remained until 1989. It was in 1878 that

William Frederick Yeames RA first exhibited his painting with this title at the Royal Academy; the original is now in the Walker Art Gallery, Liverpool.

The title of the painting has become a kind of joke catchphrase, sometimes used nudgingly, and often allusively – as in the title of Christopher Hampton's 1964 play *When Did You Last See My Mother?* and the 1986 farce by Ray Galton and John Antrobus, *When Did You Last See Your . . . Trousers?* Tom Lubbock writing in the *Independent On Sunday* (8 November 1992) commented on the fact that the title tends to be remembered wrongly: 'But the *And* matters. It turns the title from an abrupt demand into a slyly casual inquiry . . . [But] the title will probably outlast the image, just as a form of words that rings some distant bell. On green cashpoint screens you now find the query "When did you last update your insurance?" I'm sure the forgotten Yeames is ultimately responsible.'

and when the music stops . . . See under ARE YOU SITTING COMFORTABLY? . . .

and why not? A verbal tic of the British broadcaster Barry Norman who has been reviewing films on BBC TV since the 1970s with a conversational, colloquial style. This particular phrase – if he ever actually said it – was seized upon *c* 1986 by the impressionist Rory Bremner who turned it into Norman's hallmark.

and with that, I return you to the studio. See under BEYOND OUR KEN.

Angel of Death, the. A nickname bestowed in the Second World War upon Dr Joseph Mengele, the German concentration camp doctor who experimented on inmates – 'for his power to pick who would live and die in Auschwitz by the wave of his hand' (*Time*, 17 June 1985).

'Angel of death' as an expression for a bringer of ill is not a biblical phrase and does not appear to have arisen until the eighteenth century. Samuel Johnson used it in *The Rambler* in 1752.

angels one five. In Royal Air Force jargon, 'angels' means height measured in units of a thousand feet; 'one five' stands for fifteen; so '20 MEs at Angels One Five' means 'Twenty Messerschmitts at 15,000 feet'. *Angels One Five* was the title of a film (UK, 1952) about RAF fighter pilots during the Second World War.

angles. See KNOW ALL THE ~ .

Anglo-Saxon attitudes. Typically English behaviour. The title of Angus Wilson's novel (1956) about a historian investigating a possible archaeological forgery comes from Lewis Carroll's *Through the Looking Glass*, Chap. 7 (1872). Alice observes the Messenger 'skipping up and down, and wriggling like an eel, as he came along'. When she expresses surprise, the King explains: 'He's an Anglo-Saxon Messenger – and those are Anglo-Saxon attitudes.' Harry Morgan Ayres in *Carroll's Alice* suggests that the author may have been spoofing the Anglo-Saxon scholarship of his day.

angry young man, an. Any writer from the mid-1950s who showed a social awareness and expressed dissatisfaction with conventional values and with the ESTABLISHMENT – John Osborne, Kingsley Amis and Colin Wilson among them – was likely to be so labelled.

Leslie Paul, a social philosopher, had called his autobiography *Angry Young Man* in 1951, but the popular use of the phrase stems from *Look Back in Anger*, the 1956 play by John Osborne which featured an anti-hero called Jimmy Porter. The phrase did not occur in the play but was applied to the playwright by George Fearon in publicity material from the Royal Court Theatre, London. Fearon later told the *Daily Telegraph* (2 October 1957): 'I ventured to prophesy that [Osborne's] generation would praise his play while mine would, in general, dislike it . . . "If this happens," I told him, "you would become known as the Angry Young Man." In fact, we decided then and there that henceforth he was to be known as that.'

animals. See ALL ~ ARE EQUAL . . . ; NEVER WORK WITH CHILDREN OR ~ .

animal, vegetable and/or mineral. Not a quotation from anyone in particular, merely a way of describing three types of matter. And yet, why does the phrase trip off the tongue so? Edward Phillips, *The New World of English Words* (ed. Kersey)(1706) has: 'Chymists . . . call the three Orders of Natural Bodies, viz. Animal, Vegetable, and Mineral, by the name of Kingdoms.' But why not 'animal, *mineral*, vegetable'? Or '*vegetable*, animal, mineral'? Perhaps because these variants are harder to say, although in W.S. Gilbert's lyrics for *The Pirates of Penzance* (1879), Major-General Stanley does manage to sing:

> But still in matters vegetable, animal, and mineral,
> I am the very model of a modern Major-General.

For BBC television viewers, the order was clearly stated in the title of the long-running archaeological quiz *Animal, Vegetable, Mineral?* (established by 1956) in which eminent university dons had to identify ancient artefacts just by looking at them.

The trio of words was also evoked in the long-running radio series *Twenty Questions*. This originated on the Mutual Radio Network in the US in 1946, having been created by Fred Van De Venter and family – who transferred with the show to NBC TV, from 1949 to 1955. The programme ran on BBC radio from 1947 to 1976, though I'm not sure it was ever tried out on British TV. Panellists simply had to guess the identity of a 'mystery object' by asking up to twenty questions. A fourth category – 'abstract' – was added later. In 1973/4 I recall taking part as a panellist in a version of the game made for BBC World Service which was actually called *Animal, Vegetable or Mineral*.

The key to the matter is that the original American show was admittedly based on the old parlour game of 'Animal, Vegetable [and/or] Mineral'. This seems to have been known on both sides of the Atlantic in the nineteenth century. In *Charles Dickens: His Tragedy and Triumph* by Edgar Johnson, we find (1839–41): 'Dickens was brilliant in routing everybody at "Animal, Vegetable, or Mineral", although he himself failed to guess a vegetable object mentioned in "mythological history" and belonging to a queen, and was chagrined to have it identified as the tarts made by the Queen of Hearts.'

In the same book, in a chapter on the period 1858–65, we also read: '[Dickens] was swift and intuitive in "Twenty Questions" . . . On one occasion, he failed to guess "The powder in the Gunpowder Plot", although he succeeded in reaching Guy Fawkes.'

Presumably, then, the game was known by both names, though Dickens also refers to a version of it as 'Yes and No' in *A Christmas Carol* (1843). 'Twenty Questions' is referred to as such in a letter from Hannah Moore as early as 1786. Yet another name for this sort of game (by 1883) appears to have been 'clumps' or 'clubs'.

Animated Meringue, the. Nickname of Barbara Cartland (*b* 1901), British romantic novelist and health food champion, who employs a chalky style of make-up in addition to driving around in a pink and white Rolls-Royce. She was thus dubbed by Arthur Marshall who said that far from taking offence, Miss Cartland sent him a telegram of thanks.

Anne. See QUEEN ~'S DEAD.

Annie. See LITTLE ORPHAN ~; UP IN ~'S ROOM . . .

another. See THERE'LL NEVER BE ~.

another country. Julian Mitchell's play *Another Country* (1981; film UK, 1984) shows how the seeds of defection to Soviet Russia were sown in a group of boys at an English public school. The title comes not, as might be thought, from the celebrated line in Christopher Marlowe's *The Jew of Malta* (*c* 1592):

Fornication: but that was in another country;

And besides the wench is dead.

Rather, as the playwright has confirmed to me, it is taken from the second verse of Sir Cecil Spring Rice's patriotic 'Last Poem' (1918), which begins 'I vow to thee, my country' and continues:

And there's another country, I've heard of long ago –
Most dear to them that love her, most great to them that know.

In the original context, the 'other country' is Heaven, rather than the Soviet Union, of course. *Another Country* had earlier been used as the title of a novel (1962) by James Baldwin.

another day – another dollar! What one says to oneself at the conclusion of toil. Obviously of American origin, but now as well known in the UK where there does not appear to be an equivalent expression using 'pound' instead of 'dollar'. Partridge/*Catch Phrases* dates it from the 1940s in the UK and from *c* 1910 in the US.

another little drink wouldn't do us any harm. This boozer's jocular justification for another snort is, in fact, rather more than a catchphrase. Allusion is made to it in Edith Sitwell's bizarre lyrics for 'Scotch Rhapsody' in *Façade* (1922):

There is a hotel at Ostend
Cold as the wind, without an end,
Haunted by ghostly poor relations . . .
And 'Another little drink wouldn't do us any harm,'
Pierces through the sabbatical calm.

The actual origin is in a song with the phrase as title, written by Clifford Grey to music by Nat D. Ayer, and sung by George Robey in the show *The Bing Boys Are Here* (1916). It includes a reference to the well-known fact that Prime Minister Asquith was at times the worse for drink when on the Treasury Bench:

Mr Asquith says in a manner sweet and calm:
And another little drink wouldn't do us any harm.

another opening, another show! Show business exclamation – possibly said ironically, as with ON WITH THE MOTLEY! 'Another Op'nin, Another Show' is the title of a song sung by the members of a theatrical troupe in Cole Porter's musical *Kiss Me Kate* (1948).

another page turned in the book of life, that's. One of the numerous clichés of bereavement, designed to keep the awfulness of death at bay by means of comfortingly trite remarks. However, the notion of life as a book whose pages turn can be invoked on other occasions as well. On 1 September 1872, the Rev. Francis Kilvert wrote in his diary: 'Left Clyro for ever. A chapter of life closed and a leaf in the Book of Life turned over.' In its original biblical sense, the said book is a record of those who will inherit eternal life (as in Philippians 4:3 and Revelation 20:12).

answer. See I THINK THE ∼ LIES IN THE SOIL under *BEYOND OUR KEN*; LOVE IS THE ∼ ; 'NO ∼' CAME THE STERN REPLY; THERE'S NO ∼ TO THAT! under *MORECAMBE AND WISE SHOW*.

Anthony Eden, an. A black felt hat – also known as a Homburg, after the German health spa – popularized in the 1930s by Anthony Eden (later Lord Avon) when he was Foreign Secretary and one of the best-dressed members of the House of Commons.

any colour so long as it's black. An expression to convey that there is no choice, this originated with Henry Ford who is supposed to have said it about the Model T Ford which came out in 1909. Hill and Nevins in *Ford: Expansion and Challenge* (1957) have him saying: 'People can have it any colour – so long as it's black.' However, in 1925, the company had to bow to the inevitable and offer a choice of colours.

any gum, chum? Remark addressed to American G.I.s in Britain during the Second World War. Norman Longmate, *How We Lived Then* (1971): 'Crowds of small boys gathered outside American clubs to pester them for gifts, or called out as American lorries passed: "Any gum, chum?" which rapidly became a national catchphrase.'

any more fer sailing? See BY GUM; SHE'S A . . .

anyone for tennis? This perkily expressed inquiry from a character entering through

French windows and carrying a tennis racquet has become established as typical of the 'teacup' theatre of the 1920s and 1930s (as also in the forms **who's for tennis?** and **tennis, anyone?**). A clear example of it being used has proved elusive, however, although there is any number of near misses. The opening lines of Part II of Strindberg's *Dance of Death* (1901) are (in translation): 'Why don't you come and play tennis?' A *very* near miss occurs in the first act of Shaw's *Misalliance* (1910) in which a character asks: 'Anybody on for a game of tennis?' An informant assures me that the line was used in one of the shows presented by Edward Laurillard and George Grossmith – which must have been in the years 1914–21. Gladys Cooper is held definitely to have said it the musical *The Dollar Princess* (1909), but there is no tangible evidence for this. Teddie in Somerset Maugham's *The Circle* (1921) always seems on the verge of saying it, but only manages, 'I say, what about this tennis?' Myra in Noel Coward's *Hay Fever* (1925) says, 'What a pity it's raining, we might have had some tennis.' Another informant suggested it could be found in Terence Rattigan's *French Without Tears* (1936) – which sounded a very promising source – but it does not occur in the printed text.

Perhaps it was just another of those phases which was never actually said in the form popularly remembered. Unfortunately, a terrible wild-goose chase was launched by Jonah Ruddy and Jonathan Hill in their book *Bogey: The Man, The Actor, The Legend* (1965). Describing Humphrey Bogart's early career as a stage actor (c 1921) they said: 'In those early Broadway days he didn't play menace parts. "I always made my entrance carrying a tennis racquet, baseball bat, or golf club. I was the athletic type, with hair slicked back and wrapped in a blazer. The only line I didn't say was, 'Give me the ball, coach, I'll take it through.' Yes, sir, I was Joe College or Joe Country Club all the time."

'It was hard to imagine him as the originator of that famous theatrical line – "Tennis anyone?" – but he was.'

It is clear from this extract that the authors were merely adding their own gloss to what Bogart had said. Bartlett (1968)

joined in and said it was his 'sole line in his first play'. But Bogart (who died in 1957) had already denied ever saying it (quoted in Goodman, *Bogey: The Good-Bad Boy* and in an ABC TV film of 1974 using old film of him doing so). Alistair Cooke in *Six Men* (1977) is more cautious: 'It is said he appeared in an ascot and blue blazer and tossed off the invitation Tennis, anyone?' – and adds that Bogart probably did not coin the phrase.

In British show business, it has been suggested that Leon Quatermaine, a leading man of the 1920s and 30s, was the first man to say the phrase. Alan Melville, the playwright and revue artist, commented (1983): 'I know who *claimed* to have said it in a play first: Freddy Lonsdale. But he was such a delightful liar he probably invented the invention. Years ago, just after the war, down in the South of France, he maintained that he'd first put it in a play – when quizzed, he couldn't remember which one – and was quite miffed that it had gone into general circulation without due acknowledgement being made to him as the creator.' Alas, Frances Donaldson, Lonsdale's daughter, told me in 1983 that she was pretty sure he hadn't coined the phrase – or even used it, as 'it's not his style'.

In the form 'Anyone for tennis?' the phrase was used by J.B. Priestley as the title of a 1968 television play, and in 1981 it was converted into *Anyone for Denis?* by John Wells as the title of a farce guying Margaret Thatcher's husband.

any port in a storm. Meaning, metaphorically, 'any roof over your head is better than none' or 'you can't be choosy in adversity'. The phrase makes an early appearance in John Cleland's *Fanny Hill* (1749): 'I feeling pretty sensibly that it [her lover's wherewithal] was going by the right door, and knocking desperately at the wrong one, I told him of it: "Pooh, says he, my dear, any port in a storm."'

anything can happen and probably will. See under TAKE IT FROM HERE.

anything for the weekend, sir? See SOMETHING FOR THE ~.

anything you say may be taken down and used in evidence against you. The police 'caution' to a person who may be charged with a crime has had various forms in the UK. The version you might expect from reading fiction would go something like: 'You are not obliged to say anything unless you wish to do so but, I must warn you, whatever you do say will be taken down and may be given in evidence *against you.*' But this does not conform with modern practice. British police are advised that care should be taken to avoid any suggestion that evidence might only be used *against* a person, as this could prevent an innocent person making a statement which might help clear him of a charge.

Old habits die hard, however. The phrase is etched on the national consciousness, and it must have been said at one time. Charles Dickens in *Our Mutual Friend* (1864–5) has Mr Inspector (an early example of a police officer in fiction) give 'the caution' (which he refers to as such) in these words: 'It's my duty to inform you that whatever you say, will be used against you' (Bk. 4, Chap. 12). Examples of the 'against you' caution also appear in Sherlock Holmes short stories by Conan Doyle (1905 and 1917).

In the US, the phrase may still be found. In *Will* (1980), G. Gordon Liddy describes what he said during a raid on Dr Timothy Leary's house in connection with drugs charges (in March 1966): 'I want you to understand that you don't have to make any statement, and any statement you do make may be used against you in a court of law.' A decision in the US Supreme Court (*Miranda v. Arizona*, 1966) – known as the Miranda Decision – requires law enforcement officials to tell anyone taken into custody that, *inter alia*, anything the person says can be used against them.

any time, any place, anywhere. A line from Martini ads since the early 1970s. Barry Day of the McCann-Erickson advertising agency which coined the phrase agrees there is more than a hint of Bogart in the line, but adds: 'As a Bogart fan of some standing, with my union dues all paid up, I think I would have known if I had lifted from one of his utterances, but I honestly can't place it.' Possibly there is a hint of

Harry Lime, too. In the film *The Third Man* (1949), Lime says (in the run-up to the famous cuckoo-clock speech): 'When you make up your mind, send me a message – I'll meet you any place, any time . . . ' Two popular songs of the 1920s were 'Anytime, Any Day, Anywhere' and 'Anytime, Anywhere, Any Place – I Don't Care'. The exact phrase 'any time, any place, anywhere' had occurred earlier, however, in the song 'I Love To Cry at Weddings' from the musical *Sweet Charity* (1966).

In April 1987, a woman called Marion Joannou was jailed at the Old Bailey for protecting the man who had strangled her husband. She was nicknamed 'Martini Marion' because, apparently, she would have sex 'any time, any place, anywhere'.

a-okay. Another way of saying 'OK' or 'All systems working'. From NASA engineers in the early days of the US space programme 'who used to say it during radio transmission tests because the sharper sound of A cut through the static better than O' (Tom Wolfe, THE RIGHT STUFF, 1979). Now largely redundant, it seems never to have been used by astronauts themselves. President Reagan, emerging from a day of medical tests at a naval hospital in June 1986, pronounced himself 'A-OK'. Another derivation is a melding of 'A1' and 'OK'.

appeal. See LAST ~ TO REASON.

appeals. See CHILD IN ALL OF US . . .

'appen. 'It may happen, happen it may, maybe, perhaps' – a North of England dialect expression, used for example by Uncle Mort (Robin Bailey), the scuffling, seedy, old misogynist in Peter Tinniswood's funereal Yorkshire comedy series *I Didn't Know You Cared* (BBC TV, 1975).

apple. See BIG ~ .

apple of one's eye, the. What one cherishes most. The pupil of the eye has long been known as the 'apple' because of its supposed round, solid shape. To be deprived of the apple is to be blinded and lose something extremely valuable. The

Bible has: 'He kept him as the apple of his eye' (Deuteronomy 32:10).

apple pie. See AMERICAN AS ~ .

apple-pie order, in. Meaning 'with everything in place; smart', this expression (known since 1780) possibly derives from the French *cap-à-pied*, wearing armour 'from head to foot'. Another suggested French origin is from *nappe pliée*, a folded tablecloth or sheet (though this seems a more likely source for the term **apple-pie bed**, known since 1781, for one made so that you can't get into it). On the other hand, a folded cloth or napkin does convey the idea of crispness and smartness.

appointment in Samarra, an. An appointment with Death, or one which simply cannot be avoided. The novel *Appointment in Samarra* (1934) by John O'Hara alludes to the incident – described also by W. Somerset Maugham in his play *Sheppey* (1933) – in which a servant is jostled by Death in the market at Baghdad. Terrified, he jumps on a horse and rides to Samarra (a city in northern Iraq) where he thinks Death will not be able to find him. When the servant's master asks Death why he treated him in this manner, Death replies that he had merely been surprised to encounter the servant in Baghdad . . . 'I had an appointment with him tonight in Samarra.'

appreciate. See 2-4-6-8, WHO DO WE ~ .

après nous le déluge [after us, the flood]. The Marquise de Pompadour's celebrated remark to Louis XV was made on 5 November 1757 after Frederick the Great had defeated the French and Austrian armies at the Battle of Rossbach. It carries with it the suggestion that nothing matters once you are dead and has also been interpreted as a premonition of the French Revolution. Bartlett notes that this 'reputed reply' by the king's mistress was recorded by three authorities, though a fourth gives it to the king himself. Bartlett then claims the saying was not original anyway, but 'an old French proverb'. However, the *ODP* has as an English proverb, 'After us the deluge', deriving from Mme de Pompadour. Its only citation is Burnaby's 1876 *Ride to Khiva*: 'Our rulers did not trouble their heads much about the matter. "India will last my time . . . and after me the Deluge."' Metternich, the Austrian diplomat and chancellor, may later have said '*après moi le déluge*', meaning that everything would grind to a halt when he stopped controlling it. The deluge alluded to in both cases may be a dire event like the Great Flood or 'universal deluge' of Noah's time.

Aquarius. See AGE OF ~.

Arabs. See FOLD ONE'S TENT LIKE THE ~.

Arcadia ego, et in. This inscription on a tomb means either that, in death, the dead person is in Arcadia, or that he was formerly there. '*Et in Arcadia ego vixi*' [I lived] or '*Et in Arcadia fui pastor*' [I was a shepherd] are variants. Or, more likely, it is Death itself speaking – 'Even in Arcadia, I, Death, cannot be avoided.' Arcadia is the Greek name for a place of rural peace and calm taken from an actual area in the Peloponnese but used generally since classical times. '*Et in Arcadia ego*' is a phrase associated with tombs, skulls and Arcadian shepherds in classical paintings, but not before the seventeenth century. Most notably the phrase occurs in two paintings by the French artist Nicolas Poussin (1594–1665), both of which depict shepherds reading the words carved on a tomb.

Archers, The. The BBC's agricultural soap opera – **an everyday story of country-folk** – has been running on national radio since 1951. The nearest it has come to a catchphrase has been **oooo arr, me ol' pal, me ol' beauty!** said distinctively by Chriss Gittins (d 1988) in the part of the old yokel Walter Gabriel (and, no doubt, adopted from traditional yokel-ese). The phrase was already established by June 1961 when Tony Hancock as Joshua in a TV parody called *The Bowmans* had the line, 'Me old pal, me old beauty.'

Norman Painting, who has written many of the episodes as well as playing Phil Archer throughout the existence of the series, said in 1983 that a number of expository cliché/catchphrases have crept in, namely, **why are you telling me all this?** and **I see what you mean.**

aren't plums cheap? Catchphrase of the British music-hall 'Naval Comic', Bob Nelson, of whom no other information is to hand. In *The Bandsman's Daughter* (1979), Irene Thomas recalls 'one comedian acrobat who towards the end of his act used to do a handstand balanced on the back of a chair. Then, upside down, he'd turn his poor old beetroot coloured face towards the audience and croak, *apropos* nothing, "Aren't plums cheap today?"'

aren't we all? In Frederick Lonsdale's play *Aren't We All?* (1924) – the title proving that the phrase was well established by then – the Vicar says, 'Grenham, you called me a bloody old fool,' and Lord Grenham replies, 'But aren't we all, old friend?' Ray Henderson composed the song 'I'm a Dreamer, Aren't We All' in 1929. The collusive use has possibly weakened and the phrase become a simple jokey retort or a way of coping with an unintentional *double entendre*: 'I'm afraid I'm coming out of my trousers' – 'Aren't we all, dear, aren't we all?'

Compare THERE'S A LOT OF IT ABOUT.

are there any more at home like you? Partridge/*Catch Phrases* traces this chat-up line to the musical comedy *Floradora* (1899) which contains the song (written by Leslie Stuart), 'Tell Me, Pretty Maiden (Are There Any More At Home Like You?)' Partridge adds that the line was 'obsolete by 1970 – except among those with long memories'. Indeed, Tom Jones may be heard saying it to a member of the audience on the album *Tom Jones Live at Caesar's Palace Las Vegas* (1971).

are we downhearted? – no! A morale-boosting phrase connected with the early stages of the First World War but which had political origins long before that. The politician Joseph Chamberlain said in a 1906 speech: 'We are not downhearted. The only trouble is, we cannot understand what is happening to our neighbours.' The day after he was defeated as candidate in the Stepney Borough Council election of 1909, Clement Attlee, a future British Prime

Minister, was greeted by a colleague with the cry, 'Are we downhearted?' (He replied, 'Of course, we are.') On 18 August 1914, the *Daily Mail* reported: 'For two days the finest troops England has ever sent across the sea have been marching through the narrow streets of old Boulogne in solid colums of khaki . . . waving as they say that new slogan of Englishmen: "Are we downhearted? . . . Nooooo!" "Shall we win? . . . Yessss!"' Horatio Nicholls (Lawrence Wright) incorporated the phrase into a song (1917).

are yer courtin? See under HAVE A GO.

are you all right? Fanny's all right! Stock phrase of the American actress, comedienne and singer, Fanny Brice (1891–1951).

are you going to pardon me? See under RAY'S A LAUGH.

are you looking for a punch up the bracket? See under HANCOCK'S HALF-HOUR.

are you married? See OOOH, YOU ARE AWFUL.

are you now or have you ever been ('a member of the Communist Party')? The stock phrase of McCarthyism, the pursuit and public ostracism of suspected US Communist sympathizers at the time of the war with Korea in the early 1950s. Senator Joseph McCarthy was the instigator of the 'witch hunts' which led to the blacklisting of people in various walks of life, notably the film business. Those appearing at hearings of the House of Representatives Committee on UnAmerican Activities (1947–c 1957) were customarily challenged with the full question. *Are You Now Or Have You Ever Been?* was the title of a radio/stage play (1978) by Eric Bentley.

are you ready, Eddie? Not an immortal slogan, but worth mentioning for what it illustrates about advertising agencies and the way they work. In 1986, *Today*, a new national newspaper using the latest production technology, was launched by Eddie Shah, hitherto known as a union-busting printer and publisher of provincial papers. In its collective wisdom, the Wight Collins Rutherford Scott agency, charged with promoting the new paper's launch, built the whole campaign round the above slogan. Why had they chosen it? Starting with the name 'Eddie' – Mr Shah being thought of as a folk hero in some quarters – the agency found that it rhymed with 'ready'. So the man was featured in TV ads surrounded by his staff being asked this important question.

Unfortunately, the ad agency had zeroed in all too well on the most pertinent aspect of the new paper's launch. *Today* was *not* ready, and the slogan echoed hollowly from the paper's disastrous start to the point at which Mr Shah withdrew to lick his wounds.

The phrase had earlier been used as the title of a track on the Emerson, Lake and Palmer album *Tarkus* (1971), where it referred to the recording engineer, Eddie Offord (to whom it had, presumably been addressed).

The same rhyme occurs in **ready for Freddie**, meaning 'ready for the unexpected, the unknown or the unusual' (*DOAS*), an American phrase that came out of the 'L'il Abner' comic strip in the 1930s. 'Are You Ready for Freddy?' was also used as a slogan to promote *Nightmare on Elm Street – Part 4* (1989) – referring to Freddy Krueger, a gruesome character in the film.

are you sitting comfortably? Then I'll/we'll begin. This was the customary way of beginning stories on BBC radio's daily programme for small children, *Listen with Mother*. The phrase was used from the programme's inception in January 1950. Julia Lang, the original presenter, recalled in 1982: 'The first day it came out inadvertently. I just said it. The next day I didn't. Then there was flood of letters from children saying, "I couldn't listen because I wasn't ready."' It remained a more or less essential part of the proceedings until the programme ended in 1982. In the *Times* obituary (18 January 1988) of Frieda Fordham, an analytical psychologist, it was stated that *she* had actually coined the phrase when advising the BBC's producers.

From the same programme came the

stock phrase **and when it/the music stops,** [Daphne Oxenford, or some other] **will be here to tell you a story.**

arf a mo, Kaiser! A recruiting poster in the First World War showed a British 'Tommy' lighting a pipe prior to going into action, with this caption underneath. The phrase took off from there. I have seen a photograph of a handwritten sign from the start of the Second World War saying, ''Arf a mo, 'itler!'

Argyll. See GOD BLESS THE DUKE OF ∼.

ark. See OUT OF THE ∼.

arm. See IT'S WHAT YOUR RIGHT ∼'S FOR; LONG ∼ OF THE LAW.

armpit. See MAKES YOUR ∼ . . .

arms and the man. The title of George Bernard Shaw's play *Arms and the Man* (1894) comes from the first line of Virgil's *Aeneid*: '*Arma virumque cano*' [Of arms and the man, I sing] or rather from Dryden's translation of the same: 'Arms, and the man I sing.' Earlier, Thomas Carlyle, suggesting in *Past and Present* (1843) that a true modern epic was technological rather than military, had written: 'For we are to bethink us that the Epic verily is not *Arms and the Man*, but *Tools and the Man*.'

Shaw's play was later turned into a musical known as *The Chocolate Soldier* (New York, 1909 – after the original German *Der Tapfere Soldat* [*Brave Soldier*], 1908). The story concerns Captain Bluntschli, a Swiss officer, who gets the better of a professional cavalry soldier. Shaw's phrase for Bluntschli was, rather, 'the **chocolate** cream **soldier**'.

Ian Fleming, the creator of James Bond, was nicknamed the **chocolate sailor** during the Second World War because as a Commander of the RNVR he never actually went to sea.

army. See DAD'S ∼; FORGOTTEN ∼; under F.T.A.; JOIN THE ∼ . . .

army game, the. *The Army Game* was an immensely popular British TV comedy series (1957–62). Its title homed in on a

phrase that seemed to sum up the attitude of those condemned to spend their lives in the ranks. Apparently of American origin, possibly by 1900, 'it's the old army game' refers to the military system as it works to the disadvantage of those in the lower ranks. From Theodore Fredenburgh's *Soldiers March* (1930: 'I get the idea. It's the old army game: first, pass the buck; second, . . . ' Compare **war game** (known by 1900), a theoretical way of fighting battles (and a type of chess). *The War Game* (1965) was the title of a TV film by Peter Watkins that was for a long time not shown because of its vivid depiction of the effect of nuclear war on the civilian population.

See also I ONLY ARSKED.

arrived. See I'VE ∼ AND TO PROVE IT . . . under *EDUCATING ARCHIE.*

arse. See KNOW ONE'S ∼ FROM . . . ; SHINING LIKE A TANNER . . .

ars gratia artis. Motto of the Metro-Goldwyn-Mayer film company since *c* 1916. Howard Dietz, director of publicity and advertising with the original Goldwyn Pictures company, had left Columbia University not long before. When asked to design a trademark, he based it on the university's lion and added the Latin words meaning 'art for art's sake' underneath. The trademark and motto were carried over when Samuel Goldwyn retired to make way for the merger of Metropolitan with the interests of Louis B. Mayer in what has become known since as Metro-Goldwyn-Mayer.

Arthur. See BIG-HEARTED ∼ under *BAND WAGGON.*

Arthur's bosom. A malapropism for ABRAHAM'S BOSOM from Shakespeare's *King Henry V*, II.iii.9, 1599). The Hostess (formerly Mistress Quickly) says of the dead Falstaff: 'Nay, sure, he's not in hell: he's in Arthur's bosom, if ever man went to Arthur's bosom.'

artist descending a staircase. The title of a radio play (1972) by Tom Stoppard, involving three avant-garde artists, is *Artist Descending a Staircase*. It is derived from the titles of Cubo-Futurist or Dadaist paintings by Marcel Duchamp: 'Nude Descending a Staircase 1 & 2' (1911, 1912).

art mistress. See AS THE ∼ SAID . . .

art of the possible, the. What politics is said to be. A phrase used as the title of the memoirs (1971) of R.A. (Lord) Butler, the British Conservative politician. In the preface to the paperback edition of *The Art of the Possible*, Butler noted that this definition of politics appears first to have been used in modern times by Bismarck in 1866. Others who had touched on the idea included Cavour, Salvador de Madriaga, Pindar, and Camus.

arts. See LIVELY ∼.

art thou weary ('art thou languid,/Art thou sore distressed')? From a hymn 'translated from the Greek' by the Revd J.M. Neale (1818–66). Compare: 'Art thou troubled?/Music will calm thee . . . ' – an aria from Handel's opera *Rodelinda* (1725), with libretto by Salvi.

as busy as a one-armed paperhanger with the itch. Mencken listed this in 1942 as an 'American saying' and most similar colourful comparisons must be of American origin. The supply is endless, but here are a few more:

> **as useless as a chocolate kettle** (of a UK football team, quoted on BBC Radio *Quote . . . Unquote* 1986).
> **as scarce as rocking-horse manure** (an example from Australia).
> **as lonely as a country dunny** (ditto).
> **as mad as a gumtree full of galahs** (ditto).
> **as inconspicuous as Liberace at a wharfies' picnic** (ditto).
> **as black as an Abo's arsehole** (ditto).
> **as easy as juggling with soot.**
> **as jumpy as a one-legged cat in a sandbox.**
> **as much chance as a fart in a windstorm.**
> **as much use as a one-legged man at an arse-kicking contest.**
> **as likely as a snowstorm in Karachi.**
> See also CLOCKWORK ORANGE; LIKE

TAKING MONEY FROM BLIND BEGGARS; NO MORE CHANCE THAN A SNOWBALL IN HELL.

as Dorothy Parker once said . . . The title of a stage show (c 1975), devoted to the wit of Dorothy Parker and performed by Libby Morris, is testimony to the fact that Parker is undoubtedly the most quoted woman of the twentieth century. (George Bernard Shaw is probably the most quoted man – though his remarks are usually prefaced with 'I think it was Bernard Shaw who once said . . . ') It is probably an allusion to the verse to Cole Porter's song 'Just One of Those Things' (1935), which begins: 'As Dorothy Parker once said to her boy friend, "Fare thee well" . . .'

'as 'e bin in, whack? *Club Night* was a radio comedy series produced in the BBC's North Region in 1955/6 and was hosted by the pebble-lensed 'manager', Dave Morris. He would be pestered repeatedly by an eccentric figure who asked, ''As 'e bin in, whack?' ('E never 'ad, of course.) Morris also originated the saying **meet the wife – don't laugh!** What the real Mrs Morris thought of this is something we may perhaps never know.

as every schoolboy knows. Robert Burton wrote 'Every schoolboy hath . . .' in *The Anatomy of Melancholy* (1621) and Bishop Jeremy Taylor used the expression 'every schoolboy knows it' in 1654. In the next century, Jonathan Swift used 'to tell what everybody schoolboy knows'. But the most noted user of this rather patronizing phrase was Lord Macaulay, the historian, who would say things like, 'Every schoolboy knows who imprisoned Montezuma, and who strangled Atahualpa' (essay on 'Lord Clive', January 1840). But do they still?

Ashes, the. The 'trophy' played for in Test cricket matches between England and Australia. Whichever side wins is said to have 'retained' or 'regained the Ashes', although the trophy itself never leaves the pavilion at Lord's cricket ground in London. However, it was allowed to be taken to Australia during the country's bicentennial celebrations in 1988. The nickname dates from 1882 when an

Australian team won for the first time in England – by seven runs in an exciting game. A group of supporters of the English team inserted a following mock death notice for 'English cricket' in the *Sporting Times*, concluding, 'The body will be cremated, and the ashes taken to Australia.'

The following winter, when England defeated Australia and retrieved its honour, a group of women in Melbourne burned some straw and placed the ashes in a small urn. They then presented this – saying it contained the ashes of the stumps and bails – to the English captain who duly carried it back to Lord's.

as if I cared . . . From the 1940s BBC radio series *ITMA*. Sam Fairfechan (Hugh Morton) would say, 'Good morning, how are you today?' and immediately add, 'As if I cared . . . ' The character took his name from Llanfairfechan, a seaside resort in North Wales, where Ted Kavanagh, *ITMA*'s scriptwriter, lived when the BBC Variety Department was evacuated to nearby Bangor during the early part of the Second World War.

as it happens. A verbal tic of the British disc jockey Jimmy Savile (later Sir James Savile OBE) (*b* 1926). He used it as the title of his autobiography in 1974. However, when the book came out in paperback it had been changed to *Love is an Uphill Thing* because (or so it was explained) the word 'love' in a title would ensure extra sales.

After dance-hall exposure, Savile began his broadcasting career with Radio Luxembourg in the 1950s. His other stock phrase **how's about that then, guys and gals?** started then. For example, on Radio Luxembourg, *The Teen and Twenty Disc Club*, he certainly said, 'Hi, there, guys and girls, welcome to the . . . '

as I was saying before I was so rudely interrupted . . . A humorous phrase used when resuming an activity after interruption. In September 1946, 'Cassandra' (William O'Connor) resumed his column in the *Daily Mirror* after the Second World War, with: 'As I was saying when I was interrupted, it is a powerful hard thing to please all the people all the time.' In June of that same year, announcer Leslie

Mitchell is reported to have begun BBC TV's resumed transmissions with: 'As I was saying before I was so rudely interrupted.' The phrase sounds as if it might have originated in music-hall routines of the I DON'T WISH TO KNOW THAT, KINDLY LEAVE THE STAGE type. Compare A.A. Milne, *Winnie-the-Pooh* (1926): '"AS – I – WAS – SAYING," said Eeyore loudly and sternly, "as I was saying when I was interrupted by various Loud Sounds, I feel that – ."' Fary Luis de León, the Spanish poet and religious writer, is believed to have resumed a lecture at Salamanca University in 1577 with, '*Dicebamus hesterno die . . .* ' [We were saying yesterday]. He had been in prison for five years.

asked. See I ONLY ARSKED.

ask the Man from the Pru. The Prudential Assurance Co. Ltd was founded in Britain in 1848. The phrase 'The Man from the Pru' evolved naturally from what people would call the person who came to collect their life-insurance premiums. It had become a music-hall joke by the end of the century but there was no serious use of it as a company slogan until the late 1940s, when it appeared in ads as 'Ask the Man from the Pru'.

ask the man who owns one. This slogan for Packard motors, in the US from *c* 1902, originated with James Ward Packard, the founder of the company, and appeared for many years in all Packard advertising and sales material. Someone had written asking for more information about his motors. Packard told his secretary: 'Tell him that we have no literature – we aren't that big yet – but if he wants to know how good an automobile the Packard is, tell him to ask the man who owns one.' A 1903 placard is the first printed evidence of the slogan in use. It lasted for more than 35 years.

as/like the man said. See THAT IS WHAT THE SOLDIER SAID.

as pleased as Punch. The earliest citation for this phrase in *OED2* is in a letter from Thomas Moore to Lady Donegal in 1813: 'I was (AS THE POET SAYS) as pleased as Punch.' Obviously this alludes to the appearance of Mr Punch, a character known in England from the time of the Restoration (1660). As his face is carved on wood, it never changes expression and is always beaming. The *Longman Dictionary of English Idioms* (1979) is thus clearly wrong in attributing the *origin* of the phrase to 'the cheerful pictures of the character Punch, who appeared on the covers of *Punch* magazine in the 1840s'.

Even earlier, there was the expression, **as proud as punch.** A description of a visit by George III and his Queen to Wilton House in 1778 is contained in a letter from a Dr Eyre to Lord Herbert, dated 1 January 1779. He says: 'The Blue Closet within was for her Majesty's private purposes, where there was a red new velvet Close Stool, and a very handsome China Jordan, which I had the honour to produce from an old collection, & you may be sure, I am proud as Punch, that her Majesty condescended to piss in it.'

This version – 'as proud as Punch' – would now seem to have died out, more or less, although Christy Brown, *Down All the Days*, Chap. 17 (1970) has, 'Every man-jack of them sitting there proud as punch with their sons . . . '

as seen on TV. A line used in print advertising to underline the connection with products already shown in TV commercials. Presumably of American origin and dating from the 1940s/50s. Now also used to promote almost anything – books, people – which has had the slightest earlier TV exposure. From *Joyce Grenfell Requests the Pleasure* (1976): 'There was sponge cake of the most satisfactory consistency. Unlike the bready stuff that passes for sponge cake today (machine-made, packaged to be stirred up, as seen on TV) . . . '

as sure as eggs is eggs. Meaning, 'absolutely certain'. *A New Dictionary of the Terms Ancient and Modern of the Canting Crew* by 'B.E.' has 'As sure as eggs be eggs' in 1699. There is no very obvious reason why eggs should be 'sure', unless the saying is a corruption of the mathematician or logician's '*x* is *x*'. But by the eighteenth

century, the saying was being shortened to 'as sure as eggs', which might dispose of that theory.

as the art mistress said to the gardener! Monica (Beryl Reid), the posh schoolgirl friend of Archie Andrews in EDUCATING ARCHIE used this as an alternative to the traditional **as the Bishop said to the actress!** (or *vice versa*) for turning a perfectly innocent preceding remark into a *double entendre* (e.g. 'I've never seen a female "Bottom" . . . as the Bishop said to the actress'). This older phrase was established by 1931 when Leslie Charteris wrote in chapter 13 of *She Was a Lady* (later titled *The Saint Meets His Match*): 'I'm strong for having everything in its right place.'

as the monkey said . . . Introductory phrase to a form of Wellerism. For example, if a child says it can't wait for something, the speaker would comment: 'Well, as the monkey said when the train ran over its tail, "It won't be long now."' According to Partridge/*Slang* there is any number of 'as the monkey said' remarks where there is always a simple pun at stake: e.g. '"They're off!" shrieked the monkey, as he slid down the razor blade.'

as the poet has it/says. Quoter's phrase, exhibiting either a knowing vagueness or actual ignorance. 'As the poet says' was being used in 1608. When Margaret Thatcher was British Prime Minister, she was interviewed on the radio (7 March 1982) about her feelings when her son, Mark, was believed lost on the Trans-Sahara car rally. She realized then, she said, that all the little things people worried about really were not worth it . . . 'As the poet said, "One clear morn is boon enough for being born," and so it is.' (In this case, she might be forgiven for using the phrase, as the authorship of the poem is not known.)

The phrase can also be used to dignify a quotation (rather as PARDON MY FRENCH excuses swearing): P.G. Wodehouse, *Mike* (1909): 'As the poet has it, "Pleasure is pleasure, and biz is biz."'

as the saying is. Boniface, the landlord, in Farquhar's play *The Beaux' Stratagem* (1707) has a curious verbal mannerism. After almost every phrase, he adds, 'As the saying is . . . ', but this was a well-established phrase even then. In 1548, Hugh Latimer in *The Sermon on the Ploughers* had: 'And I fear me this land is not yet ripe to be ploughed. For as the saying is: it lacketh weathering.'

Nowadays, we are probably more inclined to use 'as the saying goes'. Another, less common, form occurs in Mervyn Jones, *John and Mary*, Chap. 1 (1966): 'She gave herself, as the phrase goes. It wouldn't normally be said that I gave myself: I took her, as the phrase goes.'

— as we know it. 'Politics as we know it will never be the same again' – *Private Eye* (4 December 1981). The simple intensifier has long been with us, however. From *Grove's Dictionary of Music* (1883): 'The Song as we know it in his [Schubert's] hands . . . such songs were his and his alone.' From a David Frost/Peter Cook on sport clichés (BBC TV *That Was the Week That Was*, 1962–3 series): 'the ghastly war which was to bring an end to organised athletics as we knew it.'

See also END OF CIVILIZATION AS WE KNOW IT.

as we say in the trade. A slightly self-conscious (even camp) tag after the speaker has uttered a piece of jargon or something unusually grandiloquent. First noticed in the 1960s and probably of American origin. From the record album *Snagglepuss Tells the Story of the Wizard of Oz* (1966): ' "ONCE UPON A TIME", as we say in the trade . . .'

Compare the older **as we say in France** after slipping a French phrase into English speech (from the nineteenth century) – and see also THAT'S YOUR ACTUAL FRENCH.

as you may know or as you may not know. See GOD, WHAT A BEAUTY!

at, where it's. See under — IS THE NAME OF THE GAME.

A-team, the. A group of people brought in to tackle a difficult task and seen as superior to non-existent 'B-' and 'C-' teams. Originally from sports usage, the phrase was reinforced by the American TV series *The A-Team* (which began in 1983) about a group of Vietnam War heroes who go to the aid of various victims of injustice.

at General Electric progress is our most important product. Not a slogan to trip lightly off the tongue, but memorable chiefly because of the man who said it. In 1955, Ronald Reagan became host of the popular programme *General Electric Theatre*. Each edition concluded with him intoning the line.

Athens of the North. A nickname for Edinburgh, presumably earned by the city as a seat of learning, with many long-established educational institutions and a university founded in 1583. When the 'New Town' was constructed in the early 1800s, the city took on a fine classical aspect. As such, it might remind spectators of the Greek capital with its ancient reputation for scholastic and artistic achievement.

Calling the Scottish capital either 'Athens of the North' or 'Modern Athens' seems always to have occasioned some slight unease. James Hannay writing 'On Edinburgh' (*c* 1860), said:

> Pompous the boast, and yet a truth it speaks:
> A Modern Athens – fit for modern Greeks.

Paris has been called the 'Athens of Europe', Belfast the 'Athens of Ireland', Boston, Mass. the 'Athens of the New World', and Cordoba, Spain, the 'Athens of the West'.

at one with the universe. Meaning, 'in harmony with the rest of mankind' or, at least, 'in touch with what is going on in some larger sphere'. When the Quaker George Fox (1624–91) consented to take a puff from a tobacco pipe, he said no one could accused him of 'not being at one with the universe'. Sometimes, the phrase is 'at-oneness with the universe'.

Compare, from Gore Vidal, *Myra Breckinridge*, Chap. 13 (1968): '[With a hangover from gin and marijuana] I lay in that empty bathtub with the two rings, [and] looking up at the single electric light bulb, I did have the sense that I was at one with all creation.'

at play in the fields of the Lord. The title of Peter Matthiessen's novel *At Play In the Fields of the Lord* (1976; film US, 1992) appears to be original. The story tells of American missionaries and mercenaries amid the Amazonian rain forests of Brazil.

at 60 miles an hour the loudest noise in this new Rolls-Royce comes from the electric clock. The best-known promotional line for a motor car was devised not by a copywriter but came from a car test of the 1958 Silver Cloud by the technical editor of *The Motor.* David Ogilvy, who had the idea of using it in advertisement copy, recalls presenting it as a headline to a senior Rolls-Royce executive in New York who shook his head sadly and said: 'We really ought to do something about that damned clock.'

Even the anonymous motoring journalist had not been entirely original. A 1907 review of the Silver Ghost in *The Autocar* read: 'At whatever speed the car is driven, the auditory nerves when driving are troubled by no fuller sound than emanates from the 8-day clock.'

Rolls-Royce originally used as a slogan (and sometimes still do) **the Best Car in the World** (current by 1929, and also quoting a journalist – in a 1908 edition of *The Times.*)

attention all shipping! For many years on BBC radio, the shipping (weather) forecasts were preceded by this call when rough seas were imminent. Then: 'The following Gale Warning was issued by the Meterological Office at 0600 hours GMT today . . .' (or similar).

at the drop of a hat. Originally an American expression meaning, 'at a given signal' – when the dropping of a hat was the signal to start a fight or race. The phrase has come to mean something more like 'without needing encouragement, without delay': 'He'll sit down and write a witty song for you at the drop of a hat.' Hence, the title of a revue *At the Drop of a Hat* (1957) featuring Michael Flanders and Donald Swann – who followed it up with *At the Drop of Another Hat* (1963).

at the end of the day. This must have been a good phrase once – alluding perhaps to the end of the day's fighting or hunting. It appeared, for example, in Donald O'Keeffe's 1951 song, 'At the End of the Day, I Kneel and Pray'. But it was used in epidemic quantities during the 1970s and 1980s, and was particularly beloved of British trade unionists and politicians, indeed anyone wishing to tread verbal water. It was recognized as a hackneyed phrase by 1974, at least.

Anthony Howard, a journalist, interviewing some BBC bigwig in *Radio Times* (March 1982), asked, 'At the end of the day one individual surely has to take responsibility, even if it has to be after the transmission has gone out?'

Patrick Bishop, writing in the *Observer* (4 September 1983), said: 'Many of the participants feel at the end of the day, the effects of the affair [the abortion debate in the Irish Republic] will stretch beyond the mere question of amendment.'

And, Queen Elizabeth II, opening the Barbican Centre in March 1982, also used it. But it *is* the Queen's English, so perhaps she is entitled to do what she likes with it.

at this moment/point in time. i.e. 'now'. Ranks with the previous entry at the top of the colloquial clichés poll. From its periphrastic use of five words where one would do, it would be reasonable to suspect an American origin. Picked up with vigour by British trade unionists in ad lib wafflings, it was already being scorned by 1972/3. Only occasionally to be found committed to paper – e.g. in R. McGowan and J. Hands, *Don't Cry for Me, Sergeant Major* (1983): 'The Marines, of course, had other ideas, but fortune was not favouring them at this moment in time.'

Most clichés, to qualify as such, must have been good phrases once. But there was never any point to this one.

au contraire, mon frère. See under SIMPSONS, THE.

auld lang syne. Meaning 'long ago' (lit. old long since). 'Syne' should be pronounced with an 's' sound and not as 'zyne'. In 1788, Robert Burns adapted 'Auld Lang Syne' from 'an old man's singing'. The title, first line and refrain had all appeared before as the work of other poets. Nevertheless, what Burns put together is what people should sing on New Year's Eve. Here is the first verse and the chorus:

> Should auld acquaintance be forgot,
> And never brought to min[d]?
> Should auld acquaintance be forgot,
> And days of o' lang syne.
> (*Chorus*) For auld lang syne, my dear
> For auld syne,
> We'll take a cup o' kindness yet
> For auld lang syne.

'For *the sake of* auld lang syne' should *not* be substituted at the end of verse and chorus.

aunt. See AGONY ~; MY GIDDY ~.

Aunt Edna. During the revolution in British drama of the 1950s, this term was called into play by the new wave of ANGRY YOUNG dramatists and their supporters to describe the more conservative theatre-goer – the type who preferred comfortable three-act plays of the Shaftesbury Avenue kind.

Ironically, the term had been coined in self-defence by Terence Rattigan, one of the generation of dramatists they sought to replace. In the preface to Vol. II of his *Collected Plays* (1953) he had written of: 'A nice, respectable, middle-class, middle-aged maiden lady, with time on her hands and the money to help her pass it . . . Let us call her Aunt Edna . . . Now Aunt Edna does not appreciate Kafka . . . She is, in short, a hopeless lowbrow . . . Aunt Edna is universal, and to those who may feel that all the problems of the modern theatre might be solved by her liquidation, let me add that . . . she is also immortal.'

Auntie/Aunty BBC (or plain **Auntie/ Aunty**). The BBC was mocked in this way by newspaper columnists, TV critics and her own employees, most noticeably from about 1955 at the start of commercial television – the BBC supposedly being staid, over-cautious, prim and unambitious by comparison. A BBC spokesman countered with, 'An Auntie is often a much-loved member of the family.' The corporation assimilated the nickname to such effect that when arrangements were made to supply wine to BBC clubs in London direct from vineyards in Burgundy, it was bottled under the name *Tantine*.

In 1979, the comedian Arthur Askey suggested that he had originated the term during the BAND WAGGON programme as early as the late 1930s. While quite probable, the widespread use of the nickname is more likely to have occurred at the time suggested above. Wallace Reyburn in his book *Gilbert Harding – A Candid Portrayal* (1978) ascribes the phrase to the 1950s radio and TV personality. The actor Peter Bull in *I Know the Face, But . . .* (1959) writes: 'I would be doing my "nut" and probably my swansong for Auntie BBC.' The politician Iain Macleod used the phrase when editing *The Spectator* in the 1960s. Jack de Manio, the broadcaster, entitled his memoirs *To Auntie With Love* (1967) and the comedian Ben Elton had a BBC TV show *The Man from Auntie* (1990–).

au reservoir! A jokey valediction (a variation of *au revoir*) popularized by E.F. Benson in his *Lucia* novels of the 1920s. It may have existed before this, possibly dating from a *Punch* joke of the 1890s.

Austin Reed service. See IT'S ALL PART OF THE SERVICE.

Australia. See ADVANCE ~ FAIR.

average. See SMARTER THAN THE ~ BEAR.

avoid 'five o'clock shadow'. The expression 'five o'clock shadow' for the stubbly growth that some dark-haired men acquire on their faces towards the end of the day would appear to have originated in adverts for Gem Razors and Blades in the US before the Second World War. A 1937 advert added: 'That unsightly beard growth which appears prematurely at about 5 pm looks bad.'

The most noted sufferer was Richard Nixon, who may have lost the TV debates in his US presidential race against John F. Kennedy in 1960 as a result. In his *Memoirs*

(1978), Nixon wrote: 'Kennedy arrived . . . looking tanned, rested and fit. My television adviser, Ted Rodgers, recommended that I use television make-up, but unwisely I refused, permitting only a little "beard stick" on my perpetual five o'clock shadow.'

avoid — like the plague, to. i.e. to avoid completely, to shun. The *OED2* finds the poet Thomas Moore in 1835 writing, 'Saint Augustine . . . avoided the school as the plague'. The fourth-century St Jerome is also said to have quipped, 'Avoid as you would the plague, a clergyman who is also a man of business.'

A well-established cliché by the mid-twentieth century. It may have been Arthur Christiansen, one of the numerous former editors of the *Daily Express* about that time, who once posted a sign in the office saying: 'ALL CLICHÉS SHOULD BE AVOIDED LIKE THE PLAGUE.'

Avon calling! A slogan first used in the US in 1886. The first Avon Lady, Mrs P.F.A. Allre, was employed by the firm's founder, D.H. McConnell, to visit customers at home and sell them cosmetics.

away. See AND AWA-A-AAY WE GO!; GET ~ FROM IT ALL; UP, UP AND AWA-A-A-AY under *SUPERMAN*.

aw, don't embarrass me! British ventriloquist Terry Hall (b 1926) first created his doll, Lenny the Lion, from a bundle of fox fur and papier-mâché – with a golf ball for a nose – in 1954. He gave his new partner a gentle lisping voice, and added a few mannerisms and a stock phrase which emerged thus:

> He's ferocious! (*drum roll*)
> He's courageous! (*drum roll*)
> He's the king of the jungle! (*drum roll*)
> – Aw, don't embarrass me! (*said with a modest paw over one eye*).

Unusually for the originator of a successful phrase, Terry Hall said (in 1979) that he made sure he did not over use it and rested it from time to time.

awful. See OOOH, YOU ARE ~ . . . .

awkward squad, a member of the. Of military origin and used to denote a difficult, uncooperative person, the phrase originally referred to a squad which consisted of raw recruits and older hands who were put in it for punishment. Sloppy in *Our Mutual Friend* (1864–5) is described by Charles Dickens as 'Full-Private Number One in the Awkward Squad of the rank and file of life'. The dying words of the Scots poet Robert Burns in 1796 are said to have been, 'John, don't let the awkward squad fire over me' – presumably referring to his fear that literary opponents might metaphorically fire a volley of respect, as soldiers sometimes do over a new grave.

AWOL. 'Absent WithOut Leave' – unwarranted absence from the military for a short period, but not desertion. This expression dates from the American Civil War when offenders had to wear a placard with these initials printed on it. During the First World War, the initials were still being pronounced individually. Not until just before the Second World War was it pronounced as the acronym 'Awol'. It does not mean 'absent without *official* leave'.

axe to grind, to have an. The expression meaning 'to have an ulterior motive, a private end to serve', would appear to have originated in an anecdote related by Benjamin Franklin in his essay 'Too Much for Your Whistle'. A man showed interest in young Franklin's grindstone and asked how it worked. In the process of explaining, Franklin – using much energy – sharpened up the visitor's axe for him. This was clearly what the visitor had had in mind all along. Subsequently, Franklin (d 1790) had to ask himself whether other people he encountered had 'another axe to grind'.

Axis Sally. See LORD HAW-HAW.

aye, aye, taxi! See THEY'RE WORKING WELL TONIGHT.

aye, aye, that's yer lot! Jimmy Wheeler (1910–73) was a British Cockney comedian with a fruity voice redolent of beer, jellied eels and winkles. He would appear in a bookmaker's suit, complete with spiv moustache and hat, and play a violin. At the end of his concluding fiddle piece, he would break off his act and intone these words.

aye, caramba! See under SIMPSONS, THE.

ay thang yew! See under BAND WAGGON.

· B ·

Babe, (the). Nickname given to George Herman Ruth (1895–1948), the US professional baseball player. He also became known as the **Sultan of Swat** in about 1920 because of the way he slugged at the ball. There had been a real Sultan (or more properly, Akhoond) of Swat, now part of Pakistan, in the 1870s whose death had given rise to doggerel by Edward Lear. The most popular baseball player in the history of the game was so famous that a battle cry of Japanese soldiers first heard in the Pacific in 1942 was: 'Go to hell, Babe Ruth – American, you die.'

babies scraped. See HEAVENS, ELEVEN O'CLOCK . . .

baby. See BURN, ∼, BURN!; DON'T THROW THE ∼ AWAY . . . ; WHO LOVES YA, ∼?; YOU'VE COME A LONG WAY, ∼.

baby boomer. A person born just after the Second World War during the 'baby boom'. This US term was hardly known in Britain until a 'Baby Boomer' edition of the TRIVIAL PURSUIT board game arrived in 1986. It was intended to appeal to those who had reached maturity during the 1960s. For a while, British journalists took to using the phrase 'baby boom' and even 'baby boomers' in preference to the **bulge** or **post-war bulge** which had been used hitherto (a much better way, surely, to describe a pregnancy-related phenomenon). In fact, both 'baby boom' and 'bulge' had been used to describe the rise in births after the *First* World War and, specifically, the effect this had when those children became of school age. The Japanese also have a phrase for the phenomenon: *dankai no sedai* [the cluster generation].

Baby Ruth. The name of the popular US candy bar does *not* derive from the foregoing BABE Ruth, though one story has

it that the manufacturers had wanted to call the bar a 'Babe Ruth'. They offered him $20,000 but he held out for $50,000. So they settled instead for an approximation and did not have to pay a nickel.

The bar is also said to have taken its name from President Grover Cleveland's daughter, Ruth, who was born in the White House. However, that event took place in 1891 and the bar did not make its first appearance until the 1920s.

More probably, it was thus dubbed by Mrs George Williamson, whose husband was president of the Williamson Candy Company which originally made the bar. As Burnam (1980) suggests, she named it after a granddaughter. Babe Ruth himself had to be content with giving his name to a home run in baseball.

back. See I'LL BE ∼.

backing. See I LIKE THE ∼ under I'LL GIVE IT FOIVE.

bacon. See BRING HOME THE ∼.

backroom boys. A nickname given to scientists and boffins – and specifically to those relied on to produce inventions and new gadgets for weaponry and navigation in the Second World War. Compare *The Small Back Room*, the title of the novel (1943) by Nigel Balchin.

The phrase was originated, in this sense, by Lord Beaverbrook as Minister of Aircraft Production when he paid tribute to his research department in a broadcast on 19 March 1941: 'Let me say that the credit belongs to the boys in the backrooms [*sic*]. It isn't the man who sits in the limelight who should have the praise. It is not the men who sit in prominent places. It is the men in the backrooms.' In the US, the phrase 'backroom boys' can be traced at least to the 1870s, but Beaverbrook can be credited with the modern application to scientific and technical boffins. His inspiration quite obviously was his favourite film *Destry Rides Again* (1939) in which Marlene Dietrich jumped on the bar of the Last Chance saloon and sang the Frank Loesser song 'See What the Boys in the Back Room Will Have'.

back to basics. John Major, the British Prime Minister, launched this ill-fated slogan in a speech to the Conservative Party Conference in 1993: 'The message from this Conference is clear and simple. We must go back to basics . . . The Conservative Party will lead the country back to these basics, right across the board: sound money, free trade; traditional teaching; respect for the family and the law.' A number of government scandals in the ensuing months exposed the slogan as hard to interpret or, at worst, suggesting rather a return to 'the bad old days'.

The alliterative phrase (sometimes 'back to *the* basics') may first have surfaced in the US where it was the mid-1970s slogan of a movement in education to give priority to the teaching of the fundamentals of reading, writing and arithmetic.

backs to the wall, with our. This expression, meaning 'up against it' dates back to 1535 at least, but was memorably used when the Germans launched their last great offensive of the First World War. On 12 April 1918, Sir Douglas Haig, the British Commander-in-Chief on the Western Front, issued an order for his troops to stand firm: 'Every position must be held to the last man: there must be no retirement. With our backs to the wall, and believing in the justice of our cause, each one us must fight on to the end.' A.J.P. Taylor in his *English History 1914–45* (1966) commented: 'In England this sentence was ranked with Nelson's last message. At the front, the prospect of staff officers fighting with their backs to the walls of their luxurious chateaux had less effect.'

back to normalcy. Together with 'Return to normalcy with Harding', this was a slogan effectively used by President Warren G. Harding. Both were based on a word extracted from a speech he had made in Boston during May 1920: 'America's present need is not heroics but healing, not nostrums but normalcy, not revolution but restoration, not agitation but adjustment, not surgery but serenity, not the dramatic but the dispassionate, not experiment but equipoise, not submergence in internationality but sustainment in triumphant nationality.' Out of such an alliterative bog stuck the word 'normalcy' – a perfectly good Americanism, though it has been suggested that Harding was actually mispronouncing the word 'normality'. He himself claimed that 'normalcy' was what he had meant to say, having come across it in a dictionary.

back to square one. Meaning 'back to the beginning', this phrase is sometimes said to have gained currency in the 1930s onwards through its use by British radio football commentators. *Radio Times* used to print a map of the football field divided into numbered squares, to which commentators would refer thus: 'Cresswell's going to make it – FIVE. There it goes, slap into the middle of the goal – SEVEN. Cann's header there – EIGHT. The ball comes out to Britton. Britton manoeuvres. The centre goes right in – BACK TO EIGHT. Comes on to Marshall – SIX' (an extract from the BBC commentary on the 1933 Cup Final between Everton and Manchester City). The idea had largely been abandoned by 1940. Against this proposition is the fact that square 'one' was nowhere near the beginning. The game began at the centre spot, which was at the meeting point of squares three, four, five and six.

Indeed, Partridge/*Catch Phrases* prefers an earlier origin in the children's game of hopscotch or in the board game Snakes and Ladders. If a player was unlucky and his or her counter landed on the snake's head in Square 97 or thereabouts, it had to make the long journey 'back to square one'.

back to the drawing board! Meaning 'we've got to start again from scratch', this is usually said after an original plan has been aborted. It is just possible that this began life in the caption to a cartoon by Peter Arno which appeared in the *New Yorker* during the early 1940s. An official, with a rolled-up engineering plan under his arm, is walking away from a recently crashed plane, and saying: 'Well, back to the old drawing board.'

back to the jungle. A return to primitive conditions, nearly always used figuratively (like 'a return to the Dark Ages'). Winston Churchill, in a speech about post-Revolution Russia on 3 January 1920, referred to a recent visitor to that country: 'Colonel John Ward . . . has seen these things for many months with his own eyes . . . [and] has summed all up in one biting, blasting phrase – "Back to the jungle".'

back to the land. The cry 'Back to the land!' was first heard at the end of the nineteenth century when it was realized that the Industrial Revolution and the transfer of the population towards non-agricultural labour had starved farming of labour. At about this time, a Wickham Market farmer wrote to Sir Henry Rider Haggard, who was making an inventory of the decline, published as *Rural England* (1902): 'The labourers "back to the land". That is the cry of the press and the fancy of the people. Well, I do not think that they will ever come back; certainly no legislation will ever bring them. Some of the rising generation may be induced to stay, but it will be by training them to the use of machinery and paying them higher wages. It should be remembered that the most intelligent men have gone: these will never come back, but the rising generation may stay as competition in the town increases, and the young men of the country are better paid.'

The *OED2* cites an 1894 formulation of the idea, from *The Times* (25 October): 'All present were interested in the common practice that it was desirable, if possible, to bring the people back to the land.' By 1905, the *Spectator* (23 December) was saying: '"Back-to-the-land" is a cry full not only of pathos, but of cogency.'

In the 1980s, a TV comedy series was called *Backs to the Land*, playing on the phrase to provide an innuendo about its heroines – 'Land Girls', members of the Women's Land Army conscripted to work on the land during the Second World War (though the WLA was first established in the First World War.)

bacon. See BRING HOME THE ∼.

bad. See I'M A BA-A-A-AD BOY!

badger. See BALD AS A ∼.

bad name, kind of thing that gives — a. A quite frequent format where the missing word is ironically inserted. Critic Walter Kerr (b 1913) on *Hook and Ladder* (untraced): 'It is the sort of play that gives failure a bad name.' Critic Clive Barnes on the revue *Oh! Calcutta!*: 'This is the kind of show that gives pornography a dirty name' (*New York Times*, 18 June 1969).

bag. See GLADSTONE ∼; HOLDING THE ∼; LET THE CAT OUT OF THE ∼; PAPER ∼ under COULDN'T RUN A WHELK-STALL.

bag lady. Meaning, 'a female tramp', this nickname refers to the vagrant's habit of carrying all her possessions about in the bags (made of plastic) supplied by supermarkets. The term has been part of American English since the 1970s and was in British English by 1986, usually as a pejorative term to describe any woman who looked a mess. Naturally, it is not a POLITICALLY CORRECT term: Rosalie Maggio's *The Nonsexist Word Finder: A Dictionary of Gender-Free Usage* (1988) warns: 'The gender-fair use of "bag woman" and "bag man" (avoid the nonparallel lady/man) is sometimes appropriate, although we tend to hear a great deal more about the bag woman than we do about the bag man, even though statistically more men than women are forced into this lifestyle.'

Variations include 'shopping-bag lady' and, inevitably, 'bagperson'. The term 'bagman' has been used in Australian English to denote a (usually male) tramp who carries possessions in a bag since the late 1890s. 'Street person' has been suggested as a PC term for all these people.

baker's daughter, the. 'They say the owl was a baker's daughter' Ophelia says mystifyingly in Shakespeare's *Hamlet*, IV.v.43 (1600). The reference is to an old English legend about Christ going into a baker's shop and asking for something to eat. A piece of cake is put in the oven for Him, but the baker's daughter says it is too large and cuts it in half. The dough swells up to an enormous size, she exclaims 'Woo! Woo!' and is turned into an owl.

baker's dozen, a. In use by the sixteenth century, this phrase to denote the number thirteen may date from the medieval baker's habit of giving away an extra loaf with every twelve to avoid being fined for providing underweight produce. The surplus was known as 'inbread' and the thirteenth loaf, the 'vantage loaf'. A **devil's dozen** is also thirteen – the number of witches who would gather when summoned by the devil.

baker's wife, the. *The Baker's Wife* was the title of a musical by Stein & Schwartz (first produced in Los Angeles, 1976) based on Marcel Pagnol's film *La Femme du Boulanger* (France, 1938) about village infidelity. Also in France, Louis XVI had been known as 'The Baker' and thus his Queen, 'The Baker's Wife', because of their action in giving bread to starving Parisians at Versailles in October 1789.

balance of power, the. The promotion of peace through parity of strength in rival groups – an expression used by the British Prime Minister, Sir Robert Walpole, in the House of Commons (13 February 1741). Safire (1978) states that the phrase had earlier been used in international diplomacy by 1700. Initially, the phrase appears to have been 'the balance of power in Europe'. In 1715, Alexander Pope wrote a poem with the title 'The Balance of Europe': 'Now Europe's balanc'd, neither side prevails;/For nothing's left in either of the scales.'

bald. See FIGHT BETWEEN TWO ∼ MEN . . .

bald as a badger/bandicoot/coot. Phrases used to mean 'completely bald'. 'Bald as a coot' has been known since 1430. The aquatic coot, known as the Bald Coot, has the appearance of being bald. The Australian marsupial, the bandicoot, is not bald but presumably is evoked purely for the alliteration and because the basic coot expression is being alluded to. As for badger, the full expression is 'bald as a badger's bum'. There was once a belief that

bristles for shaving brushes were plucked from this area.

Christy Brown, *Down All the Days* (1970) has, rather, 'bald as a baby's bum'.

baldheaded, to go at something. Meaning 'to act without regard for the consequences, to go at something full tilt' – e.g. from J.R. Lowell, *The Biglow Papers* (1848):

I scent what pays the best, an' then Go into it baldheaded.

This is an American expression, dating from the nineteenth century. The suggestion is that of a man who would tackle a problem as though he had just rushed out of the house without putting on his wig, or without wearing a hat.

Earlier sources have been suggested – notably that the Marquis of Granby, a colonel of the Blues, led a cavalry charge at the Battle of Warburg (1760) despite his hat and wig falling off. He was an enormously popular figure (hence the number of British pubs named after him), but it is unlikely that his fame was sufficient to have led to the expression being used in the US.

Balfour must go. See — MUST GO!

Balfour's poodle, Mr. A reference to the House of Lords. David Lloyd George spoke in the House of Commons on 26 June 1907 in the controversy over the power of the upper house. He questioned the Lords' role as a 'watchdog' of the constitution and suggested that A.J. Balfour, the Conservative leader, was using the party's majority in the upper chamber to block legislation by the Liberal government (in which Lloyd George was president of the Board of Trade). He said: '[The House of Lords] is the leal and trusty mastiff which is to watch over our interests, but which runs away at the first snarl of the trade unions. A mastiff? It is the Right Honourable Gentleman's poodle. It fetches and carries for him. It bites anybody that he sets it on to.'

ball(s). See COLD ENOUGH TO FREEZE THE ∼ . . . ; YOU PLAY ∼ WITH ME . . .

ball game. See WHOLE NEW ∼.

balloon's gone up, the. Current by 1924 and meaning 'the action or excitement has commenced', particularly in military activities, this expression derives from the barrage balloons introduced during the First World War to protect targets from air raids. The fact that these balloons – or observation balloons – had 'gone up' would signal that some form of action was imminent. C.H. Rolph in *London Particulars* (1980) suggests that the phrase was in use earlier, by 1903–4.

balls. See GREAT ∼ OF FIRE.

banality of evil, the. 'The fearsome word-and-thought-defying banality of evil' was how the German-born philosopher Hannah Arendt summed up the lessons to be learned from the trial of Adolf Eichmann, the Nazi official, who was executed in Israel as a war criminal in 1962. Her book *Eichmann in Jerusalem* (1963) was subtitled 'A Report on the Banality of Evil' and caused controversy because it seemed to suggest that Eichmann was not personally responsible for his deeds during the HOLOCAUST.

banana. See HAVE A ∼; UNZIPP A ∼.

Band Aid. See — AID.

Band Waggon. Arthur Askey (1900–82) has good cause to be acclaimed as the father of the British radio catchphrase. He had such a profusion of them from *Band Waggon* onwards that he may be said to have popularized the notion that broadcast comedians were somehow incomplete *without* a catchphrase.

'There had been radio comedians before this who used catchphrases,' he told me in 1979, 'like Sandy Powell, but ours was the first show which really made a thing of them. I was the one who was on the air most and kept banging them in.'

Band Waggon was the first BBC comedy show specifically tailored for radio – as opposed to being made up of variety acts. The basic format was that of a magazine, but the best-remembered segment was that in which Askey shared a flat with Richard Murdoch (1907–90) on the top of Broadcasting House in London, bringing

added meaning to the term 'resident comedians'.

A catchphrase that stayed with Askey for the rest of his life was spoken in the first edition of *Band Waggon* on 5 January 1938: **Big-hearted Arthur, that's me!** – 'I have always used this expression – even when I was at school. When playing cricket, you know, if the ball was hit to the boundary and nobody would go and fetch it – I would . . . saying "Big-hearted Arthur, that's me!"'

Another early coinage was **hello, playmates!** though, as Askey pointed out, this was originally **hello, folks!** When he used 'Hello, folks!' in the first broadcast of *Band Waggon*, he received a call from Tommy Handley telling him to lay off as the other comedian considered it to be *his* catchphrase. So, Askey changed it to 'Hello, playmates!' (with *Hello Playmates!* becoming the title of another of his radio shows in the mid-1950s.)

Handley continued to use 'Hello, folks!' throughout ITMA. After which, the GOON SHOW took up the cry and gave it a strangulated delivery. Harry Secombe extended this to **hello, folks, and WHAT ABOUT THE WORKERS?!** and Eric Morecambe gave it a sexual connotation when he referred to **a touch of hello folks and what about the workers?!**

Askey's third most illustrious phrase was **ay thang yew!** – a distinctive pronunciation of 'I thank you!' picked up from the cry of London bus conductors. 'I didn't know I was saying it till people started to shout it at me.' Later, as *I Thank You*, it became the title of one of Askey's films (1941).

Other *Band Waggon* phrases included:

doesn't it make you want to spit! Askey was rapped over the knuckles for introducing this 'unpleasant expression'. '[Sir John] Reith [the BBC Director-General] thought it a bit vulgar but I was in the driving seat. The show was so popular, he couldn't fire me. I suppose I said it all the more!'

(ah,) happy days! Sighed nostalgically by Askey and Murdoch in unison when reminiscing about their early days in the flat. The phrase is also well known in other contexts. By the early twentieth-century it was a popular drinker's toast, deriving from the form that Tennyson included in *In Memoriam* (1850): 'Drinking health to bride and groom/We wish them store of happy days.' The song 'Happy Days Are Here Again' appeared in 1930. 'Happy days, happy days!' is a line in J.B. Priestley's play *When We Are Married* (1938). In 1974 *Happy Days* was taken as the title of a long-running US TV series which looked back nostalgically to the 1950s.

it'll be all right with a bit of doing up. Askey, clearing out the flat at the top of Broadcasting House: 'Shall we throw this out?' 'No, it'll be all right with a bit of doing up.'

light the blue touchpaper and retire immediately. The firework instruction was first used on a Guy Fawkes night broadcast and subsequently when withdrawing from any confrontation with Mrs Bagwash.

serve that lady with a crusty loaf! 'Why I said that, I've no idea,' Askey remarked. 'It came out of the blue when some woman was laughing very loud in the studio audience. Perhaps it goes back to the days when I used to do the shopping for my mum in Liverpool and picked it up then.'

what would you do, chums? A regular feature of *Band Waggon* was a tale told by the actor Syd Walker (1887–1945) in the character of a junkman. He would pose some everyday dilemma and end with this query – or a variation upon it. It was used as the title of a film in 1939. George Orwell in his essay on 'The Art of Donald McGill' (1942) mentions a comic postcard he had seen which showed Hitler 'with the usual hypertrophied backside' bending down to pick a flower. The caption was: 'What would *you* do, chums?' From Tony Benn's diary entry for 23 January 1958 (published in *Years of Hope*, 1994): 'It is wiser for us not to attack the Government too hard at this moment. The people are sick of the Government, anyway . . . What they want is a clear

answer to the question: "What would you do, chum?" '

you silly little man! As, for example:

> *Murdoch (instructing Askey how to court Nausea Bagwash, with whom he was supposed to be in love)*: You say, 'Darling Nausea, your lips are like petals . . .'
> *Askey*: Nausea, darling, your lips are like petals. Bicycle petals.
> *Murdoch*: No, no, no, you silly little man!

The final edition of *Band Waggon* was broadcast on 2 December 1939. See also HERE AND NOW, BEFORE YOUR VERY EYES; SPEAK AS YOU FIND, THAT'S MY MOTTO.

bandwagon, to climb/jump on the. Principally in the US, circuses had bandwagons. They had 'high decks so that musicians could be seen and heard by street crowds', according to Flexner (1982). Barnum and Bailey had an elaborately decorated one in 1855 for use in circus parades.

Politicians in the US also had bandwagons which would lead the procession when votes were being canvassed. Those who jumped, climbed or hopped aboard were those who were leading the support for the candidate.

Since then, a slight shift in meaning has bandwagon-jumpers cashing in on something which is already an established success.

bang. See BIG ∼; NOT WITH A ∼ . . .

bang goes/went sixpence! A lightly joking remark about one's own or another person's unwillingness to spend money. The origins of this lie in the caption to a *Punch* cartoon (5 December 1868). A Scotsman who has just been on a visit to London says: 'Mun, a' had na' been the-rre abune two hours when – bang – went saxpence!' Benham (1948) has it that the story was communicated to the cartoonist Charles Keene by Birket Foster who had it from Sir John Gilbert. The saying was repopularized by Sir Harry Lauder, the professional stage Scotsman (1870–1950).

bang to rights. As in 'You've got me bang to rights!' said by a criminal to an arresting policeman, this is an alternative to 'It's a fair cop!' [You are quite right to have caught me, constable!]. There is also an element of 'You've caught me red-handed, in an indefensible position'. Partridge/*Slang* dates this from the 1930s, but *OED2* finds a US example in 1904. Possibly derived from nineteenth-century usage – from the idea of being 'bang-on right' in absolute certainty. Compare the somewhat rare Americanism 'bang' for a criminal charge or arrest, as in 'it's a bum bang', perhaps having some connection with the banging of a cell door.

banjaxed, to be. An Irishism meaning 'banged about; smashed' and introduced into popular British speech by the broadcaster Terry Wogan in the early 1970s. Possibly from Dublin slang of the 1920s. When he wrote a book called *Banjaxed* (1979), Wogan supplied this definition of the verb: 'To hornswoggle, corpse, knacker, rasher, caramelize, malfooster, malavogue, powfagg, keelhaul, macerate, decimate, pulverize, make rawmeish of. Hence *banjaxed*, reduced to the condition of a pig's breakfast, and *banjaxing*, tearing a plaster from a hairy leg.'

bank. See CRY ALL THE WAY TO THE ∼.

Bankhead. See WELL, NOW THEN, SIR . . .

ban the bomb. One of the simplest and best-known alliterative slogans, current in the US from 1953 and sometime marginally afterwards in the UK. The Campaign for Nuclear Disarmament – whose semi-official slogan it became – was not publicly launched until February 1958. The phrase was in use by 1960. (Richard Crossman referred to 'Scrap the Bomb' in a 1957 press article.)

Banzai! From a hundred war films and cheap comics we are familiar with the cry used by Japanese forces in the Second World War, meaning '[May you live] ten thousand years!' During the war – and after it – this traditional cry came to mean 'Ten thousand years to the Emperor' or to 'Japan'.

In a letter to me (1986), M.R. Lewis observed that, 'The root of the problem is that a language written in the Chinese ideographic characters is often difficult to translate sensibly into a West European language, because it is often not apparent when the literal meaning is intended and when the figurative. "*Banzai*" literally means no more than "ten thousand years", but what it more usually means is "for a long time". So, a pen in Japanese is, when literally translated, a "ten thousand year writing brush", which is gibberish in any language! What it actually means is "a long-lasting writing instrument" . . .

'For the suicide pilots, the ritual shout of "*Banzai!*" swept up many layers of meaning, of which the most immediate was undoubtedly "*Tenno heika banzai*" – "Long live the Emperor", a phrase which goes back into the mists of Japanese history, despite its appropriation by the nationalist movements of the 1930s. The phrase is still in use on such occasions as the Emperor's birthday, as I can testify from recent experience. When he stepped out on to the balcony and the shouts rose around me, I began to feel that I was in the wrong movie!

'As for the oddity of the phrase – if literally translated, is it really so different from: "Zadok the priest, and Nathan the prophet, anointed Solomon king. And all the people rejoiced and said, God save the king. Long live the king, *may the king live for ever*. Amen. Alleluia." – which has been sung at the coronation of almost every English sovereign since William of Normandy was crowned in Westminster Abbey on Christmas Day 1066?'

Jonathan Swift includes **may you live a thousand years** among the conversational chestnuts in *Polite Conversation* (1738). The Sergeant in Charles Dickens, *Great Expectations*, Chap. 5 (1860–1) incorporates it in a toast.

barbarians (are) at the gate(s), the. Meaning 'the END OF CIVILIZATION is at hand'. Hyperbole. In 1990 *Barbarians at the Gate* was used as the title of a book by Bryan Burrough (subtitled 'The Fall of RJR Nabisco') about goings-on in Wall Street – suggesting that unregulated, or at least ungentlemanly, behaviour had broken out.

Appropriately enough, the phrase is used literally in Edward Gibbon's *Decline and Fall of the Roman Empire*, I.303 (1776–88): 'Such was the public consternation when the barbarians were hourly expected at the gates of Rome.'

Bardney?, do you come from. Steve Race, the musician and broadcaster, wrote (1994): 'Small boys brought up in the city of Lincoln, as I was, will testify that if one left a door open, someone would be sure to say, "Do you come from Bardney?" Bardney is nine miles south-east of Lincoln and there was formerly an Abbey there, presumably with an "ever-open door".' G.L. Apperson in his *English Proverbs and Proverbial Phrases* (1929) finds this expression being discussed in *Notes and Queries* by 1905 (in the form 'I see you come from Bardney'.)

Bard of Avon, the. One of several sobriquets for William Shakespeare and alluding to the river running through his birthplace at Stratford in Warwickshire. 'Pen introduced [Shakespeare because he] professed an uncommon respect for the bard of Avon,' wrote William Thackeray in *Pendennis*, Chap. 6 (1848–50). Ben Jonson called Shakespeare 'Sweet Swan of Avon' (in a verse prefacing the First Folio of plays, 1623) and David Garrick, who excelled in Shakespearean parts at the Drury Lane Theatre, London, felt intimate enough to nickname him 'Avonian Willy'. **The Bard** on its own is also, unfortunately, common, though anything is better than the assumed familiarity, chiefly among actors, of 'Will' or 'Bill' Shakespeare.

bargepole, not to touch someone/thing with a. i.e. to keep one's distance, avoid at all costs. From the *length* of the bargepole used to propel a barge. Known by 1893.

bark. See DOGS ~ BUT THE CARAVAN . . .

Barker. See STEADY, ~!

bark up the wrong tree, to. This phrase meaning 'to follow a false scent' is of US origin (by 1832) and *appears* to come from racoon hunting. As this is done at night (racoons being nocturnal animals) and as, if chased, racoons run up trees, it would be quite possible for a dog to bark mistakenly under the wrong tree.

barmy. See GINGER, YOU'RE ~!

barn. See LET'S DO THE SHOW . . .

barn door. See SHINING LIKE SHIT . . .

Barnet. See WOGS BEGIN AT B.

barnstorm, to. (1) (Of actors) to perform unsubtly (2) (Of US politicians) to give speeches drumming up votes in rural areas.

The word originated in the US in the early nineteenth century when actors did indeed go bustling around the countryside performing in barns and similar informal venues. Their style was akin to that found in melodrama.

It was possibly more the makeshift, improvised nature of the touring which led to the word being used (from the 1890s) in connection politicians who stumped about seeking votes. In time, 'barnstorming' was largely superseded by 'WHISTLE-STOP touring'.

baron. See RED ~.

barrel. See LOCK, STOCK AND ~.

bash/flog the bishop, to. Meaning 'to masturbate'. Partridge/*Slang* dates this from the late nineteenth century and suggests it derives from the resemblance between the penis and a chess bishop or a bishop in ecclesiastical mitre.

It was unfortunate, therefore, that Labour MPs should have accused the Conservative minister, John Selwyn Gummer MP, of **bishop-bashing** when he was involved in criticisms of various Anglican bishops in March 1988.

The suffix **-bashing** had been used before, of course – as in the practice of **Paki-bashing** *c* 1970 (i.e. subjecting Pakistani immigrants to physical assault), and as in the old 'square-bashing' (army slang for drill).

basics. See BACK TO ~.

Basie. See COUNT ~.

bath. See DON'T THROW THE BABY . . .; under UP AND UNDER.

bath, early. See under UP AND UNDER.

Batman. Batman and Robin were characters created by Bob Kane in 1939 and featured in comic books before being portrayed by Adam West and Burt Ward in a filmed series for TV (1966–8). The putting of the prefix **Holy —!** in exclamations was a hallmark of the programme – 'Holy flypaper!'/'Holy cow!'/'Holy schizophrenia!' etc. Also used were **quick thinking, Batman!** – a typically crawling remark from sidekick Robin – and **boy wonder!** – Batman's commendation in return.

(The on-screen titles 'Pow!' 'Biff!' 'Thwack!' 'Crunch!' 'Rakkk!' 'Oooofff!' and 'Bonk!' could also be said to be a kind of catchphrase.)

bats in the belfry, to have (or **bats/batty, to be**). Meaning, 'to be mentally deficient, harmlessly insane, or mad', these expressions convey the idea that a person behaves in a wildly disturbed manner, like bats disturbed by the ringing of bells. Stephen Graham wrote in *London Nights* (1925): 'There is a set of jokes which are the common property of all the comedians. You may hear them as easily in Leicester Square as in Mile End Road. It strikes the unwonted visitor to the Pavilion as very original when Stanley Lupino says of some one: "He has bats in the belfry." It is not always grasped that the expression belongs to the music hall at large.'

Attempts have been made to derive 'batty', in particular, from the name of William Battie (1704–76), author of a *Treatise on Madness*, though this seems a little harsh, given that he was the psychiatrist and not the patient. On the other hand, there was a Fitzherbert Batty, barrister of Spanish Town, Jamaica, who made news when he was certified insane in London in 1839. The names of these two gentlemen merely, and coincidentally, reinforced the 'bats in the belfry' idea – but there do not seem to be any examples of either expression in use before 1900.

battle. See LOSE A ~ . . . ; NEVER-ENDING ~ FOR TRUTH . . . under *SUPERMAN*.

Battle of Britain, the. The urge to give names to battles – even before they are fought and won – is well-exemplified by Winston Churchill's coinage of 18 June 1940: 'What General Weygand called the Battle of France is over. I expect that the Battle of Britain is about to begin.' It duly became the name by which the decisive overthrowing of German invasion plans by the FEW is known. The order of the day, read aloud to every pilot on 10 July, contained the words: 'The Battle of Britain is about to begin. Members of the Royal Air Force, the fate of generations is in your hands.' Another Churchill coinage – 'The Battle of Egypt' (speech, 10 November 1942) – caught on less well.

battle royal, to wage a. Meaning, 'to take part in a keenly fought contest; a general free-for-all', this term originated in cockfighting, or at least has been specifically used in that sport. In the first round, sixteen birds would be put into a pit to fight each other, until only half the number was left. The knock-out competition would then continue until there was only one survivor. *OED2* finds the phrase in 1672, general use; 1860 for cockfighting.

batty. See BATS IN THE BELFRY.

BBC. See AUNTIE.

beach. See GERMANS FIRST ON THE ~ ; under LIFE'S A DITCH . . .

be a good bunny! Sign-off by Wendy Barrie, on her US TV chat show *c* 1949.

beaujolais nouveau. Selling Beaujolais wine during the first year of a vintage became a marketing ploy in the early 1970s. For a number of years, a race was held to see who could bring the new stock most quickly from France to Britain. The slogan was '*Le Beaujolais Nouveau est arrivée!* . . . '

beam me up, Scotty. The US TV science-fiction series *Star Trek* (1966–9), though short-lived, nevertheless acquired a considerable afterlife through countless repeats (not least in the UK) and the activities of 'trekky' fans. It was the series whose spoken introduction proposed **to**

boldly go where no man has gone before! (In one of the feature films that belatedly spun off from the series – the 1988 one – the split infinitive remained but feminism, presumably, had decreed that it should be 'where no *one* has gone before'.)

According to Trekkers, Capt. Kirk (William Shatner) never actually said to Lt. Commander 'Scotty' Scott, the chief engineer, 'Beam me up, Scotty!' – which meant that he should transpose body into matter, or transport someone from planet to spaceship, or some such thing. In the fourth episode, however, he may have said, 'Scotty, beam me up!' The more usual form of the injunction was, 'Enterprise, beam us up' or, 'Beam us up, Mr Scott.'

beans. See HOW MANY ∼ MAKE FIVE?; SPILL THE ∼.

Beanz meanz Heinz. This slogan for Heinz Baked Beans in the UK (from 1967) is the type of advertising line that drives teachers into a frenzy because it appears to condone wrong spelling. Johnny Johnson wrote the music for the jingle that went:

> A million housewives every day
> Pick up a tin of beans and say
> Beanz meanz Heinz.

'I created the line at Young & Rubicam,' copywriter Maurice Drake stated in 1981. 'It was in fact written – although after much thinking – over two pints of bitter in the Victoria pub in Mornington Crescent.'

bear. See EXIT PURSUED BY A ∼; SMARTER THAN THE AVERAGE ∼.

bear shit in the woods?, does a. See IS THE POPE A CATHOLIC?

beast. See NATURE OF THE ∼.

Beast of —. Used as a nickname formula. (1) The 'Beast of Belsen' was Josef Kramer, German commandant of the Belsen concentration camp during the worst period of its history from December 1944 to the end of the Second World War. He was executed for his crimes in 1945. (2) The 'Beast/Bitch of Buchenwald' was Ilse Koch (*d* 1967), wife of the commandant of the concentration camp near Weimar.

Infamous for having had lampshades made out of the skin of her victims. (3) The 'Beast of Bolsover' is Dennis Skinner (*b* 1932), the aggressive and outspoken Labour MP for Bolsover in Derbyshire (since 1970). Noted for interrupting speeches and making loud comments. (4) The 'Beast of Jersey' was E.J.L. (Ted) Paisnel, who was convicted of 13 sex offences against children and sentenced to 30 years imprisonment in 1971. The name was applied to him during the 11 years he evaded arrest on the island.

Beast 666, the (or **the Great Beast**). Nicknames of Aleister Crowley (*c* 1876–1947), satanist, who experimented in necromancy and the black arts, sex and drugs. He called himself the mystical 'Beast 666' after the man referred to in Revelation 13:18: 'Let him that hath understanding count the number of the beast: for it is the number of a man: and his number is six hundred threescore and six.' Newspapers called Crowley the **Wickedest Man in the World**, though he fell short of proving the claim.

beat. See IF YOU CAN'T ∼ 'EM . . .; IT ∼S AS IT SWEEPS . . .

beat a path to someone's door, to. Sarah Yule claimed (1889) that she had heard Ralph Waldo Emerson say this in a lecture: 'If a man write a better book, preach a better sermon, or make a better mousetrap than his neighbour, 'tho he build his house in the woods, the world will make a beaten path to his door.' Elbert Hubbard also claimed authorship. Either way, this is a remark alluded to when people talk of 'beating a path to someone's door' or a **better mousetrap**. In his journal for February 1855, Emerson had certainly entertained the thought: 'If a man . . . can make better chairs or knives . . . than anybody else, you will find a broad hard-beaten road to his house, though it be in the woods.'

Beat Generation, the. 'Beatniks' were young people who opted out of normal society in the 1950s (first of all in the US) because they were unable or unwilling to conform to conventional standards. Careless of appearance, critical of the

ESTABLISHMENT, they were less intellectual than the average ANGRY YOUNG MAN, but rebellious like teddy boys who preceded them (in the UK) and the hippies who followed.

The name with its Yiddish or Russian suffix (compare the Russian *sputnik* satellite orbiting the earth in 1957) derived from the phrase 'Beat Generation' which was probably coined by Jack Kerouac, although in his book *The Origins of the Beat Generation*, he admitted to borrowing the phrase from a drug addict called Herbert Huncke. In Randy Nelson's *The Almanac of American Letters* (1981), there is a description of the moment of coinage. Kerouac is quoted as saying: 'John Clellon Holmes . . . and I were sitting around trying to think up the meaning of the LOST GENERATION and the subsequent existentialism and I said: "You know, this is really a beat generation," and he leapt up and said: "That's it, that's right."' Holmes himself attributed the phrase directly to Kerouac in the *New York Times* Magazine of 16 November 1952.

beating. See WHEN DID YOU STOP ~ YOUR WIFE?

Beatles, the. The British pop group – the most famous in the world (1962–70). They were originally the 'Silver Beatles' (no such insect exists, it was a simple 'beat/beetle' pun – though coincidentally echoing 'Bootle', the district of Liverpool/ Merseyside, near from which they hailed). See also FAB FOUR; FIFTH BEATLE; WHO ARE THE BEATLES?; YEH-YEH-YEH.

beautiful. See ALL THINGS BRIGHT AND ~; ~ DOWNTOWN BURBANK under *LAUGH-IN*; BLACK IS ~; BUT MISS – YOU'RE ~; IF I SAID YOU HAD A – BODY; IT'S B'OOTIFUL . . . ; SMALL IS ~.

beautiful people, the. Coinage of this term is credited in *Current Biography* (1978) to the American fashion journalist, Diana Vreeland (c 1903–89). Whether she deserves this or not is open to question, although she does seem to have helped launch the similar term SWINGING LONDON. The earliest OED2 citation with capital letters for each word is from 1966, though there is a *Vogue* use from

15 February 1964 which would appear to support the link to Vreeland. The *OED2* makes the phrase refer primarily to ' "flower people", hippies' though the 1981 *Macquarie Dictionary*'s less narrow definition of 'fashionable social set of wealthy, well-groomed, usually young people' is preferable. The Lennon and McCartney song 'Baby You're a Rich Man' (released in July 1967) contains the line 'How does it feel to be one of the beautiful people?'

William Saroyan's play *The Beautiful People* had first been performed long before all this, in 1941, and Oscar Wilde in a letter to Harold Boulton (December 1879), wrote: 'I could have introduced you to some very beautiful people. Mrs Langtry and Lady Lonsdale and a lot of clever beings who were at tea with me.'

Compare GETAWAY PEOPLE.

beauty. See AGE BEFORE ~; ME OL' ~! under ARCHERS.

b/Beaver. (1) The cry identifying a man with a beard appears to have been common among children in the 1910s and 20s, though now redundant. But why *beaver*? Flexner notes the use of the animal's name to describe a high, sheared-fur hat in the US. The beaver's thick dark-brown fur, he says, also refers 'to a well-haired pudendum or a picture showing it, which in pornography is called a "beaver shot"'. Beaver for beard may derive rather from the Middle Ages when the 'beaver' was the part of a soldier's helmet which lay around the chin as a face-guard (the 'vizor' was the bit brought down from the forehead). In Shakespeare's *Hamlet*, I.ii.228 (1600), the Prince asks: 'Then saw you not his face?' (that of his father's ghost). Horatio replies: 'O yes, my lord, he wore his beaver up.'

(2) Nickname of William Maxwell Aitken, 1st Baron Beaverbrook (1879–1964), newspaper magnate and politician in Britain. He took his title from the town in New Brunswick, Canada, where he had a home. Called 'Max' by his friends, he was known to his staff as 'the Beaver', a name explained by Tom Driberg (his first 'William Hickey' columnist on the *Daily Express*) as conveying a 'zoological symbol of tireless industry'.

be British. Jingoistic phrase. In 1912, Captain Edward Smith reputedly said, 'Be British, boys, be British' to his crew some time in the hours between his command, the *Titanic*, hitting the iceberg and his going down with the ship. Michael Davie in his book on the disaster describes the evidence for this as 'flimsy', but the legend was rapidly established. 'Be British! was the cry as the ship went down' was the first line of a commemorative song 'Be British', written and composed by Lawrence Wright and Paul Pelham. In 1914, when a statue to Smith in Lichfield was erected, it had 'Be British' as part of the inscription.

because. See AND ALL ～ . . .

because it's there. As a flippant justification for doing anything, this makes use of a phrase chiefly associated with the British mountaineer, George Leigh Mallory (1886–1924). He disappeared on his last attempt to climb Mount Everest. The previous year, during a lecture tour in the US, he had frequently been asked why he wanted to achieve this goal. He replied, 'Because it is there.'

The saying has become a catchphrase in situations where the speaker wishes to dismiss an impossible question about motives and also to express acceptance of a challenge that is in some way daunting or foolish.

There have been many variations (and misattributions). Sir Edmund Hillary repeated it regarding his own successful attempt on Everest in 1953.

Becket, to do a Thomas à. This phrase is used to suggest a possible course of action in a general sense, which is then interpreted by others more positively than might have been the speaker's actual intention. King Henry II's rhetorical question regarding Thomas à Becket, 'Will no man rid me of this **turbulent priest**?' (which was acted upon by the Archbishop's murderers in 1170) is ascribed to 'oral tradition' by *ODQ* in the form: 'Will no one revenge me of the injuries I have sustained from one turbulent priest?' The young king, who was in Normandy, had received reports that the Archbishop was ready 'to tear the crown from' his head. 'What a pack of fools and

cowards I have nourished in my house,' he cried, according to another version, 'that not one of them will avenge me of this turbulent priest!' Yet another version has, 'of this upstart clerk'.

An example of the phrase used allusively in a tape-recorded conversation was played at the conspiracy-to-murder trial involving Jeremy Thorpe MP in 1979. Andrew Newton was heard to say, speaking of the alleged plot: 'They feel a Thomas à Becket was done, you know, with Thorpe sort of raving, "Would nobody rid me of this man?"'

bed. See APPLE-PIE ORDER; HE CAN LEAVE HIS BOOTS UNDER . . .; I SHOULD OF STOOD IN BED under WE WUZ ROBBED!; SOMEBODY GOT OUT OF ～ . . .; 'TIME FOR ～', SAID ZEBEDEE.

Bedfordshire. See UP THE WOODEN HILL TO ～.

bee. See SPELLING ～.

beef. See WHERE'S THE ～?

Bee Gees, the. The name of a British pop group, popular in the 1960s and 70s, derived from 'the BGs' – 'the Brothers Gibb' – which they were.

beeline. See MAKE A ～ FOR.

been. See 'AS 'E BIN IN, WHACK?

been there, done that. 'Michael Caine was once asked if he had a motto: "Yeah – Been There, Done That. It'll certainly be on my tombstone. It'll just say, 'Been There, Done That'"' – quoted in Elaine Gallagher *et al*, *Candidly Caine* (1990). This is what might be called a T-shirt motto and is certainly not original to Caine. Ian Dury used the phrase 'been there' in the song 'Laughter' (*The Ian Dury Songbook*, 1979) to indicate that a seduction has been accomplished, but the motto is not solely concerned with sex. It can cover all human activity. About 1989 there were T-shirts for jaded travellers with the words: 'Been there, done that, **got the T-shirt.**'

beer. See I'M ONLY HERE FOR THE ～; LIFE ISN'T ALL ～ AND SKITTLES; YOUR ～ IS SOUR.

beer and sandwiches at No. 10. An encapsulation of the informal (and often eleventh-hour) style of negotiations held at senior level (and quite often at the Prime Minister's residence) between British trade unionists and politicians to avert threatened strikes and stoppages. These only really took place under the Labour Prime Ministerships of Harold Wilson (1964–1970, 1974–6). Nothing like it was known under Margaret Thatcher, who seldom, if ever, conversed with union leaders, let alone offered them any form of hospitality.

Some called it a pragmatic approach; others viewed it less favourably. Phillip Whitehead (a one-time Labour MP) was quoted in the *Independent* (25 April 1988) as having said of Wilson that he, 'bought the hours with beer and sandwiches at No. 10 and the years with Royal Commissions'.

beer and skittles, life isn't all. An apparently late-appearing proverb (not until 1855), urging that life is not just about simple pleasures or unalloyed enjoyment – specifically the drinks and games you would find in a pub, the British yeoman's idea of HEAVEN ON EARTH.

beers. See HEINEKEN REFRESHES THE PARTS . . .

beer that made Milwaukee famous, the. The Schlitz Brewing Company had its roots in an operation begun in Milwaukee in 1849. By 1871, the year of the great Chicago fire, it was a thriving concern. The fire left Chicago thirsty; the city was desperately short of drinking water and its breweries had virtually been destroyed. So Joseph Schlitz floated a shipload of beer down Lake Michigan to refresh his parched neighbours. They liked and remembered Milwaukee beer long after the crisis passed. It is not known who coined the phrase but this is the incident which led to it. The slogan was incorporated and registered in 1895, and was in use until production ceased in the 1980s.

bee's knees, to be the. Used to mean 'the very best around; absolutely top hole'. There has always been a fascination with bees' knees. In the eighteenth century there was the expression, 'as big as a bee's knee'

and, in the nineteenth, 'as weak as a bee's knee'. But the bee whose knees became celebrated in US slang by 1923 was probably only there because of the rhyme. At about the same time, we find the **kipper's knickers**, the **cat's whiskers** (perhaps because of the importance of these in tuning wireless crystal sets in the 1920s), the **cat's pyjamas** (still new enough to be daring), 'the cat's miaow/eyebrows/ankles/ tonsils/adenoids/ galoshes/cufflinks/roller skates'. Not to mention 'the snake's hips', 'the clam's garter', 'the eel's ankle', 'the elephant's instep', 'the tiger's spots', 'the flea's eyebrows', 'the canary's tusks', 'the leopard's stripes', 'the sardine's whiskers', 'the pig's wings' – 'and just about any combination of animal, fish, or fowl with a part of the body or clothing that was inappropriate for it' (Flexner, 1976).

before/as quick as one can say 'Jack Robinson'. This expression meaning 'immediately; straight away', appears to have been alluded to by Richard Brinsley Sheridan in the House of Commons (some time after 1780) to avoid using a fellow member's name (as was, and is partly still, the custom). Having made a derogatory reference to the Secretary to the Treasury, John Robinson, and been asked by members shouting 'Name, name' to disclose the person he was referring to, Sheridan said, 'You know I cannot name him, but I could as soon as I can say Jack Robinson.'

Clearly, Sheridan was alluding to an already established expression. Neil Ewart in *Everyday Phrases* (1983) cites the theory that it 'refers to an erratic [eighteenth-century] gentleman of that name who rushed around to visit his neighbours, rang the front-door bell, and then changed his mind and dashed off before the servant had time to announce his name'. Eric Partridge in his *Name Into Word* (1949) suggests that it was a made-up name using very common first and last elements.

Fanny Burney has 'I'll do it as soon as say Jack Robinson' in her novel *Evelina* (1778), so that pushes back the date somewhat. A promising explanation is that the phrase may have something to do with Sir John Robinson who was Officer Commanding the Tower of London from 1660–79. In that case, the original reference may have been to the speed of beheading with an axe (discussed in the *Observer*, 24 April 1988).

before your very eyes. See HERE AND NOW . . .

beggars. See LIKE TAKING MONEY FROM BLIND ∼.

begin. See under ARE YOU SITTING COMFORTABLY?; LIFE ∼ S AT FORTY.

beginning of the end, not the. In a speech on the progress of the war on 10 November 1942, Winston Churchill said: 'Now this [success in the Battle of Egypt] is not the end. It is not even the beginning of the end. But it is, perhaps, the end of the beginning'. The formula seems to have a particular appeal to people, judging by the number of times it has been recalled. Talleyrand had only gone halfway when he said, 'It is the beginning of the end [*Voilà le commencement de la fin*],' either after Napoleon's defeat at Borodino (1812) or during the Hundred Days (20 March – 28 June 1815).

In *F.E. Smith, First Earl of Birkenhead* (1983), John Campbell observes that Churchill was sitting next to F.E. when Smith addressed an all-party meeting in London on 11 September 1914. The battle of the Marne, he said, was not the beginning of the end, 'it is only the end of the beginning'.

be good to yourself. Sign-off from Don McNeill, homely American radio star, on the air from 1934–68.

behind. See ∼ YOU! under OH NO, THERE ISN'T; GET THEE ∼ ME SATAN; I'M ALL ∼ LIKE THE COW'S TAIL.

behind every — man stands a — woman. A much-used and much-parodied format. An early example of the basic expression occurs in an interview with Lady Dorothy, wife of the then just retired British Prime Minister Harold Macmillan (7 December 1963). In the *Daily Sketch*, Godfrey Winn concluded his piece with the (for him) typical sentiment (his capitals): 'NO MAN SUCCEEDS WITHOUT A GOOD WOMAN BEHIND HIM. WIFE OR MOTHER. IF IT IS BOTH, HE IS TWICE BLESSED INDEED.'

In *Love All*, a little known play by Dorothy L. Sayers, which opened at the Torch Theatre, Knightsbridge, London, on 9 April 1940 and closed before the end of the month, was this: 'Every great man has a woman behind him . . . And every great woman has some man or other in front of her, tripping her up.'

being for the benefit of —. A standard nineteenth-century phrase used in advertising 'testimonial' performances. The title of Chapter 48 of *Nicholas Nickleby* (1838–9) by Charles Dickens is: 'Being for the benefit of Mr Vincent Crummles, and Positively his last Appearance on this Stage.' 'Being for the Benefit of Mr Kite' is the title of a track on the Beatles' *Sgt Pepper* album (1967). The lyrics, largely written by John Lennon, though credited jointly to him and Paul McCartney, derive almost word for word, as Lennon acknowledged, from the wording of a Victorian circus poster dated 1843.

belfry. See BATS IN THE ∼.

believe. See I DON'T BELIEVE IT!; WOULD YOU ∼?; YOU'D BETTER ∼ IT.

believed. See I'VE NEVER ∼ IN ANYTHING SO MUCH . . .

believe it or not! This exclamation was used as the title of a long-running syndicated newspaper feature, and radio and TV series, in the US. Robert Leroy Ripley (1893–1949) created and illustrated a comic strip, *Ripley's Believe It or Not* (c 1923), but citations for the phrase before this are lacking.

believe only half of what you see and nothing that you hear. Mencken (1942) finds an early quotation of this proverbial saying in *A Woman's Thoughts* by Dinah Mulock Craik (1858) where it is already described as a 'cynical saying, and yet less bitter than at first appears'. As such, it builds upon the simpler 'Don't believe all you hear' which *CODP* finds in some form before 1300, perhaps even as a proverb of King Alfred the Great's.

believing. See SEEING IS ~.

Belisha beacon, a. An orange glass globe atop a pole which is painted in black and white bands and situated on both sides of a pedestrian crossing in Britain as a warning to motorists. The beacon was introduced in 1934 when Leslie Hore-Belisha (created Baron, 1954) was Minister of Transport. On 27 January 1935, Chips Channon noted in his diary: 'Belisha Beacons, unheard of a few weeks ago, are now world famous,' and on 31 January: 'He is the most advertised man in England today.'

be like dad, keep mum. British security slogan of the Second World War, emanating from the Ministry of Information in 1941. Another version was **keep mum, she's not so dumb** and showed a very un-Mum-like blonde being ogled by representatives of the three services. The security theme was paramount in both the UK and US wartime propaganda. Civilians as well as military personnel were urged not to talk about war-related matters lest the enemy somehow got to hear.
Compare MUM'S THE WORD.

bell, I'll give you a (or **I'll bell you**). Meaning, 'I will ring you on the telephone', a promise to keep in touch. Came into British colloquial use c 1981.

bell, book and candle. Phrase from a solemn form of excommunication from the Roman Catholic Church. Bartlett (1980) says the ceremony has been current since the eighth century AD. There is a version dating from 1200 AD which goes: 'Do to the book [meaning, close it], quench the candle, ring the bell.' These actions symbolize the spiritual darkness the person is condemned to when denied further participation in the sacraments of the church. Sir Thomas Malory in *Le Morte d'Arthur* (1485) has: 'I shall curse you with book and bell and candle.' Shakespeare has the modern configuration in *King John*, III.ii.22 (1595): 'Bell, book and candle shall not drive me back.'
Bell, Book and Candle was the title of John Van Druten's play (1950; film US, 1958)

about a publisher who discovers his girlfriend is a witch.

bells. See KNOCK SEVEN ~ OUT OF; PUT THE ~ AND WHISTLES ON.

bells and smells. Phrase characterizing Anglo-Catholicism or the 'High' Anglican church with its emphasis on incense-burning and other rites more usually associated with the Roman Catholic church. Sometimes given as 'bells and *spells*', the phrase was established by the early 1980s. Such rites (and their adherents) are also described as **way up the candle.**

belongs. See TOMORROW ~ TO ME.

beloved. See BEST ~.

belt and braces. The name applied to a system with its own back-up, suggesting that if one part falls down, the other will stay up, a double check. An engineer's expression, used for example by a BBC man to describe the two microphones placed side-by-side when broadcasting the sovereign's Christmas message. In the days when this was broadcast live, it ensured transmission. Belt and Braces was also the name of a British theatre group of the 1970s.
An Australian engineer commented (1993) that some of his colleagues would talk of 'belt, braces and bowyangs, too' – 'bowyangs' being ties round a worker's trousers to keep out cold and mud.

be my guest. *American Speech* in 1955 had 'be my guest' as a way of saying 'go right ahead; do as you wish'. Hilton hotels may also have used 'be my guest' as a slogan at some time. Certainly, *Be My Guest* was the title of a book (1957) by the hotelier, Conrad Hilton. What is not obvious is when the phrase originated.

Ben. See BIG ~.

bench. See NO MORE LATIN . . .

bend. See CLEAN(S) ROUND THE ~.

Bendor. The nickname for the 2nd Duke of Westminster (*d* 1953), commemorated a defeat in heraldic law for his ancestor, Sir Robert Grosvenor, over the coat of arms he could bear. In 1389 the Court of Chivalry ruled in favour of Sir Richard le Scrope in his action over the right to arms 'Azure, a bend or' [a blue shield with a diagonal gold bar]. Grosvenor refused to accept this and appealed to Richard II. The monarch also ruled against him and Grosvenor was forced to bear the costs of the action. He ended up using 'Azure, a garb or' [a blue shield with a golden sheaf of corn].

Robert Lacey in *Aristocrats* (1983) suggests, however, that the nicknaming was not direct and that the 2nd Duke was so called via the colt that won the Derby for his grandfather, Hugh Lupus, in 1880. 'According to family legend, some similarity of colour was discerned between the chestnutty animal and the reddish fluff on the head of the baby born within a few months of the horse's first successes on the turf.'

benedictus. See MASS PHRASES.

benefit. See BEING FOR THE ∼ OF —.

Bennett. See GORDON ∼!

Bennies. The inhabitants of the Falkland Islands were so named by British forces stationed there following the 1982 conflict with Argentina. The uncomplimentary reference is to a not-very-bright character in the ITV soap opera *Crossroads*. When reprimanded for the coinage, troops resorted to calling the islanders 'Stills' (for 'Still Bennies'). An even later variant by sections of the occupying forces for some of the islanders, was 'Bubs' [Bloody Ungrateful Bastards]. The islanders responded by calling the soldiers 'Whennies' – from their constant references to past exploits: 'When I was in Belize, when I was in Cyprus . . .'

Bentley. See under TAKE IT FROM HERE.

be prepared. The motto of the Boy Scout movement (founded 1908), which shares its initials with the movement's founder, Sir Robert Baden-Powell. With permission, the words were subsequently used as an advertising slogan for Pears' soap.

berk, a (right). Morris (1977) cites Dudley Moore as saying of Peter Cook (in a magazine interview): 'It is hard to distinguish sometimes whether Peter is being playful or merely a berk.' Morris then goes on, coyly, to say '*berk* is British slang – originally a bit of Cockney rhyming slang – meaning "fool"' – and leaves it at that. In fact, 'berk' is short for 'Berkeley/Berkshire Hunt' ('cunt'). Spelling the word 'birk' or 'burk(e)' helps obscure the origin. Theoretically, if it comes from this source, the word should be pronounced 'bark'. The use probably does not date from before 1900.

Bermuda Triangle, the. An area of sea between Bermuda and Florida where a number of ships and aircraft inexplicably disappeared. So described by the early 1960s. Then, allusively, the name given to any thing or place into which people or things simply vanish.

Bernie, the bolt! Bob Monkhouse, host of ATV's game show *The Golden Shot* from 1967–75, explained in 1979: 'Lew Grade had bought the Swiss-German TV success *The Golden Shot* and the host had to repeat one line in each show – the word of instruction to the technician to load the dangerous crossbow and simultaneously warn the studio of the fact that the weapon was armed . . . "Heinz, the bolt!" [was the original phrase].

'When I took over in 1967, Heinz went home. He stayed long enough to train an ATV technician, Derek Young. I said, '"Derek, the bolt' sounds lousy. Let's make it alliterative. What's funny and begins with B?" We were reckoning without the man himself. Derek liked Derek. "Well, you think of a name that begins with B and won't embarrass you," I said. And Bernie it became. I found out later that his wife liked it. Certainly the audience did. Only blokes called Bernie grew to loathe it. Thousands of letters were addressed simply to "Bernie the Bolt, ITV".' The phrase stayed the same even when Derek was replaced by another technician.

At one time, viewers watching the programme at home could ring and instruct the operator to aim the gun. Hence: **Left a bit, – stop! Down a bit, – stop! Up a bit,**

– **stop! Fire!** This acquired a kind of catchphrase status, not least because of the possible *double entendre*.

Bertha. See BIG ∼.

Bertie. See BURLINGTON ∼.

be soon! See under SHE KNOWS, YOU KNOW!

best. See AND THE ∼ OF LUCK!; ∼ CAR IN THE WORLD under AT 60 MILES AN HOUR . . . ; ∼ FRIEND under *EDUCATING ARCHIE*; EVEN YOUR ∼ FRIENDS . . .; I ALWAYS DO MY ∼ . . . under *ITMA*; PROBABLY THE ∼ LAGER . . .; WHY NOT THE ∼? under JIMMY WHO?; YOU WANT THE ∼ SEATS . . .

best and the brightest, the. This alliterative combination is almost traditional: 'Political writers, who will not suffer the best and brightest of characters . . . to take a single right step for the honour or interest of the nation' (*Letters of Junius*, 1769); 'Best and brightest, come away!' (Shelley, 'To Jane: The Invitation', 1822); 'Brightest and best of the sons of the morning' (the hymn by Bishop Heber, 1827); 'The best, the brightest, the cleverest of them all!' (Trollope, *Dr Thorne*, Chap. 25, 1858).

In David Halberstam's book *The Best and the Brightest* (1972), the phrase applies to the young men from business, industry and the academic world whom John F. Kennedy brought into government in the early 1960s but who were ultimately responsible for the quagmire of American involvement in the Vietnam War.

best beloved. Term of endearment (also 'O My Best Beloved' and 'O Best Beloved') addressed to the reader of Rudyard Kipling's *Just So Stories* (1902). These comic fables explaining the distinguishing characteristics of animals ('How the Camel Got His Hump' and so on) were originally told by Kipling to his own children.

best foot forward, to put one's. Meaning 'to walk as fast as possible; to make a good impression', this probably derives from an earlier form: 'to put one's best foot/leg foremost'. In Shakespeare's

King John (1595) we find: 'Nay, but make haste; the better foot before' (IV.ii.170). The *right* foot has from ancient times been regarded as the best foot, right being associated with rationality, the left with emotion. To put your right foot forward is thus to guard against ill-luck.

best fucks are always after a good cry, the. A seldom-recorded observation. In *Peter Hall's Diaries* (for 22 May 1979) it is quoted as having been said at Glyndebourne after Elizabeth Söderström had burst into tears at being given tough direction and then gone on to give 'a very good first act'.

best of order. See GIVE ORDER.

best possible taste. See IT'S ALL DONE . . .

best Prime Minister we have, the. (or **never had**). R.A. (later Lord) Butler (*d* 1982) has sometimes been known as 'the best Prime Minister we never had' (as have others, like Denis Healey, for example), and it is to Butler we probably owe both formats. In December 1955, having (not for the last time) been passed over for the Conservative leadership, he was confronted by a Press Association reporter just as he was about to board an aircraft at London airport. As criticism was growing over the performance of Anthony Eden, the Prime Minister, the reporter asked: 'Mr Butler, would you say that this [Eden] is the best Prime Minister we have!' Butler assented to this 'well-meant but meaningless proposition . . . indeed it was fathered upon me. I don't think it did Anthony any good. It did not do me any good either' (*The Art of the Possible*, 1973).

best shot, to give something one's. To try as hard as possible. An American idiom (known by 1984) but now verging on the cliché. Presumably this comes from the sporting sense of 'shot' (as in golf) rather than the gun sense. The US film *Hoosiers* (1986), about a basketball team, was also known as *Best Shot*. From the *Washington Post* (13 February 1984): ' "We're not able to adequately counsel the farmer with the present plan," he said. "With this, we'll be able to give him our best shot." ' From the

Guardian (14 May 1984): 'The editor must keep his powder dry. He is there to sell newspapers and his best shot is to find and project material denied to his rivals.'

best swordsman in all France, the. (also **finest swordsman . . .**) A cliché of swashbuckling epics. 'Don't worry . . . my father was the best swordsman in France' is said to be spoken in the film *Son of Monte Cristo* (1940), though this is unverified. In 1984, a book by Keith Miles on the subject of clichés in general was given the title *The Finest Swordsman in All France*. A relatively unself-conscious use occurs in Charles Dickens, *Barnaby Rudge*, Chap. 27 (1841): 'I have been tempted in these two short interviews, to draw upon that fellow, fifty times. Five men in six would have yielded to the impulse. By suppressing mine, I wound him deeper and more keenly than if I were the best swordsman in all Europe.' Completely straightforward is John Aubrey's use in his *Lives* (c 1697): 'Sir John Digby yielded to be the best swordsman of his time.'

best thing. See GREATEST THING SINCE . . .

best things in life are free, the. A modern proverb which really does seem to have started life with the song of the title (1927) by De Sylva, Brown and Henderson – featured in the show *Good News* (filmed US 1930 and 1947).

best years of — life. See HAPPIEST DAYS OF YOUR LIFE; I'VE GIVEN YOU THE ~.

better. See EVERY DAY AND IN EVERY WAY . . . ; NO ~ THAN SHE SHOULD BE.

better mousetrap, a. See BEAT A PATH TO ONE'S DOOR, TO.

better red than dead. A slogan used by some (mainly British) nuclear disarmers. Bertrand Russell wrote in 1958: 'If no alternative remains except communist domination or the extinction of the human race, the former alternative is the lesser of two evils'. The counter cry: 'Better dead than red' may also have had some currency. (In the film *Love With a Proper Stranger* (US, 1964) Steve McQueen proposed to Natalie Wood with a picket sign stating 'Better Wed Than Dead'.)

Betty. See OOH, ~!

Betty Martin. See ALL MY EYE AND ~.

between a rock and a hard place. In a position impossible to get out of, literally or metaphorically. Popular in the 1970s and almost certainly of North American origin. An early appearance occurs in John Buchan, *The Courts of the Morning* (1929) but the phrase was being discussed in *Dialect Notes*, No. 5 (1921) where it was defined as 'to be bankrupt . . . Common in Arizona in recent panics; sporadic in California'.

bet you can't eat just one. A slogan for Lay's potato chips in the US (quoted in 1981). By 1982, **bet you can't eat three** was being used by the cricketer Ian Botham to promote Shredded Wheat in the UK.

bet your sweet bippy. See under LAUGH-IN.

Beulah. See SOMEBODY BAWL FOR ~?

Beulah – peel me a grape! A catchphrase expressing dismissive unconcern first uttered by Mae West to a black maid in the film *I'm No Angel* (1933) after a male admirer has stormed out on her. It has had some wider currency since then but is nearly always used as a quotation.

Be Upstairs Ready My Angel. See BURMA.

bewdy Newk! Translated from the Australian, this means 'What a beauty, Newcombe!', referring to the tennis player, John Newcombe. **Life. Be in it** was the slogan of a campaign which began in the State of Victoria and then spread across Australia in the late 1970s, aiming to get people involved in healthy activities like tennis. One TV commercial showed 'Norm', a fat armchair sportsman (or COUCH POTATO, as he would later have been described), watching Newcombe and cheering him on with the phrase.

Beyond Our Ken. Kenneth Horne (1900–69) was a bald, benign and urbane figure who had little of show business about him. He was not a stand-up comedian. He seemed to have drifted into the radio studio from a busy life elsewhere as a company director (and until ill-health forced him to choose broadcasting in favour of business, this was indeed the case).

From 1958–64, Horne presided over a radio show called *Beyond Our Ken*. This was basically a sketch show, scripted by Eric Merriman and Barry Took, and performed by some able supporting actors. One of these was Kenneth Williams (1926–88) who created a professional countryman figure with a loam-rich voice (perhaps based on Ralph Wightman or A.G. Street) and called Arthur Fallowfield who appeared in an *Any Questions* spoof. **I think the answer lies in the soil** was his comment on every problem. He also had the lament, **I'm looking for someone to love**. In addition, Williams played an ancient gentleman who, when asked how long he had been doing anything, would reply, forthrightly, **35 years!**

In the same show, Hugh Paddick played Cecil Snaith, a hush-voiced BBC outside broadcasts commentator. After some disaster in which he had figured, he would give, as the punchline, in a deadpan manner, **and with that, I return you to the studio!** Kenneth Horne apparently suggested the line. In its straight form, many TV and radio news reporters use the phrase in live spots even today.

Paddick and Williams also played two frightfully correct types who would greet each other with: **Hello, Rodney!/Hello, Charles!**

The announcer would conclude the show with: **'You have either been listening to – or have just missed . . .'**

Compare ROUND THE HORNE.

Beyond the Fringe. The title of a trend-setting revue presented in the West End in 1961 and then on Broadway. It had first been shown, however, at the 1960 Edinburgh Festival as part of the main programme of events, and had thus been 'beyond' the unofficial series of theatrical manifestations at Edinburgh known as the 'Fringe'. Note also an allusion to the following:

beyond the pale. Meaning, 'outside the bounds of acceptable behaviour'. The Pale was the area of English settlement around Dublin in Ireland, dating from the fourteenth century, in which English law had to be obeyed, but there have also been areas known as pales in Scotland, around Calais, and in Russia. The derivation is from Latin *palus*, meaning 'a stake'. Anyone who lived beyond this fence was thought to be beyond the bounds of civilization. The allusive use does not appear earlier than the mid-nineteenth century.

B.F.N. – bye for now! See under MORNING ALL!

Bic. See FLICK YOUR ∼.

big. See BOOTS, TO BE TOO ∼ FOR ONE'S; HE WAS A ∼ MAN . . .; MR ∼.

Big Apple, the. As a nickname for New York City, this expression seems to have arisen in the 1920s/30s. There are various possible explanations: the Spanish word for a block of houses between two streets is *manzana* which is also the word for apple; in the mid-1930s there was a Harlem night club called 'The Big Apple' which was a mecca for jazz musicians; there was also a jitterbugging dance from the swing era (c 1936) which took its name from the nightclub; 'big apple' was racetrack argot and New York City had a good reputation in this field – hence, the phrase was used to describe the city's metropolitan racing (as in 'On the Big Apple', a column by John J. Fitzgerald in the *Morning Telegraph*, mid-1920s.)

OED2 has 'Big Apple' for New York City in 1928 *before* the dance explanation, but Safire plumps for the jazz version, recalling a 1944 jive 'handbook' defining 'apple' as: 'the earth, the universe, this planet. Any place that's large. A big Northern city'. Hence, you called New York City the Big Apple if you considered it to be the centre of the universe. In 1971, Charles Gillett, president of the New York Convention and Visitors Bureau, attempted to revitalize

NYC's economy by re-popularizing it as 'the Big Apple' (compare I LOVE NEW YORK).

In the eighteenth century, Horace Walpole called London 'The Strawberry' because of its freshness and cleanliness in comparison with foreign cities.

Big Bang. On 27 October 1986, the London Stock Exchange deregulated the British securities market in a sweeping move to which the light-hearted appellation 'Big Bang' was applied by those hoping for a 'boom' and fearing a 'bust' (which duly followed a year later). The system of fixed commissions on stock trading was eliminated in favour of negotiated rates. At the same time, the practice of separating brokers (who take orders and execute trades on behalf of investors) from jobbers (who buy and sell stock on their own account in order to make a market in that stock) was abolished. The previous March, banks and brokerages, domestic and foreign, were allowed to become members of the exchange in a move dubbed 'Little Bang'. The so-called 'Big Bang' theory of the beginning of the universe had been discussed during 1950 by Fred Hoyle in his book *The Nature of the Universe* and the phrase obviously predated the specific application to deregulation in the City.

Big Ben. Although used to refer to the whole of the clock tower of the Houses of Parliament, London, the nickname is more correctly applied to just the bell. Weighing 13½ tons, it was named after Sir Benjamin Hall who was the Commissioner of Works when it was hung in 1856.

Big Bertha. A soldiers' nickname for a German long-range gun of the First World War. It was used to shell Paris in 1918. Bertha, the only child of Friedrich Alfred Krupp, who had inherited the great engineering and armaments undertaking, married in 1906 and her husband became head of the firm.

Big Brother is watching you. A fictional slogan from George Orwell's novel *Nineteen Eighty-Four* (1948). In a dictatorial state, every citizen is regimented and observed by a spying TV set in the home. The line became a popular catchphrase following a sensational BBC TV dramatization of the novel in 1954.

Aspects of the Ministry of Truth in the novel were derived not only from Orwell's knowledge of the BBC (where he worked) but also from his first wife Eileen's work at the Ministry of Food, preparing 'Kitchen Front' broadcasts during the Second World War (c 1942–4). One campaign used the slogan 'Potatoes are Good for You' and was so successful that it had to be followed by 'Potatoes are Fattening'.

big butter and egg man, a. As a description of small-town businessman trying to prove himself a big shot in the city, the phrase was much used by Texas Guinan, the US nightclub hostess (d 1933). Cyril Connolly in his *Journals* (1983) characterized the man in question as a small-town success, often a farmer who produced such commodities as butter and eggs, and who attempts to pass for a sophisticate in the big city. Finding it first in the 1920s, *OED2* emphasizes that the man in question – 'wealthy, unsophisticated' – spends his money freely.

Big Chill generation, the. A term alluding to those who grew up in the 1960s, and taken from the title of *The Big Chill* (film US, 1983), 'the story of eight old friends searching for something they lost, and finding that all they needed was each other'. Hence, the *Washington Post* for 1 August 1985 talked of: 'A performance by the Temptations or the Four Tops is always a big thrill for the "Big Chill" generation.' A report of Douglas Ginsburg's rejected nomination as a member of the US Supreme Court in *Time* Magazine (16 November 1987) contained the following: 'Although Ginsburg's indiscretion may have been common among members of the Big Chill generation, his confessions fatally undermined his support among the Capitol Hill conservatives who had lobbied so hard for his nomination.'

big deal! A deflating (mostly American) exclamation. *DOAS* has it in 'wide student use since c 1940' and 'popularized by comedian Arnold Stang in the Henry Morgan network radio program c 1946 and on the Milton Berle network program *c* 1950'. Leo Rosten in *Hooray for Yiddish!* (1982) emphasizes a similarity with sarcastic, derisive, Jewish phrases and notes how 'it is uttered with emphasis on the "big", in a dry disenchanted tone'.

Big Enchilada, the. Nickname of John Mitchell (1913–88), US Attorney General, who led President Nixon's re-election campaign in 1972 and subsequently was sentenced to a gaol term for associated offences. An enchilada is a Mexican dish. The term was evoked (like 'Big Cheese') by a Nixon aide, John Ehrlichman, during a 1973 taped conversation in the White House. He sought to describe the size of the sacrificial victim who was being thrown to the wolves.

bigger. See CLOUD NO ~ THAN A MAN'S HAND; IS IT ~ THAN A BREADBOX?; THIS THING IS ~ THAN BOTH OF US.

Bigger Splash, A. Title of a 1973 British documentary for the cinema about the artist David Hockney which did not neglect his homosexual lifestyle. Taken from Hockney's 1967 painting with the title – one of his swimming pool series.

bigger they come, the harder they fall, the. A proverbial phrase often attributed to Bob Fitzsimmons (1862–1917), a British-born boxer in the US, referring to an opponent of larger build (James L. Jeffries), by 1900. Also attributed to the boxer John L. Sullivan, but probably of earlier proverbial origin in any case.

big girl's blouse, a. Phrase used about a man who is not as manly as he might be. A rather odd expression, possibly of Welsh origin, and to do with what an effeminate football or rugby player might wear instead of a proper jersey. *Street Talk, the Language of Coronation Street* (1986) states, rather, that it 'describes an adult male who has a low pain threshold, a "sissy". When trying to remove a splinter someone might say: "Hold still you big girl's blouse. It won't hurt."' The phrase has also been associated with the British comedienne Hylda Baker (1908–86) which, if the case, would take back its use to the early 1970s, at least.

From the *Guardian* (20 December 1986) –

about a nativity play: 'The house is utterly still (except where Balthazar is trying to screw the spout of his frankincense pot into Melchior's ear, to even things up for being called a big girl's blouse on the way in from the dressing room.)' From the Glasgow *Herald* (20 October 1994): 'His acid-tongued father [Prince Philip] might be reinforced in his view of him as a big girl's blouse, but Prince Charles is actually a big boy now. His children, locked away in the posh equivalent of care, are not.' From the *Sunday Times* (6 November 1994): 'Men, quite naturally, are equally unwilling to accept paternity leave, because of the fear that this will mark them for ever as a great big girl's blouse.'

big-hearted Arthur, that's me! See under *BAND WAGGON*.

Big Lie, the. From the German *grosse Lüge* – a distortion of the truth so brazen that it cannot fail to be accepted, a technique that was the cornerstone of Nazi propaganda. Adolf Hitler wrote in *Mein Kampf* (1925): 'The great mass of the people . . . will more easily fall victims to a big lie than to a small one.' Together with Josef Goebbels, his propaganda chief, Hitler perceived that the bigger a lie was and the more frequently it was told, the greater was the likelihood of its mass acceptance.

big money! See under LOADSAMONEY!

big one, the. This boast, beloved – in particular – of a certain type of advertiser, almost certainly dates back to 1907 when, in the US, Ringling Brothers Circus bought up its rival, Barnum and Bailey. The two together were billed, understandably, as 'The Big One'. When the outfit closed in 1956, the *New York Post* had the headline, 'THE BIG ONE IS NO MORE!' The term may be applied to any product or event that any advertiser wishes to promote as important. From the BBC radio show *ROUND THE HORNE* (14 May 1967): 'Rousing fanfare: "This is the big one" – "Watch out for it" – "It's coming your way" – "It's coming soon" – "Don't miss it".'

DOAS points out that a 'big one' is also a $1,000 bill (from gambling) [£100 in the UK] and a nursery euphemism for a bowel movement. Partridge/*Slang* has 'big one' or 'big 'un' for 'a notable person' and dates it 1800–50. Pierce Egan in *Boxiana* (1829) has: 'Jem had now reduced the "big one" to his own weight, and had also placed him upon the stand-still system.'

The British TV commentator David Vine caused a good deal of inappropriate laughter around 1974 when, at athletic competitions, he would talk of competitors 'pulling out the big one' – i.e. making the supreme effort.

Since the 1960s at least, the phrase 'Big One' has also been applied to the feared and inevitable major earthquake expected in southern California, of which there have been several harbingers. From the *Washington Post* (2 October 1987): 'Shaken Californians' Thoughts Turn To The Future "Big One" – . . . Southern Californians spent most of their day today reliving the earthquake and almost everybody's wild fear that this would be what is generally referred to in this state as "the Big One" . . . a reference to the earthquake all Californians know has been building for decades along the San Andreas Fault, and which is predicted, when it hits, to cause massive devastation along the West Coast.'

big sleep, the. A synonym for death, as in the title of the novel *The Big Sleep* (1939; films US, 1946 and 1977) by Raymond Chandler.

bike. See MIND MY ∼; ON YOUR ∼.

Bill. See BUFFALO ∼; BUNGALOW ∼; OLD ∼; OVER WILL'S MOTHER'S WAY . . .

Billy. See SILLY ∼.

Bing. See OLD GROANER.

Bingo! A generalized exclamation on achieving anything, similar to 'Eureka!'. In 1919, at a carnival near Jacksonville, Florida, Edwin Lowe saw people playing what they called 'bean-o' – putting beans on a numbered card. This game of chance was already established elsewhere under the names 'Keno', 'Loo', and 'Housey-Housey'. Lowe developed the idea and launched a craze which netted him a fortune. One of

his friends stuttered, 'B . . . b . . . bingo!' on winning, and that is how the game is said to have got its name. The word had already been applied to brandy in the seventeenth century, but – as a result of this development from 'bean-o' – it turned not only into an exclamation on winning Lowe's game but also into a generalized cry.

Binkie Beaumont. For many years in British theatrical circles, this nickname meant only Hugh Beaumont, managing director of H.M. Tennent, the play production company. He was the most influential force in West End theatre from the 1940s to the 70s, and was always known thus within the profession, as he disliked his given name. There is an echo of 'Dandie Dinmont', the terrier named after a character in one of Sir Walter Scott's novels, but according to Richard Huggett's biography (1989), Beaumont became 'Binkie' as a baby when two women from the seamy side of Cardiff gazed into his pram and said: 'Oh, he's a proper little binkie, isn't he?' The word was local slang for black, negro, dirty or unwashed, and the remark was heavy with irony, because the baby was never anything but blond, pink and immaculate.

bippy. See YOU BET YOUR SWEET ∼ under *LAUGH-IN*.

bird. See I'LL BE A DIRTY ∼; IT'S A ∼ under *SUPERMAN*.

bird, to get the. Meaning, 'to be rejected by an audience'. Originally the expression was 'to get the big bird', and has been used as such since the nineteenth century. What do audiences do when they do not like something? They boo or they hiss, sounding something like a flock of geese, perhaps.

birdie. See WATCH THE ∼.

birds. See BOX OF ∼; HELLO ∼ . . .; STRICTLY FOR THE ∼.

Birds Eye. It may come as a surprise to consumers of the frozen foods sold under this brand name that the allusion is to one Clarence Birdseye (*d* 1956). An American, he thought up the freezing process while fur-trapping in Labrador. In 1923, he launched Birdseye Seafoods Inc in New York. Eventually the company was absorbed by General Foods Corporation. The two-word form of the name may be appropriate as family tradition holds that it was given to an English ancestor, a royal page at court, who once shot a hawk through the eye.

birds of the air, the. This is essentially a biblical phrase: e.g. Matthew 8:20, 'the foxes have holes, and the birds of the air have nests'. However, it makes a later notable appearance in the rhyme 'Who Killed Cock Robin?' (first recorded in the eighteenth century): 'All the birds of the air/Fell a-sighing and a-sobbing,/When they heard the bell toll/For poor Cock Robin.' Used as the title of a novel (1980) by Alice Thomas Ellis.
   A variant is 'fowl(s) of the air' (Genesis 1:26), though much more commonly one finds 'fowls of the heavens' in (mostly) the Old Testament. The 'fish(es) of the sea' occurs at least three times in the Old Testament (e.g. Genesis 1:26). 'All the beasts of the forest' is biblical too (Psalms 104:20), though more frequent is **beasts of the field** (e.g. Psalms 8:7).

biscuit factory, to go to the. 'To go to the (men's) lavatory'. A minor, dated, but charming Australianism, current at one time in South Australia. The derivation is simple. There was a brand of biscuit made by W. Menz and Co. Ltd of Adelaide, from the 1850s on. Thus 'to go to the biscuit factory' was the same as 'to go to the men's'.

bishop. See AS THE ~ SAID under AS THE ART MISTRESS . . . ; BASH THE ~; ~ OF NORWICH see DO YOU KNOW . . .

bishop-bashing. See BASH/FLOG THE BISHOP.

Bismarck a herring?, is. See IS THE POPE A CATHOLIC?

Bisto. See AHH, ~!

bit. See LEFT A ~ under BERNIE, THE BOLT!

bitch. See under BEAST OF —; LIFE'S A ~ AND THEN YOU DIE; SON OF A ~.

bite the dust. See KICK/LICK THE DUST.

bitter end, the. Meaning 'the last extremity; the absolute limit', and a common phrase by the mid-nineteenth century. Bitterness doesn't really enter into it: the nautical 'bitt' is a bollard on the deck of a ship, on to which cables and ropes are wound. The end of the cable that is wrapped round or otherwise secured to the bollard is the 'bitter end'. On the other hand, ends have – for possibly longer – been described as bitter in other senses. Proverbs 5:4 has: 'But her end is bitter as wormwood, sharp as a two-edged sword'.

black. See ANY COLOUR SO LONG AS IT'S ~; ~ BOMBER under BROWN BOMBER; LITTLE ~ DRESS; SAY IT LOUD . . .; YOUNG, GIFTED AND ~.

Black and Tans, the. Members of a special armed force (made up of ex-servicemen) sent to Ireland in 1920 by the British government. Their purpose was to put down Republican rebels, which they attempted to do with much bloodshed. The name was derived from the colour of their mixed uniforms – army khaki combined with the black belts and dark green caps of the Royal Irish Constabulary – but also from the name of a pack of hounds in County Tipperary. Earlier, during the Reconstruction period after the American Civil War, the name had been given to Republicans unwilling to abandon the negro as a basis of the party's power in Alabama; also to a type of terrier dog and to a drink of porter and ale.

black as Newgate knocker, as. This comparison meaning 'extremely black' and known by 1881 alludes to Newgate gaol, the notorious prison for the City of London until 1880. It must have had a very formidable and notable knocker because not only do we have this expression but a 'Newgate knocker' was the name given to a lock of hair twisted to look like a knocker.

blackboard jungle, the. One of several phrases which suggest that there are urban areas where the 'law of the jungle' may apply – in this case, the educational system. *The Blackboard Jungle* was the title of a novel (1954; film US, 1955) by Evan Hunter. Earlier, there had been W.R. Burnett's novel *The Asphalt Jungle* (1949), though *OED2* finds that phrase in use in 1920. A little after, in 1969, come references to 'the concrete jungle'.

Compare BACK TO THE JUNGLE.

black box, a. After a plane crash there is usually a scramble to retrieve the aircraft's 'black box' – or, more properly, its 'flight data recorder'. This contains detailed recordings of the aircraft's performance prior to the crash and can be of value in determining what went wrong. The name has been used since the Second World War. Originally it was RAF slang for a box containing intricate navigational equipment. Flight recorders are in fact *orange* so as to be more easily seen. The popular name arose probably because black is a more mysterious colour, appropriate for a box containing 'secret' equipment (Pye produced a record player with the name in the 1950s), and because of the alliteration.

black-coated workers. Referring to prunes as laxatives, this term, of earlier origin, was popularized from 1941 onwards in an early-morning BBC programme *The Kitchen Front* by the 'Radio Doctor', Charles (later Lord) Hill, who noted in his autobiography *Both Sides of the Hill* (1964): 'I remember calling on the Principal Medical Officer of the Board of Education . . . At the end of the interview this shy and solemn man diffidently suggested that the prune was a black-coated worker and that this phrase might be useful to me. It was.' Earlier, Chips Channon (8 April 1937) was using the phrase in a literal sense concerning the clerical and professional class when he wrote: 'The subject was "Widows and Orphans" the Old Age Pensions Bill, a measure which affects Southend and its black-coated workers' (*Chips: The Diaries of Sir Henry Channon*, ed. Robert Rhodes James, 1967).

black dog, the. Used notably by Winston Churchill to describe the fits of depression to which he was sometimes subjected, this is an old phrase. It was known by the late eighteenth century, as in the country/ nursery saying about a sullen child: 'The black dog is on his back'. Brewer has the alternative, 'a black dog has walked over him'. The reference here is to the devil, as in J.B. Priestley's *The Good Companions* (1929): 'He [Jess Oakroyd] was troubled by a vague foreboding. It was just as if a demoniac black dog went trotting everywhere at his heels.'

A perfect explanation appears in a letter from Samuel Johnson to Mrs Thrale (28 June 1783): 'The black Dog I hope always to resist, and in time to drive though I am deprived of almost all those that used to help me . . . Mrs Allen is dead . . . Mrs Williams is so weak that she can be a companion no longer. When I rise my breakfast is solitary, the black dog waits to share it . . .'

Black Friday. Originally this was a description of Good Friday, when clergymen wore dark vestments. However, there have been any number of specific 'Black Fridays', so designated. In Britain, on one such day (15 April 1921), certain trade unions withdrew support from the hard-pressed miners, a general strike was cancelled, and this is recalled in the Labour movement as a day of betrayal. In the US, the 'first' Black Friday was on 24 September 1929 when panic broke out on the stock market.

During the Wall Street crash there were similarly a **Black Wednesday**, a **Black Thursday** – the actual day of the crash – and a **Black Tuesday**. In 1988, on stock markets round the world, there was a **Black Monday** (October 19) and another Black Thursday (October 22).

black hole, a. A term in astronomy for what is left when a star collapses gravitationally, thus leaving a field from which neither matter nor radiation can escape. The term was in use by 1968, and is sometimes used figuratively to describe the place into which a person is presumed to have disappeared.

Black Hole of Calcutta, the. In 1756, 146 Europeans, including one woman, were condemned by the Nawab of Bengal to spend a night in the 'Black-Hole' prison of Fort William, Calcutta, after it had been captured. Only 23, including the woman, survived till morning. Subsequently the phrase has been applied to any place of confinement or any airless, dark place. From Francis Kilvert's diary entry for 27 October 1874 (about a Church Missionary Society meeting): 'The weather was close, warm and muggy, the room crowded to suffocation and frightfully hot, like the Black Hole of Calcutta, though the doors and all the windows were wide open' (*Kilvert's Diary*, Vols.1–3, ed. William Plomer, 1961).

blacking. See NOT WORTH – UP FOR!

Black is beautiful. The Rev. Dr Martin Luther King Jnr launched a poster campaign based on these words in 1967 but Stokely Carmichael had used the phrase earlier at a Memphis Civil Rights rally in 1966 and it had appeared in *Liberation* (N.Y.) on 25 September 1965. It may have its origins in the Song of Solomon 1:5, 'I am black, but comely.'

Black Maria, a. An American explanation for this name as applied to a police van is that a brawny black woman called Maria Lee kept a lodging house in Boston and helped bundle arrested people into the police van. The term was known in the US by 1847 and in the UK by 1869.

black mark, Bentley! See under TAKE IT FROM HERE.

Black Panther, the. Nickname of the British criminal, Donald Nielsen, convicted of the kidnap and murder of Lesley Whittle and of the killing of three sub-post officials in 1975. During the nine-month police search for him, he was so dubbed by the popular press on account of the black hood he wore to disguise himself. The inadvisability of the indiscriminate use of such sobriquets was demonstrated during Nielsen's trial when a BBC Radio newsreader accounced: 'At Oxford Crown Court today, the jury was told that Donald Nielsen denies being the *Pink* Panther.'

In the mid-1960s, the name 'Black Panther' was taken by members of a militant American negro organization. In the animal kingdom the name is given to a black-coated form of the leopard.

Black power. A slogan encompassing just about anything that people want it to mean, from simple pride in the Black race to a threat of violence. Adam Clayton Powell Jr, the Harlem congressman, said in a baccalaureate address at Howard University in May 1966: 'To demand these God-given rights is to seek black power – what I call audacious power – the power to build black institutions of splendid achievement.'

On 6 June the same year, James Meredith, the first black student to integrate the University of Mississippi (in 1962), was shot and wounded during a civil rights march. Stokely Carmichael, heading the Student Non-violent Coordinating Committee, continued the march, during which his contingent first used the phrase as a shout. Carmichael used it in a speech at Greenwood, Mississippi, the same month. It was also adopted as a slogan by the Congress for Racial Equality. However, the notion was not new in the 1960s.

Langston Hughes had written in *Simple Takes a Wife* (1953): 'Negro blood is so powerful – because just *one* drop of black blood makes a coloured man – *one* drop – you are a Negro! . . . Black is powerful.'

Black September. The name of a Palestinian terrorist group, established after the PLO's eviction from its strongholds in Jordan in September 1970. The name was known by the autumn of 1972.

black velvet. A drink made up of equal parts champagne and and stout (especially Guinness) and which derives from its appearance and taste. Also used to describe the sexual attributes of a black woman, according to Partridge/*Slang*. Compare BLUE VELVET and see also LITTLE GENTLEMAN IN ~.

blah-blah-blah. 'Blah' or 'blah-blah', signifying 'empty talk; airy mouthings', are phrases that have been around (originally in the US) since the end of the First World War. More recently the tripartite version (although known by 1924) has become marginally more frequent to denote words omitted or as another way of saying 'and so on'. Ira and George Gershwin wrote a song called 'Blah, Blah, Blah' for a film called *Delicious* (1931) which contains such lines as 'Blah, blah, blah, blah moon . . . Blah, blah, blah, blah croon'.

Other examples of the phrase's use are: '*Burt* [a journalist]: "You wouldn't object to that angle for the piece? Here's what he says: The Family bla-bla-bla, here's how he lives . . ."' (Peter Nichols, *Chez Nous*, 1974); 'Saul Kelner, 19 . . . was the first person in line to see the president. He arrived at the White House . . . 11½ hours before the open house was to begin. "We didn't sleep," he said. "What we did, we circulated a list to ensure our places on line. 'We the people, blah, blah, blah,' and we all signed it"' (*Washington Post*, 22 January 1989); 'Bush referred to the diplomatic language [after a NATO summit conference in Bonn] in casual slang as "blah, blah"' (*Washington Post*, 31 May 1989). The latter caused foreign journalists problems: 'After all, how do you translate "blah, blah" into Italian?'

bless his little cotton socks. A pleasant remark to make about a child, meaning, 'Isn't he sweet, such a dear little thing'. As 'bless your little cotton socks', it just means 'thank you'. Partridge/*Slang* dates it from the turn of the century and labels it heavily 'middle-class'.

blessing in disguise, a. Meaning, 'a misfortune which turns out to be beneficial', this phrase has been in existence since the early eighteenth century. A perfect example is provided by the noted exchange between Winston Churchill and his wife, Clementine. She attempted to console him after his defeat in the 1945 General Election saying: 'It may well be a blessing in disguise.' To which he replied: 'At the moment, it seems quite effectively disguised.' Despite this comment, Churchill seems to have come round to something like his wife's point of view. On 5 September 1945, he wrote to her from an Italian holiday: 'This is the first time for very many years that I have been completely out of the world . . . Others having to face the hideous problems of the

aftermath . . . It may all indeed be "a blessing in disguise".'

blind. See LIKE TAKING MONEY FROM ~ BEGGARS.

blind, in the country of the. ('. . . the one-eyed man is king'.) A phrase often ascribed to H.G. Wells because of its use by him in the story 'The Country of the Blind' (1904) – though he quite clearly labels it an old proverb. As indeed it is, and in many languages. An early appearance is in a book of *Adages* by Erasmus (d 1536): '*In regione caecorum rex est luscus.*'

blind leading the blind, the. Ineffectual leadership. 'They be blind leaders of the blind. And if the blind lead the blind, both shall fall into the ditch' (Matthew 15:4). This famous observation from the gospels seems to cry out to be tampered with. In 1958, Kenneth Tynan wrote: 'They say the *New Yorker* is the bland leading the bland. I don't know if I'm bland enough.'

Blitz. See IT WAS WORSE THAN THE ~.

block. See CHIP OF(F) THE OLD/SAME ~.

blonde bombshell, a. A journalistic cliché now used to describe *any* (however vaguely) blonde woman but especially if a dynamic personality and usually a film star, show business figure, or model. In June 1975, Margo Macdonald complained of being described by the *Daily Mirror* as 'the blonde bombshell M.P.' who 'hits the House of Commons today'. The original was Jean Harlow who appeared in the 1933 film *Bombshell*. In Britain – presumably so as not to suggest that it was a war film – the title was changed to *Blonde Bombshell*.

blondes. See IS IT TRUE ~ HAVE MORE FUN?

blood. See RIVERS OF ~.

blood and fire, (through). The motto of the Salvation Army, founded by General William Booth in 1878. The conjunction of blood and fire has appropriate biblical origins. In Joel 2:30, God says: 'And I will shew wonders in the heavens and in the earth, blood, and fire, and pillars of smoke.'

blood libel. The name given to accusations by medieval anti-Semites that Jews had crucified Christian children and drunk their blood at Passover. In September 1982, following allegations that Israeli forces in Lebanon had allowed massacres to take place in refugee camps, the Israeli government invoked the phrase in a statement headed: 'BLOOD LIBEL. On the New Year (Rosh Hashana), a blood libel was levelled against the Jewish state, its government and the Israel Defense Forces . . .'

blood, sweat and tears. In his classic speech to the House of Commons on 13 May 1940 upon becoming Prime Minister, Winston Churchill said: 'I would say to the House, as I said to those who have joined this Government: I have nothing to offer but blood, toil, tears and sweat.' Ever since, people have had difficulty getting the order of his words right. The natural inclination is to put 'blood', 'sweat' then 'tears' together – as did Byron in 1823 with 'blood, sweat and tear-wrung millions' and as did the Canadian/US rock group Blood Sweat and Tears in the late 1960s and 70s.

Much earlier, however, there had been yet another combination of the words in John Donne's *An Anatomy of the World* (1611): ' 'Tis in vain to do so or to mollify it with thy tears, or sweat, or blood.' Churchill seemed consciously to avoid these configurations. In 1931, he had written of the Tsarist armies: 'Their sweat, their tears, their blood bedewed the endless plain.' Having launched his version of the phrase in 1940, he referred to it five more times during the course of the war.

Bloody Sunday. As with BLACK FRIDAY, there has been a number of these. On 13 November 1887, two men died during a baton charge on a prohibited socialist demonstration in Trafalgar Square, London. On 22 January 1905, hundreds of unarmed peasants were mown down when they marched to petition the Tsar in St Petersburg. In Irish history, there was a Bloody Sunday on 21 November 1920 when, among other incidents, fourteen undercover British intelligence agents in Dublin were shot by Sinn Fein. More recently, the name was applied to Sunday

30 January 1972 when British troops killed thirteen Catholics after a protest rally in Londonderry, Northern Ireland. Perhaps the epithet sprang to mind readily on this occasion because of the film *Sunday Bloody Sunday* (1971).

Later (1973) the UK/US group Black Sabbath released an album with the title *Sabbath Bloody Sabbath*. Since the nineteenth century there has been the exclamation 'Sunday, *bloody* Sunday!' to reflect frustration at the inactivity and boredom traditionally associated with the Sabbath.

bloom. See MAKE THE DESERT ∼.

Bloomsbury Group, the. (or Set.) A tag applied to a group of mildly Bohemian writers, artists and thinkers who either lived or met in the Bloomsbury district of London in the early decades of the twentieth century. They included Leonard and Virginia Woolf, Duncan Grant, J.M. Keynes and David Garnett. Their well-documented personal relationships gave rise to a torrent of biographies in the second half of the century. Keynes was using the phrase 'Bloomsbury Set' by 1914. Harold Nicolson (who was loosely connected with the circle through his wife, Vita Sackville-West) noted in his diary for 2 September 1940: 'Vita says that our mistake was that we remained Edwardian for too long, and that if in 1916 we had got in touch with Bloomsbury, we should have profited more than we did by carrying on with . . . the Edwardian relics. We are amused to confess that we had never even heard of Bloomsbury in 1916.'

Blossom. See under JOHN HENRY, COME HERE!

blow. See KNOCK-OUT ∼.

blow hot and cold, to. Meaning, 'to vacillate between enthusiasm and apathy', this expression has been known in English since 1577 and comes from one of Aesop's *Fables* . On a cold day, a satyr comes across a man blowing his fingers to make them warm. He takes the man home and gives him a bowl of hot soup. The man blows on the soup, to cool it. At this, the satyr throws him out, exclaiming that he wants nothing to do with a man who can 'blow hot and cold from the same mouth'.

blow one's own trumpet, to. Meaning, 'to boast of one's own achievements', this is sometimes said to have originated with the statue of 'Fame' on the parapet of Wilton House, near Salisbury. The figure – positioned after a fire in 1647 – originally held a trumpet in each hand. But why does one need a precise origin – except that *OED2* cannot find a use of the phrase in this particular form earlier than 1854? Henry Fielding, *Joseph Andrews*, Chap 5. (1742) has 'Fame blew her brazen trumpet'.

Brewer, more reasonably, states that the 'allusion is to heralds, who used to announce with a flourish of trumpets the knights who entered a list' (as, for example, in jousting). Lord Beaverbrook used to say that if you did not blow your own trumpet, no one else would do it for you (quoted in the *Observer*, 12 March 1989).

blow some my way. A slogan used, from 1926 (some would say suggestively) when a woman made her first appearance in US cigarette advertising. The brand was Chesterfield.

blow the gaff, to. An earlier (eighteenth-century) form was 'to blow the gab' meaning 'to blab about something; to let the secret out; give the game away' and, conceivably, 'gaff' could have developed from that. 'Gaff' may here mean 'mouth' (like gab/gob) and, coupled with 'blow', this gives the idea of expelling air through it and letting things out.

blow the whistle on, to. Meaning 'to call a halt to something by exposing it' (alluding to the police use of whistles). The *OED2* finds a 1934 use in P.G. Wodehouse. More recently, the *Listener* of 3 January 1980 reported: 'English as she is murdered on radio became an issue once more. Alvar Lidell stamped his foot and blew the whistle in the *Listener*.' Sir Robert Armstrong was quoted in the *Observer* (2 March 1986) as saying: 'I do not think there could be a duty on a civil servant to blow the whistle on his Minister.'

blue. See ALICE ~ GOWN; ENOUGH ~ TO MAKE A . . . ; LIGHT THE ~ TOUCHPAPER under *BAND WAGGON*; ONCE IN A ~ MOON; SOMETHING OLD . . .

blue-blooded. This phrase is used to mean 'aristocratic; socially superior'. Human blood is red, but during the fifteenth century many Spanish aristocrats had fair complexions which made their veins appear bluer than those of darker-skinned Moorish people. Thus they were said to have blue blood.

blue for a boy, pink for a girl. Colour coding for babies along these lines may be comparatively recent. Although the *Daily Chronicle* (18 November 1909) had 'Brief drawing-room appearances in a nurse's arms with robes and tie-ups – blue for a boy, pink for a girl', according to the *Independent* (7 February 1994) 'there are also indications that the Women's Institute were advising *blue* for girls and *pink* for boys as late as 1920'. Indeed, blue has for centuries been the colour of the Virgin Mary's robe.

Possibly it is the case that greetings card manufacturers happened upon the revised guidelines by emphasizing the alliterative qualities of 'blue for a boy'.

Blue Meany, a. In the Beatles' animated film *Yellow Submarine* (1968) the music-hating baddies are called Blue Meanies. There may have been limited use of this pejorative thereafter, perhaps aimed in a general sense at anyone not liked, but particularly the **boys in blue** (the police).

blue pencil, to. To censor. In the BBC wartime radio series *Garrison Theatre* (first broadcast 1939), Jack Warner as 'Private Warner' helped further popularize this well-established synonym (the *OED2*'s first citation is an American one from 1888). In reading blue-pencilled letters from his brother at the Front, expletives were deleted ('not blue pencil likely!') and Warner's actual mother boasted that, 'My John with his blue-pencil gag has stopped the whole nation from swearing.'

In his autobiography, Warner recalled a constable giving evidence at a London police court about stopping 'Mr Warner', a lorry driver. The magistrate inquired, 'Did

he ask what the blue pencil you wanted?'
'No, sir,' replied the constable, 'this was a
different Mr Warner . . .'

It is said that when the Lord
Chamberlain exercised powers of
censorship over the British stage (until
1968), his emendations to scripts were,
indeed, marked with a blue pencil.

blue stocking, a. Denoting 'a literary or
studious woman', this phrase derived from
the gatherings of cultivated females and a
few eminent men at the home of Elizabeth
Montagu in London around 1750. Boswell
in his *Life of Johnson* (1791) explains that a
certain Benjamin Stillingfleet was a popular
guest, soberly dressed but wearing blue
stockings: 'Such was the excellence of his
conversation, that his absence was felt as so
great a loss, that it used to be said, "We can
do nothing without the blue stockings,"
and thus by degrees the title was
established.'

blue velvet. A film (US, 1986), directed by
David Lynch, about drugs and menace has
the title *Blue Velvet*. This alludes firstly to
the song 'Blue Velvet' (1951) written by
Wayne and Morris, which is sung by the
night-club singer heroine in the film, and
secondly – as *DOAS* describes – to the
name for 'a mixture of paregoric, which
contains opium and . . . an antihistamine,
to be injected', which is also relevant to the
film.

BO. See BODY ODOUR.

**BOAC takes good care of you (all over
the world).** A slogan for British Overseas
Airways Corporation, from 1948, and
adapted when the airline became British
Airways to **we'll take *more* care of you**.
Japan Air Lines began to say they would
take 'Good care of you, too' but were
persuaded to drop the line, although they
had used the punning **love at first flight** a
dozen years before BOAC took up that
slogan. In its time, BA has ranged from the
patriotic **fly the flag**, through **try a little
VC 10derness** (echoing the song 'Try a
Little Tenderness'(1933), to **the world's
favourite airline** (from the late 1980s
onwards).

Bob's your uncle! An almost meaningless
expression of the type that takes hold from
time to time. It is another way of saying
'there you are; there you have it; simple as
that'. It was current by the 1880s but
doesn't appear to be of any hard and fast
origin. It is basically a British expression –
and somewhat baffling to Americans.
There is the story of one such who went
into a London shop, had it said to him, and
exclaimed: 'But how did you know – I do
have an Uncle Bob!?' In 1886, Arthur
Balfour was appointed Chief Secretary for
Ireland by his uncle, *Robert* Arthur Talbot
Gascoyne-Cecil, 3rd Marquis of Salisbury,
the Prime Minister. Could this be a possible
source?

bodies. See KNOW WHERE THE ∼ ARE
BURIED.

body. See IF I SAID YOU HAD A BEAUTIFUL
∼ . . .; YOU, TOO, CAN HAVE A ∼ LIKE MINE.

body count. A phrase from the Vietnam
War, referring to the number of enemy
dead (in use by 1968). From *Time* Magazine
(15 April 1985): 'In the field, the Americans
were encouraged to lie about their "body
counts" (measuring progress in the war by
lives taken, not land taken).' Later, used less
literally to describe the number of people
(not necessarily dead) in a specific situation.

In 1981, the American horror film *Friday
the 13th Part 2* was promoted with the line,
'The body count continues'.

body fascism. In July 1980, Anna Ford,
then a television newcaster with ITN,
popularized this phrase in a speech given to
the Women in Media group in London.
Attacking the obsession with the looks and
clothes of women who appear on television,
she added: 'Nobody takes pictures of
Richard Baker's ankles or claims that Peter
Woods only got his job because of the bags
under his eyes.'

Ford did not invent the feminist phrase,
however. It is not a very clear phrase, except
that 'fascism' is often invoked simply to
describe something that the speaker
dislikes. 'Sexism' and 'lookism' would have
conveyed what Ford meant; possibly even
'glamour-ABUSE'.

body odour. (or **B.O.**) This worrying concept was used to promote Lifebuoy soap, initially in the US, and was current by 1933. In early American radio jingles, the initials 'B.O.' were sung *basso profundo*, emphasizing the horror of the offence:

> Singing in the bathtub, singing for joy,
> Living a life of Lifebuoy –
> Can't help singing, 'cos I know
> That Lifebuoy really stops B.O.

In the UK, TV ads showed pairs of male or female friends out on a spree, intending to attract partners. When one of the pair was seen to have a problem, the other whispered helpfully, 'B.O.'

bogey. See COLONEL ~.

bogey man. See HUSH, HUSH, HUSH, HERE COMES THE ~.

Bohemian life, the. Life as lived by artists and writers, often poverty-stricken and amoral. Puccini's opera *La Bohème* (1896) was based on Henry Murger's novel *Scènes de la Vie de Bohème* (1847), set in the Latin Quarter of Paris. At first, the term 'Bohemian' was applied to gypsies because they were thought to come from Bohemia (in what is now the Czech Republic) or, at least, because the first to come to France had passed through Bohemia. The connection between the irregular life of gypsies and that of artists is just about understandable.

bold. See OOH, BOLD! under *ROUND THE HORNE*.

boldly go, to. See under BEAM ME UP, SCOTTY.

boldness be my friend. Used as the title of a book (1953) by Richard Pape about his exploits in the Second World War, this phrase is taken from what Iachimo says when he sets off to pursue Imogen in Shakespeare's *Cymbeline*: 'Boldness be my friend!/Arm me, Audacity, from head to foot' (I.vii.18). In 1977, Richard Boston wrote a book called *Baldness Be My Friend*, partly about his own lack of hair.

bolt. See BERNIE, THE ~!

bomb. See BAN THE ~.

bomber. See BROWN ~.

Bomber Harris. Nickname of Marshal of the Royal Air Force, Sir Arthur Harris Bt (1892–1984), aggressive commander-in-chief of Bomber Command in the Second World War. An advocate of strategic bombing, he directed the great bomber offensive from Britain, a relentless night-by-night attack on German cities, manufacturing centres, ports and railways, and on other enemy territory. His policy has since been much criticized and its effects questioned. Known as 'Bert' or 'Butch' (short for 'Butcher') to his colleagues, the 'Bomber' came from a more public perception.

bombshell. See BLONDE ~.

BOMFOG. An acronym for a pompous, meaningless generality. When Governor Nelson Rockefeller was competing against Barry Goldwater for the US Republican nomination in 1964, reporters latched on to a favourite saying of the candidate – 'the brotherhood of man under the fatherhood of God' – and rendered it with the acronym BOMFOG. In fact, according to Safire, they had been beaten to it by Hy Sheffer, a stenotypist on the Governor's staff who had found the abbreviation convenient for the previous five or six years. The words come from a much-quoted saying of John D. Rockefeller: 'These are the principles upon which alone a new world recognizing the brotherhood of man and the fatherhood of God can be established . . .' Later, BOMFOG was used by feminists to denote use of language that demeaned women by reflecting patrician attitudes. The individual phrases 'brotherhood of man' and 'fatherhood of God' do not appear before the nineteenth century.

bond. See MY WORD IS MY ~.

Boneless Wonder, the. A spineless character named after a fairground freak, notably evoked by Winston Churchill in an attack on Ramsay MacDonald (28 January 1931). During a debate on the Trades Disputes Act, Churchill referred to recent efforts by the Prime Minister to conciliate Roman Catholic opinion regarding education reform (including the lowering of the school-leaving age to fifteen): 'I remember when I was a child, being taken to the celebrated Barnum's Circus which contained an exhibition of freaks and monstrosities, but the exhibit on the programme which I most desired to see was the one described as the Boneless Wonder. My parents judged that the spectacle would be too revolting and demoralizing for my youthful eyes, and I have waited fifty years to see the Boneless Wonder sitting on the Treasury bench.'

Bones. See OL' BLUE EYES.

bones, to make no. See MAKE NO BONES.

Boney will get you! A curiously enduring threat. Although Napoleon died in 1821 (and all possibility of invasion had evaporated long before that), the threat was still being made in the early twentieth century. In 1985, the actor Sir Anthony Quayle recalled it from his youth and, in 1990, John Julius Norwich remembered the husband of his nanny (from Grantham) saying it to him in the 1930s. He added: 'And a Mexican friend of mine told me that when she was a little girl her nanny or mother or whoever it was used to say, "*Il Drake* will get you" – and that was Sir Francis Drake!'

Bonfire of the Vanities, The. The title of Tom Wolfe's 1987 novel is derived from Savonarola's 'burning of the vanities' in Florence, 1497. The religious reformer – 'the puritan of Catholicism' – enacted various laws for the restraint of vice and folly. Gambling was prohibited and Savonarola's followers helped people burn their costly ornaments and extravagant clothes.

bonkers. See STARK STARING ∼.

Booboo. See SMARTER THAN YOUR AVERAGE BEAR.

book(s). See under ANOTHER PAGE TURNED . . . ; LITTLE RED ∼ ; EVERYBODY HAS ONE ∼ IN THEM; READ ANY GOOD ∼ S LATELY? under

MUCH BINDING IN THE MARSH; TURN UP FOR THE ∼ .

book 'em, Danno! A stock phrase from the American TV series *Hawaii Five-O* (1968–80). On making an arrest, Det. Steve McGarrett (Jack Lord) would say to Det. 'Danno' Williams (James MacArthur), 'Book 'em, Danno!' – adding 'Murder One' if the crime required that charge.

Booker T. and the MGs. The name of a US pop group of the 1960s and 70s. If it had been 'Model T and the MGs' one might have thought there was a motoring theme afoot: the US 'Model T Ford' (1909) coupled with the UK 'MG' (1922) from 'Morris Garages'. Or could it have something to do with 'MGs' meaning Machine Guns or Gunners. But no. Booker T. Washington (*d* 1915) was a former slave who became a leading black educationalist in the US. In fact, the keyboard player was Booker T. Jones and the 'MG' stood for 'Memphis Group'.

boom, boom! The verbal underlining to the punchline of a gag. Ernie Wise suggested to me (1979) that it was like the drum-thud or trumpet-sting used, particularly by American entertainers, to point a joke. Music-hall star Billy Bennett (1887–1942) may have been the first to use this device, in the UK, to emphasize his comic couplets. The *MORECAMBE AND WISE SHOW*, Basil Brush (the fox puppet on British TV), and many others, took it up later.

'Boom boom' has also been used as a slang/*lingua franca* expression for sexual intercourse, especially by Americans in South-East Asia during the Vietnam War.

Bootle. See I'VE GOT A LETTER FROM A BLOKE IN ∼ .

boots. See HE CAN LEAVE HIS ∼ . . .

boots, to be too big for one's. Meaning 'to be conceited'. An example: in 1948, reports of a speech by Harold Wilson, then president of the Board of Trade, wrongly suggested he had claimed that when he was at school some of his classmates had gone barefoot. Ivor Bulmer-Thomas consequently remarked at the 1949 Conservative Party Conference: 'If ever he went to school without any boots it was because he was too big for them.' This remark is often wrongly attributed to Harold Macmillan.

boots on, to die with one's. (sometimes **to die in one's boots/shoes**.) Meaning to die violently, or to be hanged summarily. *OED2* finds this in England by the eighteenth century, and in the American West by 1873. It was firmly ensconced in the language by the time of the 1941 Errol Flynn film *They Died With Their Boots On*, about General Custer and his death at Little Big Horn, and the title of a porn film with Vivien Neves is *She Died With Her Boots On* (UK, 1970s). In one sense, the phrase can suggest an ignominious death (say, by hanging) but in a general way it can refer to someone who dies 'in harness', going about his work, like a soldier in the course of duty.

'To die with one's boots *off*' suggests, rather, that one dies in bed.

bored/boring! See under *LAUGH-IN*.

bored stiff. Meaning extremely bored (possibly a pun on 'stiff as a board'). Known by 1918, according to the *OED2*, which is unable to find citations for any of the various boredom phrases before the twentieth century: **bored rigid** (earliest citation 1972), **bored to death** (1966), **bored to hell** (1962), **bore the pants off** (1958) and **crashing bore** (1928). There are no citations at all for **bored to tears**, **bored out of one's mind/skull, bored to distraction.**

What does this have to tell us? – that before this century there was no expectation that you shouldn't be bored? Or were the Victorians so bored that they couldn't even be bothered to find words for it? Either way, there are one or two relatively new arrivals in the field. To say that something is **as exciting as watching paint dry**, though popular, does not seem very old. The earliest citation to hand is of a graffito from 1981 which stated that 'Living in Croydon is about as exciting as watching paint dry'.

As for **boring as a wet weekend in**

Wigan, referring to the town in the north-west of England, the earliest use found is in the *Today* newspaper for 16 July 1991. As so often, alliteration is the main force behind this piece of phrase-making. 'Wet weekends' have long been abhorred but Wigan appears to have been tacked on because it has a downbeat sound and because people recall the old music-hall joke about there being a WIGAN PIER.

Lastly, some mention must be made of the reputation of Grantham as the **most boring place in the universe**. Famous only as a place you speed through on the railway going north to Scotland – and latterly as the birthplace of Margaret Thatcher – Grantham seems to have acquired the title as the result of an opinion poll conducted for some radio station (which was apparently rigged by mass voting from schoolchildren in Grantham, anyway). The earliest reference found is from the *Sunday Times* (31 July 1983).

born-again. Applied to evangelical and fundamentalist Christians in the Southern US since the 1960s, this adjective derives from the story of Jesus Christ and Nicodemus in John 3 ('Ye must be born again'). Originally suggesting a re-conversion or conversion to Christianity, the phrase took on a figurative sense of 're-vitalized', 'zealous', 'newly converted' around the time when Jimmy Carter, from a born-again Baptist background in the South, was running for the US presidency in 1976. Hence, 'born-again automobiles' (for reconditioned ones) and such like.

born 1820 – still going strong. Johnnie Walker whisky has used this advertising line since 1910. There *was* a John Walker but he was not born in 1820 – that was the year he set up a grocery, wine and spirit business in Kilmarnock. In 1908, Sir Alexander Walker decided to incorporate a portrait of his grandfather in the firm's advertising. Tom Browne, a commercial artist, was commissioned to draw the firm's founder as he might have appeared in 1820. Lord Stevenson, a colleague of Sir Alexander's, scribbled the phrase 'Johnnie Walker, born 1820 – still going strong' alongside the artist's sketch of a striding, cheerful Regency figure. It has been in use ever since.

From Randolph Quirk, *Style and Communication in the English Language* (1983): 'English lexicography knocks Johnnie Walker into a tricuspidal fedora. Over four hundred years, and going stronger than ever.'

born every minute. See THERE'S A SUCKER ~.

born yesterday. See I WASN'T ~.

borrowed. See SOMETHING OLD . . .

B/bosie. (1) The nickname of Lord Alfred Douglas (*d* 1945), poet, friend of Oscar Wilde and ultimate cause of that writer's downfall. He was known as 'Bosie', a corruption of 'Boysie', the name given to him by his indulgent mother. (2) An Australian cricketing nickname (also spelt **bosey**) from the 1900s for the googly, a method of bowling a ball, named after its inventor, the Middlesex and England player, Bernard Bosanquet.

bosom. See ABRAHAM'S ~; ARTHUR'S ~.

boss, boss, sumpin' terrible's happened! See under *ITMA*.

Boston Strangler, the. Nickname of Albert de Salvo who strangled thirteen women during 1962–4 in the Boston, Mass. area. Not forgotten, the man's reputation led to the creation of a joke format: from *Today* (24 May 1987), 'Liberal David Steel said earlier this year: "Mrs Thatcher seems to have done for women in politics what the Boston Strangler did for door-to-door salesmen."' From the *Independent* (20 January 1989): 'Mr Healey also had a pithy word for President Reagan: "He has done for monetarism what the Boston Strangler did for door-to-door salesmen."' From the *Washington Post* (16 October 1991): 'Shields introduced Hatch, the starched shirt of the Senate hearings, as "the man who has done for bipartisanship what the Boston Strangler did for door-to-door salesmen".' From the *Sunday Times* (9 February 1992): 'Denis Healey, who claimed to have tried to do for economic forecasters what the

Boston Strangler did for door-to-door salesmen . . .'

bottle. See MILK'S GOTTA LOTTA ~.

bottle-washer. See CHIEF COOK AND ~.

bottomless pit, the. A description of Hell from Revelation 20:1: 'And I saw an angel come down from heaven, having the key of the bottomless pit'; also in Milton *Paradise Lost* (Bk.6, line 864):

> Headlong themselves they threw
> Down from the verge of Heaven, eternal wrath
> Burnt after them to the bottomless pit

William Pitt the Younger, British Prime Minister (1783–1801, 1804–06) was nicknamed the **Bottomless Pitt**, on account of his thinness. A caricature with this title attributed to Gillray shows Pitt as Chancellor of the Exchequer introducing his 1792 budget. His bottom is non-existent.

bottom line. The ultimately important outcome. Initially referring to the last line of a financial statement which shows whether there has been profit or loss – and still very much in use ('They're only interested in the bottom line, those investors') – also used in a figurative sense. In the 1970s, Henry Kissinger spoke of the 'bottom line' as the eventual outcome of political negotiations, disregarding the intermediate arguments.

bound. See WITH ONE ~ HE WAS FREE.

bountiful. See LADY ~.

Bovril prevents that sinking feeling. Slogan for Bovril (meat extract) in the UK. On H.H. Harris's cheery poster of a pyjama-clad man astride a jar of Bovril in the sea, this line first appeared in 1920. However, the slogan was born in a golfing booklet issued by Bovril in 1890 which included the commendation: 'Unquestionably, Bovril . . . supplies . . . the nourishment which is so much needed by all players at the critical intermediate hour between breakfast and luncheon, when the *sinking feeling* engendered by an empty stomach is so distressing, and so fruitful of deteriorated play.' It is said that Bovril had intended to use the phrase earlier but withheld it because of the *Titanic* disaster of 1912. With updated illustrations, it lasted until 1958.

Heading from the *Independent* (12 April 1989): 'Crucible challenge for a champion [Steve Davis, snooker player] who thinks rivals under the table before relishing that sinking feeling.'

bowdlerize, to. Meaning 'to expurgate', this verb derives from the name of Thomas Bowdler who published *The Family Shakespeare* (1818), a ten-volume edition of the dramatist's works with all the dirty bits left out (or, as he put it, those words 'which cannot be read aloud in a family'). 'Out damn'd spot' became 'Out crimson spot', and so on. Dr Bowdler, in consequence, has given his name to any form of literary expurgation. Possibly the word 'bowdlerize' caught on because of its resemblance to 'disembowel'. It was already current by 1836.

bowl of cherries. See LIFE IS JUST A ∼.

box. See OPEN THE ∼.

box, the. A slightly passé term for a TV set (having earlier been applied to wirelesses and gramophones), and one of several derogatory epithets which were applied during the medium's rise to mass popularity in the 1940s and 50s. Groucho Marx used the expression in a letter (1950). Maurice Richardson, sometime TV critic of the *Observer*, apparently coined the epithet **idiot's lantern** prior to 1957. See also BLACK BOX.

box of birds/box of fluffy ducks, it's a. A New Zealandism/Australianism for 'fine, excellent, OK'. Known by 1943.

boy(s). See BACKROOM ∼; BLUE FOR A ∼; FINGER IN THE DIKE . . .; GOLDEN ∼ ; ∼ IN BLUE under BLUE MEANY; OLD ∼ NETWORK.

boycott, to mount a. 'The lively Irish have invented a new word; they are saying now to "boycott" someone, meaning to ostracize him' – translated from *Le Figaro* (24 November 1880). Captain Charles

Boycott was an ex-British soldier who acted as an agent for absentee landlords in Co. Mayo, Ireland, during the late nineteenth century. He was extremely hard on the poor tenants and dispossessed them if they fell behind with their rents. By way of retaliation, the tenants isolated him and refused to have any dealings with him or his family. They were encouraged in this by Charles Parnell of the Irish Land League who said that those who grabbed land from people evicted for non-payment of rent should be treated like 'the leper of old'. Eventually, the tenants brought about Boycott's own downfall by leaving his harvest to rot and he fled back to England where he died in 1897. Note that the verb 'to boycott' describes what was done *to* him rather than what was done *by* him.

boy done well, the. Although now used in any context (for example as the headline to an article about Rod Stewart, the singer, in the *Independent* on 4 April 1991), this phrase of approbation is unquestionably of sporting origin. The question is, which sport?

It sounds like the kind of thing a boxer's manager might say – 'All right, he got K.O.'d in the first round – but my boy done well . . .' but the citations obtained so far are from every sport *but* boxing. Working backwards:

'Back on dry land he took victory well and, like all good managers had words of praise for his team, in this case Derek Clark. "It's a good result, they done well the lads," he said. "Class will always tell and it did today but everything happened that quick I didn't have time to enjoy it." The boy Ron done well' – 'Cowes Diary' (yachting), *The Times* (7 August 1991)

'Particularly noteworthy were two goals by Mark Robins, one with his right, then a left-foot chip. It prompted manager Alex Ferguson to utter the immortal words: "The boy has done well"' – 'Football Focus', *The Sunday Times* (9 September 1990)

'The boy Domingo done good. The boy Carreras done well. The boy Pavarotti done great' – TV operatic concert review, the *Guardian* (9 July 1990)

'Institutional investors that were previously sceptical about Ashcroft's staying power have moved in, propelling ADT's shares from 118p in January to last week's high. As a well-known football commentator might say, "the boy Ashcroft done good"' – 'City Viewpoint' (financial), *The Sunday Times* (13 August 1989).

'It wasn't all death and destruction . . . England reached the quarter finals of the World Cup [football]. The boy Lineker – the competition's top scorer – done well . . . The boy Andrew done well, too. Sarah Ferguson, proved a popular bride' – 'Review of the Year', the *Guardian* (31 December 1986)

Quite the best suggestion for an origin was Fagin in *Oliver Twist*, but, no, he did not say it.

boy meets girl. Neat summary of what might seem to be the most popular plot in all fiction (but see SIX BASIC JOKES/PLOTS). Known by 1945 and possibly originating in discussion of Hollywood movies in the 1930s.

boy next door, the. Admirably defined by *Photoplay* (October 1958) as: 'The boy who's within reach of every girl fan' – hence, a straightforward, unsophisticated young man figuring in a conventional romance, particularly on the cinema screen. The female equivalent, **girl next door** seems to have emerged a fraction later. From the *Times Educational Supplement* (23 February 1968): 'Diana Quick's Ophelia was very much the girl-next-door.'

boys will be boys! A comment on the inevitability of youthful behaviour. Thackeray has it in *Vanity Fair* (1848).

boy wonder! See under BATMAN.

bra. See BURN YOUR ~!; I DREAMED I . . .

braces. See BELT AND ~.

bracing. See IT'S SO ~.

bracket. See PUNCH UP THE ~ under *HANCOCK'S HALF–HOUR.*

Brains Trust, a. *The Brains Trust* was the title of a BBC radio discussion programme (1941 onwards), originating from the American term for a group of people who give advice or who comment on current issues. In his first campaign in 1932, President Franklin D. Roosevelt set up a circle of advisers which became known as his '*brain* trust'. In Britain, the term was borrowed and turned into '*brains* trust'. Curiously, the Roosevelt coinage, attributed to James Michael Kieran Jnr, was at first 'the *brains* trust' also.

bran(d) new. This expression for 'very new' comes from the old word meaning 'to burn' (just as a 'brand' is a form of torch). A metal that was brand (*or* bran) new had just been taken out of the flames, having just been forged. Shakespeare has the variation 'fire-new', which points more directly to the phrase's origin.

brandy-y-y-y! under *GOON SHOW.*

brass. See COLD ENOUGH TO FREEZE . . .; KNOBS ON, WITH.

brass tacks, to get down to. Probably of US origin, this phrase means 'to get down to essentials' and has been known since 1897, at least. There are various theories as to why we say it, including: (1) In old stores, brass tacks were positioned a yard apart for measuring. When a customer 'got down to brass tacks', it meant he or she was serious about making a purchase. (2) Brass tacks were a fundamental element in nineteenth-century upholstery, hence this expression meant to deal with a fault in the furniture by getting down to basics. (3) 'Brass tacks' is rhyming slang for 'facts', though the version 'to get down to brass nails' would contradict this.

brat pack. Name for a group of young Hollywood actors in the mid-1980s who tended to behave in a spoiled, unruly fashion. Coined by David Blum in *New York Magazine* (10 June 1985) and fashioned after **rat pack,** the name given in the 1950s to the then young Frank Sinatra, Peter Lawford, Sammy Davis Jnr etc. Also applied to other young cliques of writers, performers etc. The original **brat-packers**, including Emilio Estevez, Matt Dillon, Patrick Swayze and Tom Cruise had all appeared together in Francis Ford Coppola's film *The Outsiders* (1983).

brave new world, a. Nowadays a slightly ironic term for modern life. *Brave New World* was the title of a novel (1932) by Aldous Huxley. It is taken from Miranda's exclamation in Shakespeare's *The Tempest* (1612): 'O brave new world,/That has such people in't!' (V.i.183).

Bray. See VICAR OF ~.

breach. See CUSTOM MORE HONOUR'D IN THE ~ . . .

bread. See GREATEST THING SINCE SLICED ~.

breadbox. See IS IT BIGGER THAN A ~?

bread never falls but on its buttered side. See IF ANYTHING CAN GO WRONG . . .

break a butterfly upon a wheel, to. See WHO BREAKS A BUTTERFLY UPON A WHEEL?

break a leg! A traditional theatrical greeting given before a performance, especially a first night, because it is considered bad luck to wish anyone 'good luck' directly. Another version is **snap a wrist!** Partridge/*Slang* has 'to break a leg' as 'to give birth to a bastard', dating from the seventeenth century, but that is probably unconnected. As also is the fact that John Wilkes Booth, an actor, broke his leg after assassinating President Lincoln in a theatre. Morris has it based on a German good luck expression, *Hals und Beinbruch* [May you break your neck and your leg]. Perhaps this entered theatrical speech (like several other expressions) via Yiddish.

Other theatrical good-luck expressions include *merde!* [French: 'shit!'], in *bocca del lupo* [Italian: 'into the wolf's jaws'] and TOY! TOY!

breakfast. See DOG'S ~ . . . ; CONDEMNED MAN ATE A HEARTY ~.

breakfast of champions. An advertising line used to promote Wheaties breakfast cereal in the US, since 1950 at least. In the 1980s, a series of ads featuring sporting champions showed, for example, 'Jackie Robinson – one of the greatest names in baseball . . . this Dodgers star is a Wheaties man: "A lot of us ball players go for milk, fruit and Wheaties," says Jackie . . . Had *your* Wheaties today?'

Kurt Vonnegut used the phrase as the title of a novel (1973). In 1960s Australia it was also used as a slang expression for sexual intercourse on awakening – specifically cunnilingus.

breaking of nations, the. The title of Thomas Hardy's poem 'In Time of "The Breaking of Nations"' (conceived during the Franco-Prussian War of 1870 and written during the First World War) alludes to Jeremiah 51:20: 'Thou art my battle axe and weapons of war: for with thee will I break in pieces the nations, and with thee will I destroy kingdoms.'

break the mould, to. 'To start afresh from fundamentals'. When the Social Democratic Party was established in 1981, there was much talk of it 'breaking the mould of British politics' i.e. doing away with the traditional system of a government and one chief opposition party. But this was by no means a new way of describing political change and getting rid of an old system for good, in a way that prevents it being reconstituted. In *What Matters Now* (1972), Roy Jenkins, one of the new party's founders, had quoted Andrew Marvell's 'Horatian Ode Upon Cromwell's Return from Ireland' (1650):

And cast the kingdoms old,
Into another mould.

In a speech at a House of Commons Press Gallery lunch on 8 June 1960, Jenkins had also said: 'The politics of the left and centre of this country are frozen in an out-of-date mould which is bad for the political and economic health of Britain and increasingly inhibiting for those who live within the mould. Can it be broken?'

A.J.P. Taylor in his *English History 1914–1945* (1965), had earlier written: 'Lloyd George needed a new crisis to break the mould of political and economic habit'. The image evoked, as in the days of the Luddites, is of breaking the mould from which iron machinery is cast – so completely that the machinery has to be re-cast from scratch.

Br'er fox – he lay low. An expression used to suggest that doing or saying nothing for the moment is the best course. It comes from the 'Tar-Baby Story' in *Uncle Remus. Legends of the Old Plantation* (1881) by Joel Chandler Harris: 'Tar-Baby ain't sayin' nuthin', en Brer Fox, he lay low.'

brewery. See under COULDN'T RUN A WHELK–STALL.

Brian. See WELL, ∼.

brick(s) short of a full load. See under FEW VOUCHERS.

bride. See OFTEN A BRIDESMAID . . .

bridegroom on the wedding cake, the. A memorable insult, this phrase is usually attributed to Alice Roosevelt Longworth (1884–1980). She said that Thomas Dewey, who was challenging Harry S Truman for the US presidency in 1948, looked like the 'bridegroom' or just 'the man' 'on the wedding cake'. Dewey did indeed have a wooden, dark appearance, and a black moustache.

bridesmaid. See OFTEN A ∼.

bridge too far, a. Phrase sometimes used allusively when warning of an unwise move, e.g.: 'A BRIDGE TOO NEAR. A public inquiry opened yesterday into plans to re-span the Ironbridge Gorge in Shropshire' (*The Times*, 20 June 1990); 'Ratners: A bid too far?' (*Observer*, 8 July 1990).

Cornelius Ryan's book *A Bridge Too Far* (1974; film UK/US, 1977) was about the 1944 airborne landings in Holland. These were designed to capture eleven bridges needed for the Allied invasion of Germany – an attempt which came to grief at Arnhem, the Allies suffering more casualties than in the invasion of Normandy. In advance of the action, Lieut.-General Sir Frederick Browning protested to Field-Marshal Montgomery, whose brainchild the scheme was: 'But, sir, we may be going a bridge too far.'

bright. See ALL THINGS ∼ AND BEAUTIFUL; ALWAYS MERRY AND ∼.

brightest. See BEST AND THE ∼.

bright-eyed and bushy-tailed. Alert, especially like a squirrel. This expression appears to have been used in connection with US astronauts (*c* 1967). Partridge/*Slang* suggests a Canadian 1930s origin. But the great popularizer must have been B. Merrill's song with the phrase as its title in 1953:

> If the fox in the bush and the squirr'l in the tree be
> Why in the world can't you and me be
> Bright eyed and bushy tailed and sparkelly as we can be?

bright young things. Young socialites of the 1920s and early 1930s whose reaction to the rigours of the First World War was to give parties and dance away the night, copied in more modest style by their poorer contemporaries. During a short period of frivolity, such people disregarded the poverty and unemployment around them and flouted convention. The females were also known as **flappers**. Known as such by 1927, the 'B.Y.T.s' were described by Barbara Cartland in *We Danced All Night* (1970), although she referred to them as 'bright young *people*'.

brill. An abbreviation for 'brilliant' that quite happily crosses British class boundaries. It was used in the late 1970s by the comedy team Little and Large; equally, in the early 1980s, by the journalist Emma Soames, daughter of Lord Soames and grand-daughter of Sir Winston Churchill, and by others in her then fashionable set.

Another example of a similar cross-class colloquialism from the same period is **roller**, short for 'Rolls-Royce' and just as likely to fall from the lips of an East End entrepreneur as from those of a SLOANE RANGER.

bring back the cat. Long the cry of corporal punishment enthusiasts in Britain demanding the return of beating as an official punishment. Usually associated with right-wing 'hangers and floggers' within the Conservative Party who seldom miss their chance to utter the cry (though not in so many words) at their annual conference. The cat-o'-nine-tails was the nine-thong whip once used to enforce discipline in the Royal Navy.

bring home the bacon, to. Meaning, 'to be successful in a venture', this may have to do with the **Dunmow Flitch**, a tradition established in 1111 at Great Dunmow in Essex. Married couples who can prove they have lived for a year and a day without quarrelling or without wishing to be unmarried can claim a gammon of bacon. Also, country fairs used to have competitions which involved catching a greased pig. If you 'brought home the bacon', you won.

In 1910, when Jack Johnson, the American negro boxer, won the World Heavyweight boxing championship, his mother exlaimed: 'He said he'd bring home the bacon, and the honey boy has gone and done it.' The *Oxford Companion to American History* suggests that this 'added a new phrase to the vernacular'. Unlikely, given the Dunmow Flitch connection, and yet the *OED2*'s earliest citation is not until 1924 (in P.G. Wodehouse).

Bristols. Rhyming slang provides this word meaning 'breasts', the origin of which is otherwise far from obvious. The rhyme is 'Bristol Cities' [titties] – a use more or less restricted to the UK. As Paul Beale suggests in his revision of Partridge/*Slang*, the football team Bristol City probably only gets invoked because of the initial similarity of the words 'Bristol' and 'breasts'.

Britain. See CARRY ON, ~!; KEEP ~ TIDY.

Britain can take it. During the Second World War, slogans rained down upon the hapless British as profusely as German bombs. The Ministry of Information, in blunderbuss fashion, fired away with as much material as possible in the hope of hitting something. Some of the slogans were brilliant, others were quite the reverse – hence the Ministry's abandonment of 'Britain can take it' in December 1941.

'While the public appreciated due recognition of their resolute qualities,' wrote Ian McLaine in *Ministry of Morale* (1979), 'they resented too great an emphasis on the stereotyped image of the Britisher in adversity as a wise-cracking Cockney. They were irritated by the propaganda which represented their grim experience as a sort of particularly torrid Rugby match.'

The notion was resurrected by Winston Churchill in May 1945 in a tribute to Cockney fortitude: 'No one ever asked for peace because London was suffering. London was like a great rhinoceros, a great hippopotamus, saying: "Let them do their worst. London can take it." London could take anything.'

British. See under AND THE BEST OF LUCK; BE ~!; THIS HAS RESTORED MY FAITH IN ~ JUSTICE.

broad sunlit uplands. In Winston Churchill's long speaking career, there was one thematic device he frequently resorted to for his perorations. It appears in many forms but may be summarized as the 'broad, sunlit uplands' approach. In his collected speeches, there are some thirteen occasions when he made use of the construction. 'The level plain . . . a land of peace and plenty . . . the sunshine of a more gentle and a more generous age' (1906); 'I earnestly trust . . . that by your efforts our country may emerge from this period of darkness and peril once more in the sunlight of a peaceful time' (at the end of a speech on 19 September 1915 when Churchill's own position was precarious following the failure of the Gallipoli campaign); in his 'finest hour' speech, Churchill hoped that, 'The life of the world may move forward into broad, sunlit uplands' (1940); 'it is an uphill road we have to tread, but if we reject the cramping, narrowing path of socialist restrictions, we shall surely find a way – and a wise and tolerant government – to those broad uplands where plenty, peace and justice reign' (1951, prior to the General

Election). See also LET US GO FORWARD
TOGETHER.

broken. See IF IT AIN'T ∼; NIGHT OF ∼
GLASS.

broken reed, a. A weak support;
something not to be trusted or leant on. In
Isaiah 36:6, it is said that Hezekiah could
not put his trust in Egypt if the Assyrians
made war on Jerusalem: 'Lo, thou trustest
in the staff of this broken reed . . . whereon
if a man lean, it will go into his hand, and
pierce it.' In II Kings 18:21, a similar passage
has 'bruised reed'.

Bronx cheer, a. A noise of derisive
disapproval. *DOAS* suggests that this form
of criticism (known by 1929) originated at
the National Theater in the Bronx, New
York City, although the Yankee baseball
stadium is also in the same area. The UK
equivalent is 'to blow a **raspberry**', from
rhyming slang, 'raspberry tart' [= fart].

bronzed. See LOOKING ∼ AND FIT.

brother. See BIG ∼; HE AIN'T HEAVY, HE'S
MY ∼; WE BRING YOU MELODIES . . .

b/Brown. See CAPABILITY ∼; DON'T SAY ∼
. . . ; HOW NOW, ∼ COW?

Brown Bomber, (the). A nickname
which denotes colour and power. The
original holder of this 'title' was Joe Louis,
world heavyweight boxing champion from
1937 until his retirement in 1949. He was
noted for his large number of knockouts.
The nickname was also applied to a
Burmese cat at stud in West London in
1983.
     A **black bomber** is an amphetamine
drug, first called this in the 1960s.

browned off. See CHEESED OFF.

Brown Eminence. See under GREY
EMINENCE.

brownie points, to earn/win.
Originating in American business or the
military, and certainly recorded before
1963, this has nothing to do with Brownies,
the junior branch of the Girl Guides, and

the points they might or might not gain for
doing their 'good deed for the day'. Oh no!
This has a scatological origin, not
unconnected with brown-nosing, brown-
tonguing, arse-licking and other unsavoury
methods of sucking up to someone
important.
     Note also the American term 'Brownie',
an award for doing something *wrong*.
According to *DOAS*, 'I got a pair of
Brownies for that one' (1942) refers to a
system of disciplinary demerits on the
railroads. The name was derived from the
inventor of the system.

brush. See DAFT AS A ∼.

brush, to live/get married over the (or
jump over the broomstick). Meaning 'to
live together as though married', this
expression possibly derives from some form
of informal ceremony which involved the
couple jumping over a stick.

brush off, a. Meaning 'a rebuff', this noun
is said to derive from a habit of Pullman
porters in the US who, if they thought you
were a poor tipper, gave you a quick brush
over the shoulders and passed on to the
next customer. However, perhaps the mere
action of brushing unwanted dirt off
clothing is sufficient reason for the
expression.

brute force and ignorance. What is
needed to get, say, a recalcitrant machine
working again. Sometimes pronounced
'hignorance'; sometimes abbreviated to 'BF
& I'. Known by 1930.

bucket. See KICK THE ∼.

buck stops here, the. Harry S Truman
(US President 1945–53) had a sign on his
desk bearing these words, indicating that
the Oval Office was where the passing of
the buck had to cease. It appears to be a
saying of his own invention. 'Passing the
buck' is a poker player's expression. It refers
to a marker that can be passed on by
someone who does not wish to deal. Later,
Jimmy Carter restored Truman's motto to
the Oval Office.
     When President Nixon published his
memoirs (1978), people opposed to its sale

went around wearing buttons which said 'The book stops here'.

buff. (1) An enthusiast, e.g. 'film-buff', 'opera-buff', etc. This use came from people who liked to watch fires being extinguished or who helped to extinguish them in an amateur capacity in New York City. They were called 'buffs' (by 1903) either because of their buffalo uniforms or because the heavy buffalo robes they wore to keep them warm in winter (before the fires were started, presumably) somewhat hindered their usefulness. In which case, the term was used as a mild form of rebuke by the real fire-fighters. (2) Naked, as in the phrase **in the buff**. This seems to derive from the buff-coloured leather shorts down to which people in the services were sometimes stripped. Although strictly speaking they were not naked, the term was extended to apply to those who were completely so. An English regiment has been known as 'The Buffs' for over three hundred years – not because it goes naked but because of the colour of its uniform.

Buffalo Bill. This was the nickname applied to William Frederick Cody, the showman, in 1869 by Ned Buntline who made Cody the hero of a series of dime novels. It alludes to his early days as a buffalo hunter. Cody organized his first 'wild west show' in 1883, with cowboys and Indians, and brought it to England in 1887 with spectacular success.

bug. See SNUG AS A ∼ IN A RUG.

Buggins's turn, it is. This expression gives the reason for a job appointment having been made – when it is somebody's turn to get the job rather than because the person is especially well-qualified to do so. The name Buggins is used because it sounds suitably dull and humdrum ('Joseph Buggins, Esq. J.P. for the borough' appears in one of G.W.E. Russell's *Collections and Recollections*, 1898. Trollope gave the name to a civil servant in *Framley Parsonage*, 1861. The similar sounding 'Muggins', self-applied to a foolish person, goes back to 1855, at least).

The earliest recorded use of the phrase 'Buggins's turn' is by Admiral Fisher, later

First Sea Lord, in a letter of 1901. Later, in a letter of 1917 (printed in his *Memories*, 1919), he said: 'Some day the Empire will go down because it is Buggins's turn.' It is impossible to say whether Fisher coined the phrase, though he always spoke and wrote in a colourful fashion.

But what do people with the name Buggins think of it? In February 1986, a Mr Geoffrey Buggins was reported to be threatening legal action over a cartoon which had appeared in the London *Standard*. It showed the husband of Margaret Thatcher looking through the New Year's Honours List and asking, 'What did Buggins do to get an MBE?' She replies: 'He thought up all those excuses for not giving one to Bob Geldof' (the pop star and fund raiser who only later received an Honorary KBE).

The real-life Mr Buggins (who had been awarded an MBE for services to export in 1969), said from his home near Lisbon, Portugal: 'I am taking this action because I want to protect the name of Buggins and also on behalf of the Muddles, Winterbottoms and the Sillitoes of this world.'

The editor of the *Standard* said: 'We had no idea there was a Mr Buggins who had the MBE. I feel sorry for his predicament, but if we are to delete Buggins's turn from the English language perhaps he could suggest an alternative.'

build. See IF YOU ∼ IT HE WILL COME.

Bulge, the. See BABY BOOMER.

bull. See COCK AND ∼ STORY; LIKE A RED RAG TO A ∼.

bulldog breed. In 1857, Charles Kingsley wrote of: 'The original British bulldog breed, which, once stroked against the hair, shows his teeth at you for ever afterwards.' In 1897, the British were called 'boys of the bulldog breed' in a music-hall song, 'Sons of the Sea, All British Born' by Felix McGlennon. At the outbreak of the First World War in 1914, Winston Churchill spoke at a 'Call to Arms' meeting at the London Opera House. 'Mr Churchill has made a speech of tremendous voltage and carrying power,' the *Manchester Guardian* reported. 'His comparison of the British navy to a bulldog – "the nose of the bulldog has been turned backwards so that he can breathe without letting go" – will live. At the moment of delivery, with extraordinary appositeness, it was particularly vivid, as the speaker was able by some histrionic gift to suggest quite the bulldog as he spoke.'

Indeed, during the Second World War, small model bulldogs were manufactured bearing Churchill's facial pout and wearing a tin helmet.

John Bull as a symbol and personification of Britain (sometimes shown accompanied by a bulldog) dates from before John Arbuthnot's *The History of John Bull* (1712).

bullet(s). See FASTER THAN A SPEEDING ~ under *SUPERMAN*; UP TO MY NECK IN MUD AND ~ .

bumper bundle, a. See under *FAMILY FAVOURITES*.

Bungalow Bill. Nickname applied to a man called Bill Wiggins who achieved a certain amount of media fame in 1987–8 simply by being an amour of the actress Joan Collins. 'The Continuing Story of Bungalow Bill' (a joke upon BUFFALO BILL, of course) was the title of a Lennon and McCartney song (1968). However, it was also alleged that Mr Wiggins got his nickname because he did not have 'much up top'.

bunk(um), to talk. In 1820, Felix Walker, a Congressman from Buncombe County, North Carolina, made a totally worthless speech in the House of Representatives. He justified himself by saying he was not speaking to the House, 'but to Buncombe', and the name has come to mean 'worthless rubbish' ever since, though the spelling has been simplified and shortened.

Hence, also, **to debunk**, meaning 'to draw attention to nonsense' or 'to deflate a reputation'. This was the creation of William E. Woodward in his book *Bunk* (c 1920), an exposé of Henry Ford (famous for saying: 'History is more or less bunk').

bunny. See BE A GOOD ~ .

Bunny. Nickname of Robertson Hare (1891–1979), the British comedy actor (see

also INDUBITABLY!). An inevitable nickname for anyone called Hare and, perhaps more frequently, an inseparable nickname for people called Warren. (It was also, incidentally, Jackie Kennedy's pet name for her husband, President John F. Kennedy.)

Burbank. See THIS IS BEAUTIFUL DOWNTOWN ~ under *LAUGH-IN*.

buried. KNOW WHERE THE BODIES ARE ~ ; THEY CAME . . .

Burleigh's nod. (or **Burghley's**). Referring to William Cecil (1st Lord Burleigh), the English courtier and politician (1520–98). Within R.B. Sheridan's play *The Critic* (1779), there is a performance of a mock-tragedy on the Spanish Armada. Burleigh is represented as too preoccupied with affairs of state to be able to say anything, so he shakes his head and the character Puff explains what he means: 'Why by that shake of the head, he gave you to understand that even though they had more justice in their cause and wisdom in their measures – yet, if there was not a greater spirit shown on the part of the people – the country would at last fall a sacrifice to the hostile ambition of the Spanish monarchy . . .' 'The devil! – did he mean all that by shaking his head?' 'Every word of it – if he shook his head as I taught him.'

Hence, also, the expression 'To be as significant as the shake of Lord Burleigh's head'.

Burlington Bertie. A swell gentleman, named after the one with the 'Hyde Park drawl and the Bond Street crawl' commemorated in a song with words and music by Harry B. Norris (first published 1900) and performed by Vesta Tilley. Not to be confused with 'Burlington Bertie from Bow', a parody written in 1915 by William Hargreaves for his wife, Ella Shields, the male impersonator. In this song, now the better remembered of the two, Bertie is a more down-at-heel character.

BURMA. Meaning, 'Be Upstairs Ready My Angel'. Lovers' acronym for use in correspondence and to avoid military censorship. Probably in use by the First World War.

burn, baby, burn! A black extremists' slogan that arose from the August 1965 riots in the Watts district of Los Angeles when 34 people were killed and entire blocks burnt.

The 1974 song with the title by Hudson-Ford had other connotations. Indeed, it has been suggested that the phrase arose as a joke expression of sexual encouragement a year or so before the riots. Popularized by the Black disc jockey Magnificent Montague, it was called out by audiences to singers and musicians.

burns. See FIDDLE WHILE ROME ~.

burn your bra! A feminist slogan from America *c* 1970, encouraging women to destroy an item of apparel quite clearly designed by a male chauvinist and likely to make a woman more of a sex object. The analogy is with the burning of draft-cards as a protest against the Vietnam War.

bury the hatchet, to. Meaning, to settle an argument – after the American Indian ritual of burying *two* axes to seal a peace treaty. Recorded by 1680.

Burton. See GONE FOR A ~.

buses. See NEVER CHASE GIRLS OR ~.

bush telegraph. See GRAPEVINE, TO HEAR . . .

bushy-tailed. See BRIGHT-EYED AND ~.

business. See IT'S THE ~.

business as usual. The standard declaration posted when a shop has suffered some misfortune like a fire or is undergoing alterations. However, in the First World War the phrase was adopted in a more general sense. H.E. Morgan, an advertising man, promoted this slogan which had quite a vogue until it was proved to be manifestly untrue. In a Guildhall speech on 9 November 1914, Winston Churchill said: 'The maxim of the British people is "Business as usual".'

busman's holiday, a. A holiday or break spent doing much the same as you do for a living – as though a bus driver went on a motoring holiday. Recorded by 1893. Oddly, the word 'busman' has virtually no existence outside this phrase.

busy. See AS ~ AS . . .

Butch Cassidy and the Sundance Kid. Title of a film (US, 1969) using the nicknames of Robert LeRoy Parker and Harry Longbaugh, American outlaws, who both died in 1909. Parker/Cassidy was called 'Butch' because he had once been a butcher (not because he was manly, in the later sense of the term, though this is how that term probably arose) and Longbaugh had once carried out a daring bank raid in the town of Sundance, Arizona.

Butcher, the. Nickname of Ulysses S. Grant (1822–85), commander-in-chief of Union forces in the American Civil War and 18th President of the USA (1869–77). His opponents in the north called him this because they thought he was careless of the lives of men in his army. Critics opposed to tyrannical ways and his running for a third presidential term dubbed him **American Caesar.**

Butcher of Lyons, the. Nickname given to Klaus Barbie (1913–91), head of the German Gestapo in Lyons from 1942–4. He was so called because of his alleged cruelty, torture, and murder of French Resistance fighters and others. Twice tried *in absentia*, Barbie was brought back to Lyons from exile in Bolivia in 1983 and tried again in 1987. Patrick Marnham in the *Independent* (18 March 1987) protested that Barbie had never been known thus in Lyons and that his actual nickname was '*Le Bourreau*' [the executioner]. Other 'Butchers' include: Ulysses S. Grant, as above; Alexander Woollcott, drama critic – 'The Butcher of Broadway'; the Duke of Cumberland, second son of George II – 'The Butcher of Culloden'; and General Gholam Ali Ovessi (*d* 1984), 'the Butcher of Tehran' under the Shah of Iran's rule.

but I'm all right now. See under *ITMA*.

butler. See WHAT THE ∼ SAW.

butler did it! the. The origins of this phrase – an (often ironic) suggested solution to detective stories of the 1920s and 30s – remain a complete blank. However, a correspondent (1983) recalled hearing it spoken by a member of the audience after a showing of the last episode of the film series *The Exploits of Elaine* at a London cinema in c 1916. Joseph R. Sandy noted: 'The detective was called Craig Kennedy and the butler's name was Bennet. I do not remember who played the parts (except the heroine, who was Pearl White) or anything much more about the serial.'

So maybe the phrase was current by that date. But why did it enter common parlance? One of the conventions of whodunnit writing of the period we are talking about is that the butler or servants seldom, if ever, did 'do it'. Father Ronald Knox, compiling a list of rules for this kind of fiction in his introductions to *The Best Detective Stories of the Year, 1928,* noted: 'The only person who is really scratch on morals is the aged butler. I cannot off-hand recall any lapse of virtue on the part of a man who has been with the family for sixteen years. But I may be wrong; I have not read all the detective stories.' Later, however, in Patricia Wentworth's *The Ivory Dagger* (1951) the butler really *did* do it.

The earliest use of the phrase it is possible to give chapter and verse for is the film *My Man Godfrey* (1957 – not the 1936 original) which is not even a whodunnit: 'The butler did it! He made every lady in the house, oh, so very happy!' In 1956, one year before this, Robert Robinson made an allusion in his Oxford thriller *Landscape With Dead Dons*: ' "Well, well," said the Inspector, handing his coffee cup to Dimbleby, who was passing with a tray, "it always turns out to be the butler in the end." '

Alan Melville remembered (1983): 'Years ago, a repertory actor up in Scotland ruined every available Agatha Christie or other crime drama by saying the line straight out to the audience when he was slightly pissed – "No need to wait to the end, the butler did it." He was sacked, poor soul, but the sad thing is that the week he got his cards the play he was appearing in, however

unsteadily, was one in which the butler really did do it.'

There is talk of a pre-1939 cartoon in *Punch* showing a smug man buttoning up his gloves as he descends the steps outside a cinema, and announcing to the patient queues, 'The butler did it!' The Georgette Heyer thriller *Why Shoot a Butler?* (1933) manages to avoid any mention of the phrase. It became the title of an instrumental number written, and performed on drums, by Frank Butler (naturally) in 1958.

but Miss —, you're beautiful! A cliché of the cinema. Uttered by the boss when his hitherto bespectacled secretary reveals her natural charms. No citation to hand, but one feels that Cary Grant or Clark Gable was probably around at the time.

butter. See BIG ∼ AND EGG MAN; CAN YOU TELL STORK FROM ∼?; GUNS BEFORE ∼.

buttered side. See IF ANYTHING CAN GO WRONG . . .

butterfly. See WHO BREAKS A ∼ UPON A WHEEL.

butterfly effect, the. 'Predictability: Does the Flap of a Butterfly's Wings in Brazil Set Off a Tornado in Texas?' The title of a paper on predicability in weather forecasting delivered to the American Association for the Advancement of Science, Washington D.C., on 29 December 1979 by Edward Lorenz (b 1917), an American meteorologist. Apparently, Lorenz originally used the image of a *seagull*'s wing flapping. What is now called 'The Butterfly Effect' – how small acts lead to large – appeals to chaos theorists, who view the physical universe as largely irregular and unpredictable. J. Gleick gives another example in *Chaos: Making a New Theory* (1988), also from weather forecasting: 'The notion that a butterfly stirring the air today in Peking can transform storm systems next month in New York.'

but that's another story. Phrase with which (amusingly) to break off a narrative on the grounds of assumed irrelevance. The popularity of this catchphrase around 1900 derived from Rudyard Kipling. He used it in *Plain Tales from the Hills* (1888), but it had appeared earlier elsewhere. For example, in Laurence Sterne's *Tristram Shandy* (1760), it is intended to prevent one of the many digressions of which that novel is full.

button. See YOU PRESS THE ∼ . . .

buttonhole, to. In the sense, 'to detain a reluctant listener', this verb does not derive from 'buttonhole', the hole through which a button passes, nor from the flower, so called, worn in the slit on a coat lapel. The verb is really 'to button*hold*', to stop persons going away by holding on to one of their buttons. By 1716. An earlier form was, 'to take by the button'.

buy. See STOP ME AND ∼ ONE.

buy some for Lulu. See WOTALOTIGOT.

by and large. Meaning, 'generally speaking'. Originally this was a nautical term: to sail by and large meant to keep a ship on course so that it was sailing at a good speed even though the direction of the wind was changing. Brewer defines it thus: 'To sail slightly off the wind, making it easier for the helmsman to steer and less likely for the vessel to be taken aback.' The nautical sense was current by 1669, the general sense by 1706.

— by Christmas. At first, it was not thought that the First World War would last very long. Having started in August 1914, it would be 'over by Christmas', hence the anti-German slogan 'Berlin by Christmas'. The fact that this promise was not fulfilled did not prevent Henry Ford from saying, as he tried to stop the war a year later: 'We're going to try to get the boys out of the trenches before Christmas. I've chartered a ship, and some of us are going to Europe.' He was not referring to American boys because the United States had not joined the war at this stage. The *New York Tribune* announced: 'GREAT WAR ENDS CHRISTMAS DAY. FORD TO STOP IT.'

In her *Autobiography* (1977), Agatha Christie remembered that the South

African War would 'all be over in a few weeks'. She went on: 'In 1914 we heard the same phrase. "All over by Christmas". In 1940, "Not much point in storing the carpets with mothballs." – this when the Admiralty took over my house – "It won't last over the winter".'

In *Tribune* (28 April 1944), George Orwell recalled a young man 'on the night in 1940 when the big ack-ack barrage was fired over London for the first time' insisting, 'I tell you, it'll all be over by Christmas.' In his diary for 28 November 1950, Harold Nicolson wrote, 'Only a few days ago [General] MacArthur was saying, "Home by Christmas," and now he is saying, "This is a new war [Korea]."' As Flexner comments in *I Hear America Talking*: '*The war will be over by Christmas* was a popular 1861 expression [in the American Civil War]. Since then several generals and politicians have used the phrase or variations of it, in World War I, World War II, and the Korean war – and none of the wars was over by Christmas.' (Clever-clogs are apt to point out, however, that all wars are eventually over by *a* Christmas . . .)

bye-bye, everyone, bye-bye! See IZZY-WIZZY, LET'S GET BUSY.

bye for now. See under MORNING ALL!

by gum, she's a hot 'un! Characteristic phrase of the (very) North of England comedian, Frank Randle (1901–57), one of whose turns was as a randy old hitchhiker chiefly interested in girls' legs and ale. Randle was an earthy Lancastrian who did not travel well as a performer but has acquired something of a cult following now that he is safely dead. His other phrases included: **any more fer sailing?** and **by gum, ah've supped sum ale toneet** (compare WE'VE SOOPED SOME ALE . . .) Also: **would y'care for a Woodbine?** a cigarette-offering joke, believed to have been perpetrated by Randle in the film *Somewhere in England* (UK, 1940). A correspondent suggests that what he actually said was 'Would you care for a Woodbine? Go on, take a big one' – and then offered a tin full of fag-ends.

For 'by gum', see EE, BAH GUM.

by half. See TOO CLEVER ~.

by hook or by crook. *OED2*, while finding a couple of references in the works of John Wycliffe around 1380, states firmly that while there are 'many theories', there is no firm evidence for the origin of this phrase which means 'by some means or another'. In fact, the only real theory is the one about peasants in feudal times being allowed only to take for firewood those tree branches which they could pull down 'by hook or by crook' – 'crook' here meaning the hooked staff carried by shepherds (and also, symbolically, by bishops).

'By hook or by crook **I'll be last in this book**' is the cliché you append to the final page of an autograph book when asked to contribute a little something more than your signature.

by Jingo! Now a mild and meaningless oath, this phrase derived its popularity from G.W. Hunt's notable anti-Russian music-hall song 'We Don't Want to Fight (But By Jingo If We Do . . .)' (1877). The song gave the words 'jingo' and 'jingoism' their modern meaning (excessive patriotism), but the oath had existed before this. *Punch* (3 February 1872) has a cartoon caption, 'Ghosts, by Jingo!' Motteux in his translation of Rabelais in 1694 put 'by jingo' for '*par dieu*' and there is some evidence to show that 'jingo' was conjuror's gibberish dating from a decade or two before. It is impossible to say whether there is any connection with Jingo, the legendary Empress of Japan who invaded Korea victoriously in the second century.

by Jove, I needed that! Used, as though after long-awaited alcoholic refreshment, by several comedians. Ken Dodd has said it (1960s/70s) after a quick burst on the banjo, to relieve tension. It also appeared in the *GOON SHOW*.

by that time you'll be dead and your arse cold. See IT WILL ALL BE THE SAME . . .

by the stork. See CABBAGE PATCH KIDS.

by the sword divided. In dealing with the Civil War period, Macaulay in his *History of England*, Chaps. 1–2 (1848), had earlier written: 'Thirteen years followed during which England was . . . really governed by the sword'; 'the whole nation was sick of government by the sword'; 'anomalies and abuses . . . which had been destroyed by the sword'.

A BBC TV historical drama series (1983–5) set in the English Civil War was created by John Hawkesworth who commented (1991): 'When I first wrote down the idea for a story about the Civil War I called it *The Laceys of Arnescote* . . . [but] I decided the title didn't convey the sort of Hentyish swashbuckling style that we were aiming at, so I thought again. The title *By the Sword Divided* came to me as I was walking along a beach in Wales.'

· C ·

C&A. A joke explanation of this clothing store's name in Britain, usually put in the mouth of a London bus conductor, is that the initials stand for 'Coats and 'Ats'. In full, 'C&A Modes', the name comes from the first names of Clemens and August Brenninkmeyer, the Dutch brothers who founded the business in 1841.

cab. See under FOLLOW THAT TAXI . . .

Cabbage Patch Kids. Millions of soft, ugly dolls with this name were sold in 1983–4. Created by American entrepreneur Xavier Roberts, they became a craze around the world. People did not purchase them but, tweely, 'adopted' them.

Whereas, in Britain, babies that are not delivered **by the stork** are found **under a gooseberry bush**, in the US, they are found in 'cabbage patches'. The 'stork' and 'cabbage-patch' theories of childbirth were known by 1923; the 'gooseberry-bush' by 1903.

Compare *Mrs Wiggs of the Cabbage Patch* (1901), the title of a US children's novel by Alice Hegan Rice.

cabbages and kings. Phrase from Lewis Carroll's 'Walrus and the Carpenter' episode in *Through the Looking Glass and What Alice Found There* (Chap. 4, 1871):

'The time has come,' the Walrus said,
'To talk of many things:
Of shoes — and ships — and
    sealing-wax —
Of cabbages and kings . . .'

The US writer O. Henry took *Cabbages and Kings* as the title of his first collection of short stories (1904) and there is a book *Of Kennedys and Kings: making sense of the Sixties* by Harris Wofford (1980). However, the conjunction of 'cabbages' and 'kings' pre-dates Carroll. In Hesketh Pearson's *Smith of Smiths*, a biography of Rev.

Sydney Smith (*d* 1845), he quotes Smith as saying about a certain Mrs George Groce: 'She had innumerable hobbies, among them horticulture and democracy, defined by Sydney as "the most approved methods of growing cabbages and destroying kings".'

cabin. See LOG ~ TO WHITE HOUSE.

cads. See PLAY THE GAME, ~.

Caesar. See AMERICAN ~.

Caesar's wife must be above suspicion. An example of this phrase in use occurs in Lord Chesterfield's letters (c 1740): 'Your moral character must be not only pure, but, like Caesar's wife, unsuspected.' Originally, it was Julius Caesar himself who said this of his wife Pompeia when he divorced her in 62 BC. In North's translation of Plutarch's *Lives* – which is how the saying came into English in 1570 – Caesar is quoted thus: 'I will not, sayd he, that my wife be so much as suspected.' Pompeia was Caesar's second wife and according to Suetonius, in 61 BC she took part in the women-only rites of the Feast of the Great Goddess. But it was rumoured that a profligate called Publius Clodius attended, wearing women's clothes, and that he committed adultery with Pompeia. Caesar divorced Pompeia and at the subsequent inquiry into the desecration was asked why he had done so. 'Caesar's wife must be above suspicion,' he replied. He later married Calphurnia.

café society. See NESCAFÉ SOCIETY.

cage. See PLAY THE MUSIC . . . under MUM, MUM, THEY ARE LAUGHING AT ME.

Cain. See RAISE ~.

cake. See PIECE OF ~.

cakes and ale. A synonym for 'enjoyment', as in the expression 'Life isn't all cakes and ale'. On 4 May 1876, the Rev. Francis Kilvert wrote in his diary: 'The clerk's wife brought out some cakes and ale and pressed me to eat and drink. I was to have returned to Llysdinam to luncheon ... but as I wanted to see more of the country and the people I decided to let the train go by, accept the hospitality of my hostess and the cakes and ale which life offered, and walk home quietly in the course of the afternoon' – a neat demonstration of the literal and metaphorical uses of the phrase. *Cakes and Ale* is the title of a novel (1930) by W. Somerset Maugham.

The phrase comes from Sir Toby Belch's remark to Malvolio in Shakespeare's *Twelfth Night* (1600): 'Does thou think, because thou art virtuous, there shall be no more cakes and ale?' (II.iii.114). The Arden edition comments that cakes and ale were 'traditionally associated with festivity, and disliked by Puritans both on this account and because of their association with weddings, saints' days, and holy days'.

Compare LIFE ISN'T ALL BEER AND SKITTLES.

cake-hole. See SHUT YOUR ~.

Calabash. See GOODNIGHT, MRS ~.

Calais. See under WOGS BEGIN AT BARNET.

calamity. See OII, ~!

Calamity Jane. The nickname for a female prophet of doom derives from that of Martha Jane Canary (1852–1903) of Deadwood, South Dakota. She behaved like a cowboy but was generally unlucky in nefarious activities and brought catastrophe on her associates. Eleven of her twelve husbands died untimely deaths. She dressed, swore, and shot like a man, eventually went into show business, and threatened 'calamity' to any man who offended her.

Calcutta. See BLACK HOLE OF ~ ; OH! ~!

calibre. See A MAN OF MY ~ under *HANCOCK'S HALF-HOUR*.

call. See DON'T ~ US . . . ; THEY ~ —.

calling. See AVON ~!

calling all cars, calling all cars! What the police controller says on the radio to patrolmen in American cops and robbers films and TV series of the 1950s. For some reason, it is the archetypal cop phrase of the period, and evocative. However, the formula had obviously been known before this if the British film titles *Calling All Stars* (1937), *Calling All Ma's* (1937) and *Calling All Cars* (1954) are anything to go by.

call me Madam. When Frances Perkins was appointed Secretary of Labor by President Roosevelt in 1933, she became the first US woman to hold Cabinet rank. It was held that when she had been asked *in Cabinet* how she wished to be addressed, she had replied: 'Call me Madam.' She denied that she had done this, however. It was *after* her first Cabinet meeting when reporters asked how they should address her. The Speaker-elect of the House of Representatives, Henry T. Rainey, answered for her: 'When the Secretary of Labor is a lady, she should be addressed with the same general formalities as the Secretary of Labor who is a gentleman. You call him "Mr Secretary". You will call her "Madam Secretary". You gentlemen know that when a lady is presiding over a meeting, she is referred to as "Madam Chairman" when you rise to address the chair' (quoted in George Martin, *Madam Secretary – Frances Perkins*, 1976). Some of the reporters put this ruling into Perkins's own mouth and that presumably is how the misquotation occurred.

Irving Berlin's musical *Call Me Madam* was first performed on Broadway in 1950, starring Ethel Merman as a woman ambassador appointed to represent the US in a tiny European state. It was inspired by the case of Pearl Mesta, the society hostess, whom Harry Truman had appointed as ambassador to Luxembourg.

Calvins. See YOU KNOW WHAT COMES BETWEEN ME AND MY ~?

Camay. See YOU'LL LOOK A LITTLE LOVELIER . . .

came. See THEY ~ . . . ; THIS IS WHERE WE ~ IN.

camel. See EASIER FOR A ~ TO . . .

camera cannot lie/never lies, the. An 'old saying', but one which has to be a twentieth-century proverb, though its origins are unrecorded. In the script for the commentary of a film ('Six Commissioned Texts', I., 1962), W.H. Auden wrote: 'The camera's eye/Does not lie,/But it cannot show/The life within.' 'The camera cannot lie. But it can be an accessory to the untruth' – Harold Evans, *Pictures on a Page* (1978).

came the dawn. (or **comes the dawn.**) A stock phrase of romantic fiction in the early twentieth century – also, probably, a subtitle or inter-title from the early days of cinema. 'Came the Dawn' was the title of a P.G. Wodehouse short story reprinted in *Mulliner Omnibus* (1927). Before the coming of film sound, it was possible for a catchphrase to emerge from this kind of use. In *A Fool There Was* (1914), Theda Bara 'spoke' the inter-title **kiss me, my fool**, and this was taken up as a fad expression. Similarly, Jacqueline Logan 'said' **harness my zebras** in Cecil B. De Mille's 1925 *King of Kings*. This became a fad expression for 'let's leave' or as a way of expressing amazement – 'Well, harness my zebras!'
See also MEANWHILE BACK AT THE RANCH.

can. See CARRY THE ~.

can a (bloody) duck swim! (sometimes **does/will a fish swim!**) This is said by way of meaning 'You bet!', 'Of course, I will'. *ODP* has 'Will a duck swim?' in 1842. Winston Churchill claimed he said the 'can' version to Stanley Baldwin when Baldwin asked if he would accept the post of Chancellor of the Exchequer in the 1924 government. Lady Violet Bonham Carter used the phrase to Churchill when he asked her to serve as a Governor of the BBC in 1941. Thence he proceeded to refer to her as his 'Bloody Duck' and she had to sign her letters to him, 'Your BD'.
Compare IS THE POPE (A) CATHOLIC?

candid camera. See SMILE, YOU'RE ON ~.

can dish it out but can't take it in, **(s)he.** Said of people who can't accept the kind of criticism they dispense to others. A reader's letter to *Time* (4 January 1988) remarked of comedienne Joan Rivers's action in suing a magazine for misquoting her about her late husband: 'For years she has made big money at the expense of others with her caustic remarks. Obviously Rivers can dish it out but can't take it in.'
The contrast was established by the 1930s. In the film *49th Parallel* (1941), Raymond Massey as a Canadian soldier apparently plays with the phrase when he says to a Nazi, 'When things go wrong, we can take it. We can dish it out, too.'

candle. See HOLD A ~ TO SOMETHING.

can I do you now, sir? One of the great catchphrases – from *ITMA*. Said by 'Mrs Mopp' (Dorothy Summers), the hoarse-voiced charlady or 'Corporation Cleanser', when entering the office of Tommy Handley, as the Mayor. Curiously, the first time Mrs Mopp used the phrase, on 10 October 1940, she said, 'Can I do *for* you now, sir?' This was soon replaced by the familiar emphases of 'Can I *do* you *now*, sir?' that people can still be heard using today.
Bob Monkhouse recalled (1979) Dorothy Summers saying: 'Oh, I do wish people wouldn't expect me to be only Mrs Mopp. That awful char. I never wanted to say it in the first place. I think it was rather distasteful.' She seems to have been the only person to detect any double meaning in it.

cannon. See LOOSE ~.

cannot you stay till I eat my porridge? See YOUR BEER IS SOUR.

can't pay, won't pay. Slogan adopted by those objecting to the British government's Community Charge or 'poll tax' in 1990 and by other similar protest groups. *Can't Pay, Won't Pay* was the English title of the play *Non Si Paga! Non Si Paga!* (1974) by Dario Fo, as translated by Lino Pertile (1981).

can we talk? Stock phrase of Joan Rivers, the American comedienne and TV chat-show host, by 1984.

can you hear me, mother? The British comedian, Sandy Powell (1900–82), recalled in 1979: 'It was in about 1932/3, when I was doing an hour's show on the radio, live, from Broadcasting House in London. I was doing a sketch called "Sandy at the North Pole". I was supposed to be broadcasting home and wanting to speak to my mother. When I got to the line, "Can you hear me, mother?" I dropped my script on the studio floor. While I was picking up the sheets all I could do was repeat the phrase over and over. Well, that was on a Saturday night. The following week I was appearing at the Hippodrome, Coventry, and the manager came to me at the band rehearsal with a request: "You'll say that, tonight, won't you?" I said, "What?" He said, "'Can you hear me, mother?' Everybody's saying it. Say it and see." So I did and the whole audience joined in and I've been stuck with it ever since. Even abroad – New Zealand, South Africa, Rhodesia, they've all heard it. I'm not saying it was the first radio catchphrase – they were all trying them out – but it was the first to catch on.'

can *you* tell Stork from butter? A slogan for Stork margarine in the UK from c 1956. One of the earliest slogans on commercial TV, it was invariably alluded to in parodies of TV advertising. In the original ads, housewives were shown taking part in comparative tests and tasting pieces of bread spread with real butter and with Stork.

cap. See FEATHER IN ONE'S OWN ∼.

Capability Brown. Lancelot Brown (*d* 1783) was an architect and landscape gardener, noted for planning a naturalistic type of garden for the great houses of England, with vistas of trees, lakes, and flower-beds. His usual comment after carrying out a survey was: 'It's capable' or 'It has capabilities'.

car. See BEST ∼ IN THE WORLD under AT 60 MILES AN HOUR . . . ; CALLING ALL ∼S; HOLE HEALS UP . . . ; WOULD YOU BUY A USED ∼ . . .

caravan. See DOGS BARK BUT THE ∼ . . .

carborundum. See ILLEGITIMI NON ∼.

carbuncle. See MONSTROUS ∼.

carcase. See HAVE HIS ∼.

care. See BOAC TAKES GOOD ∼ OF YOU; OH, I SAY, I RATHER ∼ FOR THAT!; NO ONE LIKES US WE DON'T ∼; TENDER LOVING ∼.

cared. See AS IF I ∼.

careful. See IF YOU CAN'T BE GOOD . . .

carelessness kills. See KEEP DEATH OFF THE ROAD.

caring and sharing. The word 'caring' – to describe official 'care' of the disadvantaged – was stretched almost to breaking point during the 1980s to embrace almost anybody concerned with social and welfare services. Marginally worse was the facile rhyme of 'caring and sharing' used, for example, to promote a Telethon-type fund-raiser in Melbourne, Australia (November 1981). The phrase is probably of American origin: 'The love I feel for our adopted children is in no way less strong than the love I feel for the three children in our family who were born to us . . . It is the caring and sharing that count' – Claudia L. Jewett, *Adopting the Older Child*, Boston, Mass., 1978.

Carlos the Jackal. See JACKAL, THE.

carpe diem. It is a motto meaning 'enjoy the day while you have the chance' or 'make the most of the present time, seize the opportunity' – quoted from the *Odes* of the Roman poet, Horace. Another translation of the relevant passage is:

> While we're talking, envious time is fleeing:
> Seize the day, put no trust in the future.

carry on, —! It is fitting that the injunction to 'carry on', a staple part of several catch- and stock phrases, should have been celebrated in virtually all the more than thirty titles of British film comedies in the *Carry On* series. The very first of the films showed the origin: *Carry On, Sergeant* (1958) was about a sergeant attempting to discipline a platoon of extremely raw recruits. 'Carry on, sergeant' is what an officer would say, having addressed some homily to the ranks, before walking off and leaving the sergeant to get on with his drill, or whatever. The actual services origin of the phrase is, however, nautical. From the *Daily Chronicle* (24 July 1909): '"Carry on!" is a word they have in the Navy. It is the "great word" of the service . . . To-morrow the workaday life of the Fleet begins again and the word will be, "Carry on!"'

Other citings: in 1936, when President F.D. Roosevelt was seeking re-election, a Democratic slogan was **Carry on, Roosevelt**. A cable from the Caribbean was received in Whitehall during the summer of 1940: '**Carry on, Britain!** Barbados is behind you!' When Sub-Lieut. Eric Barker (1912–90) starred in the Royal Navy version of the BBC radio show *Merry Go Round* (c 1945), his favourite command to others was, **carry on, smokin'**!

Jimmy Jewel (*b* 1912) of the double-act Jewel and Warriss, would refer to Ben Warriss (*d* 1993) as 'Harry Boy' and say '**Carry on, 'Arry Boy!** Tell 'em, boy. Has Harry Boy been up to something naughty?' When some dreadful tale had been unfolded, Jewel would cap it with **what a carry on!** This last phrase became the title of a film the two comedians made in 1949. In his autobiography (1982), Jewel remarked that Tommy Trinder 'stole' the line 'and later we almost came to blows over it'.

See also CARRY ON, LONDON! under *IN TOWN TONIGHT*.

carry the can, to. Meaning 'to bear responsibility; take the blame; become a scapegoat', this is possibly a military term, referring to the duties of the man chosen to get beer for a group. He would have to carry a container of beer to the group and then carry it back when it was empty. Some consider it to be precisely naval in origin; no example before 1936. Alternatively, it could refer to the man who had to remove 'night soil' from earth closets – literally, carrying the can – and leaving an empty can in its place. Or then again, it could have to do with the 'custom of miners carrying explosives to the coal face in a tin can (hence everyone's reluctance to "carry the can")' – *Street Talk, the Language of Coronation Street* (1986).

cart, to be in the. Meaning 'to be in trouble', this expression may come from the fact that prisoners used to be taken in a cart to punishment or execution, or from when a horse was put in a cart (because it was ill or dead), the owner being left in a spot.

Casbah. See COME WITH ME TO THE ∼.

cash. See IN GOD WE TRUST . . .

cash/throw in one's chips/checks, to. Meaning, originally, 'to stop gambling', but then 'to die', and, as *DOAS* has it: 'to terminate a business transaction, sell one's share of, or stock in, a business, or the like, in order to realize one's cash profits'.

It also may mean 'to make a final gesture' – Tom Mangold wrote in the *Listener* (8 September 1983), concerning the US arms race in space: 'Under malign command, a technological guarantee of invulnerability could induce the holder to cash his chips and go for a pre-emptive first strike.'

cast of thousands, with a. Now only used jokingly and ironically, this type of film promotion line *may* have made its first appearance in connection with the 1927 version of *Ben Hur* where the boast was, 'Cast of 125,000'!

cat. See BRING BACK THE ∼; LET THE ∼ OUT OF THE BAG; LIKE THE BARBER'S ∼; ONE-LEGGED ∼ under AS BUSY AS . . .

catch. See FIRST ∼ YOUR HARE.

Catch-22. Phrase encapsulating the popular view that 'there's always a catch' – some underlying law which defeats people by its brutal, ubiquitous logic. *Catch-22* was the title of a novel (1961, film US, 1970) by Joseph Heller about a group of US fliers in the Second World War. 'It was a Catch-22 situation,' people will say, as if resorting to a quasi-proverbial expression like 'Heads you win, tails I lose' or 'Damned if you do, damned if you don't', though, oddly, Heller had originally numbered it 18 (apparently *Catch-18* was dropped to avoid confusion with Leon Uris's novel *Mila-18*). In the book, the idea is explored several times. Captain Yossarian, a US Air Force bombardier, does not wish to fly any more missions. He goes to see the group's MO, Doc Daneeka, about getting grounded on the grounds that he is crazy:

> Daneeka: There's a rule saying I have to ground anyone who's crazy.
> Yossarian: Then why can't you ground me? I'm crazy.
> Daneeka: Anyone who wants to get out of combat duty isn't really crazy.

This is the catch – Catch-22.

cat got your tongue?, (has the) Question put to a person (usually young) who is not saying anything, presumably through guilt. Since the mid-nineteenth century and a prime example of nanny-speak.

cat has nine lives, a. A proverbial saying (known by 1546). But why so many? While cats have an obvious capacity for getting out of scrapes – literally 'landing on their feet' in most cases – in ancient Egypt, they were venerated for ridding the country of a plague of rats and were linked to the trinity of Mother, Father and Son. 'To figure out how many extra lives the cat had, the Egyptians multiplied the sacred number three, three times, and arrived at nine' – Robert L. Shook, *The Book of Why* (1983).

cat house, a. A brothel. In *Catwatching* (1986), Desmond Morris traces this term (mostly US use) from the fact that prostitutes have been called 'cats' since the fifteenth century, 'for the simple reason that the urban female cat attracts many toms when it is on heat and mates with them one after the other'. As early as 1401, Morris adds, men were warned of the risk of chasing 'cat's tail' – women. Hence the slang word **tail** to denote the female genitals (compare 'pussy').

cat in hell's chance, not to have a. Meaning 'to have no chance whatsoever', the full expression makes the phrase clear: 'No more chance than a cat in hell *without claws*' – which is recorded in Grose, *Dictionary of the Vulgar Tongue* (1796).

cat on a hot tin roof, to be like a. From the (mostly US) expression 'as nervous as a cat on a hot tin roof', which derives from the common English expression 'like a cat on hot bricks', meaning 'ill-at-ease, jumpy'. John Ray in his *Collection of English Proverbs* (1670–8) has, 'to go like a cat upon a hot bake stone'. Another English proverbial expression (known by 1903) is 'Nervous as cats'. In the play *Cat On a Hot Tin Roof* (1955; film US, 1958) by Tennessee Williams, the 'cat' is Maggie, Brick's wife, 'whose frayed vivacity', wrote Kenneth Tynan, 'derives from the fact that she is sexually ignored by her husband'.

cats. See RAINING ∼ AND DOGS.

cat's paw, a. Meaning 'someone used as a tool by another', this term was known in Britain by 1657, and chiefly derives from one of La Fontaine's fables (1668–94), 'The Monkey and the Cat', in which a monkey persuades a cat to pick up chestnuts off a hot stove. 'The Cat's Paw' is the title of a painting (1824) by Sir Edwin Landseer, illustrating the story. In nautical use, a 'cat's paw' is the mark made by a puff or gust of wind on an otherwise calm sea – possibly an allusion to cats dabbing at the surface of fish ponds.

cat's pyjamas/whiskers. See BEE'S KNEES.

cat that walks alone, a. A self-possessed, independent person. 'I am the cat that walks alone' was a favourite expression of the newspaper magnate Lord Beaverbrook (1879–1964). He was alluding to 'The Cat That Walked By Himself' in *The Just-So Stories* (1902) by Rudyard Kipling.

Caudle lecture. See CURTAIN LECTURE.

caviare to the general. A famously misunderstood phrase meaning 'of no interest to common folk', this has nothing to do with giving expensive presents of caviare to unappreciative military gentlemen. In Shakespeare's *Hamlet*, II.ii.434, the Prince refers to a play which, he recalls: 'pleased not the million, 'twas caviare to the general' (the general public, in other words). The Arden edition notes that in c 1600, when the play was written, caviare was a novel delicacy. It was probably inedible to those who had not yet acquired a taste for it.

Cazaly. See UP THERE, ~!

Cecil. See AFTER YOU, CLAUDE . . .

Celtic fringe. (or **edge.**) The area
occupied by the Celtic peoples of Ireland,
Scotland, Wales and Cornwall, seen –
usually derogatively – as being on the
fringes of the British Isles (compare LUNATIC
FRINGE). The phrase arose in the late
nineteenth century.

Celtic twilight, the. The atmosphere and
preoccupations of Celtic Britain –
particularly in the sense that these are/were
on the way out (compare TWILIGHT OF
EMPIRE). *The Celtic Twilight* was the title of a
collection of stories on Celtic themes (1893)
by the Irish writer and poet, W.B. Yeats.

Central Casting. See STRAIGHT OUT OF ~ .

century. See — OF THE ~ .

certain substances. A police euphemism
for drugs, chiefly used in the UK where
restrictions are placed on the reporting of
criminal activity before a charge has been
made. Starting in the 1960s, newspapers
would report raids on pop stars' houses and
conclude: 'Certain substances were taken
away for analysis.' From the episode of TV's
MONTY PYTHON'S FLYING CIRCUS broadcast
on 16 November 1969: *Policeman*: 'I must
warn you, sir, that outside I have police dog
Josephine, who is not only armed, and
trained to sniff out certain substances, but is
also a junkie.'

Chad, the. (or **Mr Chad.**) The large-
nosed, bald, little figure peering over a wall
with his hands resting either side of his
head was drawn to accompany the message
KILROY WAS HERE and is known in the US as
'Chad', 'Mr Chad', or 'the Chad'. In the
UK, the figure is more associated with the
slogan 'WOT NO —?' than with Kilroy.
Various suggestions have been advanced as
to how the little figure took the form it did,
most probably in the early part of the
Second World War (one of the most
persistent is that it is an adaptation of a
piece of electrical circuitry).
    But why was he called Chad, particularly
when in other parts of the world (notably

Canada and Australia) he acquired the
names Flywheel, Clem, Private Snoops, the
Jeep, or Phoo? A correspondent suggests
that the Women's Auxiliary Air Force
(WAAFs) had links with a building called
Chadwick House in Bolton. Brewer says the
name comes from 'Chat' the cartoonist
(George Edward Chatterton) who appears
to have created a similar figure in 1938. Or
possibly the name comes from the film
Chad Hanna which was released in Britain
in June 1941 just as the craze was taking off.

Chairman of the Board. See OL' BLUE
EYES.

chalk. See LONG ~ .

-challenged. A suffix designed to convey a
personal problem or disadvantage in a more
positive light. Originating in the US, the
first such coinage would appear to have
been 'physically challenged' in the sense of
disabled: 'This bestselling author [Richard
Simmons] of *The Never Say Diet Book*
creates a comprehensive fitness program for
the physically challenged' – *Publishers
Weekly* (10 January 1986).
    Actual '-challenged' coinages are now far
out-numbered by jocular inventions, many
aimed at discrediting the proponents of
POLITICALLY CORRECT terminology. Among
the many suggested in Britain and the US
are: 'aesthetically challenged' for 'ugly';
'chronologically challenged' for 'old'; and,
'follicularly challenged' for 'bald'.

Cham. See GREAT ~ .

Chamberlain, Neville. See UMBRELLA.

champagne socialism. The holding of
socialist beliefs by people who are
conspicuous consumers of the good things
in life. The most obvious example of a
champagne socialist is John Mortimer,
the prolific British playwright, novelist and
lawyer (*b* 1923), who may indeed have used
it about himself. The earliest use of the term
appears to have been in connection with,
'Robert Maxwell, *Daily Mirror* newspaper
tycoon and possibly the best known Czech
in Britain after Ivan Lendl, [who] has long
been renowned for his champagne socialist
beliefs (*The Times*, 2 July 1987). However, a

similar appellation was earlier applied to the Labour politician Aneurin Bevan. Randolph Churchill (who was, rather, a champagne *Conservative*) recalled how Brendan Bracken had once attacked Bevan: ' "You Bollinger Bolshevik, you ritzy Robespierre, you lounge-lizard Lenin," he roared at Bevan one night, gesturing, as he went on, somewhat in the manner of a domesticated orang-utang. "Look at you, swilling Max [Beaverbrook]'s champagne and calling yourself a socialist." ' (*Evening Standard*, 8 August 1958).

champions. See BREAKFAST OF ~.

chance. See under AS BUSY AS . . . ; CAT IN HELL'S ~; NO MORE ~ THAN A SNOWBALL IN HELL.

Chanel. See COCO ~.

change. See NEVER SWAP HORSES IN MIDSTREAM; WIND OF ~; YOU MUST HAVE SEEN A LOT OF ~ S.

changed. See ONLY THE NAMES HAVE BEEN ~ under *DRAGNET*.

chapter of accidents, a. 'A series of unforeseen happenings or misfortunes'. The 4th Earl of Chesterfield used the phrase in a letter to his son in 1753; in 1837, John Wilkes was quoted by Southey as saying: 'The chapter of accidents is the longest chapter in the book'. A *Chapter of Accidents* was the title of the autobiography (1972) of Goronwy Rees, the writer.

charge. See I'M IN ~.

Charles, hello. See under *BEYOND OUR KEN*.

Charley. See CLAP HANDS, HERE COMES ~.

Charlie. See CHASE ME, ~; COME TO ~; VAS YOU DERE, ~?; and under *RAY'S A LAUGH*.

Charlie. A 'Charlie' (as in CHARLIE FARNSBARNS, CHASE ME CHARLIE, PROPER CHARLIE and RIGHT CHARLIE) has long been a slightly derogative name to apply to anyone. In Australia, it may also be a

shortening of 'Charlie Wheeler', rhyming slang for 'Sheila', a girl (recorded in Sydney Baker, *The Australian Language*, 1945).

Charlie Farnsbarns. A twit whose name one can't remember. Noting that this moderately well-known expression had escaped Eric Partridge and his reviser, Paul Beale, I mentioned it to Beale in November 1985, suggesting that it sounded military, even pre-Second World War, though I had heard the comedian Ronnie Barker use it in a monologue quite recently. Beale came back with: 'Charlie Farnsbarns was a very popular equivalent of e.g. "Mrs Thing" or "Old Ooja", i.e. "Old whatsisname". Much play was made with the name in *MUCH BINDING IN THE MARSH*, but whether murdoch and horne actually invented it, or whether they borrowed it "out of the air", i'm afraid i don't know. they would mention especially, i remember, a magnificent motorcar called a "farnsbarns special" or something like, say, a "farnsbarns straight eight". this was in the period, roughly, 1945–50, while i was at school – i recall a very jolly aunt of mine who was vastly amused by the name and used it a lot.'

CHARLIE (as above) is a name given to an ordinary bloke; 'Farnsbarns' has the numbing assonance needed to describe a bit of a nonentity. I suspect the phrase came out of the services (probably RAF) in the Second World War. Denis Gifford, incidentally, in *The Golden Age of Radio* (1985), says the name was used by 'Sam Costa in *Merry-Go-Round* (1946)' – but the RAF edition of that show was the forerunner of *MUCH BINDING IN THE MARSH*.

charm offensive. A happy coinage (along the lines of 'peace offensive') for the the gregarious and open tactics towards the West of the Soviet leader, Mikhail Gorbachev, around 1986. These tactics contrasted greatly with the frosty style of his predecessors.

Chase. See CHEVY ~.

chase me, (Charlie). 'Chase me' has been the catchphrase of the camp British comedian, Duncan Norvelle, since before 1986. 'Chase me, Charlie', the title of a song from Noël Coward's *Ace of Clubs* (1950) was not original. It had also been the title of a popular song current in 1900.

chattering classes, the. A term for those newspaper journalists and broadcasters who are paid to discuss topics of current interest, the opinion-formers, but also those – usually of a liberal bent – who are simply likely to talk about them. The phrase first registered on me when Alan Watkins used it in the *Observer* (4 August 1985): 'At the beginning of the week the *Daily Mail* published, over several days, a *mélange* of popular attitudes towards Mrs Thatcher. Even though it contained little that was surprising or new, it was much discussed among the chattering classes.'

And the following weekend (on 11 August), a *Sunday Times* editorial went thus: 'The BBC and the weather have been the only two stories in town this silly season. But the outlook for British broadcasting is actually rather cheery, despite all the wailing and gnashing of teeth among the chattering classes.'

Subsequently, Watkins described (in the *Guardian*, 25 November 1989) how the phrase had been coined by the rightish political commentator, Frank Johnson, in conversation with Watkins in the early years of Margaret Thatcher's prime ministership (i.e. *c* 1980).

Chatterley. See LADY ∼.

Chaunt, Mrs Ormiston. See MRS GRUNDY.

chauvinist. See MALE ∼ PIG.

cheap. See AREN'T PLUMS ∼?; PILE IT HIGH . . .

check. See JOE BOB SAYS ∼ IT OUT.

checkmate. See END GAME.

checks. See CASH ONE'S ∼.

Cheeky Chappie. See HERE'S A FUNNY THING . . .

cheeky monkey! See under RIGHT MONKEY!

cheer. See BRONX ∼.

cheered. See THOUSANDS ∼.

cheerful. See IT'S BEING SO ∼ under ITMA.

cheerful Charlie. See PROPER CHARLIE.

cheerio, cads, and happy landings! See PLAY THE GAME, CADS!

cheers. See CUP THAT ∼.

cheesed/browned off, to be. 'To be fed up'. 'Cheese' and 'off-ness' rather go together, so one might think of cheese as having an undesirable quality. Also, when cheese is subjected to heat, it goes brown, or gets 'browned off'. On the other hand, the phrase could derive from 'cheese off', an expression like 'fuck off', designed to make a person go away. 'Cheesed off' may just be a state of rejection, like 'pissed off'.

chemistry. See SEXUAL ∼.

cheque. See THERE'S A ∼ IN THE POST.

Chernobyl factor. See FALKLANDS FACTOR.

cherries. See LIFE IS JUST A BOWL OF ∼.

che sera sera. The proverbial saying 'What must be, must be' can be found as far back as Chaucer's 'Knight's Tale' (*c* 1390): 'When a thyng is shapen, it shal be.' But of this foreign version, as sung, for example, by Doris Day her 1956 hit song 'Whatever Will Be Will Be'? She also sang it in the remake of Alfred Hitchcock's *The Man Who Knew Too Much* in the same year. Ten years later, Geno Washington and the Ram Jam Band had a hit with a song entitled '*Que Sera Sera*'.

So is it *che* or *que*? There is no such phrase as *che sera sera* in modern Spanish or Italian, though *che* is an Italian word and *sera* is a Spanish one. What we have is an Old French or Old Italian spelling of what would be, in modern Italian *che sara, sara*. This is the form in which the Duke of Bedford's motto has always been written.

Chevy Chase. Assumed name of the US comedy actor who came to the fore in the 1970s. He appeared on *Saturday Night Live* on TV and in films such as *Foul Play*. He was born Cornelius Crane Chase in 1943, so why did he adopt the name 'Chevy' – except to get away from Cornelius? Could it be that he wanted to allude to Chevy as in the abbreviated form of **Chevrolet,** the US motor car which derives its name from Louis Chevrolet, a Swiss engineer? Or could he have wanted to allude to the fifteenth-century ballad 'Chevy Chase' which describes an old dispute between the Percy and Douglas families on the Scottish border, arising from a hunting accident? ('Chevy' or 'chivvy' is a huntsman's call meaning 'chase or harass the fox'.) More likely it comes from the suburb of Washington DC known as Chevy Chase, though this was probably named after the fifteenth-century ballad by colonists who settled there.

'Chevy Chase' is also rhyming slang for 'face' (recorded by 1857).

chewed every mouthful . . . See GLADSTONE ~.

chew gum. See HE CAN'T FART AND ~ . . .

chew the rag, to. 'To chew something over; to grouse or grumble over something at length, to discuss matters with a degree of thoroughness' (compare 'to chew the fat'). As in the expression 'to chew something over', the word 'chew' here means simply 'to say' – that is, it is something that is carried on in the mouth like eating. The 'rag' part relates to an old meaning of that word, in the sense 'to scold' or 'reprove severely'. 'Rag' was also once a slang word for 'the tongue' (from 'red rag', probably).

Compare CUD, TO CHEW THE.

chicken. See IS THAT A ~ JOKE under LAUGH-IN; RUBBER ~.

chickens have lips?, do. See IS THE POPE A CATHOLIC?

chief cook and bottle-washer. (sometimes **head cook . . .**) 'A person put in charge of running something ; a factotum' (known by 1887). What may be

an early form of the phrase occurs in Schikaneder's text for Mozart's *Die Zauberflöte* (1791). Papageno says: 'Here's to the head cook and the head butler' [*Der Herr Koch und der Herr Kellermeister sollen leben!*] (II.xix).

chiefly, yourselves! See under YOUR OWN, YOUR VERY OWN!

chiefs. See TOO MANY ~ . . .

child. See GIVE US A ~ . . .

child in all of us, appeals to the. A cringe-making assertion made about certain types of entertainment or about occasions like Christmas. Noticed with some frequency in the 1980s. From the *Sunday Times* (18 August 1985): 'In *Back to the Future*, [Robert Zemeckis] scores by adhering to the first rule of [Steven] Spielbergism: appeal to the child in all of us.' From the *Sunday Times* (22 June 1986): '*The Wind in the Willows* appeals to the child in all of us, so we adults have accorded it the status of "a children's classic".' From the *Guardian* (28 July 1986): 'Growing up tends to hurt. And the child in all of us wants a Daddy/Mummy figure to rub our legs and give us aspirin when growing pains become acute.'

children. See GOODNIGHT ~ EVERYWHERE; NEVER WORK WITH ~ OR ANIMALS; WOMEN AND ~ FIRST.

children should be seen and not heard. This proverbial expression was, according to CODP, originally applied to young *women*. 'A mayde schuld be seen, but not herd' was described as an 'old' saying in *c* 1400. It was not until the nineteenth century that a general application to children of both sexes became common, though Thackeray in *Roundabout Papers* (1860–3) still has: 'Little boys should not loll on chairs . . . Little girls should be seen and not heard.'

children's hour, the. When the long-running and fondly-remembered BBC radio programme *Children's Hour* began in 1922, it was known as 'The Children's Hour', which suggests that it ultimately derived from the title of a poem by Longfellow (1863):

> Between the dark and the daylight,
>   When the night is beginning to
>   lower,
> Comes a pause in the day's
>   occupations,
>   That is known as the Children's
>   Hour.

This became the name for the period between afternoon tea and dressing for dinner, particularly in Edwardian England. Lillian Hellman also wrote a play called *The Children's Hour* (1934), variously filmed, about a schoolgirl's allegations of her teachers' lesbianism.

chill. See BIG ~ GENERATION.

chilly! See NAY, NAY ~ THRICE AGAIN NAY!

chimney sweep. See NEVER WRESTLE WITH A ~.

China. NOT FOR ALL THE TEA IN ~; OIL FOR THE LAMPS OF ~.

Chinaman. See NOT VERY GOOD DETECTIVE . . .

Chinese. See DAMN CLEVER THESE ~ under *GOON SHOW*; OUT OF YOUR TINY ~ MIND.

Chinese whispers. 'Inaccurate gossip' – a phrase deriving from the name of a children's party game. Seated in a circle, the children whisper a message to each other until it arrives back at the person who started, usually changed out of all recognition. An alternative name for the game is 'Russian Scandal', which *OED2* finds in 1873, (or 'Russian Gossip' or 'Russian Rumour(s)'). Presumably, Russian and Chinese are mentioned because of their exotic nineteenth-century connotations, the difficulty of both languages, and because the process of whispering might sound reminiscent of the languages when spoken.

From McGowan & Hands's *Don't Cry for Me, Sergeant-Major* (1983) (about the Falklands war): 'The words "Air Red, Air Red," had become confused as they were passed down the line, and by the time they reached the end had been changed to "Galtieri dead, Galtieri dead" . . . It was later pointed out that a message had been similarly misjudged in an earlier war. "Send reinforcements, the regiment is going to advance," had been received as "Send three and four pence, the regiment is going to a dance".'

chip of(f) the old/same block, a. Referring to a child having the same qualities as its parent, the use of this expression was established by the 1620s. Edmund Burke said of the first speech in the House of Commons by William Pitt the Younger (1781): 'Not merely a chip of the old "block", but the old block itself' (that is, Pitt the Elder, 1st Earl of Chatham).

chip on one's shoulder, to have a. Meaning 'to bear a grudge in a defensive manner', the expression originated in the US where it was known by the early nineteenth century. A boy or man would, or would seem, to carry a chip (of wood) on his shoulder daring others to dislodge it, looking for a fight.

c/Chips. See CASH ONE'S ~; MR ~.

chips are down, when the. Meaning 'at a crucial stage in a situation', the phrase alludes to the chips used in betting games. The bets are placed when they are down but the outcome is still unknown.

chips with everything. Phrase descriptive of British working-class life and used as the title of a play (1962) by Arnold Wesker about class attitudes in the RAF during National Service. Alluding to the belief that the working classes tend to have chips (potatoes) as the accompaniment to almost every dish. Indeed, the play contains the line: 'You breed babies and you eat chips with everything.' Earlier, in an essay published as part of *Declaration* (1957), the film director Lindsay Anderson had written: 'Coming back to Britain is always something of an ordeal. It ought not to be, but it is. And you don't have to be a snob to feel it. It isn't just the food, the sauce bottles on the cafe tables, and the chips with everything. It isn't just saying goodbye to wine, goodbye to sunshine . . .'

chivalry. See under AGE OF MIRACLES IS NOT PAST.

chocolate kettle. See under AS BUSY AS . . .

chocolate soldier. See under ARMS AND THE MAN.

Christian. See MISTER ∼, I'LL HAVE YOU HUNG . . .

Christmas. See — BY ∼; DO THEY KNOW IT'S ∼?; POST EARLY FOR ∼; SHOPPING DAYS TO ∼; WHITE ∼.

Christmas has come early this year.
Meaning 'we have had some welcome [usually financial] news'. Beginning a report in the *Guardian* (8 April 1988), Michael Smith wrote of the Volvo purchase of the Leyland Bus operation: 'Christmas has come early for management and staff at Leyland Bus, the sole UK manufacturers of buses which changed hands last week' – they stood to enjoy a windfall of £19 million. The previous week, Lord Williams had said of another sale – that of Rover to British Aerospace: 'Christmas has come rather early this year.'
From McGowan & Hands's *Don't Cry for Me, Sergeant-Major* (1983) (about the Falklands war): 'De-briefings afterwards . . . related that the SAS "thought Christmas had come early". They couldn't believe their luck. There were at least eleven Argentine aircraft virtually unguarded.'
Compare the expression to the effect that **all one's Christmasses have come at once** (when one has benefited from lots of luck or been snowed under with gifts).

chuck it —! Meaning, 'abandon that line of reasoning, that posturing'. An example from the BBC's *World at One* radio programme in May 1983 during the run-up to a General Election: Roy Hattersley complained that he was only being questioned on the ten per cent of the Labour Party manifesto with which he disagreed. Robin Day, the interviewer, replied: 'Chuck it, Hattersley!' This format was used earlier and notably by G.K. Chesterton. In his 'Antichrist, or the Reunion of Christendom' (1912), he satirized the pontificating of F.E. Smith

(later 1st Earl of Birkenhead) on the Welsh Disestablishment Bill:

> Talk about the pews and steeples
> And the cash that goes therewith!
> But the souls of Christian peoples . . .
> Chuck it, Smith!

chuffed, to be. (1) To be leased. (2) To be fed up. This is called a Janus word because it has two opposite meanings. The first meaning possibly predominates. When Paul McCartney of the Beatles returned to Liverpool to receive the Freedom of the City in November 1984, he declared that he was 'well chuffed'. Paul Beale in Partridge/*Slang* suggests a development (in military circles) from the word 'chow' (meaning food in general). This might indeed account for the pleased or well-sated meaning. The opposite 'fed up' may derive from a dialect use of 'chuff' (dating from 1832) meaning 'churlish, gruff, morose'.

chum. See ANY GUM, ∼?

chums. See WHAT WOULD YOU DO, ∼? under BAND WAGGON.

chunder, to. 'To be sick'. This Australian word is of uncertain origin, according to the *Macquarie Dictionary* (1981). According to the *Dictionary of Australian Quotations* (1984), 'Barry Humphries states that, to the best of his knowledge, he introduced the words "chunder" and "chundrous" to the Australian language [by 1964 at least]. Previously "chunder" was known to him only as a piece of Geelong Grammar School slang.' But this ignores the fact that 'chunda' appears in Neville Shute's novel *A Town Like Alice* (1950).
The usual derivation concerns the cry 'Watch under!' made by those about to be sick over the side of a ship to those on lower decks. Partridge/*Slang* has that it is rhyming slang for Chunder Loo ('spew'), from Chunder Loo of Akin Foo, 'a cartoon figure in a long-running series of advertisements for Cobra boot polish in the *Bulletin* [Australia] from 8 April 1909'.

church. See SEE YOU IN ∼; THAT'LL STOP YOU FARTING IN ∼.

Cicciolina, La. Sobriquet of Ilona Staller, a soft porn actress who was elected to the Italian parliament in 1987. It means 'the little fleshy one'.

cigarette. See AH, WOODBINE . . .

circle. See MAGIC ∼; WHEEL HAS COME FULL ∼.

circumstances. See DUE TO ∼ . . .

citizen of the world, a. Cicero has this phrase as '*civem totius mundi*', meaning 'one who is cosmopolitan, at home anywhere'. Similarly, Socrates said, 'I am citizen, not of Athens or Greece, but of the world.' The *OED2* finds the English phrase in Caxton (1474) and, 'If a man be gracious and courteous to strangers, it shows he is a citizen of the world' in Francis Bacon's 'Goodness, and Goodness of Nature' (1625).

The Citizen of the World was the title of a collection of letters by Oliver Goldsmith purporting to be those of Lien Chi Altangi, a philosophic Chinaman living in London and commenting on English life and characters. They were first published as 'Chinese Letters' in the *Public Ledger* (1760–1), and then again under this title in 1762.

James Boswell, not unexpectedly, in his *Journal of a Tour to the Hebrides* (1786) reflects: 'I am, I flatter myself, completely a citizen of the world . . . In my travels through Holland, Germany, Switzerland, Italy, Corsica, France, I never felt myself from home; and I sincerely love "every kindred and tongue and people and nation".'

city. See THIS IS THE ∼ under *DRAGNET*.

civilization. See END OF ∼ . . .

clanger. See DROP A ∼.

Clapham. See MAN ON THE ∼ OMNIBUS.

clap hands, here comes Charley. This apparently nonsensical catchphrase, popular at one time in Britain, appears to derive from its use in the signature tune of Charlie Kunz (1896–1958). Born in America, Kunz became a feathery-fingered, insistently rhythmic pianist popular on British radio in the 1930s/40s. The song went, 'Clap hands, here comes Charley . . . here comes Charley now.' With lyrics by Billy Rose and Ballard MacDonald, and music by Joseph Meyer, it was first recorded in the US in 1925.

According to *The Book of Sex Lists*, the song was written 'in honour of a local chorine, first-named Charline, who had given many of the music publishers' contact men (song pluggers) cases of gonorrhoea – a venereal disease commonly known as "the clap"'. Partridge/*Slang* adds that 'to do a clap hands Charlie' was 1940s RAF slang for flying an aircraft in such a way as to make the wings seem to meet overhead.

clapometer. See SWINGOMETER.

classes. See CHATTERING ∼.

clean(s). See ∼ ROUND THE BEND; IT BEATS AS IT SWEEPS . . . ; MR ∼.

cleanliness is next to godliness. Although this phrase appears in Sermon 88 'On Dress' by John Wesley, the Methodist evangelist (1703–91), within quotation marks, it is without attribution. Brewer claims that it is to be found in the writings of Phinehas ben Yair, a rabbi. Thomas J. Barratt, one of the fathers of modern advertising, seized upon it to promote Pears' Soap, chiefly in the UK in the 1880s.

cleans round the bend. Harpic lavatory cleaner used this slogan in the UK from the 1930s onwards, but it is not the origin of the idiom **round the bend**, meaning 'mad'. The *OED2* cites F.C. Bowen in *Sea Slang* (1929) as defining it thus: 'an old naval term for anybody who is mad'.

clear. See I WANT TO MAKE IT PERFECTLY ∼.

clear and present danger. Phrase taken from a ruling by the US Supreme Court justice, Oliver Wendell Holmes Jr in the case of Schenk v. United States (1919). This concerned free speech and included Holmes's claim that the most stringent protection of same would not protect a man in falsely shouting fire in a theatre and causing panic: 'The question in every case is whether the words used are used in such circumstances and are of such a nature as to create a clear and present danger that they will bring about the evils that Congress has a right to prevent.'

A film with the title *Clear and Present Danger* (US, 1994) is about a CIA agent in conflict with his political masters in Washington.

clever. See DAMN ~ , THESE CHINESE under GOON SHOW; TOO ~ BY HALF.

cleverest young man in England, the. An unofficial title bestowed semi-humorously from time to time. In 1976, the recipient was Peter Jay (*b* 1937), then an economics journalist on *The Times*. He was dubbed thus in an article so headed (with the saving grace of a question mark) by *The Sunday Times* Magazine (2 May). Two years earlier he had been included in *Time* Magazine's list of the 150 people 'most likely to achieve leadership in Europe'. He became Britain's Ambassador to Washington at the age of 40, at which point people stopped calling him one of the most promising of his generation.

In September 1938, at the League of Nations, Chips Channon had written in his diary of: 'John Foster, that dark handsome young intellectual . . . Fellow of All Souls, prospective candidate, and altogether one of the cleverest young men in England.' This was presumably the person who became Sir John Foster QC, a Tory MP.

Compare Gladstone's remark that Mary Sedgwick, mother of the fabulous Benson brothers – A.C., E.F. and so on – was 'the cleverest woman in Europe'. Also compare GREATEST LIVING —.

click. See CLUNK, ~ , EVERY TRIP.

climb. See BAND-WAGON, TO CLIMB ON THE; GRAVY TRAIN . . .

clipper. See YANKEE ~ .

Cliveden Set, the. Insofar as it actually existed, this group of people was in favour of Appeasement (the policy of conciliation and concession towards Nazi Germany, around 1938) and took its name from the seat of Lord and Lady Astor, who were at the centre of it. The name first appeared in Claud Cockburn's news sheet *The Week* (17 June 1936). Chips Channon wrote in his diary on 4 April 1938 (of a reception given by Lady Astor): 'The function will be criticised, since there is already talk of a so-called "Cliveden" set which is alleged to be pro-Hitler, but which, in reality, is only pro-Chamberlain and pro-sense.' On 8 May 1940, Channon added: 'I think [Lady Astor] is seriously rattled by the "Cliveden Set" allegations which were made against her before the war, and now wants to live them down.'

clock. See under COULD MAKE ANY ORDINARY GIRL . . .

clockwork orange, queer as a. The title of the novel *A Clockwork Orange* (1962, film UK, 1971) comes, according to its author Anthony Burgess, from a Cockney expression, 'queer as a clockwork orange' (i.e. homosexual), in use since the mid-1950s says Paul Beale in Partridge/*Slang*, though few others have heard of it. The title's relevance to the story – which has no overt homosexual element – is debatable, unless 'queer' is taken just as 'odd' and without the sexual meaning. The following passage from the novel hints at a possible reason for the choice of title: 'Who ever heard of a clockwork orange? . . . The attempt to impose upon man, a creature of growth and capable of sweetness, to ooze juicily at the last round the bearded lips of God, to attempt to impose, I say, laws and conditions appropriate to a mechanical creation, against this I raise my sword-pen.' The book describes an attempt to punish its criminal hero, Alex, by turning him into a 'mechanical man' through forms of therapy and brainwashing.

clogs. See POP ONE'S ~ .

closed. See I WENT TO NEW ZEALAND BUT . . . ; WE NEVER ~ .

close encounter of the — kind, a. An expression derived from the title of Steven Spielberg's film *Close Encounters of the Third Kind* (1977) which, in turn, is said to be taken from the categories used in the American forces to denote UFOs. A 'close encounter 1' would be a simple UFO sighting; a 'close encounter 2', evidence of an alien landing; and a 'close encounter 3', actual contact with aliens. The categories were devised by a UFO researcher called J. Allen Hynek (source: Rick Meyers, *The Great Science Fiction Films*).

Used allusively to describe intimacy: 'For a close encounter of the fourth kind, ring ****'; 'Polanski's new movie – Close Encounters with the Third Grade' – graffiti, quoted 1982.

close-run. See DAMN ~ THING.

closes. See WHEN ONE DOOR ~ . . .

closest friends won't tell you. See EVEN YOUR BEST . . .

closet. See OUT OF THE ~ . . .

close your eyes and think of England. The source that Partridge/*Catch Phrases* gives for this saying – in the sense of advice to women when confronted with the inevitability of sexual intercourse, or jocularly to either sex about doing anything unpalatable – is the *Journal* (1912) of Alice, Lady Hillingdon: 'I am happy now that Charles calls on my bedchamber less frequently than of old. As it is, I now endure but two calls a week and when I hear his steps outside my door I lie down on my bed, close my eyes, open my legs and think of England.' There *was* an Alice, Lady Hillingdon (1857–1940). She married the 2nd Baron in 1886. He was Conservative MP for West Kent (1885–92) and, according to *Who's Who*, owned 'about 4500 acres' when he died (in 1919). A portrait of Lady Hillingdon was painted by Sir Frank Dicksee PRA in 1904. The rose 'Climbing Lady Hillingdon' may have been named after her.

But where her journals are, if indeed they ever existed, I have not been able to discover. Jonathan Gathorne-Hardy repeating the quotation in *The Rise and Fall of the British Nanny* (1972) calls her Lady Hilling*ham* which only further makes one doubt whether a woman with any such a name was coiner of the phrase.

Salome Dear, Not With a Porcupine (ed. Arthur Marshall, 1982) has it instead that

the newly-wedded Mrs Stanley Baldwin was supposed to have declared: 'I shut my eyes tight and thought of the Empire.' I think we may discount Bob Chieger's assumption in *Was It Good for You, Too?* (1983) that 'Close your eyes and think of England' was advice given to Queen Victoria 'on her wedding night'. Sometimes the phrase occurs in the form **lie back and think of England** but this probably comes from confusion with SHE SHOULD LIE BACK AND ENJOY IT. In 1977, there was play by John Chapman and Anthony Marriott at the Apollo Theatre, London, with the title *Shut Your Eyes and Think of England*.

clothes. See EMPEROR'S NEW ~; I DIDN'T RECOGNIZE YOU WITH YOUR ~ ON; MOST FUN YOU CAN HAVE . . .

cloud(s). See HELLO BIRDS . . . ; LAND OF THE LONG WHITE ~.

cloud-cuckoo land, to live in. Meaning 'to have impractical ideas', the expression comes from the name *Nephelococcygia*, suggested for the capital city of the birds (in the air), in *The Birds* by Aristophanes (d c 380BC).

cloud nine, on. (or **cloud seven.**) Meaning 'in a euphoric state'. Both forms have existed since the 1950s. The derivation appears to be from terminology used by the US Weather Bureau. Cloud nine is the cumulonimbus which may reach 30–40,000 feet. Morris notes, 'If one is upon cloud nine, one is high indeed,' and also records the reason for cloud nine being more memorable than cloud seven: 'The popularity . . . may be credited to the *Johnny Dollar* radio show of the 1950s. There was one recurring episode . . . Every time the hero was knocked unconscious – which was often – he was transported to cloud nine. There Johnny could start talking again.'

cloud no bigger than a man's hand, a. When something is described as such, it is not yet very threatening – as though a man could obliterate a cloud in the sky by holding up his hand in front of his face. The phrase is biblical: 'Behold, there ariseth a little cloud out of the sea, like a man's hand' (1 Kings 18:44). The Revd Francis Kilvert, on 9 August 1871, has: 'Not a cloud was in the sky as big as a man's hand.' In a letter to Winston Churchill on 14 December 1952, Bob Boothby MP wrote of a dinner at Chartwell: 'It took me back to the old carefree days when I was your Parliamentary Private Secretary, and there seemed to be no cloud on the horizon; and on to the fateful days when the cloud was no bigger than a man's hand, and there was still time to save the sum of things.'

clowns. See SEND IN THE ∼.

clumsy clot! See under TAKE IT FROM HERE.

clunk, click, every trip. Accompanied by the sound of a car door closing and seat belt being fastened, this was used as a slogan in British road safety ads featuring Jimmy Savile from 1971. In 1979, someone wrote the slogan on a museum cabinet containing a chastity belt.

c'mere, big boy! Stock phrase of Florence Halop as 'Hotbreath Houlihan', a sex-pot in the American radio show *The Camel Caravan* (1943–7).

c'mon Colman's, light my fire. A slogan for Colman's mustard, current in the UK in 1979, accompanying a picture of a voluptuous woman on a tiger rug. A clear borrowing of the title of the Doors/Jim Morrison song '(Com' On, Baby,) Light My Fire' (1967).

coach and horses. See DRIVE A ∼ THROUGH . . .

coat. See ALL FUR ∼ . . . under ALL KID GLOVES; I WON'T TAKE MY ∼ OFF . . .

cock(s). See HANDS OFF ∼, ON WITH SOCK(s); YOUR ∼'S ON THE BLOCK.

cock-and-bull story, a. Phrase for a long, rambling, unbelievable tale, used notably in Laurence Sterne's *Tristram Shandy* (1760–7). The last words of the novel are: ' "L–d!" said my mother, "what is all this story about?" – "A cock and a bull," said Yorick, "And one of the best of its kind, I ever heard." '

Suggested origins are that the phrase comes from: old fables in general which have animals talking, going right back to Aesop – confirmed perhaps by the equivalent French phrase '*coq à l'âne*' [literally 'cock to donkey'] – someone who hated having to listen to such fables was probably the first to dub them as such; Samuel Fisher's 1660 story about a cock and a bull being transformed into a single animal – which people may have thought pretty improbable; somehow from the Cock and Bull public houses, which are but a few doors apart in Stony Stratford, Buckinghamshire; generally confused tales told first in one pub, the Cock, and then retold in another, the Bull.

The *OED2*'s earliest citation in this precise form is from the Philadelphia *Gazette of the United States* (1795): 'a long cock-and-bull story about the Columbianum' (a proposed national college).

cock a snook, to. A snook is the derisive gesture made with thumb and hand held out from the nose. 'To take a sight' is a variation. Both were known by the mid-nineteenth century, indeed *OED2* has 'cock snooks' in 1791. The game of **snooker** derives its name not from this, but rather from the military nickname for a raw recruit.

Cocker, according to. By strict calculation, exactly. Edward Cocker (1631–75) was an arithmetician who is believed to have written down the rules of arithmetic in a popular guide.

Coco. Nickname of Gabrielle Chanel, the French fashion designer (1883–1971). Hence the title *Coco* for the musical about her life (1969). See also LITTLE BLACK DRESS.

cocoa. See GRATEFUL AND COMFORTING . . . ; I SHOULD ∼.

coffee. See DAMN FINE CUP OF ∼ . . .

coffin nails. Derogatory name for a cigarette, seen in a 1957 British newsreel, but Partridge/*Slang* suggests an origin c 1885 and in catchphrase form – 'Another nail in your coffin!' (said to someone lighting up). Possibly American – Mieder & Co.'s *Dictionary of American Proverbs* (1992) has two (undated) entries of the 'Every cigarette is a nail in your coffin' type. The journal *Proverbium* (1992) also suggests that 'Cigarettes are coffin nails' may have originated in Kentucky.

coin. See SORDID MATTER OF ∼.

Coke adds life. See PAUSE THAT REFRESHES.

colander. See LIKE A FART IN A ∼.

cold. See BLOW HOT AND ∼; — WHO CAME IN FROM THE ∼.

cold enough to freeze the balls off a brass monkey. The derivation of this phrase meaning 'extremely cold' (known by 1835) probably has nothing to do with any animal. A brass monkey was the name given to the plate on a warship's deck on which cannon balls (or other ammunition) were stacked. In cold weather the brass would contract, tending to cause the stack to fall down. 'Monkey' appears to have been a common slang word in gunnery days (and not just at sea) – there was a type of gun or cannon known as a 'monkey' and a 'powder monkey' was the name for a boy who carried powder to the guns.

cold shoulder, to give someone the. Meaning 'to be studiedly indifferent towards someone'. Known by 1820, this expression is said to have originated with the medieval French custom of serving guests a hot roast. When they had outstayed their welcome, the host would pointedly produce a cold shoulder of mutton to get them on their way.

cold war, a/the. Any tension between powers, short of all-out war, but specifically that between the Soviet Union and the West following the Second World War. This latter use was popularized by Bernard Baruch, the US financier and presidential adviser in a speech in South Carolina (16 April 1947): 'Let us not be deceived – we are today in the midst of a cold war.' The phrase was suggested to him by his speechwriter Herbert Bayard Swope, who had been using it privately since 1940.

collapse of stout party. A catchphrase that might be used as the tag-line to a story about the humbling of a pompous person. It has long been associated with *Punch* and was thought to have occurred in the wordy captions given to that magazine's cartoons. But as Ronald Pearsall explains in his book *Collapse of Stout Party* (1975): 'To many people Victorian wit and humour is summed up by *Punch* when every joke is supposed to end with "Collapse of Stout Party", though this phrase tends to be as elusive as "Elementary, my dear Watson" in the Sherlock Holmes sagas.' At least *OED2* manages to find a reference to a 'Stout Party' in the caption to a cartoon in the edition of *Punch* dated 25 August 1855.

Colman's. See C'MON ∼, LIGHT MY FIRE.

Colonel Bogey. K.J. Alford's military march (1914) is the one famously whistled in the film *The Bridge on the River Kwai* (1957) and also the one to which the words HITLER HAS ONLY GOT ONE BALL were added during the Second World War. It comes from a golfing term, established by 1893. 'Colonel Bogey' is a personification of 'Bogey', formerly the lowest number of strokes with which a good player could complete a golf course or an individual hole, now a score of one above par. The aim is thus to 'beat the Colonel'. The term itself was derived from an earlier song, 'The Bogey Man'.
    Compare HUSH, HUSH, HUSH . . .

colour. See ANY ∼ SO LONG AS IT'S BLACK; HORSE OF ANOTHER ∼.

comb. See FIGHT BETWEEN TWO BALD . . . ; FINE-TOOTH ∼; KOOKIE, KOOKIE, LEND ME YOUR ∼.

come. See BIGGER THEY ∼ THE HARDER THEY FALL; DO YOU ∼ HERE OFTEN?; YOU KNOW WHAT ∼S BETWEEN ME AND MY CALVINS?; YOU'VE ∼ A LONG WAY . . .

come alive – you're in the Pepsi generation. A slogan in use in this form since 1964. The worldwide spread of the soft drinks Coca-Cola and Pepsi Cola has given rise to some difficulties in translating their slogans. It is said that 'Come alive with Pepsi' became in German, 'Come alive out of the grave', and, in Chinese, 'Pepsi brings your ancestors back from the dead'.

When Coca-Cola started advertising in Peking, **put a smile on your face** was translated as 'Let Your Teeth Rejoice'. Odder still, the famous slogan **it's the REAL THING** came out as 'The Elephant Bites the Wax Duck'.

come and talk to the listening bank. A slogan used by the Midland Bank, from 1980. It turned sour when a 21-year-old was *arrested* when she went to see a Midland manager about her overdraft (in 1981).

come back —, all is forgiven. See under WHERE ARE THEY NOW?

comedy is ended, the. The last words of François Rabelais (who died about 1550) are supposed to have been: 'Tirez le rideau, la farce est jouée' [Bring down the curtain, the farce is played out]. The attribution is made, hedged about with disclaimers, in Jean Fleury's *Rabelais et ses oeuvres* (1877) (also in the edition of Rabelais by Motteux, 1693). In Lermontov's novel *A Hero of Our Time* (1840), a character says: 'Finita la commedia'. At the end of Ruggiero Leoncavallo's opera *Il Pagliacci* [The Clowns] (1892), Canio exclaims: 'La commedia è finita' [the comedy is finished/over].

come hell and/or high water. Meaning 'come what may', this phrase is mentioned in Partridge/*Slang* as a cliché but, as such phrases go, is curiously lacking in citations. *OED2* finds no examples earlier than the twentieth century. *Come Hell or High Water* was used as the title of a book by yachtswoman Clare Francis in 1977. She followed it in 1978 with *Come Wind or Weather*. *Hell and High Water* was the title of a US film in 1954.

Graeme Donald in *Today* (26 April 1986) linked it to punishments meted out to witches in the Middle Ages: 'Lesser transgressions only warranted the miscreant being obliged to stand in boiling water, the depth of which was directly proportional to the crime. Hence the expression "From Hell and high water, may the good Lord deliver us".' This is rather

fanciful. Perhaps he was thinking of the so-called Thieves' Litany – **from Hull, Hell and Halifax, good Lord deliver us** (known by 1653, because the gibbet was much used in these places in the sixteenth and seventeenth centuries).

come here. See C'MERE . . .

comfortable. See WOULD YOU BE SHOCKED IF . . .

comforter. See JOB'S ~.

come on down! In the American TV consumer game *The Price is Right* (1957–), the host (Bill Cullen was the first) would appear to summon contestants from the studio audience by saying '[name], come on down!' This procedure was reproduced when the quiz was broadcast on British ITV from 1984–8, with Leslie Crowther uttering the words.

comes the dawn. See CAME THE DAWN.

cometh the hour, cometh the man. An expression that appears from a survey of ten British newspapers in recent years to be a weapon (or cliché), especially in the sportswriter's armoury. From *Today* (22 June 1986): 'Beating England may not be winning the World Cup, but, for obvious reasons, it would come a pretty close second back in Buenos Aires. Cometh the hour, cometh the man? Destiny beckons. England beware.' From *The Times* (13 August 1991): '"Graham [Gooch] is a very special guy," [Ted] Dexter said. "It has been a case of 'Cometh the hour, cometh the man.' I do not know anyone who would have taken the tough times in Australia harder than he did."' From the *Scotsman* (29 February 1992): 'In the maxim of "Cometh the hour, cometh the man," both the Scotland [Rugby Union] manager, Duncan Paterson, and forwards coach, Richie Dixon, indicated yesterday the need to look to the future.'

But where does the phrase come from? John 4:23 has 'But the hour cometh, and now is' and there is an English proverb 'Opportunity makes the man' (though originally, in the fourteenth century, it was 'makes the *thief*'). Harriet Martineau entitled her biography of Toussaint L'Ouverture (1840), *The Hour and the Man*. An American, William Yancey, said about Jefferson Davis, President-elect of the Confederacy in 1861: 'The man and the hour have met,' which says the same thing in a different way.

Earlier, at the climax of Sir Walter Scott's novel *Guy Mannering*, Chap. 54 (1815), Meg Merrilies says, 'Because the Hour's come, and the Man.' In the first edition and in the *magnum opus* edition that Scott supervised in his last years the phrase is emphasized by putting it in italics. Then, in 1818, Scott used 'The hour's come, but not [sic] the man' as the fourth chapter heading in *The Heart of Midlothian*, adding in a footnote: 'There is a tradition, that while a little stream was swollen into a torrent by recent showers, the discontented voice of the Water Spirit [or Kelpie] was heard to pronounce these words. At the same moment a man, urged on by his fate, or, in Scottish language, *fey*, arrived at a gallop, and prepared to cross the water. No remonstrance from the bystanders was of power to stop him – he plunged into the stream, and perished.' Both these examples appear to be hinting at some earlier core saying that remains untraced.

come to Charlie! In *c* 1952, following the success of his BBC radio show *Stand Easy* (see DON'T FORCE IT, PHOEBE), Charlie Chester had another, with the title *Come to Charlie* – which grew out of a catchphrase. He recalled (1979): 'I would talk to somebody from the stage and say, "Are you all right, Ada? Speak to Charlee-ee. Charlie spoke to *you!*" . . . You'd be surprised how many people still ask, "Say that phrase for me – say, "come to Charlee-ee!" It's just one of those things they like to hear.'

In his later role as a BBC Radio 2 presenter (1970s/80s), latterly on *Sunday Soapbox*, Chester developed an elaborate sign-off (from about 1970): **there we are, dear friends, both home, overseas and over the borders.**

come up and see me sometime. Mae West (1892–1980) had a notable stage hit on Broadway with her play *Diamond Lil* (first performed 9 April 1928). When she appeared in the 1933 film version entitled *She Done Him*

Wrong, what she said to a very young Cary Grant (playing a coy undercover policeman) was: 'You know I always did like a man in uniform. And that one fits you grand. Why don't you come up some time and see me? I'm home every evening.'

As a catchphrase, the words have been rearranged to make them easier to say. That is how W.C. Fields says them *to* Mae West in the film *My Little Chickadee* (1939), and she herself took to saying them in the rearranged version. Even so, she was merely using an established expression. The American author Gelett Burgess in *Are You a Bromide?* (1907) lists among his 'bromidioms': 'Come up and see us any time. You'll have to take pot luck, but you're always welcome.'

come with me to the Casbah. A line forever associated with the film *Algiers* (1938) and its star, Charles Boyer. He is supposed to have said it to Hedy Lamarr. Boyer impersonators used it, the film was laughed at because of it, but nowhere is it said in the film. It was simply a Hollywood legend that grew up. Boyer himself denied he had ever said it and thought it had been invented by a press agent. In *Daddy, We Hardly Knew You* (1989), Germaine Greer writes of the early 1940s: 'Frightened and revolted the Australians fled for the nearest watering-hole [in the Middle East]. "Kem wiz me to ze Casbah," Daddy used to say, in his Charles Boyer imitation. Poor Daddy. He was too frightened ever to go there.'

comfortably. See ARE YOU SITTING ~ . . . ?

comforting. See GRATEFUL AND ~ . . .

coming. See HENRY! HENRY ALDRICH! . . . ; LIKE ~ HOME.

coming in on a wing and a prayer. A popular US song of the Second World War (published in 1943) took its title from an alleged remark by an actual pilot who was coming in to land with a badly damaged plane. Harold Adamson's lyrics include the lines:

Tho' there's one motor gone, we can still carry on
Comin' In On A Wing And A Pray'r.

A US film about life on an aircraft carrier (1944) was called simply *Wing and a Prayer*.

commanding heights of the economy, the. In a speech to the Labour Party conference in November 1959, Aneurin Bevan said: 'Yesterday, Barbara [Castle] quoted from a speech which I made some years ago, and she said that I believed that socialism in the context of modern society meant the conquest of the commanding heights of the economy . . .' Alan Watkins in a throwaway line in his *Observer* column (28 September 1987) said 'the phrase was originally Lenin's'. At the Labour Party Conference in October 1989, Neil Kinnock revived the phrase in saying that education and training were 'the commanding heights of every modern economy'.

commandment. See ELEVENTH ∼.

comment. See NO ∼; YOU MIGHT THINK THAT . . .

communicate. See WHAT WE'VE GOT HERE . . .

Communist Party. See ARE YOU NOW OR HAVE YOU EVER BEEN . . .

complain. See NEVER ∼ . . .

completely. See AND NOW FOR SOMETHING ∼ DIFFERENT.

complexion. See KEEP THAT SCHOOLGIRL ∼.

concentrated cacophony. See *ITMA*.

concordia parvae res crescunt. The motto of the Merchant Taylors' Company (first incorporated in its second grant of arms, 1586) means 'in harmony small things grow'. In *The History of Myddle* by Richard Gough (begun 1700) there is a slightly different, and longer, form: '*Concordia parva* [. . .] *res crescunt, discordia magna dilabuntur.*' David Hey, the 1981 editor, translates this as, 'By agreement small things grow: by disagreement great things are cast down.' The source is Sallust's *Jugurtha* (X.vi).

condemned man ate a hearty breakfast, the. The tradition seems to have been established in Britain (and/or the Old West) that a condemned man could have anything he desired for a last meal. As to the origin of the cliché, it presumably lies in ghoulish newspaper reports of the events surrounding executions in the days of capital punishment in Britain. There was a vast amount of popular literature concerning prominent criminals and public executions, especially in the late eighteenth and early nineteenth centuries, but so far citations date only from the twentieth and tend to be of a metaphorical nature. A book of short stories about the Royal Navy called *Naval Occasions and Some Traits of the Sailor* (1914) by 'Bartimeus', has: 'The Indiarubber Man opposite feigned breathless interest in his actions, and murmured something into his cup about condemned men partaking of hearty breakfasts.' The tone of this suggests it was, indeed, getting on for a cliché even then. *The Prisoner Ate a Hearty Breakfast* is the title of a novel (1940) written by Jerome Ellison. In the film *Kind Hearts and Coronets* (1949), Louis Mazzini, on the morning of his supposed execution, disavows his intention of eating 'the traditional hearty breakfast'. In *No Chip on My Shoulder* (1957), Eric Maschwitz writes: 'Far from closing for ever, *Balalaika* [was merely to be] withdrawn for a fortnight during which time a revolving stage was to be installed at Her Majesty's! It was almost ridiculously like an episode from fiction, the condemned man, in the midst of eating that famous "hearty breakfast", suddenly restored to life and liberty.'

conditions dat prevail. See GOODNIGHT, MRS CALABASH . . .

conduct unbecoming. The full phrase is 'conduct unbecoming the character of an officer and a gentleman' and seems to have appeared first in the (British) Naval Discipline Act (10 August 1860), Article 24, though the notion has also been included in disciplinary regulations of other services, and in other countries, if not in quite these words.

Conduct Unbecoming is the title of a play by Barry England (1969; film UK, 1975) and, accordingly, came from the same source as the title of the film *An Officer and a Gentleman* (US, 1982).

conferring. See HERE'S YOUR STARTER . . .

confutatis (maledictis). See MASS PHRASES.

conscience. See STIFF PRICK HAS NO ∼.

consent. See ADVISE AND ∼.

Conservatives. See LIFE'S BETTER WITH THE ∼.

Contemptibles. See OLD ∼.

continent isolated. In Maurice Bowra's *Memories 1898–1939* (1966) he recalls how Ernst Kantorowicz, a refugee from Germany in the 1930s, 'liked the insularity of England and was much pleased by the newspaper headline, "Channel storms. Continent isolated", just as he liked the imagery in, "Shepherd's Bush combed for dead girl's body".' As an indicator of English isolationism, the first headline does indeed seem to have surfaced in the 1930s. John Gunther in his *Inside Europe* (1938 edition) has: 'Two or three winters ago a heavy storm completely blocked traffic across the Channel. "CONTINENT ISOLATED," the newspapers couldn't help saying.' The cartoonist Russell Brockbank drew a newspaper placard stating 'FOG IN CHANNEL – CONTINENT ISOLATED' (as shown in his book *Round the Bend with Brockbank*, published by Temple Press, 1948). By the 1960s and 1970s, and by the time of Britain's attempts to join the European Community, the headline was more often invoked as: 'FOG IN CHANNEL. EUROPE ISOLATED.'

continong, sur le. See under MORNING ALL!

control. See DUE TO CIRCUMSTANCES . . . ; DON'T YOU JUST LOVE BEING IN ∼?

controller. See FAT ∼.

cookie. See THAT'S THE WAY THE ∼ CRUMBLES.

Cook's tour, to go on a. To travel in an organized manner, possibly on a tour of rather greater extent than originally intended (compare MAGICAL MYSTERY TOUR). Thomas Cook was the founder of the world's original travel agency. His first tour was in 1841 when he took a party of fellow teetotallers on a railway trip in the British Midlands. Alas, there has always been a certain amount of prejudice against the organized tour. Amelia B. Edwards, the Victorian egyptologist, is suitably caustic in *A Thousand Miles Up the Nile* (1877): '[The newcomer in Cairo soon] distinguishes at first sight between a Cook's tourist and an independent traveller'.

cool as a mountain stream. A slogan for Consulate (menthol) cigarettes, in the UK from the early 1960s.

cool hundred/thousand/million, a. *OED2* says drily that the 'cool' 'gives emphasis' to the (large) amount. Is this because a large amount of money is rather chilling, lacking in warmth, or because of the calm way the money is paid out? Perhaps the word 'cool' in this context anticipates its more modern connection with jazz, as something thrilling, to be admired and approved of. In Henry Fielding's *Tom Jones* (1749) we read: 'Watson rose from the table in some heat and declared he had lost a cool hundred . . .' In Charles Dickens's *Great Expectations* (1861): 'She had wrote a little [codicil] . . . leaving a cool four thousand to Mr Mathew Pocket.' *A Cool Million* is the title of a satire by Nathaniel West (1934), and in Anthony Powell's *Hearing Secret Harmonies* (1975), Lord Widmerpool comments on a smoke-bomb let off at a literary prize-giving: 'I wouldn't have missed that for a cool million.'

coot. See under BALD AS A BADGER; QUEER AS A ∼.

corn in Egypt. See under OIL FOR THE LAMPS OF CHINA.

cop. See I'M A ∼ under *DRAGNET*.

Copper. See UP TO A POINT LORD ∼.

Corgi and Bess. Broadcasting nickname for the Christmas message given annually on radio and TV by Queen Elizabeth II (noted for her canine pets). Known by 1984 and based on *Porgy and Bess*, the title of George Gershwin's 'folk opera' (1935).

corner. See FOREIGN FIELD.

corpse, to. When actors 'corpse', it means that they have been overtaken by such involuntary laughter that they are unable to go on speaking their lines – or, if they are supposed to be lying dead on the stage, they are unable to stop shaking with mirth. Alternatively, the origin of the word lies in the actors being rendered as incapable as a dead body, or, when another actor has made them forget their lines, it is the equivalent of killing them by stopping their performance. Known by 1873.

correct. See ANATOMICALLY ~ ; POLITICALLY ~ .

corridors of power, the. A phrase that had become established for the machinations of government, especially in Whitehall, by the time C.P. Snow chose it for the title of his novel *Corridors of Power* (1964). Earlier, Snow had written in *Homecomings* (1956): 'The official world, the corridors of power, the dilemmas of conscience and egotism – she disliked them all.'

così fan tutte. 'That's what all women do' or 'women are like that' (literally 'thus do all women'), specifically referring to their infidelity. Mozart's opera with the title was first performed in 1790. The phrase had appeared earlier in Da Ponte's text for Mozart's *Le nozze di Figaro* (1778). In that opera, Don Basilio sings, 'Così fan tutte le belle, non c'è alcuna novità' [That's what all beautiful women do, there's nothing new in that].

cotton. See BLESS HIS LITTLE ~ SOCKS.

couch potato, a. A pejorative term for an addictive, uncritical (and possibly fat) TV viewer. Said to have been coined in the late 1970s by Tom Iacino in Southern California. *Sunday Today* was only getting

round to explaining the word to British readers on 27 July 1986. But why potato? Is it because of the shape of a fat person slouched on a couch? Or does it allude to the consumption of potato crisps, or to behaviour like that of a 'vegetable'? It seems the phrase is a complicated pun on the phrase 'boob-tube' (US slang for TV, not an article of clothing) and 'tuber', meaning a root vegetable.

coughin' well tonight. The British comedian, George Formby Snr (1877–1921), used to make this tragically true remark about himself. He had a convulsive cough, the result of a tubercular condition, and it eventually killed him. He was ironically known as 'The Wigan Nightingale'.

  See also JOHN WILLIE, COME ON and WIGAN PIER.

coughs and sneezes spread diseases. A British Ministry of Health warning from c 1942, coupled with the line, 'Trap the germs in your handkerchief'.

could make any ordinary girl feel like a princess. (compare **could make you feel like Cinderella before the clock struck.**) A testament to male prowess of one sort or another, though phrases likely to occur more to journalists than mere mortals. In February 1983, the Press Council reported on the curious case of Miss Carol Ann Jones and the *News of the World*. Miss Jones had been quoted as having said that Peter Sutcliffe, the Yorkshire Ripper, 'could make any ordinary girl from a mill town feel like a princess. Even now I have a place in my heart for him'. The Press Council felt that 'some words attributed to her as direct quotations were ones she was unlikely to have used'.

couldn't run a whelk-stall. A way of describing incompetence, this appears to have originated with John Burns, the Labour MP: 'From whom am I to take my marching orders? From men who fancy they are ADMIRABLE CRICHTONS . . . but who have not got sufficient brains and ability to run a whelk-stall?' (*South-Western Star*, 13 January 1894). Partridge/*Slang* has 'no way to run a whelk-stall' as the UK equivalent of the US '[that's] a hell of a way to run a railroad' (see WHAT A WAY TO RUN A —), and dates it from later, in the twentieth century. The phrases **couldn't organize a piss-up in a brewery** and **couldn't fight his/her way out of a paper bag** are more likely to be employed nowadays.

Count Basie. Sobriquet of William Basie (1904–84), the American band leader. A Kansas City radio interviewer in 1926, commenting on 'the royal family of jazz', said there was the King of Oliver and the Duke of Ellington, 'How about the Count of Basie?' Towards the end of his life, however, Basie admitted: 'I hated the name Count. I wanted to be called Buck or Hoot or even Arkansas Fats.'

counted. See I ~ THEM ALL OUT AND I ~ THEM ALL BACK; STAND UP AND BE ~ .

countries separated by a common language, two. Referring to England and America, was this said by Shaw or Wilde? Wilde wrote: 'We have really everything in common with America nowadays except, of course, language' (*The Canterville Ghost*, 1887). The 1951 *Treasury of Humorous Quotations* (Esar & Bentley), however, quotes Shaw as saying: 'England and America are two countries separated by the same language,' without giving a source. A radio talk prepared by Dylan Thomas shortly before his death (and published after it in the *Listener*, April 1954), contained an observation about European writers and scholars in America 'up against the barrier of a common language'.

country. See ~ DUNNY under AS BUSY AS . . . ; FROM A FAR ~; GOD'S OWN ~; GRATEFUL ~, FROM A; ~ OF THE BLIND; THIS IS A FREE ~; YOUR ~ NEEDS YOU.

country-folk. See EVERYDAY STORY OF ~ under ARCHERS, THE.

course you can, Malcolm. One of those advertising phrases that, for no accountable reason, caught on for a while. From British TV ads for Vick's Sinex (nasal spray). In February 1994, after the ads had been relaunched, starring the original 1970s cast, the manufacturers released a dance single

telling the adventures of Malcolm, the youth in the TV commercials.

court. See SEE YOU IN CHURCH.

courting. See ARE YER COURTIN'? under HAVE A GO.

court oath, the. See I SWEAR BY ALMIGHTY GOD . . .

courts of the morning, the. The somewhat obscure title of John Buchan's adventure novel *The Courts of the Morning* (1929) is a translation of *Los Patios de la Mañana*, a geographical hill feature in the fictitious South-American republic of Olifa, where the book is set: 'In the Courts of the Morning there was still peace. The brooding heats, the dust-storms, the steaming deluges of the lowlands were unknown. The air was that of a tonic and gracious autumn slowly moving to the renewal of spring.' Whether the name has anywhere been given to actual hills, I know not.

Coventry, to send someone to. Meaning 'to refuse to speak to a person', this expression may have originated in the old story of soldiers stationed in Coventry who were so unwelcome that the citizens carried on as if they did not exist, alternatively that if women talked to the soldiers, they were ostracized. Another version comes from the Civil War in England in the seventeenth century. When captured Royalists were sent to Coventry, a strongly Roundhead (Parliamentary) town, they were bound to be ignored. Evidently, the Roundheads sent doubtful or useless officers or soldiers to the garrison at Coventry. 'The expression is used also in America: "Send them into everlasting Coventry" – Emerson's essay, "Manners" ' – Benham (1948).

This is possibly supported by a passage in Clarendon's *History of the Rebellion* (VI:83, 1702–4): '[Birmingham] a town so wicked that it had risen upon small parties of the King's [men], and killed or taken them prisoners and sent them to Coventry.'

cow. See HOW NOW BROWN ~; I'M ALL BEHIND . . . ; WHY KEEP A ~ WHEN YOU . . .

cowabunga! This cry was re-popularized by the Teenage Mutant Ninja Turtles phenomenon of the early 1990s, but had been around since the 1950s when, in the American cartoon series *The Howdy Doody Show*, it was used as an expression of anger – 'kowa-bunga' or 'Kawabonga' – by Chief Thunderthud. In the 1960s it transferred to *Gidget*, the American TV series about a surfer, as a cry of exhilaration when cresting a wave and was taken into surfing slang. In the 1970s the phrase graduated to TV's *Sesame Street* .

cows. See TILL THE ∼ COME HOME.

cow's tail. See I'M ALL BEHIND LIKE THE ∼ .

crack. See FAIR ∼ OF THE WHIP.

crackerjack. In the US, this word has the meaning 'excellent', and has also been used as the name of a brand of popcorn and syrup. *Crackerjack* was the title of a BBC TV children's programme (from 1955) which had a noisy studio audience of youngsters who had only to hear the word 'Crackerjack' for them to scream back 'CRACKERJACK!' It was probably not a word known to them before.

crackle. See SNAP! ∼! POP!

cradle. See HAND THAT ROCKS THE ∼; OUT OF THE ∼ . . .

crazy like a fox. i.e. 'apparently crazy but with far more method than madness' (Partridge/*Catch Phrases*). Craziness is hardly a quality one associates with foxes, so the expression was perhaps merely formed in parallel with the older 'cunning as a fox'. The similar 'crazy *as* a fox', also of US origin, was known by the mid-1930s.
  Foxes always seem to get into expressions like these. Interviewing the actress Judy Carne in 1980, I asked about Goldie Hawn, her one-time colleague on *Laugh-In*. Carne said: 'She's not a dizzy blonde. She's about as *dumb* as a fox. She's incredibly bright.'
  Crazy Like a Fox was the title of a US TV series about a 'sloppy old private eye' and his 'smart lawyer son' (from 1984). Before that, it was used as the title of a book by S.J. Perelman (1945).

crazy, man, crazy! See GO, MAN, GO!

creative accountancy/accounting. A term for ingenious manipulation of accounts which may or may not actually be illegal. An early example of the phrase occurs in *The Producers* (film US, 1968): 'It's simply a matter of creative accounting. Let's assume for a moment that you are a dishonest man . . . It's very easy. You simply raise more money than you need.' The film's subject is such accountancy applied in the world of the theatrical angel.

credibility gap. The difference between what is claimed as fact and what is actually fact. It dates from the time in the Vietnam war when, despite claims to the contrary by the Johnson administration, an escalation in US participation was taking place. 'Dilemma in "Credibility Gap"' was the headline over a report on the matter in the *Washington Post* (13 May 1965) and may have been the phrase's first outing.

credit. See PLEASE DO NOT ASK FOR ∼ . . .

credo (in unum Deum). See MASS PHRASES.

Crichton. See ADMIRABLE ∼ .

cricket, it's not. 'It is not fair, proper, the done thing.' An expression suggesting that certain conduct or behaviour is not worthy of an Englishman and a gentleman. It was known in the game of cricket itself by 1851, and by 1900 in other contexts. A *Punch* headline on 15 January 1902: 'AS IT WERE NOT QUITE CRICKET'. In *First Childhood* (1934), Lord Berners comments that it 'came into vogue in the 'nineties' and gives the example: ' "I mean to say," he protested. "To kick your wife! And in public too! It's not cricket, is it?" '

crikey. See NO LIKEY? OH, ∼! under *ITMA*.

crime. See MURDERERS RETURN TO THE SCENE OF THEIR ∼ .

cringe. See CULTURAL ∼ .

crinklies. See under YUPPIE.

crocodile tears. A false display of sorrow. The legend that crocodiles shed tears in order to lure victims to their deaths was established by the year 1400. In an account of a 1565 voyage by Sir John Hawkins (published by Richard Hakluyt, 1600), there is: 'In this river we saw many crocodiles . . . His nature is ever when he would have his prey, to cry and sob like a Christian body, to provoke them to come to him, and then he snatcheth at them.' Shakespeare makes reference to crocodile tears in *Antony and Cleopatra*, *Othello* and *Henry VI*.

crook. See BY HOOK OR BY ∼.

cross of gold. William Jennings Bryan's speech to the Democratic Convention in July 1896 contained an impassioned attack on supporters of the gold standard: 'You shall not press down upon the brow of labour this crown of thorns. You shall not crucify mankind upon a cross of gold.' Bryan had said virtually the same in a speech to the House of Representatives on 22 December 1894. He won the nomination and fought the presidential election against William J. McKinley who supported the gold standard, but lost. A 'cross of gold'-type speech is sometimes called for when a politician (like Edward Kennedy in 1980) is required to sweep a convention with his eloquence.

crossroads. See DIRTY WORK AT THE ∼.

crow. See EAT ∼; JIM ∼ MUST GO.

crowd. See ROAR OF THE GREASEPAINT, THE SMELL OF THE ∼.

crow flies, as the. Phrase used when describing the shortest distance between two points. Known by 1800. In fact, crows seldom fly in a straight line but the point of the expression is to express how *any* bird might fly without having to follow the wanderings of a road (as an earthbound traveller would have to do).

crown. See JEWEL IN THE ∼.

crucial. A 1980s vogue word, used by the very young to convey the same as 'great',

'fantastic'. It came into British slang – from American hip hop, apparently – through its use as a catchphrase of 'Delbert Wilkins', a creation of the British comedian Lenny Henry (*b* 1958). As presenter of a record programme on BBC Radio 1 in 1982, Henry portrayed 'Wilkins' as a garrulous DJ from a Brixton pirate radio station. 'Well, basic, well, crucial, man!' he would say. He also used the word **wicked** to mean 'wonderful', 'splendid' and this also passed into youth slang. His exclamation **diamond!** did not.

Henry first came to notice as a 16-year-old on ITV's *New Faces*. His send-up of a woolly-hatted Rastafarian – Algernon Winston Spencer Churchill Gladstone Disraeli Pitt the Younger Razzmatazz – gave the West Indian catchphrase **Ooookaaay!** to a whole generation of schoolchildren.

On ITV's *O.T.T.* (1982), Henry introduced another black character, 'Joshua Yarlog', with the catchphrase **Katanga!** (which, as one paper commented, 'half the population already seems to have taken up in an attempt to drive the other half mad').

crumbles. See THAT'S THE WAY THE COOKIE ∼ . . .

crumblies. See under YUPPIE.

crusty loaf. See SERVE THAT LADY WITH A ∼ . . . under *BAND WAGGON*.

cry all the way to the bank, to. Meaning 'to be in a position to ignore criticism', this expression was certainly popularized, if not actually invented, by the flamboyant pianist, Liberace. In his autobiography (1973), Liberace wrote: 'When the reviews are bad I tell my staff that they can join me as I cry all the way to the bank.' (A less pointed version is, 'to *laugh* all the way to the bank'.)

The twinkly pianist (1919–87) was as famous for his phrases in the 1950s as he was for his candelabra. He seemed to say 'ladies and gentlemen' between every sentence, frequently mentioned his 'Mom', and thanked audiences on behalf of **my brother George**.

cuckoo. See CLOUD ∼ LAND.

cud, to chew the. Meaning 'to think deeply about something, especially the past'. This figurative expression (in use by 1382) refers to the ruminative look cows have when they chew their 'cud' – that is, bring back food from their first stomachs and chew it in their mouths again. 'Cud' comes from Old English *cwidu*, meaning 'what is chewed'.

cultural cringe. Referring to the belief that one's own country's culture is inferior to that of others, this phrase is probably Australian in origin, and is certainly well known in that country. Arthur Angell Phillips wrote in 1950: 'Above our writers – and other artists – looms the intimidating mass of Anglo-Saxon culture. Such a situation almost inevitably produces the characteristic Australian Cultural Cringe – appearing either as the Cringe Direct, or as the Cringe Inverted, in the attitude of the Blatant Blatherskite, the GOD'S-OWN-COUNTRY and I'm-a-better-man-than-you-are Australian bore.'

culture vulture. Slightly mocking name for a person who gobbles up artistic experiences, especially as a tourist. *DOAS* has it by 1947 and, indeed, it is probably an American coinage.

cunts. See TWO ∼ IN A KITCHEN.

cup. See DAMN FINE ∼ OF COFFEE . . .

cup runneth over, my. Meaning 'I'm overjoyed; my blessings are numerous', the expression derives from Psalms 23:5: 'Thou preparest a table before me in the presence of mine enemies: thou anointest my head with oil; my cup runneth over.' Shirley Polykoff, the advertising executive, recounts in her book *Does She . . . Or Doesn't She?* (1975) that she once jestingly proposed 'Her cup runneth over' as a slogan for a corset manufacturer. 'It took an hour to unsell him,' she adds.

cup that cheers, the. The reference here is to tea (taken in preference to alcohol). In 'The Winter Evening' from William

Cowper's *The Task* (1783), it's in the plural:

> Now stir the fire, and close the shutters fast,
> Let fall the curtains, wheel the sofa round,
> And, while the bubbling and loud-hissing urn
> Throws up a steamy column, and the cups,
> That cheer but not inebriate, wait on each,
> So let us welcome peaceful ev'ning in.

Partridge lists 'cups that cheer but not inebriate' as a cliché in his dictionary, and notes that earlier, in *Siris* (1744), Bishop Berkeley had said of tar water that it had a nature 'so mild and benign and proportioned to the human constitution, as to warm without heating, to cheer but not inebriate'.

In *Three Men In a Boat*, Chap. 2 (1889), Jerome K. Jerome puts the phrase into reverse: 'Luckily you have a bottle of the stuff that cheers and inebriates, if taken in proper quantity, and this restores to you sufficient interest in life.'

curate's egg, like the. Meaning 'patchy, good in parts', the phrase comes from the caption to a *Punch* cartoon (vol.cix, 1895) in which a Bishop is saying: 'I'm afraid you've got a bad egg, Mr Jones.' The nervous young curate, keen not to say anything critical, flannels: 'Oh no, my Lord, I assure you! Parts of it are excellent.'

cure. See DOCTOR GREASEPAINT WILL ∼ ME.

curtain lecture. (or **Caudle lecture.**) Meaning 'a private reproof given by a wife to her husband', it refers to the scolding that took place after the curtains round the bed (as on a four-poster) had been closed. It was known as such by 1633.

The 'Caudle' variation derives from Douglas Jerrold's *Mrs Caudle's Curtain Lectures*, a series published by *Punch* in 1846 in which Mr Caudle suffered the naggings of his wife after they had gone to bed. Another early version of the idea is 'boulster lecture' (1640).

Lady Diana Cooper in a letter of 12 January 1944 wrote: 'Clemmie has given him [Winston Churchill] a Caudle curtain lecture on the importance of not quarrelling with Wormwood.'

cuss. See TINKER'S ~.

customer is always right, the. Gordon Selfridge (c 1856–1947) was an American who, after a spell with the Marshall Field store in Chicago came to Britain and introduced the idea of the monster department store to London. It appears that he was the first to say 'the customer is always right' and many other phrases now generally associated with the business of selling through stores. However, the hotelier César Ritz was being credited with the saying 'the customer is never wrong' by 1908.

custom more honour'd in the breach. Usually taken to mean that whatever custom is under consideration has fallen into sad neglect. But in Shakespeare's *Hamlet* (I.iv.16), the Prince tells Horatio that the King's drunken revelry is a custom that would be *better* 'honour'd' if it were not followed at all.

customs. See OLD SPANISH ~.

cut and run, to. Meaning 'to escape; run away', the phrase has a nautical origin (recorded in 1704). In order to make a quick getaway, instead of the lengthy process of hauling up a ship's anchor, the ship's cable was simply cut. This was easy to do when the anchor was attached to a hemp rope rather than a chain. The figurative use was established by 1861.

cut off at the pass, to. Phrase from Western films where the cry would be uttered, meaning 'to intercept, ambush' (sometimes in the form **head 'em off at the pass**). It resurfaced as one of the milder sayings in the transcripts of the Watergate tapes (published as *The White House Transcripts*, 1974). As used by President Nixon it meant simply 'we will use certain tactics to stop them'. The phrase occurred in a crucial exchange in the White House

Oval Office on 21 March 1973 between the President and his Special Counsel, John Dean:

P: You are a lawyer, you were a counsel
   . . . What would you go to jail for?
D: The obstruction of justice.
P: The obstruction of justice?
D: That is the only one that bothers me.
P: Well, I don't know. I think that one . . .
   I feel it could be cut off at the pass,
   maybe, the obstruction of justice.

cut off your nose to spite your face, to. To perform a self-defeating action. The expression appears to have originated in 1593 when King Henry IV of France seemed willing to sacrifice the city of Paris because of its citizens' objections to his being monarch. One of his own men had the temerity to suggest that destroying Paris would be like cutting off his nose to spite his face. The phrase seems not to have taken hold in English until the mid-nineteenth century.

cut of someone's jib, not to like the. Meaning 'not to like the look of someone', the expression has a nautical origin – the 'cut' or condition of the 'jib' or foresail signifying the quality of the sailing vessel as a whole. Current by 1823.

cuts. See DEATH OF A THOUSAND ~.

cut the mustard, to. To succeed, to have the ability to do what's necessary. One might say of someone, 'He didn't cut much mustard.' An American phrase dating from the turn of the century when 'mustard' was slang for the 'real thing' or the 'genuine article', and this may have contributed to the coinage. From Tennessee Williams, *Sweet Bird of Youth* (1959): 'Boss Finley's too old to cut the mustard' [i.e. perform sexually].

cutting edge. A cliché expression for what is considered to be at the centre of attention or activity. 'Yet something has changed. Sex – except perhaps, and necessarily, for lesbians and gay men – is no longer at the cutting edge of politics, especially for women' – (*Guardian*, 14 March 1989).

The term is derived from the notion that the sharp edge is the most important part of a blade. Before it had been watered down by overuse, Dr Jacob Bronowski used the phrase in his TV series *The Ascent of Man* (1973): 'The hand is more important than the eye . . . The hand is the cutting edge of the mind.'

cutting room floor. See FACE ON THE ~.

Cyril. See NICE ONE, ~!

· D ·

dabra, dabra! See EYAYDON, YAUDEN . . .

dad. See BE LIKE ∼ . . . ; I'LL 'AVE TO ASK
ME ∼ under *ITMA*.

daddy. See DON'T GO DOWN THE MINE, ∼ ;
WHY-Y-Y-Y, ∼?

Daddy-o. A phrase that apparently
originated at the Gaiety Palace of Varieties
in Leicester in the 1880s. The proprietor,
Sam Torr, would dance around the stage
with a dummy horse, singing about being
'on the back of Daddy-o'. He addressed
remarks to it, rather like a ventriloquist's
dummy, and 'Daddy-o' became a well-
known catchphrase of the day. *Source*:
Howell & Ford, *The True History of the
Elephant Man* (1980).
   Compare the use of 'Daddy-o' in the
world of jazz, just a few decades later.
DOAS has it in 'bop' use by 1946 and, as 'an
affectionate term . . . for any male who is
hip . . . whether a father or not', by 1956.
'Now one of the most common -o words.'

**daddy, what did *you* do in the Great
War?** Slogan used on recruiting posters in
the First World War. The accompanying
picture showed an understandably appalled
family man puzzling over what to reply to
the daughter on his knee. It became a
catchphrase in the form, 'What did you do
in the Great War, Daddy?' and gave rise to
such responses as 'Shut up, you little
bastard. Get the Bluebell and go and clean
my medals' (Partridge/*Catch Phrases*). *What
Did You Do in the War, Daddy?* was the title
of a film (US, 1966).

Dad's Army. The long-running BBC TV
comedy series (1968–77), established in
general a nickname for the Local Defence
Volunteers (LDV), formed in Britain at the
outbreak of the Second World War and
soon renamed the Home Guard. 'Dad's

Army' was a posthumous nickname given
by those looking back on the exploits of this
civilian force (though its members were
uniformed and attached to army units).
Many of the members were elderly men.
   The TV series produced many semi-
catchphrases. Right from the first episode,
Captain Mainwaring (Arthur Lowe) was
apt to exclaim: **Stupid boy!** to Private Pike
(Ian Lavender). When Lowe died in 1982,
the *Daily Mail* reported: 'The Captain did
try to go unrecognised in private life, but
found it increasingly difficult. Often people
would come up to him in the street or in
restaurants and ask him to say "Stupid
boy!" just once.'
   In the Home Guard platoon, the elderly
Lance-Corporal Jones (Clive Dunn) would
request **Permission to speak, sir!** shout
Don't panic! and remark **They don't
like it up 'em.** John Laurie as Private
Fraser (a Scots undertaker when out of
uniform) would wail **We're doomed** or
Doomed I am, doomed. John le Mesurier
as Sergeant Wilson would quietly inquire
**Excuse me, sir, do you think that's
wise?** and Arnold Ridley as Private
Godfrey **May I spend a penny?** (see SPEND
A PENNY).

daft. See EE, AIN'T IT GRAND TO BE ∼.

daft as a brush. Meaning 'stupid', this
expression was adapted from the northern
English **soft as a brush** by the British
comedian Ken Platt, who said in 1979: 'I
started saying daft as a brush when I was
doing shows in the Army in the 1940s.
People used to write and tell me I'd got it
wrong!' (Partridge/*Slang* suggests that 'daft
. . .' was in use before this, however, and
Paul Beale reports the full version – 'daft as
a brush without bristles' – from the 1920s.)

daisy. See DARLING ∼.

damage. See WHAT'S THE DAMAGE?

damn. See FRANKLY MY DEAR.

damn clever these Chinese! See under GOON SHOW.

damn close-run thing, a. A narrow victory. What the 1st Duke of Wellington actually told the memoirist Thomas Creevey about the outcome of the Battle of Waterloo, was: 'It has been a damned serious business. Blucher and I have lost 30,000 men. It has been a damned nice thing – the nearest run thing you ever saw in your life' (18 June 1915). The *Creevey Papers* in which this account appears were not published until 1903. Somehow out of this description a conflated version arose, with someone else presumably supplying the 'close-run'.

damned if you do and damned if you don't. A modern version of 'betwixt the devil and the deep blue sea' – possibly of American origin. From the *Guardian* (1 July 1992): 'It's still very much a thing with women that you're damned if you do and damned if you don't. If women choose to stay at home and look after their children, now they're accused of opting out of the workforce and decision-making because they're afraid to look up to it.'

damn fine cup of coffee – and hot! 'Kyle Maclachlan, who plays the FBI Special Agent Dale Cooper in *Twin Peaks* ... is one of TV's true originals. His much-loved and oft-repeated catchphrase "Damn fine cup of coffee, and hot!" has indeed caught on and Maclachlan himself parodies it crisply in a TV commercial' (*Radio Times*, 15–21 June 1991). Other food-related exclamations by 'Coop' included: 'Had a slice of cherry pie – *incredible!*' and (confronted with a table of doughnuts) 'A policeman's dream!' The American TV series *Twin Peaks* was first aired in 1990.

damn is to swearing, as near as. Meaning, 'too close to call', or 'no difference'. I first heard it from an optician in Liverpool in 1963.

dancing. See THERE'LL BE ~ IN THE STREETS TONIGHT.

dander up, to get one's. Meaning 'to get ruffled or angry', the expression occurs in William Thackeray's *Pendennis*: 'Don't talk to me about daring to do this thing or t'other, or when my dander is up it's the very thing to urge me on' (Chap.44, 1848–50). Apparently of US origin (known by 1831), where 'dander' was either a 'calcined cinder' or 'dandruff'. It is hard to see how the expression develops from either of these meanings. The Dutch word *donder* meaning 'thunder', or 'dunder', a Scottish dialect word for 'ferment', may be more relevant.

danger. See CLEAR AND PRESENT ~.

dangerous age, the. The title of an early (and very mild) Dudley Moore film comedy of 1967 was *Thirty Is a Dangerous Age, Cynthia*. This would seem to allude, however distantly and unknowingly, to *Den farlige alder* [The dangerous age], a book in Danish by Karin Michaelis (1910). In that instance, the dangerous age was forty. In the Moore film, as far as I can recall, it was very important for him to write a musical, or perhaps get married, before he was *thirty*. In fact, the 'dangerous age' is whatever the speaker thinks it is. It might be said of teenagers first encountering the opposite sex, 'Well, that's the dangerous age, of course' as much as it might be said of married folk experiencing the SEVEN YEAR ITCH.

Danno. See BOOK 'EM, ~.

Darby and Joan. The term is descriptive of an old couple, happy in their long marriage, in modest but contented circumstances. A ballad on this theme was published in 1735, possibly after an actual couple with these names who are said to have lived in either London or West Yorkshire.

daring young man on the flying trapeze, the. The original of this phrase in the song 'The Man on the Flying Trapeze' by George Leybourne and Alfred Lee (1868) was Jules Léotard (d 1880), the French trapeze artist. He also gave his name to the tight, one-piece garment worn by ballet dancers, acrobats, and other performers. *The Daring Young Man on the Flying Trapeze* was the title of a volume of short stories (1934) by William Saroyan.

dark. See ALL WOMEN LOOK THE SAME IN THE ~; IT WAS A ~ AND STORMY NIGHT; KEEP IT ~; OVER WILL'S MOTHER'S WAY; TALL ~ AND HANDSOME.

dark continent/darkest Africa. In 1878, H.M. Stanley, the journalist who discovered Dr Livingstone, published *Through the Dark Continent* and followed it, in 1890, with *Through Darkest Africa*. It was from these two titles that we appear to get the expressions 'dark continent' and 'darkest — ' to describe not only Africa but almost anywhere remote and uncivilized. Additionally, Flexner (1982) suggests that 'In darkest Africa' was a screen caption in a silent film of the period 1910–14.

darken. See NEVER – MY DOOR AGAIN.

darkest hour comes just before the dawn, the. A proverb of the 'things will get worse before they get better' variety. Terence Rattigan used it in his play *The Winslow Boy* (1946). Mencken finds it in Thomas Fuller's *A Pisgah-Sight of Palestine* (1650): 'It is always darkest just before the day dawneth.' Whether there is any little literal truth in it is another matter.

dark horse, a. Figuratively, the phrase refers to a runner about whom everyone is 'in the dark' until he comes from nowhere and wins the race – of whatever kind. It is possible the term originated in Benjamin Disraeli's novel *The Young Duke: A Moral Tale Though Gay* (1831) in which 'a dark horse, which had never been thought of . . . rushed past the grandstand in sweeping triumph.' It is used especially in political contexts.

darkness at noon. *Darkness at Noon, or the Great Solar Eclipse of the 16th June 1806* was the title of an anonymous booklet published in Boston (1806). Arthur Koestler's novel *Darkness at Noon* (1940) (originally written in German, but apparently with the title in English) is about the imprisonment, trial, and execution of a Communist who has betrayed the Party. It echoes Milton's *Samson Agonistes* (1671): 'O dark, dark, dark, amid the blaze of noon.'

dark night of the soul, a/the. Denoting mental and spiritual suffering prior to some big step, the phrase '*La Noche oscura del alma*' was used as the title of a work in Spanish by St John of the Cross. This was a treatise based on his poem 'Songs of the Soul Which Rejoices at Having Reached Union with God by the Road of Spiritual Negation' (c 1578). In *The Crack-up* (1936), F. Scott Fitzgerald wrote: 'In a real dark night of the soul it is always three o'clock in the morning, day after day.' Douglas Adams wrote *The Long Dark Tea-time of the Soul* (1988), a novel.

Darling Daisy. One of the nicknames of Frances Evelyn Greville, Countess of Warwick (1861–1938), for nine years mistress of King Edward VII. He wrote to her as 'my Darling Daisy wife'. A play about their correspondence was entitled *My Darling Daisy* (1970). Daisy was also known as the **Red Countess** on account of her later conversion to socialism. Hector Bolitho said: 'Her devotion to the cause of labour was as complete as her early conquests in society.'

Darling of the Halls, the. Sir George Robey, the British music hall comedian, was often known as 'the Darling of the Halls'. The appellation derived from the possibly apocryphal exchange between the lawyer F.E. Smith (1872–1930) (later Lord Birkenhead) and a judge. In the way judges have of affecting ignorance of popular culture (compare WHO ARE THE BEATLES?), the judge asked who George Robey was and Smith replied: 'Mr George Robey is the Darling of the music halls, m'lud.' This gains added sense when you know that the judge was Mr Justice *Darling* whose own witticisms attracted much publicity.

darlings. See HELLO, MY ~.

Darth Vader. Applied to any dark, menacing person, this name derives from a character in the film *Star Wars* (US, 1977) and its sequels. He was a fallen Jedi knight who had turned to evil, appeared totally in shiny black, all skin hidden, and spoke with a distorted voice. From the *Palm Beach Post* (5 March 1989): 'Mr Lorenzo, who in some circles is viewed as the "Darth Vader" of the industry, has shown nothing but contempt for Eastern [Airlines] employees, both union and non-contract.'

date rape. A term used to identify a particular and predominant type of rape – one that involved people who were not strangers, and that took place on a date or during a similarly voluntary encounter. 'There is nothing new about ending up having sex with someone you didn't quite mean to; but calling it date rape or "acquaintance rape" is relatively recent. The concept originated in the United States in the Eighties and took hold among the politically correct movement in American universities' (*Independent*, 20 November 1991). When Dr Mary Koss of the University of Arizona laid claim to the coinage (*Ms Magazine*, 1987), it was pointed out that the phrase had in fact been used much earlier: 'He could be prosecuted if only the legal system would accept that "date rape" is possible' (*Mademoiselle*, November 1980).

As with **acquaintance rape** (which equally may occur at any time, and not just on a date) the rape may constitute no more than verbal harassment and not legally recognized rape.

dat's my boy dat said dat! See under GOODNIGHT, MRS CALABASH . . .

daughter. See IT'S NOT FOR ME, IT'S FOR MY ∼.

dawn. See CAME THE ∼.

day. See AT THE END OF THE ∼; EVERY ∼ AND IN EVERY WAY . . . ; GO AHEAD, MAKE MY ∼; HAPPIEST ∼S OF YOUR LIFE; HAPPY AS THE ∼ IS LONG; HAVE A NICE ∼; OUR ∼ WILL COME; P.O.E.T.S.' ∼; QUEEN FOR A ∼; TODAY IS THE FIRST ∼ . . . ; WHAT A DIFFERENCE A ∼ MAKES.

day for night. A film-maker's term for shooting a scene during the day and then tinting it dark to make it look like night.

Hence, *Day for Night* – the English title given to François Truffaut's film about film-making (1973) whose original title *La Nuit Américaine* [American Night], is the French equivalent.

day in the life, a. The most-remembered track from the Beatles' *Sgt Pepper* album (1967) presumably took its name from that type of magazine article and film documentary which strives to depict 24 hours in the life of a particular person or organization. In 1959, Richard Cawston produced a TV documentary which took this form, with the title *This is the BBC*. In 1962, the English title of a novel (film UK, 1971) by Alexander Solzhenitsyn was *One Day in the Life of Ivan Denisovich*. John Lennon and Paul McCartney's use of the phrase 'A Day in the Life' for the description of incidents in the life of a drug-taker may have led to the *Sunday Times Magazine* feature 'A Life in the Day' (running since the 1960s) and the play title *A Day in the Death of Joe Egg* by Peter Nichols (1967, film UK, 1971).

daylight robbery. Flagrant over-charging – a phrase in use by the 1940s and building upon the simple 'it's robbery' to describe the same thing, dating from the mid-nineteenth century. The application of the phrase in Britain to the Window Tax (1691–1851) which led to the blocking up of windows – and thus to a form of daylight robbery – appears to be merely retrospective.

day of the locust, a/the. The relevance of the title *The Day of the Locust* to Nathanael West's novel (1939) about the emptiness of life in Hollywood in the 1930s is not totally clear. Locusts are, however, usually associated with times when waste, poverty or hardship are in evidence. They also go about in swarms committing great ravages on crops. The climax of the novel is a scene in which Tod, the hero, gets crushed by a Hollywood mob. In the Bible, Joel 2:25 has: 'And I will restore to you the years that the locust hath eaten'; Revelations 9:3: 'There came out of the smoke locusts upon the earth: and unto them we give power'; Revelations 9:4: 'locusts give power to hurt only those men which have not the seal of God in their foreheads'.

day that the rains came down, the. A line from the song 'The Day the Rains Came', written by Carl Sigman and Gilbert Becaud. Jane Morgan had a hit with it in 1958.

day war broke out, the. A catchphrase from the Second World War radio monologues of the British comedian Robb Wilton (1881–1957): 'The day war broke out . . . my missus said to me, "It's up to you . . . you've got to stop it." I said, "Stop what?" She said, "The war."' Later, when circumstances changed, the phrase became 'the day *peace* broke out'.

D-Day. Meaning 'an important day when something is due to begin', the most frequent allusion is to 6 June 1944, the day on which the Allies began their landings in northern France in order to push back German forces. Like H-Hour, D-Day is a military way of detailing elements in an operation. The 'D' just reinforces the 'Day' on which the plan is to be put into effect and enables successive days to be labelled 'D-Day plus one', etc.

dead. See BETTER RED THAN ∼; DE MORTUIS . . . ; DROP ∼; QUEEN ANNE'S ∼; QUICK AND THE ∼; WHEN I'M ∼ under THERE'LL NEVER BE ANOTHER.

dead and gone. See HERE'S A FUNNY THING . . .

dead – and never called me mother. This line is recalled as typical of the three-volume sentimental Victorian novel, yet it does not appear in Mrs Henry Wood's *East Lynne* (1861) as is often supposed. Nevertheless, it was inserted in one of the numerous stage versions of the novel (that by T.A.Palmer in 1874) which were made before the end of the century. The line occurs in a scene when an errant but penitent mother who has returned in the guise of a governess to East Lynne, her former home, has to watch the slow death of her eight-year-old son ('Little Willie'), but is unable to reveal her true identity.

dead as a doornail. Completely dead. In the Middle Ages, the doornail was the name given to the knob on which the

knocker struck: 'As this is frequently knocked on the head, it cannot be supposed to have much life in it' (Brewer). The phrase occurs as early as 1350, then again in Langland's *Piers Plowman* (1362). Shakespeare uses it a couple of times, in the usual form and, as in *Henry IV, Part 2*, V.iii.117 (1597):

> *Falstaff:* What, is the old king dead!
> *Pistol:* As nail in door!

dead in the water. Helpless, lacking support, finished. Suddenly popular in the late 1980s and undoubtedly of North American origin. From the *Guardian* (2 March 1987): 'Mr John Leese, editor of both the *Standard* and the *Evening News*, replied: "This obviously means that Mr Maxwell's [news]paper is dead in the water."' In other words, an opponent or antagonist is like a dead fish. He is still in the water and not swimming anywhere.

deadlier than the male. Phrase from the poem 'The Female of the Species' (1911) by Rudyard Kipling: 'For the female of the species is more deadly than the male.' A much-quoted line, though sometimes the quoter takes the teeth out of the remark. In 1989, Margaret Thatcher said: 'The female of the species is rather better than the male.' *Deadlier Than the Male* was the title of a film (UK, 1967) and an unrelated novel (1981) by Jessica Mann. *The Female of the Species* has also been the title of a film – a 1917 silent version of *The Admirable Crichton*.

dead parrot, a. Meaning 'something that is quite incapable of resuscitation'. This expression derives from the most famous of all the MONTY PYTHON'S FLYING CIRCUS sketches (first shown on 7 December 1969) in which a man (known as 'Praline') who has just bought a parrot that turns out to be dead, registers a complaint with the pet shop owner in these words: 'This parrot is no more. It's ceased to be. It's expired. It's gone to meet its maker. This is a late parrot. It's a stiff. Bereft of life it rests in peace. It would be pushing up the daisies if you hadn't nailed it to the perch. It's rung down the curtain and joined the choir invisible. It's an ex-parrot.'

In early 1988, there were signs of the

phrase becoming an established idiom when it was applied to a controversial policy document drawn up as the basis for a merged Liberal/Social Democratic Party. Then the *Observer* commented (8 May 1988): 'Mr Steel's future – like his document – was widely regarded as a "dead parrot". Surely this was the end of his 12-year reign as Liberal leader?' In October 1990, Margaret Thatcher belatedly came round to the phrase (fed by a speechwriter, no doubt) and called the Liberal Democrats a 'dead parrot' at the Tory Party Conference. When the Liberals won a by-election at Eastbourne the same month, the Tory party chairman Kenneth Baker said the 'dead parrot' had 'twitched'.

Whether the phrase will have much further life, ONLY TIME WILL TELL.

(Compare SICK AS A PARROT under OVER THE MOON.)

dead ringer, a. Meaning 'one person closely resembling another', the expression derives from horse-racing in the US, where a 'ringer' has been used since the nineteenth century to describe a horse fraudulently substituted for another in a race. 'Dead' here means 'exact', as in 'dead heat'.

deal. See BIG ~!; FAIR ~; NEW ~.

death. See AND ~ SHALL HAVE NO DOMINION; FATE WORSE THAN ~; HIS ~ DIMINISHES US ALL; KEEP ~ OFF THE ROAD; KISS OF ~; NATURE'S WAY OF TELLING YOU TO SLOW DOWN.

deathless prose/verse. An (often ironical) description of writing, sometimes used self-deprecatingly about one's own poor stuff. 'Robert Burns once expressed in deathless verse a Great Wish. His wish, translated into my far from deathless prose, was to the effect . . .' (Collie Knox, *For Ever England*, 1943). From an actor's diary: 'The writer . . . concentrates his most vicious verbal gymnastics [in these scenes]. After we've mangled the deathless prose we have another cup of tea' (*Independent on Sunday*, 13 May 1990).

death of/by a thousand cuts. Meaning 'the destruction of something by the cumulative effect of snipping rather than by one big blow'. In February 1989, Robert Runcie, Archbishop of Canterbury, told the General Synod: 'If the Government does not take the axe to the BBC, there is surely here the shadow of death by a thousand cuts.' The allusion may be to a literal death of this kind, as shown in the proverbial saying from an English translation of Chairman Mao's *Little Red Book* (1966): 'He who is not afraid of death by a thousand cuts dares to unhorse the emperor.' An eastern source for the phrase may be hinted at in what Jaffar the villainous magician (Conrad Veidt) says in the 1940 film version of *The Thief of Baghdad*: 'In the morning they die the death of a thousand cuts.' *Carry on Up the Khyber* (1968) has the phrase, too.

Death or Glory boys, the. Regimental nickname of the 17th Lancers (later 17th/21st), formed originally in 1759. The badge replaces the word 'death' with a Death's Head (skull) and adds 'Or Glory'.

death sentence, the. i.e. the spoken order for execution. In English law, it really was a sentence, but quite a long one, and capable of variation. When William Corder was found guilty of the murder of Maria Marten at the Red Barn, Polstead, Suffolk, the Lord Chief Baron said: '. . . that sentence is, that you be taken back to the prison from which you came, and that you be taken thence, on Monday next, to the place of execution, and there be hanged by the neck till you are dead, and that your body shall afterwards be dissected and anatomized, and the Lord God Almighty have mercy on your soul' (reported in *The Times*, 9 August 1828).

By 1910, when Dr Harvey Crippen was being sentenced to death for the murder of his wife by poisoning, the Lord Chief Justice (Lord Alverstone), having assumed the black cap, was solemnly saying this: 'The sentence of the Law is that you be taken from this place to a lawful prison, and thence to a place of execution, that you be there hanged by the neck until you are dead, and that your body be buried within the precincts of the prison in which you will be confined before your execution. And may the Lord have mercy on your soul!' This formula had been adopted in 1903.

Ultimately it derives from and expands the medieval death sentence – 'Suspendatur per collum' [Let him be hanged by the neck]. Along the way, it had been able to accommodate all the grisly demands made by the Law. Thus, for example, in the seventeenth century: 'The Court doth award that you be drawn upon a hurdle to the place of execution and there shall be hanged by the neck, and, being alive, shall be cut down and your entrails to be taken out of your body, and, you living, the same to be burnt before your eyes, and your head to be cut off, your body divided into four quarters, and head and quarters to be disposed of at the pleasure of the King's Majesty: and the Lord have mercy on your soul.'

The last execution was ordered in Britain in 1964. The death penalty was abolished in 1970. The *OED2* does not find the actual phrase 'death sentence' until 1943, but in Edgar Allan Poe's story 'The Pit and the Pendulum' (1843) he writes of 'the dread sentence of death'.

death wish, a. The film *Death Wish* (US, 1974) and its several sequels is concerned with the death of others by way of retribution. In the original, psychological sense of the phrase, it may be one's own death that is being wished for. In 1913, Sigmund Freud suggested that people have an innate tendency to revert to their original state. This could be self-destructive, although the death wish towards parents might also be strong. Accordingly, the phrase in its psychological sense is a translation of the German *todeswunch*, although the two words had come together in English by 1896.

debate. See GREAT ∼.

debate continues, the. Concluding phrase from BBC radio news reports of parliamentary proceedings in the 1940s/50s. *The Debate Continues* was also used as the title of a programme in which pundits in the studio would pick over the subjects of parliamentary debates. Compare **the case/hunt/search continues** at the conclusion of similar broadcast reports on court proceedings, escaped prisoners and missing people.

decisions, decisions! What a harried person might exclaim over having to make however trivial a choice. This is listed among the 'Naff Expressions' in *The Complete Naff Guide* (1983). Partridge/Catch Phrases offers 'c 1955' as a possible starting date. Perhaps an echo of the perpetually fraught WHITE RABBIT in *Alice In Wonderland*. Although he doesn't say this, he mutters: 'Oh my ears and whiskers, how late it's getting.'

decline and fall. The title of the novel (1928) by Evelyn Waugh, was ludicrously extended to *Decline and Fall . . . of a Birdwatcher!* when filmed (UK, 1968). As with all such titles, the origin is *The History of the Decline and Fall of the Roman Empire* (1766–88) by Edward Gibbon. There are numerous variations on the 'rise and fall' theme: *The Rise and Fall of Legs Diamond* (film US, 1960); *The Rise and Fall of the Man of Letters* (a book by John Gross, 1969); *The Fall and Rise of Reginald Perrin* (BBC TV comedy series, 1976–80; *The Rise and Rise of Michael Rimmer* (film UK, 1970).

decus et tutamen. The inscription found on the rim of the British pound coin which replaced the banknote of that denomination in 1983. The same words, suggested by John Evelyn the diarist, had appeared on the rim of a Charles II crown of 1662/3 (its purpose then was as a safeguard against clipping). Translated as 'an ornament and a safeguard' – referring to the inscription rather than the coin – the words come from Virgil's *Aeneid* (Bk.5) '*Decus et tutamen in armis*'. In its full form, this is the motto of the Feltmakers' Company (incorporated 1604).

deed. See NO GOOD ∼ GOES UNPUNISHED.

deep blue sea. See DEVIL AND THE ∼.

— deeply regret(s) any embarrassment/inconvenience caused. Now a cliché of apology. The standard form is something like: 'British Rail apologizes for the late running of this train and for any inconvenience that may have been caused' (never mind the pain of having to listen to the apology being trotted routinely out).

Incidentally, when giving apologies it is important never to be explicit as to the cause. If trains arrive late it is 'because of late departure' (but no apology for that); at airports, planes are late taking off 'because of the late arrival of the incoming plane'. Or, in other words, things happen – or, rather, don't happen, 'for operational reasons'.

Lieut. Col. Sitiveni Rabuka, leader of a coup in Fiji (May 1987) was quoted as saying, 'We apologize for any inconvenience caused.'

deep-six, to. Meaning 'to dispose of; destroy', the expression is of nautical origin – from men who took soundings. When they said 'by the deep six', they meant six fathoms (36 feet). In naval circles, 'to deep-six' equally means 'to jettison overboard'. *DOAS* notes an extension to this meaning in jive and jazz use since the 1940s where 'the deep six' means 'the grave'. During Watergate, former presidential counsel John Dean told of a conversation he had had with another Nixon henchman, John Ehrlichman: 'He told me to shred the documents and "deep-six" the briefcase. I asked him what he meant by "deep-six". He leaned back in his chair and said, "You drive across the river on your way home tonight, don't you? Well, when you cross over bridge . . . just toss the briefcase into the river."' (Erhlichman, before going to prison, denied that this conversation ever took place.)

Deep Throat, a. Meaning 'a person within an organization who supplies information anonymously about wrongdoing by his colleagues', the phrase comes from the nickname given to the source within the Nixon White House who fed *Washington Post* journalists Carl Bernstein and Bob Woodward with information which helped in their Watergate investigations (1972–4). It has been suggested that 'Deep Throat' never existed but was a cover for unjustified suppositions. The nickname was derived from *Deep Throat* (US, 1972), a notorious porno movie concerning a woman, played by Linda Lovelace, whose clitoris is placed in the back of her throat.

DEF II. This was the title given to a 'strand' of youth programming on BBC2 TV from May 1988. Janet Street-Porter, the executive in charge, said that it was a graffito meaning 'I *defy* you *to* erase this'. On the other hand, the *Guardian*, writing about a young London graffiti artist on 14 October 1987, glossed his use of 'def' as signifying approval of a piece of lettering. Paul Beale in the *Concise Slang* wonders, on this basis, whether it is short for 'definitely'. In American hip-hop talk (by 1987), 'def' was short for 'definitive' (i.e. brilliant, excellent, cool).

degrades. See THIS AD INSULTS WOMEN.

degree. See NTH ~.

deliberate. See DID YOU SPOT . . . ?

delightful weather we're having for the time of year. Genteel conversational gambit, possibly from the nineteenth century. In parody, often used as a way of changing the subject from something embarrassing. An example occurs in J.B. Priestley, *When We Are Married*, Act I (1938).

déluge. See APRES NOUS LE ~.

De Mille. See READY WHEN YOU ARE, MR ~.

de mortuis nil nisi bonum [Of the dead, speak kindly or not at all]. Sometimes ascribed to Solon (c 600 BC), 'Speak not evil of the dead' was also a saying of Chilo(n) of Sparta (one of the Seven Sages (sixth century BC). Later Sextus Propertius (d AD 2) wrote: 'Absenti nemo non nocuisse velit' [Let no one be willing to speak ill of the absent]. Sometimes simply referred to in the form 'de mortuis . . . ', it is a proverb which appears in some form in most European languages.

depends. See IT ALL ~ WHAT YOU MEAN BY . . .

depressed. See TIRED, ~, IRRITABLE?

De Profundis. The title of Oscar Wilde's letter of self-justification following his imprisonment (published 1905) comes from the Latin words for 'out of the depths' (Psalm 130).

Derby, the. The very first of all the races called 'Derby' was named in 1780 by the 12th Earl of Derby who is said to have discussed the idea of a flat race for three-year-old fillies, over dinner with his friend, Sir Charles Bunbury. Tradition has it that they tossed a coin over which of them the race should be named after and Derby won. The idea of a race called the 'Kentucky Bunbury' would have been a little hard to take seriously.

desert. See MAKE THE ~ BLOOM.

Desert Fox, the. Nickname of the German Field Marshal Erwin Rommel (1891–1944), noted for his audacious generalship in North Africa during the Second World War. A fox known as the pale fox does inhabit North Africa, so presumably this is the one that attracted the original sobriquet.

deserting. See LIKE RATS ~ A SINKING SHIP.

Desert Rats, the. Nickname of the British 7th Armoured Division which served throughout the North Africa campaign in the Second World War and adopted the badge of a desert rat (the jerboa). The division made use of 'scurrying and biting' tactics in desert warfare and later fought in the invasion of occupied Europe, from Normandy onwards.

Desert Storm. 'Operation Desert Storm' was the code name bestowed by its American leadership on the Allied military operation whose aim was to reverse the 1990 Iraqi occupation of Kuwait. Curiously, a desert storm is the worst climatic condition under which to launch a military operation. The conflict came to be more widely known as the **Gulf War** (by 22 January 1991) and was concluded by March 1991.

designer —. This adjective was applied to clothes and fashion accessories in the 1960s/70s. It suggested that they carried the label of a particular designer, were not just mass-produced and, consequently,

had prestige and were worth coveting. 'Designer jeans' (by 1978) were what probably caused people to notice the usage, bringing together, as they did the extremes of a 'name' designer and mass production.

Then came the jokes: fashionable Perrier was being called 'designer water' by 1984; careful undershaving by men was known as 'designer stubble' by 1989.

desist! (' —, curb your hilarity' or ' —, refrain and cease'). One of a number of mock-disapproving phrases employed by the British music-hall comedian Sir George Robey (1869–1954), the **Prime Minister of Mirth.** When disapproving of ribald laughter he had provoked, he would say things like: 'If there is any more hilarity, you must leave. Pray temper your hilarity with a modicum of reserve. Desist! And I am surprised at you, Agnes [pronounced "Ag-er-nes"]!' Also 'Go *out!*' or 'Get *out!*' or simply '*Out!*'

See also I MEANTER SAY and DARLING OF THE HALLS.

despatched. See HATCHED, MATCHED AND ~.

desperate diseases require desperate remedies. Proverbial saying commonly ascribed to Guy Fawkes on 6 November 1605 (when he was arrested the day after attempting to blow up the Houses of Parliament): 'A desperate disease requires a dangerous remedy' (the version according to the *DNB*) was apparently said by him to James I, one of his intended victims. The king asked if he did not regret his proposed attack on the Royal Family. Fawkes replied that one of his objects was to blow the Royal Family back to Scotland. He was subsequently tried and put to death. What he said, however, appears to have been a version of an established proverbial saying. In the form: 'Strong disease requireth a strong medicine', *ODP* traces it to 1539. In Shakespeare's *Romeo and Juliet* (1594), there is:

I do spy a kind of hope,
Which craves as desperate an execution
As that which we would prevent
(IV.i.68).

Shakespeare also alludes to the saying on two other occasions.

desperation, pacification, expectation, acclamation, realization – 'it's Fry's'. In the UK, advertisements for Fry's chocolate for many years after the First World War featured the faces of five boys anticipating a bite and coupled them with these descriptive words.

despondency. See SPREAD ALARM AND ∼.

destiny. See MAN OF ∼.

detective. See NOT VERY GOOD ∼ . . .

deviation. See WITHOUT HESITATION . . .

devices and desires. Phrase from the General Confession in the Prayer Book: 'We have followed too much the devices and desires of our own hearts.' *Devices and Desires* was the title of a crime novel (1989) by P.D. James.

devil and the deep blue sea, betwixt the. Meaning 'having two courses of action open, both of them dangerous' (as with the mythological Scylla and Charybdis), the phrase should not be taken too literally. The 'devil' here may refer to the seam of a wooden ship's hull or to a plank fastened to the side of a ship as a support for guns. Either of these was difficult of access, a perilous place to be, but better than in the deep blue sea. Current by 1894 (with the 'blue' omitted).

devil can cite scripture for his own purposes, the. Meaning 'an ill-disposed person may turn even good things to his own advantage', and in this precise form, this an allusion to Antonio the Merchant, in Shakespeare's *The Merchant of Venice*, I.iii.93 (1596) who says this because Shylock has just been doing so.

Devil made me do it!, the. The American comedian Flip Wilson became famous for saying this, wide-eyed, about any supposed misdemeanour, when host of a TV comedy and variety hour (1970–4).

devil's dozen. See BAKER'S DOZEN.

Dexy's Midnight Runners. The name of a British pop group of the early 1980s is derived from the slang term for pills containing the amphetamine Dexedrine, a drug popular in the 1950s and 60s.

diamond. See CRUCIAL!; DOUBLE ∼ WORKS WONDERS.

diamond is forever, a. In 1939, the South African-based De Beers Consolidated Mines launched a campaign to promote further the tradition of diamond engagement rings. The N.W. Ayer agency of Chicago (copywriter B.J. Kidd) came up with this line. It passed easily into the language, having an almost proverbial ring. Anita Loos in *Gentlemen Prefer Blondes* (1925) had enshrined something like the idea in: 'Kissing your hand may make you feel very, very good but a diamond and safire bracelet lasts for ever.' Ian Fleming gave a variation of the phrase as the title of his 1956 James Bond novel *Diamonds are Forever*.
    Technically speaking, however, they are not. It takes a very high temperature, but, being of pure carbon, diamonds *will* burn.

Di(ana). See DON'T DO IT, ∼.

Dick. See QUEER AS ∼'S HATBAND; SAY GOODNIGHT, ∼ under *LAUGH-IN*.

dickens. See WHAT THE ∼!

Dick Whittington. See STREETS PAVED WITH GOLD.

Dick(y). See TRICKY ∼.

dicky bird. See WATCH THE BIRDIE.

dictator. See TIN-POT ∼.

diddy. See HOW TICKLED I AM.

did I ever tell you about the time I was in Sidi Barrani? See under *MUCH BINDING IN THE MARSH*.

didjavagoodweekend? 'No, I forgot the Aerogard.' A briefly memorable exchange from Australian advertisements for an insect repellent in the early 1980s.

The initial phrase, said with a strong Aussie accent, passed into the language Down Under, not least because it was a useful thing for people to say themselves in conversation.

didn't he do well? See under GENERATION GAME.

did she fall or was she pushed? The original form of this inquiry is said to date from the 1890s when it had to do with loss of virginity. Then it was supposedly used in newspaper reports (c 1908) of a woman's death on cliffs near Beachy Head (Thorne Smith alluded to the phrase in the title of a novel *Did She Fall?*, 1936). The line 'Was she pushed or did she jump?' occurs in the song 'Well! Well! Well! (My Cat Fell Down the Well)' by Shand/Moll/Robertson (1970s).

Now applied to men or women, the formula usually inquires whether they departed from a job of their own volition or whether they were eased out by others. (Hence, the 1970s graffito, 'Humpty Dumpty was pushed . . . by the CIA'.)

did the earth move for you? Jokily addressed to one's partner after sexual intercourse, this appears to have originated as 'Did thee feel the earth move?' in Ernest Hemingway's novel *For Whom the Bell Tolls* (1940). I have not been able to find it in the 1943 film version, however. Headline from the *Sport* (22 February 1989): 'SPORT SEXCLUSIVE ON A BONK THAT WILL MAKE THE EARTH MOVE'.

did you spot this week's deliberate mistake? As a way of covering up a mistake that was *not* deliberate, this expression arose from the BBC radio series *Monday Night at Seven* (later *Eight*) in c 1938. Ronnie Waldman had taken over as deviser of the 'Puzzle Corner' part of the programme which was presented by Lionel Gamlin. 'Through my oversight a mistake crept into "Puzzle Corner" one night,' Waldman recalled in 1954, 'and when Broadcasting House was besieged by telephone callers putting us right, Harry Pepper [the producer] concluded that such "listener participation" was worth exploiting as a regular thing. "Let's always

put in a deliberate mistake," he suggested.'

Waldman revived the idea when he himself presented 'Puzzle Corner' as part of *Kaleidoscope* on BBC Television in the early 1950s and the phrase 'this week's deliberate mistake' has continued to be used jokingly as a cover for ineptitude.

die. See EAT, DRINK AND BE MERRY . . . ; LIFE'S A BITCH AND THEN YOU ~; NEVER SAY ~; OLD SOLDIERS NEVER ~; WE'LL ALL LIVE TILL WE ~ . . .

die is cast, the. The fateful decision has been made, there is no turning back now. Here 'die' is the singular of 'dice' and the expression has been known in English since at least 1634. When Julius Caesar crossed the Rubicon, he is supposed to have said '*Jacta alea est*' – 'the dice have been thrown' (although he actually said it in Greek).

dies irae. See MASS PHRASES.

die with one's boots on, to. See BOOTS ON, TO DIE WITH ONE'S.

difference. See WHAT A ~ A DAY MAKES.

different. See AND NOW FOR SOMETHING COMPLETELY ~.

different drummer, to march to a. To act in a way expressive of one's own individualism. The concept comes from Henry David Thoreau in *Walden* (1854): 'If a man does not keep pace with his companions, perhaps it is because he hears a different drummer. Let him step to the music which he hears, however measured or far away.' Hence, presumably: *Different Drummer*, a ballet (1984) choreographed by Kenneth MacMillan; *The Different Drum* (1987), a work of popular psychotherapy by M. Scott Peck; and *Different Drummer*, a BBC TV series (1991) about eccentric American outsiders.

different strokes for different folks. This means 'different people have different requirements' (a slight sexual connotation here). The proverb is repeated several times in the song 'Everyday People' (1968) sung by Sly and the Family Stone. *Diff'rent Strokes* was the title of a US TV series (from 1978 onwards) about a widowed millionaire who adopts two black boys.

difficulties, little local. Phrase used dismissively to show a lack of concern. In 1958, as Prime Minister, Harold Macmillan made a characteristically airy reference to the fact that his entire Treasury team, including the Chancellor of the Exchequer, had resigned over disagreement about budget estimates. In a statement at London airport before leaving for a tour of the Commonwealth on 7 January, he said: 'I thought the best thing to do was to settle up these little local difficulties, and then turn to the wider vision of the Commonwealth.'

difficult we do immediately – the impossible takes a little longer, the. Bartlett (1980) reported that the motto, now widespread in this form, was used by the US Army Service Forces. The idea has, however, been traced back to Charles Alexandre de Calonne (d 1802), who said: 'Madame, si c'est possible, c'est fait; impossible, impossible? cela se fera' [Madame, if it is possible, it is done; if it is impossible, it will be done]. Henry Kissinger once joked: 'The illegal we do immediately, the unconstitutional takes a little longer' (quoted in William Shawcross, Sideshow, 1979).

dig for victory. Shortage of foodstuffs was an immediate concern in the UK upon the outbreak of the Second World War. On 4 October 1939, Sir Reginald Dorman Smith, the Minister of Agriculture, broadcast these words: 'Half a million more allotments, properly worked, will provide potatoes and vegetables that will feed another million adults and one-and-a-half million children for eight months out of twelve . . . So, let's get going. Let "Dig for victory" be the motto of everyone with a garden and of every able-bodied man and woman capable of digging an allotment in their spare time.'

A poster bearing the slogan showed a booted foot pushing a spade into earth. Consequently, the number of allotments rose from 815,000 in 1939 to 1,400,000 in 1943.

dignity of labour, the. The phrase refers especially to manual labour but citations have proved elusive. Booker T. Washington, the US negro writer, alludes to the notion in *Up from Slavery* (1901): 'No race can prosper till it learns that there is as much dignity in tilling a field as in writing a poem.' The similar **honest toil** is almost as elusive. Thomas Gray in his 'Elegy' (1751) spoke of the **useful toil** of the 'rude forefathers' in the countryside. *Useful Toil* was the title of a book comprising 'autobiographies of working people from the 1820s to the 1920s' (published 1974). The *OED2* finds 'honest labour' in 1941. Thomas Carlyle spoke of 'honest work' in 1866. 'Honourable toil' appears in the play *Two Noble Kinsmen* (possibly by John Fletcher and William Shakespeare, published 1634).

dike. See FINGER IN THE ∼ . . .

dim. See MY EYES ARE ∼ .

dinkies. See YUPPIE.

dinner. See ALL GONG AND NO ∼; under DOG'S BREAKFAST . . .

dinners. See HOT ∼ , I'VE HAD AS MANY . . .

dipstick. See YER PLONKER.

dirt before the broom. See under AGE BEFORE BEAUTY.

dirty. See YOU ∼ OLD MAN; YOU ∼ RAT!; YOU ∼ ROTTEN SWINE, YOU! under GOON SHOW.

dirty bird. See I'LL BE A ∼ .

dirty old man. See DOM.

dirty work at the crossroads. Meaning 'despicable behaviour; foul play' (in any location), this is mostly a Hollywood idiom, but not quite a cliché. The earliest film citation found is from *Flying Down to Rio* (1933), although P.G. Wodehouse had it in the book *Man Upstairs* in 1914 and Walter Melville, a nineteenth-century melodramist, is said to have had it in *The Girl Who Took the Wrong Turning, or, No Wedding Bells for Him* (no date). A *Notes and Queries* discussion of the phrase in 1917 threw up the view that it might have occurred in a music-hall sketch of the 1880s and that the chief allusion was to the activities of highwaymen. Brewer suggests that it might have something to do with the old custom of burying people at crossroads.

discontent. See WINTER OF ∼.

discumknockerating. See HOW TICKLED I AM.

discuss Ugandan affairs, to. To have sexual intercourse. In *Private Eye* No. 293 (9 March 1973), there appeared a gossip item which launched a euphemism for sexual intercourse: 'I can reveal that the expression "Talking about Uganda" has acquired a new meaning. I first heard it myself at a fashionable party given recently by media-people Neal and Corinna Ascherson. As I was sipping my Campari on the ground floor I was informed by my charming hostess that I was missing out on a meaningful confrontation upstairs where a former cabinet colleague of President Obote was "talking about Uganda".

'Eager, as ever, to learn the latest news from the Dark Continent I rushed upstairs to discover the dusky statesman "talking about Uganda" in a highly compromising manner to vivacious former features editor, Mary Kenny . . . I understand that 'Long John' and Miss Kenny both rang up later to ascertain each other's names.'

Later, references to 'Ugandan practices' or 'Ugandan discussions' came to be used – though whether far beyond the readership of *Private Eye*, I doubt. In a letter to *The Times* (13 September 1983), Corinna Ascherson (now signing herself Corinna Adam) identified the coiner of the phrase as the poet and critic James Fenton. She also claimed that the phrase had been included in '*The Oxford Dictionary of Slang*', whatever that might be. It is not in Partridge/*Slang*.

Richard Ingrams (editor of *Private Eye* at the time) added the interesting, er, footnote in the *Observer* (2 April 1989) that the original Ugandan was 'a one-legged former Minister in President Obote's Government. When the *New Statesman* found out that the *Eye* was going to refer to the incident, representations were made to the effect that the Minister, on the run from Obote, would

be in danger if identified. The detail of the wooden leg was therefore omitted, but the expression passed into the language.'

As a further, er, footnote, Nicholas Wollaston wrote to the *Observer* (9 April 1989) and pointed out that the one-legged performer *wasn't* on the run from President Obote but 'the much-loved chairman of the Uganda Electricity Board, also of the Uganda Red Cross, and an exile for seven years from the tyranny of Idi Amin. When he died in 1986, it was reported that 10,000 people attended his funeral . . . and a memorial service at St Martin-in-the-Fields was packed with his friends, among them several who remembered their discussions on Uganda with him, the artificial limb notwithstanding, with much pleasure.'

diseases. See COUGHS AND SNEEZES . . . ; DESPERATE ∼ . . .

disgraceful. See IT IS ∼, IT OUGHT NOT TO BE ALLOWED!

disguise. See BLESSING IN ∼.

disgusted, Tunbridge Wells. When it was announced in February 1978 that a Radio 4 programme was to be launched with the title *Disgusted, Tunbridge Wells* (providing a platform for listeners' views on broadcasting), there was consternation in the Kent township (properly, Royal Tunbridge Wells). The title was intended to evoke the sort of letter fired off to the press between the wars when the writer did not want to give his/her name and so signed 'Mother of Three', 'Angry Ratepayer', 'Serving Policeman', etc. Tunbridge Wells has long been held as the source of reactionary, blimpish views. Derek Robinson, the presenter of the programme while disliking its title, told me (1989): 'Why Tunbridge Wells was considered to be stuffier than, say, Virginia Water or Maidenhead, I don't know. It's just one of those libels, like tightfisted Aberdeen, that some places get lumbered with.'

The *Kent Courier* (24 February 1978) reported the 'disgust' that the 'Disgusted' label had stirred up in the town. Some people interviewed thought the tag had originated with Richard Murdoch in *MUCH BINDING IN THE MARSH* in which 'he made much use of his connections with the town' and was always mentioning it. I think someone else suggested that the phrase – capturing a certain type of outraged tone of voice – might equally have arisen in TAKE IT FROM HERE. Can the phrase ever have been seriously used, however? Earlier citations are lacking.

dish. See CAN ∼ IT OUT . . .

disposition. See NOT SUITABLE FOR THOSE . . .

distinction. See FOR MEN OF ∼.

diver. DON'T FORGET THE ∼.

divorce. See WE'LL GET MARRIED JUST AS SOON . . .

do. See I ∼.

doc. See WHAT'S UP, ∼?

doctor. See IS THERE A ∼ IN THE HOUSE?

Doctor Greasepaint/Theatre will cure me. Both versions of this theatrical saying were quoted in obituaries for the actress Irene Handl in November 1987 as phrases that had been used by her. The saying suggests that acting is not only a cure for ailments, but also that actors *have* to be well most of the time to be able to perform their function. The actor Bernard Bresslaw told me in 1991 that his preference was for **Doctor Footlights will cure me.**
    Compare Swift's observation: 'The best doctors in the world are Doctor Diet, Doctor Quiet and Doctor Merryman'; and the nickname 'Dr Brighton' for the healthy seaside resort.

doctors wear scarlet. Phrase put on invitations to university gatherings – 'Evening dress with decorations, doctors wear scarlet' – referring to the scarlet academic robes worn by doctors of law and divinity, and so on. *Doctors Wear Scarlet* is the title of a novel (1960) by Simon Ravens and is set in Cambridge University, hinting at certain bloody goings-on within.

dodgy! Rather as the British upper classes tend to rely on two adjectives – 'fascinating' and 'boring' so, too, did the comedian Norman Vaughan (*b* 1927) in the 1960s. Accompanied by an upward gesture of the thumb, his **swinging!** was the equivalent of upper-class 'fascinating' and (with a downward gesture of the thumb) his 'dodgy!', the equivalent of their 'boring'. Norman told me in 1979: 'The words "swinging" and "dodgy" came originally from my association with jazz musicians and just seemed to creep into everyday conversation. Then when I got the big break at the Palladium [introducing ITV's *Sunday Night at the London Palladium* in 1962] they were the first catchphrases that the papers and then the public seized upon.'
    According to *The Making of the Prime Minister 1964* by Anthony Howard and Richard West, the Labour Party considered using the word 'swinging' with an upraised thumb as the basis of its advertising campaign prior to the 1964 General Election. However, doubts were expressed whether everyone would get the allusion and only the thumb was used. Although not, of course, the first person to use the word, Norman's use of 'swinging' helped to characterize an era – the SWINGING SIXTIES.
    During his Palladium stint he also introduced the format phrase, **a touch of the** — ('A touch of the Nelson Riddles' etc.) Later, he had a TV series called *A Touch of the Norman Vaughans*. This was established by May 1965 when I entitled an undergraduate revue at Oxford *A Touch of the Etceteras* ('The Etceteras' being a hoped-for Oxford equivalent of the Cambridge Footlights).

does he dance at the other end of the ballroom? See IS SHE A FRIEND OF DOROTHY?

does he take sugar? A principal failing of people when dealing with the physically disabled is encapsulated in the title of the BBC Radio series *Does He Take Sugar?* This phrase, pinpointed originally by social workers in the title of a booklet, 'Does he take sugar in his tea?', has been used since the programme's inception in 1978. It represents the unthinking attitude that leads people to talk to the companions or relatives of those with physical disabilities rather than directly to the people themselves.

From 'Guide to the Representation of People With Disabilities in Programmes' (compiled by Geoffrey Prout, BBC, 1990): 'For the record, [the title] has nothing to do with diabetes. It refers to the tendency of able-bodied people to speak over the heads of those with a disability and assume that they are brain-dead. In fact the vast majority of people, no matter what their disability, are perfectly able and willing to speak for themselves. In particular, we should not assume that people with a mental handicap are inarticulate.'

I wonder if anyone in the ranks of the POLITICALLY CORRECT has ever objected to the blatant sexism of the title?

doesn't it make you want to spit! See under BAND WAGGON.

doesn't time fly when you're having fun/enjoying yourself? Nowadays, an expression more often used ironically when work is hard, boredom rife or there is some other reason for not using the expression straightforwardly. Even in Act II of W.S. Gilbert's The Mikado (1885), it is used ironically. Yum-Yum is to marry Nanki-Poo but her joy is somewhat tempered by the thought that he is to be beheaded at the end or the month. Nanki-Poo tries to cheer her up by saying that they should call each hour a day, each day a year – 'At that rate we've about thirty years of married happiness before us!' Yum-Yum ('*still sobbing*') says: 'Yes. How time flies when one is thoroughly enjoying oneself.'

From the Scotsman (21 November 1991): 'Can it really be a year since [Margaret Thatcher] became politically semi-detached . . . Doesn't time fly when you're having more fun than you've been allowed for a decade and more.' Another laconic use of the phrase, from The Times (30 October 1985): 'I go home and look for the invoice. Find it. It was not three months ago but ten months. Doesn't time fly when your car is falling to bits?'

Of course, 'Doesn't time fly?', on its own, is a version of the ancient tempus fugit [time flies], and the original 'doesn't time fly when . . .' is an old thought. In

Shakespeare's Othello (II.iii.369; 1604), Iago says: 'Pleasure, and action, make the hours seem short.'

does she . . . or doesn't she? This innuendo-laden phrase began life selling Clairol hair colouring in 1955. The brainchild of Shirley Polykoff (who entitled her advertising memoirs Does She . . . or Doesn't She? in 1975), the question first arose at a party when a girl arrived with flaming red hair. Polykoff involuntarily uttered the line to her husband, George. As she tells it, however, her mother-in-law takes some of the credit for planting the words in her mind some twenty years previously. George told Shirley of his mother's first reaction on meeting her: 'She says you paint your hair. Well, do you?'

When Ms Polykoff submitted the slogan at the Foote Cone & Belding agency in New York (together with two ideas she wished to have rejected) she suggested it be followed by the phrase 'Only her mother knows for sure!' or 'So natural, only her mother knows for sure'. She felt she might have to change 'mother' to 'hairdresser' so as not to offend beauty salons, and **only her hairdresser knows for sure** was eventually chosen.

However, it was felt that the double meaning in the main slogan would cause the line to be rejected. Indeed, Life magazine would not take the ad. But subsequent research at Life failed to turn up a single female staff member who admitted detecting any innuendo and the phrases were locked into the form they kept for the next 18 years.

'J' did find a double meaning, as shown by this comment from The Sensuous Woman (1969): 'Our world has changed. It's no longer a question of "Does she or doesn't she?" We all know she wants to, is about to, or does.' A New York graffito, quoted in 1974, stated: 'Only his hairdresser knows for sure.'

See also IS SHE . . . OR ISN'T SHE?

does your mother know you're out? See MOTHER KNOW YOU'RE OUT . . .

dog. See BLACK ~; EVERY ~ HAS ITS DAY . . . ; ~ FOLLOWS ITS MASTER under AGE BEFORE BEAUTY; GIVE A ~ A BAD NAME; IN AND OUT

LIKE A ~ AT A FAIR; LOVE ME LOVE MY ~; MY ~ HAS FLEAS; PUT ON THE ~; THERE'S LIFE IN THE OLD ~ YET.

dog days. Nothing to do with dogs getting hot under the collar, contracting rabies, or anything like that. The ancients applied this label to the period between 3 July and 11 August when the Dog-star, Sirius, rises at the same time as the sun. At one time, this seemed to coincide with the overwhelmingly hot days of high summer.

dog have fleas?, does a. See IS THE POPE A CATHOLIC?

dog house, to be in the. To be in disgrace, out of favour. An American expression (known by 1932), as is shown by the use of 'dog house' rather than 'kennel'. It seems to be no more than coincidence that in J.M. Barrie's *Peter Pan and Wendy* (1911), it is said of Mr Darling, who literally ends up in a dog house: 'In the bitterness of his remorse he swore that he would never leave the kennel until his children came back.'

dogs, to go to the. To go downhill, down the drain, and end up in a bad state. This form (known by 1619) appears to have grown out of, or alongside, the expression to the effect that something is only fit for 'throwing to the dogs' (which Shakespeare uses on several occasions). The suggestion that it is a corruption of a Dutch business maxim: '*Toe goe, toe de dogs*' [Money gone, credit gone] is probably fanciful.

dogs bark – but the caravan passes by, the. Meaning 'critics make a noise, but it does not last'. Sir Peter Hall, the theatre director, was given to quoting this 'Turkish proverb' during outbursts of public hostility in the mid-1970s. In *Within a Budding Grove* – the 1924 translation of Marcel Proust's *A l'Ombre des Jeunes Filles en Fleurs* (1918) – C.K. Scott Moncrieff has: 'the fine Arab proverb, "The dogs may bark; the caravan goes on!"' Truman Capote entitled a book, *Dogs Bark: Public People and Private Places* (1973).

dog's breakfast/dinner, looking/ dressed up like a. When the first saying

(known by 1937) suggests something *scrappy* and the second (known by 1934) something *showy*, what are we led to conclude about the differing nature of a dog's breakfast and dinner? A dog's breakfast might well have consisted (before the invention of tinned dog food) of the left-over scraps of the household from the night before. So that takes care of that, except that there is also the phrase **cat's breakfast**, meaning a mess. Could both these derive from a belief that dogs and cats on occasions appear to eat their own sick?

A dog's dinner might well not have differed very much (and, on occasions, can mean the same as a dog's breakfast) except for the case described in 2 Kings 9 where it says of Jezebel that, after many years leading Ahab astray, she 'painted her face and tired her head', but failed to impress Jehu, whose messy disposal of her fulfilled Elijah's prophecy that the 'dogs shall eat Jezebel by the wall of Jezreel'.

Quite how one should distinguish between the two remains a problem, as is shown by this use of both phrases in a letter from Sir Huw Wheldon (23 July 1977), published in the book *Sir Huge* (1990) and concerning his TV series *Royal Heritage*: 'It was very difficult, and I feared it would be a Dog's Dinner. There was so much . . . to draw upon . . . I think it matriculated, in the event, into a Dog's Breakfast, more or less, & I was content.'

dogs of war, the. Phrase from Shakespeare's *Julius Caesar* (1599): 'Cry havoc and let slip the dogs of war' (III.i.273). Used as the title of a Frederick Forsyth novel (1974, film UK, 1980). Compare the title of the book *Cry Havoc!* (1933) by Beverley Nichols and the 1943 US film *Cry Havoc*.

doing. See HOW'M I ~?

doing up. See IT'LL BE ALL RIGHT . . . under *BAND WAGGON*.

— do it —ly. On 26 April 1979, the British *Sun* newspaper was offering a variety of T-shirts with nudging 'do it' slogans inscribed upon them. The craze was said to have started in the US. Whatever the case, scores of slogans 'promoting' various groups with this allusion to performing the sexual act appeared over the next several years on T-shirts, lapel-buttons, bumper-stickers and car-window stickers. In my *Graffiti* books (1979–86) I recorded some seventy, among them: 'Charles and Di do it by Royal Appointment'; 'Donyatt Dog Club does it with discipline and kindness'; 'Linguists do it orally'; 'Footballers do it in the bath afterwards'; 'Gordon does it in a flash'; 'Chinese want to do it again after twenty minutes'; 'City planners do it with their eyes shut'; 'Builders do it with erections'; 'Windsurfers do it standing up'; 'Printers do it and don't wrinkle the sheets'.

All this from simple exploitation of the innuendo in the phrase 'do it', which had perhaps first been seized on by Cole Porter in the song 'Let's Do It, Let's Fall in Love' (1928):

In shady shoals, English soles do it,
Goldfish in the privacy of bowls do it . . .

and then in a more personal parody by Noël Coward (in the 1940s):

Our leading writers in swarms do it
Somerset and all the Maughams do it . . .

Much later came the advertising slogan 'You can do it in an M.G.' (quoted in 1983).

Dolce Vita, La. The title of Federico Fellini's 1960 Italian film passed into English as a phrase suggesting a high-society life of luxury, pleasure, and self-indulgence. Meaning simply 'the sweet life', it is not clear how much of a set phrase it was in Italian (compare **dolce far niente** [sweet idleness]) before it was taken up by everybody else.

dollar. See ANOTHER DAY ANOTHER ∼; SIXTY–FOUR ∼ QUESTION.

Dolly Varden. A name given to a youthful style of girls' clothing, including slim-waisted, flowered-print dresses and flower-bedecked hats worn coquettishly tilted, with a ribbon under the chin. It comes from a character in the Charles Dickens novel *Barnaby Rudge* (1841) who was 'the very impersonation of good-humour and blooming beauty'. 'She's a regular Dolly Varden' was an expression, derived from the same character, for any

girl like that or who wore similar clothes. Rev. Francis Kilvert wrote in his diary: 'Dora looked very pretty in her Dolly Varden dress with blue scarf and blue veil' (18 September 1871).

Has sometimes been used as rhyming slang for 'garden'.

DOM. '*Deo, Optimo, Maximo*' [To God, most good, most great] – what you would find on bottles of Benedictine liqueur since the sixteenth century. Also short for 'Dirty Old Man'.

Domestos. See NINETY–NINE PER CENT . . .

Domine Deus. See MASS PHRASES.

dominion. See AND DEATH SHALL HAVE NO ∼.

domino theory. The old metaphor of falling over 'like a stack of dominoes' was first used in the context of Communist takeovers by the American political commentator, Joseph Alsop. Then President Eisenhower said at a press conference in April 1954: 'You have broader considerations that might follow what you might call the "falling domino" principle. You have a row of dominoes set up. You knock over the first one, and what will happen to the last one is that it will go over very quickly.' In South-East Asia, the theory was proved true to an extent in the 1970s. When South Vietnam collapsed, Cambodia then fell to the Khmer Rouge and Laos was taken over by the Communist-led Pathet Lao. In 1989 when one Eastern European country after another *renounced* Communism, there was talk of 'reverse domino theory'.

done. See BEEN THERE, ∼ THAT . . .

donkey's years. As in, 'I haven't seen her for donkey's years' – i.e. for a very long time (current by 1916). It is not very hard to see that what we have here is a distortion of the phrase 'donkey's ears' (which are, indeed, long). As such, what we have is a form of rhyming slang: donkey's = donkey's ears = years.

This also helps to explain the alternative expression, 'I haven't seen her **for yonks**', where 'yonks' may well be a distortion of year and donk(ey)s. Brewer, however, gives the less enjoyable explanation that 'donkey's years' is an allusion to the 'old tradition' that one never sees a dead donkey.

do not adjust your set (there is a fault). In the early days of British television, particularly in the late 1940s and early 1950s, technical breakdowns were a common feature of the evening's viewing. The BBC's caption **normal service will be resumed as soon as possible** became a familiar sight. The wording is still sometimes used in other contexts. As standards improved, it was replaced by the (usually more briefly displayed) phrase, 'There is a fault – do not adjust your set'. *Do Not Adjust Your Set* was the title of a children's comedy series on ITV in 1968, devised in part by some of the future MONTY PYTHON team.

do not fold, spindle or mutilate. When punched computer cards began to accompany bills and statements in the 1950s, computerization was looked on as a harbinger of the BRAVE NEW WORLD (though Bartlett used to date this somewhat bossy injunction to the 1930s). By the 1960s, the words evoked a machine age that was taking over. By the 1980s, the cards were no longer necessary. A slogan of the 1960s student revolution was: 'I am a human being – do not fold, spindle or mutilate me.' A graffito (quoted 1974) read: 'I am a masochist – please spindle, fold or mutilate.'

Do Not Fold Spindle or Mutilate was the title of a film (US, 1971).

do not pass 'Go'. A *Sunday Mirror* editorial (3 May 1981) stated: 'The laws of contempt are the ones under which editors and other media folk can be sent straight to jail without passing Go.' A businessman said to a woman who had paid for her husband to be beaten up (report of trial, *The Times*, 30 November 1982): 'If the police find out you are paying, you will go to jail, directly to jail, you will not pass "go" or collect £200.'

These two citations are testimony to the enduring use of Monopoly phraseology. Monopoly is the name of a board game

invented by an unemployed salesman, Charles Darrow, in 1929, the year of the Wall Street crash, and is based on fantasies of buying up real estate in Atlantic City. Players begin on the square marked 'Go', may possibly return to that square to 'collect $200 salary as you pass', or land on the 'Go to jail' square, or draw a 'Chance' card with the penalty:

GO TO JAIL
MOVE DIRECTLY TO JAIL
DO NOT PASS 'GO'
DO NOT COLLECT $200.

In the UK version, the sum is £200.

don't ask the price – it's a penny. The great British stores institution, Marks & Spencer, had its origins in a stall set up in Leeds market in 1884 by a 21-year-old Jewish refugee from Poland. Michael Marks's slogan has become part of commercial folklore. It was written on a sign over the penny section – not all his goods were that cheap. He had simply hit upon the idea of classifying goods according to price.

don't be fright! Catchphrase of Sirdani, the British radio magician (*sic*) in c 1944.

don't be vague – ask for Haig. The slogan for Haig whisky since c 1936. The origin is to some extent lost in a Scotch mist because many of the John Haig & Co. archives were destroyed during the Second World War. However, the agency thought to be responsible was C.J. Lytle Ltd. An ad survives from 1933 with the wording 'Don't be vague, order Haig'; another from 1935 with, 'Why be vague? Ask for Haig'; and it seems that the enduring form arose in about 1936.

It has been jocularly suggested that Haig's premium brand, Dimple (which is sold as Pinch in North America), should be promoted with the slogan, 'Don't be simple, ask for Dimple'.

don't call/ring us, we'll call/ring you. Verging on the cliché: what theatre directors say to auditionees, the implication being that 'we' will never actually get round to calling 'you'. Now more widely applied to anyone unwelcome seen to be asking a favour. The *OED2* finds no example before 1969. However, a *Punch* cartoon on 11 October 1961 showed the European Council of Ministers saying to a British diplomat: 'Thank you. Don't call us: we'll call you.'

Also used in this situation: **we'll let you know.**

don't do anything I wouldn't do. See under IF YOU CAN'T BE GOOD . . .

don't do it, Di. Slogan on a feminist badge issued in Britain prior to the wedding of Lady Diana Spenser to the Prince of Wales in 1981.

don't eat oysters unless there's an R in the month. 'The oyster is unseasonable and unwholesome in all months that have not the letter R in their name,' wrote Richard Buttes in *Diet's Dry Dinner* (1599). 'Though politics, like oysters, are only good in the R months . . .' – *Lord Chesterfield's Letters to Lord Huntingdon* (for 30 August 1769)(1923).

This is an old belief, hard to dispose of, but no longer tenable. Before modern refrigeration came along, oysters did 'go off' in the warmer months from May to August which, as it happens, do not have an R in them. Now oysters may be eaten at any time. As it was, some people allowed themselves to eat oysters in August by spelling it 'Orgust'.

don't force it, Phoebe! A catchphrase from British comedian Charlie Chester's BBC radio show *Stand Easy* (1946–50). From that show also came the name **Whippit Kwick**, a cat burglar in a 'radio strip cartoon'. Leslie Bridgmont, the producer, recalls in *Leslie Bridgmont Presents* (1949) how the name swept the country. Wherever he went on bus, Tube or train he would hear someone say, 'Who's that over there?', to which the reply would come, 'Whippit Kwick!' Chester remembered (1979): 'Bruce Woodcock, the boxer, used to run around the streets chanting the jungle chants from the same strip cartoon: **Down in the jungle, living in a tent,/Better than a pre-fab – no rent!** – that sort of thing. Once at Wembley, just before he threw a right to put the other fellow out for the

count, some wag in the audience yelled out, "Whippit Kwick!" he did – and it went in.'

Also from *Stand Easy* came **wotcher, Tish!/wotcher, Tosh!** – an exchange between two barrow boys, and yet another catchphrase: 'This was really a joke on my missus. My wife broke her arm and was sitting in the audience. I told Len Marten to keep coming up to me with the line **I say, what a smasher!** Then, at the end of the programme, the resolving gag was: "Len, what do you mean by all this, 'I say, what a smasher' business?" He said, "The blonde in the third row!" And there's this broken arm sticking out like a beacon. Strangely enough, I went down to Butlin's not long after and somebody dropped a pile of crockery. Of course the noise resounded all over the place and everybody shouted "I say, what a smasher!"'

Partridge/*Catch Phrases* finds the phrase earlier in a 1940 ad for Kolynos toothpaste and Partridge's *Dictionary of Forces' Slang* (1948) has the word 'smasher', meaning an attractive girl, as coming from the Scots 'a wee smasher'. Iona and Peter Opie in *The Lore and Language of Schoolchildren* (1959) show how the phrase penetrated, firstly, to 'Girls, 13, Swansea, 1952' who recited: 'I say, what a smasher,/Betty Grable's getting fatter,/Pick a brick and throw it at her./If you wish to steal a kiss,/I say, what a smasher.' And, secondly, to 'Boy, 11, Birmingham': 'I say what a smasher/Pick it up and slosh it at her./If you miss/Give her a kiss/I say what a smasher.'

Chester also used **I can hear you!** which arose when he noticed somebody talking about him in a rehearsal room.

don't forget the diver! Of all the many catchphrases sired by the BBC radio show ITMA, the one with the most interesting origin was spoken by Horace Percival as the Diver. It was derived from memories that the star of the show, Tommy Handley, had of an actual man who used to dive off the pier at New Brighton in the 1920s/30s. 'Don't forget the diver, sir, don't forget the diver,' the man would say, collecting money. 'Every penny makes the water warmer, sir.'

The radio character first appeared in 1940 and no lift went down for the next few years without somebody using the Diver's main catchphrase or his other one, **I'm going down now, sir!** – which bomber pilots in the Second World War would use when about to make a descent.

don't forget the fruit gums, mum! A slogan for Rowntree's Fruit Gums, 1958–61, and coined by copywriter Roger Musgrave at the S.T. Garland agency. Market research showed that most fruit gums were bought by women but eaten by children. Later on, the line fell foul of advertising watchdogs keen to save parents from nagging: accordingly, 'Mum' became 'chum'.

don't get mad, get even. This is one of several axioms said to come from the Boston-Irish political jungle or, more precisely, from Joseph P. Kennedy (1888–1969), father of President Kennedy. *Don't Get Mad Get Even* is the title of a book (1983) – 'a manual for retaliation' – by Alan Abel.

don't get me mad, see! Frequently used by those impersonating the actor James Cagney (1899–1986) in gangster mode, but I am unable to say which of his films he says it in. Sometimes remembered as, 'Jest don't make me mad, see!'

don't go down the mine, Daddy. A phrase used when warning anyone against doing anything. When Winston Churchill visited Berlin in 1945 and was preparing to enter Hitler's bunker, his daughter Mary said to him, 'Don't go down the mine, Daddy.' It comes from a tear-jerking ballad popular with soldiers during the First World War and written by Will Geddes and Robert Donnelly in 1910. The title is, correctly, 'Don't Go Down In the Mine, Dad'.

don't go near the water. Phrase (one of two) derived from the nursery rhyme (best known in the US):

> Mother, may I go out to swim?
> **Yes, my darling daughter**;
> Hang your clothes on a hickory limb,
> But don't go near the water.

Even Peter and Iona Opie were unable to date this rhyme. It may not go back beyond

1900. *Don't Go Near the Water* was the title of a film (US 1957) about sailors stationed on a South Pacific island – based on a William Brinkley novel. 'Yes, My Darling Daughter' was a popular song of 1941 – the Andrews Sisters recorded it – and there was also a play with the title in the late 1930s, subsequently filmed (US, 1939). *No, My Darling Daughter* was the title of a British film comedy (1961).

don't have a cow, man! See under SIMPSONS, THE.

don't leave home without it. See THAT'LL DO NICELY, SIR.

don't let Labour ruin it. See LIFE'S BETTER WITH THE CONSERVATIVES.

don't panic! (1) See under DAD'S ARMY. (2) Words written on the cover of the eponymous fictional guide featured in *The Hitch Hiker's Guide to the Galaxy*, the radio series (1978) by Douglas Adams.

don't read it – measure it. See ALL PUBLICITY IS GOOD . . .

don't say Brown – say Hovis. A slogan for Hovis bread, from the mid-1930s. One of the firm's paper bags of that period shows a radio announcer saying, 'Here's a rather important correction . . . I should have said Hovis and not just "brown".' The slogan was used in its final form from 1956 to 1964. It still reverberates: in May 1981, when a British golfer, Ken Brown, was deserted by his caddie during a championship, a *Sunday Mirror* headline was, 'Don't Say Brown, Say Novice'.

don't some mothers have 'em? The British comedian Jimmy Clitheroe (1916–73) was a person of restricted growth and with a high-pitched voice who played the part of a naughty schoolboy until the day he died. The BBC radio comedy programme *The Clitheroe Kid* which ran from 1957–72 popularized an old Lancashire – and possibly general North Country – saying, 'Don't some mothers have 'em?' In the form, 'Some mothers do 'ave 'em', the phrase was used in the very first edition of TV's *Coronation Street* in

1960 and later as the title of a Michael Crawford series on BBC TV (1974–9).

don't spit – remember the Johnstown flood. This turn-of-the-century Americanism is an admonition against spitting. The Johnstown flood of 31 May 1889 entered US folklore when a dam burst near Johnstown, Pennsylvania, and 2200 died. A silent film, *The Johnstown Flood*, was made in the US in 1926. Partridge/*Catch Phrases* finds that notices bearing this joke were exhibited in bars before Prohibition started in 1919. Safire quotes William Allen White's comment on the defeat of Alfred Landon in the 1936 US presidential election: 'It was not an election the country has just undergone, but a political Johnstown flood.'

don't teach your grandmother to suck eggs. Meaning 'don't try to tell people things which, given their age and experience, they might be expected to know anyway'. According to Partridge/*Slang*, variations of this very old expression include advice against instructing grandmothers to 'grope ducks', 'grope a goose', 'sup sour milk', 'spin', and 'roast eggs'. In 1738, Jonathan Swift's *Polite Conversation* had 'Go teach your grannam to suck eggs'.

I have heard it suggested that, in olden days, sucking eggs would be a particularly important thing for a grandmother to be able to do because, having no teeth, it would be all she was capable of.

don't throw the baby out with the bath water. Meaning 'don't get rid of the essential when disposing of the inessential'. There are several similar English expression, including 'to throw away the wheat with the chaff', 'to throw away the good with the bad', but this one seems to have caught on following its translation from the German by Thomas Carlyle in 1849. According to Wolfgang Mieder (*Western Folklore*, October 1991), the first written occurrence appears in the satirical book *Narrenbeschwörung* (1512). Chapter 81 is entitled '*Das kindt mit dem bad vß schitten*' [To throw the baby out with the bath water].

don't worry, be happy. Bobby McFerrin's song with this title became George Bush's unofficial campaign theme in the presidential election of 1988 and won the Grammy award for the year's best song. 'The landlord says the rent is late, he might have to litigate, but don't worry, be happy,' sang McFerrin, in a song which became a minor national anthem, reflecting a feeling in the US at the time.

The Times (8 March 1989) noted: 'The song has spawned a whole "happy" industry and re-launched the Smiley face emblem that emerged in America in the late 1960s and was taken up in Britain by the acid-house scene last year. Bloomingdales, the Manhattan department store, now features a "Don't worry, be happy shop".'

'Be happy, don't worry' was earlier a saying of Meher Baba (1894–1969), the so-called Indian God-Man.

don't you just love being in control? Originally a slogan from TV advertising for British Gas from 1991, this soon acquired catchphrase status in the UK, not least because of its scope for sexual innuendo. From the *Independent* (19 October 1992): 'England signally failed to achieve their stated [rugby union] goals. Perhaps disarranged by their new surroundings, England, who just love being in control, were frustrated by the resilience and organisation of the Canadians.' From the *Daily Telegraph* (5 April 1993): 'Most annoying of all is the circle of fire [in a National Theatre production of *Macbeth*], like a giant gas ring, which whooshes into jets of flame at certain key moments. It is ludicrously obtrusive and sometimes it doesn't seem to be working properly, adding to the viewer's sense of fretful alienation. As Alan Howard stands in the middle of it, looking haggard, you suddenly wonder if the whole dire production is actually an advertisement for British Gas. Will he suddenly flick his thumb and say "Don't you just love being in control?"'

Originally, the control element came from the fact that a gas appliance responds more quickly to its operator's demands than does an electrical one.

don't you know there's a war on? A response to complaints used by (Will)

Hatton and (Ethel) Manners portraying a Cockney chappie and a Lancashire lass in their British variety act of the 1940s. Fairly widely taken up, ironically *after* the Second World War. Somehow or other it found its way into the script of the US film *It's A Wonderful Life* (1946), where it is exclaimed by James Stewart. Partridge/*Catch Phrases* has the similar 'Remember there's a war on' dating from the First World War.

doobry, a. A 'thingy', a 'thingamy', a 'thingumajig', a 'thingumabob', a 'whatsit' – a word for when you can't think what to call an object (usually). Paul Beale in Partridge/*Slang* has it as **doobri**, 'an elaboration of *doofah*, a gadget' or, applied to a person, as the short form of 'doobri-firkin'. I think it was being said at Oxford in the 1960s and was certainly in use by the 1980s. It is ignored by the *OED2*.

dood. See I ~ IT.

dooks. See DUKES.

doom. See GLOOM AND ~.

doomed. See WE BE ~ under *ROUND THE HORNE*.

doomed I am, doomed. See under *DAD'S ARMY*.

door. See EVER-OPEN ~; NEVER DARKEN MY ~; OPEN THE ~, RICHARD under *ITMA*; SHUT THAT ~; WHEN ONE ~ CLOSES . . .

doornail. See DEAD AS A ~.

doors of perception, the. Phrase from William Blake, *The Marriage of Heaven and Hell* (c 1790): 'If the doors of perception [i.e. the senses] were cleansed, every thing would appear to man as it is, infinite.' This view was seized upon by proponents of drug culture in the 1960s. *The Doors of Perception* had been the title given to Aldous Huxley's book (1954) about his experiments with mescalin and LSD. From it was also derived the name of the US vocal/instrumental group The Doors.

doots. See I HAE ME ~.

Dorian Gray, a. A person who looks unnaturally young and well preserved. From the hedonistic character in Oscar Wilde's novel *The Picture of Dorian Gray* (1890; film US, 1945). He achieves eternal youth by the fact that his portrait ages on his behalf. Hence, also, those references to 'having a **portrait in the attic**' which tend to be made about such people.

Dorothy. See IS SHE A FRIEND OF ~?

do the right thing. *Do the Right Thing* was the title of film (US, 1989) about Black people in a Brooklyn slum. From *Harper's Index* (January 1990): 'Number of times the phrase "do the right thing" has been used in Congress since Spike Lee's film was released last June: 67/Number of times the phrase was used in reference to congressional pay rise: 16/Number of times it was used in reference to racial issues: 1.'

The British English equivalent would be **do the decent thing** (known by 1914), although 'do the right thing' seems almost as well established (known by the 1880s).

Is there a connection with First World War epitaphs, 'He trusted in God and tried to do the right' or with the older motto 'Trust in God, and do the Right'?

Double Diamond works wonders, a. A slogan for Double Diamond beer in the UK, from 1952. The double alliteration may have a lot to do with it, but it was also the singing of the slogan to the tune of 'There's a Hole in my Bucket' that made it one of the best-known of all.

double-o seven. See LICENSED TO KILL.

double your pleasure, double your fun. A slogan for Wrigley's Doublemint chewing gum, in the US, from 1959. However, about the same time, the signature tune of ITV's *Double Your Money* quiz included the line, 'Double your money, and double your fun'. The show was first transmitted in 1955.

doubt. See IF IN ~ . . .

Doubting Thomas, a. A sceptic who has to be given evidence in order to believe. An allusion to Saint Thomas, the apostle, who would not believe that Christ had risen from the dead until he had actually seen and touched the wounds from the Crucifixion (John 20:25). A relatively late coinage (known by 1883), having been preceded by such usages as 'wavering Thomas' and 'unbelieving Thomas'.

down a bit. See under BERNIE, THE BOLT!

downhearted. See ARE WE ~?

down in the forest something stirred. A gently mocking suggestion merely that something has happened (perhaps after prolonged inactivity) – and not without possible innuendo. The line comes from the song 'Down in the Forest' (1915) with words by H. Simpson and music by Sir Landon Ronald. And what was it that stirred? 'It was only the note of a bird.'

down in the jungle . . . See under DON'T FORCE IT, PHOEBE.

down memory lane. Once a pleasant phrase, now a journalistic cliché: 'The Ding-Dong special that spelled love for Sid and Jan Parker will take a trip down memory lane . . . to celebrate their 25th wedding anniversary. The happy couple will kiss and cuddle on the top deck of the No. 44 bus, just like they did when they were courting' (*Sun*, 15 October 1983).

The phrase seems to have developed from 'Memory Lane', the title of a popular waltz (1924) written by Buddy De Sylva, Larry Spier, and Con Conrad – not to be confused with 'Down Forget-Me-Not Lane' by Horatio Nicholls, Charlie Chester and Reg Morgan (1941). *Down Memory Lane* was the title of a compilation of Mack Sennett comedy shorts (US, 1949). *OED2* gives 'Down Memory Lane' as a 'title by Dannet and Rachel' (1954).

Accepting the GOP presidential nomination at Dallas, Texas (23 August 1984), Ronald Reagan said: 'Our opponents began this campaign hoping that America has a poor memory. Well, let's take them on a little stroll down memory lane. Let's remind them of how a 4.8 per cent inflation in 1976 became . . .'

down the hatch! Drinker's phrase before pouring the liquid down the throat. Possibly ex-Navy. Recorded by 1931.

— down, — to go! See IS IT BIGGER THAN A BREADBOX?

down to the (real) nitty-gritty. See LET'S GET DOWN . . .

do you come from Bardney? See BARDNEY.

do you come here often? Traditional chatting up line, common by the 1920s/30s. For a response, see under GOON SHOW.

do you know *me*? See THAT'LL DO NICELY, SIR.

do you know —?/No, but if you hum it, I'll pick out the tune/fake it. A comic exchange, current in the US and the UK by the 1960s. From BBC radio ROUND THE HORNE (29 May 1966): 'Do you know Limehouse?'/'No, but if you hum a few bars, I'll soon pick it up.' Compare the caption from a cartoon in *Punch* (26 October 1872) in which a 'Kirk Elder' asks, 'My friend, do you know the chief end of man?' A Scots piper replies, 'Na, I dinae mind the chune! Can you whistle it?'

do you know the Bishop of Norwich? A question traditionally addressed to a port drinker who is holding on to the bottle and not passing it round. Partridge/*Slang* lists a 'norwicher' as 'one who drinks too much from a shared jug . . . an unfair drinker'. Perhaps this is a subtle way of calling somebody such? Brewer also has the version: 'Do you know Dr Wright of Norwich?' Had there been a Dr Wright who was Bishop of Norwich? The nearest was Dr White (d 1632).

do you mind? See under RAY'S A LAUGH.

Do You Sincerely Want To Be Rich? The title of a book (1972) by Charles Raw *et al*, it was the question posed to his salesmen, during training, by Bernie Cornfeld (1928–95) who made his name and fortune selling investment plans in the 1960s. He spent 11 months in a Swiss jail before fraud charges against him were dropped.

dozen. See NINETEEN TO THE ∼.

drag (someone/thing) kicking and screaming into the twentieth century, to. For a well-known phrase, this is curiously little documented. The only example I have found in this precise form comes from an article by Kenneth Tynan written in 1959 and collected in *Curtains* (1961): 'A change, slight but unmistakable, has taken place; the English theatre has been dragged, as Adlai Stevenson once said of the Republican Party, kicking and screaming into the twentieth century.'

Tony Benn said during a by-election, fought on his right to renounce a peerage, in May 1961: 'It is given to Bristol in this election to wrench the parliamentary system away from its feudal origins, and pitchfork it kicking and screaming into the twentieth century.' Nobel chemist, Sir George Porter, said in a speech in September 1986: 'Should we force science down the throats of those that have no taste for it? Is it our duty to drag them kicking and screaming into the twentieth century? I am afraid it is.'

Obviously, this is a 'format' phrase that lends itself to subtle modification. From a sketch by Keith Waterhouse and Willis Hall in BBC TV *That Was the Week That Was* (1962–3 *seres*): 'The loveable cockney sparrer . . . drags us kicking and screaming back into the nienteenth century.' From the *Daily Telegraph* (11 September 1979): 'Mr Ian McIntyre, whose ambition was to bring Radio 4 kicking and screaming into the 1970s . . .'; from the *Washington Post* (19 January 1984): 'All [President Reagan] said before he was dragged kicking and screaming into the East Room was that he wouldn't call the Soviet Union an "evil empire" any more'; and from the same paper (19 December 1988): 'Still, Jones and Hawke, prodded by other corporate-minded partners, have dragged Arnold & Porter – sometimes kicking and screaming – into a 21st century mode of thinking, which they believe will position the firm to compete with firms that already have more than 1,000 lawyers.'

The nascent form can be found in a 1913 article by J.B. Priestley in *London Opinion*: '[By listening to ragtime] he felt literally dragged out of the nineteenth into the twentieth century.' (His use of 'literally' suggests that the idea of dragging from one century to another was already an established one.)

Dragnet. The American TV series *Dragnet* was made between 1951 and 1958 and revived 1967–9. It was largely the creation of Jack Webb (1920–82) who produced, directed and starred in it. As Police Sergeant Joe Friday he had a deadpan style which was much parodied. The show had first appeared on radio in 1949 and was said to draw its stories from actual cases dealt with by the Los Angeles police – hence the famous announcement: 'Ladies and gentlemen, the story you are about to hear is true. **Only the names have been changed to protect the innocent.**'

The signature tune was almost a catchphrase in itself – 'Dum-de-dum-dum'. Joe Friday had a staccato style of questioning: **just the facts, ma'am** or **all we want is the facts, ma'am**. These were probably the first big phrases to catch on in Britain from the onset of commercial TV in 1955.

And to add to the list of memorable phrases, here is the opening narration from a typical TV episode: 'Ladies and gentlemen, the story you are about to see is true, the names have been changed to protect the innocent . . . **This is the city.** Everything in it is one way or the other. There's no middle ground – narrow alleys, broad highways; mansions on the hill, shacks in the gulleys; people who work for a living and people who steal. These are the ones that cause me trouble. **I'm a cop.** It was Monday April 17. We were working the day-watch on a forgery detail. My partner: Frank Smith. The boss is Captain Welch. **My name's Friday . . .**'

The phrase 'all we want is the facts' was already a cliché when importunate journalists were represented in theatrical sketches. In 'Long-Distance Divorce', a revue sketch from *Nine Sharp* (1938), Herbert Farjeon put it in the mouth of a British reporter interviewing a Hollywood star.

Dragon Lady. Nancy Reagan, when US First Lady in the 1980s, attracted criticism for what was perceived as being her manipulative and frosty style and was given this nickname, as were also Imelda Marcos, wife of Ferdinand Marcos, ruler of the Philippines until his ousting in 1986, and Michele Duvalier, wife of 'Baby Doc' Duvalier, ruler of Haiti until his fall from power, also in 1986. The original 'Dragon Lady' was a beautiful Chinese temptress in the American comic strip 'Terry and the Pirates' (1934–73).

dragon's teeth, to sow. To stir up trouble – especially by doing something which appears intended to bring about the opposite. From the Greek myth of Cadmus who, having killed the dragon guarding the fountain of Dirce, sowed its teeth. These sprang up as fierce warriors. Milton alludes to the story in *Areopagitica* (1644).

draw. See HANG, ~ AND QUARTER.

drawers. See ALL KID GLOVES . . .

drawing. See BACK TO THE ~ BOARD; ELEPHANT IN YOUR ~ ROOM.

dreaded lergy, the. See under *GOON SHOW.*

dream. See LIKE A ~ COME TRUE.

dreaming. See I'M ~ OH MY DARLING LOVE OF THEE!

dream is over, the. A phrase very much associated with John Lennon. He used it in his song 'God' (1970): 'And so, dear friends, you'll just have to carry on, the dream is over.' Also, in the 1970s he reflected on the split-up of the Beatles and the end of the 1960s: 'And so, dear friends, you'll just have to carry on. The dream is over . . . nothing's changed. Just a few of us are walking around with longer hair.'
Compare the **dream is ended.** From C.S. Lewis, *The Last Battle* (1956): 'The term is over: the holidays have begun. The dream is ended: this is the morning.' Compare also PARTY'S OVER, THE.

dream on, baby, dream on. Meaning, 'if you really believe that, then carry on kidding yourself'. From the *Independent on Sunday* (24 November 1991), here is the country and western singer Tammy Wynette talking about an embarrassing encounter with an ex-husband who came up and asked her to autograph a photo for him: 'I thought, "Now what do I say here?" and then it hit me like a light and I wrote – "Dream on, baby, dream on!" . . . Sweet revenge at last.'
I would suspect a black American blues origin, if not in fact a country and western one. As simply, *Dream On* the phrase became the title of an 'American adult [TV] comedy series', with David Bowie and Tom Berenger, broadcast in the UK in 1991, while 'Dream On' has been the title of songs from Lynn Anderson (1990) right back to Herman's Hermits (1965). 'Dream On Baby' was recorded by Rosco Gordon in Memphis, Tenn. in the 1950s, while 'Dream On, My Love, Dream On' was recorded by The Four Lads in 1955.

dreams. See SUCH STUFF AS ~ ARE MADE ON.

dream the impossible dream, to. The expression derives from a line in the song 'The Impossible Dream' in the musical about Don Quixote, *Man of La Mancha* (1965, film US, 1972).

dress. See LITTLE BLACK ~; PLEASE ADJUST YOUR ~ BEFORE LEAVING; WHEN ARE YOU GOING TO FINISH OFF THAT ~?

dressed. See ALL ~ UP AND NOWHERE TO GO.

dressed up to the nines. i.e. 'very smartly dressed'. This may have come to us via a pronunciation shift. If you were to say dressed up 'to then eyne', that would mean, in Old English, 'dressed up to the eyes' (*eyne* being the old plural of eye). The snag with this is that no examples of the phrase occur before the eighteenth century.
I do not accept the *Longman Dictionary of English Idioms* (1979) definition which suggests that it refers to the setting of a standard with ten as the highest point one can reach. (If you were up to nine, you were

very nearly the best. Compare the catchphrase, 'How would you rate it/her/ anything ON A SCALE OF ONE TO TEN?' or 'she's a ten' which was all the rage after the film *10* in 1979.)

Nor do I agree with Neil Ewart, *Everyday Phrases* (1983) that it has anything to do with setting oneself up to match the Nine Muses of classical mythology; nor with Partridge/*Slang* that it has to do with the mystic number nine; nor with whoever suggested that as the 99th Regiment of Foot was renowned for smartness of dress, anyone well turned out was 'dressed up [to equal] the nines'.

The origin remains a bit of a mystery.

dribble. See WIZARD OF THE ∼.

drink. See ANOTHER LITTLE ∼ . . . ; EAT ∼ AND BE MERRY; I'LL ∼ TO THAT.

Drinka Pinta Milka Day. The target was to get everyone drinking one pint of milk a day and the slogan was a piece of bath-tub inspiration that came from the client, namely Bertrand Whitehead, executive officer of the National Milk Publicity Council of England and Wales in 1958. The creative department of Mather & Crowther took an instant dislike to it, but Francis Ogilvy, the agency chairman, insisted on it being used despite the protests.

It was the kind of coinage to drive teachers and pedants mad, but eventually 'a pinta' achieved a kind of respectability when accorded an entry in *Chambers' Twentieth Century Dictionary* and others (the *OED2* in due course).

drive a coach and horses through something, to. Meaning 'to overturn something wantonly, and to render it useless'. Sir Stephen Rice (1637–1715), a Roman Catholic Chief Baron of the Exchequer is quoted as saying in 1672: 'I will drive a coach and six horses through the Act of Settlement.'

In 1843, Charles Dickens wrote in *A Christmas Carol*: 'You may talk vaguely about driving a coach-and-six up a good old flight of stairs, or through a bad young Act of Parliament . . .' (which might seem to allude to the first example).

From an editorial in *The Times*

concerning the premature police jubilation over the arrest of a man suspected of being the YORKSHIRE RIPPER in January 1981 – jubilation which was 'to drive a number of coaches and horses through the contempt laws: the popular press seems to have decided that this was such a fantastic story that they would publish what they wanted and let the lawyers pick up the pieces later'.

From *The Times* (22 October 1983): 'Labour lawyers argued that Mr Justice Mervyn Davies had "driven a coach and horses" through Conservative legislation designed to limit the scope of trade disputes and outlaw political strikes, by refusing to ban the "blacking" of Mercury.'

drive/go/ride/sail off into the sunset, to. To end happily, and probably romantically. Derived from the visual cliché of the silent film era when a united couple would often do just this at the end of a story. Used inevitably when Ronald Reagan retired from the White House: 'As Reagan rides off into the sunset we offer two opposing verdicts on his eight years in office . . .' (*Observer*, 15 January 1989). *OED2*'s first citation is from 1967.

Dr Livingstone, I presume? Now a catchphrase used on meeting someone unexpectedly or after an arduous journey, this famous greeting was put by Sir Henry Morton Stanley, the British explorer and journalist, to the explorer and missionary Dr David Livingstone at Ujiji, Lake Tanganyika on 10 November 1871. Stanley had been sent by the *New York Herald* to look for Livingstone who was missing on a journey in central Africa. In *How I Found Livingstone* (1872), Stanley described the moment: 'I would have run to him, only I was a coward in the presence of such a mob – would have embraced him, only, he being an Englishman, I did not know how he would receive me; so I did what cowardice and false pride suggested was the best thing – walked deliberately to him, took off my hat and said: "Dr Livingstone, I presume?" "Yes," said he, with a kind smile, lifting his cap slightly.'

droit de seigneur. Phrase used when a man tries to exercise some imagined 'right' in order to force a woman to go to bed with him, as perhaps a boss might do with a secretary. The general assumption is that this 'right' dates from the days when medieval barons would claim first go at the newly-wedded daughters of their vassals – the so-called *ius primae noctis* [law of the first night]. In the play *Le Mariage de Figaro* (1784) by Beaumarchais, the Count has just renounced his right and is beginning to regret it. In March 1988, it was reported that Dr Wilhelm Schmidt-Bleibtreu of Bonn had looked into the matter very thoroughly and discovered there was never any such legal right and that reliable records of it ever happening were rare. He concluded that the whole thing was really a male fantasy – and it was exclusively men who had used the phrase – though he didn't rule out the possibility that sex of the kind *had* taken place between lords and brides in one or two cases, legally or otherwise.

drop. See GOOD TO THE LAST ~; TURN ON, TUNE IN, ~ OUT.

drop a clanger, to. 'To say something socially embarrassing or commit an act of similar kind'. According to a photograph caption in the *Sunday Times* Magazine (30 January 1983): 'The nerveless men who worked on the construction of New York's Woolworth Building in 1912 had nightmares of dropping a girder, or "clanger" in the phrase they gave to the language.' Partridge/*Slang* calls 'clanger' here a synonym for 'testicle', but derives it from the inoffensive 'drop a brick'. *OED2*'s first citation is from 1958.

drop dead! Said by (mostly) young persons in almost any situation to someone with whom they are in disagreement. Partridge/*Catch Phrases* correctly notes that it is short for 'Why don't you drop dead!' and dates it from the US in the late 1930s. The earliest *OED2* citation is from a John O'Hara story of 1934.

Leo Rosten in *Hooray for Yiddish* (1982) draws attention to the Yiddish equivalent *Ver derharget!*, meaning 'get yourself killed'. As he also suggests, this is a vigorous version of 'Fuck you!' and the more useful because its component words are perfectly respectable. He points to the enormously impactful use of the phrase as the Act Two

curtain line of Garson Kanin's play *Born Yesterday* (1946). Judy Holliday said 'Du-rop du-ead!' – and 'the slow, sweet, studied rendition was stupendous. Waspish ladies have been tossing "Drop dead!" into their phones (to obscene callers) and as retorts (to abusive cabbies) ever since.'

Latterly, the expression **drop-dead gorgeous** has become popular, presumably American, perhaps from a film script, to describe (usually) a woman's good looks – the sort sufficient to stop the traffic if not actually stun the beholder with extreme prejudice. From the *Washington Post* (23 December 1986): 'In *No Mercy* . . . Jillette, a maverick Chicago cop . . . hears that the woman (Kim Basinger) is drop-dead gorgeous. That's all Jillette needs to hear. He's that kind of guy.' From the *Guardian* (16 June 1990): 'Today's 12-year-olds . . . [have] an insatiable appetite for snog-worthy dream-guys. All groovin', slammin', drop-dead gorgeous kickin' lads – for in the stylised world of the teenage magazines, no young man is ever simply good-looking.' From the *Sunday Telegraph* (5 January 1992): 'Take the issue of [Michelle Pfeiffer's] beauty, for example. She is indeed drop-dead-gorgeous with flawless, natural beauty which is different from the striking, often eccentric looks you find among top models.'

dropping the pilot. Used to mean 'dispensing with a valued leader', this phrase comes from the caption to a *Punch* cartoon that appeared on 29 March 1890 and showed Kaiser Wilhelm II leaning over the side of a ship as his recently disposed-of Chancellor, Otto von Bismarck, dressed as a pilot, walked down steps to disembark. Bismarck had been forced to resign following disagreements over home and foreign policy. The phrase was also used as the title of a poem on the same subject. From the *Independent* (12 May 1990): 'Kenneth Baker, the Conservative chairman, yesterday called on Tories to stop idle speculation about the party leadership . . . "We have moved through difficult waters . . . We should not, we must not, we will not drop the pilot."'

drop the gun, Looey! Alistair Cooke writing in *Six Men* (1977) remarked of Humphrey Bogart: 'He gave currency to another phrase with which the small fry of the English-speaking world brought the neighbourhood sneak to heel: "Drop the gun, Looey!"'

Quite how Bogart did this, Cooke does not reveal. We have Bogart's word for it: 'I never said, "Drop the gun, Louie"' (quoted in Ezra Goodman, *Bogey: The Good-Bad Guy*).

It's just another of those lines that people would like to have heard spoken but which never were. At the end of *Casablanca* (1942) what Bogart says to Claude Rains (playing Captain Louis Renault) is: 'Not so fast, Louis.' Ironically, it is *Renault* who says: 'Put that gun down.'

drowning man, his whole life passes before the eyes of a. A common belief, origins unknown. 'It is said that a drowning man sees the whole of his life in a flash,' – James Agate, *Ego* (1935). '[Attended] *a ball*, my dearest Colonel . . . I must say I felt like a drowning man, the whole of my past life was there' – letter from Nancy Mitford (3 February 1946).

drugs. See SEX'N'DRUGS'N'ROCK'N'ROLL.

drum. See PUT A PENNY ON THE ~.

drummed out of. See FACE THE MUSIC.

drummer. See DIFFERENT DRUMMER . . .

dry. See NOT A ~ EYE IN THE HOUSE.

Dubuque. See LITTLE OLD LADY FROM ~.

Duchess. See 'HELL,' SAID THE ~ . . .

duck. See CAN A ~ SWIM?; DYING ~ IN A THUNDER STORM; LAME ~ ; IF IT LOOKS LIKE A ~ . . . ; WANNA BUY A ~?

duck soup. An American phrase meaning 'anything simple or easy, a cinch' or 'a gullible person, easily victimized, a pushover'. When *Duck Soup* was used as the title of a Marx Brothers' movie (US, 1933), Groucho admitted that he did not understand it. Nevertheless, he explained: 'Take two turkeys, one goose, four cabbages, but no duck, and mix them together. After one taste, you'll duck soup

for the rest of your life.' The film's director Leo McCarey had earlier made a Laurel and Hardy picture with the same title.

due to circumstances beyond our control. Now, a cliché of apology. The 1st Duke of Wellington used the phrase, 'Circumstances over which I have no control' in an 1839 letter. Charles Dickens had Mr Micawber talk of 'circumstances beyond my individual control' in *David Copperfield* (1849–50). The broadcaster Fred W. Friendly entitled a critical survey of American TV, *Due to Circumstances Beyond Our Control* (1967), presumably from the TV announcer's, 'We regret we are unable to proceed with the scheduled programme, due to . . .'

dukes/dooks up, to put one's. To put one's fists up as though preparing for a fight. Describing a summit between Soviet and US leaders, *Time* (20 October 1986) stated: 'Reagan and Gorbachev both came to office not with their hands outstretched but with their dukes up.' If 'dukes' means 'fists', why so? One theory is that because the 1st Duke of Wellington had such a large nose, a 'duke' became a synonym for one. Then, so this theory goes, a man's fist became a 'duke buster'. In time this was shortened, and fists became 'dukes'.

Morris prefers another theory: that the use derives from Cockney rhyming slang, viz. 'Duke of York's' ('forks' meaning 'fingers' – standing for the whole hand or fist). *OED2* has the expression by 1874. Winston Churchill neatly played on the phrase in a public speech about House of Lords reform on 4 September 1909: 'In the absence of any commanding voice, the Tory party have had to put up their "dooks".' A report of the speech adds: 'Great laughter and a voice: "What about your grandfather?"' (Churchill's grandfather was the Duke of Marlborough).

Dulce et decorum est pro patria mori. Meaning 'it is sweet and honourable to die for one's country'. From Horace, *Odes*, III.ii.13. Frequently put in the shortened form '*pro patria mori*' on the graves of those killed on active service. Also a family motto. Wilfred Owen treated the saying with savage irony in his 1917 poem 'Dulce et Decorum est':

> If you could hear, at every jolt, the blood
> Come gargling from the froth-corrupted lungs,
> Obscene as cancer, bitter as the cud
> Of vile, incurable sores on innocent tongues, -
> My friend, you would not tell with such high zest
> To children ardent for some desperate glory,
> The old Lie: Dulce et decorum est
> Pro patria mori.

dull it isn't. A slogan for London's Metropolitan police, 1972. The day after the brief TV and poster campaign using this curiously memorable slogan started, it was apparent that the phrase was catching on. A senior Scotland Yard officer told me that a young policeman went to break up a fight at White Hart Lane football ground. Having seized a young hooligan, the constable emerged, dishevelled but triumphant from the mêlée. A voice from the crowd cried out, 'Dull it effing isn't, eh?'

The format sometimes recurs: '*Casualty* it isn't' – from the front cover of *Radio Times* (16 April 1994).

dumb. See KEEP MUM, SHE'S NOT SO ~ under BE LIKE DAD . . .

Dunkirk spirit, the. *OED2* does not find this phrase until 1956, though it does find 'to do a Dunkirk' (meaning 'to extract oneself from disaster') as early as 1944. Both phrases allude to the evacuation from the northern French town of Dunkerque/Dunkirk in May/June 1940. Retreating in the face of the German advance, British and Allied troops had a remarkable escape in an *ad hoc* rescue by small boats. About 338,000 were rescued in this way. It was, in anybody's language a defeat, but almost at once was seen as a triumph. Harold Nicolson wrote to his wife on 31 May: 'It is a magnificent feat once you admit the initial misery of the thing.' Winston Churchill, in his 'We shall never surrender' speech to the House of Commons on 4 June, warned: 'We must be very careful not to assign to this deliverance the attributes of a victory. Wars are not won by evacuations. But there was a

victory inside this deliverance which should be noted.'

Harold Wilson said in the House of Commons, on 26 July 1961: 'I have always deprecated . . . in crisis after crisis, appeals to the Dunkirk spirit as an answer to our problems.' No sooner had he become the British Prime Minister than he said in a speech to the Labour Party Conference (12 December 1964): 'I believe that the spirit of Dunkirk will once again carry us through to success.'

Dunmow Flitch. See BRING HOME THE BACON.

dunny, country. See under AS BUSY AS . . .

Duran Duran. The name of a British vocal/instrumental group that flourished in the early 1980s, derives from the name of a character – a lost scientist – in the French comic strip *Barbarella* (1962). He also featured in the film (1967).

dust. See ~ BEFORE THE BROOM under AGE BEFORE BEAUTY; PALM WITHOUT THE ~ .

dustbin of history, the. (sometimes **dustheap/scrapheap**). The fate to which you might wish to consign your opponents or their ideas. The phrase was used by Trotsky in his *History of the Russian Revolution*, Vol. 3, Chap. 10 (1933): 'You [the Mensheviks] are pitiful isolated individuals; you are bankrupts; your role is played out. Go where you belong from now on – into the dustbin of history.'

In a similar coinage, Charles Dickens reflected on Sir Robert Peel's death in 1850: 'He was a man of merit who could ill be spared from the Great Dust Heap down at Westminster.' Augustine Birrell, politician and writer (d 1933), wrote of 'that great dust-heap called "history"' in his essay on Carlyle.

dwarfs. See SEVEN ~ .

dying duck in a thunderstorm, like a. As a description of a person's forlorn appearance, *OED2* finds 'like a duck in thunder' in 1802, and the more familiar form in Sir Walter Scott's *Peveril of the Peak* in 1822. By 1843-4, the phrase was sufficiently well known for Charles Dickens to allude to it in *Martin Chuzzlewit*: 'His eye . . . with something of that expression which the poetry of ages has attributed to a domestic bird, when breathing its last amid the ravages of an electric storm' (Chap. 10).

dynamite. See THESE ARE ~!

· E ·

each and every one of us/you. Mostly American and especially political periphrastic use – dating from the Nixon era at least. Harold Washington on becoming Mayor of Chicago in May 1983: 'I'm a peacemaker who reaches out to each and every one of you.'

eagle. See LEGAL ∼.

eagle day. (1) An American term for 'pay day', dating from the armed forces use in the Second World War. As with the expressions **when the eagle flies** and the **day the eagle shits**, the reference is to the eagle emblem on US currency. (2) Eagle Day [*Adler Tag*] was the German code word that would have signalled an invasion of Britain, mooted in 1940 but never launched. The main attack plan was known as *Adlerangriff* [Attack of the Eagle]. The overall operation was code-named *Seelöwe* [Sea Lion].

Eagle has landed, the. In July 1969, when the lunar module bearing Neil Armstrong touched down for the first ever moon visit, he declared: 'Tranquillity Base here – the Eagle has landed' ('Eagle' was the name of the craft, after the US national symbol). Subsequently and rather inappropriately, *The Eagle Has Landed* became the title of a novel (1975; film UK, 1976). Jack Higgins fancifully suggested in an Author's Note that Heinrich Himmler was informed on 6 November 1943 that 'The Eagle has landed' – meaning that a small force of German paratroops had safely landed in England in order to kidnap Winston Churchill.

A headline from the *Observer* Magazine, 24 June 1990 (on a profile of the tycoon and crook, Robert Maxwell): 'The Ego Has Landed'.

ear. See EYES AND ∼S OF THE WORLD; IN YOUR SHELL-LIKE ∼; WALLS HAVE ∼S.

early. See CHRISTMAS HAS COME ∼ . . . ; ∼ BATH under UP AND UNDER.

earner. See NICE LITTLE ∼.

earth. See DID THE ∼ MOVE . . . ; GONE TO ∼; GREATEST SHOW ON ∼.

easier for a camel to go through the eye of a needle, it is. This biblical phrase from Matthew 19:24 and Mark 10:25 continues: '. . . than for a rich man to enter into the kingdom of God'. The Koran contains a similar view and in Rabbinical writings there is the similar expression 'to make an *elephant* pass through the eye of a needle' – which also appears in an Arab proverb. So why this camel/elephant confusion? Probably because the word for 'camel' in older Germanic languages, including Old English, was almost like the modern word for 'elephant' (OE *olfend* 'camel'). In this biblical saying, however, it is probable that neither camel nor elephant was intended. The original Greek word should probably have been read as *kamilos* 'a rope', rather than *kamelos*, 'a camel'. The difficulty of threading a rope through the eye of a needle makes a much neater image. (Compare ELEPHANT NEVER FORGETS).

eastern. See FULL OF ∼ PROMISE.

East is red, the. A theme song of the Chinese Cultural Revolution (1966–9) was 'The East Is Red'. When the first Chinese space satellite was launched in April 1970, it circled the earth, broadcasting the message: '*Tung fang hung – Mao Tse-tung*' [The east is red – Mao Tse-tung]. The song begins:

The East turns red, day is breaking,
Mao Tse-tung arises over Chinese soil . . .

East of Suez. Territory, especially that belonging to the British Empire as it was in

India and the East, and which was usually reached through the Suez Canal (opened in 1869). In the poem 'Mandalay' (1892), Rudyard Kipling wrote: 'Ship me somewhere east of Suez', and that would appear to be the origin of the phrase. John Osborne entitled a play set on a 'sub-tropical island neither Africa nor Europe', *West of Suez* (1971).

easy. See under AS BUSY AS . . . ; LIFE WASN'T MEANT TO BE ∼.

ea-sy, ea-sy! Crowd chant. I recall it being used by supporters of candidates at the declaration in the Hillhead, Glasgow by-election of 1982. More usually to be heard from football crowds. The Scotland World Cup Squad recorded a song called 'Easy, Easy' in 1974.

eat. See BET YOU CAN'T ∼ JUST ONE; YOU ARE WHAT YOU ∼.

eat crow, to. Meaning 'to have to do something distasteful', it refers to an incident in the British-American war of 1812–14. During a ceasefire, a New England soldier went hunting and crossed over into British lines where, finding no better game, he shot a crow. An unarmed British officer encountered the American and, by way of admiring his gun, took hold of it. He then turned it on him and forced him to eat part of the crow.

eat, drink and be merry (for tomorrow we die). From Isaiah 22:13: 'Let us eat and drink, for tomorrow we shall die.' Brewer comments: 'A traditional saying of the Egyptians who, at their banquets, exhibited a skeleton to the guests to remind them of the brevity of life.' Ecclesiastes 8:15 has: 'A man hath no better thing under the sun, than to eat, and to drink, and to be merry,' and Luke 12:19: 'Take thine ease, eat, drink and be merry.'

eat humble pie, to. Meaning 'to submit to humiliation', the 'humbles' or 'umbles' were those less appealing parts of a deer (or other animal) which had been killed in a hunt. They would be given to those of lower rank and perhaps served as 'humble pie' or 'umble pie'. A coincidence then that

'humble pie' should have anything to do with being 'humble'. Appropriately, it is Uriah Heep in Charles Dickens, *David Copperfield*, Chap. 39 (1849–50), who says: 'I got to know what umbleness did, and I took to it. I ate umble pie with an appetite.'

Eating People is Wrong. The title of Malcolm Bradbury's novel (1959) comes from the song 'The Reluctant Cannibal' by Michael Flanders and Donald Swann, featured in the revue *At the Drop of a Hat* (1956).

eat my shorts! See under SIMPSONS, THE.

—, eat your heart out! A minor singer having just finished a powerful ballad might exult defiantly, 'Frank Sinatra, eat your heart out!' Partridge/*Catch Phrases* glosses it as: 'Doesn't *that* make you jealous, fella!' As something said *to* another person, this expression acquired popularity in the mid-twentieth century largely, I would say, through its American show business use.

As such, it is probably another of those Jewish expressions popularized by showbiz. Originally, 'to eat one's (own) heart out', simply meaning 'to pine', it was current in English by the sixteenth century, and Leo Rosten in *Hooray for Yiddish* (1983) finds it in the Yiddish *Es dir oys s'harts*. Apparently, Diogenes Laertius ascribed to Pythagoras the saying 'Do not eat your heart' meaning 'do not waste your life in worrying'.

Ebenezer. See RAISE ONE'S ∼.

Eccles, shut up. See under GOON SHOW.

ecky thump! (1) Supposedly a North of England exclamation uttered in place of an actual oath. From the *Guardian* (21 March 1991): 'Jackanory stuff is for wimps,' says [Bernard] Manning]. "Grown men that work on building sites don't want to hear ecky thump and ooh dammit. They don't talk like that on building sites."' I have no idea what the derivation of this euphemistic phrase is. (2) An adjectival phrase used to describe whatever is characteristic of North of England culture – i.e. brass bands, slag heaps, flat caps, *Coronation Street*, black puddings, ferrets down the trouser, and so on. In about 1974, I recall hearing a senior

BBC executive who, like several of his ilk, was a Hungarian refugee, opining that something was 'a bit ecky thump'. I concluded that he had been completely assimilated into our culture.

J. Wright's *English Dialect Dictionary* (c 1900) gives 'ecky' as a 'mild oath or rather meaningless expression . . . "the ecky", "go to ecky" . . .', but gives no clue as to how the 'thump' came to be grafted on to the expression. Note, however, that 'thump' is a Yorkshire word for a festival, wake, feast and there is also an obsolete expression (though not Yorkshire) 'to cry thump', meaning 'to make a thumping sound'.

economical with the truth, to be. To dissemble, tell a lie. On 18 November 1986, the British Cabinet Secretary, Sir Robert Armstrong, was being cross-examined in the Supreme Court of New South Wales. The British Government was attempting to prevent publication in Australia of a book about MI5, the British Secret Service. Defence counsel Malcolm Turnbull asked Sir Robert about the contents of a letter he had written which had been intended to convey a misleading impression. 'What's a "misleading impression"?' inquired Turnbull. 'A sort of bent untruth?' Sir Robert replied: 'It is perhaps being economical with the truth.' This explanation was greeted with derision not only in the court but in the world beyond, and it looked as though a new euphemism for lying had been coined.

In fact, Sir Robert had prefaced his remark with, 'As one person said . . .' and, when the court apparently found cause for laughter in what he said, added: 'It is not very original, I'm afraid.' In March 1988, (by now) Lord Armstrong said in a TV interview that he had no regrets about using the phrase. He said, again, it was not his own, but Edmund Burke's, though an earlier use is by Samuel Pepys in 1669/70.

economy. See COMMANDING HEIGHTS OF THE ~.

ecstasy. See AGONY AND THE ~.

Eddie. See ARE YOU READY, ~?

Eddie the Eagle. Nickname of Michael David 'Eddie' Edwards (b 1964), a short, myopic British plasterer, who finished 56 out of 56 in the ski jump at the 1988 Winter Olympics and became briefly something of a hero – for trying against all the odds and still coming last.

Eden. See ANTHONY ~; under — MUST GO!

edge. See CUTTING ~.

Edge, Celtic. See CELTIC FRINGE.

Edinburgh. See ATHENS OF THE NORTH.

Edmond. TEA ~? under MILK?

Edna. See AUNT ~.

Educating Archie. Bizarre though the idea of ventriloquism on radio may be, this show, starring Peter Brough and his wooden dummy Archie Andrews, was first broadcast by the BBC on 6 June 1950 and ran for ten years. It was a noted breeding ground for young entertainers, and catchphrases abounded.

The 'catchphrase of the year' in 1951, according to Peter Brough, was spoken by Tony Hancock as one of the dummy's long line of 'tutors'. **Flippin' kids!** he would say. Indeed, 'The Lad 'imself' was billed as 'Tony (Flippin' Kids) Hancock' before moving on to his own shows, which more or less eschewed the use of catchphrases.

During his period as Archie's tutor, Max Bygraves made a splash with **I've arrived – and to prove it, I'm here!** (which formed part of his bill matter when he appeared at the London Palladium in 1952) and **a good idea . . . son!** (also incorporated in a song). Bygraves told me (1980): 'None of them were planned. They just came up in the reading. When Archie read a line, it was so stilted, I would ape him. This happened a couple of times and people sensed I was reading the line rather than saying it. They're still saying it today, a lot of people.'

Robert Moreton (1922–c 1952) had a brief taste of fame as another of the tutors and was noted for his *Bumper Fun Book*, out of which he would quote jokes. His catchphrase was **Oh, get in there,**

Moreton! Alas, after only a year he was dropped from the show, was unable to get other work and committed suicide.

For a while, Beryl Reid played Monica – Archie's posh, toothy, schoolgirl friend, who would introduce herself by saying **my name's Monica!** and would declare **Priscilla – she's my best friend and I** *hate* **her!** (See also AS THE ART MISTRESS SAID TO THE GARDENER!) Beryl told me in 1979: 'Even though I've done so many other things, straight acting parts and so on, people always remember these little phrases and want me to say them still.'

Above all, Beryl's Monica seems to have given rise to the expression **jolly hockey sticks!** – first used as an exclamation and then adjectivally to describe a type of woman – public school, gushing, games-playing and enthusiastic. Beryl claims to have coined it: 'I can't write comedy material . . . but I know what sort of thing my characters should say!' In this case she seems to have lighted upon a masterly phrase which has entered the language (compare OH, JOLLY D!)

Having established Monica, Beryl wanted to find another character from a different social class. This turned out to be Marlene from Birmingham, complete with Brum accent and girlfriend, Deirdre. She helped establish the American import IT SENDS ME! as the archetypical 1950s phrase for the effect of music on the hearts and minds of the young. She also had a wonderful way of saying **good evening, each!** and **it's terrific!** (pronounced 'turreefeek').

Following his success as the gormless private in TV's *The Army Game*, Bernard Bresslaw was a natural choice as another of Archie's educators. Usually preceded by the sound of heavy footsteps he would arrive and give his 'thicko' greeting, **hello, it's me – Twinkletoes!**

Towards the end of the run, Dick Emery made his mark as more than one character in the show. As Mr Monty, he would say, **we've got a right one 'ere!** – a familiar phrase also employed at one time and another by Tony Hancock, Frankie Howerd and Bruce Forsyth. In 1959, Emery was saying, as 'grimble', **oh, I was livid – livid I was – I wasn't half livid!**

ee, bah gum! A Lancastrian/North of England version – though probably more often attributed mockingly by outsiders – of the old oath 'by gum' (possibly a contraction of 'by God Almighty', known by 1806). The Yorkshire comedian Dick Henderson used it in a monologue about first meeting his wife (probably 1920s): 'Apart from that she has one very good point – ee, by gum, she can cook.' In 1994, I was told what was described as a 'Yorkshire playground rhyme': 'Eeh bah gum/I saw me father's bum./I carved a slice/And it were nice/Eeh bah gum!'

ee, in't it grand to be daft. Said by Albert Modley (1901–79), the Northern English comedian who achieved nationwide fame through radio's *Variety Bandbox* in the late 1940s. A former railway porter, he employed several Northern expressions of the 'Heee!' and 'Flippin' 'eck!' variety. In *Roy Hudd's Book of Music-Hall, Variety and Showbiz Anecdotes* (1993), the phrase is given, rather, as 'Eeeh, intit grand when you're daft!'

Towards the end of Modley's life, he referred (on TV's *Looks Familiar, c* 1979) to an inexplicable catchphrase he had used on BBC radio's *Variety Bandbox*: **ninety-two!**

ee, it was agony, Ivy! See under RAY'S A LAUGH.

ee, wot a geezer! The Glasgow-born comedian Harold Berens (1903–95), often believed to be a Cockney, became known through the late 1940s BBC radio show *Ignorance is Bliss*. He said (1979) that when he was living near the Bayswater Road in London he would buy his daily newspaper from a vendor who always asked him what the latest joke was. When told, his customary reaction was, 'Ee, wot a geezer.' Berens acquired another of his catchphrases from a woman who used to sell him carnation buttonholes. To everything he said she would reply, **now, there's a coincidence!**

effect is shattering, the. See under I THOUGHT — UNTIL I DISCOVERED —.

efficiency's the ticket, the. See EYAYDON, YAUDEN . . .

effluent society. See AFFLUENT SOCIETY.

egg(s). See AS SURE AS ~ IS ~; CURATE'S ~;
DON'T TEACH YOUR GRANDMOTHER . . . ; GO
TO WORK ON AN ~; LAY AN ~; YOU CAN'T
MAKE AN OMELETTE . . .

eggs is eggs, as sure as. Meaning
'absolutely certain', the derivation for this
expression is obscure, unless it is a
corruption of the mathematician or
logician's '*x* is *x*'. It occurs in Charles
Dickens, *The Pickwick Papers*, Chap.43
(1836–7).

ego. See ARCADIA EGO.

Egypt. See FLESHPOTS OF ~; LITTLE ~.

eight. See ONE OVER THE ~.

eighty in the shade. A phrase used to
express extreme temperature. A song
'Charming Weather' in *The Arcadians*
(1908) has the lines:

Very, very warm for May
Eighty in the shade they say,
Just fancy!

However, one notes that it is alluded to
comically with regard to age rather than
temperature in Gilbert and Sullivan's *The
Mikado* (1885). Ko-Ko asks Katisha:

Are you old enough to marry, do you
think?
Won't you wait till you are eighty in the
shade?

Eighty in the Shade is the title of a play by
Clemence Dane (published 1959).

elbow. See MORE POWER TO YOUR ~.

elbow/big E, to give someone the. To
dispose of someone's services, to get rid of
them, i.e. by elbowing them aside. I first
heard the 'big E' version in a show business
context about 1971.

elegant. See EXCELLENT SUFFICIENCY.

elementary, my dear Watson! The
Sherlock Holmes phrase appears nowhere
in the writings of Sir Arthur Conan Doyle
(1859–1930), though the great detective

does exclaim 'Elementary' to Dr Watson in
The Memoirs of Sherlock Holmes ('The
Crooked Man', 1894) and 'Ho! (*Sneer.*)
Elementary! The child's play of deduction!'
in the play *Sherlock Holmes* written with
William Gillette in 1901 (1922 revision).

Conan Doyle brought out his last
Holmes book in 1927. His son Adrian (in
collaboration with John Dickson Carr) was
one of those who used the phrase in follow-
up stories – as have adapters of the stories in
film and broadcast versions. In the 1929
film *The Return of Sherlock Holmes* – the first
with sound – the final lines of dialogue are:

Watson: Amazing, Holmes!
Holmes: Elementary, my dear Watson,
elementary.

elephant, to see the. According to John
D. Unruh Jr, *The Plains Across: The
Overland Emigrants and the Trans-Mississippi
West, 1840–60* (1979), 'seeing the elephant'
was a popular expression in the US,
'connoting, in the main, experiencing
hardship and difficulty and somehow
surviving'. The source of a longer version –
'I've seen the elephant, and I've heard the
owl, and I've been to the other side of the
mountain' – is untraced. Another
unidentified source suggests that at the time
of the American Civil War, the expression
'I've seen the elephant' was used by both
Union and Confederate troops to mean
that the speaker was an experienced soldier
who had seen active service, and not a
gullible raw recuit. In other words, it was an
expression of seniority.

Brewer defines 'to see the elephant' as 'to
see all there is to see'. Edwin Radford, *To
Coin a Phrase* (1974), suggests that the
original form, dating from the 1830s, was:
'"That's sufficient," as Tom Haynes said
when he saw the elephant.' J.M. Dixon,
English Idioms (c 1912), has the definition:
'To be acquainted with all the latest
movements; to be knowing', which
sharpens the idea somewhat. Partridge/
Slang has, 'To see the world; gain worldly
experience' and dates it to *c* 1840 in the US,
1860 in the UK.

Elephant and Castle, the. Name given to
a British public house in central London,
south of the River Thames, and hence to

the adjoining area (not before the seventeenth century). The sign of the pub (now pulled down) probably showed an elephant with a fortified howdah containing armed soldiers on its back, as was customary in ancient times. A suggestion that the phrase is a corruption of *Infanta de Castile* – Eleanor of Castile, wife of Edward I – is entertaining but fanciful. 'The Elephant' (simply) was known as a pub name by Shakespeare's time and one is mentioned in *Twelfth Night* (1600).

elephant in your drawing room, the. An Ulster expression, quoted in the *Guardian* (26 June 1988), is that **the Troubles** are 'the elephant in your drawing room' – referring to the debilitating effect of sectarian hostility and violence in the province. Before the present round of civil strife in Northern Ireland started in 1969, 'The Troubles' had been applied specifically to the outburst of Civil War in southern Ireland (1919–23), but was also applied generally to any nationalist unrest – even to events as far back as 1641.

elephant never forgets, an. What one might say of oneself when complimented on remembering a piece of information forgotten by others, it is based on the view that elephants are supposed to remember trainers, keepers, and so on, especially those who have been unkind to them. A song with the title 'The Elephant Never Forgets' was featured in the play *The Golden Toy* by Carl Zuckmayer (London, 1934) and recorded by Lupino Lane. *Stevenson's Book of Proverbs, Maxims and Familiar Phrases* (1949) has that it derives from a Greek proverb: 'The camel [*sic*] never forgets an injury.' Compare 'Saki', *Reginald* (1904): 'Women and elephants never forget an injury.'

elephants' graveyard, an. A place to which people go to retire, or more loosely, to any place where the formerly important now languish. Partridge/*Slang*, more precisely, prefers 'the elephants' burial ground', referring to Petersfield in Hampshire where 'vast legions of retired admirals' live (an expression dating from the 1940s). The allusion is probably to the known death rituals of elephants, who tend to congregate when one of their number is on the way out – sometimes standing around and providing the pachyderm equivalent of hospital screens.

eleven o'clock. See HEAVENS, ~ . . .

eleventh commandment, the. Mencken has that this is 'Mind your own business' as 'borrowed from Cervantes, *Don Quixote*, 1605', but he also records 'The Eleventh Commandment: Thou shalt not be found out – George Whyte-Melville, *Holmby House*, 1860', and that is the much more usual meaning. *OED2* adds from the *Pall Mall Gazette* (10 September 1884): 'the new and great commandment that nothing succeeds like success' and from *Paston Carew* (1886) by Mrs Lynn Lynton that the eleventh commandment was 'do not tell tales out of school'. In 1850, Charles Kingsley suggested that it was: **buy cheap, sell dear.** The 1981 remake of the film *The Postman Always Rings Twice* was promoted with the slogan: 'If there was an 11th Commandment, they would have broken that too'.

eleventh hour, at the. Meaning 'at the last moment', this phrase's origin is the parable of the labourers, of whom the last 'were hired at the eleventh hour' (Matthew 20:9). It was used with a different resonance at the end of the First World War. The Armistice was signed at 5 a.m. on 11 November 1918 and came into force at 11 a.m. – 'at the eleventh hour of the eleventh day of the eleventh month'.

Elizabeth. See QUEEN ~ SLEPT HERE.

Elvis the Pelvis. Sobriquet of Elvis Presley (1935–77), the waggling of whose hips in rock'n'roll performances earned him this journalistic tag, though sometimes he was simply known as **the Pelvis.** Also simply as the **King (of Rock'n'Roll).**

embarrass. See AW, DON'T ~ ME.

embarrassing moments. See under HAVE A GO.

embarrassment. See DEEPLY REGRET ANY ~ . . .

éminence grise. This nickname is given to any shadowy figure who exercises power or influence. It was first applied to François Leclerc du Tremblay (*d* 1638), known as Père Joseph, private secretary to Cardinal Richelieu. Richelieu, statesman and principal adviser to Louis XIII of France, was something of an '*éminence grise*' himself and virtually ruled France from 1624 till his death. He was known, however, as the **Red Cardinal** or as '*L'Eminence Rouge*'. Du Tremblay, who dressed in grey, became known, first of all, as 'the Grey Cardinal' because – although not a cardinal – he exercised the power of one through his influence on Richelieu. Later, the Nazi Martin Bormann was sometimes known as the **Brown Eminence**, perhaps because of his 'Brownshirt' background.

Emma Peel. The name of a self-sufficient female character (played by Diana Rigg) in the British TV series *The Avengers*. The part was introduced in *c* 1965 and the name derives from the producers' desire to give the programme 'M appeal' (or **man appeal**, as a phrase from Oxo advertising had been putting it since 1958).

emotional. See TIRED AND ∼.

emperor's (new) clothes, the. Describing a person's imaginary qualities whose fictitiousness other people forbear to point out, the origin of this expression lies in a story called 'The Emperor's New Clothes' (1835) by Hans Christian Andersen, in which tailors gull an emperor into wearing a new suit of clothes, invisible to unworthy people but which do not, in fact, exist at all. None of the emperor's subjects dares point out that this renders him naked – until an innocent boy does just that.

enchilada. See BIG ∼.

empire. See EVIL ∼.

Empire Strikes Back, The. Title of a sci-fi movie (US, 1980), the first sequel to George Lucas's STAR WARS. This was the fictional EVIL EMPIRE vaguely alluded to by Ronald Reagan in his remarks about the Soviet Union. The phrase caught on in

other ways, too. In *c* 1981, the proprietors of an Indian restaurant in Drury Lane, London, considered it as a name before rejecting it in favour of 'The Last Days of the Raj'. See also YOU CANNOT BE SERIOUS!

empire upon which the sun never sets, the. The phrase refers to the British Empire, which was so widespread at its apogee that the sun was always up on some part of it. 'John Wilson' (Christopher North) wrote in *Noctes Ambrosianae*, No.20 (April 1829) of: 'His Majesty's dominions, on which the sun never sets.' Earlier, the idea had been widely applied to the Spanish Empire. In 1641, the English explorer and writer Captain John Smith (of Pocahontas fame) asked in *Advertisements for the Unexperienced, Etc.*: 'Why should the brave Spanish soldier brag the sun never sets in the Spanish dominions, but ever shineth on one part or other we have conquered for our king?' Ascribed to 'Duncan Spaeth' (is this John Duncan Spaeth, the US educator?) in Nancy McPhee *The Book of Insults* (1978) is the saying: 'I know why the sun never sets on the British Empire: God wouldn't trust an Englishman in the dark.'

enchilada. See BIG ∼.

encounter. See CLOSE ∼.

end. See ALL GOOD THINGS COME TO AN ∼; AT THE ∼ OF THE DAY; BEGINNING OF THE ∼; BITTER ∼; LIGHT AT THE ∼ OF THE TUNNEL.

end game. An expression describing the final stages of a chess game when few pieces remain. *End Game* is the English title of *Fin de Partie*, a play (1957) by Samuel Beckett. Compare **checkmate** – also used as the title of a ballet by Ninette de Valois and Arthur Bliss (1937) – from the term for the actual end of a game of chess, which has been etymologized as from the Arabic *Shahmat* [the Shah/King is dead].

end is nigh, the. The traditional slogan of placard-bearing religious fanatics refers to the end of the world and the day of judgement. But, although 'nigh' is a biblical word, this phrase does not occur as such in the Authorized Version. Rather: 'The day of the Lord . . . is nigh at hand' (Joel 2:1);

'the kingdom of God is nigh at hand' (Luke 21:31); 'the end of all things is at hand' (1 Peter 4:7).

end of civilization as we know it, the. A supposed Hollywood cliché (and the title of an announced but unreleased film, US, 1977) – the kind of thing said when people are under threat from invaders from Mars, or wherever: 'This could mean the end of civilization as we know it . . .'

I don't have an example from sci-fi films, but the deathless phrase does get uttered in *Citizen Kane* (1941). Orson Welles as the newspaper magnate Kane is shown giving a pre-war press conference: 'I've talked with the responsible leaders of the Great Powers – England, France, Germany, and Italy. They're too intelligent to embark on a project which would mean the end of civilization as we now know it. You can take my word for it: there'll be no war!'

From the *Independent* Magazine (4 February 1989): '[A second Danish television channel] was about to take to the air, with the certain result that culture would be relegated to the dustbin . . . In short, it will be for Danes the end of civilisation as they know it.'

See also AS WE KNOW IT.

end of history, the. A concept which was promoted by Francis Fukuyama, a US State Department official, in a 1989 article to describe Western democracy's perceived triumph over Communism in Eastern Europe: 'What we may be witnessing is not the end of the Cold War but the end of history as such: that is, the end point of man's evolution and the universalisation of Western liberal democracy.'

Compare the title of Daniel Bell's book *The End of Ideology* (1960).

enemies. See WITH FRIENDS LIKE THESE . . .

enemy. See PUBLIC ~ NO. 1; SLEEPING WITH THE ~; WE HAVE MET THE ~ AND HE IS US.

enemy within, the. An internal rather than external threat. *ODCIE* suggests that it is a shortened version of 'the enemy/traitor within the gate(s)' – 'one who acts, or is thought to act, against the interests of the family, group, society, etc. of which he is a member'.

As for its particular modern use: on 22 January 1983, *The Economist* wrote of the industrial relations scene in Britain: 'The government may be trusting that public outrage will increasingly be its ally. Fresh from the Falklands, Mrs Thatcher may even relish a punch-up with the enemy within to enhance her "resolute approach" further.' Seven months later, Mrs Thatcher was using exactly the same phrase and context regarding the British miners' strike. She 'told Tory MPs that her government had fought the enemy without in the Falklands conflict and now had to face an enemy within . . . she declared that the docks and pit strikers posed as great a threat to democracy as General Galtieri, the deposed Argentine leader' (*Guardian*, 20 July 1984).

Earlier, in 1980, Julian Mitchell had used the phrase as the title of a play about anorexia. It was also the title of a Tony Garnett BBC TV play in 1974, of a stage play by Brian Friel in 1962, and of a 1960 book by Robert F. Kennedy about 'organized corruption' in the US labour movement. In 1940, Winston Churchill said of the BBC that it was 'an enemy within the gates, doing more harm than good'. The earliest citation of the phrase in the *OED2* dates from 1608.

England. See CLEVEREST YOUNG MAN IN ~; CLOSE YOUR EYES . . . ; FALLING TOWARDS ~; GOTT STRAFE ~; GOOD EVENING, ~; GRANDPAPA ~; SOMEWHERE IN ~; THINGS I'VE DONE FOR ~; WAKE UP, ~!

England expects. Admiral Horatio Lord Nelson's signal to the English fleet before the Battle of Trafalgar on 21 October 1805 was 'England expects that every man will do his duty'. Mencken found a US saying from 1917 – during the First World War: 'England expects every American to do his duty'. In Britain at about the same time, there was a recruiting slogan: 'England Expects that Every Man Will Do His Duty and Join the Army Today'.

England, my England. Phrase from a poem by W.E. Henley called 'For England's Sake' (1892):

What have I done for you,
England, my England?
What is there I would not do,
England, my own?

England My England was used as the title of a book of short stories by D.H. Lawrence (1922). Compare A.G. MacDonell's satire on country life, *England, Their England* (1933), and a book of George Orwell's essays, *England, Your England* (1953).

English as she is spoke. Phrase now used to show how the language might be spoken by foreigners or the illiterate. Its origin lines in an English edition of a book of selections (1883) from the notorious French-Portuguese phrasebook *O Novo Guia da Conversacão em frances e portuguez* by José da Fonseca, which had been published in Paris in 1836. The original text was in parallel columns; then, in 1865, a third column, carrying English translations, was added by one Pedro Carolino. Field and Tuer's English book *English As She Is Spoke* took its title from a phrase in the chapter on 'Familiar Dialogues'. In 1883, Mark Twain also introduced an edition of the complete work in the US.

Englishman. See GREATEST LIVING ～.

enjoy. See SHE SHOULD LIE BACK AND ～ IT; YOURS TO ～ IN THE PRIVACY . . .

enjoying. See DOESN'T TIME FLY WHEN . . .

Enola Gay. Name of the US aircraft from which the atomic bomb which destroyed Hiroshima was dropped in 1945. Taken from the name of the mother of its pilot, Colonel Paul W. Tibbets, it was also used as the title of a TV movie (US, 1980) about the plane and its crew.

enough blue to make a pair of sailor's trousers. This saying is listed in *Nanny Says* (1972) as an example of 'nanny philosophy': 'If there's enough blue sky to make a pair of sailor's trousers then you can go out.' Brewer glosses it as 'two patches of blue appearing in a stormy sky giving the promise of better weather' and notes the alternative 'Dutchman's breeches' for 'sailor's trousers'.

enough is enough! A basic expression of exasperation, this is often trotted out in political personality clashes – though usually without result. 'What matters is that Mr Macmillan has let Mr [Selwyn] Lloyd know that at the Foreign Office, in these troubled times, enough is enough' (*The Times*, 1 June 1959). Having fed the story to *The Times*, Macmillan was prevented by the fuss it caused from firing Lloyd and the Foreign Secretary remained in place for a further year. On 10 May 1968, the *Daily Mirror* carried a front page headline: 'Enough is Enough', referring to the Labour government of Harold Wilson. It was over an article by Cecil H. King, Chairman of the International Publishing Corporation, but it led to *his* fall from power, however, and not the government's.

enough to make a parson swear, it's. A mild way of expressing genuine aggravation, annoyance or irritation. Edward Ward used it in *Hudibras Redivivus* (1706): 'Your Folly makes me stare;/Such talk would make a Parson swear.'

ENSA. The Entertainments National Service Association was an organization set up at the start of the Second World War to send groups of performers to entertain British and Allied troops in the war zones. The fare was not always of the highest quality, and so the acronym has been reinterpreted as 'Every Night Something Awful/Atrocious' and 'Even NAAFI Stands Aghast'.

Entertainer, The. Title of a play (1957) by John Osborne. It may not seem like a quotation but Osborne says he took it from a particular source: Bunk Johnson's 1947 recording of a tune called 'The Entertainer', often ascribed to Scott Joplin, though also to J.R. Johnson (no relation to Bunk).

Entertainment National Services Association. See ENSA.

equal. See ALL ANIMALS ARE ～ . . .

equal pay for equal work. A modern feminist slogan dating from the 1970s, though echoing a cry of teachers' organizations in the late nineteenth century. The phrase 'equal pay' on its own was known by 1923.

Eric Pode of Croydon. See ISN'T HE A PANIC?

'er indoors. Meaning 'the wife' (unseen, but domineering), this expression was popularized by George Cole as Arthur Daley in the ITV series *Minder* (1979–). The series, which was created by Leon Griffiths, had a field day with (predominantly) South London slang. When he died (10 June 1992), his obituarist in the *Independent* wrote: 'Once Griffiths gave me the inside story on the expression "'Er indoors". A taxi-driver drinking companion of his always referred to his never-to-be-seen wife as "'Er Indoors" . . . When the series was eventually screened, Griffiths was terrified the taxi-driver would be upset. He need not have bothered for he soon realised that the taxi-driver firmly believed all husbands never took their wives to a pub and always called them "'Er Indoors". I even know someone who pays tribute to Griffiths by calling his cat "'Er Outdoors".'
'I'm talking about Lodge Hill estate, in Bucks. This lies cheek-by-jowl with Chequers . . . the country seat of Her Indoors [i.e. Mrs Thatcher], and it's up for sale' – (*Guardian*, 25 January 1989).

Ernie. See ACRONYMS.

-erooni. See under THIRSTEROONI.

Essex Man. An uncouth, uneducated person of right-wing sympathies who may have done well out of the Thatcher years. He is likely to be found dwelling in Essex (a county just to the east of London) – some would say in company with East End criminals.

Establishment, the. Nickname for a conservative, partly hereditary, secretive, self-perpetuating ruling class. In Britain, it was brought to prominence by Henry Fairlie in a series of articles for the *Spectator* in 1955. Hugh Thomas, editing a book on the phenomenon and called *The Establishment* (1959), stated: 'The word was, however, in use among the thoughtful at least a year previously; I recall myself

employing it while passing the Royal Academy in a taxi in company with Mr Paul Johnson of the *New Statesman* in August 1954.' An earlier example of use of the phrase among the 'thoughtful' has, indeed, come to light in A.J.P. Taylor's *Essays in English History*. In one on William Cobbett (originally a review in the *New Statesman* in 1953) he wrote: 'Trotsky tells how, when he first visited England, Lenin took him round London and, pointing out the sights, exclaimed: "That's *their* Westminster Abbey! That's *their* Houses of Parliament!" Lenin was making a class, not a national emphasis. By "them" he meant not the English, but the governing classes, the Establishment so clearly defined and so complacently secure.' *OED2* has other citations of the phrase in its modern sense going back to 1923, to which might be added one in George Eliot's *Daniel Deronda*, Bk. 2, Chap. 12 (1876).

estate. See FOURTH ~.

Eth, yes. See under TAKE IT FROM HERE.

et in Arcadia ego. See ARCADIA EGO.

Eurocrap. 'Euro-' is a prefix used to denote absolutely anything of European origin. The form spread like a disease about the time of British entry into the European Common Market (January 1972). *OED2* finds its earliest example (which it compares to Anglo-, Austro- etc.) in 1928. 'Eurocrat', 'Euro-dollar', 'Eurospeak', and 'Eurocommunism' are but some of the scores that have followed. The *Guardian* of 17 December 1973 was already using the word 'Eurocrap'. However, the first real imposition of this rather medical-sounding (compare neuro-) tag had occurred with the setting up of **Eurovision** (1951), the television network for the production and exchange of programmes, most notably the 'Eurovision Song Contest' (first shown 1956). The coinage of this word is attributed (in Asa Briggs, *History of Broadcasting in the United Kingdom*, Vol. III) to George Campey, a BBC publicity executive.

even. See DON'T GET MAD, GET ~.

even Homer nods. See HOMER NODS.

evenin' all! Accompanied by a shaky salute to the helmet, PC George Dixon (Jack Warner) would bid viewers welcome with this phrase through several decades of *Dixon of Dock Green* on BBC TV (1955–76). His farewell, **mind how you go!**, achieved equal status as the phrase that all real policemen ought to say, even if not all of them do.

eventually – why not now? A slogan for Gold Medal Flour in the US, from *c* 1907. The story has it that when Benjamin S. Bull, advertising manager of the Washburn Crosby company requested members of his department to suggest catchphrases to be used in support of the flour, nobody came up with anything worthwhile. Mr Bull demanded, 'When are you going to give me a decent slogan?' His underlings staved him off by saying, 'Eventually.' 'Eventually!' thundered Mr Bull, 'Why not now?'

even your best friends won't tell you. A line which originated in the famous Listerine mouthwash advertisement headed OFTEN A BRIDESMAID BUT NEVER A BRIDE (US, 1920s), though the idea may have been used to promote another such product in the UK – Lifebuoy soap, according to *ODCIE* – in the late 1950s? Originally, the line in the Listerine copy was **and even your closest friends won't tell you.** Partridge/*Catch Phrases* suggests that it became a catchphrase in the form **your best friend(s) won't tell you** (= 'you stink!').

In the film *Dangerous Moonlight* (UK, 1941), the Anton Walbrook character says to a man putting on hair oil (in New York), 'Even your best friend won't *smell* you.' This helps with the dating, but does not really confirm the American origin as the film was made and scripted in England.

A similar idea was used by Amplex, the breath purifier, in advertisements (current in the UK, 1957) showing two people reacting to a smelly colleague with the slogan **someone isn't using Amplex** (or perhaps it was 'somebody's not using Amplex'?).

ever after. See AND THEY ALL LIVED HAPPILY ∼.

ever-open door, the. A slogan phrase used to describe Dr Barnado's Homes, the orphaned children's charity in the UK (by the 1950s). However, I can recall it being applied to the insatiable mouth, representing the appetite of an un-orphaned youth (me), also in the 1950s. A correspondent recalls a mother calling her son (*b* 1900), 'the ever-open door'. And note this, from Alexander Pope's translation of the *Iliad*, VI.14 (1715–20):

> He held his seat; a friend to human race
> Fast by the road, his ever-open door
> Obliged the wealthy and relieved the
> poor.

every. See EACH AND ∼ ONE OF US.

everybody. See IS ∼ HAPPY?

everybody has one book in them. A cliché of the publishing world – or perhaps not, for it advances a popular belief which publishers might well disagree with. Presumably, the idea behind the saying is that all people have one story that they alone can tell – namely, the story of their life.

From a George Orwell review in *New Statesman and Nation* (7 December 1940): 'It is commonly said that every human being has in him the material for one good book, which is true in the same sense as it is true that every block of stone contains a statue.' From a *Punch* book review: 'Every one, it is said, has one good book inside him, and, if this be so, it would be unkind to suggest that Mr James Agate is the exception that proves the rule. All one can in fairness say is that his good book is not among the thirty-six he has so far produced' (quoted in Agate, *Ego 6*, for 12 November 1942).

everybody out! *The Rag Trade* (written by Ronald Wolfe and Ronald Chesney) had the unusual, though not unique, experience of running on BBC TV from 1961–5 and then being revived on London Weekend Television from 1977. Miriam Karlin in her best flame-thrower voice as Paddy, the Cockney shop steward, would shout the phrase at every opportunity. Now connected in the public mind with all strike-happy trade union leaders.

everybody wants to get into the act!
See GOODNIGHT, MRS CALABASH . . .

**every day and in every way I am
getting better and better** (sometimes
every day in every way . . . or **day by
day in every way** . . .) The French
psychologist Emile Coué was the originator
of a system of 'Self-Mastery Through
Conscious Auto-Suggestion' which had a
brief vogue in the 1920s. His patients had to
repeat this phrase over and over and it
became a popular catchphrase of the time,
though physical improvement did not
necessarily follow. The French original was:
'Tous les jours, à tous les points de vue, je vais
de mieux en mieux.' Couéism died with its
inventor in 1926, though there have been
attempted revivals. John Lennon alludes to
the slogan in his song 'Beautiful Boy' (1980).

everyday story of country-folk, an. See
ARCHERS.

**every dog has its day – and a bitch two
afternoons!** G.L. Apperson in his English
Proverbs and Proverbial Phrases (1929) finds
the second half of this proverbial saying
being added by 1896 and – earlier, by 1864 –
the 'Essex saying', 'Every dog has his day,
and a cat has two Sundays.'

every — gets the — it deserves. A
format phrase that probably derives from a
quotation. ODQ cites Joseph de Maistre as
saying, 'Every country has the government
it deserves' in Lettres et Opscules Inédits (15
August 1811). From Today (10 June 1993),
concerning Jeffrey Archer: 'It's said that a
nation gets the politicians it deserves . . .'

Every Good Boy Deserves Favour. A
mnemonic for remembering, in ascending
order, the five horizontal black lines of the
treble clef – signifying the notes E, G, B, D,
and F. The four spaces between the lines are
for the notes F, A, C, and E, which hardly
need a mnemonic. Also used as the title of a
Moody Blues LP (1971) and of a Tom
Stoppard play for speaker and orchestra
(1977).

every home should have one. An all-
purpose slogan probably deriving from
American advertising in the 1920s/30s.

Used as the title of a British film about an
advertising man in 1970. Against the
American origin, I would mention that
Punch (18 October 1905) had a cartoon
whose caption contained the interesting
variation: 'The Portable Gramophone . . .
no country house should be without it.'

every inch a gentleman. A complete
gentleman. This basic expression occurs, for
example, in William Thackeray, Pendennis,
Chap. 54 (1848–50). Shakespeare, King
Lear, IV.vi.107 (1605) has 'Every inch a
king'.
  Every Other Inch a Lady was the title of
the autobiography (1973) of Beatrice Lillie,
the actress who was Lady Peel in private life.
'For all his reputation [he] is not a bounder.
He is every other inch a gentleman' – R.E.
Drennan in Wit's End (1973) quotes
Woollcott as having said this of Michael
Arlen. The same remark about Arlen has
also been attributed to Rebecca West (by
Ted Morgan in Somerset Maugham, 1980).

**every little helps – as the old lady said
when she piddled into the sea.** A pretty
common saying of the 'Wellerism' type.
British use, since the 1910s/20s?

every man has his price. Mencken says
of this proverb: 'Ascribed to Robert
Walpole c 1740 in William Coxe, Memoirs of
the Life and Administration of Robert Walpole,
1798.' There the form was: 'All those men
have their price.' But CODP finds W.
Wyndham in The Bee (1734) saying: 'It is an
old Maxim, that every Man has his Price, if
you can but come up to it.'

every picture tells a story. A modern
proverb and used to promote Doan's
Backache Kidney Pills (not 'Sloane's', as in
the PDMQ, 1980), and was current in 1904.
The picture showed a person bent over with
pain. In 1847, Charlotte Brontë had placed
the same thought in Jane Eyre: 'The letter-
press . . . I cared little for . . . Each picture
told a story.'

everything. See CHIPS WITH ~; MAN WHO
HAS ~; PLACE FOR ~ . . .

everything in the garden's lovely.
Meaning 'all is well', in a general sense, the

saying comes from the title of a song made popular by Marie Lloyd (d 1922). *Everything in the Garden* was the title of a stage play (1962) by Giles Cooper, about suburban housewives turning to prostitution.

Everything London. The one-time telegraphic address of Harrods department store in London (unverified). Certainly, 'Harrods for everything' was a promotional slogan quoted in 1925. Harrods motto is also said to be *Omnia omnibus ubique*. Advertising slogans have included 'Harrods Serves the World' (this was pre-1881) and 'Enter a different world' (current in the 1980s).

everything's coming up roses. All is well, prospects are good, everything's blooming. The phrase is used as the title of a song with words by Stephen Sondheim in the musical *Gypsy* (1959). But did the expression exists before this? It is possibly adapted from the expression, 'to come out of something smelling of roses', but there do not even seem to be any examples of *that* in use before the date of the Sondheim song.

everything you always wanted to know about — but were afraid to ask. A format phrase inspired by the title *Everything You Always Wanted To Know About Sex But Were Afraid to Ask*, a book (published in 1970) by David Reuben MD (b 1933). The use was popularized even further when Woody Allen entitled a film *Everything You Always Wanted To Know About Sex, But Were Afraid To Ask* (US, 1972) – though, in fact, he simply bought the title of the book and none of its contents.

The format soon became a cliché and almost any subject you can think of has been inserted into the sentence. An advertisement for the UK *Video Today* magazine (December 1981) promised: 'All you ever wanted to know about video but were afraid to ask.' In 1984, I drew up this short list from the scores of books that bore similar titles: *Everything That Linguists Have Always Wanted to Know About Logic But Were Ashamed To Ask*; *Everything You Always Wanted to Know About Drinking Problems And Then a Few Things You Didn't Want to Know*; *Everything You Always*

Wanted to Know About Elementary Statistics But Were Afraid to Ask; *Everything You Always Wanted to Know About Mergers, Acquisitions and Divestitures But Didn't Know Whom to Ask*; *Everything You Wanted to Know About Stars But Didn't Know Where to Ask*; *Everything You Wanted to Know About the Catholic Church But Were Too Pious to Ask*; *Everything You Wanted to Know About the Catholic Church But Were Too Weak to Ask* . . .

In 1988, the publishers of this dictionary brought out a paperback edition of a book by Robert Goldenson and Kenneth Anderson called *Everything You Ever Wanted to Know About Sex – But Never Dared Ask* – which is surely where we came in.

evidence. See ANYTHING YOU SAY . . . ; ANYTHING YOU SAY . . . ; I SWEAR BY ALMIGHTY GOD . . .

evil. See BANALITY OF ∼; HEAR ALL . . . ; WE MUST STAMP OUT THIS ∼ IN OUR MIDST.

evil empire. The Soviet Union was so described by President Reagan in a speech to the National Association of Evangelicals at Orlando, Florida (8 March 1983): 'In your discussions of the nuclear freeze proposals, I urge you to beware the temptation of pride – the temptation blithely to declare yourselves above it all and label both sides equally at fault, to ignore the facts of history and the aggressive impulses of an *evil empire* . . .' It is a reasonable assumption that the President's use of the phrase '*evil empire*' was influenced by George Lucas's film STAR WARS (1977) in which reference is made to an 'evil galactic empire'.

From the *Independent* (19 May 1990): 'Frank Salmon, an East End protection racketeer who built an "evil empire" on violence and fear, was yesterday jailed for 7 years at the Old Bailey.'

evil under the sun. See NOTHING NEW UNDER THE SUN.

excellent! See WAYNE'S WORLD.

excellent sufficiency, an. When declining an offer of more food, my father

(1910–89) would say, 'No, thank you, I have had an excellent sufficiency' Paul Beale's *Concise Dictionary of Slang* . . . (1989) has this, rather, as 'an **elegant sufficiency** . . . Jocular indication, mocking lower-middle-class gentility, that one has had enough to eat or drink, as "I've had an elegant sufficiency, ta!" since *c* 1950.'

excuse. See IF YOU'LL ∼ THE PUN; OUR REPORTER MADE AN ∼ . . .

excuse me, is this the place? See I'VE GOT A LETTER FROM A BLOKE IN BOOTLE.

excuse me, sir, do you think that's wise? See under DAD'S ARMY.

excuse my French. See PARDON MY FRENCH.

excuse stinkers. Smoker's phrase from the 1920s/30s when lighting up an inferior brand. As Robert Graves and Alan Hodge explain in *The Long Week-End* (1940), cigarettes made from Virginia tobacco were, at that time, considered by fashionable women to be a little vulgar. A common catchphrase when offering them was was 'I hope you don't mind; it's only a Virgin', or, more pointedly, 'Excuse stinkers'.

exercise the ferret, to. Euphemism for sexual intercourse, recorded in 1985.

exit pursued by a bear. A famous stage direction, from Shakespeare, *The Winter's Tale*, III.iii.58 (1611). It refers to the fate of Antigonus who is on the (in fact, non-existent) sea coast of Bohemia. Most of Shakespeare's stage directions are additions by later editors, but this one may be original. The bear could have been real (as bear-baiting was common in places adjacent to Shakespeare's theatres) or a man in costume.

exit stage left. See under HEAVENS TO MURGATROYD.

expectation. See DESPERATION . . .

expects. See ENGLAND ∼ . . .

experience. See GROWING ∼ .

experience, the —. A cliché of 1980s marketing, particularly of 'heritage' material. It suggests that by going to some historical site or theme park you will have a life-enhancing visit and not just an ordinary day out. From the *Independent on Sunday* (25 April 1993): 'At Land's End, for instance, there's the *Land's End Experience*, a multi-media retelling of our island story, in which visions of Excalibur gleam through dry ice, waves crash and – for that extra tang of actuality – visitors are lightly-moistened with simulated sea-spray. A curious thing: to go to the sea-side to get wet indoors.' A few miles away it was possible, in the same year, to have the *Minack Experience* – a rather unnecessary indoor display attached to a wonderful open-air theatre (which truly is an experience).
    From the *Independent* (20 August 1992): 'The *Dracula Experience* exhibition in Whitby, North Yorkshire, is for sale . . . The exhibit, in the town that inspired Bram Stoker, author of the legend, attracts 80,000 visitors a year.'

expletive deleted. The American way of indicating that an obscenity or blasphemous remark has been left out of a printed document. The phrase became famous elsewhere during Watergate upon the release of transcripts of conversations between President Nixon and his aides – published as *The White House Transcripts* (1974). The documents also used 'expletive removed', 'adjective omitted', 'characterization omitted'. British practice had been to rely on **** (asterisks) or . . . . (dots) or ---- (dashes) for sensitive deletions.
    I note this in a 1937 *Time* review of Hemingway's *To Have and Have Not*: 'No matter how a man alone ain't got no bloody (Obscenity deleted) chance.'
    For a while after Watergate people even exclaimed 'Expletive deleted!' instead of swearing.

exporting is fun. A Harold Macmillan slogan that misfired, though in this instance he never actually 'said' it. The phrase was included in a 1960 address to businessmen by the British Prime Minister, but when he came to the passage he left out what was later considered to be a rather patronizing remark. The press, however, printed what was in the advance text of the speech as though he had actually said it. Compare the earlier **we must export – or die**, which arose out of a severe balance of payments problem under the Labour government in 1945/6.

exterminate, exterminate! The science fiction TV series *Dr Who* has given rise to numerous beasties since its inception on BBC TV in 1963 but none more successful than the Daleks (who arrived in 1964) – deadly, mobile pepperpots whose metallic voices barked out 'Exterminate, exterminate!' as they set about doing so with ray guns. Much imitated by children.

extra mile. See GO THE ~.

— extraordinaire! A format phrase, current by 1940, and now a cliché. '[Culture Club's] flexible eight-piece includes Steve Grainger's sax, Terry Bailey's trumpet, Phil Pickett's keyboards, and their secret weapon, Helen Terry, a backing singer extraordinaire' – *The Times*, 27 September 1983.

eyaydon, yauden, yaydon, negidicrop dibombit! In the Navy version of BBC radio's *Merry Go Round* (1943–8), Jon Pertwee portrayed Svenson, a Norwegian stoker, whose cod Norwegian (based on close scrutiny of wartime news broadcasts) always ended up with these words. Paul Beale in Partridge/*Catch Phrases* adds that this was 'much imitated at the time'.

In the same show, Pertwee also played Weatherby Wett (who later became Commander Weatherby in *The Navy Lark*). He would say **dabra, dabra!** (followed by stuttering). Then there was an inefficient character whose watchword was **the efficiency's the ticket**, and, in *Mediterranean Merry Go Round*, a Devonshire bugler at Plymouth barracks who eventually became a postman in *Waterlogged Spa* – not to mention thirteenth trombonist in the Spa Symphony Orchestra. At one concert he became bored with the slow movement of a symphony and broke into 'Tiger Rag'. When Eric Barker remonstrated with him,

he said: 'Ah, me old darling, but it tore 'em through, didn't it?' Barker: 'Well, er, yes . . .' 'Postman: 'Well, **what does it matter what you do as long as you tear 'em up?'** Pertwee explained in *Pick of the Week* (4 July 1975), that all this was derived from a character he had known as a boy in the West Country, a postman who used to get drunk on cider and throw all the letters away.

eye. See ALL MY ~ AND . . . ; APPLE OF ONE'S ~ ; I SPY WITH MY LITTLE ~ ; NOT A DRY ~ IN THE HOUSE; ~ OF A NEEDLE under EASIER FOR A CAMEL . . .

eyeball to eyeball. Meaning 'in close confrontation'. Use of this expression is of comparatively recent origin. In the missile crisis of October 1962, the US took a tough line when the Soviet Union placed missiles on Cuban soil. After a tense few days, the Soviets withdrew. Safire records that Secretary of State Dean Rusk (1909–94) was speaking to an ABC news correspondent, John Scali, on 24 October and said: 'Remember, when you report this, that, eyeball to eyeball, they blinked first.' Columnists Charles Bartlett and Stewart Alsop then helped to popularize this as, 'We're eyeball to eyeball and the other fellow just blinked.'

Before this, 'eyeball to eyeball' was a Black American serviceman's idiom. Safire quotes a reply given by the all-black 24th Infantry Regiment to an inquiry from General MacArthur's HQ in Korea (November 1950): 'Do you have contact with the enemy?' 'We is eyeball to eyeball.'

eyeless in Gaza. Phrase from John Milton's *Samson Agonistes* (1671): 'Ask for this great deliverer now, and find him/ Eyeless in Gaza, at the mill with slaves.' *Eyeless in Gaza* is the title of a book (1936) by Aldous Huxley.

eyes. See CLOSE YOUR ~ . . . ; HERE AND NOW, BEFORE . . . ; MY ~ ARE DIM.

eyes and ears of the world, the. A slogan promoting the cinema newsreel, Paramount News, from 1927–57. Not Gaumont British News, as in Partridge/ *Slang*.

· F ·

Fab Four, the. An early nickname of the BEATLES pop foursome (1962–70). 'Fab' was a vogue word, short for fabulous, and current by 1963. It is said by some to have originated in Liverpool lingo but Partridge/ *Slang* had it in general teenage use by the late 1950s.

face(s). See CUT OFF YOUR NOSE . . . ; HIS/ HER ~ IS HIS/HER FORTUNE; IN YER ~ ; MAN OF A THOUSAND ~ ; UNACCEPTABLE ~ OF —.

— faces of —, the. Journalistic format phrase with the number of faces variable. The origin is the book and film title *The Three Faces of Eve* (US, 1957) – a story concerning a schizophrenic. (In Fritz Spiegl's splenetic *Keep Taking the Tabloids*, 1983, he concludes wrongly that the film title was *The Four Faces of Eve* on the basis of a newspaper headline, 'THE FOUR FACES OF STEVE'.)
   When BBC2 TV started transmissions in 1964 each evening's viewing had its own theme – education, entertainment, minorities – and this scheduling was billed as 'The Seven Faces of the Week' (and was soon abandoned, as it was ratings death). Walter Terry in the *Daily Mail* (19 June 1964) listed the 'ten faces of Harold' [Wilson] – 'Little Englander Harold, Capitalist Harold, Russian Harold . . .' etc.

face on the cutting-room floor, the. An actor or actress cut out of a film after it has been completed. Used as the title of a novel by Cameron McCabe in 1937 and possibly related to the ballad known as 'The Face on the Bar-room Floor' by H. Antoine d'Arcy (though he insisted the title was simply 'The Face on the Floor'). Now the 'cutting-room floor' tends to be invoked as the place where any unwanted material ends up – and not only in reference to media matters. From Josephine Tey, *A Shilling for Candles*

(1936): 'Treating me like bits on the cutting-room floor.'

face that launch'd a thousand ships, the. An impressive compliment to female beauty, much alluded to. Originally, Christopher Marlowe's mighty line in *Dr Faustus* (c 1594) referred to Helen of Troy: 'Was this the face that launch'd a thousand ships?' Earlier, Marlowe had said something similar in *Tamburlaine the Great* (1587): 'Helen, whose beauty . . . drew a thousand ships to Tenedos.' Shakespeare must have been alluding to Marlowe's line when, in *Troilus and Cressida* (c 1601) he said of Helen:

> Why she is a pearl
> Whose price hath launch'd above a
>   thousand ships.

He also alludes to it in *All's Well That Ends Well* (1603). The consistent feature of these mentions is the figure of a 'thousand' which was a round number probably derived from the accounts of Ovid and Virgil. Chips Channon records (23 April 1953) in the House of Commons: '[Aneurin] Bevan looked at poor, plain Florence Horsburgh [Independent MP for the Combined English Universities] and hailed her with the words "That's the face that sank a thousand scholarships".' To Jack de Manio, the broadcaster, is attributed a more recent version. Of Glenda Jackson, the actress, he is alleged to have said, in the 1970s: 'Her face could launch a thousand dredgers.'

face the music, to. Meaning 'to face whatever punishment is coming' and known by 1850, this saying has two possible origins. An actor or entertainer must not only accept the judgement of the audience but also of the (often hard-to-impress) musicians in the orchestra in front of him. He literally faces the music. More likely is the second explanation, that it is akin to the expression 'to be **drummed out of**' something. At one time, if a soldier was dismissed from the army for dishonourable conduct, he would be drummed out in a ceremony which included having a description of his crime read out and his insignia stripped from his uniform.

face to face. Looking another person in the face, possibly close up. Known since 1300. In the 1960s, the phrase was used as the title of a BBC Television interview series, conducted by John Freeman, in which the interviewer was not seen, only his subject. An appropriate use as there is a proverb which states, in full, 'Face to face, the truth comes out' (known by 1732).

facilis descensus Averno [it is easy to go down into Hell]. From Virgil's *Aeneid* (VI.126), this phrase is employed when wanting to suggest that humankind is readily inclined towards evil deeds. Avernus, a lake in Campania, was a name for the entrance to Hell. The epic poem continues with:

    Noctes atque dies patet atri ianua Ditis;
    Sed revocare gradum superasque evadere ad
      auras,
    Hoc opus, hic labor est

[Night and day, the gates of dark Death stand wide; but to climb back again, to retrace one's steps to the upper air – there's the rub, that is the task].

-factor. See FALKLANDS FACTOR.

facts. See JUST THE ∼, MA'AM under *DRAGNET*; NEVER LET THE ∼ STAND IN THE WAY . . .

fade. See OLD SOLDIERS NEVER DIE . . .

failure. See IT WENT FROM ∼ TO CLASSIC . . . ; WHAT WE'VE GOT HERE . . .

fair. See ALL'S ∼ IN LOVE, WAR . . . ; IN AND OUT LIKE A DOG AT A ∼.

fair crack of the whip, a. What one should give to people in order that they may have a fair chance or, at least, an opportunity to do something. Known by 1929. The origin is obvious: in the days of horse-drawn transport, whoever had the whip was also holding the reins and therefore in charge of the vehicle's progress.

fair day's wages for a fair day's work, a. Slogan of nineteenth-century British origin. T. Attwood in a speech in the House of Commons (14 June 1839) said: 'They only ask for a fair day's wages for a fair day's work.' This is picked up by Charles Dickens in *Our Mutual Friend*, Bk. I, Chap. 13 (1864–5): 'A fair day's wages for a fair day's work is ever my partner's motto.'

fair deal. 'Every segment of our population and every individual has a right to expect from this government a Fair Deal' – from President Truman's State of the Union message, 1949, introducing a package of measures including legislation on civil rights and fair employment practices. The two words had, however, been together since 1600.

fairy-tale. See LIKE A ∼ PRINCESS.

fais ce que voudras. See FAY . . .

faith. See KEEP THE ∼, BABY; THIS HAS RESTORED MY ∼ . . .

faithful unto death. Epitaphic phrase of biblical origin – Revelation 2:10 has: 'Be thou faithful unto death and I will give thee a crown of life.' The phrase was also used as the title of a famous painting (1865) by Sir Edward John Poynter PRA which shows a centurion staying at his sentry post during the eruption of Vesuvius which destroyed Pompeii in AD 79. In the background, citizens are panicking as molten lava falls upon them. The picture was inspired by the discovery of an actual skeleton of a soldier in full armour excavated at Pompeii in the late eighteenth or early nineteenth century. Many such remains were found of people 'frozen' in the positions they had held as they died. Bulwer-Lytton described what might have happened to the soldier in his *Last Days of Pompeii* (1834). The painting hangs in the Walker Art Gallery, Liverpool.

Falklands factor, the. The supposed improvement in Margaret Thatcher's fortunes in the 1983 British General

Election following her 'victory' in the previous year's 'war' with Argentina over the Falklands.

In the 1980s, almost any phenomenon was liable to be dignified by the *-factor* suffix. It gave a spurious sense of science – or at least journalistic weight – to almost any theory or tendency that had been spotted. Hence, also: from the *Observer* (19 August 1984): '[Geraldine] Ferraro's **"sleaze factor"** . . . Anything questionable which emerges subsequently about their background becomes known as the "sleaze factor"'; 'The **Chernobyl factor** appears to have cast its shadow over not just British lamb, but the homes of those unfortunate to live near the four areas shortlisted for the NIREX nuclear dumping site' – *Daily Telegraph* (3 July 1986); the **F-factor** for the 'fanciability' (or indeed 'fuckability') factor as a key element in the success or otherwise of presenters on GMTV breakfast television, January 1993.

fall. BIGGER THEY COME, THE HARDER THEY ∼; DID SHE ∼ OR WAS SHE PUSHED?

fall and rise. See DECLINE AND FALL.

fallen. See GOOD MAN ∼ AMONG . . .

fallen in the water. See under GOON SHOW.

falling towards England. Phrase probably derived from W.H. Auden's poem 'O Love, the interest itself' (1936): 'And make us as Newton was, who in his garden watching/The apple falling towards England, became aware between himself and her of an eternal tie.' Used as the title of the second volume of memoirs (1985) by the Australian-born writer, Clive James.

Julian Mitchell's 1994 play about a family in the early part of the twentieth century has the similar title, *Falling Over England*.

fame is the spur. Phrase from Milton's 'Lycidas' (1637):

Fame is the spur that the clear spirit doth raise
(That last infirmity of noble mind)
To scorn delights, and live laborious days.

Used as the title of a novel (1940; film UK, 1946) by Howard Spring, about an aspiring politician.

families. See ACCIDENTS WILL OCCUR . . .

family. See I WOULD LIKE TO SPEND MORE TIME WITH . . .

Family Favourites. A potent memory of Sunday mornings in the 1950s and early 1960s: the smell of roast and gravy wafting out of the kitchen and from the radio, **it's twelve o'clock in London, one o'clock in Cologne – at home and away it's time for** *Two-Way Family Favourites* (or words to that effect), followed by the sweeping strings of the signature tune – the André Kostelanetz version of Rodgers and Hart's 'With a Song in My Heart' . . .

The BBC programme began on 7 October 1945 as a link between home and the British occupying troops in Germany. Cliff Michelmore, who used to introduce the programme from Hamburg, and later met and married the London presenter, Jean Metcalfe, recalls the origin of the phrase **bumper bundle**: 'It was invented by Jean. Her road to Damascus was at the crossroads on Banstead Heath one Sunday morning when driving in to do the programme. It was used to describe a large number of requests all for the same record, especially "Top Ten" hits, *circa* 1952–3.'

The programme took various forms and had various presenters before closing in the 1970s. The title change to *Two-Way Family Favourites* was in 1960 (giving rise to a slang expression for a type of sexual intercourse).

Family Hold Back. See FHB.

family newspaper, not in a. Journalistic humbug of the OUR REPORTER MADE AN EXCUSE AND LEFT variety. The reporter sails as close to the wind as he can and then states, 'she committed an act which we cannot describe in a family newspaper', or some such. Claud Cockburn in *I, Claud* (1967) said, 'the Bowdlers – "can't put that in a family newspaper" – were on the job everywhere, swabbing down the lavatory walls'. The idea of a 'family' newspaper goes back as far as the first edition of the *Observer* (4 December 1791) in which the

'Address to the Public' stated: 'Servants also, as the *Observer* cannot fail of becoming a favourite family Paper, will find it their peculiar interest to give it their decided preference.'

The notion has now spread to broadcasting – 'This is a family show, so I couldn't possibly tell you what happened . . .'

family silver. See SELL OFF THE ~.

famous. See RICH AND ~; YOU'RE ~ WHEN . . .

famous for being famous. Dating, I would guess, from the 1960s/70s – a phrase used to describe people who are celebrated by the media although it is difficult to work out precisely what it is they have done to deserve such attention. Nowadays, these people appear as guests on TV quiz shows, participate in charity telethons, and – as they have always done – feature on guest-lists for first nights and film premieres. From the *Daily Mail* (4 March 1989): 'With Christine Keeler in person . . . and with the attendant chorus of showbiz froth and nonentities famous for being famous, the film's premiere brazenly upheld all the meretricious values.'

Daniel J. Boorstin in *The Image* (1962) noted: 'The celebrity is a person who is known for his well-knownness.'

famous for fifteen minutes, to be. Meaning, 'to have transitory fame' of the type prevalent in the twentieth century, this expression comes from the celebrated words in a catalogue for an exhibition of Andy Warhol's work in Stockholm (1968). The artist wrote: 'In the future everyone will be world-famous for fifteen minutes.' It is often to be found used allusively, e.g.: 'He's had his fifteen minutes', etc. *Famous for Fifteen Minutes* was the title of a series of, naturally, fifteen-minute programmes on BBC Radio 4 (from 1990) in which yesterday's headline-makers were recalled from obscurity.

famous last words! This is the kind of response given to someone who has just made a rash statement of the type: 'I always drive better when I've got a few drinks inside me.' There is a book entirely made up

of such motorists' boasts called **You Have Been Warned** (1936) with illustrations by Fougasse. This second phrase comes from the 1930s' 'familiar police admonition' (Partridge/*Catch Phrases*).

fancy. See LITTLE OF WHAT YOU ~.

Fanny. See ARE YOU ALL RIGHT?

Fanny Adams. See SWEET ~.

far. See FROM A ~ COUNTRY; THUS ~ SHALT THOU GO.

farewell. See AND SO WE SAY ~; SO, ~ THEN.

far from the madding crowd. Phrase from Thomas Gray's 'Elegy Written in a Country Church-Yard' (1751):

Far from the madding crowd's ignoble strife
Their sober wishes never learn'd to stray.

Hence, the title of Thomas Hardy's novel (1874; film UK, 1967). 'Madding' here means 'frenzied, mad' – not 'maddening'.

Farmer Giles. The personification of the (British) country farmer, possibly named after the subject of Robert Bloomfield's poem *The Farmer's Boy* (1800) (although he is a labourer rather than a farmer). Coincidentally or not, Isaac Bickerstaff in *The Maid of the Mill* (1765) has: 'I am determined farmer Giles shall not stay a moment on my estate, after next quarter day.' *Farmer Giles of Ham* was the title of a story (1949) by J.R.R. Tolkien.

Accordingly, 'farmers' is rhyming slang for piles (haemorrhoids).

Farnsbarns. See CHARLIE ~.

fart. See HE CAN'T ~ AND CHEW GUM . . . ; LIKE A ~ IN A COLANDER.

fart in a wind-storm. See under AS BUSY AS . . .

farting. See THAT'LL STOP YOU ~ IN CHURCH.

fascism. See BODY ~.

fashion victim. A person (usually female) who wears clothes solely to be fashionable and without any reference to whether the particular items are suitable for her figure. Possibly a coinage of the American journal *Women's Wear Daily* and current by the early 1970s.

There is also the phrase **a martyr to be smarter** which Partridge/*Slang* locates mid-century and which seems to be describing the same affliction.

fast and loose. See PLAY ~ .

faster than a speeding bullet! See under *SUPERMAN*.

fast lane. See LIVING LIFE IN THE ~ .

Fat Controller, the. Name of a character in the *Thomas the Tank Engine* children's books by the Revd W(ilbert) Awdry (*b* 1911). He has twice undergone a name change. From the Introduction to *James the Red Engine* (1948): 'We [British Rail] are nationalised now, but the same engines still work the Region. I am glad, too, to tell you that the Fat Director, who understands our friends' ways, is still in charge, but is now the Fat Controller.' Initially, indeed, he was shown very much as a director of a private railway company, wearing striped pants, tail coat and top hat.

In the 1990s, when a hugely successful TV film version was made of the stories, sales to the politically correct US market necessitated that the character be known as 'Sir Topham Hat'.

fate. See FLYING FICKLE FINGER OF ~ under *LAUGH-IN*.

fate worse than death, a. Originally referring to rape or loss of virginity, this is an expression dating from the days when such dishonour for a woman would, indeed, have seemed so. In John Cleland's *Memoirs of a Woman of Pleasure* (1748–9), Fanny Hill talks of a 'dread of worse than death'. *OED2* has the phrase in its original sense by 1810.

In *The Trumpet-Major* (1882), Thomas Hardy reproduces what purports to be a document headed 'Address to All Ranks and Descriptions of Englishmen' dating from the time of Napoleonic invasion scares: 'You will find your best Recompense,' it concludes, '. . . in having protected your Wives and Children from death, or worse than Death, which will follow the Success of such Inveterate Foes.'

Now used jokingly of any situation one might wish to avoid.

fat, hairy legs. See under MORECAMBE AND WISE SHOW.

father. See AND WHEN DID YOU LAST SEE YOUR ~?; HOW'S YOUR ~; LLOYD GEORGE KNEW MY ~ .

fat lady sings. See OPERA AIN'T OVER . . .

fattening. See ILLEGAL IMMORAL OR ~ .

favourite airline. See THE WORLD'S ~ under BOAC TAKES GOOD CARE OF YOU.

fay ce que voudras (or *fais ce que voudras*). Meaning '**do what you will**; do as you please', this is an appealing motto and one that has been adopted by more than one free-living soul. It appeared first in Bk. I of *Gargantua and Pantagruel* (1532) by Rabelais. Then, in the eighteenth century it was the motto of the Monks of Medmenham, better known as the Hell Fire Club. Sir Francis Dashwood founded a mock Franciscan order at Medmenham Abbey in Buckinghamshire in 1745 and the members of the Club were said to get up to all sorts of disgraceful activities, orgies, black masses, and the like. The politician John Wilkes was of their number. The motto was written up over the ruined door of the abbey.

Aleister Crowley (*c* 1876–1947), the satanist who experimented in necromancy, the black arts, sex and drugs, also picked up the motto. Of his 'misunderstood commandment', Germaine Greer comments in *The Female Eunuch* (1970): '*Do as thou wilt* is a warning not to delude yourself that you can do otherwise, and to take full responsibility for what you do. When one has genuinely chosen a course for oneself it cannot be possible to hold another responsible for it.'

fear. See FLIGHT FROM ~ .

Fear and Loathing in Las Vegas. Title of a book (1972) by the US writer Hunter S. Thompson, describing a visit to the gambling resort while under the influence of a variety of mind-expanding drugs. Apart from having a much-quoted title, the book is a prime example of what Thompson calls **gonzo journalism**, in which the writer chronicles his own role in the events he is reporting and doesn't worry too much about the facts. The word may be the same as Italian *gonzo* [a fool; foolish].

feast. See SPECTRE AT THE ~.

feather in one's cap, to have a. Meaning 'to have an honour or achievement of which one can be proud', the expression (known by 1700) probably dates from 1346, when the Black Prince was awarded the crest of John, King of Bohemia, which showed three ostrich feathers, after he had distinguished himself at the Battle of Crécy. This symbol has since been carried by every Prince of Wales. Later, any knight who had fought well might wear a feather in his helmet.

feeding frenzy. Meaning 'furious media attention', the image here is of fish swimming to retrieve bait thrown to them by a fisherman, or of homing in on any potential food. An article by Prof Perry W. Gilbert in *Scientific American* (July 1962) has this: 'As the blood and body juices of the marlin flow from the wound, the other sharks in the pack become more and more agitated and move in rapidly for their share of the meal. Frequently three or four sharks will attack the marlin simultaneously. A wild scene sometimes called a "feeding frenzy" now ensues.' As William Safire observed in the *New York Times* Magazine in (September 1988), packs of journalists in the US had come to be described by that time as 'in a piranha-like feeding frenzy' or behaving like 'sharks in a feeding frenzy'. Alliteration rules once more: '[Hunter S. Thompson's] forthcoming trial has the makings of an international media circus – or "feeding frenzy", as Thompson would put it' (*Independent*, 14 April 1990).

feel. See HOW DID YOU ~?

feeling is the truth. See SEEING IS BELIEVING.

feeling one's oats. See SOW ONE'S WILD OATS.

feet. See HOW'S YOUR POOR OLD ~.

fellows. See I SAY YOU ~ under YAROOOO!

female of the species. See under DEADLIER THAN THE MALE.

Ferguson's. See FINE SETS THESE ~.

ferret. See EXERCISE THE ~.

Few, the. Name given to fighter pilots of the RAF at the height of the German air attacks on London and the south-east of England in 1940 during what came to be known as the BATTLE OF BRITAIN. Although greatly outnumbered, they wreaked havoc on the Luftwaffe, with heavy losses to themselves. Paying tribute to these airmen, Winston Churchill, Prime Minister, said in the House of Commons on 20 August 1940: 'Never in the field of human conflict was so much owed by so many to so few.' Here we have an echo of Shakespeare's Henry V speaking to his men before the Battle of Agincourt and talking of: 'We few, we happy few, we band of brothers' – *Henry V*, IV.iii.60 (1599). Benham quotes Sir John Moore after the fall of Calpi (where Nelson lost an eye): 'Never was so much work done by so few men.'

Another pre-echo may be found in Vol. 2 of Churchill's own *A History of the English-Speaking Peoples* (1956, but largely written pre-war). Describing a 1640 Scottish incursion in the run-up to the English Civil War, he writes: 'All the Scots cannon fired and all the English army fled. A contemporary wrote that "Never so many ran from so few with less ado".' In a speech on the Government of Ireland Bill, in the House of Commons (30 April 1912), Churchill himself had said: 'Never before has so little been asked; and never before have so many people asked for it.' It is interesting to note that Harold Nicolson, noting Churchill's 1940 speech in his diary (20 August), slightly misquotes the passage: '[Winston] says, in referring to the RAF, "never in the history of human conflict has so much been owed by so many to so few".' By 22 September, Churchill's daughter, Mary, was uttering a *bon mot* in his hearing about the collapse of France through weak leadership: 'Never before has so much been betrayed for so many by so few' (recorded by John Colville, *The Fringes of Power*, Vol. 1, 1985).

few and far between. 'Our semi-tautological phrase "few and far between" is a corrupt formulation by the nineteenth-century Scottish poet Thomas Campbell of an old folk saying to the effect that the visits of angels to our world are "brief and far between"' – *Observer*, 26 June 1988. To be precise, Campbell's reference in *The Pleasures of Hope*, II.372 (1799) was:

. . . my winged hours of bliss have been,
Like angel-visits, few and far between.

This was an echo of what Robert Blair had written in *The Grave* (1743):

Its Visits Like those of Angels' short, and
far between.

Even so, something like the phrase had existed before this. R. Verney wrote a letter in *c* July 1668 saying 'Hedges are few and between' (*Memoirs of the Verney Family*, IV.iii.89).

few vouchers short of a pop-up toaster, a. One of those phrases used to describe mental shortcomings, or 'a deficiency in the marbles department' of someone who is 'not all there' and has either 'a screw loose' or 'a bit missing'. I first noticed this one being used around May 1987. Another version: 'Not quite enough coupons for the coffee percolator and matching set of cups'. More venerable idioms for the same thing would include: that a person is 'eleven pence half-penny' [i.e. not the full twelve pence of a shilling]; 'not the full shilling'; 'tuppence short of a shilling'; 'ninepence to the shilling'; 'one apple short of a full load'; 'one grape short of a bunch'; 'rowing with one oar in the water'; 'not playing with a full deck'; 'operating on cruise control'; 'one brick/a few bricks short of a (full) load'; 'a couple of bales shy of a full trailer load'; 'two sticks short of a bundle'; 'one pork pie/two sandwiches short of a picnic'; 'one card

short of a full deck'; 'fifty cards in the pack'; 'one can short of a six-pack'; 'ball doesn't bounce very high'; 'got off two stops short of Cincinnati'; 'the stairs do not reach all the way to the attic'; 'the lift/elevator doesn't go to the top floor/all the way up'; and 'the light's on, but no one's in'.

Moving a shade to one side, I can but print my favourite description of a TV producer (now dead) who was not at his best after lunch. Said his assistant, apologetically, at that time, 'by three o'clock he transmits, but he doesn't receive'.

F-Factor. See under FALKLANDS FACTOR.

FHB. Meaning, 'Family Hold Back' – a social instruction to members of the family not to eat all the food (which may be in short supply) before guests have had their fill. Probably only British middle-class use. Probably known by the 1950s.

fickle finger of fate. See under LAUGH–IN.

fiddle. See FIT AS A ∼.

fiddler on the roof, a. An opportunist, one who takes life easy, one who does what he pleases, a happy-go-lucky person. Popularized by *Fiddler on the Roof*, a musical (1964; film US, 1971), from a book by Joseph Stein and with lyrics by Sheldon Harnick. This tells the story of Tevye, a Jewish milkman in pre-Revolutionary Russia, who cheerfully survives family and political problems before emigrating to America. Based on Sholom Aleichem's collected stories *Tevye and His Daughters*, the title is used allusively to describe the easy-going nature of the hero. The title-song merely asks the question, why is the fiddler playing up on the roof all day and in all weathers? It concludes: 'It might not mean a thing/But then again it might!'

'Fiddling on the roof' is, however, one of the proverbial expressions portrayed (literally) in the painting known as 'The Proverbs' by David Teniers the Younger (*d* 1690) which hangs in Belvoir Castle, England. In the key to these Flemish proverbs, 'fiddling on the roof' is compared to 'eat, drink and be merry'. In Marc Chagall's painting 'The Dead Man' (1908), he shows – literally – a fiddler on a roof. Chagall often drew on Russian folktales in his work, and the character also turns up in his painting 'The Fiddler' (1912–13). Werner Haftmann in his book on the artist calls the fiddler on the roof, 'representative of the artist; a solitary individual, isolated by the strangeness and mystery of his art . . . a metaphorical figure who can be identified with . . . Chagall himself'. One source tells me that the writers of the musical were definitely thinking of this second picture when they came to settle on their title. A further attempt at explanation can be found in *Gänzl's Book of the Musical Theatre* (1988) where Tevye is described as: 'the epitome of the Jewish people of Anatevka who each scratch out a living, as the fiddler scratches out his tune, while perilously perched on the edge of existence as represented by the unsafe roof'. Another correspondent is certain that 'fiddler on the roof' is a Jewish euphemism for 'God'.

fiddle while Rome burns, to. Meaning 'to do something irrelevant while there are important matters to be dealt with'. For example, in early 1979, the Kuwaiti Ambassador to the UN told the Security Council, referring to Cambodia, 'Rome is burning, children are being orphaned, women widowed, and we haggle.'

The allusion is to the Emperor Nero's behaviour when Rome burned for several days and was two-thirds destroyed in AD 64. It is possible that he knew what he was doing, however. It has been suggested that the fire was started on his orders, as part of what we would now call an 'urban renewal programme'. Nevertheless, being a shrewd politician he blamed the Christians and persecuted them. As to the fiddling: Suetonius states that Nero watched the conflagration, then put on his tragedian's costume and sang the *Fall of Ilium* from beginning to end. The fiddle as we know it had not been invented, so if he played anything it was probably the lyre. Tacitus says, rather, that Nero went on his private stage and 'sang' of the (comparable) destruction of Troy.

The phrase is in English by 1649, when George Daniel wrote in *Trinarchodia*: 'Let Nero fiddle out Rome's obsequies.' Benjamin Haydon (*d* 1846) painted a vast

canvas with the title 'Nero playing his Lyre while Rome is burning'.

fiddling and fooling. This was the billing of the British comedian/violinist Ted Ray (1909–77) by the late 1940s. But the alliteration had appealed long before. Jonathan Swift in *Polite Conversation* has: 'For my Part, I believe the young Gentleman is his Sweet-heart; there's such fooling and fiddling betwixt them.'

fields. See AT PLAY IN THE ∼ OF THE LORD.

fifteen. See FAMOUS FOR ∼ MINUTES.

Fifth Beatle, the. Murray the K, the American disc jockey, applied this term to himself, on the basis of his presumed friendship with the BEATLES during the group's visit to the US in 1964 – much to the annoyance of Brian Epstein, their manager. The tale is recounted in an essay entitled 'The Fifth Beatle' in Tom Wolfe's *The Kandy-Kolored Tangerine-Flake Streamline Baby* (1966).

Others could more fittingly have merited the title – Stu Sutcliffe, an early member of the group who was eased out and died before fame struck; Pete Best, who was replaced as drummer by Ringo Starr; Neil Aspinall, road manager, aide and friend; and George Martin, the group's arranger and record producer. And others have had it applied to them with less reason. From a *New York Times* review (25 October 1991) of the Paul McCartney concert movie *Get Back*, directed by Richard Lester: 'Stitched-together . . . scrambled, incoherent . . . All this is the doing of Richard Lester, who still has "Help!" and "A Hard Day's Night" to his credit but hereby forefeits any claim he ever had to being the Fifth Beatle.' In addition, even if he wasn't actually called it at the time, the footballer George Best is looked upon as qualifying for the title in retrospect. In his Sixties heyday, Best flourished in Manchester (which is almost Liverpool, after all), had something approximating to a Beatles haircut, and was certainly the first British footballer to be accorded pop star status.

There is a secondary meaning, referring to someone who has missed out on the success of something he was once a part of.

This was certainly true in the case of Stu Sutcliffe and Pete Best. I can recall it being applied, for example, by a former *Observer* TV critic to Robert Hewison, the writer, who could be said to have missed out on the success of the MONTY PYTHON TV comedy team. At one time, Hewison worked closely at developing the Python type of humour with some of the other members of the group, though he never profited from it himself. Similarly, both Michael Bentine and Graham Stark have been referred to as 'the Fourth Goon' of the GOON SHOW – and with some justification.

When I was discussing this phrase on LBC Radio in 1989, a phone-in listener cleverly suggested that the 'fifth Beatle' was the Volkswagen Beetle which figures on the group's *Abbey Road* album sleeve.

fifth column, a. A group of traitors, infiltrators. In October 1936, during the Spanish Civil War, the Nationalist General, Emilio Mola, was besieging the Republican-held city of Madrid with four columns. He was asked in a broadcast whether this was sufficient to capture the city and he replied that he was relying on the support of the *quinta columna* [the fifth column], which was already hiding inside the city and which sympathized with his side. *The Fifth Column* was the title of Ernest Hemingway's only play (1938).

fifty million Frenchmen can't be wrong. As a slightly grudging argument this appears to have originated with US servicemen during the First World War, justifying support for their French allies. The precise number of millions varies. A song with the title (by Billy Rose, Willy Raskin and Fred Fisher) was recorded by Sophie Tucker in 1927. Cole Porter's musical *Fifty Million Frenchmen* opened in New York in 1929.

Where confusion has crept in is that Texas Guinan, the New York nightclub hostess, was refused entry into France with her girls in 1931 and said: 'It goes to show that fifty million Frenchmen *can* be wrong.' She returned to the US and renamed her show *Too Hot for Paris*. George Bernard Shaw also held out against the phrase. He insisted: 'Fifty million Frenchmen can't be right.'

57 varieties. See HEINZ.

fight and fight and fight again, to. Oratorical expression of determination. Hugh Gaitskell, leader of the British Labour Party, used a similar construction memorably at the Party Conference on 3 October 1960. When, against the wishes of the Party leadership, the conference looked like taking what Gaitskell called the 'suicidal path' of unilateral disarmament 'which will leave our country defenceless and alone', he was faced with making the most important speech of his life – for his leadership was at issue. 'There are some of us, Mr Chairman,' he said, 'who will fight and fight and fight again to save the Party we love.' Many delegates who were free to do so changed their votes, but the Party executive was still defeated. Nevertheless, Gaitskell reduced his opponents to a paper victory and the phrase is often recalled in tribute to a great personal achievement.

Earlier, when Austrian armies had threatened France, the revolutionary leader Danton (1759–94) had exhorted his fellow countrymen to: 'Dare! and dare! and dare again!'

fight between two bald men over a comb, a. A proverbial saying, possibly of Russian origin, and meaning 'an unnecessary struggle'. The Argentinian novelist, Jorge Luis Borges, was quoted as saying of the 1982 Falklands War between Britain and Argentina: 'The Falklands thing was a fight between two bald men over a comb.'

fight his/her way out of a paperbag. See under COULDN'T RUN . . .

fight on flab, the. Term for physical jerks used by the Irish-born disc jockey Terry Wogan (*b* 1938) on BBC Radio 2 in the early 1970s. He himself managed to lose two of the sixteen stone he weighed on first arriving in Britain, though whether this achievement was permanent is doubtful.

film. See GETS RID OF ~ ON TEETH.

final solution, the [German, *Endlösung*]. Euphemistic name given to Hitler's plan to exterminate the Jews of Europe and used by

Nazi officials from the summer of 1941 onwards to disguise the enormity of what they intended. A directive (drafted by Adolf Eichmann) was sent by Hermann Goering to Reinhard Heydrich on 31 July 1941: 'Submit to me as soon as possible a draft showing . . . measures already taken for the execution of the intended final solution of the Jewish question.' Gerald Reitlinger in *The Final Solution* (1953) says that the choice of phrase was probably, though not certainly, Hitler's own. Before then it had been used in a non-specific way to cover other possibilities – like emigration, for example. It is estimated that the 'final solution' led to the deaths of up to six million Jews. Compare HOLOCAUST.

find. See SPEAK AS YOU ∼ . . .

fine mess. See HERE'S ANOTHER ∼ . . .

fine sets these Ferguson's. A curiously memorable slogan for Ferguson radio sets (current in the UK in the 1950s). The advertisments carried what looked like a wood-cut of a pipe-smoking man listening to one of the sets.

finest. See BEST SWORDSMAN IN ALL FRANCE.

Finest, the. Nickname for New York City police, from about 1930 onwards. Later the use became ironic, as in: 'New York's finest – the best that money can buy.'

finest hour, their. Phrase of Winston Churchill's which delivered in his speech to the House of Commons (18 June 1940): 'Let us therefore brace ourselves to our duties, and so bear ourselves that, if the British Empire and its Commonwealth last for a thousand years, men will say, "This was their finest hour."'
    The Finest Hours was the title of a documentary film (UK, 1964) about Churchill's life.

fine-tooth comb, to go through (something) with a. 'To examine very closely' (known by 1891). Note, it is 'a fine-tooth comb' rather than 'fine tooth-comb' – the comb has fine teeth (enabling the smallest pieces of dirt to be removed) and isn't necessarily excellent.

fine weather for ducks. See LOVELY . . .

finger in the dike, boy who put his. A reference to the legendary Dutch boy who spotted a tiny hole in a canal dike, stuck his finger in it and stayed put all night, stopping a flood from happening. The story is related in Chapter 18 of *Hans Brinker, or the Silver Skates* (1865) by the American author, Mary Mapes Dodge (who had never actually been to Holland). Her novel includes a recollection of this 'Hero of Haarlem', whose story, she suggests, had long been known to Dutch children. It is not clear whether she was making this up or not. What is clear, however, is that only as a result of the success of her book did various Dutch towns claim the boy as their own. A small statue was erected to him at Harlingen. Whatever the case, he was never more than a legend. Sometimes, erroneously, he is given the name 'Hans Brinker' out of confusion with the hero of Dodge's book.
    Hence, the figure of speech for someone who staves off disaster through a simple (albeit temporary) gesture. From *The Times* (9 October 1986): 'To try to stand in front of the markets like the Little Dutch Boy with his finger in the dike would have been an act of folly if the Government were not convinced that the dike was fundamentally sound', (27 July 1989): ' "It was finger-in-the-dike stuff for us throughout the match," the Oxbridge coach, Tony Rodgers, said. "Ultimately the flood walls cracked." '

fingerlickin'. See IT'S ∼ GOOD.

finger of fate. See FLYING FICKLE ∼ AWARD under *LAUGH–IN*.

fingers. See LET YOUR ∼ DO THE WALKING.

Fings Ain't Wot They Used T'be. See THINGS AIN'T . . .

finish. See I'VE STARTED SO I'LL ∼!; NICE GUYS ∼ LAST; WHEN ARE YOU GOING TO ∼ OFF THAT DRESS?

fire. See BLOOD AND ∼; C'MON COLMAN'S . . . ; GREAT BALLS OF ∼; HANG ∼; SET THE THAMES ON ∼.

fire and ice. This word combination has appealed to many over the ages. It is the title of a short poem (1923) by Robert Frost: 'Some say the world will end in fire,/Some say in ice.' Here fire = desire, ice = hate, either of which is strong enough to kill. A.E. Housman in *A Shropshire Lad* (1896) has: 'And fire and ice within me fight/ Beneath the suffocating night.' Dante's *Inferno* has: 'Into the eternal darkness, into fire and into ice.' Psalm 148:7 in the Book of Common Prayer has 'fire and hail'.

Latterly, the phrase has been used to refer to the death of the planet Earth by atomic warfare or a new ice age. The ice skaters Jayne Torville and Christopher Dean had a routine with the title in the late 1980s.

first. See LOVE AT ∼ FLIGHT under BOAC TAKES GOOD CARE OF YOU; TODAY IS THE ∼ DAY . . . ; WOMEN AND CHILDREN ∼.

first among equals. As *primus inter pares*, this is an anonymous Latin saying. It has been used about the position of politicians in a number of countries and also of the Pope. *ODCIE* defines it as an idiom meaning 'the one of a group who leads or takes special responsibility but who neither feels himself, nor is held by others to be, their superior'. The Round Table in Arthurian legend was meant to show not only that there was no precedence among the knights who sat at it but also that King Arthur was no more than first among equals.

Used specifically regarding the British Prime Minister within the Cabinet, the phrase cannot pre-date Sir Robert Walpole (in power 1721–42) who is traditionally the first to have held that position. Lord Morley may have been the first to use the phrase in this context in his life of Walpole (1889) where he says: 'Although in Cabinet all its members stand on an equal footing, speak with equal voice, and, on the rare occasions when a division is taken, are counted on the fraternal principle of one vote, yet the head of the Cabinet is *primus inter pares*, and occupies a position which, so long as it lasts, is one of exceptional and peculiar authority.' In 1988, Julian Critchley MP was quoted as having referred to Margaret Thatcher as '*prima donna inter pares*'.

First Among Equals was the title of Jeffrey Archer's novel (1984) about the pursuit of the British Prime Ministership.

first catch your hare. Proverb indicating that you can't begin to do something until you have acquired a certain necessary element (which may be difficult to acquire). *CODP* finds the equivalent thought in *c* 1300, translated from the Latin: 'It is commonly said that one must first catch the deer, and afterwards, when he has been caught, skin him.' For a long time, however, the saying was taken to be a piece of practical, blunt good sense to be found in Mrs Beeton's *Book of Household Management* (1851), but it does not appear there. However, in Mrs Hannah Glasse's earlier *The Art of Cookery made plain and easy* (1747), there is the similar: 'Take your hare when it is cased [skinned].' It was known in the familar form by 1855 when it appeared in Thackeray's *The Rose and the Ring*. Similar proverbs include: 'Catch your bear before you sell its skin', 'Never spend your money before you have it' and 'Don't count your chickens before they are hatched'.

firstest with the mostest. To describe anything as 'the mostest' might seem an exclusively US activity. However, *OED2* finds English dialect use in the 1880s and Partridge/*Slang* recognizes its use as a jocular superlative without restricting it to the US. As such, it is a consciously ungrammatical way of expressing extreme degree. Whether this was consciously the case with the Confederate General, Nathan B. Forrest (*d* 1877) is very much in doubt. He could hardly read or write but he managed to say that the way to win battles was to be 'firstest with the mostest', or that you needed to 'git thar fustest with the mostest'. Bartlett gives this last as the usual rendering of the more formally reported words: 'Get there first with the most men.' In Irving Berlin's musical *Call Me Madam* (1950) there is a song with the title 'The Hostess with the Mostes' on the Ball'. One assumes that Berlin's use, like any evocation of 'the mostest' nowadays, refers back to Forrest's remark.

First Hundred Thousand, The. Title of a war novel (1915) by Ian Hay, which is subtitled 'Adventures of a typical regiment in Kitchener's army'. The book begins with a poem (Hay's own, presumably):

We're off a hundred thousand strong.
And some of us will not come back.

A.J.P. Taylor in his *English History 1914–45*, describing a period of 'patriotic frenzy' in the Great War, says that the 'spirit of 1915 was best expressed by Ian Hay, a writer of light fiction, in *The First Hundred Thousand* – a book which treated soldiering as joke, reviving "the best days of our lives" at some imaginary public school'.

first past the post. Electoral arrangements (as in Britain) where the candidate or party with the largest number of votes wins, as compared, say, to the system known as proportional representation. W.P. Brown of Aberdeen commented (1993): 'Note how the felicitous phrase attaches the warm glow of Great British Sportsmanship (Derby Day, the Boat Race, *Chariots of Fire*, etc.) to a voting system whose defining characteristic is the absence of anything corresponding to a winning post. It is merely a case of "first past the second" after all.'

There was no need for this comforting metaphor until the Westminster system was under attack by the advocates of electoral reform. The earliest citations in the *OED2* date from 1952/65 and come from Australia, one of them referring back to Queensland in 1892. Is this significant?

First World War, the. Known at first as the 'European War', it became known quite rapidly as the **Great War**. By 10 September 1918, Lieut.-Col. C. à Court Repington, was referring to it in his diary as the 'First World War', thus: 'I saw Major Johnstone, the Harvard Professor who is here to lay the bases of an American History. We discussed the right name of the war. I said that we called it now *The War*, but that this could not last. The Napoleonic War was *The Great War*. To call it *The German War* was too much flattery for the Boche. I suggested *The World War* as a shade better title, and finally we mutually agreed to call it *The First World War* in order to prevent the millennium folk from forgetting that the history of the world was

the history of war.' Repington's book entitled *The First World War 1914–18* was published in 1920. Presumably this helped popularize the name for the war, while ominously suggesting that it was the first of a series.

first — years are the hardest, the. A format phrase usually employed in connection with marriage or jobs – suggesting, in an ironical way, that the initial stages of anything are the most difficult. It probably derives from the Army saying, 'Cheer up – the first seven years are the worst!' from *c* the First World War, referring to the term of a regular soldier's service. Partridge/*Catch Phrases* also finds 'the first hundred years are the hardest/worst' from about the same period.

Compare SEVEN YEAR ITCH.

fish. See under CAN A (BLOODY) DUCK SWIM; HERE'S A PRETTY KETTLE OF ~; NEITHER ~, FLESH . . .

Fisher King, the. Name of a mythical figure from the legend of the Holy Grail, where he is the uncle of Sir Percevale. His story is alluded to in T.S. Eliot's poem *The Waste Land* (1922). In Anthony Powell's novel *The Fisher King* (1986), he appears as a sexually impotent photographer, wounded in the Second World War, who takes part in a modern-day quest. In the unrelated film with the title (US, 1991), he appears as a hallucinating down-and-out (played by Robin Williams) who aids a suicidal talk-show host.

fist. See HAND OVER ~; IRON ~.

fit. See ALL THE NEWS THAT'S ~; LOOKING BRONZED AND ~.

fit as a fiddle, to be. A fiddler, when playing quickly, has to be so dextrous with his fingers and bow that he is assumed to be especially lively and awake. Could, then, the phrase that we have be a contraction of 'fit as a fiddler'? It was current by 1616.

fit to a T, to. 'To fit perfectly'. A T-square is used by draughtsmen to draw parallel lines and angles, though it seems 'to a T' was in use by 1693 and before the T-square got its name. Perhaps the original expression was 'fit to a tittle' – a tittle being the dot over the letter i – so the phrase meant 'to a dot, fine point'. There are other theories, none of them conclusive.

five. See HOW MANY BEANS MAKE ∼; I'LL GIVE IT FOIVE.

5–4–3–2–1. A case of life imitating art? It is said that the backwards countdown to a rocket launch was originated by the German film director Fritz Lang (1890–1976). He thought it would make things more suspenseful if the count was reversed – 5–4–3–2–1 – so, in his 1928 film *By Rocket to the Moon* (sometimes known as *Frau im Mond* or 'The Woman in the Moon', from the German title), he established the routine for future real-life space shots. I await challenges to this theory. However, I note that the 1931 American novel with the title *By Rocket to the Moon* (by Otto Willi Gail) does not appear to include the phrase.

five o'clock shadow. See AVOID ∼.

fix. See IF IT AIN'T BROKEN . . .

Fixit. See MR ∼.

flab. See FIGHT ON ∼.

flag. See FLY THE FLAG under BOAC TAKES GOOD CARE OF YOU.

flagpole, run it up the. See under LET'S — AND SEE IF —.

flaming Nora! See under RUDDY NORA!

flanelled fool. Phrase from the poem 'The Islanders' (1902) by Rudyard Kipling: 'Flannelled fools at the wicket or the muddied oafs at the goals' – where the 'fools' are, of course, cricketers. Used as the title of a book (1967), 'a slice of life in the 30s', by the critic, T.C. Worsley.

flappers. See BRIGHT YOUNG THINGS.

Flash Harry. Nickname of Sir Malcolm Sargent (1895–1967), the orchestral conductor. It is said to have originated with a BBC announcer after Sargent had

appeared on the radio *Brains Trust* and was also about to be heard in the following programme. Listeners were told that they were to be taken over to a concert conducted by Sargent in Manchester. It sounded as if he had gone there straightaway, in a flash. This is the version given by Sargent himself in the *Sunday Times* (25 April 1965). However, the nickname also encapsulated his extremely debonair looks and manner – smoothed-back hair, buttonhole, gestures and all. When Sir Thomas Beecham heard that Sargent was conducting in Tokyo, he remarked: 'Ah! Flash in Japan!' In due course, Sir Alexander Gibson (*b* 1926), conductor of the Scottish National Orchestra, was dubbed **Flash Haggis**.

It has been suggested that 'Flash Harry' was originally the name given to the man who would 'flash' the furnaces every morning in Midlands factories – which might go some way to explain why the 'Harry' was inserted in the Malcolm Sargent nickname. Other similar coinages noted by Partridge/*Slang* are 'Flash Alf' and 'Flash Jack'.

flaunt. See WHEN YOU GOT IT, ∼ IT.

flavour of the month. Originally a generic advertising phrase aimed at persuading people to try new varieties of ice cream and not just stick to their customary choice (in the US, by 1946). Latterly, it has become an idiom for any fad, craze or person that is quickly discarded after a period of being in the news or in demand. From the *Longman Register of New Words* (1989): 'The metaphorical possibilities of the word *ambush* are catching on in several areas of activity in the USA, making it the lexical flavour-of-the-month in American English.'

fleas. See MY DOG HAS ∼.

fleet. See HEAVENS, ELEVEN O'CLOCK . . .

Fleet's lit up, the. The most famous British broadcasting boob came from Lieut.-Cdr Tommy Woodrooffe (1899–1978), a leading BBC radio commentator of the 1930s. On the night of 20 May 1937 he was due to give a 15–minute description of the 'illumination' of the Fleet after the Coronation Naval Review at Spithead. What he said, in a commentary that was faded out after less than four minutes, began: 'At the present moment, the whole Fleet's lit up. When I say "lit up", I mean lit up by fairy lamps. We've forgotten the whole Royal Review. We've forgotten the Royal Review. The whole thing is lit up by fairy lamps. It's fantastic. It isn't the Fleet at all. It's just . . . fairy land. The whole fleet is in fairy land . . .'

Eventually the commentary was taken off the air. Naturally, many listeners concluded that Woodrooffe himself had been 'lit up' as the result of enjoying too much hospitality from his former shipmates on board HMS *Nelson* before the broadcast. But he denied this. 'I had a kind of nervous blackout. I had been working too hard and my mind just went blank.' He told the *News Chronicle*: 'I was so overcome by the occasion that I literally burst into tears . . . I found I could say no more.'

The BBC took a kindly view and the incident did not put paid to Woodrooffe's broadcasting career. But the phrase became so famous that it was used as the title of a 'musical frolic' at the London Hippodrome in 1938 and Bud Flanagan recorded a song written by Vivian Ellis called 'The Fleet's Lit Up'.

The Second World War song 'I'm Going to Get Lit Up When the Lights Go Up in London' by Hubert Gregg (1943) probably owes something to the Woodrooffe affair, though use of 'lit up' to mean 'tipsy' dates back to 1914, at least.

fleshpots of Egypt, the. Meaning 'any place of comparative luxury', it was originally said by the Israelites (Exodus 16:3): 'Would to God we had died by the hand of the Lord in the land of Egypt, when we sat by the flesh pots, and when we did eat bread to the full.' Clementine Churchill wrote to Winston on 20 December 1910: 'I do so wish I was at Warter with you enjoying the Flesh Pots of Egypt! It sounds a delightful party . . .' (quoted in *Clementine Churchill* by Mary Soames, 1979).

flick your Bic. Originally a slogan for Bic cigarette lighters, this was coined by US copywriter Charlie Moss in 1975 and

occurred in an ad that showed how smart sophisticated people didn't use lighters – they simply 'flicked their Bics'. The phrase caught on and was picked up by many comedians. During the energy crisis, Bob Hope said: 'Things are getting so bad that the Statue of Liberty doesn't light up any more. She just stands there and flicks her Bic.'

flies. See AS THE CROW ~.

flight. See LOVE AT FIRST ~ under BOAC TAKES GOOD CARE OF YOU.

flight from fear, a. A cliché of journalism, demonstrating the lure of alliteration yet again. 'TO BRITAIN ON FLIGHT FROM FEAR. A flight from fear ended at Heathrow Airport yesterday for passengers on the first plane to arrive from Poland since martial law was proclaimed at the weekend' (*Daily Mail*, 18 December 1981).

flippin' kids! See under EDUCATING ARCHIE.

flog the bishop. See BASH THE BISHOP.

flood, Johnstown. See DON'T SPIT . . .

floor. See FACE ON THE CUTTING ROOM ~; GOLDEN ~.

Floreat Etona [May Eton flourish]. Motto of Eton College (founded 1440) in Berkshire. It is spoken by the villain 'Captain Hook' (presumably an Old Etonian), just before he is eaten by a crocodile in J.M. Barrie's play *Peter Pan* (1904). (In Barrie's novel, *Peter Pan and Wendy* (1911) he merely cries, 'Bad form.') It was earlier used as the title of a painting (1882) by Elizabeth, Lady Butler depicting a British attack on the Boers in South Africa at Laing's Neck in 1881, after this eyewitness account: 'Poor Elwes fell among the 58th. He shouted to another Eton boy (adjutant of the 58th, whose horse had been shot) "Come along, Monck! Floreat Etona! we must be in the front rank!" and he was shot immediately.'

Flower Power. A hippy slogan – formed, no doubt, in emulation of BLACK POWER, to describe the beliefs of the so-called Flower Children. Flowers were used as a love and peace symbol when the phrase came into use *c* 1967.

flowers. See SAY IT WITH ∼.

fluffy ducks. See BOX OF BIRDS . . .

flute. See MAN WITH THE GOLDEN . . .

fly by the seat of one's pants, to. To perform any function relying on instinct and experience without scientific support or knowledge. Originally applied to flying (in the US, by 1942) and now figuratively.

flying. See DARING YOUNG MAN ON . . .

flying fickle finger of fate award, the. See under LAUGH-IN.

fly me. See I'M —.

Flynn. See IN LIKE ∼.

fly the flag. See under BOAC TAKES GOOD CARE OF YOU.

fog. See NIGHT AND ∼.

fogey. See YOUNG ∼.

Foggy Bottom. The nickname for the US Department of State comes from the name of a marshy part of Washington DC where its offices are located. Compare the similar locational nicknames for: the British Foreign Office, **Whitehall**; the French, **Quai d'Orsay**; and the Russian, **Gorky Street**.

fog in Channel. See CONTINENT ISOLATED.

fold one's tents like the Arabs, to. Meaning 'to bring to a conclusion unostentatiously', the expression comes from Longfellow's 'The Day is Done':

And the night shall be filled with music
And the cares that infest the day
Shall fold their tents, like the Arabs,
And as silently steal away.

Alas, at the conclusion of his case for the

defence in the Jeremy Thorpe trial (1979), Mr George Carman QC said to the jury: 'I end by saying in the words *of the Bible* [*sic*]: "Let this prosecution fold up its tent and quietly creep away." '

folks. See HELLO, FOLKS under BAND WAGGON; THAT'S ALL, ∼!

follows. See HE WHO LOVES ME, ∼ ME.

follow that cab/taxi/van! A cliché of the cinema. Said to a taxi driver by the hero/ policeman in pursuit of a villain. Few people can ever have said it in real life. (It is as much of a cliché as the ability film actors have, on getting *out* of taxis, to tender exactly the right change to the driver.) In *Top Hat* (US, 1935), Eric Blore as a butler says 'Follow that cab' when he is shadowing Ginger Rogers. In *Let's Dance* (US, 1950), Fred Astaire says 'follow that cab' in order to chase Betty Hutton. The film *Amsterdamned* (1989), a cop thriller set amid the canals of the Dutch capital, includes the memorable injunction, 'Follow those bubbles!'

food for thought. Something that requires reflection and consideration. Known by 1825.

food shot from guns. Slogan for Quaker Puffed Wheat and Puffed Rice, current since the early 1900s. Claude C. Hopkins (1867–1932), one of the great American advertising gurus, wrote: 'I watched the process where the grains were shot from guns. And I coined the phrase. The idea aroused ridicule. One of the greatest food advertisers in the country wrote an article about it. He said that of all the follies evolved in food advertising this certainly was the worst the idea of appealing on "Food shot from guns" was the theory of an imbecile. But the theory proved attractive. It was such a curiosity arouser that it proved itself the most successful campaign ever conducted in cereals.'

fooling. See FIDDLING AND ∼.

foolish things. See THESE ∼.

fools. See ONLY ∼ AND HORSES WORK.

foot. See BEST ∼ FORWARD; I'LL GO TO THE ∼ OF OUR STAIRS; ONE ∼ IN THE GRAVE.

footlights. See DOCTOR GREASEPAINT . . .

force. See BRUTE ∼ AND IGNORANCE; DON'T ∼ IT, PHOEBE; MAY THE ∼ BE WITH YOU.

foreign field, some corner of a. See FOREVER ENGLAND.

forest. See DOWN IN THE ∼ SOMETHING STIRRED.

forever. See DIAMOND IS ∼; NOW AND ∼.

forever England. Phrase from Rupert Brooke's 1914 poem 'The Soldier':

> If I should die, think only this of me:
> That there's some corner of a foreign field
> That is for ever England.

Forever England was the UK title given to the reissue of the film version of C.S. Forester's novel *Brown on Resolution* (1929; film UK, 1935). In the US, the film had been known all along as *Born for Glory*. An anthology, *For Ever England*, edited by Collie Knox, was published in 1943.

forget. See DON'T ∼ THE DIVER!; DON'T ∼ THE FRUIT GUMS, MUM; I'LL ∼ MY OWN NAME under *ITMA*.

forgets. See AN ELEPHANT NEVER ∼

forgiven. See ALL IS ∼ under WHERE ARE YOU NOW?

forgotten. See GONE BUT NOT ∼.

Forgotten Army, the. Nickname given to the British Army in India and South-East Asia, and more precisely, Burma and Malaya during the Second World War. According to John Connell, *Auchinleck* (1959), the phrase was mentioned in a despatch by Stuart Emeny, a *News Chronicle* war correspondent, in the summer of 1943, but the idea behind it had long been current with the soldiers. Lord Louis Mountbatten, supreme Allied commander in S-E Asia (1943–45) is said to have 'reassured' his men with the words,

'You are not the Forgotten Army – nobody's even heard of you!'

fork. See MORTON'S ∼.

forked tongue. See WHITE MAN SPEAK WITH ∼.

for men of distinction. Slogan for Lord Calvert custom-blended whiskey in the US, current 1945. 'For years,' the copy ran, 'the most expensive whiskey blended in America, Lord Calvert is intended especially for those who can afford the finest.' Marshall McLuhan wrote in *The Mechanical Bride* (1951): 'Snob appeal might seem to be the most obvious feature of this type of ad, with its submerged syllogism that since all sorts of eminent men drink this whiskey they are eminent because they drink it. Or only this kind of whiskey is suited to the palate of distinguished men, therefore a taste for it confers, or at least displays an affinity for, distinction in those who have not yet achieved greatness.'

Former Naval Person. In his wartime cables as Prime Minister to President Roosevelt, Winston Churchill used this code name. He had sent his telegrams to the President as 'Naval Person' when First Lord of the Admiralty at the beginning of the Second World War.

for — of — opportunity knocks. See OPPORTUNITY KNOCKS.

for Pete's sake. A mild oath, known in the US since 1903, possibly derived from 'for pity's sake'.

fort. See HOLD THE ∼.

Forth Bridge. See PAINTING THE ∼.

Forties, Roaring. See ROARING TWENTIES.

fortifies. See PHYLLOSAN ∼ THE OVER-FORTIES.

fortune. See HIS/HER FACE IS HIS/HER ∼; I CAME TO LONDON TO SEEK MY ∼.

fortune(s) of war. Olivia Manning's 'Balkan' and 'Levant' trilogies of novels form a single narrative. When BBC TV adapted the six books under the title *Fortunes of War* (1985), this became the overall name of the cycle. The earliest citation in *OED2* for the phrase 'fortunes of war' is 1880, but it had long been known in the singular: 'After uncertain fortune of war, on both sides' was written by John Selden in 1612; Charles Dickens, *Sketches by Boz*, Chap. 12 (1833–6) has this cry from a street game: 'All the fortin of war! this time I vin, next time you vin'; the war memorial at the cemetery of El Alamein (following the battle of 1942) is dedicated 'to whom the fortune of war denied a known and honoured grave'.

forty. See LIFE BEGINS AT ~.

forty acres and a mule. See TEN ACRES AND A MULE.

forward. See ONE STEP ~ . . . ; BEST FOOT ~.

for yonks. See DONKEY'S YEARS.

for you, Tommy, the war is over! Said by a German capturing a British soldier ('Tommy Atkins' being the traditional nickname for such), presumably in fiction, but no citation is to hand. Partridge/*Catch Phrases* has it as said, rather, by Italians to British prisoners of war in 1940–5 and without the 'Tommy'. In McGowan & Hands's *Don't Cry for Me, Sergeant-Major* (1983)(about the Falklands war), a British radio officer is asked what Spanish voices are saying over the air waves and 'could hardly keep the smile from his lips as he replied in a phoney Spanish accent, "They're saying, 'Buenos dias, senors, for you the war is over!'"'

four. See GANG OF ~.

four hundred, the. Name given to the top stratum of New York society in 1888 by its leader, Ward McAllister. 'There are only about four hundred people in fashionable New York society,' he told the *Tribune*. 'If you go outside that number you strike people who are either not at ease in a ballroom or else make other people not at ease.' Mrs Ward Astor asked McAllister to help prune her invitation list down to four hundred when giving a ball in a room which could only comfortably hold that number. Earlier, the top level had been called the Upper 10,000 or Upper Ten.

The Four Hundred became the title of a novel (1979) by Stephen Sheppard on this subject.

four more years! In US presidential elections where the incumbent seeks, or is being urged to seek, a further term, this is the standard cry. His supporters chanted it of Richard Nixon in 1972, and look what happened. With it, several times, Ronald Reagan's supporters interrupted his remarks accepting the GOP presidential nomination in Dallas, Texas, on 23 August 1984. Their prayer was answered.

four-square?, are you. Aimée Semple McPherson (*d* 1944), the Canadian-born revivalist, had the Angelus Temple in LA as the centre for her 'Foursquare Gospel'. This phrase was the greeting and slogan of her followers – and was used to mean, 'are you solid, resolute?' Being 'square', in this sense, dates from at least 1300. Compare Theodore Roosevelt's campaign promise in 1901: 'We demand that big business give people a **Square Deal** . . . If elected I shall see to it that every man has a Square Deal, no more and no less.' Meaning 'a fair deal', this phrase of US origin was current by 1876.

fourth estate, the. The British press. In 1828, Thomas Macaulay wrote of the House of Commons: 'The gallery in which the reporters sit has become the fourth estate of the realm' – that is to say, after the Lords Spiritual, the Lords Temporal, and the Commons – and Macaulay has often been credited with coining this expression. But so have a number of others. The phrase was originally used to describe various forces outside Parliament – such as the Army (as by Falkland in 1638) or the Mob (as by Fielding in 1752). When William Hazlitt used it in 'Table Talk' in 1821, he meant not the Press in general but just William Cobbett. Two years later, Lord Brougham is said to have used the phrase in the House of Commons to describe the Press in general. So by the time Macaulay used it in the *Edinburgh Review* in 1828, it was obviously an established usage. Then Thomas Carlyle used it several times – in his article on Boswell's *Life of Johnson* in 1832, in his history of the *The French Revolution* in 1837, and in his lectures 'On Heroes, Hero-Worship, & the Heroic in History' in 1841. But, just to keep the confusion alive, he attributed the phrase to Edmund Burke, who died in 1797 and is said to have pointed at the press gallery and remarked: 'And yonder sits the fourth estate, more important than them all.'

It has been suggested that the BBC (or the broadcast media in general) now constitute a *fifth* estate, as also, at one time, the trades unions.

fox. See CRAZY LIKE A ~; DESERT ~.

Frankie Goes To Hollywood. Name of a British pop vocal group *c* 1983/4, which derived from a newspaper headline referring to Frank Sinatra. A tantalizing T-shirt slogan (referring to the group) **Frankie Say Relax** was taken up by the comedian Frankie Howerd (also on a T-shirt) in the form 'Frankie Says Relax'.

frankly my dear I don't give a damn. In the last scene of the film *Gone With the Wind* (1939), Scarlett O'Hara is finally abandoned by her husband Rhett Butler. Although she believes she can get him back, there occurs the controversial moment when Rhett replies with these words to her entreaty: 'Where shall I go? What shall I do?' They were only allowed on to the soundtrack after months of negotiation with the Hays Office which controlled film censorship. In those days, the word 'damn' was forbidden in Hollywood under Section V (1) of the Hays Code, even if it was what Margaret Mitchell had written in her novel (though she hadn't included the 'frankly'). Accordingly, Clark Gable, as Rhett, had to put the emphasis unnaturally on 'give' rather than on 'damn'.

Freddie. See READY FOR ~ under ARE YOU READY, EDDIE?

Fred Karno. An adjective meaning 'inept, disorganized', this was applied humorously

to the new British army raised to fight in the First World War. The name comes from the leader (actually, Fred Westcott, *d* 1941) of a music-hall comedy troupe which was popular in the early years of the century. Hence: 'Fred Karno's Army', 'Fred Karno outfit', etc.

free. See BEST THINGS IN LIFE ARE ~; I'M ~!; I'M NOT A NUMBER . . . ; NO SUCH A THING AS A ~ LUNCH; THIS IS A ~ COUNTRY; WITH ONE BOUND HE WAS ~.

Freedom Now. In the early 1960s, a black litany went:

Q. What do you want?
A. Freedom!
Q. Let me hear it again – what do you want?
A. Freedom!
Q. When do you want it?
A. Now!

This format may have arisen from a petition delivered to Governor George Wallace of Alabama in March 1965. On this occasion, Martin Luther King Jr and other civil rights leaders led some 3,000 people in a 50-mile march from Selma to Montgomery. The petition began: 'We have come to you, the Governor of Alabama, to declare that we must have our *freedom now*. We must have the right to vote; we must have equal protection of the law, and an end to police brutality.'

free, gratis, and for nothing. A double tautology. Partridge/*Slang* quotes Thomas Bridges as saying in 1770 that 'the common people' always put 'free' and 'gratis' together; and notes that the longer version occurs in an 1841 book. In fact, 'free, gratis' was current by 1682 and the longer version occurs a little earlier than 1841. Charles Dickens in *The Pickwick Papers*, Chap. 26 (1836–7) has Sam Weller's father say 'free gratis for nothin''. In *Usage and Abusage*, Partridge decides that it is a cliché, only excusable as a jocularity.

free the —. This all-purpose slogan came into its own in the 1960s – usually in conjunction with a place and number. Hence: 'Free the Chicago 7' (charged with creating disorder during the Democratic

Convention in 1968), 'Free the Wilmington 10', and so on. Dignifying protesters with a group name incorporating place and number began with the 'Hollywood 10' (protesters against McCarthyite investigations) in 1947.

The format has now become a cliché of sloganeering. Various joke slogans from the late 1970s demanded: 'Free the Beethoven 9/the Heinz 57/the Intercity 125/the Chiltern Hundreds/the Indianapolis 500/ the Grecian 2000.'

free, white, and 21. 'Having reached the age of consent and in charge of one's own life, especially sex life.' Known in US and the UK, the first recorded use of this expression appears to be in John Buchan, *The Courts of the Morning* (1929). A minor American gangster states that someone is 'free, white, twenty-one and hairy-chested'.

French. See under NO MORE LATIN . . . ; PARDON MY ∼; THAT'S YOUR ACTUAL ∼ under *ROUND THE HORNE*.

Frenchmen. See FIFTY MILLION ∼.

frenzy. See FEEDING ∼.

Friday. See MY NAME'S ∼ under *DRAGNET*.

Friday night is Amami night. A slogan for Amami hair products, current in UK in the 1920s. Presumably this inspired the title of the long-running BBC radio show *Friday Night is Music Night* (from 1953).

friend. See EVEN YOUR BEST ∼ S . . . ; GUIDE PHILOSOPHER AND ∼; IS SHE A ∼ OF DOROTHY?; SHE'S MY BEST ∼ under *EDUCATING ARCHIE*; MY ∼; SOME OF MY BEST ∼ S . . . ; WE ARE JUST GOOD ∼ S; WITH A LITTLE HELP FROM . . . ; SOME OF MY BEST ∼ ARE . . . ; WITH ∼ S LIKE THAT . . .

friendly. See YOUR ∼ NEIGHBOURHOOD —.

friends . . . and you are my friends . . . Pat Patrick as 'Ersil Twing' in the American radio show *The Chase and Sanborn Hour* (1937–48).

fright. See DON'T BE FRIGHT.

frogs have watertight assholes?, do. See IS THE POPE A CATHOLIC?

From a Far Country. Title of a TV film (1981) of dramatized episodes from the early life of Pope John Paul II. The source seems to lie in the Old Testament where there are several examples of 'from a far land' and 'from a far country' (Deuteronomy 29:22, 2 Kings 20:14, Isaiah 39:3, etc.) but, perhaps most felicitously, there is 'good news from a far country' (Proverbs 25:25).

Compare *Crowned In a Far Country*, a book (1986) by Princess Michael of Kent about people who had married into the British Royal Family. William Caxton in England's first printed book, *Dictes or Sayengis of the Philosophres* (1477), has: 'Socrates was a Greek born in a far country from here.' H.D. Thoreau, *On the Duty of Civil Disobedience* (1849) has: '[On going to prison] It was like travelling into a far country, such as I had never expected to behold, to lie there for one night.' Poem X. in the Edith Sitwell/William Walton entertainment *Façade* (1922) is entitled 'A Man From a Far Countree'.

— from Hell. The origin of this idiom – meaning 'ghastly' or 'hellish' would seem to lie in the neighbouring fields of horror movies and rock albums. A writer in the *Independent* (24 September 1988) joked about videos with titles like *Mutant Hollywood Chainsaw Hookers From Hell!* Pantera recorded 'Cowboys from Hell' in 1990 and Original Sin recorded 'Bitches from Hell' in 1986.

Henry McNulty listed some examples of this suddenly ubiquitous phrase: from his own paper the *Hartford Courant* (in Connecticut) (7 February 1992), a description of US figure-skating champion Christopher Bowman as 'Hans Brinker from Hell'; in the *New York Times* (9 May 1993), 'Lisa Samalin's painting of grandma from hell' and (13 June 1993), a mention of Hillary Clinton, 'She is alternately deified and vilified as nun or Lady Macbeth, Florence Nightingale or Yuppie From Hell.' Mr McNulty tried also to crisp up the definition of the phrase: 'In my view, the situation or person being described must be extremely, even exaggeratedly characteristic of the type, but strongly emphasizing the negative qualities. Thus, the grandma from Hell would need to exhibit all the traits that would lead others to describe her as "a typical grandmother", but only in the pejorative sense. Something or somebody said to be "the — from Hell" has not just gone wrong, but has done so specifically by inflating the negative characteristics of the species.'

(In the First World War, kilted Scottish regiments were apparently known as 'ladies from hell'.)

from log cabin to White House. See LOG CABIN . . .

from sea to shining sea. A line from the poem 'America the Beautiful' (1893) by Katharine Lee Bates:

> America! America!
> God shed his grace on thee
> And crown thy good with brotherhood
> From sea to shining to shining sea!

These words have also been set to music. The motto of the Dominion of Canada (adopted 1867) is '*A mari usque ad mare*' [From sea to sea], which came from Psalm 72:8: 'He shall have dominion also from sea to sea.'

from your mouth to God's ear. Meaning 'I hope what you say will come true by being acted upon by God'. I first heard this expression used by Joan Collins in a TV interview in 1982. Probably of Jewish/American origin.

from — with love. The obvious inspiration for *From Russia With Love*, Ian Fleming's James Bond novel (1957, film UK, 1963), is the simple form of wording used to accompany a present. But, as a format phrase, it has launched any number of allusions of the 'from — with —' variety. Compare *To Paris With Love* (film UK, 1954) and *To Sir With Love* (book by E.R. Braithwaite, 1959, film UK, 1967). In *Keep Taking the Tabloids* (1983), Fritz Spiegl noted these headline uses: 'From the Rush Hour with Love', 'From Maggie without love!'

front. See SECOND ~ NOW.

frontier. See NEW ~.

frozen mit, to give someone the. Meaning 'to freeze out; give the cold shoulder to someone; exclude' (from 'mit', 'mitten', thence 'hand'). Lady Diana Cooper writing to Duff Cooper on 14 September 1925 (in a letter printed in *A Durable Fire*, 1983) said: 'Duffy, don't be deathly proud, my darling . . . you probably dish out the frozen mit to all, and I want all men to love and admire you.' Partridge/*Slang* finds it in *Punch* in 1915. 'To give someone the mitten', meaning to reject a lover (especially) was known by 1838.

fruit gums. See DON'T FORGET THE ~, MUM!

fruits ye shall know them, by their. 'By their — ye shall know them' has become almost a format phrase. The original version occurs in Matthew 7:20 in the part of the Sermon on the Mount advising the hearers to beware false prophets.

FTA (Fuck The Army). Much used in the US Army, especially as graffiti. *DOAS* adds: 'Since *c* 1960, as a counter expression to disliked orders, rules etc.' *F.T.A.* was the title of an anti-Vietnam War film made by Jane Fonda in 1972.

The 'initial' strategy has also been used regarding the Pope ('FTP') and the Queen ('FTQ') especially in Northern Ireland (both types recorded in Belfast, 1971)

fuck(s). See BEST ~ ARE ALWAYS AFTER . . . ; I SUPPOSE A ~'S OUT OF THE QUESTION; WHO DO I HAVE TO ~ . . .

fudge and mudge, to. Meaning 'to produce the appearance of a solution while, in fact, only patching up a compromise', these verbs (and associated nouns) were often wheeled out in discussions of the Social Democratic and the Liberal parties in Britain in the 1980s. One of the SDP's GANG OF FOUR, Dr David Owen, had used it earlier in his previous incarnation, as a member of the Labour Party. He told Labour's Blackpool Conference (2 October 1980): 'We are fed up with fudging and mudging, with mush and slush.'

full circle. See WHEEL HAS COME FULL CIRCLE.

full-frontal nudity. Referring to nudity which allows a man or woman's sexual parts to be seen. Before the 1960s, naked people when being photographed had a way of holding large beach balls in front of themselves, but with the advent of naked actors in such shows as *Hair* (1967) and OH! CALCUTTA! (1969) a term obviously had to be invented for this great leap forward in civilized behaviour. *OED2* does not find the term until 1971, but in my diary for 25 March 1970, I find myself going to see Ken Russell's film *Women in Love* and noting: 'full frontal nudity, too, as they call it, though I don't feel a better man for having seen Oliver Reed's genitals'. The episode of TV's MONTY PYTHON'S FLYING CIRCUS broadcast on 7 December 1969 was entitled 'Full Frontal Nudity'.

full monty, the. Meaning, 'the full amount, everything included' – a phrase suddenly popular in British English in the early 1990s but known since the early 1980s. Its appearance in *Street Talk, the Language of* Coronation Street (1986) shows that it was established in the North of England/Lancashire soap opera by that date. The dictionary explains: 'To avoid the awkwardness of stumbling through an unfamiliar menu, someone might tell the waiter: "We'll have the full monty"' (though the expression **full house** might just as easily be used in that context). From the *Guardian* (28 September 1989): ' "What we're after is a live skeleton – the full monty," said the stage manager.' The somewhat Cockney comedian Jim Davidson entitled his autobiography *The Full Monty* in 1993.

   Could it be a corruption of the 'full amount'? Or could it have something to do with 'monty' (from the Spanish *monte*), a card game, or a complete suit of clothes from Montague Burton, the English drapers?

full of Eastern promise. A slogan for Fry's Turkish Delight, current in the late 1950s. One of the longest-running British TV ads, appealing to escapist fantasies. An early example showed a male slave

unrolling a carpet containing a woman captive in front of an eastern potentate. From the *Independent on Sunday* (5 April 1992): 'Benny Hill was fired by Thames in 1989 when ratings slumped after decades of . . . the Crimplene eroticism of Hill's Angels – those willing young ladies with the bee-stung mouths, full of East End promise.'

full of plumptiousness. See HOW TICKLED I AM.

full of wind and water. See LIKE THE BARBER'S CAT . . .

fully paid-up member of the human race, a. A complimentary phrase to describe a person who has human qualities and is three dimensional in character terms. Of the British Conservative politician Kenneth Clarke, the *Observer* wrote (31 July 1988): 'He is always well-informed (or anyway well-briefed), always reasonable and equable. He seems to be a fully paid-up member of the human race.'

—fulness is terrific, the. See under YAROOOO!

fun. See DOESN'T TIME FLY WHEN . . . ; DOUBLE YOUR PLEASURE . . . ; GETTING THERE IS HALF THE ~; MOST ~ I'VE HAD . . . ; MOST ~ YOU CAN HAVE . . . ; SPOT OF HOMELY ~ under HAVE A GO;

Funf. See THIS IS ~ SPEAKING.

Funk and Wagnalls. See under LAUGH-IN.

funny. See HERE'S A ~ THING . . .

funny is money. An old Hollywood expression, quoted in Steven M.L. Aronson, *Hype* (1983) – meaning that it is more profitable to deal in comedy than the more serious reaches of dramatic art.

funny peculiar. Phrase from the basic distinction made clear by Ian Hay in his play *Housemaster* (1936):

   That's funny.
   What do you mean, funny? Funny-peculiar, or funny ha-ha?

Funny Peculiar was the title of a play (1976) by Mike Stott, and also of an (unrelated) series of compilations of newspaper clangers and oddities by Denys Parsons beginning with *Funny Ha Ha and Funny Peculiar* (1965).

funny thing happened (to me) on the way to the theatre tonight . . ., a. The uninspired comedian's preliminary to telling a joke, and dating presumably from music-hall/vaudeville days. Compare the titles of a book by Nancy Spain – *A Funny Thing Happened on the Way* (1964) – and of the comedy musical *A Funny Thing Happened on the Way to the Forum* (filmed 1966) set in ancient Rome, based on Plautus (but the phrase can't be *quite* as old as that, surely?). Following one of his election defeats in the 1950s, Adlai Stevenson remarked, 'A funny thing happened to me on my way to the White House.'

fur coat. See ALL ∼ . . . under ALL KID GLOVES . . .

further. See THUS FAR SHALT THOU GO . . .

future. See YOUR ∼ IS IN YOUR HANDS.

· G ·

gaff. See BLOW THE ~.

gag. See MAN THEY COULDN'T ~.

gag me with a spoon. See VALLEY GIRL.

gaiety of nations, the. Phrase from one of the finest obituary tributes ever penned – Samuel Johnson's lament for his friend, the actor David Garrick (d 1779). In his 'Life of Edmund Smith', one of the *Lives of the English Poets* (1779), Johnson wrote: 'At this man's table I enjoyed many cheerful and instructive hours . . . with David Garrick, whom I hoped to have gratified with this character of our common friend; but what are the hopes of man! I am disappointed by that stroke of death, which has eclipsed the gaiety of nations, and impoverished the public stock of harmless pleasure.'
    When Charles Dickens died in 1870, Thomas Carlyle wrote: 'It is an event world-wide, a *unique* of talents suddenly extinct, and has "eclipsed" (we too may say) "the gaiety of nations".'

gains. See NO PAINS NO ~.

galahs, gumtree full of. See under AS BUSY AS . . .

Gallagher. See ABSOLUTELY, MR ~ . . .

gallery. See ROGUE'S ~.

Galloping Gourmet, the. The professional sobriquet of Graham Kerr, a jokey, British-born cookery demonstrator whose TV programmes were made in Canada but seen in many countries during the late 1960s and early 70s. He was billed as such because he did everything very quickly (and was also very popular with the ladies).

Galore. See PUSSY ~.

gals. See HOW'S ABOUT THAT THEN . . . under AS IT HAPPENS.

game. See END ~; ONLOOKER SEES MORE OF THE ~; ~S FINISHED under THERE'LL NEVER BE ANOTHER; GOOD ~ under *GENERATION GAME*; I DO NOT LIKE THIS ~ under *GOON SHOW*; — IS THE NAME OF THE ~; under IT ISN'T OVER TILL IT'S OVER; PLAY THE ~, CADS . . .

Game for a Laugh. Title of a British TV show (from London Weekend Television, 1981 onwards) which had elements of *Candid Camera* (and several others) as it persuaded members of the public to take part in stunts both in and out of the studio. The title – much-repeated by the presenters of the show, as in 'Let's see if so-and-so is *game for a laugh . . .*' – was apparently a conflation of the phrases 'game for anything' and 'good for a laugh' (the latter phrase itself used as the title of a book by Bennett Cerf in 1952).

gangbusters, to come on like. Meaning 'to perform in a striking manner', the expression comes from the US radio series *Gangbusters* which ran from c 1945–57 and used to begin with the sound of screeching tyres, machine guns, and police sirens, followed by the announcement: '*Gangbusters!* With the co-operation of leading law enforcement officials of the United States, *Gangbusters* presents facts in the relentless war of the police on the underworld, authentic case histories that show the never-ending activity of the police in their work of protecting our citizens.'
    'He [counsel investigating Jim Wright, Speaker of the House of Representatives] came in like gangbusters. He came in full of enthusiasm' – *New York Times* (12 May 1989); 'At the interview, this guy [Anthony Cheetham] was coming across like

gangbusters. We told him we'd let him know' – *Observer* (30 August 1992).

gang of four, a/the. Now meaning 'any group of four people working in concert', the original 'Gang of Four' was led by Jiang Qing, the unscrupulous wife of Chairman Mao Tse-tung, and so labelled in the mid-1970s when the four were tried and given the death sentence for treason and other crimes (later commuted to life imprisonment). The other three members were Zhang Chunqiao, a political organizer in the Cultural Revolution; Wang Hogwen, a youthful activist; and Yao Wenyuan, a journalist. Chairman Hua Kuo-feng attributed the phrase to his predecessor. Apparently on one occasion, Mao had warned his wife and her colleagues: 'Don't be a gang of four.' The nickname was later applied to the founders of the Social Democratic Party in Britain in 1981 – Roy Jenkins, David Owen, William Rodgers, and Shirley Williams.

gap. See CREDIBILITY ∼.

garbage in, garbage out. A term from computing, known by 1964 (and sometimes abbreviated to **GIGO**, pronounced 'guy-go'). Basically, it means that if you put bad data into a computer, you can come up with anything you want but what comes out will be useless and meaningless. In the wider sense it conveys the simple idea that what you get out of something depends very much on what you put into it.

garden. See EVERYTHING IN THE ∼; I NEVER PROMISED YOU A ROSE ∼; OVER THE ∼ WALL.

gardener. See AS THE ART MISTRESS SAID . . .

Garnet. See ALL SIR ∼.

gauntlet. See RUN THE ∼.

—gate. See WATERGATE.

gates. See BARBARIANS (ARE) AT THE ∼.

gaudy. See NEAT BUT NOT ∼.

gay. See SAY IT LOUD.

Gay Gordons, the. (1) Sobriquet of the Gordon Highlanders regiment, in particular the 2nd Battalion, the 92nd Highlanders, and apparently derived from an old song, 'Gay Go the Gordons To a Fight'. Known by 1925. Their reputation for 'cheerful belligerence' may have derived in part from an assault on the Heights of Dargai on the North-West Frontier of India in 1896, when Piper Findlater (later awarded the VC) continued to play lively regimental pibrochs though shot in both legs (comment from the *Independent*, 1994). (2) A dance popular in modern and old-time dancing, known as such by 1947, and presumably taking its name from (1).

Gay Nineties. See NAUGHTY NINETIES.

gazumped, to be. Meaning 'to lose out on a house purchase agreement, when the vendor accepts a bid higher than that agreed with the earlier purchaser', this specific meaning became popular in England and Wales during the early 1970s. The process can only occur in those countries where vendors are allowed to break a verbal agreement to sell if they receive a later, better offer. In Scotland where the 'sealed bid' system operates, gazumping is not possible.

But why the word 'gazump' – alternatively 'gazoomph', 'gasumph', 'gazumph', 'gezumph'? *OED2* has citations from English sources from 1928 onwards suggesting that the word has always had something to do with swindling. It occurs to me that it might come from 'goes up!' – meaning the price – along the lines of the term 'gazunder' for 'chamberpot' (because it 'goes under' the bed). Another suggestion is that it is a Yiddish word, *gezumph*.

GBH (Grievous Bodily Harm). British legal term for an offence of which there are other grades (e.g. Actual Bodily Harm). This expression, used almost invariably in its initials form, has been known and used outside the legal field since about 1950.

geddit? Meaning, 'Do you get it?' and said after a poor joke. Popularized from the early 1980s onwards by the 'Glenda Slag' column in *Private Eye*.

geezer. See EE, WOT A ~.

general. See CAVIARE TO THE ~.

General Electric. See AT ~ . . .

generation. See BIG CHILL ~; COME ALIVE . . . ; LOST ~.

Generation Game, The. As host of BBC TV's hugely popular silly games show of the 1970s, Bruce Forsyth (b 1928) soon had the nation parroting his catchphrases. **Didn't he do well?** first arose when a contestant recalled almost all the items that had passed before him on a conveyor belt (in a version of Kim's Game). However, it is also said to have originated c 1973 with what a studio attendant used to shout down from the lighting grid during rehearsals. **Good game . . . good game!** was encouragement to contestants. **Nice to see you, to see you . . . /Nice!** was the opening exchange of greetings with the studio audience (which supplied the last word). Forsyth would also say **Anthea, give us a twirl** – an invitation to the hostess, Anthea Redfern (to whom he was briefly married) to show off her skirt of the week.

When Larry Grayson took over the presentation of the show from 1978, a stock phrase when chatting to contestants was, **she seems like a nice girl, doesn't she?** or **he seems like a nice boy, doesn't he?** – 'It's the expression mothers always use when they describe their daughter's boyfriend and I never dreamt it would catch on like it did.'

Genghis Khan. See SOMEWHERE TO THE RIGHT OF ~.

gentle giant. The alliteration is important and the application to any tall, strong person has become a journalistic cliché. A policeman killed by an IRA bomb outside Harrods store in London (December 1983) was so dubbed. Terry Wogan used the expression allusively in the early 1980s to describe the BBC's Radio 2 network (compare the BIG ONE, beloved of advertising folk). Larry Holmes (b 1950), world heavyweight boxing champion, is another to whom the label has been affixed, as also James Randel Matson (b 1945), the US track and field champion.

In 1967, there was an American film entitled *The Gentle Giant*. This was about a small boy in Florida who befriends a bear which later saves the life of the boy's disapproving father. In the 1930s, Pickfords Removals were promoted with the rhyme:

A note from you, a call from us,
The date is fixed, with no worry or fuss,
A Pickfords van, a gentle giant,
The work is done – a satisfied client.

Going back even further, the journalist William Howard Russell wrote of Dr Thomas Alexander, a surgeon who served in the Crimean War, as a 'gentle giant of a Scotchman'.

gentleman. See ALMOST A ~; EVERY INCH A ~.

gentleman and a scholar, a. (or – equally well-known – **a scholar and a gentleman**.) Paul Beale notes in Partridge/*Catch Phrases* that he was familiar with this compliment in the British army (c 1960) in the form: 'Sir, you are a Christian, a scholar, and a gentleman.' It was 'often used as jocular, fulsome, though quite genuine, thanks for services rendered'. Partridge, earlier, had been tracking down a longer version – 'A gentleman, a scholar, and a fine judge of whiskey' – but had only been able to find the 'gentleman and scholar' in Robert Burns (1786):

His locked, lettered, braw brass collar
Shew'd him the gentleman an' the scholar.

It looks, however, as though the conjunction goes back even further. *OED2* has a citation from 1621: 'As becommed a Gentleman and a Scholer'. The phrase was probably born out of a very real respect for anyone who could claim to have both these highest of attributes. Equally as old is the combination 'a gentleman and a soldier'.

gentleman's agreement, a. Meaning 'an agreement not enforceable at law and only binding as a matter of honour' – of US origin and not known before the 1920s. A.J.P. Taylor in *English History 1914-1945* (1965) says: 'This absurd phrase was taken by [von] Papen from business usage to describe the agreement between Austria and Germany in July 1936. It was much used hereafter for an agreement with anyone who was obviously not a gentleman and who would obviously not keep his agreement.'

gentlemen. See I ALWAYS DO MY BEST . . . under *ITMA*.

gentlemen – be seated! A stock phrase from the days of black minstrels in the US, 1840–1900. 'Mr Interlocutor' the white compère, would say this to the minstrels.

Gentlemen Prefer Blondes. Title of a novel (1925) by Anita Loos (to which the sequel was *But Gentlemen Marry Brunettes*, 1928). Loos is presumed to have originated the phrase, though a lesser-known Irving Berlin song with this title was being performed in 1926, and in the same year there was another song with the title by B.G. De Sylva and Lewis Gensler.

gently, Bentley! See under *TAKE IT FROM HERE*.

George. See LET ~ DO IT; LLOYD ~ KNEW MY FATHER.

George – don't do that! A quotation from Joyce Grenfell's 'Nursery School Sketches' (1953). Grenfell (1910–79), the British monologist, would do entire solo evenings of monologues and songs. This line came from a sketch in which she played a slightly harrassed but unflappable teacher. Part of its charm lay in the audience's never knowing precisely what it was that George was being asked not to do.

George Washington slept here. See QUEEN ELIZABETH SLEPT HERE.

Germans first on the beach. A popular perception of German tourists' behaviour in the holiday resorts of the Mediterranean (mostly) is that they rise early, get down to the beach before anyone else and occupy all the sun-loungers long before members of less efficient nationalities do. Probably from the 1960s when German tourism (always a popular activity) began once more to be noticed elsewhere in Europe. From the

diary of Kenneth Williams (for 14 June 1965): '[In Crete] we went for a swim but the krauts had grabbed all the best places on the plage.'

germs. See NINETY–NINE PER CENT OF ALL KNOWN ~ .

Geronimo! It was during the North African campaign of November 1942 that US paratroopers are said first to have shouted 'Geronimo!' as they jumped out of planes. It then became customary to do so and turned into a popular exclamation akin to 'Eureka!' A number of American Indians in the paratroop units coined and popularized the expression, recalling the actual Apache Geronimo who died in 1909. It is said that when he was being pursued by the army over some steep hills near Fort Sill, Oklahoma, he made a leap on horseback over a sheer cliff into water. As the troops did not dare follow him, he cried 'Geronimo!' as he leapt. Some of the paratroopers who were trained at Fort Bragg and Fort Campbell adopted this shout, not least because it reminded them to breathe deeply during a jump. In 1939, there had been a film entitled *Geronimo*, which may have reminded them. From Christy Brown, *Down All the Days* , Chap. 6 (1970) we have: 'He heard his brothers cry out in unison: "The dirty lousy bastards – hitting a cripple! Geronimo! . . ." And off they flew in maddened pursuit of the ungentlemanly enemy.'

gerrymander something, to. Meaning, 'to manipulate in order to bring about a desired position' and, more particularly in politics, 'to redraw the boundaries of voting districts in the interests of a particular party or candidate'. The word derives from the activities of Elbridge Gerry, the Governor of Massachusetts in 1812. His administration enacted a law redrawing the state's senatorial districts, giving disproportionate representation to Democratic-Republicans. Gilbert Stuart, an artist working for the Boston *Sentinel*, altered one district's outline into a salamander. The paper's editor said: 'Better say a gerrymander.'

gertcha! This word had a burst of popularity in about 1980 when it was used in TV advertisements for Courage Best Bitter in the UK. Various grim-faced drinkers sat around in an East End pub and shouted it out during breaks in the music. Dave Trott, the copywriter responsible for using the word, suggested it derived from 'Get out of it, you!' This is supported by Partridge/*Slang* who was on to it – as 'gercher' – in 1937. The *OED2* has 'get away/along with you' as a 'derisive expression of disbelief'. The line got into the commercial from a song composed by the Cockney singers Chas and Dave. They originally pronounced it 'Wooertcha'. (See also RABBIT, RABBIT).

Gesundheit! An exclamation made when someone sneezes, this is German for 'health', but it also has the rhythm of 'God bless you' and of a musical finish (as to a music-hall joke). Sneezing was believed to be the expulsion of an evil spirit, hence the need for such an exclamation. The Romans cried **absit omen!** [flee, omen!].

get. See GOAT, GET (SOME)ONE'S . . .

get a life! Admonition suggesting that the person addressed should find him/herself a worthwhile, focused role to play in life. Suddenly popular in the early 1990s, probably from the US (does it sound a touch Jewish?). From the *Independent* (27 July 1991): 'Disney is used to taking flak for its cartoons . . . A spokesman said: "These people need to get a life. It's a story. It's fiction."' Also in the form **get yourself a life!** From the *Daily Mail* (27 February 1993): '[Pam Ferris, actress] is not a fan [of the part she plays on TV]. "Ma Larkin," she says, "is a male chauvinist's dream, constantly available and even celebrating her husband's conquests of other women. I'd like to educate Ma a bit. Give her some Germaine Greer to read. Tell her: 'Get yourself a life!' I'd probably split up the Larkins' marriage, be a real cat among the pigeons."'

get away from it all, to. Cliché of travel journalism/ advertising, and meaning 'to have a rest, holiday'. From an advertisement for the Moroccan National Tourist Office (February 1989): 'In 1943 where did Churchill go to get away from it all?'

getaway people, the. Denoting glamorous, dashing folk, akin to the BEAUTIFUL PEOPLE, they were so dubbed in an advertising campaign for National Benzole petrol in the UK, from 1963. Bryan Oakes of the London Press Exchange agency told the authors of *The Persuasion Industry* (1965): 'They were the jet set, clean-limbed beautiful girls, the gods and goddesses who did exotic things. We used expensive cars – E-type Jaguars and Aston Martins – and the promise was that, if you get this petrol, you're aligning yourself with those wonderful people, midnight drives on the beach and so on.'

get away with something scot-free, to. 'If we could do that, she might go scot-free for aught I cared' wrote Charles Dickens in *The Old Curiosity Shop* (1840–1). Not 'scot', as in Scotland, but *sceot*, a medieval municipal tax paid to the local bailiff or sheriff, so it means in a sense, 'tax-free; without penalty'. Known in its modern figurative sense by 1700.

get back on your jam jar. Said dismissively to someone who is behaving objectionably. This appears to be rhyming slang for 'get back on your tram-car' (i.e. go away). It is not in origin a racist slur alluding to the golliwog figure who appears on jars of Robertson's Jam (although such a use was reported in 1985).

get out of one's pram, to. Meaning 'to get angry, over-excited'. Learned debate over this phrase followed in the wake of Labour leader Neil Kinnock's use of 'Schultz got out of his pram' to describe US Secretary of State George Schultz during the Labour leader's visit to Washington in February 1984. Mr Kinnock said: 'It's a colloquialism. I believe it is becoming more common in its usage. It means Mr Schultz was departing from his normal diplomatic calm. Nothing so undiplomatic as losing his temper.'

Nevertheless, other forms are more widely known. London East End and Glasgow slang both have, 'Don't get out of your pram about it', when someone is 'off his head' about something. A touch of OFF ONE'S TROLLEY seems to be involved, too.

gets rid of film on teeth. Slogan for Pepsodent, current in the US in the early 1900s. It was another of Claude C. Hopkins's great coups – to claim something that every toothpaste could claim, and get away with it. He said: 'People do not want to read of penalties. They want to be told of rewards . . . People want to be told the ways to happiness and cheer . . . I resolved to advertise this toothpaste as a creator of beauty.'

get thee behind me Satan! Nowadays an exclamation used in answer to the mildest call to temptation, it came originally from St Matthew 16:23, where Jesus Christ rebukes Peter with the phrase for something he has said.

getting. See WE'RE ~ THERE.

getting there is half the fun. This expression sloganizes Robert Louis Stevenson's views: 'I travel not to go anywhere, but to go' and 'to travel hopefully is a better thing than to arrive'. It also reflects 'the journey not the arrival matters' (an expression used as the title of an autobiographical volume by Leonard Woolf, 1969). I believe that, as a slogan, it may have been used to advertise Cunard steamships in the 1920s/30s. It was definitely used to promote the Peter Sellers film *Being There* (1980) in the form, 'Getting there is half the fun. Being there is all of it.'

In *Up the Organisation* (1970), Robert Townshend opined of getting to the top: 'Getting there isn't half the fun – it's all the fun.'

get up them stairs! A reference to the prospect of sexual intercourse. Partridge/*Catch Phrases* finds it in 1942 with 'Blossom' added. Denis Gifford in *The Golden Age of Radio* (1985) gives it as comedian Hal Monty's catchphrase (noting that it seems to have escaped the BBC's BLUE PENCIL).

get your hair cut! A catchphrase from British music-hall. Some say it was the property of the comedian George

Beauchamp (1863–1901) who sang it in a song, 'Johnnie Get Your Hair Cut'. Others would have that it comes from a song popularized by Harry Champion (written by Fred Murray) (see GINGER, YOU'RE BARMY!) Either way, it seems to have been current 1880–1900, especially so at the end of the period. It was eventually, of course, the sort of thing sergeant-majors would bawl at new recruits, though perhaps originally it might been addressed to long-haired aesthetes of the 1880s/90s.

get yourself a life! See GET A LIFE!

ghost walks (on Friday), the. Meaning 'it's pay day' (for actors), the expression (current by 1833) is said to date from a touring company's production of *Hamlet*. The cast had been unpaid for many weeks and when Hamlet said of his father's ghost: 'Perchance 'twill walk again,' the ghost replied: 'Nay, 'twill walk no more until its salary is paid.' Consequently, a theatrical manager who hands out the pay has sometimes been called a 'ghost'.

giant. See GENTLE ~; HE WAS A BIG MAN; ONE SMALL STEP . . .

Gibbs. See AND NOW, HER NIBS, MISS GEORGIA ~.

giddy. See MY ~ AUNT.

gift. See MAN WHO HAS EVERYTHING.

gifted. See YOUNG, ~ AND BLACK.

gift horse. See LOOK A ~ IN THE MOUTH.

gifts. See GREEKS BEARING ~.

gild the lily, to. Meaning 'to attempt to improve something that is already attractive and risk spoiling it', the allusion is to Shakespeare's *King John*, IV.ii.11 (1596) where, in fact, the line is: 'to gild refined gold, to paint the lily'. Arden notes that 'to gild gold' was a common expression by Shakespeare's time.

Giles. See FARMER ~.

Ginger, you're barmy! Addressed to any red-headed male, this street cry merely means he is stupid or crazy. It may date from the early 1900s and most probably originated in the British music-hall song with the title sung by Harry Champion (1866–1942). Originally, the following phrase was 'getcher 'air cut' [GET YOUR HAIR CUT]; a later version appears to have been, '. . . you ought to join the army'. *Ginger, You're Barmy* was used as the title of a novel (1962) by David Lodge.

Separately, the word 'ginger' has been applied in the UK to male homosexuals (since the 1930s, at least) on account of the rhyming slang, 'ginger beer = queer'.

Gioconda Smile, the. What you may see in Leonardo da Vinci's portrait of a young woman, known as 'Mona Lisa' (c 1503), now in the Louvre, Paris, which has a curious, enigmatic, unsmiling smile, almost a smirk. '*La Gioconda*' and '*La Joconde*', the titles by which the painting is also known may either be translated as 'the jocund lady', as might be expected, or refer to the sitter's actual surname – she may have been the wife of Francesco del Giocondo (whose name does, however, derive from 'jocund').

The smile was already being mentioned by 1550 in Giorgio Vasari's life of the painter. Vasari probably made up the story that Leonardo employed 'singers and musicians or jesters' to keep the sitter 'full of merriment'. Any number of nineteenth-century writers were fascinated by the smile, some seeing it as disturbing and almost evil. In the twentieth century Laurence Durrell commented: 'She has the smile of a woman who has just dined off her husband,' and Cole Porter included 'You're the smile/On the Mona Lisa' in his list song 'You're the Top!' (1934). Ponchielli's opera *La Gioconda* (1876) – after Victor Hugo's drama – and D'Annunzio's play (1898) are not connected with da Vinci's portrait (except in that they feature jocund girls). 'The Gioconda Smile' was the title of an Aldous Huxley short story which was included in *Mortal Coils* (1922) and dramatized in 1948.

Gipper. See WIN THIS ONE FOR THE ~ .

girl. See BLUE FOR A BOY . . . ; COULD MAKE ANY ORDINARY ~ . . . ; NEVER CHASE ~ S OR BUSES; PAGE THREE ~ ; VALLEY ~ ; WHAT'S A NICE ~ LIKE YOU . . .

girl in every port, a. This phrase was used as the title of a film (US, 1928) with Louise Brooks. The more venerable version of the benefit supposedly enjoyed by sailors is a **wife in every port,** which occurs for example in the caption to a *Punch* cartoon (22 May 1907) and as far back as Isaac Bickerstaffe's play *Thomas and Sally* (1761). In Charles Dibdin's 'Jack in his Element' (1790) also, there is:

> In every mess I find a friend,
> In every port a wife.

And in John Gay's *Sweet William's Farewell to Black-Eyed Susan* (1720):

> They'll tell thee, sailors, when away,
> In ev'ry port a mistress find.

Girl in the Red Velvet Swing, the. Sobriquet of Evelyn Nesbit (c 1885–1967), American dancer and former 'Gibson Girl', who married the industrialist Harry K. Thaw. In 1906, Thaw shot Stanford White for what the newspapers called his 'exotic house-keeping' with the 22-year-old woman. Used as the title of film (US, 1955) about the case.

girl next door. See under BOY NEXT DOOR.

girl said (at the picnic). See under THAT IS WHAT THE SOLDIER SAID.

gi'us a job, I could do that (or **gizza job** . . .). A rare example of a catchphrase coming out of a TV *drama* series. Alan Bleasdale's *The Boys from the Blackstuff* (about unemployment in Liverpool) was first shown on BBC TV in 1982 and introduced the character of Yosser Hughes. His plea became a nationally repeated catchphrase, not least because of the political ramifications. It was chanted by football crowds in Liverpool and printed on T-shirts with Yosser confronting Prime Minister Margaret Thatcher. From the *Observer* (30 January 1983): 'At Anfield nowadays whenever the Liverpool goalkeeper makes a save, the Kop affectionately chants at him the catch-phrase of Yosser Hughes: "We could do that." It's a slogan which might usefully rise to the lips of the chairbound viewer just as often.' In fact, there were *two* phrases here, sometimes used independently, and sometimes together in a different form, 'I can do that. Gi'us a job.'

give a dog a bad name. Meaning 'say bad things about a person and they'll stick', this possibly comes from the longer 'Give a dog a bad name and hang him', suggesting that if a dog has a reputation for ferocity, it might as well be killed because no one will trust it.

give 'im the money, Barney/Mabel! See under HAVE A GO.

give me a note please. See I'VE GOT A LETTER FROM A BLOKE IN BOOTLE.

give order! The injunction 'Give order – thank you, please!' became nationally known when Colin Crompton used it to members of Granada TV's *Wheeltappers and Shunters Social Club*, on ITV 1974–7. 'I had been including the club chairman character in my variety act for some years,' Crompton said in 1979, 'before Johnny Hamp of Granada suggested that we build a sketch round it for inclusion in the stage version of *The Comedians*. This led to *Wheeltappers*. Like most successful catchphrases it was manufactured. It has been used by club concert chairmen for years – and still is.' Crompton also used the version **best of order**! In Christy Brown's novel *Down All the Days*, Chap. 15 (1970) we have the cry (at a social gathering): 'Best of order now for the singer!'

Then there was his phrase, **On behalf of the committee-ee!** Crompton said: 'Letters by the score told me my catchphrases were a schoolteacher's nightmare. And we had so many children outside the house, shouting them out, that we were forced to move to a quieter neighbourhood! Although it is several years since the last programme was transmitted, the phrases have remained popular and I'm flattered that most impressionists include them in their acts.'

give over! See RIGHT MONKEY!

give us a child until it is seven and it is ours for life. This saying has been attributed to the Jesuits, founded in 1534 by St Ignatius Loyola, but was possibly wished on to them by their opponents. Another version is: 'Give us the child, and we will give you the man.' Compare what Lenin may have said to the Commissars of Education in Moscow (1923): 'Give us the child for eight years and it will be a Bolshevik for ever.' Muriel Spark in her novel *The Prime of Miss Jean Brodie* (1962) has her heroine, a teacher, say: 'Give me a girl at an impressionable age and she is mine for life.'

gladdies. See WAVE YOUR ~.

Gladstone chewed each mouthful of food 32 times before swallowing. William Ewart Gladstone (1809–98) was four times British Liberal Prime Minister and dominated the political scene during the second half of the nineteenth century. Most famously, he was held up as an example to countless generations of children as the man who chewed his food properly. In the BBC TV programme *As I Remember* (30 April 1967), Baroness Asquith (Lady Violet Bonham Carter) recalled having had a meal with Gladstone, when she was a little girl, at which he did no such thing. Quite the reverse in fact: he bolted his food.

Confirmation of this deplorable fact also came in a lecture given by George Lyttelton at Hawarden (Gladstone's old home) on 24 June 1955: 'More than one lynx-eyed young spectator [has discovered] that Mr Gladstone did *not* chew every mouthful thirty-two times . . . though I am not sure that Mr Gladstone himself might not have made some weighty and useful observations on the common and deplorable gap between principle and practice.'

glad we could get together! Sign-off by the American radio and TV newscaster John Cameron Swayze (*b c* 1913) in the 1940s/50s. His customary opening remark was **and a good evening to you!**

glasses. See HEY, YOU DOWN THERE WITH THE ∼.

Glimmer Twins, the. A nickname for two members of the Rolling Stones pop group. From the *Independent* (26 March 1990): 'There were times when Dr Runcie [Archbishop of Canterbury] and Dr John Habgood, the Archbishop of York, seemed "the glimmer twins" of the Church of England, as the Rolling Stones' foremost members liked to refer to themselves: Runcie up front like Mick Jagger, all lips and charm, while Habgood lurked in the dark, like Keith Richard, ready to kick intruders off the stage.'

glisters. See GLITTERS.

glittering prizes. Phrase from the Rectorial Address at Glasgow University by F.E. Smith, 1st Earl of Birkenhead (7 November 1923): 'The world continues to offer glittering prizes to those who have stout hearts and sharp swords.' *The Glittering Prizes* was the title of the BBC TV drama series (1976) by Frederic Raphael, about a group of Cambridge graduates.

glitters/glisters is not gold, all that. Meaning 'appearances may be deceptive', the allusion is to Shakespeare's *The Merchant of Venice*, II.vii.65 (1596):

All that *glisters* is not gold,
Often have you heard that told.

As indicated, the proverb was common by Shakespeare's time. *CODP* quotes a Latin version – '*Non omne quod nitet aurum est*' [not all that shines is gold] and also an English one in Chaucer. The now obsolete word 'glisters' rather than 'glitters' or 'glistens' was commonly used in the saying from the seventeenth century onwards, though in poetic use, Thomas Gray, for example, used 'glisters' in his 'Ode on the Death of A Favourite Cat drowned in a Tub of Gold Fishe' (1748).

global village, the. Phrase from Marshall McLuhan's dictum that: 'The new electronic interdependence recreates the world in the image of a global village' (*The Gutenberg Galaxy*, 1962). From 1979, *David Frost's Global Village* was the title of an occasional Yorkshire TV series in which Frost discussed global issues with pundits beamed in by satellite.

gloom and doom. A rhyming phrase (sometimes reversed) that became especially popular in the 1980s: 'Amongst all the recent talk of doom and gloom one thing has been largely overlooked' (*Daily Telegraph*, 7 November 1987). An early appearance was in the musical *Finian's Rainbow* (1947, film 1968) in which Og, a pessimistic leprechaun, uses it repeatedly, as in: 'I told you that gold could only bring you doom and gloom, gloom and doom.'

gloria (in excelsis Deo). See MASS PHRASES.

Glorious Revolution, the. When King James II was removed from the English throne in 1688 and replaced by William and Mary of Orange, the process came to be variously described as the 'bloodless' and 'glorious' revolution. But by whom first and when? By 1749, Henry Fielding was writing in *Tom Jones* (Bk. 8, Chap. 14): 'I remained concealed, til the news of the Glorious Revolution put an end to all my apprehensions of danger.' Before that, *OED2* finds only other epithets: 'great revolution' in 1689 and 'prodigious revolution' in 1688 itself. 'That glorious Revolution' was, however, applied in 1725 to the overthrow of the Rump Parliament in 1660. By *c* 1690 a club was founded in Northampton to celebrate the William and Mary 'glorious revolution' and by 1692 'Glorious' had acquired a capital G. If this is true, it would confirm that the phrase arose very early on – but not in a form which can be attributed to any particular person or source.

Glorious Twelfth, the (or simply **the Twelfth**). This name for 12 August, when grouse-shooting legally begins in Britain, was current by 1895, and was possibly devised in emulation of 'The Glorious First of June', a sea-battle in the French revolutionary war (and known as such since 1794). Compare 'the Twelfth' (of July), celebrated by Protestants in Northern Ireland to commemorate the Battle of the Boyne (1 July 1690, Old Style) at which

William III defeated James II.

gloves. See ALL KID GLOVES . . .

glow. See HORSES SWEAT . . .

Gnomes of Zurich, the. A term used to disparage the tight-fisted speculators in the Swiss financial capital who questioned Britain's creditworthiness and who forced austerity measures on the Labour government of Prime Minister Harold Wilson when it came to power in 1964. George Brown, Secretary of State for Economic Affairs, popularized the term in November of that year. Wilson himself had, however, used it long before in a speech to the House of Commons (12 November 1956), referring to 'all the little gnomes in Zurich and other financial centres'. In 1958, Andrew Shonfield wrote in *British Economic Policy Since the War*: 'Hence the tragedy of the autumn of 1957, when the Chancellor of the Exchequer [Peter Thorneycroft] adopted as his guide to action the slogan: I must be hard-faced enough to match the mirror-image of an imaginary hard-faced little man in Zurich. It is tough on the Swiss that William Tell should be displaced in English folklore by this new image of a gnome in a bank at the end of a telephone line.' ('Lord Gnome', the wealthy and unscrupulous supposed proprietor of *Private Eye* was presumably named after the 1964 use.)

go. See ALL DRESSED UP AND NOWHERE TO ∼; AND AWA-A-AAY WE ∼!; DO NOT PASS ∼; HERE WE ∼ . . . ; I ∼, I COME BACK under *ITMA*; LET US ∼ FORWARD; — MUST ∼; MUST YOU ∼?; TO BOLDLY ∼ under BEAM ME UP, SCOTTY; WHERE DO WE ∼ FROM HERE?

go ahead, make my day. 'Do what you like, see if I care, BE MY GUEST' – a laconicism. In March 1985, President Ronald Reagan told the American Business Conference, 'I have my veto pen drawn and ready for any tax increase that Congress might even think of sending up. And I have only one thing to say to the tax increasers. Go ahead – make my day.'

For once, he was not quoting from one of his own film roles, or old Hollywood. The line was originally spoken by Clint Eastwood, himself brandishing a .44 Magnum, to a gunman he was holding at bay in *Sudden Impact* (1983). At the end of the film he says (to another villain, similarly armed), 'Come on, make my day.' In neither case does he add 'punk', as is sometimes supposed. (This may come from confusion with *Dirty Harry* in which he holds a .44 Magnum to the temple of a criminal and says 'Well, do ya [feel lucky], punk?')

The phrase may have been eased into Reagan's speech by having appeared in a parody of the New York *Post* put together by editors, many of them anti-Reagan, in the autumn of 1984. Reagan was shown starting a nuclear war by throwing down this dare to the Kremlin (information from *Time*, 25 March 1985).

goal. See OWN ∼.

goalposts. See MOVE/SHIFT THE ∼.

goat, to get (some)one's. Meaning, 'to annoy/be annoyed by something'. Apparently another Americanism that has passed into general use (and current by 1910), this expression can also be found in French as *prendre la chèvre*, 'to take the milch-goat'. One is always suspicious of explanations that go on to explain that, of course, goats were very important to poor people and if anyone were to get a man's goat . . . etc. One is even more unimpressed by the explanation given by Morris: 'It used to be a fairly common practice to stable a goat with a thoroughbred [horse], the theory being that the goat's presence would help the high-strung nag to keep its composure. If the goat were stolen the night before a big race, the horse might be expected to lose its poise and blow the race.'

Robert L. Shook in *The Book of Why* (1983) wonders, interestingly, whether it has anything to do with a 'goatee' (a beard like a goat's). If you got someone by the 'goat', it would certainly annoy them.

All one can do is to point to the number of idioms referring to goats – 'act the goat', 'giddy goat', 'scapegoat', and, once more, emphasize the alliteration. Another version is 'to get one's nanny-goat'.

God. See FROM YOUR MOUTH TO ~'S EAR; IF ~ HAD INTENDED US TO . . . ; IN ~ WE TRUST . . . ; PREPARE TO MEET THY ~ .

—, God Bless 'er/'im. Originally, a toast to Royalty, this gradually turned into a more general, genial way of referring to such people and others. From George Eliot, *Felix Holt* (1866): 'You'll rally round the throne – and the King, God bless him, and the usual toasts.' From *Punch*, Vol. CXX (1902): 'The Queen God Bless 'Er.' Robert Lacey revived the custom in 1990 with a book entitled *The Queen Mother, God Bless Her*. The American cartoonist Helen Hokinson had one of her collections entitled *The Ladies, God Bless 'Em* (1950), which takes the toast out into a broader field.

God bless the Duke of Argyll! What Scots Highlanders were supposed to exclaim when scratching themselves. Why? Because a Duke of Argyll is said to have erected scratching posts on his estates for cattle and sheep. His herdsmen would use the posts for the same purpose and give this shout by way of thanks for the relief they afforded.

Goddess. See GREEN ~ .

God go with you. See GOODNIGHT, GOOD LUCK . . .

God Is an Englishman. Title of a novel (1970) by R.F. Delderfield, which may derive from an untraced saying of George Bernard Shaw (*d* 1950): 'The ordinary Britisher imagines that God is an Englishman.' But the view is of longstanding. Harold Nicolson recorded on 3 June 1942 that three years before, R.S. Hudson, the Minister of Agriculture, was being told by the Yugoslav minister in London of the dangers facing Britain. 'Yes,' replied Hudson, 'you are probably correct and these things may well happen. But you forget that God is English.'

Godiva, Lady. See PEEPING TOM.

godliness. See CLEANLINESS IS NEXT TO ~ .

God love you. The Most Reverend Fulton J. Sheen (1895–1979) was Auxiliary (Roman Catholic) Bishop of New York and presented highly-popular religious TV shows called *Life Is Worth Living* and *The Bishop Sheen Program* in the period 1952–68. This was his famous sign-off.

God moves in a mysterious way. A direct quotation from No. 35 of the *Olney Hymns* (1779) by William Cowper, the hymn continues: '. . . His wonders to perform'.

god protect me from my friends. The full expression is: 'I can look after my enemies, but God protect me from my friends.' *CODP* traces it to 1477 in the forms 'God keep/save/defend us from our friends' and says it is now often used in the abbreviated form, 'Save us from our friends.' It appears to be common to many languages. *God Protect Me from My Friends* was the title of a book (1956) by Gavin Maxwell about Salvatore Giuliano, the Sicilian bandit. The diarist Chips Channon (21 February 1938) has: 'This evening a group of excited Communists even invaded the Lobby, demanding Anthony [Eden]'s reinstatement. God preserve us from our friends, they did him harm.' Morris seems to confuse this saying with the similar WITH FRIENDS LIKE THESE . . . , but finds a quotation from Maréchal Villars who, on leaving Louis XIV, said: 'Defend me from my friends; I can defend myself from my enemies'.

God's own country. Referring to one's own country, if one is fond of it, there can be few countries which have not elected to call themselves this.

Of the United States: OED2 provides an example from 1865, and tags the phrase as being of US origin. Flexner says that in the Civil War the shorter 'God's country' was the Union troops' term for the North, 'especially when battling heat, humidity, and mosquitoes in the South. Not until the 1880s did the term mean any section of the country one loved or the open spaces of the West'. A 1937 US film had the title *God's Country and the Woman*.

Of Australia: Dr Richard Arthur, a State politician and President of the Immigration

League of Australasia, was quoted in *Australia Today* (1 November 1911) as saying: 'This Australia is "God's Own Country" for the brave.' The *Dictionary of Australian Quotations* (1984) notes that at the time 'Australia was frequently referred to as "God's Own Country", the phrase drawing satirical comments from the foreign unenlightened.'

Of South Africa/Ireland: one has heard both these countries so dubbed informally (in the 1970s), with varying degrees of appropriateness and irony.

Also Yorkshiremen describe their homeland as 'God's own *county*'. 'Yorkshire's natural reluctance to play second fiddle to London has faced some difficulty in the matter of house prices . . . God's own county is at the centre of things yet again' (*Guardian*, 23 January 1989).

God, what a beauty! The British 'Coster Comedian' Leon Cortez (1898–1970) was associated with this cry, as also **as you may know . . . or as you may not know . . .**

go for gold. A slogan meaning, literally, 'aim for a gold medal'. As far as I can tell, this slogan was first used by the US Olympic team at the Lake Placid Winter Olympics in 1980. (*Going for Gold* became the title of an Emma Lathen thriller set in Lake Placid, published in 1983, and there was a TV movie *Going for the Gold* in 1985). Other teams, including the British, had taken it up by the time of the 1984 Olympics. A BBC TV quiz called *Going for Gold* began in 1987.

Just to show, as always, that there is nothing new under the sun: in 1832, there was a political slogan 'To Stop the Duke, Go for Gold' – which was somehow intended, through its alliterative force, to prevent the Duke of Wellington from forming a government in the run up to the Reform Bill. The slogan was coined by a radical politician, Francis Place, for a poster, on 12 May 1832. (It was intended to cause a run on the Bank of England – and succeeded.)

go for it! A popular slogan from the early 1980s, mostly in America – though any number of sales managers have encouraged their teams to strive this way in the UK, too.

In June 1985, President Reagan's call on tax reform was, 'America, go for it!' Victor Kiam, an American razor entrepreneur, entitled his 1986 memoirs *Going For it!*; and 'Go for it, America' was the slogan used by British Airways in the same year to get more US tourists to ignore the terrorist threat and travel to Europe. Lisa Bernbach in *The Official Preppie Handbook* (1980) pointed to a possible US campus origin, giving the phrase as a general exhortation meaning 'Let's get carried away and act stupid'. At about the same time, the phrase was used in aerobics. Jane Fonda in a work-out book (1981) and video (c 1983), cried, 'Go for it, **go for the burn!**' (where the burn was a sensation felt during exercise). There was also a US beer slogan (current 1981), 'Go for it! Schlitz makes it great'. Media mogul Ted Turner was later called a 'go-for-it guy', and so on.

Partridge/Slang has 'to go for it' as Australian for being 'extremely eager for sexual intercourse' (c 1925).

go forth to war, to. The 1989 BBC TV comedy series *Black Adder Goes Forth* was set during the First World War. The phrase this title embodied was as used by Bishop Heber in his hymn (1812) beginning: 'The Son of God goes forth to war/A kingly crown to gain.'

Earlier, it was known in the Bible, occurring in Numbers 1:3 and 2 Chronicles 25:5.

going. See WHEN THE ~ GETS TOUGH . . .

going back to the wagon. See I'M ~ . . .

gold. See CROSS OF ~; GO FOR ~; STREETS PAVED WITH ~; THERE'S ~ IN THEM THAR HILLS.

golden arm. See MAN WITH THE ~.

golden age, a/the. The original golden age was that in which, according to Greek and Roman poets, men lived in an ideal state of happiness. It was also applied to the period of Latin literature from Cicero to Ovid (which was followed by the lesser, silver age.) Now the phrase is widely used in such clichés as 'the Golden Age of Hollywood' to describe periods when a country or a creative field is considered to have been at the height of its excellence or prosperity.

golden boy, a. Meaning 'a young person with talent', it derives chiefly from its use as the title of a play, *Golden Boy* (1937; film US, 1939) by Clifford Odets, in which the violinist hero becomes a successful boxer instead. It was also the title of a cinema short (*c* 1962) about the singer, Paul Anka, possibly remembering the term golden/gilded youth and Shakespeare's *Cymbeline*, IV.ii.262 (1609):

> Golden lads and girls all must,
> As chimney-sweepers, come to dust.

golden floor, the. Meaning 'Heaven' and possibly derived from 'threshing floor', as in various Old Testament verses. Current by 1813 (Shelley, 'Queen Mab'), the phrase also occurs in the Harvest Festival hymn 'Come ye thankful people, come'. The poet A.E. Housman said to the doctor who told him a risqué story to cheer him up before he died: 'That is indeed very good. I shall have to repeat that on the Golden Floor' (quoted in the *Daily Telegraph*, 21 February 1984).

golden rule, the. Nowadays, any guiding principle that the speaker wishes to nominate as especially important. By the seventeenth century, 'Do as you would be done by' (based on Matthew 7:12, from Christ's Sermon on the Mount) was known as 'The Golden Rule' or 'The Golden Law'. But the 'rule of three' in mathematics was, however, known as the Golden Rule the century before that.

go, man, go! A phrase of encouragement originally shouted at jazz musicians in the 1940s. Then it took on wider use. At the beginning of the number 'It's Too Darn Hot' in Cole Porter's *Kiss Me Kate* (film version, 1953) a dancer cried, 'Go, girl, go!'

TV newscaster Walter Cronkite reverted famously to 'Go, baby, go!' when describing the launch of Apollo XI in 1969 and this form became a fairly standard cry at rocket and missile departures thereafter. *Time* Magazine reported it being shouted at a test firing of a Pershing missile (29 November 1982). **Crazy, man, crazy!** originated at about the same time. One wonders whether

T.S. Eliot's 'Go go go said the bird' ('Burnt Norton', *Four Quartets*, 1935) or Hamlet's 'Come, bird, come' (the cry of a falconer recalling his hawk) relate to these cries in any way . . . ?

gone. See WHERE HAVE ALL THE — ~?

gone but not forgotten. A sentiment displayed on tombstones, memorial notices and such, and used as the title of a Victorian print showing children at a grave or similar.

The earliest example of its use I have found (in a far from exhaustive search) is on the grave of William Thomas Till (*d* 1892, aged 28 years) in the churchyard of St Michael on Greenhill, Lichfield. Ludovic Kennedy in his autobiography *On My Way to the Club* (1989) suggests that it is an epitaph much found in the English graveyard at Poona, India.

In 1967, there was a Parlophone record album of the BBC Radio GOON SHOW entitled, *Goon . . . But Not Forgotten*.

gone for a Burton. Early in the Second World War, an RAF expression arose to describe what had happened to a missing person, presumed dead. He had 'gone for a Burton', meaning that he had gone for a drink (*in the drink* = the sea) or, as another phrase put it, 'he'd bought it'.

Folk memory has it that during the 1930s 'Gone for a Burton' had been used in advertisements to promote a Bass beer known in the trade as 'a Burton' (though, in fact, several ales are produced at Burton-on-Trent). More positive proof is lacking. An advert for Carlsberg in the 1987 Egon Ronay *Good Food in Pubs and Bars* described Burton thus: 'A strong ale, dark in colour, made with a proportion of highly-dried or roasted malts. It is not necessarily brewed in Burton and a variety of strong or old ales were given the term.'

Other fanciful theories are that RAF casualty records were kept in an office above or near a branch of Burton Menswear in Blackpool, and that Morse Code instruction for wireless operators/air gunners took place in a converted billiards hall above Burtons in the same town (and failure in tests meant posting off the course – a fairly minor kind of 'death'). Probably no more than a coincidental use of the name Burton.

gone to earth! The huntsman's traditional cry when the fox has disappeared into the earth or the quarry escapes to its lair. Used as the title of a novel (1917; film UK, 1948) by Mary Webb about a Shropshire girl who is pursued by the local squire. In the story, the heroine has a pet fox, a hunting scene is the climax, and both the pursued end up down a disused mine shaft.

gone to the big/great — in the sky. This format phrase is used to announce lightly that someone has died. Thus, an actor might go to 'the great Green Room in the sky', a surgeon to 'the great operating theatre in the sky', a boozer to 'the great saloon bar in the sky', etc. From *Joe Bob Goes to the Drive-in* (1987): 'Ever since Bruce Lee went to the big Tae Kwon Do Academy in the sky'. Compare HAPPY HUNTING GROUND.

gone with the wind. Phrase from Ernest Dowson's poem '*Non Sum Qualis Eram*' (1896): 'I have forgot much, Cynara! Gone with the wind . . .' As the title of Margaret Mitchell's novel *Gone With the Wind* (1936; film US, 1939), the phrase refers to the Southern United States before the American Civil War, as is made clear by the on-screen prologue to the film: 'There was a land of Cavaliers and Cotton Fields called the Old South. Here in this patrician world the Age of Chivalry took its last bows. Here was the last ever seen of the Knights and their Ladies fair, of Master and Slave. Look for it only in books, for it is no more than a dream remembered, a Civilization gone with the wind . . .'

gong. See ALL ∼ AND NO DINNER; WHEN YOU HEAR THE ∼.

go now, pay later. An advertising inducement that has developed into a format phrase. Daniel Boorstin in *The Image* (1962) makes oblique reference to travel advertisements using the line 'Go now, pay later'. Was hire purchase ever promoted with 'Buy now, pay later'? It seems likely. These lines – in the US and UK – seem to be the starting point for a construction

much used and adapted since. *Live Now Pay Later* was the title of Jack Trevor Story's 1962 screenplay based on the novel *All on the Never Never* by Jack Lindsay. As a simple graffito, the same line was recorded in Los Angeles (1970), according to *The Encyclopedia of Graffiti* (1974). The same book records a New York subway graffito on a funeral parlour ad: 'Our layaway plan – die now, pay later.' 'Book now, pay later' was used in an ad in the programme of the Royal Opera House, Covent Garden, in 1977.

gonzo. See FEAR AND LOATHING IN LAS VEGAS.

good. See ALL ∼ THINGS MUST COME TO AN END; ALL PUBLICITY IS ∼ PUBLICITY; BE ∼ TO YOURSELF; ∼ GAME under GENERATION GAME; GUINNESS IS ∼ FOR YOU; HE'S VERY ∼, YOU KNOW under GOON SHOW; IF YOU CAN'T BE ∼ . . . ; IT'S LOOKING ∼; TWELVE ∼ MEN AND TRUE; WAS IT ∼ FOR YOU, TOO?; WE ARE JUST ∼ FRIENDS; YOU'RE ONLY AS ∼ AS YOUR LAST —; YOU'VE NEVER HAD IT SO ∼.

good and the great, the. Those who are on a British Government list from which are selected members of Royal Commissions and committees of inquiry. In 1983 the list stood at some 4,500 names. For the previous eight years custodians of the list had sought more women, more people under 40 and more from outside the golden triangle of London and the South-East in an attempt to break the stereotype enshrined in Lord Rothschild's parody of it as containing only 53-year-old men 'who live in the South-East, have the right accent and belong to the Reform Club'.

In the 1950s, the Treasury division which kept the list was actually known as the 'G and G'. On one occasion, it really did nominate two dead people for service on a public body (*The Times*, 22 January 1983).

good-bye-ee! Catchphrase of the British music-hall comedian Harry Tate (1872–1940) who is also said to have been the first to sing the song with this title which became very popular during the First World War. The song was written by R.P. Weston and Bert Lee in 1917.

good evening. See HELLO, ~, AND WELCOME; ~, EACH! under *EDUCATING ARCHIE*.

good evening, cads, your better selves are with you once again! See PLAY THE GAME, CADS!

good evening, England! This is Gillie Potter speaking to you in English. Customary beginning of BBC radio talks by Gillie Potter (1887–1975), the English humorist. Delivered in an assumed pedagogic and superior air, Potter's talks recounted the doings of the Marshmallow family of Hogsnorton Towers – a delight from the 1940s and early 50s. He would conclude with **goodbye, England, and good luck!**

good evening, everyone. The customary salutation of A.J. Alan, the radio storyteller of the 1920s and 30s. He was a civil servant (real name, Leslie Lambert) who eschewed personal publicity and always broadcast wearing a dinner jacket. He never went into a BBC studio without having a candle by him in case the lights fused. *Good Evening, Everyone* was the title of a book by him (1928).

good evening, Mr and Mrs North America and all the ships at sea – let's go to press. Walter Winchell (1892–1972) was an ex-vaudevillian who became a top radio newscaster. This was how he introduced his zippy 15-minute broadcast on Sunday nights, starting in 1932. By 1948 it was the top-rated radio show in the US with an average audience of 20 million people. A TV version ran 1952–5 in which Winchell entertained viewers by wearing his hat throughout. A variation of his greeting was 'Mr and Mrs North *and South* America'. Winchell also ran a syndicated newspaper gossip column and narrated the TV series *The Untouchables*. Many of his stories were pure fabrication.

good idea. See ~, SON under *EDUCATING ARCHIE*; IT SEEMED LIKE A ~ AT THE TIME.

Good — Guide, the. A format for book titles, which is obviously helped by the alliteration. The first in the field was *The*

Good Food Guide, edited by Raymond Postgate (1951). Subsequently, there have been Good – Book, Cheese, Hotel, Museums, Pub, Reading, Sex, Skiing, Software, Word – Guides, and many others.

good idea . . . son!, a. See under *EDUCATING ARCHIE*.

good man fallen among —, a. A construction which would appear to be based on 'a good man fallen among thieves' which may allude to Luke 10:30 in the parable of the good Samaritan: 'A certain man went down from Jerusalem to Jericho, and fell among thieves.'
Arthur Ransome, *Six Weeks in Russia* (1919) quotes Lenin as having called Bernard Shaw, 'A good man fallen among Fabians.' From R.M. Wardle, *Oliver Goldsmith* (1957): 'It was Goldsmith's misfortune that he was a jigger fallen among goons.' John Stonehouse called Edward Heath, 'A good man fallen among bureaucrats' (House of Commons, 13 May 1964). And when former journalist Michael Foot was leader of the British Labour Party, the *Daily Mirror* described him in an editorial (28 February 1983) as 'a good man fallen among politicians'.

good man is hard to find, a. Is this the same as the proverb 'Good men are scarce' found by *CODP* in 1609? In the present form, it was the title of a song by Eddie Green (1919). Nowadays, it is most frequently encountered in reverse. 'A hard man is good to find' was used, nudgingly, as the slogan for Soloflex body-building equipment in the US (1985). Ads showed a woman's hand touching the bodies of well-known brawny athletes. In this form the saying is sometimes attributed to Mae West.

good morning, boys! Opening line from the British comedian Will Hay (1888–1949) in his schoolmaster persona. He would say this as the Headmaster of St Michael's. His pupils would reply wearily, 'Good morning, sir!' Used as the title of a film (UK, 1937).

good morning . . . nice day! See under *ITMA*.

good morning, sir! Was there something? See under MUCH BINDING IN THE MARSH.

goodness gracious me! The key phrase in Peter Sellers's Indian doctor impersonation which all citizens of the subcontinent subsequently rushed to emulate. It occurred in a song called 'Goodness Gracious Me' (written by Herbert Kretzmer and Dave Lee) recorded by Sellers and Sophia Loren in 1960 and based on their characters in the film of Shaw's *The Millionairess*.

goodnight. See AND A SPECIAL ~; IT'S ~ FROM ME . . . ; SAY ~, DICK under *LAUGH-IN*.

goodnight . . . and good luck. Sign-off by Edward R. Murrow (1908–65), the American broadcaster, particularly on *See It Now* which has been called 'the prototype of the in-depth quality television documentary' (CBS TV, 1951–8).

goodnight, Chet/goodnight, David. Famous exchange between Chet Huntley and David Brinkley, co-anchors on NBC TV News and *The Huntley-Brinkley Report* from *c* 1956 to Huntley's retirement in 1970.

goodnight, children . . . everywhere! The stock phrase of Derek McCulloch (Uncle Mac) who was one of the original Uncles and Aunts who introduced BBC radio *Children's Hour* from the 1920s onwards. He developed this special farewell during the Second World War when many of the programme's listeners were evacuees. Vera Lynn recorded a song with the title (1939). J.B. Priestley wrote a war-time play with the title, also.

goodnight, everybody . . . goodnight! Distinctive pay-off at the end of the day's broadcasting from Stuart Hibberd (even in the days when BBC radio announcers were anonymous). Hibberd (1893–1983) would count four after the initial two words in order that listeners could say 'goodnight' back to him if they felt like it.

goodnight, gentlemen, and good sailing! Another example of informality from a BBC announcer in the otherwise starchier days of presentation – the customary end to a shipping forecast read by Frank Phillips (1901–80).

goodnight . . . God bless. Comedian Benny Hill (1925–92), as himself, at the end of his TV comedy shows in the UK from 1969 on. Latterly, Hill became equally well known in the US, where this farewell was once associated with comedian Red Skelton.

goodnight, good luck, and may your God go with you. Customary farewell from Dave Allen (*b* 1934), the Irish-born comedian, on British and Australian TV from the 1970s onwards.

goodnight, Mrs Calabash . . . wherever you are! Jimmy 'Schnozzle' Durante (1893–1980), the big-nosed American comedian, had a gaggle of phrases – including **I'm mortified** and an exasperated **everybody wants to get into the act!** and (after a successful joke), **I've got a million of 'em!** (also used in the UK by Max Miller and others).

He used to sign off his radio and TV shows in the 1940s and 1950s with the Calabash phrase. It was a pet name for his first wife, Maud, who died in 1943. The word comes from an American idiom for 'empty head', taken from the calabash or gourd. For a long time, Durante resisted explaining the phrase. His biographer, Gene Fowler, writing in 1952, could only note: 'When he says that line his manner changes to one of great seriousness, and his voice takes on a tender, emotional depth . . . when asked to explain the Calabash farewells, Jim replied, "That's my secret – I want it to rest where it is." '

Of Gary Moore, the MC on American radio's *The Camel Caravan* (1943–7) – and 22 years his junior – Durante would say **dat's my boy dat said dat!** Yet more phrases: **stop da music! stop da music!** and **dem's de conditions dat prevail!** or **dese are de conditions dat prevail!** or **it's da conditions dat prevail!**

good old Charlie-ee! See MUCH BINDING IN THE MARSH.

good riddance to bad rubbish. A gentle/good/fair riddance has been wished to an unwanted departing person since the sixteenth century but in this particular form, the earliest example appears to be in Charles Dickens, *Dombey and Son*, Chap. 44 (1848), precisely as: 'A good riddance *of* bad rubbish.'

good, the bad and the ugly, the. Colonel Oliver North giving evidence to the Washington hearings on the Irangate scandal in the summer of 1987, said: 'I came here to tell you the truth – the good, the bad, and the ugly.' *The Good, the Bad and the Ugly* was the English-language title of the Italian 'spaghetti Western', *Il Buono, il Bruto, il Cattivo* (1966).

good time was had by all, a. When the poet Stevie Smith entitled a collection of her poems *A Good Time Was Had By All* (1937), Eric Partridge asked her where she had taken the phrase from. She replied: from parish magazines where reports of church picnics or social evenings invariably ended with the phrase.

good to the last drop. A slogan for Maxwell House coffee, in the US, from 1907. President Theodore Roosevelt was visiting Joel Cheek, perfector of the Maxwell House blend. After the President had had a cup, he said of it that it was 'Good . . . to the last drop'. It has been used as a slogan ever since, despite those who have inquired what was wrong with the last drop. Professors of English have been called in to consider the problem and ruled that 'to' can be inclusive and not just mean 'up to but not including'.

good war, a. I don't know who first started talking about having had a 'good or bad war' but I think it has *usually* been said by survivors of the Second World War. Lord Moran in *Churchill: The Struggle for Survival* made a 1943 reference: 'But it was [Lord] Wavell who said to me, "I have had a bad war."' In Henry Reed's radio play of 1959, *Not a Drum Was Heard: the War Memoirs of General Gland*, Gland says: 'It was, I think a *good* war, one of the best there have so far been. I've often advanced the view that it was a war deserving of better generalship than it received on either side.' Usually, however, it is a good war in the sense of a

personally successful or enjoyable one that is being talked about.

Recent uses have been mostly figurative. In his *European Diary*, Roy Jenkins has this entry for 19 February 1979: 'Bill Rodgers . . . clearly thought he had had, as Peter Jenkins put it, "a good war" during the strike period and was exhilarated by having made a public breakthrough.' From Julian Critchley MP in the *Guardian* (3 May 1989): 'I well remember some years ago at the Savoy a colleague who had had a good war leaping to his feet (before the Loyal Toast) in order to pull back the curtains which separated the party from the outside world . . .' From the *Independent* (13 July 1989): 'British Rail has not had a good war. The public relations battle in the industrial dispute seems to have been all but lost.'

good work. See KEEP UP THE ∼.

goody-goody gumdrops! Used by Humphrey Lestocq, host of BBC TV's children's show *Whirligig* in the early 1950s, though he did not originate it. Harold Acton in his book *Nancy Mitford: a Memoir* (1975) quotes 'goody-goody gum-*trees*' as being a favourite of Noël Coward in the late 1920s.

Goon Show, The. The Goons – Peter Sellers, Harry Secombe and Spike Milligan – first appeared in a BBC radio show called *Crazy People* in May 1951. At that time, Michael Bentine was also of their number. *The Goon Show* proper ran from 1952–60, with one extra programme in 1972, and numerous re-runs.

The humour was zany, often taking basic music-hall jokes and giving them further infusions of surrealism. The cast of three did all the funny voices, though Harry Secombe concentrated on the main character, Neddie Seagoon. Catchphrases included:

and this is where the story really begins/starts . . .

brandy-y-y-y! Accompanied by the sound of rushing footsteps, this was the show's beloved way of getting anybody out of a situation that was proving too much for him.

damn(ed) clever these Chinese! A Second World War phrase taken up from time to time by the Goons. (Or 'dead clever chaps/devils these Chinese!') Referring to a reputation for wiliness rather than skill. Compare the line 'Damn clever, these *Armenians*' uttered by Claudette Colbert in the film *It Happened One Night* (US, 1934).

dreaded lergy, the. Pronounced 'lurgy' (hard 'g'), and = allergy (soft 'g').

have a gorilla! Neddie Seagoon's way of offering a cigarette, to which the reply might be 'No, thank you, I'm trying to give them up' or 'No, thanks, I only smoke baboons!'

he's fallen in the water! Said by Little Jim (Milligan):

> *Voice:* Oh, dear, children – look what's happened to Uncle Harry!
> *Little Jim (helpfully, in simple sing-song voice):* He's fallen in the wa-ter!

he's very good, you know! Ironic commendation, spoken by various characters.
I do not like this game! Said by Bluebottle (Sellers):

> *Seagoon:* Now, Bluebottle, take this stick of dynamite.
> *Bluebottle:* No, I do not like this game!

it's all in the mind, you know. Convincing explanation of anything heard in the show – often said as a final word by Wallace Greenslade, the announcer.

I've been sponned! Oddly, this phrase does not actually occur in the episode called 'The Spon Plague' broadcast in March 1958, but I clearly remember running around saying it at school. The symptoms of sponning included bare knees – of which we had quite a few in those days. In 'Tales of Men's Shirts' (December 1959), however, Sellers's 'Mate' character gets clobbered and says, 'Ow! I've been sponned from the film of the same name' and proceeds to write his memoirs, 'How I was sponned in action.'

Earlier, in August 1957, Peter Sellers used the exact phrase as the tag line for his recording of 'Any Old Iron'.

needle, nardle, noo! Nonsense phrase, spoken by various characters.

only in the mating season. The Goons' response to the traditional chatting-up line, DO YOU COME HERE OFTEN?

sapristi! (as in 'sapristi nuckoes!' etc). Count Jim Moriarty (Milligan) used this fairly traditional exclamation of surprise – a corruption of the French '*sacristi*' and current by 1839. Some will remember it being said, also, by Corporal Trenet, friend of 'Luck of the Legion' in the boys' paper *Eagle*, also in the 1950s.

shut up, Eccles! Said by Seagoon, repeated by Eccles (Milligan), and then taken up by everyone.
ying-tong-iddle-i-po! All-purpose nonsense phrase, notably incorporated in 'The Ying Tong Song'.

you can't get the wood, you know! Said by Minnie Bannister or Henry Crun.

you dirty rotten swine you! Bluebottle on being visited by some punishment or disaster.

See also AND THERE'S MORE . . . ; BY JOVE, I NEEDED THAT!; I DON'T WISH TO KNOW THAT . . . ; 2–4–6–8 . . .

gooseberry, to play. To act as an unwanted chaperon or third party so that two young lovers can be together with propriety. Current by 1837, this expression has no obvious derivation, though one is that the chaperon might find him/herself filling in time by picking gooseberries while the couple is more romantically engaged.
  On the other hand, playing gooseberry is not a very enviable or enjoyable job and the chaperon may well feel a bit of a *fool* and 'gooseberry' is a slang word for 'fool', derived of course from the pudding known as 'gooseberry fool' (or from the supposedly comic appearance of gooseberries) since the

early eighteenth century. Could this have something to do with it?

gooseberry bush. See CABBAGE PATCH KIDS.

Gordon Bennett! A euphemistic exclamation. My inquiries into this odd expletive began in about 1982. The first person I consulted – a cheery Londoner with the absolute confidence of the amateur etymologist – assured me that it was short for 'Gawd and St Benet!' Quite who St Benet was, and why people invoked his name, I never found out. Except that in Shakespeare's *Twelfth Night* (1600), 'the bells of Saint Bennet' (= Saint Benedict, or possibly St Bennet Hithe, Paul's Wharf, opposite the Globe Theatre) is alluded to at V.i.37.

Then, shortly afterwards, on a visit to Paris, I found myself staring up in amazement at a street sign which bore the legend 'Avenue Gordon-Bennett'. I felt like exclaiming, '*Mon Dieu et St Benet!*'

Reading Churchill's *History of the Second World War*, I came across one Lieut. Gen. Gordon Bennett. Knowing how many slang expressions have come out of the services, I wondered whether he had done something to impress himself upon the language.

Next, I talked to a man at the annual convention of the Institute of Concrete Technology. He told me he thought the expression was current in the 1930s. Hadn't Gordon Bennett been a comedian? Indeed, there were comedians called Billy Bennett, Wheeler and Bennett, Bennett and Moreny, Bennett and Williams, though why any of *them* should have been commemorated by having a street named after then in Paris (even had their first names been Gordon) is anybody's guess

'Ah,' said the concrete man, 'the *French* Gordon Bennett was probably the man who gave his name to a motor race in the early 1900s.'

In fact, he wasn't French at all, but American, and there were two of him. James Gordon Bennett I (1795–1872) was a Scot who went to the US and became a megalomaniac newspaper proprietor. James Gordon Bennett II (1841–1918) was the even more noted editor-in-chief of the *New York Herald* and the man who sent Henry Morton Stanley to find Dr Livingstone in Africa.

But why should either of these gentlemen have a street named after him in Paris, not to mention a motor race, as well as bequeath his moniker as a British expletive?

James Gordon Bennett II (for we must concentrate on him) was quite a character. He was exiled to Paris after a scandal but somehow managed to run his New York newspaper from there (the cable bills ran up and up, so he bought the cable company). He disposed of some $40 million in his lifetime. He offered numerous trophies to stimulate French sport and, when the motor car was in its infancy, presented the Gordon Bennett cup to be competed for. On one occasion, he tipped a train guard $14,000 and, on another, drew a wad of 1,000 franc notes from his back pocket (where they had been causing him discomfort) and threw them on the fire. He became, as the *Dictionary of American Biography* puts it, 'one of the most picturesque figures of two continents'.

This, if anything does, probably explains why it was *his* name that ended up on people's lips and why they did not go around exclaiming, 'Gordon of Khartoum!' or 'Gordon Selfridge!' or anything else. Gordon Bennett was a man with an amazing reputation.

I don't take very seriously the suggestion that stunned members of the public shouted 'Gordon Bennett!' when Stanley found Livingstone. Nor that there were cartoons of Stanley phoning his editor (from the jungle?) and shouting, 'Gordon Bennett, I've found him!' The truth of the matter seems to be that people found some peculiar appeal in the name Gordon Bennett – but the important thing is that the first name was 'Gordon'.

Understandably, people shrink from blaspheming. 'Oh Gawd!' is felt to be less offensive than 'Oh God!' At the turn of the century it was natural for people facetiously to water down the exclamation 'God!' by saying 'Gordon!' The name Gordon Bennett was to hand. The initial letters of the name also had the explosive quality found in 'Gorblimey! [God blind me!]'.

A decade or two later, in similar fashion – and with a view to circumventing the strict Hollywood Hay's Code – W.C. Fields would exclaim 'Godfrey Daniel!', a 'minced oath' in place of 'God, damn you!'

But who was Godfrey Daniel . . . ?

gorilla. See HAVE A ∼ under *GOON SHOW.*

Gorki Street. See FOGGY BOTTOM.

got. See THAT ALMOST ∼ AWAY; WHEN YOU ∼ IT, FLAUNT IT.

gotcha! The *OED2* has an example of this form of 'got you' from 1966. The headline 'GOTCHA!' was how the *Sun* newspaper 'celebrated' the sinking of the Argentine cruiser *General Belgrano* during the Falklands war (front page, 4 May 1982). But it was retained for the first edition only.

Gotham City. Name of the city featured in the *BATMAN* cartoon strip, possibly deriving from 'Gotham' as the name for New York City in Washington Irving's *Salmagundi* (1807).

Could this in turn be derived from the name of a village in Nottinghamshire, England, noted for the (sometimes calculated) folly of its inhabitants? Their reputation was established by the fifteenth century, as in the nursery rhyme:

Three wise Men of Gotham
Went to sea in a bowl,
If the bowl had been stronger,
My story would have been longer.

go the extra mile, to. To make an extra special effort to accomplish something. President George Bush used this American military/business expression at the time of the Gulf War (1991), referring to his attempts to get a peaceful settlement before resorting to arms. Later that same year, Bush, expressing sorrow for baseball star Magic Johnson who had been found HIV-positive, said: 'If there's more I can do to empathize, to make clear what AIDS is and what it isn't, I want to go the extra mile' (*Independent*, 9 November 1991).

The expression had been around long before that, however. Even in a revue song by Joyce Grenfell, 'All We Ask Is Kindness' (1957), there is: 'Working like a beaver/Always with a smile/Ready to take

the rough and smooth/To go the extra mile.'

Gothic. See AMERICAN ∼.

go to it! In the summer of 1940, the Minister of Supply, Herbert Morrison, called for a voluntary labour force in words that echoed the public mood after Dunkirk. The slogan was used in a campaign run by the S.H. Benson agency (which later indulged in self-parody on behalf of Bovril, with 'Glow to it' in 1951–2). 'Go to it', meaning 'to act vigorously, set to with a will' dates at least from the early nineteenth century. In Shakespeare, it means something else, of course:

Die for adultery! No:
The wren goes to't, and the small gilded
fly
Does lecher in my sight.
King Lear, IV.vi.112 (1605)

go to the biscuit factory. See BISCUIT FACTORY . . .

go to work on an egg. In 1957, Fay Weldon (*b* 1932), later known as a novelist and TV playwright, was a copywriter on the British Egg Marketing Board account at the Mather & Crowther agency. In 1981 she poured a little cold water on the frequent linking of her name with the slogan: 'I was certainly in charge of copy at the time "Go to work on an egg" was first used as a slogan as the main theme for an advertising campaign. The phrase itself had been in existence for some time and hung about in the middle of paragraphs and was sometimes promoted to base lines. Who invented it, it would be hard to say. It is perfectly possible, indeed probable, that I put those particular six words together in that particular order but I would not swear to it.'

gotta. See I ∼ HORSE; MAN'S ∼ DO . . . ; MILK'S ∼ LOTTA BOTTLE.

gottle o' geer. The standard showbiz way of mocking the inadequacies of many ventriloquist acts. It represents 'bottle of beer', said with teeth tightly clenched. Known by the 1960s, at least.

Gott strafe England! 'God punish England' – a German propaganda slogan from the First World War. It apparently originated, or at least made an early appearance, in a book called *Schwert und Myrte* (1914) by Alfred Funke.

gourmet. See GALLOPING ∼.

government health warning. Now, any warning which suggests that a person, thing or activity should be avoided – as, for example, 'Mind yourself with him; he ought to carry a government health warning.'

The phrase came originally from cigarette advertising and packets which, in the UK from 1971, have carried a message to this effect: 'DANGER. H.M. GOVERNMENT HEALTH DEPARTMENT'S WARNING: CIGARETTES CAN SERIOUSLY DAMAGE YOUR HEALTH'. The 'seriously' was added in 1977; the 'danger' in 1980.

In the US, from 1965, packs carried the message: 'CAUTION: CIGARETTE SMOKING MAY BE HAZARDOUS TO YOUR HEALTH'. Five years later, this was strengthened to read: 'WARNING; THE SURGEON-GENERAL HAS DETERMINED THAT CIGARETTE SMOKING IS DANGEROUS TO YOUR HEALTH'.

Gov'nor, the. See OL' BLUE EYES

go West, young man. The saying 'Go west, young man, and grow up with the country', was originated by John Babsone Lane Soule in the Terre Haute, Indiana, *Express* (1851) when, indeed, the thing to do in the US was to head westwards, where gold and much else lay promised. However, Horace Greeley repeated it in *his* New York newspaper, the *Tribune*, and being rather more famous as he was also a candidate for the presidency, it stuck with him. Greeley reprinted Soule's article to show where he had taken it from, but to no avail.

Go West Young Man became the title of a film (1936), which was a vehicle for *Mae West* rather than anything to do with *the* West. *Go West Young Lady* followed in 1940.

There have been two films called simply *Go West*, notably the 1940 one often referred to as *The Marx Brothers Go West*.

To **go west**, meaning 'to die' is a completely separate coinage. It dates back to the sixteenth century and alludes to the setting of the sun and may have entered American Indian usage by 1801.

grace. See AMAZING ∼.

grace under pressure. The Latin tag '*Suaviter in modo, fortiter in re*' [gentle in manner, resolute in action] was reduced to the definition of 'guts' as 'grace under pressure' by Ernest Hemingway in a *New Yorker* article (30 November 1929). It was later invoked by John F. Kennedy in *Profiles in Courage* (1956).

gracious. See GOODNESS ∼ ME!

grain of salt, to take something with a. Meaning, 'to treat something sceptically', just as food is sometimes made more palatable by the addition of a pinch of salt. This comes from the Latin *cum grano selis*.

grand. See EE, AIN'T IT ∼ TO BE DAFT; SERIOUSLY, THOUGH, HE'S DOING A ∼ JOB.

grandmother. See DON'T TEACH YOUR ∼ . . . ; I HAVEN'T BEEN SO HAPPY SINCE . . . ; I WOULD WALK OVER MY ∼.

grandfather. See AND THAT, MY DEARS . . .

Grand Old Man (or **GOM**). The nickname of W.E. GLADSTONE is believed to have been coined by either Sir William Harcourt or Lord Rosebery or the Earl of Iddesleigh. The latter who said in an 1882 speech (when Gladstone was 73): 'Argue as you please, you are nowhere; that grand old man, the Prime Minister, insists on the other thing.'

Grandpapa England. King George V (1865–1936) was reputedly known as this to his granddaughters, the Princesses Elizabeth and Margaret. However, in a 1983 biography of Queen Elizabeth II (by Elizabeth Longford), Princess Margaret was quoted as denying that she or her sister had ever used the nickname: 'We were much too frightened of him to call him anything but Grandpapa.'

grape. See BEULAH, PEEL ME A ∼.

grapeshot. See WHIFF OF ∼.

grapevine, to hear something on the. Meaning, 'to acquire information by word of mouth, through intermediaries, rather than directly from the original source' – how gossip and rumour usually travel. In the American Civil War, the method was known as 'the grapevine telegraph'. Presumably the allusion is to a network running about the place like the branches of a vine.

Compare the Australian **bush telegraph**, a name given to the system of unofficial warnings of police movements given by bushrangers to each other (known by 1878), and now used generally.

grass is greener, the. The *ODP* (1970) ignored the proverb 'The grass is always greener on the other side of the fence', in this form, preferring to cite a sixteenth-century translation of a Latin proverb, 'The corn in another man's ground seemeth ever more fertile than doth our own'. By 1956, the time of the Hugh and Margaret Williams play *The Grass is Greener*, the modern form – sometimes ending 'on the other side of the hedge' – was well established. Wolfgang Mieder in *Proverbium* (1993) questions whether the two proverbs are in fact related but finds an earlier citation of the modern one: an American song with words by Raymond B. Egan and music by Richard A. Whiting entitled 'The Grass is Always Greener (In the Other Fellow's Yard)', published in 1924.

grassroots, from the. A political cliché of the early 1970s, used when supposedly reflecting the opinions of the 'rank and file' and the 'ordinary voter' rather than the leadership of the political parties 'at national level'. Katherine Moore writing to Joyce Grenfell in *An Invisible Friendship* (letter of 13 October 1973): 'Talking of writing – why have roots now always got to be *grass* roots? And what a lot of them seem to be about.' A BBC Radio programme

From the Grassroots started in 1970. The full phrase is 'from the grassroots up' and has been used to describe anything of a fundamental nature since *c* 1900 and specifically in politics from *c* 1912 – originally in the US.

grass widow, a. A divorced woman or one apart from her husband because his job or some other preoccupation has taken him elsewhere. It originally meant an unmarried woman who had sexual relations with one or more men – perhaps on the grass rather than in the lawful marriage bed – and had had a child out of wedlock. This sense was known by the sixteenth century. Later it seems to have been applied to women in British India who were sent up to the cool hill country (where grass grows) during the hottest season of the year. An alternative derivation is from 'grace widow' or even 'Grace Widow', the name of an actual person.

grass will grow in the streets. A popular warning of the decay that will inevitably follow the pursuit of certain policies. 'The grass will grow in the streets of a hundred cities, a thousand towns,' said President Hoover in a speech (31 October 1932) on proposals 'to reduce the protective tariff to a competitive tariff for revenue'. The image had earlier been used by William Jennings Bryan in his 'Cross of Gold' speech (1896): 'Burn down your cities and leave our farms, and your cities will spring up again as if by magic; but destroy our farms and the grass will grow in the streets of every city in the country.'

Compare, from Anthony Trollope, *Dr Thorne*, Chap. 15 (1858): 'Why, luke at this 'ere town . . . the grass be a-growing in the very streets; – that can't be no gude.'

grateful and comforting like Epps's Cocoa. In Noël Coward's play *Peace In Our Time* (1947) one character says, 'One quick brandy, like Epps's Cocoa, would be both grateful and comforting.' When asked, 'Who is Epps?' he replies, 'Epps's cocoa – it's an advertisement I remember when I was a little boy.' The slogan has, indeed, been used since *c* 1900.

grateful country/nation, from a. A memorial phrase especially popular in the nineteenth century. At St Deiniol's, W.E. Gladstone's library in the village of Hawarden, Wales, where the British Prime Minister (1809–98) had his family home for almost fifty years, there is a plaque saying it was 'erected to his memory by a grateful nation'. W.M. Thackeray, writing in *The Virginians*, Chap. XXXV (1859), has: 'The late lamented O'Connell . . . over whom a grateful country has raised such a magnificent testimonial.' On the statue to General Havelock (1795–1857) in Trafalgar Square, London, is written: 'Soldiers! Your valour will not be forgotten by a grateful country.' The notable Alexander Column in the square outside the Winter Palace at St Petersburg was completed in 1834. On the base was the inscription (in Russian): 'To Alexander the First from a Grateful Russia.'

Nowadays, the phrase is invariably used with irony. From the *Independent* (23 July 1992): 'There have been loads of Roy Orbisons and Neil Diamonds and Gene Pitneys, and, after Elvis, the man most often impersonated by a grateful nation . . . Cliff Richard.'

gratias agimus tibi. See MASS PHRASES.

gratis. See FREE, ~ , AND FOR NOTHING.

grave. See ONE FOOT IN THE ~ ; TURN OVER IN ONE'S ~ .

graveyard. See ELEPHANTS' ~ .

gravy train, to climb aboard the. To obtain access to a money-spinning scheme. This was an American expression originally – *DOAS* suggests that it started in sporting circles. An alternative version is 'to climb aboard the gravy *boat*', which is a bit easier to understand. Gravy boats exist for holding gravy in and take their name from their shape. So, if money is perceived as being like gravy, it is not hard to see how the expression arose.

According to *Webster's Dictionary*, the 'train' and 'boat' forms are equally popular in the US (and have been since the 1920s). 'Boat' is probably less popular in the UK.

Gray, Dorian. See DORIAN ~ .

greasepaint. See DOCTOR ~ WILL CURE ME; ROAR OF THE ~ . . .

greasy pole, the. Referring to politics at a high level, this term comes from the remark made by Benjamin Disraeli to friends when he first became British Prime Minister in 1868: 'Yes, I have climbed to the top of the greasy pole.' The allusion is to the competitive sport, once popular at fairs and games, of climbing up or along a greasy pole without slipping off.

great. See AH, WOODBINE . . . ; GOOD AND THE ~ ; under BEAST 666; LATE ~ —; THIS ~ MOVEMENT OF OURS.

great balls of fire! To those who are most familiar with this exclamation from the Jerry Lee Lewis hit song of 1957 (written by Jack Hammer and Otis Blackwell) or the Lewis biopic (1989), it should be pointed out that, of course, it didn't begin there.

In fact, it occurs several times in the script of the film *Gone With the Wind* (1939), confirming what I would suspect are its distinctly Southern US origins. While the *OED2* and other dictionaries content themselves with the slang meaning of 'ball of fire' (glass of brandy/a person of great liveliness of spirit), even Partridge/*Slang* and American slang dictionaries avoid recording the phrase.

I mean, goodness gracious . . .

Great Cham (of Literature), the. Nickname applied to Dr Samuel Johnson by Tobias Smollett in a letter to John Wilkes in 1759. 'Cham' is a form of 'khan' (as in Genghis Khan) meaning 'monarch' or 'prince'.

great debate. Politicians like to apply this dignifying label to any period of discussion over policy. The rhyming phrase goes back to 1601, at least. 'The Conservative leaders now decided to bring a vote of no confidence against the Government [on its Defence Programme], and on February 15 [1951] the "Great Debate" as it was known in Tory circles was opened, by Churchill himself' (Martin Gilbert, *Never Despair*,

1988). From BBC TV, MONTY PYTHON'S
FLYING CIRCUS (4 January 1973): 'Stern music
as the lights come on. SUPERIMPOSED
CAPTIONS: "THE GREAT DEBATE"
"NUMBER 31" "TV4 OR NOT TV4". In a
speech at Ruskin College, Oxford, in
October 1976, James Callaghan, as Prime
Minister, called for a 'national debate' on
education policy which also became known
as a 'Great Debate'.

greatest. See I AM THE ~; WORLD'S ~
ENTERTAINER.

greatest living —, the. A (mostly)
journalistic tag applied to people since at
least the 1850s, and latterly with irony.
David Lloyd George used to annoy
C.P.Scott, editor of the *Manchester
Guardian* in the 1910s/20s by always
referring to him at public meetings as 'the
world's greatest living journalist'. James
Agate, writing in *Ego 3* (on 5 December
1936) of King Edward VIII and the
Abdication, said: 'Everybody is impressed
by Rothermere's letter saying that
Baldwin is in too much of a hurry, and
that "the greatest living Englishman
cannot be smuggled off his throne in a
week-end".' The term 'Greatest
Englishman of his Age' was much used of
Sir Winston Churchill about the time of
his death in 1965 – also ironically of Cyril
Connolly, the writer and critic. In the
1970s, Nigel Dempster, the gossip
columnist who contributed to *Private Eye*
pseudonymously as part of the 'Grovel'
column, promoted himself as 'the
Greatest Living Englishman' or 'GLE'.

greatest show on earth, the. A slogan
used by P.T. Barnum (d 1891) to promote
the circus formed by the merger with his
rival, Bailey's, in the US, from 1881. It is
still the slogan of what is now Ringling Bros
and Barnum & Bailey Circus. It was used as
the title of a Cecil B. de Mille circus film in
1952.

greatest thing since sliced bread, the.
(sometimes **best/hottest**). A 1981 ad in the
UK declared: 'Sainsbury's bring you the
greatest thing since sliced bread. Unsliced
bread' – neatly turning an old formula on
its head. Quite when the idea that pre-sliced

bread was one of the landmark inventions
arose is not clear. Sliced bread had first
appeared on the market by the 1920s – so a
suitable period of time after that.

Great Fatherland/Patriotic War. See
WORLD WAR II.

Great Helmsman, the. A dignified
sobriquet for Chairman Mao Tse-tung
during the Cultural Revolution in China of
the 1960s. It was applied, jokingly, to
Edward Heath, when British Prime
Minister (1970–76) because of his
enthusiasm for yachting.

Great Leap Forward, the. Chairman
Mao Tse-tung's phrase for the enforced
industrialization in China in 1958. It is now
used ironically about any supposed move in
the right direction.

great majority, the. (or simply **the
majority**.) A term for the dead, since the
eighteenth century (compare SILENT
MAJORITY). Edward Yonge's *The Revenge*
(1719) has: 'Death joins us to the great
majority.' In the Epistle Dedicatory of *Urn-
Burial* (1658), Sir Thomas Browne writes
of: 'When the living might exceed, and to
depart this world could not be properly
said to go unto the greatest number.'
There is also the Latin phrase *abiit ad
plures*.

    The dying words of Lord Houghton in
1884 were: 'Yes, I am going to join the
Majority and you know I have always
preferred Minorities.' *Punch* (19 June 1907)
carries an exchange between a parson and a
parishioner after a funeral: 'Joined the great
majority, eh?' 'Oh, I wouldn't like to say
that, Sir. He was a good enough man as far
as I know.'

great morning. Possibly a phrase from
hunting. *Great Morning* is the title of a
volume of memoirs (1947) by Osbert
Sitwell. It occurs earlier in Shakespeare's
Troilus and Cressida (1601) and *Cymbeline*
(1609) (where it means 'broad daylight').
Compare the title *Bright Day*, a novel (1946)
by J.B. Priestley.

great Scott! As with GORDON BENNETT,
one is dealing here with a watered-down

expletive. 'Great Scott!' clearly sounds like 'Great God!' and yet is not blasphemous. Morris says the expression became popular when US General Winfield Scott was the hero of the Mexican War (1847) and 'probably our most admired general between Washington and Lee'. No rival candidate seems to have been proposed and the origination is almost certainly American. *OED2*'s earliest British English example dates from 1885.

Great Society, the. The name of President Lyndon Johnson's policy platform in the US. In a speech at the University of Michigan (May 1964) he said: 'In your time, we have the opportunity to move not only toward the rich society and the powerful society but upward to the Great Society.'

Great Train Robbery, the. Journalistic tag given to the spectacular hold-up of a Glasgow-to-London train in Buckinghamshire (1963), when £2,500,000 was stolen from a mail van. Those who committed the robbery were consequently dubbed 'the Great Train Robbers'.
The Great Train Robbery had earlier been the title of a silent film (US, 1903) which is sometimes considered to be the first 'real' movie. The 1963 robbery was, in turn, appropriately 'celebrated' in the films *Robbery* (1967) and *Buster* (1988).

Great Unwashed, the. Meaning 'working-class people; the lower orders', this term was originally used by the politician and writer Edmund Burke (*d* 1797), perhaps echoing Shakespeare's reference to 'another lean unwash'd artificer' – *King John*, IV.ii.201 (1596). Lytton in *Paul Clifford* (1830) uses the full phrase.

Great War. See DADDY WHAT DID YOU DO IN THE ∼ ?; under FIRST WORLD WAR.

Great Wen, the. In *Rural Rides* (1830), William Cobbett asked of London: 'But what is to be the fate of the great wen of all? The monster, called . . . "the metropolis of empire"?' A 'wen' is a lump or protuberance on a body; a wart. Compare MONSTROUS CARBUNCLE.

Great White Way, the. Nickname for Broadway, the main theatre zone of New York City – alluding to the brightness of the illumination, and taken from the title of a novel (1901) by Albert Bigelow Paine. For a while, Broadway was also known as 'the Gay White Way', though for understandable reasons this is no longer so.

Greeks bearing gifts, beware. A warning against trickery, this is an allusion to the most famous Greek gift of all – the large wooden horse which was built as an offering to the gods before the Greeks were about to return home after besieging Troy unsuccessfully for ten years. It was taken within the city walls of Troy, but men leapt out from it, opened the gates and helped destroy the city. Virgil in the *Aeneid* (II.49) has Laocoon warn the Trojans not to admit the horse, saying *timeo Danaos et dona ferentes* [I still fear the Greeks, even when they offer gifts].

Greeks had a word for it, the. An expression used, a trifle archly, when one wishes to express disapproval – as one might say: 'there's a name for that sort of behaviour'. From the title of a US play (1930) by Zoë Akins, although, as she said, the 'phrase is original and grew out of the dialogue', it does not appear anywhere in the text. The 'it' refers to a type of woman. One character thinks that 'tart' is meant, but the other corrects this and says 'free soul' is more to the point.

green. See SEE YOU ON THE ∼.

green cheese. See MOON IS MADE OF ∼.

greener. See GRASS IS ∼.

green-eyed monster, the. Jealousy. From Shakespeare's *Othello*, III.iii.170 (1604), where Iago says to Othello, 'O, beware jealousy;/It is the green-ey'd monster, which doth mock/That meat it feeds on.'

Green Goddess. An alliterative nickname which has been applied variously to Second World War fire engines (painted green), Liverpool trams, a crème de menthe cocktail, a lettuce salad, and a lily. In 1983, Diana Moran, a keep-fit demonstrator on a BBC TV breakfast programme, was so billed. She wore distinctive green exercise clothing. Perhaps all these uses derive from William Archer's play entitled *The Green Goddess* (1923; film US, 1930).

green grow the rushes, oh. One of the many almost impenetrable phrases from one of the most-quoted folk songs. A pamphlet from the English Folk Dance and Song Society (*c* 1985) remarks: 'This song has appeared in many forms in ancient and modern languages from Hebrew onwards, and it purports in almost all cases to be theological.' *Green Grow the Rushes* was used as the title of a film (UK, 1950).

Here is what some of the other phrases in the song *may* be about:

I'll sing you one oh,
Green grow the rushes oh,
One is one and all alone and evermore
    shall be so.
            [Refers to God Almighty.]

Two, two for the **lilywhite boys,**
Clothed all in green oh.
            [Christ and St John the
            Baptist as children (though
            what the green refers to is not
            clear). Compare the title of
            Christopher Logue's 1950s
            play *The Lily-White Boys*.]

Three, three for the rivals
            [The Trinity? The Three Wise
            Men?]

Four for the Gospel makers
            [Matthew, Mark, Luke, and
            John?]

Five for the **symbol at your door**
            [The Pentagram or five-
            pointed star inscribed on the
            threshold to drive away the
            evil one.]

Six for the **six proud walkers**
            [The six *waterpots* used in the
            miracle of Cana of Galilee.
            Compare the title of Donald

Wilson's detective series on BBC TV (1954, 1964), *The Six Proud Walkers*.]

Seven for the seven stars in the sky
            [The group in Ursa Major
            called Charley's Wain; or the
            seven days of the week; or
            Revelation 1:16: 'And he had
            in his right hand seven stars
            and out of his mouth went a
            two-edged sword.']

Eight for the eight bold rainers/rangers/
    archangels
            [Bold rainers, i.e. angels? But
            why eight? There are only
            four archangels, so why
            double? A 1625 version refers
            to the people in Noah's Ark
            who might well be described
            as 'bold rangers'.]

Nine for the nine bright shiners
            [The nine choirs of angels?
            The nine months before
            birth?]

Ten for the ten commandments
            [Obvious, this one.]

Eleven for the eleven that went up to
    heaven
            [The Apostles without Judas
            Iscariot.]

Twelve for the twelve apostles.
            [Or the tribes of Israel.]

Greening of America, The. Title of a book (1971) by Charles Reich. Here, the 'greening' is not of the environmental kind (that sense was, however, already emerging in Europe in the early 1970s), but rather of the maturing of the US through a new anti-urban counter-culture and consciousness. 'The extraordinary thing about this new consciousness,' Reich concludes, 'is that it has emerged out of the wasteland of the Corporate State. For one who thought the world was irretrievably encased in metal and plastic and sterile stone, it seems a remarkable greening of America.' Oddly, of course, 'to be green' can also mean 'to be immature, inexperienced'.

green room, a/the. A place where actors and other performers retire when they are not appearing on the stage or in their dressing rooms. Originally known as their 'tiring room'. A common explanation for the term is that such rooms were originally painted green to rest the eyes of those who had been in the glare of harsh stage lighting – but the expression was known in times when stages were candle-lit and hardly a strain on anybody's eyes. The earliest reference in a play occurs in Thomas Shadwell's *The True Widow* (1678). Eleven years before this, Samuel Pepys was entertained backstage by an actress at the Dorset Garden Theatre in what he calls the 'scene room'. Subsequently, the two terms have been used almost interchangably, and possibly 'green' is no more than a rhymed equivalent of 'scene'. Compare SEE YOU ON THE GREEN.

green shoots. A phrase used to indicate that something is about to bud or bloom. As Britain's Chancellor of the Exchequer, Norman Lamont was earnestly endeavouring to convince his audience that Britain was coming out of a recession when he used this horticultural metaphor in a speech to the Conservative Party Conference at Blackpool on 9 October 1991: 'The turn of the tide is sometimes difficult to discern. What we are seeing is the return of that vital ingredient – confidence. The green shoots of economic spring are appearing once again.' In a letter to a lover (6 May 1962), the poet Philip Larkin wrote: 'Spring comes with your birthday, and I love to think of you as somehow linked with the tender green shoots I see on all the trees and bushes . . . I wish I could be with you and we could plunge into bed.'

grey. See MAN IN A ~ SUIT.

grind. See AXE TO ~.

groaner. See OLD ~.

grody to the max. 'Vile, grotty to the maximum degree' – from American 'Valspeak', the slang of teenage girls living in the San Fernando Valley area of Southern California. The phrase first became known to the outside world in 1982, especially following its inclusion in the record 'Valley Girl', performed by Moon Unit, the daughter of Frank Zappa. See also VALLEY GIRL.

Grog, Old. Nickname of the British Admiral Edward Vernon (1684–1757), because of his fondness for a cloak made of grogram, a coarse material of silk and wool. In 1740, he introduced a ration of rum diluted with water in an attempt to prevent scurvy among his crewmen. It did not work, but the name 'grog' was given to the drink and then, by sailors, to public houses ashore – hence 'grog shops', places where spirits were sold.

groovy baby! This was given added impetus as a catchphrase c 1968 through its use by the disc jockey Dave Cash on BBC Radio 1. He would play a brief clip of an actual baby boy, referred to as 'Microbe', saying it. As a result, 'Groovy baby' stickers were much in demand and Blue Mink incorporated 'Microbe' saying the phrase on a record with the title (1969).

'Groovy' meaning 'very good' (particularly of music) was, in any case, already popular in the 1960s, although *DOAS* traces it back to the mid-1930s and its use among 'swing' musicians and devotees. It comes from 'in the groove', referring to the way a gramophone or phonograph stylus or needle fits neatly into the groove on a record.

grotty, to be (dead). Meaning, 'to be seedy; down-at-heel; crummy; unpleasant; nasty; unattractive,' this was a trendy word in the 1960s (compare the 1980's NAFF). It is short for 'grotesque' and is very much associated with the Mersey culture that accompanied the Beatles out of Liverpool in 1962–3. Alun Owen put it in his script for the first Beatles film, *A Hard Day's Night* (1964) but the word was in general Scouse (Liverpudlian) use before that.

As for **grotesque** itself, it has been jokingly derived from the name of Mrs Grote, the wife of a nineteenth-century historian. The Rev. Sydney Smith said of her turban: 'Now I know the meaning of the word grotesque.' She was peculiar in other ways, too. She 'dressed in discordant colours, with her petticoats aranged to show her ankles and feet'; she wore a man's hat and a coachman's cloak when driving her dogcart; and, she had 'unwholesome attachments to other women' (Ronald Pearsall, *Collapse of Stout Party*, 1975). This, alas, is more a case of life imitating the dictionary than the other way round. 'Grotesque' is a word of Italian and Greek origin and is derived from the 'grotto' style of ornamentation.

ground. See HIT THE ~ RUNNING.

groves of Academe, the. The world of scholarship; the academic community. A translation of Horace's phrase *silvas Academi*. Popular in its English form since the mid-nineteenth century.

growing experience, a. Meaning 'an experience which leads to the positive development of your character'. When the American film people David and Talia Shire were experiencing 'a very loving separation', said she, 'We're going to rotate the house and we even rotate the car. We've been separated for four months and it's a growing experience' (quoted in William Safire, *On Language*, 1980).

grub. See LOVELY ~ under *ITMA*.

Grundy. See MRS ~.

guide philosopher and friend, my. An ingratiating form of address (compare GENTLEMAN AND A SCHOLAR), it originally came from Alexander Pope's *An Essay of Man* (1733):

Shall then this verse to future age pretend
Thou wert my guide, philosopher and friend?

guilty. See WE NAME THE ~ MEN.

Guinness is good for you. After 170 years without advertising, Arthur Guinness, Son & Company, decided to call in the image-makers for their beer in 1929.

So, Oswald Greene at the S.H. Benson agency initiated some consumer research (unusual in those days) into why people did drink Guinness. It transpired that they thought it did them good.

Today, ask British people to give you an example of an advertising slogan and the chances are they are likely to quote 'Guinness is Good for You'. It is etched on the national consciousness although the slogan was discontinued *c* 1941 and has not been revived since 1963.

Gulf War. See DESERT STORM.

gum. See ANY ~, CHUM?

gumdrops. See GOODY, GOODY, ~.

gumtree full of galahs. See under AS BUSY AS . . .

gun. See DROP THE ~, LOOEY; HAVE ~ WILL TRAVEL; SMOKING ~.

gung-ho. Meaning 'enthusiastic, if carelessly so', the phrase derives from Chinese *kung* plus *ho* meaning 'work together'. Lieut. Gen. Evans F. Carlson of the US Marines borrowed these words to make a slogan during the Second World War. In 1943, a film about the Marines had the title *Gung Ho!*

gunpowder. See PLEASE TO REMEMBER . . .

guns. See FOOD SHOT FROM ~.

guns before butter. Political slogan associated with Joseph Goebbels, the German Nazi leader, though there are other candidates. When a nation is under pressure to choose between material comforts and some kind of war effort, the choice has to be made between 'guns *and* butter'. Some will urge 'guns *before* butter'. From a translation of a speech Goebbels gave in Berlin (17 January 1936): 'We can do without butter, but, despite all our love of peace, not without arms. One cannot shoot with butter, but with guns' Later that same year, however, Hermann Goering said in a broadcast, 'Guns will make us powerful; butter will only make us fat,' so he may also be credited with the 'guns or butter' slogan. But there is a third candidate. Airey Neave in his book *Nuremberg* (1978) stated of Rudolf Hess: 'It was he who urged the German people to make sacrifices and coined the phrase: "Guns before butter".'

guys. See HOW'S ABOUT THEN . . . under AS IT HAPPENS; NICE ～ FINISH LAST.

· H ·

habeas corpus. See HAVE HIS CARCASE.

Hades. See NO MORE CHANCE THAN . . .

hae. See I ~ ME DOOTS.

haggis. See FLASH HARRY.

ha! ha! – joke over! Stock phrase of the British music-hall entertainer Dick Henderson Snr (1891–1958) after telling an obvious or failed joke. Partridge/*Catch Phrases* also has 'joke over' as a sarcastic catchphrase addressed to the maker of a feeble witticism from '*c* 1925'.

ha-harr, Jim, lad! Nowadays used to indicate how any piratical old sea dog would talk, but originally an impersonation of Robert Newton as Long John Silver in the film *Treasure Island* (1950). The British comedian Tony Hancock may actually have attempted the impersonation on stage but the phrase tended to be trotted out in HANCOCK'S HALF–HOUR (BBC radio and TV, 1950s) in emulation of *bad* impressionism.

Haig. See DON'T BE VAGUE . . .

hair. See GET YOUR HAIR ~; THERE'S ~.

hairdresser. See ONLY HER ~ . . . under DOES SHE . . . OR DOESN'T SHE?

hair in the gate, (there's a). A joke explanation for almost anything that goes wrong. It comes from filming, where this is the most frequent setback. J.K. Galbraith, recalling his participation in a documentary film, in *A Life in Our Times* (1981), says: 'A "hair in the gate" means that, on post-operative inspection, the camera lens – or something else shows some defect. A retake is required. Briefing me on what I could expect in my new career, David Niven had warned, "Just remember that when the cameraman or the technicians bitch up, they will always say there's a hair in the gate." '

hair of the dog (that bit me), the. Meaning 'another drink of the same to help cure a hangover', it comes from the old belief that a bite from a mad dog could be cured if you put hair from the same dog's tail on the wound. Known by 1760.

hairy legs. See under MORECAMBE AND WISE SHOW.

half. See BELIEVE ONLY IN . . . ; GETTING THERE IS ~ THE FUN; HOW THE OTHER ~ LIVES.

halls. See DARLING OF THE ~.

halt and the blind, the. Phrase for any group of unfortunate people. From the parable of the great supper in St Luke 14:21: 'Go out quickly into the streets and lanes of the city and bring in hither the poor, and the maimed, and the halt and the blind.' 'Halt' here means 'lame, crippled, limping'.

***Hamlet* without the Prince.** An event without the leading participant. Byron wrote in a letter on 26 August 1818: 'My autobiographical essay would resemble the tragedy of Hamlet . . . recited "with the part of Hamlet left out by particular desire".' This and other early uses of the phrase may possibly hark back to the theatrical anecdote (as told in the *Morning Post*, 21 September 1775): 'Lee Lewes diverts them with the manner of their performing Hamlet in a company that he belonged to, when the hero who was to play the principal character had absconded with an inn-keeper's daughter; and that when he came forward to give out the play, he added, "the part of Hamlet to be left out, for that night".' Compare the title of Philip

King's play *Without the Prince* (1946). In 1938, James Agate headed his review of a Ralph Richardson performance: 'Othello Without the Moor'.

Hancock. See JOHN ∼.

Hancock's Half-Hour. Co-scriptwriter Ray Galton has said of this BBC radio show's start in 1954: 'Alan Simpson and I wanted a show without breaks, guest singers and catchphrases – something that hadn't been done before. After the first week with Kenneth Williams in the show, bang went out the idea of no funny voices and no catchphrases!'

Although Williams's cameos occupied a very tiny part of the show, they were enough to start him on an outrageous career (see also *BEYOND OUR KEN* and *ROUND THE HORNE.*) His **stop messin' abaht!** began with the Hancock show and was later used as the title of a radio show of which Williams, by that time, was the star. Williams also had an expression, **it's a disgrace!** which he used personally all the time (see *The Kenneth Williams Diaries*, 1993, *passim*) but also in character.

Hancock himself had not so much catchphrases as distinctive phraseology, on radio and in the TV series (from 1956): **a man of my calibre** (pronounced 'cal-aye-ber'), **are you looking for a punch up the bracket?** and **stone me!**

See also *EDUCATING ARCHIE.*

hand(s). See CLAP ∼ , HERE COMES CHARLEY; CLOUD NO BIGGER THAN . . . ; IRON ∼ under IRON FIST; LEFT ∼ DOWN A BIT; LOOK, MA, NO ∼!, SAFE PAIR OF ∼ , YOUR FUTURE IS IN YOUR ∼ .

hand over fist. As in 'to make money hand over fist'. A similar expression, 'pulling it in', provides the origin here. If you are pulling in a rope or hoisting a sail on board ship, you pass it between your two hands and, in so doing, unavoidably put one hand over the fist of the other hand. Current by 1825.

hands off cock(s), on with sock(s). As though delivered as a wake-up call to a men's dormitory (in the army, Boy Scouts, or wherever), I first encountered this cry in a play called *Is Your Doctor Really Necessary?* at the Theatre Royal, Stratford East in 1973. Partridge/*Catch Phrases* suggests an early twentieth-century British Army origin and the slightly more elaborate form: 'Hands off your cocks and pull up your socks!' I expect the female equivalent is **all hands above the bedclothes, girls** which Edward V. Marks of Banstead told me (1994) he overheard said by one of three women in their late twenties who were in a tea-shop in Kensington on their way to an old girls' reunion.

handsome. See TALL, DARK AND ∼ .

hand that rocks the cradle, the. (. . . 'is the hand that rules the world'). This tribute to motherhood comes from 'What Rules the World' by the US poet William Ross Wallace (d 1881). *The Hand That Rocks the Cradle* was the title of a film (US, 1992).

hang on to your Hollyhocks! See NOW THERE'S A BEAUT . . .

hang fire, to. To be hesitant, hold back. This expression comes from gunnery – when the gun is slow to fire, or there is a delay between the fuse being ignited and the weapon firing. Current by 1781 and, figuratively, by 1801.

hang, draw and quarter, to. To execute for treason using a method last carried out in the UK in 1867 and known by the mid-seventeenth century. The order of procedure is actually 'drawn, hanged, and quartered' as is plain from the words of a British judge sentencing Irish rebels in 1775: 'You are to be *drawn* on hurdles to the place of execution, where you are to be *hanged* by the neck but not until you are dead; for, while you are still living, your bodies are to be taken down, your bowels torn out and burned before your faces; your heads then cut off, and your bodies *divided each into four quarters*, and your heads and quarters to be then at the King's disposal; and may the Almighty God have mercy on your souls.'

hangs. See AND THEREBY ∼ A TALE.

hang the Kaiser! Given the role played in the First World War by Kaiser Wilhelm II, there was pressure for retribution at the war's end during the 1918 British General Election. The demand was largely fuelled by the press and had this cry as a slogan. The Treaty of Versailles (1919) committed the Allies to trying the Kaiser (who was forced to abdicate), but the government of the Netherlands refused to hand him over. He lived until 1941.

happen. See ACCIDENT WAITING TO ∼; ANYTHING CAN ∼ .... under *TAKE IT FROM HERE*; IT CAN'T ∼ HERE.

happened. See WHATEVER ∼ TO —?

happening. See IT'S ALL ∼.

happens. See AS IT ∼.

happiest days of one's life, the. The traditional platitude intoned by the old buffer who gives away prizes at school speech days is that his listeners will agree that schooldays are 'the happiest days of your life'. The expression of this sentiment pre-dates *The Happiest Days of Your Life*, a famous play by John Dighton (produced in London in 1948; film UK, 1950.) However, the schoolchildren in that work may have had special cause to believe the catchphrase as the plot hinges on war-time confusion in which a boys' school and a girls' school are lodged under the same roof. Winston Churchill wrote in *My Early Life* (1930): 'I was told that "school days were the happiest time in one's life".' Lord Berners wrote in *A Distant Prospect* (1945): 'Accounts I had been given of Eton – not by the kind of old gentleman who says that his schooldays were his happiest . . .'

The Best Years of Our Lives is the title of an American film (1946) about what happens to a group of ex-servicemen when they return from the war – presumably having 'given the best years of their lives' to their country. The phrase **best years of one's life** dates from at least 1827. Groucho Marx says in *Monkey Business* (1931): 'Oh, so that's it. Infatuated with a pretty uniform! We don't count, after we've given you the best years of our lives. You have to have an officer.' 'The best *days* of our lives' is also an expression used in this kind of context.

I tend to remark that I have spent the best years of my life waiting for lifts/ elevators.

happily. See AND THEY ALL LIVED ∼ . . .

happiness is —. Samuel Johnson declared in 1766, 'Happiness consists in the multiplicity of agreeable consciousness,' but he was not the first to have a go at defining happiness, nor the last. In 1942, along came E.Y. Harburg with the lyrics to his song 'Happiness is a Thing Called Joe'. However, it was Charles M. Schultz (b 1922) creator of the Peanuts comic strip, who really launched the 'Happiness is ——' format.

In c 1957 he had drawn a strip 'centring around some kid hugging Snoopy and saying in the fourth panel that "Happiness is a warm puppy."' This became the title of a best-selling book in 1962 and let loose a stream of promotional phrases using the format, including: 'Happiness is egg-shaped', 'Happiness is a cigar called Hamlet', 'Happiness is a warm ear-piece' (UK ad slogans); 'Happiness is being elected team captain – and getting a Bulova watch', 'Happiness is a $49 table' (both US ad slogans); 'Happiness is seeing Lubbock, Texas, in the rear view mirror' (line from a Country and Western song); 'Happiness is a Warm Gun' (song title), 'Happiness is Wren-shaped', and many, many more.

By which time one might conclude that 'Happiness is . . . a worn cliché'.

happy. See DON'T WORRY, BE ∼; HE WON'T BE ∼ TILL HE GETS IT; I HAVEN'T BEEN SO ∼ SINCE . . . ; IS EVERYBODY ∼?; YOU'VE MADE AN OLD MAN VERY ∼.

happy as a sandboy, as. (or **jolly as . . .**) Presumably these expressions refer to the boy who used to hawk sand from door to door but why he was especially remarkable for his happiness is hard to say. The *OED2* finds a quotation from Pierce Egan (1821): 'As happy as a sandboy who had unexpectedly met with good luck in disposing of his hampers full of the above household commodity.' Dickens in *The Old Curiosity Shop* (1840–1) has 'The Jolly Sandboys' as the name of a pub, with a sign, 'representing three Sandboys increasing their jollity with as many jugs of ale and bags of gold'. Angus Easson in his Penguin edition, notes: 'Sand was sold for scouring, as a floor cover to absorb liquids, and for bird cages. Sandboys were proverbially happy people, as indeed they might be in 1840 when they could buy a load of about 2 tons for 3s. 6d. (17p), and take £6 or £7 in a morning . . . .During the century, sawdust tended to replace sand for floors . . . and, by 1851, those in the trade were much less happy.'

happy as Larry, as. Meaning 'extremely happy'. Brewer has it as an Australian expression and supposedly referring to the boxer Larry Foley (1847–1917). The first OED2 citation (indeed Australian) is from 1905. Another suggestion is that the phrase derives from the Australian 'larrikin', meaning 'lout, hoodlum, mischievous young person'.

happy as the day is long, as. Current by 1786, this expression was much used, for example, by Charles Dickens who, nevertheless, occasionally varied it. In *David Copperfield*, Chap. 41 (1849–50), he wrote: 'We . . . were happy as the week was long.' In 1820, Lord Norbury joked of Caroline of Brunswick's behaviour with the *dey* (governor) of Algiers: 'She was happy as the dey was long.'

happy birthday to you. The most frequently sung phrase in English, according to *The Guinness Book of Records 1985* (which also lists 'For He's a Jolly Good Fellow' and 'Auld Lang Syne' as the most-performed songs of all time). It started out as 'Good Morning to All' with words by Patty Smith Hill and music by Mildred J. Hill in *Song Stories for the Kindergarten* (1893). 'Happy Birthday to You' is the first line of the second stanza, but was not promoted to the title until 1935. The song has had a chequered legal history, due to the erroneous belief that it is in the public domain and out of copyright.

happy clappy. Name for a type of religious worship or worshipper identified in Britain in the early 1990s. From the clapping along with bouncy hymns used especially in 'evangelical' church services. From the

Independent (9 March 1991): 'The parish church has a knack of attracting those whose approach is more casual or nervous, and gently drawing them to faith. While it cannot be good if the end product of the system is semi-commitment, it certainly is good if this low-key style attracts many who would run a mile from a "Happy Clappy" congregation'; (17 April 1991): '[George Carey, Archbishop of Canterbury] attempted to distance himself from the "evangelical" tag he has attracted, and emphasised that he wanted to affirm all traditions in the Church. "I am not a 'happy clappy' person, and I am not a fundamentalist," he said.'

happy days! See under BAND WAGGON.

happy hunting ground. A translation of the North American Indian name for 'heaven, paradise', the phrase is now used of any field that appears fruitful.

Happy Warrior. The nickname of Alfred E. Smith, US Democrat politician, so dubbed by Franklin D. Roosevelt in 1924: 'He is the Happy Warrior of the political battlefield.' It comes from William Wordsworth's 'Character of the Happy Warrior' (1807):

> Who is the happy Warrior? Who is he
> That every man in arms should wish to be?

hard. See BETWEEN A ROCK AND A ∾ PLACE.

Hard Day's Night, A. This title for the Beatles' first feature film (UK, 1964) was apparently chosen towards the end of filming when Ringo Starr used the phrase to describe a 'heavy' night (Ray Coleman, *John Lennon*, 1984). What, in fact, Ringo must have done was to use the title of the Lennon and McCartney song (presumably already written if it was towards the end of filming) in a conversational way. Indeed, Hunter Davies in *The Beatles* (1968) notes: 'Ringo Starr came out with the phrase, though John had used it earlier in a poem.' It certainly sounds like a Lennonism and may have had some limited general use subsequently as a catchphrase meaning that one has had 'a very tiring time'.

hardest. See FIRST — YEARS ARE THE ∼.

hard-faced men who had done well out of the war. The members of the House of Commons who had been returned in the 1918 General Election were so described by a 'Conservative politician', according to John Maynard Keynes, the economist, in *The Economic Consequences of Peace* (1919). Stanley Baldwin, a future Conservative Prime Minister, was the one who said it. In the biography of Baldwin by Keith Middlemas, he is also quoted as having noted privately on 12 February 1918: 'We have started with the new House of Commons. They look much as usual – not so young as I had expected. The prevailing type is a rather successful-looking business kind which is not very attractive.'

hard knocks. See SCHOOL OF ∼.

hard man is good to find, a. See GOOD MAN IS HARD TO FIND.

hare/Hare. See BUNNY; FIRST CATCH YOUR ∼.

harm. See ANOTHER LITTLE DRINK . . .

harness my zebras. See under CAME THE DAWN.

harp. See I TOOK MY ∼ TO A PARTY.

Harris. See BOMBER ∼.

Harry. See FLASH ∼; KNOW WHAT I MEAN, ∼?

(H)arry Boy! See CARRY ON —.

harvest home. Name for the bringing in of the last load of corn, accompanied by a special song, or the harvest supper laid on at this time. According to the *DNB*, the *Church* use of 'harvest home' was originated by George Anthony Denison (*d* 1896), Archdeacon of Taunton. According to Brewer, the Church 'harvest thanksgiving' (or now more usually, 'harvest festival') originated with the Rev. R.S. Hawker, Vicar of Morwenstow, Cornwall, in 1843.

Simply meaning the bringing in of the harvest or the celebrations surrounding that event, the phrase goes back to the sixteenth century. Shakespeare, *Henry IV, Part 1*, I.iii.33 (1597) has: 'His chin reap'd/ Show'd like a stubble-land at harvest-home.'

harvest moon. See SHINE ON ∼.

Harvey Smith. Meaning 'a V-SIGN gesture given as a signal of disapproval', it owes its name to the British showjumping champion, Harvey Smith, who gave it in view of the TV audience at Hickstead in 1971. It looked like contempt of Hickstead's owner, Douglas Bunn, but Smith argued that it was as in V FOR VICTORY.

hasn't it been a funny day today? See I WON'T TAKE ME COAT OFF . . .

hasta la vista, baby. The Spanish for 'goodbye, au revoir, until we meet again' was given a distinctive twist by Arnold Schwarzennegger in the film *Terminator II: Judgement Day* (US, 1991).

hat. See IF YOU WANT TO GET AHEAD . . .; KEEP IT UNDER YOUR ∼; WHERE DID YOU GET THAT ∼?

hatband. See QUEER AS DICK'S ∼.

hatch. See DOWN THE ∼.

hatched, matched and despatched columm. Nickname given to the births, marriages and deaths column of a newspaper. The phrase was referred to in a poem in *Punch* (17 August 1904).

hatchet. See BURY THE ∼.

hate. See MAN YOU LOVE TO ∼; SHE'S MY BEST FRIEND . . . under *EDUCATING ARCHIE*.

hatter. See MAD AS A ∼.

hat-trick, to perform a. Meaning, in cricket, three wickets taken with successive balls – which *OED2* finds by 1877. The player so doing is entitled to be awarded a new hat – 'or equivalent' – by the club. The expression went on to mean any three-in-a-row achievement. Another suggested origin: the Barons of Kingsale – in the Irish peerage – have long maintained that they can remain covered in the presence of the Sovereign. Almericus, the 18th Baron Kingsale, 'walked to and fro with his hat on his head' in the presence chamber of William III, claiming he was asserting an ancient privilege. He did it three times, the original hat-trick (Simon Winchester, *Their Noble Lordships*, 1981). (I rather doubt this explanation.)

have. See I'LL ~ WHAT SHE'S HAVING.

have a banana! Britain became 'banana conscious' in the early years of the twentieth century following the appointment of Roger Ackerley as chief salesman of Elders & Fyffes, banana importers, in 1898. The phrase 'have a banana!' – never a slogan as such – was popularly interpolated at the end of the first line of the song 'Let's All Go Down the Strand', which was published in 1904. It had not been put there by the composer, but was so successful that later printings of the song always included it. Every time it was sung, the phrase reinforced the sales campaign free of charge. A slight sexual innuendo, of course, as in the song 'Burlington Bertie from Bow' (1914) 'I've had a banana with Lady Diana'.

have a Coke and a smile. See PAUSE THAT REFRESHES.

Have a Go. 'Ladies and gentlemen of Bingley, 'ow do, 'ow are yer?' – that was how Wilfred Pickles introduced the first edition of this folksy, travelling BBC radio show in 1946. Within 12 months, it had an audience of 20 million and ran for another 20 years. It was to the 1940s and 50s what TV's *GENERATION GAME* was to the 1970s – a simple quiz which enabled the host, accompanied by his wife, to indulge in folksy chatting to contestants.

Indeed, Pickles (1904–78) spent most of the programme fishing for laughs with questions like **have you ever had any embarrassing moments?** One reply he received was from a woman who had been out with a very shy young man. Getting desperate for conversation with him she had said, 'If there's one thing I can't stand,

it's people who sit on you and use you as a convenience.'

Chatting up unmarried women, of any age from NINETEEN TO NINETY, Pickles would ask, **are yer courtin'?** But, after all, this was what the programme set out to provide: **a spot of homely fun, presenting the people to the people.**

Winners of the quiz took away not cars or consumer goods or holidays abroad but pots of jam and the odd shilling or two. **Give 'im/'er the money, Barney!** was the cry when a winner was established (sometimes with a good deal of help from Pickles). The 'Barney' in question was Barney Colehan, a BBC producer (*d* 1991). Later, Mrs Pickles supervised the prizes – hence the alternative **give 'im/'er the money, Mabel!** and the references to **Mabel at the table** and the query **what's on the table, Mabel?**

The original phrase 'have a go' – meaning 'make an attempt' (dating from the nineteenth century, at least), was used in a rather different context in 1964 when Sir Ranulph Bacon, then Assistant Commissioner at Scotland Yard, urged members of the public to 'have a go' if they saw an armed robbery. His advice caused a storm of protest, and was labelled 'madness' and 'suicidal' by the British Safety Council, but the phrase is still used in this sense.

have a good/happy/nice day. William Safire traces the origins of this pervasive American greeting in his book *On Language* (1980). Beginning with an early flourish in Chaucer's 'The Knight's Tale' ('Fare well, have good day') he jumps to 1956 and the Carson/Roberts advertising agency in Los Angeles. 'Our phone was answered "Good morning, Carson/Roberts. Have a happy day,"' recalled Ralph Carson. 'We used the salutation on all letters, tie tacks, cuff buttons, beach towels, blazer crests, the works.' Shortly after this, WCBS-TV weather-girl Carol Reed would wave goodbye with 'Have a happy'.

In the 1960s, 'Have a good day' was still going strong. Then, the early 1970s saw 'Have a nice day' push its insidious way in, although Kirk Douglas had got his tongue round it in the 1948 film *A Letter to Three Wives*. 'Have a nice city' was a slogan in the 1970 Los Angeles mayoral election.

From all this, it may be understood that the usage seems likely to have been a Californian imposition upon the rest of the US. In 1992, it emerged that, as a valediction, 'have a nice day' was being coupled with **missing you already!** Terrible.

have a gorilla. See under GOON SHOW.

have gun, will travel. Best known as the title of a Western TV series (made in the US, 1957–64), this led to a format phrase capable of much variation. The hired-gun hero of the series had on his business card, 'Have gun. Will travel. Wire Paladin. San Francisco'. Later, the phrase turned up in many ways – as joke slogans ('Have pill, will'; 'Have wife, must travel') and even as the UK title of another TV series (1981) *Have Girls, Will Travel* (but known as *The American Girls* in the US).

Have His Carcase. Title of a detective novel (1932) by Dorothy L. Sayers. An old joke upon the Latin legal phrase *habeas corpus* [you have the body]. Sam Weller makes the joke in *The Pickwick Papers*, Chap. 40 (1836–7) by Charles Dickens. A Habeas Corpus is a writ ordering someone who is keeping another in custody to produce him in court. Its aim is to stop people being imprisoned on mere suspicion or kept waiting unduly for trial.

haves and the have-nots, the. Phrase referring to the advantaged and disadvantaged in society. Motteux's 1700 translation of Cervantes's *Don Quixote* has Sancho Panza saying: 'There are only two families in the world, the Haves and the Have-Nots' (Spanish *el tener* and *el no tener*). Edward Bulwer-Lytton in *Athens* (1836) wrote: 'The division . . . of the Rich and the Poor – the havenots and the haves.'

have you ever had any embarrassing moments? See under HAVE A GO.

have you met my niece? A well-known British political figure arriving at some function with a nubile young girl on his arm tends to introduce her by asking, 'Have you met my niece?' He is not alone. According to the *Independent*'s obituary of film producer Nat Cohen (11 February 1988), 'He was much loved – not least by the young ladies usually introduced as "Have you met my niece?"'

According to *Soho* by Judith Summers (1989), the first Lord Beaverbrook habitually dined upstairs at the French [restaurant] with sundry 'nieces' – 'He had more nieces than any man I've known,' one Gaston confided to the author. And the film *Pretty Woman* (1990) contains an entertaining disquisition between a hooker and a hotel manager on 'niece' being used in this sense. From BBC radio ROUND THE HORNE (26 March 1967): [A butler announces] 'Lord Grisley Makeshift and his niece – he says – Mrs Costello Funf.'

The lines 'Moreover, if you please, a niece of mine/ Shall there attend you' – Shakespeare, *Pericles*, III.iv.14 (1609)- are unfortunately not connected.

having a wonderful time. See under WISH YOU WERE HERE.

hawae the lads! This cry of encouragement (like 'come on!') is from the North-East of England, also in the forms 'Haway' (or 'Howay') or 'Away' (or 'A-wee'). According to the Frank Graham's *New Geordie Dictionary* (1979), it is a corruption of 'hadaway' as in 'hadaway wi'ye', which actually means the opposite, 'begone!'

Haw-Haw, Lord. See LORD HAW-HAW.

hay. See AND THAT AIN'T ∼.

haywire, to go. To behave in an uncontrolled and crazy manner. This phrase is of American origin – *c* 1900, perhaps – and seemingly derives from the wire used to hold bales of hay together. If cut, the wire can whip round in a fearsome way.

According to *DOAS*, there is another use of the word 'haywire' in American slang. Something is described as 'haywire' if it is dilapidated and might be held together with such, just as in British English one might say something is 'held together with bits of string'.

he. See WHO ∼?

head. See HOLE IN THE ~; TALKING ~S.

head cook and bottle-washer. See CHIEF COOK AND BOTTLE-WASHER.

he ain't heavy, he's my brother. King George VI concluded his 1942 Christmas radio broadcast by reflecting on the European allies and the benefits of mutual cooperation, saying: 'A former President of the United States of America used to tell of a boy who was carrying an even smaller child up a hill. Asked whether the heavy burden was not too much for him, the boy answered: "It's not a burden, it's my brother!" So let us welcome the future in a spirit of brotherhood, and thus make a world in which, please God, all may dwell together in justice and peace.'

Benham (1948) suggests that the American President referred to must have been Lincoln – though it has not been possible to trace a source for the story. In fact, the King's allusion seems rather to have been a dignification of an advertising slogan and a charity's motto. As an advertising headline, 'He ain't heavy . . . he's my brother' the expression may have been used first by Jack Cornelius of the BBD&O agency in a 1936 American advertisement for the 'Community Chest' campaign ('35 appeals in 1'). But it is difficult to tell what relationship this has, if any, with the similar slogan used to promote the Nebraska orphanage and poor boys' home known as 'Boys' Town'.

In the early 1920s, the Rev. Edward J. Flanagan – Spencer Tracy played him in the film *Boys' Town* (1938) – admitted to this home a boy named Howard Loomis who could not walk without the aid of crutches. The larger boys often took turns carrying him about on their backs. One day, Father Flanagan is said to have seen a boy carrying Loomis and asked whether this wasn't a heavy load. The reply: 'He ain't heavy, Father . . . he's m'brother.' In 1943, a 'two brothers' logo (similar to, though not the same as, the drawing used in the Community Chest campaign) was copyrighted for Boys' Town's exclusive use. Today, the logo and the motto (in the 'Father/m'brother' form) are registered service marks of Father Flanagan's Boys' Home (Boys' Town).

My feeling is that the saying probably *does* predate the Father Flanagan story, though whether it goes back to Lincoln is anybody's guess. More recent applications have included the song with the title, written by Bob Russell and Bobby Scott, and popularized by the Hollies in 1969. Perhaps the brief Lennon and McCartney song 'Carry that Weight' (September 1969) alludes similarly? – 'Boy – you're gonna carry that weight,/Carry that weight a long time.'

head 'em off at the pass. See CUT OFF AT THE PASS.

heals. See HOLE ~ UP . . .

health. See WHAT ME, IN MY STATE OF ~? under *ITMA*; GOVERNMENT ~ WARNING.

heap. See STRUCK ALL OF A ~.

hear. See BELIEVE ONLY HALF . . . ; CAN YOU ~ ME, MOTHER?; GRAPEVINE, TO ~ . . . ; under OH ARR . . .

hear all – see all – say nowt. The motto of Yorkshiremen is said to be:

Hear all, see all, say nowt,
Aight all, sup all, pay nowt,
And if ever tha does owt for nowt
Do it for thisen.

A Noel Gay song written in 1938 for Sandy Powell, the Yorkshire comedian, had the title: 'Hear all, see all, say nowt'. Compare **hear no evil, see no evil, speak no evil** which Bartlett describes as a legend related to the Three Wise Monkeys carved over the door of the Sacred Stable, Nikko, Japan in the seventeenth century. The monkeys are represented having their paws over respectively, ears, eyes, and mouth. 'Hear, see, keep silence' (often accompanied by a sketch of the Three Wise Monkeys) is the motto of the United Grand Lodge of Freemasons – in the form *Audi, Vide, Tace.*

Compare also, from the Second Book of Hermas, 2:2 in the Apocryphal New Testament: 'Especially see that thou speak evil of none, nor willingly hear anyone speak evil of any.'

heard. See under YOU AIN'T SEEN NOTHIN' YET.

heart. See EAT YOUR ~ OUT; IN YOUR ~ YOU KNOW . . . ; WHERE THE ~ IS.

hearts and flowers. Title of a popular, sentimental song of the early 1900s. The tune was often played to accompany the weepy bits of silent movies. Accordingly, the phrase is used to describe anything of tear-jerking appeal.

hearts and minds. A description of what had to be won in the Vietnam War by the US Government – almost of slogan status. John Pilger, writing on 23 August 1967, reported: 'When Sergeant Melvin Murrell and his company of United States Marines drop by helicopter into the village of Tuylon, west of Danang, with orders to sell "the basic liberties as outlined on page 233 of the Pacification Programme Handbook" and at the same time win the hearts and minds of the people (see same handbook, page 86 under WHAM) they see no one: not a child or a chicken' (quoted in *The Faber Book of Reportage*, 1987).

The origins of the phrase go back to Theodore Roosevelt's day when Douglas MacArthur, as a young aide, asked him (in 1906) to what he attributed his popularity. The President replied: '[My ability] to put into words what is in their hearts and minds but not in their mouths.'

Safire also points out that, in 1954, Earl Warren ruled in the case of Brown *v* Board of Education of Topeka: 'To separate [Negro children] from others of similar age and qualifications solely because of their race generates a feeling of inferiority as to their status in the community that may affect their hearts and minds in a way unlikely ever to be undone.'

The Blessing in the Holy Communion service of the Prayer Book is: 'The peace of God, which passeth all understanding, keep your hearts and minds in the knowledge and love of God, and of his Son Jesus Christ Our Lord.' This is drawn from the Epistle of Paul the Apostle to the Philippians 4:7.

hearty. See CONDEMNED MAN ATE A ~ BREAKFAST.

heat. See IF YOU CAN'T STAND THE ~ . . . ; IT'S NOT THE ~, IT'S THE HUMIDITY.

Heath Robinson. Adjectival phrase applied to complicated, ingenious, and sometimes amateur and makeshift contraptions. It is derived from the name of W. Heath Robinson (1872–1944) whose drawings of such things appeared in *Punch* and elsewhere. The use was established by 1917.

heaven. See ALL THIS AND ~ TOO; MORE STARS THAN THERE ARE IN ~.

heavenly twins, the. Complimentary phrase applied to a well-meaning couple, usually of the same sex. Possibly alluding to the Gemini twins in astrology and perhaps popularized by its use as the title of a novel by 'Sarah Guard' (1893).

heaven on earth. Ideal conditions, a pleasant state of affairs. From the *Guardian* (3 September 1974): ' "In educational terms," he says of his current post, "it's heaven on earth" '; (5 June 1986): 'The Prime Minister [Mrs Thatcher] yesterday promised her party "a little bit of heaven on earth" produced by further tax cuts.' An early use of the phrase occurs in the title of T. Brooks's *Heaven on Earth, or a Serious Discourse touching a well-grounded Assurance of Mens Everlasting Happiness* (1654).

heavens, eleven o'clock and not a whore in the house dressed! A domestic cry, acknowledging that progress is not being made in carrying out household duties. British use, possibly of theatrical origin in the 1920s and capable of immense variation. One continues '. . . **not a po emptied, and the streets full of Spanish sailors . . .**' The time can, of course, vary, as also the precise nature of the potential users of the brothel: 'the street full of sailors', 'the Spanish soldiers in the courtyard', 'a street full of matelots', 'a troopship in the bay', and 'the Japanese fleet in town'.

Partridge/*Slang* only examines the comparatively simple phrase 'eleven o'clock and no pos emptied' – though **no potatoes peeled** and **no babies scraped** are mentioned as variants. In Paul Beale's revision of Partridge/*Catch Phrases*, there is a 1984 reference to the version used by Terry Wogan on his breakfast radio show (after giving a time-check) – '[It's eight twenty-five] . . . and not a child in the house washed.' In the 1980s, the comedian Les Dawson in drag is reliably reported to have uttered the 'no pos emptied' line. Rupert Hart-Davis in *The Lyttelton Hart-Davis Letters* (Vol.3, 1981) writes in a letter dated 9 June 1958: 'In the words of the harassed theatrical landlady, "Half-past four, and not a po emptied."'

The 'whores/pos/sailors' version is possibly a colourful elaboration of this basic expression.

heaven's gate. The idea of a 'gate to heaven' goes back to the Bible, e.g.: 'This is none other but the house of God, and this is the gate of heaven' (Genesis 28:17), and, 'He commanded the clouds from above, and opened the doors of heaven' (Psalm 78:23).

Shakespeare twice uses the phrase. In *Cymbeline*, II.iii.20 (1609), there is the song: 'Hark, hark, the lark at heaven's gate sings' and Sonnet 29 (1590s) has:

> Like to the lark at break of day arising
> From sullen earth sings hymns at
>   heaven's gate.

In *Heaven's Gate*, the title of a film (US, 1980) directed by Michael Cimino, 'Heaven's Gate' is the name of a roller-skating rink used by settlers and immigrants in Wyoming in 1891. Conceivably, the name is meant to be taken as an ironic one for the rough situation many of the characters find themselves in as they arrive to start a new life. Steven Bach in *Final Cut* (1985), a book about the making of the film, cites two more possible sources. William Blake in *Jerusalem* (1820) wrote:

> I give you the end of a golden string;
> Only wind it into a ball,
> It will lead you in at Heaven's gate,
> Built in Jerusalem's wall.

Robert Browning also uses the phrase and there is a poem by Wallace Stevens with the title, 'The Worms at Heaven's Gate'.

heavens to Murgatroyd! Catchphrase of a rather camp cartoon lion called Snagglepuss, created by the Hannah-Barbera studios in the 1960s. He made his first appearance in *The Yogi Bear Show*, but his catchphrase was apparently not original. An American correspondent noted (1993): 'It was a favorite expression of a favorite uncle of mine in the 1940s, and my wife also remembers it from her growing-up years in the '40s.'

Snagglepuss also used to say **exit stage left** – a self-imposed stage direction.

heavy. See HE AIN'T ~ . . .

heavy, man! Stock phrase of the lugubrious, long-haired student Neil (Nigel Planer) in BBC TV's *The Young Ones* (1982–4). This use was a parody of earlier hip/hippie slang. 'Heavy' meaning 'profound, serious, intense, meaningful, important' was established in the jazz world by the 1930s. But, just as much, the meaning can be akin to 'it's a drag', or the opposite of 'groovy'.

heavy metal. The type of music known as heavy metal – very loud, amplified, clashing – was first described as such in the late 1960s following the group Steppenwolf's use of the phrase 'heavy metal thunder' in the song 'Born To be Wild' (written by M. Bonfire, 1968). This was apparently derived from the writings of the American novelist William Burroughs who wrote, for example, in *Nova Express* (1964) of 'Ukrainian Willy the Heavy Metal Kid'.

In science, 'heavy metal' also refers to uranium and the transuranic elements (such as plutonium). There have also been other uses of the phrase: from P.G. Wodehouse, *Summer Lightning*, Chap. 4.iv (1929: 'Anybody who has ever been bounced from a restaurant knows that commissionaires are heavy metal.'

he can leave his boots/shoes under my bed anytime. 'I find him sexually attractive'. A reasonably common expression. I recall it being said to me by a small lady of Iranian extraction regarding Robert Redford in April 1970. As far as I know, she still hasn't even met him.

he can't fart and chew gum at the same time. Meaning 'he's stupid'. This is the correct version – advanced on the authority of John Kenneth Galbraith – of what President Lyndon Johnson once said about Gerald Ford, and is rather more colourful than 'he can't *walk* and chew gum at the same time', the version quoted when Ford became president in 1974. Like much of Johnson's earthy speech, I think it might have been an established Texan expression rather than of his own invention.

hedgehog and the fox, the. The Greek poet Archilochus (*fl.* seventh Century BC) said, 'The fox knows many things – the hedgehog one *big* thing.' This view was expanded on by the philosopher, Isaiah Berlin, in his book called *The Hedgehog and the Fox* (1953): 'There exists a great chasm between those, on one side, who relate everything to a single central vision . . . and, on the other side, those who pursue many ends, often unrelated and even contradictory . . . The first kind of intellectual and artistic personality belongs to the hedgehogs, the second to the foxes.'

In other words, there are those who have one big idea – like the hedgehog rolling itself up into a ball to save itself (and this is the one way in which it takes on the world) – and there are others who dart hither and yon all over the place like foxes, but who do not have any single big idea.

heels. See ROUND ∼.

heights. See COMMANDING ∼.

Heineken refreshes the parts other beers cannot reach. Slogan for Heineken lager, chiefly in the UK, and used on and off since 1975. 'I wrote the slogan,' said Terry Lovelock, 'during December 1974 at 3 a.m. at the Hotel Marmounia in Marakesh. After eight weeks of incubation with the agency [Collett, Dickenson, Pearce], it was really a brainstorm. No other lines were written. The trip was to refresh the brain, but it worked.'

The resulting sentence – though not tripping easily off the tongue – became one of the most popular slogans ever used in Britain and is still revived from time to time. The refreshing qualities of the lager were always demonstrated with amusing accompanying visuals: the 'droop-snoot' of

Concorde raised by an infusion of the brew; a piano tuner's ears sharpened; a policeman's toes refreshed. There has also been a strong topical element. When Chia-Chia, a panda from London Zoo, was sent off in 1981 to mate with Ling-Ling in Washington, a full-page press ad merely said 'Good Luck Chia-Chia from Heineken', the slogan being understood.

Much parodied – in graffiti: 'Courage reaches the parts other beers don't bother with', 'Joe Jordan [Scottish footballer] kicks the parts other beers don't reach', 'Hook Norton ale reaches the parts Heineken daren't mention', 'Mavis Brown reaches parts most beers can't reach', 'Vindaloo purges the parts other curries can't reach'; in political speeches: 'When I think of our much-travelled Foreign Secretary [Lord Carrington] I am reminded of . . . the peer that reaches those foreign parts other peers cannot reach' (Margaret Thatcher, Conservative Party Conference, 1980).

Compare the American proverb first recorded by Gelett Burgess in *Are You a Bromide?* (1907): 'The Salvation Army reaches a class of people that churches never do.'

Heinz 57 Varieties. A brand name which amounts to a slogan, and used for Heinz canned foods since 1896. In that year, Henry Heinz was travelling through New York City on the overhead railway. He saw a street-car window advertising 21 styles of shoe; the idea appealed to him and, although he could list 58 or 59 Heinz products, he settled on 57 because 'it sounded right'. Heinz commented later: 'I myself did not realize how successful a slogan it was going to be.' In housey-housey or bingo, 'all the beans' is now the cry for '57'.

Partridge/*Slang* has 'Heinz' and '57 Varieties' as expressions for a 'mongrel dog'. See also BEANZ MEANZ HEINZ.

heir. See SON AND ∼.

he knows whereof he speaks/spoke. A conscious archaism used in place of 'he knows what he's talking about, he has a particular reason for saying that'. From the song 'Homeward Through the Haze' (1975) by David Crosby and Graham Nash:

How could he know whereof he spoke,
When all of his wheels are turning him
    into a joke?

From Hendrik Van Loon, *The Story of
Mankind* (1922): '[Erasmus] had travelled a
great deal and knew whereof he wrote.'

hell. See ALL ∼ BROKE LOOSE; CAT IN ∼'S
CHANCE; COME ∼ OR HIGH . . . ; I'M MAD AS
∼ . . . ; NO MORE CHANCE THAN . . .

hell for leather, to go. 'To go fast, flat
out' – originally on horseback. Known by
1889, this expression is not totally
explicable. One suggestion has been that it
is a corruption of 'all of a lather', but from
some association with leather saddles seems
more likely.

**hello birds, hello trees, hello clouds,
hello sky!** A joke expression of joy in
nature, as though spoken by a poet,
aesthete or other fey character. I am
uncertain of its origin – possibly in a revue
sketch or song – but am told that the phrase
was used in some form in a Warner Bros.
cartoon film dating from 1941. An
approximate appearance occurs in *How To
Be Topp* (1954) by Geoffrey Willans and
Ronald Searle. The (British) schoolboy
character Nigel Molesworth writes: 'There
is no better xsample of a goody-goody than
fotherington-tomas in the world in space.
You kno he is the one who sa Hullo Clouds
Hullo Sky and skip about like a girly.'
Indeed, the most prominent British use has
been in the Molesworth books. Again, from
Back in the Jug Agane (1959): 'And who is
this who skip weedily up to me, eh? "Hullo
clouds, hullo sky," he sa. "Hullo birds, hullo
poetry books, hullo skool sossages, hullo
molesworth 1." You hav guessed it is dere
little basil fotherington-tomas.'

hello, everybody. Not much of a phrase,
you may think, but it is still associated with
the British radio comedian John Henry.
From the *Independent* (2 August 1988):
'Here was the first radio catch-phrase,
remembered by "Blossom", stage-wife of the
Yorkshire comedian, John Henry. "I think
he said 'Ah Well'. He used to say that a lot.
'Ah Well.' 'Hello, everybody' of course, that
became very well known . . . he used to

come on, he never had any make-up on at
all, always a dinner jacket, and he just said
'Hello, everybody', and as soon as he said
that there used to be a round of applause.
Just sheer personality – very ugly man – but
sheer personality." '
    Henry is sometimes called 'the first
wireless comedian'. **John Henry, come
here!/Coming, Blossom** is remembered
by some as the archetypal exchange
between wife and hen-pecked husband. On
the BBC from 1925.

**hello, everyone – old ones, new ones,
loved ones, neglected ones.** The pianist
Semprini's opening patter (referring to the
music he was going to play) on his BBC
radio shows in the 1960s and 70s.

hello, folks! See under BAND WAGGON.

hello, good evening, and welcome! A
greeting well known on TV on both sides of
the Atlantic. It derives from the period
when the British broadcaster Sir David
Frost (*b* 1939) was commuting back and
forth to host TV chat shows in London and
New York, and in particular was presenting
ITV's *The Frost Programme* (1966). It may
have been contrived to say three things
where only one was needed but it became
an essential part of the Frost impersonator's
kit (not to mention the Frost self-
impersonator's kit). He was still saying it in
1983 when, with a small alteration, it
became 'Hello, good *morning*, and welcome!'
at the debut of TV-am, the breakfast TV
station.
    The original phrase was used as the title
of a BBC TV 'Wednesday Play' on 16
October 1968.
    For a while, Frost used a variation on the
traditional lead-in to a commercial break –
'We'll be right back after this break/after
this word/don't go away' – which was,
we'll be back in a trice!

**hello, hello, and a very good, good
morning to you all!** Edmundo Ros, the
Venezuelan-born band leader who came to
Britain in 1937, introduced Latin-American
music programmes on BBC radio until the
mid-1970s. He would say things like,
'You're listening to a programme of Latin-
American music played by my ballroom

orchestra – which we most sincerely hope you are enjoying.' Whatever type of dance music he was about to lead the orchestra into, he always seemed to say, 'Ah, three-four!'

hello, honky-tonks! See OOOH, YOU ARE AWFUL.

hello, I'm Julian . . . See under ROUND THE HORNE.

hello, it's me – Twinkletoes! See under EDUCATING ARCHIE.

hello, John, got a new motor? The use of 'John' as a mode of address to any man (in England) was drawn attention to by the comedian Alexei Sayle in about 1980. Compare the use of 'Jimmy' in Scotland and 'Boyo' in Wales. ' 'Ullo, John, got a new motor?' was the full catchphrase, echoing East End of London and Essex use, and, in this form, was the title of a record by Sayle, released in 1984.

hello, me old mates! Presenter/disc jockey Brian Matthew on early BBC radio pop programmes in the 1960s, like *Easy Beat* and *Saturday Club*. In 1983, he was still referring to himself on the air as 'Your old mate, Brian Matthew'.

hello, Mrs! See HOW TICKLED I AM.

hello, my darlings! From the early 1950s, this was the greeting of comedian Charlie Drake (*b* 1925). Perhaps it was rendered more memorable because of the husky, baby-voiced way in which it is spoken.

hello, playmates! See under BAND WAGGON.

hello, Rodney!/ hello, Charles! See BEYOND OUR KEN.

hello, sailor! Originally this must have been something that a prostitute would call out to a potential customer in somewhere like Portsmouth, along the lines of, 'Like a nice time, dearie?' Indeed, the phrase must have long been around – with varying degrees of heterosexual and homosexual emphasis – before becoming a camp

catchphrase in the early 1970s, reaching a peak in 1975/6, and promoted by various branches of the media.

The first appearance of the phrase that I have come across is in a reminiscence of Graham Payn singing the song 'Matelot' in Noël Coward's *Sigh No More* in 1945. The chorus is said to have muttered 'Hello, sailor!' whenever Payn appeared.

Next, in Spike Milligan's script for 'Tales of Men's Shirts' in the GOON SHOW (31 December 1959), 'Hello, sailor!' is spoken, for no very good reason, by Minnie Bannister. Milligan told me in 1978 that he thought he had started the 70s revival of the phrase in one of his Q TV shows. To fill up time, he had just sat and said it a number of times. However, it was spoken in MONTY PYTHON on 12 October 1969 and the cast of radio's *I'm Sorry I'll Read That Again* promoted it heavily – perhaps influenced by there being a number of newsworthy sailors about in the early 1970s, including Prince Philip, Prince Charles and the Prime Minister, Edward Heath.

In the end, it was most often used by the speaker to indicate that the person being addressed was homosexual.

hello there, record-lovers everywhere and welcome to the show. Former British bandleader Jack Jackson (1906–78) was latterly a disc jockey. His show on BBC Radio 2 chiefly consisted of pop music intercut with extracts from comedy records. This was his familiar greeting.

hello, twins! In the very early days of BBC radio's *Children's Hour*, Derek McCulloch and Mary Elizabeth Jenkin were 'Mac' and 'Elizabeth' among the original 'Uncles' and 'Aunts' who presented the programmes. In the 1920s, birthday greetings were read out over the air (until they were dropped in 1932 because they took up nearly half the 'hour') and the joint cry of 'hello . . . twins!' or, less frequently, 'hello . . . triplets!' became a catchphrase.

'Hell!' said the Duchess . . . The opening lines of Agatha Christie's *The Murder on the Links* (1923): 'I believe that a well-known anecdote exists to the effect that a young writer, determined to make the commencement of his story forcible and original enough to catch the attention of the most blasé of editors, penned the first sentence: "'Hell!' said the Duchess." Note also, *Hell! Said the Duchess*, 'A Bed-time Story' by Michael Arlen (1934). Partridge/*Catch Phrases* dates the longer phrase: 'Hell! said the Duchess when she caught her teats in the mangle' to *c* 1895 (compare I HAVEN'T BEEN SO HAPPY . . .).

Similarly, there is a suggested newspaper headline containing all the ingredients necessary to capture a reader's attention (sex, royalty, religion, etc.): 'Teenage Sex-change Priest in Mercy Dash to Palace' (a joke current by 1976).

helmet. See OH, MY SUNDAY ∼!

helmsman. See GREAT ∼.

help. See WITH A LITTLE ∼ FROM . . .

helper. See MOTHER'S LITTLE ∼.

helping the police with their inquiries. A journalistic stock phrase, now a a cliché. When a suspect is being interviewed by the British police but has not yet been charged with any offence, this rather quaint euphemism is trotted out and eagerly passed on by the media. It is quite possible, of course, that the suspect in question is, in fact, being quite unhelpful to the police in their inquiries and they are being impolite to him in equal measure. Current by 1957.

helps. See EVERY LITTLE ∼.

Henry. See JOHN ∼, COME HERE!

Henry! Henry Aldrich!/Coming, Mother! The television version of the long-running American radio show *The Aldrich Family* ran from 1949–53. The plots concerned a teenager from a typical American family. This was the opening exchange between mother and son.

Henry Hall. THIS IS ∼ SPEAKING . . .

here. See I'M ONLY ∼ FOR THE BEER; QUEEN ELIZABETH SLEPT ∼; WISH YOU WERE ∼!

here and now, before your very eyes! When the British comedian Arthur Askey

moved from radio to TV in the early 1950s, his first series was called *Before Your Very Eyes*. Indeed, he was one of the first comedians to address the viewer through the camera in an intimate way rather than just do a variety act as if to a theatre audience. Arthur registered the title in conversation with the BBC's Ronnie Waldman, even before he had been given the series – although, in the end, it was made by ITV. He would say the phrase to emphasize that the show was, indeed, done live. The basic expression 'before your very eyes' predates the Askey use – perhaps it comes from the patter of magicians, showmen, etc. – and was current by 1835.

here come de judge. See under *LAUGH-IN*.

here is the news – and this is Alvar Liddell reading it. Until the Second World War, and for about 20 years after it, newsreaders on BBC radio were anonymous, but for a period during the war they did identify themselves. This was to lessen the possibility of impersonation by English-speaking newsreaders on German propaganda stations or if Britain was invaded. Hence, when Alvar Liddell (1908–81), a regular broadcaster from 1932 to his retirement in 1969, died, it was suggested that it was he who had made the format famous. Indeed, he may well have done so, being the possessor of one of the most famous of the old-style BBC voices and having read the news at some key points in the course of the war.

here's a funny thing. The flamboyant British comedian Max Miller 'The Cheeky Chappie' (1895–1963) had stock phrases rather than phrases that caught on. *Here's a Funny Thing* was the title of a stage show about Miller, written by B. W. Shakespeare, in *c* 1981. Hence, 'Now this *is* a funny thing. I went home the other night. *There*'s a funny thing!' Partridge/*Catch Phrases* has **now there's a funny thing** current by the late nineteenth century.

When I'm dead and gone, the game's finished! was another rather ingratiating phrase – also, 'Miller's the name, lady. **There'll never be another!'**

Not forgetting, **you're the kind of people who give me a bad name!** –

when an audience perceived a double entendre without him having to emphasize it.

here's another fine/nice mess you've gotten me into! Oliver Hardy's exasperated cry to his partner Stan Laurel after yet another example of the latter's ineptitude has come to light was spoken in several of the comedians' American films. Oddly, both the *Oxford Dictionary of Modern Quotations* (1991) and *ODQ* (1992) place the saying under Laurel's name while acknowledging that it was always said *to* him. It is one of the few film catchphrases to register – because there was a sufficient number of Laurel and Hardy features for audiences to become familiar with it. Latterly, it has often been remembered as 'another *fine* mess', possibly on account of one of the duo's 30-minute features (released in 1930) being entitled *Another Fine Mess*. The *Independent* (21 January 1994) carried a letter from Darren George of Sheffield – clearly a Laurel and Hardy scholar – which stated that 'nice mess' was what was 'invariably' spoken and that in *Another Fine Mess* 'the duo inexplicably misquote themselves'. A graffito, reported during the Falklands war of 1982, declared: 'There's another fine mess you got me into, [Port] Stanley.'

here's a pretty kettle of fish! That Queen Mary did indeed exclaim 'Here's a pretty kettle of fish' to Prime Minister Stanley Baldwin at the time of the Abdication crisis, is not in doubt. However, a differently worded version has turned up with a precise date. Nancy Dugdale (d 1969) wrote a diary from data supplied by her husband, Thomas (Parliamentary Private Secretary to Baldwin from 1935 to 1937). On Tuesday 17 November 1936 she wrote: 'Mr Baldwin went today to see the Queen, who enchanted him by the sentence with which she greeted him: "This is a nice kettle of fish, isn't it?" She was naturally very upset . . .'

On the broader question of why we use the expression 'kettle of fish' in this way: in the 1740s, Henry Fielding uses 'pretty kettle of fish' in both *Joseph Andrews* and *Tom Jones*, so it was obviously well established by then. Brewer has a plausible explanation,

saying that 'kettle of fish' is an old Border country name for a kind of *fête champêtre*, or riverside picnic, where a newly caught salmon is boiled and eaten. 'The discomfort of this sort of party may have led to the phrase, "A pretty kettle of fish", meaning an awkward state of affairs, a mess, a muddle.'

A 'fish kettle' as the name of a cauldron for cooking fish has been a term used since the seventeenth century, though this appears not to have much to do with the expression.

Rather preferable is the explanation given in *English Idioms* published by Nelson (c 1912) that kettle comes from 'kiddle' = a net. So all one is saying is, 'here is a nice net of fish', as one might on drawing it out of the sea, not being totally sure what it contains.

here's Johnny! Said with a drawn-out, rising inflection on the first word, this was Ed McMahon's introduction to Johnny Carson on NBC's *Tonight* show from its inception in 1961: '[*Drum roll*] And now . . . heeeeere's Johnny!' It was emulated during Simon Dee's brief reign as a chat-show host in Britain during the 1960s. The studio audience joined in the rising inflection of the announcer's **it's Siiimon Dee!** Jack Nicholson playing a psychopath chops through a door with an axe and cries 'Here's Johnny!' in the film *The Shining* (1981).

here's looking at you, kid! From the film *Casablanca* (1942), a line based on existing drinking phrases and turned into a catchphrase by Humphrey Bogart impersonators. 'Here's Looking At You' had earlier been the title of one of the first revues transmitted by the BBC from Alexandra Palace in the early days of television (c 1936).

here's one I made earlier. (or **one I prepared earlier . . .**) This curiously popular catchphrase in Britain originated with 'live' TV cookery demonstrations in the 1950s in which it was important that the showing of the finished product was not left to chance. But the phrase was also borrowed by presenters of BBC TV's children's programme *Blue Peter* (from 1963 onwards) who had to explain how to make models of the Taj Mahal out of milk-bottle tops, for example, but wouldn't actually be seen doing so there and then.

Headline from the *Independent* (14 December 1991) – over a gardening article – 'And here's one I made earlier . . .'

here's to our next merry meeting! As a catchphrase, this might seem at first to be linked to Henry Hall's signature theme 'HERE'S TO THE NEXT TIME' for the BBC Dance Orchestra (which Hall took over in March 1932):

> Here's to the next time and a merry meeting,
> Here's to the next time, we send you all our greeting,
> Set it to music, sing it in rhyme,
> Now, all together, Here's to the next time!

And BBC Radio's electronic organist, Robin Richmond, for many years presenter of *The Organist Entertains*, used the phrase as his weekly sign-off.

But the alliterative lure of 'merry meetings' was in evidence long before these two gentlemen. King Richard III has 'Our stern alarums chang'd to merry meetings' in the famous opening speech to Shakespeare's play (1592). *Punch* for 27 July 1904 has in the caption to a cartoon accompanying 'Operatic Notes' 'TO OUR NEXT MERRY MEETING!'

Even more significantly, the *Punch Almanack* for 1902 has a cartoon of two foxes drinking in a club, celebrating the fact that all the best hunting horses are away in the Boer War. One fox is saying, 'To our next merry meeting!' Does this indicate that this was an established toast? Does it also suggest that the original 'meeting' referred to in the phrase was the kind you have in fox-hunting?

here's to the next time. See under THIS IS HENRY HALL SPEAKING . . .

here's your starter for ten (and no conferring). Stock phrases from the British TV quiz *University Challenge* (1962–87, 94–) and forever associated with the original chairman, Bamber Gascoigne.

here today, gone tomorrow. Applied to any short-lived, transitory phenomenon or person, an early use of this old proverbial expression occurs in Aphra Benn's *Luckey Chance* (1687): 'Faith, Sir, we are here to Day and gone to Morrow.'

here we are again! Possibly the oldest catchphrase it is possible to attach to a particular performer. Joseph Grimaldi (*d* 1837) used it as Joey the Clown in pantomime and it has subsequently been used by almost all clowns on entering the circus ring.

here we go, here we go, here we go! This chant, sung to the tune of Sousa's 'Stars and Stripes for Ever', is one beloved of British football supporters, though it does have other applications. It suddenly became very noticeable at the time of the Mexico World Cup in June 1986. The previous year, the Everton football team had made a record of the chant, arranged and adapted by Tony Hiller and Harold Spiro. This version included an excursion into Offenbach's famous Can-Can tune.

here we go round the mulberry bush. From the refrain sung in the children's game (first recorded in the mid-nineteenth century, though probably earlier) in which the participants hold hands and dance in a ring. There are numerous variations, using various fruits.

One theory of the rhyme's origin is that a mulberry tree stood in the middle of the exercise yard at Wakefield Prison in Yorkshire. The prisoners would have to go round and round it on a 'cold and frosty morning'. This may, however, be no more than a coincidence.

Here We Go, Round the Mulberry Bush (with the comma) was the title of a novel (1965; film UK, 1967) by Hunter Davies.

her indoors. See 'ER INDOORS.

hero. See under HOME IS THE SAILOR; MY ~!

Herod, to out-Herod. To go beyond the extremes of tyranny as usually perceived. The allusion is to Herod's slaughter of all the children of Bethlehem (Matthew 2:16).

The precise formulation of the phrase occurs in Shakespeare's *Hamlet* (1600) when the Prince is instructing the actors not to go OVER THE TOP (III.ii.8): 'O! it offends me to the soul to hear a robustious periwig-pated fellow tear a passion to tatters . . . I would have such a fellow whipped for o'erdoing Termagant; it out-herods Herod: pray you, avoid it.'

Termagant and Herod both featured in medieval mystery plays as noisy violent types.

hero from zero, a. A fairly meaningless rhyming phrase suggesting that a person has come from humble beginnings. It was used as the title of a document produced in 1988 by the British industrialist Tiny Rowlands in a prolonged war of words with Mohamed Al-Fayed. The Egyptian businessman had been able to gain control of the House of Fraser stores group (which includes Harrods) and thwarted Mr Rowlands's ambitions in that direction.

The phrase was derived from an alleged tape recording of a conversation between Fayed (who was presumably talking about himself) and two Indian gurus said to have links with the Sultan of Brunei.

he's fallen in the water! See under GOON SHOW.

hesitation. See WITHOUT ~ . . .

he's loo-vely, Mrs 'Oskin . . . See under RAY'S A LAUGH.

he's very good, you know! See under GOON SHOW.

he was a big man in every sense of the word/a giant among men. Clichés of obituary. From *Money-Brief* (issued by stockbrokers Gerrard Vivian Gray, April 1989): 'Roddy was an excellent stockbroker and wonderful friend. His memorial service . . . was a marvellous tribute to a man who was larger than life in every way.'

From Marmaduke Hussey's appreciation of Sir Michael Swann in the *Independent* (24 September 1990): 'Michael Swann, a big man in every way, was a RENAISSANCE figure, scholar, scientist, soldier . . .'

he who is not with us is against us. This view is popularly ascribed to the Russian leader, Joseph Stalin. *Time* (11 August 1986) noted a corollary attributed to the Hungarian Communist Party leader, Janos Kadar: 'He who is not against us is with us.' In fact Stalin was quoting Jesus Christ who said: 'He that is not with me is against me' (Luke 11:23) and Kadar was also quoting Christ who provided the corollary: 'He that is not against us is for us' (Luke 9:50). It is not surprising that Stalin quoted Scripture. He went from a Church school at Guri to the theological seminary at Tiflis to train for the Russian Orthodox priesthood.

he who loves me follows me. Slogan for Jesus Jeans, in various countries, from 1970. In that year, Maglificio Calzificio Torinese, an Italian clothing manufacturer, launched an advertising campaign showing the rear view of a young girl in a tight-fitting pair of the company's new Jesus Jeans, cut very short. The slogan echoed the New Testament, as also did another one, **thou shalt have no other jeans before me.**

Later, a spokesman for the company explained in the *International Herald Tribune* (12 January 1982): 'We were not looking for a scandal. It's just that it was the late 1960s and Jesus was emerging increasingly as a sort of cult figure. There was the Jesus generation and *Jesus Christ Superstar*. There was this enormous protest, in Italy and around the world, and Jesus looked to a lot of people like the biggest protester ever . . . It's funny, we had no trouble in Mediterranean countries, but the biggest resistance came in the protestant countries, in North America and northern Europe.'

Jesus Jeans were eventually only sold in Italy, Greece and Spain. In Greece, there was a threat of prosecution for 'insulting religion and offending the Christian conscience of the public'. In France, complaints of blasphemy and sacrilege flooded in when the slogan '*Qui m'aime me suive*' was tried out in 1982, similarly located on a girl's behind.

he who runs may read. This expression is an alteration of Habbakuk 2:2, 'That he may run that readeth it', but is no more easily understandable. The New English Bible translates it as 'ready for a herald to carry it with speed' and provides the alternative 'so that a man may read it easily'. The *OED2* has citations from 1672, 1784 and 1821, but possibly the most famous use is in John Keble's hymn 'Septuagesima' from *The Christian Year* (1827):

> There is a book, who runs may read,
> Which heavenly truth imparts,
> And all the lore its scholars need,
> Pure eyes and Christian hearts.

Given the obscurity, one of the most unlikely uses of the phrase has been as an advertising slogan for *The Golden Book* in the 1920s (according to E.S. Turner, *The Shocking History of Advertising*, 1952).

he won't be happy till he gets it. A slogan for Pears' soap, current 1888 and coupled with a picture of a baby stretching out of its bath to pick up a cake of the soap. Cartoonists made much play with this idea – changing the baby into the Tsar or Kaiser and the soap into various disputed territories. In early editions of *Scouting for Boys* (c 1908) Robert Baden-Powell used the slogan (with acknowledgement to Pears) to refer to the achievement of a first-class badge. There was also a companion advertisement with the slogan **he's got it and he's happy now.**

hey, are you putting it around I'm barmy? See I'VE GOT A LETTER FROM A BLOKE IN BOOTLE.

hey, you down there with the glasses (on)! From BBC radio's *The Billy Cotton Band Show* (1949–68) (see WAKEY!–WAKEY!) The words were addressed to Cotton by a voice which sounded as though it was being spoken from a plane. The opening gambit to some comedy crosstalk.

hidden agenda. The true meaning behind words and actions, often and contradicting them. The expression is believed to have emerged following discussions in British educational circles in the late 1960s and early 1970s when the concept of a 'hidden curriculum' in schools (going against the actual curriculum that was taught) was much talked about.

From the *Financial Times* (5 October

1983): 'Those who vote Yes for the new constitution will vote ostensibly for reform in South Africa but will in effect be voting for the permanent rejection of the black majority – unless, as the Government repeatedly denies, there is a "hidden agenda" for dramatic new reforms after the vote is won.' From the *Sunday Telegraph* (29 March 1992): 'A Labour government, grabbing vast new powers and dispensing patronage on a scale never seen before, will give [political correctness] impetus, official backing and legislative authority. Here indeed is the hidden agenda, which does not figure in the manifesto because much of it will be enacted by private member's bills in a parliament with a "progressive" majority.'

In 1990, a British film about the 'shoot-to-kill' policy of security forces in Northern Ireland was given the title *Hidden Agenda*.

The phenomenon is also sometimes referred to currently as the **subtext**.

hide. See YOU CAN RUN BUT YOU CAN'T ~ .

hi-de-hi! For several years from 1980 onwards, BBC TV had a long-running situation comedy series set in a 1950s holiday camp called *Hi-de-hi*. The title probably came to be used in this way from a camper's song special to Butlin's:

> Tramp, tramp, tramp, tramp,
> Here we come, to jolly old Butlin's every year.
> All come down to Butlin's, all by the sea.
> Never mind the weather, we're as happy as can be.
> Hi-de-hi! Ho-de-ho!
> > (quoted in the *Observer* magazine, 12 June 1983)

This possibly dates from the late 1930s. In May 1937, Stanley Holloway recorded a song called 'Hi-de-hi' (his own composition) on a promotional record for Butlin's Holiday Camps, though the lyrics differ from the above.

The origin of the phrase lies, however, in the dance band vocals of the 1920s/30s – the 'Hi-de-ho, vo-de-o-do' sort of thing. In particular, Cab Calloway's song 'Minnie the Moocher' (1931) contains the refrain, 'Ho-de-ho, hi-de-hi'. The line 'Hey, ho-de-ho, hi-de-hi!' also occurs in the Ira

Gershwin lyrics for the song 'The Lorelei' (1933). In addition, according to Denis Gifford's *The Golden Age of Radio*, 'Hi-de-hi! Ho-de-ho!' was the catchphrase of Christopher Stone, the BBC's first 'disc jockey', when he went off and presented *Post Toasties Radio Corner*, a children's programme for Radio Normandy in 1937.

Shortly after this last, the phrase achieved notoriety when a commanding officer in the army faced a court of inquiry or court martial for making his troops answer 'Ho-de-ho' when he (or his fellow officers) yelled 'Hi-de-hi'. I don't know when this case was, but it was well in the past when *Notes and Queries* got around to it in 1943–44, and there was a revue with the title at the Palace Theatre, London, in 1943. Gerald Kersh referred to army use of the exchange (though not to the specific case) in *They Die with their Boots Clean* in 1941.

hiding to nothing, to be on a. Meaning 'to be in a no-win situation'; to be confronted with a thrashing without the chance of avoiding it, to face impossible odds', the origin of this expression is obscure, but possibly comes from horse racing. In use by 1905.

hi, gang! Ben Lyon's greeting to the audience of his wartime BBC radio programme of the same name, first broadcast on 26 May 1940. The former Hollywood star would shout, 'Hi gang!' The audience would reply, 'Hi, Ben!' At the end of the show, he would say, 'So long, gang!' and they would reply, 'So long, Ben!'

An incidental line of Lyon's, addressed to members of the studio audience was: **not you, momma, siddown!** (once reported as having appeared as a graffito on the underside of a train lavatory seat).

high. See COME HELL AND ~ WATER; PILE IT ~; SET 'EM UP ~.

higher the fewer, because the. See WHY IS A MOUSE WHEN IT SPINS?

high noon. In the straightforward sense, 'high noon' is simply a way of describing the time when the sun is high in the heavens. John Milton, *Paradise Lost*, V.174 (1667)

has, 'Sun . . . sound his praise . . . both when thou climb'st, And when high Noon hast gain'd.'

The film Western *High Noon* (US, 1951) concerns a sheriff (played by Gary Cooper) who, alone, faces up to four outlaws threatening to take over his town. The climax of the film is a confrontation between the sheriff and the leader of the outlaws in the town square at high noon. Consequently, the phrase 'high noon' is used in situations where anyone is standing up a fight against lawlessness or where there is a fatal/final confrontation.

high off the hog, to eat/live. Meaning, 'to live prosperously, in luxury'. It is an expression, as Morris (1977) puts it, 'quite literally accurate, since you have to go pretty high on the hog to get tender – and expensive – loin chops and roasts.' Of American origin and known by 1946.

high profile. When people are said to be maintaining or keeping one of these, it means that they are actively seeking publicity or attention and are not hiding away – which would involve, rather, maintaining a **low profile**. From the *Washington Post* (29 September 1991): 'Dean Robinson Replies: "Stinson's high profile at DCSL is Exhibit 1 for the case that there is no rigid political orthodoxy at the school"'; (3 November 1991) 'There have been times, however, when the council's politics have dictated that Atwell take a low profile on a controversial issue.'

It is likely that 'high profile' was created in response to the popularity of 'low profile' which had become a way of describing the Nixon administration's attitude in certain policy matters in about 1970. It is probably of US military origin and soon became incorporated into 'Pentagonese' (the jargon of defense). As Safire (1978) points out, in tank warfare, a low vehicle presents less of a target for artillery. He also quotes presidential assistant Leonard Garment as saying in early 1970: 'I've kept my profile so low for so long, I've got a permanent backache.'

The use of the British term 'low profile' in connection with motor-car tyres, a year or two before this, appears to be a coincidental coinage.

high water. See COME HELL . . .

hills. See OVER THE ~ AND FAR AWAY; THERE'S GOLD IN THEM THAR ~.

HILTHYNBIMA. 'How I Love To Hold Your Naked Body In My Arms' – lovers' code in correspondence to avoid military censorship. Dating from the Second World War, or earlier.

Him. See TO KNOW ~ IS TO LOVE ~.

him bad man, kemo sabe! See HI-YO, SILVER!

hinc illae lacrimae [hence all those tears]. Said by way of explanation as to the real cause of something. From *Andria* by Terence (d 159 BC).

his death diminishes us all. A cliché of obituaries, this possibly derives from John Donne's *Devotions*, XVII (1624): 'Any man's death diminishes me, because I am involved in Mankind: and therefore never send to know for whom the bell tolls; it tolls for thee.'

his/her face is his/her fortune. Old saying. 'My face is my fortune' occurs, for example, in the (laundered) sea shanty 'Rio Grande' (trad./anon.) to be found in various students' song-books. 'What is your fortune, my pretty maid?/My face is my fortune, sir, she said' is in a c 1800 nursery rhyme ('Where are you going to, my pretty maid?') which is a version of an earlier, more lubricious, folk song.

his master's voice. Occasionally used to describe 'the voice of authority' or the practice of only carrying out what one is instructed to do – or of not revealing one's own thoughts, only those of one's superiors. From M.A. von Arnim, *Enchanted April* (1922): '"Francesca!" shouted Briggs. She came running . . . "Her Master's Voice," remarked Mr Wilkins.'

The phrase comes from the trademark and brand name of the HMV record company. In 1899, the English painter Francis Barraud approached the Gramophone Company in London to borrow one of their machines so that he

could paint his fox terrier, Nipper, listening to it. Nipper was accustomed, in fact, to hearing a *phonograph* but his master thought that the larger horn of the gramophone would make a better picture. Barraud entitled the finished work, 'His Master's Voice'.

Subsequently, the Gramophone Company bought the painting and adapted and adopted it as a trademark. In 1901, the Victor Talking Machine Company ('Loud enough for dancing' was its slogan) acquired the US rights. The company later became RCA Victor and took Nipper with them. Nowadays Britain's EMI owns the trademark in most countries, RCA owns it in North and South America, and JVC owns it in Japan. It was used until 1991.

history. See END OF ~; REST IS ~.

history man, a. Following the BBC TV adaptation in 1981 of the novel *The History Man* (1975) by Malcolm Bradbury, the phrase 'history man' has been used to describe a particular type of scheming, unidealistic, university lecturer. In fact, the title of the novel describes a character who does not appear, but it was taken to mean the left-wing sociology don 'hero' – and from that, any similar don at a 'new' university.

hit. See YOU DON'T REWRITE A ~.

hi-tiddly-i-ti, brown bread! A snappy ending from children's singing games, vocalizing the familiar musical phrase 'om-tiddly-om-pom, pom pom', which is said first to have occurred in Fischler's 'Hot Scotch Rag' of 1911. The phrase 'Hi-tidli-i-ti/-i-ti-hi' had already occurred, however, in *Punch* in 1900. Other versions: 'Tripe and bananas, fried fish!' 'Guard to the guard-room, dismiss!' 'Shave and a haircut, five bob/two bits!' Also extended to: '. . . I look at your father's – bald head!' It has been suggested that the most common conclusion to the phrase used in British music hall was '—, cream cheese' and that the comedian Harry Champion (1866–1942) may first have used the 'brown bread' version, either because of the alliteration or through irony – a restaurant or pub advertising its wares in nineteenth-century

Britain that advertised brown bread through such a cry would be offering very meagre fare indeed.

hit the ground running, to. From the *Independent* (29 March 1989): '*The Late Show* has so far generated an overwhelmingly favourable response . . . "To hit the ground running with four shows a week," said Alex Graham, editor of *The Media Show* on Channel 4, "that's really impressive."' I think this phrase comes from the military – leaping from assault craft and helicopters, even landing by parachute, immediately running off, and, without preamble, successfully getting straight on with the business in hand. Current by 1985.

Compare **up and running,** meaning 'to be under way', current by 1987.

hi-yo, Silver (away)! 'Who *was* that masked man? . . . A fiery horse with the speed of light, a cloud of dust, and a hearty "Hi-yo, Silver!" The Lone Ranger! With his faithful Indian companion Tonto, the daring and resourceful masked rider of the plains led the fight for law and order in the early western United States. Nowhere in the pages of history can one find a greater champion of justice. **Return with us now to those thrilling days of yesteryear** . . . From out of the past come the thundering hoofbeats of the great horse Silver. **The Lone Ranger rides again!**
'"Come on, Silver! Let's go, big fellow! Hi-yo, Silver, away!"'
The above was more or less the introduction to the masked Lone Ranger and his horse, Silver, in the various American radio, cinema and TV accounts of their exploits – accompanied, of course, by Rossini's 'William Tell' overture.
Groucho Marx used to say that George Seaton (the first Lone Ranger on radio from 1933) invented the call 'Hi-yo, Silver!' because he was unable to whistle for his horse. It seems, indeed, that the phrase was minted by Seaton and not by Fran Striker, the chief scriptwriter in the early days.
The Lone Ranger's Indian friend, Tonto (which is Spanish for 'fool'), wrestled meanwhile with such lines as, **him bad man, kemo sabe!** ('kemos sabe' – whichever way you spell it – is supposed to

mean 'trusty scout' and was derived from the name of a boys' camp at Mullet Lake, Michigan, in 1911).

Hobson's choice. No choice at all. Thomas or Tobias Hobson (*d* 1631) hired horses from a livery stable in Cambridge. His customers were always obliged to take the horse nearest the door. The man's fame was considerable, the expression was recorded by 1649, and Hobson was celebrated in two epitaphs by Milton. *Hobson's Choice* was the title of a play (1915; film UK, 1953) by Harold Brighouse.

hockey-sticks. See JOLLY ∼.

hog. See HIGH OFF THE ∼.

ho-ho, *very* satirical. Expressing ironical appreciation of a satirical joke. Probably a reaction to the 'satire boom' of the early 1960s, but still alive. A 'Mini-Trog' cartoon in the *Observer* of 17 July 1988, at a time of long delays at British airports, shows a little man looking at an advertisement jokily promoting Gatwick as 'Gatqwick'. He is saying to himself, '*Very* satirical.'
In fact, the phrase originated on the cover of one of the very first issues of *Private Eye* (7 February 1962). It is a comment on a piece of artwork showing the Albert Memorial as 'Britain's first man in space'.
Compare this from a letter written by Nancy Mitford on 26 December 1940: 'These ton bombs are [Hitler's] new joke . . . so one has great fun guessing where they will land. Ha ha ha *such* a little comedian.'

hoist with one's own petard, to be. Meaning 'to be caught in one's own trap' – but, in origin, nothing to do with being stabbed by one's own knife (poniard = dagger), or hung with one's own rope. The context in which Hamlet uses it in Shakespeare's play (III.iv.209; 1600) makes the source clear:

For 'tis the sport to have the engineer Hoist with his own petard.

A petard was a newly invented device in Shakespeare's day, used for blowing up walls, etc. with gunpowder. Thus the image is of the operative being blown up into the air by his own device. Compare the more recent expression 'to score an OWN GOAL'.

hokey-pokey. See OKEY-POKEY.

hold a candle to someone/thing, unable to. In the pre-electric light era, an apprentice might have found himself holding a candle so that a more experienced workman could do his job. Or, in the days before street lighting, a linkboy would carry a torch for another person. Holding a candle, in either of these ways, was a necessary but menial task. If a person was so incompetent that he could not even do that properly, then he really was not fit for anything.

There seems to have been no suggestion of anything to do with examining eggs by holding them up to the light (as has been suggested) or even of one person being *compared* with another. The meaning of the phrase is better expressed as 'not fit to hold a candle *for* another'. It has been known since the sixteenth century.

Hold Back the Dawn. As the title of a film (US, 1941), this is apparently an original phrase, as are also *Hold Back the Night* (US, 1956) and *Hold Back Tomorrow* (US, 1956), and Barbara Taylor Bradford's novel *Hold the Dream* (1985).

holding the bag, to be left. Meaning, to be left in an incriminating position and having to CARRY THE CAN. But what bag? One suggestion is that, in the sixteenth century, 'giving the bag' was an expression used to describe a servant who ran off with his master's cash, leaving behind only an empty purse or bag. In time, 'giving' became 'holding'.

hold it against me. See IF I SAID YOU HAD A BEAUTIFUL BODY . . .

hold it up to the light, not a stain, and shining bright. A slogan for Surf washing powder and current in the late 1950s. This was a line from the 'Mrs Bradshaw' series of British TV ads in which the eponymous lady never appeared but her male lodger did. (From an edition of the GOON SHOW of the same period: 'The BBC – hold it up to the light – not a brain in sight!')

hold the fort. This phrase has two meanings: 'Look after this place while I'm away' and 'Hang on, relief is at hand'. In the second sense, there is a specific origin. In the American Civil War, General William T. Sherman signalled words to this effect to General John M. Corse at the Battle of Allatoona, Georgia (5 October 1864). What he actually semaphored from Keneshaw Mountain was: 'Sherman says hold fast. We are coming' (Mencken) or 'Hold out. Relief is coming' (Bartlett). The phrase became popularized in its present form as the first line of a hymn/gospel song written by Philip Paul Bliss in *c* 1870 ('Ho, My Comrades, See the Signal!' in *The Charm*). This was introduced to Britain by Moody and Sankey during their evangelical tour of the British Isles in 1873 (and not written by them, as is sometimes supposed):

'Hold the fort, for I am coming,'
Jesus signals still;
Wave the answer back to heaven,
'By thy grace we will.'

More recently, perhaps thanks to a pun on 'union' (as in the American Civil War and trade union), the song has been adapted as a trade union song in Britain:

Hold the fort, for we are coming
Union men be strong
Side by side keep pressing onward.
Victory will come.

hole(s). See ACE IN THE ~; BLACK ~; BLACK ~ OF CALCUTTA; KNOW ONE'S ARSE FROM A ~ IN THE GROUND; IF YOU KNOW A BETTER ~ . . . ; TOP ~.

hole heals up as soon as you leave the car park, the. Meaning 'one will not be missed, no one is irreplaceable'. Broadcasting executive Michael Grade said it on leaving the BBC for Channel 4 in November 1987 and called it a 'BBC saying'.

hole in the head, to need something like a. Meaning 'not to need something at all'. Leo Rosten in *Hooray for Yiddish* (1982) describes this phrase as 'accepted from Alaska to the Hebrides' and states that it comes directly from the Yiddish *lock in kop*: 'It was propelled into our vernacular by the play *A Hole in the Head* (1957) by Arnold Schulman and more forcibly impressed upon mass consciousness by the Frank Sinatra movie (1959).' *OED2* finds it by 1951.

holiday. See BUSMAN'S ∼.

Holocaust, the. This is the phrase applied to the mass murder of Jews and the attempted elimination of European Jewry by the German Nazis during the 1939–45 war. A holocaust is an all-consuming conflagration and is not perhaps the most obvious description of what happened to the estimated six million Jews under the Nazis, though many were burned after being gassed or killed in some other way (compare FINAL SOLUTION).

The term seems to have arisen because 'genocide' hardly sounded emotive enough. The popular use of 'the Holocaust' for this purpose dates only from 1965 when Alexander Donat published a book on the subject entitled *The Holocaust Kingdom*. However, *OED2* has it in this sense in the *News Chronicle* by 1942, as well as various other 1940s citations. As early as 1951, the Israeli Knesset had 'The Holocaust and Ghetto Uprising Day' – translated from *Yom ha-Sho'ah*. The use was finally settled when a US TV mini-series called *Holocaust* (1978) was shown and caused controversy in many countries. Well before *that* happened, Eric Partridge was advising in his *Usage and Abusage* (1947): 'Holocaust is "destruction by fire": do not synonymize it with *disaster*. Moreover, it is properly an ecclesiastical technicality.'

In fact, the word derives from the Greek words *holos* and *kaustos* meaning 'wholly burnt' and was for many years used to describe a sacrifice or offering that was burnt. Some translations of the Bible use it to describe Abraham's preparations to slay his son Isaac. The term has latterly been used to describe what happened to the people of Cambodia at the hands of the Khmer Rouge in the 1970s, and also to the Vietnamese boat people.

holy — ! See under BATMAN.

home. See ARE THERE ANY MORE AT ∼ LIKE YOU; AT ∼ AND AWAY . . . under FAMILY

FAVOURITES; DON'T LEAVE ∼ WITHOUT IT; EVERY ∼ SHOULD HAVE ONE; HARVEST ∼; I THINK I GO ∼; LIKE COMING ∼; NO PLACE LIKE ∼; TILL THE COWS COME ∼; WHERE THE HEART IS; YOURS TO ENJOY IN THE PRIVACY . . .

home! a home!, a. The Scottish Home family's traditional war-cry or slogan not only identified it but spurred its soldiers on to action – despite the legend that on hearing it at the Battle of Flodden Field in 1513, they turned tail and headed for home.

home is the sailor, home from sea. In Robert Louis Stevenson's poem 'Requiem' (1887), it is definitely 'home from sea' – without the definite article, but his grave in Samoa has (incorrectly) 'home from *the* sea'. 'Home from sea' is also the title of a painting (1862) by Arthur Hughes, showing a young sailor and (probably) his sister at their mother's grave (also known as 'The Sailor Boy' and 'Mother's Grave'). Compare *Home Is the Hero*, the title of a film (UK, 1959) based on Walter Macken's play.

home is where the heart is. See WHERE THE HEART IS.

home, James, and don't spare the horses. A catchphrase used jocularly, as if talking to a driver, telling someone to proceed or get a move on. From the title of a song (1934) by the American songwriter Fred Hillebrand and recorded by Elsie Carlisle in that year and by Hillebrand himself in 1935. The component 'Home, James!' had existed long before – in the works of Thackeray, for example.

homely fun. See under A SPOT OF . . . under HAVE A GO.

Homer nods, even. Meaning 'even the greatest, best and wisest of us can't be perfect all the time, and can make mistakes'. Current by the eighteenth century at least: 'Let Homer, who sometimes nods, sleep soundly upon your shelf for three or four years' (letter of Lord Chesterfield to Lord Huntingdon, 31 August 1749). Mencken has 'even Homer sometimes nods' as an English proverb derived from Horace, *De Arte Poetica* (c 8 BC): 'I am indignant when worthy Homer nods', and familiar since the

seventeenth century. Longinus (c 213–
273AD) evidently added: 'They say that
Homer sometimes nods. Perhaps he does –
but then he dreams as Zeus might dream.'

home rule (for ever). A slogan first used
about 1860 in its usual sense of self
government for Ireland, then under British
rule. The Home Rule Movement led by
Sinn Fein ultimately led to the founding of
the Irish Free State – with Northern Ireland
remaining part of the UK.

honest toil. See under DIGNITY OF LABOUR.

honey. See LAND FLOWING WITH MILK
AND ~.

honeymoon, to go on. The name for the
holiday taken by a bride and groom after
their wedding comes from the old custom of
newly married couples drinking mead (wine
made with honey) for a month after the
ceremony. Other languages follow the same
pattern: French *lune de miel*, Italian *luna di
miele*.

Hood, Robin. See ROBIN HOOD.

hook. See BY ~ OR BY CROOK.

Hooray Henry. Denoting 'a loud-
mouthed upper-class twit' (in Britain), the
phrase was coined by Jim Godbolt in 1951
to describe the upper-class contingent
attracted to the jazz club at 100, Oxford
Street, London by the Old Etonian
trumpeter, Humphrey Lyttelton. It derives
from a character in Damon Runyon's story
'Tight Shoes' who is described as 'strictly a
Hurrah Henry'.

hoots mon! The 1958 British hit
instrumental record 'Hoots Mon',
performed by Lord Rockingham's XI, was
punctuated at strategic points by the
speaking of the cod Scotticisms, 'Hoots
Mon, there's a moose loose aboot this
hoose' and **it's a braw bricht moonlicht
nicht**.
    The last phrase also occurs in the song
'Just a wee deoch-an-duoris' that Sir Harry
Lauder performed and which he wrote in
1912 in collaboration with G. Grafton, R.F.
Morrison and Whit Cunliffe.

As for 'hoots mon' (i.e. 'man') on its own,
the *Collins English Dictionary* describes
'hoot/s' as 'an exclamation of impatience or
dissatisfaction; a supposed Scotticism –
C17: of unknown origin'.
    The *OED2* weighs in with the word
being 'of Scottish and Northern England
use', comparing the Swedish *hut* [begone],
the Welsh *hwt* [away], and the Irish '*ut*'
[out], all used in a similar sense.
    In 1982, I put the phrase to a panel
including such noted Scottish word-persons
as John Byrne, Cliff Hanley and Jimmy
Reid. One thought it was a greeting with
the meaning, 'How's it going, man?'
Another thought it might mean 'Have a big
dram, man' – a 'hoot' being a drink. Finally,
Jimmy Reid dismissed it as 'stage Scots . . .
bastardized Scots, for the placation of
Sassenachs'.

Hoover. See IT BEATS AS IT SWEEPS AS IT
CLEANS.

hope. See LAST BEST ~ ON EARTH.

Horace. See WHAT DID ~ SAY?

Horlicks. See under NIGHT STARVATION;
THINKS . . . THANKS TO ~.

horny-handed sons of toil. Denis
Kearney popularized the expression
denoting labourers bearing the marks of
their trade, in a speech at San Francisco (c
1878). Irish-born Kearney led a
'workingman's protest movement against
unemployment, unjust taxes, unfair
banking laws, and mainly against Chinese
labourers' (Flexner, 1982). Earlier, J.R.
Lowell had written in 'A Glance Behind the
Curtain' (1843): 'And blessèd are the horny
hands of toil', and Lord Salisbury, the
British Conservative Prime Minister, was
quoted as having used the precise phrase in
the *Quarterly Review* (October 1873).

horrible. See YOU 'ORRIBLE LITTLE MAN.

horror. See SHOCK, ~!

horse(s). See DARK ~; HOME, JAMES, AND
DON'T SPARE THE ~; I GOTTA ~; NEVER
CHANGE ~ IN MID STREAM; ONLY FOOLS AND
~S WORK; STALKING ~.

horse of another/different colour, a.
Meaning 'something is of another matter
altogether, of a different complexion
entirely'. Known by 1798. Note the related
'horse of the *same* colour' known by 1601.
Some etymologists have gone to
unnecessary lengths to find an origin for a
perfectly simple phrase. One even says it
could have grown out of the White Horse of
Berkshire, an English archaeological
phenomenon, carved in a chalk hillside.
From time to time, it was customary for
neighbourhood volunteers to clean the
weeds away, thus making it 'a horse of a
different colour' . . .

horse's mouth, straight from the. To
hear something directly from the person
concerned and not garbled by an
intermediary. The horse itself is not doing
any speaking, of course. A horse's age can
be judged best by looking at its teeth (which
grow according to a strict system). So, if you
are buying a horse, you do better to look at
its teeth than rely on any information
about its age that the vendor might give
you. Known by 1928.

**horses sweat, men perspire – and
women merely glow.** A saying used to
reprove someone who talks of 'sweating'. It
is listed as a nanny's reprimand in *Nanny
Says* (1972) in the form: 'Horses sweat,
gentlemen perspire, but ladies only gently
glow.' J.M. Cohen includes it in *Comic and
Curious Verse* (1952–9) as merely by Anon,
in the form: 'Here's a little proverb that you
surely ought to know:/ Horses sweat and
men perspire, but ladies only glow.'

hostile. See NATIVES ARE ~.

hot. See BLOW ~ AND COLD; BY GUM, SHE'S
A ~'UN; LONG ~ SUMMER.

**hot dinners, I've had as many — as
you've had.** An exaggerated form of
boasting, originally in the form, 'I've had
as many women as you've had hot
dinners.' Established by the time of the
Second World War, then subjected to
endless variation. 'I've had more gala
luncheons than you've had hot dinners'
(*MONTY PYTHON'S FLYING CIRCUS*, 12
October 1969).

Hot Lips Houlihan. The name of a
formidable female character in the film
M*A*S*H (1970) and the subsequent TV
series, she was played by Sally Kellerman in
the film and by Loretta Swit on TV. Earlier,
in the US radio series *Camel Caravan*
(1943–7), there had been a sex-pot character
with the name 'Hotbreath Houlihan'.

hottest. See GREATEST THING SINCE . . .

hour. See COMETH THE ~, COMETH THE
MAN; DARKEST ~ . . . ; ELEVENTH ~.

house. See FULL ~ under FULL MONTY; IS
THERE A DOCTOR IN THE ~?

house of mirth, the. Phrase from
Ecclesiastes 7:3–4: 'Sorrow is better than
laughter: for by the sadness of the
countenance is the heart made better. The
heart of the wise is in the house of
mourning; but the heart of fools is in the
house of mirth.' Hence, *The House of Mirth*,
title of an Edith Wharton novel (1905)
about a failed social climber.

Hovis. See DON'T SAY BROWN . . .

how about that (then)! Probably an
American expression of surprise or
wonderment dating from the 1930s. I
noticed it being used in the UK particularly
in the late 1950s and mid-1960s. Before the
BBC really began to use disc jockeys, in the
modern sense of the word, there were one
or two announcers or 'introducers' who
developed distinctive ways. Roger Moffatt
(1927–86) was a staff announcer in
Manchester with the necessary plummy
voice for reading the news. He also had a
long and fruitful relationship with the BBC
Northern Dance Orchestra (originally
Variety Orchestra). After some dazzlingly
impressive instrumental number, he was
inclined to exclaim: 'Well, how about that
then!' (See also Jimmy Savile's version of
the phrase under AS IT HAPPENS.)
   Incidentally, when introducing a
programme called *Make Way for Music*
(broadcast simultaneously on radio and TV
in the early 1960s), Moffatt had another
stock phrase: **wherever you are,
whoever you are, why not make way
for music?**

how did you feel when —? An appallingly clichéd question from TV newsgathering, especially in the UK – 'How did you feel when your daughter was raped before your eyes/ your house was blown up/you'd forgotten to post the pools coupon and lost your next-door neighbour a million pounds?' It may be necessary for the question to be asked in order to elicit a response but the nearest any of the newsgatherers has come to doing anything about it is to suggest that, while asking the question is a legitimate activity, the question itself shouldn't actually be broadcast – only the answer. Noticed since the mid-1970s.

When Thurgood Marshall was retiring from the US Supreme Court in 1992, he was asked at a press conference, 'How do you feel?' He replied, 'With my hands.'

how do? See 'ow DO under *HAVE A GO*.

how do you do? The traditional polite greeting (established by the seventeenth century) has been treated as a catchphrase or stock phrase by a number of entertainers particularly in the Britain of the 1940s and 50s. The comedian Arthur Askey used it as the title of a BBC radio series in 1949 and a film. Terry-Thomas used the phrase at the start of monologues (and in the early 1950s had a TV show called *How Do You View?*). Comedian Jimmy James had a distinctive way of saying it, as did Carroll Levis (see below). In any number of editions of radio's *Desert Island Discs*, Roy Plomley began, 'How do you do, ladies and gentlemen, our castaway this week is . . .' (how old-fashioned). The goofy comedian Cardew Robinson (1917–92) inevitably had the version, **this is Cardew the Cad saying Car-dew do!**

See also under I'VE GOT A LETTER FROM A BLOKE IN BOOTLE.

how *do* you do, ladies and gentlemen, how *do* you do? Carroll Levis, a Canadian-born showman, introduced a talent contest on British radio for a number of years. From a typical edition broadcast in 1946: after a fanfare, the announcer said: 'The Carroll Levis Show! We're back again with our feast of fun for everybody, bringing you the family show which is equally welcome to outlaws and in-laws. The founder of the feast, Carroll Levis!' Levis would then intone his welcome. Along the way he called people 'Brother' and would refer to 'my brother Cyril's favourite comedy couple . . .'. At the end of the show he said: '**Same day, same time, same spot on the dial** . . . so long, good luck and happy listening.'

How I Love To Hold Your Naked Body In My Arms. See HILTHYNBIMA.

how is a man when he's out? See WHY IS A MOUSE WHEN IT SPINS?

how's about that then, guys and gals? See under AS IT HAPPENS.

how long is a piece of string? See HOW MANY BEANS MAKE FIVE?

how many beans make five? A joke riddle, but also a catchphrase uttered as an answer to an impossible question (along the lines of **how long is a piece of string?** etc). Miss Alice Lloyd was singing a music-hall song in November 1898 which contained these lines:

> You say you've never heard
> How many beans make five?
> It's time you knew a thing or two -
> You don't know you're alive!

The phrase was also recorded 12 years earlier and seems to come from the heyday of Victorian humour. Miss M.L. King of London SW3 told me that one possible answer was: 'Two in each hand and one in the mouth.'

how'm I doin'? Ed Koch was Mayor of New York City from 1977–89. He helped balance the books after a period of bankruptcy on the city's part by drastically cutting services. His catchphrase during this period was 'How'm I doing?' He would call it out as he ranged round New York. 'You're doing fine, Ed' the people were supposed to shout back. An old song with the title was disinterred in due course. Unfortunately for him, Koch's achievements in NYC did not carry him forward to the State governorship as he had hoped and finally everything turned sour on him. A 1979 cartoon in the *New Yorker* showed a woman answering the phone and saying to her husband: 'It's Ed Koch. He wants to know how he's doin'.' A booklet of Koch's wit and wisdom used the phrase as its title.

how now, brown cow? This phrase has long been used as an elocution exercise in the UK, and regarded as the paradigm thereof. It was not included along with the **rain in Spain stays mainly in the plain** and 'in Hertford, Hereford and Hampshire hurricanes hardly ever happen' in the elocution song in *My Fair Lady* (1956), though these two may have been manufactured especially for the song, in any case.

The earliest trace I have found of the phrase is in a reminiscence of the Oxford University Dramatic Society in the 1920s by Osbert Lancaster in *With an Eye to the Future* (1967). Of an OUDS Last Night party, he writes: 'The principal entertainment was provided by musical members past and present repeating the numbers which they had composed for OUDS smokers, many of which – such as "How now brown cow" – had, after some slight modification of the lyrics at the request of the Lord Chamberlain, reappeared in West End revues.' Indeed, 'How Now Brown Cow' with words by Rowland Leigh and music by Richard Addinsell was sung by Joyce Barbour in the revue *RSVP* at the Vaudeville theatre on 23 February 1926 and was recorded by her. (Incidentally, the *OED2* has an example of the simple interjection 'How now?', meaning 'How goes it?', dating from 1480.)

The rhyming of 'rain' and 'Spain' seems a venerable activity, too. In *Polite Conversation* (1738), Jonathan Swift has this exchange:

I see 'tis raining again.
Why then, Madam, we must do as they do in Spain.
Pray, my Lord, how is that?
Why, Madam, we must let it rain.

'Rain, rain, go to Spain' was a proverbial expression current by 1659.

Yet another speaking exercise appears in *Little Dorrit* by Charles Dickens (1857). Mrs General opines, 'Papa, potatoes, poultry, prunes and prism, are all very good words for the lips: especially prunes and prism.'

Two undated speaking exercises from the schooldays of the actress Eleanor Bron (shall we say 1950s?) went: 'Lippy and Loppy were two little rabbits – lippity, lippity, lippity, lop', and, 'They put the lady in the tar. They said that she was in their power. They left her there for half-an-hour'.

how's about that then, guys and gals? See under AS IT HAPPENS.

how sweet it is! See under AND AWA-A-AAY WE GO!

how's your father? A catchphrase associated with the British music-hall comedian Harry Tate (1872–1940). Apparently, he would exclaim it as a way of changing the subject and in order to get out of a difficult situation (compare READ ANY GOOD BOOKS LATELY?). The phrase either subsequently or simultaneously took on a life of its own, meaning the same as a 'thingummy' or anything the speaker did not wish to name. From that, in phrases like 'indulging in a spot of how's-your-father', it became a euphemism for sexual activity.

how's your poor old feet? Referred to by Ted Ray in his book *Raising the Laughs* (1952). From nineteenth-century music hall? Possibly, but Benham (1948) has a version without the 'old' dating from *c* 1851 – 'alleged to have been a jocular saying in allusion to the fatigue resulting from visiting the Great Exhibition [in London] of 1851'. Partridge/*Catch Phrases* suggests that, as a catchphrase, it was 'rampant' in 1862 and popular until 1870.

how the money rolls in. This alludes to the last line of each verse in a bawdy, anonymous song (included, for example, in *Rugby Songs*, 1967), telling of the various fund-raising activities of a family. A typical verse:

My brother's a poor missionary,
He saves fallen women from sin,
He'll save you a blonde for a guinea,
My God how the money rolls in.

T.R. Ritchie in *The Singing Street* seems to favour 'By God . . .' in the last line.

how the other half lives. Meaning 'how people live who belong to different social groups, especially the rich', the expression was used as the title of a book (1890) by Jacob Riis, an American newspaper reporter. He described the conditions in which poor people lived in New York City. Indeed, the expression seems basically to have referred to the poor but has since been used about any 'other half'. Riis alluded to the core saying in these words: 'Long ago it was said that "one half of the world does not know how the other half lives".' OED2 finds this proverb in 1607 in English, and in French, in *Pantagruel* by Rabelais (1532). Alan Ayckbourn entitled a play (1970) *How the Other Half Loves*.

how tickled I am! 'I was once a salesman and I've always been fascinated by sales techniques,' the British comedian Ken Dodd (*b* 1927) told me in 1979, 'and catchphrases are like trade marks – they are attention-getting details which in my case make people exclaim, "Ah yes, Ken Dodd." The disadvantage of catchphrases is that they get worn – like tyres. So I wanted a catchphrase that was better than a catchphrase . . . I narrowed it down to the fact that it had to be a greeting like HELLO, FOLKS or something like Fanny Brice's ARE YOU ALL RIGHT? FANNY'S ALL RIGHT. I thought of the word "tickled" and all the permutations and combinations one could get from that. So I devised "How tickled I am" as a phrase that could be varied by the addition of a joke – "Have you ever been tickled, Mrs?" and so on. But it was out of the need for a catchphrase that the Tickling Stick actually came.' [**Hello, Mrs** is also a hangover from Dodd's days as a travelling hardware salesman.]

Dodd had a whole series of BBC radio comedy shows from 1963 into the 70s. 'Like most performers, I'm always trying out material on friends and relatives. One night after recording my radio show in London, we rushed to catch the train back to Knotty Ash [in Liverpool] from Euston. I was trying on various daft voices and saying, "Where's me case? **Where's me shirt?**" and the people who were with me laughed – so it went into the next show.' The pronunciation is approximately 'whairs me shairt?' and Dodd recorded a song with the

title. From the same source: **I'm a shirt** [shairt] **short.**

Other Doddisms on stage and on radio included:

diddy Adjective used to describe anything 'quaint, small and lovable'. In the eighteenth century a 'diddy' was a woman's breast or nipple (or that of an animal) – compare 'titty'. 'Diddy Uncle Jack' was how the family used to describe Dodd's great-uncle. 'My family,' he said, 'always impressed on me the importance of being original in my act and I suppose these words I use, like "diddy", **full of plumptiousness** and **tattifalarious**, are an attempt at having something which is mine and nobody else's.'

discumknockerating means that something bowls you over.

nikky-nokky-noo – nonsense phrase. 'Humour is anarchic, I suppose. So, like a child, from time to time you revolt against the discipline of words and just jabber!'

tatty-bye (everybody)! – Dodd inherited this form of farewell from his father.

what a beautiful day for — is another example of a catchphrase which allows for variety by the addition of a new punchline.

(See also BY JOVE, I NEEDED THAT!)

On 31 December 1981, the *Liverpool Echo* reported Dodd's reaction to being awarded the OBE: 'I am delighted. It's a great honour and wonderful news. I am full of plumptiousness. The jam butty workers are discumknockerated and the Diddymen are diddy-delighted.'

How To Succeed in Business Without Really Trying. The title of a business handbook (1953) by Shepherd Mead, it is more widely known as the title of Frank Loesser's musical (1961; film US, 1967).

How To Win Friends and Influence People. This was title of a book (1936) by Dale Carnegie. Carnegie's courses incorporating his self-improvement plan had already been aimed at business people for a quarter of a century before the book came out.

Hoyle, according to. Meaning 'exactly; correctly; according to the recognized rules; according to the highest authority', the phrase comes from the name of the one-time standard authority on the game of whist (and other card games). Edmond Hoyle was the author of *A Short Treatise on the Game of Whist* (1742).

hubba! hubba! (or **hubba! bubba!**) Said, echoing a wolf-whistle, to a pretty girl. Popular in the US military, 1940s, and used by Bob Hope in radio shows of that period. Said to be based on the Chinese cry *how-pu-how*.

Hull, Hell and Halifax . . . , from. See under COME HELL AND/OR HIGH WATER.

hum. See DO YOU KNOW . . .

human. See ALL ~ LIFE IS THERE; FULLY PAID-UP MEMBER OF THE ~ RACE.

humble pie. See EAT ~.

humidity. See IT'S NOT THE HEAT, IT'S THE ~.

hundred. See COOL ~; IT WILL ALL BE THE SAME IN A ~ YEARS' TIME.

hundred days, a/the. This phrase is used to refer to a period of intense political action (often immediately upon coming to power). During the 1964 General Election, Harold Wilson said Britain would need a 'programme of a hundred days of dynamic action' such as President Kennedy had promised in 1961. In fact, Kennedy had specifically ruled out a hundred days, saying in his inaugural speech that even 'a thousand days' would be too short (hence the title of Arthur M. Schlesinger's memoir, *A Thousand Days*, 1965, referring also to the 1,056 days of Kennedy's presidency). The allusion was to the period during which Napoleon ruled between his escape from Elba and his defeat at the Battle of Waterloo in 1815.

hundredth. See OLD ~.

hunting ground. See HAPPY ~.

hurry on down. The epigraph of John Wain's 1953 novel *Hurry on Down* simply has 'Hurry on down to my place, baby,/ Nobody home but me. – *Old Song*'. In fact it was a song (1947) written and performed by Nellie Lutcher, the American entertainer. Wain's novel was lumped together with others in the Angry Young Men school of the early 1950s. It was about a man hurrying down from university and doing rather unlikely jobs.

hurts me more than it hurts you, this. The traditional line spoken by teacher or parent administering corporal punishment to a child. An early occurrence is in Harry Graham's *Ruthless Rhymes* (1899):

> Father, chancing to chastise
> His indignant daughter Sue,
> Said: 'I hope you realize
> That this hurts me more than you.'

A *Punch* cartoon (11 April 1905) has the politician Augustine Birrell saying to a boy representing 'the Education Act 1902' (which Birrell was reforming): 'My boy, this can't hurt you more than it's going to hurt me.'

Also turned on its head from time to time: from James Agate's *Ego 4* (1940): '*Nouveaux Contes Scabreux*, No. 7. This is a tale of a rosy-cheeked schoolboy who turns his head to the master flogging him and winningly remarks, "Excuse me, sir, but this is pleasing me more than it is hurting you!"'

husband. See MY ~ AND I.

hush, hush, hush, here comes the bogey man. Compton Mackenzie recalled going to pantomimes in the 1890s and, in particular, hearing the Demon King sing:

> Hush, hush, hush!
> Here comes the bogey man,
> Be on your best behaviour,
> For he'll catch you if he can.

He adds (in *Echoes*, 1925): 'At these words children were fain to clutch parent or nurse or governess in panic, and I remember hearing it debated whether a theatre management was justified in terrifying children with such songs.'

I first encountered the song on the B-side of the famous Henry Hall recording of 'The Teddy Bears' Picnic' (1932).

The golf term 'bogey' apparently was derived from 'bogey-man' (as recounted in *OED2*) on an occasion in 1890. 'Bogey' meaning 'goblin, phantom or sprite' is very old indeed.

Compare COLONEL BOGEY.

hush, keep it dark! See KEEP IT DARK.

hush puppies. (1) Deep-fried corn meal batter, often served with fried fish in the Southern US. The food may have got its name from pieces being tossed to hounds with the admonition, 'Hush, puppy!' (2) Soft shoes, popular in the 1960s in the US and UK. In 1961, the Wolverine Shoe and Tanning Corp registered 'Hush Puppies' as a trade name in the US. Adrian Room in his *Dictionary of Trade Name Origins* (1982) suggests the name was adopted because it conjures up softness and suppleness. Pictures of beagle-like dogs were shown on the display material. The only connection between the food and the shoe seems to have been a would-be homeliness.

Hyde. See JEKYLL AND ~.

· I ·

I. See MY HUSBAND AND ~.

I always do my best for all my gentlemen. See *ITMA*.

I am the greatest. Muhammad Ali, formerly Cassius Clay (*b* 1942), became world heavyweight boxing champion in 1964. He admitted that he copied his 'I am the greatest . . . I am the prettiest' routine from a wrestler called Gorgeous George he had once seen in Las Vegas: 'I noticed they all paid to get in – and I said, this is a good idea!' In a moment of unusual modesty, Ali added: 'I'm not really the greatest. I only say I'm the greatest because it sells tickets.'

I am what I am. See I YAM WHAT I YAM.

I came to London to seek my fortune. 'I therefore came to London last Tuesday – as the old saying goes – "to seek my fortune" ' – Tom Driberg in a letter dated 5 June 1955 (quoted in Francis Wheen's biography, 1990). Indeed, it is an old saying (though more usually applied to young people) and probably derives from the same source as STREETS PAVED WITH GOLD – namely, the legend of Dick Whittington. Swift wrote *c* 1745: 'His father dying, he was driven to London to seek his fortune.'

I can hear you! See DON'T FORCE IT, PHOEBE.

I can't believe I ate the whole thing. See TRY IT ~ YOU'LL LIKE IT.

ice. See FIRE AND ~.

iceberg. See TIP OF THE ~.

icing on the cake, the. What finishes off something and brings it to perfection (while at the same time being a bit of an unnecessary luxury and no more than 'the trimmings'). This figurative use may only date from the mid-twentieth century. From the *Observer* (7 January 1990), concerning the imprisonment of a dictator: ' "A political jackpot" is how Lee Atwater, Bush's chief Republican campaign adviser, sees the outcome of the Panamanian invasion. "The icing on the cake," was the description of Dick Cheney, the Defence Secretary.'

I could do that. See GI'US A JOB.

I counted them all out and I counted them all back. This was, 'An elegant way of telling the truth without compromising the exigencies of military censorship,' according to the BBC's Director-General Alasdair Milne in *DG: The Memoirs of a British Broadcaster* (1988). 'I'm not allowed to say how many planes [Harrier jets from HMS *Hermes*] joined the raid, but I counted them all out and I counted them all back,' said Brian Hanrahan, a British journalist, in a report broadcast by BBC Television on 1 May 1982. Hanrahan was attempting to convey the success of a British attack on Port Stanley airport during the Falklands War. The phrase stuck.

I Cover the Waterfront. Title of a film (US, 1933) about a newspaper reporter exposing corruption, based on a book (1932) by Max Miller, a 'waterfront reporter' on the *San Diego Sun*. Hence 'cover' is in the journalistic sense. The song with this title (by John W. Green and Ed Heyman), sung notably by Billie Holiday, is unconnected with the film and sounds as if it might be about laying paving stones or some other activity. It was so successful, however, that it was later added to the soundtrack.

Since the film, 'to cover the waterfront' has meant 'to cover all aspects of a topic' or merely 'to experience something'. A woman going in to try a new nightclub in the film *Cover Girl* (US, 1944) says: 'This is it. We cover the waterfront.' In *The Wise Wound* (1978) by Penelope Shuttle and Peter Redgrove, 'she's covering the waterfront' is listed among the many slang expressions for menstruation.

idea. See A GOOD ∼, SON under *EDUCATING ARCHIE*; IT SEEMED LIKE A GOOD ∼ AT THE TIME.

I didn't get where I am today . . . In BBC TV's *The Fall and Rise of Reginald Perrin* (1976–80), 'C.J.', the boss (John Barron) would thus frequently muse. This popularized a characteristic phrase of the pompous.

I didn't know you cared! Phrase spoken after an unexpected gesture or compliment but, often ironically, when the compliment is double-edged or outright critical. Known by the 1940s. *I Didn't Know You Cared* was taken as the title of a BBC TV comedy series (1975) set in a dour North Country family.

I didn't oughter 'ave et it! The British actor and entertainer Jack Warner recounts in his book *Jack of All Trades* (1975) the occasion when this catchphrase was born. He was leaving Broadcasting House in London with Richard Murdoch: 'I had to step over the legs of a couple of fellows who were sitting in the sunshine with their backs against the wall eating their lunches from paper bags. As we passed, I heard one say to the other, "I don't know what my old woman has given me for dinner today but I didn't oughter 'ave et it." I remarked to Dickie, "If that isn't a cue for a song, I don't know what is!" It provided me with my first catchphrase to be picked out by members of the public.'

I didn't recognize you with your clothes on. A frisky line addressed to a member of the opposite sex (sometimes in jokes about doctors meeting patients at parties). Compare Groucho Marx's line in *Go West* (1940): 'Lulubelle, it's you! I didn't recognize you standing up.'

idiot('s) lantern. See BOX, THE.

idle on parade. A parade-ground, sergeant-major's term for when a soldier makes the slightest wrong movement. Paul Beale compares it with **naked on parade**, similar sergeant-major's hyperbole for, say, one button left undone in an otherwise immaculately smart turn-out. Both phrases were probably current in the 1930s. *Idle on Parade* is the title of a film (US, 1959) with Anthony Newley as a rock singer in what has been described as a 'kind of folksy British parody of Elvis Presley's controversial drafting into the US Army'.

I'd like to buy the world a Coke. See PAUSE THAT REFRESHES.

I do/I will. When taking marriage vows, which reply is correct? In the Anglican Prayer Book, the response to 'Wilt thou have this man/woman to thy wedded husband/wife . . . ?' is obviously, 'I will.' In the Order of Confirmation, to the question: 'Do ye renew the solemn promise and vow that was made . . . at your baptism?' the response is obviously, 'I do.' But in some US marriage services, the question is posed: 'Do you take so-and-so . . . ?' to which the response has to be, 'I do.' 'Will you . . .' is said to be more popular with American clergy, 'Do you . . .' at civil ceremonies. Jan de Hartog's play *The Four Poster* was turned into a musical with the title *I Do! I Do!* (1966).

I do not like this game. See under *GOON SHOW*.

I don't *believe* it! Anybody's exclamation but one that achieved catchphrase status in 1993 when spoken in a distinctive, strangulated Scots accent by the actor Richard Wilson as 'Victor Meldrew' in BBC TV's blackish comedy *One Foot In the Grave*, written by David Renwick. Meldrew, coping with enforced retirement, was in a state of permanent exasperation at modern life and at all the extraordinary misfortunes that befell him.

I don't get no respect. Catchphrase of Rodney Dangerfield (*b* 1921), US comedian popular in the 1970s/80s.

I don't mind if I do! See under *ITMA*.

. . . I *don't* think! Catchphrase reversing the statement that precedes it (compare NOT! under *WAYNE'S WORLD*). Charles Dickens in *Pickwick Papers*, Chap. 38 (1837) has: ' "Amiably disposed . . . I don't think," resumed Mr Weller in a tone of moral reproof.' *Punch* (7 April 1909) refers to it as a 'popular slang phrase'.

I don't wish to know that, kindly leave the stage. The traditional response to a corny joke in music hall, variety and, presumably, vaudeville. Usually said by a person who has been interrupted while engaged in some other activity on stage. Impossible to say when, and with whom, it started, but in the 1950s the phrase was given a new lease of life by the *GOON SHOW* on radio and by other British entertainers who still owe much to the routines and spirit of music hall. In the 1930s, the phrase was associated with Murray and Mooney (later, Mooney and King), but may have been used earlier by Dave and Joe O'Gorman. Dan Rowan used to say to Martin on *LAUGH-IN*, 'I don't want to hear about it,' in similar circumstances.

See also I SAY, I SAY, I SAY!

I dood it. The catchphrase of 'Junior, the Mean Widdle Kid' – as portrayed by Red Skelton on American radio in the 1930s. This was how he owned up to mischief. Used as the title of a Red Skelton film in 1943. The character also appeared in the *Red Skelton Show* on TV (1951–71).

I dreamed I — in my Maidenform bra. A classic slogan from the days when bras were not for burning but for dreaming about. The series, devised by the Norman Craig & Kummel agency in the US, ran for 20 years from 1949. Maidenform offered prizes up to $10,000 for dream situations that could be used in the advertising, in addition to: 'I dreamed I took the bull by the horns/Went walking/Stopped the traffic/Was a social butterfly/Rode in a gondola/Was Cleopatra . . . in my Maidenform bra.' 'I dreamed I went to blazes . . .' was illustrated by a girl in bra, fireman's helmet and boots, swinging from a fire engine.

if anything can go wrong, it will. Most commonly known as **Murphy's Law** (and indistinguishable from **Sod's Law** or **Spode's Law**), this saying dates back to the 1940s. *The Macquarie Dictionary* (1981) suggests that it was named after a character who always made mistakes, in a series of educational cartoons published by the US Navy.

CODP suggests that it was invented by George Nichols, a project manager for Northrop, the Californian aviation firm, in 1949. He developed the idea from a remark by a colleague, Captain Edward A. Murphy Jnr of the Wright Field-Aircraft Laboratory, 'If there is a wrong way to do something, then someone will do it.'

The most notable demonstration of Murphy's Law is that a piece of bread when dropped on the floor will always fall with its buttered side facing down (otherwise known as the Law of Universal Cussedness). This, however, pre-dates the promulgation of Murphy's Law. In 1867, A.D. Eichardson wrote in *Beyond Mississippi*: 'His bread never fell on the buttered side.' In 1884, James Payn composed the lines:

> I never had a piece of toast
> Particularly long and wide,
> But fell upon the sanded floor
> And always on the buttered side.

Brewer calls this an 'old north country proverb'. The corollary of this aspect of the Law is that bread always falls buttered side down *except when demonstrating the Law*!

Some have argued that the point of Captain Murphy's original observation was constructive rather than defeatist – it was a prescription for avoiding mistakes in the design of a valve for an aircraft's hydraulic system. If the valve could be fitted in more than one way, then sooner or later someone would fit it the wrong way. The idea was to design it so that the valve could only be fitted the right way.

Film titles have included *Murphy's Law* (US, 1986) and *Murphy's War* (UK, 1971).

if — did not exist, it would have to be invented. This format phrase originated with Voltaire's remark: '*Si Dieu n'existait pas, il faudrait l'inventer*' [If God did not exist, it would be necessary to invent him] (*Epîtres*, xcvi, 1770). Other examples include: 'If Austria did not exist it would have to be invented' (Frantisek Palacky, *c* 1845); 'If he [Auberon Waugh, a literary critic] did not exist, it would be unnecessary to invent him' (Desmond Elliott, literary agent, *c* 1977); 'What becomes clear is that Olivier developed his own vivid, earthy classical style as a reaction to Gielgud's more ethereal one . . . So if Gielgud did not exist would Olivier have found it necessary to invent himself?' (review in the *Observer*, 1988); 'If Tony Benn did not exist, the old Right of the Labour Party would have had to invent him' (the *Observer*, 15 October 1989).

if God had intended us to — he wouldn't have —. This format phrase is used as an argument against doing or using something, especially the aeroplane: 'If God had intended us to fly, He'd never have given us the railways' (Michael Flanders, *At the Drop of Another Hat*, 1963). In the final chapter of David Lodge's novel, *Changing Places* (1975), Morris Zapp, after a close air miss, comments: 'I always said, if God had meant us to fly, he'd have given me guts.' Attributed to Mel Brooks is the observation: 'If God had intended us to fly, He would have sent us tickets.'

From Lord Berners, *First Childhood* (1934): 'My [model flying machine] elicited a reproof from the Headmaster, who happened to see it [in *c* 1893]. "Men," he said, "were never meant to fly; otherwise God would have given them wings." The argument was convincing, if not strikingly, having been used previously, if I am not mistaken, by Mr Chadband.' (Sort of: Dickens, *Bleak House*, Chap. 19 (1853): '[Chadband] "Why can't we not fly, my friends?" [Mr Snagsby] "No wings."') In turn, one can imagine the remark being adjusted to dismiss the railway train and the motor car.

From J.B. Priestley's play *When We Are Married*, Act II (1938): *Ruby*: 'Me mother says if God had intended men to smoke He'd have put chimneys in their heads.' *Ormonroyd*: 'Tell your mother from me that if God had intended men to wear clothes He'd have put collar studs at back of their necks.'

if in doubt, strike it out. A piece of (I would say) journalist's lore is, 'If in doubt, strike it out' – meaning 'if you're not sure of a fact or about the wisdom of including an item of information or opinion, leave it out'. It may be that the advice was more specific, originally. Mark Twain in *Pudd'nhead Wilson* (1894) says: 'As to the adjective, when in doubt strike it out.' Ernest Hemingway recommended striking out adverbs, I believe.

Compare this with the advice Samuel Johnson quoted from a college tutor (30 April 1773): 'Read over your compositions, and where ever you meet with a passage which you think is particularly fine, strike it out.' Which might be recommended to journalists also.

The precise phrase appears in the notorious 'Green Book' issued *c* 1949 to guide BBC Light Entertainment producers as to which jokes were, or were not, then permissible on the radio: 'Material about which a producer has any doubts should, if it cannot be submitted to someone in higher authority, be deleted, and an artist's assurance that it has been previously broadcast is no justification for repeating it. "When in doubt, take it out" is the wisest maxim.'

Partridge/*Slang* has 'when/if in doubt, toss it out' as, curiously, a 'pharmaceutical catchphrase C20'. 'When in doubt, do nowt' is a northern English (I would say) proverb which *CODP* first finds in 1884.

if I said you had a beautiful body, would you hold it against me? A simple punning question became the title of a hit song by the American duo, the Bellamy Brothers, in 1979 (though they sang 'have' instead of 'had'). *The Naff Sex Guide* (1984) then listed it among 'Naff Pick-Up Lines'.

MONTY PYTHON used the line on 15 December 1970 (adding 'I am not infected') but, not unexpectedly, the British comedian Max Miller ('The Cheeky Chappie') (1895–1963), seems to have got there first. In a selection of his jokes once published by the *Sunday Dispatch* (and reprinted in *The Last Empires*, ed. Benny Green, 1986) we find: 'I saw a girl who was proud of her figure. Just to make conversation I asked her, "What would you do if a chap criticised your figure?" "Well," she said, "I wouldn't hold it against him."'

if it ain't broke(n), why fix it? A very modern proverb indeed. I came across it several times in late 1988, without having registered it before. In the *Independent* (3 November), a TV reviewer asked it of the Government's plans to deregulate broadcasting. On 12 November, in the same paper, this appeared about changes made in the musical *Chess* once it had opened: 'Tim Rice [the writer, said], "The notices were very good and people liked it, so we could have said, 'If it ain't broken, don't fix it.' But we felt that certain aspects weren't quite right." '

Safire, however, attributes it to Bert Lance, President Carter's Director of the Office of Management and Budget (1977), speaking on the subject of governmental reorganization.

if it's h-h-hokay with you, it's h-h-hokay with me. The stuttering catchphrase of Tubby Turner (1882–c 1935), the Lancashire-born music-hall performer.

if it's —, this must be —. *If It's Tuesday, This Must be Belgium* was the title of a 1969 film about a group of American tourists rushing around Europe. It popularized a format phrase which people could use when they were in the midst of some hectic activity, whilst also reflecting on the confused state of many tourists superficially 'doing' the sights without really knowing where they are. A *Guardian* headline (7 April 1989) on a brief visit to London by Mikhail Gorbachev: 'If It's Thursday, Then It Must Be Thatcherland'.

if it was raining . . . A series of moans by the terminally miserable/unfortunate/disaster-prone. In 1983, I heard 'if it was raining palaces I'd end up with a toilet at the bottom of the garden'. Compare the Australian: 'if it was raining palaces, I'd be hit on the head with the handle of a dunny [privy] door'; 'if it was raining pea soup, I'd only have a fork'; 'if it was raining virgins, I'd end up with a poofter'.

if seven maids with seven mops . . . In a letter to her daughter, Clementine Churchill described Tunis (23 December 1943): 'It is really a particularly dirty and unattractive town. I do not believe if seven hundred thousand mops "swept it for half a year, that they could get it clean" . . .' (Mary Soames, *Clementine Churchill*, 1979). The allusion is to Lewis Carroll, *Through the Looking-Glass* (1872), when the Walrus and the Carpenter are reflecting on 'such quantities of sand':

'If seven maids with seven mops
Swept it for half a year,
Do you suppose,' the Walrus said,
'That they could get it clear?'

if you build it, he will come. The *Observer* (5 June 1994) quoted James Cosgrove of 'telecoms giant' AT&T: 'In the movie *Field of Dreams* there is the phrase "If you build it they will come".' Not quite, there isn't. In the 1989 US movie, Kevin Costner plays an Iowa farmer who hears a voice (played by 'Himself' according to the credits) which tells him repeatedly, 'If you build it, *he* will come.' So Costner creates a baseball pitch in a field so that 'Shoeless Joe' Jackson, the discredited Chicago White Sox player of 'Say it ain't so, Joe' fame, can come back from the dead and be rehabilitated. Subsequent messages received – and too complicated to explain here – are 'Ease his pain' and 'Go the distance'.

A neat allusion to the main phrase occurred in the second *WAYNE'S WORLD* movie (1994) in which the ghost of rock star Jim Morrison inspires the teenagers to put on a rock concert called 'Waynestock'. When Morrison is asked whether big name groups will actually show up, he intones, 'If you book them, they will come.'

if you can't beat 'em, join 'em. A familiar proverb, probably American in origin in the alternative form, 'If you can't lick 'em, join 'em'. The earliest citation in the *CODP* is from Quentin Reynolds, the American writer, in 1941. Mencken had it in his dictionary, however, by 1942.

Safire calls it 'a frequent bit of advice, origin obscure, given in areas dominated by one (political) party . . . The phrase, akin to the Scottish proverb "Better bend than break", carries no connotation of surrender; it is used to indicate that the way to take over the opposition's strength is to adopt their positions and platform'.

ODCIE (1985) takes in a broader view of the phrase's use: 'If a rival faction, political party, business firm, foreign power, etc. continues to be more successful than one's own, it is better to go over to their side and get what advantages one can from the alliance.'

if you can't be good, be careful! Mencken calls it an American proverb, though *CODP*'s pedigree is mostly British, finding its first proper citation here in 1903 (from A.M. Binstead, *Pitcher in Paradise*). But in 1907, there was an American song called 'Be Good! If You Can't Be Good, be Careful!'

It is a nudging farewell, sometimes completed with 'and if you can't be careful, name it after me' – or 'buy a pram'. The same sort of farewell remark as **don't do anything I wouldn't do!**

if you can't stand the heat, get out of the kitchen. In 1960, former US President Harry S Truman said: 'Some men can make decisions and some cannot. Some men fret and delay under criticism. I used to have a saying that applies here, and I note that some people have picked it up.'

When Truman announced that he would not stand again as President, *Time* (28 April 1952) had him give a 'down-to-earth' reason for his retirement, quoting a favourite expression of his military jester Major General Harry Vaughan', namely, 'If you can't stand the heat, get out of the kitchen.'

The attribution is usually given to Truman himself but it may not be what he said at all. 'Down-to-earth' is not quite how I would describe this remark, but that would do very nicely for 'If you can't stand the stink, get out of the shit-house'. I have only hearsay evidence for this, but given Truman's reputation for salty expressions, it is not improbable.

Bartlett quotes Philip D. Lagerquist of the Harry S Truman Library as saying, 'President Truman has used variations of the aphorism . . . for many years, both orally and in his writings' (1966). Note the 'variations'.

if you know a better 'ole – go to it. This comes from the caption to a cartoon (1915) by the British cartoonist, Bruce Bairnsfather, depicting 'Old Bill', up to his waist in mud on the Somme during the First World War. Two films (UK, 1918; US, 1926), based on the strip, were called *The Better 'Ole* and followed a musical with the title staged in London and New York (1917–18).

if you know what I mean, and I think you do. See JOE BOB SAYS CHECK IT OUT.

if you'll excuse the pun! Of the kind used by the humourless, when having sunk to one. So ghastly, I feel like calling it a cliché, which it isn't really. Alternatives are **pardon the pun** and **no pun intended.** Nothing new about it: in *Pictures from Italy* (1846), Charles Dickens wrote, 'The ten fingers, which are always – I intend no pun – at hand.'

if you've never been to Manchester, you've never lived! See under RAY'S A LAUGH.

if you want anything, just whistle. This is not a direct quotation, but is derived, from lines in the film *To Have and Have Not* (1945). What Lauren Bacall says to Humphrey Bogart (and not the other way round) is: 'You know you don't have to act with me, Steve. You don't have to say anything, and you don't have to do anything. Not a thing. Oh, maybe just whistle. You know how to whistle, don't you, Steve? You just put your lips together and blow.'

if you want to get ahead, get a hat. A slogan for the (British) Hat Council – and curiously memorable. Quoted in 1965, but also remembered from the early 1950s, and perhaps even dating from the 1930s.

ignorance. See BRUTE FORCE AND ~.

I go – I come back! See under ITMA.

I gotta horse! 'Ras Prince Monolulu' was a British racing tipster who flourished – perhaps the only nationally famous one of his kind – from the 1930s to the 1950s. His real name was Peter Carl McKay, he was black, and he used to wander around dressed up like a Masai warrior, or similar. He died in 1965.

Partridge/*Catch Phrases* renders his cry as 'I got an 'orse!' or 'I gotta norse!' and finds that it was coined when Monolulu was trying to outdo a racetrack evangelist who carried the placard 'I got Heaven'.

There seem to be many ways of reproducing the cry. However, there is a record on which he sings it – Regal MR 812 – but I've not been able to trace a copy – and there the title is given as 'I got a 'orse'.

I've Got a Horse appears to have been the title of a Noel Gay revue in London (1938) and definitely of a British film, featuring the singer Billy Fury, in 1965. A black version of Cinderella, originally entitled *I Gotta Shoe*, was presented in London in 1976 and may distantly allude to this phrase.

I hae me doots. Scottish pronunciation of 'I have my doubts' – slightly affected, patronizing and irritating. In a Joyce Grenfell sketch, 'Head Girl' from *The Little Revue* (1939): 'It would be great fun to give Miss Torpor a present . . . Mavis suggests silver candlesticks . . . if we get enough £.s.d . . . about which I Hae Me Doots.'

I hate J.R. See WHO SHOT J.R.?

I have seen the elephant. See ELEPHANT, TO SEE THE.

I haven't been so happy since my grandmother caught her tit in a mangle. Daley Thompson, the British athlete, actually had the nerve to say this on winning a gold medal in the decathlon at the 1984 Los Angeles Olympics.

More commonly, it would go, 'I haven't *laughed* so much since . . .' The rest can vary. It might be 'mother/aunt' and 'left tit/tits'. There is a version in Nicholas Monsarrat's *The Cruel Sea* (1951), which hints at a probable origin in the services. Alan Bennett in *Forty Years On* (1968) has a victorious rugby team sing:

> I haven't laughed so much since
> Grandma died
> And Aunty Mabel caught her left titty in
> the mangle
> And whitewashed the ceiling.

See under HELL! SAID THE DUCHESS . . . for an 1890s citation.

I hear you. See OH ARR . . .

I just don't care any more! See SHUT THAT DOOR!

Ike. See I LIKE ~ .

I know I packed it. See NIGHT STARVATION.

I like Ike. These words began appearing on buttons in 1947 as the Second World War US General, Dwight David Eisenhower, began to be spoken of as a possible presidential nominee (initially as a Democrat). By 1950, Irving Berlin was including one of his least memorable songs, 'They Like Ike', in *Call Me Madam*, and 15,000 people at a rally in Madison Square Gardens were urging Eisenhower to return from a military posting in Paris and run as a Republican in 1952, with the chant 'We like Ike'. It worked. The three sharp monosyllables, and the effectiveness of the repeated 'i' sound in 'I like Ike', made it an enduring slogan throughout the 1950s.

I like the backing. See under I'LL GIVE IT FOIVE.

I'll 'ave to ask me Dad. See under ITMA.

I'll be a dirty bird!, well. Catchphrase of the American comedian George Gobel, star of *The George Gobel Show* (1954–60) on NBC TV and then CBS TV. According to Brooks & Marsh, *The Complete Directory to Prime Time Network TV Shows* (1981), 'low-key comedian George Gibel, known affectionately as "Lonesome George" . . . [was] for a time one of TV's top hits, and his familiar sayings ("Well, I'll be a dirty bird!", **"You don't hardly get those no more"**) became bywords.'

I'll be back! A phrase that caught on following its menacing use by Arnold Schwarzenegger in *The Terminator* (1984), in which he plays a time-travelling robot who terminates his opponents with extreme prejudice (ripping their hearts out, etc.). Coincidentally, the last words of the film

Pimpernel Smith (UK, 1941) are: 'I'll be back . . . we'll all be back.' These are spoken by Leslie Howard as a professor of archaeology who goes into war-torn Europe to rescue refugees.

I'll be last in this book. See BY HOOK OR BY CROOK . . .

I'll be leaving you now, sir . . . The stock phrase when anticipating a tip – given new life by Claud Snudge (Bill Fraser) in Granada TV's *Bootsie and Snudge* (1960–62). He was a doorman at a London club. The phrase was a stock one by 28 June 1911 when a caption to a *Punch* cartoon read: 'Foreign Waiter (who has forgotten the right formula for the usual hint, "I am leaving you now, Sir," to startled guest. "YOU WILL NEVARE SEE ME NO MORE, SIR." '

I'll drink to that! 'I agree with what you say or the course of action you propose' – but used only in light-hearted situations. American origin, by the 1950s. Had something of a revival when Dick Martin took to saying it to Dan Rowan in *Rowan and Martin's Laugh-In* (NBC TV, 1960s).

illegal immoral or fattening. Alexander Woollcott wrote in *The Knock at the Stage Door* (1933): 'All the things I really like to do are either illegal, immoral, or fattening.' Compare the song, 'It's Illegal, It's Immoral Or It Makes You Fat' by Griffin, Hecht, and Bruce and popularized in the UK by the Beverley Sisters (1950s).

illegitimi non carborundum. This cod-Latin phrase – supposed to mean 'Don't let the bastards grind you down' – was used by US General 'Vinegar Joe' Stilwell as his motto during the Second World War, though it is not suggested he devised it. Partridge/*Catch Phrases* gives it as '*illegitimis*' and its origins in British army intelligence very early on in the same war. Something like the phrase has also been reported from 1929.

'Carborundum' is, in fact, the trade name of a very hard substance composed of silicon carbide, used in grinding.

The same meaning is also conveyed by the phrase **nil carborundum . . .** (as in the title of a play by Henry Livings, 1962) – a

pun upon the genuine Latin *nil desperandum* [never say die – lit.: there is nought to be despaired of] which comes from '*nil desperandum est Teucro duce et auspice Teucro*' [nothing is to be despaired of with Teucer as leader and protector] (Horace, *Odes*, I.vii.27).

Perhaps because it is a made-up one, the phrase takes many forms, e.g.: '*nil illegitimis* . . .', '*nil bastardo illegitimi* . . .', '*nil bastardo carborundum* . . .' etc. When the Rt Rev. David Jenkins, the Bishop of Durham, was unwise enough to make use of the phrase at a private meeting in March 1985, a cloth-eared journalist reported him as having said, '*Nil desperandum illegitimi* . . .'

I'll forget my own name in a minute. See under ITMA.

I'll give it five. That rarity – a catchphrase launched by a member of the British public. Not that Janice Nicholls, a Birmingham girl conscripted on to the 'Spin-a-Disc' panel of ABC TV's pop show *Thank Your Lucky Stars* in c 1963 could avoid a type of celebrity for long. Awarding points to newly-released records in her local dialect ('five' was pronounced 'foyve') and declaring (as if in mitigation for some awful performance) 'but **I like the backing . . .**', she became a minor celebrity herself. She even made a record called 'I'll Give it Five' (coupled with 'The Wednesbury Madison') – which later she was prepared to admit was worth about *minus* five.

When she started appearing, Janice was only sixteen, had just left school and was working as a junior clerk/telephonist at a local factory. She was soon meeting 'all the stars except Elvis' and became the pin-up of three ships, a submarine and a fire station. Janice told me in 1980: 'I think it was just the accent really. It's a broad Black Country accent, y'know. I think it must have took the fancy of a lot of people. So they just kept asking me to go back and it ended up being three years before I finished.'

I'll give you a bell. See BELL, I'LL . . .

I'll give you the results in reverse order. Eric Morley founded the Miss World beauty contest in 1951. He assured himself a small measure of fame each year by appearing in the TV show and announcing the winners in the order No. 3, No. 2, No. 1. In consequence, whenever anyone has to give similar results in this way, it is said they are being given **in Miss World order**.

I'll go to bed at noon. Phrase from the Fool's last words in Shakespeare's *King Lear*, III.vi.83 (1605): 'And I'll go to bed at noon,' after Lear has said: 'We'll go to supper i'th'morning.' Used as the title of a book (1944), subtitled 'A Soldier's Letters to His Sons', by the actor Stephen Haggard, published posthumously. Haggard had played the Fool in the 1940 Old Vic production of *Lear* with John Gielgud.

I'll go to the foot of our stairs! An old northern English expression of amazement – meaning, presumably, that the short walk to the place mentioned will allow the speaker to recover equanimity. Used by Tommy Handley in BBC radio's *ITMA* (1940s) and elsewhere.

I'll have what she's having. A quotation hovering on the edge of becoming a catchphrase. In the film *When Harry Met Sally* (US, 1989), Meg Ryan fakes an orgasm in the middle of a crowded restaurant. The punch line to the scene is provided by Estelle Reiner as an older woman sitting at a nearby table. When a waiter asks what she would like to order, she says, 'I'll have what she's having.'

I'll try anything once. Meaning, 'there's always a first time' and often said somewhat fatalistically. Mencken has 'I am always glad to try anything once' as an 'American saying not recorded before the nineteenth century'. Certainly current by 1921.

I Love/♥ —. In June 1977, the New York State Department of Commerce launched a campaign to attract tourists. The first commercial showed people enjoying themselves in outdoor activities – fishing, horseback riding, camping, and so forth. Each one said something like, 'I'm from New Hampshire, but I love New York,' 'I'm from Cape Cod, but I love New York,' and ended with a man in a camping scene

saying, 'I'm from Brooklyn, but I loooove New York.'

Since then 'I Love New York' has become one of the best-known advertising slogans in the world but has been swamped by the use of the 'I Love —' formula on stickers and T-shirts to promote almost every other place in the world (and much else), particularly with the word 'love' replaced by a heart shape.

Charlie Moss at the Wells, Rich, Greene agency is credited with having coined the phrase – though maybe he had heard the song 'How About You?' (lyrics by Ralph Freed, music by Burton Lane) which includes the line 'I like New York in June' and was written for the Garland/Rooney film *Babes on Broadway* (1941). Earlier, Cole Porter had written 'I Happen to Like New York' for his show *The New Yorkers* (1930).

I love it but it doesn't love me. A cliché of conversation – what people say to soften the refusal of what they have been offered – usually food or drink. And they have been using it for many a year. Jonathan Swift lists it in *Polite Conversation* (1738):

> *Lady Smart*: Madam, do you love bohea tea?
> *Lady Answerall*: Why, madam, I must confess I do love it; but it does not love me . . .'

I love my wife, but oh you kid! An American expression addressed to an attractive girl – possibly amounting to a not very serious 'pass', but indicating that despite the tug of marital fidelity it is still possible for a married man to dream a little. Popular 1916–40, though Flexner (1976) has it by 1908. 'Oh you kid!' has had a life of its own as a rather meaningless exclamation.

I'm a ba-a-a-ad boy! Shy admission from chubby American comedian Lou Costello (1906–59) to his partner Bud Abbott (1895–1974) in their many films of the 1940s. Quoted by Eric Morecambe in *There's No Answer To That* (1981) as 'H'im a bad boy!'

I'm a cop. See under DRAGNET.

I'm all behind – like the cow's tail. What people say when they are behind with their tasks, and have done so since the nineteenth century. 'C.H. Rolph' wrote in *London Particulars* (1980): 'Grandma Hewitt [his grandmother] was a walking repository, rather than a dictionary, of clichés and catchphrases; and I have often wished she could have been known to Mr Eric Partridge during the compilation of his delectable dictionaries. Both she and I . . . could pre-date many of [his] attributions. Here are four examples . . . all of which were common currency in my Edwardian childhood: "Just what the doctor ordered", "Are you kidding?", "Cheats never prosper", and "All behind like a cow's tail".'

This last is one of a number of ritual additions (like AS THE ART MISTRESS SAID . . ., but without the innuendo). Others are KNICKERS ON THE LINE and EVERY LITTLE HELPS. . . .

I'm all right, Jack. Partridge/*Catch Phrases* suggests that this saying may have arisen c 1880 in the form 'Fuck you, Jack, I'm all right'. Bowdlerized versions 'typified concisely the implied and often explicit arrogance of many senior officers towards the ranks', in the *Navy*, hence the use of 'Jack', the traditional name for a sailor since c 1700. Hence, the example included in Sir David Bone's *The Brassbounder* (1910), one of Bone's many novels set on the sea and based on his own experiences (he rose to be Commodore of the Anchor Line): 'It's "Damn you, Jack – I'm all right!" with you chaps.'

In the mid-twentieth century, the phrase came to represent the selfish, uncaring attitude of any person or group of people. *I'm All Right Jack* was the title of a British film (1959) satirizing labour relations, bosses and the trade unions.

I'm a shirt short! See HOW TICKLED I AM.

I'm as mad as hell and I'm not taking any more! Political slogan adopted in 1978 by Howard Jarvis (1902–86), the California social activist, when campaigning to have property taxes reduced. Jarvis entitled a book *I'm Mad as Hell* but duly credited Paddy Chayevsky with the coinage. Chayevsky wrote the film *Network* (1976) in which Peter Finch played a TV pundit-cum-evangelist who exhorted his viewers to get mad: 'I want you to get up right now and go to the window, open it and stick your head out and yell: "I'm as mad as hell, and I'm not going to take this any more!" '

I'm a stranger here myself, (no, I'm sorry). Excuse given for inability or unwillingness to be of assistance to someone who comes up to you in the street asking, say, for directions. 'I'm a stranger 'ere myself' occurs in the caption to a *Punch* cartoon (16 July 1881). 'I don't know why-a-no-chicken. I'm a stranger here myself' is a Groucho Marx line from *Cocoanuts* (US, 1929). *I'm a Stranger Here Myself* is the title of a book (1938) by Ogden Nash and also of a later song with lyrics by Nash and music by Kurt Weill from the show *One Touch of Venus* (1943). It is also a line spoken in Nicholas Ray's camp Western *Johnny Guitar* (1953) and the title of books by John Seymour (1978), 'the story of a Welsh farm', and by Deric Longden (1994) – described as a view of 'Huddersfield seen as a foreign country'.

I'm Bart Simpson, who the hell are you? See under SIMPSONS, THE.

I'm black and I'm proud. See SAY IT LOUD.

I'm dreaming, oh, my darling love, of thee! The British comedy performer Cyril Fletcher (*b* 1913) recalls in *Nice One, Cyril* (1978) how he was persuaded to broadcast Edgar Wallace's poem 'Dreaming of Thee'/ 'The Lovesick Tommy's Dream of Home' in 1938. He did it in an extraordinary voice – a Cockney caricature – and the constant refrain of each verse got 'yells of delight'. It 'made' him, he says, and later when he returned to London for a repeat performance he was on a bus and the conductor was saying 'Dreaming of thee' to every passenger, in a passable imitation of Fletcher's funny voice, as he gave them their tickets.

Fletcher's customary cry when embarking on one of his Odd Odes was **pin back your lugholes!** (i.e. 'lend me your ears')(by 1939). Other Fletcherisms have included **thanking you!** (pronounced 'thenking yew', and as *Thanking Yew* used as the title of a BBC radio series, 1940). As 'yerse, thanking ycw!', the phrase was first spoken by the character 'Percy Parker' in a mid-1930s series of sketches, *The Lodger*. Also **ours is a nice 'ouse ours is** – from the possibly Cockney and ironic description which Partridge/*Catch Phrases* dates from 1925. The sort of argument a respectable matron might advance to prevent any behaviour in the home of which she might disapprove.

I'm/I'll be a monkey's uncle, well. Expressing astonishment, surprise. *OED2* finds it established in a 1926 'wise-crack' dictionary, which rather rules out one origin I have been given for it – that it had something to do with the famous 'Scopes' or 'Monkey Trial' (of a teacher who taught evolutionary theory in Tennessee.) As the trial only took place the year before, the connection is unlikely. As, too, is anything to with the fact that in London East End slang a 'monkey' = £500 and an 'uncle' = pawnbroker. Partridge/*Slang* has it of American origin.

I meanter say! This was one of the phrases used by the British music-hall comedian, Sir George Robey (1869–1954). Neville Cardus recalled him arriving on a stage filled with girls posing as nude Greek statues: 'I can see now his eyebrows going up and him saying, "Well, I mean to say, I mean to say."'

But it is quite a common expression (and spelt this way to emphasize the pronunciation) as a kind of slightly exasperated apology or exclamation. I have come across it in a Frank Richards 'Billy Bunter' story in a 1915 edition of *The Magnet*. It is also used by Joe Gargery in Charles Dickens, *Great Expectations*, Chap. 27 (1860–61).

I mean that most sincerely, folks. When Hughie Green was introducing *Opportunity Knocks*, the British TV talent show (1956–77), he may never have said this (or 'sincerely, friends'). The point is that everyone thought he had and it seemed typical of his manner. I believe that the impressionist Mike Yarwood claimed on the *Parkinson* TV chat show that he had invented the phrase as part of his take-off of Green.

I'm —, fly me. A slogan for National Airlines in the US, current in *c* 1971 – e.g. 'I'm Margie, fly me', referring to (supposedly actual) air hostesses whose pictures appeared in the advertisements. The campaign aroused the ire of feminist groups (another suggestive line used was, 'I'm going to fly you like you've never been flown before'). The group 10 CC had a hit with 'I'm Mandy Fly Me', obviously inspired by the slogan, in 1976. Wall's Sausages later parodied it in Britain with, 'I'm meaty, fry me' (current 1976).

I'm free! From the BBC TV comedy series *Are You Being Served?* (1974–84). The lilting cry of Mr Humphries (John Inman), the lighter-than-air menswear salesman of Grace Bros. store. In the *Independent* (10 April 1994), it was reported: 'Early on, everyone got to say it. You were meant to look left, look right, then say, "I'm free." But in one episode a colonel turned up and asked for a woman's dress. Inman threw his ties in the air: "*I'm freeeee!!!*" From then on, the writers always gave him the line.'

I'm going down now, sir! See under DON'T FORGET THE DIVER!

I'm goin' back to the wagon, boys – these shoes are killin' me. Grand Old Opry, the Nashville country and western venue, was featured in network radio broadcasts until 1957. At one time, the *Grand Ole Opry* show featured an MC, Whitey Ford, who was known as the 'Duke of Paducah'. And this was his catchphrase.

I'm going to make him an offer he can't refuse. In 1969, Mario Puzo (*b* 1920) published his novel about the Mafia called *The Godfather*. It gave to the language a new expression which, as far as one can tell, was Mr Puzo's invention. Johnny Fontane, a singer, desperately wants a part in a movie and goes to see his godfather, Don Corleone, for help. All the contracts have been signed and there is no chance of the studio chief changing his mind. Still, the godfather promises Fontane he will get him the part. As he says of the studio chief, 'He's a businessman. I'll make him an offer he can't refuse.'

In the 1971 film, this was turned into the

following dialogue: 'In a month from now this Hollywood big shot's going to give you what you want.' 'Too late, they start shooting in a week.' 'I'm going to make him an offer he can't refuse.'

In 1973, Jimmy Helms had a hit with the song 'Gonna Make You An Offer You Can't Refuse'.

I'm in charge! The British entertainer Bruce Forsyth (*b* 1928) first achieved fame as an entertainer when host of the ATV show *Sunday Night at the London Palladium* (from 1958). One night he was surpervising 'Beat the Clock', a game involving members of the audience. A young couple was in a muddle, throwing plates at a see-saw table. Bruce Forsyth recalled (1980): 'We had a particularly stroppy contestant. In the end I just turned round and told him, "Hold on a minute . . . I'm in charge!" It just happened, but the audience loved it and it caught on.' Lapel badges began appearing with the slogan, foremen had it painted on their hard hats. The phrase suited Forsyth's mock-bossy manner to a tee.

See also *GENERATION GAME*.

I'm looking for someone to love. See under *BEYOND OUR KEN*.

immoral. See ILLEGAL ∼ OR FATTENING.

I'm mortified! See GOODNIGHT, MRS CALABASH . . .

I'm not a number, I'm a free man. First shown on British TV in 1967, *The Prisoner*, Patrick McGoohan's unusual series about a man at odds with a '*1984*'-type world, acquired a new cult following in the late 1970s. The McGoohan character was 'Political Prisoner Number Six'. **Six of one** was another phrase from the series. The Six of One Appreciation Society had 2000 members in 1982. (The saying 'Six of one, half a dozen of the other' was current by 1836.)

I'm only here for the beer. In 1971, a visiting American advertising copywriter, Ros Levenstein, contributed this phrase to a British campaign for the Double Diamond brand. It passed into the language as an inconsequential catchphrase, though – from the advertiser's point of view – it was not a good slogan because it came detached from the particular brand of beer.

ODCIE glosses it thus: 'We don't pretend to be present in order to help, show goodwill, etc. but just to get the drink, or other hospitality.' Indeed, in September 1971, Prince Philip attended a champagne reception at Burghley. 'Don't look at me,' he was quoted as saying, 'I'm only here for the beer.'

See also DOUBLE DIAMOND WORKS WONDERS, A.

important. See — IS TOO ∼.

impossible. See DREAM THE ∼ DREAM; MISSION ∼.

impossible takes a little longer. See DIFFICULT . . .

I'm sorry, I'll read that again. The BBC radio newsreader's traditional apology for a stumble was registered as a cliché when the phrase was taken as the title of a long-running radio comedy show (1964–73) featuring ex-Cambridge Footlights performers.

I must love you and leave you. See under LOVE ME OR LEAVE ME.

I'm worried about Jim. Ellis Powell played the eponymous heroine of BBC radio's *Mrs Dale's Diary* (1948–69) and this is what she always seemed to be confiding to that diary about her doctor husband. Although she may not have spoken the phrase very often, it was essential in parodies of the programme. Her successor in the part, Jessie Matthews, definitely once had the line, 'I'm afraid one thing's never going to change: I shall always worry about you, Jim.'

in and out – like a dog at a fair. Irritating – like a child running in and out of the house. It appears in R.H. Barham's poem 'The Jackdaw of Rheims', published with *The Ingoldsby Legends* in 1840. The eponymous bird busies itself on the Cardinal's table:

In and out
Through the motley rout,
That little jackdaw kept hopping about:
Here and there,
Like a dog at a fair,
Over comfits and cates [dainties],
And dishes and plates . . .

Barham seems, however, to have been using an already-established expression. G.L. Apperson in his *English Proverbs and Proverbial Phrases* (1929) finds 'As sprites in the haire, Or dogges in the ffayre' by 1520. G.L. Gower's *Glossary of Surrey Words* (1893) has the version: 'They didn't keep nothing reg'lar, it was all over the place like a dog at a fair.'

in bed with my favourite Trollope. An archetypal punning joke. Chips Channon, the diarist, writes on 4 April 1943: 'At Wells we went over the Cathedral, and then to the Palace where we lunched with the Bishop . . . Much talk of Barchester, "there is nothing I like better than to lie on my bed for an hour with my favourite Trollope", the Bishop said, to everybody's consternation.' ('Trollop' has meant a 'slut, morally loose woman' since the seventeenth century.) Kenneth Horne got into trouble on *Beyond Our Ken* (BBC radio, early 1960s) when he said that there was nothing he liked more of a cold winter's evening than to curl up on the hearth rug with Enid Blyton.

inch. See EVERY ~ A GENTLEMAN.

include me out! A famous and typical 'Goldwynism', that is a remark made by the Hollywood film producer Samuel Goldwyn (1882–1974), and meaning, 'Leave me out of your plan'. Goldwyn had a habit of massacring the English language in a way that nonetheless conveyed vividly what he wanted to say. This phrase apparently arose when Goldwyn and Jack L. Warner were in disagreement over a labour dispute. Busby Berkeley, who had made his first musical for Goldwyn, was discovered moonlighting for Warner Brothers. Goldwyn said to Warner: 'How can we sit together and deal with this industry if you're going to do things like this to me? If this is the way you do it, gentlemen, include me out!'

Many Goldwynisms are invented, but Goldwyn himself might appear to have acknowledged this one when speaking at Balliol College, Oxford, on 1 March 1945: 'For years I have been known for saying "Include me out" but today I am giving it up for ever.'

inconspicuous. See under AS BUSY AS . . .

inconvenience. See DEEPLY REGRET ANY ~ . . .

indeedy-doody! American affirmative, noted in TV's *The Muppet Show* (1980 series). *DOAS* finds 'indeedy' on its own by 1856, as in 'yes, indeedy' or 'no, indeedy'.

India. See WHEN PEOPLE ARE STARVING IN ~.

Indians. See TOO MANY CHIEFS . . .

indoors. See 'ER ~.

indubitably! See under OH, CALAMITY!

industrial action. Used in British journalism for a strike or stoppage, and thus something of a cliché denoting, rather, 'inaction'. An odd coinage, which was established by 1970. There even used to be the occasional 'Day of Action' on which no one did any work.

I never promised you a rose garden. Used by Joanne Greenberg ('Hannah Green') as the title of a best-selling (American) novel in 1964 (film US, 1977), and as a line in the song 'Rose Garden' in 1968. I take it to mean: 'It wasn't going to be roses, roses all the way between us – or a bed of roses – but maybe it's still acceptable.'

Fernando Collor de Mello, President of Brazil, said in a TV address (reported 26 June 1990) to his shaken countrymen: 'I never promised you a rose garden . . . following the example of developed countries, we are also cutting state spending.'

infant phenomenon, an. From the stage billing of Ninetta Crummles (who has been ten years old for at least five years) in

Nicholas Nickleby (1838–9) by Charles Dickens. The term also appears earlier in *Pickwick Papers*, Chap. 26, (1836–7) when Sam Weller says to Master Bardwell: 'Tell her I want to speak to her, will you my hinfant fernomenon?' This suggests that the phrase was in general use or was something Dickens had picked up from an actual case. In 1837, the eight-year-old Jean Davenport was merely billed as 'the most celebrated juvenile actress of the day'. George Parker Bidder (*b* 1806) who possessed extraordinary arithmetical abilities had been exhibited round the country as a child, billed as 'the calculating phenomenon'.

in God we trust – all others pay cash. After the Washington summit between Mikhail Gorbachev and Ronald Reagan in December 1987, the US Secretary of State George Schultz commented on a Russian slogan that Reagan had made much of: '"Trust but verify" is really an ancient saying in the United States, but in a different guise. Remember the storekeeper who was a little leery of credit, and he had a sign in his store that said, IN GOD WE TRUST – ALL OTHERS CASH?' Referring to the verification procedures over arms reductions signed by the leaders in Washington, Shultz said, 'This is the cash.'

Mencken in 1942 was listing 'In God we trust; all others must pay cash' as an 'American saying'. 'In God we trust' has been the official national motto of the United States since 1956, when it superseded '*E Pluribus Unum*', but had been known since 1864 when it was first put on a two-cent bronze coin.

There is a similar joke in the British Isles – of the type printed on small cards and sold for display in pubs and shops. It made an appearance as a quote in the early 1940s in Flann O'Brien's column for the *Irish Times*: 'We have come to an arrangement with our bankers. They have agreed not to sell drink. We, on our part, have agreed not to cash cheques.'

ingredient. See PRICELESS ~.

in like Flynn. Someone who is 'in like Flynn' is a quick seducer – at least, according to the Australian use of the

phrase. Appropriately, it is derived from the name of Errol Flynn (1909–59), the Australian-born film actor. It alludes to his legendary bedroom prowess, though the phrase can also mean that a person simply seizes an offered opportunity (of any kind).

According to *The Intimate Sex Lives of Famous People* (Irving Wallace *et al*, 1981), Flynn frowned on the expression when it became popular, especially among servicemen, in the Second World War. It 'implied he was a fun-loving rapist', though 'in fact, Flynn's reputation stemmed partly from his having been charged with statutory rape'. After a celebrated trial, he was acquitted. Nevertheless, he 'boasted that he had spent between 12,000 and 14,000 nights making love'.

Rather weakly, a US film of 1967 was entitled *In Like Flint*.

Partridge/*Catch Phrases* turns up an American version which refers to Ed Flynn, a Democratic machine politician in the Bronx, New York City, in the 1940s. Here the meaning is simply 'to be in automatically' – as his candidates would have been.

in Miss World order. See I'LL GIVE YOU THE RESULTS . . .

innocent. See ONLY THE NAMES HAVE BEEN CHANGED . . . under DRAGNET.

in office but not in power. When Norman Lamont was sacked as Britain's Chancellor of the Exchequer in June 1993, he caused a slight stir in the House of Commons during his 'resignation' statement, by saying of the Government: 'We give the impression of being in office but not in power.' A shaft, but not a new one. As A.J.P. Taylor noted in his *English History 1914–45*, writing of Ramsay MacDonald as Prime Minister of a minority government in 1924: 'The Labour government recognized that they could make no fundamental changes, even if they knew what to make: they were "in office, but not in power".'

inquiries. See HELPING THE POLICE WITH THEIR ~.

in song and story. A somewhat literary tag, probably best known from W.S. Gilbert's lyrics for *The Pirates of Penzance* (1879):

> Go, ye heroes, go to glory,
> Though you die in combat gory,
> Ye shall live in song and story.

An earlier occurrence is in Charles J. Lever, *Jack Hinton the Guardsman* (1843): 'To lighten the road by song and story.'

Instant Sunshine. Name of a British cabaret group (formed 1966) which sings its own humorous songs echoes the title of a Cambridge undergraduate revue *Instant Laughter – Just Add Water*, performed not long before. 'Instant Karma' became the title of a John Lennon song (1970). The group was also 'instant' in that it was formed very quickly when the cabaret booked for a hospital ball failed to materialize. The first of all the many 'instant' things – coffee, soup, tan – was probably Instant Postum, the American breakfast cereal (1912). In February 1980, Margaret Thatcher told TV viewers, 'We didn't promise you instant sunshine.' The phrase is also used in the RAF as a euphemism for the explosion of a nuclear device. Hence the dropping of nuclear bombs can be described as 'releasing buckets of instant sunshine'.

instinctively. See ONE ~ KNOWS . . .

integrity. See IT'S ABSOLUTELY VITAL . . .

interrupted. See AS I WAS SAYING . . .

in the buff. See BUFF.

in the pipeline. Meaning 'in train, on the way', this idiom is now a cliché. The *OED2* finds it in used by 1955. 'We have several more [test-tube] babies in the pipeline' – said a doctor on BBC Radio in 1985.

In Town Tonight. From 1933 to 1960 this was the nearest BBC radio came to a chat show. It was introduced by what now sounds a very quaint montage of 'The Knightsbridge March' by Eric Coates, traffic noises, the voice of a woman selling violets in Piccadilly Circus, and then a stentorian voice – which I always believed (wrongly) to be that of Lord Reith – shouting '**Stopppp!**' Then an announcer would intone: '**Once again we stop the mighty roar of London's traffic and from the great crowds we bring you some of the interesting people who have come by land, sea and air to be "In Town Tonight".**'

At the end of the programme, to get the traffic moving again, the stentorian voice would bellow, '**Carry on, London!'** Various people were 'The Voice' but I am told that Freddie Grisewood was the first.

in your face (usually **in yer face**). An adjectival phrase meaning 'upfront, not hidden' and, reflecting aggressive behaviour, perhaps derived from 'I'll shove this fist right in your face'. An 'in yer face' performance at a theatre would be one where the actor confronted the audience directly. A buzz-phrase of the early 1990s, it made an early appearance in March 1991 as the title of the theme tune from the Channel 4 TV programme *The Word*, recorded by 808 State. From the *Sunday Times* (28 February 1993): 'This country has never particularly enjoyed its sex "in yer face", as young folk say nowadays. Behind your back, under your heaving stays, beyond the twitching curtains of Bennettland fine, but not explicit.'

in your heart you know I'm/he's right. Senator Barry Goldwater's much-parodied slogan when he attempted to unseat President Lyndon Johnson in the 1964 US presidential election. Come-backs included: 'In your guts, you know he's nuts' and 'You know in your heart he's right – far right'.

in your shell-like (ear). A phrase used when asking to have a 'quiet word' with someone: '(let me have a word) in your ear' is all it means, but it makes gentle fun of a poetic simile. Thomas Hood's *Bianca's Dream* (1827) has: 'Her small and shell-like ear'. *The Complete Naff Guide* (1983) has 'a word in your shell-like ear' among 'naff things schoolmasters say'.

I only a(r)sked! Quite the most popular British catchphrase of the late 1950s. Bernard Bresslaw (1934–93) played a large, gormless army private – 'Popeye' Popplewell – in Granada TV's *The Army Game* from 1957 to 1962. This was his response when anyone put him down and the phrase occurred in the very first episode. A feature film for the cinema called *I Only Arsked* was made in 1958.

Irish Question, the. The political/ historical term for the issue of whether Ireland should be granted Home Rule by the British in the nineteenth century. W.E. Gladstone in the House of Commons (4 April 1893) declared: 'We say that the Irish question is the curse of this House.' Sellar and Yeatman in *1066 and All That* (1930) write: '[Gladstone] spent his declining years trying to guess the answer to the Irish question; unfortunately, whenever he was getting warm, the Irish secretly changed the question.'

Iron Curtain, the. The imaginary dividing line between East and West blocs in Europe, caused by the hard-line tactics of the Soviet Union after the Second World War. In a speech at Fulton, Missouri (5 March 1946) Winston Churchill said: 'From Stettin in the Baltic to Trieste in the Adriatic, an iron curtain has descended across the Continent.' The phrase in this context dates back to the 1920s, and Churchill had already used it in telegrams to President Truman and in the House of Commons.

iron fist/hand in a velvet glove, an. Unbending ruthlessness or firmness covered by a veneer of courtesy and gentle manners. Thomas Carlyle in *Latter-Day Pamphlets* (1850) writes: 'Soft speech and manner, yet with an inflexible rigour of command . . . "iron hand in a velvet glove", as Napoleon defined it.' The Emperor Charles V may have said it earlier.

Iron Lady, the. Nickname of Margaret Thatcher, British Prime Minister from 1979–90. On 19 January 1976, she said in a speech: 'The Russians are bent on world dominance . . . the Russians put guns before butter.' Within a few days, the Soviet Defence Ministry newspaper *Red Star* had accused the 'Iron Lady' of seeking to revive the Cold War. The article wrongly suggested that she was known by this nickname in the UK at that time, although the headline over a profile by Marjorie Proops in the *Daily Mirror* of 5 February 1975 had been 'The IRON MAIDEN'.

Iron Maiden. The name of a British heavy metal group of the 1980s derived from 'The Iron Maiden of Nuremberg', a medieval instrument of torture in the form of a woman-shaped box with spiked doors which closed in on the victim.

— is —. A cliché of sloganeering. The film *You Only Live Twice* (1967) was promoted with the slogan, 'Sean Connery *is* James Bond' – surely, a debatable proposition at the best of times and only likely to encourage a regrettable tendency, particularly among journalists, to confuse actors with their roles. Other examples: 'Michael Caine is Alfie is wicked!' (1966); 'Paul Hogan *is* Crocodile Dundee' (1987); 'Phil Collins *is* Buster' (title of a video about the making of the film *Buster*, 1988); 'Domingo *is* Otello' [*sic*], advertisement in *Los Angeles* Magazine, March 1989; 'Jessye Norman *is* Carmen', ad on LBC radio, August 1989.

I said a subtle! See NOW THERE'S A BEAUT . . .

— is a long time in —. In 1977, when I asked Harold Wilson (1916–95), later Lord Wilson, when he first uttered the much-quoted dictum, 'A week is a long time in politics', he was uncharacteristically unable to remember. He also challenged the accepted interpretation of the words – which most people would think was along the lines of 'What a difference a day makes', 'Wait and see', and 'Don't panic, it'll all blow over'. 'It does not mean I'm living from day to day,' he said, but was intended as 'a prescription for long-term strategic thinking and planning, ignoring the day-to-day issues and pressures which may hit the headlines but which must not be allowed to get out of focus while longer-term policies are taking effect'.

Inquiries among political journalists led to the conclusion that in its present form the phrase was probably first used at a meeting between Wilson and the

Parliamentary lobby correspondents in the wake of the sterling crisis shortly after he first took office as Prime Minister in 1964.

From the late 1980s onwards, Channel Four carried a weekly review with the title *A Week in Politics*, clearly alluding to Wilson's phrase – which provides an easily variable format. From the *Independent* (19 May 1989), on the outgoing editor of the TV programme *Forty Minutes*: 'His successor will have to work hard, though, to keep the formula fresh. 2,400 seconds is a long time in television.'

I say, I say, I say! Hard to know whether Murray and Mooney, the British variety duo, invented this interruption, but they perfected the routine in their act during the 1930s. Mooney would interrupt with 'I say, I say, I say!' To whatever he had to impart, Murray would reply with the traditional I DON'T WISH TO KNOW THAT, KINDLY LEAVE THE STAGE. Harry Murray died in 1967; Harry Mooney in 1972.

I say it's spinach. Meaning 'nonsense', the phrase comes from a caption devised by Elwyn Brooks White for a cartoon by Carl Rose which appeared in the issue of the *New Yorker* of 8 December 1928. It shows a mother at table saying: 'It's broccoli, dear.' Her little girl replies: 'I say it's spinach, and I say the hell with it.' Ross, then editor of the magazine, remembered that when White asked his opinion of the caption the writer was clearly uncertain that he had hit on the right idea. 'I looked at the drawing and the caption and said, "Yeh, it seems okay to me," but neither of us cracked a smile.' The use of the word 'spinach' to mean 'nonsense' stems from this (mostly in the US), as in the title of Irving Berlin's song 'I'll Say It's Spinach' from the revue *Face the Music* (1932) and the book *Fashion is Spinach* by Elizabeth Dawes (1933).

I say, what a smasher! See under DON'T FORCE IT, PHOEBE.

I say you fellows! See under YAROOOO!

I see what you mean. See under ARCHERS.

I'se regusted! When the long-running *Amos'n'Andy* US radio series of the 1930s

and 40s was transferred to TV in 1951–53, black actors had to be found to play the characters originally portrayed by whites. The catchphrases and stock phrases were carried over intact, however. They included: '**Holy mackerel, Andy!** We's all got to stick together in dis heah thing . . . remember, we is brothers in that great fraternity, the Mystic Knights of the Sea'; **check and double check;** and **now ain't dat sump'n?**

is everybody happy? The traditional holiday camp cry and the rallying call of several entertainers. The American comedian Harry Brown was been mentioned as using it in c 1906. Ian Whitcomb, *After the Ball* (1972) states: 'Ted Lewis, ex-clarinettist of the Earl Fuller Jazz Band [post 1919], toured as the "Top-Hatted Tragedian of Jazz", the Hamlet of the Halls, posing the eternal question, "Is everybody happy?"' 'Is Everybody Happy Now?' was a popular song in the US (1927) – was this the one that Florrie Forde (*d* 1940) is said to have sung? – and *Is Everybody Happy?* was the title of an early sound film (US, 1929, remade 1943) recounting the life of Ted Lewis and featuring him.

is he one of us? Asked concerning anyone being considered for membership of a select group, but specifically said to have been a frequent test of her colleagues' loyalty by Margaret Thatcher (by 1985). I don't know whether this has spread much beyond No. 10 Downing Street, where it became known quite early on in the Thatcher years. From the *Independent* (28 January 1989): 'Mr [Kenneth] Clarke also failed the is-he-one-of-us? test applied by Mrs Thatcher to favoured colleagues.' Hugo Young's biography of Mrs Thatcher (1989) had the title *One of Us*.

I should cocoa! A slightly dated British English exclamation meaning 'certainly not!' Longman's *Dictionary of English Idioms* (1979) adds a word of caution: 'This phrase is not recommended for use by the foreign student.'

But why 'cocoa'? As always when in difficulty with a phrase origin, turn to rhyming slang. 'Cocoa' is from 'coffee and cocoa', almost rhyming slang for 'I should hope so!' Often used ironically. Current by 1936.

I should of stood in bed. See under WE WUZ ROBBED!

is it bigger than a breadbox? Since 1950, the Goodson-Todman production *What's My Line* has remained the archetypal TV panel game. Guessing the jobs of contestants and then donning masks to work out the identity of a visiting celebrity turned panellists into national figures in the US and UK. Attempting to establish the size of an article made by one contestant, Steve Allen formulated the classic inquiry 'is it bigger than a breadbox?'

From 'Tinseltown' in Armistead Maupin, *Further Tales of the City* (1982): ' "Right . . . how big was his dick again? . . . Bigger than a breadbox?" '

Other *What's My Line?* phrases included: **would the next challenger sign in please!** – the chairman inviting a contestant to indicate something or other by the way he or she wrote their name. Then **a spot of mime for the panel** would be largely mystifying. The chairman, trying to get the contestant to answer 'No' to ten of the panel's questions would score: **and that's three down, seven to go!** If ten was scored: **you've beaten the panel!** In the UK, the game ran from 1951–63, with brief revivals in the 1970s and 80s.

is it true . . . blondes have more fun? A slogan, devised by Shirley Polykoff, for Lady Clairol in the US from 1957. Chosen from ten suggestions, including 'Is it true that blondes are never lonesome?' and 'Is it true blondes marry millionaires?' 'Blondes have more fun' entered the language and had great persuasive effect. The artist David Hockney once told on TV of how and why he decided to bleach his hair and become the blond bombshell he is today. It was in response to a television advertisement he saw late one evening in New York City. 'Blondes have more fun,' it said. 'You've only one life. Live it as a Blonde!' He immediately jumped up, left the apartment, found an all-night hairdresser and followed the advice of the advertiser.

The TV jingle managed to become a hit in the USSR *c* 1965.

isn't he a panic? Aside uttered by Fred Harris about Eric Pode of Croydon (Chris Emmett) in the BBC Radio series *The Burkiss Way* (1976–80). Incidentally, when the grotty scumbag introduced himself as **Eric Pode of Croydon**, there was always ecstatic cheering, applause, the 'Hallelujah Chorus' and much more.

I spy (with my little eye). The exclamation 'I spy!' appeared in *Punch* (14 September 1910) and apparently means, simply, 'I've seen/spotted something'. In the 1950s, there was a British craze for 'I Spy' which extended the game of trainspotting to other fields. According to the subject of the little book being used, the spotter would score points for having observed different breeds of animal, types of building, and so on. The craze was presided over by 'Big Chief I Spy' in the *Daily Express*.

The origin of the phrase probably lies in the simple children's game of 'I spy' or 'Hy-spy' (known in the eighteenth century), a form of hide and seek. Then there is also the children's game of 'I spy with my little eye . . . something beginning with [P] . . .', in which the guessers have to work out what object this initial letter refers to.

Might there also be an allusion to the nursery rhyme 'Who Killed Cock Robin?' (1740s) in which the question 'Who saw him die?' is answered with, 'I said the fly,/ With my little eye.'

I spy strangers! Procedural phrase in the House of Commons which draws attention to the presence of outsiders with a view to having them excluded. A bizarre device used to delay controversial legislation or to embarrass the Government by forcing a division. The 'strangers' may be members of the public in the galleries, reporters or journalists. The device can be blocked, but succeeded on 18 November 1958.

is she a friend of Dorothy? i.e. 'Is he [*sic*] a homosexual?' Probably this originated among American homosexuals. It was current by 1984. Dorothy was the put-upon heroine of *The Wizard of Oz* and was played in the film by Judy Garland, a woman much revered in male homosexual circles.

A similar expression, probably current at about the same time, was **does he dance at the other end of the ballroom?**

is she . . . or isn't she? A slogan for Harmony hairspray, in the UK, current in 1980. Nothing to do with DOES SHE . . . OR DOESN'T SHE?, but a deliberate echo – as, presumably, was the line 'Is she or isn't she a phoney?', spoken in the film *Breakfast at Tiffany's* (1961).

The ad went on: 'Harmony has a ultra-fine spray to leave hair softer and more natural. She *is* wearing a hairspray but with Harmony it's so fine you're the only one that knows for sure.'

is that a chicken joke? See under LAUGH-IN.

— is the name of the game. An overused phrase from the mid-1960s, meaning '. . . is what it's all about'. Partridge/*Catch Phrases* finds an example in 1961. US National Security Adviser McGeorge Bundy talking about foreign policy goals in Europe in 1966 said: 'Settlement is the name of the game.' In time, almost everything was, following the title of an American TV movie called *Fame Is the Name of the Game* (1966). Then followed several series of TV's *The Name of the Game* (1968–71). The expression was replaced for a while by **— is where it's at.**

is the Pope (a) Catholic? Partridge/*Catch Phrases* lists this as one of its 'American response to stupid questions', along with: **do chickens have lips?, can snakes do push-ups?, do frogs have watertight assholes?** and **does a bear shit in the woods?** It may date from c 1950, but is now quite well established in the UK: 'Is Melvyn [Bragg] vain? Is the Pope Catholic?' – *Independent on Sunday* (17 June 1990). In the *Midwestern Journal of Language and Folklore* (1975), Charles Clay Doyle described these phrases as 'sarcastic interrogative affirmatives'. Robert L. Chapman, *New Dictionary of American Slang* (1986) provides further examples (in addition to the variations, 'Is the Pope Polish/Italian?': **does a wooden horse have a hickory dick?, does a dog have fleas?, is**

Bismarck a herring?, does Muhammad Ali own a mirror?**

Compare CAN A BLOODY DUCK SWIM?

is there a doctor in the house? The traditional cry, usually in a theatre or at some other large gathering of people, when a member of the audience is taken ill. One suspects it dates from the nineteenth century, if not before. The *Daily Mirror* (10 October 1984) reported a member of the audience passing out during the film *1984*: 'There was a kerfuffle as people rallied round and an excited rustle as the traditional call went out: "Is there a doctor in the house?" . . . Dr David Owen, a few rows away, continued to be transfixed by the activities on the screen.'

Sir Ralph Richardson used to tell of an actor who was taking part in a very bad play. Halfway through he turned to the audience and asked, 'Is there a doctor in the house?' When one stood up, the actor said, 'Doctor, isn't this show *terrible*!'

Doctor in the House (1952) was the title of a novel by Richard Gordon (but is also a play on the term 'house doctor').

is there life after —? Presumably derived from the question of life after death, there seems no end to the variations on this theme. On 14 October 1984, the *Sunday Times* Magazine had: 'Is there life after redundancy?' and the *Sunday People*: 'Can there be life after Wogan?' An American book with the title *Is There Life After Housework?* (1981) was written by Don A. Aslett and films (US, 1971 and 1973) had the titles *Is There Sex After Death?* and *Is There Sex After Marriage?*

The original question was posed, for example, in MONTY PYTHON'S FLYING CIRCUS: 'Tonight on "Is There" we examine the question, "Is there a life after death?" And here to discuss it are three dead people.'

The variant 'Is there life *before* death?' was recorded as a graffito in Ballymurphy, Ireland in c 1971 and is confirmed by Seamus Heaney's poem 'Whatever You Say Say Nothing' from *North* (1975) which has:

Is there a life before death? That's chalked up
In Ballymurphy . . .

But as if this underlines the saying's Irish origins too well, bear in mind that 'Is there life before death?' had earlier been the epigraph to Chapter 9 of Stephen Vizinczey's novel *In Praise of Older Women* (1966). There, it is credited to 'Anon. Hungarian'.

is this a record? The traditional cry of people writing to newspapers with claims of various kinds. A letter to *The Times* (18 September 1951)(and written from the Reform Club) stated: 'I have just been asked "Any money for the guy?" Is this a record?'

is this the party to whom I am speaking? See under LAUGH-IN.

I suppose a fuck's out of the question? A sly, sideways chat-up line (or 'no chance of a fuck, I suppose?'). I first became aware of it, perhaps as a cartoon caption, in *c* 1981. What the precise allusion is, if any, still escapes me. A British cinema commercial (1994) included the obvious reference, 'I suppose a plumber's out of the question?' From the *Independent* (23 July 1994): '[A chat-up from a] man I met at a recent dinner party. "Can I have your home number?" "No." "How about your home address?" "No," I repeated. "Does that mean a fax is out of the question?"'

I swear by Almighty God that the evidence . . . There are many versions of the oath sworn by witnesses in courts of law. A composite formed from countless viewings of fictional courts in the UK and the US, might be: 'I swear by Almighty God that the evidence I shall give will be the **truth, the whole truth and nothing but the truth. So help me God.**' The last phrase has never been part of the English court oath, however, but is common in the US (and has occurred, for example, in oaths of allegiance to the British Crown). The emphatic repetition of 'the truth' is common to many countries. In Cervantes, *Don Quixote* (1605–15), we find: 'I must speak the truth, and nothing but the truth'. *Nothing But the Truth* has been the title of three films (US, 1920, 1929, 1941) based on James Montgomery's play (pre-1920). *The Whole Truth* was also the title of a film (UK, 1958).

is your journey really necessary? A slogan first devised in 1939 to discourage evacuated civil servants from going home for Christmas. 'From 1941, the question was constantly addressed to all civilians, for, after considering a scheme for rationing on the "points" principle, or to ban all travel without a permit over more than fifty miles, the government had finally decided to rely on voluntary appeals, and on making travel uncomfortable by reducing the number of trains' (Norman Longmate, *How We Lived Then*, 1973).

it ain't over till it's over. See IT ISN'T . . .

it all depends what you mean by . . . *The Brains Trust* was a discussion programme first broadcast by the BBC in 1941, taking its title from President Roosevelt's name for his circle of advisers (in America, more usually, '*brain* trust'). A regular participant, who became a national figure, was C.E.M. Joad (1891–1953) – often called 'Professor', though not entitled to be. His discussion technique was to jump in first and leave the other speakers with little else to say. Alternatively, he would try and undermine arguments by using the phrase with which he became famous. When the chairman once read out a question from a listener, Mr W.E. Jack of Keynsham – 'Are thoughts things or about things?' – Joad inevitably began his answer with 'It all depends what you mean by a "thing".' A more precise dating of when the phrase had 'caught on' is contained in a letter to James Agate, dated 15 October 1943 and included in his *Ego 6*: ' "Is *Responsibility* a work of art?" Well, as Joad would say, that depends on your definition of a work of art.'

Joad's broadcasting career ended rather abruptly when he was found travelling by rail using a ticket that was not valid. The BBC banished him.

It Always Rains On Sunday. The title of a British film (1948, from a novel by Arthur La Bern) is apparently original but has a nice proverbial feeling to it. The melodramatic story was about an escaped convict in London's East End.

ITALY. 'I Treasure/Trust And Love You'. Lover's acronym in correspondence, used to avoid military censorship and probably current by the Second World War.

it beats as it sweeps as it cleans. A slogan for Hoover carpet sweepers, in the US from 1919, and still current in the UK in the 1980s. Coined by Gerald Page-Wood of the Erwin Wasey agency in Cleveland, Ohio. The exclusive feature of Hoovers was that they gently beat or tapped the carpet to loosen dirt and grit embedded in it. An agitator bar performed this function, together with strong suction with revolving brushes – giving the Hoover the 'triple action' enshrined in the slogan. The words 'Hoover' and **to hoover** became generic terms for vacuum cleaners and for vacuuming. Meaning 'to use a vacuum cleaner' the verb is after William H. Hoover who marketed, but did not invent, the original Hoover model. James Murray Spengler invented the 'triple action' machine 1908. Alas for him, we don't say we are going to 'spengler' the carpet.

it can't happen here. A self-deluding catchphrase. Not unexpectedly for such a short-sighted view of external threats, it appears to have arisen in the 1930s. Sinclair Lewis's novel *It Can't Happen Here* was published in 1935 and adapted for the stage the following year. It warned against fascism in the United States.

Appropriately, Kevin Brownlow and Andrew Mollo's film about what would have happened if the Germans had invaded England in 1940 was entitled *It Happened Here* (UK, 1963).

itch. See AS BUSY AS . . . ; SEVEN YEAR ∼.

it floats. See 99 44/100 PER CENT . . .

It Girl, the. Nickname of Clara Bow (1905–65), the popular actress of the silent film era who appeared in the film *It* (1928), based on an Elinor Glyn story. 'It' was the word used in billings to describe her vivacious sex appeal. Earlier, 'It' was the title of a song in *The Desert Song* (1926). Elsewhere 'it' has had more basic sexual connotations, such as survive in the expression 'to have it off'. In 1904, Rudyard Kipling wrote in *Traffics and Discoveries*: ''Tisn't beauty, so to speak, nor good talk

necessarily. It's just It. Some women'll stay in a man's memory if they once walk down a street.' *Punch* commented on an 'It' craze (18 March 1908), which may be relevant.

it goes with the territory. A late-twentieth-century expression (sometimes 'comes with the territory'), meaning 'it's all part and parcel of something, what is expected'. From the *Washington Post* (13 July 1984): '[Geraldine Ferraro as prospective Vice-President] will have to be judged on her background, training and capacity to do the job. That goes with the territory.' In the film *Father of the Bride* (1991), Steve Martin says: 'I'm a father. Worrying comes with the territory.' From the London *Evening Standard* (17 February 1993): 'Why go on about the latest "award-winning documentary maker"? If you get a documentary on television, you win an award: it goes with the territory.'

Since at least 1900, 'territory' has been the American term for the area a salesman covers and it seems quite likely that the origin of the 'goes with' phrase is the 'Requiem' scene at the end of Arthur Miller's play *Death of a Salesman* (1948): 'For a salesman, there is no rock bottom to the life . . . He's a man way out there in the blue, riding on a smile and a shoeshine . . . A salesman is got to dream, boy. It comes with the territory.'

I think I go home. At one time, 'I tink I go home', spoken in a would-be Swedish accent, was as much part of the impressionist's view of Greta Garbo as I WANT TO BE ALONE. One version of how the line came to be spoken is told by Norman Zierold in *Moguls* (1969): 'After such films as *The Torrent* and *Flesh and the Devil*, Garbo decided to exploit her box-office power and asked Louis B. Mayer for a raise – from three hundred and fifty to five thousand dollars a week. Mayer offered her twenty-five hundred. "I tink I go home," said Garbo. She went back to her hotel and stayed there for a full seven months until Mayer finally gave way.'

Alexander Walker in *Garbo* (1980) recalls, rather, what Sven-Hugo Borg, the actress's interpreter, said of the time in 1926 when Mauritz Stiller, who had come with her from Sweden, was fired from directing

The Temptress: 'She was tired, terrified and lost . . . as she returned to my side after a trying scene, she sank down beside me and said so low it was almost a whisper, "Borg, I think I shall go home now. It isn't worth it, is it?"'

Walker comments: 'That catch-phrase, shortened into "I think I go home", soon passed into the repertoire of a legion of Garbo-imitators and helped publicize her strong-willed temperament.'

A caricatured Garbo was shown hugging Mickey Mouse in a cartoon film in the 1930s. 'Ah tahnk ah kees you now' and 'ah tink ah go home', she said. This cartoon was, incidentally, the last item to be shown on British television before the transmitters were closed down on the brink of war on 1 September 1939.

I think that shows we're getting it about right. A cliché of argument. For example, when defending itself in the 1980s, the BBC was in the habit of pointing out that half the letters of complaint it received about a particular programme were critical, the other half supportive. 'I think that shows we're getting it about right . . .'

I think the answer lies in the soil. See under BEYOND OUR KEN.

I think we should be told. By 1980, *Private Eye* was running a regular parody of the opinion column written by John Junor for the *Sunday Express*. It frequently included the would-be campaigning journalist's line, 'I think we should be told'. In 1985, Sir John – as he was by then – told me that he had never once used the phrase in his column. He did, however, admit to having used the *Eye* parody's other stock phrase – **pass the sick-bag, Alice** – though only once.

I thought — until I discovered —. The common advertising notion of a way of life or a belief being swept away by some sudden revelation. From a David Frost/Christopher Booker parody of political advertisements (BBC TV *That Was the Week That Was*, 1962–3 series): 'I was a floating Voter until they discovered Wilson – now I'm sunk.' The format was used memorably from 1970 to 1975 in a series of

slogans for Smirnoff vodka. The variations included:

> I thought . . . St Tropez was a Spanish monk . . .
> . . . accountancy was my life . . .
> . . . I was the mainstay of the public library . . .
> . . . the Kama Sutra was an Indian restaurant . . .
> . . . until I discovered Smirnoff.

David Tree, an art director at the Young & Rubicam agency, recalled how he and John Bacon, the copywriter, had struggled for weeks to get the right idea. One day, after a fruitless session, he was leaving for lunch when he happened to glance at a magazine pin-up adorning the wall of their office. 'If we really get stuck,' he said, 'we can always say, "I was a boring housewife in Southgate until . . ."' (Southgate was where he was living at the time.)

The end-line to the ads was the **effect is shattering**.

it is a disgrace. See under HANCOCK'S HALF–HOUR.

it is disgraceful, it ought not to be allowed! A popular ingredient of BBC radio *Children's Hour* between 1929 and 1963 was the dramatizations of S.G. Hulme Beaman's *Tales of Toytown*. Mr Growser's 'It is disgr-r-raceful . . .' (spoken by Ralph de Rohan) and the bleatings of **Laaaa-rry the Laaa-amb!** (played by Derek McCulloch) became famous expressions.

it'll all come out in the wash. That is, the truth will emerge in due course, a situation will be resolved. Anthony Trollope was using the expression in 1876: 'The effects which causes will produce, the manner in which this or that will come out in the washing, do not strike even Cabinet Ministers at a glance.' The phrase appears to have been put into common parlance by Rudyard Kipling through its use as a refrain in his 1903 poem 'Stellenbosch':

> And it all goes into the laundry,
> But it never comes out in the wash . . .

it'll be all right on the night. Theatrical phrase, and dating from the late nineteenth century, at least. Curiously – when the phrase has to be invoked – things quite often *are* better on the subsequent (first) night. In the same way, a disastrous dress rehearsal is said to betoken a successful first night. It was the title of a song by Alan Melville and Ivor Novello in the musical *Gay's the Word* (1950).

British ITV hijacked the phrase for a long-running series of TV 'blooper' programmes in the 1980s, though witlessly spelt it 'alright'.

it'll be all right with a bit of doing up. See under BAND WAGGON.

it'll play in Peoria. In about 1968, during the Nixon election campaign, John Ehrlichman is credited with having devised a yardstick for judging whether policies would appeal to voters in 'Middle America'. They had to be judged on whether they would 'play in Peoria'. Ehrlichman later told William Safire, 'Onomatopoeia was the only reason for Peoria, I suppose. And it . . . exemplified a place, far removed from the media centres of the coasts where the national verdict is cast.' Peoria is in Illinois and was earlier the hometown of one of Sgt Bilko's men in the 1950s TV series – so was picked on humorously even then.

it looks like something out of *Quatermass*. This alludes to *The Quatermass Experiment* (BBC TV, 1953) – the first in a series of science-fiction drama series by Nigel Kneale involving a certain Professor Quatermass. In this one, viewers were held enthralled by the tale of a British astronaut who returned from a space trip and started turning into a plant. Eventually, he holed up in Poets' Corner at Westminster Abbey, by which time he was a mass of waving fronds. Although the phrase was not used in the programme, it gave rise to an expression still to be heard in the 1990s, and used to describe any peculiar – but especially rambling and leafy – specimen.

ITMA. It is appropriate that *ITMA*, the BBC radio programme incorporating more catchphrases per square minute than any other, before or since, should have had as its title an acronym based on a catchphrase. **It's that man again!** was a late 1930s

expression, often used in newspaper headlines, for Adolf Hitler, who was always bursting into the news with some territorial claim or other. Winston Churchill was to speak often of Hitler as 'that man'.

ITMA was first broadcast in July 1939 and ran until January 1949, when its star, Tommy Handley, died. What did the show consist of? There would be a knock on the famous *ITMA* door, a character would engage in a little banter with Tommy Handley, the catchphrase would be delivered (usually receiving a gigantic ovation), and then the next one would be wheeled in. Given this format, it is not easy now to appreciate why the show was so popular. But the laughter undoubtedly took people's minds off the war and the programmes brought together the whole country, fostering a family feeling and a sense of sharing which in turn encouraged the spread of catchphrases. The writing is not to everyone's taste nowadays (it relied heavily on feeble rather than atrocious puns) but Handley's brisk, cheerful personality was the magic ingredient that held the proceedings together.

Characters came and went over the years, the cast fluctuated, and catchphrases changed. But here are some of the more than fifty I have pinned down:

ain't it a shame, eh? ain't it a shame? Spoken by Carleton Hobbs as the nameless man who told banal tales ('I waited for hours in the fish queue . . . and a man took my plaice') – always prefaced and concluded with, 'Ain't it a shame?'

boss, boss, sumpin' terrible's happened! Spoken in a gangster drawl by Sam Scram (Sydney Keith), Handley's henchman.

but I'm all right now. Sophie Tuckshop (Hattie Jacques) was always stuffing herself and giggling and pretending to suffer. Then, with a squeal, she would say this.

concentrated cacophony! Deryck Guyler's archetypical scouser 'Fisby Dyke' found this a bit hard to understand. After a noisy burst of music, Handley said, 'Never in the whole of my three hundred *ITMA*'s have I ever heard such a piece of concentrated cacophony.' Dyke: 'What's "concentrated cacophony"?'

good morning . . . nice day! Said by Clarence Wright as a commercial traveller who never seemed to sell anything.

I always do my best for all my gentlemen. Mrs Lola Tickle (Maurice Denham) appeared within six weeks of the start of the show in 1939. As office charlady to Mr ITMA (Handley), she was the precursor by a full year of Mrs Mopp.

I don't mind if I do! The immortal reply of Colonel Chinstrap (Jack Train) whenever a drink was even so much as hinted at. The idea first appeared in 1940–41 in the form, 'Thanks, I will!' The Colonel was based on an elderly friend of John Snagge's – a typical ex-Indian Army type, well pleased with himself. The phrase had existed before, of course. *Punch* carried a cartoon in 1880 with the following caption:

> *Porter:* Virginia Water!
> *Bibulous old gentleman (seated in railway carriage):* Gin and water! I don't mind if I do!

ITMA, however, secured the phrase a place in the language, as the Colonel doggedly turned every hint of liquid refreshment into an offer:

> *Handley:* Hello, what's this group? King John signing the Magna Carta at Runnymede?
> *Chinstrap:* Rum and mead, sir? I don't mind if I do!

I go – I come back! Said in a horse whisper by Ali Oop (Horace Percival), the saucy postcard vendor. First used in the summer of 1940.

I'll 'ave to ask me Dad. The point of this phrase was that it was spoken by a character who sounded about 100 years old. He was called the Ancient Mark Time. Randolph Churchill, speaking at a general election meeting in 1945, was heckled with the remark, 'He'll have to ask *his* Dad!'

I'll forget my own name in a minute. The nameless man from the ministry (Horace Percival). An old phrase to show the limits of one's forgetfulness. It occurs in Charles Dickens, *The Chimes* (First Quarter, 1844) as 'I'll forget my own name next.' James Boswell said to Samuel Johnson (on 19 August 1773, recorded in *Journal of a Tour to the Hebrides*), 'A worthy gentleman of my acquaintance actually forgot his own name.' Johnson replied, 'Sir, that was a morbid oblivion.' Even earlier, in the Motteux translation of Cervantes, *Don Quixote* (1605) there is: 'My memory is so bad that many times I forget my own name!'

it's being so cheerful as keeps me going. Said by Mona Lott (Joan Harben), the gloomy laundrywoman. When told to keep her pecker up by Handley, she would reply, 'I always do, sir, it's being so cheerful as keeps me going.' Her family was always running into bad luck, so she had plenty upon which to exercise her particular form of fortitude. Something like the phrase had earlier appeared in a *Punch* cartoon of 27 September 1916: 'Wot a life. No rest, no beer, no nuffin. It's only us keeping so cheerful as pulls us through.'

it's me noives! Lefty (Jack Train), friend of Sam Scram. An unexpected complaint for a gangster to have.

lovely grub, lovely grub! Said by George Gorge (Fred Yule), the 'greediest man ever to have two ration books'. He used to say it smacking his lips.

nobody tells me nothing! (or, 'nobody tells no one nothing') – Dan Dungeon, the gloomy Liverpudlian (Deryck Guyler).

no likey? oh, crikey! Usually said by Ali Oop (Horace Percival), the show's saucy postcard vendor who frequently rhymed English idioms like 'very jolly – oh golly!' or 'Your hands are grimy/ Grimy? Oh, blimey!' Peter Black, the TV critic, once wrote: 'This lunatic exchange sank so deeply into the minds of the girl I was to marry and myself that we still use it thirty years later.'

open the door, Richard! A line from the popular American song (1947), first sung in Britain on *ITMA*.

TTFN. ('Ta-ta for now') The farewell of Mrs Mopp (Dorothy Summers) after having presented her weekly gift to Mayor Handley. It is said that during the war, quite a few people died with the phrase on their lips. Still quite widely in use today.

vouz pouvez cracher. ITMA did skits on pre-war Radio Luxembourg and called it 'Radio Fakenburg'. 'Ici Radio Fakenburg,' the announcer would say, 'mesdames et messieurs, défense de cracher' (no spitting). Each episode would end: 'Mesdames et messieurs, vous pouvez cracher!'

what me – in my state of health? Charles Atlas (Fred Yule).

See also AFTER YOU, CLAUDE/NO, AFTER YOU, CECIL!; AS IF I CARED . . . ; CAN I DO YOU NOW, SIR?; DON'T FORGET THE DIVER!; THIS IS FUNF SPEAKING!

it never rains but it pours. John Arbuthnot, the pamphleteer, entitled a piece thus in 1726, and since then the phrase has gained proverbial status, meaning 'misfortunes never come singly'. A famous US advertising slogan was **when it rains, it pours** which was used from 1911 by Morton salt. The logo showed a girl, sheltering the salt under her umbrella, and capitalized on the fact that the Morton grade ran freely from salt-cellars even when the atmosphere was damp. The film *Cocktail* (US, 1989), about a barman, was promoted with the line: 'When he pours, he reigns.'

I took my harp to a party (but nobody asked me to play). Meaning 'I went prepared to do something, but wasn't given the opportunity'. From a song by Desmond Carter and Noel Gay, popularized by Gracie Fields and Phyllis Robins, 1933/4.

it pays to advertise. A proverbial saying which almost certainly originated in the US. Indeed, Mencken in 1942 lists it simply as an 'American proverb'.

Bartlett quotes the anonymous rhyme:

The codfish lays ten thousand eggs,
The homely hen lays one.
The codfish never cackles
To tell you what she's done.
And so we scorn the codfish,
While the humble hen we prize,
Which only goes to show you
That it pays to advertise.

I feel sure, though, that this rhyme came after the proverb or slogan was established.

It is possible to push back the dating of the phrase rather more positively. There was a play co-written by Walter Hackett (1876–1944) which had it for a title in 1914, and this was turned into a film in 1931. Back even earlier, Cole Porter entitled one of his earliest songs 'It Pays to Advertise'. The song alludes to a number of advertising lines that were current when he was a student at Yale (c 1912):

I'd walk a mile for that schoolgirl complexion,
Palmolive soap will do it every time.
Oh cream, oh best cigar!
Maxwell Motor Car!
Do you have a baby vacuum in your home?
Gum is good for you,
Try our new shampoo,
Flit will always free your home of flies.
If you travel, travel, travel at all,
You know, it pays to advertise.
(included in *The Complete Lyrics of Cole Porter*, ed. Robert Kimball, 1983).

This suggests to me that the phrase, though not Porter's own, was not too much of a cliché by 1912. Ezra Pound wrote in a letter to his father in 1908 about the launch of his poems: 'Sound trumpet. Let rip the drum & swatt the big bassoon. It pays to advertise.'

We are probably looking for an origin in the 1870s to 1890s when advertising really took off in America (as in Britain). Indeed, Benham (1960) lists an 'American saying c 1870' – 'The man who on his trade relies must either bust or advertise' – and notes that 'Sir Thomas Lipton [d 1931] is said to have derived inspiration and success through seeing this couplet in New York about 1875'.

I Treasure/Trust And Love You. See ITALY.

it's a bird . . . it's a plane . . . See under SUPERMAN.

it's a braw bricht moonlicht nicht. See HOOTS MON.

it's absolutely vital both to the character and to the integrity of the script. Actresses (and, I suppose, occasionally actors) invariably answer something to this effect when asked whether there is any nudity in the play or film they are about to appear in and whether there is any justification for taking their clothes off. When I consulted Glenda Jackson about it in 1983, she suggested that the remark was usually made in reply to a reporter's question, 'Is there any nudity in this film?' – 'Yes, but it is absolutely vital to the character and the part.' *The Naff Sex Guide* (1984) gave as one of the 'naff things starlets say': 'Yes, I would appear nude, as long as I trusted the director and the integrity of the script demanded it.'

MONTY PYTHON was already guying the answer on 7 February 1969. A policeman stated: 'I would not appear in a frontal nude scene unless it was valid'; and a woman: 'Oh, no, no, no . . . unless it was artistically valid.' Other responses to the nudity question include, 'I don't mind if it's *relevant* to the script' or '. . . .if it's done in a meaningful way'. Lord Delfont, the impresario, is quoted by Hunter Davies in *The Grades* (1981) as saying: 'I do allow four-letter words and nudity in my films, if they are in the right context, if it has integrity.'

Compare IT'S ALL DONE IN THE BEST POSSIBLE TASTE.

it's a cracker! See IT'S THE WAY I TELL 'EM.

it's a disgrace! See under HANCOCK'S HALF-HOUR.

it's all done in the best possible taste. This was spoken by the British comedy performer Kenny Everett (1944–95), with beard, playing a large-breasted Hollywood actress, Cupid Stunt, being 'interviewed' by a cardboard cut-out Michael Parkinson in *The Kenny Everett Television Show* (after 1981). 'She' was explaining how she justified playing in some forthcoming film of less than award-winning potential (see IT'S ABSOLUTELY VITAL . . .).

According to the co-scriptwriter Barry Cryer, 'she' was never intended to be Dolly Parton. He had heard these very words said in an interview by an American actress whose name he has since, fortunately, forgotten. (In *Time* magazine, 20 July 1981, I did, however, come across John Derek, director of *Tarzan the Ape Man* declaring almost the same thing: 'The sacrifice scene was done in the finest of taste – taste the Pope would applaud.')

As an illustration of how a good catchphrase is seized upon by the media, I noted that in the *Scottish Daily Express* of 28 April 1982, there were two separate stories making use of this one: 'Pia [Zadora] . . . in the best possible taste' and 'Spicy Geraldine . . . in the best possible taste.'

Understandably, too, Wills Tobacco began to promote Three Castles brand with the slogan 'In the best possible taste'.

it's all happening! A rather 1960s phrase intended to suggest that life is very exciting, swinging, and what have you. A British film with the title came out in 1963. It was about a talent scout for a record company and starred Tommy Steele. The title was changed to *The Dream Maker* in the US. Also in c 1965 there was a BBC TV show called *Gadzooks It's All Happening* (yes, really).

In the same period, Norman Vaughan used the stock phrase **it's all been happening this week!** to introduce topical gags when he was compering TV's *Sunday Night at the London Palladium* (from 1962).

it's all in the mind, you know. See GOON SHOW.

it's all part of life's rich pageant. Peter Sellers as Inspector Clouseau has just fallen into a fountain in *A Shot in the Dark* (1964) when Elke Sommer commiserates with him: 'You'll catch your death of pneumonia.' Playing it phlegmatically, Clouseau replies, 'It's all part of life's rich pageant.'

The origin of this happy phrase – sometimes 'pattern' or 'tapestry' is substituted for 'pageant' – was the subject of an inquiry by Michael Watts of the *Sunday Express* in 1982. The earliest citation he came up with was a record called 'The Games Mistress', written and performed by Arthur Marshall (1910–89) in *c* 1935. The monologue concludes, 'Never mind, dear – laugh it off, laugh it off. It's all part of life's rich pageant.' Consequently, Arthur called his autobiography, *Life's Rich Pageant* (1984).

In 1831, Thomas Carlyle talked of 'the fair tapestry of human life'. The phrase **life's rich tapestry** appears in BBC radio's ROUND THE HORNE (16 May 1965).

it's all part of the service! Response to an expression of gratitude from a customer. Spoken by a tradesman it suggests that thanks (or further payment) is not necessary as he has 'only been doing his job'. Elevated to a slogan by Austin Reed, the British menswear stores, in 1930, as: **it's just a part of the Austin Reed service.**

it's always August under your armpits. See MAKES YOUR ARMPIT . . .

it's a-one for the money, a-two for the show ('. . . three to get ready, now go, cat, go!') The start to the Carl Perkins song 'Blue Suede Shoes' (immortalized by Elvis Presley in 1956) is based on the form of words that children traditionally use at the start of races. A version used in Britain and dating from 1888 is, 'One for the money, two for the show, three to make ready, and four to go.' Another version from 1853, is, 'One to make ready, and two to prepare; good luck to the rider, and away goes the mare.'

it's a wrap. 'That's it, we've finished for the day'. From film/TV slang, after the expression 'to wrap it up', for to put an end to something, presumably because wrapping up is the last thing you do when a goods purchase has been completed. Noted by 1974.

it says here . . . Phrase that distances the reader of a document from the contents thereof. Arthur Mullard, the British actor who specialized in 'thicko' parts, would add 'It sez 'ere' after reading with apparent difficulty some definition on TV's *Celebrity Squares* (1976–80).

it's being so cheerful as keeps me going. See under ITMA.

it's b'ootiful, really b'ootiful! From the *Sunday Times* (21 December 1980): 'No surer test of fame exists than the school playground . . . Small boys narrow their eyes, flatten their voices to a Norfolk burr like Bernard Matthews's and repeat what Matthews says of his Golden Norfolk turkey, "It's b'ootiful. Really b'ootiful." ' It is an axiom of the advertising world that, when in doubt, one should allow the client to appear in the ads for his product. Matthews has endured for more than 15 years, promoting his products – turkey roll, sausages, frankfurters, and so on – in his own distinctive way.

it seemed like a good idea at the time. Partridge/*Catch Phrases* has this limp excuse for something that has gone awry as dating back to the 1950s. But Halliwell found it in a 1931 film called *The Last Flight*. In this story of a group of American airmen who remain in Europe after the First World War. One of them is gored to death when he leaps into the arena during a bullfight. Journalists outside the hospital ask his friend why the man should have done such a thing. The friend (played by Richard Barthelmess) replies: 'Because it seemed like a good idea at the time.'

it sends me! The 1950s way for young people to describe the effect of popular music on their souls. But earlier, in a letter to *The Times* (18 December 1945), Evelyn Waugh was writing: 'He [Picasso] can only be treated as crooners are treated by their devotees. In the United States the adolescents, speaking of music, do not ask: "What do you think of So-and-so?" They say: "Does So-and-so *send* you?" '

Indeed, *OED2* finds this use in the early 1930s.

See also *EDUCATING ARCHIE*.

it's fingerlickin' good! A slogan for Kentucky Fried Chicken, current by 1958. Several songs/instrumental numbers with the title 'Fingerlickin' Good' appear to have been inspired by this advertising use. In addition, Lonnie Smith had a record album called 'Fingerlickin' Good Soul Organ' in 1968. In 1966, 'Finger Lickin'', on its own, was the title of a (guitar) instrumental by Barbara Clark. But was the word 'fingerlickin'' an established Southern US/possibly Black/musicians' phrase before being made famous by the slogan? 'Licking good', on its own, was a phrase current by the 1890s.

it's for yoo-hoo! In c 1985, British Telecom made advertising use of the familiar phrase of someone answering the phone and finding it is for another, 'It's for you'. But it was pronounced in a distinctive way which no doubt led to it catching on.

According to the *Guardian* (24 October 1985), detectives seeking a man on assault charges – a man known to be a keen Chelsea supporter – put an 'urgent message for Graham Montagu' sign on the electronic scoreboard at Stamford Bridge football ground. Thousands of fans spontaneously sang out, 'Montagu, it's for yoo-hoo!', the man fell for the ruse, and was arrested.

it's goodnight from me/and it's goodnight from him! A stock exhange from the BBC TV comedy series *The Two Ronnies* (1971–88). Ronnie Corbett and Ronnie Barker always ended editions with a gentle poke at a cliché of TV presentation. Ronnie C. would feed Ronnie B. with, 'It's goodnight from me . . .' And Ronnie B. would sabotage this with, 'And it's goodnight from him.' See also AND IN A PACKED PROGRAMME TONIGHT . . .

it's just a trick of the light. See ROUND THE HORNE.

it's make-your-mind-up time. See OPPORTUNITY KNOCKS.

it's me noives. See under ITMA.

it's not cricket. See CRICKET, IT'S NOT.

it's not for me, it's for my daughter. What people almost invariably say when asking famous people for an autograph. From the *Guardian*'s obituary of Arthur Marshall (28 January 1989): 'One of his favourite stories was about how, on coming out of the BBC TV centre, he was once accosted and asked for an autograph. The woman making the request explained that she wanted it for her daughter . . .'

it's not over till it's over (sometimes **the game isn't over . . .**) A warning comparable to the OPERA AIN'T OVER TILL THE FAT LADY SINGS and of American origin also. From the *Independent* (27 February 1991): 'Brigadier General Richard Neal, the US spokesman in Riyadh, warned "let there be no mistake the [Gulf] war is over. Parts of the Iraqi army are still in Kuwait City" . . . He added: "It's not over until it's over."'

it's not the heat, it's the humidity. An expression certainly current in the Second World War but of earlier and most probably American origin. One of S.J. Perelman's prose pieces had the punning title 'It's Not the Heat, It's the Cupidity'. What was the allusion there? Presumably the same as contained in the title of a revue put on by the British Combined Services Entertainment in the Far East (c 1947) and featuring the young actor Kenneth Williams. It was called 'It's Not So Much the Heat, It's the Humidity', though in his memoirs he simply calls it *Not So Much the Heat*. Whatever the form, was this a common expression around the time of the Second World War?

Ted Bell of Reading, who served with the RAF in the Middle East in 1945–7, confirmed (1992) that it was indeed a common expression then and thereabouts: 'What I heard (among *all* ranks; most of my time was in the Sergeants' Mess) was usually an *exaggerated* omission of the aspirate. The saying was often in the form of a piece of folklore recalling the long tradition of British service in those parts, notably in the period between the two World Wars. So the expression would be something like: "Hot? Very hot, but as they always say there, 'It's not the 'eat, it's the 'yoomidity.'"' You might have expected expletives to precede the abstract nouns, but most people appreciated that if used they spoilt the effect. I am pretty sure you would have to go back to the 1920s or beyond to approach the origins of the expression; it is clearly part of the very strong oral RAF and RFC tradition, and it is just possible that it might be traceable to an individual, whom I picture as a Warrant Officer 2nd class, with a mottled face, a bulbous nose and a bushy moustache.'

The case for supporting an American origin is this: in the first paragraph of P.G. Wodehouse's novel *Sam the Sudden* (1925), he describes the inhabitants of New York on a late August afternoon: '[One half] crawling about and asking those they met if this was hot enough for them, the other maintaining that what they minded was not so much the heat as the humidity.'

American use of the phrase may be further confirmed by Thomas Tryon's novel *The Other* which, though not published until 1971, is set in the New England of the mid-1930s. Several times it has characters saying, 'It ain't the heat, it's the humidity,' in circumstances suggesting that it was a conversational cliché of the time and place.

In addition, Leonard Miall, who was the BBC's first peacetime correspondent in Washington D.C. after the Second World War, recalls the expression commonly being used in complaints about the climate of the US capital, and adds that around 1953, when McCarthyism was at its height, the saying was changed to, 'It's not so much the heat, it's the humiliation.'

The clincher is that in his booklet *Are You a Bromide?* (1907), the American author Gelett Burgess lists 'it isn't so much the heat (or the cold), as the humidity in the air' as the sort of thing a 'bromide' (someone addicted to clichés and platitudes) would say.

it's only rock'n'roll. Meaning 'It doesn't matter; the importance should not be exaggerated'. The title of a Mick Jagger/ Keith Richard composition of 1974 has entered the language to a certain extent. In a 1983 *Sunday Express* interview, Tim Rice was quoted as saying, "It would be nice if [the musical *Blondel*] is a success but I won't be upset if it isn't. It is only rock'n'roll after all and it doesn't really matter a hoot.'

it's page one. 'It's elementary, fundamental, what you start from'. Noted in broadcasting, 1986. In the film *Wilt* (UK, 1989), a police inspector says 'Page one! Page one!', with the same meaning.

it's showtime, folks! An exclamation used by theatrical people, sometimes to remind themselves that now is the time to get out there on the stage and shine, sometimes a touch sarcastically. Also used in other fields where an element of performance or presentational glitter is required. In the film *All That Jazz* (US, 1979), Roy Scheider playing a choreographer ritually says the line before getting on with whatever has to be done in his life.

it's Siiimon Dee! See HERE'S JOHNNY!

it's/Skegness is so bracing! Skegness, the seaside resort in Lincolnshire, was so promoted along with the London & North Eastern Railway company in advertisements current from 1909. The slogan is inseparable from the accompanying portrait of a jolly fisherman drawn by John Hassall (1868–1948). Actually, Hassall did not visit Skegness until 28 years after he drew the poster. His first visit was when he was made a freeman of the town.

it's terrific! See under *EDUCATING ARCHIE*.

it's that man again! See under *ITMA*.

it's the business. Meaning, 'it's the real thing, the genuine article, not a fake' or 'the very best, the acme of excellence.' Current in the UK by 1990.

it's the real thing. See under COME ALIVE . . . and REAL THING.

it's the refreshing thing to do. See PAUSE THAT REFRESHES.

it's the way I tell 'em! Almost any comedian could say this of a joke that has just gone down well (and no doubt most of them would agree with the observation) but Frank Carson, the Ulster comedian (b 1926) managed to make the catchphrase his own

(from the mid-70s). In full, the line is:
'You've heard them all before, but . . . it's
the way I tell 'em.' Another of his fillers has
been **it's a cracker!** (pronounced
'crocker').

it's turned out nice again! The British
North Country entertainer George Formby
(1904–61) disclaimed any credit for
originating the phrase with which he always
opened his act. 'It's simply a familiar
Lancashire expression,' he once said.
'People use it naturally up there. I used it as
part of a gag and have been doing so ever
since' – particularly in his films when
emerging from some disaster or other. It was
used as the title of one of these films in 1941
(as well as being the punchline of it) and as
the title of a song.
   Formby was not exactly a comedian but
he exuded persoanlity and, singing slightly
naughty songs to a ukelele accompaniment,
he became one of the great stars of the
variety stage between the wars. He also
appeared in a highly successful series of
films. In these there was another
catchphrase: **ooh, mother!** – said when
scuttling away from trouble.

it's twelve o'clock in London . . . See
under FAMILY FAVOURITES.

it's what your right arm's for. Slogan for
Courage Tavern (ale), current in the UK by
1972. Although this line became a popular
catchphrase, it risks being applied to rival
products. Possibly of earlier origin.

it takes two to tango. A modern
proverbial expression which appears to
derive solely from the song 'Takes Two to
Tango' (1952) by Al Hoffman and Dick
Manning, popularized by Pearl Bailey.
President Ronald Reagan cited it when
commenting (11 November 1982) on the
future of Soviet-American relations
following the death of Leonid Brezhnev.
Possibly based on the earlier proverb, 'It
takes two to quarrel' (known by the early
eighteenth century).

it was a dark and stormy night . . . As a
scene-setting, opening phrase, this appears
to have been irresistible to more than one
storyteller over the years and has now

become a joke. At some time unknown, this
phrase became part of a children's 'circular'
storytelling game, 'The tale without an
end'. Iona and Peter Opie in *The Lore and
Language of Schoolchildren* (1959) describe
the workings thus: 'The tale usually begins:
"It was a dark and stormy night, and the
Captain said to the Bo'sun, 'Bo'sun, tell us a
story,' so the Bo'sun began . . ." Or it may
be: "It was a dark and stormy night, the
rain came down in torrents, there were
brigands on the mountains, and thieves,
and the chief said unto Antonio: 'Antonio,
tell us a story.' And Antonio, in fear and
dread of the mighty chief, began his story:
'It was a dark and stormy night, the rain
came down in torrents, there were brigands
on the mountains, and thieves . . .'" And
such is any child's readiness to hear a good
story that the tale may be told three times
round before the listeners appreciate that
they are being diddled.'
   The Opies noted that each of these
variations was also current in the US,
'except that in the first tale American
children say: "It was a dark and stormy
night, some Indians were sitting around the
camp fire when their chief rose and said . . ."'
   The phrase had been used in all
seriousness by the English novelist Edward
Bulwer-Lytton at the start of *Paul Clifford*
(1830): 'It was a dark and stormy night, the
rain falling in torrents – except at
occasional intervals, when it was checked
by a violent gust of wind which swept up
the streets and then (for it is in London that
our scene lies), rattling along the housetops,
and fiercely agitating the scanty flames of
the lamps that struggled against the
darkness.'
   Stephen Leacock, the Canadian
humorist (1869–1944), went for something
similar to start his *Gertrude the Governess*
(1911): 'It was a wild and stormy night on
the West Coast of Scotland. This, however,
is immaterial to the present story as the
scene is not laid in the West of Scotland.'
By the time P.G. Wodehouse wrote *Summer
Lightning*, Chap. 4 (1929) it had become
firmly a joke: 'It was a dark and stormy
night . . . No, I'm a liar. The moon was
riding serenely in the sky.'
   In the 1960s, it became the title of one of
Charles M. Schultz's books in which the
line is given to the character Snoopy in his

doomed attempts to write the Great American Novel. Consequently, the dog is acclaimed as author of the world's greatest one-line novel. Paradoxically, Schultz's own book *It Was a Dark and Stormy Night* was a best-seller.

The culmination of all this has been the Annual Bulwer-Lytton Fiction Contest, founded by Dr Scott Rice, a professor of English literature at San Jose State University, California. Contestants are asked to compose truly atrocious opening sentences to hypothetical bad novels. Rice was quoted in *Time* (21 February 1983) as saying, 'We want the kind of writing that makes readers say, "Don't go on." ' Some of the entries have now been published in book form – with the authors given every inducement not to keep on writing . . .

it was going to be a long night. 'He was doing the crossword from *The Washington Star*. He had finished three clues; it was going to be a long night' – Jeffrey Archer, *Shall We Tell the President* (1977), but a cliché of earlier origin.

it was just like a fairy tale. See LIKE A FAIRY-TALE . . .

it was like an Aladdin's cave in there! What – according to the press – ordinary members of the (British) public invariably say when they stumble upon a burglar's horde, or similar. 'Aladdin's cave' as a phrase signifying a place of vast stores of wealth was already established by 1922.

Compare, from *Good Housekeeping* (May 1986): 'Down in London's Soho is . . . an Aladdin's cave of cotton jerseys, silks, velvets and unusual cloths.'

it was worse than the Blitz. What – according to the press – ordinary members of the (British) public invariably say when involved in bomb incidents, train crashes, etc. Note, however, this interesting variation apropos an incident in which police rained shots on an innocent man: 'Mr David Steele . . . in a Volkswagen van which was behind the Mini carrying Mr Waldorf [when asked about the number of police officers he saw, said]: "I saw one, then two, then it was World War Two all over again." ' (*Daily Telegraph*, 14 October 1983).

it's terrific! See under EDUCATING ARCHIE.

it will all be the same in a hundred years(' time). Consolatory or dismissive catchphrase – 'why worry?', 'who will care in time?' As 'it will all be one in a hundred/thousand years', the saying was recorded in various versions between 1611 and 1839. Bill Wilkes told Paul Beale (1994) that his mother, originally from Norfolk, used the expression **by that time you'll all be dead and your arse cold** in the same sense. Compare Samuel Johnson's excellent advice for putting a distressful situation in perspective: 'Consider, Sir, how insignificant this will appear a twelvemonth hence' (Boswell's *Life of Johnson*, for 6 July 1763).

I've arrived – and to prove it – I'm here! See under EDUCATING ARCHIE.

I've been sponned! See under GOON SHOW.

I've given you the best years of my life! What one half of a fictional couple is apt to say when they are splitting up or having a row. In the film *Monkey Business* (US, 1931), Groucho Marx says to a woman: 'Oh, so that's it. Infatuated with a pretty uniform! We don't count, after we've given you the years of our lives. You have to have an officer.' From J.B. Priestley, *When We Are Married*, Act II (1938): 'And after giving you the best years of our life – without a word o' thanks.' Something like the line is spoken in the film *Mr and Mrs Smith* (US, 1941). Compare *The Best Years of Our Lives* under HAPPIEST DAYS OF YOUR LIFE.

I've got a letter from a bloke in Bootle. This was one of a number of expressions used by the great British comedian Jimmy James (1892–1965). Others were: **excuse me, is this the place? Are you the bloke?**; **somebody come** (said by James in his 'drunk' bedroom sketch – though he himself was a teetotaller); **give me a note please . . . er-fa-a-fa-a fah . . . fah . . . fah** (trying to get the note at the start of a song, when drunk); and **how do you do?** – said with a slight nod.

One of his team – the splendidly named Hutton Conyers – would say to James: **hey,**

are you putting it around that I'm barmy?

I've got a million of 'em! See
GOODNIGHT, MRS CALABASH . . .

I've got his pecker in my pocket.
Meaning, 'he is under obligation to me',
this was one of Lyndon B. Johnson's earthy
phrases from his time as Senate Majority
leader in Washington. 'Pecker' means
'penis' in North America (rather less so in
Britain) – though this should not inhibit
people from using the old British expression
keep your pecker up, where the word has
been derived from 'peck' meaning appetite.
In other words, this second phrase is merely
a way of wishing someone good health,
though *OED2* has 'pecker' meaning
'courage, resolution' in 1855.

**I've never believed in anything so
much in all my life.** Something of a cliché
of film scriptwriting, though perhaps not
too painful as clichés go. An example occurs
in *Dangerous Moonlight* (UK, 1941).
Compare what Mickey Rooney says to Judy
Garland in *Strike Up the Band* (US, 1940):
'Mary, I was never more sure of anything in
my life'; and what Fred Astaire says to Rita
Hayworth in *You'll Never Get Rich* (US,
1941): 'I was never so sure of anything in my
life.'
    But it is an old format. In Henry
Fielding's *Tom Jones* (1749) there is: 'D–n
me if ever I was more in earnest in my life'.
In Conan Doyle's 'The Priory School'
(1905): 'I was never more earnest in my life';
and in 'The Cardboard Box' (1917): 'I was
never more serious in my life.'

I've only got four minutes . . . The
Australian actor/comedian Bill Kerr,
chiefly remembered now as one of the
supporting characters in HANCOCK'S HALF-
HOUR, began his career in Britain doing
stand-up routines on BBC radio's *Variety
Bandbox* (from 1948). **I don't want to
worry you . . .** (concerning the imminent
collapse of the theatre) and 'I've only got
four minutes' were all part of his assumed
depressive act.

I've started so I'll finish! In BBC TV's
Mastermind quiz (first broadcast in 1972),

the chairman, Magnus Magnusson, would
say this if one of his questions was
interrupted when the time ran out. It
became a figure of speech – sometimes also
given a double meaning.
    From the same programme came **Pass!**
Noted *The Times* (8 November 1977): 'For
proof of how . . . *Mastermind* is catching on,
I would refer you to this story sent in by a
reader from London NW6. He was accosted
by a small lad, asking for a penny for the
guy. On being asked if he knew who Guy
Fawkes was, the lad replied with engaging
honesty, "Pass."'
    The word is used by participants in the
quiz when they do not know the answer to
a question and wish to move on to the next,
so as not to waste valuable time. It is not the
most obvious of things to say. 'Next
question' or 'I dunno' would spring more
readily to mind but, so deep has this phrase
penetrated the public consciousness that
when I was chairing a TV quiz called
Challenge of the South in 1987/8, I found
that contestants automatically reached for
'Pass'.
    In 1981, London Transport
advertisements showed an empty studio
chair, of the type used in the programme,
with the query, 'How can you save money
on bus fares?' The answer was, 'Correct.
The London Bus pass.'

ivory tower, to live in an. Meaning 'to
live in intellectual seclusion and protected
from the harsh realities of life', the
expression comes from Sainte-Beuve
writing in 1837 about the turret room in
which the Comte de Vigny, the French
poet, dramatist, and novelist, worked. He
described it as his *tour d'ivoire*, possibly after
the Song of Solomon 7:4: 'Thy neck is as a
tower of ivory; thine eyes like fishpools . . .'

I wanna tell you a story! Launched on a
sea of catchphrases in EDUCATING ARCHIE,
Max Bygraves (b 1922) later became
associated with a phrase wished upon him
by an impersonator. It is possible that he
may have said of his own accord, 'I wanna
tell you a story' (with the appropriate hand-
gestures – as if shaking water off them) but
it was Mike Yarwood who capitalized on it
in his impersonation. Bygraves then used
the phrase himself in self-parody and chose

it as the title of his autobiography (1976). Still, as he says, he once went into a competition for Max Bygraves impressionists – and came fifth.

Of having successful catchphrases in general, Bygraves told me (1980): 'It's like having a hit record!'

I want me tea! *The Grove Family* was the first British TV soap opera – or something approaching one – and ran for three years from 1953. It told of a suburban family that included a wonderfully irritable Grandma Grove (Nancy Roberts) who used to make this demand. There are still families which consciously repeat her phrase (I belong to one).

I want to be alone. Greta Garbo (1905–90) claimed that what she said was 'I want to be *let* alone' – i.e. she wanted privacy rather than solitude. Oddly, as Alexander Walker observes in *Sex in the Movies* (1968): 'Nowhere in anything she said, either in the lengthy interviews she gave in her Hollywood days when she was perfectly approachable, or in the statements on-the-run from the publicity-shy fugitive she later became, has it been possible to find the famous phrase, "I want to be alone". What one can find, in abundance, later on, is "Why don't you let me alone?" and even "I want to be left alone", but neither is redolent of any more exotic order of being than a harassed celebrity. Yet the world prefers to believe the mythical and much more mysterious catchphrase utterance.'

What complicates the issue is that Garbo herself *did* use the line several times on the screen. For example, in the 1929 silent film *The Single Standard* she gives the brush-off to a stranger and the subtitle declares: 'I am walking alone because I want to be alone.' And, as the ageing ballerina who loses her nerve and flees back to her suite in *Grand Hotel* (1932), she actually *speaks* it. Walker calls this 'an excellent example of art borrowing its effects from a myth that was reality for millions of people'.

The phrase was obviously well established by 1935 when Groucho Marx uttered it in *A Night at the Opera*. Garbo herself says, 'Go to bed, little father. We want to be alone' in *Ninotchka* (1939). So it is not surprising that the myth took such a

firm hold, and particularly since Garbo became a virtual recluse for the second half of her life.

I want to make it perfectly clear. Politicians' cliché. Often said when doing quite the opposite. Much used by William Whitelaw, British Conservative politician – especially when Home Secretary in the early 1980s.

I was amazed! See NAY, NAY – THRICE AGAIN NAY!

I was a seven-stone weakling. See YOU, TOO, CAN HAVE A BODY LIKE MINE.

I wasn't born yesterday. OED2 has 'I wasn't born yesterday', meaning 'I'm not as innocent as you take me for', as an established saying by 1757. Modern use must have been encouraged by the Garson Kanin play *Born Yesterday* (1946, film US, 1951), an excellent vehicle for Judy Holliday, about an ignorant girl who wins out in the end.

I was only obeying orders! Much-parodied self-excusal from responsibility for one's actions. The Charter of the International Military Tribunal at Nuremberg (1945–6) specifically excluded the traditional German defence of 'superior orders'. But the plea was, nevertheless, much advanced. As early as 1940, Rex Harrison says in the UK film *Night Train to Munich*: 'Captain Marsen was only obeying orders.' Kenneth Mars as a mad, Nazi-fixated playwright in *The Producers* (US, 1967) says, 'I only followed orders!'

Not that everyone seemed aware of the parodying. From the *New York Times* (6 July 1983): 'Herbert Bechtold, a German-born officer in the [US] counter-intelligence who became [the "handler" of Klaus Barbie, the Nazi war criminal] was asked if he questioned the morality of hiring a man like Barbie by the United States. "I am not in a position to pass judgement on that," Mr Bechtold replied, "I was just following orders."'

I went to New Zealand but it was closed. A joke remark which gets rediscovered every so often. The Beatles found it in the 1960s; slightly before, Anna Russell, the musical comedienne, said it on one of her records. It has also been attributed to Clement Freud. But William Franklyn, son of the Antipodean actor, Leo Franklyn, tells me that his father was saying it in the 1920s.

I expect W.C. Fields began saying 'I went to Philadelphia and found that it was closed' about the same time (if indeed he did).

I wonder if they are by any chance related? It is an obsession with some to make assumptions about people being related to one another on the basis that they look similar or have names in common. For many years from the 1970s, *Private Eye* ran a feature in which people would write in, under a pseudonym, drawing attention to facial similarities – almost always ending up with the line, 'I wonder if they are by any chance related?' (e.g. Lyndon Johnson/Mrs Golda Meir; Alfred Brendel/Roy Hudd). The US magazine *Spy* has run a similar feature headed **Separated at Birth?**

I won't take me coat off – I'm not stopping. Ken Platt (*b* 1922), the nasal-voiced, somewhat lugubrious British North Country comedian, was handed this catchphrase on a plate by Ronnie Taylor, producer of BBC radio's *Variety Fanfare* in January 1951. Platt told me (1979): 'I told him rather grudgingly that I thought it was "as good as anything" . . . and I've been stuck with it ever since. People are disappointed if I don't say it.' Also in the show he would comment **hasn't it been a funny day, today?**
See also DAFT AS A BRUSH.

I would like to spend more time with my (wife and) family. A cliché of British political resignations. In March 1990, two of Prime Minister Thatcher's ministers – Norman Fowler and Peter Walker – withdrew from the Cabinet, both giving as their reason for going that they wished to 'spend more time with their families'. Fowler, in his resignation letter, wrote: 'I have a young family and for the next few years I should like to devote more time to them while they are still so young.' Prime

Minister Thatcher replied: 'I am naturally very sorry to see you go, but understand your reasons for doing this, particularly your wish to be able to spend more time with your family.'

Subsequently, Gordon Brown, the Labour MP, suggested in the House of Commons that Nicholas Ridley might care to follow suit. But the Secretary of State for Industry was having none of it. 'The last thing I want to do,' he said, 'is spend more time with my family' (quoted in the *Independent*, 14 July 1990).

I would walk over my grandmother ('to achieve something'). When Richard Nixon sought re-election as US president in 1972, he surrounded himself with an unsavoury crew including Charles W. Colson, a special counsel and White House hatchet man. 'I would walk over my grandmother if necessary to get Nixon re-elected!' was his declared point of view. Subsequently convicted of offences connected with Watergate, he described in his book *Born Again* (1977) how a memo to his staff containing the offensive boast had been leaked to the press: 'My mother failed to see the humour in the whole affair, convinced that I was disparaging the memory of my father's mother . . . Even though both of my grandmothers had been dead for more than twenty-five years (I was very fond of both).'

Earlier, the editor of the *Pall Mall Gazette*, W.T. Stead, famous for his exposé of the child prostitution racket, once said: 'I would not take libel proceedings if it were stated that I had killed my grandmother and eaten her.' Another earlier image often invoked was of 'selling one's grandmother'.

I yam what I yam . . . ('and that's all that I yam'). The personal philosophy of Popeye, the one-eyed, pipe-smoking, spinach-eating sailor originally appeared in strip cartoons but is best-known through the many short animated films made for cinema and TV. Created by Elzie Crisler Sefar, Popeye first appeared in a syndicated strip 'Thimble Theatre' in the 1930s. His slender, shrewish girlfriend was Olive Oyl.

I Zingari. The name of this itinerant British cricket team (founded 1845) which has no ground of its own, comes from the

Italian for 'the gypsies'. It is also the title of a one-act opera by Leoncavallo (1912).

izzy-wizzy, let's get busy! Harry Corbett's little bear puppet, Sooty, first appeared on British TV screens in 1952 and has been there ever since, latterly with Harry's son Matthew with his hand up the back. This was the magic spell for conjuring tricks. The programmes invariably ended with Sooty squirting water at, or throwing a custard pie in, Harry's face ('Ooh, 'e's a scamp, 'e is really!'). Harry would then intone the famous farewell in his flat Lanacashire vowels, **bye-bye, everyone, bye-bye!**

· J ·

Jack. See BEFORE ONE CAN SAY ~
ROBINSON; I'M ALL RIGHT, ~; JOLLY ~;
under WITH ONE BOUND . . .

Jackal, the. Nickname of Ilich Ramirez
Sanchez (*b* 1949), a Venezuelan-born
assassin, who worked with various terrorist
gangs in several countries before being
apprehended in 1994. A journalistic tag, it
derived from the *nom de guerre* of the would-
be assassin of Charles de Gaulle in
Frederick Forsyth's novel *The Day of the
Jackal* (1971, film UK/France, 1973). It was
frequently coupled with a code name,
'Carlos'. As if to confirm the artificial
nature of this sobriquet, Christopher
Dobson and Ronald Payne writing in *The
Carlos Complex* (1977) refer, rather, to 'a
young Venezuelan named Ilich Ramirez
Sanchez, better known as Carlos the Killer'.

jack in office, a. Meaning 'a self-
important petty official' this term was
known by 1700. Sir Edwin Landseer
entitled a painting (1833): 'A Jack in Office',
which showed a terrier guarding the barrow
of a cat-and-dog-meat salesman while four
mangy, obsequious dogs eyed the barrow.

Jack the Lad. Name given to a (possibly
harmless) ruffian – 'a bit of a lad' – and
latterly to a promiscuous young man. Such
a venerable-sounding phrase may, however,
be of comparatively recent origin – first
becoming apparent in the 1970s. 'I was
always Jack the Lad – the one everyone
liked but nobody wanted to know' (*New
Society*, 4 June 1981). The phrase is said to
have originated in Liverpool working-class
argot, referring to an outstanding
individual in a group.

Jack the Ripper. Nickname of the
unknown murderer of some eight
prostitutes in the East End of London
(1887–9), who mutilated his victims. He
may have been a sailor, a butcher, or even a
member of the Royal Family, according to
various theories. The first time the name
was used was in a letter signed by a man
claiming to be the killer, which was sent to
a London news agency in September 1888.
The murders were such a long-lasting
sensation that the nickname 'Ripper' has
been bestowed on subsequent perpetrators
of similar crimes (compare YORKSHIRE
RIPPER).

jam. See ALL ~ AND JERUSALEM.

James. See HOME, ~, AND DON'T SPARE THE
HORSES.

jam jar. See GET BACK ON YOUR . . .

jam tomorrow, and never jam today.
An allusion to Lewis Carroll's *Through the
Looking Glass* (1871): the White Queen
wants Alice to be her maid and offers her
twopence a week and jam every other day,
except that she can never actually have any
– it's never jam today. An early version of
CATCH-22. The Queen explains: 'The rule is,
jam to-morrow and jam yesterday – but
never jam to-day.' Quite often the phrase is
used in connection with the unfulfilled
promises of politicians.

Jane. See ME, TARZAN . . .

JAP. Initials standing for 'Jewish American
Princess' – the nickname for a type of
upwardly-mobile woman who wants to be
rich and well married and believes that
there is a formula for achieving this. She is
notable, therefore, for wearing the right
clothes, for her lacquered hair and carefully
tended fingernails, and for her jewellery.
Perhaps she would once have liked to
emulate that (non-Jewish) princess, Jackie
Kennedy Onassis – indeed, she does not
have to be Jewish or even American, the

type occurs in most societies. Identified by 1985, at least. There is a male equivalent.

jazz. See AND ALL THAT ∼.

Jazz Age, the. Another sobriquet for the ROARING TWENTIES, this one comes from the title *Tales of the Jazz Age* (1922) by F. Scott Fitzgerald.

Jeez, Wayne! From McPhail and Gadsby's New Zealand TV show, set in the bar of a hotel. Current in 1980.

Jekyll and Hyde, a. Term for a person displaying two completely different characters, one respectable, the other not. After the eponymous character in R.L. Stevenson's *The Strange Case of Dr Jekyll and Mr Hyde* (1886) who, by means of a drug, can switch between the good and evil in his own nature. Consequently, a 'Jekyll and Hyde —' is something that is a mixture of contrasting elements or switches between two such elements. G.K. Chesterton wrote in 1927: 'Jekyll and Hyde have become a proverb and a joke; only it is a proverb read backwards and a joke that nobody sees.'

Jelly Roll Morton. This was the stage name of Ferdinand Le Menthe Morton (*d* 1941), a pianist, and one of the creators of New Orleans jazz. 'Jelly roll' was Southern Negro slang for the vagina, for a virile man, and for sundry sexual activities. A jelly roll was an item of food which you would get from a baker's shop (like a Swiss Roll), and the word 'jelly' could refer to the meat of the coconut when it is still white and resembling semen.

Jemmy Twitcher. Nickname of John Montagu, 4th Earl of Sandwich (1718–92), after whom the food was named. He was an extremely unpopular man, partly because of widespread corruption in the Navy when he was First Lord of the Admiralty, partly because he turned against and betrayed his friend, John Wilkes. The nickname was taken from a character in John Gay's *The Beggar's Opera* (1728). He is one of Captain Macheath's associates but betrays him.

Jennifer! See under RAY'S A LAUGH.

Jerry. See STICK IT, ∼!; TOM AND ∼.

jerry-built. Meaning 'built badly of poor materials', the phrase was in use by 1869 (which rules out any connection with buildings put up by German or 'Jerry' prisoners-of-war). There are various suggestions as to its origin: that it has to do with the walls of Jericho which came tumbling down; or that there were two brothers called Jerry who were notoriously bad builders in Liverpool; or that it has to do with the French *jour* [day] – workers paid on a daily basis were unlikely to make a good job of things. Or that, as with the nautical term 'jury' ('jury-rigging', 'jury mast') it is something temporary.

Jersey Lily. Sobriquet of Lily Langtry (1852–1929), a beautiful actress, born in Jersey, daughter of a Dean, who made her London debut in *She Stoops to Conquer* in 1881. She became a mistress of Edward VII when he was Prince of Wales. Anita Leslie in *Edwardians in Love* (1972) notes that she was painted by Millais holding a lily.

Jerusalem. See ALL JAM AND ∼.

Jesus wept! John 11:35 is the shortest verse in the Bible (the shortest sentence would be 'Amen.'). It occurs in the story of the raising of Lazarus. Jesus is moved by the plight of Mary and Martha, the sisters of Lazarus, who break down and weep when Lazarus is sick. When Jesus sees the dying man he, too, weeps.

Like it or not, the phrase has become an expletive to express exasperation. The most notable uttering was by Richard Dimbleby, the British TV commentator, on 27 May 1965. In a broadcast in which everything went wrong during a Royal visit to West Germany, Dimbleby let slip this oath when he thought his words were not being broadcast.

A graffito from the 1970s, from the London advertising agency which lost the Schweppes account, was: 'Jesus wepped'.

Jethro Tull. This British pop group, successful in the early 1970s, took its name from the English agriculturalist (*d* 1741) who invented the seed drill.

Jew. See WANDERING ～.

jewel in the crown, the/a. Meaning, 'a bright feature, an oustanding part of something.' In the space of a single day – 2 March 1988 – I read in the *Guardian*, 'Poor David Steel. He's bound for Southport on Saturday for a regional conference in what ought to be one of the precious few jewels in the Liberals' dented crown'; in *Harpers & Queen*, 'Annecy is considered to be the jewel in the Savoyard crown'; and in Michael Powell's book *A Life in Movies* (published two years before), 'Sir Thomas Beecham, Bart., conducting the "Ballet of the Red Shoes" would be the final jewel in our crown.'

It would be reasonable to suppose that the 1984 television adaptation of Paul Scott's 'Raj Quartet' of novels had something to do with the popularity of this phrase. The first of Scott's novels (published in 1966) is called *The Jewel in the Crown* and gave its name to the TV series. 'The Jewel in *Her* Crown' [my italics] is the title of a 'semi-historical, semi-allegorical' picture referred to early on in the book. It showed Queen Victoria, 'surrounded by representative figures of her Indian Empire: Princes, landowners, merchants, money-lenders, sepoys, farmers, servants, children, mothers, and remarkably clean and tidy beggars . . . An Indian prince, attended by native servants, was approaching the throne bearing a velvet cushion on which he offered a large and sparkling gem'. (In fact, Victoria, like Disraeli, who is also portrayed, never set foot in India.)

Children at the school where the picture was displayed had to be told that, 'the gem was simply representative of tribute, and that the jewel of the title was India herself'. The picture must have been painted *after* 1877, the year in which Victoria became Empress of India. I imagine it was an actual picture, no doubt much reproduced, but I have no idea who painted it.

The *OED2* refers only to the 'jewels of the crown', as a rhetorical phrase for the colonies of the British Empire, and has a citation from 1901. The specifying of India as *the* jewel is understandable. The Kohinoor, a very large oval diamond of 108.8 carats, from India, has been part of the British crown jewels since 1849.

Many writers have used the phrase in other contexts. In *Dombey and Son*, Chap. 39 (1844–6), Charles Dickens writes: 'Clemency is the brightest jewel in the crown of a Briton's head.' Earlier, in *The Pickwick Papers*, Chap. 24 (1836–7), he has (of Magna Carta): 'One of the brightest jewels in the British crown.' In the poem 'O Went Thou in the cauld blast', Robert Burns has: 'The brightest jewel in my crown/Wad be my queen.'

Jewish. See ～ AMERICAN PRINCESS under JAP; SOME OF MY BEST FRIENDS ARE . . . ; YOU DON'T HAVE TO BE ～.

jib. See CUT OF SOMEONE'S ～.

Jim. See I'M WORRIED ABOUT ～; SUNNY ～.

Jim Crow must go. i.e., racial segregation must be abolished. An early 1960s US chant, with 'clap, clap' between the second and third words. The phrase 'Jim Crow' became common in the 1880s but goes back to the 1730s when blacks were first called 'crows'. By 1835, 'Jim Crow' or 'Jim Crowism' meant segregation.

Jimmy who? The question was posed when James Earl Carter (*b* 1924) came from nowhere to challenge Gerald Ford, successfully, for the US presidency in 1976. It had almost the force of a slogan. Carter's official slogan, used as the title of a campaign book and song, was **why not the best?** This came from an interview Carter had had with Admiral Hyman Rickover when applying to join the nuclear submarine programme in 1948: 'Did you do your best [at Naval Academy]?' Rickover asked him. 'No, sir, I didn't *always* do my best,' replied Carter. Rickover stared at him for a moment and then asked: 'Why not?'

jingo. See BY ～!

job. See GI'US A ～; SERIOUSLY, THOUGH, HE'S DOING A GRAND ～.

Job's comforter. An expression used to describe one who seeks to give you comfort but who, by blaming you for what has happened, makes things worse. It comes from the rebukes Job received from his friends, to whom he says: 'miserable comforters are ye all' (Job 16:2).

Joe Bob says check it out. 'Joe Bob Briggs' was the pseudonymous drive-in movie critic of the *Dallas Times Herald* from 1982–5. Written by John Bloom, the reviews represented the views of a self-declared redneck. They frequently caused offence, not least because they tended to rate movies according to the number of 'garbonzas' (breasts) on display. Joe Bob had a battery of stock phrases (not all original to him, by any means), including **no way, Jose**; **if you know what I mean, and I think you do**; and the inevitable closing comment: 'Joe Bob says check it out'. The column was eventually dropped when Briggs poked fun at efforts to raise money for starving Africans. The columns were published in book form as *Joe Bob Goes to the Drive-In* (1989).
See also NIPPLE COUNT.

Joe Miller, a. At first a joke, then a worn-out joke – a 'chestnut' from long usage – named after Joe Miller (1684–1738), a popular British comedian. Published in 1739, the year after Miller died, *Joe Miller's Jests* was compiled by a man called John Mottley and included the kind of jokes that Miller had liked to tell. Things being the way they often are, it turned into something of a backhanded compliment, as a 'Joe Miller' became the nickname for a joke that had so many whiskers on it that it must have been old enough to have appeared in the jest book.

John. See HELLO, ~, GOT A NEW MOTOR?

John Bull. See under BULLDOG BREED.

John Hancock. This US nickname for a signature or autograph derives from John Hancock, a Boston merchant, who was one of the first signatories of the Declaration of Independence in 1776. His signature is quite the largest on the document and he is variously reported to have made it that way 'so the King of England could read it without spectacles' and said: 'There! I guess King George [or John Bull] will be able to read that!'

John Henry come here! See HELLO, EVERYBODY . . .

Johnnie Walker. See BORN 1820 . . .

Johnny. See HERE'S ~.

Johnstown Flood. See DON'T SPIT . . .

John Willie, come on! The British comedian George Formby Snr (1877–1921) included in his act monologues from a typical Lancashire character called 'John Willie'. The phrase 'John Willie, come on' swept the country. Audiences waited for the line and knew just when it was coming – so they could join in. See also COUGHIN' WELL TONIGHT and WIGAN PIER.

join. See IF YOU CAN'T BEAT 'EM . . . ; YOU CAN'T SEE THE ~. under MORECAMBE AND WISE SHOW.

joint. See WHAT'S A NICE GIRL LIKE YOU . . .

join the Army/Navy and see the world. The Army version of this slogan seems to have been used in both Britain and the US in the 1920s and 30s. Partridge/*Slang* dates the riposte '. . . the next one' as *c* 1948. In the song 'Join the Navy' from the musical *Hit the Deck* (1927), there appears the line 'Join the Navy and see the world'. In the film *Duck Soup* (1933), Harpo Marx holds up a placard which says, 'Join the Army and See the Navy'. Irving Berlin's song 'We Saw the Sea' from *Follow the Fleet* (US, 1936) goes, 'I joined the Navy to see the world. And what did I see? I saw the sea.' 'I joined the Navy to see the world' is quoted ironically, by a sailor in the film *In Which We Serve* (UK, 1942).

joke. See HA! HA! ~ OVER!; THAT'S A ~, SON!

jokes, five basic. See under SIX BASIC PLOTS.

jolly D. See OH, ~! under MUCH BINDING IN THE MARSH.

jolly good show! A very English phrase of approbation, recorded by 1934. Terry-Thomas (1911–90), the gap-toothed comedian used it, as also **oh, good show!** in his late 1940s and early 1950s monologues.

jolly hockey sticks! See under EDUCATING ARCHIE.

Jolly Jack. The nickname given to the Yorkshire-born writer J.B. Priestley (1894–1984) was an ironic coinage, as he was a champion grumbler. According to his widow, it was first conceived by the staff of the *New Statesman* at a time when he had fallen into a prolonged gloomy mood (quoted in Vincent Brome, *J.B. Priestley*, 1988).

Joneses. See KEEP UP WITH THE ~.

Josephine. See NOT TONIGHT, ~.

jot and tittle, a. Meaning 'the least item or detail', the words come from Matthew 5:18: 'Till heaven and earth pass, one jot or one tittle shall in no wise pass from the law, till all be fulfilled.' 'Jot' is *iota*, the smallest Greek letter (compare 'not one iota') and 'tittle' is the dot over the letter *i* (Latin *titulus*).

journey. See IS YOUR ~ REALLY NECESSARY?

journey into the unknown, a. Journalistic cliché. At the beginning of the Falklands War, for example: 'To the strains of "We are Sailing", the ropes were slipped and *Canberra* was off into the unknown' (J. Hands & R. McGowan, *Don't Cry for Me, Sergeant-Major*, 1983). *Journey To the Unknown* was the title of a TV suspense series (US, produced in England, 1968–9).

Jove. See BY ~, I NEEDED THAT!

joy of —, the. A cliché, mostly of book-titling. First on the scene were I.S. Rombauer and M.R. Becker, American cookery experts, with *The Joy of Cooking* (1931). A US film was entitled *Joy of Living* in 1938. Then, in 1972, along came Alex Comfort with *The Joy of Sex* and even *More Joy of Sex*. Then everyone joined in, so that we have had books about the 'joys' of computers, chickens, cheesecake,

breastfeeding and geraniums, among many others.

In 1984, I published *The Joy of Clichés* – which I thought would be seen to be ironical – though Fritz Spiegl seems to have had no compunction in naming a book *The Joy of Words* (1986) or Gyles Brandreth *The Joy of Lex* (1980).

JR. See WHO SHOT ~?

Judas Priest. A euphemism for the oath 'Jesus Christ!' Of American origin and recorded by 1914. Judas Priest was taken as the name of a UK pop group of the 1980s. Compare GORDON BENNETT!

judge. See HERE COME DE ~ under LAUGH-IN.

Judy! . . . Judy! . . . Judy! Impersonators always put this line in the mouth of Cary Grant, but the actor always denied that he had ever said it and had a check made of all his films (in which, presumably, if he was referring to Judy Garland in character, he wouldn't have been calling her by her actual name, anyway). According to Richard Keyes, *Nice Guys Finish Seventh* (1992), Grant once said: 'I vaguely recall that at a party someone introduced Judy by saying, "Judy, Judy, Judy," and it caught on, attributed to me.'

There may be another explanation. Impersonators usually seek a key phrase which, through simple repetition, readily gives them the subject's voice. It is possible that one of these impersonators found that saying 'Judy' helped summon up Grant's distinctive tones, and it went on from there. Besides, many an impersonator, rather than ape his subject, simply impersonates fellow impersonators.

Did Bette Davies ever say, similarly, 'Peter . . . Peter . . . Peter!'?

juggling with soot. See under AS BUSY AS . . .

Julian. See OH, HELLO, I'M ~ under ROUND THE HORNE.

jump on to the band-wagon. See BAND-WAGON, TO CLIMB . . .

jump over the broomstick. See BRUSH, TO LIVE OVER THE.

jumpy. See under AS BUSY AS . . .

jungle. See BACK TO THE ~; BLACKBOARD ~; under DON'T FORCE IT, PHOEBE.

jungle fresh. A gloriously meaningless advertising line used to promote Golden Wonder salted peanuts in the UK, current late 1970s.

jury is (still) out on —, the. A mostly journalistic cliché, noticeable from the late 1980s, meaning that no final conclusion can be drawn, minds are not yet made up. From Andrew Morton, *Diana: Her True Story* (1993): 'The royal family now face an unenviable task in adapting themselves to the challenges of the twenty-first century. The jury is out and it is by no means certain that the verdict will be favourable to the monarchy.' Compare **a question-mark still hangs over . . .**

just and lasting settlement, a. A cliché of politics. As Safire notes, President Eisenhower spoke in Geneva (1955) of 'a just and durable peace' and later said, 'we will make constantly brighter the lamp that will one day guide us to our goal – a just and lasting peace'. The 'settlement' version became boringly popular with regard to the Palestinian problem after 1973. When the IRA announced its 'ceasefire' in Northern Ireland (31 August 1994), its statement managed to include the phrase twice: 'the desire for peace based on a just and lasting settlement cannot be crushed . . . We believe that an opportunity to secure a just and lasting settlement has been created'.

Whichever version is used, however, it does come with the Abraham Lincoln seal of approval. He talked of a 'just and lasting peace' in his Second Inaugural address (4 March 1865), referring to the end of the American Civil War.

just do it. Slogan for Nike sportsware, especially shoes, current by August 1989. Hardly meaningful (though it has been glossed as 'If a thing's worth doing, it's worth doing well') but a slogan that 'had become second nature to an entire

generation', according to the *International Herald Tribune* (June 1994).

just fancy that! Often ironical exclamation after a revelation has been made which – to the speaker – was eminently predictable given what was known about the person/people involved beforehand. Since the 1880s, and revived as a catchphrase by *Private Eye* in the 1970s – often as a headline over a story of curious malfeasance.

just how serious . . . ? A cliché of broadcast journalism, the invariable start to a thrusting, probing question. In the mid-1970s, Michael Leapman, as diarist on *The Times*, invented a character called 'Justow Serious'.

justice. See AND ~ FOR ALL; THIS HAS RESTORED MY FAITH . . . ; TRUTH, ~ AND THE AMERICAN WAY under *SUPERMAN*.

just like a fairy tale. See LIKE A FAIRY TALE (PRINCESS).

just like that! Said in gruff tones and accompanied by small paddling gestures, this was the catchphrase of the British comedian Tommy Cooper (1922–84) – and a gift to mimics. It was not a premeditated catchphrase, he said. He only noticed it when impressionists and others singled it out from his mad 'failed conjuror' act. Inevitably, the phrase was used by Cooper as the title of his autobiography. There is also a song incorporating it.

just one of those things. Meaning 'something inexplicable or inevitable'. The *OED2* finds the first modern use in John O'Hara's story *Appointment in Samarra* (1934), and in the following year as the title of the Cole Porter song which undoubtedly ensured its enduring place in the language. Five years earlier, however, Porter had used the title for a completely different song which was published, though dropped from the show it was supposed to be in. The form of words had been existence, however, by 1875.

just say no. Slogan of the anti-drug abuse campaign in the US, supported by Nancy

Reagan when First Lady. From the *Washington Post* (22 February 1985): 'The 8-year-old [Soleil Moon Frye] is honorary national chairperson of the Just Say No Club movement organized by three elementary school youngsters in Oakland to encourage kids to say no to drugs instead of giving in to peer pressure. The program attracted the attention of Mrs Reagan last summer when she visited the participants.'

just the facts, ma'am. See ALL I WANT IS THE FACTS . . . under *DRAGNET*.

just when you thought it was safe to —. The film *Jaws 2* (US, 1978) – a sequel to the successful shark saga – was promoted with the line, 'Just when you thought it was safe to go back in the water . . .' A graffito reported to me in 1979 was 'Jaws 3 – just when you thought it was safe to go to the toilet'. Headline from the *Observer* (16 July 1989): 'Just when you thought it was safe to get back in a bikini . . .'

· K ·

Kaiser. See ARF A MO ~ ; HANG THE ~.

kangaroo court. The name applied to a self-appointed court which has no proper legal authority – as in the disciplinary proceedings sometimes to be found among prisoners in gaol. Recorded by 1853. Ironically, *Macquarie* (1981), the Australian dictionary, calls this an American and British colloquialism, but surely it must have something to do with the land of the kangaroo? Perhaps it alludes to the vicious streak that such animals sometimes display?

Kansas. See TOTO, I HAVE A FEELING WE'RE NOT IN ~ ANY MORE.

Karachi. See SNOWSTORM IN ~ UNDER AS BUSY AS; YOU'RE FAMOUS WHEN . . .

Karno, Fred. See FRED KARNO.

Katanga! See CRUCIAL!

keen as mustard. Extremely keen. According to the *Independent* (3 November 1993), the Thomas *Keen*, who is buried in West Norwood Cemetery, near London, is the one 'whose family firm made mustard and whose activities led to the phrase "keen as mustard."' A nice thought, but 'the keenest mustard' was a phrase by 1658.

keep Britain tidy. The simplest of messages and one of the most enduring. Promoted through the Central Office of Information, it first appeared in their records as a sticker produced for the Ministry of Housing and Local Government in 1952. However, it was probably coined about 1949.

keep death off the road (carelessness kills). Nobody knows who created this message – the best-remembered of any used in British government-sponsored advertising campaigns through the Central Office of Information. It was used in the memorable poster by W. Little featuring the so-called 'Black Widow' in 1946.

Discussing the pointlessness of the campaign in *Tribune* (8 November 1946), George Orwell referred to 'Keep Death off the *Roads*', though the poster version in fact used the singular.

keep it dark! A security slogan from the Second World War (in the UK), appearing in more than one formulation, and also in verse:

> If you've news of our munitions
> KEEP IT DARK
> Ships or plans or troop positions
> KEEP IT DARK
> Lives are lost through conversation
> Here's a tip for the duration
> When you've private information.
> KEEP IT DARK.

Shush, Keep It Dark was the title of a variety show running in London during September 1940. Later, the naval version of the BBC radio show *Merry Go Round* (1943–8) featured a character called Commander High-Price (Jon Pertwee) whose catchphrase was, 'Hush, keep it dark!'

None of this had been forgotten by 1983, apparently, when Anthony Beaumont-Dark, a Tory candidate in the General Election, campaigned successfully for re-election with the slogan, 'Keep it Dark'.

keep it under your hat/stetson. Security slogans from the Second World War for the UK and US, respectively. *Under Your Hat* had been the title of a Cicely Courtneidge/ Jack Hulbert musical comedy in the West End (1938).

keep mum, she's not so dumb. See BE LIKE DAD, KEEP MUM.

keep on muddling through. See
MUDDLING THROUGH.

keep on truckin'. This expression,
meaning that you've got to 'persevere' or
'keep on keeping on' is described in Bartlett
as the 'slogan of a cartoon character'
created by Robert Crumb (b 1943). Crumb
drew 'dirty' cartoons for a number of
underground periodicals like *Snatch* and
created 'Fritz the Cat', later the subject of a
full-length cartoon film.

There were a number of records with
the title by 1970, and there was certainly
a vogue for the phrase in the 1960s and
70s. I notice, however, that there was a
song called simply 'Truckin'' in 1935
(words by Ted Koehler and music by
Rube Bloom) and that the *OED2* finds
'the truck' or 'trucking' as a jerky dance
that came out of Harlem in the summer of
1934. Partridge/*Catch Phrases* plumps for a
suggestion that the phrase, while of Negro
dance origin, came out of the great
American dance marathons of the 1930s,
though one of Partridge's contributors
hotly disputes this.

Flexner (1982) discussing 'hoboes,
tramps and bums' on the American
railroad probably gets nearest to the
source. He defines 'trucking it' thus:
'Riding or clinging to the trucking
hardware between the wheels. This may
have contributed to the jitterbug's use of
trucking (also meaning 'to leave or move
on' in the 1930s) and to the 1960 students'
phrase *keep on trucking*, keep moving, keep
trying, keep "doing one's (own) thing" with
good cheer.'

keep taking the tablets. Traditionally
what doctors advise patients to do and what
anybody might say particularly to someone
who is getting on in years and needs to have
medication in order to keep on going.
Possibly turned into a catchphrase by the
BBC radio *GOON SHOW*, though this is
unverified. An edition of BBC radio *ROUND
THE HORNE* (5 March 1967) includes the
remark, 'Good luck, Bishop, and keep
taking the tablets.' There is a lino-cut by
Gertrude Elias, dated 1950, entitled 'Keep
on taking the tablets' (reproduced in
Women's Images of Men, ed. Kent &
Morreau, 1985).

It is also the punch line of a sort of joke.
When James Callaghan, the British Labour
Prime Minister, was compared by his son-
in-law Peter Jay to Moses in 1977,
Margaret Thatcher, then Leader of the
Opposition, sought to make capital out of
it by jesting in her speech to that year's
Conservative Party Conference, 'My
advice to Moses is: keep taking the tablets.'
This was a venerable jest even then. 'What
Moses said to David Kossoff was
"Continue taking the tablets as before"'
was mentioned on BBC Radio *Quote . . .
Unquote* (1976). Even so, according to an
account given by Alan Watkins in *The
Observer* (27 May 1988), the joke very
nearly misfired. When Sir Ronald Millar,
Mrs Thatcher's speech-writer, presented
her with the effort, she 'pronounced the
joke funny but capable of improvement.
Would it not be more hilarious for her to
say "Keep taking the pill"?' And, indeed,
'Keep taking the Pils' was used as an
advertising slogan for Pilsener lager in the
late 1970s.

keep that schoolgirl complexion. A
slogan used to promote Palmolive soap, in
the US, from 1917. Coined by Charles S.
Pearce, a Palmolive executive. Beverley
Nichols wrote in *The Star-Spangled Manner*
(1928) that in his 'riotous youth' he had
been comforted through 'numberless orgies'
only by the conviction that if he used a
certain soap he would retain his schoolboy
complexion: 'It did not matter how much I
drank or smoked, how many nameless and
exquisite sins I enjoyed – they would all be
washed out in the morning by that magical
soap . . . I bought it merely because years
ago a bright young American sat down in
an office on the other side of the Atlantic
and thought of a slogan to sell soap. And he
certainly sold it.'

During the Second World War,
Palmolive was still plugging the old line in
the UK: 'Driving through blitzes won't spoil
that schoolgirl complexion'.

keep the ball rolling, to. See TO KEEP THE
BALL ROLLING.

keep the faith, baby. A slogan adopted
by Black activists in the US in the 1960s –
designed to encourage fellow Blacks to carry

on the struggle for civil rights whatever the setbacks. Popularized by the Congressman Adam Clayton Powell.

keep the wolf from the door, to. Meaning, 'to keep poverty and hunger at bay, to find the elementary necessities needed for survival'. The literal expression occurs in the *OED2* as long ago as 1470! Groucho Marx had a song called 'Toronto' which incorporated an elaborate joke about keeping (Jewish) people called Woolf from the door. In the film *She Done Him Wrong* (US, 1933), Mae West has the line: 'The wolf at my door? Why, I remember when he came right into my room and had pups!'

keep up the good work! A phrase of encouragement, probably current in the UK before 1939. The *OED2* has an American citation, dated 1953, from Eugene O'Neill's *Long Day's Journey Into Night*. I would have plumped for a services origin myself. Surely, it is the sort of thing likely to be uttered by any officer before, after, or instead of, saying, 'CARRY ON, Sergeant!'

keep up with the Joneses, to. Meaning 'to strive not to be outdone by one's neighbours', the expression comes from a comic strip by Arthur R. 'Pop' Momand entitled *Keeping up with the Joneses*, which appeared in the New York *Globe* from 1913 to 1931. It is said that Momand had at first intended to call his strip 'Keeping up with the Smiths' but refrained because his own neighbours were actually of that name and some of the exploits he wished to report had been acted out by them in real life.

keep your pecker up. See I'VE GOT HIS PECKER IN MY POCKET.

Kemo Sabe. See HI-YO, SILVER.

Kensington Gore. The name given to a type of artificial blood used in theatricals and the making of horror films. Derived from the short stretch of road in London near the Royal Albert Hall which was named, in turn, after Gore House, formerly on the site.

kettle. See CHOCOLATE ~ under AS BUSY AS . . . ; HERE'S A PRETTY ~ OF FISH.

Keynsham – that's K-E-Y-N-S-H-A-M . . . Listeners to Radio Luxembourg in the 1950s and 60s remember the rolling, West Country accent of Horace Batchelor (1898–1977) who appeared in commercials for his own method of winning the football pools. At his death it was said he had netted £12 million for his clients. His usual message was something like: 'Good evening, friends. This is Horace Batchelor at the microphone – the inventor of the Infra-Draw Method for the Treble Chance. I have myself, with my own coupon entries, won 1012 first Treble Chance top dividends. And my ingenious method can help you to win also. Don't send any money – just your name and address.'

Then came the high spot of his ads: 'Send now to Horace Batchelor, Department One, Keynsham – spelt K-E-Y-N-S-H-A-M, Bristol.'

kibosh on something, to put the. Meaning 'to squelch; put an end to; spoil; veto', this expression was current by 1884. It possibly comes from the Gaelic *cie bais*, meaning 'cap of death', but it is also known in Yiddish. An extraordinary (and unverified) explanation is that 'kibosh' was the name of the black cap worn by a British judge when pronouncing sentence of death.

kicking. See DRAGGED ~ AND SCREAMING . . .

kick the bucket/dust, to. All these euphemisms for 'to die', derive from either the suicide's kicking away the bucket on which he/she is standing, in order to hang him/herself, or from the 'bucket beam' on which pigs were hung *after* being slaughtered. The odd *post mortem* spasm would lead to the 'bucket' being kicked.

'Kick the dust' for 'to die' is nicely illustrated by a passage from Thoreau's *Walden* (1854): 'I was present at the auction of a deacon's effects . . . after lying half a century in his garret and other dust holes . . . When a man dies he kicks the dust.' The *OED2* mentions neither this expression, nor 'kiss the dust', though it does find **bite the dust** in 1856.

Psalm 72:9 has **lick the dust**: 'They that dwell in the wilderness shall bow before him; and his enemies shall lick the dust' – though this is suggesting humiliation rather than death.

kid. See ALL ∼ GLOVES . . . ; HERE'S LOOKING AT YOU, ∼!

killing fields. *The Killing Fields* was the title of a film (UK, 1984) concerning the mass murders carried out by the Communist Khmer Rouge, under Pol Pot, in Cambodia between 1975–8, when possibly three million were killed. The mass graves were discovered in April 1979.

In the film, the phrase was seen to refer, literally, to paddy fields where prisoners were first forced to work and where many of them were then callously shot. The film was based on the article 'The Death and Life of Dith Pran' by Sydney Schanberg, published in the *New York Times Magazine* (20 January 1980), which tells of the journalist's quest for reunion with his former assistant. The article has the phrase towards the beginning, thus: 'In July of 1975 – two months after Pran and I had been forced apart on April 20 – an American diplomat who had known Pran wrote me a consoling letter. The diplomat, who had served in Phnom Penh, knew the odds of anyone emerging safely from a country that was being transformed into a society of terror and purges and "killing fields".' So it appears that the coinage is due to the unnamed diplomat. Haing S. Ngor, who played Pran in the film, wrote a book called *Surviving the Killing Fields* (1988).

William Shawcross, author of two notable books on Cambodia, said (1990) that he had never heard the phrase until the film was in preparation. It is now widely used allusively to describe any place given over to mass executions, e.g. 'How Ridley saved his killing fields' [where a British politician went shooting game] (the *Observer*, 23 July 1989); and: 'The killing fields revisited' [headline to a travel article about the battlefield of Waterloo] (*Observer*, 25 February 1990).

The phrase **killing ground(s)** has also entered the military vocabulary as a strategic term for an area into which you manouevre the enemy before finishing them off and which has been current since the Second World War. In a non-military sense, the phrase was used by Rudyard Kipling in his poem 'The Rhyme of the Three Sealers' (1893) about seal hunting.

It is difficult to say whether there is any connection with the US term **killing floor**, originally referring perhaps to an abbatoir but in the 1960s used for a place where sexual intercourse took place.

Kilroy was here. The most widely known of graffiti slogans, was brought to Europe by American GIs (*c* 1942). The phrase may have originated with James J. Kilroy (*d* 1962), a shipyard inspector in Quincy, Mass., who would chalk it up to indicate that a check had been made by him. It was also the title of a film (US, 1947).

Kinder, Kirche, Küche. 'Children, church, kitchen' – it became a German Nazi doctrine that a woman's place in the state should be confined to these so-called womanly occupations – noted by Dorothy L. Sayers in *Gaudy Night*, Chap. 22 (1935). In fact, the idea is a good deal older than that. In the 1890s, it also had a fourth K at the end – '*Kleider*' [dress].

kindly leave the stage. See I DON'T WISH TO KNOW THAT . . .

king. See under ELVIS THE PELVIS; SPORT OF ∼S; TRUE, O ∼!

king and country. The alliterative linking of these two words is of long standing. Francis Bacon (1625) wrote: 'Be so true to thyselfe, as thou be not false to others; specially to thy King, and Country.' Earlier, Shakespeare, *Henry VI, Part 2*, I.iii.157 (1597) has:

> But God in mercy so deal with my soul
> As I in duty love my king and country!

King and Country was the title of a film (UK, 1964), coming from the First World War slogan 'Your King and Country Need You' (see also YOUR COUNTRY NEEDS YOU). In that war, 'For King and Country' was the official reply to the question: 'What are we fighting for?'

king of terrors, the. Death, as in Job 18:14. Thomas Carlyle, *The History of French Revolution*, I.i.iv (1837) has: 'Frightful to all men in Death; from of old named King of Terror.' The phrase was used as the title of Henry Scott Holland's sermon (1910) from which the passage beginning 'Death is nothing at all' is taken.

king of the road. Phrase used in the UK as a slogan for Lucas bicycle lamps in the 1920s. In the song 'A Transport of Delight' (1957), Flanders and Swann refer to a London bus as a 'monarch of the road'. Also used as the title of a song written and performed by Roger Miller (US, 1965), by way of allusion to hoboes and tramps, who have more usually been known as **knights of the road**. In England, 'knight of the road' has also referred to a highwayman since 1665.

King over the water!, the. A toast using the name given to the exiled James II after his departure from the English throne in 1688 (also to his son and grandson, the Old Pretender and the Young Pretender). Jacobites would propose the toast while passing the glass over a water decanter.

kipper's knickers. See under BEE'S KNEES.

kiss. See WHERE DID YOU LEARN TO ∼ LIKE THAT?

kiss and tell. As in 'kiss and tell memoirs', used to describe the situation where one half of a couple sells an account of their affair (invariably over by this stage) to a newspaper. An older phrase than you might think: William Congreve in *Love for Love* (1695) has: 'Oh, fie, Miss, you must not kiss and tell.' Bernard Shaw in a letter to Mrs Patrick Campbell (30 December 1921) writes: 'A gentleman does not kiss and tell.' A headline from the *Sunday Telegraph* (17 May 1992): 'KISS IF YOU MUST, BUT PLEASE DON'T TELL'.

kisses. See STOLEN ∼.

kiss me, my fool. See under CAME THE DAWN.

kiss my grits! Meaning, 'to hell with you', a catchphrase from the TV situation comedy *Alice* (US, 1976–80). Flo Castelberry, a Southern-born, man-hungry waitress (played by Polly Holliday), uttered the phrase and later had her own series, *Flo* (1980–81).

kiss of death/life, the. The 'kiss of death' derives from the kiss of betrayal given by Judas to Christ which foreshadowed the latter's death. In the Mafia, too, a kiss from the boss is an indication that your time is up. Compare *Kiss of Death*. the title of a gangster film (US, 1947). Safire defines the political use of the phrase as 'unwelcome support from an unpopular source, occasionally engineered by the opposition'. He suggests that Governor Al Smith popularized the phrase in 1926, when he called William Randolph Hearst's support for Smith's opponent, Ogden Mills, 'the kiss of death'. In Britain, Winston Churchill used the phrase in the House of Commons on 16 November 1948. Nationalization and all its methods were a 'murderous theme'; the remarks of Government spokesman about the control of raw materials, 'about as refreshing to the minor firms as the kiss of death'.

'Kiss of life' as the name of a method of mouth-to-mouth method of artificial respiration was current by the beginning of the 1960s. On one unfortunate occasion I heard a BBC Radio 4 newsreader confuse the two. 'Having been pulled out of the river,' he said, 'the boy did not survive, despite being given the kiss of death by a passing policeman.'

kissy-kissy. Come-on of 'Miss Piggy', the resident porcine vamp of TV's *The Muppet Show* (UK, 1976–81).

kitchen. See IF YOU CAN'T STAND THE HEAT . . .

Kite. See BEING FOR THE BENEFIT OF . . .

kittens, to have. To act nervously, behave in a hysterical manner. Originally American and known by 1900. Morris explains that, in medieval times, if a pregnant woman was having pains, it was 'believed she was bewitched and had kittens clawing at her inside her womb'. Witches could provide lotions to destroy the imagined 'litter'. As late as the seventeenth century an 'excuse for obtaining an abortion was given in court as "removing cats in the belly"'.

kitty, in the. Money is put in the kitty or 'the pool' in card games and the expression has been known since 1887. Robert L. Shook in *The Book of Why* (1983) suggests that it comes from 'kit', short for 'kitbag', which was used among soldiers as a receptacle in which to pool their money. I can find no support for this theory, but no one seems to have a better idea.

knees. See BEE'S ~.

knickers. See ALL FUR COAT AND NO ~ under ALL KID GLOVES . . .

(K)nickers Off Ready When I Come Home. See NORWICH.

knickers/breeches on the line, hang your. In our household, when someone asks, 'What's the time?' and the answer happens to be (as it does, frequently, for some reason), 'Half past nine,' the first person says, 'Knickers on the line.' One of a number of ritual additions, this was imported by my wife from her Buckinghamshire childhood in the 1950s. A possible origin? In a section called 'Crooked Answers' in *The Lore and Language of Schoolchildren* (1959), Iona and Peter Opie print two versions of a rhyme from Alton, Hampshire:

> What's the time?
> Half past nine
> Put the napkins on the line.
> When they're dry
> Bring them in
> And don't forget the safety pin.

And:

> What's the time?
> Half past nine

> Hang your breeches on the line.
> When the copper
> Comes along
> Pull them off and put them on.

knife. See MAC THE ~.

knight of the shires, a. A British political term for the type of Conservative back-bench Member of Parliament who is awarded a knighthood simply for long and devoted service. He then continues to represent the safe, conservative interests of 'Middle England' in which perhaps he once used to be a landowner. From the *Financial Times* (12 May 1983): 'Those traditional Tory stalwarts, the knights of the shires – and suburbs – may be becoming an endangered species. At least 26 Tories have announced they are going, and this includes 17 with knighthoods.'

knights of the road. See under KING OF THE ROAD.

knives. See NIGHT OF THE LONG ~.

knobs on, with. As in the similar phrases **with bells on** and **with brass knobs on**, this is a way of saying (somewhat ironically) that something comes with embellishments. British use only, I think. *OED2* has a 1931 citation from J.J. Farjeon. I have found a 1932 one in a theatre review by Herbert Farjeon (perhaps if they were related, it was a family expression!). It goes: 'A massive company has been assembled at His Majesty's Theatre to restore what is called "the Tree tradition" with an overwhelming production of *Julius Caesar*, which I need hardly tell anyone who knows anything about the Tree tradition means plenty of lictors and vestal virgins or, to sum the matter up in the base vernacular, *Julius Caesar* with knobs on.'

knock. See SET 'EM UP HIGH . . .

knocker. See AS BLACK AS NEWGATE ~.

knock, knock! (1) Catchphrase said to have been used in the UK by the British music-hall comedian Wee Georgie Wood (1895–1979). He used it in a radio programme in 1936. This was possibly an imported American device to warn that a dubious joke was coming up. From *Variety* (19 August 1936): 'Manager Russell Bovim of Loew's Broad, Columbus, cashed in handsomely on the "Knock Knock" craze now sweeping the country.' (2) Name given to a type of (usually punning) joke popular especially in the UK and US by the 1950/60s and repopularized by *LAUGH-IN*, e.g.:

Knock, knock!
Who's there? Sam and Janet.
Sam and Janet who?
'Sam and Janet evening . . .'

knock off work, to. i.e. to finish work for the day. Morris explains that this dates from the days of slave galleys. The man who beat time to keep the oarsmen pulling in unison would give a special knock to indicate when there was to be a change of shift. Good try. Not recorded before 1902 (in the UK).

knock-out blow, a. The final thrust that settles everything. As Britain's Secretary of State for War, David Lloyd George gave an interview to Roy W. Harris, president of the United Press of America. It was printed in *The Times* (29 September 1915). Lloyd George was asked to 'give the United Press, in the simplest possible language, the British attitude toward the recent peace talk'. He answered: 'Sporting terms are pretty well understood wherever English is spoken . . . Well, then. The British soldier is a good sportsman . . . Germany elected to make this a finish fight with England . . . The fight must be to a finish – to a knock out.' In his memoirs, Lloyd George entitled one chapter 'The Knock-out Blow' – which is how this notion was popularly expressed. In boxing, the expression had been known since the 1880s.

knocks. See OPPORTUNITY ~; SCHOOL OF HARD ~.

knock seven bells out of —, to. To beat severely, if not actually knock someone out. It is nautical in origin (and known by 1929), but why seven out of the eight bells available aboard ship?

know. See AS EVERY SCHOOLBOY ~S; AS WE ~ IT; DO YOU ~ . . . ; DO THEY ~ IT'S

CHRISTMAS?; END OF CIVILIZATION AS WE ~ IT; EVERYTHING YOU ALWAYS WANTED TO ~; I DON'T WISH TO ~ THAT . . . ; NOT MANY PEOPLE ~ THAT; ONE INSTINCTIVELY ~S; SHE ~S, YOU KNOW.

know all the angles, to. Meaning, 'to have experience, be professional'. The earliest *OED2* citation is from Nevil Shute's *Pastoral* (1944): 'The old stagers . . . the men who knew all the angles, who had great experience.' But where does the expression come from – geometry/gunnery/snooker/billiards?

know one's arse from a hole in the ground, to. 'To be sufficiently clued up to be able to make this distinction.' Almost certainly American in origin and possibly current by the early 1900s. Is often presented in a negative and allusive form, as in *Mr Smith Goes to Washington* (film US, 1939): 'doesn't know — from a hole in the ground'.

know what I mean, 'Arry? Post-boxing match interview phrase supposedly used by the British fighter Frank Bruno in reply to Harry Carpenter, for many years BBC TV's chief match commentator. Established by 1986. Carpenter himself commented (*Sunday Times*, 19 April 1992): 'I only have to walk down the street or stand in a bar to have someone say to me: "Where's Frank?" or "Know what I mean, 'Arry?" (Strange how people always drop the aitch when they say that. Frank never does.)'

know where the bodies are buried, to. To know the secrets of an organization and thus to be in a position where you are not likely to be 'let go'. Used from the 1980s onwards in the US and UK. From the *Sunday Times* (29 September 1985): 'A senior member of the PLP [in the Bahamas] said: "If he is sent to America, he will sing like a canary – and this guy knows where the bodies are buried."' From the *Financial Times* (9 June 1986): 'Like Martha Mitchell, the political wife who spilled the beans, she knows where the bodies are buried in the Rose Garden.'

Kookie, Kookie (lend me your comb).
This was the title of a song (1960), featuring
Ed Byrnes and Connie Stevens, using a
stock phrase from the American TV cop
show *77 Sunset Strip* (1958–63). Byrnes played
'Kookie', a fast-talking parking lot attendant
who became a teen idol wearing slick shirts,
tight pants, and a 'wet look' hairstyle. He
had a habit of constantly combing his hair,
and this was celebrated in the hit song.

kosher nostra. See under TAFFIA.

kyrie eleison. See MASS PHRASES.

· L ·

labonza. See under AND AWA-A-AAY WE GO!

labour/Labour. See DIGNITY OF ~; under LIFE'S BETTER WITH THE CONSERVATIVES.

Labour isn't working. A noted British Conservative political slogan. It first appeared in 1978 on posters showing a long queue outside an employment office. Created by the Saatchi & Saatchi agency, the poster was later widely used in the 1979 General Election that took Margaret Thatcher to Downing Street. When unemployment continued to rise under the Conservatives, the slogan was, of course, recalled with irony.

lacrimae. See HINC ILLAE ~.

lacrimosa (dies illa). See MASS PHRASES.

laddie. See ACTOR ~.

ladies and gentle-men! See NAY, NAY ~ THRICE AGAIN NAY!

lads. See HAWAE THE ~.

lady. See AND ALL BECAUSE . . . ; BAG ~; WHAT'S THAT MAN/ ~ FOR?; WHO WAS THAT ~ . . .

lady bountiful, a. Applied (now only ironically) to a woman who is conspicuously generous to others less fortunate than herself (particularly within a small community or village). The expression comes from the name of a character in George Farquhar's play *The Beaux' Stratagem* (1707).

Lady Chatterley. Usually, when this name is invoked, it is not so much the particular character but the whole phenomenon of the book *Lady Chatterley's Lover* by D.H. Lawrence that is being referred to. In October 1960, when Penguin Books Ltd were cleared of publishing an obscene work in the unexpurgated edition of the novel, a landmark in publishing and sexual freedom was established. Philip Larkin, in his poem 'Annus Mirabilis' (1974), said:

Sexual intercourse began
In nineteen sixty-three
. . . Between the end of the *Chatterley* ban
And the Beatles' first LP.

Lady Godiva. See PEEPING TOM.

Lady in Red. See WOMAN IN RED.

Lady with a/the Lamp, the. This was the nickname given to Florence Nightingale, the philanthropist and nursing pioneer, in commemoration of her services to soldiers at Scutari during the Crimean War (1853–6). She inspected hospital wards at night, carrying a lamp – a Turkish lantern consisting of a candle inside a collapsible shade. The phrase 'lady with *a* lamp' appears to have been coined by Longfellow in his poem *Santa Filomena* (1858 – i.e. very shortly after the events described). On her death, Moore Smith & Co. of Moorgate, London, published a ballad with the title 'The Lady with *the* Lamp'. The film biography (1951), with Anna Neagle as Miss Nightingale, was called *The Lady with a Lamp* and was based on a play (1929) by Reginald Berkeley. Very occasionally one finds 'The Lady *of* a Lamp'.

lager. See PROBABLY THE BEST ~ IN THE WORLD.

lager lout. Term for a young person in the UK, noted for lager consumption and a tendency to violence, particularly when attending football matches. The species was identified in 1988, the name clearly owing much to alliteration. According to Simon Walters, political correspondent of the *Sun*, in a letter to the *Independent* (13 April 1989): 'It dates back to last August when the Home Office referred to the "lager culture" among young troublemakers . . . from that I coined the term "lager lout" to give it more meaning.'

lame duck. Referring to someone or something handicapped by misfortune or by incapacity, this was the name originally given to a defaulter on the London Stock Exchange in the nineteenth century. In William Thackeray's *Vanity Fair*, Chap. 13 (1847–8), the money-conscious Mr Osborne is suspicious of the financial position of Amelia's father: 'I'll have no lame duck's daughter in my family.' It is said that people who could not pay their debts would 'waddle' out of Exchange Alley in the City of London – hence perhaps, the 'duck'.

In the US, the term has come to be applied to a president or other office-holder whose power is diminished because he is about to leave office or because he is handicapped by some scandal. In *c* 1970, the term was also applied by British politicians to industries unable to survive without government financial support.

lamp. See LADY WITH A ~.

lamps. See OIL FOR THE ~ OF CHINA.

land. See BACK TO THE ~.

—land. A format phrase, as in 'radioland', 'listenerland' 'viewerland' – a suffix construction originating, I would say, in the US. 'Hi there, all you folks out their in radioland!' a presenter might well have said in the 1930s/40s. In the late 1950s/early 1960s, Granada TV in the UK was promoted via a series of print ads giving facts about 'Granadaland', the area covered by the company and then comprising Lancashire and Yorkshire. From the American *Spy* magazine (February 1989): 'And from the *Spy* mailroom floor: The Unsoliciteds out in Returnenvelopeland continue to ply us with free verse and promises of loose fiction.'

landed. See EAGLE HAS ~.

land flowing with milk and honey, a. Referring to any idyllic, prosperous situation, the origin of the phrase is to be found in Exodus 3:8: 'And I am come to deliver them out of the hand of the Egyptians . . . unto a land flowing with milk and honey.'

land of Nod, to go into the. To fall/be asleep (compare 'to nod off'). Jonathan Swift has the expression in *Polite Conversation* (1738). As such, this is a pun on the land of Nod ('on the East of Eden'), to which Cain was exiled after he had slain Abel (Genesis 4:16).

lang may yer lum reek. 'May you have long life', in Scots dialect. A 'lum' is a chimney, 'reek' is smoke – so the phrase literally means: 'long may your chimney smoke'.

language. See COUNTRIES SEPARATED BY A COMMON ~.

large. See BY AND ~.

large lumps! An expression used by the British comedian Dickie Hassett, who flourished *c* 1940. He was even given a BBC radio show with the title. Remembered by some as 'large lumps – they're lovely!' and explained by others as having appeared in a sketch about London street cries: 'Don't fergit yer mohair laces . . . Sarsparillar . . . Mmatches, two fer a h'penny!' 'Large lumps' was the cry of the iced coconut man.

larks. See WHAT ~, PIP!

larovers for meddlers and crutches for lame ducks. A way of not giving an answer to an inquisitive person, especially a child. If someone asks, 'What have you got there?' this is the reply with which to fob them off. Possibly a Northern English dialect expression originally, but now quite widespread. Could 'meddlers' be 'medlars' (i.e. the fruit – also, as it happens, a term for the female genitals)?

Philip N. Wicks of Wellingborough, Northamptonshire, recalled (1994): 'When as a small child I asked my Mother [who hailed from Norfolk], "What's in there?" regarding the contents of any unreadable packet or blank blue grocer's bag, she would reply secretively, "Leerooks for meddlers and beans for gooses eyes." I've wondered for forty years what she meant.'

Partridge/*Catch Phrases* finds a version already in use by 1668. G.L. Apperson in his *English Proverbs and Proverbial Phrases* (1929) explains 'larovers' as 'lay-overs' – things laid over, covered up, to protect them from meddlers – and concludes: 'Almost every county has its variation probably of this phrase. The most common form in which it survives, however, is "Layers for meddler".' Other versions include 'larrows to catch meddlers', 'layversfor meddlers' and 'lay-o for meddlars'.

Another explanation is that 'lay-holes for medlars' are what you put the fruit in to ripen. Partridge also gives the variant: 'Crutches for meddlers and legs for lame ducks'. No easy solution to this one.

Larry. See HAPPY AS ~.

last. See AND WHEN DID YOU ~ SEE . . .; FAMOUS ~ WORDS; NICE GUYS FINISH ~.

last best hope of earth, the. Referring to the act of giving freedom to the slaves by the US, the phrase comes from Abraham Lincoln's Second Annual Message to Congress (1 December 1862): 'We shall nobly save or meanly lose the last, best hope of earth'.

last chance trendy, a. (sometimes abbreviated to **LCT**.) A species of male, identified in the UK, who – faced with the onset of his fortieth birthday, or thereabouts – attempts to look and behave younger than he is, with inappropriate results. At the time this man was celebrated (Fred Wedlock's disc 'The Oldest Swinger in Town' was a hit in 1981; Christopher Matthew used the phrase 'Last-Chance Trendy' in his book *How To Survive Middle Age* in 1983), the symptoms of such behaviour included wearing tight trousers, long hair carefully styled to cover bald spots, and sporting gold medallions and other equipment unsuitable for a man of this vintage. The LCT also attempts to pursue younger women, often dumping his wife in the process, and exhibits many of the hallmarks of the mid-life crisis.

last drop. See GOOD TO THE ~.

last hurrah, the. A politician's final flourish or farewell. From *The Last Hurrah*, the title of a novel (1956; film US, 1958) by Edwin O'Connor, about an ageing Boston-Irish politician making his last electoral foray.

lasting. See JUST AND ~ SETTLEMENT.

lastlies. See NINTHLIES AND ~.

Last of England, The. Title of a painting by Ford Madox Brown (1855) which shows a young man and woman huddled together on a boat, as they emigrate from England. It was inspired by the departure of Thomas Woolner, the Pre-Raphaelite sculptor, who left England for Australia in order to join the gold rush. 'The Last of England' also became the title-poem of a collection (1970) by the Australian poet, Peter Porter ('You cannot leave England, it turns/A planet majestically in the mind').

Last of the Red-Hot Mamas, the. The stage sobriquet of Sophie Tucker, the singer, taken from the title of a song by Jack Yellen, which was introduced by her in 1928.

last of the (summer) wine, the. *The Last of the Summer Wine* is the title of a BBC TV comedy series (1974 onwards) about a trio of old school friends in a Yorkshire village, finding themselves elderly and unemployed. According to Roy Clarke, the programme's writer (in *Radio Times*, February 1983), the phrase is, 'not a quotation, merely a provisional title which seemed to suit the age group and location. I expected it to be changed but no one ever thought of anything better'.

The phrase 'last of the wine' had earlier been used to describe things of which there is only a finite amount or of which the best has gone. From a programme note by composer Nicholas Maw for *The Rising of the Moon*, Glyndebourne Festival Opera, 1970: 'In a recent television interview, Noël Coward was asked if he thought it still possible to write comedy for the stage. Did his own generation not have the "last of the wine"?' In the 1950s, Robert Bolt wrote a radio play with the title *The Last of the Wine* and Mary Renault, a novel (1956).

last resort, a/the. Positively the last place wherein to seek help or the ultimate chance to rescue a situation. Originally a legal expression for the supreme court of appeal. From Sir Walter Scott, *The Bride of Lammermoor*, Chap. 16 (1819): ' "No, my lord," answered Underwood; "it is in the House of British Peers, whose honour must be equal to their rank – it is in the court of last resort, that we must parley together." '

Probably French in origin – in the seventeenth century, they talked of *dernier ressort*.

last supper, the. The name given to the meal shared by Jesus Christ and his disciples the night before he was crucified and thus, the origin of the Eucharist, Lord's Supper, Holy Communion, and Mass. The phrase does not appear as such in the Bible, but may have become known chiefly through its use as the English title of the painting (1494–7) by Leonardo da Vinci in Milan. This is known in Italian simply as '*La Cena*' [The Supper], though sometimes '*L'Ultima Cena*'.

late. See TOO LITTLE, TOO ~.

late great —, the. A cliché, mostly used by disc jockeys and pop promoters. That death can confer status on a pop star, and do wonders for record sales, is certainly true – however, one feels that the use of 'great' here has often rather more to do with the demands of rhyme than truth.

later. See GO NOW, PAY ~.

late unpleasantness, the. A euphemism for the previous war or recent hostilities, it was introduced by the US humorist David Ross Locke in *Ekkoes from Kentucky* (1868). Writing as 'Petroleum V. Nasby', he referred to the recently ended Civil War as 'the late onpleasantniss' and the coinage spread. It still survives: 'Here, for instance, is Dan Rather, America's father-figure, on the hot-line to Panama during the late

unpleasantness [an invasion] . . .' (*Independent*, 20 January 1990).

Latin. See NO MORE ~.

laudamus te. See MASS PHRASES.

laugh. See ~ ALL THE WAY TO THE BANK under CRY ALL THE WAY . . . ; GAME FOR A ~; MEET THE WIFE . . . under 'AS 'E BIN IN, WHACK?; NO, DON'T ~ under NAY, NAY ~ THRICE AGAIN NAY!

laughed. See THEY ~ WHEN I SAT DOWN . . .

Laugh-In. A quintessential late 1960s sound was announcer Gary Owens, with hand cupped to ear, intoning, **this is beautiful downtown Burbank** – an ironic compliment to the area of Los Angeles where NBC TV's studios are located and where *Rowan and Martin's Laugh-in* was recorded. An enormous hit on US television from its inception in 1967, *Laugh-In* lasted until 1973 and was briefly revived, without Rowan and Martin, and with little success, in 1977. The original was a brightly coloured, fast-moving series of sketches and gags, with a wide range of stock characters, linked together by the relaxed charm of Dan Rowan (1922–87) and Dick Martin (*b* 1923).

For a while, the whole of America was ringing to the programme's catchphrases. The most famous of these was **sock it to me!** spoken by the English actress, Judy Carne (*b* 1939) who became known as the Sock-It-To-Me Girl. She would appear and chant the phrase until – ever unsuspecting – something dreadful happened to her. She would be drenched with a bucket of water, fall through a trap door, get blown up, or find herself shot from a cannon.

The phrase 'to sock it to someone' originally meant 'to put something bluntly' (and was used as such by Mark Twain). Black jazz musicians gave it a sexual meaning, as in 'I'd like to sock it to *her*'.

The precise way in which this old phrase came to be adopted by *Laugh-In* was described to me by Judy Carne in 1980: 'George Schlatter, the producer, had had great success in America with a show starring Ernie Kovacs in the 1950s. The wife on that show used to get a pie in the face every week and got enormous sympathy mail as a result. So George wanted a spot where an actress would have *horrendous* things done to her each week – a sort of "Perils of Pauline" thing – and then find a catchphrase to fit it.'

In the summer of 1967, Aretha Franklin had a hit record with 'Respect' which featured a chorus repeating 'Sock it to me' quite rapidly in the background. The previous year there had been a disc called 'Sock it to 'em, J.B.' by Rex Garvin with Mighty Craven, and in February 1967 an LP entitled 'Sock it to me, baby' had come from Mitch Ryder and the Detroit Wheels. But Aretha Franklin's record was where the *Laugh-In* catchphrase came from. 'George came up with the idea of making it literal. I said, "Well it should be Cockney." He said, "How far are you prepared to go?" And I said, "I'll do anything for a laugh. If I'm safe, I don't mind what you do to me."

'It all happened very fast . . . in about three weeks we were No. 1 with 50 million people watching. The sayings caught on at exactly the same time the show did . . . It had a dirty connotation and it was also very clean and was great for the kids. That's why I think that it took off the way it did – because it appealed to everyone at one level or another.' On being known as the Sock-It-To-Me Girl: 'It got in the way for a while. You have to go through a period of living a tag like that down, and proving that you are not just a saying. The main thing is not to identify with it, not to sit about worrying that people think of you as a saying. But better they think of you as a saying than not at all.'

Among the guests on the show who spoke the line were John Wayne, Mae West, Jack Lemmon, Jimmy Durante, Marcel Marceau (even) and Richard Nixon. The latter, running for the US presidency, said it on the show broadcast 16 September 1968. He pronounced it in a perplexed manner: 'Sock it to *me*?' And, lo, they finally did.

The next most famous phrase from the show was probably, **very interesting . . . but stupid!** ('but stinks', or some other variant). This was spoken in a thick accent by Arte Johnson as a bespectacled German soldier wearing a helmet and peering through a potted plant.

The third notable phrase was **you bet your sweet bippy!** – usually spoken by Dick Martin.

Other phrases from the show included:

bored! Jo Ann Worley used to exclaim this loudly. Could this be connected with 'bor-ring!' said in a sonorous, two-note sing-songy way by people also at about this time?

Flying Fickle Finger of Fate Award, the. This was the name of the prize in a mock talent contest segment of the show ('who knows when the Fickle Finger of Fate may beckon *you* to stardom?') According to Partridge/*Slang*, 'fucked by the Fickle Finger of Fate' was a Canadian armed forces' expression in the 1930s.

here come de judge! The old vaudeville phrase had a revival when Dewey 'Pigmeat' Markham, a black vaudeville veteran, was brought back to take part in a series of blackout sketches to which the build-up was the chant, 'Here comes de judge!'

> *Judge*: Have you ever been up before me?
> *Defendant*: I don't know – what time do you get up?

In July 1968, Pigmeat and an American vocalist called Shorty Long both had records of a song called 'Here Come(s) the Judge' in the US and UK charts.

is that a chicken joke? Asked by Jo Ann Worley (presumably alluding to the age-old variety, Q. Why did the chicken cross the road? A. To get to the other side/For some foul reason, etc).

is this the party to whom I am speaking? Ernestine, the rude, snobbish, nasal switchboard operator (Lily Tomlin), c 1969.

look that up in your Funk and Wagnalls! Referring to the American dictionary.

say goodnight, Dick/goodnight, Dick! Rowan and Martin's concluding exchange was a straight lift from the old

George Burns and Gracie Allen sign-off on *The Burns and Allen Show* (1950–58):

> Burns: Say goodnight, Gracie.
> Allen: Goodnight,Gracie!

Compare IT'S GOODNIGHT FROM ME/AND IT'S GOODNIGHT FROM HIM!

laughing. See MOST FUN I'VE HAD WITHOUT ~; MUM, MUM, THEY ARE ~ AT ME; THAT'LL STOP YOU ~ IN CHURCH.

laughs. See LORRA LORRA . . .

laughter is the best medicine. A fairly modern proverbial expression that relates a way of healing the psychosomatic illnesses of the body (compare 'fretting cares make grey hairs', 'a merry heart makes a long life'). Recorded in *Proverbium* (1991). Was it also the title of a long-running *Reader's Digest* feature? Compare the title of Irvin S. Cobb's joke miscellany: *A Laugh a Day Keeps the Doctor Away* (1921).

law. See LONG ARM OF THE ~.

law and order. An inevitable coupling, together by 1598 at least. In 1846, the 'Law and Order' Party existed in the US. By the 1970s, it was such a plank of British (Conservative) politics that a joke pronunciation 'Laura Norder' was introduced.

lay an egg, to. Although *OED2* says the source is American, Morris and other transatlantic sources give the English game of cricket as the origin of this expression meaning 'to fail'. A zero score was called a 'duck's egg' because of the obvious resemblance between the number and the object. In the US in baseball there developed a similar expression, 'goose egg'.

lay it on with a trowel, to. Benjamin Disraeli is said to have told Matthew Arnold: 'Everyone likes flattery; and when you come to Royalty you should lay it on with a trowel.' But the figure of speech was an old one even in the nineteenth century. 'That was laid on with a trowel' appears in Shakespeare's *As You Like It*, I.ii.98 (1598) which the Arden edition glosses as 'slapped on thick and without nicety, like mortar'.

The trowel in question is not a garden one, but of the kind used by painters for spreading paint thickly.

LCT. See LAST CHANCE TRENDY.

leader. See TAKE ME TO YOUR ~.

leading. See WHERE IS ALL THIS ~ US under MORNING ALL!

lead on Macduff! Meaning 'you lead the way!; let's get started!' the expression is from Shakespeare's *Macbeth*, V.iii.33 (1606): 'Lay on, Macduff;/And damn'd be he that first cries, "Hold enough!"'

There has been a change of meaning along the way. Macbeth uses the words 'lay on', defined by *OED2* as: 'to deal blows with vigour, to make vigorous attack, assail'. The shape of the phrase was clearly so appealing that it was adapted to a different purpose.

leaks. See under LET'S — AND SEE IF —.

leap. See GREAT ~ FORWARD; and under ONE SMALL STEP . . .

leather. See HELL FOR ~.

leather personnel carrier. See LCT.

leave. See DON'T ~ HOME WITHOUT IT, LOVE ME, OR ~ ME.

leave no stone unturned, to. Meaning 'to search for something with complete thoroughness', the expression was used by President Johnson in 1963 when announcing the terms of the Warren Commission's investigations into the cause of President Kennedy's assassination. Another example of the phrase's use is from an anonymously published attack on dice-playing, c 1550: 'He will refuse no labour nor leave no stone unturned, to pick up a penny.' Diana Rigg neatly twisted the phrase for her collection of theatrical reviews – *No Turn Unstoned* (1982).

leaving. See I'LL BE ~ YOU NOW, SIR . . .; PLEASE ADJUST YOUR DRESS BEFORE ~.

Led Zeppelin. The name of the British rock group (formed c 1968) presumably alludes to the type of airship, named after Count Ferdinand von Zeppelin (d 1917), the German aeronautical pioneer who designed and built them (c 1900), and combines this with the expression to '**go down like a lead balloon**', meaning 'to flop'. The spelling of 'led' was designed to reduce the likelihood of mispronunciation, especially in the US.

left a bit . . . See under BERNIE, THE BOLT!

left and right. See RIGHT AND LEFT.

left hand down a bit. From the standard instruction to people with their hands on the steering wheel of a vehicle. Meaning, 'to turn in an anti-clockwise direction'. Applied to navigation in many editions of *The Navy Lark* on BBC Radio (1960s/70s). Leslie Phillips would say it as a naval officer steering a boat. Jon Pertwee would reply, 'Left hand down it is, sir!'

leg. See BREAK A ∼; SHORT, FAT, HAIRY ∼S under *MORECAMBE AND WISE SHOW.*

legal, decent, honest, truthful. A slogan of the Advertising Standards Authority (founded 1962), reflecting the British Code of Advertising Practice view that the essence of good advertising is that 'all advertisements should be legal, decent, honest and truthful'. Originally, this was 'Legal, *Clean*, Honest, Truthful' (according to J. Pearson and G. Turner, *The Persuasion Industry*, 1965). *Legal Decent Honest Truthful* was, accordingly, the title of a BBC Radio 4 comedy series about advertising (mid-1980s).

legal eagle. For many years in the 1980s, Jimmy Young (see MORNING ALL) referred to his visiting legal expert thus (also 'legal beagle', I believe). Obviously, the rhyme dictates the 'eagle' bit, though this might be an appropriate epithet for one playing a look-out role. Partridge/*Slang* dates it from 'late 1940s, ex US'.

There was a US film with the title *Legal Eagles* in 1986.

legend. See WHAT BECOMES A ∼ MOST?

legend in one's own lifetime/living legend, a. Both of these phrases are now clichés of tribute. Even *The Oxford Companion to English Literature* (1985) has this: 'In 1888 [Robert Louis] Stevenson had set out with his family entourage for the South Seas, becoming a legend in his lifetime.' In a speech marking the retirement of George Thomas, Speaker of the House of Commons, in May 1983, Mrs Margaret Thatcher said: 'A great many have occupied your chair but it is a measure of your Speakership that you have become a legend in your own lifetime.' A joke reported to me in 1981 was, 'Is Michael Foot a leg-end in his own lifetime?'

On 25 August 1984, the *Guardian* reported that Tony Blackburn, the disc jockey, was writing his autobiography: ' "It's called The Living Legend – The Tony Blackburn Story," he explains more or less tongue-in-cheek. "They call me the Living Legend at Radio One . . . I'm known as the Survivor around there." '

Where did it all begin? A possibility exists that the first person to whom both versions of the epithet were applied (and within a couple of pages of each other), actually deserved them. Lytton Strachey in *Eminent Victorians* (1918) wrote of Florence Nightingale: 'She was a legend in her lifetime, and she knew it . . . Once or twice a year, perhaps, but nobody could be quite certain, in deadly secrecy, she went for a drive in the park. Unrecognised, the living legend flitted for a moment before the common gaze.'

I recall that in about 1976, Christopher Wordsworth, reviewing a novel by Clifford Makins, a sporting journalist, described the author as having been a **legend in his own lunchtime**, and this epithet is now quite frequently applied to other journalists of a certain type. According to Ned Sherrin, *Theatrical Anecdotes* (1991), 'David Climie, the witty revue and comedy writer . . . claims to have invented the phrase "A legend in his own lunchtime" and to have lavished it on the mercurial BBC comedy innovator, Dennis Main Wilson.'

leotard. See under DARING YOUNG MAN . . .

lergy, dreaded. See under *GOON SHOW.*

less is more. A design statement made by the German-born architect Mies van der Rohe (*d* 1969), meaning that less visual clutter makes for a more satisfying living environment. Robert Browning had used the phrase in a different artistic context in 'Andrea del Sarto' (1855).

lest we forget. Phrase from Rudyard Kipling's 'Recessional' (1897), written as a Jubilee Day warning that while empires pass away, God lives on. Kipling himself, however, may have agreed to the adoption of 'Lest we forget' as an epitaph at the time of his work for the Imperial War Graves Commission after the First World War. *Lest We Forget* was the title of the Fritz Lang film *Hangmen Also Die* (US, 1943) when it was re-issued.

let George do it! Meaning, 'let someone else do it, or take the responsibility', this catchphrase was in use by 1910 and is possibly of American origin.

let me tell you! See under RAMSBOTTOM, ENOCH AND ME.

let's — and see if —. In business and advertising, this construction is much used to indicate how an idea should be researched and tested, or rather, simply put to the public to see what reaction will be. Some of the versions:

Let's . . .
   . . . run it up the flagpole and see if anyone salutes it.
   . . . put it on the porch and see if the cat will eat it.
   . . . put it on the train and see if it gets off at Westchester.
   . . . leave it in the water overnight and see if it springs any leaks.

Not forgetting: 'Let me just pull something out of the hat here and see if it hops for us.' All these were known by the early 1980s.

let's do the show (right here in the barn)! This is taken to be a staple line in the films featuring the young Mickey Rooney and Judy Garland from 1939 onwards. It had several forms: 'Hey! I've got it! Why don't we **put on a show**?'/'Hey kids! We can put on the show in the

backyard!' – but a precise example has proved hard to find.

In *Babes in Arms* (1939), Rooney and Garland play the teenage children of retired vaudeville players who decide to put on a big show of their own. Alas, they do not actually say any of the above lines, though they do express their determination to 'put on a show'. In *Strike Up the Band* (1940), Rooney has the line: 'Say, that's not a bad idea. We could put on our own show!' – though he does not say it to Garland. In whatever form, the line has become a film cliché, now used only with amused affection.

let's get America moving again. A recurring theme in election slogans is that of promising to move forward after a period of inertia. John F. Kennedy used this one in 1960 – Walt Rostow is credited with suggesting it (sometimes it was '. . . this country moving again'). It is a short step from this to Ronald Reagan's 'Let's make America great again' in 1980.

There is also a format phrase: **let's get — moving again.** The Irish politician Jack Lynch ran in 1980 under the banner 'Get our country moving'. So, interchangeable slogans and formats that could be made to apply to any politician, party or country.

let's get down to the (real) nitty-gritty. Meaning, 'let's get down to the real basics of a problem or situation' (like getting down to BRASS TACKS). Sheilah Graham, the Hollywood columnist, in her book *Scratch an Actor* (1969) says of Steve McQueen: 'Without a formal education – Steve left school when he was fifteen – he has invented his own vocabulary to express what he means . . . His "Let's get down to the nitty-gritty" has gone into the American language.'

All she meant, I feel, is that McQueen popularized the term, for it is generally held to be a Black phrase and was talked about before the film star came on the scene. It seems to have had a particular vogue among BLACK POWER campaigners *c* 1963, and the first *OED2* citation is from that year. In 1963, Shirley Ellis recorded a song 'The Nitty Gritty' to launch a new dance (like 'The Locomotion' before it). The opening line of the record is, 'Now let's get down to the real nitty-gritty'.

Flexner (1982) comments: 'It may have originally referred to the grit-like nits or small lice that are hard to get out of one's hair or scalp, or to a Black English term for the anus.'

let's get myself comfy! See NAY, NAY ~ THRICE AGAIN NAY!

let's get on with it! British husband and wife entertainers, Nat Mills (1900–93) and Bobbie (*d* 1955), flourished in the 1930s and 1940s portraying 'a gumpish type of lad and his equally gumpish girlfriend'. Nat recalled (in 1979): 'It was during the very early part of the war. We were booked by the BBC to go to South Wales for a *Workers' Playtime*. Long tables had been set up in front of the stage for the workers to have lunch on before the broadcast. On this occasion, a works foreman went round all the tables shouting, "Come on, let's get on with it," to get them to finish their lunch on time. I was informed he used this phrase so many times, the workers would mimic him among themselves. So I said to Bobbie, "You start the broadcast by talking to yourself and I'll interject and say, 'Let's get on with it.''' Lo and behold it got such a yell of laughter we kept it in all our broadcasts. Even Churchill used our slogan to the troops during the early part of the war.'

let's get outta here! A survey of 350 feature films, made in the US between 1938 and 1985, revealed that the cry 'Let's get outta here!' was used at least once in 81 per cent of them and more than once in 17 per cent. In reporting this, the *Guinness Book of Movie Facts and Feats* (1993) adds that a film critic, David McGillivray, has disputed the finding. He asserted that no single phrase had been so overworked in film scripts as **try to get some sleep now.**

let's get this show on the road. Now used as an encouragement to get started on any activity, this phrase was originally from American show business. Perhaps originally from circus and travelling theatre use, it probably moved into the mainstream through the military and business. From J. Blish, *Fallen Star* (1957): ' "That's enough," Jayne said at last. "Let's get this show on the road." '

let's put on a show! See LET'S DO THE SHOW . . .

letter. See SOMEONE, SOMEWHERE . . .

let the cat out of the bag, to. Meaning 'to reveal a secret' this saying derives from the trick played on unsuspecting purchasers of sucking-pigs at old English country fairs. The pig would be shown to the buyer, then put in a sack while the deal was finalized. A quick substitution of a less valuable *cat* would then be made, and this is what the buyer would take away. When he opened the sack, he would 'let the cat out of the bag'.

let us go forward together. A political cliché, it was chiefly made so by Winston Churchill: 'I can only say to you let us go forward together and put these grave matters to the proof' (the conclusion of a speech on Ulster, 14 March 1914); 'Let us go forward together in all parts of the Empire, in all parts of the Island' (speaking on the war, 27 January 1940); and 'I say, "Come then, let us go forward together with our united strength"' (in his BLOOD, SWEAT AND TEARS speech, 13 May 1940).

let your fingers do the walking. A slogan for Yellow Pages (classified phone directories) from American Telephone & Telegraph Co., current from the 1960s. Also used in the UK and elsewhere.

level playing field, to start from a. Meaning 'to begin an enterprise with no participant having an advantage over another or with no unfairness involved'. Known in the US by 1988. From the *Independent on Sunday* (2 May 1993): 'Tears flowed when the axe fell. "The programme [TV soap *Eldorado*] had a lot of baggage attached to it," said Ms Hollingworth. "We did not start from a level playing field because there was so much antipathy."'

The British Foreign Secretary, Douglas Hurd, made an unfortunate play on words when, in a letter to the *Daily Telegraph* (5 April 1993) on lifting the arms embargo in Bosnia in favour of Muslims only, he wrote:

'We would in effect be saying "Here are the arms: fight it out". That is the policy of the level KILLING FIELD.'

Liberace at a wharfies' picnic. See under AS BUSY AS . . .

licensed to kill. What the British secret service agent James Bond is said to be, in the novels by Ian Fleming. The first of the series is *Casino Royale* (1953). Bond's identifying number – **007** – is linked to this: 'The licence to kill for the Secret Service, the double-o prefix, was a great honour' – *Dr No* (1958), though another explanation is given in *Live and Let Die* (1954): 'You have a double-o number, I believe – 007, if I remember right. The significance of that double-o number, they tell me, is that you have had to kill a man in the course of some assignment.'

lick the dust. See under KICK THE BUCKET.

lie. See BIG ∼; BR'ER FOX . . . ; under CLOSE YOUR EYES AND THINK . . . ; CAMERA CANNOT ∼; LIVING A ∼; SHE SHOULD ∼ BACK AND ENJOY IT.

lie down, I think I love you. This was considered a sufficiently well-established, smart, jokey remark to be listed by the *Sun* (10 October 1984) as one of 'ten top chat-up lines'. I have a feeling it may also have been used in a song or cartoon just a little before that. Indeed, there was a song entitled 'Lie Down (A Modern Love Song)' written and performed by the British group Whitesnake in 1978. Before that, 'Sit Down I Think I Love You', written by Stills, was performed by The Mojo Men in 1967. An article 'Down with sex' was published in collected form (1966) by Malcolm Muggeridge in which he wrote: 'I saw scrawled on a wall in Santa Monica in California: "Lie down! I think I love you." Thus stripped, sex becomes an orgasm merely.'

And then again, there was the Marx Brothers' line from *The Cocoanuts* (1929), 'Ah, Mrs Rittenhouse, won't you . . . lie down?' As ever, there is nothing new under the sun. Horace Walpole, in a letter to H.S. Conway on 23 October 1778, wrote: 'This sublime age reduces everything to its quintessence; all periphrases and expletives are so much in disuse, that I suppose soon the only way to making love will be to say "Lie down".'

life. See ALL HUMAN ∼ IS THERE; ANOTHER PAGE TURNED IN THE BOOK OF ∼ ; under BEER AND SKITTLES . . . ; BEST THINGS IN ∼ ARE FREE; BOHEMIAN ∼; DAY IN THE ∼; under DROWNING MAN . . .; GET A ∼; HAPPIEST DAYS OF YOUR ∼; IS THERE ∼ AFTER —; KISS OF DEATH; IT'S ALL PART OF ∼S RICH PAGEANT; LIVING ∼ IN THE FAST LANE; PRIVATE ∼ OF —; SUCH IS ∼; THAT'S ∼; THERE'S ∼ IN THE OLD DOG YET; THIS IS YOUR ∼; YOUR MONEY OR YOUR ∼.

life begins at forty. In 1932, William B. Pitkin (1878–1953), Professor of Journalism at Columbia University, New York, published a book called *Life Begins at Forty* in which he dealt with 'adult reorientation' at a time when the problems of extended life and leisure were beginning to be recognized. Based on lectures Pitkin had given, the book was a hearty bit of uplift: 'Every day brings forth some new thing that adds to the joy of life after forty. Work becomes easy and brief. Play grows richer and longer. Leisure lengthens. Life's afternoon is brighter, warmer, fuller of song; and long before shadows stretch, every fruit grows ripe . . . Life begins at forty. This is the revolutionary outcome of our new era . . . TODAY it is half a truth. TOMORROW it will be an axiom.' It is certainly a well-established catchphrase. Helping it along was a song with the title by Jack Yellen and Ted Shapiro (recorded by Sophie Tucker in 1937).

life. Be in it. See under BEWDY NEWK!

life is just a bowl of cherries. A modern proverbial expression that apparently originated in the song by Lew Brown (music by Ray Henderson), first heard in the American musical *Scandals of 1931*.

life isn't all beer and skittles. A proverbial expression warning that life does not solely consist of the enjoyment of simple pleasures, such as those of the typical English yeoman in his tavern (compare CAKES AND ALE). An established 'saw' by the 1850s when it appeared, for example, in

Thomas Hughes, *Tom Brown's Schooldays* (1857).

life of Reilly/O'Reilly/Riley, to live the. Meaning, 'to have a high old time, wallow in luxury, live it up, without much effort – have an easy life'. *The Life of Riley* was used as the title of an American TV sitcom with Jackie Gleason (1949–50). Partridge/*Catch Phrases* guesses an Anglo-Irish origin *c* 1935. In 1939, US adverts for Coronada, 'the air-cooled suit that resists wrinkles', were on the theme 'A Day in the Life of Reilly' (Jim Reilly Jr). In 1919 (also in the US) there was a song by Harry Pease with the title 'My Name Is Kelly' which went, 'Faith and my name is Kelly, Michael Kelly,/But I'm living the life of Reilly just the same.' This seems to be using an established phrase.

Morris thinks the name was 'O'Reilly' and that the association arose from a US vaudeville song about such a character, from the 1880s – though it doesn't appear to incorporate the line as we know it. Bartlett, however, quotes from the chorus of an 1882 song with the title 'Is That Mr Reilly' and adds that this is the 'assumed origin of "the life of Riley"'. It tells of what the hero would do if he struck it rich. Another song sometimes mentioned as a source is from *c* 1900: 'Best of the House is None Too Good for Reilly'.

life's a bitch, and then you die. This is a popular saying of untraced origin, though probably North American. A development of it, known both in the US and the UK, is 'Life's a bitch, *you marry a bitch*, and then you die.' Citations in print are few. Working backwards: during the summer of 1991, the Body Shop chain in the UK was promoting suntan products with a window display under the punning slogan, 'Life's a beach – and then you fry'. A caption to an article in the London *Observer* (23 September 1990) about frozen food was the equally punning, 'Life's a binge and then you diet'. In Caryl Churchill's play about the City, *Serious Money* (first performed March 1987), we find: 'I thought I'd be extremely rich./You can't be certain what you'll get./I've heard the young say Life's a bitch.' The earliest citation I have found comes from the

Sunday Times of 21 December 1986: 'Life is a bitch, then you die. So says the pilot of a flying fuel tank who, last week took off to circumnavigate the globe with his girlfriend.'

Life's a beach seems to have taken on a life of its own as a slogan, especially in Australia, but probably developed from 'Life's a bitch', rather than the other way round.

Attention might be drawn to *An Essay on Woman* by 'Pego Borewell Esq.' which was published in about 1763 as a bawdy parody of Alexander Pope's *An Essay on Man*. It is thought to have been written by the politician John 'Friend of Liberty' Wilkes and one Thomas Potter, working in some form of collaboration. Interestingly, it starts like this:

Let us (since life can little more supply
Than just a few good fucks, and then we
    die)
Expatiate freely . . .

Something of the same spirit comes through here.

life's better with the Conservatives – don't let Labour ruin it. A Tory slogan that helped bring the party a further period in office after the 1959 General Election – a poll in which many broadcasting and advertising techniques were applied to UK politics for the first time. There was much to justify the claim: material conditions had improved for most people; the balance of payments surplus, gold and dollar reserves were at a high level; wages were up; and taxation had gone down. The slogan emerged from consultations between Central Office and the Colmam, Prentis & Varley agency. In his book *Influencing Voters* (1967), Richard Rose says he knows of four people who claimed to have originated it. Ronald Simms was the PR chief at Central Office from 1957 to 1967. He is said to have come up with 'Life is good with the Conservatives, don't let the Socialists support it'. Lord Hailsham wanted 'better' instead of 'good' and CPV changed 'spoil' to 'ruin'. On the other hand, Maurice Smelt wrote (1981): 'The slogan was so successful that many people have claimed it (that always happens): but it was just a perfectly routine thing I did one afternoon in 1959 as the copywriter on the Conservative account at CPV. The brief from Oliver Poole [party chairman] was to say something like "YOU'VE NEVER HAD IT SO GOOD" but with less cynicism and more bite. The first five words were the paraphrase: and the whole ten told what I still think was a truth for its time. It's the slogan I am proudest of.'

Life the Universe and Everything. The title of a novel (1982) by Douglas Adams, this was blended with an allusion to his first work *The Hitch-Hiker's Guide to the Galaxy* (BBC Radio programme, 1978; novel 1979) to form an advertising slogan for the *Daily Telegraph* (current 1988): 'The Earth Dweller's Guide to Life the Universe and Everything'. From an untraced source, it is used to signify absolutely everything. Compare the all-embracing title of my own *The Quote . . . Unquote Book of Love, Death and the Universe* (1980).

lifetime. See LEGEND IN ONE'S OWN ∼.

life wasn't meant to be easy. Malcolm Fraser, Prime Minister of Australia 1975–83, was noted, among other things, for having said: 'Life wasn't meant to be easy.' The phrase was used as the title of a book about him by John Edwards in 1977. Fraser replied to a question from *The Times* (16 March 1981), as to whether he had ever actually said it: 'I said something very like it. It's from *Back to Methusaleh* [1918–20] by Bernard Shaw.' Indeed it is: 'Life is not meant to be easy, my child; but take courage: it can be delightful.' In a Deakin lecture on 20 July 1971, which seems to have been his first public use of the phrase, Fraser made no mention of Shaw, however. It is not, anyway, a startlingly original view. In one of A.C. Benson's essays in *The Leaves of the Tree* (1912), he quotes Brooke Foss Westcott, Bishop of Durham, as saying: 'The only people with whom I have no sympathy . . . are those who say that things are easy. Life is not easy, nor was it meant to be.'

lift-off. See WE HAVE ∼.

light. See HOLD IT UP TO THE ∼ . . . ; C'MON COLMAN'S . . . ; ∼ THE BLUE TOUCHPAPER . . .

under *BAND WAGGON*; WHERE WERE YOU WHEN THE ∼S WENT OUT?

light at the end of the tunnel, the. Meaning, a sign that some long-awaited relief or an end to some problem is at hand. Mostly used in politics, this is an idiom that has become a cliché. The *OED2*'s earliest citation is from 1922, and in a non-political context, though George Eliot had expressed the idea of coming out of a tunnel of darkness into daylight in a letter of 1879. In June 1983, the diarist of *The Times* tried to find the first Tory politician to have used the phrase. Stanley Baldwin in 1929 was the first, it turned out, followed by Neville Chamberlain at a Lord Mayor's banquet in 1937.

As for Churchill – well, John Colville, his private secretary, seems to quote a French source in his diary for 13 June 1940 ('some gleam of light at the far end of the tunnel'), quotes Paul Reynaud, the French PM on 16 June ('the ray of light at the end of the tunnel'), and himself uses it on 31 May 1952, 'I think it is more that he [Churchill] cannot see the light at the end of the tunnel.' But I have been unable to locate the source of Churchill's reported use of the cliché on 3 May 1941.

The old expression was later dusted down and invoked about an end to the Vietnam War. In 1967, New Year's Eve invitations at the American Embassy in Saigon bore the legend: 'Come and see the light at the end of the tunnel.' President Kennedy nearly employed the expression apropos something else at a press conference on 12 December 1962: 'We don't see the end of the tunnel, but I must say I don't think it is darker than it was a year ago, and in some ways lighter.'

Somewhere about this time, a joke was added: 'If we see the light at the end of the tunnel, it's the light of the oncoming train.' Though not original to him, the line appears in Robert Lowell's poem 'Day by Day' (1977). In 1988, I heard of a graffito in Dublin which ran: 'Because of the present economic situation, the light at the end of the tunnel will be switched off at weekends.'

lightning never strikes twice in the same place. Actually it can and does, but what the phrase seeks to suggest is that misfortune really ought not to revisit its victims. From the *Financial Times* (7 Aug 1984): 'Their disastrous mutual involvement in the affairs of Sun Hung Kai in Hong Kong seems not to have soured relations between Merrill Lynch and Paribas one jot. Presumably operating on the assumption that lightning never strikes twice in the same partnership, Merrill has agreed to take Becker Paribas, the Wall Street securities business, off the hands of the French bank'; (5 November 1984): 'What should the fund manager do now? . . . Lightning never strikes the same place twice, and the interest-rate play may be nearing its finish.'

light on one's feet, to be. To display the attributes of the homosexual, to be camp. A relatively inoffensive characterization. British, mid-twentieth century? From *Roy Hudd's Book of Music-Hall, Variety and Showbiz Anecdotes* (1993): 'This same infamous loo was, for many years, a meeting place for those whose were a bit light on their feet – all right, then – "ginger".'

like. See I ~ IKE; SOMEONE UP THERE ~ S ME; WE SHALL NOT SEE HIS ~ AGAIN.

like a dream come true. What any stroke of luck is to an ordinary member of the public, when reported by journalists, and thus an idiom that has turned into a cliché. Examples: 'British radio hams are to be able to talk to an astronaut on board the latest US space shuttle . . . Dr Garriott said: "This will be a dream come true. I have had this project on my mind since I first became an astronaut"' (*The Times*, October 1983); 'A club cricket enthusiast has inherited a fortune and his own village cricket club from an elderly widow who was a distant relative he never knew . . . Mr Hews, aged 68, a retired company representative, lives in a semi-detached house in Arnold Avenue, Coventry. "It's like a dream come true," he said' (*The Times*, 22 October 1983).

like a fairy tale (princess). Another journalistic cliché. The urge to say that everything in sight was 'like a fairy tale' was, of course, rampant at the nuptials of the Prince of Wales and Lady Diana Spencer in July 1981. Tom Fleming, the BBC TV commentator for the fixture, said the bride was 'like a fairy-tale princess'. Even Robert Runcie, Archbishop of Canterbury, began his address at St Paul's: 'Here is the stuff of which fairy tales are made.'

It was just like a fairy tale is also a cliché (current by 1860) and now put into the mouths of unsuspecting members of the public by popular journalists when they are trying to describe some rather pleasant thing that has happened to them. As Iona and Peter Opie point out, however, in *The Classic Fairy Tales* (1974), this is a very partial way of looking at such matters: 'When the wonderful happens, when a holiday abroad is a splendid success or an unlikely romance ends happily, we commonly exclaim it was "just like a fairy tale", overlooking that most events in fairy tales are remarkable for their unpleasantness, and that in some of the tales there is no happy ending, not even the hero or heroine escaping with their life.'

like a fart in a colander. Indecisive; all over the place. Partridge/*Catch Phrases* suggests an origin sometime in the 1920s. The complete expression, which makes its meaning clear, may be something like: 'He's like a fart in a colander – can't make up his mind which hole to come out of!'

like a red rag to a bull. Meaning, 'obviously provocative'. Christy Brown in *Down All the Days*, Chap. 13 (1970) has: 'Sure they [breasts] only get you into trouble, woman dear . . . Showing them off to a man is like waving a red cloth at a bull.' Caption from a Du Maurier cartoon in *Punch* (26 July 1879): '*Jordan Jones (to whom a picture by R. Robinson is as a red rag to a bull, as B.B. knows)* . . . '

There is no example to hand of the phrase in use before 1873, but John Lyly in *Euphues and His England* (1580) has: 'He that cometh before [a bull] will not wear . . . red', based on the belief that bulls are aggravated by the colour. In fact, they are colour blind. In all probability, if they do react, it is simply the *movement* of material in a bright colour that causes the animal to charge. Charles Dickens in *Bleak House*, Chap.43 (1853) seems to allude to the saying in: 'You know my old opinion of him . . . An amiable bull, who is determined to make every colour scarlet.'

like a vicarage tea-party, makes — look. Such critical similes may verge on the cliché but can still be fun. One which lingers in my memory is from a *Daily Telegraph* review of Alan Sillitoe's novel *Saturday Night and Sunday Morning* (1958): 'A novel of today, with a freshness and raw fury that makes *Room at the Top* look like a vicarage tea-party.' The quote was used on the cover of the paperback of Sillitoe's novel.

When Jacqueline Suzann's *Valley of the Dolls* came out in 1966, a publication called *This Week* noted that it made '*Peyton Place* look like a Bobbsey Twins escapade' (the Bobbsey Twins were nice, clean-cut Americans who got into and out of scrapes in juvenile fiction). From the *Washington Post* (19 April 1986): ' "After the Mexican earthquake, they were all jumping up and down saying 'Are we prepared?' The next BIG ONE here is going to make Mexico look like a Sunday afternoon tea party," Shah said.'

The *Sunday Times* (21 August 1988), quoting an earlier *Sun* profile, said of Charles Saatchi that his advertisements 'Made previous campaigns look like Mary Poppins'. From the *Sun* (16 March 1989), quoting the reported words of Pamella Bordes during a political/sexual scandal: 'The City would grind to a standstill if I spoke out. What I could reveal would make the film *Scandal* look like a teddy bears' picnic.'

See also under WOULD YOU BE MORE CAREFUL IF . . .

like coming home. Meaning 'what is appropriate for one; what one feels completely natural doing' – an idiom, almost a cliché. Winston Churchill said at a Conservative rally in 1924 (having left the Liberal Party): 'It's all very strange for [his wife]. But to me, of course, it's just like coming home.' Other examples are from the *Independent* (31 October 1989): 'For Douglas Hurd, it was just like coming home . . . [he] took his place behind the Foreign Secretary's desk'; and from the *Independent on Sunday* (17 June 1990): [Melvyn Bragg] 'Actually I found arriving at the BBC was

like arriving home . . . It was a job I knew I wanted to do.'

likely. See under AS BUSY AS . . .

like mother makes/used to make, just. i.e. like home cooking and very acceptable. This expression seems to have acquired figurative quotation marks around it by the early years of this century. As such, it is of American origin and was soon used by advertisers as a form of slogan (compare the US pop song of the Second World War, 'Ma, I Miss Your Apple Pie'). 'The kind mother used to make' was used as a slogan by New England Mincemeat around 1900.

Vance Packard in *The Hidden Persuaders* (1957) records an example of the phrase's effectiveness when slightly altered: 'When the Mogen David wine people were seeking some way to add magic to their wine's sales appeal, they turned to motivation research via their agency. Psychiatrists and other probers listening to people talk at random about wine found that many related it to old family-centred or festive occasions. The campaign tied home and mother into the selling themes. One line was: "the good old days – the home sweet home wine – the wine that grandma used to make." As a result of these carefully "motivated" slogans, the sales of Mogen David doubled within a year.'

So, one of numerous advertising lines playing on assumptions about the goodness of home produce and the good old days, and reminding one of the advertisement which proclaimed:

BUCK WHEAT CAKES
Like mother used to bake – $1.25
Like mother thought she made – $2.25.

like one o'clock half struck. Immobile, hesitating. As in 'don't stand there like one o'clock half struck; do something'. Known by 1876.

like rats deserting/leaving a sinking ship. i.e. hurriedly, desperately. This comes from the English proverb to the effect that 'rats desert/forsake/leave a falling house/ sinking ship.' *ODP* finds an example of the 'house' version in 1579 and of the 'ship' (in Shakespeare) in 1611. Brewer adds: 'It was an old superstition that rats deserted a ship before she set out on a voyage that was to end in her loss.'

'Rat' to mean 'a politician who deserts his party' was used by the 1st Earl of Malmesbury in 1792 (*OED2*). In the US it made its first appearance in the saying 'like a rat deserting a sinking ship' around 1800 (Safire).

A number of good jokes have grown from this usage. In Malcolm Muggeridge's diary for 14 February 1948 (published 1981), he notes: 'Remark of Churchill's was quoted to me about the Liberal candidature of Air Vice-Marshal Bennett in Croydon. "It was the first time," Churchill said, "that he had heard of a rat actually swimming out to join a sinking ship."'

In his diary for 26 January 1941, John Colville noted that Churchill had reflected on the difficulty of 'crossing the floor' (changing parties) in the House of Commons: 'He had done it and he knew. Indeed he had re-done it, which everybody said was impossible. They had said you could rat but you couldn't re-rat.'

(When TV-am, the breakfast television company, had a disastrous start in 1983 and was pulled round, in part, by the introduction of a puppet called Roland Rat, an unnamed spokesman from the rival BBC said, 'This must be the first time a rat has come to the aid of a sinking ship.')

likes. See NO ONE ~ US WE DON'T CARE.

like taking money from blind beggars. Meaning 'achieving something effortlessly, by taking advantage.' Compare, 'as easy as taking/stealing pennies from a blind man' or 'sweets/candy/money from a child' ('like taking candy from a baby' occurs in the film *Mr Smith Goes to Washington*, US, 1939).

I first heard the head-phrase form in *c* 1962 – said by my English teacher who had just given a talk to a (wildly impressed) Women's Institute or some such. But it is an old idea. Charles Dickens in *Nicholas Nickleby*, Chap. 59 (1838–9) has Newman Noggs say: 'If I would sell my soul for drink, why wasn't I a thief, swindler, housebreaker, area sneak, robber of pence out of the trays of blind men's dogs . . .'

like the barber's cat – full of wind and water. (to rhyme with 'hatter'). Dismissive phrase, used as when the opinion of another is adduced: 'Oh, he's . . .' Partridge/*Slang* has 'like the barber's cat – all wind and piss', and dates it from the late nineteenth century.

likey. See NO, ~ under *ITMA*.

lilacs. See WHEN ~ LAST IN THE DOORYARD . . .

lily. See GILD THE ~; JERSEY ~.

Lily-White Boys, the. See GREEN GROW THE RUSHES.

line. See BOTTOM ~; THIN RED ~.

lion. See MARCH COMES IN LIKE A ~.

lips. See READ MY ~.

lips are sealed, my. Meaning 'I am not giving anything away', and deriving originally perhaps, from the expression to seal up *another* person's lips, mouth, to prevent him betraying a secret (*OED2* has this by 1782). 'My lips are not yet unsealed' was said during the Abyssinia Crisis of 1935 by the British Prime Minister, Stanley Baldwin. He was playing for time, with what he subsequently admitted was one of the stupidest things he had ever said. The cartoonist Low portrayed him for weeks afterwards with sticking plaster over his lips.

listen! See NAY, NAY ~ THRICE AGAIN NAY!

listening. See COME AND TALK TO THE . . . ; under *BEYOND OUR KEN*.

listen very carefully, I shall say this only once. A line from the BBC TV comedy series *'Allo, 'Allo* (1984–) about Resistance workers in occupied France during the Second World War (*sic*). Used by Michelle, an agent of the Resistance, it somehow contrived to catch on. Jeremy Lloyd, one of the show's co-scriptwrters, used it as the title of his autobiography (1993).

lit. See FLEET'S ~ UP.

little. See TOO ~ , TOO LATE.

little black book, a. There have been many 'black books' over the centuries containing authoritative records or lists of people in disgrace. The 'little' ones, however, are now more usually those containing lists of girls' telephone numbers such as might be kept by a promiscuous male. 'Guess you got back to my name in your little black book' is a line from the song 'Running Out of Fools' (by K.Rogers and R.Ahlert) recorded by Aretha Franklin in 1964. But note, from the *Independent* (30 June 1990): 'Never the most elegant or fastidious of [football] defenders, Jack [Charlton] kept an infamous little black book for noting opponents he "owed one".'

little black dress, a. A simple frock suitable for most social occasions and sometimes abbreviated to 'lbd', that was popular from the 1920s and 30s onwards. The original, a creation of COCO Chanel, was sold at auction for £1500 in 1978. In Britain, the designer Molyneux perfected the dress as the ideal cocktail party wear of the between-the-wars years.

Little Egypt. This was the stage name of Catherine Devine who made the Coochee-Coochee dance famous at the Chicago Colombian Exposition in 1893. She had a tendency to dance in the nude and was celebrated in the song 'Little Egypt' (1961) by Lieber and Stoller (sung by The Coasters and Elvis Presley). *Little Egypt* was also the title of a film (US, 1951) about a girl posing as an Egyptian princess at the Chicago World Fair.

One etymology of the word 'gypsy' is that it derives from 'Little Egypt', the fictional Middle Eastern homeland of the gypsies.

little fish are sweet. See OIL FOR THE LAMPS OF CHINA.

little gentleman in (black) velvet!, the. This was a Jacobite toast to the mole whose hillock caused King William III's horse to stumble in 1702. William died soon afterwards, partly from the injuries sustained. Compare KING OVER THE WATER!

little learning, a. Phrase from Alexander Pope's *An Essay on Criticism* (1711):

A little learning is a dang'rous thing;
Drink deep, or taste not the Pierian
Spring
[Pieria, home of the Greek
Muses].

Hence, the title of a volume of Evelyn Waugh's autobiography (1964).

little local difficulties. See DIFFICULTIES.

Little Nell. Nickname of Nell Trent, child heroine of *The Old Curiosity Shop* (1840–41) by Charles Dickens. She attempts to look after her inadequate grandfather and to protect him from various threats, but her strength gives out. According to one account, 'Does Little Nell die?' was the cry of 6000 book-loving Americans who hurried to the docks in New York to ask this question of sailors arriving from England. Another version is that it was longshoremen who demanded 'How is Little Nell?' or 'Is Little Nell dead?' As the novel was serialized, they were waiting for the arrival of the final instalment of the magazine to find out what had happened to the heroine. Little Nell's death came to typify the heights of Victorian sentimental fiction. Oscar Wilde later commented: 'One must have a heart of stone to read the death of Little Nell without laughing.'

little of what you fancy does you good, a. A nudging point of view from a song by Fred W. Leigh and George Arthurs. It was popularized, with a wink, by Marie Lloyd (1870–1922) in the 1890s.

little old lady from Dubuque, the. When Harold Ross founded the *New Yorker* in 1925, he said it would 'not be edited for the old lady from Dubuque' but for caviare sophisticates. Dubuque, Iowa, thus became involved in another of those yardstick phrases of non-cosmopolitanism – like IT'LL PLAY IN PEORIA – on account of it being representative of MIDDLE AMERICA.

Little Orphan Annie. Name of the irrepressible, red-haired waif, who stands up to the world, succoured by millionaire Daddy Warbucks. She originally appeared in a poem by J.W. Riley in 1913 ('Little Orphant Annie's come to our house to stay') but then became the heroine of a comic strip created by Harold Gray (in the US, from 1924) and of versions in virtually every other medium. Consequently, any waif-like person is so known.

Little Red Book, the. This is the name given to the collected thoughts of Chairman Mao Tse-tung which were published in this form (and brandished by Red Guards) during the Chinese Cultural Revolution of the 1960s. An English-language version was published as *Quotations from Mao Tse-tung* by the Foreign Language Press, Peking (1972).

Little Tich. Stage name of Harry Relph (1868–1928), a popular British music-hall comedian. Probably invented by his family when he was a baby, the nickname derived from the sensational Tichborne case – about the claim made in 1866 by a man from Australia that he was the missing heir to a Hampshire baronetcy and fortune. The Tichborne Claimant (Arthur Orton), who was imprisoned for perjury, was plump – as no doubt was Harry Relph as a little boy. Relph remained small in stature and, at first, called himself 'Little Tichborne'. 'Tich' then became the nickname for anyone small.

Live Aid. See — AID.

live and let live. A plea for what has come to be known as peaceful co-existence, and recorded in 1622. An obvious play upon the expression is *Live and Let Die*, the title of a James Bond novel by Ian Fleming (1954, filmed UK 1973).

lived. See AND THEY ALL ~ HAPPILY . . .

lively arts, the. A curious phrase which must have been used for any number of broadcast programmes about the arts, not all of which needed to be described as other than boring. A possible origin is Billy Rose's stage show *The Seven Lively Arts* (New York, 1944) which included ballet among its number.

live now, pay later. See GO NOW, PAY LATER.

lives. See CAT HAS NINE ~ .

livid. See under EDUCATING ARCHIE.

living. See ALIVE AND WELL AND ~ IN . . . ; GREATEST ~ . . . ; LEGEND IN ONE'S OWN . . . ; WORLD OWES ONE A ~ .

living life in the fast lane. A cliché of journalism, meaning 'living expensively, indulgently and dangerously', and current by 1978. From the association of such a lifestyle with 'fast cars' and such. Used with plodding literalness in these two examples: 'Controversial racing car genius Colin Chapman lived life in the fast lane' – *Daily Star*, 11 October 1984; 'Jackie Stewart lives life in the fast lane. Like any businessman, really' – advertisement for Toshiba computer, February 1989.

Livingstone, Dr. See DR ~ .

Lizzie. See TIN ~ .

Lloyd George knew my father. Even before David Lloyd George's death in 1945, Welsh people away from home liked to claim some affinity with the Great Man. In time, this inclination was encapsulated in the singing of the words 'Lloyd George knew my father, my father knew Lloyd George' to the strains of 'Onward Christian Soldiers', which they neatly fit.

In Welsh legal and Liberal circles the credit for this happy coinage has been given to Tommy Rhys Roberts QC (1910–75) whose father did indeed know Lloyd George. Arthur Rhys Roberts was a Newport solicitor who set up a London practice with Lloyd George in 1897. The partnership continued for many years, although on two occasions Lloyd George's political activities caused them to lose practically all their clients.

The junior Rhys Roberts was a gourmet, a wine-bibber and of enormous girth. Martin Thomas QC, a prominent Welsh liberal of the next generation, recalled (1984): 'It was, and is a tradition of the Welsh circuit that there should be, following the after-dinner speeches, a full-blooded sing-song. For as long as anyone can remember, Rhys Roberts's set-piece was to sing the phrase to the tune of "Onward

Christian Soldiers" – it is widely believed that he started the practice . . . By the 50s it had certainly entered the repertoire of Welsh Rugby Clubs. In the 60s, it became customary for Welsh Liberals to hold a Noson Lawen, or sing-song, on the Friday night of the Liberal Assemblies. It became thoroughly adopted in the party. I recall it as being strikingly daring and new in the late 60s for Young Liberals to sing the so-called second verse, "Lloyd George knew my mother". William Douglas-Home's play *Lloyd George Knew My Father* was produced in London in 1972. One of the leading Welsh Silks recalls persuading Rhys Roberts to see it with him.'

From Robert Robinson, *Landscape with Dead Dons* (1956): 'He had displayed a massive indifference to the rollicking scientists who would strike up *Lloyd George Knew My Father* in a spirit of abandoned wickedness.'

loadsamoney! 'Loadsamoney' was the name of a character portrayed by the British comedy performer Harry Enfield, chiefly in the Channel 4 TV series *Friday Night Live* in 1987–8. A 'monster son of the enterprise culture', as he was described, the character waved wads of tenners about, proclaimed his belief in what he referred to as 'dosh' (money), and said 'Loadsamoney!' or **show us your wad!** a lot.

A *Guardian* editorial on 30 April 1988 noted that, 'to his horror (for in private life Mr Enfield is a politics graduate of impeccable left-wing persuasions) a creation intended to be a satire of the money-worshipping philistinism of Thatcher's Britain appears to be savoured and loved. Real yobs all over the City, according to eye-witness reports, have begun appearing in pubs brandishing bundles of genuine bank notes and screaming "loadsamoney, loadsamoney".'

As sometimes happens, a satirical invention threatened to become a role model instead, and Mr Enfield took steps to abandon the character. The following month, Neil Kinnock, the Labour Party leader, was telling a conference at Tenby, 'We've got the loadsamoney economy – and behind it comes loadsatrouble.' And there were signs of a format phrase in the making: 'Loadsa-sermons won't stop the Thatcherite

rot' – *Sunday Times* headline, 29 May 1988; 'Loadsateachers' – *Daily Mail* headline, 25 July 1989.

Earlier constructions on the same theme have included **big money!** (said by Max Bygraves of what contestants stood to win in the ITV quiz *Family Fortunes*, current 1985) and *Tons of Money*, the title of a long-running stage farce (and film) of the 1920s.

In BBC TV shows in the early 1990s, Enfield created a whole series of characters whose names or catchphrases neatly defined them – Mr **You Don't Want To Do That**, Tim Nice But Dim, a *nouveau riche* Midlands couple who said, **We appear to be considerably richer than you**, the Lovely Wobbly Randy Old Ladies who exclaimed **Young man!**, and so on. See also POPTASTIC!

loaf. See SERVE THAT LADY WITH A CRUSTY ~ under BAND WAGGON.

Lobby Lud. See YOU ARE MR ~.

local. See SUPPORT YOUR ~ —.

lock stock and barrel. Meaning, 'the whole lot', this term comes to us from the armoury where the lock (or firing mechanism), stock and barrel are the principal parts of a gun.

locust. See DAY OF THE ~.

Log Cabin to White House, From. The title of a biography of President James Garfield (1881) by Rev. William Thayer. Earlier presidents Henry Harrison and Abraham Lincoln had used the log cabin as a prop in their campaigns. Subsequently almost all presidential aspirants have sought a humble 'log cabin' substitute to help them on their way.

London. See under GREAT WEN; I CAME TO ~ TO SEEK MY FORTUNE; THIS . . . IS . . . ~; SWINGING ~.

lonely. See under AS BUSY AS . . .

lonelyhearts column. See MISS LONELYHEARTS.

Lone Ranger. See ∼ RIDES AGAIN under
HI-YO, SILVER!

long. See HOW ∼ IS A PIECE . . . UNDER HOW
MANY BEANS . . . ; — IS A ∼ TIME IN —; IT
WAS GOING TO BE A ∼ NIGHT; NIGHT OF THE
∼ KNIVES.

Long and the Short and the Tall, The.
The title of the play (1959; film UK, 1960)
by Willis Hall comes from the song 'Bless
'em all' (1940) by Jimmy Hughes and Frank
Lake: 'Bless 'em all, bless 'em all,/The long
and the short and the tall' (or its parody
version 'Sod 'Em All'). The film's US title
was *Jungle Fighters*.

long and the short of it, the. The old
phrase meaning 'in brief, in a nutshell' or
'the essence, all that need be said' was
known *c* 1330. Inevitably, it became the bill
matter of British music-hall entertainers
Ethel Revnel and Gracie West (*fl.* 1930s/
40s), one of whom was short and one
wasn't.

long arm of the law, the. The title of a
film (UK, 1956 – *The Third Key* in the US)
about a Scotland Yard superintendent
solving a series of robberies. It comes from
the idea that the law is an arm and that it is
a long one, rooting out the guilty however
far away they may hide. Charles Dickens in
The Pickwick Papers (1836–7) has: 'Here was
the strong arm of the law, coming down
with twenty gold-beater force,' and in *The
Mystery of Edwin Drood* (1870): 'The arm of
the law is a strong arm, and a long arm.' In
Shakespeare's *Richard II* (1595), Aumerle is
quoted as saying (IV.i.11):

> Is not my arm of length, That reacheth
> from the restful English court
> As far as Callice, to mine uncle's head?

It is possibly a development of the proverb
'Kings have long arms/hands/many ears
and many eyes', found by *ODP* in Ovid,
and in English by 1539.

long chalk, not by a. Meaning 'not by
any means', this probably refers to the
method of making chalk marks on the floor
to show the score of a player or team. A
'long chalk' would mean a lot of points, a
great deal.

long hot summer, a/the. A cliché of
journalism. 'It looks as if it will be a long hot
summer for the dons of Christ's College,
Cambridge, who are once again faced with
the tricky business of electing a Master'
(Lady Olga Maitland, *Sunday Express*, 11
July 1982).

This once-bright phrase rapidly turned
into a journalist's cliché following the 1967
riots in the Black ghettos of 18 US cities,
notably Detroit and Newark. In June of
that year, the Rev. Dr Martin Luther King
Jnr warned: 'Everyone is worrying about
the long hot summer with its threat of riots.
We had a long cold winter when little was
done about the conditions that create riots.'

The Long Hot Summer was the title of a
1958 film based on the stories of William
Faulkner and also of a spin-off TV series
(1965–6). The film was based on 'The
Hamlet', a story published by Faulkner in
1928, which contains the chapter heading
'The Long Summer' (*sic*). So it is not correct
to say that Faulkner 'coined' the longer
phrase. Bartlett (1980 and 1992) claims,
however, that there was a film with the
longer title in 1928. Some mistake surely?

Claud Cockburn's *I, Claud* (1967) has a
chapter entitled 'Long Cold Winter'.

long in the tooth. Old people suffer from
receding of the gums and so their teeth
appear to have got longer. The same
probably applies to horses, so compare
LOOK A GIFT HORSE IN THE MOUTH.

long time no see. The *OED2* calls this a
'jocular imitation of broken English' and
has citations showing that the phrase was in
use, more or less, by 1900. It appears fully
formed in Raymond Chandler, *Farewell,
My Lovely* (1940) and as a title in Ed
McBain's *Long Time No See* (1977).

loo, to go to the. A euphemism for going
to the lavatory, established in well-to-do
British society by the early twentieth
century and into general middle-class use
after the Second World War. Of the several
theories of its origin, perhaps the most well
known is that the word comes from the
French *gardez l'eau* [mind the water], dating
from the days when chamber pots or dirty
water were emptied out of the window into
the street and recorded by Laurence Sterne

as *garde d'eau* in *A Sentimental Journey* (1768). This cry was also rendered 'gardyloo' in old Edinburgh and recorded by Tobias Smollett as such in *Humphrey Clinker* (1771).

However, Professor A.S.C. Ross who examined the various options in a 1974 issue of *Blackwood's Magazine* favoured a derivation, 'in some way which could not be determined', from *Waterloo*. At one time people probably said: 'I must go to the water-closet' and, wishing not to be explicit, substituted 'Water-loo' as a weak little joke. The name 'Waterloo' was there, waiting to be used, from 1815 onwards – just as it was in MEET ONE'S WATERLOO.

look a gift horse in the mouth, to. Meaning 'to spoil an offer by inquiring too closely into it', the proverb alludes to the fact that the age of horses is commonly assessed by the length of their teeth. If you are offered the gift of a horse, you would be ill-advised to look in its mouth. You might discover information not to your advantage.

looking. See HERE'S ∼ AT YOU; WHO YOU ∼ AT?

looking bronzed and fit. A cliché of journalism, current by 1961. An inevitable pairing when someone (often a politician) 'returns to the fray' having acquired a suntan, perhaps after earlier being ill, and having enjoyed the inevitable 'well-earned rest.' A variation: 'Eric Burdon: Tan, fit and living in the desert' (*San Diego Union*, 25 March 1989).

Alternatively, people in this situation look 'relaxed'. A T-shirt jokingly promoted an ex-President for a return to the White House: 'He's tanned, he's rested, he's ready: Nixon in '88.'

For 'tanned, rested and fit' see under AVOID FIVE O'CLOCK SHADOW.

looking good, (it's). Obviously, to say that something 'looks good' is an old expression, but this particular version was popularized by participants in and commentators on the US space programme in the 1960s/70s. The optimism that things are going smoothly is tempered by the unstated addition '. . . so far'. A British TV

fitness programme in *c* 1989 was entitled *Looking Good, Feeling Great.*

look, Ma, no hands! The American version of the British 'look, Mum, no hands!' or 'look, no hands!' when a child (usually) is demonstrating some feat to its elders, like riding a bicycle. Now used allusively about any activity to which the doer seeks to draw attention. Lesley Storm's comedy *Look, No Hands!* opened in London in July 1971, but the phrase probably dates back to the 1950s at least (from when I seem to a recall a joke about a German boy shooting his mother – 'Look, Hans – no Ma!').

looks even better on a man. An advertising line for Tootal shirts in the UK, from 1961. The poster featured a girl wearing an oversize man's shirt.

look that up in your Funk and Wagnalls! See under LAUGH-IN.

looney tune. Meaning 'mad person' or, as an adjective, 'mad'. President Reagan commented on the hijacking of a US plane by Shi-ite Muslims: 'We are not going to tolerate these attacks from outlaw states run by the strangest collection of misfits, looney tunes, and squalid criminals since the advent of the Third Reich' (8 July 1985). The phrase had earlier been used in the Mel Brooks film *High Anxiety* (1977).

The reference is to the cinema cartoon comedies called Looney Tunes which have been produced by Warners since the 1940s.

loose. See FAST AND ∼.

loose cannon, a. A person who is not attached to a particular faction and acts independently and, possibly, unreliably. Of American origin. From the *Observer* (26 July 1987): 'GUNG-HO, loose cannon, cowboy, Jesus freak – there is already a cottage industry manufacturing Ollie epithets. Lynching [Oliver] North is quickly becoming a national sport.'

The reference is either to a cannon that is not properly secured to the deck of a ship or to an artillery man who is working independently during a land battle.

loose talk costs lives. A security slogan (US only) from the Second World War.

Lord. See PRAISE THE ~ AND PASS THE AMMUNITION.

Lord Haw-Haw. William Joyce broadcast Nazi propaganda from Hamburg during the Second World War, was found guilty of treason (on the technicality that he held a British passport at the beginning of the war) and was hanged in 1946. He had a threatening, sneering, lower-middle-class delivery, which made his call-sign sound more like 'Jarmany calling'. Although Joyce was treated mostly as a joke in wartime Britain, he is credited with giving rise to some unsettling rumours. No one seemed to have heard the particular broadcast in question, but it got about that he had said the clock on Darlington Town Hall was two minutes slow, and so it was supposed to be.

His nickname of 'Lord Haw-Haw' was inappropriate as he did not sound the slightest bit aristocratic. *That* sobriquet had been applied by Jonah Barrington, the *Daily Express* radio correspondent, to Joyce's predecessor who *did* speak with a cultured accent but lasted only a few weeks from September 1939. This original was Norman Baillie-Stewart. He is said to have sounded like the entertainer Claud Hulbert or one of the Western Brothers. An imaginary drawing appeared in the *Daily Express* of a Bertie Woosterish character with a monocle and receding chin. Baillie-Stewart himself said that he understood there was a popular English song called 'We're Going to Hang Out the Washing on the Siegfried Line' which ended 'If the Siegfried Line's still there'. 'Curiously enoff,' he said, 'the Siegfried Line is still they-ah.'

The US equivalents were **Tokyo Rose**, the nickname given to the US-born Iva Ikuko Toguri D'Aquino who broadcast to US servicemen over Japanese radio advising them to give up the unequal struggle; and **Axis Sally**, a US-born Nazi broadcaster who urged US withdrawal from the Second World War. She has been variously identified as Mildred Gillars and Rita Louise Zucca.

Lord of the Flies. The title of the novel (1954; films UK, 1963, US, 1990) by William Golding comes from the literal meaning of the Hebrew word 'Beelzebub', the devil.

lord of words, a. A complimentary title bestowed upon a 'master of language', it was used to describe the broadcaster, Sir Huw Wheldon, and the playwright, Samuel Beckett, at their deaths in 1986 and 1989, respectively. The phrase **lord of language** may be older. In *Ego 8* (for 2 May 1945), James Agate discusses a passage in *De Profundis* in which Oscar Wilde says of himself, 'I summed up all systems in a phrase and all existence in an epigram.' Agate writes: 'The boast about being "a lord of language". Wilde was that very different thing – the fine lady of the purple passage.' Whence, however, the 'lord of language'? In Tennyson's poem 'To Virgil' (1882) – 'written at the request of the Mantuans for the nineteenth centenary of Virgil's death' – the Mantuan poet is described, in a rush of alliteration, as 'landscape-lover, lord of language'.

lorra lorra laffs. In *c* 1987, when the singer Cilla Black was presenting a programme called *Surprise, Surprise* for London Weekend Television, her way of saying, '[There'll be a] lot of, lot of laughs' somehow became the key phrase for impressionists to skewer her very wonderful Liverpool accent.

lose a battle but not the war, to. Charles de Gaulle in his proclamation dated 18 June 1940 and circulated among exiled Frenchmen, said: '*La France a perdu une bataille! Mais la France n'a pas perdu la guerre*' [France has lost a battle, but France has not lost the war!]. Earlier, on 19 May 1940, Winston Churchill, in his first broadcast to the British people as Prime Minister, had said: 'Our task is not only to win the battle – but to win the war' (meaning the battle *for* Britain, which he was later to call the BATTLE OF BRITAIN). Later, in 1962, Harold Macmillan used the formula after a by-election defeat at Orpington: 'We have lost a number of skirmishes, perhaps a battle, but not a campaign.'

lost generation, the. This phrase refers to the large number of promising young men who lost their lives in the First World War, and also, by extension, to those who were *not* killed in the war but who were part of a generation thought to have lost its values. Gertrude Stein recorded the remark made by a French garage owner in the Midi just after the war. Rebuking an apprentice who had made a shoddy repair to her car, he said: 'All you young people who served in the war' are from 'a lost generation' [*une génération perdue*]. Ernest Hemingway used this as the epigraph to his novel *The Sun Also Rises* (1926) and referred to it again in *A Moveable Feast* (1964).

lot. See AYE, AYE, THAT'S YER ∼!; NOT A ∼; THERE'S A ∼ OF IT ABOUT.

loudest noise. See AT 60 MILES AN HOUR . . .

Louis. See DROP THE GUN, LOOEY!

lout. See LAGER ∼.

love. See ALL'S FAIR IN ∼ . . . ; DON'T YOU JUST ∼ BEING IN CONTROL?; I ∼ IT, BUT . . . ; I ∼ —; I ∼ MY WIFE BUT OH YOU KID!; LIE DOWN, I THINK I ∼ YOU; I'M LOOKING FOR SOMEONE TO ∼ under BEYOND OUR KEN; I MUST ∼ YOU AND LEAVE YOU; MAKE ∼ NOT WAR; MAN YOU ∼ TO HATE; NEVER ∼ A STRANGER.

love among the —. A format used in titles, especially among the **ruins**. The notion of love among classical ruins seems hauntingly appealing, rather as do the reminders of time and decay in Arcadia (compare ET IN ARCADIA EGO). 'And found young Love among the roses' is a line from an old ballad alluded to by Charles Dickens in *Barnaby Rudge* (1841), and *Love Among the Haystacks* is the title of a collection of short stories (1930) by D.H. Lawrence. Evelyn Waugh entitled one of his shorter novels *Love Among the Ruins: A Romance of the Near Future* (1953), and Angela Thirkell used the title for a novel about the aristocracy in the post-war period, in 1948 (of which the title only was borrowed in 1974 for a TV movie, with Laurence Olivier and Katharine Hepburn). Earlier than this, there is the painting by Sir Edward Burne-Jones where the lover and his lass embrace among fallen pillars and stones with mysterious inscriptions on them, hemmed in by the briar rose which rambles over all, and search for the way to Cythara where in the end they must separate. The subject comes from the Italian romance *Hypnerotomachia* (1499). The painting dates from 1870–3 and hangs in Wightwick Manor. Earlier still is Robert Browning's poem with the title in *Men and Women* (1855).

love at first flight. See under BOAC TAKES GOOD CARE OF YOU.

loved. See WHOEVER ∼ THAT ∼ NOT . . .

love in a — ∼. This format is used in several titles and phrases. William Thackeray refers to 'love in a cottage' in *Pendennis* (1848–50) and Keats has 'love in a hut' in 'Lamia' (1820). Both these deal with the romantic fantasy of love in poverty. *The Comical Revenge, or Love in a Tub* was the title of a play by George Etherege (1664); *Love In a Wood*, a play by William Wycherley (1671); and *Love in a Village*, a comic opera by Isaac Bickerstaffe (1762). *Love in a Cold Climate*, the novel (1949) by Nancy Mitford caused Evelyn Waugh to write to her (10 October): '[It] has become a phrase. I mean when people want to be witty they say I've caught a love in a cold climate and everyone understands.' Earlier, Robert Southey, the poet, writing to his brother Thomas (28 April 1797) had said: 'She has made me half in love with a cold climate.'

Love In a Mist (from the popular name for the misty blue plant *Nigella*) was the title of a silent film (1916) with two popular British stars, Stewart Rome and Alma Taylor, and of several popular songs, especially one in the musical comedy *Dear Love* (London, 1929). It was also the title of a play by Kenneth Horne (the writer not the comedian), staged in London (1942). This last is a light comedy about two couples who find themselves fog-bound in a duck farm on Exmoor. The film *Love in a Goldfish Bowl* followed in the US (1961).

love is the answer. A line from John Lennon's song 'Mind Games' (1973) which itself became the title of a song written by Ralph Cole and performed by Island Lighthouse (1974). The line 'Is love the answer?' occurs in Liz Lochhead's poem 'Riddle-Me-Ree' (1984). A much-alluded to view: 'Love is the answer, but while you are waiting for the answer, sex raises some pretty good questions' – Woody Allen, 1975; 'If love is the answer, could you rephrase the question?' – Lily Tomlin, 1979; both quoted in Bob Chieger, *Was It Good For You Too?* (1983).

lovelier. See YOU'LL LOOK A LITTLE ~ EACH DAY . . .

lovely. See HE'S LOO-VELY, MRS HARDCASTLE . . . under *RAY'S A LAUGH.*

lovely grub, lovely grub! See under *ITMA.*

lovely jubbly. See under YER PLONKER!

lovely weather for ducks! What you say when it is raining. Although it must be ancient, I have not found a citation in this precise form before 1985. However, **nice weather for ducks** was recorded in 1973 and G.L. Apperson in his *English Proverbs and Proverbial Phrases* (1929) finds 'another fine week for the ducks' in Charles Dickens, *The Old Curiosity Shop* (1840) and suggests that the predominant form is **fine weather for ducks.**

love me, love my dog. Meaning 'if you are inclined to take my side in matters generally, you must put up with one or two things you don't like at the same time', it comes from one of St Bernard's sermons: '*Qui me amat, amat et canem meum*' [Who loves me, also loves my dog]. A good illustration comes from an article by Valerie Bornstein in *Proverbium* (1991): 'I told my mother that she must love my father a lot because she tolerated his snoring! . . . She became aggravated with me and stated the proverb "*Aime moi, aime mon chien*". She told me that when you love someone, you accept all the things that go along with them, their virtues and faults.'

Alas, this was a different St Bernard to the one after whom the breed of Alpine dog is named. It was said (or quoted) by St

Bernard of Clairvaux (*d* 1153) rather than St Bernard of Menthon (*d* 1008).

love me, or leave me. During the Vietnam War, one of the few memorable patriotic slogans, current from 1969, was 'America, Love It or Leave It'. This was perhaps inspired by the song 'Love Me or Leave Me' (1928, hit version 1955), although since the nineteenth century there has been the semi-proverbial, semi-jocular farewell, **I must love you and leave you.** *Love 'Em and Leave 'Em* was the title of a Louise Brooks film (US, 1927).

Love, Pain and the Whole Damn Thing. The English title of a collection (1989) of four short stories by the German writer and film director, Doris Dorrie. Earlier, in 1972, there had been Alan J. Pakula's US film with the title *Love and Pain and the Whole Damn Thing.*

lover. See ALL THE WORLD LOVES A ~.

lovers. See PARIS IS FOR ~.

loves. See HE WHO ~ ME, FOLLOWS ME.

loves ya. See WHO ~, BABY?

love that man! See SOMEBODY BAWL FOR BEULAH?

love you madly. Duke Ellington (1899–1974), the composer, pianist and band-leader, used to say, 'We'd like you to know that the boys in the band all *love you madly!*' Also the title of one of his songs.

loving. See TENDER ~ CARE.

low. See BR'ER FOX HE LAY ~.

low profile. See under HIGH PROFILE.

LPC. Initials for 'Leather Personnel Carrier', i.e. a British army boot. Quoted with regard to the Falklands campaign (*Sunday Times*, 19 July 1982 – where use was specifically ascribed to Brigadier Julian Thompson).

LS/MFT. A slogan for Lucky Strike cigarettes, in the US, current in the 1940s.

The initials, spoken in radio ads, meant 'Lucky Strike Means Finer Tobacco'. A graffito collected in my *Graffiti 4* (1982) translated the initials as 'Let's Screw, My Finger's Tired', though this merely reproduces 'oral tradition'.

luck. See AND THE BEST OF ~!

lucky/Lucky. See REACH FOR A ~ INSTEAD OF A SWEET; YOU ~ PEOPLE.

lucky Jim. Titlte of a US song by Frederick Bowers (*d* 1961) and his vaudeville partner Charles Horwitz (though it is usually ascribed to Anon). It tells of a man who has to wait for his childhood friend to die before he can marry the girl they were once both after. Then, married to the woman and not enjoying it, he would rather he was dead like his friend: 'Oh, lucky Jim, how I envy him.'
   Lucky Jim became the title of a comic novel (1953) by Kingsley Amis, about a hapless university lecturer, Jim Dixon.

lugger. See ONCE ABOARD THE ~.

Lulu. See BUY SOME FOR ~ UNDER WOTALOTIGOT.

lum. See LANG MAY YER ~ REEK.

lumps. See LARGE ~.

lunatic fringe. Referring to a minority group of extremists, usually in politics, the phrase gained currency after Theodore Roosevelt said in 1913: 'There is apt to be a lunatic fringe among the votaries of any forward movement.'

lunch. See SUCH THING AS A FREE ~.

lunchtime. See LEGEND IN ONE'S OWN ~.

lust. See SAVAGE STORY OF ~ AND AMBITION.

Luton Airport. See under NICE 'ERE, INNIT?

lux aeterna. See MASS PHRASES.

lynch mob, a. A group of people administering summary justice by execution. There are several candidates for the origin of this name. Most likely is Colonel William Lynch (*d* 1820) of Pittsylvania County, Virginia, who certainly took the law into his own hands, formed a vigilante band and devised what became known as the Lynch Laws. However, as Burnam (1980) points out, even he did not really behave in the way 'to lynch' came to mean. There was also an old English word *linch*, meaning punishment by whipping or flogging, and this was sometimes imposed by the 'Lynch' courts of Virginia.

Lyons. See BUTCHER OF ~.

· M ·

ma'am. See JUST THE FACTS, ~ under *DRAGNET*.

Mabel. See ~ AT THE TABLE; GIVE 'IM THE MONEY, ~!, WHAT'S ON THE TABLE, ~? under *HAVE A GO*.

Macbeth. See SCOTTISH PLAY.

McCoy. See REAL ~.

Macduff. See LEAD ON ~.

McGregor. See WHERE ~ SITS IS THE HEAD OF THE TABLE.

MacGuffin, the. This was the name given by the film director Alfred Hitchcock to the distracting device, the red herring, in a thriller upon which the whole plot appears to turn but which, in the end, has no real relevance to the plot or its solution. For example, the uranium in *Notorious* (1946) turns out to be less important than the notorious woman falling for the US agent.

Mac the Knife. The English name of the character Mackie Messer in *The Threepenny Opera* (1928) by Brecht and Weill, derived from the name MacHeath in Gay's *The Beggar's Opera* (1728). It is now a nickname applied to people with a name beginning Mac/Mc who behave ruthlessly, e.g. Harold Macmillan at the time of the NIGHT OF THE LONG KNIVES, and Ian MacGregor at the National Coal Board when making large-scale redundancies in the 1980s.

Macwonder. See under SUPERMAC.

mad. See under AS BUSY AS . . . ; DON'T GET ~ . . .

mad as a hatter. The Hatter in Lewis Carroll's ALICE IN WONDERLAND (1865) is not described as the *Mad* Hatter, though he is undoubtedly potty. His behaviour encapsulates a once-popular belief that people working as hat-makers could suffer brain damage by inhaling the nitrate of mercury used to treat felt. In fact, Carroll may not have been thinking of a hatter at all but rather of a certain Theophilus Carter, a furniture dealer of Oxford, who was notable for the top hat he wore, was also a bit potty and known as the Mad Hatter. And it is the March Hare who is marginally more mad (after the much older expression 'mad as a march hare').

Morris favours a derivation from the Anglo-Saxon word *atter*, meaning poison (and closely related to the adder, the British snake whose bite can cause fever). The phrase 'mad as a hatter' is not recorded before the 1830s. On the other hand, by 1609, there was a phrase 'mad as a weaver' which takes us back to the peculiarity of specific tradespeople.

mad as hell and I'm not going to take this any more, I'm. See I'M AS MAD AS HELL . . .

made. See HERE'S ONE I ~ EARLIER.

madly. See LOVE YOU ~.

Mad Monk, the. Nickname of Grigori Efimovich (c 1871–1916), otherwise known as Rasputin. Of Siberian peasant origin, he was a self-styled holy man, but was famous for his debauchery and the influence he exercised over Tsarina Alexandra. He was murdered by a group of Russian noblemen. *Rasputin the Mad Monk* was the title used in the UK for the 1932 US picture *Rasputin and the Empress*.

In the early 1980s, the nickname was also applied by *Private Eye* magazine to Sir Keith Joseph (1918–94), who was something of an EMINENCE GRISE to Prime Minister Margaret Thatcher.

Mad Mullah, the. This nickname was shared by two Mohammedan leaders of revolt against British rule: one, the 'Mad Mullah of Swat' in the Indian uprisings of 1897–8, the other, the better-known Mohammed bin Abdullah, who created terror for tribes friendly to the British in Somaliland (1899–1920). In the plural, the name was reapplied to Iranian religious leaders in the turmoil following the fall of the Shah (1979) and the rise of Ayatollah Khomeini.

mad woman's underclothes. See ALL OVER THE PLACE LIKE . . .

maestro. See MUSIC, ∼, PLEASE!

Mae West. The nickname for an inflatable life jacket issued to the services in the Second World War, it gets its name from the curvaceous American film star, Mae West. It was in use by May 1940.

Maggie May. This character in a Liverpool song, dating from at least 1830, is a prostitute who steals sailors' trousers, but: 'a policeman came and took that girl away./ For she robbed a Yankee whaler,/She won't walk down Lime Street any more'.

A number of groups (including the Beatles) revived the song at the time of Liverpool's resurgence in the early 1960s. Lionel Bart and Alun Owen wrote a musical based on her life called *Maggie May* in 1964. Margaret Thatcher unwisely alluded to the song in April 1983 when wishing to appear coy about whether she would be calling a general election soon: 'Some say Maggie may, or others say Maggie may not. I can only say that when the time comes, I shall decide.'

magic! In Yorkshire Television's mid-1970s series *Oh, No, It's Selwyn Froggit*, Bill Maynard in the cheerful title role would exclaim this about almost anything he encountered. Now quite a common adjectival exclamation.

magical mystery tour, a. Name given to a winding journey, caused by the driver not knowing where he is going. A 'Mystery Tour' is a journey undertaken in a coach from a holiday resort when the passengers are not told of the intended destination (and known as such, I should think, from the 1920s onwards). The 'magical' derives from the Beatles' title for a largely unsuccessful attempt at making their own film in 1967. In *Next Horizon* (1973), Chris Bonington writes: 'Climbing with Tom Patey was a kind of Magical Mystery Tour, in which no one, except perhaps himself, knew what was coming next.' From the *Daily Express* (12 April 1989): 'On and on went the city bus driver's magical mystery tour. Passengers point out their way home – and get a lift to the door.' From McGowan & Hands's *Don't Cry for Me, Sergeant-Major* (1983) (about the Falklands war): 'Then at Midnight *Canberra* slipped out, or as Lt Hornby so eloquently put it, "buggered off on the second leg of our magical mystery tour".'

magic circle (sometimes **of Old Etonians**). In British politics this phrase was introduced by Iain Macleod in an article in the *Spectator* (17 January 1964), about the previous year's struggle for the leadership of the Conservative Party. He was describing the way in which the leader, although supposedly just 'emerging', was in fact the choice of a small group of influential Tory peers and manipulators: 'It is some measure of the tightness of the magic circle on this occasion that neither the Chancellor of the Exchequer nor the Leader of the House of Commons had any inkling of what was happening.' A year or two later, and as a result of this experience, the Tory leadership came to be decided instead by a ballot of Conservative MPs.

Presumably, Macleod was influenced in his choice of phrase by the magicians' Magic Circle (founded 1905) and the ancient use of the term in necromancy. The phrase has continued to be applied to other semi-secret cabals to which those wishing to belong are denied access.

magnificent. See MEAN! MOODY! ∼!

maiden. See IRON ∼.

Maidenform bra. See I DREAMED I . . .

maids. See IF SEVEN ∼ WITH SEVEN MOPS . . .

mail must get/go through, the. A slogan of probable North American origin – as indicated by use of the word 'mail' rather than 'post'. Though 'Royal Mail' is still very much used in the UK, the older term 'post' predominates. There is no citation of the precise slogan being used in Britain. As for the US, the Longman *Chronicle of America* reports (as for 13 April 1860) the arrival in Sacramento, California, of the first Pony Express delivery – a satchel with 49 letters and three newspapers that had left St Joseph, Missouri, 11 days previously. 'The pace is an astounding improvement over the eight-week wagon convoys. But the brave riders, who vow "the mail must get through" despite all kinds of dangers ranging from hostile Indians on the prairie to storms in the mountains, may only be a temporary link [as the Iron Horse makes progress].'

The *Chronicle* does not provide a solid basis for invoking the slogan at this point but the connection with Pony Express seems very likely. It would be good to have an actual citation from the period. Raymond and Mary Settle in *The Story of the Pony Express* (1955) point out that the organization flourished only in the years 1860–61, soon being overtaken by telegraph and railroad, and add: 'A schedule, as exacting as that of a railroad timetable, was set up, and each rider was under rigid orders to keep it, day and night, fair weather or foul. Allowance was made for nothing, not even attack by Indians. Their motto was, "The mail must go through", and it did except in a very few, rare cases.'

majority. See GREAT ∼.

make. See GO AHEAD, ∼ MY DAY; LIKE MOTHER . . . ; THEY DON'T ∼ — LIKE THAT . . .

make a beeline for, to. Meaning 'to go directly', from the supposition that bees fly in a straight line back to the hive.

make-do and mend. Popularized during the Second World War, when there were Make-do-and-Mend departments in some stores, this phrase was designed to encourage thrift and the repairing of old garments, furniture, etc., rather than expenditure of scarce resources on making

new. It was possibly derived from 'make and mend' which was a Royal Navy term for an afternoon free from work and devoted to mending clothes.

make 'em laugh, make 'em cry, make 'em wait. This was a suggested recipe for writing novels to be published in serial form (as done by Charles Dickens and many others in the nineteenth century). Charles Reade, who wrote *The Cloister and the Hearth* (1863), came up with it.

make love, not war. A 'peacenik' and 'flower power' slogan of the mid-1960s. It was not just applied to the Vietnam War but was used to express the attitude of a whole generation of protest. It was written up on the walls (in English) at the University of Nanterre during the French student revolution of 1968. Coinage has been attributed to 'G. Legman', a sexologist with the Kinsey Institute, though this is also the name of the editor of *The Limerick* (1964/9).

In the 1970/80s, it was still current, as part of a well-known car-sticker joke: 'Make love not war – see driver for details'.

make no bones about, to. Meaning 'to get straight to the point; not to conceal anything', the expression refers either to drinking a bowl of soup in which there are no bones, which is easy to swallow and there is nothing to complain about; or, from 'bones' meaning 'dice'. Here 'making no bones' means not making much of, and not attempting to coax the dice in order to show favour.

makes — look like a —. See LIKE A VICARAGE TEA-PARTY.

makes you feel like a queen. A slogan for Summer County margarine, current in UK in the 1960s. Barry Day, vice-chairman of McCann-Erickson Worldwide, pointed out to me in 1985 that this slogan was originally used in the US for Imperial Margarine (also a Unilever product). 'The sudden magical appearance of the crown on the mother clever enough to use the brand made more sense. It was considered to be a successful brand property and used on several brands in other markets, irrespective of brand name. In none of the other cases was it markedly successful. The device seems to have been a piece of Americana that did not travel well.'

The idea is not new. In November 1864, Tolstoy's wife Sonya wrote to him, 'Without you, I am nothing. With you, I feel like a queen' – though this is from a translation for an American edition of a French biography (1967).

make(s) your armpit your charmpit. In about 1953, Lady Barnett, the British TV personality, paid a visit to the United States and came across a most ladylike advertising slogan for a deodorant spray called Stopette. It was: 'Make the armpit the charm pit!' (related in her book *My Life Line*, 1956). Compare this: arriving in Los Angeles after flying on an inaugural flight over the Pole (1940s?), Wynford Vaughan-Thomas, the Welsh broadcaster, was – unusually – rendered speechless by an American colleague. V-T's description of the Greenland icecap apparently made the American broadcaster remember his sponsors, who were makers of deodorants. Said he: 'It may be December outside, but **it's always August under your armpits.**' (Related in V-T's *Trust to Talk*, 1980.)

However, *News Review* (13 November 1947) reproduced from the *Evening Standard*: 'He [John Snagge] had been against commercial broadcasting ever since he heard a Toscanini radio concert in New York interrupted by the sponsor's slogan "It may be December outside, ladies, but it is always August under your armpits".'

According to Miles Kington in the *Independent* (13 May 1994), when W.H. Auden was Professor of Poetry at Oxford (early 1960s), he said in a lecture: 'Never underestimate advertisers. One of the most impressive lines of poetry I have ever come across was contained in an ad for a deodorant. This was the line: "It's always August underneath your arms . . ."'

make's you think. See THIS IS IT!

make the desert bloom. The modern state of Israel has made this injunction come true, but it 'dates from Bible times', according to Daniel J. Boorstin in *The Image* (1960). Adlai Stevenson also alluded to the phrase in a speech at Hartford, Connecticut (18 September 1952): 'Man has wrested from nature the power to make the world a desert or to make the deserts bloom.' The exact phrase does not appear in the Bible, though Isaiah 35:1 has: 'The desert shall rejoice, and blossom as the rose,' and 51:3 has: 'For the Lord shall comfort Zion . . . and he will make . . . her desert like the garden of the Lord.' Cruden's *Concordance* points out: 'In the Bible this word [desert] means a deserted place, wilderness, not desert in the modern usage of the term.'

Malaprop. See MRS ~.

male chauvinist (pig) (or **MCP**). This phrase for a man who is sunk in masculine preoccupations and attitudes erupted in 1970 at the time of the launch of the women's movement in the US and elsewhere. The optional use of 'pig' was a reversion to the traditional, fat, porky use of the word after the recent slang borrowing to describe the police (mostly in the US).

'Chauvinism' itself is a venerable coinage and originally referred to excessive patriotism. Nicolas Chauvin was a French general during Napoleon's campaigns who became famous for his excessive devotion to his leader.

malice aforethought. English legal term (current by 1670) for a wrongful act carried out against another person *intentionally*, without just cause or excuse (originally Old French *malice prepense*). *Malice Aforethought* was the title of a crime novel (1931) by Francis Iles.

malice in wonderland. Expression obviously playing upon ALICE IN WONDERLAND. It has been used as the title of a novel (1940) by 'Nicholas Blake' (C. Day Lewis), and also of an unrelated TV movie (US, 1985) about Hollywood gossip columnists. It was also the title of a record album by the UK group Nazareth (1980).

In his diary for February 1935, Cecil Beaton, the photographer, writes: 'Cocteau says I am Malice in Wonderland and I have succeeded in spending my life in an unreality made up of fun.'

man. See COMETH THE HOUR, COMETH THE ∼; EVERY ∼ HAS HIS PRICE; GO, ∼, GO!; GRAND OLD ∼; IT'S THAT ∼ AGAIN under *ITMA*; MOUNTIES ALWAYS GET THEIR ∼; RENAISSANCE ∼; WHAT'S THAT ∼ /LADY FOR?; YOU 'ORRIBLE LITTLE ∼!

man alive! An expression of surprise, a mild expletive, recorded by 1845 and building on the older usage 'any man alive' when referring to 'any living man whatever'. *Man Alive* was the title of a long-running BBC TV documentary series (from 1965 on).

man appeal. See under EMMA PEEL.

Manchester. See IF YOU'VE NEVER BEEN . . . under *RAY'S A LAUGH*; under WHAT — DOES TODAY. . . .

man for all seasons, a. Robert Bolt's title for his 1960 play about Sir Thomas More (filmed 1967) has provided a popular phrase for an accomplished, adaptable, appealing person. As such it also founded a phrase format, more than verging on the cliché, whereby almost anything can be described as 'a — for all seasons'. From Laurence Olivier, *On Acting* (1986): '[Ralph Richardson] was warm and what the public might call ordinary and, therefore, quite exceptional. That was his ability, that was his talent; he really was a man for all seasons.' Jean Rook wrote of Margaret Thatcher in the *Daily Express* (in 1982/3): 'She has proved herself not the "best man in Britain" but the "Woman For All Seasons".'

Bolt found his play-title in a description of More (1478–1535) by a contemporary, Robert Whittington: 'More is a man of angel's wit and singular learning; I know not his fellow. For where is the man of that gentleness, lowliness and affability? And as time requireth, a man of marvellous mirth and pastimes; and sometimes of as sad a gravity: as who say a man for all seasons.'

Whittington (c 1480 – c 1530) wrote the passage for schoolboys to put into Latin in his book *Vulgaria* (c 1521). It translates a comment on More by Erasmus – who wrote in his preface to *In Praise of Folly* (1509) that More was '*omnium horarum hominem*'.

Man From —, the. There has been an intermittent tendency to describe US presidents as if they were tall-walking characters from Westerns. Thus Harry Truman was dubbed 'The Man from Missouri', Dwight Eisenhower 'The Man from Abilene', and Jimmy Carter 'The Man from Plains'. None of this was very convincing and the craze is best left to the cinema whence we have had *The Man from Bitter Ridge/Colorado/Dakota/Del Rio/Laramie/the Alamo/Wyoming*, not to mention, any number of 'The Man Who —''s and 'A Man Called — ''s.

See also the next two listings and compare THE MAN WHO —.

man from the Pru, the. See ASK ∼.

Man from UNCLE, The. The title of a US TV series (1964–7) about an international spy organization. The letters stood for 'United Network Command for Law and Enforcement'. Any number of BBC stars have been dubbed 'the Man from AUNTIE' in consequence.

Manhattan Transfer. The name of the US vocal group (*fl.* 1977)(sometimes with the definite article attached), was taken from the novel *Manhattan Transfer* (1925) by John Dos Passos, depicting the 'shifting and variegated life of New York City' which was in turn named after the station on the Pennsylvania Railroad in New Jersey which enabled passengers between NYC and points south and west to change trains.

man in a grey/dark suit. From *Broadcast Magazine* (1987): 'With this latest career move can we expect to see the wunderkind [John Birt] transformed into the proverbial Man In A Grey Suit?' Such a man is a colourless administrator or technocrat and is probably as grey in his personality as in the colour of his suit. When the Beatles set up the Apple organization in the 1960s, John Lennon said this was an attempt 'to wrest control from the **men in suits**'. Sometimes such people are simply called 'suits'. From the *Observer* (29 October 1989): '[John] Major's spectacular ordinariness – the Treasury is now led by a "man in a suit" whose most distinguishing feature is his spectacles.'

The plural **men in grey suits** are, however, something a little different. In the November 1990 politicking which saw the British Prime Minister Margaret Thatcher eased out of office by her own party, there was much talk of the 'men in (grey) suits', those senior members of the Tory party who would advise Mrs Thatcher when it was time for her to go. Here, although still referring to faceless administrative types, the term is not quite so pejorative. In the *Observer* (1 December 1990), Alan Watkins adjusted the phrase slightly: 'I claim the paternity of "the men in suits" from an *Observer* column of the mid-1980s. Not you may notice, the men in dark suits, still less those in grey ones, which give quite the wrong idea.'

man in the street, the. A cliché of journalism, as in: 'Let's find out what the man in the street wants to know/really thinks'. Not a modern phrase. Fulke Greville, the English diarist, used it (entry dated 22 March 1830). Compare MAN ON THE CLAPHAM OMNIBUS.

manners, please – tits first. Used by the seducer's victim, when she considers that foreplay has started in the wrong place. Current in the 1960s and probably a bit earlier.

Man of a Thousand Faces, the. Sobriquet of Lon Chaney (1883–1930), the American film actor and master of macabre make-up. A 1957 biopic with the title *The Man of a Thousand Faces* starred James Cagney.

Man of Destiny, the. The nickname for Napoleon Bonaparte was used as the title of a play about him (1895) by George Bernard Shaw. Sir Walter Scott had earlier used the phrase in his *Life of Napoleon Bonaparte* (1827).

man of my calibre, a. See under HANCOCK'S HALF-HOUR.

man on the Clapham omnibus, the. i.e. the ordinary or average person, the MAN IN THE STREET, particularly when his/her point of view is instanced by the Courts, newspaper editorials, etc. This person was first evoked in 1903 by Lord Bowen when hearing a case of negligence: 'We must ask ourselves what the man on the Clapham omnibus would think.'

Quite why he singled out that particular route we shall never know. It sounds suitably prosaic, of course, and the present 77A to Clapham Junction (1995) does pass though Whitehall and Westminster, thus providing a link between governors and governed.

There is evidence to suggest that the 'Clapham omnibus' in itself had already become a figure of speech by the mid-nineteenth century. In 1857, there was talk of the 'occupant of the knife-board of a Clapham omnibus'.

man's gotta do what a man's gotta do, a. Partridge/*Catch Phrases* dates this from *c* 1945. Donald Hickling tells me he recalls hearing it in a war-time concert party, and suggests it came out of some late 1930s Western (Hopalong Cassidy?) or from an American strip cartoon.

The only printed reference to a definite source for the phrase in this precise form I have found is to the Alan Ladd film *Shane* (1953), which was based on a novel by Jack Shaeffer, though – on checking – neither book nor film contains the exact line. Ladd says: 'A man has to be what he is, Joey.' Another male character in the film says: 'I couldn't do what I gotta do if . . .' And a woman notes: 'Shane did what he had to do.' In the novel, we find only: 'A man is what he is, Bob, and there's no breaking the mould.'

Perhaps the phrase was used in promotional material for the film? Other suggested residing places of the phrase include *High Noon*, *The Sheepman* and *Stagecoach*. In the latter, John Wayne gets to say something like, 'There are some things a man just has to do.' By the 1970s, several songs had been recorded with the title.

So, the origin remains obscure, but an early example has now been found in John Steinbeck's novel *The Grapes of Wrath*, Chap. 18 (1939): 'I know this – a man got to do what he got to do.'

Man They Couldn't Gag, the. Nickname/by-line of Peter Wilson (d 1981), a sports journalist on the *Daily Mirror* who was famous for his hard-hitting style and outspoken opinions. A line from BBC radio's ROUND THE HORNE (19 March 1967) about two camp journalists: 'We're from the *Daily Palare*. He's the man you follow around and I'm the one you can't gag.'

manure, rocking-horse. See under AS BUSY AS . . .

Man Who —, the. This was a format title for a cartoon series of the 1920s/30s by H.M. Bateman, which showed people who had committed some solecism or other. Among them: 'The Man Who Missed the Ball on the First Tee at St Andrews', 'The Man Who Lit His Cigar Before the Royal Toast', 'The Girl Who Ordered a Glass of Milk at the Café Royal', and, 'The Man Who Asked for "A Double Scotch" in the Grand Pump Room at Bath'.

man who has everything, for the. Ex-America in the 1920s/30s? Promoting some odd luxury gift-item, inessential and overpriced – like a gold remover of fluff from belly-buttons, or the like. A salesman at the eponymous jewellery store in *Breakfast at Tiffany's* (film US, 1961) produces something, 'For the lady and gentleman who has everything'.

In *Sunday Today* (4 January 1987), Alana Stewart was quoted as saying of her ex-husband, singer Rod: 'What do you give to the man who's had everyone?'

man with the golden arm/flute/gun/ orchid-lined voice/trumpet, the. A medley of sobriquets. *The Man With the Golden Arm* was the title of a novel by Nelson Algren (1949; film US, 1956) about a poker dealer who kicks the drug habit. The Man With the Golden Flute is the Ulster-born flautist James Galway (b 1939). *The Man With the Golden Gun* is the title of a James Bond novel by Ian Fleming (1965; film UK, 1974). The Man With the Orchid-Lined Voice was the Italian tenor Enrico Caruso (1873–1921) – a phrase coined by his publicist Edward L. Bernays. The Man With the Golden Trumpet was the British musician Eddie Calvert (1922–78).

man with the plan, the. Political slogan used by the British Labour Party in the 1959 General Election. Posters carried the line under a picture of the party leader, Hugh Gaitskell, who did not win the election.

many, many times! See under ROUND THE HORNE.

man you love to hate, the. Coming across a 1979 film with this title, made as tribute to the Hollywood director Erich Von Stroheim (1885–1957) I was curious to know where the phrase came from. In fact, it was a billing phrase applied to Von Stroheim himself when he appeared as an actor in the 1918 propaganda film *The Heart of Humanity*. In it, he played an obnoxious German officer who not only attempted to violate the leading lady but nonchalantly tossed a baby out of the window. At the film's premiere in Los Angeles, Von Stroheim was hooted and jeered at when he walked on stage. He had to explain that he was only an actor – and was himself an Austrian.

March comes in like a lion. On 1 March 1876, the Rev. Francis Kilvert, the English diarist, wrote: 'March came in like a lion with wild wind and rain and hail.' It is from the saying: 'March comes in like a lion and goes out like a lamb,' proverbial by 1625.

marches. See TIME ∼ ON.

Maria. See BLACK ∼.

Marines, tell it to the. Meaning 'don't expect us to believe that'. This apparently dates from the days, in Britain, when Marines were looked down upon by ordinary sailors and soldiers. Working on land and sea, the Marines were clearly neither one thing nor the other, and thus stupid. So perhaps they would believe a piece of unbelievable information. The phrase was current by 1806. In 1867, *Notes and Queries* discussed it in the form, 'Tell that to the Marines for the sailors won't believe it.'

Brewer derives it from an occasion when Samuel Pepys was regaling Charles I with stories from the Navy. An officer of the Maritime Regiment of Foot (the precursors of the Marines) gave his support to Pepys when doubt was cast on the existence of flying fish. Said the King, 'Henceforeward ere ever we cast doubts upon a tale that lacks likelihood we first "Tell it to the Marines".' In fact, this story was originated by Major W.P. Drury in *The Tadpole of an Archangel* (1904). He subsequently admitted that it was an invention and a 'leg pull of my youth'.

The phrase is also well known in the US. Sometimes it takes the form, 'Tell *that* to the Marines'; sometimes, 'Tell that to the *horse*-marines.'

Mark Twain. See TWAIN.

Marples must go. See — MUST GO!

married. See WE'LL GET ∼ JUST AS SOON . . .

marry. See AND THAT, MY DEARS . . .

marrying. See NOT THE ∼ SORT.

Mars are marvellous. Slogan for the chocolate-coated soft-toffee bar, manufactured in the UK from 1932, and named after Forrest Mars, an American, who founded the company which makes it. Another notable advertising line for the product has been **a Mars a day helps you work, rest and play** (since 1960).

In the 1960s, Mars Bars became unforgettably associated with Marianne Faithfull, the singer, who was the girlfriend of Mick Jagger 1967–70. For the uses to which one was supposedly put, see Philip Norman, *The Rolling Stones*, Chap. 9 (1984). In *Faithfull* (1994), the singer dismisses the myth of the Mars Bar event as 'a very effective piece of demonising that was such a malicious twisting of the facts – a cop's idea of what people do on acid'.

Martha, rather a. The nickname given to a housewifely woman, derives from the biblical Martha, sister of Lazarus and Mary. While Mary sat listening to Jesus, her sister got on with the housework – 'distracted with much serving' – and Martha complained to Jesus, who nevertheless supported Mary (Luke 10:38–42). A modern example of the word's use occurs in *One of Us* by Hugo Young (1989): 'There was an almost obsessive reluctance to refer to [Margaret Thatcher's mother] . . . If she

was alluded to at all, it was under the patronizing designation of "rather a Martha".'

Martin, Betty. See ALL MY EYE . . .

Martini – shaken not stirred, a. This example of would-be sophistication became a running joke in the immensely popular James Bond films of the 1960s and 70s. The idea stems from the very first of Ian Fleming's Bond books, *Casino Royale* (1953), in which Bond orders a cocktail of his own devising. It consists of one dry Martini 'in a deep champagne goblet', three measures of Gordon's gin, one of vodka – 'made with grain instead of potatoes' – and half a measure of Kina Lillet. 'Shake it very well until it's ice-cold.' Bond justifies this fussiness a page or two later: 'I take a ridiculous pleasure in what I eat and drink. It comes partly from being a bachelor, but mostly from a habit of taking a lot of trouble over details. It's very pernickety and old-maidish really, but when I'm working I generally have to eat all my meals alone and it makes them more interesting when one takes trouble.'

This characteristic was aped by the writers of the first Bond story to be filmed – *Dr No* (1962). A West Indian servant brings Bond a vodka and Martini and says: 'Martini like you said, sir, and not stirred.' Dr No also mentions the fad, though the words are not spoken by Bond. In the third film, *Goldfinger* (1964), Bond (played by Sean Connery) does get to say 'a Martini, shaken not stirred' – he needs a drink after just escaping a laser death-ray – and there are references to it in *You Only Live Twice* (1967) and *On Her Majesty's Secret Service* (1969), among others.

The phrase was taken up in all the numerous parodies of the Bond phenomenon on film, TV and radio, though – curiously enough – it may be a piece of absolute nonsense. According to one expert, shaking a dry Martini 'turns it from something crystal-clear into a dreary frosted drink. It should be stirred quickly with ice in a jug'.

The *Oxford Dictionary of Modern Quotations* (1991) proudly claims to have discovered the source for this remark actually in one of Fleming's novels – *Dr No*

(1958) ('Bond said . . . Martini – with a slice of lemon peel. Shaken and not stirred, please.'). But, actually, it appears in the novels earlier than that: 'The waiter brought the Martinis, shaken and not stirred, as Bond had stipulated' (*Diamonds are Forever*, 1956).

martyr to be smarter. See under FASHION VICTIM.

Marx Brothers. Each member of the famous US family of comedians who appeared on stage and in films used a name other than the one he was born with. The nicknames were acquired at a poker game (*c* 1918): Leonard became Chico; Adolph became Harpo (he played the harp); Julius became Groucho; Milton became Gummo (though he left the act early on); and Herbert became Zeppo (though he also left in due course). On the record album *An Evening with Groucho Marx* (1972), Groucho attempts to explain the nicknames. Chico was a 'chicken-chaser'; Zeppo was 'after the Zeppelin which arrived in Lakehurst, New Jersey, at the time he was born' (1901); and Gummo 'wore gumshoes'. As for Groucho, 'I never did understand . . .'

In *The Marx Bros Scrapbook* (1974), Groucho gives a slightly different account – the stage names were given by a 'monologist named Art Fisher . . . I think Fisher got the names from a cartoon that was appearing in the papers. *The Monk Family* or something like that.' And as for Groucho? 'He named me because I was stern and rather serious.'

MASH. Acronym standing for 'Mobile Army Surgical Hospital' and made famous by the film *M*A*S*H** (US, 1970) and the subsequent sardonic TV series (1972–82) about one such American unit in the Korean War.

Mass, Phrases from the. These names are commonly given to parts of the Mass, especially to their musical settings, and all are Latin with the exception of *kyrie eleison*, which is Greek. Some of the phrases only occur in requiem masses. They are listed here in alpabetical sequence, not the order in which they are sung.

agnus dei: lamb of God.
benedictus: blessed (is He).
confutatis (maledictis): (when the damned) are cast away.
credo (in unum Deum): I believe (in one God).
dies irae: day of wrath.*Domine Deus*: O Lord God.
et incarnatus est: and was incarnate.
gloria (in excelsis Deo): glory (be to God on high).
gratias agimus tibi: we give thanks to Thee.
kyrie eleison: Lord, have mercy.
lacrimosa (dies illa): (this day full of) tears.
laudamus te: we praise Thee.
lux aeterna: eternal light.
pie Jesu: gentle Jesus.
qui tollis peccata mundi: (Thou) that takest away the sins of the world.
quoniam tu solus Sanctus: for Thou only art holy.
recordare: remember.
rex tremendae (majestatis): king of awful majesty.
Sanctus: Holy.
tuba mirum (spargens sonum): the trumpet, scattering its awful sound.

master. See DOG FOLLOWS ITS ~ under AGE BEFORE BEAUTY; WE ARE THE ~S NOW.

Master, the. Nickname of Sir Noël Coward (*d* 1973), actor and writer, who was known thus throughout the theatrical profession from the 1940s, but not by those close to him. He professed to dislike the name (perhaps because it had already been applied to D.W. Griffith, the film pioneer, and W. Somerset Maugham, the writer) and, when asked to explain it, replied: 'Oh, you know, jack of all trades, master of none . . .' Sir John Mills in his autobiography *Up In the Clouds, Gentlemen, Please* (1980) claims to have been the first to give Coward the name when they were both involved in a production of *Journey's End*.

mastermind. (1) Since 1720, a term for someone of commanding intellect, but also often given to the supposed progenitor of criminal acts who (usually) is not directly involved in their execution – Trollope has one in *The Eustace Diamonds* (1872). (2) Senior Service cigarettes were promoted in the UK, sometime before 1950, with the curious line **a product of the mastermind.** (3) A sort of catchphrase from the BBC radio comedy series RAY'S A LAUGH. From the edition of 1 April 1954, 'Mrs Easy', the home help (Patricia Hayes): 'Now, don't you take that tone of voice with me, Mastermind!' (4) The title of a long-running general and specialist knowledge quiz (1972–) on BBC TV (see I'VE STARTED SO I'LL FINISH).

matched. See HATCHED, – AND DESPATCHED.

mates. See HELLO ME OLD ~.

mating. See ONLY IN THE ~ SEASON under GOON SHOW.

max. See GRODY TO THE ~.

maybe. See AND I DON'T MEAN ~.

May-December romance, a. A relationship in which there is a wide age gap. Probably originating in American show business. From the *Independent* (5 July 1992): 'In the novel [*Grand Hotel*] the big love affair involves a couple with a big age disparity. But in the movie they cast Garbo and John Barrymore. No May-December.' From the *Washington Post* (28 December 1991): 'Martha Raye's 75, he's 42 . . . as for the romantic side of their May-December matchup, she says, "After all those years, I almost forgot how to "do it."' *May to December* has been the title of a BBC TV situation comedy (1989–) about such an age-gap relationship: Anton Rodgers with a young-enough-to-be-his-daughter girlfriend.

Possible inspiration for the phrase may be: the James Walker/Ernest R. Ball song 'Will You Love Me in December As You Do in May' (1905); the Maxwell Anderson/Kurt Weill 'September Song' (1938): 'Oh, it's a long, long while/From May to December,/But the days grow short/When you reach September.' Compare this, from 'To the most Courteous and Fair Gentlewoman, Mrs Elinor Williams' by Rowland Watkyns (d 1664): 'For every marriage then is best in tune,/When that the wife is May, the husband June.' In

Chaucer's 'The Merchant's Tale', a 60-year-old bachelor called *January* marries a young thing called *May*. She is unfaithful, as is perhaps sometimes the case.

Sometimes also **a spring and winter romance.** From Ned Sherrin, *Theatrical Anecdotes* (1991): 'She [Coral Browne] showed the same frankness when commenting on a spring and winter romance between Jill Bennett and Sir Godfrey Tearle: "I could never understand what he saw in her," she drawled, "until I saw her eating corn on the cob at the Caprice."'

may I spend a penny? See under DAD'S ARMY.

may the Force be with you! This benediction/valediction is a delicious piece of hokum from the film *Star Wars* (1977). At one point, Alec Guinness explains what it means: 'The Force is what gives the Jedi its power. It's an energy field created by all living things. It surrounds us, it penetrates us, it binds the galaxy together.'

The phrase turned up in Cornwall a short while after the film was released in Britain – as a police recruiting slogan. Later, President Reagan, promoting his 'Star Wars' weapon system, said: 'It isn't about fear, it's about hope, and in that struggle, if you'll pardon my stealing a film line, "The force is with us."'

Compare 'The Lord be with you' from, for example, Morning Prayer in the Anglican Prayer Book.

MCP. See MALE CHAUVINIST PIG.

mean. See I MEANTER SAY!; I ~ THAT MOST SINCERELY . . . ; I SEE WHAT YOU ~ under ARCHERS; IT ALL DEPENDS WHAT YOU ~ BY . . . ; WE HAVE WAYS AND ~S OF MAKING YOU TALK.

mean! moody! magnificent! A slogan from the most notorious of all film advertising campaigns – for the Howard Hughes production of *The Outlaw* in 1943. As if 'The Two Great Reasons for Jane Russell's Rise to Stardom' (skilfully supported by the Hughes-designed cantilever bra) were not enough, there were various pictures of the skimpily clad new star. One version had her reclining with a long whip. It's a very tame film, but the campaign has to be an early example of promotional hype.

mean streets. A noted phrase used by Raymond Chandler in 'The Simple Art of Murder' (1950): 'Down these mean streets a man must go who is not himself mean; who is neither tarnished nor afraid' (referring to the heroic qualities a detective should have). However, in 1894, Arthur Morrison had written *Tales of Mean Streets* about impoverished life in the East End of London. *Mean Streets* was also the title of a film (US, 1973) about an Italian ghetto in New York.

meanter/mean to. See I ~ SAY.

meanwhile back at the ranch . . . One of the caption/subtitles/intertitles from the days of the silent cinema. I think it may also have been used in US radio 'horse operas', when recapping the story after a commercial break.

medicine. See LAUGHTER IS THE BEST ~.

meet. See ~ THE WIFE UNDER 'AS 'E BIN IN, WHACK?; PREPARE TO ~ THY GOD.

meeting. See HERE'S TO OUR NEXT MERRY ~.

megaphone diplomacy. Referring to political 'dialogue' which consists of shouted sloganeering rather than a genuine meeting of minds, the phrase was used (by 1985) in particular to describe the abusive tone of relations between the US and the USSR, prior to the *rapprochement* of the late 1980s.

member of the human race. See FULLY PAID-UP MEMBER . . .

memory. See DOWN ~ LANE.

men. See FOR ~ OF DISTINCTION; YESTERDAY'S ~.

mend. See MAKE-DO AND ~.

men in white coats. Doctors and orderlies (especially from mental hospitals) whose appearance on the scene suggests that someone is about to be taken away for treatment. The cry 'Send for the men in white coats' might have preceded their arrival. *OED2* finds the term 'whitecoat' for such a person in use by 1911.

merde! See under BREAK A LEG.

Meredith we're in! This shout of triumph originated in a music-hall sketch called 'The Bailiff' (or 'Moses and Son'), performed by Fred Kitchen, the leading comedian with FRED KARNO's company. The sketch was first seen in 1907 and the phrase was uttered each time a bailiff and his assistant looked like gaining entrance to the house. Reportedly, Kitchen even had it put on his gravestone.

meringue. See ANIMATED ~.

merry. See ALWAYS ~ AND BRIGHT; EAT, DRINK AND BE ~; HERE'S TO OUR NEXT ~ MEETING.

mess. See HERE'S ANOTHER NICE ~ . . .

message of —, the. Cliché of (mostly British) politics. ' "The SDP bubble has burst," crowed Fallon. "That is the message of Darlington" ' (*Time*, 4 April 1983).

messing. See STOP MESSIN' ABAHT! under HANCOCK'S HALF-HOUR.

mess of potage, a. 'To sell one's birthright for a mess of potage', meaning 'to sacrifice something for material comfort', has biblical origins but is not a direct quotation from the Bible. 'Esau selleth his birthright for a mess of potage' appears as a chapter heading for Genesis 25 in one or two early translations of the Bible, though not in the Authorized Version of 1611. The word 'mess' is used in its sense of 'a portion of liquid or pulpy food'. 'Potage' is thick soup (compare French *potage*).

metal. See HEAVY ~.

Me, Tarzan – you, Jane. A box-office sensation of 1932 was the first Tarzan film with sound – *Tarzan the Ape Man*. It spawned a long-running series and starred Johnny Weissmuller, an ex-US swimming champion, as Tarzan, and Maureen O'Sullivan as Jane. At one point the ape man whisks Jane away to his tree-top abode and indulges in some elementary conversation with her. Thumping his chest, he says, 'Tarzan!'; pointing at her, he says, 'Jane!' So, in fact, he does not say the catchphrase commonly associated with him – though I suppose he might have done in one of the later movies. Interestingly, this great moment of movie dialogue appears to have been 'written' by the British playwright and actor Ivor Novello. In the original novel, *Tarzan of the Apes* (1914), by Edgar Rice Burroughs, the line does not occur – not least because, in the jungle, Tarzan and Jane are only able to communicate by writing notes to each other.

methinks she doth protest too much. Gertrude's line from Shakespeare's *Hamlet*, III.ii.225 (1600) is often evoked to mean 'there's something suspicious about the way that person is complaining – it's not natural'. However, what Hamlet's mother is actually doing is giving her opinion of 'The Mousetrap', the play-within-a-play. What she means to say is that the Player Queen is overdoing her protestations, and uses the word 'protest' in the sense of 'state formally', not 'complain'.

Mexican wave, a. Stadium crowds have long entertained themselves (and observers) by rising up and down from their seats in an orderly sequence, thus giving the impression (when viewed from a distance) of a rippling wave or flag. The name 'Mexican wave' was given to the practice following much use of it during the football World Cup in Mexico in 1986.

mickey. See TAKE THE ~.

mickey finn. Anything slipped into people's drinks in order to knock them out. *DOAS* claims that, to begin with, the term meant a laxative for horses. The original Mickey Finn may have been a notorious bartender in Chicago (d 1906) who proceeded to rob his unconscious victims.

Middle America. Originally a geographical expression, this phrase was applied to the US conservative middle class in 1968 during Richard Nixon's campaign for the presidency. It corresponded to what he was later to call the SILENT MAJORITY and was what was alluded to in the expression IT'LL PLAY IN PEORIA. The expression is said to have been coined by the journalist Joseph Kraft.

middle name is —, [a person's]. An American way of defining a person's outstanding characteristic (often negatively). From P.G. Wodehouse, *Damsel in Distress* (1919): 'Everyone told me your middle name was Nero.' From Sinclair Lewis, *Main Street* (1920): ' "Like fishing?" "Fishing is my middle name." ' From Thomas Tryon, *All That Glitters* (1987): 'Belinda Carroll had a middle name, but you never saw it in print or on a theatre marquee. Her middle name was trouble with a capital "T".' 'Trouble Is My Middle Name' was the title of a song (US, 1963) by Nader & Gluck.

middle way, the. A middle course in politics, occupying 'the middle ground' between extremes. The concept is an ancient one and also occurs in some religions. Winston Churchill had earlier ended an election address on 11 November 1922 by saying: 'What we require now is not a period of turmoil, but a period of stability and recuperation. Let us stand together and tread a sober middle way.' *The Middle Way* was the title of a book (1938) by Harold Macmillan, setting out the arguments for the politician approach.

midstream. See NEVER SWAP/CHANGE HORSES IN ~.

mighty roar. See STOP THE ~ under *IN TOWN TONIGHT*.

mile, to go the extra. See GO THE EXTRA MILE.

miles. See NOT A MILLION ~ FROM . . .

milk. See DRINKA PINTA ~ A DAY; LAND FLOWING WITH ~ AND HONEY; under WHY KEEP A COW . . . ?

milk? Pronounced 'mil-uck' on a rising inflection by Hermione Gingold, making tea for Alfred Marks in a feature called 'Mrs Doom's Diary' on the BBC radio show *Home at Eight* (first broadcast 21 April 1952 and the catchphrase certainly established by 1955). According to the *Independent* obituary of the show's scriptwriter Sid Colin (28 December 1989): 'Sid ingeniously combined Mrs Dale with Charles Addams in a series of sketches . . . [the Dooms] lived in a suburban castle with Fido, their pet alligator, and Trog, their giant speechless servant. At tea-time, people all over Britain were parroting the words that closed every Dooms sketch: "**Tea, Edmond?**" "Yes, thank you, dear – thank you." "Mil-uck?"'

milk from contented cows. A slogan for Carnation Milk, from 1906. Elbridge A. Stuart launched Carnation evaporated milk in 1899. Seven years later he went to the Mahin agency in Chicago to lay on an advertising campaign. The copywriter was Helen Mar: 'Mr Stuart gave me a description of the conditions under which Carnation was produced . . . the ever-verdant pastures of Washington and Oregon, where grazed the carefully-kept Holstein herds that supplied the raw milk. He described in a manner worthy of Burton Holmes the picturesque background of these pastures from which danced and dashed the pure, sparkling waters to quench the thirst of the herds and render more tender the juicy grasses they fed on. He spoke of the shade of luxuriant trees under which the herds might rest. Remembering my lectures in medical college and recalling that milk produced in mental and physical ease is more readily digested – I involuntarily exclaimed, "Ah! The milk of contented cows!" . . . "That's our slogan" [said Mr Stuart].'

And so it has remained or almost. The words on the can have usually been, 'From contented cows.'

In *The Cocoanuts* (US, 1929), Groucho Marx gets to say: 'There's more than two hundred dollars worth of milk in those cocoanuts – and *what* milk, milk from contented cow-co-nuts.'

milk's gotta lotta bottle. A slogan promoting milk consumption in Britain, *c* 1982. Milk comes in bottles, of course, but why was the word 'bottle' used to denote courage or guts in this major attempt to get rid of milk's wimpish image? Actually, the word 'bottle' has been used in this sense since the late 1940s at least. To 'bottle out' consequently means to shrink from, e.g. in *Private Eye* (17 December 1982): 'Cowed by the thought of six-figure legal bills and years in the courts, the Dirty Digger has "bottled out" of a confrontation with Sir Jams.'

One suggestion is that 'bottle' acquired the meaning through rhyming slang: either 'bottle and glass' = 'class' (said to date from the 1920s, this one); 'bottle and glass' = 'arse'; or, 'bottle of beer' = fear. But the reason for the leap from 'class/arse' to 'courage', and from 'fear' to 'guts', is not terribly clear, though it has been explained that 'arse' is what you would void your bowels through in an alarming situation. And 'class' is what a boxer has. If he loses it, he has 'lost his bottle'.

Other clues? Much earlier, in *Swell's Night Guide* (1846), there had occurred the line: 'She thought it would be no bottle 'cos her rival could go in a buster,' where 'no bottle' = 'no good'. In a play by Frank Norman (1958), there occurs the line: 'What's the matter, Frank? Your bottle fallen out?' There is also an old-established brewers, Courage Ltd, whose products can, of course, be had in bottles.

The way forward for the 1982 advertising use was probably cleared by the ITV series *Minder* which introduced much south London slang to a more general audience.

Milk Tray. See AND ALL BECAUSE . . .

mill. See TROUBLE AT T' ~ .

Miller. See JOE ~ .

million. See COOL ~ ; I'VE GOT A ~ OF 'EM! under GOODNIGHT, MRS CALABASH . . . ; NOT A ~ MILES FROM ── .

mills of God grind slowly, the ('. . . yet they grind exceeding small'). The meaning of this saying is that the ways in which reforms are brought about, crime is punished, etc., are often slow, but the end result may be perfectly achieved. The saying comes from Longfellow's translation of Friedrich von Logau, a German seventeenth-century poet.

Milwaukee. See BEER THAT MADE ~ FAMOUS.

mind. See HEARTS AND ~S; I DON'T ~ IF I DO under *ITMA*; IT'S ALL IN THE ~ under *GOON SHOW*; OUT OF YOUR TINY CHINESE ~S; PS AND QS, ~ YOUR.

mind how you go! See under EVENIN' ALL!

mind my bike! The British actor and entertainer Jack Warner (1895–1981) wrote in his autobiography, *Jack of All Trades* (1975): 'When I dropped the phrase for two weeks, I had 3,000 letters from listeners asking why . . . the only other complaint came from a father who wrote, "I am very keen on your *Garrison Theatre* show, but I have spent several hundreds of pounds on my son's education and all he can do is shout "Mind my bike!" in a very raucous Cockney voice. I'm trying to break him of the habit, so will you please stop saying it?"' *Garrison Theatre* was broadcast on BBC radio from 1939 onwards.
    See also BLUE PENCIL.

mine. See DON'T GO DOWN THE ~ . . .

mineral. See ANIMAL, VEGETABLE OR ~.

Minnie(s). See MOANING ~.

minute(s). See FAMOUS FOR FIFTEEN ~; I'VE ONLY GOT FOUR ~; see THERE'S A SUCKER BORN EVERY ~.

miracles. See AGE OF ~ IS NOT PAST.

mirrors. See ALL DONE WITH ~.

misrule. THIRTEEN YEARS OF TORY ~.

missed, just. See under *BEYOND OUR KEN.*

missing you already. See HAVE A GOOD DAY.

mission. See WE'RE ON A ~ FROM GOD.

mission impossible. The title of the US TV series *Mission Impossible* (1966–72) has achieved catchphrase status. The original show dealt with government agents in the Impossible Missions Force. See also SELF-DESTRUCT IN FIVE SECONDS.
    'Yet another journalist brought on to the set! He said "I want to write about all the fun that goes on *behind* the scenes . . ." and Kenny Connor said "Mission impossible"' (from *The Diaries of Kenneth Williams*, for 20 March 1975). 'When Kissinger took the commission post, his associates warned that it was mission impossible' (*Washington Post*, 3 January 1984); 'Hostage rescue is mission impossible' (headline in the *Observer*, 19 August 1990).

Miss Lonelyhearts. Name given to writers of advice columns for the lovelorn (chiefly in the US), taken from the title of a novel (1933) by Nathanael West, about a man who writes such a column under this pen name. In the UK (mostly), the term **lonelyhearts column** has come to mean not an advice column but a listing service for men and women seeking partners.

Miss World order. See under I'LL GIVE YOU THE RESULTS . . .

mist. See under LOVE IN A ~.

mistake. See DID YOU SPOT . . . ?, SHOME ~, SHURELY?

Mis-ter Chris-tian . . . I'll have you hung from the high-est yard-arm in the Navy! An impersonation of the lines delivered by Charles Laughton as Captain Bligh in the film *Mutiny on the Bounty* (1935). The British comedian Tony Hancock made something of a speciality of the impersonation in *HANCOCK'S HALF-HOUR* (BBC TV and radio, from 1954 onwards).

mit. See FROZEN ~.

Mitty. See WALTER.

mix and match, to. A way of selecting clothes for wearing (chiefly by women and in the US). From *McCall's Sewing* (1964): 'Separates are the answer to the schoolgirl's needs. Skirts, sweaters, jackets and blouses that can mix and match are ideal.' Sometimes used allusively in other fields.

mix and mingle, to. To socialize formally as part of a programme, especially when a celebrity allots time to meet the public or press. Chiefly an American expression. From the *Washington Post* (19 July 1985): 'Reagan will join everybody later at dinner . . . Afterward, forgoing the entertainment by opera singer Grace Bumbry and the "mix and mingle" over after-dinner coffee, he will return to the family quarters'; (13 July 1986): 'At Buckingham Palace there's the party within the party. Only those bidden to the royal tea tent actually get to mix and mingle with the royals.'

mo. See ARF A ∼, KAISER.

Moaning Minnie(s). On 11 September 1985, the British Prime Minister Margaret Thatcher paid a visit to Tyneside and was reported as accusing those who complained about the effects of unemployment of being 'Moaning Minnies'. In the ensuing uproar, a Downing Street spokesman had to point out that it was the reporters attempting to question her, rather than the unemployed, on whom Mrs Thatcher had bestowed the title.

As a nickname, it was not an original alliterative coinage. Anyone who complains is a 'moaner' and a 'minnie' can mean a lost lamb which finds itself an adoptive mother. From the *Observer* (20 May 1989): 'Broadcasters are right to complain about the restrictions placed on them for the broadcasting of the House of Commons . . . But the Moaning Minnies have only themselves to blame.'

The original 'Moaning Minnie' was something quite different. In the First World War, a 'Minnie' was the slang name for a German *minenwerfer*, a trench mortar or the shell that came from it, making a distinctive moaning noise. In the Second World War, the name was also applied to air-raid sirens which were also that way inclined.

Mobile Army Surgical Hospital. See MASH.

mojo working?, got your. In 1960, Muddy Waters, the American blues singer (1915–83) was singing a song with the refrain, 'Got my mojo workin', but it just don't work on you.' He knew what he was singing about because he had written the song under his real name, McKinley Morganfield. *DOAS* defines 'mojo' simply as 'any narcotic' but a sleeve note to an album entitled *Got My Mojo Workin'* (1966) by the jazz organist Jimmy Smith is perhaps nearer to the meaning of the word in the song. It describes 'mojo' as 'magic – a spell or charm guaranteed to make the user irresistible to the opposite sex'.

Indeed, it seems to me that 'mojo' could well be a form of the word 'magic' corrupted through Black pronunciation, though the *OED2* finds an African word meaning 'magic, witchcraft' that is similar. The *OED2* derives the narcotic meaning of the word from the Spanish *mojar*, 'to celebrate by drinking'.

mole, to infiltrate as a. The name 'mole' is applied to one who 'tunnels' into a large organization, but particularly a spy who is placed in another country's intelligence network often years before being needed. The CIA term for this process is 'penetration' and former CIA chief Richard Helms told Safire he had never encountered use of the word 'mole' in this regard. Although flirted with by other writers (as early as Francis Bacon), the term was introduced by John Le Carré in his novel *Tinker, Tailor, Soldier, Spy* (1974). In a BBC TV interview in 1976, he said he *thought* it was a genuine KGB term which he had picked up.

Molotov cocktail, a. The incendiary device, similar to a petrol bomb, acquired its name in Finland during the early days of the Second World War. V.M. Molotov had become Soviet Minister for Foreign Affairs in 1939. The Russians invaded Finland and these home-made grenades proved an effective way for the Finns to oppose their tanks.

Moltke, a. Name given to a taciturn, unsmiling person. Michael Wharton ('Peter Simple' columnist in the *Daily Telegraph*) was so nicknamed by his German grandfather after the famous general, Helmuth Graf von Moltke (d 1891): 'who seldom spoke and was said to have smiled only twice in his life'. Walter Bagehot quotes a remark that Moltke was 'silent in seven languages'.

moment. See ARF A MO KAISER; AT THIS ~ IN TIME.

moment of truth, the. Meaning, 'a decisive turning point; a significant moment', the phrase comes from '*el momento de la verdad*' in Spanish bullfighting – the final sword-thrust that kills the animal. *Il Momento della Verità* was the title of an Italian/Spanish film (1964) on a bullfighting theme. In *I, Claud* (1967), Claud Cockburn said of European intellectuals who had fought in the Spanish Civil War: 'They proclaimed, however briefly, that a moment comes when your actions have to bear some kind of relation to your words. This is what is called the Moment of Truth.'

monarch of all one surveys. Nowadays used as a light-hearted proprietorial boast, this phrase comes from William Cowper's 'Verses Supposed to be Written by Alexander Selkirk' (the original of 'Robinson Crusoe), c 1779:

> I am monarch of all I survey,
> My right there is none to dispute;
> From the centre all round to the sea
> I am lord of the fowl and the brute.

Kenneth Tynan, writing about Noël Coward (in *Panorama*, Spring 1952) said: 'He is, if I may test the trope, monocle of all he surveys.'

Monday. See BLACK ~.

money. See FUNNY IS ~; GIVE 'IM THE ~ under HAVE A GO; HOW THE ~ ROLLS IN; LIKE TAKING ~ FROM BLIND BEGGARS; SERIOUS ~; TAKE THE ~ AND RUN; YOUR ~ OR YOUR LIFE.

money does not smell. See PECUNIA NON OLET.

money makes the world go (a)round. With this phrase, as with TOMORROW

BELONGS TO ME, we may have to thank the writers of the musical *Cabaret* (1966) for either creating an instant 'saying' or, perhaps in this instance, for introducing to the English language something that has been known in others. 'Money makes the world go around' is clearly built on the well-established proverb ' 'Tis love, that makes the world go round', but is not recorded in either the *ODP* or the *CODP* (the nearest they get is, 'Money makes the mare to go').

I see that it appears in the English-language key to the Flemish Proverbs picture by David Teniers the Younger (1610–90), at Belvoir Castle. The painting shows an obviously wealthy man holding a globe. How odd that it should, apparently, have taken a song in a 1960s musical to get this expression into English.

Monica. See MY NAME'S ~ under *EDUCATING ARCHIE*.

monk. See MAD ~.

monkey. See AS THE ~ SAID; COLD ENOUGH TO FREEZE . . . ; I'M A/I'LL BE A ~'S UNCLE; RIGHT ~; SOFTLY, SOFTLY, CATCHEE ~.

monster. See GREEN-EYED ~.

monstrous carbuncle. In June 1984, Prince Charles described a proposed design for a new wing of the National Gallery in London as: 'a kind of vast municipal fire station . . . I would understand better this type of high-tech approach if you demolished the whole of Trafalgar Square, but what is proposed is like a monstrous carbuncle on the face of a much loved and elegant friend.' (In the same speech he called a planned Mies van der Rohe office building in London a 'glass stump', and opening a factory in May 1987 he likened the new building to a 'Victorian prison'.)

The Prince of Wales's ventures into architectural criticism have not gone unnoticed and the image of a 'monstrous carbuncle' ('a red spot or pimple on the nose or face caused by habits of intemperance' OED2) has become part of the critical vocabulary. A report in the *Independent* (1 March 1988) about plans for a new lifeboat station dominating the harbour at Lyme

Regis concluded by quoting a local objector: 'They've called this building a design of the age. What we've got here is a Prince Charles Carbuncle, and we don't like carbuncles down on Lyme harbourside.' The Prince's step-mother-in-law, the Countess Spencer, had earlier written in a book called *The Spencers on Spas* (1983) of how 'monstrous carbuncles of concrete have erupted in Gentle Georgian squares'. In *Barnaby Rudge*, Chap. 54 (1841), Charles Dickens writes: 'Old John was so red in the face . . . and lighted up the Maypole Porch wherein they sat together, like a monstrous carbuncle in a fairy tale.'

Even before this, in 1821, William Cobbett had characterized the whole of London as 'the **great wen** of all' – a 'wen' being a lump or protuberance on a body, a wart.

month. See FLAVOUR OF THE ~.

monty. See FULL ~.

Monty Python's Flying Circus. The BBC TV comedy series was first aired 1969–74 and a feature film of highlights was released in 1971. Like most graduate comedy shows of the 1960s and 70s, *Monty Python* rather frowned upon the use of catchphrases as something belonging to another type of show business. However, **naughty bits!**, from a lecture on parts of the body (24 November 1970), caught on as a euphemism for the genitals. So also did **nudge-nudge, wink-wink. Know what I mean? Say no more!** following Eric Idle's use of the words as the prurient character 'Norman' (later known as 'Nudge') who accosted people with remarks like, 'Is your wife a goer, then? Eh, eh?' His phrases were spoken in any order (firstly on 19 October 1969).

Graham Chapman played a bossy Colonel who would interrupt sketches – if not provide them with an ending – and say that they were **silly!** His tenor, two-note enunciation of this word was much imitated (in my house, anyway).

See also AND NOW FOR SOMETHING COMPLETELY DIFFERENT . . . ; DEAD PARROT.

moo. See SILLY (OLD) ~.

moody. See MEAN! ~! MAGNIFICENT!

moon. See ONCE IN A BLUE ~ ; OVER THE ~ .

moon is made of green cheese, the. One of the most frequently found sayings in sixteenth- and seventeenth-century literature. 'You would have us believe that the moon is made of green cheese' is an old riposte to someone inclined to make far-fetched remarks.

mop flops. See THAT'S THE WAY THE COOKIE CRUMBLES.

mops. See IF SEVEN MAIDS WITH SEVEN ~ . . .

more. See ALL ANIMALS ARE EQUAL . . .; AND THERE'S ~ ; ARE THERE ANY ~ AT HOME LIKE YOU?; LESS IS ~ .

Morecambe and Wise Show, The. The long-running double-act of comedians Eric Morecambe (1926–84) and Ernie Wise (*b* 1925) began on the variety stage, went through a period on ITV, and finally achieved the status of a national institution on BBC TV from the late 1960s to the late 1970s. Then, once more, they returned to ITV. The essence of their crosstalk was the inconsequentiality of Eric's interruptions of the relatively 'straight' Ernie's posturings. Their many phrases included:

> **short, fat, hairy legs.** Applied by Eric to Ernie's, in contrast to his own long, elegant legs. Ernie says that this emerged, like most of their phrases, during rehearsals – particularly during their spell on ITV. I have heard of people who refer to short trousers that reveal hairy legs as 'Morecambes'.

> **there's no answer to that!** Eric's standard innuendo-laden response to such comments as: 'Casanova (Frank Finlay) "I'll be perfectly frank with you – I have a long felt want."'

> **this play what I have wrote.** From the long-running joke that Ernie was capable of writing plays (in which guest stars would perform on the show).

what do you think of it [the show] so far?/Rubbish! Eric's customary inquiry of audiences animate or inanimate. He said he got the idea from his family and it was first put into a famous sketch about Antony and Cleopatra (featuring Glenda Jackson) in 1971. Eric recalled (1980): 'I said it during rehearsals in a sketch with a ventriloquist's dummy. It got such a laugh that we kept it in . . . but it's bounced back on me more than once. When I was a director of Luton Town, I dreaded going to see away games. If we were down at half time, home fans would shout up to me, "What do you think of it so far?"'

you can't see the join. Eric to Ernie, concerning his (presumed) hair-piece. Ernie recalled (1979) the origin of this: 'We shared digs in Chiswick with an American acrobat who had a toupee which – like all toupees – was perfectly obvious as such. We would whisper to each other, out of the side of our mouths, "You can hardly see the join!"'

See also BOOM, BOOM! and WHAT ABOUT THE WORKERS?

more efficient conduct of the war, a. (sometimes **energetic . . .**) This almost became a slogan of the First World War for what was required of the British Government (c 1916) prior to the replacement of Prime Minister Asquith by Lloyd George. However, the coalition government announced by Asquith on 26 May 1915 had claimed that this was what it was promoting.

Compare, from Lord Home, *The Way the Wind Blows* (1976): 'Sir Roger Keyes [in 1939] . . . made an impassioned speech in favour of more urgent conduct of the war.'

more in sorrow than in anger, to do something. Meaning, that you are doing something – like meting out punishment – in a rational rather than hot-headed way. An allusion to Shakespeare, *Hamlet*, I.ii.231 (1600) where Horatio explains that the Ghost of Hamlet's father exhibited, 'A countenance more in sorrow than in anger.' From the *Independent* (23 April 1992): 'I told an Essex Girl Joke. A young woman turned on me as if I came from another, less advanced planet, and, more in sorrow than in anger, said she didn't think what I'd said was frightfully RIGHT-ON.'

more power to your elbow. A phrase of encouragement (only used when an enterprise is laudable). But where does it come from – archery, gambling, weight-lifting or drinking? Brewer suggests the latter and there is an obvious link to the beer slogan IT'S WHAT YOUR RIGHT ARM'S FOR. *OED2*'s earliest citation (1832) is Irish: 'More power to your honour's elbow', which might support the drinking connection. There are also the expressions 'to shake the elbow' for 'to gamble' and 'knight of the elbow' for 'gambler'.

But the phrase may be no more than a connection between 'elbow' and 'effort', as in the expression 'apply a little elbow-grease'. I would also like to think that it had something to do with writing – vigorous movement of the elbow when scribbling in long-hand.

more stars than there are in heaven. A slogan for the MGM studios in Hollywood, and created by Howard Dietz (1896–1983), the writer and film executive, in the 1920s/30s. See ARS GRATIA ARTIS.

more tea, Vicar? Phrase for use after a fart, or to cover any kind of embarrassment. British use, from the 1920s/30s? Paul Beale has collected various forms for a revision of Partridge/*Catch Phrases*, including: 'good evening, vicar!'; 'no swearing, please, vicar' (said facetiously to introduce a note of the mock-highbrow into a conversation full of expletives); 'another cucumber sandwich, vicar' (after an involuntary belch); 'speak up, Padre!/Brown/Ginger (you're through)' (as a response to a fart).

more — than you can shake a stick at. i.e. uncountable numbers – as in, 'Hell, there's more deer in those woods than you can shake a stick at.' From the US, originally – e.g. the Lancaster, Pa. *Journal* (5 August 1818): 'We have in Lancaster more Taverns as you can shake a stick at.' In the film *Monkey Business* (US, 1931), Groucho Marx says to a sea captain: 'If you were a man you'd go in business for yourself. I know a fella started only last year with just a canoe. Now he's got more women than you could shake a stick at, if that's your idea of a good time.'

Moreton. See OH, GET IN THERE, ~ under *EDUCATING ARCHIE*.

morituri te salutant [those who are about to die salute you]. These words were addressed to the emperor by gladiators in ancient Rome on entering the arena. The practice seems to have been first mentioned in *Claudius* by Suetonius (AD 75–160). In time, the phrase was extended to anyone facing difficulty, and then ironically so.

morning. See GOOD ~ . . . NICE DAY under *ITMA*; GREAT ~ ; NEVER GLAD CONFIDENT ~ .

morning all! Jimmy Young (*b* 1923), one-time crooner, became an unlikely recruit to BBC Radio 1 as a disc-jockey in the late 1960s, and became hugely popular with the mainly female morning audience. He would begin with a routine like this: 'Morning all! I hope you're all leaping about to your entire satisfaction, especially those **sur le continong** . . . and **orft we jolly well go!**'

The pronunciation 'continong', approximating to the French, was established by the turn of the century. Marie Lloyd had a song called 'The Naughty Continong'. Charles Dickens in *Little Dorrit*, Bk I, Chap. 2 (1857) wrote, '[Marseilles] sent the most insurrectionary tune into the world [the *Marseillaise*]. It couldn't exist without allonging [*allons*] and marshonging [*marchons!*] to something or other.'

Young would also frequently wonder **where is it all leading us, I ask myself?** before concluding with **BFN – 'bye for now!** (perhaps harking back to 'TTFN' in *ITMA*.).

His recipe spot was heralded by a chipmunk-voiced character called 'Raymondo' who asked **what's the recipe today, Jim?** Jim would then recite the ingredients, after which Raymondo would intone **and this is what you do!** Jim would also chat to listeners on the phone, which he would refer to in curious Euro-lingo as being **sur le telephoneo.**

In the mid-1970s, Young transferred to Radio 2, became more involved with current affairs subjects, and virtually dropped all his stock phrases (but see LEGAL EAGLE).

Morton's fork, to apply. A kind of test where there is no choice, dating from England in the fifteenth century. John Morton (*c* 1420–1500) was Archbishop of Canterbury and a minister to Henry VII. As a way of raising forced loans he would apply his 'fork' – the argument that if people were obviously rich, then they could afford to pay. And, if people looked poor, then they were obviously holding something back and so could also afford to pay. An early form of CATCH-22.

mortuis. See *DE MORTUIS*.

Moses. See OH, ~ !

mostest. See FIRSTEST WITH THE ~ .

most fun I've had without laughing, the. This is how the Woody Allen character compliments the Diane Keaton character in the film *Annie Hall* (1977). As a description of sex it clearly complements the next entry. However, Mencken was recording, 'Love [he probably meant sex] is the most fun you can have without laughing' in 1942. And I have seen 'Nothing beats making love – it's the most fun you can have without laughing' attributed to Humphrey Bogart.

most fun you can have with your clothes on, the. Of something other than sex (naturally). I feel this probably predates the above, though the earliest example I have is from Jerry Della Femina in *From Those Wonderful Folks Who Gave You Pearl Harbor* (1970): 'Advertising is the most fun you can have with your clothes on.' People are still drawn to play with the phrase: 'Touch Dancing is the closest you can get to making love with a stranger without actually taking your clothes off' (London *Evening Standard*, 20 October 1987).

mother. See CAN YOU HEAR ME, ~ ; DEAD AND NEVER CALLED ME ~ ; DON'T SOME ~ S HAVE 'EM; LIKE ~ USED TO MAKE; OVER

WILL'S ~'S WAY; YOUR ~ WOULDN'T
LIKE IT.

mother know you're out?, does your.
A chat-up line now addressed to a
seemingly under aged girl but, originally, to
a foolish person of either sex. From the title
of a comic poem published in the *Mirror* (28
April 1838) but popular even before that.

mother of the nation, the. Sobriquet of
Winnie Mandela (*b* 1934), the South
African political activist and estranged wife
of the first black president of that country.
From the *Financial Times* (1 February 1989):
'Mrs Mandela, who earned respect for her
dignified resistance to years of official
harassment, internal exile and separation
from her husband, was given the honorary
title 'Mother of the Nation' by many in the
black community on her defiant return to
Soweto during the 1984–86 township
revolt. But she soon gave the impression of
being out of her depth and subject to
manipulation by feuding factions.'
    A book by Nancy Harrison with the title
Winnie Mandela, Mother of a Nation was
published in 1985.

Mother Shipton. The prophecies
attributed to 'Mother Shipton' are suspect,
yet she herself appears to have existed.
Ursula Southeil was born in a cave in
Knaresborough, Yorkshire in 1488. She
married Toby Shipton in 1512 and gained a
reputation as a fortune-teller, if not as the
witch she physically resembled. She was
said to have predicted both the Civil War
and the Great Fire of London, so much so
that when Prince Rupert heard of the fire he
said: 'Now Shipton's prophecy is out!'
However, her alleged anticipation of
railway trains and the telegraph appears to
have been the work of Charles Hindley, a
London bookseller, who brought out *The
Prophecies of Mother Shipton* (1862–71).

mother's little helper. Might now be
applied to a small child literally being of
assistance to its mother around the house,
but originally referred to the 'uppers' that
enabled a tired housewife to get through
her daily tasks. Celebrated in a song poking
fun at such pill-addiction – 'Mother's Little
Helper', written and performed by the

Rolling Stones on the *Aftermath* album
(1966).

Mother Teresa. Mother Teresa (*b* Agnes
Gonxha Bojaxhiu, 1910, in Skopje,
Yugoslavia) received the Nobel Peace
Prize (1979) for her charitable works,
notably running a mission among the
starving in Calcutta, and her name has
now become a byword for goodness. For
example, the *Independent* (6 June 1990),
quoting a lawyer for arrested Panamanian
defendants in the US : 'If you had Mother
Theresa sitting at the table next to
[General] Noriega, she'd have trouble
getting past the jury.'

motion. See POETRY OF ~ .

motley. See ON WITH THE ~ .

motley to the view, a. Harold Nicolson
wrote in *The Spectator* (19 March 1948):
'The attention aroused by a bye-election
renders even the most sedate candidate a
motley to the view.' The allusion is to
Shakespeare, Sonnet 110 (1590s): 'Alas 'tis
true, I have gone here and there,/And
made myself a motley to the view', i.e.
'made a fool of myself in public', 'motley'
here meaning 'fool, jester'.

motto. See SPEAK AS YOU FIND . . .

motor. See HELLO, JOHN, GOT A NEW ~ ?

mould. See BREAK THE ~ .

mountain stream. See COOL AS A ~ .

Mounties always get their man, the.
The unofficial motto of the Royal Canadian
Mounted Police. John J. Healy, editor of the
Fort Benton (Montana) *Record*, wrote on 13
April 1877 that the Mounties 'Fetch their
man every time'. The official motto since
1873 has been 'Maintain the right'
[*Maintiens le droit*].

mouse. See WHY IS A ~ . . .

mousetrap. See BEAT A PATH . . .

mouth. See FROM YOUR ~ TO GOD'S EAR;
HORSE'S ~ ; LOOK A GIFT HORSE IN THE ~ .

mouthful. See GLADSTONE CHEWED EACH ∼ . . .

move. See DID THE EARTH ∼ FOR YOU?

moveable feast, a. In the ecclesiastical world, a moveable feast is one which does not fall on a fixed date but – like Easter – occurs according to certain rules. *A Moveable Feast*, as the title of a book (1964) by Ernest Hemingway, is explained by the author in an epigraph: 'If you are lucky enough to have lived in Paris as a young man, then wherever you go for the rest of your life, it stays with you, for Paris is a moveable feast.'

moved. See WE SHALL NOT BE ∼.

move 'em on, head 'em up ('head 'em up, move 'em on,/Move 'em on, head 'em up . . . Rawhide!') *Rawhide*, the American Western TV series (1959–66), was notable for its Frankie Laine theme song over the credits. From McGowan & Hands's *Don't Cry for Me, Sergeant-Major* (1983) (about cattle and sheep in the Falklands war): '"I can just imagine the orders for the Gazelle pilot," smiled an officer as soon as the farmer was out of earshot. "Proceed to grid reference so-and-so, then head 'em on and move 'em on. Most urgent, keep them dogeys movin'."'

movement. See THIS GREAT ∼ OF OURS.

movers and shakers. People who get things done, innovators and activists. From the *Guardian* (10 November 1986): 'Nancy Reagan, Nancy Kissinger . . . and their friends, the movers and the shakers in fund-raising galas and behind-the-scenes politics.' The phrase comes from Arthur O'Shaughnessy's *Ode* (1874): 'We are the music-makers,/And we are dreamers of dreams . . . /Yet we are the movers and shakers/Of the world for ever, it seems.' Clearly he was thinking of less worldly people than the phrase is nowadays usually applied to.

moves. See GOD ∼ IN A MYSTERIOUS WAY.

move/shift the goalposts, to. Meaning, 'to change the rules or conditions after something has been started, in order to upset the "players"'.

'Barenboim had been appointed under the *ancien régime* of Chirac. Now that Michel Rocard is Prime Minister, the goalposts have been moved and Barenboim has found himself the target of the new order's distrust of the Bastille [Paris opera house] edifice' (*Independent*, 21 January 1989).

'The people of Kent vote solidly for the Conservative Party . . . Why are these people, therefore, trying to attempt to move the goalposts after the football match has started? [by imposing a new rail line through the county]' – (*Guardian*, 1 March 1989).

movie. See —: THE MOVIE.

moving. See LET'S GET AMERICA ∼ AGAIN.

Mr —. Cliché of journalism. Any 'supremo' automatically gets dubbed one of these. *Private Eye* jokingly pointed to the trend by inventing 'Soccer's Mr Football'. Actual examples: 'London's new Mr Railway, David Kirby, likes messing about in boats and singing in the choir' (*The Times*, 8 December 1981); 'Last week it was disclosed that Mewmarch is to be the new chief executive of the Prudential – or, put another way, Mr Insurance UK' (*Observer*, 9 April 1989).

Mr Big. As a name for the supposed MASTERMIND behind substantial crimes (for example, the Great Train Robbery of 1963), I once thought this phrase originated in Ian Fleming's second novel *Live and Let Die* (1954). 'Mr Big', a Black gangster, lives in Harlem: 'Because of the initial letters of his fanciful name, Buonaparte Ignace Gallia, and because of his huge height and bulk, he came to be called, even as a youth "Big Boy" or just "Big". Later this became "The Big Man" or "Mr Big".'

OED2, however, finds 'Mr Big' not only in a Groucho Marx letter of 1940 but, more significantly, in Raymond Chandler's *The Long Goodbye* (1953), though I am not sure that either of these uses is specifically criminal. *Mister Big* was the title of a 1943 B-movie starring Donald O'Connor.

Now, the phrase is also used to denote any major criminal. From the *Observer* (6 August 1989): ' "MR BIG" HELD. Customs officers have arrested a man they believe to be one of London's top criminals.'

Mr Chad. See CHAD.

Mr Chips. A name applied to an elderly schoolmaster, once feared but now revered. It derives from the character in the novel *Goodbye, Mr Chips* (1934) by James Hilton.

Mr Christian. See MISTER CHRISTIAN . . .

Mr Clean. Originally the name of an American household cleanser, this is a fairly generally applied nickname. 'The Secretary of State, James Baker, always regarded as Mr Clean among several highly-placed roguish officials in Ronald Reagan's administration . . .' (*Independent*, 15 February 1989). Others to whom it has been applied are: Pat Boone (*b* 1934), the US pop singer and actor noted for his clean image and habits (he would never agree to kiss in films); John Lindsay (*b* 1921), Mayor of New York (1965–73); Elliot Richardson (*b* 1920), US Attorney-General who resigned in 1973 rather than agree to the restrictions President Nixon was then placing on investigations into the Watergate affair.

Mr Fixit. A nickname for one who has a reputation for solving problems. Chips Channon wrote in his diary (30 November 1936) of the Abdication: 'Beaverbrook, while enjoying his role of Mr Fixit, and the power he now holds in his horny hands, is now nearly distraught.' *OED2* finds 'Mr and Mrs Fix-It' as the title of a Ring Lardner story in 1925.

Mr Nice Guy. See NO MORE ~.

Mr Nyet. Nickname applied to Andrei Gromyko (1909–89), long-serving Soviet foreign minister (from 1957 almost to his death) because of his liberal use of the veto at the United Nations. Also known by British officials as **Grim Grom** because of his solemn expression.

Mr Sands is in the —. Coded warning – a way of informing the staff and actors in a theatre over a public address system that a fire has broken out but without alarming the audience. Hence 'Mr Sands is in the scene dock' or, indeed, any mention of 'Mr Sands' would do the trick. Source untraced, but mentioned in the *Independent* (27 July 1992).

Mrs Calabash. See GOODNIGHT, ~ . . .

Mrs Girochie? SOS! See WHERE'VE YOU BEEN . . .

Mrs Grundy. Meaning 'a censorious person; an upholder of conventional morality', the name comes from Thomas Morton's play *Speed the Plough* (1798) in which a character frequently asks: 'What will Mrs Grundy say?' Compare the later names of **Mrs Ormiston Chaunt**, an actual woman who campaigned in the late nineteenth century against immorality in the music-hall, and **Mrs (Mary) Whitehouse** who attempted to 'clean up' British TV from 1965 onwards.

Mrs Hardcastle. See HE'S LOO-VERLY, ~. under RAY'S A LAUGH.

Mrs Malaprop. The name of a character in *The Rivals* (1775) by Richard Brinsley Sheridan after whom 'malapropisms' are called. 'Her select words [are] so ingeniously *misapplied*, without being *mispronounced*' (II.ii.) Among her misapplied but inspired words are: '*pineapple* of politeness', 'a nice *derangement* of epitaphs' and 'as headstrong as an *allegory* on the banks of the Nile'. She was not the first character to have such an entertaining affliction: Shakespeare's Dogberry and Mistress Quickly are similarly troubled. After the French phrase *mal à propos* ('awkward, inopportune').

Mrs Worthington. The name for the archetypal aspiring actress's mother comes from Noël Coward's song 'Mrs Worthington' (1935) which contains the refrain: 'Don't put your daughter on the stage, Mrs Worthington.'

MTF. Social typing phrase, for identifying the type of man who 'Must Touch Flesh' belonging usually to the opposite sex – a compulsion falling somewhat short of outright perversion. Probably only British middle-class use. Known by the 1950s?

Much Binding in the Marsh. This BBC radio programme grew out of the air-force edition of *Merry-Go-Round* in 1947 and ran until 1953. The programme starred the urbane Kenneth Horne and Richard Murdoch and incorporated the following examples of regular phraseology, among much else:

did I ever tell you about the time I was in Sidi Barrani? Horne to Murdoch, by way of introduction to a boring anecdote.

good morning, sir! Was there something? Sam Costa's entry line. He played a kind of batman to Horne and Murdoch.

good old Charlie-ee! A Murdoch interjection, given with especial relish at the birth of Prince Charles in 1948. The phrase was an old one, used for example in *Punch* (2 February 1910).

oh, jolly D! (short for 'jolly decent') was said by Maurice Denham as 'Dudley Davenport'. Probably taken from public school or RAF usage, though from not much earlier than the Second World War. The same character would also cry, **oh, I say, I am a fool!** A Methodist minister in Brighton once advertised it as the title of a sermon. Ken Platt later used the shorter, 'Oh, I am a fool!'

read any good books lately? Murdoch's way of changing the subject:

> Horne: One of the nicest sandwiches I've ever had. What was in it, Murdoch?
> Murdoch: Well, there was – er – have you read any good books lately?
> Horne: I thought it tasted something like that.

It is also what you might say to someone who, for no obvious reason, is staring at you. An old phrase, of course. It also occurs, for example, in the Marx Brothers' *A Night at the Opera* (1935) and had been used in BBC radio's *BAND WAGGON*. Presumably it had once been used in all seriousness as a conversational gambit.

muck and bullets. See UP TO MY NECK IN ～.

muddling through, to keep on. Supposedly what the British have a great talent for. Mencken has 'The English always manage to muddle through' – 'author unidentified; first heard c 1885'. Ira Gershwin celebrated the trait in the song 'Stiff Upper Lip' from *A Damsel in Distress* (1937). He remembered the phrase 'Keep muddling through' from much use at the time of the First World War, but knew that it had first been noted in a speech by John Bright MP in c 1864 (though, ironically, Bright was talking about the Northern States in the American Civil War).

mudge. See FUDGE AND ～.

mufti, dressed in. This phrase is used for plain clothes or 'civvies' – as when a military person is not wearing uniform. A 'mufti' is a doctor in Muslim law. Perhaps an English officer put on the robes as disguise, for some reason, and the word stuck as a way of describing the 'clothes that you don't usually wear'.

Muhammad Ali own a mirror?, does. See IS THE POPE A CATHOLIC?

mullah. See MAD ～.

mum. See BE LIKE DAD . . .

mum, mum, they are laughing at me! The British comedian Arthur English (1919–95) was famous in the late 1940s for his spiv character with pencil moustache and big tie. Arthur told me (1979) that this line was ad-libbed in his first broadcast: 'I had my big tie rolled up and proceeded to unfurl it. There was a great laugh and, to cover it, I said, "Mum, mum, they are laughing at me."'

A necessary exhortation to audiences from the same spiv character was **sharpen up there, the quick stuff's coming!** He would spiel at some three hundred words a minute. Before this, at the Windmill Theatre, he had been stuck for a finish to his act: 'So I started rambling on with the senseless chatter I became known for . . . [but] I suddenly realised I had no finish to the chatter. I don't know what made me say it, but I said, "I don't know what the devil I'm talking about. **Play the music and open the cage!**" and ran off.' The phrase stuck.

mum's the word. Meaning 'we are keeping silent on this matter'. No mother is invoked here: 'mum' is just a representation of 'Mmmm', the noise made when LIPS ARE SEALED. The word 'mumble' obviously derives from the same source. Shakespeare has the idea in *Henry VI, Part 2*, I.ii.89 (1590): 'Seal up your lips and give no words but mum.'

Compare BE LIKE DAD, KEEP MUM.

murderers return to the scene of the crime. There is no obvious source for this proverbial saying. A French propaganda poster from the First World War has the slogan: '*Les assassins reviennent toujours . . . sur les lieux de leur crime.*' In fiction, Raskolnikov does indeed return to the scene of his crime in Dostoevsky's *Crime and Punishment* (1866), though the phrase is not used.

Murder She Wrote. The title of a US TV series (1984 onwards), with Angela Lansbury as Jessica Fletcher, a widowed best-selling crime writer who becomes involved in solving actual murder cases. Modelled on Miss Marple perhaps, there is another nod in the direction of Agatha Christie in the title. *Murder She Said* was the title given to a film version (UK, 1961) of Christie's Miss Marple story *4.50 From Paddington*. In turn, that echoed *Murder He Says* (film US, 1945) and 'Murder, He Says', the curious Frank Loesser lyric to music by Jimmy McHugh which was sung by Betty Hutton in the film *Happy Go Lucky* (1942).

Murgatroyd. See HEAVENS TO ~.

Murphia. See under TAFFIA.

Murphy's Law. See IF ANYTHING CAN GO WRONG, IT WILL.

mush!, 'ere. See NAY, NAY ~ THRICE AGAIN NAY!

music. See AND WHEN THE ~ STOPS . . . under ARE YOU SITTING COMFORTABLY?; FACE THE ~; PLAY THE ~ . . . under MUM, MUM, THEY ARE LAUGHING AT ME!; SINGING FROM THE SAME SHEET OF ~.

music-lovers. See THANK YOU, ~.

music, maestro, please! Stock phrase of the British band leader Harry Leader (*d* 1987), who broadcast from 1933 onwards. Leader had had two signature tunes before he adopted this one while he was resident at the Astoria, Charing Cross Road, in 1943. It appears to have come from a song with the title by Herb Magidson and Allie Wrubel, featured by Flanagan and Allen in the revue *These Foolish Things* (1938).

mustard. See CUT THE ~; KEEN AS ~.

— must go! A slogan incorporating the cry that he or she 'must go' is liable to pursue any prominent politician who falls seriously out of favour. To date, A.J. Balfour, Prime Minister 1902–6, is the first British example I have found. In his case, the cry was sometimes abbreviated to 'BMG.' After losing the 1906 election, Balfour lingered on as leader of his party. Leo Maxse, editor of the *National Review*, wrote an article in the September 1911 edition in the course of which, demonstrating that the Conservative Party needed a new leader, he invented the slogan, 'Balfour must go'. And he went in November.

'Eden Must Go' arose during Sir Anthony Eden's inept premiership (1955–7) when he instigated the disastrous landings in Egypt to 'protect' the Suez canal. On the evening of 4 November 1956, while he met with his Cabinet ministers in 10 Downing Street, he could hear roars of 'Eden Must go!' from an angry mass meeting in

Trafalgar Square. He went under the guise of illness early the following year.

The most notable such campaign in British politics was directed at Ernest Marples, an energetic Minister of Transport (1959–64). The slogan arose in October 1962 when he intervened in the build-up of opposition to sweeping cuts in the railway service (announced the following year in the Beeching Report). However, it was because of motoring matters that the slogan was taken up at a more popular level. He introduced various unpopular measures including, in the summer of 1963, a 50 mph speed limit at peak summer weekends in an effort to reduce the number of road accidents. It was this measure that produced a rash of car stickers bearing the cry. It appeared daubed on a bridge over the M1 motorway in August (and remained visible for many years).

'The Saloon Must Go' was the slogan of the Anti-Saloon League in the United States – a temperance movement, organized 18 December 1895, and a precursor of Prohibition.

must touch flesh. See MTF.

must you go, can't you stay? First recorded, I think, by G.W.E. Russell in his *Collections and Recollections* (1898), this was a helpful remark of Dr Vaughan, Head Master of Harrow, designed to get rid of boys he had entertained at breakfast. 'When the muffins and sausages had been devoured . . . and all possible school-topics discussed, there used to ensue a horrid silence . . . Then the Doctor would approach with cat-like softness, and, extending his hand to the shyest and most loutish boy, would say, "Must you go? Can't you stay?" and the party broke up with magical celerity.'

It was later twisted to, 'Must you stay? Can't you go?' For example, as the caption to a *Punch* cartoon in the edition dated 18 January 1905. The Governor of Madagascar is saying it, referring to the prolonged stay of the Russian Admiral Rodjestvensky at Madagascar when on his way to meet the Japanese Fleet.

my aunt (Fanny)! See under MY GIDDY AUNT.

my brother George. See under CRY ALL THE WAY TO THE BANK.

my dog has fleas. Title of a little tune that gives you the tuning notes (A, D, F♯, E) for a ukelele or banjo. Has been called the 'international call-sign of the ukelele-player'.

my eyes are dim – I cannot see . . . '. . . I have not got my specs with me'. From the anonymous song, 'In the Quartermaster's Stores', first performed I know not when, although a version was copyrighted in 1940.

my friends . . . Cliché of politics. It always presumes rather a lot when politicians make use of this phrase. Safire asserts that the first American to do so – noticeably, at any rate – was Franklin D. Roosevelt who acquired the salutation in 1910 from Richard Connell who was running for Congress at the same time. But Abraham Lincoln had used this form of address on occasions.

During a party political broadcast on 4 June 1945, Winston Churchill said, 'My friends, I must tell you that a Socialist policy is abhorrent to the British idea of freedom.' This was the occasion on which he made the notorious suggestion that a Labour government would require 'some form of Gestapo' to put down criticism.

Anthony Eden, in his pained TV broadcast during the Suez crisis (3 November 1956) used the phrase, ingratiatingly, too. But I don't think any British prime minister has done so since. It is hard to imagine Margaret Thatcher ever getting her tongue round it. Nor has anyone tried to find an equivalent of the standard 'My fellow Americans', beloved of US presidents.

my giddy aunt! This is one of those trivial exclamations – others include **my sainted aunt!** and **my Aunt Fanny!** or simply **my aunt!** – which seem to have arisen in the mid-nineteenth century. They appear to have been especially popular among schoolboys. 'My sainted aunt!' pops up quite frequently in the Billy Bunter of Greyfriars stories by Frank Richards (e.g. in *The Magnet*, No. 401, 16 October 1915).

In a wry note in Partridge/*Slang*, Paul Beale wonders whether 'My aunt!' was originally a euphemism for *my arse*. He may well be right, though he adds, '. . . or have I been working on this Dictionary too long!'

my hero! The quintessential cry of the female in romantic fiction when her beau has just rescued her or overcome some formidable obstacle to their love. Unfortunately, I do not seem able to find an actual example.

So perhaps it only actually appears in parodies – as in P.G. Wodehouse, *Aunts Aren't Gentlemen* (1975)? Raina says it a number of times in Shaw's *Arms and the Man* (1894), but that is really a parody, too. Burns in *The Jolly Beggars* (1785) has a woman say to a soldier: 'But whilst with both hands I can hold the glass steady/ Here's to thee, my hero, my sodger laddie!' So that will have to do.

my husband and I. Queen Elizabeth II's father, King George VI, had quite naturally spoken the words 'The Queen and I' but something in Elizabeth's drawling delivery turned her version into a joke. It first appeared during her second Christmas broadcast (made from New Zealand) in 1953 – 'My husband and I left London a month ago' – and still survived in 1962: 'My husband and I are greatly looking forward to visiting New Zealand and Australia in the New Year.' By 1967, the phrase had become 'Prince Philip and I'. At a Silver Wedding banquet in 1972, the Queen allowed herself a little joke: 'I think on this occasion I may be forgiven for saying "My husband and I".'

In 1988, the phrase was used as the title of an ITV comedy series with Mollie Sugden.

my lips are sealed. See LIPS ARE SEALED.

my little perforations. Phrase from Lyons Quick Brew Tea Bags commercials in the UK, early 1970s: 'It's not me, ma'am, it's me little perforations.' 'You have to admit,' said the British comedian Roy Hudd, who spoke the line, 'that any business which allows a catch-phrase such as "*yer little perforations*" to turn you into a household name, buy you a house in the country and give a certain amount of financial security to you and your

family, *has* to be crazy.' He also added: 'For some reason, the tea people thought it sounded too rude. Don't ask me why, but they did' (*Sunday Express*, 4 December 1977).

my name is mud. This exclamation might be uttered as an acknowledgement that one has made a mistake and is held in low esteem. When John Wilkes Booth was escaping from the Washington DC theatre in which he had just assassinated President Lincoln in 1865, he fell and broke his leg. A country doctor called Dr Samuel Mudd tended Booth's wound without realizing the circumstances under which it had been received. When he did realize, he informed the authorities, was charged with being a co-conspirator, and sentenced to life imprisonment.

As Morris points out, however, 'mud' in the sense of scandalous and defamatory charges, goes back to a time well before the Civil War. There had been an expression 'the mud press' to describe mud-slinging newspapers in the US before 1846, so it seems most likely that the expression was well established before Dr Mudd met his unhappy fate. Indeed, *OED2* has an 1823 citation from 'Jon Bee' in *Slang* for 'And his name is mud!' as an ejaculation at the end of a silly oration, and also by then from *A Dictionary of the Turf* as a name for a stupid fellow.

my name's Friday. See under DRAGNET.

my name's Monica! See under *EDUCATING ARCHIE*.

my regiment leaves at dawn. A line spoken by Groucho Marx in the film *Monkey Business* (1931), preceded by the words, 'Come, Kapellmeister, let the violas throb!' Presumably this is a cliché of operetta, but no precise example has been traced. It was certainly the situation in many romantic tangles, even if the line itself was not actually spoken.

my sainted aunt! See MY GIDDY AUNT!

mysterious way. See GOD MOVES IN A ~ .

mystery tour. See MAGICAL ~ .

my word is my bond. The motto of the London Stock Exchange (since 1801), where bargains are made 'on the nod', with no written pledges being given and no documents being signed. Its Latin form is: *'Dictum meum pactum'*.

naff off! Euphemistic expletive (echoic of 'eff off!') which was once used notably by Princess Anne to press photographers at the Badminton horse trials (April 1982). Probably derived from the adjective 'naff', meaning 'in poor taste; unfashionable; bad' and largely restricted to British use. This word had a sudden vogue in 1982. Keith Waterhouse had used the participle 'naffing' in his novel *Billy Liar* (1959), remembering it from his service in the RAF (c 1950). That novel also includes the 'naff off!' expletive. Attempts have been made to derive the word 'naff' from 'fanny' in back-slang, from the acronym NAAFI, and from the French 'rien à faire', none very convincingly. In the BBC radio series *ROUND THE HORNE*, the word 'naph' (as it was spelt in the scripts) enjoyed another revival as part of camp slang. From the edition of 30 April 1967: 'Don't talk to us about Malaga!' – 'Naph, is it?' – 'He's got the palare off, hasn't he?' – 'I should say it is naph, treashette. Jule had a nasty experience in Malaga . . .'

nah . . . Luton airport! See under NICE 'ERE, INNIT?

nail. See ON THE ~.

nails. See COFFIN ~.

naked on parade. See under IDLE ON PARADE.

naked truth, the. This was the title of a film (UK, 1957) and as a phrase for 'the absolute truth', it comes from an old fable which tells how Truth and Falsehood went swimming and Falsehood stole the clothes that Truth had left upon the river bank. Truth declined to wear Falsehood's clothes and went naked. Known in English by 1600, in Latin, as in the works of Horace, the phrase is 'nudas veritas'.

namby-pamby. Meaning 'insipid; wishy-washy; soft', the phrase derives from Ambrose Philips (d 1749), a writer and politician whom the dramatist Henry Carey ridiculed with this nickname after Philips had written some insipid verses for children.

name. See BAD ~, KIND OF THING . . .; GIVE A DOG A BAD ~; I'LL FORGET MY OWN ~ . . . under *ITMA*; — IS THE ~ OF THE GAME; MIDDLE ~ IS —; MY ~'S FRIDAY AND ONLY THE ~S HAVE BEEN CHANGED under *DRAGNET*; NO ~S NO PACKDRILL; WE ~ THE GUILTY MEN; WHAT A ~ TO GO TO BED WITH.

name your poison! 'What would you like to drink?' Mostly British use. Recorded by 1951.

nanu, nanu! In the US TV series *Mork and Mindy* (1978–81), Robin Williams played Mork, an alien from the planet Ork. This was his farewell.

Naples. See SEE ~ AND DIE.

nasty. See SOMETHING ~ IN THE WOODSHED.

nation. See GRATEFUL ~ . . .

nations. See GAIETY OF ~.

nation shall speak peace unto nation. The motto of the BBC (1927) echoes Micah 4:3: 'Nation shall not lift up a sword against nation.' In 1932, however, it was decided that the BBC's primary mission was to serve the home audience and not that overseas. Hence, **Quaecunque** [whatsoever] was introduced as an alternative reflecting the Latin inscription (composed by Dr Montague Rendall) in the entrance hall of Broadcasting House, London, and based on Philippians 4:8: 'Whatsoever things are

beautiful and honest and of good report . . .'
In 1948, the original motto was
reintroduced. '*Quaecunque*' was also taken
as the motto of Lord Reith, the BBC's first
Director-General.

natives are hostile/restless!, the. What
someone might say, with literal meaning, in
British imperial fiction – but probably best
known through parodies of same. Could
now be used to convey that any group of
people is hostile or impatient or whatever –
a queue in a canteen, an audience in a
theatre. The 'hostile' version is uttered in
Target for Tonight (UK, 1942), the film
about RAF Bomber Command. Compare
PEASANTS ARE REVOLTING.

nature of the beast, that is the. 'That is
the way things are because of the type of
person (or situation or circumstance) we are
dealing with.' Probably implying there is
not much one can do to change it. 'It's the
nature o' th' beast' was listed as an English
proverbial expression in 1678. From Val
Gielgud, *Necessary End* (1969): 'Barry
Compayne never made any bones about . . .
the number of girls that he had "laid" . . .
Anthea had chosen deliberately to put
down such exploits to "the nature of the
beast".'

**nature's way of telling you to slow
down, death is.** A joke current in the US
by 1960 (as in *Newsweek*, 25 April). It has
been specifically attributed to Severn
Darden (*b* 1937), the American film
character actor. It is capable of infinite
variation: from *Punch* (3 January 1962):
'Some neo-Malthusians have been heard to
suggest that the bomb is Nature's way . . . of
checking . . . the over-spawning of our
species.' In 1978, the American cartoon
strip Garfield produced a bumper-sticker
with the slogan: 'My car is God's way of
telling you to slow down.' In McGowan &
Hands's *Don't Cry for Me, Sergeant-Major*
(1983) (about the Falklands war), a Marine
corporal says, 'This is nature's little way of
telling you you are going to die.'

naughty bits. See under *MONTY PYTHON'S
FLYING CIRCUS*.

naughty but nice. Alliteration rules. The
phrase was used in British advertisements,
originated by the Ogilvy and Mather
agency, for fresh cream cakes in 1981–84.
Also for the National Dairy Council's
cream adverts in the late 1980s. But the
phrase has been much used elsewhere. A
1939 US film had the title. It was about a
professor of classical music who accidentally
wrote a popular song.

The catchphrase in full is 'It's naughty
but it's nice'. Partridge/*Slang* glosses it as 'a
reference to copulation since *c* 1900 ex a
song that Minnie Schult sang and
popularized in the USA, 1890s'.

There have since been various songs with
the title, notably one by Johnny Mercer
and Harry Warren, 'Naughty but Nice', in
The Belle of New York (film, 1952). Compare
also, 'It's Foolish But It's Fun' (Gus Kahn/
Robert Stolz) sung by Deanna Durbin in
Spring Parade (1940).

Naughty Nineties, the. (also **Gay
Nineties**.) Referring to the 1890s in
England, when VICTORIAN VALUES softened
somewhat in the face of hedonism in
certain circles. The most characteristic
figure was that of Oscar Wilde. *OED2* does
not find the term in use until 1925.

Naval Person. See FORMER ∼.

navy. See JOIN THE ARMY . . . ;

Navy's here!, the. Phrase indicating that
rescue is at hand, everything is going to be
all right, be assured. From an actual use of
the words during the Second World War.
On the night of 16 February 1940, 299
British seamen were freed from captivity
aboard the German ship *Altmark* as it lay in
a Norwegian fjord. The destroyer *Cossack*,
under the command of Captain Philip
Vian, had managed to locate the German
supply ship and a boarding party discovered
that British prisoners were locked in its
hold. As Vian described it, Lieutenant
Bradwell Turner, the leader of the boarding
party, called out: 'Any British down there?'
'Yes, we're all British,' came the reply.
'Come on up then,' he said, 'The Navy's
here.' The identity of the speaker is still in
some doubt, however. *The Times* on 19
February 1940 gave a version from the lips

of one of those who had been freed and who had actually heard the exchange: 'John Quigley of London said that the first they knew of their rescue was when they heard a shout of "Any Englishmen here?" They shouted "Yes" and immediately came the cheering words, "Well, the Navy is here." Quigley said – "We were all hoarse with cheering when we heard those words."'

nay, nay – thrice again nay! Towards the end of his life, this emerged as one of the most typical of the stock phrases used by the British comedian Frankie Howerd (c 1917–92). Howerd himself referred to his phrases as 'verbal punctuation marks'. They did not exactly catch on but they were certainly characteristic. 'While other shows used catchphrases almost as characters, I was a character who used catchphrase,' was the way he put it. **Ladies and gentlemen!** was an opening phrase to which he gave special emphasis.

Howerd explained that when he was starting in radio just after the Second World War he thought a good gimmick would be for him to give unusual emphasis to certain words. Hence **I was a-mazed!**

Other Howerdisms included: **not on your Nellie!** (though Partridge/*Catch Phrases* dates this from the 1930s and says it is abbreviated rhyming slang for 'puff – breath – as in 'Not on your Nellie Duff!' meaning 'not on your life'. Howerd undoubtedly popularized the expression in the 1940s, however); **no, don't laugh!**, **titter ye not!**, **chilly!**, **'ere, mush!**, **listen!**, **let's get myself comfy!**, **please yourselves!** (also used as the title of a radio series) and **poor soul – she's past it!** (said of his supposedly deaf accompanist), alternatively, **poor old thing – she'll have to go!**, not to be confused with **er, Thing, you know**, when speaking of the person responsible for or in charge of the show.

Shut your face! perhaps demonstrates what Howerd was all about – taking phrases that are already in circulation (this one was known by 1893) and somehow giving them a special twist. The phrase was also given a going over on a hit single by Joe Dolce, an American singer pretending to be Italian: 'Shaddap Your Face' in 1981.

See also AND THE BEST OF BRITISH LUCK!

neat but not gaudy. Quirky comment coupled with some outlandish image (or an AS THE MONKEY SAYS Wellerism). 'Neat but not gaudy – like a bull's arse tied up with a bicycle chain' was told to me by a (sensibly) anonymous correspondent from the Cotswolds in 1994. Partridge/*Catch Phrases* suggests that the initial phrase 'neat but not gaudy' was established by c 1800, though in 1631 there had been the similar 'Comely, not gaudy'. Then variations were introduced – as by John Ruskin, writing in the *Architectural Magazine* (November 1838): 'That admiration of the "neat but gaudy [sic]" which is commonly reported to have influenced the devil when he painted his tail pea green.' Indeed, Partridge cites: 'Neat, but not gaudy, as the monkey said, when he painted his tail-sky blue' and '. . . painted his bottom pink and tied up his tail with pea-green'.

necessary. See IS YOUR JOURNEY REALLY ~?

nectar. See AMBER ~.

needle, eye of a. See EASIER FOR A CAMEL . . .

needle, nardle, noo! See under GOON SHOW.

needs. See FROM EACH ACCORDING TO HIS ABILITIES . . . ; WITH ― LIKE THAT, WHO ~.

neighbourhood. See YOUR FRIENDLY ~ ―.

neither fish, flesh, nor good red herring. Meaning 'neither one thing nor another; suitable to no class of people', the phrase sometimes occurs in the form: 'neither fish, flesh, nor fowl', where the origin of the expression (which dates from the Middle Ages) is that whatever is under discussion is unsuitable food for a monk (fish), for people generally (flesh), or for the poor (red, smoked, herring).

A 'red herring' in the sense of a distraction, diversion or false clue, derives from the practice of drawing the strongly-smelling fish across the path of foxhounds to put them off the scent.

Nell. See LITTLE ~.

Nellie. See NOT ON YOUR ~.

Nelson touch, the. Denoting any action bearing the hallmark of Horatio Nelson, his quality of leadership and seamanship, this term was coined by Nelson himself before the Battle of Trafalgar (1805): 'I am anxious to join the fleet, for it would add to my grief if any other man was to give them the Nelson touch.' The *Oxford Companion to Ships and the Sea* (1976) describes various manoeuvres to which the term could be applied, but adds, also: 'It could have meant the magic name of his name among officers and seamen of his fleet, which was always enough to inspire them to great deeds of heroism and endurance.' The British title of the film *Corvette K-225* (US, 1943) was *The Nelson Touch.*

ne plus ultra [not further beyond]. The supposed inscription on the Pillars of Hercules in the Strait of Gibraltar preventing ships from going further. It subsequently came to mean 'the furthest attainable point; the acme of something'.

Nero. See FIDDLE WHILE ROME BURNS.

nerves. See IT'S ME NOIVES under *ITMA*.

nervous. See NOT SUITABLE FOR THOSE . . .

Nescafé Society. A coinage by Noël Coward, recalled by Alec Guinness in *Blessings in Disguise* (1985): 'Thumbing through a smart social magazine he suddenly read loud, "Mrs So-and-So, a well-known figure in Café Society." Pause. "Nescafé Society."' Presumably, Coward was referring to a denizen of a downmarket type of **café society**, the American coinage (by 1937) for people who frequent fashionable restaurants and other watering-holes.

network. See OLD BOY ~.

never. See THERE'LL ~ BE ANOTHER!; WILL ~ BE THE SAME AGAIN; YOU'VE ~ HAD IT SO GOOD.

never again! A sort of slogan used during and after the First World War, although the phrase was in use against the Germans by 1915. T.F.A. Smith wrote in *Soul of Germany* that year: 'The oft-quoted phrase is applicable to the case: Never again!' Winston Churchill in his *The Second World War* (Vol. 1, 1948) says of the French: 'with one passionate spasm [they cried] never again'. Later, in the mid-1960s, it became the slogan of the militant Jewish Defence League – referring to the Holocaust. A stone monument erected near the birthplace of Adolf Hitler at Braunau, Austria, in 1989 (the centenary of his birth) bore the lines 'For Peace, Freedom and Democracy – Never Again Fascism [*Nie wieder Faschismus*] – Millions of Dead are a warning'. Compare NO MORE WAR.

The film *Never Say Never Again* (UK, 1983) which marked Sean Connery's return to the part of James Bond was so called because he had declared 'never again' after playing Bond in *Diamonds Are Forever* in 1971.

never chase girls or buses (there will always be another one coming along soon). Turn of the century? Partridge/ *Catch Phrases* dates it to the 1920s and derives it from the early US version with 'streetcars' instead of 'buses'. Compare this allusion to the saying by Derick Heathcoat-Amory when British Chancellor of the Exchequer (1958–60): 'There are three things not worth running for – a bus, a woman or a new economic panacea; if you wait a bit another one will come along.'

never darken my door again. Meaning 'never cross the threshold of my house again'. In James Boswell's journal for 5 December 1786 (included in *Boswell: The English Experiment*) he writes: 'Satterthwaite used the expression "Never darkened his door". Lonsdale said he had never heard it before, and he durst say it was not in print. I said, "It is in an Irish song" (see it also in Shadwell's *Hasty Wedding*, Act III).'

Shadwell died in 1692, so that takes us back to the seventeenth century. Shakespeare does not use the phrase. Nearer to Boswell's time, the *OED2* finds Benjamin Franklin in the US using it in

1729, and Samuel Richardson in his 1749 novel *Clarissa*.

never-ending battle. See under *SUPERMAN*.

never give a sucker an even break. Meaning 'don't pass up the opportunity to take advantage of a fool'. This saying has been attributed to various people (Edward Francis Albee and P.T. Barnum among them) but has largely become associated with the American comedian W.C. Fields. He is believed to have ad-libbed it in the musical *Poppy* (1923) and certainly spoke it in the film version (1936). The words are not uttered, however, in the film with the title *Never Give a Sucker an Even Break* (1941).

never glad confident morning (again). A much-quoted phrase of disappointment with respect to a person's performance. The origin is Robert Browning's poem 'The Lost Leader' (1845) in which he regretfully portrays William Wordsworth as a man who had lost his revolutionary zeal. A correct – and devastating – use of the phrase came on 17 June 1963 when the British Government under its Prime Minister Harold Macmillan was rocking over the Profumo scandal. In the House of Commons, Tory MP Nigel Birch quoted the lines at Macmillan:

Let him never come back to us!
There would be doubt, hesitation and pain.
Forced praise on our part – the glimmer of twilight,
Never glad confident morning again!

In November 1983, on the twentieth anniversary of President Kennedy's assassination, Lord Harlech, former British Ambassador in Washington, paid tribute thus in the *Observer* Magazine: 'Since 1963 the world has seemed a bleaker place, and for me and I suspect millions of my contemporaries he remains the lost leader – "Never glad confident morning again".' Harlech may have wanted to evoke a leader who had been lost to the world, but surely it was a mistake to quote what is a criticism of one? Also in November 1983, in the *Observer*, Paul Johnson wrote an attack

(which he later appeared to regret) on Margaret Thatcher: 'Her courage and sound instincts made her formidable. But if her judgement can no longer be trusted, what is left? A very ordinary woman, occupying a position where ordinary virtues are not enough. For me, I fear it can never be "glad confident morning again".'

never knowingly undersold. This was a line formulated by the founder of the John Lewis Partnership, John Spedan Lewis, in about 1920, to express a pricing policy which originated with his father, who first opened a small shop in Oxford Street, London, in 1864. The slogan is believed to have been used within the firm before it was given public expression in the 1930s, in the form: 'If you can buy more cheaply elsewhere anything you have just bought from us we will refund the difference.' The firm does not regard the undertaking as an advertising device in the generally accepted sense, although it is displayed on its vans and on sales bills. As John Lewis merchandise is not advertised, the phrase has an almost mystical significance to the Partnership.

never let the facts stand in the way of a good story. A cynical journalistic saying. *The Paper* (film US, 1994) used the promotional line: 'Never let the truth get in the way of a good story.' To the British journalist James Cameron (1911–85) is attributed the similar: 'It was long ago in my life as a simple reporter that I decided that facts must never get in the way of truth.'

never love a stranger. Title of a Harold Robbins novel (1948; film US, 1958). Possibly derived from the English poet Stella Benson (d 1933). In 'To the Unborn', *This Is the End* (1917) she writes: 'Call no man foe, but never love a stranger.'

never mind the quality, feel the width. This was used as the title of a British 'multi-ethnic' TV comedy series (1967–9) about 'Manny Cohen' and 'Patrick Kelly' running a tailoring business in the East End of London. Supposedly the sort of thing a street-tradesman (or Jewish tailor) might say. Paul Beale in Partridge/*Catch Phrases* suggests that this 'mid-C20' saying had, by the later twentieth century come to be used in more serious contexts – 'e.g. the necessity of eking out meagre resources of government aid to cover an impossibly large and neglected field.' Indeed. Headline from *Observer* editorial (29 January 1989) on a National Health Service where 'the pressure will be on to cut overheads and generally sacrifice quality for price' – 'NEVER MIND THE QUALITY'. From the *Independent* (1 March 1989): 'England's senior chief inspector of schools warned . . . "Nor must there be attempts, in trying to reduce shortages, to dilute standards by taking a 'never mind the quality, feel the width' approach."'

never more. In the Courtauld Institute Gallery, London, there is a painting of a nude by Gauguin which has the title 'Nevermore'. What bird would you say features in it? Well, no, not a raven, it is a devil's bird. You might expect it to allude to Edgar Allan Poe's poem 'The Raven' (1845): 'Quoth the Raven "Nevermore"', but Gauguin quite clearly stated that this was not the case.

Never Never. (1) The land where the Lost Boys live in J.M. Barrie's *Peter Pan* (1904), 'Never Never Never Land' in early versions, but simply 'Never Land' in the published text. Not an original coinage: a play by Wilson Barrett was called *The Never Never Land* (1902). Later, Winston Churchill said in the House of Commons (5 April 1906): 'That constitution now passes away into the never never land, into a sort of chilly limbo . . .' 'Never Never Land' was the English title of a song *Naar de Specituin* (1954) by Beryenberg and Froboess. (2) The Australian outback, as in *We of the Never Never* by Mrs Aeneas Gunn in 1908, though known as such by 1882. (3) Alternative name for hire purchase, as in 'the never-never' (by 1926).

never say die! This exclamation, meaning 'never give in' was much used by Charles Dickens in his writings, starting with 'Greenwich Fair' in *Sketches by Boz* (written 1833–6) – though it is presumably not original to him. It occurs in *The Pickwick Papers* (1836–7) and is notably the

catchphrase of Grip, the raven, in *Barnaby Rudge* (1841).

never swap/change horses in midstream. Meaning 'don't alter course in the middle of doing something', Mencken has 'Never swap horses crossing a stream' as an 'American proverb, traced to c 1840'. *CODP*'s earliest citation is Abraham Lincoln saying in 1864: 'I am reminded . . . of a story of an old Dutch farmer, who remarked to a companion once that "it was best not to swap horses when crossing streams".' This would seem to confirm the likely US origin. 'Don't change barrels going over Niagara' was a slogan attributed (satirically) to the Republicans during the presidential campaign of 1932, and is clearly derived from the foregoing.

never underestimate the power of a woman. A slogan for *Ladies' Home Journal*, from c 1941. Gordon Page of the N.W. Ayer agency recalled: 'It came off the back burner of a creative range where ideas simmer while the front burners are preoccupied with meeting closing dates . . . it was just a more direct way of stating the case for the leading woman's magazine of the day. But always believing that you can do things with a twinkle that you can't do with a straight face, it was trotted to Leo Lionni . . . it's largely *his* fault that you can't say "never underestimate the power of *anything*" today without echoing the line.' Even in 1981, the following ad was appearing in the *New York Times*: 'Ladies' Home Journalism – Never Underestimate Its Power'.

never work with children or animals. A well-known piece of show-business lore, from American vaudeville originally, I should think – and, occasionally, adapted: '"Never work with children, dogs, or Denholm Elliott," British actors are said to advise one another' (*Guardian*, 29 April 1989).

Phyllis Hartnoll in *Plays and Players* (1985) has: 'W.C. Fields is quoted as saying, "Never act with animals or children."' Although this line reflects his known views, I suspect the attribution may result from confusion with 'Any man who hates dogs and babies can't be all bad' (which he didn't say either: it was said by Leo Rosten *about* him at a dinner in 1939).

Similar sentiment is contained in Noël Coward's remark about the child actress Bonnie Langford, who appeared along with a horse in a West End musical version of *Gone With the Wind* in 1972. Inevitably, there came the moment when the horse messed up the stage. Coward said: 'If they'd stuffed the child's head up the horse's arse, they would have solved two problems at once.'

Sarah Bernhardt had a pronounced aversion to performing with animals (as to children, I know not). When she received an offer to appear in music hall in a scene from *L'Aiglon*, she replied, 'Between monkeys, *non!*'

never wrestle with a chimney sweep. From the *Observer* Magazine (4 July 1993) on Tony Benn MP: 'Now he is older he finds himself repeating advice his father offered him as a child like "never wrestle with a chimney sweep", which means don't soil yourself by responding to your opponents' dirty tricks. "The whole wisdom of humanity is summed up in these phrases," he muses.'

Benn earlier used the phrase for his own purposes. From Ben Pimlott, *Harold Wilson* (1992): 'For the Labour Party to rub its hands with glee, as Wedgwood Benn put it [about the Profumo Affair, 1963] would be like wrestling with a chimney sweep.'

new. See BRAND ~; NOTHING ~ UNDER THE SUN; under SOMETHING OLD . . . ; SO WHAT'S ~? under 'TWAS EVER THUS; WHAT'S ~, PUSSYCAT?

New Deal. The slogan of Franklin D. Roosevelt (though Abraham Lincoln had used it on occasions). To the 1932 Democratic Convention which had just nominated him, Roosevelt said: 'I pledge you, I pledge myself to a New Deal for the American people . . . a new order of competence and courage . . . to restore America to its own people.'

New Frontier. A slogan of John F. Kennedy which he first used on accepting the Democratic nomination in 1960: 'We stand today on the edge of a New Frontier.

The frontier of the 1960s . . . is not a set of promises – it is a set of challenges. It sums up not what I intend to offer the American people, but what I intend to ask of them.' In 1964, Harold Wilson said in a speech in Birmingham: 'We want the youth of Britain to storm the new frontiers of knowledge.'

Newgate. See BLACK AS ~ KNOCKER.

New Journalism, the. Name given to a type of heavily subjective writing practised in the US by Tom Wolfe and Gay Talese and, in the UK, by Nicholas Tomalin and others during the late 1960s. The term was known by 1970 although, as might be expected, it had been used less specifically before then about other innovative types of journalism. An anthology entitled *The New Journalism*, edited by Tom Wolfe and E.W. Johnson, was published in 1973.

Newk. See BEWDY ~!

news. See AH, THERE'S GOOD ~ TONIGHT!; AND THAT'S THE TOP OF THE ~ . . . ; HERE IS THE ~ AND THIS IS . . .

newspaper. See FAMILY ~.

newt. See PISSED AS A ~.

New York. See I LOVE —.

New Zealand. See I WENT TO ~ BUT . . .

next. See AND THE ~ OBJECT . . . ; AND THE ~ TONIGHT . . .

next year in Jerusalem! A familiar Jewish toast. In the Diaspora, it was the eternal hope – expressed particularly at the Feast of the Passover – that all Jews would be reunited, 'next year in Jerusalem'. Passover originally celebrated the exodus of the Jews from Egypt and their deliverance from enslavement some 3,200 years ago. In the centuries of the Diaspora, the central Jewish dream was of being reunited in the land of Israel. In June 1967, following the Six Day War, when the modern state of Israel encompassed once more the old city of Jerusalem, all Jews could, if they were able, end their exile and make this dream more of a reality.

NIBMAR. 'No Independence Before Majority (African) Rule'. Acronym encapsulating the British Labour government's terms when dealing with the illegal Rhodesian regime following its UDI (Unilateral Declaration of Independence) in 1965.

nibs. See AND NOW, HER ∼ , MISS GEORGIA GIBBS.

nice. See GOOD MORNING . . . ∼ DAY under *ITMA*; under HAVE A GOOD DAY; IT'S TURNED OUT ∼ AGAIN!; NAUGHTY BUT ∼ ; NO MORE MR ∼ GUY; WHAT'S A ∼ GIRL LIKE YOU . . .

nice 'ere, innit? From a British TV advertisement in 1976: on a balcony in Venice, an elegant-looking girl sips Campari and then shatters the atmosphere by saying in a rough Cockney voice, 'Nice 'ere, innit?' In the follow-up ad, a smooth type asks the same girl, 'Were you truly wafted here from Paradise?' She replies: '**Nah . . . Luton Airport.**' These nothing phrases were crafted by copywriter Terry Howard and let fall by Lorraine Chase. Campari sales rose by a record 35 per cent in a single year. Lorraine went on to record a song called 'It's Nice 'Ere, Innit?' (1979) and Cats UK recorded 'Luton Airport' the same year. Next step was for the personality to be written into a TV sitcom called *The Other 'Arf* (from 1980).

nice guys finish last. During his time as manager of the Brooklyn Dodgers baseball team (1951–4), Leo Durocher (*b* 1906) became known for this view – also in the form, 'Nice guys don't finish first' or '. . . don't play ball games'. Partridge/*Catch Phrases* dates the popular use of the phrase from July 1946. Used as the title of a book by Paul Gardner, subtitled 'Sport and American Life', in 1974.

In his autobiography with the title *Nice Guys Finish Last* (1975), Durocher recalled that what he had said to reporters concerning the New York Giants in July 1946, was: 'All nice guys. They'll finish last. Nice guys. Finish last.' However, Frank Graham of the New York *Journal-American* had written down something slightly different: 'Why, they're the nicest guys in the world! And where are they? In seventh place!' Hence, the title of Ralph Keyes's book on misquotations, *Nice Guys Finish Seventh* (1992).

nice little earner, a. Much used by George Cole in the character of 'Arthur Daley' in British TV's *Minder* series (from the late 1970s on). 'Earner' on its own, for 'money earned' (often shadily), may go back to the 1930s.

From the *Independent* (27 April 1989): '[On a large number of claims for tripping over broken paving stones in Northern Ireland] That, said Michael Latham, Tory MP for Rutland, meant that either the state of local pavements was "exceptionally disgraceful . . .", or the locals saw a "nice little earner there and are trying it on".'

nicely. See THAT'LL DO ∼ , SIR.

nice one, Cyril! The story of this phrase is a classic instance of a line from an advertisement being taken up by the public, turned into a catchphrase, and then as suddenly discarded. Its origins were quite soon obscured, and then forgotten. The line, apparently written by Peter Mayle, caught the imagination of British TV viewers in a 1972 advertisement for Wonderloaf. Two bakers were shown wearing T-shirts labelled 'Nottingham' and 'Liverpool' respectively. 'All our local bakers reckon they can taste a Wonderloaf and tell you who baked it,' purred a voice-over commentary. 'It was oven-baked at one of our local bakeries.' The following exchange then took place between the bakers:

> *Liverpool:* Leeds? High Wycombe? It's one of Cyril's. Mmm. Good texture, nice colour, very fresh . . .
> *Nottingham:* Cyril . . . I think it's one of Frank's down at Luton . . . it's definitely saying Newcastle to me . . .

The voice-over then intervened: 'The truth is, they can't say for sure. But we can say . . .': *Nottingham:* 'Nice one, Cyril!'

As a phrase, why did 'Nice one, Cyril!' catch on? It had a sibilant ease; it was fun to say. More importantly it could be used in any number of situations, not least sexual ones. In 1973, the phrase was taken up by Tottenham Hotspur football supporters who were fans of the player Cyril Knowles. They even recorded a song about him which went:

Nice one, Cyril
Nice one, son.
Nice one, Cyril,
Let's have another one.

Comedian Cyril Fletcher inevitably used it as the title of his 1978 autobiography. The following year the word 'Cyril' was observed scrawled on the first kilometre sign outside a certain seaside resort in the South of France. Shortly afterwards the phrase disappeared almost completely from use, although in February 1989 posters appeared for a credit card company which showed Sir Cyril Smith, the obese politician, attempting to touch his toes. The slogan was: 'Nice one, Sir Cyril . . . but Access is more flexible.'

Compare, **nice one, Stew!** from a children's programme on New Zealand TV in the mid-70s. Stew Dennison, the host, wore a schoolboy's cap and would say it to himself. Kids around him would then echo it.

nice place you got here. Dick Vosburgh and Trevor Lyttleton included this film phrase in their delightful catalogue song 'I Love a Film Cliche', which was included in the Broadway hit, *A Day in Hollywood, A Night in the Ukraine* (1980). In it, they gave the longer version – the one uttered by a gangster with a lump in his jacket, viz: 'Nice place you got here, blue eyes. Be too bad if something was to . . . happen to it!' At this point, the heavy usually knocks over an ornament, as a warning.

Often, one hears the version 'nice *little* place you've got here' – used with equal amounts of irony about a dump or somewhere impressively grand. However, in the film *Breakfast at Tiffany's* (1961), it is said almost straight. Partridge/*Catch Phrases* seems to think it all started in Britain in the 1940s, but I feel sure the film use must have started in the US in the 1930s. It is also said to have been popularized around 1942 by the BBC radio show *ITMA*, following a visit to Windsor Castle by the star Tommy Handley.

From the *Independent* (13 May 1989): 'To this day [Stevie] Wonder habitually talks about "seeing" and catches out sighted friends by walking into unfamiliar rooms, taking a "look" around and saying: "Hey, nice place you've got here." '

nice —, shame about the —. 'Nice Legs, Shame About Her Face' was the title of a briefly popular song recorded by The Monks in 1979. The title launched a format phrase which appeared, for example, in a take-off by TV's *Not the Nine O'Clock News* team – 'Nice video, shame about the song' and in a slogan for Hofmeister lager, 'Great lager, shame about the . . .' (both in 1982). Just before this, I think Listerine ran an ad with the slogan 'Nice Face, Shame About the Breath'.

Headline to an *Independent* piece on the hundredth birthday of the 'The Red Flag': 'Good tune, shame about the words' (9 February 1989). Headline from the *Observer* (9 April 1989): 'Nice prints, shame about the books'. Also used loosely: 'Victoria Wood is almost perfect. Lovely lady, pity about the voice' (*Cosmopolitan*, February 1987); headline to an *Observer* report on puny car horns (January 1989): 'NICE CAR, BUT WHAT A VOICE!'

nice to see you . . . to see you . . . /Nice! See under GENERATION GAME.

nice weather for ducks. See LOVELY . . .

nick, nick! One-time catchphrase of the British Cockney comedian Jim Davidson (b 1954), providing an aural counterpart to the revolving blue light on the top of police vehicles. In c 1978, he commented, 'As kids we all shouted it whenever OLD BILL appeared on the horizon.' Presumably, it is derived from 'You're nicked' (i.e. caught) which is what British policemen do actually sometimes say when making an arrest. In November 1980, having been fined for using threatening behaviour at a football match and for obstructing the police, Davidson announced that he was giving up the phrase and replacing it with **too risky!** (which also became the title of a song and of an album that same year).

niece. See HAVE YOU MET MY ~?

nigger in the woodpile, a/the. Meaning 'something surprising hidden, a concealed factor'. Mencken has: 'There's a nigger in the woodpile – American saying, traced by Thornton to 1864, and probably older.' The *OED2* finds it in Kansas in 1852. Nowadays considered an unacceptable usage.

nigh. See END IS ∼.

night. See DARK ∼ OF THE SOUL; FRIDAY ∼ IS . . . ; IT'LL BE ALL RIGHT ON THE ∼ ; IT WAS GOING TO BE A LONG ∼ ; TAKE BACK THE ∼ .

night and fog. *Nacht und Nebel* was the name of a 1941 decree issued under Hitler's signature. It described a simple process: anyone suspected of a crime against occupying German forces was to disappear into 'night and fog'. Such people were thrown into the concentration camp system, in most cases never to be heard of again. Alain Resnais, the French film director, made a cinema short about a concentration camp called *Nuit et Brouillard* (1955). The phrase comes from Wagner's opera *Das Rheingold* (1869): '*Nacht und Nebel niemand gleich*' is the spell that Alberich puts on the magic Tarnhelm which renders him invisible and omnipresent. It means approximately, 'In night and fog no one is seen'.

night is young, the. 'The Night is Young (and You're So Beautiful)' is the title of a song by Billy Rose and Irving Kahal (1936). The previous year 'The Night Is Young (And So Are We)' had been written by Oscar Hammerstein II and Sigmund Romberg and included in the film *The Night is Young*. Hence, presumably, the expression, 'The night is young!' – the sort of thing one says when attempting to justify another drink. From Frank Brady, *Citizen Welles* (1989): 'At three in the morning, when a few people decided to leave, Orson, stepping into the role of clichéd host from a Grade B movie, would not hear of it: "You're not leaving already, my friends. The night is still young. Play, Gypsies! Play, play, play!" '

night of broken glass, the.
[*Kristallnacht*]. A euphemism attributed to

Walther Funk to describe the Nazi pogrom against Jews in Germany on the night of 9/10 November 1938.

night of the long knives, a/the. During the weekend of 29 June/2 July 1934, there occurred in Nazi Germany *Die Nacht der Langen Messer* – the Night of the Long Knives, a phrase that has passed into common use for any kind of surprise purge (but one in which, usually, no actual blood is spilt). It was applied, for example, to Harold Macmillan's wholesale reorganization of his Cabinet in 1962. When Norman St John Stevas was dropped from his Cabinet post in a 1981 reshuffle, one wit described the changes as Mrs Thatcher's 'night of the long hatpin'.

On the original occasion, Hitler, aided by Himmler's black-shirted SS, liquidated the leadership of the brown-shirted SA. These latter undisciplined storm-troopers had helped Hitler gain power but were now getting in the way of his dealings with the German army. Some 83 were murdered on the pretext that they were plotting another revolution.

'It was no secret that this time the revolution would have to be bloody,' Hitler explained to the Reichstag on 13 July. 'When we spoke of it, we called it "The Night of the Long Knives" . . . in every time and place, rebels have been killed . . . I ordered the leaders of the guilty shot. I also ordered the abscesses caused by our internal and external poisons cauterised until the living flesh was burned.' It seems that in using the phrase Hitler may have been quoting from an early Nazi marching song.

night starvation, Horlicks guards against. Horlicks milk drink used this slogan in the UK from 1930. The J. Walter Thompson agency evolved the concept of 'night starvation' to add to the worries of the twentieth century – nobody had been aware of it before: 'Right through the night you've been burning up reserves of energy without food to replace it. Breathing alone takes twenty thousand muscular efforts every night.' Partridge/*Slang* records that the phrase became a popular term for sexual deprivation. Horlicks had advertised before this with the memorable picture of a man turning out his suitcase and the slogan **I know I packed it.**

During the 1950s, JWT ran comic-strip sagas of the refreshing qualities of Horlicks for tired housewives, run-down executives, etc., which customarily ended with the hero/heroine offering thanks within a think bubble **thinks . . . thanks to Horlicks.** But the idea was an old one. 'Thinks . . . thanks to *Radio Times*' was running in the 1930s.

night-time in Italy. See WHEN IT'S ~ . . .

nikky-nokky-noo! See under HOW TICKLED I AM.

nil carborundum. See *ILLEGITIMI* . . .

Nimby, a. Word from the acronym 'NIMBY', meaning 'not in my back yard' and used to describe people who object to have having unpleasant developments near their homes but, by implication, don't mind them being sited elsewhere. In 1988, the British Environment Secretary, Nicholas Ridley, was so named when he objected to housing developments near his own home when he had previously criticized people who took this attitude. In fact, 'NIMBY' was an American coinage *c* 1980, for people who objected to the siting of something like a nuclear waste dumping site or a sewage treatment plant. 'TRENDY DINERS TURN NIMBY OVER NEW YORK DRUGS CLINIC' (headline in the *Guardian*, 12 November 1991).

nine days' wonder, a. Referring to something of short-lived appeal and soon forgotten, the expression comes from an old proverb: 'A wonder lasts nine days, and then the puppy's eyes are open' – alluding to the fact that dogs (like cats) are born blind. After nine days, in other words, their eyes are open to see clearly. The saying was known in this form by 1594.

Another etymologist finds a link with the old religious practice of selling indulgences, one of which – guaranteeing the purchaser nine days' worth of prayers – was called a *novem*. The indulgence was held to be a bit suspect – rather like this explanation.

Chaucer expressed the old proverb thus: 'For wonder last but nine night never in

town.' Surely, we need look no further for the origin of an expression of which the truth is self-evident: wonder dies in time.

Incidentally, there is an Italian proverb: 'No wonder can last more than three days.'

nine/nineteen to ninety. Cliché of broadcasting, mostly. 'This show will appeal to everyone from nine to ninety.' Sometimes 'nineteen . . .', if the entertainment in question is a touch more adult.

nine out of ten —. A formula beloved of advertisers. 'Nine out of ten screens stars use Lux Toilet Soap for their priceless smooth skins' – so ran a famous campaign that lasted for 20 years from 1927. Among the stars who were listed as Lux users were Fay Wray, Clara Bow and Joan Crawford. *ROUND THE HORNE* (1 May 1966) called itself 'the show that nine out of ten horses prefer', and a 1987 graffito read, 'Bestiality – nine out of every ten cats said their owners preferred it', indicating that the format must have been used to promote pet food in the UK.

Compare '4 out of 5 people say Big John's Beans taste better' (US ad, quoted 1977).

nines. See DRESSED UP TO THE ~.

nine tailors. In bell-ringing it was possible to indicate the age or sex of a dead person for whom the bells were being tolled. Three times one for a child, three twos for a woman and three threes for a man (hence 'nine tellers' or 'nine tailors' – strokes – meant a man). In Dorothy L. Sayers's novel The Nine Tailors (1934), the bell is called 'Tailor Paul' and does indeed toll nine times for a man found dead in the belfry.

But the phrase also appears to be from a proverb in contempt of tailors: 'It takes nine tailors to make a man', which apparently came from the French *c* 1600. The meaning of this seems to be that a man should buy his clothes from various sources. G.L. Apperson in his *English Proverbs and Proverbial Phrases* (1929) shows that, until the end of the seventeenth century, there was some uncertainty about the number of tailors mentioned. In *Westward Hoe* by John Webster and Thomas Dekker (1605) it appears as three.

nineteen to the dozen, to talk. i.e., very quickly. A very literal derivation comes from the Cornish tin mines of the eighteenth century. When pumps were introduced to get rid of flooding, they were said to pump out 19,000 gallons of water for every 12 bushels of coal needed to operate the engines.

But, surely, one can be even more basic than that: to speak 19 words where only 12 are needed gets across the idea very nicely. Nineteen may be a surprising number to choose. Oddly, however, it sounds right and better than any other number. 'Twenty to the dozen', for example, sounds rather flat. The phrase was in use by 1785.

nineties. See NAUGHTY ~.

99 44/100 per cent pure. A slogan for Ivory Soap, in the US, from c 1882. One of the clumsiest but most enduring slogans of all. Nobody remembers who first coined this bizarre line but it has stuck, along with the claim that **it floats.** A story has it that the floating character of the soap was not recognized until a dealer asked for another case of 'that soap that floats'. An advertisement for *Swan* soap in the UK is featured in Vol. 122 of *Punch*, 1902, also using 'it floats'.

In 1974, an American gangster film with Richard Harris was entitled *99 And 44/100 Per Cent Dead*. For the benefit of non-Americans who would not understand the allusion, the film was tardily retitled *Call Harry Crown*. But *Variety* opined crisply that even the original version was 'as clumsy as its title'.

ninety-nine per cent of all known germs, Domestos kills. The domestic cleaning agent and disinfectant appears to have used several versions of this slogan. In 1959, 'Domestos kills all known germs in one hour'. In 1967, 'Domestos kills all known germs – dead!'

From BBC radio's ROUND THE HORNE (13 March 1966): 'Ladies and gentlemen – the programme that contains ninety-nine percent of all known jokes . . .'

ninety-two! See under EE, IN'T IT GRAND TO BE DAFT!

ninthlies and lastlies. Ronald Knox's *Juxta Salices* (1910) includes a group of poems he had written when still at Eton and is prefaced with this remark: 'As no less than three of [these poems] wear the aspect of a positively last appearance [i.e. a promise not to write more], they have been called in the words of so many eminent preachers "ninthlies and lastlies".' Earlier, the OED2 has Thomas B. Aldrich writing in *Prudence Palfrey* (1874–85) of: 'The poor old parson's interminable ninthlies and finallies,' and there is a 'fifthly and lastly' dated 1681. Benjamin Franklin, in 1745, concludes his *Reasons for Preferring an Elderly Mistress* with: 'Eighth and lastly. They are so grateful!!' Ultimately, the origin for all this must be the kind of legal nonsense-talk parodied by Shakespeare's Dogberry in *Much Ado About Nothing* (c 1598): 'Marry, sir, they have committed false report; moreover, they have spoken untruths; secondarily, they are slanders; *sixthly and lastly*, they have belied a lady; thirdly, they have verified unjust things; and to conclude, they are lying knaves.'

nipple count. This phrase came into use in 1970s Britain when the *Sun* and other newspapers began a 'war' in which the number of pin-ups' nipples shown per issue was of importance (compare BODY COUNT in the Vietnam War). The American drive-in movie critic, Joe Bob Briggs, who wrote for the *Dallas Times Herald* in the 1980s (see JOE BOB SAYS CHECK IT OUT), literally counted the breasts he saw and rated the films accordingly. He did not actually use this phrase, though.

nitty-gritty. See LET'S GET DOWN TO THE ~.

'no answer' came the stern reply! An ironic comment on the fact that no one has replied or said a word. Known by the 1930s but in various forms, including: ' "No answer, no answer" came the loud reply' and ' "shrieks of silence" was the stern reply'. If these are quotations, the original source has not been identified.

no better than she should be. A famous line of understated criticism, established by 1815 and probably much older. Motteux's translation (1712) of Cervantes's *Don Quixote* (Bk. III, Chap. 20) has: 'The shepherd fell out with his sweetheart . . . thought her no better than she should be, a little loose in the hilts, and free of her behaviour.' A construction almost invariably applied to women.

no blade of grass. A turn of phrase with no precise origin. The nearest the Bible gets is Isaiah 15:6: 'The grass faileth, there is no green thing.' Lord Palmerston, quoted by the *Daily Telegraph* (1864), said: 'I had at one time nearly 1,000 acres of blowy sand where no blade of grass grew.' Amelia B. Edwards in *A Thousand Miles Up the Nile* (1877) writes: 'The barren desert hems us in to right and left, with never a blade of green between the rock and the river.' A 1902 citation of an old Turkish proverb in *ODP* is: 'Where the hoof of the Turkish horse treads, no blade of grass ever grows.' Other examples are found in Agatha Christie's *Autobiography* (1977): 'There was no scrap of garden anywhere. All was asphalt. No blade of grass showed green,' and from *The Life of Kenneth Tynan* by Kathleen Tynan (1987): 'I felt there was nothing about the country in Ken at all. Not a blade of grass . . .' *No Blade of Grass* was used as the title of a film (UK, 1970) about worldwide food shortages brought about by industrial pollution, and based on a book by John Christopher called *The Death of Grass* (1956).

nobody's perfect. A pleasant way of excusing (usually) another's failings. From George Eliot, *Middlemarch*, Chap. 25 (1871–2): ' "I'm afraid Fred is not to be trusted, Mary," said the father . . . "Well, well, nobody's perfect, but . . ." ' The last lines of the film *Some Like It Hot* (US, 1959) have Tony Curtis (in drag) explaining to a potential husband why they should not marry. 'She' is not a woman. Unflustered by this, Joe E. Brown as an old millionaire says, 'Nobody's perfect.'

nobody tells me nothing. See under *ITMA*.

no comment. This useful phrase, when people in the news are being hounded by journalists, has not quite been condemned as a cliché. After all, why should people in such a position be required to find something original to say? Nevertheless, it has come to be used as a consciously inadequate form of evasion, often in an obviously jokey way (compare WE ARE JUST GOOD FRIENDS).

From the *Guardian* (25 January 1989): 'Mr [Norman] Willis [TUC General Secretary at book award ceremony] is not going to rock the boat by descending to literary chat. "No comment," he says vigorously when asked if he has read any of the short-listed books.'

I suppose the phrase arose by way of reaction to the ferretings of Hollywood gossip columnists in the 1920s and 30s, though perhaps it was simply a general reaction to the rise of the popular press in the first half of the century.

Winston Churchill appears not to have known it until 1946, so perhaps it was not generally known until then, at least not outside the US? After a meeting with President Truman, Churchill said, 'I think "No Comment" is a splendid expression. I got it from Sumner Welles.' Also in 1946, critic C.A. Lejeune's entire review of the US film *No Leave, No Love* was 'No comment'.

A good example of the phrase in something like straightforward use can be found in a terse broadcast interview conducted with Kim Philby on 10 November 1955 after the diplomat had been cleared of being the THIRD MAN in the Burgess/Maclean spy case. He later defected to Moscow in 1963 and was shown to have been a liar and a spy all along:

> *Interviewer:* Mr Philby, Mr Macmillan, the Foreign Secretary, said there was no evidence that you were the so-called 'third man' who allegedly tipped off Burgess and Maclean. Are you satisfied with that clearance that he gave you?
> *Philby:* Yes, I am.
> *Interviewer:* Well, if there was a 'third man', were you in fact the 'third man'?
> *Philby:* No, I was not.
> *Interviewer:* Do you think there was one?
> *Philby:* No comment.

Martha 'The Mouth' Mitchell, the blabber who helped get the Watergate investigations under way and who was the wife of President Nixon's disgraced Attorney-General, once declared: 'I don't believe in that "no comment" business. I always have a comment.' Desmond Wilcox, a TV executive, came up with a variant for the TV age in 1980. When ducking a question, he said, 'Sorry, your camera's run out of film.' The *Financial Times* for many years has used the slogan 'No *FT* . . . no comment' (current 1982).

no conferring. See HERE'S YOUR STARTER . . .

nod/Nod. See BURLEIGH'S ~; HOMER ~S; LAND OF ~.

no good deed goes unpunished. A consciously ironic rewriting of the older expression 'No *bad* deed goes unpunished' – (surely proverbial but unrecorded in *ODP* or *CODP*.)

Joe Orton recorded in his diary for 13 June 1967: 'Very good line George [Greeves] came out with at dinner: "No good deed ever goes unpunished."' Earlier, before opening in Noël Coward's *Waiting in the Wings*, Marie Lohr went to church and prayed for a good first night. On her way to the theatre she slipped and broke her leg. 'No good deed ever goes unpunished,' was Coward's comment.

I have also seen the remark ascribed to Oscar Wilde and, whether or not it is one of his, it is a perfect example of the inversion technique used in so many of his witticisms.

No Independence Before Majority (Africa) Rule. See NIBMAR.

noise and the people!, the. A mock exclamation of dismay at crowded conditions, derived from what a certain Captain Strahan supposedly said after the Battle of Bastogne (1944) or, more probably, after the evacuation of Allied forces from Dunkirk (1940). Often introduced with, 'Oh, my dear fellow . . . !', with the inference that the speaker has a blasé attitude to the dangers and a disdain of the common soldiery he is being forced to mix with. It was already being quoted in 1942.

noise, loudest. See AT 60 MILES AN HOUR . . .

no likey? oh, crikey! See under ITMA.

no man's land. From the old expression (current by 1320) for unowned, waste land, it has also been used to describe the space between entrenched armies (as in the First World War). The title of a play (1974) by Harold Pinter, and an unrelated film (US, 1987).

no more chance than (or **as much chance as**) **a snowball/snowflake in Hell/Hades.** Mencken (1942) has the first of these versions listed as an 'American saying'. It had been recorded by 1931. In the form 'Gloom hasn't got a snowball's chance in Hades' the line occurs in Stephen Graham, *London Nights* (1925). Either way, Partridge/*Catch Phrases* thinks the expression dates from the turn of the century.

no more Latin, no more French,/no more sitting on a hard board bench (or **the old school bench**). I learnt this rhyme at school in the 1950s – the sort of thing you said before the holidays began. It turns out to be the second half of a verse which – in the US – begins, 'No more lessons, no more books./ No more teacher's sassy looks' – at least in the 'schoolboy's song, *c* 1850' quoted by Mencken.

In the *Lore and Language of Schoolchildren* (1959), Iona and Peter Opie print two lengthy 'breaking up' rhymes current in Britain this century. Both include these two lines.

no more Mr Nice Guy. 'Mr Nice Guy' is a nickname applied to 'straight' figures (especially politicians) who may possibly be following someone who is palpably not 'nice' (Gerald Ford after Richard Nixon, for example). They then sometimes feel the need to throw off some of their virtuous image, as presidential challenger Senator Ed Muskie did in 1972 – and his aides declared, 'No more Mr Nice Guy.' In April 1973, Alice Cooper had a song entitled 'No More Mr Nice Guy' in the British charts.

Safire dates to the 'mid-1950s' the joke about Hitler agreeing to make a comeback with the words, 'But this time – no more Mr Nice Guy.'

no more war. A recurring slogan, mostly twentieth century. At the UN in 1965, Pope Paul VI quoted President Kennedy 'four years ago' to the effect that 'mankind must put an end to war, or war will put an end to mankind . . . No more war, never again war.' (He said this in Italian.)

Earlier, the phrase was used by Winston Churchill at the end of a letter to Lord Beaverbrook in 1928 (quoted in Martin Gilbert's biography of Churchill, Vol. 5). A.J.P. Taylor in his *English History 1914–45* suggests that the slogan was 'irresistible' at the end of the First World War.

In *Goodbye to Berlin* (1939), Christopher Isherwood describes a Nazi book-burning. The books are from a 'small liberal pacifist publisher'. One of the Nazis holds up a book called '*Nie Wieder Krieg*' as though it were 'a nasty kind of reptile'. 'No More War!' a fat, well-dressed woman laughs scornfully and savagely, 'What an idea!'

Compare NEVER AGAIN.

no, my darling daughter. See DON'T GO NEAR THE WATER.

no names, no packdrill. i.e., I am not going to betray any confidences by mentioning names. Somehow this alludes to a one-time British army punishment when soldiers were made to march up and down carrying a heavy pack – a very physical punishment for use in the field where fines or confinement to barracks would be meaningless or impossible. It is probably a short form of saying, 'As long as I don't give away any names, I won't get punished for it – that's why I am not telling you.' Recorded by 1923.

Paul Beale gave this even lengthier paraphrase (1988): 'I will tell you this discreditable story, because it is a good story and shows the criminal ingenuity, or at least low cunning, of some people I know. But I won't tell you their names (even though you might guess who they are) because I don't want *them* to get into trouble – after all they are my mates, my muckers, and I'm only telling you so that you can admire their cleverness: it's all "off the record".' Beale added: 'Only secondarily was there any implication of "I don't want to get punished", except in as far as "the mates" might round on an informant. It's really an expression of the old army muckers-stick-together, and to hell with anyone of any rank higher than private/trooper/gunner/sapper or effing fusilier.'

noofter. See YER PLONKER!

nookie, I like. 'Nooky/nookie' has been a slang word for sexual activity since at least 1928 and is of American origin. In the 1970s, a British ventriloquist called Roger de Courcey (*b* 1944) had some success with a teddy bear with the name Nookie. T-shirts appeared with pictures of the bear and the slogan 'I like Nookie'.

no one likes us, we don't care. Phrase from the new lyrics sung by fans of Millwall football club to the tune of Rod Stewart's song 'Sailing'. Millwall fans are famous in London for their vocal and physical forcefulness. *No One Likes Us, We Don't Care* was, consequently, the title given to a Channel 4 TV documentary about them in January 1990.

no pain(s), no gain(s). Adlai Stevenson said in his speech accepting the Democratic Presidential nomination (26 July 1952): 'Let's talk sense to the American people. Let's tell them the truth, that there are no gains without pains.' 'No pains, no gains, no sweat, no sweet' is, indeed, a proverb best known in the US, though it can be dated back in England to 1648, and in a simpler form to 1577.

The same message was relayed by John Major when he delivered a speech at Northampton (27 October 1989) on suddenly becoming Britain's Chancellor of the Exchequer following the resignation of Nigel Lawson. It had probably been written for his predecessor. He said: 'The harsh truth is that if the policy isn't hurting it isn't working. I know there is a difficult period ahead but the important thing is that we cannot and must not fudge the determination to stop inflation in its tracks.'

no place like home, there's. A quotation from the song 'Home, Sweet Home' from the opera *Clari* (1823) by the American playwright and actor, J.H.

Payne: ' 'Mid pleasures and palaces though we may roam,/Be it ever so humble, there's no place like home.' This appears to build on the earlier proverb (1546), 'Home is home though it's never so homely.'

An advertising slogan, quoted in 1982, was: 'Come to Jamaica, it's no place like home' which (I think) nicely plays upon the other, derogatory, view of home.

no pockets in shrouds, there are no. Rebuke to a person who believes that money is for hoarding, not spending. R.C. Trench, *On Lessons in Proverbs* (1854) refers to an Italian proverb: 'With an image Dantesque in its vigour, that "a man shall carry nothing away with him when he dieth", take this Italian, *Our last robe* . . . is made *without pockets*.' In English nowadays, this proverb is more usually: 'Shrouds have no pockets.'

no Popery (no tyranny, no wooden shoes). The writer Daniel Defoe (1660–1731) said that there were a hundred thousand fellows in his time ready to fight to the death against Popery – without knowing whether Popery was a man or a horse. After the initial impact of the Restoration had worn off, this was the cry that came to be heard. The wife of Charles II, Catherine of Braganza, was a Roman Catholic and so was his brother (later James II), and they were surrounded by priests. The Great Fire of London (1666) was said to have been caused by papist action and foreign interference. Hence, the anti-Roman Catholicism of the slogan coupled with a general English distrust of foreigners (wooden shoes = French *sabots*). The variation **no Jews = no wooden shoes** (obviously rhyming slang) arose in 1753 when an anti-Jewish Bill was before Parliament.

The cry 'No Popery' is chiefly associated, however, with the Gordon Riots of 1780, when Lord George Gordon fomented a violent protest against legislation which had lightened penalties on Roman Catholics. The riots in London were put down by George III's troops (and form the background to Charles Dickens's novel *Barnaby Rudge*). The slogan was again used by supporters of the Duke of Portland's government opposed to Catholic Emancipation, in 1807.

no pun intended. See IF YOU'LL EXCUSE . . .

no questions asked. A promise of collusion over a deal which probably involves wrongdoing. Apparently the British Larceny Act of 1861 banned anew the use of this phrase in newspaper personal columns. Modern use is more generally applied in situations where people are being told they will not have to account for their conduct. From P.G. Wodehouse, *The Indiscretions of Archie* (1921): 'Nine out of ten of them had views on Art which would have admitted them to any looney-bin, and no questions asked.'

Nora. See RUDDY ~!

normal service will be resumed as soon as possible. See under DO NOT ADJUST YOUR SET.

normalcy. See BACK TO ~.

north by north-west. Meaning 'mad', and used obliquely as the title of Alfred Hitchcock's film *North by Northwest* (US, 1959) in which Cary Grant feigns madness. The phrase is a slight adjustment of Hamlet's words in Shakespeare's play (II.ii.374; 1600): 'I am but mad north-north-west. When the wind is southerly, I know a hawk from a handsaw.'

North of Watford. Meaning 'beyond the edge of civilization' and referring to a town on the north-west of the London conurbation. The *OED2* definition is unbeatable: 'Used with allusion to the view (attributed to Londoners) that north of the metropolis there is nothing of any signifcance to English national or cultural life.' Recorded by 1973. Compare WOGS BEGIN AT BARNET.

North-South divide, the. This is a political phrase for (1) the perceived difference in living standards between the developed nations (mostly to be found in the northern hemisphere) and the underdeveloped nations in the southern hemisphere. Recorded by 1980. (2) the division between the prosperous south of England and the rest of the country. In a speech on 4 February 1927, Winston

Churchill said: 'I saw a comparison made in the "Nation" newspaper of the conditions prevailing north and south of a line which the writer had drawn across the country from Cardiff to Hull.'

NORWICH. Meaning '(K)Nickers Off Ready When I Come Home'. Lovers' acronym for use in correspondence and to avoid military censorship. In use by the First World War?

See also DO YOU KNOW THE BISHOP OF ∼?

nose. See CUT OFF YOUR ∼ TO SPITE YOUR FACE; PAY THROUGH THE ∼; POWDER ONE'S ∼; SKIN OFF MY ∼, NO.

no sex please we're British. Derived from the title of a long-running farce (1971; film UK, 1973) by Anthony Marriott and Alastair Foot. Much alluded to by headline writers and such. From the *Independent* (23 April 1992): 'As Ken Livingstone said, "One of the things missing from this election was a sense of humour." No jokes, please, we're British.' Chapter heading in *The State of the Language* (ed. Ricks & Michaels, 1991): 'No Opera Please – We're British'. Headline from *Harpers & Queen* (September 1994): 'No pecks [kisses] please, we're British'.

nosey parker. Meaning 'an interfering, inquisitive person', from the fact that the nose has long been associated with an inquisitive nature. Traditionally, a link has been suggested with Matthew Parker, Elizabeth I's Archbishop of Canterbury. But Partridge/*Slang* wonders whether the word 'parker', meaning 'park-keeper', might also have described someone who enjoyed spying on love-making couples in London's Hyde Park.

no such thing as a free lunch, there is. This old American expression meaning, 'There's no getting something for nothing' dates back to the mid-nineteenth century. Flexner puts an 1840s date on the supply of a 'free lunch' – even if no more than thirst-arousing snacks like pretzels – in saloon bars. This was not strictly speaking 'free' because you had to buy beer to obtain it. The precise phrase was quoted by Burton Crane in *The Sophisticated Investor* (1959). It

was also attributed to the University of Chicago school of economists by Paul Samuelson in *Newsweek* (29 December 1969).

Indeed, the notion was given a new lease of life in the 1970s by the economist Milton Friedman, therefrom, and the saying was sometimes ascribed to him by virtue of the fact that he published a book with the title, and wrote articles and gave lectures incorporating the phrase. When Margaret Thatcher and Ronald Reagan attempted to embrace, up to a point, Friedman's monetarist thinking, the phrase was trotted out by their acolytes (in Thatcher's case, according to press reports, specific instructions were given for ministers to drop it into their speeches).

In July 1989, US Representative Richard Gephardt, commenting on the announcement of a new American goal in space, commented: 'We don't have the economic strength we need to make it a reality . . . there is no such thing as a free launch.'

no surrender! In 1689, the year after the Catholic King James II was replaced with the Protestant William of Orange on the British throne, forces still loyal to James maintained a siege against the citizens of Derry in Ulster. The siege was raised after a month or two. 'No surrender!' was the Protestant slogan and 'Long Live Ulster. No surrender' is still a Loyalist slogan. Another version is: 'NO POPERY, no surrender.' *No Surrender* was the title of a 1985 film written by Alan Bleasdale about warring Protestant and Roman Catholic factions in Liverpool.

not —. This construction might seem to have been launched by *Not the Nine O'Clock News* (1979–82) which was broadcast on BBC2 opposite the *Nine O'Clock News* on BBC1. Accordingly, there were several British derivatives, e.g. *Not Private Eye* (1986), a spoof of the satirical magazine brought out by some of its supposed victims, and *Not Yet the Times* – when the actual newspaper *The Times* was not being published in 1978–9.

In fact, the model for all these titles was *Not the New York Times*, a spoof on the newspaper, published in 1978.

—, not! See under *WAYNE'S WORLD*.

not a dry eye in the house. Exaggerated comment on an effective performance or speech that has palpably moved an audience to tears. From William H. Prescott, *Philip II* (1855): 'They were deeply affected, and not a dry eye was to be seen in the assembly.' P.G. Wodehouse, *Very Good, Jeeves!* (1930): ' "Held them spellbound" . . . "Cold," said young Tuppy, "Not a dry eye." '

not a lot. The Yorkshire magician and comedian Paul Daniels (*b* 1938) said in 1979 that he had found this catchphrase early on in his career. He was being heckled by someone who didn't like his act. 'A pity,' he said, 'because I like your suit. Not a lot, but I like it.'

not a million miles from —. Much used in *Private Eye* since the 1960s, this is, however, a venerable form of ironic exaggeration meaning 'very close to'. Nelson's *English Idioms* (referring to about 1890) explains 'not a hundred miles off/from' thus: 'A phrase often used to avoid a direct reference to any place. The place itself or its immediate neighbourhood is always intended . . . the phrase is also used of events not far distant in time.' And the example given is from H. Rider Haggard: 'From all of which wise reflections the reader will gather that our friend Arthur was not a hundred miles off an awkward situation.' From Charles Dickens, *Bleak House*, Chap. 51 (1853): 'Mr C's address is not a hundred miles from here, sir.'

Another, almost facetious variant, appears in the *Eye* phrase, 'a sum not unadjacent to . . .'

not a po emptied. See HEAVENS, ELEVEN O'CLOCK . . .

no taxation without representation. A slogan current before the American War of Independence and, in the form 'Taxation without representation is tyranny', attributed to the lawyer and statesman James Otis in 1763. He opposed British taxation of the American colonies on the grounds that they were not represented in the British House of Commons. (Echoed in 1947 by Arnold Toynbee, pressing for a greater British role in the UN: 'No annihilation without representation.')

not for all the tea in China. 'Under no circumstances, not for anything'. A nineteenth-century phrase which Partridge/*Slang* (1937 edition) seemed to think was Australian in origin and *OED2* took this up, but with no firm evidence. Compare OIL FOR THE LAMPS OF CHINA.

nothing but the truth. See I SWEAR . . .

nothing over sixpence. The first British Woolworth's opened in 1909 and was described as a 'threepence and sixpence' store, the equivalent of the 'five-and-ten' (cent) stores in the US. Hence the phrase 'nothing over sixpence' arose and endured until the Second World War, when prices could no longer be contained below this limit. A song 'There's Nothing Over Sixpence in the Store' (1927), written by W.S. Frank & Frank S. Wilcock, includes the lines:

> To Woolworth's, Hobbs and Sutcliffe
> always go to get their bats,
> Stan Baldwin gets his pipes there, and
> Winston gets his hats;
> And the Prince would never think of
> going elsewhere for his spats -
> And there's nothing over sixpence in the
> stores!

Aneurin Bevan once said (1930s): 'Listening to a speech by [Neville] Chamberlain is like paying a visit to Woolworth's – everything in its place and nothing above sixpence.'

nothing venture, nothing win. The first recorded use of the proverb in this precise form is in Sir Charles Sedley's comedy *The Mulberry Garden* (1668). However, the variants 'nothing venture, nothing gain' and 'nothing venture, nothing have' go back further, and may derive from a Latin original. W.S. Gilbert used this form in the 'proverb' song in Act II of *Iolanthe* (1882) and Sir Edmund Hillary, the mountaineer, used it as the title of his autobiography (1975).

Not In My Back Yard. See NIMBY.

not many dead. See SMALL EARTHQUAKE...

not many people know that. It is rare for a personal catchphrase to catch on (as opposed to phrases in entertainment, films, advertising that are engineered to do so). But it has certainly been the case with the one that will always be associated with the actor Michael Caine (*b* 1933). Peter Sellers started the whole thing off when he appeared on BBC TV's *Parkinson* show on 28 October 1972. The edition in question was subsequently released on disc (*Michael Parkinson Meets the Goons*), thus enabling confirmation of what Sellers said: ' "Not many people know that" . . . this is my Michael Caine impression . . . You see Mike's always quoting from *The Guinness Book of Records*. At the drop of a hat he'll trot one out. "Did you know that it takes a man in a tweed suit five-and-a-half seconds to fall from the top of Big Ben to the ground? Now there's not many people know that!" ' Earlier that year, on 30 April 1972, Sellers apparently ad-libbed a 'There's not many people know that' during the recording of BBC Radio's *The Last Goon Show Of All*.

It was not until 1981–2 that the remark really caught on. Caine was given the line to say as an in-joke (in the character of an inebriated university lecturer) in the film *Educating Rita* (1983), and he put his name to a book of trivial facts for charity with the slight variant *Not a Lot of People Know That!* in 1984.

not necessarily in that order, but/ though. 'They married and had a number of children, though not necessarily in that order' – nowadays a mostly humorous (and possibly meaningless) addition to a statement, using the old rather pedantic formula. From the *Morecambe Guardian* (7 December 1976): 'With that film is *The Swiss Conspiracy* which is all about people who tax dodge, and blackmail, are blackmailed and murdered, not necessarily in that order.' And Carol Burnett quoted in *American Film* (1982): 'The first time someone said, "What are your measurements?" I answered, "Thirty-seven, twenty-four, thirty-eight – but not necessarily in that order." '

Not Only . . . But Also. See under NOT SO MUCH A —.

not on your Nellie! See under NAY, NAY ~ THRICE . . .

Not Quite Top Drawer. See NQTD.

Not (Quite) Our Class, Dear. See N(Q)OCD.

Not Safe in Taxis. See NSIT.

not so much a —, more a —. Use of this format was encouraged by the title of BBC TV's late-night-satire-plus-chat show (from 13 November 1964), *Not So Much a Programme, More a Way of Life*.

However, earlier that year, I find in my personal diary for 20 February that an actress at Oxford who was taking part in an undergraduate show, *Hang Down Your Head and Die*, told me that it was going to Stratford and then on to the West End: 'She concluded, "Not just a show, a way of life." '

This would suggest that the construction was in the air at that time, before the TV show took it up. In 1965, Peter Cook and Dudley Moore chose the loosely similar title *Not Only . . . But Also* for their BBC2 series. From BBC radio's *ROUND THE HORNE* (28 March 1965): 'This is the part of the show designed for trendy young moderns – the people who are not only but also, and indeed, scarcely.'

not suitable for those of a nervous disposition. This warning was used in the 1950s on British television – the announcer would say: 'The programme that follows is not suitable . . .' Curiously, the phrase lingers. A 1982 ad for the video of *Macabre* has 'WARNING. UNSUITABLE FOR THOSE OF A NERVOUS DISPOSITION.' Such phraseology, acting as a come-on, almost amounts to a slogan.

not the marrying sort. In Anthony Powell's autobiographical volume *Infants of the Spring* (1976), he writes of an entertainer called Varda that she 'had been married for a short time to a Greek surrealist painter, Jean Varda, a lively figure . . . but not the marrying sort'. It is not quite clear what is to be inferred from this. However, when Hugh Montefiore, an Anglican clergymen and later a bishop, wondered at a conference in Oxford (26 July 1967), 'Why did He not marry? Could the answer be that Jesus was not by nature the marrying sort?' – people were outraged at the suggestion that Christ might have been a homosexual.

Usually encountered in the negative sense, 'marrying sort' has nevertheless existed in its own right. From Shaw's *Pygmalion* (1916): (Prof. Higgins to Liza) 'All men are not confirmed old bachelors like me and the Colonel. Most men are the marrying sort (poor devils!).'

not tonight, Josephine. Napoleon Bonaparte did not, so far as we know, ever say the words which have become linked with him. The idea that he had better things to do than satisfy the Empress Josephine's famous appetite, or was not inclined or able to, must have grown up during the nineteenth century. There was a saying, attributed to Josephine, '*Bon-a-parte est Bon-à-rien*' [Bonaparte is good for nothing].

The catchphrase probably arose through music hall in Victorian times. A knockabout sketch filmed for the Pathé Library in *c* 1932 has Lupino Lane as Napoleon and Beatrice Lillie as Josephine. After signing a document of divorce (which Napoleon crumples up), Josephine says, 'When you are refreshed, comes as usual to my apartment.' Napoleon says (as the tag to the sketch), 'Not tonight, Josephine,' and she throws a custard pie in his face.

not very good detective, just lucky old Chinaman. A line from the 1930s American radio series *Charlie Chan*, about a Chinese detective (based on the character created by Earl Derr Biggers in *The House Without a Key*, 1925).

See also NUMBER ONE SON.

not with a bang but a whimper. This phrase is used to express an anticlimax and alludes to T.S. Eliot, *The Hollow Men* (1925): 'This is the way the world ends/Not with a bang but a whimper'. Frequently alluded to: from Richard Aldington, *The Colonel's Daughter* (1931): 'I wish you'd all shoot yourselves with a bang, instead of

continuing to whimper.' From *The Times* (16 December 1959): 'Here the world ends neither with a bang nor a whimper, but with a slow, resigned sigh at its own criminal imbecility.'

Not With a Bang was the title of an ITV series (1990), and the *Observer* (8 July 1990) reported: 'After some 70 hours Ernest Saunders finally left the Southwark witness box on Thursday afternoon not with a bang or whimper but more with a chorus of the familiar refrains which had echoed . . .'

not worth blacking up for! British show business expression for anything that is not worth the trouble – but especially an audience that is not worth performing in front of. According to *Roy Hudd's Book of Music-Hall, Variety and Showbiz Anecdotes* (1993), the phrase arose when Billy Bennett was on a variety bill preceding the West Indian entertainer 'Hutch'. As Bennett came off the stage at the end of his act, Hutch asked him what the audience was like. Bennett snorted: 'Not worth blacking up for.'

not you, Momma – siddown! See under HI, GANG!

now. See GO ~, PAY LATER.

now and forever. *Cats*, the longest-running musical in the West End, has used the promotional line since at least 1987. Three films have been made with this title: 1934, with Gary Cooper; 1956, with Janette Scott; and 1983, with Cheryl Ladd. Not having seen them, I take it that it was 'love' which was 'now and forever' in each case. Vera Lynn had a hit in 1954 with a song called this, translated from the German. Indeed, the phrase enshrines an idea common to other languages. Basques demanding that Eta should not keep up its terror campaign (March 1989) bore a banner with the words; '*Paz ahora y para*' [Peace now and forever].

The conjunction of words is an old one. Daniel Webster proclaimed: 'Liberty and union, now and forever, one and inseparable' (26 January 1830). '*Et nunc et semper*' at the end of the Gloria in religious services is sometimes translated as 'now and forever [world without end. Amen]' but also (as in the Anglican prayer book) 'now and ever shall be'.

no way, Jose. See under JOE BOB SAYS CHECK IT OUT.

no way!/way! See under WAYNE'S WORLD.

nowhere to go. See ALL DRESSED UP AND ~.

now is the time for all good men to come to the aid of the party. This typewriter exercise was possibly originated by Charles E. Weller, a court reporter in Milwaukee (1867) to test the efficiency of the first practical typewriter, which his friend, Christopher L. Scholes, had made. Unfortunately, he did not do a very good job because the phrase only contains 18 letters of the alphabet. **The quick brown fox jumps over the lazy dog,** on the other hand, has all 26. This was once thought to be the shortest sentence in English containing all the letters of the alphabet but it was superseded by: 'Pack my box with five dozen liquor jugs' (which is three letters shorter overall) and 'Quick blowing zephyrs vex daft Jim' (which is even shorter). Even more concise 'pangrams' have been devised but they are also shorter on sense and memorability.

now then, sir, Miss Bankhead. See WELL, NOW THEN . . .

now there's a beaut if ever there was one. A failed catchphrase is a contradiction in terms. If a catchphrase does not catch on it is not a catchphrase. Perhaps it should be called a 'drop phrase'. However, here are some phrases which were contrived so that they might take off but lacked some essential ingredient to help them do so. The prominence of Bob Monkhouse in this section is not significant – he just had the courage to remember more than others.

He remembered (1979): 'As a comedian in the early 1950s, I had one unique aspect. I was without a catchphrase. Radio producers sympathized and made suggestions. Charlie Chester even offered to give me one. "Every time you score a big laugh," he said, "just remember to dance a little jig and say: 'Now there's a beaut if ever

there was one!"' I tried it out on a *Variety Ahoy!* down at Portsmouth. I got a big laugh which I killed by suddenly shuffling inexplicably and shouting this catchphrase at the audience who were understandably baffled. So they stopped laughing at once. I politely declined and Charlie, never to waste comic material, repeated it in his next series until its persistent failure to please drove him to ad-lib another line, a plea for audience response – "Speak to Charlee-ee!" – which proved to be a genuine winner.' (Compare COME TO CHARLIE.)

Monkhouse also tried to launch **I said a subtle** when, for some reason a joke failed. And another trick that Denis Goodwin and he both used, if a gag really died, was to give a complicated explanation of the joke, ending with, 'That's what the joke means, **and I wish I was dead.**'

Later, at the time of his *Golden Shot* appearances on TV (see BERNIE, THE BOLT!), Monkhouse had the idea that a phrase like **hang on to your hollyhocks!** would work. 'During the warm-ups I would tell a joke "I'd been told not to tell" – Lady Chatterley is in bed with a light cold. Through the French windows comes Mellors the gamekeeper, his hands full of hollyhocks, freshly picked from the garden, to present to her ladyship. She says, "Thank you for the hollyhocks. And I would appreciate your attention for I have never been bed-ridden before." "Haven't you?" says Mellors. "Then hang on to your hollyhocks!" I could then place that phrase anywhere in the show with a hundred per cent certainty of getting a roar of laughter . . . and I waited and waited for the nation to be aware of this phrase. A year later I quietly dropped it . . .'

Ted Ray recalled two failed catchphrases from *RAY'S A LAUGH* in about 1950: **what about Rovers?** – as in the exchange, 'Unlucky? – what about Rovers?' 'Unlucky – you don't know you're born.' Also: **he's one of Nature's!** – as in Martha about Albert: 'Don't you insult my husband, he's one of Nature's . . .'

Peter Cook remembered (1979) that the exclamation **funny!** – delivered in a strangulated Dud and Pete voice between himself and Dudley in BBC2 TV's *Not Only . . . But Also* in the late 1960s – caught on with the performers if not with the public at large. I think he may underestimate the extent to which the pronunciation of the word *did* catch on. Later, Fozzy Bear had something similar in *The Muppet Show* (1976–81), pronouncing the word 'fun-neeee!'

Max Bygraves told me (1980) that in his 1979 TV series, 'I had Geoff Love keep walking on. He'd get a big laugh and I'd turn to the audience and say **You can't help loving him, can you?** It happened in the studio, but it didn't happen with the public.'

On the *GENERATION GAME* in the early 1970s, Bruce Forsyth tried **Tell me – who's to know?**, while Larry Grayson tried unsuccessfully to follow Forsyth's 'DIDN'T HE DO WELL?' with **what a lot you've got!**

now there's a coincidence. See under EE, WOT A GEEZER.

N(Q)OCD. Social typing phrase, for identifying the type of person who is 'Not (Quite) Our Class, Dear'. Probably only British middle-class use. Known by the 1950s?

NQTD. Social typing phrase, for identifying the type of person who is 'Not Quite Top Drawer' – i.e. a bit common. Probably only British middle-class use. Known by the 1950s?

NST. Social typing phrase, for identifying the type of man who is 'Not Safe in Taxis', i.e. a threat to women. Probably only British middle-class use. Known by the 1950s?

nth degree, to the. i.e. 'to any extent'. This derives from the mathematical use of 'n' to denote an indefinite *number*. From the *Sunday Express* (18 March 1928): 'In America the film-cutter is a man with a sub-editorial mind developed to the nth degree.'

nudge-nudge. See under MONTY PYTHON'S FLYING CIRCUS.

nudity. See FULL-FRONTAL.

nuff said! Short for 'nough said' and used when bringing a topic of discussion to a close on the grounds that there is no more to be said about it. The earliest recorded examples are from the US in the 1840s where also 'nuff ced', 'NC' and 'NS' are also found.

number. See I'M NOT A ∼ . . .

Number One. See PUBLIC ENEMY ∼.

number one son. This nickname for an eldest son, in imitation of Chinese speech, was popularized in the many American radio shows and films about Charlie Chan which featured an oriental detective (who had a large family), in the 1930s.

Number Ten. See BEER AND SANDWICHES AT ∼.

· O ·

Oates, 'Titus'. See I'M JUST GOING OUTSIDE . . .

oath, court. See I SWEAR . . .

oats. See SOW ONE'S WILD ∼.

obeyed. See SHE WHO MUST BE ∼.

obeying. See I WAS ONLY ∼ ORDERS.

object. See AND THE NEXT ∼.

odour. See BODY ∼.

ODEON. Slogan-acronym standing for 'Oscar Deutsch Entertains Our Nation'. Although the word 'Odeon' came to refer to any typical British cinema, it originally referred to those in a chain built by Oscar Deutsch and company in the 1930s. He had come across the word *odeion*, for amphitheatre, on a visit to Greece. It had already been taken up by the French as a word for 'concert hall' and thence into American English as part of 'nickelodeon' (first as a word for a coin-operated player piano, then for cinemas which charged a nickel). Later, someone suggested it could also be an acronym for 'Oscar Deutsch Entertains Our Nation'.

OE. Meaning, 'overseas experience' – the name given in New Zealand to the time spent working and travelling abroad by young people. First heard by me in 1981.

offer. See I'M GOING TO MAKE HIM AN ∼ . . .

offensive. See CHARM ∼.

office. See IN ∼ BUT NOT IN POWER; JACK IN ∼.

officer and a gentlemen. See CONDUCT UNBECOMING.

off one's trolley, to be. Meaning 'to be mad', *DOAS* finds this (in the US) by 1909 and calls it 'probably the oldest of the "off [one's] —" = crazy terms', but 'off one's head' and 'rocker' are a little older. *OED2* finds it by 1896.

An entertaining but coincidental derivation of the phrase comes from the days of the Acoustic Recording Machine (*c* 1910). The best effects were obtained not by the use of a volume control, but by physically adjusting the distance between the singer and the machine according to the noise the singer was making. A trolley was employed to effect this. If a singer flounced off from the arrangement, she was said to be 'off her trolley'.

off we go and the colour's pink! In 1980, Anthony Smith of Pinner, Middlesex queried the origin of this phrase which he said was used when restarting some social activity/topic of conversation/fresh round of drinks. Many years later, Donald Hickling of Northampton commented: 'I heard this catchphrase in "Metroland" (to the north of Pinner and slightly to the left) in a respectable hostelry one Saturday lunchtime when the host or master of ceremonies, a WW2 naval officer, was remembering how a liberal supply of pink gins kept him going, and he assumed that everyone in his company appreciated "pinkers". And, in the context of family sayings, I can quote the parent of a friend who was wont to exclaim, "Up she goes and her knickers are pink." Metroland again!'

off with his head – so much for Buckingham! The second of these two phrases was a wonderfully dismissive addition by the playwright Colley Cibber to his 1700 edition of Shakespeare's *Richard III*. The extension of Shakespeare's simple 'Off with his head' proved a popular and lasting emendation. In 'Private Theatres' (1835), one of the *Sketches by Boz*, Charles Dickens describes the roles on offer to amateur actors who at that time could pay to take certain roles in plays: 'For instance, the Duke of Glo'ster is well worth two pounds . . . including the "off with his head!" – which is sure to bring down the applause, and it is very easy to do – "Orf with his ed" (very quick and loud; – then slow and sneeringly) – "So much for Bu-u-u-uckingham!" Lay the emphasis on the "uck;" get yourself gradually into a corner, and work with your right hand, while you're saying it, as if you were feeling your way, and it's sure to do.'

The extra phrase was also included in Laurence Olivier's film of Shakespeare's play (UK, 1955). The simple 'Off with his head!', as an abrupt command, has probably been more associated latterly with the Queen of Hearts in Lewis Carroll's *Alice's Adventures in Wonderland* (1865).

often a bridesmaid, but never a bride. Slogan for Listerine mouthwash, in the US, from *c* 1923. One of the best known lines in advertising, written by Milton Feasley, though there is an echo of the British music-hall song 'Why Am I Always the Bridesmaid?' made famous by Lily Morris (1917).

— of the century. Promotional cliché. There was a British TV quiz called *Sale of the Century* (1970s/80s). The 1981 Royal nuptials were dubbed by *Time* 'the wedding of the century'. I even wrote a book called *Sayings of the Century* (1984). But, going back, one finds two films, both called *Crime of the Century*, in 1933 and 1946. The Australian film *Robbery Under Arms* (1907) was promoted on a Melbourne poster as 'The Picture of the Century'. The Empire Hotel, Bath (opened 1901) had lavatory bowls with the slogan 'The Closet of the Century' written around the rim. And, in the previous century, a review of Amanda M. Ros's novel *Irene Iddesleigh* in the magazine *Black and White* (19 February 1898) was headed 'The Book of the Century'. The *San Francisco Examiner* (13 April 1895) described the murder of two pretty girls by a Sunday school superintendent as 'THE CRIME OF A CENTURY'. This last points to a likely American origin for the format.

oggi, oggi, oggi/oi, oi, oi! I first encountered this as a chant at Rugby Union matches in the late 1970s. It was also featured in the routines of the Welsh comedian (and rugby enthusiast) Max Boyce about the same time.

Its use may be much broader than this, especially among children. In 1986, I heard of a Thames River police inspector who believed that the shout (as used by children) was similar to that used by watermen to warn their thieving mates of approaching police.

A correspondent suggests that it could also be related to the Cornish 'oggy' or 'oggie' or 'tiddy-oggie', nicknames for a pasty. Partridge/*Slang* has this nickname and adds that 'Oggy-land' is a name for Cornwall itself. Another correspondent, also from Cornwall, states that 'oggi-oggi-oggi' was long a rallying cry in those parts before being taken up in Wales and elsewhere.

The chant familiar from demos against the Thatcher Government, 'Maggie-Maggie-Maggie, Out-Out-Out!', clearly derives from it.

oh arr . . . A non-commital response to something said that is considered unlikely or preposterous or dubious. It sounds like an imitation of a country yokel determinedly unimpressed by what he has been told. I first heard it from my wife (yes!) in the 1980s. This is possibly an example: from P.G. Wodehouse, *Summer Lightning*, Chap. 18 (1929): ' "Ronald has just announced his intention of marrying a chorus-girl." "Oh, ah?" said Lord Emsworth.'

Compare **I hear you**, a Scots expression meaning that a remark is not worth considering or is untrue or is certainly not going to be responded to – used by Lord Reith to fob off suggestions by Malcom Muggeridge in the BBC TV programme *Lord Reith Looks Back* (1967).

oh, calamity! The comic actor Robertson Hare (1891–1979) used to exclaim this. It came from an Aldwych farce of long ago – perhaps one in which the put-upon little man had to lose his trousers – but even he was unable to recall which. His other characteristic utterance was **indubitably!** He called his autobiography *Yours Indubitably*. In *Up In the Clouds, Gentlemen, Please* (1980), John Mills relates an occasion when Hare had to utter the word – and jump in the air – in the play *Aren't Men Beasts* (1936). Unfortunately, as he did so, Hare let out 'one of the loudest and most spectacular farts it has ever been my pleasure to hear'.

oh! Calcutta! The title of Kenneth Tynan's sexually explicit stage revue (Broadway, 1969) derives from a curious piece of word play, being the equivalent of the French 'Oh, *quel cul t'as*' [Oh, what a lovely bum you've got]. French *cul* is derived from the Latin *culus* 'buttocks' but, according to the context, may be applied to the female vagina or male anus. In her *Life of Kenneth Tynan* (1987), Kathleen Tynan states that she was writing an article on the surrealist painter Clovis Trouille, one of whose works was a naked odalisque lying on her side to reveal a spherical backside. The title was 'Oh! Calcutta! Calcutta!': 'I suggested to Ken that he call his erotic revue *Oh! Calcutta!* . . . I did not know at the time that it had the further advantage of being a French pun.'

oh, get in there, Moreton! See under *EDUCATING ARCHIE*.

oh, good show! See JOLLY GOOD SHOW!

oh, hello, I'm Julian . . . See under *ROUND THE HORNE*.

oh, I say, I am a fool! See under *MUCH BINDING IN THE MARSH*.

oh, I say, I rather care for that! Hahaha-haa-ha! In the BBC radio comedy show *Waterlogged Spa* (from 1946), Humphrey Lestocq played Flying Officer Kite, an ex-RAF officer, complete with handlebar moustache and varsity accent. Lestocq recalled (1980): 'When the show started, I'd just left the RAF. I was madly air-force – "Whacko!" "Good-o!" "Bang-on!" . . . all that sort of thing – and this really fascinated Eric Barker [the writer and

star of the show]. So he went away and found this character for me.'
After many a 'Wizard prang!' Barker would slap Kite down in some way, but Kite would only roar: 'Oh, I say, I rather care for that, hahaha-haa-ha!' The producer, Leslie Bridgmont, once commented: 'When we introduced the character we worked out this pay-off very carefully . . . the rhythm of the laugh, for instance, had to be exactly the same each time. It is this inexorable sameness that establishes a phrase.'

oh, I was livid – livid I was . . . ! See under *EDUCATING ARCHIE*.

oh, jolly D! See under *MUCH BINDING IN THE MARSH*.

oh, Moses! Pauline Devaney and Edwin Apps who scripted the late 1960s BBC TV comedy series about clerical folk, *All Gas and Gaiters*, remembered (in 1979): 'Derek Nimmo who played Noot, the Bishop's chaplain, was always asking for a catchphrase and we always resisted the suggestion until one day a neighbour who a pillar of the church, discussing something over the garden wall, said "Moses!" and we wrote it into the script. Derek leapt on it and thereafter used it with such frequency that we eventually got a notice to the effect that it was time the writers stopped putting in "Moses" whenever they couldn't think of anything funny!' Usually remembered as 'Oh, Moses!', I think.

oh, my Sunday helmet! Brian Reece (1913–62) played a somewhat silly-ass police constable in the BBC radio series *PC 49* (from 1946). The constable's name was Archibald Berkeley Willoughby and his exclamation was 'Oh, my Sunday helmet!', as also in the film *A Case for PC 49* (1951). Reece appears to have died at the age of 49, too.

oh no, there isn't! In British pantomime, there is always a scene in which an actor speaks to the audience with his back to someone or something which he denies exists. The following kind of ritual exchange then takes place: 'There isn't a bear behind me, is there, children?' Audience: **'oh yes, there is!'** There will also be cries of **'behind you!'** (The phrase 'Oh, no there isn't!' was also used as bill matter by the Two Pirates variety act.)

There is the story of a curtain speech by the manager of a provincial theatre halfway through a panto: 'I'm very sorry, ladies and gentlemen, but we cannot continue the performance as our leading lady has just died.' Children in the audience: 'Oh, no, she hasn't!'

oh, Ron/Yes, Eth? See under TAKE IT FROM HERE.

oh yes, there is! See OH NO, THERE ISN'T!

oh, you kid! See I LOVE MY WIFE BUT ∼.

oi! The British comedian Bud Flanagan (1896–1968) had a way of rounding off a joke or explanation in his routines with Chesney Allen by saying, 'Oi!' Or if he fluffed a line or committed a malapropism, he would at last correct himself with Allen's help, shout, 'Oi!', and the orchestra would repeat it. Used as the title of a biographical show about Flanagan and Allen on the London stage in 1982. The phrase was also used by Lupino Lane.

oi, oi, oi. See OGGI . . .

oil for the lamps of China. An old expression said about anything won or received as a windfall. Other similar expressions include **corn in Egypt** and the proverbial (by 1830) **little fish are sweet**, said particularly about receiving a small something. *Oil for the Lamps of China* was the title of a novel by Alice Tisdale Hobart (1933; film US, 1935) about an American oil man out East.

OK. See — RULES ∼.

OK! The origin of this expression has occasioned more debate than any other in this dictionary. Here are some of the suggested origins, though one probably need go no further than explanations (1) and (2).

(1) President Andrew Jackson (*d* 1837), when a court clerk in Tennessee, would mark 'OK' on legal documents as an

abbreviation for the illiterate 'Oll Korrect'. The first recorded use in the US of this jocular form is in the Boston *Morning Post* (23 March 1839).

(2) It was used by President Martin van Buren as an election slogan in 1840. The initials stood for 'Old Kinderhook', his nickname, which derived from his birthplace in New York State.

(3) Inspectors who weighed and graded bales of cotton as they were delivered to Mississippi river ports for shipment would write *aux quais* on any found faulty (i.e. this meant they were not OK and had to be sent back to the jetty).

(4) It comes from Aux Cayes, a port in Haiti famous for its rum.
(5) It is an anglicization of the word for 'good' in Ewe or Wolof, the West African language spoken by many of the slaves taken to the Southern US.

(6) It derives from the Greek words *ola kala* meaning 'all is fine; everything is good'.

(7) In the First World War, soldiers would report each night the number of deaths in their group. 'OK' stood for 'O killed'.

(8) A railroad freight agent, Obadiah Kelly, used his initials on bills of lading.

(9) An Indian chief, Old Keokuk, used his initials on treaties.

(10) It stood for 'outer keel' when shipbuilders chalked it on timbers.

(11) Teachers used it instead of *omnes korrectes* on perfect exam papers.

(12) From boxes of Orrins-Kendall crackers, popular with Union troops in the Civil War.

(13) From an English word 'hoacky', meaning 'the last load of a harvest'.

(14) From a Finnish word *oikea* meaning 'correct'.

(15) From a Choctaw word *okeh* [it is] or *hoke*.

See also IF IT'S H-H-HOKAY WITH YOU . . .; OK, YAH!

okey-pokey/hokey-pokey. The name of imitation ice cream made from shaved ice mixed with syrup was current by 1900. Perhaps it was thought that the imitation was a form of hocus-pocus or trickery, or else it could have been a corruption of '*ecce, ecce!*', the cry with which Italian street vendors would call attention to their wares. Iona and Peter Opie in *The Lore and Language of Schoolchildren* (1959) wonder whether it could derive from Italian '*O che poco!*' [O how little!] though why anyone should say that they do not explain.

OK, yah! An agreeing noise characteristic of the – especially female – SLOANE RANGER and remarked upon in the mid-1980s. The London *Evening Standard* wrote of the show *The Sloane Ranger Revue* at the Duchess Theatre, 'OK Yah, that's BRILL!' (quoted in *Harpers & Queen*, January 1986).

Ol' Blue Eyes. A (rather commercial rather than natural) sobriquet of the American popular singer, Frank Sinatra (*b* 1915). In his twenties, he was a teenage idol. His slight, boyish appearance gave him the first of several nicknames – **Bones**. Next, in the 1940s, he became known as the **Voice**. As he prospered – and perhaps because of his alleged underworld connections – he became known as the **Chairman of the Board** or the **Gov'nor**. After a temporary retirement in the 1970s, he returned touting the slogan 'Ol' Blue Eyes is back'.

old. See SOMETHING ∼ . . .

old as my tongue and a little older than my teeth, as. This is what nannies (and other older folk) traditionally reply when asked how old they are by young NOSEY PARKERS. Jonathan Swift has it in *Polite Conversation* (1738).

Old Bill. A nickname for the police (and in particular, the Metropolitan Police of London). So many policemen wore walrus moustaches after the First World War that

they reminded people of Bruce Bairnsfather's cartoon character 'Old Bill'. He was the one who said: 'IF YOU KNOW A BETTER 'OLE – GO TO IT'. Partridge/*Slang*, which provides this explanation, also wonders whether there might be some connection with the US song 'Won't You Come Home, Bill Bailey' (*c* 1902) or with the Old Bailey courts. 'The Bill' is an abbreviation of the name and was used as the title of an ITV cops series (from *c* 1990).

old boy net(work), the. British term for the informal system of support given to one another by men who once attended the same school. Not recorded before the 1950s but said to have been known in the Second World War, where the 'old boy *net*' referred to use of the wireless 'net' to organize military support from old friends and colleagues. Here the meaning of 'old boy' seems to move away from that of 'former schoolboy' to anyone you might address using the words, 'I say, old boy . . .'

From Claud Cockburn, *In Time of Trouble* (1956): 'My father . . . knew quite enough about the working of what is nowadays called "The Old Boy Net" to realize that as things now stood he had considerably less chance of entering the Indian Civil Service than he did of entering the Church of England and becoming a Bishop.'

Old Contemptibles, the. This nickname was gladly taken unto themselves by First World War veterans of the British Expeditionary Force who crossed the English Channel in 1914 to join the French and Belgians against the German advance. It was alleged that Kaiser Wilhelm II had described the army as 'a contemptibly little army' (referring to its size rather than its quality). The British press was then said to have mistranslated this so that it made him appear to have called them a 'contemptible little army'. The truth is that the whole episode was a propaganda ploy masterminded by the British.

older. See YOU KNOW YOU'RE GETTING ∼ . . .

Old Grey Whistle Test, The. The title of this BBC TV pop music series (from the 1970s) came from the alleged practice in TIN

PAN ALLEY of trying new pop songs out on the elderly grey-haired doormen. If they could pick up the tune to the extent of being able to whistle it, the song stood a chance.

Old Groaner, the. Sobriquet of Harry Lillie Crosby (1904–77), better known by his other nickname **Bing** or (in German) **Der Bingle**. Oddly, he had rather a smooth, low voice rather than a groaning one (Sinatra had that sort). As one of the first crooners, however, inevitably the name stuck.

Old Hundred(th), the. Name given to the tune of the hymn 'All people that on earth do dwell' (words written by William Kethe and first appearing in the Geneva Psalter, 1561) because it is a setting of Psalm 100. In the 1696 Psalter, the name was given to the tune to indicate that the earlier version was being retained.

old lady from Dubuque. See LITTLE ~.

old man. See YOU'VE MADE AN ~ VERY HAPPY.

old ones, new ones, loved ones, neglected ones . . . See under HELLO, EVERYONE!

old school tie, the. A symbol of the clannishness and loyalties involving those who attended British Public Schools (i.e. private schools). One of the features of 'old boys'' associations is that they sell ties which make the affiliation of the wearer immediately apparent to others of the same background. An early use of the phrase was by Rudyard Kipling in *Limits & Renewals* (1932).

Often used in a critical sense, hence the more recent expression **strangled by the old school tie.** From *The Times* (27 September 1986): '[Trevor Howard] broke new ground, away from the English studio stereotypes of silly-ass eccentrics or decent but wooden chaps strangled by a combination of old school tie and stiff upper lip.' A key use of the term appeared in the politician Norman Tebbit's autobiography, as quoted in the *Independent* (14 October 1988): 'Some thought my

willingness to stand toe-to-toe against the more thuggish elements of the Labour Party and slug it out blow for blow rather vulgar. Others, especially in the country at large, seemed delighted at the idea of a Tory MP unwilling to be strangled by the old school tie . . .'

Old Slow Hand. Nickname of Eric Clapton, the British rock guitarist (*b* 1945) – either because of his distinctive way of producing a twangy guitar sound or from the expression 'a slow hand-clap'.

Old Sod, the. A term for Ireland, more usually spelt 'ould', to represent the Irish pronunciation. 'Sod' here means a piece of earth to which natives will return and is presumably so used because of the close identification between Ireland, green grass and turf. Recorded by 1812.

old soldiers never die, they simply fade away. A notable use of this saying was made by General Douglas MacArthur when, following his dismissal by President Truman, he was allowed to address Congress on 19 April 1951. He ended: 'I still remember the refrain of one of the most popular barrack ballads of that day [turn of the century], which proclaimed, most proudly, that "Old soldiers never die. They just fade away." And like the old soldier of that ballad. I now close my military career and just fade away . . .'

The origins of the ballad he quoted lie in a British army parody of the gospel hymn 'Kind Words Can Never Die' which (never mind MacArthur's dating) came out of the First World War. J. Foley copyrighted a version of the parody in 1920.

The format has appealed to many jokers over the years. From the early 1980s come these examples: 'Old soldiers never die, just their privates'; 'Old professors . . . just lose their faculties'; 'Old golfers . . . just lose their balls'; 'Old fishermen never die, they just smell that way'.

old Spanish customs. The phrase refers to practices which are of long standing but are unauthorized. Although the journal *Notes and Queries* was vainly seeking the origin of the phrase in 1932, the term came to prominence in the 1980s to describe the irregular behaviour of British newspaper production workers in Fleet Street (cheating over pay-packets, especially). From Simon Jenkins, *Newspapers: The Power and the Money* (1979): 'The biggest internal cost is production wages . . . embroidered round with "old Spanish customs", which was regarded as virtually outside management control.' I would say the use was mainly British, though this does not explain how Groucho Marx came to make the pun 'old Spinach customs' in *Animal Crackers* (1930).

Why the Spanish are blamed is not clear, except that Spaniards tend to attract pejoratives – not least with regard to working practices (the *mañana* attitude). In Elizabethan times, William Cecil is quoted as saying of Sir Thomas Tresham, architect of Rushton Triangular Lodge, that he was not given to **Spanish practices** (i.e. Roman Catholic ones). In 1584, also, Lord Walsingham referred to 'Spanish practices' in a way that meant they were 'deceitful, perfidious and treacherous'. This could provide us with an origin for the modern phrase. Indeed, latterly (late 1980s), the two have been used interchangeably in the newspaper context.

Old Vic, the. When the Royal Coburg theatre, south of the River Thames in London, was redecorated in 1833, it was renamed the Victoria and was popularly referred to as the 'Vic' by 1858. In time it became known as 'the Old Vic'. In 1914, Lilian Baylis formed the Old Vic Shakespeare Company to perform in the theatre and between then and 1963 when the company was disbanded, the phrase 'the Old Vic' was applied rather more to the distinguished theatrical organization than to the building itself. Subsequently the building has housed the National Theatre and then other companies.

omelette. See YOU CAN'T MAKE AN ~ . . .

omnibus. See MAN ON THE CLAPHAM ~ .

omnium gatherum. A mock Latin term for a gathering of all sorts, a miscellaneous jumble, a mixture. Recorded by 1530. In the novels of Anthony Trollope there is a character called the Duke of Omnium who lives in Gatherum Castle.

on a scale of one to ten. A popular system of rating things – also used allusively, e.g 'a ten', 'a two'. In the introduction to the song 'Tits and Ass' in the musical *Chorus Line* (1975), a character says (of an audition), 'On a scale of ten, he gave me . . .' In a West Coast party scene in the film *Annie Hall* (1977), a character says of a woman, 'She's a ten,' indicating that she is his ideal. This usage was further popularized by the film *10* (1979) in which the sexual allure or performance of the hero's girlfriends was so rated. Some people still use it. *The Naff Sex Guide* (1984) quoted an unidentified celebrity as having said: 'On a scale of one to ten I'd give him a two, but that's only because I've never met a one.'

An ad in the *New York Times* (26 March 1989) quoted Gary Franklin of KABC-TV as rating the film *Heathers*, 'A 10! Absolutely brilliant, a remarkable film.'

Perhaps the usage derives from the Richter scale of measuring the severity of earthquakes (1 to 10), named after Charles F. Richter who began devising the scale in 1932, or simply from the old school habit of marking things out of ten. 'Ten' also equals intercourse on the schoolboy/girl petting scale.

on behalf of the committ-ee! See under GIVE ORDER!

on behalf of the working classes . . . At first this was a phrase used literally by people purporting to represent the case of this sector of society; Robert Owen, the social reformer, used the title *Two Memorials on behalf of the Working Classes* in 1816.

The phrase later became the bill matter of the British music-hall comedian Billy Russell (1893–1971).

once. See I'LL TRY ANYTHING ~ .

once a — always a —. This format derives from an old series of proverbs, 'Once a knave/whore/captain, always a . . .' S.T. Coleridge wrote an article with the title *Once a Jacobin Always a Jacobin* (21 October

1802). William Cobbett quoted 'once a parson always a parson' in his *Rural Rides* (for 11 October 1826). Charles Dickens in *Little Dorrit*, Chap. 28 (1857) has, 'Once a gentleman, and always a gentleman.' Mary O'Malley wrote a play called *Once a Catholic* (1971) and this specific example appears in full in Angus Wilson's novel *The Wrong Set* (1949).

Partridge/*Slang* finds more recently, 'Once a teacher/policeman . . .' To which I would add, 'Once a Marine, always a Marine' from the US (current in 1987) and the joke (which I first noted in 1967): 'Once a knight, always a knight – and **twice a night, you're doing all right!**' Partridge/ *Catch Phrases*, however, finishes the joke off: '. . . twice a night, dead at forty' and dates it *c* 1950 'but probably from at least fifty years earlier'.

once aboard the lugger and the girl is mine! 'A male catchphrase either joyously or derisively jocular' notes Partridge/*Catch Phrases*. It came originally from a late Victorian melodrama – either My *Jack and Dorothy* by Ben Landeck (*c* 1890) or from a passage in *The Gypsy Farmer* by John Benn Johnstone (*d* 1891) – 'I want you to assist me in forcing her aboard the lugger; once there, I'll frighten her into marriage.' In 1908, A.S.M. Hutchinson called a novel *Once Aboard the Lugger – the History of George and Mary*. The phrase occurs in the music-hall song 'On the Good Ship Yacki-Hicki-Doo-La', written and composed by Billy Merson in 1918. Benham (1948) has a different version, as often. According to him: 'Once aboard the lugger and all is well' was said to have been an actor's gag in *Black Eyed Susan*, a nautical melodrama (*c* 1830).

once again we stop the mighty roar . . . See under IN TOWN TONIGHT.

once in a blue moon. Meaning 'very rarely, if ever', the notion of a 'blue moon' being something you *never* saw and could not believe in, was current by 1528. However, given that in some circumstances the moon can appear blue, this less stringent expression had established itself by 1821. Also, a blue moon is the second full moon within a given month (something

that happens about once every two years – but still, obviously, a rare event).

once upon a time . . . 'Never, in all my childhood, did any one address to me the affecting preamble, "Once upon a time!" ' wrote Edmund Gosse in *Father and Son*, 1907. Poor deprived thing. The traditional start to 'fairy' stories has existed as a phrase for a very long time. George Peele has the line in his play *The Old Wives' Tale* (1595). The Old Woman begins a story she is telling with, 'Once upon a time there was a King, or a Lord, or a Duke . . .' – which suggests that it was a 'formula' phrase even then. No less than 13 of the 24 *Classic Fairy Tales* collected in their earliest English versions by Iona and Peter Opie (1974) begin with the words. Mostly the versions are translations from the French of Charles Perrault's collected *Histories, or Tales of Past Times* (1697). The ready-made English phrase is used to translate his almost invariable, '*Il estoit une fois.*' 'There was once upon a time a King and a Queen . . .'; 'Once upon a time, and be sure 'twas a long time ago . . .'; 'Once upon a time, and twice upon a time . . .'; 'Once upon a time, and a very good time it was . . .' – all these variants hark back to a mythical past. The Opies comment that fairy stories, 'are the space fiction of the past. They describe events that took place when a different range of possibilities operated in the unidentified long ago; and this is part of their attraction . . . The stories would, curiously, not be so believable if the period in which they took place was specified.'

The Nelson *English Idioms* (*c* 1912) calls it 'a somewhat old-fashioned and pedantic phrase used to introduce an incident or story which took place at some indefinite time in the past'.

one. See ALL FOR ~ . . . ; AT ~ WITH THE UNIVERSE; BIG ~ ; IS HE ~ OF US?; JUST ~ OF THOSE THINGS; SEEN ~ SEEN 'EM ALL; TAKES ~ TO KNOW ~ .

one and only, the. Might be used as a promotional phrase about anything or anyone, but Phyllis Dixey, the noted British striptease artist of the 1940s, was billed as 'The One and Only', as was Max Miller, the comedian. The Gershwins wrote a song

'My One and Only' for *Funny Face* (1927).

one-armed paperhanger. See under AS BUSY AS . . .

one day all this will be yours, my son. I'm not sure where this cliché began. It is, of course, spoken by a proud father gesturing proprietorially over his property. The only examples I have are recent adaptations of the formula: 'One day my son all this might *not* be yours' (headline to Albany Life assurance advertisement, December 1981); 'One day, my boy, all this *won't* be yours' (headline to National Provident life assurance ad, the same month); 'One day, my son, all this will be yours – but not just yet' (Glenmorangie whisky ad, December 1982).

Paul Beale drew my attention to this passage from Rudyard Kipling's story 'The Brushwood Boy' (1895): ' "Perfect! By Jove, it's perfect!" Georgie was looking at the round-bosomed woods beyond the home paddock, where the white pheasant-boxes were ranged . . . Georgie felt his father's arm tighten in his.

' "It's not half bad – but *hodie mihi, eras tibi* [what's mine today will be yours], isn't it? I suppose you'll be turning up some day with a girl under your arm . . ." '

one foot in the grave, to have. Meaning 'to be near death', the earliest citation in the *OED2* is from Burton's *Anatomy of Melancholy* (1621): 'An old acherontic dizzard that hath one foot in his grave.' The idea is older, however, and occurs in Barclay's *Ship of Fools* (1509) and the precise phrase is in J. Case, *Praise of Music* (1586). Swift in *Gulliver's Travels* (1726) uses the phrase in connection with the immortal Struldbruggs of Laputa. There is also a punning inscription upon the grave of the actor and dramatist, Samuel Foote (d 1777), in Westminster Abbey:

Here lies one Foote, whose death may
    thousands save,
For death has now one foot within the
    grave.

David Renwick wrote a BBC TV comedy series *One Foot in the Grave* (1993–) about a man having to endure premature retirement (see I DON'T BELIEVE IT!).

one for the money. See IT'S A-ONE . . .

one instinctively knows when something is right. A line from advertisements (current in the UK, 1982) for Croft Original Port. It has had some afterlife elsewhere.

one-legged cat. See under AS BUSY AS . . .

one man, one vote. A slogan first coined in the nineteenth century for a campaign led by Major John Cartwright (1740–1824), a radical MP ('the Father of Reform'), in the fight against plural voting. It was possible in those days for a man to cast two votes, one on the basis of residence and the other by virtue of business or university qualifications. This right was not abolished until 1948. The phrase arose again during the period of the (illegal) Unilateral Declaration of Independence in Rhodesia (1965–80) to indicate a basic condition required by the British government before the breakaway could be legitimized. The phrase has also been used in the US, in civil rights contexts.

In 1993, when the British Labour Party was trying to overthrow the 'block votes' that gave its trade union membership a disproportionate say in the formulation of policy, the phrase was rendered by the acronym **OMOV**.

one o'clock. See LIKE ∼ HALF STRUCK.

one of these days . . . one of these days! See under AND AWA-A-AAY WE GO!

one of our aircraft is missing. The title of a film (UK, 1941). In *A Life in Movies* (1986), Michael Powell writes of a moment in the Second World War: 'After I returned from Canada and I had time to listen to the nine o'clock news on the BBC, I had become fascinated by a phrase which occurred only too often: "One of our aircraft failed to return." ' He determined to make a film about such a failed bombing mission. 'Our screenplay, which was half-finished, was entitled *One of Our Aircraft is Missing*. We were never too proud to take a tip from distributors, and we saw that the original title, *One of Our Aircraft Failed to Return*, although evocative and euphonious, was downbeat.' In 1975, Walt Disney came up with a film called *One of Our Dinosaurs is Missing*.

one over the eight. This expression for 'drunk' is services' slang, but not before the twentieth century. For some reason, eight beers was considered to be a reasonable and safe amount for an average man to drink. One more and you were incapable.

one small step for —, one giant leap for —. What Neil Armstrong claimed he said when stepping on to the moon's surface for the first time on 20 July 1969 was 'That's one small step for a man, one giant leap for mankind'. The indefinite article before 'man' was, however, completely inaudible, thus ruining the sense.

Many reference books have been thrown into confusion since. Several follow the version – 'One small step for [. . .] man, one big step for mankind' (*sic*) – which appeared in the magazine *Nature* in 1974. The *Observer* 'Sayings of the Week' column in the week after the landing had, 'That's one small step for [. . .] man, one giant leap for all [*sic*] mankind.'

Either way, Armstrong launched an imperishable format: 'SMALL STEP FOR NON-WHITE MANKIND' (*The Times*, 29 October 1983); 'UP TO 10.75% – ONE SMALL STEP FOR YOUR MONEY, ONE GIANT LEAP FOR YOUR INTEREST RATE. You'll be over the moon to discover you only need £1,000 to open a Capital Choice account at the Alliance & Leicester' (advertisement, July 1989); 'A SMALL STEP FOR MAN; A GIANT LEAP FOR PLASTIC FROGS' (*Independent*, 9 May 1992).

The correct version has even been set to music. I have heard the Great Mormon Tabernacle Choir sing: 'One small step for a man, one giant leap for mankind -/It shows what a man can do, if he has the will.'

one step forward two steps back. In 1904, Lenin wrote a book about 'the crisis within our party' under this title [*Shag vpered dva shaga nazad*], but note that in *Conducted Tour* (1981), Bernard Levin refers to Lenin's 'pamphlet' under the title *Four Steps Forward, Three Steps Back*. Vilmos Voigt pointed out in *Proverbium Yearbook of*

International Proverb Scholarship (1984) that just after the publication of his work, Lenin referred to the 'current German form, *Ein Schritt vorwärts, zwei Schritte zurück* [one step forwards, two steps back]', and Voigt wondered what precisely the source of Lenin's phrase was and in what language it had been.

I once regularly used to interview an expert on Portugal (in the early 1970s) who invariably made use of this phrase to describe the Caetano regime and its moves, such as they were, towards any form of liberalization. From Russell Grant, the astrologer, in the *Chiswick and Brent Gazette* (22 September 1983): 'GEMINI. It's been a one-step-forward-two-steps-backwards time.'

Variations occur, of course. From *Cosmopolitan* (February 1987): 'Alternatively, try retro-dressing. It's here again. One step forward, thirty years back. The Fifties look is determined to make a comeback . . .'

onlooker sees more/most of the game, the. A little-recorded proverb, expressing the view that when you are in the thick of something you don't get the whole picture. From *Macmillan's Magazine* (November 1884): 'It is the onlooker that sees most of the game.'

only. See ONE AND ∼ .

only fools and horses work. The BBC TV comedy series with the title *Only Fools and Horses*, written by John Sullivan, has been on the air since 1981 and concerns itself with a pair of 'wide boy' brothers sparring together in London. The title must have puzzled many people. Although unrecorded in reference books, it apparently comes from an old Cockney expression, 'Only fools and horses *work*.' Compare 'Only fools and fiddlers sing at meals,' known by 1813.

only her hairdresser knows for sure. See under DOES SHE . . . OR DOESN'T SHE?

only in America . . . ! Used as the title of a TV series in 1980, this exclamation means 'Only in America is this possible'. Leo Rosten in *Hooray for Yiddish!* (1982) writes:

'Not a week passed during my boyhood (or two weeks, since then) without my hearing this exclamation. It is the immigrants' testament, an affirmation of the opportunities imbedded in that Promised Land . . . America. Scarcely a new shop, new product, a new journal or school or fad could appear without ecstatic *Only in America!s*.'

only in the mating season. See under GOON SHOW.

only the names have been changed to . . . See under DRAGNET.

only time will tell. A cliché especially of broadcast news journalism and used by reporters to round off a story when they can't think of anything else to say. *Time* (March 1984) quoted Edwin Newman, a former NBC-TV correspondent, on a continuing weakness of TV news: 'There are too many correspondents standing outside buildings and saying, "Time will tell."' (Indeed, the 'only' is often omitted.) The proverbial expression has existed since 1539.

only when I larf. Used (with this spelling) as the title of novel (1968; film UK, 1968) by Len Deighton. As *Only When I Laugh* it was the title of an ITV comedy series (1979–84), set in a hospital, and of a film (US, 1981) which was released in the UK as *It Hurts Only When I Laugh* – which points to its origin. There is an old joke about an English soldier in Africa who gets pinned to a tree by an assegai. When asked if it hurts, he replies with this stiff-upper-lip statement.

on one's tod, to be. Meaning 'to be on one's own', this expression derives from rhyming slang: Tod Sloan was a noted US jockey (d 1933). The expression was recorded by 1934.

on song. On top form or in top condition. Although recorded in 1971, this phrase suddenly had a vogue in the 1980s especially among sports commentators and journalists. From the *Daily Telegraph* (2 April 1986): 'Once the turbo [of a Saab Turbo] is "on song", the power comes in

with a blood-tingling rush and catapult acceleration.'

The origin of the phrase would seem to lie in birdsong. Compare, therefore, the line 'then she went *off* song' in the music-hall song 'She Was One of the Early Birds' (c 1900).

on the con-positively-trary! See SOMEBODY BAWL FOR BEULAH?

on the nail. Promptly, when asked – usually of the making of a payment. Known by the 1590s. The port of Bristol is often given as the source for this saying. Outside the Corn Exchange there, merchants are said to have placed cash on flat-topped pillars (known as 'nails') to settle bargains. The *OED2*, however, points out that the explanations linking the phrase to exchanges at Bristol (and Limerick) are 'too late to be of any authority in deciding the question'. In fact, the phrase *may* have more to do with 'fingernail', as in the French expression *sur l'ongle*, 'precisely, exactly'.

onwards and upwards! Perhaps this humorously uplifting phrase, designed to encourage, derives from a religious notion of striving onwards and upwards through the everlasting night? In James Russell Lowell's *The Present Crisis* (1844) we find: 'They must upward still, and onward, who would keep abreast of truth.' The first lines of the nineteenth-century hymn 'Onward! Upward!' (words by F.J. Crosby, music by Ira D. Sankey) are:

Onward! upward! Christian soldier.
Turn not back nor sheath thy sword;
Let its blade be sharp for conquest
In the battle for the Lord.

Sankey also set the words of Albert Midlane in 'Onward, Upward, Homeward!', of which the refrain is:

Onward to the glory!
Upward to the prize!
Homeward to the mansions
Far above the skies!

Or could the words be from a motto? The Davies-Colley family of Newfold, Cheshire, have them as such in the form 'Upwards and Onwards'. 'Nicholas Craig' in *I, An Actor* (1988) asks of young actors: 'Will you be able to learn the language of the profession and say things like "onwards and upwards", "Oh well, we survive" and "Never stops, love, he *never stops*".'

'Onwards and upwards' as such was recorded by 1901.

on with the motley! Partridge/*Catch Phrases* suggests that this is what one says to start a party or trip to the theatre. It may also mean 'on with the show, in spite of what has happened'. Either way, the allusion is to the Clown's cry – '*vesti la giubba*' – in Leoncavallo's opera *I Pagliacci* (1892). The Clown has to 'carry on with the show' despite having a broken heart. So it might be said jokingly nowadays by anyone who is having to proceed with something in spite of difficulties. The English translation was undoubtedly popularized by Enrico Caruso's 1902 gramophone recording of the song (the first million-selling disc to be made).

Laurence Olivier used the phrase in something like its original context when describing a sudden return dash home from Ceylon during a crisis in his marriage to Vivien Leigh: 'I got myself on to a plane . . . and was in Paris on the Saturday afternoon. I went straight on home the next day as I had music sessions for *The Beggar's Opera* from the Monday; and so, on with the motley' (*Confessions of an Actor*, 1982).

'*Giubba*' in Italian, means simply 'jacket' (in the sense of costume), and 'the motley' is the old English word for an actor or clown's clothes, originally the many-coloured coat worn by a jester or fool (as mentioned several times in Shakespeare's *As You Like It*).

on your bike! Newly appointed as Britain's Employment Secretary, Norman Tebbit (*b* 1931) addressed the Conservative Party conference on 15 October 1981. He related how he had grown up in the 1930s when unemployment was all around. '[My father] did not riot. He got on his bike and looked for work. And he kept on looking till he found it.'

This gave rise to the pejorative catchphrase 'on your bike' or 'get on your bike' from the lips of Mr Tebbit's

opponents, and gave a new twist to a saying which Partridge/*Slang* dates from *c* 1960, meaning 'go away' or 'be off with you'.

Tebbit later pointed out that he had not been suggesting that the unemployed should literally get on their bikes, but claimed to find the catchphrase 'fun'.

ooh, an 'e was strong! See under RIGHT MONKEY!

ooh, Betty! Became a key phrase for impersonators of the accident-prone Frank Spencer (Michael Crawford) in the BBC TV series *Some Mothers Do 'Ave 'Em* which ran from 1974 to 1979. In particular, the catchphrase was extended to include, 'Ooh, Betty, the cat's done a whoopsie!'

ooh, bold! very bold! See under ROUND THE HORNE.

ooh, I say! Dan Maskell's voice in his Wimbledon tennis commentaries during the 1970s and 80s was an essential part of the occasion. 'Ooh, I say! There's a *dream volleh*!' was remarked by TV critic Clive James in the *Observer* (1 July 1979) and, a year later, 'Ooh, I *say*! That's as brave a coup as I've seen on the Centre Court in *yers*.' Accordingly, *Ooh, I say!* became the title of a BBC TV programme to mark Maskell's eightieth birthday in 1988. He died in 1992.

ooh, mother! See under IT's TURNED OUT NICE AGAIN.

oooh, you are awful . . . but I like you! In TV series of the 1970s, one of the characters played by the comedian Dick Emery (1917–83) was Mandy, a man-hungry spinster. The last word of the phrase was followed by a quick bash with her handbag. Also the title of a song and of a feature film (1980). Another of his characters – Hetty, an equally amorous character – would inquire **are you married?**, and Clarence, a camp gentleman would greet with **hello, honky-tonks!** Either as a result of this, or coincidentally, 'honky-tonk' became one of the names for a homosexual in the Britain of the mid-1970s. Hitherto, of course, the word had described a jangly type of piano, or anything that was shoddy, and as plain 'honky' it had been a Black American racist slur against white men (said to derive from the fact that they would honk the horns of their motors when picking up Black girlfriends).

oookaay! See CRUCIAL!

oooo arr, me ol' pal, me ol' beauty! See under ARCHERS.

opening. See ANOTHER ~, ANOTHER SHOW.

open sesame! Meaning, 'open up (the door)!' or as a mock password, the phrase comes from the tale of 'The Forty Thieves' in the ancient Oriental *Tales of the Arabian Nights*.

Sesame seed is also famous for its other opening qualities, as a laxative.

open the box! Contestants in the old British TV quiz *Take Your Pick* – which ran on ITV for almost 20 years from 1955 – were given the option of opening a numbered box (which might contain anything from air-tickets to Ena Sharples's hairnet) or accepting a sum of money which might turn out to be worth more – or less – than what was in the box. The studio audience would chant its advice – 'take the money' or, more usually, 'open the box!'

When the host, Michael Miles ('Your Quiz Inquisitor'), died, it was said that his funeral was interrupted by the congregation shouting, 'Open the box! Open the box! . . .'

open the door, Richard! See under ITMA.

opera ain't/isn't over till the fat lady sings, the. Relatively few modern proverbs have caught on in a big way but, of those that have, this one has produced sharp division over its origin. It is also used with surprising vagueness and lack of perception. If it is a warning 'not to count your chickens before they are hatched', it is too often simply employed to express a generalized view that 'it isn't over till it's over'.

So how did the saying come about? A report in the *Washington Post* (13 June 1978) had this version: 'One day three years ago [i.e. 1975], Ralph Carpenter, who was then Texas Tech's sports information director,

declared to the press box contingent in Austin, "The rodeo ain't over till the bull riders ride." Stirred to that deep insight, San Antonio sports editor Dan Cook countered with, "The opera ain't over till the fat lady sings."'

Two days before this (i.e. 11 June 1978), the *Washington Post* had more precisely quoted Cook as coming up with his version *the previous April*, 'after the basketball playoff game between the San Antonio Spurs and the Washington Bullets, to illustrate that while the Spurs had won once, the series was not over yet. Bullets coach Dick Motta borrowed the phrase later during the Bullets' eventually successful championship drive, and it became widely known and was often mistakenly attributed to him.'

Another widely shared view is that the saying refers to Kate Smith, a handsomely-proportioned American singer in the 1930s and 1940s. Her rendition of Irving Berlin's 'God Bless America' signified the end of events like the political party conventions and World Series baseball games. Hence, possibly, the alternative version: the **game's not over till the fat lady sings.** On the other hand, it has been argued that American national anthems ('The Star-Spangled Banner', 'America the Beautiful' among others) are usually sung at the *start* of baseball games, which would remove the point from the saying.

If the 'opera' version can actually be said to mean anything, it derives from a hazy view of those sopranos with a 'different body image' who get to sing a big number before they die and thus bring the show to a close. But they do not do this invariably. In *Tosca*, for example, the heroine makes her final death plunge over the battlements without singing a big aria.

Whatever the case, allusive use of the proverb is widespread – especially just the second part of it. The Fat Lady Sings is the name of an Irish (pop) band, formed *c* 1990. After winning the US presidential election in November 1992, Bill Clinton appeared at a victory party in Little Rock bearing a T-shirt with the slogan 'The Fat Lady Sang', which presumably meant no more than, 'It's over.' In July 1992, tennis champion Andre Agassi, describing the surprise climax of his Wimbledon final, said, 'I knew that it might just go to 30–30 with two more aces. I didn't hear the fat lady humming yet.' The American singers En Vogue had a song called 'It ain't over till the fat lady sings' about this time, and there were several books with approximate versions of the phrase for their titles.

As is to be expected with a proverbial expression, the *idea* behind 'the fat lady' is nothing new. In Eric Maschwitz's memoir *No Chip on My Shoulder* (1957), he recalled Julian Wylie, 'The Pantomime King': 'He had a number of favourite adages about the Theatre, one of which I have always remembered as a warning against dramatic anti-climax: "Never forget," he used to say "that once the giant is dead, the pantomime is over!" Which is a corollary if there was one.'

That there were earlier American versions of the saying appears to be confirmed by *A Dictionary of American Proverbs* (1992), which lists both 'The game's not over until the last man strikes out' and 'Church is not out 'til they sing'. Bartlett (1992) finds in *Southern Words and Sayings* by F.R. and C.R. Smith, the expression 'Church ain't out till the fat lady sings'. As the Smiths' book was published in 1976, this would seem to confirm that the 'opera' version of the proverb is only a derivative.

opportunity knocks. A talent contest with this title ran on British TV from 1956 to 1977. Introducing contestants, the host, Hughie Green, would say: **for — of —, opportunity knocks!** and so characteristic was the pronunciation that the phrase became his. It derives, of course, from the rather more restrictive proverbial expression, 'Opportunity knocks *but once*'. As *CODP* notes, 'fortune' occurs instead of 'opportunity' in earlier forms of the proverb and slightly different ideas are expressed – 'opportunity is said to knock once or more, but in other quotations, once only'. From Sir Geoffrey Fenton's *Bandello* (1567) comes the example: 'Fortune once in the course of our life, doth put into our hands the offer of a good turn.'

In the TV show, Green would also say **it's make-your-mind-up time** when the audience was asked to vote on the various contestants. He is also reported to have said, **this is your show, folks – and I do**

mean you. See also I MEAN THAT MOST SINCERELY, FOLKS.

orange. See QUEER AS A CLOCKWORK ~.

orchid-lined. See under MAN WITH THE GOLDEN . . .

order. See APPLE-PIE ~; GIVE ~; NOT NECESSARILY IN THAT ~.

order, order! The traditional call to order given by the Speaker of the House of Commons. George Thomas (later Viscount Tonypandy)(*b* 1909) made it very much his own as he was in office when radio broadcasts of the proceedings began for the first time on 3 April 1979. From the *Sunday Express* (19 June 1983): 'George Thomas gave the last Parliament its verbal hallmark. "*Order, order*" was the catchphrase from the Speaker's chair that swept the country – delivered in that soft, distinctive Welsh lilt.'

orders. See I WAS ONLY OBEYING ~.

orft we jolly well go! See under MORNING ALL!

orphan. See LITTLE ~ ANNIE.

orphans of the storm. How one might describe, humorously, any bedraggled, rain-soaked people. The phrase was the title of a famous silent film (US, 1921), with Lillian and Dorothy Gish as two sisters caught up in the French Revolution (a somewhat different type of storm). Before this, it had been the title of a play by Adolph Ennery.

Oscar Deutsch Entertains Our Nation. See ODEON.

OTT. See OVER THE TOP.

our day will come. This is an English translation of the Provisional IRA slogan, which is in Gaelic '*Tiocfaidh Ar La*'. Relatives of those accused of trying to blow up the British Prime Minister at Brighton in 1984 shouted it out as the defendants were being sentenced in court on 23 June 1986. The phrase had existed independently of this, of course.

It is also the title of a song performed by

the American vocal group Ruby and the Romantics (1963). Compare 'Our day is come', as it appears in Lord Lytton's novel, *Leila* (1838).

our mutual friend. Used as the title of a novel (1864) by Charles Dickens and referring to its hero, John Harmon, who feigns death and whose identity is one of the mysteries of the plot. This is a rare example of Dickens using an established phrase for a title (he usually chooses the invented name of a character). 'Our mutual friend' was an expression established by the seventeenth century but undoubtedly Dickens encouraged its further use. Some would object that 'mutual friend' is a solecism, arguing that it is impossible for the reciprocity of friendship to be shared with a third party. Even before Dickens took it for a title, a correspondent was writing to the journal *Notes and Queries* in 1849, asking: 'Is it too late to make an effective stand against the solecistic expression "mutual friend"?' The *Oxford Dictionary for Writers and Editors* (1981) points out that it is an expression used also by Edmund Burke, George Eliot and others, but 'the alternative "common" can be ambiguous'.

our reporter made an excuse and left. With the rise of the mass-circulation British newspaper came the rise of a two-faced mode of reporting which sought to depict vice and crime in a titillating way while covering itself with righteous condemnation and crusading zeal. The *People*, which was founded in 1881 as a weekly (and became the *Sunday People* in 1971), was one of those muck-raking papers that developed a method of reporting sexual scandals which sometimes involved a reporter setting up a compromising situation – e.g. provoking prostitutes and pimps to reveal their game – and then making it clear that, of course, the journalist had taken no part in what was on offer. Having found out all that was needed, 'our reporter made an excuse and left' – a classic exit line, probably from the 1920s onwards. It was still going strong, more or less, in the *News of the World* (12 March 1989): 'Our investigator declined her

[Pamella Bordes's] services and she put her clothes back on.'

où sont les neiges d'antan?, mais [but where are the snows of yesteryear?] A line, now used only in mock-yearning, which occurs as a refrain in the 'Ballade des Dames du Temps Jadis' from *Le Grand Testament* (1461) by the French poet François Villon.

out of —. A small epidemic of 'out of's spread with the release of the film *Out of Africa* (US/UK, 1985) based in part on Isak Dinesen's 1938 book (originally, in Danish, *Den Afrikanske Farm*). In 1986, the *Independent* launched a series of weekly columns entitled 'Out of Europe/Asia/etc'. The same year, Ruth Prawer Jhabvala and Tim Piggot-Smith both brought out books called *Out of India*.

Perhaps the original had something to do with Pliny's version of a Greek proverb, '*Ex Africa semper aliquid novi*' [there is always something new out of Africa], in his *Natural History*, VIII.17.

The title of the 1932 Noah Beery film *Out of Singapore* would seem to derive from the shipping use of 'out of', meaning the port from which a ship has sailed.

out of the Ark. Meaning, 'something that is very old indeed', alluding to the antiquity of Noah's Ark. Thackeray in *Roundabout Papers* (1860–63) has: 'We who lived before railways, and survive out of the ancient world, are like Father Noah and his family out of the Ark.'

out of the closet (and into the street). Slogan for the US homosexual rights organization known as the Gay Liberation Front, *c* 1969. The starting point was the term 'closet homosexual' or 'closet queen' for one who hid his inclinations away in a closet ('cupboard' in American usage rather than 'lavatory' or 'small room', as in British English).

out of the cradle endlessly rocking. A silent film subtitle occurring in D.W. Griffith's epic *Intolerance* (1916) accompanies a shot of Lillian Gish rocking a cradle, and is repeated many times during the course of the long film. It comes from the title of a poem (1859) by Walt Whitman.

out of your tiny Chinese mind, you must be. Meaning 'mad'. Gratuitously offensive but I suspect that the only reason for 'Chinese' is because it chimes with 'tiny'. Probably dates from the 1950s, at the earliest. The simpler 'out of your tiny mind' *may* be the older expression, though it is not recorded until 1965. Compare DAMN CLEVER THESE CHINESE! under GOON SHOW.

The phrase caused inevitable offence when used by Britain's Labour Chancellor of the Exchequer, Denis Healey, in February 1976 about left-wing opponents of his public expenditure cuts. In his book *The Time of My Life* (1989), he writes: 'I accused Ian Mikardo of being "out of his tiny Chinese mind" – a phrase of the comedienne Hermione Gingold, with which I thought everyone was familiar. On the contrary, when he leaked it to the press, the Chinese Embassy took it as an insult to the People's Republic.'

outta. See LET'S GET ~ HERE!

over. See IT'S NOT ~ TILL IT'S ~; WAR'S ~, YOU KNOW.

overcome. See WE SHALL ~.

over-forties. See PHYLLOSAN FORTIFIES THE ~.

overseas experience. See OE.

over the garden wall. A phrase evoking neighbourliness and especially gossipy conversation. It is the title of a painting by Helen Allingham (c 1880) and was also used to describe particular British variety sketches performed by the comedian Norman Evans (1901–62) in the character of 'Fanny Fairbottom', a garrulous woman.

over the hills and far away. Escaped far distant. One of the most used phrases by poets and songwriters over several centuries – Alfred Tennyson, Robert Louis Stevenson, John Gay among them. In Farquhar's *The Recruiting Officer* (1706), is the exact phrase:

> For now he's free to sing and play,
> Over the hills and far away.

But the words are already being alluded to

in a ballad 'The Wind Hath Blown My Plaid Away' (c 1670 and possibly as old as 1549):

> My plaid awa, my plaid awa,
> And ore the hill and far awa,
> And far awa to Norrowa.

The tune with the title 'Over the Hills and Far Away', dates from about 1706. The song now known by this title was written by John Gay and adorns *The Beggar's Opera* (1728).

over the moon. In about 1978, two cliché expressions became notorious in Britain if one wished to express either pleasure or dismay at the outcome of anything, but especially of a football match. The speaker was either 'over the moon' or **sick as a parrot.**

It probably all began because of the remorseless post-game analysis by TV football commentators and the consequent need for players and managers to provide pithy comments. Liverpool footballer Phil Thompson said he felt 'sick as a parrot' after his team's defeat in the 1978 Football League Cup Final.

Ironically, *Private Eye* fuelled the cliché by constant mockery, to such an extent that by 1980 an 'instant' BBC Radio play about the European Cup Final (written on the spot by Neville Smith according to the outcome) was given the alternative titles *Over the Moon/Sick as a Parrot.*

Some failed to note the cliché. *The Times* (21 January 1982) reported the reaction of M. Albert Roux, the London restaurateur, on gaining three stars in the *Michelin Guide*: '"I am over the moon," M. Roux said yesterday . . . he quickly denied, however, that his brother [another celebrated restaurateur] would be "sick as a parrot".'

'Over the moon' is probably the older of the two phrases. Indeed, in the diaries of May, Lady Cavendish (published 1927) there is an entry for 7 February 1857 saying how she broke the news of her youngest brother's birth to the rest of her siblings: 'I had told the little ones who were first utterly incredulous and then over the moon.' The family of Catherine Gladstone (*née* Gwynne), wife of the Prime Minister, is said to have had its own idiomatic language and originated the phrase. However, the nursery rhyme 'Hey diddle diddle/The cat and the fiddle,/The cow jumped over the moon' dates back to 1765 at least and surely conveys the same meaning. Besides, the Rev. Sydney Smith was reported in 1833 as having said 'I could have jumped over the moon'.

The specific application to football was already in evidence in 1962, when Alf Ramsey (a team manager) was quoted as saying, on one occasion, 'I feel like jumping over the moon.'

What may be an early version of 'sick as a parrot' appears in Robert Southey's Cumbrian dialect poem *The Terrible Knitters e' Dent* (1834). There, 'sick as a peeate' (pronounced 'pee-at') means a feeling like a heavy lump of peat in the stomach – the equivalent of having a heart feeling 'as heavy as lead' perhaps? A more likely origin is in connection with psittacosis or parrot disease/fever. In about 1973, there were a number of cases of people dying of this in West Africa. It is basically a viral disease of parrots (and other birds) but can be transmitted to humans. Even so, there may be an older source. In the seventeenth and eighteenth centuries, there was an expression 'melancholy as a (sick) parrot' (in the plays of Aphra Behn, for example). And Desmond Morris in *Catwatching* (1986) claims that the original expression was 'as sick as a parrot with a rubber beak', meaning that the animal was incapacitated without a sharp weapon, as also in the saying, 'no more chance than a cat in hell with no claws'.

Another use for the phrase is to describe post-alcoholic dejection. Parrots will eagerly feed on rotting – and therefore alcoholic – fruit or fruit pulp. Hence 'pissed as a parrot' and, next day, 'sick as a parrot'.

over the top. (or **OTT.**) i.e. exaggerated in manner of performance; 'too much'. The expression 'to go over the top' originated in the trenches of the First World War. It was used to describe the method of charging over the parapet and out of the trenches on the attack.

In a curious transition, the phrase was later adopted for use by show business people when describing a performance that has gone beyond the bounds of restraint, possibly to the point of embarrassment. In

1982, a near-the-bone TV series reflected this by calling itself *OTT*. After which, you heard people saying that something was 'a bit OTT' instead of the full expression. On 15 February 1989, the *Independent* quoted from a play called *State of Play* at the Soho Poly theatre: 'Look at sport – I'm sure you'll agree:/ It's much more fun when it's OTT.'

over Will's/Bill's mother's way, it's dark/black. Paul Beale in his revision of Partridge/*Catch Phrases* mentions the expression 'it's a bit black over Bill's mother's' (referring to the weather, when rain threatens) and gives an East Midlands source. H.S. Middleton of Llanyblodwel, Shropshire, formerly of Aylestone Park, Leicester, and whose brother was called Bill, wrote (1994) to say how, in the early 1920s, a certain Len Moss had looked through the sitting room window in the direction of Mr Middleton's home and said, 'It looks black over Bill's mother's.' Was this the origin of the phrase (which sometimes occurs elsewhere as 'over *Will's* mother's way')?

All I was able to tell Mr Middleton was that in 1930, the journal *Notes and Queries* carried a query about this phrase in the form 'it looks pretty black over Will's Mother's'. It was described as an 'old Sussex' saying. And there was no response. Barry Day of New York, NY, recalled that 'It's a bit black over Bill's mother's' used to be said a great deal by *his* mother when he was growing up in Derbyshire. 'It was always said ironically,' he added. 'So I can confirm its Midlands usage.'

I first heard about it on a London radio phone-in (June 1990), in the form, 'It looks like rain . . . over Will's mother's way.' In *Verbatim* (Autumn 1993), Alan Major discussed a number of 'Kentish sayings' and included, 'Out Will's mother's way', meaning 'somewhere else, in the distance, on the horizon'. Major added: 'Who Will's mother was is unknown, but there are several similar expressions, with word variations, used in other English counties. In Gloucestershire, the expression is "It's dark over our Bill's Mum's mind".'

The Rev. P.W. Gallup of Winchester wrote that he had traced the saying in eleven counties and commented on its age: 'I have friends in their late eighties [in 1994] who as children knew it well from their parents and say that it was then widely known and used. This suggests that the saying has been used at least by several generations.'

'ow do, 'ow are yer? See under HAVE A GO.

owes. See WORLD ∼ ONE A LIVING.

own. See YOUR ∼, YOUR VERY ∼.

own goal, to score an. Meaning to bring harm upon oneself ('Ozal risks own goal in move to kick life into slack

election' [by attending a Turkish football team's foray into European soccer – when it might have lost the game] – *Guardian*, 20 March 1989).

The phrase (based on football) came originally from the security forces in Northern Ireland (by 1978) and was used to describe what happened when a terrorist blew himself up with his own bomb. It is a very similar coinage to 'shooting oneself in the foot' or 'being HOIST WITH ONE'S OWN PETARD'.

owns. See ASK THE MAN WHO ∼ ONE.

oysters. See DON'T EAT ∼ UNLESS . . .

· P ·

pacification. See DESPERATION . . .

packdrill. See NO NAMES NO ∼.

packed. See AND IN A ∼ PROGRAMME . . .

page. See ANOTHER ∼ TURNED IN . . .

pageant. See IT'S ALL PART OF LIFE'S RICH ∼.

page one. See IT'S ∼.

Page Three girl. Meaning 'a topless photographic model', the allusion is specifically to the kind once regularly featured on page three of the *Sun* newspaper, but can be broadly applied to any nude model. Larry Lamb, the editor, introduced the feature within a year of the paper's relaunch on 17 November 1969, following its acquisition by Rupert Murdoch, the Australian-born newspaper proprietor.

paid-up member. See FULLY PAID-UP . . .

pains. See NO ∼ NO GAINS.

painting in the attic. See DORIAN GRAY.

painting the Forth Bridge, like. An expression used to describe an endless task. It is popular knowledge that since it was constructed in the 1880s, the steel rail bridge over the Firth of Forth in Scotland has been continuously repainted. That is to say, when they got to the end of it, the painters immediately started all over again (though in 1993 a 'maintenance holiday' was declared and the traditional on average four-yearly application of paint to each part of the structure looked likely to lapse).

From the *Financial Times* (25 July 1984): 'Because of the mismatch in the computer criteria used by Western governments and industry, a nightmarish task is now involved in explaining the new CoCom rules to companies . . . There is talk in CoCom of making its list review a continuous process – "like painting the Forth Bridge, the minute you finish, you start again," one official says.' From the *Guardian* (2 August 1984): 'In the far future, small free-roaming insectoids could be set to handle continuous tasks such as cleaning the outside of skyscrapers, or painting the Forth Bridge. Miniature versions could be put to work cleaning pavements and gutters, or the inside of your house.'

Paki-bashing. See BASH/FLOG THE BISHOP.

pal. See ME OL' ∼ under ARCHERS.

pale. See BEYOND THE ∼.

palm without the dust, the. It was said of Lord Rosebery, the British Liberal Prime Minister in the 1890s, that 'he wanted the palm without the dust', an allusion to Horace, the Roman author, who talked of 'the happy state of getting the victor's palm without the dust of racing'. '*Palma non sine pulvere*' [no palm without labour] is a motto of the Earls of Liverpool, among others.

pan. See FLASH IN THE ∼.

panic. See ISN'T HE A ∼?

panther. See BLACK ∼.

pants. See FLY BY THE SEAT OF ONE'S ∼; TAKE A KICK IN THE ∼.

paperbag. See under COULDN'T RUN A WHELK-STALL . . .

paperhanger. See under AS BUSY AS . . .

paper tiger, a. A person who appears outwardly strong but is, in fact, weak. It was popularized by the Chinese leader, Mao Tse-tung, who told a US interviewer in 1946: 'All reactionaries are paper tigers. In appearance, the reactionaries are terrifying, but in reality they are not so powerful.' *Paper Tiger* was used as the title of a film (UK, 1975) about a coward who pretends to be otherwise.

pardon my French. (or **excuse ...**) What you can say after using bad language. The use of 'French' to mean 'bad language' was known by 1895 when the 'excuse my French' version appeared in *Harper's Magazine.* 'Pardon my French' was recorded in 1936. Possibly use of this British and American phrase was encouraged by forces' use in France during the First World War.

pardon the pun. See IF YOU'LL EXCUSE THE PUN.

Paris by night. A kind of promotional tag for tourism in the French capital, in use since the 1950s at least. A London West End revue used the somewhat nudging phrase as its title in 1955. The title of a David Hare film (1989). From the 1930s onwards there was a cheap perfume, available from Woolworth and manufactured by Bourjois (*sic*), called 'Evening in Paris' – which also traded on the city's reputation for sophisticated pleasures.

Paris is for lovers. This phrase, spoken in Billy Wilder's film *Sabrina* (*Sabrina Fair* in the UK, 1954), almost has the ring of an official slogan, though this was long before the days of such lines as 'I LOVE New York' (1977) and 'Virginia is for Lovers' (1981).

Nor have I found a song including the phrase or using it as a title, though Cole Porter's Broadway musical *Silk Stockings* (US, 1955) has one called 'Paris Loves Lovers'.

parker. See NOSEY ~.

Parker, Dorothy. See AS ~ ONCE SAID.

Parkinson's Law. The observation that 'work expands so as to fill the time available for its completion' was first promulgated by Professor C. Northcote Parkinson in the *Economist* Magazine (1955).

parrot. See DEAD ~; SICK AS A ~ under OVER THE MOON.

parson. See ENOUGH TO MAKE A ~ SWEAR.

part. See IT'S ALL ~ OF LIFE'S RICH PAGEANT; IT'S ALL ~ OF THE SERVICE!; HEINEKEN REFRESHES THE ~S . . .

partridge in a pear tree, a. The lines from the old Christmas carol/nursery rhyme, 'The first day of Christmas,/My true love sent to me/A partridge in a pear tree' have been questioned, chiefly because the game bird is a famously low flyer and is never seen in trees. A popular suggestion (which also explains some of the other gifts listed in the song) is that a 'partridge in a pear tree' is a corruption of the Latin *parturit in aperto* [she gave birth in the open], referring to Mary's delivery of Christ in a stable. Similarly, the shepherds coming down from the hills [*descendens de collibus*] could explain the phrases 'three French hens' and 'four colly/calling birds'.

The rhyme, which is also known in French, was first recorded in English in *c* 1780.

party. See COLLAPSE OF STOUT ~; I TOOK MY HARP TO A ~.

party on! See under *WAYNE'S WORLD.*

party's over, the. A phrase used to describe the end of absolutely anything, but inevitably used in political contexts. On 4 June 1990, the *Daily Express*, *Sun*, and the *Daily Mirror* all used it in headlines regarding the collapse of the British Social Democratic Party. In 1975, Anthony Crosland, the Labour minister, said that local government was 'coming to realize that, for the time being at least, the party is over'. On 12 October 1963, the BBC TV satirical show *That Was the Week That Was* marked the resignation of Prime Minister Harold Macmillan with William Rushton singing the *song* with this title in a broken-voice. In fact, there are two songs: Noël Coward's 'The Party's Over Now' from *Words and Music* (1932) or 'The Party's

Over' from *Bells Are Ringing* (1956) by
Comden, Green and Styne.

Pasionaria, La [Passion flower].
Nickname of Dolores Ibarruri (d 1990), the
Spanish Communist leader at the time of
the Civil War. Margaret Thatcher was
dubbed 'La Pasionaria of Privilege' in 1975
by Denis Healey, the Labour minister.

pass. See AND THIS TOO SHALL ∼; under
I'VE STARTED SO I'LL FINISH; CUT OFF AT
THE ∼; DO NOT ∼ GO; ∼ THE SICKBAG,
ALICE under I THINK WE SHOULD BE TOLD.

passage. See RIGHTS OF ∼.

passed. See TIME HAS ∼ BY —.

pass the buck, to. Meaning 'to shift
responsibility on to someone else', the
phrase derives from some card games,
where a marker called a 'buck' is put in
front of the dealer to remind players who
the dealer is. When it is someone else's turn,
the 'buck' is 'passed'. The original marker
may have been a buckthorn knife or, in the
Old West, a silver dollar – hence the
modern use of the word 'buck' for a dollar.

Patagonia. See WHEN I WAS IN ∼.

pause that refreshes, the. A phrase used
to advertise Coca-Cola since 1929. Other
Coke slogans, out of scores, include: **thirst
knows no season** (from 1922); **it's the
refreshing thing to do** (current 1937);
things go better with Coke (from 1963);
I'd like to buy the world a Coke (from
1971 – the jingle became a hit in its own
right when retitled 'I'd Like to Teach the
World to Sing'); **Coke adds life** (from
1976); **have a Coke and a smile** (current
1980).
    See also under COME ALIVE . . . and REAL
THING.

paved. See STREETS ∼ WITH GOLD.

paw. See CAT'S ∼.

pay. See EQUAL ∼ FOR EQUAL WORK; GO
NOW, ∼ LATER; IT ∼S TO ADVERTISE.

pay freeze/pause. See under WAGE FREEZE.

pay through the nose, to. Meaning 'to
pay heavily', one possible explanation for
the origin of the phrase lies in the 'nose' tax
levied upon the Irish by the Danes in the
ninth century. Those who did not pay had
their noses slit.

PC Plod. Like OLD BILL, this is another
critical nickname for the British police,
perceived as having lumbering ineptitude in
the catching of criminals and a plodding
walk while on the beat. The most likely
allusion is to a character in the 'Noddy'
children's books which first appeared in
1949. From the *Independent* (10 April 1992):
'The BBC is reviving Noddy this autumn,
but would Enid Blyton recognise the lad? . . .
Grumpy old PC Plod will be "less
aggressive", while the golliwogs will be
replaced by monkeys and gremlins.'

peace at any price. 'Peace at any price;
peace and union' was the slogan of the
American (Know-Nothing) Party in the
1856 US presidential election. The party
supported ex-President Fillmore and the
slogan meant that it was willing to accept
slavery for blacks in order to avoid a civil
war. Fillmore lost to James Buchanan.
    It has been suggested that the phrase had
been coined earlier (in 1848 or 1820) by
Alphonse de Lamartine, the French foreign
affairs minister in his *Méditations Poétiques*
in the form: '*La paix à tout prix*'. However,
the Earl of Clarendon quoted an
'unreasonable calumny' concerning Lord
Falkland in his *History of the Rebellion*
(written in 1647): 'that he was so
enamoured on peace, that he would have
been glad the king should have bought it at
any price'. When Neville Chamberlain
signed his pact with Hitler in 1938, many
praised him for trying to obtain 'peace at
any price'.

peace for/in our time. On his return from
signing the Munich agreement with Hitler
in September 1938, the British Prime
Minister Neville Chamberlain spoke from a
window at 10 Downing Street ('not of
design but for the purpose of dispersing the
huge multitude below' [according to his
biographer Keith Feiling]). He said: 'My
good friends, this is the second time in our
history that there has come back from

Germany to Downing Street PEACE WITH HONOUR. I believe it is peace for [sic] our time. Go home and get a nice quiet sleep.' His phrase 'peace for our time' is often misquoted as 'peace *in* our time' – as by Noël Coward in the title of his 1947 play set in an England after the Germans have conquered. Perhaps Coward, and others, were influenced by the phrase from the Prayer Book: 'Give Peace in our time, O Lord'.

peace is our profession. Motto (by 1962) of the US Strategic Air Command. In 1972, there was a US film called *Lassie: Peace Is Our Profession*.

peace with honour. When Benjamin Disraeli returned from the Congress of Berlin (1878), which had been called to settle the 'Balkan question' – this was what he claimed to have achieved. Two days before Neville Chamberlain returned from signing the Munich agreement with Hitler, someone had suggested that he might like to use the Disraeli phrase. He impatiently rejected it, but then, according to John Colville, *Footprints in Time* (1976), he used the phrase at the urging of his wife (see PEACE FOR/IN OUR TIME).

pearls before swine. Referring to things of quality put before the unappreciative, the source is Matthew 7:6: 'Give not that which is holy unto the dogs, neither cast ye pearls before swine.' See also AGE BEFORE BEAUTY.

pear tree. See PARTRIDGE IN A ∼.

peasants are revolting, the. As with the NATIVES ARE HOSTILE/RESTLESS!, this is a jocular way of describing almost any form of unrest among people. It also harks back to what imperialist Britons (or medieval tyrants) *might* be supposed to have said, if only in historical fiction. The actual Peasants' Revolt (against taxes) took place in southern England in 1381.

pecker. See I'VE GOT HIS ∼ IN MY POCKET.

peculiar. See FUNNY ∼.

pecunia non olet [money does not smell]. Meaning 'don't concern yourself with the

source of money. Don't look a gift horse in the mouth'. A quotation from the Emperor Vespasian. In about AD 70, when Vespasian imposed a tax on public lavatories, his son Titus objected on the grounds that this was beneath the dignity of the state. The Emperor – according to Suetonius, *Lives of the Ceasars* – took a handful of coins and held them under his son's nose, and asked if they smelt. On being told they didn't, Vespasian said, '*Atque et lotio est*' [Yes, that's made from urine].

As a result, public urinals in France are still sometimes called *Vespasiennes*.

peel. See BEULAH, ∼ ME A GRAPE!

peeping Tom, a. The name given to voyeurs of any kind and deriving from Tom the Tailor who was struck blind because he peeped when **Lady Godiva** rode by. In the legend, Lady Godiva's husband, the Lord of Coventry, only agreed to abolish some harsh taxes if she would ride naked through the town. The townspeople responded to her request that they should stay behind closed doors – all except Peeping Tom. This element of the story was probably grafted on to the record of an actual happening of the eleventh century. *Peeping Tom* was the title of a film (UK, 1959), about a man who films his victims while murdering them.

peg. See SQUARE ∼ IN A . . . ; TAKE SOMEONE DOWN A ∼.

peel. See BEULAH, ∼ ME A GRAPE.

pelvis. See ELVIS THE ∼.

pencil. See BLUE ∼.

Pen In Top Pocket. See PITP.

penny. See DON'T ASK THE PRICE, IT'S A ∼; SPEND A ∼; PUT A ∼ ON THE DRUM.

penny plain and twopence coloured. Plain and fancy. 'A Penny Plain and Twopence Coloured' was the title of a noted essay (in *The Magazine of Art*, 1884) by Robert Louis Stevenson on the toy theatres or 'juvenile drama' of his youth. The expression referred to the prices of characters and scenery you could buy either already coloured or in black and white to colour yourself.

As a phrase, *ODCIE* has that it means 'in cheap or more expensive (attractive or merely showy) form (from, formerly, paper cut-outs of characters and scenery for toy theatres)'. On the other hand, the *Longman Dictionary of English Idioms* (1979) takes things a little further: '*rather old-fash.*: [meaning] although one of two similar things may be more attractive or bright in appearance than the other, they both basically have the same use or value'.

Stevenson popularized the phrase but it undoubtedly existed before. George Augustus Sala, *Twice Round the Clock* (1859) has: 'The Scala [theatre, Milan] . . . with its rabbit-hutch-like private boxes, whose doors are scrawled over with the penny plain and twopence coloured-like coats of arms of the . . . Lombardian nobility.'

Tuppence Coloured (on its own) was the title of a theatrical novel by Patrick Hamilton (1927) and of a revue (with Joyce Grenfell and others) in 1947.

people. See BEAUTIFUL ∼; GETAWAY ∼; NOISE AND THE ∼; NOT MANY ∼ KNOW THAT; TOP ∼ TAKE *THE TIMES*; WE THE ∼; WHEN ∼ ARE STARVING IN INDIA.

People Like Us. See PLU.

Peoria. See IT'LL PLAY IN ∼.

Pepsi. See COME ALIVE . . .

Pepsodent. See YOU'LL WONDER WHERE THE YELLOW WENT . . .

perfect. See NOBODY'S ∼; PERFICK!

perfectly. See I WANT TO MAKE IT ∼ CLEAR; SMALL, BUT ∼ FORMED.

perfect stranger, a. The phrase 'perfect stranger' – as in 'I'm a perfect stranger to this part of the world' (meaning 'complete, entire' rather than 'possessing perfection') can already be found in Vanbrugh, *The False Friend* (1699). From Wilkie Collins, *No Name*, Sc. 2, Chap. 1 (1862–3): ' "You are mistaken," she said quietly. "You are a perfect stranger to me." '

The Perfect Stranger was the title of a volume of autobiography by P.J. Kavanagh (1966), dealing in part with the death of his young wife. He prefaces it with a quotation from Louis MacNeice: 'Or will one's wife also belong to that country/And can one never find the perfect stranger?'

perfick! A Kentish pronunciation of 'perfect' as found particularly in H.E. Bates, *The Darling Buds of May* (1958) and subsequent stories. In Chapter 1 of that first book, Pa Larkin talks of 'perfick wevver', for 'perfect weather'. The expression 'perfick!' again had a vogue in the spring of 1991 when the stories were dramatized for British TV with huge success. At that time, 'Perfick' was the *Sun*'s headline over a front-page story about the new council tax (Pa Larkin is a notable income tax dodger); the Family Assurance Society promoted a tax-free investment with the word as headline in newspaper adverts in May 1991 (revealing, at the same time, that the word had been registered as a trade mark by Yorkshire Television, the programme's producer).

perforations. See MY LITTLE ∼.

performance. See WHAT A ∼!

permission to speak, sir! See under *DAD'S ARMY*.

Persil washes whiter. See under WHITER THAN WHITE.

perspire. See HORSES SWEAT . . .

petard. See HOIST WITH ONE'S OWN ∼.

Pete. See FOR ∼'S SAKE.

Peter Principle, the. The observation that 'in a hierarchy every employee tends to rise to his level of incompetence' was first promulgated by Dr Laurence J. Peter in *The Peter Principle – Why Things Go Wrong* (written with R. Hull) (1969).

pew. See TAKE A ∼.

phenomenon. See INFANT ∼.

phew, what a scorcher! *Private Eye*'s joke headline (since the 1960s) for hot-weather reports from tabloid newspapers. Presumably it did once appear in an actual newspaper. A 'scorcher' was common usage in the 1930s. In Patrick Hamilton's radio play *Money with Menaces* (1937) the events take place in a heatwave: 'Weather hot enough for you, sir?' – 'Yes, it's a scorcher, isn't it?' In fact, *OED2* finds 'scorcher' as early as 1874.

philosopher. See GUIDE ∼ AND FRIEND.

Phoebe. See DON'T FORCE IT, ∼.

phrase. See REARRANGE THE FOLLOWING . . . ; TO COIN A ∼.

Phyllosan fortifies the over-forties. A slogan for Phyllosan tonic, current in the UK from the 1940s. (This gave rise to the BBC saying of the 1970s, 'Radio 4 over-fortifies the over-forties'.)

piano. See THEY LAUGHED WHEN I SAT DOWN . . .

pick. See YOU CAN ALWAYS LOOK DOWN . . .

picnic, wharfies. See under AS BUSY AS . . .

picture. See EVERY ∼ TELLS A STORY.

pidgin English. Jargon made up of mainly English words but arranged according to Chinese methods and pronounced in a Chinese way. It arose to facilitate communication between Chinese and Europeans at seaports and has nothing to do with 'pigeon'. Rather, it is the Chinese pronunciation of 'business'. Nowadays, 'pidgin' can be formed from any two languages and is not restricted to Chinese and English.

pie. See EAT HUMBLE ∼.

piece of cake, (it's a). Meaning that something is simple, no bother, and easily achieved. Comparisons are inevitable with other food phrases like 'easy as pie' and 'money for jam', but the general assumption seems to be that it is a shortened form of 'it's as easy as eating a piece of cake'. The earliest *OED2* citation is American and from 1936, though the phrase may not be of actual US origin. It was especially popular in the RAF during the Second World War, hence the appropriate title *Piece of Cake*, applied by Derek Robinson to his novel (1983) about RAF fliers in the Second World War and which was turned into a TV mini-series in 1988. In 1943, C.H. Ward-Jackson published *It's a Piece of Cake*.

piece of string. See under HOW MANY BEANS.

pie Jesu. See MASS PHRASES.

Piff(e)y, to sit like. As when a person is left in an isolated, useless position for some time and asks, 'Why am I sat here like Piffy?' British North Country usage. A longer version is, 'Sitting like Piffy on a rock-bun', remembered from the 1930s. And never send to ask who the original Piffy was.

pig. See MALE CHAUVINIST ∼.

pig in a poke, to buy a. To buy something sight unseen. 'Poke' here means 'bag' [of which a 'pock-et' is a small one], which immediately explains the meaning of the term: if you bought a pig hidden in a bag you would not know whether it was worth buying or not. Recorded by 1536. From H.G. Wells, *The History of Mr Polly* (1910): 'Never was bachelor married yet that didn't buy a pig in a poke.'

pig's bum. See YUM YUM, ∼.

pile it high, sell it cheap. Sir John Cohen (1898–1979), founder of Tesco supermarkets in the UK, built his fortune upon this golden rule and it became a sort of unofficial slogan for his organization.

pillars of society. People who are the main supporters of church, state, institutions or principles (compare 'pillars of state', 'pillar of faith'). Derived from the English title of Henrik Ibsen's play *Samfundets Stotter* (1877), in the translation by William Archer. (When the play was first produced in London in 1880 it was, however, called *Quicksands*.) In the play, the 'pillars of society' are described as being 'the spirit of truth and the spirit of freedom'.

pillar to post, from. Originally 'from post to pillar', this expression derives from the game of 'real tennis' and suggests that whoever is being driven or bounced or chased from one place to other is being harrassed. In use by 1420.

pilot. See DROPPING THE ~.

Piltdown Man. See SELSDON MAN.

pin back your lugholes! See under I'M DREAMING . . .

Pincher Martin. 'Pincher' has become an inseparable nickname for anyone surnamed 'Martin' ever since the days of Admiral Sir William F. Martin (c 1860). He was a strict disciplinarian who insisted on ratings being put under arrest (or 'pinched') for even minor offences. *Pincher Martin* is the title of a novel (1956) by William Golding, about a drowning sailor.

pink. See under BLUE FOR A BOY . . .; OFF WE GO AND THE COLOUR'S ~; SHOCKING ~.

Pink Camay. See YOU'LL LOOK A LITTLE LOVELIER . . .

Pinta. See DRINKA ~ MILKA DAY.

pin to an elephant, from a. Whiteley's, first in Westbourne Grove and later in Queensway, introduced department store shopping to London in 1863. William Whiteley (1831–1907), the self-styled **Universal Provider**, claimed to be able to supply anything, hence this slogan. One morning, as Whiteley described it: 'An eminent pillar of the Church called upon me and said, "Mr Whiteley, I want an elephant." "Certainly, sir. When would you like it?" "Oh, today!" "And where?" "I should like it placed in my stable." "It shall be done!" In four hours, a tuskiana was placed in the reverend gentleman's coach-house.

'Of course, this was a try-on designed to test our resources, and it originated in a bet. The Vicar confessed himself greatly disconcerted because, as he frankly avowed,

he did not think we would execute the order. He displayed the utmost anxiety lest I should hold him to the transaction. But I let him down with a small charge for pilotage and food only, at which he confessed himself deeply grateful' (quoted in R.S. Lambert, *The Universal Provider*, 1937).

pipeline. See IN THE ~.

pips. See SQUEEZE TILL THE ~ SQUEAK.

Pip, Squeak and Wilfred. A term you might apply to any set of three people or things. Derived from the names of cartoon characters in the newspaper strip with this name, featured in the *Daily Mirror* from 1920 to the 1940s. Pip was a dog, Squeak a female penguin, and Wilfred a baby rabbit.

Gilbert Harding, the television personality, was invited to the official opening of the BBC Television Centre in London (1960) and observed the Director-General, Hugh Greene, talking in a group with two of his predecessors, Sir William Haley and Sir Ian Jacob. 'Ah,' said Harding, 'either the Holy Trinity or Pip, Squeak and Wilfred.' Then he added: 'The latter, I fear' (quoted in Paul Ferris, *Sir Huge*, 1990).

pissed as a newt. i.e. 'very drunk', recorded by 1957. Partridge/*Slang* gives various metaphors for drunkenness from the animal kingdom – 'pissed as a coot/rat/parrot' among them. None seems particularly apposite. And why 'newt'? Could it be that the newt, being an amphibious reptile, can submerge itself in liquid as a drunk might do? Or is it because its tight-fitting skin reflects the state of being 'tight'?

We may never know, though the alternative (and, according to Partridge, original) expression 'tight as a newt' has a pleasing sound to it. Folk expressions have been coined with less reason. (Partridge's reviser Paul Beale wrote to me in December 1987: 'The great thing about newts is the characteristic they share with fishes' arse'oles: they are watertight. And you can't get tighter than that!')

There is any number of other explanations, most based on mishearings of words.

Compare OVER THE MOON.

piss off. See POETS' DAY.

piss-up in a brewery. See under
COULDN'T RUN A WHELK–STALL.

pit/Pitt. See BOTTOMLESS ~.

PITP. Social typing phrase, for identifying
the type of man who carries his 'Pen In Top
Pocket' and thus is considered inferior.
Probably only British middle-class use.
Known by the 1950s?

place. See ANY TIME . . . ; NICE ~ YOU GOT
HERE; NO ~ LIKE HOME.

**place for everything and everything in
its place, a.** The writer Charles Osborne
who grew up in Australia in the 1930s
remembers being an untidy child and his
mother's nannyish admonition, 'A place for
everything and everything in its place.'
Quite a well-known saying it is, too –
Samuel Smiles quotes it in *Thrift*, 1875.

place in the sun, a. The phrase for what
German colonial ambitions in East Asia
were meant to secure was coined by
Bernard von Bülow, the German
Chancellor, in a speech to the Reichstag in
1897: 'In a word, we desire to throw no one
into the shade, but we also demand our
own place in the sun [*Platz an der Sonne*].' In
1901, Kaiser Wilhelm II took up the theme
in a speech at Elbe: 'We have fought for our
place in the sun and won it. Our future is
on the water.' The notion was much
referred to in the run-up to the First World
War. An early appearance occurs in the
Pensées of Blaise Pascal (Walker's
translation, 1688): 'This Dog is mine, said
those poor Children; That's my place in the
Sun. This is the beginning and Image of the
Usurpation of all the Earth.' The phrase is
now hardly ever used in this precise sense,
but simply to indicate a rightful piece of
good fortune, a desirable situation, e.g.: 'Mr
Frisk could bring Aintree punters their
place in the sun' (headline from the
Independent on Sunday, 1 April 1990). *A
Place in the Sun* was the title given to the
1951 film of Theodore Dreiser's *An
American Tragedy*.

place is alive! See under SHUT THAT DOOR!

plague. See AVOID — LIKE THE ~.

plan. See MAN WITH THE ~.

plane. See IT'S A ~. under SUPERMAN.

play. See AT ~ IN THE FIELDS OF THE LORD;
IT'LL ~ IN PEORIA; SCOTTISH ~; THIS ~
WHAT I HAVE WROTE under *MORECAMBE AND
WISE SHOW*; THEY LAUGHED WHEN I SAT
DOWN . . . .

play fast and loose, to. i.e. to mess
another person about, to resort to deceit, to
act in a slippery fashion. The expression
was known by the sixteenth century, as was
a game called Fast-and-loose – though
which came first is hard to say. The game,
also called 'Pricking the Belt', was an old
fairground trick akin to 'Find the Lady' (the
so-called Three-Card Trick). The victim
was incited to pin a folded belt to the table.
The operator would then show that the belt
was not (held) 'fast' but 'loose'. So the
victim would lose the bet.

playing our tune. See THEY'RE ~,
DARLING.

play it again, Sam. AS EVERY SCHOOLBOY
KNOWS by now, neither Humphrey Bogart
nor Ingrid Bergman actually used this
phrase in the film *Casablanca* (1942). All
one need say now is that the saying was
utterly well established by the time Woody
Allen thus entitled his play (1969; film US,
1972) about a film critic who is abandoned
by his wife and obtains the help of Bogart's
'shade'. By listing it under Allen's name,
Bartlett might be thought to suggest that
Allen coined the phrase. It would be
interesting to know by which year it had
really become established.

playmates. See HELLO, ~ under *BAND
WAGGON*.

play the game, you cads! The British
variety performers The Western Brothers
(Kenneth and George – who were in fact
cousins) had an act in which they sang
songs to the piano in the 1930s/40s. They
played clubbish, bemonocled toffs and

would begin with something to the effect: **good evening, cads, your better selves are with you once again!** and end with **cheerio, cads, and happy landings!**

play the music and open the cage! See under MUM, MUM, THEY ARE LAUGHING AT ME.

play what I have wrote, this. See under MORECAMBE AND WISE SHOW.

please adjust your dress before leaving. From notices in men's British public lavatories (nineteenth century onwards?). 'Adjust' is a perfectly normal word for 'arranging' one's clothes (and has been since the early eighteenth century), but here it is euphemistic. The 'dress' is a little worrying: Arthur Marshall in *Sunny Side Up* (1987) recalls querying this and other aspects of the wording, possibly in the 1910s. An uncle promised to write to the authorities proposing instead: 'Before leaving please engage all trouser buttons securely and return hands to normal position.'
Winston Churchill denied (1941) having said of a long-winded memorandum from Anthony Eden that, 'as far as I can see, you have used every cliché except "God is love" and "Please adjust your dress before leaving."' A graffito (reported 1980): 'Please adjust your dress before leaving – as a refusal often offends.'

pleased. See AS ~ AS PUNCH.

please do not ask for credit as a refusal often offends. Notice in shops since the 1920s/30s? A more recent variant, mentioned by Bernard Levin in *The Times* (16 August 1984), and deplored, was taken from a photocopying shop in London W1: 'We do NOT give facilities for change, telephone books, or anything not directly pertaining to this business.' From the same decade – a 'Bureau de Change' at Waverley Station, Edinburgh, had a notice in the window, 'We do not give change'.

please to remember/the Fifth of November/Gunpowder treason and plot. (Continuing: 'I see no reason/Why gunpowder treason/Should ever be forgot.')

Rhyme commemorating the arrest of Guy Fawkes and others who had planned to blow up the House of Parliament at Westminster, on the occasion of the opening of parliament by King James I (set for 5 November 1605). In fact, Fawkes was arrested shortly before midnight on the 4 November. He has been burned in effigy on bonfires ever since on the 5 November. Something like the above rhyme was recorded in 1742: 'Don't you remember/The fifth of November/'Twas Gun-Powder Treason Day . . .' Nowadays, most people would probably say 'Remember, remember, the Fifth of November . . .'
The cry **penny for the guy!** when soliciting contributions ahead of the effigy being burned must date back at least to that time.

please yourselves! See NAY, NAY ~ THRICE AGAIN NAY!

pleasure. See DOUBLE YOUR ~ . . .

plenty. See STARVATION IN THE MIDST OF ~ .

Plinge. See WALTER ~ .

plod. See PC ~ .

plonker. See YER ~!

plots. See SIX BASIC ~ .

plot thickens!, the. Used seriously in nineteenth-century melodramas, but now jokingly in conversation of any turn of events that appears to be significant or which betrays some complicating feature. In *The Rehearsal* by George Villiers (1671), a character said, perhaps for the first time, 'Ay, now the plot thickens very much upon us.'

ploughman's lunch, a. The coinage of this term for a meal of bread, cheese, and pickle, though redolent of olden days, was in fact a marketing ploy of the English Country Cheese Council in the early 1970s. *The Ploughman's Lunch* was then the title of a film (UK, 1983), about how history gets rewritten.

PLU. 'People Like Us.' Social typing phrase, for identifying the type of people who share one's outlook on life, one's interests and, probably, one's behavioural patterns. British middle-class use – and known by the 1950s?

plume de ma tante, la. As 'the cat sat on the mat' is to learning the English language, so '*je n'ai pas la plume de ma tante*' is to learning French. It must have occurred in some widely used French grammar in British schools – possibly just prior to the First World War. In Terence Rattigan's play *French Without Tears* (1936) a character says: 'If a Frenchman asked me where the pen of his aunt was, the chances are I could give him a pretty sharp comeback and tell him it was in the pocket of the gardener.' A revue with the title played at the Garrick Theatre in 1955.

plums. See AREN'T ∼ CHEAP?

pocket. See I'VE GOT HIS PECKER IN MY ∼; NO ∼S IN SHROUDS.

poet. See AS THE ∼ HAS IT . . .

poet though I didn't know it, I am a. Said by a person accidentally making a rhyme. An old one this: Swift's *Polite Conversation* (1738) has this exchange:

> *Neverout:* Well, miss . . .
> *Miss Notable:* Ay, ay; many a one says well, that thinks ill.
> *Neverout:* Well, miss; I'll think of this.
> *Miss Notable:* That's rhyme, if you take it in time.
> *Neverout:* What! I see you are a poet.
> *Miss Notable:* Yes, if I had but the wit to show it.

poetry of motion, the. A phrase known by the seventeeth century when it referred to dancing (also called **poetry of the foot**), but particularly popular c 1900 in connection with railways and motor vehicles. On the other hand, 'Poetry *in* Motion' is the title of a pop song recorded by Johnny Tillotson in 1960. And Charles Sprawson, *Haunts of the Black Masseur* (1992) has: 'The style of [American swimmer] Martha Norelius . . . was

described by a Parisian as "poetry in motion", and her coach . . . never tired of watching her.'

Poets' Day. Phrase from the acronym 'POETS' for 'Piss/Push Off Early Tomorrow's Saturday' – indicating a frequent inclination of workers on Friday afternoons. Perhaps quite recent – by 1960.
Compare TGIF.

Pogues, The. The name of an Irish pop group (*fl.* 1989), originally called 'Pogue Mahone', from the Gaelic for 'kiss my arse'.

point(s). See under AT THIS MOMENT IN TIME; BROWNIE ∼S; UP TO A ∼ LORD COPPER.

poison. See NAME YOUR ∼.

poison(ed) dwarf, the. A name given to any unpleasant person of small stature. According to episode one of the ITV series *The World at War* (1975), this was a popular German nickname in the late 1930s for Hitler's diminutive propaganda chief, Joseph Goebbels. The literal German *Giftzwerg* is defined by the Collins German dictionary as 'poisonous individual; spiteful little devil'. In Wagner's *Das Rheingold* (1869), however, Wellgunde calls Alberich 'Schwefelgezwerg' (literally 'sulphurous dwarf'). Knowing how a Wagnerian phrase like NIGHT AND FOG was adapted in the Nazi era, this seems a likely source for the phrase.
From the *Independent on Sunday* (5 July 1992): 'The regiment involved in the unhappy events at Minden some 30 years ago, which provoked the local inhabitants to nickname its soldiers "The Poison Dwarves" was The Cameronians (The Scottish Rifles).'
In c 1979, Terry Wogan, the BBC Radio 2 disc jockey, helped ensure the success in Britain of the imported American TV series *Dallas*. He poked fun at it and, in particular, drew attention to the diminutive proportions of the actress Charlene Tilton who played the character Lucy Ewing by referring to her as 'the poison dwarf'.
Compare, from John Osborne, *Almost a Gentleman* (1991): 'Ronald Duncan

(dubbed "the **Black Dwarf**" by Devine and Richardson, because of his diminutive height and poisonous spirit) . . .' Sir Walter Scott published *The Black Dwarf* in 1816.

poke. See PIG IN A ~.

pole. See GREASY ~.

police. See HELPING THE ~ WITH THEIR INQUIRIES.

police caution, the. See ANYTHING YOU SAY MAY BE TAKEN DOWN . . .

policeman. See RAIN IS THE BEST ~ . . .

policemen. See YOU KNOW YOU'RE GETTING OLDER . . . ; YOUR ~ ARE WONDERFUL.

polish you off, oh I should love to. A British actor with the wonderful name of Tod Slaughter (1885–1956) was noted for his performances as Sweeney Todd, 'the demon barber of Fleet Street'. This line came from the rather melodramatic version he performed and which was filmed in 1936. The words were addressed to his victims who, of course, were subsequently turned into meat pies.

To 'polish something off', meaning to finish it quickly, began as boxing slang (recorded in 1829) but latterly has often been applied to food. Compare the hangman's phrase for his job in Charles Dickens, *Barnaby Rudge* (1841): he talks of 'working someone off'.

politically correct, to be. To avoid actions or words which might exclude or reflect badly upon minorities or groups perceived as being disadvantaged. These groups might be identified on the grounds of their race, sex, sexual orientation, class or politics. People in the US started talking about **political correctness** in the current, specific sense, in about 1984. From the *Washington Post* (12 March 1984): 'Langer . . . is saying that novelists have a duty higher than the one they owe to their art and their private vision of the world; they have a duty to be politically correct . . . In thus construing, Langer reveals herself to be a captive of the assumption, widespread among the academic and literary left, that art exists to serve politics.' By the following year, the phrase in its modern sense is fully formed and stands alone in the same paper (11 March 1985): 'It is the only caffeinated coffee served by the "wait-persons", as they are called, at the politically correct Takoma Cafe in Takoma Park.'

Really, 'politically correct' and 'political correctness' are the wrong terms for the idea, in that they may make people think it has to do with Politics with a capital P, whereas it has much more to do with social concerns. Why not 'socially correct', then? – because that would make it sound as though it had something to do with manners and etiquette.

'Ideologically correct' would give the game away, of course, and leads us back to politics. As it is, 'political' hints at the coercion that is all too much part of the PC movement.

politics. See ART OF THE POSSIBLE.

pomp and circumstance. The title of five marches by Sir Edward Elgar (Nos. 1–4 composed 1901–7, and No.5 in 1930, comes from Shakespeare's *Othello*, III.iii.360 (1604):

> O farewell . . .
> Pride, pomp, and circumstance of
>   glorious war!

poodle. See BALFOUR'S ~.

poor. See HOW'S YOUR ~ OLD FEET?

poor are always with you, the. This biblical phrase is to be found in Matthew 26:11, Mark 14:7, and John 12:8: 'For the poor always ye have with you.' *The Rich Are Always With Us* was the title of a film (US, 1932) and *The Rich Are With You Always*, the title of a novel (1976) by Malcolm Macdonald.

poor little rich girl, a. Phrase used about any young woman whose wealth has not brought her happiness. *The Poor Little Rich Girl* was the title of a novel (1912) by the American writer Eleanor Gates, filmed (US, 1917) starring Mary Pickford, remade

(US, 1936) with Shirley Temple. It is the story of a rich society girl who lives an isolated life and is kept apart from her parents. Later, the title of a song (1925) by Noël Coward.

poorly. See PROPER ~.

poor man's —, the. Gently derogatory way of indicating that someone is cheaper (in some sense) and probably inferior to what is named. Hence, 'Joan Collins is the poor man's Marlene Dietrich' or 'Norman Hunt is the poor man's Robert McKenzie' (broadcasting psephologists) (as the *New Statesman* put it in the early 1970s). William Inge (1860–1954), Dean of St Pauls', is supposed to have described women as 'the poor man's men'. Armadillo was known as 'poor man's pork' in the Southern US (because of its taste).

From the *Financial Times* (4 June 1982): 'In Britain at present mussels are a specialised taste, a sort of poor man's oyster, not an item of general diet at all'; (15 July 1982) 'The Bank of England is being called in to advise on what controls should be put into place and unless an effective system can be paid for, the Isle of Man could be stuck with the image of a poor man's Jersey.' From the *Daily Mail* (5 November 1993): 'With his burgeoning talent for comic impersonations, scathing one-liners and extravagant predictions of fistic mayhem, [boxer] Riddick Bowe is expanding into a poor man's Cassius Clay. Or rather, in these pay-TV days with 11 million $ per fight, a rich pretender to being the fastest lip in the ring.'

This continues a tradition going back to the mid-nineteenth century of referring mostly to *things* in this way. In Canada, a plate of dried beans was 'the poor man's piano' – on account of the noise that it provoked. An Italian expression is said to have been, 'Bed is the poor man's opera.'

poor old thing – she'll have to go! See NAY, NAY ~ THRICE AGAIN NAY!

poor soul – she's past it! See NAY, NAY ~ THRICE AGAIN NAY!

poor thing but mine own, a. In 1985, a painter called Howard Hodgkin won the

£10,000 Turner prize for a work (of art) called 'A Small Thing But My Own'. It was notable that he used the word 'small' rather than 'poor'. Nevertheless, he was presumably alluding to Touchstone's line in Shakespeare's *As You Like It*, V.iv.57 (1598): 'A poor virgin, sir, an ill-favoured thing, sir, but mine own.' Here Touchstone is not talking of art but of Audrey, the country wench he woos. The line is nowadays more likely to be used (in mock modesty) about a thing rather than a person.

pop. See SNAP! CRACKLE! ~!; SWEET AS THE MOMENT WHEN THE POD WENT ~.

Pop Art. Lawrence Alloway invented this designation for art that refers to popular culture (comic strip images, etc.), in the mid-1950s, although originally he used it as a synonym for 'popular culture'. The first recorded use of the word 'Pop' *in* art is in Eduardo Paolozzi's picture 'I Was a Rich Man's Plaything' (c 1947) which is a modest collage of advertisements and the cover of *Intimate Confessions*. A pistol, pointed at a pin-up, is going 'Pop!'

Popery. See NO ~.

pop goes the weasel. At some time in the nineteenth century, possibly in 1853, W.R. Mandale may have written the celebrated words:

> Up and down the City Road,
> In and out of the Eagle,
> That's the way the money goes –
> Pop goes the weasel!

He may have put these words to a country dance tune that already existed, but what did he mean by them? What is plain is that 'the Eagle' refers to the Eagle Tavern, then a theatre and pub in the City Road, London (the present tavern was built at the turn of the century). Those who went 'in and out', spent plenty of money and were forced to 'pop', or pawn, something. But what was the 'weasel' they pawned? A kind of tool used by a carpenter or a hatter, a tailor's flat iron, a coat (from rhyming slang 'weasel and stoat'), have all been suggested. As for 'pop goes the weasel' meaning an orgasm, this is probably a later play on the established phrase.

According to Morris, there is an American version of the song which goes:

Every night when I come home,
The Monkey's on the table.
I take a stick and knock him off
And pop goes the weasel!

pop one's clogs, to. Meaning 'to die'. Judging from its absence from Partridge/ *Slang* and *OED2*, this must be a fairly recent blending of 'to pop off', 'to die with one's boots on/off' (see BOOTS ON) and possibly 'pop' in the sense of 'to pawn' (see POP GOES THE WEASEL). An unconfirmed eighteenth-century use has been reported. *Street Talk, the Language of* Coronation Street (1986) has it.

poptastic! In 1993–4, the British comedy performers Harry Enfield and Paul Whitehouse created for BBC TV the characters of 'Smashie' and 'Nicey', two brilliant parodies of ageing disc jockeys at one time to be heard on BBC Radio 1 but who at about this time were being put out to grass. Specifically, they bore a strong resemblance to Alan Freeman and Mike Reid. 'Poptastic' is but an example of the lacklustre verbal invention that their kind indulged in.

pop-up toaster. See FEW VOUCHERS SHORT OF A ~ .

porch, put it on the. See under LET'S — AND SEE IF — .

porridge, to do. The term 'porridge' for 'time spent in prison' has been current since the 1950s at least. It is supposedly from rhyming slang 'borage and thyme' (time) though I have always thought this a little unlikely. The porridge-stirring connection with the (more American) expressions 'stir' (meaning 'prison'), 'in stir' (in prison) and 'stir crazy' (insane as a result of long imprisonment) may just be coincidental. These terms are said to derive from the Anglo-Saxon word *styr*, meaning 'punishment', reinforced by the Romany *steripen*, meaning 'prison'

(*DOAS*). On the other hand, if porridge was once the prisoner's basic food – and it was known as 'stirabout' – it may be more than coincidence that we have here. *Porridge* was the title of a BBC TV comedy series (1974–7) about prison life. In *Something Nasty in the Woodshed* (1976), Kyril Bonfiglioli provides another angle: '"Porridge" . . . means penal servitude. There is a legend . . . that if . . . on the last morning of your "stretch", you do not eat up all your nice porridge, you will be back in durance vile within the year.'

port. See ANY ~ IN A STORM; WIFE IN EVERY ~ .

Port Out Starboard Home. The mythical etymology for the word 'posh', meaning 'smart, grand', is that it is an acronym for 'Port Out Starboard Home', as the requirement for the most desirable staterooms on ships travelling to and from British India. But the P&O Line, which was the principal carrier, has no evidence of a single 'POSH' booking, nor would it have made much difference to the heat of the cabin which side you were on. *OED2* has no citations before the twentieth century. However, meaning 'dandy' or 'money' the word was nineteenth-century thieves' and especially Romany slang. It is not hard to see either of these meanings, or both combined, contributing to what we now mean by 'posh'.

possible. See ART OF THE ~ .

post early for Christmas. An enduring slogan of the British Post Office, intended to reduce the pressure on mail services caused by the weight of Christmas cards and parcels. Date of inception unknown – possibly 1920s. The simple non-seasonal **Post Early** on its own was apparently new in June 1922. In the Second World War, there was the similar injunction **Post Early – before noon,** not to mention the very bald **Telegraph less.**

positively. See ABSOLUTELY, MR GALLAGHER . . .

possums. See WAVE YOUR GLADDIES, ~ .

post. See FIRST PAST THE ∼; THERE'S A
CHEQUE IN THE POST.

post-war bulge. See BABY BOOMER.

potato. See COUCH ∼.

potatoes peeled. See under HEAVENS,
ELEVEN O'CLOCK . . .

potage. See MESS OF ∼.

pours. See IT NEVER RAINS BUT IT ∼.

powder one's nose, to. Euphemism for a
woman's going to the lavatory. *OED2*
doesn't find it before 1921 when Somerset
Maugham daringly put it in his play *The
Circle*. Cole Porter put it in *The New
Yorkers, 1930* – though there is some doubt
whether the song was actually used in the
show: 'The girls today/ Have but one thing
to say,/ "Where can one powder one's
nose?"'

power. See BLACK ∼; FLOWER ∼.

power to the people. A slogan shouted –
with clenched fist raised – by the Black
Panther movement and publicized as such
by its leader Bobby Seale, in Oakland,
California, in July 1969. It was also used by
other dissident groups, as illustrated by
Eldridge Cleaver: 'We say "All power to the
people" – Black Power for Black People,
White Power for White People, Brown
Power for Brown People, Red Power for Red
People, and X Power for any group we've
left out.' It was this somewhat generalized
view of 'People Power' that John Lennon
appeared to promote in the 1971 song
'Power to the People (Right On!)'. 'All
Power to the Soviets' was a cry of the
Bolsheviks during the Russian Revolution
of 1917.

pow! right in the kisser! See AND ∼ WE
GO.

power. See BALANCE OF ∼; IN OFFICE BUT
NOT IN ∼; MORE ∼ TO YOUR ELBOW.

**praise the Lord and pass the
ammunition!** A phrase of religious
pragmatism. Said in 1941, and

subsequently used as the title of a song by
Frank Loesser (1942), the authorship of this
saying is disputed. It may have been said by
an American naval chaplain during the
Japanese attack on Pearl Harbor. Lieut.
Howell M. Forgy (1908–83) is one
candidate. He was on board the US cruiser
New Orleans on 7 December 1941 and
encouraged those around him to to keep up
the barrage when under attack. His claim is
supported by a report in the *New York
Times* (1 November 1942).

Another name mentioned is that of
Captain W.H. Maguire. At first Captain
Maguire did not recall having used the
words but a year later said he might have
done. Either way, the expression actually
dates from the time of the American Civil
War.

pram. See GET OUT OF ONE'S ∼.

prayer. See COMIN' IN ON A WING AND A ∼;
SAYS ANYTHING BUT HIS/HER ∼S; TORY
PARTY AT ∼.

pregnant. See WOULD YOU BE MORE
CAREFUL IF . . .

prejudice. See TERMINATE WITH
EXTREME ∼.

prepared. See BE ∼.

prepare to meet thy God. This
slogan, unlike the END IS NIGH, another
favourite of placard-bearing religious
fanatics, does actually come from the
Bible: Amos 4:12.

presidency. See HEARTBEAT AWAY FROM
THE ∼.

press. See YOU ∼ THE BUTTON . . .

press, let's go to. See GOOD EVENING . . .

pressure. See GRACE UNDER ∼.

pretty. See HERE'S A ∼ KETTLE OF FISH.

pretty amazing! When Lady Diana
Spencer (*b* 1961) was asked in 1981 what
her first impression of the Prince of Wales,
her intended husband, had been, she

replied, 'Pretty amazing!' This innocuous verdict on their encounter in a freshly-ploughed field during 1977 briefly achieved catchphrase status.

price. See DON'T ASK THE ~ . . . ; EVERY MAN HAS HIS ~; WHAT ~ —?

priceless ingredient, the. ('. . . of every product is the honor and integrity of its maker'.) A slogan for Squibb drug products, in the US, from 1921. Before that year, Squibb had never advertised to the public. The problem given to Raymond Rubicam, then a writer at the N.W. Ayer & Son agency, was to produce a series of advertisements which would sell Squibb to the public and not offend the publicity-sensitive medical profession. David Ogilvy commented: 'Raymond Rubicam's famous slogan . . . reminds me of my father's advice: when a company boasts about its integrity, or a woman about her virtue, avoid the former and cultivate the latter.'

price of eggs. See WHAT'S THAT GOT TO DO WITH THE ~.

prick. See STIFF ~ HAS NO CONSCIENCE.

prick up one's ears, to. To become attentive, as a dog or horse would. Known by 1626.
   As for *Prick Up Your Ears*, the title of a film (UK, 1987) about the life and murder of Joe Orton, the playwright: in his diary for 18 February 1967, Orton wrote: 'Started typing up my final version [of the first draft] of *Up Against It*. Kenneth suggested that I call it *Prick Up Your Ears*. But this is much too good a title to waste on a film.' The 'Kenneth' was Kenneth Halliwell, Orton's flatmate who murdered him later that year. It was indeed too good a title to waste on the abortive *Up Against It*, Orton's planned film for the Beatles. In 1978, John Lahr used the phrase as the title of his biography of Orton. In his edition of *The Orton Diaries* (1986), Lahr noted: 'The title is a triple-pun, "ears" being an anagram of "arse". Orton intended using it as the title for a farce about the backstage goings-on prior to a coronation.' When the film *Prick Up Your Ears* came out, there were reports of

enthusiastic punsters in London climbing up to rearrange the lettering of the last word over cinema doors. In c 1974, a *Financial Times* crossword clue was: 'Listen carefully, or a sexual perversion (5,2,4,4).'

Prime Minister. See BEST ~ . . .

Prime Minister of Mirth. See under DESIST!

prince. See HAMLET WITHOUT THE ~.

princess. See COULD MAKE ANY ORDINARY GIRL . . . ; LIKE A FAIRY- TALE ~.

print. See ALL THE NEWS THAT'S FIT TO ~.

Priscilla, she's my best friend and I hate her . . . See under *EDUCATING ARCHIE.*

prison-house. See SHADES OF THE ~.

privacy. See YOURS TO ENJOY IN THE ~ . . .

private eye, a. Although it is true that a private investigator's job consists of keeping an eye on people, there may be more to the name than that. The term could derive from 'private investigator' or from the wide-open 'eye' symbol of the Pinkerton detective agency, founded in Chicago (1850). It went with the slogan WE NEVER SLEEP and was referred to as the 'Eye' by criminals and others. The full phrase seems to have emerged in the 1930s and 40s, particularly through the fiction of Raymond Chandler and others.
   Private Eye, the British satirical fortnightly (founded 1961) seems to have taken the title because of the investigative exposures which have always made up a portion of its contents.

private life/lives of —, the. Although Alexander Korda had directed a film called *The Private Life of Helen of Troy* (1927), the original of all the 'Private Life of . . .' books and films was surely his immensely successful *The Private Life of Henry VIII* (1933). The following year, Julian Huxley with R.M. Lockley produced a natural history film called *The Private Life of Gannets* (which won an Oscar).

Since then, in the cinema, we have had private lives of Don Juan (1934), Elizabeth and Essex (1939), Sherlock Holmes (1970), and so on. And, on TV, there have been numerous natural history films since the mid-1960s, e.g. the BBC's *The Private Life of the Kingfisher*.

There is, of course, a nudging note to the use of the phrase – as though we are not just being promised a glimpse of domestic happenings, but probably sex life, too.

probably the best lager in the world. A slogan for Carlsberg, from 1973. Even if it had not been intoned by Orson Welles in the TV ads, the 'probably' inserted into this hyperbole would still have fascinated. However, it is by no means the first product to be advertised with such caution. Zephyr, imported by A. Gale & Co. Ltd of Glasgow, was called 'Possibly the finest tobacco in the world' in ads current in 1961.

Procul Harum (also known as **Procol Harum**). The name of a British pop group (*fl.* 1967) which had a hit with 'A Whiter Shade of Pale' came from the bastard Latin for 'beyond these things'. It may, however, have been an attempt to express in Latin a more widely used phrase of the day – 'way out'.

product of the mastermind. See under MASTERMIND.

profile. See HIGH ∼ .

Profundis. See DE PROFUNDIS.

programme. See AND IN A PACKED ∼ . . .

prominent in his field. This phrase was possibly first used in hunting. As for, 'prominent, mainly because of the flatness of the surrounding countryside', it seems to be a rare joke by Karl Marx. In Vol. 1, Chap 16 of *Capital* (1867), he writes: 'On a level plain, simple mounds look like hills; and the insipid flatness of our present bourgeoisie is to be measured by the altitude of its "great intellects".' Marx comments thus after having demolished one of John Stuart Mill's arguments.

promised. See I NEVER ∼ YOU A ROSE GARDEN.

promises, promises! Dating from at least the 1960s, this expression is either a way of mocking another person's undertaking to do something or is the simple promoter of a double entendre. For example, if one person were to say, 'If you pop round later this evening, I can give you one,' then the other might say . . .

From BBC radio's ROUND THE HORNE (30 April 1967): 'You swine – you'll feel my crop for this' – 'Promises, promises.' *Promises, Promises* was the title of a musical (Broadway, 1968) based on the Billy Wilder film *The Apartment*, and may have further encouraged use of the phrase.

pro patria mori. See DULCE ET DECORUM . . .

proper Charlie, a. The phrase a **right Charlie** probably grew out of rhyming slang 'Charlie Hunt', used to describe a fool or simpleton. I think it probably arose during the Second World War – it may have been a simultaneous British and American coinage, too. 'Proper Charlie' presumably developed from the same source. It was commandeered by the comedian Charlie Chester (*b* 1914) on radio immediately after the war and later used by him as the title of a radio show.

From the *Guardian* (1 December 1988) concerning a judge, Sir Harold Cassel QC: 'He once gave a robber an hour's bail, warning: "If you do not turn up you will make me look a proper Charlie." The man never returned.'

(Charlie Chester was billed as '**cheerful Charlie** Chester'. The alliteration is all important and I think the phrase has found use elsewhere.)

proper poorly! 'I didn't feel well, I didn't. I felt poorly – proper poorly' – catchphrase of the British comedian Reg Dixon (1915–84). He was also noted, on early 1950s radio show like *Variety Bandbox*, for his theme song, 'Confidentially'.

prose. See DEATHLESS ∼ .

protest. See METHINKS SHE DOTH ∼ . . .

proud as Punch. See PLEASED AS PUNCH.

Pru. See ASK THE MAN FROM THE ~.

ps and qs, to mind one's. Meaning 'to be careful', the phrase has several suggested origins: the letters 'p' and 'q' look so alike, a child might well be admonished to be careful writing them or a printer to take care in setting them; because a well-mannered person has to be careful to remember 'pleases and thankyous'; because in a public house 'pints' and 'quarts' would be chalked up on a blackboard for future payment; and, in the days of wigs, Frenchmen had to be warned not to get their *pieds* (feet) mixed up with their *queues* (wig-tails) when bowing and scraping. Recorded by 1779.

Pseud's Corner. A feature of the British satirical magazine *Private Eye* (from 1968 onwards) has been a column listing examples of pretentious writing and thinking culled from the media. This has led to a certain self-consciousness among likely 'pseuds' who are now likely to preface their remarks with, 'I expect this'll land me in Pseud's Corner but . . .'

Apparently, the noun 'pseud', referring to a pseudo-intellectual person, was British schoolboy slang among the editors of the *Eye* in the 1950s but the prefix 'pseudo-' for 'counterfeit; spurious' is very old. The American Daniel J. Boorstin in *The Image* (1960) coined the term **pseudo-event** for an occasion laid on solely for the purpose of attracting news coverage.

PS I Love You. The title of a memoir of his father, Peter (1981) by Michael Sellers, comes from the title of a Lennon and McCartney song (1963), though there had been an earlier song with the title by Johnny Mercer and Gordon Jenkins (1934).

public enemy No. 1. John Dillinger (1903–34) was the first officially designated 'Public Enemy No. 1' in the US. He robbed banks and killed people in Illinois, Indiana and Ohio during 1933–4 to such an extent that the Attorney General, Homer Cummings, called him this. In fact, Dillinger was the only person ever so named. The FBI's 'Ten Most Wanted Men' list did not give a ranking. Dillinger's exploits and his escape from capitivity aroused great public interest. He was eventually shot dead by FBI agents outside a cinema in Chicago.

The coining of the term 'Public Enemy' in this context has been attributed to Frank Loesch, president of the Chicago Crime Commission, who had to try to deal with Al Capone's hold over the city in 1923. The idea was to try and dispel the romantic aura such gangsters had been invested with by the popular press. James Cagney starred in a gangster film called *The Public Enemy* in 1931.

The phrase soon passed into general usage. In June 1934, P.G. Wodehouse, referring in a letter to difficulties with US income-tax officials, said: 'I got an offer from Paramount to go to Hollywood at $1,500 a week and had to refuse as I am Public Enemy No. 1 in America, and can't go there.'

Other US film titles have been: *Public Hero Number One* (1935), *Public Menace* (1935), and *Public Enemy's Wife* (1936). There was a British musical called *Public Nuisance No.1* and in the musical comedy *Seeing Stars* at the Gaiety Theatre, London (1935), Florence Desmond had a hit with the song 'Public Sweetheart Number One'. In *Anything Goes* (1934), Cole Porter had a song 'Public Enemy Number One', and so did Harold Rome for the 1937 *Pins and Needles*.

The words have since been applied to any form of supposed undesirable, while Raymond Postgate, founder of the *Good Food Guide*, was dubbed 'Public Stomach No. 1', and Beverley Nichols, the author and journalist, called himself 'Public Anemone No. 1'.

publicity. See ALL ~ IS GOOD ~.

public speaking. See UNACCUSTOMED AS I AM . . .

publish and be damned! 'Go ahead and write what you want about me!' From the 1st Duke of Wellington's comment to a blackmailer who offered not to publish anecdotes of the Duke and his mistress, Harriet Wilson, in return for payment. *Publish and Be Damned* was the title of a book (1955) by the journalist Hugh Cudlipp. Richard Ingrams declared on several occasions (c 1977) that a suitable motto for *Private Eye*, of which he was editor, would be: 'Publish and Be Sued'.

pudding(s). See SOMEBODY PINCHED ME ~ .

pull the wool over someone's eyes, to. When wigs were commonly worn, they were sometimes referred to as wool (because of the resemblance, particularly the curls). Thus to pull the wool over people's eyes was to pull wigs over their eyes and render them incapable of seeing. Hence also the modern meaning 'to hoodwink'. 'To pull the wool etc.' would seem to be a phrase of American origin and was in use by 1859.

pun. See IF YOU'LL EXCUSE THE ~ !

Punch. See AS PLEASED AS ~ .

punch up the bracket. See under *HANCOCK'S HALF-HOUR*.

puppies. See HUSH ~ .

pure. See 99 44/100 PER CENT ~ .

pushed. See DID SHE FALL OR WAS SHE ~ ?

pussycat. See WHAT'S NEW, ~ ?

Pussy Galore. One of the most intriguingly named of all James Bond's women in the novels of Ian Fleming was the heroine of *Goldfinger* (1959; film UK, 1964). Other Bond women included Honeychile Rider, Kissy Suzuki, Giovanna Goodthighs, and not forgetting Miss Moneypenny and the villainous Rosa Klebb.

put a penny on the drum. Said by comedian Clay Keyes (a Liverpudlian who pretended to be an American) in a BBC radio show called *The Old Town Hall* in 1941. Members of the studio orchestra had to guess musical riddles sent in by listeners, failing which they paid a forfeit to charity, e.g.: 'Where did the salt and vinegar go?' Musical answer: 'All over the pla(i)ce.'

However, the phrase existed before this. Stanley Holloway recorded a song with the title 'Penny on the Drum' in 1937. Written by him, it was on a promotional record made for Butlin's Holiday Camps. Jean Phillips of Henley-on-Thames wrote to me (1994): 'According to my father, who was in the army in the First World War, it constituted among his fellow soldiers an invitation to take part in a game of Crown and Anchor. The person starting the game would call out, "put a penny on the drum", and anyone who did so could then take part in the game. I think the use of an actual drum had been superseded and the game may well have been played on the ground. It was a gambling game, requiring a board and some dice, marked with crown and anchor. I rather fancy that most of the soldiers who innocently put their pennies on the drum never saw them back again.'

A Canadian correspondent remembers from the 1940s an irreverent song about the Salvation Army which included the chorus: 'Hallelujah, hallelujah, throw a nickel on the drum and you'll be saved.'

put a smile on your face. See under COME ALIVE . . .

put a sock in it! 'Shut up!' 'Shut your mouth!' addressed to a noisy person. Neil Ewart in *Everyday Phrases* (1983) confidently asserts that this dates from the days of the wind-up, 'acoustic' gramophones where the sound emerged from a horn. With no electronic controls to raise or lower the volume, the only way to regulate the sound was to put in or take out an article of clothing, which deadened it. (Presumably, mutes as stuck in the horns of brass instruments were not supplied.)

The *OED2* has a citation from 1919 – an explanation of the term from the *Athenaeum* journal – which suggests the phrase was not widely known even then.

I am not totally convinced by the gramophone explanation. Partridge/*Slang* compares the earlier expression '(to) put a bung in it' – as in a bath or leak. So I reserve judgement. Why shouldn't a sock inserted in the human mouth be the origin? After all, a sock in the jaw would be the next best thing.

put a spoke in someone's wheel, to.
Meaning 'to prevent someone from doing something' this is an odd expression if one knows that bicycle wheels already have spokes in them. Here, however, what is evoked is the days when carts had solid wheels and no spokes in the modern sense. The spoke then was a pin which could be inserted into a hole on the wheel to act as a brake. The *OED2* believes that, while the expression has been known since 1583, 'spoke' may be a mistranslation of a Dutch expression including the word *spaak*, meaning 'bar, stave'.

put a tiger in your tank. The Esso Tiger had been around in the US for a long time before 1964 when a cartoon version was introduced for the first time (a year later in the UK) to promote Esso petroleum. It became a national craze, with countless tiger tails adorning the petrol caps of the nation's cars. Subsequently, with the slogan 'Put a Tiger in Your Tank', the idea spread even further afield. '*Pack den Tiger in den Tank*' appeared in Germany. '*Mettez un tigre dans votre moteur*' appeared in France (in Jean-Luc Godard's 1965 film *Pierrot Le Fou*, the Jean-Paul Belmondo character says, 'Put a tiger in my tank' to a Total service station attendant who replies, 'We don't do tigers here.').

In the US, especially, the slogan gave rise to numerous tiger derivatives: 'If you feel like a tiger is in your throat, reach for Guardets Lozenges . . .' A hamburger stand advertised, 'Put a tiger in your tummy'. Tiger Beer in the Japanese *Times* sloganned, 'Put a tiger in your tankard'. Standard Rochester Beer countered with, 'Put a tankard in your tiger'. The UK campaign ran for two years before it flagged.

Perhaps the slogan owed something to the Muddy Waters song '(I Want to Put a) Tiger in Your Tank' (by W. Dixon) which he was performing by 1960 and which gave double meanings to a number of motoring phrases (not least in the title).

put a woman on top for a change. A slogan promoting the idea of Margaret Thatcher as Prime Minister prior to the Conservative election win in 1979. Rob Hayward MP told me in 1984 that the idea first came up when he was National Vice-Chairman of the Young Conservatives. Originally, 'Have a Woman on Top' (or 'Fuck Me, I'm a Tory'), it was devised by Young Conservatives in 1976 and distributed as a sticker at the Tory Party Conference. It was taken up as an official slogan by the party.

put on (the) dog, to. Meaning 'to put on airs, fine clothes', this is a US expression dating from the 1870s, probably from among college students (especially at Yale) who had to wear stiff, high collars (jokily known as 'dog-collars') on formal occasions.

put one's best foot forward, to. See BEST FOOT FORWARD.

put one's pudding out for treacle. See SOMEBODY PINCHED ME PUDDING.

put the bells and whistles on, to. To make an elaborate fuss about something. From the *Independent* (15 March 1989): '"It's not a story you put the bells and whistles on," says Malcolm Hoddy, the news editor.' 'It's a simple message and I'm leaving out the whistles and bells' – song, 'Birdhouse in Your Soul' (1990), performed by They Might Be Giants.

In computing, 'bells and whistles' are additional but not essential features put on hardware and software to make them commercially attractive (and so used by 1984). Compare ALL-SINGING, ALL-DANCING.

The origin of the phrase in both senses appears to lie in the bells and whistles fixed to fairground organs. (Probably unconnected is the expression 'to souple the whistle and bells' that occurs in 'Todlen Hame', one of the bawdy verses by Robert Burns.)

put the screws on, to. Meaning 'to apply pressure on someone to do something', 'screws' here is short for 'thumbscrews', the ancient and medieval method of torturing prisoners. This could be why prison guards have been nicknamed 'screws', although another explanation is from screw meaning 'key'. Gaolers were sometimes known as 'turnkeys', as this was their most significant function.

put the tin hat on, to. To finish off completely, in a way that the speaker may find objectionable. Possibly from military use, where tin hat = brass hat. Current by 1919. From P.G. Wodehouse, *Summer Lightning*, Chap. 12.ii (1929): 'But this was final. This was the end. This put the tin hat on it.'

· Q ·

QE2, the. This is the popular name for the Cunard Line ship which made its maiden voyage in May 1969. It was the successor to the liner known as *Queen Elizabeth*, named after the wife of King George VI and launched by her in 1938. The idea seems to have been *not* to call the ship *Queen Elizabeth II* or *Queen Elizabeth the Second* (after HM Queen Elizabeth II), but to evoke a second *Queen Elizabeth* liner like the first. During building, it was known as 'Q3' – the third of the queens, the other having been the *Queen Mary*. Nevertheless, when the reigning Queen launched the ship in 1967, she distinctly named her the 'Queen Elizabeth the Second', as though after herself. On the bow and stern of the vessel is written '*Queen Elizabeth II*'.

Quai d'Orsay. See under FOGGY BOTTOM.

quality. See NEVER MIND THE ~ . . .

quango. The acronymous name of a type of statutory body set up outside the Civil Service but appointed by and financed by central government seems to have originated in the US in the 1960s. It became popular in the UK in the 1970s, standing for 'QUasi-Autonomous-Non-Governmental-Organization', though sometimes 'National' has been substituted for 'Non-Governmental'.

quarter. See HANG, DRAW AND ~ .

Quatermass. See IT LOOKS LIKE SOMETHING OUT OF ~ .

qué? In the BBC TV comedy series *Fawlty Towers* (1975–9), Manuel the Spanish waiter (Andrew Sachs) seemed to do very little else than ask 'What?' in Spanish. But then, as Basil Fawlty (John Cleese) would explain, 'You'll have to excuse him – he comes from Barcelona.'

queen. See MAKES YOU FEEL LIKE A ~ .

Queen Anne's dead. This phrase might be used to put down someone who has just told you some very old news or what you know already. Mencken glosses it slightly differently: 'Reply to an inquiry for news, signifying that there is none not stale.' He also supplies the alternative **Queen Elizabeth is dead** and says that both forms appear to date from *c* 1720.

In George Colman the Younger's play *The Heir-at-Law* (1797), there occurs the line: 'Tell 'em Queen Anne's dead.' She actually died in 1714. Partridge/*Slang* dates 'Queen Anne is dead' to 1722, in a ballad cited by Apperson: 'He's as dead as Queen Anne the day after she dy'd' (which doesn't seem to convey the modern meaning of the expression); and 'Queen Elizabeth is dead' to 1738 in Swift's *Polite Conversation*:

> What news, Mr Neverout?
> Why, Madam, Queen Elizabeth's dead

and puts 'My Lord Baldwin is dead' to *c* 1670–1710. A US equivalent is, 'Bryan has carried Texas' – presumably referring to William Jennings Bryan (*d* 1925) who stood three times unsuccessfully for the US presidency.

Queen Elizabeth slept here. Usually an unsubstantiated claim and a slogan that has been used to promote visits to English stately homes – and some inns – probably since such tourism began in the eighteenth century. Elizabeth I was an inveterate traveller and guest. By 1847, Thackeray was writing in *Vanity Fair*, Chap. 8: 'I think there are at least twenty bedrooms on the first floor; and one of them has the bed in which Queen Elizabeth slept.' By 1888, Jerome K. Jerome in *Three Men in a Boat* has: 'She was nuts on public houses, was England's Virgin Queen. There's scarcely a pub of any attractions within ten miles of

London that she does not seem to have looked in at, stopped at, or slept at, some time or other.'

In the US, the equivalent slogan is **George Washington slept here**, as in the title of Kauffman and Hart's play (1940, film US, 1942), which, when adapted by Talbot Rothwell for the Strand Theatre, London, later in the 1940s, was called *Queen Elizabeth Slept Here*.

queen for a day. Phrase for a woman who is being given a special treat. It derives from an American radio programme which ran for ten years in the 1940s. According to an informant, 'being a queen for a day didn't mean they gave you a country; you only got your wish, that's what. No one complained.' Adapted as a daytime TV show, it was a big hit from 1955–64, but *Halliwell's Television Companion* (1982) calls it 'the nadir of American TV'.

I note that when Radio Luxembourg adopted the format (from 1955, introduced by Richard Attenborough, sponsored by Phensic) they changed the title to *Princess for a Day*. Was this because the wishes fulfilled were more modest, the participants younger, or had the word 'queen' become too tainted by that time? In about 1970, I think there was a cinema documentary about transvestites with the title, *Queen for a Day*.

queer as a clockwork orange, to be as. See CLOCKWORK ORANGE.

queer as a coot. This pejorative phrase has been applied to 'queers' in the homosexual sense (and was so recorded in 1958), but is probably no more than an alliterative version of the older 'stupid as a coot'. Coots are probably no stupider or queerer than any other bird, but the name sounds funny. Compare BALD AS A BADGER/BANDICOOT/COOT.

queer as Dick's hatband, to be as. Dismissive phrase, remembered by many (in 1994). Tony Brisby of Little Haywood, Staffordshire, recalled: 'A sentence used by my grandmother was, "He's as queer as Dick's hatband – it went round twice and then didn't meet."' Marjorie M. Rawicz of Sandiacre, Nottinghamshire, recalled: 'As a

young person in the Twenties, I remember my Mother (Derbyshire with Yorkshire roots) saying "You're as funny as Dick's hat band" when either my sister or I was being contrary and difficult. I heard no more of this expression until the late Sixties when a Miss Emily White (from Cheshire) told me that *her* Mother finished the quote – "Funny as Dick's hat band – it went twice round and then would not tie."'

David Scott of Windermere recalled his grandmother saying in the 1930s – if things didn't work out: 'That's like Dick's hatband – it went round twice and still didn't fit!' Dorothy Hoyle of Grantham added that, in her family, it was always 'as *black* as Dick's hatband' when something was very dirty. Mrs J.M.H. Wright of Ilkley countered with: 'The correct version – "as *near* as Dick's hatband" – makes the saying self-explanatory, at least to a Yorkshire person. "Near" in Yorkshire speech as well as meaning "close to" also means "mean or stingy with money". Thus the person referred to is as "near" with money as Dick's hatband is "near" to Dick's head.'

So, lots of variations. The *OED2* gives the phrase thus: 'as queer (tight, odd, etc.) as Dick's (or Nick's) hatband', and adds: 'Dick or Nick was probably some local character or half-wit, whose droll sayings were repeated.' Partridge/*Slang* describes it as 'an intensive tag of chameleonic sense and problematic origin'. He dates the phrase from the mid-eighteenth to the early nineteenth century, finds a Cheshire phrase 'all my eye and Dick's hatband', and also a version that went, 'as queer as Dick's hatband, that went nine times round and wouldn't meet'. In Grose's *Dictionary of the Vulgar Tongue* (1796), Partridge found the definition: 'I am as queer as Dick's hatband; that is, out of spirits, or don't know what ails me.' A 'Newcastle form c 1850' is the 'nine times round and wouldn't meet', just given.

But who was Dick, if anybody? Brewer is confident that it knows the answer: Richard Cromwell (1626–1712), who succeeded Oliver, his father, as Lord Protector in 1658 and did not make a very good job of it. Hence, Brewer believes, 'Dick's hatband' was his 'crown', as in the following expressions: *Dick's hatband was made of sand* ('his regal honours were a "rope of sand"'), as queer as Dick's hatband ('few things have been more ridiculous than the exaltation and abdication of Oliver's son') and as tight as Dick's hatband ('the crown was too tight for him to wear with safety').

Queer Street, to be in. Meaning 'to be in debt'. Possibly from the tradesmen's habit of putting a 'query' next to the names of people whose creditworthiness was questionable. The expression has also been used (since 1811) to describe being in any kind of difficulty.

question. See SIXTY-FOUR DOLLAR ~.

question-mark still hangs over. See under JURY IS STILL OUT.

question of —, a. A format much used in the framing of broadcast programme titles and, by now, a cliché of same. As in A Question of Sport/Confidence/Stars/Politics etc. I was responsible for A Question of Degree (about graduate unemployment, BBC Radio, 1970) and that particular phrase has been around for a long time (Punch, 7 December 1910, for example).
  Many titles are also put in the form, The Body/The Week/Sport **In Question.**

questions. See NO ~ ASKED.

quick. See BEFORE ONE CAN SAY 'JACK ROBINSON'; SLOW, SLOW, ~, ~, SLOW.

quick and the dead, the. 'Quick' here has

the old sense of 'the living', as on several occasions in the Bible, e.g. 'judge of the quick and the dead' (Acts 10:42).

quick brown fox . . . See NOW IS THE TIME . . .

quick thinking, Batman! See under BATMAN.

qui tollis peccata mundi. See MASS PHRASES.

quoniam tu solus Sanctus. See MASS PHRASES.

Quo vadis? [Whither goest thou?] come from the Latin translation (the Vulgate) of John 13:36: 'Simon Peter said unto him, Lord, whither goest thou? Jesus answered him, Whither I go, thou canst not follow me now'; and from John 16:5 in which Christ comforts his disciples before the Crucifixion. The words also occur in Genesis 32:17 and in the Acts of St Peter among the New Testament Apocrypha in which, after the Crucifixion, Peter, fleeing Rome, encounters Christ on the Appian Way. He asks Him, '*Domine, quo vadis?*' [Lord, whither goest thou?] and Christ replies, '*Venio Romam, iterum crucifigi*' [I am coming to Rome to be crucified again.]
  Familiar from the title of a film (US, 1951, and two previous Italian ones) and an opera (1909) by Jean Nouguès, all based on the novel *Quo Vadis?* (1896) by the Pole, Henryk Sienkiewicz.

· R ·

rabbit. See SHOW US YOUR ~.

rabbit, rabbit. The singers Chas and Dave introduced this line to one of their commercials for Courage Best Bitter in the UK, *c* 1983. It emulates talkative women who interrupt the pleasures of the drinking process. 'To rabbit', meaning 'to talk', comes from rhyming slang ('rabbit and pork'). See also GER(T)CHA!

race to the sea, the. This phrase dates from the Autumn of 1914, during the early months of the First World War. In his *English History 1914–45* (1966), A.J.P. Taylor writes: 'Both combatant lines hung in the air. Some 200 miles of open country separated the German and French armies from the sea. Each side tried to repeat the original German strategy of turning the enemy line. This was not so much a "race to the sea", its usual name, as a race to outflank the other side before the sea was reached. Both sides failed.'

Martin Gilbert uses the phrase evocatively of a phase of the Second World War in the official biography of Winston Churchill (Vol. 6, Chap. 21): 'As dawn broke on May 26 [1940], the news from France dominated Churchill's thoughts, and those of his advisers and staff. The road to Dunkirk was open. The race to the sea was about to begin.' (In his own *The Second World War*, Vol. 2, Churchill entitled the chapter dealing with Dunkirk, 'The March to the Sea'.)

radical chic. The fashionable espousal of left-wing, radical causes, clothes and lifestyle by people with more money than sense. The phrase was coined in an article by Tom Wolfe describing a party given by Leonard Bernstein, the American composer and conductor, for members of the Black Panthers movement. The article was subsequently collected in Wolfe's book *Radical Chic & Mau-Mauing the Flak Catchers* (1970).

radio. See STEAM ~.

rag. See CHEW THE ~.

rags to riches. The name given to a certain type of fiction, often in publishers' blurbs, of which the novels by the American writer Horatio Alger (1832–99) are prototypical. Sometimes also to the actual stories of people who have risen from poverty to wealth. The term comes from the story of CINDERELLA. It was also the title of a popular song (1953) by Adler and Ross. *OED2*'s earliest citation is from 1947.

railroad. See WHAT A WAY TO RUN . . .

railway lines. See UP AND DOWN THE ~.

rain cats and dogs, to. Meaning 'to rain extremely heavily', there is no very convincing explanation for this phrase. According to Morris, it comes from the days when street drainage was so poor that a heavy rain storm could easily drown cats and dogs. After the storm people would see the number of dead cats and dogs and assume they had fallen out of the sky. Brewer suggests, on the other hand, that in northern mythology cats were supposed to have great influence on the weather and dogs were a signal of wind, 'thus cat may be taken as a symbol of the downpouring rain, and the dog of the strong gusts of wind accompanying a rain-storm'. Hmmm.

rain-check. See TAKE A ~.

raining. See IF IT WAS ~ . . .

rain in Spain, the. See under HOW NOW, BROWN COW?

rain is the best policeman of all. Heard from a senior police officer after the London Notting Hill Carnival had been rained off on the Late Summer Bank Holiday in August 1986. Meaning that crime falls when the rain does (as also in cold weather).

rains. See DAY THAT THE ~ CAME DOWN; *IT ALWAYS ~ ON SUNDAY*; IT NEVER ~ BUT IT POURS.

raise Cain, to. Meaning 'to make trouble, a fuss, a disturbance', the allusion here is to the biblical Cain ('the first murderer') who killed his brother Abel (Genesis 4:2–8). A person who makes trouble, 'raises the spirit' of Cain by doing so.

raise one's Ebenezer, to (sometimes **to get one's Ebenezer up**). Meaning 'to be angry', this expression was in US use by the mid-1830s, Ebenezer being a nickname for the devil. It is not to be confused with what is referred to in the hymn: 'Come Thou Fount' (R. Robinson, 1758) – 'Here I raise my Ebenezer', where Ebenezer is the Hebrew 'stone of help', as in the name of a type of chapel. Samuel raised a thanksgiving stone at Ebenezer after the defeat of the Philistines. Plenty of scope for double entendres, of course – especially, if the hymn is sung at weddings, as has been known.

Raisin in the Sun. Title of a play (1959) by Lorraine Hansberry, taken from the poem 'Harlem' (1951) by Langston Hughes: 'What happens to a dream deferred?/Does it dry up/Like a raisin in the sun?'

Ramsbottom, Enoch and me. During the Second World War, the BBC radio programme *Happidrome* featured Harry Korris as Mr Lovejoy, a theatre manager, Cecil Fredericks as Ramsbottom, and Robby Vincent as Enoch, the call-boy. hence, the phrase from the opening song, 'We three in *Happidrome*,/Ramsbottom, Enoch and me . . .' Also from the show came **take 'im away, Ramsbottom!** and **let me tell you!** Enoch would say this last before revealing some startling fact to Mr Lovejoy.

ranch. See MEANWHILE BACK AT THE ~ . . .

rape. See DATE ~ .

raspberry. See under BRONX CHEER.

rat. See DESERT ~ S; LIKE ~ S DESERTING . . .; YOU DIRTY ~ !

rat pack. See BRAT PACK.

Ray's a Laugh. Comedian Ted Ray (1909–77) served his apprenticeship around the music halls before becoming one of Britain's great radio comedians. His programme *Ray's a Laugh* ran on the BBC from 1949 to 1960. He recalled one of the most famous of the show's catchphrases in his book *Raising the Laughs* (1952). It occurred in sketches between 'Mrs Hoskin' (played by Bob Pearson) and 'Ivy' (Ted Ray): 'George Inns [the producer] agreed that the climax of their original conversation should be the mention of a mystical "Dr Hardcastle" whom Ivy secretly adored . . . From the moment Bob, in his new role, had spoken the words, "I sent for young Dr Hardcastle", and we heard Ivy's excited little intake of breath, followed by, **"He's loo-vely, Mrs Hoskin . . . he's loo-oo-vely!"** a new phrase had come into being.'

Mrs Hoskin would also say, famously, **Ee, it was agony, Ivy!** – however, it has been suggested that this had earlier origins in music hall.

Other phrases from the show:

are you going to pardon me? Charles Hawtrey as 'Mr Muggs'.
Char-har-lie!/'Allo, what do you want, Ingrid? An exchange between Pat Hayes and Fred Yule.

do you mind! Spoken by Kenneth Connor as 'Sidney Mincing'. Appearing in a different situation each week, Mincing was usually some sort of unhelpful, downbeat shop assistant and was introduced, for example, thus, by Ray in a furniture store: 'It looks like a contemptuous lamp-standard with a weird-looking shade.' Mincing: 'Do you mind! My name is Sidney Mincing and I happen to be the proprietor of this dish pans, frying pans and Peter Pans (as it's all on the Never-Never) emporium. What can I do for you?'

if you've never been to Manchester, you've never lived! Or perhaps it was, 'If you haven't been to Manchester, you haven't lived'? Either way, it was said by 'Tommy Trafford' (Graham Stark). Probably, one has here another format phrase – 'If/Until you've . . . you haven't lived.' From the *Observer* (15 January 1989) on the George Formby Appreciation Society: 'Until you have seen this herd of wallies, all long past their sell-by dates and playing their ukuleles in time to a film of their diminutive hero, you haven't lived.' Compare, too, the Spanish proverb that Mencken records: 'He who has not seen Seville has seen nothing.'

Jen-nif-er said in a special way, as I recall from the mid-1950s. This appears to have grown out of an exchange between Ted Ray and a little girl (again played by Bob Pearson). Ray would ask what her name was and she would lisp the reply.

See also MASTERMIND, YOU SHOULD USE STRONGER ELASTIC.

reach for a lucky instead of a sweet. A slogan for Lucky Strike cigarettes, current in the US from the late 1920s. George Washington Hill of the American Tobacco Company was driving through New York City one day when he noticed a stout woman waiting to cross the street, eating a big piece of candy. Alongside, a taxi pulled up in which a 'nice-looking woman' was smoking a cigarette. The contrast inspired the slogan. Understandably, the confectionery industry wasn't very pleased, but it is said that this campaign created more women smokers than any other promotion.

reach for the sky/stars! (sometimes just **reach for it!**) This is what a character in a Western movie says when, pointing a gun at an opponent, he wants him to 'put his hands up' and thus away from any weapons the opponent may have. However, when Paul Brickhill entitled his biography of Douglas Bader, the legless flying ace, *Reach for the Sky* (1954) he was no doubt alluding to the RAF motto *'per ardua ad astra'*

[through striving to the stars].

'Reach for the *Star*' was a line used in promoting the British newspaper (current February 1989).

read. See HE WHO RUNS MAY ~; I'M SORRY I'LL ~ THAT AGAIN.

read any good books lately? See under MUCH BINDING IN THE MARSH.

ready for Freddie. See under ARE YOU READY, EDDIE?

read my lips. 'Listen to what I am saying – I mean it.' Although popularized by George Bush in his speech accepting the Republican nomination on 19 August 1988, the phrase was not new. Bush wanted to emphasize his pledge not to raise taxes, whatever pressure Congress applied, so what he said was, 'I'll say no, and they'll push, and I'll say no, and they'll push again, and I'll say to them, "Read my lips, no new taxes."' According to William Safire, in an article in the *New York Times* Magazine (September 1988), the phrase is rooted in 1970s rock music (despite there being a song with the title copyrighted by Joe Greene in 1957). The British actor/singer Tim Curry used the phrase as the title of an album of songs in 1978. Curry said he took it from an Italian-American recording engineer who used it to mean, 'Listen and listen very hard, because I want you to hear what I've got to say.'

Several lyricists in the 1980s used the phrase for song titles. A football coach with the Chicago Bears became nicknamed Mike 'Read My Lips' Ditka. There has been a thoroughbred race horse so named. Safire also cites a number of American politicians using the phrase before Bush, also in the 1980s.

read the riot act, to. The meaning of this phrase is 'to make strong representations about something; express forcibly that something must cease'. The actual Riot Act passed by the British Parliament in 1714 (and finally repealed in 1973), provided for the dispersal of crowds (defined as being of more than 12 persons) by those in authority. The method used was for someone to stand up and, literally, read out the terms of the Act so that the rioters knew what law they were breaking.

ready when you are, Mr De Mille! (or ... **C.B.!**) The punchline of a rather lengthy joke, current by the 1960s at least. In short, the joke tells of the day when Cecil B. De Mille, the famed producer of biblical epics for the cinema, was directing a battle scene which involved thousands of extras and animals and probably ended with the destruction of the set. Whatever the case, it would only be possible for there to be one 'take'. And so, C.B. covered himself by having the scene filmed by four cameras. When the action was completed, the destruction wrought, and any chance of repeating the matter had been lost for all time, Mr De Mille checked with each cameraman that he had filmed the scene successfully. No, said the first, the film had jammed in the camera. No, said the second, 'THERE'S A HAIR IN THE GATE', no, said the third, the sun had shone into the lens . . . until, in desperation, the director turned to the last cameraman who said brightly, 'Ready when you are, Mr De Mille!'

Presumably this joke is popular because it portrays innocence in the face of dire calamity. The punchline hangs in the air almost joyfully. *Ready When You Are, Mr McGill* became the title of a British TV play (by Jack Rosenthal, 1976) about how a TV production is ruined by an actor who can't remember his (two) lines.

real. See WILL THE ~ . . .

realization. See DESPERATION . . .

real McCoy, the. Meaning 'the real thing'; the genuine article', the phrase *possibly* derives from 'Kid' McCoy, a US welterweight boxing champion in the late 1890s. When challenged by a man in a bar to prove he was who he said he was, McCoy flattened him. When the man came round, he declared that this was indeed the 'real' McCoy. As Burnam (1980) notes, 'Kid' McCoy promoted this story about himself.

However, Messrs G. Mackay, the Scottish whisky distillers, were apparently promoting their product as 'the real *Mackay*' in 1870, as though alluding to an established expression. This could have

derived from the Mackays of Reay in Sutherland claiming to be the principal branch of the Mackay clan. Robert Louis Stevenson used this version in an 1883 letter.

real men don't eat quiche. Used as the title of a book (1983) by Bruce Feirstein, following an article by him in *Playboy* (1982), this became a jokey yardstick of manliness of the type popular in journalistic sociological discussions. Compare the film title *Dead Men Don't Wear Plaid* (US, 1981).

real thing, it's the. There have been so many rivals to the Coca-Cola drink that there has been a continuing necessity to maintain that 'Coke' is the 'real' one. This idea appeared in 1942 in the form, 'The only thing like Coca-Cola is Coca-Cola itself.' 'It's the real thing' followed in 1970, and has proved one of the most enduring of the Coca-Cola slogans.

Tom Stoppard's play *The Real Thing* (1982) was more about love (as in 'It's the real thing this time'), but could hardly fail to remind one of the slogan. *OED2* has an example of this use – i.e. true love as distinct from infatuation – in 1857.

See also COME ALIVE – YOU'RE IN THE PEPSI GENERATION.

reappraisal. See AGONIZING ~ .

rearrange the following [words] into a well-known phrase or saying. Instruction often to be found in competitions and puzzles. The actual game of re-ordering the words on a board to make up a sentence was almost certainly played in the 'Beat the Clock' segment of the ITV show *Sunday Night at the London Palladium* (1950s/60s). From the 1970s, a graffito: 'Arrange the following words into a well-known phrase or saying: Off Piss.'

rears. See SEX ~ ITS UGLY HEAD.

recipe. See WHAT'S THE ~ TODAY, JIM? under MORNING ALL!

recognize. See I DIDN'T ~ YOU WITH YOUR CLOTHES ON.

record. See IS THIS A ~?

recordare. See MASS PHRASES.

Recording Angel, the. Referring to an angel who keeps a record of every person's good and bad deeds, this was a concept known by 1761 (in Sterne's *Tristram Shandy*), but is not mentioned as such in the Bible.

record-lovers. See HELLO THERE, ~ . . .

red. See BETTER ~ THAN DEAD; LIKE A ~ RAG TO A BULL; LITTLE ~ BOOK; THIN ~ LINE; WOMAN IN ~ .

Red Baron, the. Nickname of Manfred Freiherr von Richthofen (1892–1918), the German fighter ace of the First World War. He flew a red Fokker plane and was credited with having destroyed 80 Allied planes.

Red Cardinal. See under EMINENCE GRISE.

Red Countess. See under DARLING DAISY.

Red Dean, the. Nickname of Dr Hewlett Johnson (1874–1965), former Dean of Manchester who became Dean of Canterbury in 1931. Often the centre of controversy because of his political views and his genuine belief that the Communist ideal was akin to Christian ethics. He travelled widely, including tours of the Soviet Union and China, and his last visit to China took place when he was 90.

red herring. See NEITHER FISH . . .

red-hot mamas. See LAST OF THE ~ .

red-letter day, a. Denoting a special day, because in almanacs and old calendars, feast days and saints' days were often printed in red rather than black ink. The *OED2*'s earliest citation is from 1704 in the US.

Reds under the bed. This became a watchword of anti-Bolshevik scares, and was current within a few years of the 1917 October Revolution in Russia. A red flag was used in the 1789 French Revolution and the colour had come to be associated with revolutionary movements during the nineteenth century before being adopted by Communists and their sympathizers. It was said that originally the flag had been dipped in the blood of victims of oppression.

red tape. Referring to delay caused by bureaucrats, the allusion, dating from the eighteenth century, is to the ribbons that lawyers and other public officials still use to bind up their papers (although they look more pink than red).

reed. See BROKEN ~ .

refreshes. See HEINEKEN ~ THE PARTS . . .

refusal. See PLEASE DO NOT ASK FOR CREDIT . . .

refuse. See I'M GOING TO MAKE HIM AN OFFER . . .

regiment. See MY ~ LEAVES AT DAWN.

regret. See DEEPLY ~ ANY . . .

regusted. See I'SE ~ .

Reilly. See LIFE OF ~ .

reinvent the wheel, to. To go back to basics, with a view to doing things better or more freshly. Often used pejoratively of someone who is doing so unnecessarily or out of ignorance. Or, in the form, 'let's not reinvent the wheel', as an injunction not to waste time by going over the obvious. Probably of American origin, since the 1970s.

From the *Washington Post* (16 July 1984): ' "It used to be you almost had to reinvent the wheel to get funding," said Daniel Cobb, dean of the faculty at the small liberal arts college in West Virginia'; (12 August 1984): ' "I don't think a leader of the western world can run a foreign policy that isn't consistent without great danger," says Eagleburger, "You can't reinvent the wheel every time because people have got to have some sense of continuity." '

The notion of reinventing can also be applied to almost anything: from the *Independent* (7 March 1992): 'The blurb says of the *Vox* characters [in a novel by Nicholson Baker] that in their 166 pages of conversation they are "re-inventing sex" ';

from President Clinton's inaugural speech (20 January 1993) had: 'A spring reborn in the world's oldest democracy, that brings forth the vision and courage to reinvent America.'

rejoice! rejoice! Margaret Thatcher, the British Prime Minister, is sometimes reported as having said this to newsmen outside 10 Downing Street on 25 April 1982 following the recapture of South Georgia by British forces during the Falklands War. What she actually said was: 'Just rejoice at that news and congratulate our forces and the Marines. Goodnight. Rejoice!' Either way, can one detect signs of her Methodist upbringing? Although 'Rejoice, rejoice!' is quite a common expression, each verse of Charles Wesley's hymn 'Rejoice! the Lord is King' ends: 'Rejoice, again I say, rejoice'. This is derived from Philippians 4:4: 'Rejoice in the Lord alway: and again I say, Rejoice.' The phrase also occurs in Handel's oratorio *Messiah* ('Rejoice, rejoice, rejoice greatly, O daughter of Zion') based on Zechariah 9:9. There is also a nineteenth-century hymn (words by Grace J. Frances), 'Rejoice, Rejoice, Believer!'

related. See I WONDER IF THEY ARE . . .

relationship. See SPECIAL ~.

relax. See FRANKIE GOES TO HOLLYWOOD.

remember the — ! This is a common form of sloganeering, particularly as a way of starting conflicts or keeping them alive, especially in the US. Probably the first was **remember the River Raisin!** – a war cry of Kentucky soldiers dating from the War of 1812. In the Raisin River massacre, 700 Kentuckians, badly wounded trying to capture Detroit, were scalped and butchered by Indians who were allies of the British. Then came **remember the Alamo!**: the Alamo Mission in San Antonio, Texas, was used as a fort during the rebellion against Mexico in 1836. A garrison of 100 or so Texans, including Davy Crockett, was wiped out by a force of 3,000 Mexicans after a 13–day siege. 'Remember the Alamo' was the war-cry with which Sam Houston subsequently led the Texans to victory over the Mexicans.

Remember Goliad! comes from the same Texas/Mexican conflict. **Remember the** *Maine!* helped turn the sinking of the battleship *Maine* in Havana harbour (1898) into an excuse for the Spanish-American War (as well as for the contemporary graffito: 'Remember the Maine/To hell with Spain/Don't forget to pull the chain'). **Remember the** *Lusitania!* followed the sinking of another ship (in 1915). **Remember Belgium!** was originally a recruiting slogan of the First World War. It eventually re-emerged with ironic emphasis amid the mud of Ypres, encouraging the rejoinder: 'As if I'm ever likely to forget the bloody place!' **Remember Pearl Harbor!** followed from the 1941 incident and **remember the** *Pueblo!* commemorated the capture of the USS *Pueblo* by North Korea in 1968.

Renaissance man, a. Used to describe anyone who is accomplished in more than one field, but (these days) rather less than a polymath. Originally used to describe anyone who displayed the educated, civilized, practical virtues of the idealized Renaissance man. Now a cliché. Kenneth Tynan in *Show* (October 1961): 'Young people in their teens and twenties for whom [Orson] Welles was Renaissance man reborn.' From *Time* (8 August 1977): 'At 50, Hood is the Renaissance man of sailing; he designed, cut the sails and outfitted *Independence*, the first man in history to control every aspect of a 12–tonner from drawing-board to helm.' From a letter in *Radio Times* (11 February 1989): 'I once told him [actor David Buck] that he was "the Renaissance man of radio". He thought that uproarious.' From Marmaduke Hussey's appreciation of Sir Michael Swann in *The Independent* (24 September 1990): 'Michael Swann, a big man in every way, was a Renaissance figure, scholar, scientist, soldier . . .'

I once heard a BBC Radio 2 trailer for 'Renaissance man, Humphrey Lyttelton'. While admiring Humph's ability to play the trumpet and write and talk wittily (though not, of course, simultaneously), I couldn't help but feel this was pushing it a bit.

repetition. See WITHOUT HESITATION . . .

reply. See 'NO ANSWER' CAME THE STERN ∼ .

reporter. See OUR ∼ MADE AN EXCUSE . . .

reservoir. See AU ∼ .

resort. See LAST ∼ .

respect. See I DON'T GET NO ∼ ; WITH ∼ .

rest is history, the. An ending to a biographical anecdote, now a cliché. Russell Grant, *TV Times* (15 October 1983): 'There across all the papers was the photograph of me presenting the Queen Mother with her chart, under the caption "Astrologer Royal". Well, the rest, as they say, is history.' Alan Bennett played delightfully on the phrase in *Oxford Today* (Michaelmas 1988), having described his transition from Oxford history don to Broadway revue artist: 'The rest, one might say pompously, is history. Except that in my case the opposite was true. What it had been was history. What it was to be was not history at all.'

restless. See NATIVES ARE HOSTILE.

rest of your life, the. See TODAY IS THE FIRST DAY . . .

restored. See THIS HAS ∼ MY FAITH . . .

results. See I'LL GIVE YOU THE ∼ . . .

resumed. See NORMAL SERVICE WILL BE ∼ . . . under DO NOT ADJUST YOUR SET.

retire immediately. See LIGHT THE BLUE TOUCHPAPER . . . under *BAND WAGGON.*

retreat? hell, no! we just got here! A remark attributed Captain Lloyd S. William, an American soldier (*fl.* 1918), and made by him when advised by the French to retreat, shortly after his arrival at the Western Front in the First World War. Or, specifically referring to the retreat from Belloar (5 June 1918). Margaret Thatcher quoted it at a Confederation of British Industry dinner in 1980, a year after she had become British Prime Minister.

return with us now to those thrilling days . . . See under HI-YO, SILVER!

return you to the studio. See under *BEYOND OUR KEN.*

reverse order. See I'LL GIVE YOU THE RESULTS IN ∼ .

— revisited. A frequently used title format. In January 1989, Channel 4 showed a programme marking the fiftieth anniversary of the publication of a John Steinbeck novel, with the title *'The Grapes of Wrath' Revisited.* In 1989, the South Bank Centre ran a commemoration of the 200th anniversary of the French Revolution under the blanket title 'Revolution Revisited'.

All such uses now owe something to the title of Evelyn Waugh's novel *Brideshead Revisited* (1945), and especially to the TV adaptation in 1981, though the format was well established before Waugh got hold of it. A book by E.V.Lucas (1916) has the title *London Revisited.* Chapter 11 of Harrison Ainsworth's novel *Jack Sheppard* (1836) is entitled 'Dollis Hill Revisited'. William Wordsworth wrote poems entitled 'Yarrow Unvisited' (1803), 'Yarrow Visited' (1814), and 'Yarrow Revisited' (1831).

revolting. See PEASANTS ARE ∼ .

revolution. See GLORIOUS ∼ .

rewrite. See YOU DON'T ∼ A HIT.

rex tremendae (majestatis). See MASS PHRASES.

rhubarb, rhubarb! Actors mumble this in crowd scenes to give the impression of speech, as a background noise, without actually producing coherent sentences. I suppose some unwise actors might think they could actually get away with saying 'rhubarb', but the idea is to repeat a word, which uttered by various voices, adds together to sound like the noise a crowd makes. I am not sure that this custom dates from much before this century but it is a well-known concept now, as demonstrated by the use of the verb 'to rhubarb', meaning to talk nonsense.

Another phrase said to have been repeated by actors in this situation is 'My fiddle, my fiddle, my fiddle'. I am also assured that there is a phrase used by Russian actors meaning, literally, 'I speak and I don't speak'.

One wonders whether the adoption of the word 'rhubarb' in the English version has anything to do with its slang use to denote the male (and occasionally female) genitals. Or could there have been some rhyming slang phrase, i.e. rhubarb (tart) = fart (akin to raspberry tart = fart)? The rhyming slang books I have consulted do not support me in this, however.

rich. See DO YOU SINCERELY WANT TO BE ~ ?; IT'S ALL PART OF LIFE'S ~ PAGEANT; and under POOR ARE ALWAYS WITH YOU.

rich and famous. Designated a cliché on the basis that the words are always and inevitably put together. The first example I have noted is in the film *Breakfast at Tiffany's* (US, 1961). The usage has become completely set in concrete since a film with the title *Rich and Famous* (US, 1981). An American TV series *Lifestyles of the Rich and Famous* was established by 1986. From the *Independent* (4 April 1989): 'The [Press] Council's assistant director, said yesterday that lawyers acting for the rich and famous were becoming aware of the fast track system for getting speedy corrections of untruths.'

Richard. See OPEN THE DOOR, ~ ! under *ITMA.*

riches. See RAGS TO ~ .

riddance. See GOOD ~ TO BAD RUBBISH.

riddle of the Sphinx, the. The riddle is: 'What animal walks on four feet in the morning, two feet at noon, and on three feet in the evening – but has only one voice; its feet vary, and when it has most it is weakest.' The answer is: Man – because he crawls on all fours as an infant, walks on two feet when full grown, but in old age moves upon his feet and a staff. As mentioned in *Oedipus Rex* by Sophocles, Oedipus answered the riddle correctly when he encountered the Sphinx on the

road to Thebes. The Sphinx killed herself in despair, and the Thebans made Oedipus their king out of gratitude. If he had not answered correctly, the Sphinx would have killed him.

ride off into the sunset. See DRIVE OFF INTO THE SUNSET.

ridiculous. See SUBLIME TO THE ~ .

right. See AM I ~ OR . . . ; BANG TO ~ S; CUSTOMER IS ALWAYS ~ ; DO THE ~ THING; IN YOUR HEART YOU KNOW . . . ; I THINK THAT SHOWS . . . ; IT'S WHAT YOUR ~ ARM'S FOR; ONE INSTINCTIVELY KNOWS . . . ; ~ ONE 'ERE under *EDUCATING ARCHIE*; SOMEWHERE TO THE ~ OF GENGHIS KHAN; THAT'S ~ – YOU'RE WRONG.

right and left, a. A shot. Also used figuratively for a powerful blow or shock. From Josephine Tey, *The Singing Sands* (1952): 'His reply contained a right-and-left.' Compare **left and right**, rhyming slang for 'fight'.

right monkey! Al Read (1909–87), the northern English comedian, was big on radio in the 1950s and then disappeared almost completely. His speciality was monologues – or, rather, dialogues – with him playing all the parts. He used a number of standard Lancashire expressions and made them for a while his own – **give over!, you'll be lucky . . . I say, you'll be lucky, ooh, an' 'e was strong!** and **we've soopped soom stooff tonight** – the last as a drunk staggering homeward and shouting through his neighbours' letter boxes. Recalled by Irene Thomas in *The Bandsman's Daughter* (1981). But compare Frank Randle's similar phrase under BY GUM, SHE'S A HOT 'UN.

Above all, Read was known for two catchphrases – 'right monkey!' and **cheeky monkey!** For example: 'She said, "Did he say anything about the check suit?" and I thought, "Right monkey!"' ' From a theatre poster once seen in Blackpool: 'HENRY HALL PRESENTS AL READ IN *RIGHT MONKEY*'.

right on! According to Flexner (1976), 'Right on!' replaced TELL IT LIKE IT IS! as the

American Civil Rights shout of encouragement to speakers at demonstrations round about 1967. It is 'a general term meaning "you're absolutely right, you tell 'em"'. The *OED2* finds, however, a 1925 Black use of the phrase.

More recently, the phrase has been used adjectivally for attitudes that might equally qualify for the designation POLITICALLY CORRECT. 'My play takes a sledgehammer to the "right on" clichés that have debilitated recent radical theatre in Britain' – (*Guardian*, 7 April 1992).

rights of passage. As *rites de passage*, this was a coinage of Arnold van Gennep in the title of a book (1909) about the transitional stages through which man passes between birth and death. The most notable *rite de passage* is probably some experience (maybe of a ritual nature) that a boy has to go through before achieving manhood. It might have to do with a demonstration of his physical skills or involve some confirmation of his sexual maturity.

The concept is now well known, especially as the name given to a genre of films. From *Flicks* Magazine (April 1994): 'Brad Pitt and Craig Sheffer play Paul and Norman in Robert Redford's *A River Runs Through It*, a nostalgic "rites of passage" drama . . . it's only when they're fishing that they find the true harmony that eludes them elsewhere.'

Rites of Passage was the title of a novel (1980) by William Golding.

right stuff, the. Tom Wolfe helped re-popularize the phrase 'the right stuff' when he chose to use it as the title of a book (1979; film US, 1983). He employed it to describe the qualities needed by test pilots and would-be astronauts in the early years of the US space programme.

But the 'right (sort of) stuff' had been applied much earlier to qualities of manly virtue, of good officer material and even of good cannon fodder. Partridge/*Slang* has an example from the 1880s. In this sense, the phrase was used by Ian Hay as the title of a novel – 'some episodes in the career of a North Briton' – in 1908.

It is now a handy journalistic device. An *Independent* headline over a story about the ballet *Ondine* (13 May 1988) was, 'The Sprite Stuff'; the same month, *The Magazine* had 'The Right Stuff' as the title of an article on furnishing fabrics; in 1989, there was an ITV book programme called *The Write Stuff*.

It has also been used as an expression for alcohol (compare 'the hard stuff').

Riley. See LIFE OF ∼.

ring. See under DON'T CALL US . . .

ringer. See DEAD ∼.

ring of steel, a. Journalistic cliché. Reporter on BBC TV *Nine O'Clock News* (17 December 1981): 'The place [Warsaw] is just a ring of steel.' From a report on the Falklands War in *The Times* (30 April 1982): 'RING OF STEEL AROUND ISLANDS'. From the *Sunday Express* (8 October 1983): 'SYRIAN STEEL RINGS ARAFAT'.

Somewhat earlier, Adolf Hitler had said in a speech on the Italian armistice in 1943: 'Tactical necessity may compel us once and again to give up something on some front in this gigantic fateful struggle, but it will never break the ring of steel that protects the Reich.' (Translation from *Hitler's Words*, ed. Gordon W. Prange, 1944.)

R in the month. See DON'T EAT OYSTERS UNLESS . . .

riot. See READ THE ∼ ACT.

Ripper. See JACK THE ∼; YORKSHIRE ∼.

rise and fall. See DECLINE AND FALL.

river. See SOLD DOWN THE ∼.

rivers of blood. On 20 April 1968, Enoch Powell, the Conservative opposition spokesman for Defence, made a speech in Birmingham on the subject of immigration. He concluded with the words: 'As I look ahead, I am filled with foreboding. Like the Roman, I seem to see "the River Tiber foaming with much blood".' Later, Powell said that he should have quoted the remark in Latin to emphasize that he was only evoking a classical prophecy of doom and not actually predicting a bloodbath. In

Vergil's *Aeneid* (VI:87), the Sibyl of Cumae prophesies: '*Et Thybrim multo spumantem sanguine cerno.*' 'Rivers of blood' was thus quite a common turn of phrase before Powell made it notorious. Thomas Jefferson in a letter to John Adams (4 September 1823) wrote: 'To attain all this [universal republicanism], however, rivers of blood must yet flow, and years of desolation pass over; yet the object is worth rivers of blood, and years of desolation.' Speaking on European unity (14 February 1948), Winston Churchill said: 'We are asking the nations of Europe between whom rivers of blood have flowed, to forget the feuds of a thousand years.'

road. See KEEP DEATH OFF THE ~; KING OF THE ~.

roar. See STOP THE MIGHTY ~ under *IN TOWN TONIGHT*.

Roaring 20s, the. The decade label for the 1920s had established itself by 1939, reflecting the heady buoyant atmosphere in certain sections of society following the horrors of the First World War. The adjective 'roaring' meaning 'boisterous, riotous, noisy', had previously been applied to the 1850s and, in Australia, to the 'roaring days' of the gold-rush. The same meaning occurs in the expression 'roaring drunk'. The 1940s do not appear to have been given a label, least of all **Roaring Forties** – that term had already been applied to parts of the oceans between 40 degrees and 50 degrees south where strong westerly winds blow.
Compare SWINGING SIXTIES.

Roar of the Greasepaint – the Smell of the Crowd, The. The title of the musical (New York, 1965) by Leslie Bricusse and Anthony Newley nicely confuses two standard concepts – the 'roar of the crowd' and 'the smell of greasepaint'. From Vicente Blaco-Ibáñez, *Blood and Sand* (1908): 'It was the roar of the real, the only beast [the crowd in the arena].' From David Piper, *The Companion Guide to London* (1965): 'Other theatres cling still to real live actors and a waft of greasepaint over the footlights.'

roast. See RULE THE ROOST.

robbed. See WE WUZ ~.

robbery. See DAYLIGHT ~.

Robin. See ROUND ~.

Robin Hood, a. The name for one who robs the rich to benefit the poor comes from the English outlaw, celebrated since the fourteenth century, who may or may not have actually existed. Early versions of the tales about him were set in either Yorkshire or Nottinghamshire (particularly in Sherwood Forest, with the villainous Sheriff of Nottingham always in hot pursuit). The cast of characters surrounding Robin Hood included his love, Maid Marian, and fellow outlaws Little John, Allen-a-dale, Friar Tuck and Will Scarlet.

Robinson. See BEFORE/AS QUICK AS/ ANYONE CAN SAY JACK ~; HEATH ~.

rock. See BETWEEN A ~ AND A HARD PLACE.

rocking-horse manure. See under AS BUSY AS . . .

rock'n'roll. This name for a type of popular music was first popularized by Alan Freed, the US disc jockey, who is generally credited with first discovering and promoting it. In 1951, he was hosting *Moondog's Rock'n'Roll Party* on a radio station in Cleveland, Ohio. It was not until he moved to New York City in 1954, however, that the term took hold. Earlier, in 1934, there had been a song by Sidney Clare and Richard Whiting with the title 'Rock and Roll' in the film *Transatlantic Merry-Go-Round*, referring to a ship's movements. Earlier, the phrase may also have been Black English slang for the sexual act.
See also IT'S ONLY ~; SEX'N'DRUGS'N'~.

rock'n'roll, — is the new. A buzz phrase of *c* 1993, subsequently open to adaptation, was 'comedy is the new rock'n'roll'. In Britain at that time, such was the attention paid to comedy performers and writers in the 'alternative' and 'improvisational' fields, and such was the wealth and fame accrued by other young comedy practitioners in the media generally, that the parallel was drawn with the exciting, fashionable phenomenon of an earlier time. The phrase made an early appearance in the *Guardian* (19 October 1991): 'In this age of CDs, Discmasters, videos, prototype virtual reality, handheld computer games, all-night raves, and stand-up comedy as the new rock'n'roll, the gig has become a tedious anachronism.' From the *Herald* (Glasgow) (21 May 1994): 'This year's award recognises the way the arts can reach out and extend into new areas and to a new audience. For many who have seen it, the Citizens' Theatre production of *Trainspotting* is a reminder of how powerful drama can be. *Trainspotting* proves that theatre can be the new rock'n'roll.'

rock on, Tommy! Said by Bobby Ball (*b* 1944) of the British comedy partnership Cannon and Ball. The precise origin goes unremembered but Ball thinks it probably arose in a place like Oldham or Wigan when he was spurring on Tommy Cannon (*b* 1938). Depending on which of them is telling the story, it may also have occurred when Cannon was singing and be related to the David Essex song 'Rock on' (1973). Ball recalled (1980): 'About three years ago, Tommy was singing a rock'n'roll number. I was fooling about and just happened to say it. To my astonishment it got a big laugh, such a tremendous response that we decided to try it again.' Cannon added: 'After a couple of years we thought of dropping it because it might be losing its impact. But we decided to keep it in for our TV show. We could never drop it now.'

rocks. See HAND THAT ∼ THE CRADLE.

Rodney, hello. See under BEYOND OUR KEN.

rogue's gallery, a/the. Phrase for a group of disreputable people as shown in a photograph or picture (e.g. wanted criminals) but also used humorously of quite unoffensive people so portrayed. The criminal use was prevalent in the US in the mid- to late nineteenth century. The allusive twentieth-century UK use derives, in part, I think, from a Latin school textbook *The Rogue's Gallery* (current by the 1950s, at least) which included classical descriptions of notable Roman villains.

From an *Independent* report of a speech in the House of Lords by Lord Stevens of Ludgate (on 26 April 1989): 'For most people, the *Sun* and the *News of the World* were the starring exhibits in the Rogues Gallery of the Press, but each paper appeared to thrive on its notoriety, he said.'

roll. See under TURN OVER IN ONE'S GRAVE.

roll, on a. Enjoying a run of success. If this originally American expression came out of surfing, as seems likely, then it would seem appropriate to define it also as 'on the crest of a wave'. Recorded by 1976. From the *Independent on Sunday* (18 April 1993): 'To give ENO an extra twinge of doubt, the Royal Opera, which was so often compared unfavourably to it in the last decade, is on an artistic roll.'

roller. See BRILL.

Rolling Stones, the. The name of this enduring British pop group (formed 1962) came not directly from the proverb 'a rolling stone gathers no moss' (known by 1546) but via the title of the Muddy Waters song 'Rollin' Stone' (1950).

rolls. See HOW THE MONEY ∼ IN.

Rolls-Royce. A description of anything of the highest quality ('the Rolls-Royce of bicycles', 'a Rolls-Royce speaking voice') comes from the name of the motor car or the aero engine, after the founders of the manufacturing company, the Hon Charles Stewart Rolls and Frederick Henry Royce (who met for the first time in the Midland Hotel, Manchester, in 1904).

See also AT 60 MILES AN HOUR . . .

Rome. See FIDDLE WHILE ∼ BURNS; WHEN IN ∼.

Ron, oh. See under TAKE IT FROM HERE.

room. See UP IN ANNIE'S ∼.

room at the top. *CODP* lists this as a proverbial expression 'commonly used to encourage competition', but doesn't record the occasion when Daniel Webster (*d* 1852), the US politician, said it. Responding to a suggestion that he shouldn't become a lawyer because the profession was overcrowded, he said: 'There is always room at the top.' At one point in John Braine's novel *Room At the Top* (1957; film UK, 1958), the hero, Joe Lampton, is told: 'You're the sort of young man we want. There's always room at the top.'

room of one's own, a. The title of a feminist essay (1929) by Virginia Woolf, arguing that women will not be able to succeed in writing fiction until they have the independence demonstrated by having a room of their own to write in.

room with a view, a. The hotel guest's popular requirement. Used as the title of a novel (1908; film UK, 1985) by E.M. Forster. Noël Coward's song with this title did not appear until *This Year of Grace* (1928).

Roosevelt. See under CARRY ON —.

root, hog or die. A proverbial expression that was once described (in 1944) as the 'American national motto'. Davy Crockett used it in his memoirs (1834). It affirms the necessity of hard work and exertion to maintain life and prosperity. Here 'root' is used in the sense of rooting around and 'hog', as in 'to appropriate'.

Rosebud. The mystifying last word spoken by the eponymous hero of the film *Citizen Kane* (US, 1941): finding out what it meant to him is a theme of the picture. It is finally glimpsed written on the side of a snow-sledge – a powerful talisman of childhood innocence, or a 'symbol of maternal affection, the loss of which deprives him irrecoverably of the power to love or be loved' (Kenneth Tynan). Orson Welles himself issued a statement (14 January 1941) explaining: ' "Rosebud" is the trade name of a cheap little sled on which Kane was playing on the day he was taken away from his home and his mother. In his subconscious it represented the simplicity, the comfort, above all the lack of responsibility in his home, and also it stood for his mother's love which Kane never lost.'

rose garden. See I NEVER PROMISED YOU A ~.

rose is a rose is a rose. The poem 'Sacred Emily' (1922) by Gertrude Stein (d 1946) does not include the line 'a rose is a rose is a rose', but rather: 'Rose is a rose is a rose is a rose' (i.e. upper case 'R', no indefinite article at the start, and three, not two, repetitions). The Rose in question was not a flower but an allusion to the English painter Sir Francis Rose 'whom she and I regarded', wrote Constantine Fitzgibbon, 'as the peer of Matisse and Picasso, and whose paintings – or at least painting – hung in her Paris drawing-room while a Gauguin was relegated to the lavatory' (letter to the *Sunday Telegraph*, 7 July 1978). Stein also refers to a 'Jack Rose' (not a 'Jack' rose) earlier in the poem.

The format is now a commonplace: 'Bad reviews are bad reviews are bad reviews are bad reviews' ('Nicholas Craig', *I, An Actor*, 1989); 'A Tory is a Tory is a Tory, whatever he might think' (Hugo Young, *One of Us*, 1990).

roses. See EVERYTHING'S COMING UP ~.

rough old trade, a. Not to be confused with 'rough trade' in the homosexual sense (sadistic, violent), this tag has principally been applied in recent years to politics. From Alan Watkins, the *Observer* (21 January 1990): 'I have often remarked – it may perhaps have become something of a cliché – that politics is a rough old trade. But not since we ceased executing Ministers some time in the late seventeenth century has it been quite as rough as it is under Mrs Margaret Thatcher.'

But other jobs and professions are almost as likely to attract the tag. From the *Sunday Telegraph* (4 January 1987): 'Terry departs to Provence with more friends and fewer enemies than anyone I know in our rough old trade [literary journalism]'. From the *Independent* (1 December 1988): 'Berg, now 79 but still sprightly enough to climb unassisted into the ring and still a handsome and lucid advertisement for a rough old trade [boxing]'.

round heels, she has got. She is loose sexually. American origin, current by 1957.

A sharp image, suggesting that the woman is easy to push over backwards.

round hole. See SQUARE PEG IN A ∼.

round Robin, a. A letter where the responsibility for sending it is shared by all the signatories (known in the British Navy by 1730). In France, in the same century, petitioners would sign their names on a ribbon whose top was joined to its bottom. This was to prevent a situation where the first signatory on the list might be singled out for punishment. Nowadays, the term is often applied to a letter of protest with signatures not arranged in any special way, except perhaps alphabetically.

The term has nothing to do with the bird. 'Round' is from French *rond* and 'Robin' is a corruption of French *ruban*, meaning ribbon.

round the bend. See CLEANS ∼.

Round the Horne. More or less the same team as in BBC radio's BEYOND OUR KEN manifested itself from 1965–9 in *Round the Horne* – this time with somewhat broader and zanier scripts by Marty Feldman and Barry Took. Took told me: 'Marty and I went all out to avoid catchphrases but the cast kept pencilling them in. Eventually we gave up the unequal struggle.'

The new approach was typified by the introduction of two stock figures, the gay ex-chorus boys, Julian and Sandy. **Oh, hello, I'm Julian and this is my friend, Sandy** was how Hugh Paddick would refer to Kenneth Williams, opening the routines. From their first appearances, they larded their speech with bits of camp *parlare* (talk) from the *omipalomi* (homosexual) subculture of actors and dancers. Fantabulosa! One of their incarnations was as film producers:

> *Sandy:* Mr Horne, we are in the forefront of your *Nouvelle Vague.* **That's your actual French.**
> *Julian:* It means we are of the New Wave.
> *Sandy:* And very nice it looks on you, too.

(Peter Cook claimed to have launched **your actual** as a turn of phrase, however.) **Ooh,**

bold! Very bold! was their standard exclamation.

Betty Marsden played Lady Beatrice Counterblast (née Clissold) and would say **many, many times!** (originally in answer to a query as to how many times she had been married). Spasm, her butler (played by Kenneth Williams), would wail **we be doomed, we all be doomed!**

The writers were inordinately fond of having Kenneth Horne himself say, **it's just a trick of the light** as an amusing way of explaining away almost anything (for example, he uses it twice in the edition of 28 March 1965).

Route 66. A major US highway immortalized in the song 'Route 66' (1946), by Bobby Troup: 'If you ever plan to motor west,/Travel my way, take the highway, that's the best,/Get your kicks on Route 66.' From *TV Times* (19 October 1985): 'For years, the 2,200–odd miles of black-top, running from Chicago to Los Angeles, conjured up visions of romance and adventure.'

From the *Independent on Sunday* (21 June 1992): 'Winding through a grim, polluted landscape of new wrecks, new graffiti, new drug dealers and new prostitutes, Europastrasse-55 is the Route 66 of the lands that communism betrayed.'

Rowan and Martin's Laugh-In. See LAUGH–IN.

royal 'we', the. King Richard I is believed to have been the first monarch to use the royal 'we' (in Latin) – as a way of showing that he did not simply rule for himself but on behalf of his people. Before this, when Roman consuls *shared* power, it was appropriate for each of them to speak in this collective manner.

Some monarchs seem to have been more prone to using it than others. As is obvious from her alleged expression, 'We are not amused', Queen Victoria was one who did, but nevertheless her letters and journals are just as full of the first person singular.

However, when non-royals like Margaret Thatcher start saying things like 'We have become a grandmother' (as she did to widespread guffaws in March 1989), it is clearly time for the rest of us to desist. The actual term 'royal we', as opposed to the usage, is comparatively recent (by 1931).

rubber chicken. Name given to the circuit around which professional speakers go in the US. The meal provided is usually chicken and it usually tastes of rubber. So called by about 1985. In the UK, when the Conservative minister Michael Heseltine resigned from Margaret Thatcher's government, he embarked on a rigorous speaking programme all over the country, addressing constituency associations. In 1990, he was given the nickname 'Rubber chicken' for his pains.

rubbish! See under MORECAMBE AND WISE SHOW; GOOD RIDDANCE TO BAD ~.

Ruddy Nora! A delightful expletive, current in the UK by the late 1970s. I have absolutely no idea whence it came or to whom, if anyone in particular, it refers. *Street Talk, the Language of Coronation Street* (1986) prefers **flaming Nora!** and defines it as 'Flipping 'eck!' or, as Americans put it, 'holy cow!' The operators of the TV soap have no idea who the red-haired Nora was, either.

rug. See SNUG AS A BUG IN A ~.

rule. See GOLDEN ~.

— rules OK. This curious affirmative is said to have begun in gang speak of the late 1960s in Scotland and Northern Ireland, though some would say it dates back to the 1930s. Either a gang or a football team or the Provisional IRA would be said to 'rule OK'. Later, around 1976, this was turned into a joke with numerous variations – 'Queen Elizabeth rules UK', 'Rodgers and Hammerstein rule OK, lahoma', and so on.

It soon became an all but unstoppable cliché. In 1981, Virginian rubbed tobacco was advertised beneath the slogan, 'Virginian Rolls OK' and a French cigarette beneath '*Gauloises à rouler, OK*'. In 1982, I was asked by BBC Radio to present a series on local government. 'Yes,' I said, 'I will – as long as you don't call it "Town Hall Rules OK".' Two weeks later, they rang back to say, 'We've chosen that title you suggested.'

And they had. I only spoke it through gritted teeth.

'GOLF RULES OK?' appeared as an *Observer* headline (13 November 1983). With luck, the phrase is now on the way out.

rule the roost, to. Meaning 'to lord it over others', this possibly derives from the image of a cock's behaviour towards hens on the roosting perch. The existence of the (probably) earlier expression 'to **rule the roast**' – presiding as the head of the dinner table (as in Shakespeare, *Henry VI, Part 2*, I.i.108; 1590) – may point to a more likely source (though just possibly the two phrases developed side by side).

rum, bum and concertina. The title of a volume of British jazz singer George Melly's autobiography (1977) alludes to the old naval saying: 'Ashore it's wine, women and song, aboard it's rum, bum and concertina.' Winston Churchill's version in response to a remark about naval tradition (recounted in Harold Nicolson's diary, 17 August 1950) was: 'Naval tradition? Monstrous. Nothing but rum, sodomy, prayers and the lash.'

run. See TAKE THE MONEY AND ~; THIS ONE WILL ~ AND ~; WHAT A WAY TO ~ . . . ; YOU CAN ~ BUT YOU CAN'T HIDE.

runneth. See CUP ~ OVER.

running. See HIT THE GROUND ~.

running dogs. A phrase meaning 'lackeys' and popularized by Chairman Mao Tse-tung. In a 'Statement Supporting the People of the Congo Against US Aggression' (28 November 1964), he said: 'People of the world, unite and defeat the US aggressors and all their running dogs!' This provided a vivid weapon for use against the 'lackeys' of the US during the Vietnam War. Edgar Snow had earlier recorded Mao using the term in 1937.

runs. See HE WHO ~ MAY READ.

run the gauntlet, to. An expression meaning 'to endure something of a prolonged, testing nature, to be attacked on all sides', this has nothing to do with the type of glove but is from the Swedish *gatlop* or *gatloppe* which means 'lane run'. It carries the idea of someone having to run as a punishment (in the military) between two lines of tormentors. The literal use was recorded in English in 1676, but the transferred sense 15 years earlier.

From Oliver Goldsmith, *She Stoops to Conquer* (1773): 'He claps not only himself but his old-fashioned wife on my back . . . and then, I suppose we are to run the gauntlet through all the rest of the family.'

rushes. See GREEN GROW THE ∼, OH.

Russians with snow on their boots. In September 1914, there was an unfounded rumour that a million Russian troops had landed at Aberdeen in Scotland and passed through England on their way to the Western Front. The detail that they were seen to have had 'snow on their boots' was supposed to add credence to the report. It had to be officially denied by the War Office.

· S ·

sack, to give someone the. The suggestion is that this expression dates from the days when workers would carry the tools of their trade around with them, from job to job, in a bag which they would leave with their employer. When their services were no longer required, they would be given the bag back.

safe. See JUST WHEN YOU THOUGHT . . .

safe pair of hands, a. In political circles, a person who can be relied upon to perform a task without mistakes and without bringing down opprobrium upon a government. This expression may derive from sporting use and in particular from cricket. In 1851, someone was described as having 'the safest pair of hands in England' (meaning, presumably, that he would not drop the ball or miss a catch). From Ben Pimlott, *Harold Wilson* (1992): 'In London, morning press conferences [during the 1966 General Election] were taken by [James] Callaghan, whom Wilson considered (as he flatteringly told the Chancellor) "a safe pair of hands".' From the *Sunday Telegraph* (1 August 1993): '[Sir Norman Fowler] does the job because he had supported Mr Major's candidature (later acting as his minder during the General Election), and because he was reputed to be "a safe pair of hands".'

safety. See FOR THINE ESPECIAL ~.

safety first. A slogan that was first used in the US in connection with railroad safety. In the UK of the 1890s, this was also the original use of the slogan when a railway notice declared: 'The Safety of the Passengers is our First Concern'. In 1915, it became the motto of the National Council for Industrial Safety in the US. In 1916, the London General Bus Company formed a London 'Safety First Council'. The 1922 British general election saw the phrase in use as a political slogan for the Conservatives. Again, in 1929, it was the Tory slogan under which Stanley Baldwin fought for re-election, but it proved a loser. In 1934, the National Safety First Association was formed, concerned with road and industrial safety, and it is in this connection that the slogan has endured.

said. See NUFF ~!

sailing. See GOODNIGHT, GENTLEMEN, AND GOOD ~.

sail off into the sunset. See DRIVE OFF INTO THE SUNSET.

sailor. See CHOCOLATE ~ under ARMS AND THE MAN; under ENOUGH BLUE . . .; HELLO, ~!; under THAT IS WHAT THE SOLDIER SAID.

sainted aunt!, my. See MY GIDDY AUNT.

saloon must go, the. See — MUST GO!

saloon-bar Tory, a. 'There is in Britain a political animal known as a "saloon-bar Tory". He sits in the most comfortable bar of his local pub, sipping gin and tonic, bemoaning the state of the nation and saying how much better everything would be if only managements and everyone else would stand up to the dreadful unions' (Michael Leapman, *Barefaced Cheek*, 1983).

salt. See GRAIN OF ~; WORTH ONE'S ~ . . .

salt of the earth, the. Meaning 'the best of mankind', this expression comes from Jesus Christ's description of his disciples in Matthew 5:13: 'Ye are the salt of the earth: but if the salt have lost his savour, wherewith shall it be salted?' Which suggests, rather, that they should give the world an interesting flavour, be a ginger group, and not that they were simply jolly good chaps. The New English Bible conveys this meaning better as 'you are salt to the world'.

Sam. See PLAY IT AGAIN, ∼ .

Samarra. See APPOINTMENT IN ∼ .

same. See THEY ALL LOOK THE ∼ . . . ; WILL NEVER BE THE ∼ AGAIN.

same day, same time, same spot on the dial. See under HOW DO YOU DO, LADIES AND GENTLEMEN . . .

Sanctus. See MASS PHRASES.

sand. See SUN, ∼ AND SEA.

sand-box, cat in a. See under AS BUSY AS . . .

sandboy. See HAPPY AS A ∼ .

sands. See MR ∼ IS IN THE —.

Sandy. See OH, HELLO, I'M JULIAN . . . under ROUND THE HORNE.

san fairy ann. This expression meaning 'it doesn't matter; why worry?' dates from the First World War and is a corruption of the French *ça ne fait rien* [that's nothing, makes no odds].

sans peur et sans reproche [without fear and without reproach]. The Chevalier de Bayard (d 1524), a French knight, was known as *le chevalier sans peur et sans reproche*. Mark Twain once proposed '*sans peur et sans culottes*' [knee britches] as the motto of a gentlemen's dining club and Harry Graham of *Punch* proposed '*sans beurre et sans brioche*' [butter/brioche].

sapristi! See under GOON SHOW.

Satan. See GET THEE BEHIND ME ∼ .

Satchmo. Nickname of Louis Armstrong (1900–71), the American jazz trumpeter and singer. A contraction of 'satchel-mouth', it was consquently given to a type of fungus

which appears to exhibit a very large mouth.

satirical. See HO-HO, VERY ∼ .

savage story of lust and ambition, a. Cliché of the type used to promote films and books. This was actually used on posters for the film *Room at the Top* (1958).

say. See AND SO WE ∼ FAREWELL; ANYTHING YOU ∼ . . . ; AS WE ∼ IN THE TRADE; I MEANTER ∼; I ∼, I ∼, I ∼!; I ∼ WHAT A SMASHER; I ∼ YOU FELLOWS!; LISTEN VERY CAREFULLY . . . ; ∼ NO MORE under MONTY PYTHON'S FLYING CIRCUS.

say goodnight, Dick/Gracie. See under LAUGH-IN.

saying. See AS THE ∼ IS.

say it loud . . . 'Say it loud, **we're gay and we're proud**' was a slogan of the Gay Liberation Front in the US, *c* 1970. It was clearly derived from the James Brown song 'Say it loud, **I'm black and I'm proud**' with which he had had a hit in 1968. From *The Encyclopedia of Graffiti* (1974): 'Say it loud, I'm yellow and I'm mellow' (New York City).

say it with flowers. This slogan was originally devised for the Society of American Florists, and invented in 1917 for its chairman, Henry Penn of Boston, Massachusetts. Major Patrick O'Keefe, head of an advertising agency, suggested: 'Flowers are words that even a babe can understand' – a line he had found in a poetry book. Penn considered that too long. O'Keefe, agreeing, rejoined: 'Why, you can say it with flowers in so many words.' Later came several songs with the title.

says. See IT ∼ HERE.

says anything but his/her prayers, he/she. Dismissive phrase for when the opinion of another person is adduced. G.L. Apperson in his *English Proverbs and Proverbial Phrases* (1929) finds, 'He says anything but his prayers and then he whistles' in 1732; six years later, Jonathan

Swift has in *Polite Conversation*, 'Miss will say anything but her prayers, and those she whistles.'

scale. See ON A ∼ OF ONE TO TEN.

scarce. See under AS BUSY AS . . .

Scarface. Nickname of Al Capone (1899–1947), the gangster who terrorised Chicago during the Prohibition era. Originally, 'Scarface Al' – the scar on his left cheek (usually turned away from cameras) was caused by a razor slash he received in a Brooklyn gang fight in his younger days. According to his biographer, John Kobler, the scar in question, 'ran along his left cheek from ear to jaw, another across the jaw, and a third below the left ear . . . he was touchy about his disfigurement. He often considered plastic surgery . . . He detested the sobriquet the press had fastened on him . . . and nobody used it in his presence without courting disaster.' He allowed his intimates to call him **Snorky** – slang for elegant.

The film *Scarface* (US, 1932) pretended not to be a biopic of Capone. Difficult, given the title.

scarlet. See DOCTORS WEAR ∼.

Schmilsson. See LITTLE TOUCH OF ∼.

scholar. See GENTLEMAN AND A ∼.

school. See OLD ∼ TIE.

schoolboy. See AS EVERY ∼ KNOWS.

schoolgirl. See KEEP THAT ∼ COMPLEXION.

school of hard knocks, the. i.e. experience or hardship considered as an educative force. The *OED2* calls this 'US Slang' and finds it in 1912. *The Complete Naff Guide* (1983) has as a 'naff boast': 'But then, of course, I left university without a degree. I like to think I have a First from the School of Hard Knocks.'

Receiving an honorary doctorate in the humanities from the University of Nevada in May 1976, Frank Sinatra said, 'I am a graduate of the school of hard knocks.' In losing his job as chairman of Mecca in October 1978, Eric Morley said: 'I went to the College of Hard Knocks and last week I got my doctorate.' At least, he didn't say he had attended **the university of life.** (Partridge/*Slang* prefers 'the university of hard knocks' and dates it *c* 1910.) Robert Louis Stevenson writing in *Memories and Portraits* (1887) has: 'A man, besides, who had taken his degree in life and knew a thing or two about the age we live in.' Horatio Bottomley, addressing the Oxford Union on 2 December 1920, said: 'Gentlemen: I have not had your advantages. What poor education I have received has been gained from the University of Life.' Lord Baden-Powell wrote a book called *Lessons from the 'Varsity' of Life* (1933).

science and tenacity. A phrase that lingers from the introduction to the modest TV detective series *Fabian of Scotland Yard*, based on the work of an actual detective and first aired on British TV in 1954. The opening sequence began with Bruce Seton saying, 'This is Fabian of Scotland Yard,' then an American voice took over: 'In a nation's war on crime, Scotland Yard is the brain of Great Britain's man-hunting machine. Routine, detail, science and tenacity – these are the weapons used by squads of highly-trained men. Men like former Inspector Robert Fabian, hailed by the press as one of England's greatest detectives.' Then Seton came on again and said, 'My name is Fabian. Detective Inspector Robert Fabian.'

scot-free. See GET AWAY WITH . . .

scorcher. See PHEW, WHAT A ∼!

Scots wha hae. It sounds like an exclamation – of the WU-HEY! OR HAWAE THE LADS! sort – but it is the title of a battle song by Robert Burns (and also known as 'Robert Bruce's March to Bannockburn'). The poem begins:

Scots, wha hae [lit. who have] wi'
   Wallace bled,
Scots, wham Bruce has often led,
Welcome to your gory bed,
Or to victorie.

Scott. See GREAT ~.

Scottish play, the. Theatrical superstition is understandable in a profession so dependent on luck. However, the euphemism 'Scottish play', invariably used for Shakespeare's *Macbeth* (1606), is based on a well-documented history of bad luck associated with productions of the play. Merely to utter the name of the play would be enough to invoke misfortune.

Scotty. See BEAM ME UP, ~.

scrapheap. See DUSTBIN.

scratch'n'sniff. Name of a gimmick used originally in the cinema whereby audience members scratched cards to release smells appropriate for the scene they were watching. The first 'scratch'n'sniff' opera production may have been *The Love for Three Oranges* at the English National Opera in 1989.

The term is also applied to the kind of perfume samples supplied with magazines. From *Today* (1 April 1987): 'Using the latest refinements in tasteless high technology, Revlon is bringing out a new scratch'n'sniff range of advertisements in America's national women's magazines, under the copy line, "Where does Joan Collins become a Scoundrel?"' From the *Daily Telegraph* (8 September 1989): 'New products can be the answer and Reckitts' latest is an air freshener in a pseudo cut-glass container packaged with a scratch'n'sniff panel.'

screaming. See DRAGGED KICKING AND ~ . . .

screws. See PUT THE ~ ON.

scripture. See DEVIL CAN CITE ~ . . .

sea. See DEVIL AND THE DEEP BLUE ~ ; FROM ~ TO SHINING ~ ; SUN, SAND AND ~ ; WORSE THINGS HAPPEN AT ~ .

Seagreen Incorruptible, the. Nickname of Robespierre, the French revolutionary leader. He established the Reign of Terror (1793–4) but was executed in it himself. The name comes from Thomas Carlyle's *History*

of the French Revolution (1837). There was no connection between Robespierre's greenness and his incorruptibility. He was green because of poor digestion, and he was incorruptible because he was a fanatic.

sealed. See LIPS ARE ~ .

Sealed With A Lover's Kiss. See SWALK.

seamless robe, a. Phrase from John 19:23: 'The soldiers, when they had crucified Jesus, took . . . his coat: now the coat was without seam, woven from the top throughout.' Used as the title of a book, subtitled 'Broadcasting Philosophy and Practice' (1979) by Sir Charles Curran, a former Director-General of the BBC, it was meant to describe 'the impossibility of separating out any one strand of the job from another . . . It was impossible to disentangle, in the whole pattern, one thread from another'.

sea of upturned faces, a. Possibly now a literary and journalistic cliché but it was a fresh phrase once. From Sir Walter Scott, *Rob Roy*, Chap. 20 (1817): 'I next strained my eyes, with equally bad success, to see if, among the sea of upturned faces which bent their eyes on the pulpit as a common centre, I could discover the sober and businesslike physiognomy of Owen.' Earlier, Mrs Radcliffe, *The Italian* (1797) has, 'the thousand upturned faces of the gazing crowd'. Later, Harriet Martineau, *French Wines and Politics* (1833) has: 'A heaving ocean of upturned faces.'

Searchers, the. The name of the Liverpool pop group (*fl.* 1963–6) was taken from the title of the John Wayne film (US, 1956).

seasons. See MAN FOR ALL ~ .

seat. See FLY BY THE ~ OF ONE'S PANTS.

seated. See GENTLEMEN BE ~ .

sea, the sea!, the. Cry taken from Xenophon's story (in *Anabasis*, IV.vii.24) of how his Greek mercenaries retreated to the Black Sea following their defeat in battle (401 BC). When they reached it, the soldiers cried: '*Thalatta, thalatta!*' (Attic form of the Greek '*Thalassa, thalassa!*'). Used as the title of a novel (1978) by Iris Murdoch.

seats. See YOU WANT THE BEST ∼ . . .

Second Front Now. A demand chalked on walls in the UK (and supported by the Beaverbrook press) during 1942–3, calling for an invasion of the European mainland, particularly one in collaboration with the Soviet Union. The Allied military command disagreed with this proposal and preferred to drive Axis troops out of North Africa and the Mediterranean first. Churchill's argument against a second front was that Britain's resources were fully stretched already.

Second World War. See WORLD WAR TWO.

see. See AND WHEN DID YOU LAST ∼ . . . ; BELIEVE ONLY HALF OF WHAT YOU ∼; COME UP AND ∼ ME SOMETIME; JOIN THE ARMY AND ∼ THE WORLD; MY EYES ARE DIM . . . ; NICE TO ∼ YOU . . .

see America first. Slogan for the Great Northern Railway Co., from *c* 1914. This slogan was splashed all over the US and helped turn the tide of travel from the east to the west coast. By 1916, the phrase was being used as the title of a show and a song by Cole Porter.

seeing is believing. A proverb by 1639 and clearly derived from John 20:25 where DOUBTING THOMAS refuses to believe in Christ's resurrection until he sees him: 'Except I shall see in his hands the print of the nails . . . I will not believe.'
    A modern addition to the proverb – by 1879 – is . . . **but feeling is the truth.**

seen. See AS ∼ ON TV; CHILDREN SHOULD BE ∼ AND NOT HEARD; YOU AIN'T ∼ NOTHIN' YET!

see Naples and die. Old Italian saying suggesting that once you have been to Naples there is nothing more beautiful to be seen on earth or, more ominously, a warning dating from the time when the city was a notorious centre for typhoid, cholera

and other diseases. This extract dated 3 March 1787 from Goethe's *Italian Journey* would seem to support the first origin: 'I won't say another word about the beauties of the city and its situation, which have been described and praised so often. As they say here, "*Vedi Napoli e poi muori!*" "See Naples and die!"'

seen one —, seen 'em all. Blasé format phrase of dismissal. A development of 'when you've seen one, you've seen the lot' – said about members of the opposite sex (and possibly their sexual equipment). From Thomas Tryon, *All That Glitters* (1987): 'I guess I needn't describe the "Community Room" [in an asylum]. Seen one community room, seen 'em all.'

see you in church. Jocular farewell – usually among non-churchgoers. American origin, by the mid-century. Compare **see you in court,** a rather more menacing farewell, perhaps hinting that someone is up to no good. Also American, by the 1920s/30s.

see you later, alligator. Note how a phrase develops: according to Flexner, the simple 'See you later', as a form of farewell, entered American speech in the 1870s. By the 1930s, it had some 'jive use' as 'see you later, alligator'. To this was added the response, 'In a while, crocodile.'
    This exchange became known to a wider public through the song 'See You Later, Alligator', sung by Bill Haley and his Comets in the film *Rock Around the Clock* (1956), which recorded the origins of rock'n'roll. Princess Margaret and her set became keen users. There was even a sudden vogue for keeping pet alligators.
    The next stage was for the front and back of the phrase to be dropped off, leaving the simple 'Lay-tuh' as a way to say goodbye.

see you on the green. A theatrical slang expression meaning 'I'll see you on the stage'. Has it something to do with GREEN ROOM? Apparently not, it is simple rhyming slang: 'greengage' = stage. Recorded by 1931. Sometimes 'the greengage' is used in full to mean 'the stage'.

see you Wednesday! At the end of the British ITV pop show, *Cool for Cats* (late 1950s), the host, Kent Walton, would spin round in his chair and say, 'Happy Monday, Tuesday, see you Wednesday!' Some, however, remember it as **see you Friday!** I think the confusion comes about because Canadian-born Walton (*b* 1925) was also famous for his all-in wrestling commentries on Wednesdays and Saturdays. Hence on Saturday he would say, 'See you Wednesday' and on Wednesday 'see you Saturday'. Obviously, he had a sign-off that could be adapted to any day of the week, whatever the show.

seigneur. See DROIT DE ∼.

self-destruct in ten seconds, this — will. Originally, 'this [audio] tape [of instructions] will . . .' in the American TV spy thriller MISSION IMPOSSIBLE (1966–72), though some insist that it was *five* seconds. Each episode began with the leader of the Impossible Missions Force listening to tape-recorded instructions for an assignment. The voice on the tape would say: 'Your mission, Dan, should you decide to accept it, is . . . As always, should you or any member of your IM Force be caught or killed, the secretary will disavow any knowledge of your actions. This tape will self-destruct . . .'
  'This cubicle will self-destruct in ten seconds which will make your mission impossible' – lavatorial graffito quoted from West Germany in my *Graffiti Lives OK* (1979).

sell. See PILE IT HIGH . . .

sell down the river, to. See SOLD DOWN THE RIVER.

sell off the family silver, to. Meaning 'to dispose of valuable assets which, once gone, cannot be retrieved', this allusion was memorably used in a speech to the Tory Reform Group by the 1st Earl of Stockton (Harold Macmillan) on 8 November 1985. Questioning the British government's policy of privatizing profitable nationalized industries, he said: 'First of all the Georgian silver goes, and then all that nice furniture that used to be in the saloon. Then the Canalettos go.' This was summarized as 'selling off the family silver'.

Selsdon Man. This name for a mythical primitive beast destroying the benefits of socialism in postwar Britain, was coined in Labour Party circles (possibly by Harold Wilson) in 1970. It was applied to the Conservative Party, following a much-publicized policy-making session by Edward Heath's Shadow Cabinet, held at the Selsdon Park Hotel near Croydon. The allusion is to the **Piltdown Man**, the name given to the celebrated forgery of a prehistoric skull.

send. See COVENTRY, TO ∼ SOMEONE TO.

send in/on the clowns. The tradition that the SHOW MUST GO ON grew out of circus. Whatever mishap occurred, the band was told to go on playing and the cry went up 'send in/on the clowns' – for the simple reason that panic had to be avoided, the audience's attention had to be diverted, and the livelihood of everybody in the circus depended on not having to give the audience its money back.
  Stephen Sondheim chose the 'Send *in* . . .' form as the title of a song in *A Little Night Music* (1974). Perhaps 'send in' was right for the circus, 'send on' for the stage?

sends. See IT ∼S ME.

sensational! A word made special by British disc jockey Tony Blackburn. According to *Radio Times* (6 March 1982), his 'idiosyncratic enunciation of "sensational" has become a password for would-be DJs and impersonators'. The first to poke at the delivery may well have been the disc jockey Mike Reid in *c* 1980. (In the fullness of time his own enunciation also came in for substantial ribbing – see POPTASTIC!)

sense. See YOU KNOW IT MAKES ∼.

separated at birth. See I WONDER IF THEY ARE BY ANY CHANCE RELATED?

sera. See CHE ∼.

serious. See JUST HOW ~ . . . ?; YOU CANNOT BE ~!

seriously, though, he's doing a grand job. After a satirical attack on a person in BBC TV's *That Was The Week That Was* (1962–3), David Frost would proffer this pretend conciliation. I can remember it being taken up by clergymen and others but Ned Sherrin, the show's producer, claims that the phrase was used no more than half a dozen times in all.

serious money. Meaning 'money in excessive amounts'. The *Longman Register of New Words* (1979) correctly surmises that this 'facetious usage seems to have started life among the fast-burning earners of the post-BIG BANG, pre-Bust city of London, who when speaking of salaries in the six-figure bracket would concede that this was "serious money"'. The phrase was popularized when used as the title of Caryl Churchill's satirical play about the City (London, 1987).

The *Register* also notes that the usage was likely to spread to other areas: 'Annie's – a bar favoured by serious drinkers' (*Sunday Times*, 28 August 1988).

serve that lady with a crusty loaf! See under BAND WAGGON.

service. See IT'S ALL PART OF THE ~!; NORMAL ~ WILL BE RESUMED . . . under DO NOT ADJUST YOUR SET.

Sesame. See OPEN ~.

set. See DO NOT ADJUST YOUR ~; FINE ~S THESE FERGUSON'S.

set alarm bells ringing, to. A cliché of journalism, meaning 'to alert'. 'The trio moved off in a yellow Mini and as they drove west the resemblance between Mr Waldorf and Martin began to ring alarm bells among the police' (*The Times*, 20 October 1983). 'The committee chairman, Mr Sam Nunn . . . interrupted a committee hearing on nuclear weapons to make the announcement, immediately setting off alarm bells in Washington' (*Guardian*, 3 February 1989).

set 'em up high, then knock 'em down hard. A modern proverb in the making? 'Just ten years after they entered the public consciousness as the "alternative comedians", most of our brightest young performers and writers of the eighties seem to be inexorably passing into the second stage of that old British showbiz tradition, "Set 'em up high, then knock 'em down hard"' – (*Guardian*, 25 May 1992).

Compare Melvyn Bragg on the actor Richard Burton: 'There's nothing the British like better than a bloke who comes from nowhere, makes it and then gets clobbered' – quoted in the *Observer* (1 January 1989).

sets. See EMPIRE UPON WHICH . . .

set the Thames on fire, to. This expression is often used in the negative: 'Well, he didn't exactly set the Thames on fire' – meaning 'he failed to make an impression'. W.S. Gilbert in *Princess Ida* (1884) has:

> They intend to send a wire? To the moon
> – to the moon
> And they'll set the Thames on fire
> Very soon – very soon.

Versions of this saying date back to the eighteenth century, and similar things have been said about the Rhine, Seine and Liffey in the appropriate languages. The Romans had the expression: '*Tiberium accendere nequaquam potest*' [it isn't at all possible to set the Tiber on fire]. The Thames, famously, once used to freeze over, which would only serve to increase the achievement should anyone manage to set it on fire.

settle down, now, settle down. British comedian Ken Goodwin (*b* 1933) had a diffident catchphrase based on the observation that if you tell people not to laugh, they will only do so the more (compare George Robey's DESIST!). 'Settle down now, settle down! I don't want you to make a noise, I've got a headache' was Goodwin's attempt to quieten laughter at his own jokes. He recalled (1979): 'I first said "Settle down" in a working men's club after the so-called compère/chairman had announced me to the audience. They didn't hear him and they didn't know I was on stage till I let them know. They were so noisy that, to get attention, I said, "Come on, you lot, settle down now." One or two began to smile and say to themselves, "What's this unknown commodity?" They were all waiting for bingo! It really took off after I did the Royal Variety Show, a summer season at the Palladium and *The Comedians* on TV.'

settlement. See JUST AND LASTING ∼.

seven. See GIVE US A CHILD UNTIL IT IS ∼ . . . ; KNOCK ∼ BELLS OUT OF.

Seven Deadly Sins, the. These are pride, wrath, envy, lust, gluttony, avarice and sloth – 'mortal' sins (as opposed to 'venial', i.e. pardonable sins) which entail spiritual death. They are not listed in the Bible, and may have grown out of medieval morality plays but were known as such by the early fourteenth century.

Seven Dwarfs, the. The story of 'Snow White and the Seven Dwarfs' was one of the old fairy tales collected by the Brothers Grimm in 1823. In the Walt Disney film version (US, 1937), the dwarfs are given names: Bashful, Doc, Dopey, Grumpy, Happy, Sleepy and Sneezy.

In the US Democratic Primaries for the 1988 presidential election, the original contenders were dubbed 'the Seven Dwarfs' out of scorn for their small stature as candidates. None of them won nomination or the presidency.

sevens. See SIXES AND ∼.

seven stone weakling. See under YOU, TOO, CAN HAVE A BODY LIKE MINE.

seven year itch, the. i.e. the urge to be unfaithful to a spouse after a certain period of matrimony. The *OED2* provides various examples of this phrase going back from the mid-twentieth to the mid-nineteenth century, but without the specific matrimonial context. For example, the 'seven year itch' describes a rash from poison ivy which was believed to recur every year for a seven-year period. Then one has to recall that since biblical days

seven-year periods (of lean or fat) have had especial significance, and there has also been the Army saying, 'Cheer up – the first seven years are the worst!'

But the specific matrimonial meaning was not popularized until the phrase was used as the title of George Axelrod's play (1952) and then film (1955). 'Itch' had long been used for the sexual urge but, as Axelrod commented on my *Quote . . . Unquote* programme (BBC Radio, 1979): 'There was a phrase which referred to a somewhat unpleasant disease but nobody had used it in a sexual [I think he meant 'matrimonial'] context before. I do believe I invented it in that sense.'

Oddly, I can find no mention in any reference book of 'itch' being used in connection with venereal diseases. Nonetheless, I was interested to come across the following remark in *W.C. Fields: His Follies and Fortunes* (Robert Lewis Taylor, published as early as 1950): 'Bill exchanged women every seven years, as some people get rid of the itch.'

sex and the (single) — ∼ . Journalistic headline format derived from the book *Sex and the Single Girl* (1962 – film US, 1964) by Helen Gurley Brown. Fritz Spiegl, *Keep Taking the Tabloids!* (1983) identified it in the following actual headlines: 'Sex and the single Siberian', 'Sex and the kindly atheist', 'Sex and the girl reporter' and 'Sex and the parish priest'.

Sex, Lies and Videotape. Title of film (US, 1989) and soon a favourite allusion of headline writers. From the *Sunday Telegraph* (29 March 1992): 'FURY AT "SEX, LIES AND STEREOTYPES": GAY PROTESTERS THREATEN TO DISRUPT OSCARS CEREMONY OVER NEW MOVIE'.

sex'n'drugs'n'rock'n'roll. i.e. what young people are supposed to be preoccupied with. From a 1977 song by Ian Dury and Chaz Jankel (written as 'Sex & Drugs & Rock & Roll'), which continues, '. . . is [*sic*] all my brain and body need . . . is very good indeed'.

'Nostalgia for the 1960s, call it sex and drugs and rock and roll (and high purpose) is rife in *Hot Flashes*' (*Guardian*, 25 January

1989). 'Aurum Press is shortly to publish [Lord Whitelaw's] memoirs . . . "It's not exactly sex, drugs and rock-and-roll," Aurum's Tim Chadwick tells me' (*Observer*, 26 February 1989).

sex rears its ugly head. And how curious. Why? Because the penis rises? If so, then why ugly? A very odd usage, except that the construction 'to raise/rear its ugly head' was probably used about other matters before sex. The image is presumably of a Loch Ness-type monster, perhaps, emerging from the deep.

The 'sex' form has been current since at least 1930 when James R. Quirk used it in a *Photoplay* editorial about the film *Hell's Angels*. In Alan Ayckbourn's play *Bedroom Farce* (1975), Delia comments: 'My mother used to say, Delia, if S-E-X ever rears its ugly head, close your eyes before you see the rest of it.'

It is used both as an explanation for people's behaviour (like '*cherchez la femme*') and as a complaint of the intrusion of sex in books, TV programmes, etc. where the speaker would rather not find it.

sexual chemistry. In the period prior to the start of TV-am, the British breakfast television station, in 1983, David Frost talked about hoped-for new approaches to on-screen presentation. He either invented the phrase 'sexual chemistry', or merely endorsed it when it was suggested to him by a reporter, to describe what it was important for Frost and his colleagues to have: 'The chemistry thing is really important . . . chemistry – sexual or otherwise – that is important.'

'Personal chemistry' to describe the attraction between two people had long been remarked where it existed in other walks of life. 'Remember the nauseating way Margaret Thatcher turned into a lovesick girl during Gorbachev's visit here and all that talk in the press of "personal chemistry"?' (*Guardian*, 7 June 1989). George Bernard Shaw in *You Never Can Tell* (1898) had earlier had: 'Not love: we know better than that. Let's call it chemistry . . . Well, you're attracting me irresistibly – chemically.'

shades of the prison-house. A phrase from William Wordsworth, 'Ode, Intimations of Immortality' (1807): 'Heaven lies about us in our infancy!/Shades of the prison-house begin to close/Upon the growing boy.' Title of a book about prison life by 'S. Wood' (1932). Note also the opening lines of 'Marlborough', a poem written about his old school by John Betjeman for a TV programme (1962): 'Shades of my prison house, they come to view,/Just as they were in 1922:/The stone flag passages, the iron bars . . .'

shadow. See AVOID FIVE O'CLOCK ∼.

shake. See MORE — THAN YOU CAN ∼ . . .

shaken not stirred. See MARTINI, ∼.

shakers. See MOVERS AND ∼.

shakes. See TWO ∼ OF A LAMB'S TAIL.

shake/show a leg, to. 'Shake a leg' means either 'to dance' (by 1881) or (in the US) 'to hurry up' (by 1904). 'Show a leg' (meaning 'to get up out of bed in the morning or get a move on') dates from the days when women were allowed to spend the night on board when ships of the Navy were in port. Next morning at the cry: 'Show a leg!', if a woman's leg was stuck out of a hammock, she was allowed to sleep on. If it was a man's, he had to get up and on with his duties. No citation for this use before 1854, however.

shame of our —, the. A cliché of tabloid journalism, although 'THE SHAME OF OUR PRISONS' was a headline in the broadsheet *Observer* (3 May 1981).

Shangri-La. Name for an earthly paradise comes from the name of the hidden Tibetan lamasery in James Hilton's novel, *Lost Horizon* (1933). All who stay there enjoy long life.

sharing. See CARING AND ∼.

sharpen up there, the quick stuff's coming! See under MUM, MUM, THEY ARE LAUGHING AT ME.

shattering. See THE EFFECT IS ∼ under I THOUGHT — UNTIL I DISCOVERED —.

Shean. See ABSOLUTELY, MR GALLAGHER . . .

she done him wrong. A phrase from the refrain of the anonymous US ballad 'Frankie and Johnny' which Mencken dates c 1875 and which is sung in the film *She Done Him Wrong* (US, 1933) based on Mae West's play *Diamond Lil*. There are numerous versions of the ballad (200 is one estimate) and it may be of Black origin. 'Frankie and Johnnie were lovers' [or husband and wife] but he [Johnnie] does her wrong by going off with other women – 'He was her man, but he done her wrong'. So, to equal the score, Frankie shoots him, and has to be punished for it (in some versions in the electric chair):

Frankie walked up to the scaffold, as calm as a girl could be,
She turned her eyes to Heaven and said 'Good Lord, I'm coming to Thee;
He was my man, but I done him wrong.'

sheet of music. See SINGING FROM THE SAME ∼.

she knows, you know! Diminutive northern English comedienne Hylda Baker (1908–86) used to say this about Cynthia, her mute giraffe-like partner in sketches. Her other phrase **be soon!** was used as the title of a TV series in the 1950s.

Shell. See THAT'S ∼.

shell-like. See IN YOUR ∼ EAR.

she seems like a nice girl, doesn't she? See under GENERATION GAME .

she should lie back and enjoy it. Best described – as it is in Paul Scott's novel *The Jewel in the Crown* (1966) – as 'that old, disreputable saying'. Daphne Manners, upon whose 'rape' the story hinges, adds: 'I can't say, Auntie, that I lay back and enjoyed mine.'

It is no more than a saying – a 'mock-Confucianism' is how Partridge/*Slang* describes it, giving a date (c 1950) – and one

is unlikely ever to learn when, or from whom, it first arose.

A word of caution to anyone thinking of using it. An American broadcaster, Tex Antoine, said in 1975: 'With rape so predominant in the news lately, it is well to remember the words of Confucius: "If rape is inevitable, lie back and enjoy it."' ABC News suspended Antoine for this remark, then demoted him to working in the weather department and prohibited him from appearing on the air.

Compare CLOSE YOUR EYES AND THINK OF ENGLAND.

she who must be obeyed. The original 'she' in the novel *She* (1887) by H. Rider Haggard was the all-powerful Ayesha, 'who from century to century sat alone, clothed with unchanging loveliness, waiting till her lost love is born again'. But also, 'she was obeyed throughout the length and breadth of the land, and to question her command was certain death'.

From the second of these two quotations we get the use of the phrase by barrister Horace Rumpole with regard to his formidable wife in the 'Rumpole of the Bailey' stories by John Mortimer (in TV plays since 1978, and novelizations therefrom). Hence, too, one of the many nicknames applied to Margaret Thatcher when British Prime Minister – 'The great she-elephant, she-who-must-be-obeyed' (Denis Healey, quoted in the *Observer*, 4 March 1984).

shift the goalposts. See under MOVE THE GOALPOSTS.

shining like a tanner on a sweep's arse. Peter Foulds of Darlington, County Durham, wrote (1994): 'A Cockney cousin of mine once told me of her pleasure at receiving, from her husband, the gift of a baby grand piano. She described the beautiful lustre of the instrument with these words.' Partridge/*Slang* has 'shine like a shilling up a sweep's arse' – which is a touch more alliterative – and dates it 'early C20'.

shining like shit on a barn door. Shining admirably (as, say, after a good polishing). Partridge/*Slang* has 'shine like a shitten barn door' and finds an allusion to the phrase in Jonathan Swift's *Polite Conversation* (1738).

shining. See FROM SEA TO ~ SEA.

ship. See LIKE RATS DESERTING A SINKING ~.

shipping. See ATTENTION ALL ~.

Shipton. See MOTHER ~.

ship(s). See FACE THAT LAUNCH'D A THOUSAND ~; LIKE RATS DESERTING . . .

shirt. See under HOW TICKLED I AM; STUFFED ~.

shit. See SHINING LIKE ~ . . .

shock, horror! Reaction expressed in parody of tabloid newspaper-speak, from the 1970s onwards. In form it is, of course, similar to 'Shock, horror, probe, sensation!' promoted since the 1960s by *Private Eye* as a stock sensational newspaper headline. **Shock probe** has been, I think, a type of *News of the World* headline word.

shocked. See WOULD YOU BE ~ IF I PUT ON . . .

shocking pink. A coinage of the Italian fashion designer Elsa Schiaparelli (1896–1973). She used it in 1938 to describe a lurid pink she had created. As such it made a pleasant change from alliterative coinages and has undoubtedly stuck. In her autobiography, entitled, understandably, *Shocking Life*, Chap. 9 (1954) she notes that her friends and executives warned her off creating a 'nigger pink' but 'the colour "shocking" established itself for ever as a classic. Even Dali dyed an enormous stuffed bear in shocking pink'.

shock of the new, the. The title of a TV series and a book (1980) by the art critic, Robert Hughes, came – as acknowledged – from Ian Dunlop's 1972 study of seven historic modernist exhibitions.

shoes are killin' me. See I'M GOING BACK TO THE WAGON . . .

shome mistake shurely? (or **shurely shome mistake?**) Written as such and interpolated as an editorial query in *Private Eye* copy (from the 1980s), this reproduces the spraying vocal style of William Deedes, editor of the *Daily Telegraph* from 1974 to 1986.
Compare WHO HE?

shoots. See GREEN ~.

shoot the moon, to. An American expression meaning 'to do a moonlight flit', i.e. to leave without paying your bills, rent, etc. or to remove your goods at night in order to cheat the bailiff. Current by 1869 when it was discussed in *Notes and Queries*. *Shoot the Moon* was the title of a film (US, 1981) 'To shoot the moon' can also mean 'to go for broke' in card playing.

shopping. See under WHEN THE GOING GETS TOUGH . . .

— shopping days to Christmas. This may have been one of the coinages of H. Gordon Selfridge (1856–1947), American-born creator of Selfridges department store in London. At least, when he was still in Chicago he sent out an instruction to heads of departments and assistants at the Marshall Field store there: 'The Christmas season has begun and but twenty-three more shopping days remain in which to make our holiday sales record.'

short. See LONG AND THE ~ OF IT.

short, fat, hairy legs. See under *MORECAMBE AND WISE SHOW*.

short, sharp shock, a. A phrase used by William Whitelaw, the British Home Secretary, in a speech to the Conservative Party Conference (10 October 1979) describing a new method of hard treatment for young offenders. The expression had been used by other Home Secretaries before him and is a quotation (referring to execution) from W.S. Gilbert's lyrics for *The Mikado* (1885). Used as the title of a play (1980) by Howard Brenton and Tony Howard (originally called *Ditch the Bitch*, referring to Margaret Thatcher).

shot. See BEST ~; FOOD ~ FROM GUNS; WHO ~ J.R.?

shoulder. See CHIP ON ONE'S ~; COLD ~ . . .

show. See ANOTHER OPENING, ANOTHER ~; GREATEST ~ ON EARTH; JOLLY GOOD ~!; LET'S DO THE ~ . . . ; LET'S GET THIS ~ ON THE ROAD; ~ MUST GO ON under SEND IN THE CLOWNS; ~ US YOUR WAD under LOADSAMONEY!; YOU'RE ONLY AS GOOD . . .

show a leg. See SHAKE A LEG.

showbiz/show business. See THAT'S ~!

shower!, you're an absolute. Military rebuke to Other Ranks, best spoken in a very English upper-class voice, as by Terry-Thomas in the film *Private's Progress* (UK, 1956). He also said of the workers in *I'm All Right Jack* (UK, 1959): 'I can tell you, they're an absolute shower – a positive shower.' He was playing a personnel officer.

Partridge/*Catch Phrases* suggests that the original expression was 'what a shower!' (RAF, 1930s), short for 'a shower of shit'.

showers, send someone to the. See under UP AND UNDER.

show must go on, the. Like SEND IN THE CLOWNS, this seems to have been originally a circus phrase, though no one seems able to turn up a written reference much before 1930. It was the title of a film in 1937 and of an Ira Gershwin/Jerome Kern song in *Cover Girl* (1944). In 1950, the phrase was spoken in the film *All About Eve* and, in the same decade, Noël Coward wrote a song which posed the question '*Why* Must the Show Go On?'

shows. See I THINK THAT ~ . . .

showtime. See IT'S ~, FOLKS!

show us your rabbit! Curious but inspired phrase used by the British comedians (Raymond) Bennett and (Harry) Moreny in their variety act of the 1930s/40s.

'shrieks of silence' was the stern reply. See under 'NO ANSWER' WAS . . .

shrouds. See NO POCKETS IN ~.

shut that door! Larry Grayson (1923–95) came to prominence as a comedy personality on British TV in the 1970s. The first time he used the phrase was on stage at the Theatre Royal, Brighton in 1970, 'when I felt a terrible draught up my trouser legs. I turned to the wings and said it. I really meant it, but the only response was giggles from the wings and a roar of laughter from the audience. So I kept it in my act. I can't go anywhere now without taxi-drivers or shopkeepers telling me to "shut that door".' (Another version has him first saying it when appearing in pantomine at the Kidderminster Playhouse in the 1960s).

In the 1970s, Grayson also had any number of camp phrases like **what a gay day!, the place is alive!** and **I just don't care any more!** See also under *GENERATION GAME*.

shut up, Cecil! See under THEY'RE WORKING WELL TONIGHT.

shut up, Eccles! See under *GOON SHOW*.

shut your cake-hole. 'Cake-hole' for mouth was British servicemen's slang by 1943. 'Shut your cake-hole', meaning 'shut up, be quiet' was recorded among schoolchildren by 1959. Compare SHUT YOUR FACE under NAY, NAY – THRICE AGAIN NAY!

sick and tired. Why are these two words always put together? There is a 1783 example. In May 1988, Terry Dicks, a Conservative MP and self-proclaimed tribune of the plebs, spoke during a House of Commons debate on the arts, and said: 'Ordinary people are sick and tired of people who can well afford to pay the full going rate for attendance at the theatre and ballet getting away with being subsidized by the rest of us.' This seems a fairly classic context for the phrase to be used – and spoken by just the type of person one would expect to use it.

From the *Independent* (7 March 1989): 'President Bush complained he was "sick and tired" of attacks on Defense Secretary-designate John Tower.'

sick as a parrot. See under OVER THE MOON.

sick-bag. See PASS THE ∼, ALICE.

sic transit gloria mundi. The phrase meaning 'so passes away the glory of the world' – perhaps now mostly used ironically when something has failed – is an allusion to *Of the Imitation of Christ* (c 1420) by Thomas à Kempis ('*O quam cito transit gloria mundi*' [O, how quickly the world's glory passes away]). It is used at the coronation ceremony of Popes when a reed surmounted with flax is burned and a chaplain intones: '*Pater sancte, sic transit gloria mundi*' to remind the new 'Holy Father' of the transitory nature of human vanity. *ODQ*, however, says it was used at the crowning of Alexander V at Pisa in July 1409, and is of earlier origin, which, if so, would mean that it was à Kempis who was doing the quoting.

Sid. See TELL ∼.

Sidi Barrani. See DID I EVER TELL YOU . . . under *MUCH BINDING IN THE MARSH*.

silence is golden. This encouragement to silence is from a Swiss inscription written in German and best known in the English translation by Thomas Carlyle: '*Sprechen ist silbern, Schweigen ist golden*' [Speech is silver(n), silence is golden].

silent majority, the. On 3 November 1969, President Richard Nixon gave a TV address on Vietnam and called for the support of a particular section of US opinion – 'the great silent majority of my fellow Americans', by which he meant MIDDLE AMERICA or at least, that part of the US not involved in the vociferous anti-war protest movement. The previous year, in his speech accepting the Republican nomination, Nixon had already addressed this theme: 'The quiet voice in the tumult and the shouting . . . the voice of the great majority of Americans, the forgotten Americans – the non-shouters.'

Earlier, the phrase had been used in the nineteenth century to describe the dead – compare GREAT MAJORITY.

silly! See under *MONTY PYTHON*.

silly Billy. Nickname for a foolish person. The most notable person to be given it as a nickname was William Frederick, 2nd Duke of Gloucester (1776–1834), uncle of William IV – though it was also applied to the king himself. In the wrangles between Whigs and Tories, when the king supported the former, Gloucester is reported to have asked, 'Who's Silly Billy now?' Partridge/*Slang* has Henry Mayhew in 1851 finding 'Silly Billy . . . very popular with the audience at the fairs' (as a name used by a clown for his stooge).

In the 1970s, Mike Yarwood, the TV impressionist, put it in the mouth of the Labour politician Denis Healey, because it went rather well with the Healey persona and distinctive vocal delivery. Healey then imitated art by saying it himself.

According to Alan Watkins in the *Observer* (13 January 1985), Randolph Churchill, the Conservative politician (and son of Winston), was also noted for using the expression.

silly little man. See under *BAND WAGGON*.

silly (old) moo! Alf Garnett (Warren Mitchell) in the BBC TV comedy series *Till Death Us Do Part* would say either form of this to his wife (Dandy Nichols) – a euphemism for 'cow'. Dandy Nichols said that people used to call it out to her in the street – affectionately, nonetheless. The series ran from 1964 to 1974.

silly season, the. This phrase refers to the period of time around August/September when, for lack of hard news, newspapers traditionally fill their pages with frivolities. Although Parliament and the law courts are in recess, and Britain (like France) increasingly seems to stop work for the month of August, the fact is that important news does *not* cease happening. The Soviet invasion of Czechoslovakia took place then, as did the resignation of President Nixon, and the 1990 Gulf Crisis, not to mention the start of two world wars. The phrase was in use by 1861.

Silver/silver. See HI-YO, ~; SELL OFF THE FAMILY ~.

Simpsons, The. The first new media hero of the 1990s was Bart, the skateboard-toting teenage son of Homer and Marge, in Twentieth-Century Fox's TV cartoon series *The Simpsons*. His vocabulary was colorful, if not always comprehensible: **yo, dude!**; **aye caramba!**; **whoa, mama!**; **au contraire, mon frère**; and **don't have a cow, man!** sounded as if they had been plucked straight off the streets, but probably weren't – even if they soon found their way there on a host of T-shirts, buttons and bumper-stickers. **Eat my shorts!** became a threatening imperative (shorts = underpants), having previously been popular in the 1980s with US high school and college kids; **I'm Bart Simpson – who the hell are you?** and **underachiever and proud of it** became curiously potent slogans.

sincerely. See DO YOU ~ WANT TO BE RICH?; I MEAN THAT MOST ~ . . .

sinews of peace/war, the. Winston Churchill's speech at Fulton, Missouri, on 5 March 1946, which introduced the old phrase IRON CURTAIN to a wider audience, was entitled 'The Sinews of Peace'. This was an allusion to the phrase '*nervi belli pecunia*' from Cicero's *Philippics* where the 'sinews of war' means 'money'. The 'sinews of peace' recommended by Churchill in dealing with the Soviet Union amounted to recourse to the newly formed United Nations Organization.

singing. See ALL- ~ , ALL-DANCING.

singing from the same sheet of music, we are all. 'We are all operating according to the same plan or agreement, acting according to the same set of principles'. A phrase from British industrial and trade union parlance, possibly influenced by the Welsh choral tradition. From the *Sunday Times* (20 October 1985): 'Parker sums it up: "At Belfast shipyard we have only lost 0.05% of our man hours over the last 10 years. We are all singing from the same sheet of music.'

singing sands. Long-established term for sands which appear to make a noise. *The Singing Sands* is the title of a Josephine Tey crime novel (1952) in which the whole plot hinges on a fragment of verse scribbled on a newspaper by a dying man:

> The beasts that talk,
> The streams that stand,
> The stones that walk,
> The singing sand,
> . . .
> . . .
> That guard the way To Paradise.

The detective in question – Inspector Grant – is reduced to putting an advert in *The Times* to find the source, and thinks: 'It will serve me right if someone writes to say that the thing is one of the best-known lines of some Xanadu concoction of Coleridge's, and that I must be illiterate not to have known it.' But it does not appear to be an actual quotation.

sings. See OPERA AIN'T OVER . . .

sinking. See BOVRIL PREVENTS THAT ~ FEELING; LIKE RATS DESERTING . . .

sins. See SEVEN DEADLY ~.

sister, sob. See under AGONY AUNT.

sit. See PIFFY, TO ~ LIKE.

sitcoms. See under YUPPIE.

sitting. See ARE YOU ~ COMFORTABLY? . . . ; NO MORE LATIN . . .

— situation, a. For several years in the 1970s and 80s, *Private Eye* waged a campaign against the unnecessary addition of the word 'situation' in situations where the speaker thought it added something to the sentence. This succeeded in making the matter a well-known joke but did not entirely put an end to the practice. Two ripe examples from my own reading: an employee of the Royal Borough of Windsor and Maidenhead wrote to a householder in 1981 and asked him to trim a hedge. He did so in these words: 'Whereas a *hedge situation* at Altwood Road, Maidenhead in Berkshire, belonging to you overhangs the highway known as Altwood Road, Maidenhead aforesaid, so as to endanger or obstruct the passage of pedestrians . . .'

Yoko Ono is quoted in Peter Brown and Steven Gaines, *The Love You Make* (1983), as saying: '[John Lennon] asked if I had ever tried [heroin]. I told him that while he was in India with the Maharishi, I had a sniff of it in a *party situation* . . .'

And still it goes on: in *High Life* magazine (September 1993) there appeared this piece of tastelessness: 'Much has been learned since the first Whitbread [round-the-world yacht race] in 1973/74 when, tragically, three men died in *man overboard situations* . . .'

Oddly, as long ago as 22 August 1934, *The Times* was drawing attention to the trend: 'A popular dodge at present is to add the word "situation" or "position" to a noun; by this means, apparently, it has been discovered that the most pregnant meanings can be expressed with the least effort. The "coal situation" remains unchanged; the "herring position" is grave.'

situation hopeless but not serious. The basic format here is 'situation — but not —'. The film *Situation Hopeless But Not Serious* (US, 1965) derived its title from what has been called an Austrian saying: 'The situation in Germany is serious but not hopeless; the situation in Austria is hopeless but not serious.' Conan Doyle in 'The Second Stain' (*The Return of Sherlock Holmes*, 1905) has the basic, 'The situation is desperate, but not hopeless.'

Situation Normal All Fouled/Fucked Up. See SNAFU.

six basic plots, the. It is sometimes held that there is a fixed number of plots that provide the basis for all literature and storytelling. In the *Guardian*'s 'Notes and Queries' section in 1992, Rory Johnston postulated *eight* plots. David Cottis believed (1994) that *seven* would be more appropriate. Here is his list, together with examples of each as used:

1) Cinderella (as in most of Dickens's novels, musicals like *Annie*, or Hollywood comedies such as *Pretty Woman*).

2) Achilles (this is Aristotle's definition of tragedy: the hamartia or tragic error; see *Macbeth*, *Citizen Kane* etc).

3) Faust (*King Lear*, *Oedipus*, almost every horror film, from *Frankenstein* to *Jurassic Park*).

4) Romeo and Juliet (too numerous to mention).

5) Circe – the entrapment story (*Wall Street*, *Pravda*).

6) The Hero and the Quest (everything from Gilgamesh to *Indiana Jones*).

7) Orestes – the revenge story (*Hamlet*, *Wuthering Heights*, Sondheim's *Sweeney Todd*, *Robocop*).

Similarly there is also dispute over what may be the **five basic jokes.** Richard Janko in his book *Aristotle on Comedy* (1984) claimed to have unearthed the Greek philosopher's long-lost classification of *eight* basic jokes. On the other hand, Sully Prudhomme (French poet and winner of the first Nobel Prize for Literature) in his 1902 'Essay on Laughter' identified *twelve* 'Classes of the Laughter-Provoking', which may amount to much the same thing:

1) Novelties
2) Physical Deformities
3) Moral Deformities and Vices
4) Disorderliness
5) Small Misfortune
6) Indecencies
7) Pretences
8) Want of Knowledge or Skill
9) The Incongruous and Absurd
10) Word Play
11) The Expression of a Merry Mood
12) Outwitting or Getting the Better of a Person.

sixes and sevens, to be at. Meaning 'to be confused; in an unresolved situation', the usual origin given for this expression is that in the days when the medieval guilds of London took pride in their order of precedence, the Merchant Taylors and the Skinners could not agree who should be sixth, and who seventh. After an intervention by the Lord Mayor, they agreed to take it in turns – as they do to this day. Morris, on the other hand, supports the theory that the idiom dates from a dice game (as mentioned by Chaucer in one of his poems) in which the dice bore marks up to seven, if not further: 'Only a confused or disorganized person would roll for this point' (i.e. a 'six and seven'). This is the origin favoured by *OED2*.

Shakespeare's only use of the phrase occurs in *Richard II*, II.ii.122 (1595):

> All is uneven,
> And everything is left at six and seven.

In *Pericles* (IV.vi.74; 1609), Shakespeare may be making a punning allusion to it when (in a sexual context) Lysimachus says: 'Did you go to't [copulate] young? Were you a gamester at five or at seven?'

six of one and half a dozen of the other. Phrase describing a situation where there is no difference, especially where blame is to be laid. The Rev. Francis Kilvert, the English diarist, wrote (6 September 1878): 'There was a great deal of talk at that time in London about the quarrel between the King [George IV] and the Queen [Caroline]. There was about six for one and half a dozen for the other'.

See also under I'M NOT A NUMBER . . .

sixpence. See BANG GOES ∼; NOTHING OVER ∼.

sixties, swinging. See under SWINGING LONDON.

sixty-four (thousand) dollar question, the. 'Ah, that's the sixty-four dollar question, isn't it?' some people will exclaim, when surely they mean 'sixty-four *thousand*'. Or do they? Put it down to inflation. *Webster's Dictionary* says that $64 *was* the highest award in a CBS radio quiz called *Take It or Leave It* which ran from 1941–8 and in which the value of the prize doubled every time the contestant got a right answer (in the progression 1–2–4–8–16–32–64 – hence the title *Double Your Money* given to the first of the British TV versions). This is how the saying entered common parlance, meaning 'that is the question which would solve all our problems if only we knew the answer to it'.

An example of the original use in the 1950s is contained in a *Daily Express* article about P.G. Wodehouse written by Rene McColl (undated): ' "Wodehouse, Esq.", I

observed, "Could I, to use the vernacular of this our host nation, pop the jolly old 64–dollar question? If you were back in Germany, a prisoner, and you had it all to do again – would you do it?" '

Subsequently, in the US TV version of the show (1955–7), the top prize did go up to $64,000 – though, cunningly, when ITV imported the show for British viewers shortly afterwards, the title was simply *The 64,000 Question* or *Challenge*, making no mention of the denomination of currency involved.

In February 1989, I heard a female weather forecaster on ITV being asked, 'Is the mild weather going to continue?' She replied, 'That's the sixty-four million dollar question.' So inflation is still rampant.

Skegness is so bracing. See IT'S SO BRACING.

skin off [one's] nose, no. An expression of indifference: 'it's no skin off my nose if you choose to do . . .' The *OED2*'s earliest citation is from Sinclair Lewis in 1920, but Charles Dickens, *Hard Times*, Chap. 16 (1854) has: 'If she takes it in the fainting way, I'll have the skin off her nose at all events!' [where Mr Bounderby has armed himself with a bottle of smelling salts before imparting bad news]. The meaning of 'the skin off her nose' is not too clear here. It almost anticipates the later toast (from the 1920s), 'Here's to the skin off your nose!' This last has also been described as a theatrical greeting and said to refer to the bad old days of make-up which affected the skin. If you said it to an actor, it meant you wished he be kept in work.

skittles. See LIFE ISN'T ALL BEER AND ∼.

sky. See GONE TO THE BIG — IN THE ∼; HELLO BIRDS, HELLO ∼ . . . ; REACH FOR THE ∼.

sky through the trees, to see the. To have sex – as though one of the participants was lying on his/her back with this particular view (*al fresco*, naturally). Noted in 1985. Compare the jocular suggestion that a woman (usually) has been **studying the ceilings** in the promiscuous pursuit of sex.

sleaze factor. See FALKLANDS FACTOR.

sleep. See WE NEVER ~.

sleeping with the enemy. Originally, this phrase was used by lesbian separatists to describe their 'sisters' who persisted in heterosexual dalliances, hence the enemy was 'men'. Used as the title of a film (US, 1991) about marital violence, the enemy was an individual man.

slept. See QUEEN ELIZABETH ~ HERE.

sliced bread. See GREATEST THING SINCE ~.

Sligger Urquhart. Nickname of Francis F. Urquhart (d 1935), a noted Oxford don and dean of Balliol, and curiously interesting. Cyril Bailey in *F.F. Urquhart* (1936) thinks he got the nickname at a 'Minehead reading party in 1892'. Maurice Bowra, *Memories 1898–1939* (1966) suggests that 'Sligger' was a corruption into pre-war dialect of the 'sleek one'. In *Geoffrey Madan's Notebooks* (1981), Cyril Asquith is quoted as saying that, 'the name "Sligger" [suggests] not a golf club, or cue rest, but some instrument of a dentist: like a small chopper, with a crank appendage'.

Incidentally, Anthony Powell in *Infants of the Spring* (1976) insists that 'Sligger Urquhart' is a solecism – he was either 'Sligger' or 'Urquhart' but not the two together.

Sloane Ranger, a. Denoting a posh, upper-class woman, of good family, living (originally) in the Sloane Square area of London. The joke allusion is, of course, to the Western character, the Lone Ranger. The term was invented in 1975 by the magazine *Harpers & Queen*, and when the Princess of Wales ('Supersloane') entered public life in 1981, the term became much more widely understood.

The coinage has been attributed to the style writer Peter York but was apparently actually coined by Martina Margetts, a subeditor on the magazine.

slow down. See NATURE'S WAY OF TELLING YOU TO ~.

slow hand. See OLD ~.

slowly. See TWIST ~, ~, IN THE WIND.

slow, slow, quick, quick, slow. Dance tempo spoken by Victor Sylvester (1902–78), the British ballroom dance instructor and band leader, on radio from 1941 and on TV from the 1950s. The tempo is for the quickstep.

In December 1988, poster advertisements for the Rover 200 series compared start-up speeds for two Rover models and a BMW under the heading, 'Quick, Quick, Slow'.

small. See ONE ~ STEP FOR . . .

small, but perfectly formed. I can remember quite clearly the time when this phrase first registered with me. It was at a one-man show performed by Tim Thomas at the tiny Soho Poly theatre, London, in 1977. Addressing the diminutive audience at a lunch-hour performance, he informed us we were 'small . . . but perfectly-formed'.

As such, it was an idiom which I vaguely thought to be theatrical, possibly American show biz, in origin. I am sure, too, that I have heard variations, of the 'small, but exquisitely talented' variety.

Then, in 1983, I was intrigued when Artemis Cooper published *A Durable Fire – The Letters of Duff and Diana Cooper 1913–50*. In a letter from Duff to Diana in October 1914, he writes: 'That is the sort of party I like . . . You must think I have enjoyed it too, with your two stout lovers frowning at one another across the hearth rug, while your small, but perfectly formed one kept the party in a roar.'

From the use of fashionable slang elsewhere in the letters, I would suppose that this coinage was not original to Cooper but drawn from the smart talk of the period. If there is an earlier example of the phrase in use, however, I wait with bated breath to hear of it.

The 'small, but . . .' construction appears earlier in the German saying '*klein, aber mein*' ('small, but my own') and in the line from 'Ode to Evening' (1747) by William Collins: 'Or where the beetle winds/ His small but sullen horn' (where 'sullen' = 'of a deep, dull or mournful tone' – *OED2*). James Lees-Milne in his diary entry for 21

June 1949 (in *Midway on the Waves*, 1985) says of Princess Margaret: 'In size she is a midget but perfectly made' – which amounts to much the same thing.

I might mention, also, that Richard Lowe has sent me this entry from the Skipton Town Council Yearbook: 'The following remarkable record is taken from a gravestone at the east end of Christ Church burial ground: "In memory of Edwin Calvert, son of Richard Calvert, of Skipton, known by the title of the 'Commander in Chief'. He was the *smallest and most perfect* human being in the world, being under 36 inches in height, and weighing 25 lb. He died much lamented and deeply regretted by all who knew him, August 7th 1859, aged 17 years".'

small earthquake in Chile, a. Phrase from a famously mousey headline with which Claud Cockburn claimed to have won a competition for dullness among subeditors on *The Times* during the 1930s. It went: 'Small Earthquake in Chile. **Not Many Dead**'. The original has proved impossible to trace and may just have been a smoking-room story. However, the idea lives on: *Small Earthquake in Chile* was the title of a book (1972) by Alastair Horne about the Allende affair (in Chile), the journalist Michael Green called a volume of memoirs, *Nobody Hurt in Small Earthquake* (1990), and the cartoonist Nicholas Garland called his 'journal of a year in Fleet Street', *Not Many Dead* (1990).

small is beautiful. The title of a book published in 1973 by Professor E.F. Schumacher (1911–77) provided a catchphrase and a slogan for those who were opposed to an expansionist trend in business and organizations that was very apparent in the 1960s and 70s and who wanted 'economics on a human scale'. However, it appears that he very nearly didn't come up with the phrase. According to his daughter and another correspondent (*Observer*, 29 April/6 June 1984), the book was going to be called 'The Homecomers'. His publisher, Anthony Blond suggested 'Small*ness* is Beautiful', and then Desmond Briggs, the co-publisher, came up with the eventual wording.

smarter than the average bear, (Booboo). Said of himself by Yogi Bear to his sidekick, Booboo, in the American Yogi Bear cartoon TV series (started 1958). The character was voiced by Charles 'Daws' Butler. At his death in May 1988, it was suggested, perhaps mistakenly, that he had coined the phrase as well.

smasher. See I SAY, WHAT A ~! UNDER DON'T FORCE IT, PHOEBE.

smashing, lovely, super! A *real* catchphrase based on the enthusiastic mutterings of the British comedian Jim Bowen (*b* 1937) when hosting a darts-orientated TV game called *Bullseye* (since 1981). The order of the words was variable and when Bowen appeared in poster ads for Skol Lager (1993–4), the copy line was 'Great, smashing, super'. From the *Independent* (4 December 1992): 'Jim Bowen is a student hero. In common rooms across the country, they hunker down to watch his show . . . to see if Jim will engage his guests in the small talk beloved of his *Spitting Image* puppet: "Just look at what you could have won! Lovely, smashing, super."' Bowen admits himself to having enthused similarly when a female contestant informed him that her husband had died.

smatter wit chew? See under TAKE A KICK IN THE PANTS.

smells. See BELLS AND ~.

smile on your face. See under COME ALIVE . . .

smile, you're on *Candid Camera*! The American broadcaster Allen Funt translated his practical joke radio programme *Candid Microphone* to TV and it ran from 1948–78 (there was a British version, too). On revealing to members of the public that they had been hoaxed, this was his somewhat hopeful greeting – hopeful that they would not take it badly.

Smith. See HARVEY ~.

smoke-filled room, a. Suite 408–409–410 (previously rooms 804–5) of the Blackstone

Hotel in Chicago was the original 'smoke-filled room' in which Warren Harding was selected as the Republican presidential candidate in June 1920. The image conjured up by this phrase is of cigar-smoking political bosses coming to a decision after much horse-trading. Although he denied saying it, the phrase seems to have come out of a prediction by Harding's chief supporter, Harry Daugherty (d 1941). He foresaw that the convention would not be able to decide between the two obvious candidates and that a group of senators 'bleary-eyed for lack of sleep' would have to 'sit down about two o'clock in the morning around a table in a smoke-filled room in some hotel and decide the nomination'. This was precisely what happened and Harding duly emerged as the candidate.

smokin'. See CARRY ON —.

smoking gun/pistol, a. Meaning 'incriminating evidence', as though a person holding a smoking gun could be assumed to have committed an offence with it – as in Conan Doyle's Sherlock Holmes story 'The "Gloria Scott"' (1894): 'Then we rushed on into the captain's cabin . . . and there he lay . . . while the chaplain stood, with a smoking pistol in his hand.' The term was popularized during Watergate. For example, Representative Barber Conable said of a tape of President Nixon's conversation with H.R. Haldeman, his chief of staff, on 23 June 1972, containing discussion of how the FBI's investigation of the Watergate burglary could be limited, 'I guess we have found the smoking pistol, haven't we?'

Smuckers. See WITH A NAME LIKE ~ . . .

SNAFU. Acronym for 'Situation Normal All Fouled/Fucked Up'. American origin, probably from the services, by early in the Second World War.

snakes do push-ups?, can. See IS THE POPE A CATHOLIC?

s'n'f. ('Shopping and fucking'.) Term for a type of pulp fiction wherein the heroines devote their lives to these activities (though not simultaneously, as a rule). Sometimes known as **s'n's** – for 'sex and shopping'. In fact, shopping is not really the other activity – it is more the author's lingering descriptions of clothes and property, often with the designer labels still attached.

From the *Guardian* (6 February 1986): 'These Sidney Sheldon, Judith Krantz, Jackie Collins, Shirley Conran books have the generic title of s'n'f.'

snap a wrist! See under BREAK A LEG.

snap! crackle! pop! A slogan for Kellogg's Rice Krispies, in the US from c 1928, later in the UK. There has been more than one version. An early one: 'It pops! It snaps! It crackles!'

sneezes. See COUGHS AND ~ SPREAD DISEASES.

snook(er). See COCK A ~.

'sno use. ('It's no use'). Catchphrase of the British musichall performer Harry Weldon (1881–1930). From a Matthew Norgate theatre programme article c 1980: '[Weldon's] catch-phrase was "Sno use" with the "s" uttered in an ear-drum-piercing whistle without which Weldon could pronounce no "s". But unlike [Fred] Kitchen's [MEREDITH, WE'RE IN], his catchphrase was appropriate, and used appropriately, to every situation in which he found himself, and indicative of his claim . . . to be an artist as well as an artiste.'

snow. See RUSSIANS WITH ~ ON THEIR BOOTS.

snowball/snowflake's chance in Hades, a. See NO MORE CHANCE THAN A SNOWBALL IN HELL.

snowman. See ABOMINABLE ~.

snow-storm in Karachi. See under AS BUSY AS . . .

snug as a bug in a rug. Meaning 'well-fitting and/or extremely warm and comfortable'. Usually ascribed to Benjamin Franklin, the American writer and philosopher, who mentioned a type of epitaph in a letter to Miss Georgiana

Shipley (26 September 1772) on the death of her pet squirrel, 'Skugg': 'Here Skugg lies snug/As a bug in a rug.' But there are earlier uses. In an anonymous work *Stratford Jubilee* (commemorating David Garrick's Shakespeare festival in 1769) is: 'If she [a rich widow] has the mopus's [money]/I'll have her, as snug as a bug in a rug.' Probably, however, it was an established expression even by that date, if only because in 1706 Edward Ward in *The Wooden World Dissected* had the similar 'He sits as snug a Bee in a Box' and in Thomas Heywood's play *A Woman Killed with Kindness* (1603) there is 'Let us sleep as snug as pigs in pease-straw.'

SOB. See SON OF A BITCH.

sob sister. See under AGONY AUNT.

socialism. See CHAMPAGNE ∼.

society. See AFFLUENT ∼; GREAT ∼.

sock. See PUT A ∼ IN IT.

sock it to me! See under *LAUGH-IN*.

socks. See BLESS HIS LITTLE COTTON ∼; HANDS OFF COCKS . . .

sod. See OLD ∼.

Sod's Law. See IF ANYTHING CAN GO WRONG . . .

so, farewell then. From the drab poems of 'E.J. Thribb' which have graced *Private Eye*'s 'Poetry Corner' since the 1970s. Most of them celebrate, in an off-hand way, the recent deaths of famous people, and usually begin, 'So, farewell then . . .'
　　From the *Observer* (17 April 1988): 'So farewell then Kenneth Williams . . .'
　　Compare AND SO WE SAY FAREWELL . . .

soft as a brush. See under DAFT AS A BRUSH.

softly, softly catchee monkee. Said to be a 'Negro proverb'. Hence, the title *Softly Softly* of a BBC TV police drama series (1966–76), which came, more particularly, from the saying's use as the motto of the

Lancashire Constabulary Training School which inspired the series.

Soft Machine. The name of the UK vocal/instrumental group (*fl.* 1970) was taken from *The Soft Machine*, the title of a novel (1961) by William Burroughs.

soft underbelly, the. A vulnerable part. Speaking to the House of Commons on 11 November 1942, Winston Churchill said: 'We make this wide encircling movement in the Mediterranean . . . having for its object the exposure of the under-belly of the Axis, especially Italy, to heavy attack.' In his *The Second World War* (Vol. 4), Churchill describes a meeting with Stalin before this, in August 1942, at which he had outlined the same plan: 'To illustrate my point I had meanwhile drawn a picture of a crocodile, and explained to Stalin with the help of this picture how it was our intention to attack the soft belly of the crocodile as we attacked his hard snout.' Somewhere subsequently, the 'soft' and the 'underbelly' must have joined together to produce the phrase in the form in which it is now used.

so help me God. See under I SWEAR BY ALMIGHTY GOD . . .

soil. See ANSWER LIES IN THE ∼ under *BEYOND OUR KEN*.

sold down the river, to be. Meaning 'to be betrayed', this expression is of US origin. In the South, after 1808, it was illegal to import slaves, so they were brought down the Mississippi to the slave markets of Natchez and New Orleans. Hence, if a slave was 'sold down the river', he lost his home and family. The saying particularly relates to the practice of selling troublesome slaves to the owners of plantations on the lower Mississippi where conditions were harsher than in the Northern slave states. Mark Twain's novel *Pudd'nhead Wilson* (1894) is dominated by this theme and the expression occurs in it some 15 times, e.g.: '"Very good," said the master, putting up his watch, "I will sell you *here*, though you don't deserve it. You ought to be sold down the river."'

soldier. See CHOCOLATE ∼ under ARMS AND THE MAN; OLD ∼s NEVER DIE; THAT IS WHAT THE ∼ SAID; UNKNOWN ∼.

so long . . . until tomorrow! Sign-off from Lowell Thomas (1892–1981), a top American radio newscaster from 1930 to the mid-1970s. (Before this he had helped promote the legend of T.E. Lawrence – 'Lawrence of Arabia' – on lecture tours.)

solution. See FINAL ∼.

somebody bawl for Beulah? This was the cry of Beulah, the cheery, Black housemaid who was a supporting character in the American radio series *Fibber McGee and Molly* but went on to have her own radio show – *Beulah* – and TV series in the period 1944–54. Five people played her over the years – originally she was played by a white *man*. She would also say **on the con-positively-trary!** and **love that man!** (after laughing uproariously at one of Fibber McGee's jokes).

From the same show came wife Molly's response to jokes: **t'ain't funny, McGee!** and next-door neighbour Gildersleeve's **you're a hard man, McGee!** When Harold Peary, the actor, died aged 76, *Time Magazine* (15 April 1985) noted that, 'as "The Great Gildersleeve", the pompous windbag with a heart of gold well hidden behind a wall of bluster . . . [he had] made "You're a ha-a-ard man, McGee" and his trademark oily giggle national crazes.'

somebody come. See under I'VE GOT A LETTER FROM A BLOKE IN BOOTLE.

somebody got out of bed the wrong side today! That is, 'you *are* in a temper/bad mood'. Why this should have anything to do with the way you got out of bed is not clear. A more or less traditional saying: *Marvellous Love-Story* (1801) has, 'You have got up on the wrong side, this morning, George,' and Henry Kingsley, *Silcote of Silcotes* (1867) has: 'Miss had got out of bed the wrong side.'

somebody pinched me puddin'! British variety act Collinson and Breen (1930s/40s?) apparently used this somewhat obscure phrase. The explanation was that, 'Somebody said "All put your puddins out

for treacle", and I put mine out and somebody pinched it!'

Relevant to this or not, to **put one's puddings out for treacle** has a figurative meaning also. It is a phrase of encouragement to people to put themselves forward (as though in order to receive sauce on their dessert). In May 1994, Teresa Gorman MP accused Michael Heseltine of disloyalty to Prime Minister John Major by saying that he was 'putting his puddings out for treacle'. Mrs Gorman subsequently explained her expression to Alan Watkins in the *Independent on Sunday* (12 June 1994): '[It] was used in our neighbourhood about any woman considered to be putting herself forward for attention – or suspected of paying the tradesmen's bills in "kind"!'

somebody/someone up there likes me. Shortly before he was elected leader of the British Labour Party in 1983, Neil Kinnock emerged unscathed from his car when it inexplicably turned over on the M4 motorway. He remarked, 'My escape was miraculous. It's a word which is somewhat overused, but I know what it means. Someone up there likes me.'

Somebody Up There Likes Me was the title of a 1956 film written by Ernest Lehman. It starred Paul Newman and was based on the life of the World Middleweight Boxing Champion of 1947–8, Rocky Graziano (not to be confused with Rocky Marciano). I believe Graziano's autobiography had the same title. There was a title song from the film – also, in 1957, a song called 'Somebody Up There Digs Me'.

some like it hot. A phrase chiefly familiar as the title of a film (US, 1959) about two unemployed musicians who are accidental witnesses of the St Valentine's Day Massacre and flee to Miami disguised as members of an all-girls jazz band. So the 'hotness' may come from the jazz or the position they find themselves in. In fact, the phrase does actually occur in the film:

Tony Curtis: Syncopators? Does that mean you play very fast music . . . er . . . jazzz?
Marilyn Monroe: Yeah . . . real hot!
Tony Curtis: Oh, well, I guess some like it hot. I personally prefer classical music.

There had been an unrelated US film with the same title in 1939 (starring Bob Hope). The allusion is apparently to the nursery rhyme 'Pease porridge hot' (first recorded about 1750), of which the second verse goes:

> Some like it hot
> Some like it cold
> Some like it in the pot
> Nine days old.

This is such nonsense that it is sometimes ended with a riddle: 'Spell me that without a P' ('that' being quite easy to spell without a P). Ring Lardner's story 'Some Like Them Cold' (c 1926, collected 1935) contains a song, referring to women: 'Some like them hot, some like them cold/Some like them fat, some like them lean' (etc.)

some mothers do 'ave 'em. See under DON'T SOME MOTHERS HAVE 'EM.

some of my best friends are — (most commonly ending with **Jews/Jewish**). A self-conscious (and occasionally jokey) disclaimer of prejudice. In a May 1946 letter, Somerset Maugham replied to charges that he was anti-semitic and said: 'God knows I have never been that; some of my best friends in England and America are Jews . . .'

So, clearly, at that date the phrase could be used without irony. However, the line may – according to one source – have been rejected as a cartoon caption by the *New Yorker* prior to the Second World War and presumably dates, in any case, from the Nazi persecution of the Jews from the 1930s on.

In the (Jewish) Marx Brothers film *Monkey Business* (as early as 1931), there is the line, 'Some of my best friends are *housewives*.'

The Russian Prime Minister, Alexei Kosygin, was apparently unaware of the phrase's near-cliché status in 1971 when he said, 'There is no anti-semitism in Russia. Some of my best friends are Jews.'

The expression may be adapted, jokingly, to accommodate any group to which the speaker may be thought to be apart or a aloof from.

someone isn't using Amplex. See under EVEN YOUR BEST FRIENDS . . .

someone's mother. See under WHITER THAN WHITE.

someone, somewhere, wants a letter from you. A slogan for the British Post Office, current in the early 1960s.

someone up there likes me. See SOMEBODY . . .

something. See AND NOW FOR ~ COMPLETELY DIFFERENT; WAS THERE ~ under MUCH BINDING IN THE MARSH.

something/anything for the weekend, sir? The traditional parting question from British barbers (in the days before they became called hairdressers) inviting male customers to stock up with condoms (which, for no apparent reason, they sold). 1930s to 1950s, at a guess.

something else. A way of complimenting the indefinable. Probably from American, as in, 'Hey, lady, you're something else.' 1960s/70s. From Derek Taylor, *It Was Twenty Years Ago Today* (1987): 'Across the decreasing divide between America and Britain good things were happening . . . It wasn't pop, it wasn't poetry, it wasn't politics. It was . . . Something Else.'

something nasty in the woodshed. Phrase for an unnamed unpleasantness coined by the British novelist Stella Gibbons in *Cold Comfort Farm* (1933). In that novel, the phrase is used *passim* to refer to a traumatic experience in someone's background, e.g. from Chap. 10: 'When you were very small . . . you had seen something nasty in the woodshed.' Hence, from Beryl Bainbridge's novel *Another Part of the Wood* (1968): 'They had all, Joseph, brother Trevor, the younger sister . . . come across something nasty in the woodshed, mother or father or both, having it off with someone else.' Kyril Bonfiglioli entitled a novel *Something Nasty in the Woodshed* (1976).

something old, something new, something borrowed, something blue. The traditional ingredients of a bride's clothes, not recorded in this full form until 1883. However, blue has long been associated with truth in women (and the Virgin Mary is often clothed in this colour). If married in white, the bride usually wears a blue garter. The wearing of things old and borrowed also appears designed to bring good fortune.

somewhere in England. In 1986, I received a jokey birthday card which announced in small letters on the back that it was printed 'somewhere in England'. There was a film *Somewhere in England* (1940) which begot a series of British regional comedies (*Halliwell's Film Guide* lists *Somewhere in Camp/on Leave/in Civvies* and *in Politics*).

The construction originated in the First World War, for security reasons (e.g. 'somewhere in France', as in a letter from J.B. Priestley to his father, 27 September 1915), and its use came to be broadened to anywhere one cannot, or one does not want to, be too precise about. On 24 August 1941, Winston Churchill broadcast a report on his meeting with President Roosevelt: 'Exactly where we met is secret, but I don't think I shall be indiscreet if I go so far as to say that it was "somewhere in the Atlantic".'

somewhere to the right of Genghis Khan. A cliché description of someone's politics. Arthur Scargill, president of the National Union of Mineworkers, told John Mortimer in the *Sunday Times* (10 January 1982): 'Of course, in those days, the union leaders were well to the right of Genghis Khan.' An allusion from the *Independent* (28 January 1989): 'Close friends say he [Kenneth Clarke] has been an emollient force behind the doors of the Department of Health, but Genghis Khan would have looked like a calming influence alongside his ebullient ministers David Mellor and Edwina Currie.'

Genghis Khan (c 1162–1227) was a Mongol ruler who conquered large parts of Asia and, rightly or not, his name is always equated with terror, devastation and butchery.

son. See A GOOD IDEA . . . under *EDUCATING ARCHIE*; NUMBER ONE ~; ONE DAY ALL THIS WILL BE YOURS, MY ~.

son and heir, the. Phrase now only used jokingly to describe an eldest son. Charles Dickens has 'together with the information that the Son and Heir would sail in a fortnight' in *Dombey and Son*, Chap.17 (1846–8). Shakespeare has 'the son and heir to that same Faulconbridge' (*King John*, I.i.56; 1596) and 'son and heir of a mongrel bitch' (*King Lear*, II.ii.20; 1606) but here the quotation marks are not yet quite around the phrase.

song. See ON ~.

song and story, in. See IN ~.

son of —. Used, particularly, in the title of sequels to American films, emphasizing how they are the derivatives of (usually) superior originals. The first such *book* may have been *Son of Tarzan* (1917) by Edgar Rice Burroughs. The first such *film* was probably *Son of the Sheik* (1926), with Rudolph Valentino, following *The Sheik* (1921). Then *Son of Kong* (1933) followed *King Kong*. Others have been: *Son of Ali Baba/ Captain Blood/Dr Jekyll/Dracula/ Frankenstein/Geronimo/Lassie/ Monte Cristo/Paleface/Robin Hood/the Sheik/Zorro*.

Alternatively, you could stage a return: *The Return of Dracula/the Scarlet Pimpernel/ a Man Called Horse*. Or merely add a number. An early example of this came from TV: the BBC's *Quatermass Experiment* (1953) was followed by *Quatermass II* (1955). In the cinema, since *The Godfather, Part II* (1974), we have had not only *Rocky II – IV* but also *Jaws II*, and *French Connection II/ Death Wish II/Damien: Omen II/ Friday the Thirteenth, Part II/Crocodile Dundee 2*, and so on.

There are exceptions, of course. The sequel to *American Graffiti* was *More American Graffiti*. Forswearing 'Pink Panther 2' etc., Blake Edwards gave us *The Pink Panther Strikes Again*, *The Revenge of the Pink Panther*, *The Return of the Pink Panther*. The *Airport* sequels followed their own peculiar numerology – from *Airport 1975* to *Airport '77* and then *Airport '80 – The Concorde*.

son of a bitch. (or **SOB**). A very old term of abuse. 'Bitch-son' was in use by 1330. Shakespeare has 'son and heir of a mongrel bitch' in *King Lear* (II.ii.20; 1606). The fully-formed phrase was with us by 1707. The abbreviation was known by 1918. *S.O.B.* was the title of a film (US, 1981) where it was delicately explained as standing for 'Standard Operational Bullshit'. Other translations have included 'Silly Old Bastard'.

son of a gun. Nowadays, this is an inoffensively jocular way of addressing someone. However, in seafaring days, if a pregnant woman somehow found herself upon a warship and was ready to go into labour, the place traditionally made available to her was between two guns. If the father was unknown, the child could be described as a 'son of a gun'. Partridge/ *Slang*, however, quoting an 1823 source, defines the term as meaning a '*soldier*'s bastard', so perhaps there was an Army equivalent of the space made available.

soot, juggling with. See under AS BUSY AS . . .

sordid topic of coin, the. Delightful term for the question of payment, cash. Not from any sketch by the British monologist Joyce Grenfell but mentioned by her in discussing a woman who inspired the creation of one of her characters. In *Joyce Grenfell Requests the Pleasure* (1976), she writes about the 'wife of an Oxbridge vice chancellor who featured in three monologues called 'Eng. Lit.'. The character was based partly on Grenfell's own expression while cleaning her teeth, partly on the playwright Clemence Dane (Winifred Ashton) and partly on the idiosyncratic speech patterns of Hester Alington, wife of the Dean of Durham, and a distant relative of Grenfell's husband. 'On a postcard addressed to a shoe-shop in Sloane Street she had written: "Gently fussed about non-appearance of dim pair of shoes sent to you for heeling" . . . And when Viola [Tunnard, Grenfell's accompanist] and I went to Durham to perform in aid of one of her charities she introduced the paying of our expenses: "My dears, we have not yet touched on the sordid topic of coin . . ."'

sorrow. See MORE IN ~ THAN IN ANGER.

sorry. See I'M ~ I'LL READ THAT AGAIN.

sorry about that! See under WOULD YOU BELIEVE?

SOS. The emergency Morse Code signal, represented by the dots and dashes for the letters SOS, does not actually stand for anything, least of all 'Save Our Souls', as commonly supposed. The letters were chosen because they were easy to send in an emergency. Until about 1910, the Morse cry for help was 'C, Q, D'. Other acronyms have been devised to suit the letters SOS: e.g., '*Si Opus Sit*' [which, in medicine, means 'give relief where necessary'],'Slip On Show', 'Same Old Slush/Story/Stuff' and 'Short Of Sugar'.

soufflé rise twice, you can't make a. Meaning, 'It is pointless to try and make something happen again if it is unrepeatable.' Alice Roosevelt Longworth is supposed to have said it of Thomas E. Dewey's nomination as the Republican challenger in 1948 (Dewey had previously stood against F.D. Roosevelt in 1944). Paul McCartney has more than once used the phrase to discount the possibility of a Beatles reunion. Some say that making a soufflé rise twice is not actually impossible.

soul. See DARK NIGHT OF THE ~.

sour grapes. Explanatory phrase given for the behaviour of anyone who affects to despise something because he knows he cannot have it. The source is Aesop's fable of 'The Fox and the Grapes' in which a fox tries very hard to reach some grapes but, when he is unable to do so, says they looked sour anyway.

South will rise again, the. A slogan referring to the aftermath of the American Civil War and which presumably came out of the period that followed it, known as Reconstruction. But did any particular person say it? Was it an actual slogan? Did it make its way into *Gone With the Wind*? Curiously little information is to hand on these points.

Modern allusions: from the London

Times (18 February 1988): 'Jubilant [Bush, seeking re-election], told cheering supporters on Tuesday night: "I feel I have a lot in common with Mark Twain: reports of my death were greatly exaggerated." He said he was now going on to the South, "where we will rise again".' From the *Washington Post* (11 November 1984): 'President Reagan himself took some giant steps backward in race relations during the campaign . . . telling an audience in Macon, Ga., that "the South will rise again!", a rallying cry of segregationists in an earlier era.'

And from the *Financial Times* (7 June 1985): 'Along the 100–mile highway that now links the two old civil war capitals – Washington (The Union) and Richmond (The Confederacy) – you can stop and buy a tee-shirt that bears the proud slogan "Save your Confederate money, the South will rise again".'

sow. See under DRAGON'S TEETH . . .

sow one's wild oats, to. A wild oat is a common weed, so for anyone to sow it means that (usually) he is doing something useless or worthless. Hence, the expression is employed to describe behaviour prior to a man's 'settling down'. In use by 1576. Quite how much implication there is of him wasting his semen in unfruitful couplings is hard to judge, though the expression often has reference to sexual dissipation. Perhaps this connotation has increased with the popularity of such expressions as 'getting one's oats' (for having sex).

To **feel one's oats**, however, has nothing to do with this. It means to act in an important way as though pleased with oneself, and seems to have originated in the US. It refers to the way a horse was thought to feel friskier and more energetic after it had eaten oats.

space. See WATCH THIS ∼.

Spanish. See OLD ∼ CUSTOMS.

spare rib. The title of a British feminist magazine *Spare Rib* (founded 1972), is a punning reference to the cuts of meat known as 'spare-ribs' and also to ADAM'S RIB.

sparrow's fart. Dawn. Often mistakenly taken to be an Australianism, but it is included in Carr's *Craven Dialect* (1828) – from Yorkshire – and the definition given as, 'break of day'.

speak. See WHITE MAN ∼ WITH . . .

speak as you find, that's my motto. In a 1950s BBC radio series *Hello Playmates!* featuring Arthur Askey, this catchphrase was spoken not by him but by Nola Purvis (Pat Coombs), the daughter of the studio cleaner (Irene Handl). This was her smug excuse for the appalling insults she hurled. In 1955, *Hello Playmates!* won the *Daily Mail* Radio Award as the year's top show and the catchphrase was inscribed on the presentation silver microphone – which didn't go down too well with Askey, who had never uttered it. (Source Bob Monkhouse, who with Denis Goodwin wrote the show.)

speaks. See HE KNOWS WHEREOF HE ∼.

speak softly and carry a big stick. Speaking at the Minnesota State Fair in September 1901, President Theodore Roosevelt gave strength to the idea of backing negotiations with threats of military force when he said: 'There is a homely adage which runs "Speak softly and carry a big stick; you will go far". If the American nation will speak softly and yet build up and keep at a pitch of the highest training a thoroughly efficient navy, the Monroe Doctrine will go far.' The 'homely adage' is said to have started life as a West African proverb.

special. See AND A ∼ GOODNIGHT TO *YOU*.

special relationship, the. Term used to describe affiliations between countries (the earliest *OED2* citation is for one between Britain and Galicia in 1929) but particularly referring to that supposed to exist between Britain and the US on the basis of historical ties and a common language. The notion was principally promoted by Winston Churchill in his attempts to draw the US into the Second World War, though whether he used the phrase prior to 1941, is not clear. In the House of Commons on

7 November 1945, Churchill said: 'We should not abandon our special relationship with the United States and Canada about the atomic bomb.' In his 1946 'IRON CURTAIN' speech at Fulton, Missouri, he asked: 'Would a special relationship between the United States and the British Commonwealth be inconsistent with our overriding loyalties to the World Organization [the UN]?'

spectre at the feast, a/the. An embarrassing reminder of something that one would rather have forgotten. I suppose the allusion is simply to the appearance of Banquo's ghost in Shakespeare's *Macbeth*, III.iv (1606), where the man Macbeth has just had murdered comes back to haunt him during what is specifically called a 'feast'. But similar things happen in Mozart's *Don Giovanni* when a statue of the Commendatore (a man Don Giovanni has murdered) appears during supper and drags him off to Hell. And then there is the WRITING ON THE WALL at Belshazzar's Feast in the Book of Daniel.

The earliest use I have found of the actual expression is Charles Dickens's reference to a 'spectre at their licentious feasts' in *Barnaby Rudge*, Chap. 16 (1840). Headline from gossip item in *Today* (16 April 1988): 'Snowdon's just a spectre at Linley's feast.' From the *Independent* (3 June 1993): '"There was just one nomination for spectre at the feast," said one of the contributors to . . . BBC1's chocolate box recollection of Coronation Day. He had the Duke of Windsor in mind (who didn't turn up in the end, to everyone's relief).'

speeding bullet. See under SUPERMAN.

speed the plough/plow. A very old phrase indeed: in the form 'God speed the plough', it was what one would say when wishing someone luck in any venture (and not just an agricultural one). The phrase was in use by 1500 at least and is also the title of a traditional song and dance. *Speed the Plough* was the title of a novel (1798) by Thomas Morton which introduced the unseen character of MRS GRUNDY. *Speed-The-Plow* was the title of a play (1988) by David Mamet, about two Hollywood producers trying to get a project off the ground.

Speedy Gonzales. A person who moves fast – though sometimes used ironically of someone who is completely the reverse. Most people would think that this name originated in the pop song with which Pat Boone had a hit in 1962, but in fact the film cartoon character Speedy Gonzales ('the fastest mouse in all Mexico') came out of Warner Bros in 1955.

I see that the *Guardian*'s 'Notes and Queries' was asked in late 1992, 'Was there ever a *real* Speedy Gonzales?', but answer came there none. I wonder, though, whether the fact that Pancho Gonzales, the tennis player, was all the rage in the 1950s had anything to do with the naming of the mouse?

spelled. See THAT ~ —.

spelling bee, a. An innocent game to do with spelling, from the days when people had to make their own entertainment. A 'bee' is the American word (since 1769) for when a group of neighbours gathers to do something communally – hence, a 'harvest bee', even a 'lynching bee' – and so named after the social character of the insect.

spend a penny, to. A euphemism for 'to go to the lavatory'. The first public convenience to charge one penny opened in London in 1855. So I am curious about this from Chapter 6 of Charles Dickens's *Dombey and Son* (1846–8): 'The young Toodles, victims of a pious fraud, were deluded into repairing in a body to a chandler's shop in the neighbourhood, for the ostensible purpose of spending a penny.' (*OED2* does not find it before 1945.) See also under DAD'S ARMY.

spend more time with family. See I WOULD LIKE TO . . .

spend, spend, spend!, I'm going to. Viv Nicholson (*b* 1936) and her husband Keith, a trainee miner, were bringing up three children on a weekly wage of £7 in Castleford, Yorkshire. Then, in September 1961, they won £152,000 on Littlewoods football pools. Arriving by train to collect their prize (as Viv recalled in her autobiography, *Spend, Spend, Spend*, 1977), they were confronted by reporters. One asked: 'What are you going to do when you get all this money?' Viv said, 'I'm going to spend, spend, spend, that's what I'm going to do.' She says it was just an off-the-cuff remark, but it made newspaper headlines and was later used as the title not only of her book but of a TV play about her.

As a phrase it still lingers, not least because of the tragic overtones to Viv's use of it. Keith died in a car crash and Viv worked her way through a series of husbands until the money had all gone. From the *Daily Mail* (4 March 1989): 'The Sixties were indeed "a low dishonest decade" . . . We thought the great post-war boom would go on for ever, that both individuals and the state could spend, spend, spend without the smallest concern for tomorrow.'

Sphinx. See RIDDLE OF THE ∼.

spill the beans, to. To divulge information inadvertently. This has been traced back to the ancient Greeks who held secret ballots for membership of clubs by using beans. A white bean was a 'yes' vote, a brown bean a 'no' vote. The beans were counted in secrecy so that a prospective member would not how many people voted for or against him. If the jar containing the beans was knocked over, that secret might get out.

This is a very elaborate explanation, but the phrase only entered American speech (from whence it passed into English generally) early this century. Why did it take so long?

Another possible explanation is that gypsy fortune tellers in Turkey do not have crystal balls, neither do they read tea leaves. One of the many ways they tell fortunes is to spill beans out of a cup and interpret the resulting pattern.

spinach. See I SAY IT's ∼.

spirit of —, the. A cliché of politics. Like MESSAGE OF —, this is a highly versatile phrase. 'The Spirit of '76' came into use following the American Revolution in the eighteenth century. Later, President

Eisenhower was very fond of the format, several times speaking of 'the Spirit of Geneva' in 1955, and 'the Spirit of Camp David' in 1959. Michael Foot, the British Labour politician, combined it with another political cliché following a by-election victory in April 1983, and said that Labour would, 'get the spirit of Darlington **up and down the country**'. (The Darlington win was reversed at the General Election the following month . . .)

spit. See DOESN'T IT MAKE YOU WANT TO ∼! under *BAND WAGGON*; DON'T ∼ . . . .

spite. See CUT OFF YOUR NOSE . . .

spitting image, the. An exact likeness. Used as the title of a British TV comedy series (from 1984) using puppets to satirize current events. Given the venom involved in *Spitting Image*, it might be thought that any spitting had to do with saliva. The theories are, however, that the phrase is a corruption of 'speaking image' or 'splitting image' (two split halves of the same tree which provide an exact likeness), or a Black Southern US pronunciation of 'spirit and image' (which a true likeness might have). Current by 1901 and – as 'the spit of someone' by 1894.

splash. See BIGGER ∼.

splice the main brace, to. Meaning 'to have a drink', the expression comes from a comparison between the reviving effect of alcoholic drink and repairing or strengthening the mainbrace on board ship, where the mainbrace is the rope for holding or turning one of the sails. As used in the Navy itself, the expression refers to the rare occurrence of an extra tot of rum all round.

Spode's Law. See under IF ANYTHING CAN GO WRONG . . .

spoke. See PUT A ∼ IN.

sponned. See I'VE BEEN ∼ under *GOON SHOW*.

sponsor. See AND NOW A WORD FROM OUR ∼.

sport of kings, the. In the seventeenth century it was war-making. William Somerville described hunting as 'the sport of kings' in *The Chase*, 1735. But in the twentieth century horse racing has tended to be the sport so described. So, too, – with what justification, I know not – has surf-riding.

spot. See DID YOU ∼ THIS WEEK'S DELIBERATE MISTAKE?; ∼ OF HOMELY FUN under *HAVE A GO*; ∼ OF MIME FOR THE PANEL under IS IT BIGGER THAN A BREADBOX?

spread alarm and despondency, to. Meaning, 'to have a de-stabilizing effect, purposely or not'. During the Second World War, Lieut.-Col. Vladimir Peniakoff ran a small raiding and reconnaissnce force on the British side which became known as 'Popski's Private Army'. In his book *Private Army* (1950), he wrote: 'A message came on the wireless for me. It said 'Spread alarm and despondency . . . The date was, I think, May 18th, 1942.'

When a German invasion was thought to be imminent at the beginning of July 1940, Winston Churchill had issued an 'admonition' to 'His Majesty's servants in high places . . . to report, or if necessary remove, any officers or officials who are found to be consciously exercising a disturbing or depressing influence, and whose talk is calculated to spread alarm and despondency'. Prosecutions for doing this did indeed follow. The phrase goes back to the Army Act of 1879: 'Every person subject to military law who . . . spreads reports calculated to create unnecessary alarm or despondency . . . shall . . . be liable to suffer penal servitude.'

spring. See under WITH ONE BOUND . . .

spring/winter romance, a. See MAY TO DECEMBER ROMANCE.

spy. See I ∼ (WITH MY LITTLE EYE).

squad. See AWKWARD ∼.

square deal. See FOUR-SQUARE.

square one. See BACK TO ∼.

square peg in a round hole, a. (or *vice versa*). Meaning 'someone badly suited to his job or position'. James Agate in *Ego 5* (1942) writes: 'Will somebody please tell me the address of the Ministry for Round Pegs in Square Holes?'

Known by 1836. However, Sydney Smith, *Lectures on Moral Philosophy* (1804) has: 'If you choose to represent the various parts in life by holes upon a table, of different shapes, – some circular, some triangular, some square, some oblong, – and the persons acting these parts by bits of wood of similar shapes, we shall generally find that the triangular person has got into the square hole, and a square person has squeezed himself into the round hole.'

squeeze till the pips squeak, to. Meaning 'to extract the most [usually, money] from anything or anyone'. Apparently coined by Sir Eric Geddes, a British Conservative politician, shortly after the end of the First World War. On the question of reparations, Geddes said in an election speech in Cambridge (10 December 1918): 'The Germans, if this Government is returned, are going to pay every penny; they are going to be squeezed as a lemon is squeezed – until the pips squeak. My only doubt is not whether we can squeeze hard enough, but whether there is enough juice.' The previous night, Geddes, who had lately been First Lord of the Admiralty, said the same thing in a slightly different way as part of what was obviously a stump speech: 'I have personally no doubt we will get everything out of her that you can squeeze out of a lemon and a bit more . . . I will squeeze her until you can hear the pips squeak . . . I would strip Germany as she has stripped Belgium.'

***stabat mater (dolorosa)*.** From the hymn variously ascribed to Jacopone da Todi (c 1230–1306), Pope Innocent III and St Bonaventure: '*Stabat Mater dolorosa/Iuxta crucem lacrimosa/Dum pendebat Filius*' [There was standing the sorrowing Mother, beside the cross, weeping while her Son hung upon it].

stage. See EXIT ∼ LEFT.

stage, kindly leave the. See I DON'T WISH TO KNOW THAT . . .

stain. See HOLD IT UP TO THE LIGHT . . .

stairs. See GET UP THEM ~!; I'LL GO TO THE FOOT OF OUR ~.

stalking horse, a. A device used in hunting to get close to game which apparently sees no danger in a four-legged beast (and recorded since 1519). The wooden horse at Troy was an even more devastating form of equine deception.

Also used figuratively, by 1612. Latterly, in British politics (1990–94), the term has been applied to an MP who stands for election as leader of his party with no hope of getting the job. His role is to test the water on behalf of other stronger candidates and to see whether the incumbent leader is challengeable.

stamp. See WE MUST ~ OUT THIS EVIL IN OUR MIDST.

stand. See AMERICA CANNOT ~ PAT; WILL THE REAL —, PLEASE ~ UP.

standard by which all — will be measured. Something of a cliché of approval. Known by 1878. From *Time* Magazine (14 December 1981): 'A new standard by which all thoroughbred driving machines will be measured.'

standing prick has no conscience. See STIFF . . .

stand up and be counted, to. To declare openly one's allegiance or beliefs. American origin. From the *Hartford Courant* (Connecticut) (12 August 1904): 'Another democratic paper, the "Sacramento Bee", follows the example of the "Chicago Chronicle" and stands up to be counted for Roosevelt.'

Stand Up and Be Counted was the title of a film (US, 1971) about a woman journalist who becomes involved in Women's Lib. In 1976, the British-based entertainer Hughie Green brought out a record entitled 'Stand Up and be Counted' in which he quoted Churchill, lambasted the then Labour

Government (by implication) and told the nation to pull its socks up.

star. See YOU'RE GOING OUT A YOUNGSTER . . . ; REACH FOR THE SKY.

stark staring bonkers. A rather English expression for 'mad' and, indeed, a version of 'stark raving mad'. Mid-twentieth century. Lord Hailsham, speaking on Labour policies at a General Election press conference (12 October 1964): 'If the British public falls for this, I say it will be stark, staring bonkers.'

stars. See MORE ~ THAN THERE ARE IN HEAVEN.

stars and bars, the. Nickname for the flag of the Confederate States of the US (1861), which differed from the 'Stars and Stripes'. Used as the title of a novel *Stars and Bars* (1984; film US, 1988) by William Boyd, in which the bars were of a more alcoholic nature.

started. See I'VE ~, SO I'LL FINISH!

starter. See HERE'S YOUR ~ FOR TEN.

starts. See AND THIS IS WHERE THE STORY . . . under GOON SHOW; WEEKEND ~ HERE.

starvation in the midst of plenty. In *The Book of Cloyne* (1993), concerning the town and former seat of a Protestant bishopric in Co. Cork, Ireland, a certain George Cooper is quoted as writing in 1799: 'The peasant starves in the midst of plenty,' while George Berkeley (1685–1753), the philosopher and one-time Bishop of Cloyne, is also credited with being the first to make use of the phrase (with 'peasant' included). The *OED2*'s earliest citation (in a different context) is from 1703 and Florence Nightingale is found writing in her *Notes of Nursing* (1861): 'Thousands of patients are annually starved in the midst of plenty.'

starving. See WHEN PEOPLE ARE ~ IN INDIA.

star wars. The title of the popular sci-fi film *Star Wars* (US, 1977) was adopted as a political catchphrase following President

Reagan's speech (23 March 1983) proposing to extend the nuclear battleground into space. The President did not use the term 'Star Wars' himself but it was an inevitable tag to be applied by the media, given Reagan's own fondness for adapting lines from the movies. The proposal, properly known by its initials SDI (for Strategic Defense Initiative), eventually came to nothing.

See also EMPIRE STRIKES BACK and EVIL EMPIRE.

state of the nation, the. Used as the title of British ITV current affairs specials (from 1966), this phrase might seem to have been devised in emulation of the US president's 'State of the Union' message, his annual address to Congress, which is required of him by the 1787 Constitution. However, in John Aubrey's plans for a 'Register Generall of People' which he devised c 1684, he writes: 'The design is to have Abstracts of all the above particulars . . . so as to give the King a true State of the Nation at all times' – which may suggest that the concept was known in the seventeenth century. Edmund Burke wrote *Observations on . . . 'the Present State of the Nation'* in 1769.

states. See WAR BETWEEN THE STATES.

sta viator. The form of epitaph writing that begins or includes, 'Stop, stranger/traveller/passer-by' is of ancient origin. A common British epitaphic rhyme is: 'Stop stranger as you pass by/As you are now so once was I/As I am now so will you be/So be prepared to follow me.' James Morris in *Farewell the Trumpets* (1978) records that a Turkish poet, Mehmet Akif Ersoy, is quoted on a memorial above Kilid Bahr at Gallipoli (recalling the debacle of 1915): 'Stop, passer-by! The earth you have just unknowingly trodden is the spot where an era ended and where the heart of a nation beats.'

In Gustave Flaubert's novel *Madame Bovary* (1857), the conventional Latin inscription *Sta viator: amabilem conjugem calcas* [Hold your step, wayfarer, for you tread on a beloved wife] is put on the grave of Emma Bovary. It is chosen by Homais, the dull chemist, after Emma, a doctor's

wife, has taken her own life after committing adultery.

stay, can't you. See MUST YOU GO . . .

steady, Barker! When Sub-Lieutenant Eric 'Heartthrob' Barker (1912–90) starred in the Royal Navy version of the BBC radio comedy show *Merry Go Round* (c 1945), this was his command to himself. It was later carried over to his other show *Just Fancy* (1951–61) and became the title of his autobiography in 1956. In that book, Barker writes of the phrase: 'It could be used on so many occasions . . . it almost passed into the language. Also each time it was quoted it gave me the all-vital personal publicity . . . I have had letters from those who have said it helped them to cure a lifelong habit of swearing, as they were able to use it instead. One old lady who shared a flat with an awkward sister in Cheltenham said they had been in danger of drifting apart, but that now, lo! when they reached a point when it seemed neither could endure the bickering a moment longer, they both said, "Steady, Barker!" and it cleared the air. I also learned it was sent as a naval signal from a C-in-C to a ship whose gunfire was a little wide of the mark.'

See also under CARRY ON . . .

steam radio. This pejorative term for sound broadcasting (in Britain) is said to have been coined by Norman Collins in the early 1950s when he transferred his attentions as a broadcasting executive to television. The implicit allusion is to the rivalry between steam and electric trains.

steel. See RING OF ∼.

steel magnolia, a. *Steel Magnolias* was the title of a film (US, 1990) based on Robert Harling's off-Broadway stage play, revolving round a beauty parlour and the friendship of six women who form the backbone of society in a small Louisiana town. The women share their secrets and, presumably, the title was chosen to suggest their underlying strengths. Earlier, Rosalynn Carter, wife of President Jimmy Carter, had been nicknamed 'the Steel Magnolia'. This First Lady's role apparently went further than holding hands with her husband in public. He consulted her on policy matters and she seems to have had some influence over his decisions. The magnolia is a flower particularly associated with Southern US areas.

Compare IRON HAND IN A VELVET GLOVE.

step. See ONE SMALL ∼ . . . ; ONE ∼ FORWARDS . . .

stetson. See KEEP IT UNDER YOUR HAT.

stick. See MORE — THAN YOU CAN SHAKE A ∼ AT.

stick it, Jerry! A phrase from a sketch involving Lew Luke, the Cockney comedian. Playing a burglar, he would say it to his companion when they were throwing missiles at policemen pursuing them. Hence, the phrase of encouragement (i.e. 'stick at it . . .'), originating in the early years of the twentieth century. It was popular during the First World War but, apparently, this is not how the name 'Jerry' came to be applied to refer to Germans.

stiff prick has/hath no conscience, a. This proverbial view (sometimes completed with **and an itching cunt feels no shame,** according to Partridge/*Catch Phrases*) has been confidently ascribed to St Augustine of Hippo, the North African Christian theologian (AD 354–430). Or so John Osborne would have us believe in *Almost a Gentleman* (1991). Indeed, it would not be surprising given Augustine's interesting activities prior to conversion (compare 'Give me chastity and continency – but not yet!' from his *Confessions*, AD 397–8). But confirmation is lacking and one can only say that its proverbial status was evident by the 1880s when 'Walter' in *My Secret Life* (Vol. I, Chap. 12) has: 'I thought how unfair it was to her sister, who was in the family way by me . . . but a standing prick stifles all conscience.' Indeed **standing prick has no conscience** is an equally well-known version.

still going strong. See BORN 1820 . . .

stinkers. See EXCUSE ∼.

stir one's stumps, to. To walk or dance briskly. 'Stump' here means leg, as it has done since at least the fifteenth century.

stirred. See DOWN IN THE FOREST SOMETHING ∼; MARTINI SHAKEN NOT ∼.

stock. See LOCK ∼ AND BARREL.

Stockbroker's Tudor. A term for bogus Tudor architecture coined by Osbert Lancaster in *Pillar to Post* (1938).

stolen kisses. *Baisers Volés* was the title of a film (France, 1968) by François Truffaut and, as such, is taken from a phrase in the song, '*Que Reste-t-il de Nos Amours*' (1943), written and performed by Charles Trenet (and which is featured in the film). This phrase suggests perhaps that filched, fleeting moments of happiness are the most that can be hoped for. In English, there had earlier been a song 'A Stolen Kiss' (1923) by R. Penso; also a ballad, undated, by F. Buckley, 'Stolen Kisses are the Sweetest'. The proverbial 'stolen kisses are sweet' had appeared, for example, in R.H. Barham's *The Ingoldsby Legends* (1840).

Most probably this saying derives from the proverb **stolen fruit is sweet** which was established by the early seventeenth century and often used alluding to the temptation of Eve with the apple in Genesis 3:6. **Stolen pleasures are sweetest** was also current in the seventeenth century, perhaps reflecting Proverbs 9:17: 'Stolen waters are sweet.'

stomach. See HEART AND ∼ OF A KING.

stone. See LEAVE NO ∼ UNTURNED.

stone me! See under HANCOCK'S HALF-HOUR.

Stonewall Jackson. Thomas J. Jackson (1824–63), Confederate general in the American Civil War, won his nickname at the First Battle of Bull Run on 21 July 1861. General Barnard Bee is said to have remarked, 'See, there is Jackson, standing like a stone-wall.' He may not having been paying a tribute but complaining about Jackson's refusal to move forward.

The verb 'to stonewall', meaning to

obstruct, may derive from this image of steadfastness (and it has long been used in cricket, for example, for cautious batsmanship.)

stop. See AND WHEN THE MUSIC ~s under ARE YOU SITTING COMFORTABLY?; BUCK ~s HERE; ~ THE MIGHTY ROAR . . . under *IN TOWN TONIGHT*; WHEN DID YOU ~ BEATING YOUR WIFE?

stop da music! See under GOODNIGHT, MRS CALABASH . . .

stop – look – listen. This slogan is said to have been devised in 1912 by Ralph R. Upton, an American engineer, for use on notices at railway crossings in place of the earlier, 'Look out for the locomotive'. Certainly, on 27 December 1915 there opened a show (with music by Cole Porter) at the Globe Theater, New York, called *Stop! Look! Listen!* A George Robey song from *The Bing Boys Are Here* (1916) was entitled, 'I Stopped, I Looked, I Listened', and by 1936, an advertisement for H.H. Sullivan Inc 'Technical merchandise' (Rochester, New York) was playing with the phrase to the extent of 'Stop, look and kiss 'em' to accompany the picture of a leggy girl in cheesecake pose.

stop me and buy one. Lionel and Charles Rodd were on the board of T. Wall & Sons, the British ice cream manufacturers, and are believed to have come up with this slogan in 1923. 8,500 salesmen with the words on their tricycles pedalled round Britain out of a national network of 136 depots.

In the 1970s, there followed the graffito on contraceptive vending machines, 'Buy me and stop one.'

stop messin abaht! See under HANCOCK'S HALF-HOUR.

stopping. See I WON'T TAKE ME COAT OFF . . .

storm. See ANY PORT IN A ~; ORPHANS OF THE ~.

stork/Stork. See under CABBAGE PATCH KIDS; CAN YOU TELL ~ FROM BUTTER?

stormy night. See IT WAS A DARK AND ~.

story. See BUT THAT'S ANOTHER ~; COCK AND BULL ~; EVERY PICTURE TELLS A ~; IN SONG AND ~; I WANNA TELL YOU A ~; ~ REALLY BEGINS under *GOON SHOW*; SAVAGE ~ OF LUST . . .

stout. See COLLAPSE OF ~ PARTY.

straight from/out of Central Casting. Meaning 'a person who conforms to type, or to what you would expect'. From the *Observer* (19 March 1989): 'If you had asked Central Casting, or Equity, to provide an archetypal bigot, it's unlikely they could come up with someone as perfect as Jan van der Berg . . . owner of one of the better restaurants in Windhoek, the capital of Namibia.'

Central Casting was set up in 1926 and maintained by all major Hollywood studios as a pool for supplying extras for films. David Niven, for example, claimed to have been listed on their books in the mid-1930s as 'Anglo-Saxon Type No. 2008'.

straight from the horse's mouth. See under HORSE'S MOUTH.

Strand. See YOU'RE NEVER ALONE WITH A ~.

strange but true. The contrast of these two adjectives is recorded by 1594 but remains a potent combination. From Anon., *Collection of Epitaphs* (1806): 'Here lies one *Strange*, no *Pagan*, *Turk*, nor *Jew*,/ 'Tis *Strange*, but so *Strange* as it is true.' The first line of the song 'So In Love' from Cole Porter's *Kiss Me Kate* (1948) is, 'Strange, dear, but true, dear.' *Strange But True* was the title of a book of odd newspaper stories, edited by Tim Healey (1983). 'Interesting If True' was the title of a gossip column in the *Independent on Sunday* in 1990.

Compare the proverbial 'truth is stranger than fiction'. In Edmund Burke's *On Conciliation with America* (1775), this appears as 'Fiction lags after truth'. In Byron's *Don Juan*, xiv.ci (1819–24), he uses both forms : ' 'Tis strange, but true; for truth is always strange – /Stranger than fiction.' By the mid-nineteenth century, the version 'Fact is stranger than fiction' had also emerged.

stranger. See I'M A ∼ HERE MYSELF; NEVER LOVE A ∼; PERFECT ∼.

strangers. See I SPY ∼.

strangled by the old school tie. See under OLD SCHOOL TIE.

strangler. See BOSTON ∼.

street. See GRASS WILL GROW IN THE ∼; MAN IN THE ∼; QUEER ∼; THERE'LL BE DANCING IN THE ∼S TONIGHT.

streets paved with gold, to find the. When Hollywood was in its heyday, many writers were reluctant to go there, fearing how badly they would be treated. According to Arthur Marx in *Son of Groucho* (1973), his father tried very hard to persuade the dramatist George S. Kaufman to join him out on the West Coast.

'No, no,' said Kaufman. 'I don't care how much they pay me. I hate it out there.'

'But, George,' pleaded Groucho, 'the streets out here are paved with gold.'

There was a moment's pause, and then Kaufman said, 'You mean, you have to bend down and pick it up?'

But where did this near-cliche originate? In the story of Dick Whittington, he makes his way to London from Gloucestershire because he hears the streets are paved with gold and silver. The actual Dick Whittington was thrice Lord Mayor of London in the late fourteenth and early fifteenth centuries. The popular legend does not appear to have been told before 1605. Benham (1948) comments on the proverbial expression 'London streets are paved with gold' – 'A doubtful story or tradition alleges that this saying was due to the fact that *c* 1470, a number of members of the Goldsmiths' Company, London, joined the Paviors' Company.'

George Colman the Younger in *The Heir-at-Law* (1797) wrote:

Oh, London is a fine town,
A very famous city,
Where all the streets are paved with gold,
And all the maidens pretty.

The Percy French song 'The Mountains of Mourne' (1896) mentions 'diggin'' for gold in the streets [of London]'. From G.K. Chesterton, *William Cobbett* (1925): 'He had played the traditional part of the country boy who comes up to London where the streets are paved with gold.' In the Marx Brothers film *Go West* (US, 1940), Chico says: 'He's goin' West, and when he gets off the train he's gonna pick up some gold and send it to me. They say that the gold is layin' all over the streets.'

The streets of heaven are also sometimes said to be paved with gold – though not specifically as such in the Bible. There is, however, a 'Negro' spiritual where the 'streets in heaven am paved with gold'.

Compare I CAME TO LONDON TO SEEK MY FORTUNE.

strictly for the birds. Meaning 'of no consequence', this is a US expression (by 1951), alluding to horse manure which is only good for picking over by small birds. It was the title of a Dudley Moore instrumental number (1961), and also, rather oddly, given its origin, was used in a Rexona soap advertisement (1968).

strife. See IN PLACE OF ∼.

strike it out. See IF IN DOUBT . . .

strikes. See EMPIRE ∼ BACK.

string, piece of. See under HOW MANY BEANS . . .

strokes. See DIFFERENT ∼ . . .

struck. See LIKE ONE O'CLOCK HALF ∼.

struck all of a heap. Astounded. Gerald du Maurier, as a schoolboy, wrote to his sister about her getting engaged (30 March 1890): 'My Darling Sylvia, I am so sorry I haven't written to congratulate you, but I was "struck all of a 'eap!"' Sir Walter Scott was calling it 'that vulgar phrase' in 1817. 'Struck of a heap' was current by 1741 and Shakespeare has 'all on a heap'.

studio, return you to the. See under *BEYOND OUR KEN*.

studying the ceilings. See under SKY THROUGH THE TREES . . .

stuff. See RIGHT ~; SUCH ~ AS DREAMS ARE MADE ON; THAT'S THE ~ TO GIVE THE TROOPS.

stuffed shirt, a. A stiff, pompous person. There seems to be an urge among obituary writers to credit the recently deceased with the coining of phrases, even where the facts do not really support it. Patrick Brogan writing of Mrs Clare Boothe Luce in the *Independent* (12 October 1987) stated: 'She wrote a series of articles poking fun at the rich and pompous, coining for them the descriptive phrase "stuffed shirts", a title she used for her first book.'

That book was published in 1933, but the *OED2* has an example of the phrase dating from 1913 (when Luce was a mere ten), which makes it clear that by then it was already current US usage. So though she may have re-popularized the phrase she certainly didn't coin it.

stumps. See STIR ONE'S ~.

stupid. See VERY INTERESTING . . . BUT ~! under *LAUGH-IN*.

stupid boy! See under *DAD'S ARMY*.

sublime to the ridiculous, from the. This is usually quoted now without the final qualifying phrase: '. . . there is but one step'. The proverb most probably came to us from the French. After the retreat from Moscow in 1812, Napoleon is said to have uttered: '*Du sublime au ridicule il n'y a qu'un pas*'. However, Thomas Paine had already written in *The Age of Reason* (1795): 'The sublime and the ridiculous are often so nearly related, that it is difficult to class them separately. One step above the sublime, makes the ridiculous; and one step above the ridiculous, makes the sublime again.'

substances. See CERTAIN ~.

success. See IT WENT FROM FAILURE TO CLASSIC . . .

such is life. A reflective expression of the inevitable. Recorded by 1796 in William Temple's diary: 'This interruption is very teasing; but such is life'. From a George Eliot letter (20 December 1860): 'Our curtains are not up and our oil-cloth is not down. Such is life, seen from the furnishing point of view.' The last words of Ned Kelly, the Australian outlaw, who was hanged in Melbourne in 1880 at the age of 25, are said to have been: 'Ah well, I suppose it has come to this! . . . Such is life!' The British pop singer and political clown 'Lord' David Sutch felicitously entitled his autobiography *Sutch is Life* (1992).

such stuff as dreams are made on. If one is quoting Prospero's words from Shakespeare, *The Tempest*, IV.i.156 (1612): 'We are such stuff/As dreams are made on' – it is definitely 'on' not 'of' (though Shakespeare did use the 'of' form elsewhere). Humphrey Bogart as Sam Spade in *The Maltese Falcon* (1941) is asked: 'What is it?' before speaking the last line of the picture, and replies: 'The stuff that dreams are made of.' The title of the 1964 Cambridge Footlights revue was *Stuff What Dreams Are Made Of*.

suck eggs. See DON'T TEACH YOUR GRANDMOTHER . . .

sucker. See NEVER GIVE A ~ AN EVEN BREAK.

suck it and see. Meaning 'try out', presumably from what you would say about a sweet – 'suck it and see whether you like the taste of it'. It was used as a catchphrase by Charlie Naughton of the Crazy Gang, though possibly of earlier music-hall origin (Partridge/*Slang* dates it from the 1890s).

Suez. See EAST OF ~.

sufficiency. See EXCELLENT ~.

sugar. See DOES HE TAKE ~?

suit. See MAN IN A GREY ~.

suitable. See NOT ~ FOR THOSE . . .

Sultan of Swat. See BABE, THE.

summer. See LONG HOT ~.

sun. See EMPIRE UPON WHICH . . .

Sunday. See IT ALWAYS RAINS ON ~; OH, MY ~ HELMET!

Sunday bloody Sunday. See BLOODY SUNDAY.

sunlit. See BROAD ~.

Sunny Jim. One might say, 'Ah, there you are . . . I've been looking for you, Sunny Jim' – even if the person isn't called Jim. It is a name applied to a cheerful person. From *Lady Cynthia Asquith's Diary* (for 13 July 1918): 'I like McKenna. He is such a "Sunny Jim" and ripples on so easily.' But it can also be a slightly patronizing expression, and thus was aptly applied to James Callaghan, when Prime Minister, who was nothing if not patronizing in return with his air of a bank manager who knew best (an *Observer* headline of 18 March 1979 stated, 'Sunny Jim tires of wheeler-dealing').

Few who use the name know that it originated with a character who appeared in ads for Force breakfast cereal from about 1903. He was the invention of two young American women, a Miss Ficken and Minnie Maud Hanff (usually credited with the phrase), who came up with a jingle and rough sketch of the character for the Force Food Company.

sun, sand and sea. A cliché of travel promotion. In 1972, I interviewed a group of children born in London of West Indian parents, who were about to pay their first visit to Barbados. When I asked one of them what he expected to find there, he quite spontaneously said, 'All I know is, it's sun, sand and sea.' We used this line as the title of a BBC Radio programme which reported their reactions before and after the visit.

Clearly, the child had absorbed this alliterative phrase at an early age. It is never very far away. Several songs have the title. From a photo caption in the *Observer* (26 June 1988): 'Sun, sand and sea are no longer enough for the Yuppie generation of fun-seekers.' In the 1939 film version of *The Four Feathers*, the Sudan is referred to, with

similar alliteration, as 'sun, sweat and sunstroke'.

sunset. See DRIVE OFF INTO THE . . .

sun sinks slowly in the west, the. Cliché of the cinema travelogue, though it has not been confirmed as being in the 'Fitzpatrick Traveltalks' (1930s – see AND SO WE SAY FAREWELL).

sunt lacrimae rerum. 'There are tears shed for things' – from Virgil, *Aeneid* (i.462). Hence *lacrimae rerum* symbolize the sadness of life. They are the tears shed for the sorrows of men.

super. See SMASHING, LOVELY, ~!

Supermac. Nickname bestowed on Harold Macmillan (1894–1986), British Conservative Prime Minister (1957–63), later 1st Earl of Stockton. It was created by the political cartoonist Vicky in a drawing for the London *Evening Standard* (6 November 1958) showing Macmillan dressed as SUPERMAN. Like Aneurin Bevan's similar coinage **Macwonder,** this nickname was originally ironic in intent but came to lose that overtone in the early part of Macmillan's premiership when he exerted a great flair for relaxed showmanship.

Superman!, it's. The comic-strip hero was the brainchild of a teenage science-fiction addict, Jerry Siegel, in 1933. Five years later, Superman appeared on the cover of No. 1 of *Action Comics*. In 1940, he took to the radio airwaves in the US on the Mutual Network, with Clayton 'Bud' Collyer as the journalist Clark Kent who can turn into the Man of Steel whenever he is in a tight spot: 'This looks like a job for . . . Superman! Now, off with these clothes! **Up, up and awa-a-a-ay!**' After appearing in film cartoons, Superman finally appeared as a live-action hero on the screen in a 15–episode serial in 1948. He was still on the big screen in the 1970s and 80s.

It was from the radio series, however, that the exciting phrases came:

Announcer: Kellogg's Pep . . . the super-delicious cereal . . . presents . . . *The*

Adventures of Superman! **Faster than a speeding bullet!** [*ricochet*] More powerful than a locomotive! [*locomotive roar*] Able to leap tall buildings at a single bound! [*rushing wind*] Look! Up in the sky!

Voice 1: **It's a bird!**

Voice 2: **It's a plane!**

Voice 3: **It's Superman!**

Announcer: Yes, it's Superman – a strange visitor from another planet, who came to earth with powers and abilities far beyond those of mortal men. Superman! – who can change the course of mighty rivers, bend steel with his bare hands, and who – disguised as Clark Kent, mild-mannered reporter for a great metropolitan newspaper – fights **a never-ending battle for truth, justice and the American way.**

'Up, up, and away!' was used by Jim Webb as the title of a song in 1967 and, in the same year, was incorporated in the slogan 'Up, up and away with TWA'.

— Superstar. This suffix became fashionable following the success of the musical *Jesus Christ Superstar* (1970). Tim Rice, its lyricist, says that he and the composer, Andrew Lloyd Webber, settled on the title after seeing a 1960s Las Vegas billing for 'Tom Jones – Superstar'.

The showbiz use of the term 'superstar' although very much a 1960s thing – it was also used by Andy Warhol – has been traced back to 1925 by the *OED2* which finds in that year talk of 'cinema super-stars'.

supper. See LAST ~.

support your local —~. A slogan format, almost certainly from the US originally. Established before the 1968 film *Support Your Local Sheriff* (which was followed three years later by *Support Your Local Gunfighter*). In 1969 there was a police bumper sticker in the US, 'Support your local police, keep them independent.' Compare YOUR FRIENDLY NEIGHBOURHOOD —.

sure. See AS ~ AS EGGS IS EGGS.

sur le continong/ telephoneo. See under MORNING ALL!

surprise, surprise! What you say when giving someone an unexpected present or when arriving unexpectedly to see them. Possibly of American origin, 1950s. In the 1990s, a British TV show with the title *Surprise, Surprise* was built on the premise of surprising members of the public who had merited this treatment.

surrender. See NO ~!; UNCONDITIONAL ~.

surveys. See MONARCH OF ALL ONE ~.

suspicion. See CAESAR'S WIFE.

SWALK. Lover's acronym in correspondence, meaning 'Sealed With A Loving Kiss'. Possibly dating from the days of military censorship of letters in the First World War. *S.W.A.L.K.* was the alternative title of the film *Melody* (UK, 1971).

Swan of Pesaro, the. Sobriquet of Gioacchino Antonio Rossini (1792–1868), the composer, especially of opera, including the *Barber of Seville* and *William Tell*. He was born at Pesaro, the resort in eastern Italy.

swap. See NEVER ~/CHANGE HORSES.

swear. See ENOUGH TO MAKE A PARSON ~.

swearing. See DAMN IS TO ~ . . .

swear to tell the truth, I. See COURT OATH.

sweat. See BLOOD ~ AND TEARS; HORSES ~ . . .

Swedish Nightingale, the. Sobriquet of Jenny Lind (1820–87), whose great talents as a singer made her famous in Europe (especially Germany and Britain) and in America. She excelled in opera and Handel's *Messiah*. England was her home in the latter part of her life, and she died at Malvern. In the US, her nickname gave rise to the term the 'Irish nightingale' for a bullfrog.

Sweeney, the. The title of a British ITV drama series (1974–8) about Scotland Yard's Flying Squad comes from rhyming slang: Sweeney Todd (Flying Squad). Sweeney Todd, 'the demon barber of Fleet Street', murdered his customers in the play sometimes called *A String of Pearls, or, The Fiend of Fleet Street* (1847) by George Dibden-Pitt, though the title *Sweeney Todd, the Barber of Fleet Street* seems to have originated with a play (on the same theme) by F. Hazelton in 1865.

sweep. See SHINING LIKE A TANNER . . .

sweeps. See IT BEATS, AS IT ~ . . .

sweet. See HOW ~ IT IS under AND AWA-A-AAY WE GO!; REACH FOR A LUCKY INSTEAD OF A ~; VERY TASTY, VERY ~.

sweet as the moment when the pod went 'pop'. Slogan for Birds Eye frozen peas, in the UK, from *c* 1956. Sometimes remembered as 'fresh as the moment when . . .'

sweet Fanny Adams/sweet FA/sweet fuck-all. There actually was a person called Fanny Adams from Alton in Hampshire, who was murdered, aged eight, in 1867. At about the same time, tinned meat was introduced to the Royal Navy, and sailors – unimpressed – said it was probably made up from the remains of the murdered girl. 'Fanny Adams' became the naval nickname for mutton or stew, and then the meaning was extended to cover anything that was worthless. The abbreviation 'Sweet FA' being re-translated as 'Sweet Fuck-All' is a more recent coinage.

sweet smell of success, the. The title of a film (US, 1957), based on a short story, is apparently an original coinage of the writer, Ernest Lehman. Subsequently, Laurence Olivier was quoted as saying that 'Success smells like Brighton'.

swim. See CAN A BLOODY DUCK ~?

swine. See YOU DIRTY ROTTEN ~, YOU under *GOON SHOW*.

swing. See GIRL IN THE RED VELVET ~.

swinging! See under DODGY!

swinging London/the Swinging Sixties. 'Swinging' had been a musician's commendation for many years before it was adopted to describe the free-wheeling, uninhibited atmosphere associated with the 1960s. By extension, 'swinging' came to denote sexual promiscuity. 'A swinger' was one who indulged in such activity. One suggestion is that 'swinging' in the sense of changing partners derives from the caller's use of words in square dancing.

How the phrase caught on is not totally clear. In the early 1960s, the comedian Norman Vaughan would say it (see DODGY!). But Frank Sinatra had had an album entitled *Songs for Swinging Lovers* (1958), Peter Sellers, *Songs for Swinging Sellers* (1959), and Diana Dors *Swinging Dors*. Could the square-dancing use of 'swing your partners' have contributed to this?

The coming together of 'swinging' and 'London' may first have occurred in an edition of the *Weekend Telegraph* magazine on 30 April 1965 in which the words of the American fashion journalist Diana Vreeland (*c* 1903–89) were quoted: 'I love London. It is the most swinging city in the world at the moment.' In addition, a picture caption declared, 'London is a swinging city.' Almost exactly one year later, *Time* magazine picked up the angle and devoted a cover-story to the concept of 'London: The Swinging City' (edition dated 15 April 1966).

swingometer, on the. A 'swingometer' was a device for demonstrating the swing (transfer of votes from one party to another) in British general elections, as used by Robert McKenzie in BBC election night broadcasts (from 1959). The suffix '-ometer', for a measuring device (as in 'barometer') was not new, however. Egyptologists of the eighteenth century were using the name 'Nilometer' for a device found in ancient temples and used to measure the height of the Nile. In the 1960s, the ITV talent show *Opportunity Knocks* had a 'clapometer' which gave a visual indication of the loudness of applause given to individual acts. Hence, from the *Evening Standard* (12 October 1989): 'Nigel Lawson's speech registered well on the clapometer', and other variations of the same: 'Even recent [architecture], like a sheltered housing scheme, would score highly on the Prince Charlesometer' (the *Independent*, 20 January 1990).

swordsman. See BEST ~ IN ALL FRANCE.

· T ·

T. See FIT TO A ~.

tablets. See KEEP TAKING THE ~.

tabloid newspaper, a. The word 'tabloid' was coined by the chemist Sir Henry Wellcome in the 1880s to describe a small new medicinal tablet he had invented. 'Tabloid' was registered as a trademark, but in a short space of time came to be applied to anything that was miniature. British newspaper magnates Alfred Harmsworth and Lord Northcliffe both used the word to describe the new newspapers launched at the start of the twentieth century (with smaller pages than a 'broadsheet' and written in a downmarket, popular style), and the name stuck. Now mostly used pejoratively.

tacks. See BRASS ~.

Taffia, the. Nickname applied to a group of Welshmen looking after their own interests, since the 1970s. For example, in the media, one might have said that the founders of Harlech TV in 1968 were members of the Taffia. They included Richard Burton, Sir Geraint Evans, John Morgan and Wynford Vaughan-Thomas. The word is an obvious combination of 'Taffy' (the traditional nickname for a Welshman, from the supposed Welsh pronunciation of Davy = David) and *mafia*, the Sicilian-Italian word which means 'bragging', applied to the organized body of criminals among Italian immigrants in the US.

From the *Sun* (2 April 1979): 'Terror of the Taffia! The militants who'll black out your telly for their cause' – though is a reference to Welsh Nationalist activists (rather the opposite of the above-described HTV mob).

Similar light-hearted coinages are the **Murphia** (from Murphy, the typical Irish name and nickname of a potato), applied to the band of Irish broadcasters in the UK headed by Terry Wogan, and **kosher nostra**, for the Jewish 'mafia'.

tail. See CAT HOUSE.

tails. See WE REALLY MOVE OUR ~ FOR YOU.

t'ain't funny, McGee! See under SOMEBODY BAWL FOR BEULAH?

take. See YOU CAN'T ~ IT WITH YOU.

take a kick in the pants. Catchphrase of the British comedian George Doonan (*d* 1973). He also was wont to ask **'smatter wit chew?**

take an early bath. See under UP AND UNDER.

take a pew. Meaning, 'be seated'. Recorded by 1898 and facetiously alluding to the sort of seating you would find in a church. Alan Bennett's archetypal Anglican sermon in the revue *Beyond the Fringe* (1961) was entitled 'Take a Pew'.

take a rain-check, to. Originally, in the US, a rain-check (or -cheque) was a ticket for re-admission to a sporting event when the event had had to be postponed because of rain. The person to whom it was given would be able to produce it at a later date and claim free admission. Now broadened, the expression is used to mean 'let's put this "on hold", let's not make any arrangements about this until the time is more opportune'. Obviously, the phrase can be used as a polite way of postponing something indefinitely, but basically there is some kind of commitment to 'renegotiate' at a later date.

An Australian source states that 'rain-check' was used of someone's action in putting a licked finger on a cake to reserve it for later – 'Unhygienic, but I am talking about perhaps the late 1930s, when I was but a teenager.'

take back the night. An American slogan from the campaign to make it possible for women to go out in the dark without fear of attack or rape (by the late 1970s). **Women reclaim the night** was probably better known in the UK.

take 'im away, Ramsbottom. See under RAMSBOTTOM, ENOCH AND ME.

Take It From Here. The BBC radio comedy programme in which **anything can happen and probably will** was first broadcast on 23 March 1948 and ran until 1959. It was based on literate scripts by Frank Muir and Denis Norden, and featured Jimmy Edwards (1920–88), Dick Bentley (b 1907) and June Whitfield (b 1927) (who succeeded Joy Nichols). A few of the phrases that came out of it:

> **black mark, Bentley!** Edwards referring to Dick B. Muir told me that it arose from the use of 'black mark!' by James Robertson Justice in Peter Ustinov's film of *Vice Versa*.

> **clumsy clot!** A hangover from wartime slang.

> **gently, Bentley!** Edwards to Dick B.

> **oh, Ron!/Yes, Eth?** The immortal exchange between a swooning Whitfield and a gormless Bentley as the lovers in the segment of the show known as 'The Glums'. A stock phrase originally rather than a catchphrase, but it caught on because of Eth's rising inflection and Ron's flat response.

> **'ullo, 'ullo, 'ullo, what's this?** Edwards as Pa Glum (usually interrupting son Ron as he attempted to kiss fiancée Eth). Muir says: 'It was not meant to be a catchphrase but as Pa Glum always said it on his entrance – and it was so useful a phrase in everyday life – it caught on.' It also, of course, echoes the traditional inquiry of a

policeman encountering something suspicious going on.

wake up at the back there! Muir: 'This was a line I always used in writing Jim's schoolmaster acts. It was technically very useful in breaking up his first line and getting audience attention.'

> *Jim*: They laughed at Suez, but he went right ahead and built his canal – wake up at the back there!

Compare WAKE UP THERE! under YOU 'ORRIBLE LITTLE MAN!

take it in. See CAN DISH IT OUT . . .

take me to your leader. The traditional line spoken in cartoons by Martians having just landed on earth, or in science fiction by earth persons landing on some other planet. Echoing what explorers or invaders might have said when encountering a tribe in some distant land in imperial days. No citations, alas, but very 1950s. In the song 'Whatever Became of Hubert?' (1965), Tom Lehrer puns, 'Take me to your *lieder.*'

take my wife – please! Catchphrase of Henny Youngman (b 1906), US comic much on TV in the 1970s. However, in *Roy Hudd's Book of Music-Hall, Variety and Showbiz Anecdotes* (1993), the inventor of this gag is given as the earlier Canadian music-hall comedian, R.G. Knowles.

take someone down a peg, to. Meaning 'to humble; reduce in self-esteem', the expression derives from nautical use, in connection with flags which were raised and lowered with pegs. A flag flying high would carry more honour than one lower down.

takes one to know one, (it). Trick phrase, seizing on people's *awareness* of some interest to accuse them of being rather more involved in it than they might care to admit. Usually with reference to homosexuality, though for joking effect it can arise about almost anything. Echoic of the proverbial 'it takes a thief to catch a thief'. From Stephen Fry, *The Liar*, Chap. 3 (1991): ' "Only you would know about something as disgusting as the Biscuit Game." "Takes one to know one." '

take the mickey, to. Meaning 'to send up, tease'. Possibly from rhyming slang, 'Mickey Bliss' = 'piss', in the 1950s. But who was Mickey Bliss to be so honoured, I wonder? The Rev. Geoffrey Knee wrote to *Radio Times* (in April 1994) thus: 'I have long understood that the phrase is a less vulgar form of "Taking the p***" [his asterisks] and that it's derived from the term "p*** proud", meaning an erection caused by pressure in the bladder and not, therefore a sign of sexual prowess; hence, someone who is "p*** proud" has an exaggerated sense of his own importance. Such a one might be to told to "p*** off", meaning, not "go away", but "get rid of the p***" and stop boasting. Thus, to "take the p*** out of someone" means to deride him into lowering his self-esteem.'

However, with respect to the reverend etymologist, an earlier form – **to take the Mike** – is remembered by some from the 1920s and would seem to demolish his origin. More recently, the verbose and grandiose 'are you by any chance **extracting the Michael?**', and '**extracting the urine**' have become reasonably common. Another explanation is that the 'mickey' = 'piss' derives from the word 'micturition' (the overwhelming desire to urinate frequently).

take the money and run, to. Meaning 'to settle for what you've got and not hang about', as though advice was being given to a bank robber to take what he'd got rather than look for more and risk being caught. Or it might be advice given to a person worried about the value of a job. In which case, one might say, 'I should just take the money and run, if I were you.' I have no citations for this other than the title of Woody Allen's film 1968 film *Take the Money and Run*.

taking. See I'M MAD AS HELL AND I'M NOT ~ ANY MORE.

tale. See AND THEREBY HANGS A ~.

talent will out. A modern proverbial saying, meaning that if a person has talent,

a way of expressing it will be found. An advertisement for Lloyds Bank Young Theatre Challenge (June 1988) had: 'Talent will out, they say. But only under the right conditions.' The young Beatrix Potter in her diary for 5 June 1891 mentions: 'A theory I have seen – that genius – like murder – will out – its bent being simply a matter of circumstance.' The proverb 'murder will out' (i.e. will be found out, will reveal itself) goes back at least to 1325, and 'truth will out' to 1439. Hannah Cowley in *The Belle's Stratagem* (1782) has: 'Vanity, like murder, will out.'

talk. See CAN WE ~ ?; LOOSE ~ COSTS LIVES; NINETEEN TO THE DOZEN; WE HAVE WAYS . . .

talking heads. British broadcasting term for the type of TV programme which is composed mainly of people talking, shown in 'head and shoulder' shots and sometimes addressing the camera directly. Often used critically by those who would prefer a programme to show more physical action or to get out of the confines of the studio. Granada TV's booklet *Some Technical Terms and Slang* (1976) defined the term solely as 'a documentary programme which uses the technique of people talking directly to the camera'. Earlier (c 1968), the term 'talking head' seems to have been applied to anyone addressing a camera in a presenter's role.

The US/UK pop group with the name Talking Heads flourished from 1981.

talk telephone numbers, to. To negotiate about money where the sums involved are extremely large, perhaps in the millions and thus looking like seven-number phone numbers. Probably from American showbusiness usage, by the 1980s. An ITV game show, based on viewers' telephone numbers and called *Talking Telephone Numbers* had its debut in 1994.

tall, dark and handsome. This description of a romantic hero's attributes (as likely to be found especially in women's fiction) had surfaced by 1906. Flexner puts it in the late 1920s as a Hollywood term referring to Rudolph Valentino (though, in fact, he was not particularly tall). Sophie

Tucker recorded a song called 'He's Tall, Dark and Handsome' (by Tobias & Sherman) in 1928. Cesar Romero played the lead in the 1941 film *Tall, Dark and Handsome* which no doubt helped fix the phrase in popular use. However, in a piece called 'Loverboy of the Bourgeoisie' (collected in 1965), Tom Wolfe writes: 'It was Cary Grant that Mae West was talking about when she launched the phrase "tall, dark and handsome" in *She Done Him Wrong* (1933).'

tango. See IT TAKES TWO TO ∼.

tank. See PUT A TIGER IN YOUR ∼.

tanker. See TURNING A ∼.

tanner. See SHINING LIKE A ∼ . . .

tante. See PLUME DE MA ∼.

tapestry. See IT'S ALL PART OF LIFE'S RICH PAGEANT.

TARDIS. Acronym of 'Time And Relative Dimension In Space'. Hence the name given to the machine – disguised as an old British police (phone) box – used for travelling through time and space in the BBC TV series *Dr Who* (from 1963).

Tarzan. See ME, ∼ . . .

taste. See IT'S ALL DONE IN THE BEST POSSIBLE ∼.

tasty. See VERY ∼ . . .

tatti-bye (everybody)! See under HOW TICKLED I AM.

tattifalarious. See HOW TICKLED I AM.

tatty-bye (everybody). See HOW TICKLED I AM.

taxation. See NO ∼ WITHOUT REPRESENTATION.

taxi. See FOLLOW THAT ∼!

tea. See I WANT MY ∼; NOT FOR ALL THE ∼ IN CHINA; ∼, EDMOND? under MILK?

teach. See DON'T ∼ YOUR . . .

tea-party. See LIKE A VICARAGE ∼.

tear. See EYAYDON, YAUDEN . . .

tears. See BLOOD SWEAT AND ∼; CROCODILE ∼.

teeth. See GETS RID OF FILM ON ∼; DRAGON'S ∼; under OLD AS MY TONGUE . . .

telegraph less. See under POST EARLY FOR CHRISTMAS.

telephone numbers. See TALK ∼.

telephoneo, sur le. See under MORNING ALL!

television. See TIT, TOTE AND ∼.

tell. See EVERY PICTURE ∼S A STORY; IT'S THE WAY I ∼ 'EM!; I WANNA ∼ YOU A STORY!; ONLY TIME WILL ∼; under MARINES, ∼ IT TO THE.

telling. See WHY ARE YOU ∼ . . . under ARCHERS.

tell it like it is! Injunction to tell the truth or as you see things, popular in the 1960s addressed to speakers at American Civil Rights demonstrations. Flexner (1976) has it by 1965 and replaced by RIGHT ON! in 1967.

tell Sid. In November 1986, an advertising campaign was mounted to promote the flotation of shares in British Gas which was being privatized by the Government. A catchline involved the telling of a certain Sid (not seen, only mentioned) about the benefits to be had from subscribing. Another line, and just as irritating to most people, was **if you see Sid, tell him.** Sid, consequently, had a short after-life as journalistic shorthand for the small-scale private investor and share holder.

tell-tale tit, a. As Iona and Peter Opie record in *The Lore and Language of Schoolchildren* (1977), the rhyme:

Tell tale tit
Your tongue shall be slit,
And all the dogs in the town
Shall have a little bit

has been 'stinging in the ears of blabbers for more than two hundred years' (or since 1780, at least). *Tell-Tale Tits* was the title of the autobiography (1987) of the British soft-porn actress Fiona Richmond.

ten. See NINE OUT OF ~; ON A SCALE OF ONE TO ~.

tenacity. See SCIENCE AND ~.

ten acres and a mule. A slogan for what was sought by American slaves from 1862 onwards. They thought that their masters' plantations would be divided up to their benefit after the Civil War. However, this demanded escalated to **forty acres and a mule** when, in January 1865, General Sherman stated that 'Every family shall have a plot of not more than forty acres of tillable ground' – a promise which had nothing to do with the Federal government. Consequently, this Reconstruction slogan dwindled to **three acres and a cow.** *That* phrase had originated in John Stuart Mill's *Principles of Political Economy* (1848) – 'When the land is cultivated entirely by the spade and no horses are kept, a cow is kept for every three acres of land.' In Britain, Jesse Collings (1831–1920), a henchman of Joseph Chamberlain in the 1880s, proposed that every smallholder should have these things. He was an advocate of radical agrarian policies and the smallholding movement. He became known as 'Three Acres and a Cow Collings'.

Noël Coward once described Edith, Osbert and Sacheverell Sitwell as 'two wiseacres and a cow'.

tender loving care. Understandably, this is a phrase that appears irresistible to song-writers. The catalogue of the BBC Gramophone Library reveals a considerable list:

As 'T.L.C.', there is a song by Lehman: Lebowsky: C. Parker dating from 1960 (and translated as 'Tender loving *and*

care). Also with this title, there is a Motown song by Jones: Sawer: Jerome (1971), an instrumental by R.L. Martin: Norman Harris (1975); and a song by the Average White band and Alan Gorrie.

As 'Tender Lovin' Care' there is a song written by Brooks: Stillman (1966) and one written and performed by Ronnie Dyson (1983).

As 'Tender Loving Care', there is a song written by Mercer: Bright: Wilson, and recorded in 1966 by Nancy Wilson. It was also used as the title of an album by her.

It has also been suggested to me that 't.l.c.' was used in advertisements for BUPA, the British medical insurance scheme, or for Nuffield Hospitals. Have I imagined it being used in washing powder ads, too – for Dreft perhaps? The *OED2* recognizes the phrase as a colloquialism denoting, 'especially solicitous care such as is given by nurses' and cites the *Listener* (12 May 1977): 'It is in a nurse's nature and in her tradition to give the sick what is well called "TLC", "tender loving care", some constant little service to the sick.'

The earliest use of the phrase, in this sense, that I have come across occurs in the final chapter, 'T.L.C. TREATMENT', of Ian Fleming's *Goldfinger* (1959). James Bond says to PUSSY GALORE, 'All you need is a course of TLC.' 'What's TLC,' she asks. 'Short for Tender Loving Care Treatment,' Bond replies. 'It's what they write on most papers when a waif gets brought in to a children's clinic.'

So the phrase may be of American origin. A correspondent in the US recalls being told in the 1940s that there was a study done in foundling hospitals where the death rate was very high, which showed that when nurses picked up the babies and cuddled them more frequently, the death rate went down. This led to the prescription, 'TLC *t.i.d.*' (including the Latin abbreviation for three times a day).

Well, there's no phrase like a good phrase. In Shakespeare *Henry VI, Part 2,* III.ii.277/9 (1590) we read:

Commons. (Within): [i.e. a rabble offstage]
An answer from the King, or we will

all break in!

King: Go, Salisbury, and tell them all
from me,

I thank them for their tender loving care.

tenderness. See TRY A LITTLE VC 10DERNESS
under BOAC TAKES GOOD CARE OF YOU.

ten-four! In the American TV cop series
Highway Patrol (1955–59), Chief Dan
Matthews (Broderick Crawford) was always
bellowing this into his radio. It signifies
agreement and conforms to the 'ten-code' of
radio communication used by US police.

tennis, anyone? See under ANYONE FOR
TENNIS?

tents. See FOLD ONE'S ~ LIKE THE ARABS.

Teresa. See MOTHER ~.

terminate with extreme prejudice, to.
To kill. In the parlance of the US Central
Intelligence Agency, by 1972.

terrible. See BOSS, BOSS . . . under *ITMA*.

terrific. See THE —FULNESS IS ~ under
YAROOOO; IT'S ~ under *EDUCATING ARCHIE*.

territory. See IT GOES WITH THE ~.

terrors. See KING OF ~.

TGIF. Short for 'Thank God It's Friday',
an expression of relief especially among
office workers and schoolteachers. I heard
first it in 1967 though I am told it was
current in the 1940s. It is amusing to see
how broadcasters have shrunk from
spelling it out when using it for Friday night
programmes. Granada TV in Manchester
had *At Last It's Friday* in 1968 and Capital
Radio, *T.G.I.F.* in 1983. In the early 1970s,
on the other hand, BBC TV did have
Thank God It's Sunday, appropriately.

Visiting Dallas, Texas, in December
1980, I noticed there was a singles bar called
Thank God It's Friday – and the name
appears to have been adopted subsequently
by more than one club or restaurant (e.g.
T.G.I. Friday's) in the US and elsewhere.
Compare POETS' DAY.

Thames. See SET THE ~ ON FIRE.

thank. See AY THANG YEW under BAND
WAGGON.

thank God it's Friday. See TGIF.

thank you, music-lovers! The American
musician Spike Jones (1911–64) specialized
in comedy arrangements on radio, records
and films from the late 1930s onwards.
After massacring some well-known piece of
music like 'The Dance of the Hours' he
would come forward and acknowledge
applause with these words.

thank you, Thing. Thing was a
disembodied hand which kept popping out
of a black box in the 1964–66 live-action
American TV series *The Addams Family*
(based on the cartoons of Charles Addams).

thar. See THERE'S GOLD IN THEM ~ HILLS.

— that almost got away, the. A
journalistic cliché based presumably on
'This was the fish that almost got away'. A
British film with the title *The One That Got
Away* (about an escaped prisoner) was
released in 1957.

that and a — will get you a —. An
American format for saying that what you
are referring to is worthless. So, 'that, and a
token, will get you on the subway' or 'that,
and a dollar, will get you a cup of coffee'.
Noted by 1990. Compare Shakespeare, *A
Midsummer Night's Dream*, V.i.277 (1594):
'This passion and the death of a dear friend,
would go near to make a man look sad.'

— that is —, the. Portentous cliché.
Already identified as such in a BBC TV
That Was the Week That Was sketch about
sports journalist 'Desmond Packet': 'Plucky
British athletes . . . who ran their lion hearts
into the ground in the sizzling cauldron
that is Perth' (1962–63 series). An advert for
some old Alfred Hitchcock film shown in
London (November 1983) ran thus: 'This is
a unique opportunity to see these classic
films and either re-live or experience for the
first time *the genius that is Hitchcock*.'

Perhaps this use derives from the format
used so notably by Edgar Allan Poe in *To*

Helen (1831): 'The glory that was Greece/ And the grandeur that was Rome.'

that is what the soldier said. A throw-away humorous tag, like **that is what the girl said (at the picnic)**. These are probably earlier versions of the more recent **as/like the man said** or **as the girl said to the sailor** which are both used as throw-away remarks, though not quite to the subversive extent of AS THE BISHOP SAID TO THE ACTRESS. Partridge/*Catch Phrases* suggests that the origin is the passage from Charles Dickens, *The Pickwick Papers* (1835–37) where Sam Weller remarks during the trial of Mr Pickwick, 'Oh, quite enough to get, Sir, as the soldier said ven they ordered him three hundred and fifty lashes' and the judge interposes with, 'You must not tell us what the soldier, or any other man, said, Sir . . . it's not evidence.' (This is a Wellerism. See also AS THE MONKEY SAYS . . .)

that'll do nicely, sir. A fawning line from an American Express TV ad of the late 1970s, especially in the UK. It was in answer to an inquiry as to whether the establishment accepted the credit card in question. About the same time, another phrase used in advertising for the AmEx card was **don't leave home without it.** Bob Hope once did a parody on a TV special in which he appeared as the Pope carrying his Vatican Express Card ('Don't leave Rome without it'). Another theme used in the early 1980s was **do you know me?** in which celebrities like Robert Ludlum and Stephen King, known for what they did but not easily recognizable from how they looked, explained that relative celebrity could have its drawbacks . . . but not when you carried the card.

that'll stop you farting/laughing in church. Phrase used, say, when a father is obliged to act in order to prevent youngsters from meddling with anything dangerous or from straying beyond control. He places something beyond their reach or locks it away. Or, when a person has put right another who has chanced his arm with him.

Partridge/*Catch Phrases* suggests that the original was the less polite 'that will teach

you to fart in chapel (i.e. 'stop taking liberties') and was possibly an English public school expression of the 1930s.

that man. See under *ITMA*.

that's a joke, son. 'Senator Claghorn' in the American radio feature called 'Allen's Alley' (with Fred Allen) in *Town Hall Tonight* (1934–49). Became a national catchphrase.

that's all, folks! The concluding line – not spoken, but written on the screen – of *Merry Melodies*, the Warner Bros. cartoon series, from 1930. When Mel Blanc (1908–89), the voice behind so many cartoon characters, was asked for an epitaph, he plumped for the following 'in joined-up handwriting' – 'That's All, Folks!'

that's life! Exclamation of the *c'est la vie*, SUCH IS LIFE, THAT'S SHOW BIZ! type, used to cover disappointment at the inevitable happening. Probably established by the 1950s. *That's Life* was the title of an intolerable BBC TV programme (1975–94) that combined folksy human-interest items with consumerist campaigning.

that's my boy that said that. See DAT'S MY BOY . . .

that spelled —, the —. Journalistic cliché. From the *Sun* (15 October 1983): 'The Ding-Ding special that spelled love for Sid and Jan Parker will take a trip DOWN MEMORY LANE . . . to celebrate their 25th wedding anniversary. The happy couple will kiss and cuddle on the top deck of the No. 44 bus, just like they did when they were courting.'

that's right – you're wrong! Kay Keyser (who died aged 79 in 1985) was a bandleader and self-styled 'Old Perfessor' of American radio's *Kollege of Musical Knowledge* (1933 to 1949). His weekly mix of dance music, comedy and quiz questions is said to have drawn as many as 20 million listeners. This phrase was said in the quiz part. Also used as the title of a film (1939).

that's Shell – that was! A slogan for Shell petrol in the UK, from the early 1930s. Two one-headed men with the slogan 'That's

Shell – that is!', current in 1929, were developed into one seemingly two-headed man (his head sweeping from left-profile to right) with the more widely known slogan. A possibly apocryphal story is that the two-headed man was devised by a member of the public called Horsfield, who received £100 for his trouble.

that's show biz/show business!, well.
Exclamation is used to cover disappointment at bad luck or the failure of anything, and as such no longer limited to the world of entertainment. At the end of an article on theatrical auditions: 'That, as they say, is show business' (*Independent*, 23 May 1990). Certainly in use by the early 1960s, the expression is akin to THAT'S LIFE! The similar-sounding 'That's Entertainment' was used by Howard Dietz and Arthur Schwarz as the title of a song in the film *Band Wagon* (1953) and as the title of two films (US, 1974; 1976).

that's the stuff to give the troops.
Welcoming remark as food is placed on the table or after consuming it. Partridge/*Slang* dates this from the First World War but defines it simply as 'that's the idea, that's what we want', and not necessarily about food.

that's the way the cookie crumbles.
Meaning 'that's the way it is, there's no escaping it'. Bartlett describes this basic form as an 'anonymous phrase from the 1950s'. It was, however, given a memorable twist in Billy Wilder's film *The Apartment* (1960). The main characters make much use of the suffix '-wise', as in 'promotion-wise' and 'gracious-living-wise'. Then Miss Kubelik (Shirley MacLaine) says to C.C. Baxter (Jack Lemmon): 'Why can't I ever fall in love with somebody nice like you?' Replies Baxter: 'Yeah, well, **that's the way it crumbles, cookie-wise.**'

A joke translation of the original phrase – '*Sic biscuitus disintegrat*' – occurred in an Iris Murdoch novel, I believe, before 1978. A showbiz variant I heard in 1988 was **that's the way the mop flops.**

that's what — is all about. A journalistic cliché appearing most frequently in sporting contexts. The basic notion is 'winning is

what it's all about' (and never mind all that nonsense of the Olympic motto). Often ascribed to Vince Lombardi, coach and general manger of the Green Bay Packers pro-football team from 1959, in the form 'Winning isn't everything, it's the only thing', it had nevertheless been said earlier by John Wayne as a football coach in the 1953 movie *Trouble Along the Way*. President Nixon's notorious Committee to Re-Elect the President in 1972 had as its motto: 'Winning in politics isn't everything; it's the only thing.'

The format can be used in any sport – 'Whoever plays best is going to win . . . this is what the game is all about,' said Peter Purves, commentating on BBC TV *Championship Darts*, 22 September 1983 – and in other contexts, of course. 'That's what love is all about' is a line in the song 'The Love Bug Will Bite You' by Pinky Tomlin (1937).

that's you and me. Ingratiating parenthetical phrase that some British broadcasters use to involve the listener or viewer. e.g. 'The Chancellor of the Exchequer today imposed a swingeing new tax on everybody whoever downed a well-earned pint, put a pony on a gee-gee, or lit up a Christmas cigar – that's you and me.' Noted by 1980.

that's your actual French. See under ROUND THE HORNE.

that was no lady – that was my wife!
See WHO WAS THAT LADY . . .

that was the — that was. The BBC TV satire show *That Was The Week That Was* (1962–63) launched this one. The programme's title was apparently modelled on THAT'S SHELL – THAT WAS! and coined by the actor, John Bird. It was customarily abbreviated to *TW3*.

Headline in the *Evening Standard* (25 January 1989) about a programme to mark the tenth anniversary of Mrs Thatcher's government: 'That Was the Ten Years That Was'.

theatre. See FUNNY THING HAPPENED . . . ; under DOCTOR GREASEPAINT WILL CURE ME.

—: **the Movie.** A format phrase. Possibly
the first film to be so labelled was *Abba: The
Movie* in 1977. In these days of 'concepts'
and 'merchandising' in pop music, perhaps
the idea was to distinguish the film product
from 'the tour', 'the TV series', 'the book'
and 'the album' (and in 1978 *Abba: The
Album* did, indeed, appear). The format has
subsequently been used to poke fun at
exploitation, self-promotion, and self-
aggrandizement in certain quarters. For
example, a Cambridge Footlights show in
the mid-1980s was called *Ian Botham: The
Movie* (referring to the English cricketer and
his non-sporting activities). In 1985,
Michael Rogin, a professor of political
science at Berkeley, California, entitled his
exploration of President Reagan's
(sometimes) unattributed borrowings of
film quotes, 'Ronald Reagan: The Movie'.
Headline over an article in the *Observer* (30
April 1989) suggesting that a film would one
day be made of a certain actress's life:
'Meryl Streep: The Movie?'

Along the same lines, in 1990, a novel by
the film critic Iain Johnstone was published
with the title *Cannes: the Novel*, and a short-
lived West End musical about Martin
Luther King was dubbed *King – The
Musical*.

there. See ALL HUMAN LIFE IS ∼ ; BECAUSE IT
IS ∼ .

there ain't gonna be no war! An
optimistic catchphrase or anti-war slogan.
As Foreign Secretary to British Prime
Minister Eden, Harold Macmillan attended
a four-power summit conference at Geneva
where the chief topic for discussion was
German reunification. Nothing much was
achieved but the 'Geneva spirit' was
optimistic and on his return to London he
breezily told a press conference on 24 July
1955, 'There ain't gonna be no war.' Was
this a conscious Americanism? There had
been, at some time prior to December 1941,
an American song (by Frankl) called,
precisely, 'There Ain't Gonna Be No War':

> We're going to have peace and quiet
> And if they start a riot
> We'll just sit back and keep score.
> The only place you'll go marching to
> Will be the corner grocery store.

> So rock-a-bye, my baby
> There ain't gonna be no war.

But Macmillan was, without doubt,
quoting directly from a *c* 1910 music-hall
song, which was sung in a raucous cockney
accent by a certain Mr Pélissier (1879–1913)
in a show called 'Pélissier's Follies' during
the reign of Edward VII:

> There ain't going to be no waar
> So long as we've a king like Good King
>   Edward.
> 'E won't 'ave it, 'cos 'e 'ates that sort of
>   fing.
> Muvvers, don't worry,
> Not wiv a king like Good King Edward.
> Peace wiv honour is 'is motter [*snort*] -
> Gawd save the King!

**there ain't/is no such thing as a free
lunch.** See NO SUCH THING AS A FREE
LUNCH.

thereby. See AND ∼ HANGS A TALE.

there is no alternative. When asked for
the origin of Margaret Thatcher's famously
nannyish phrase in 1984, her then political
secretary replied: 'I am not sure that the
British Prime Minister ever actually used
the phrase . . . and my suspicion, shared by
others, is that TINA was coined by those
who were pressing for a change of policy.'

However, in 1986, I happened to stumble
upon a report of a speech that Mrs
Thatcher had made to the Conservative
Women's Conference, on 21 May 1980,
marking the end of her first year in office.
Describing the harsh economic measures
already set in train by her government, she
said: 'There is no easy popularity in that,
but I believe people accept *there is no
alternative.*'

So, there, she *had* said it, and publicly,
too. I don't know whether this was the first
time – in fact, I think she may well have said
it at some stage in 1979.

The acronym **TINA**, said to have been
coined by Young Conservatives, was
flourishing by the time of the Party
Conference in September 1981.

A correspondent suggests that I compare
it to an old Hebrew catchphrase '*ain breira*'
('there is no choice').

there'll be dancing in the streets tonight. A cliché of journalism – to signify elation at some victory. Tom Stoppard in an extended parody of sports journalism in the play *Professional Foul* (1978) has: 'There'll be Czechs bouncing in the streets of Prague tonight as bankruptcy stares English football in the face.'

there'll never be another! See under HERE'S A FUNNY THING!

there's a cheque in the post. Customary unbelieved response to a request for payment. Used as a running gag in a Spike Milligan BBC TV comedy series *Q8* in 1979.

there's 'air. (or **there's 'hair**). Comment about a girl's fashionable cut, probably from British music hall but certainly 'the latest catchword', according to *Punch* (8 August 1900) – which also featured it in a poem and referred to it as 'this fatuous catchword'.

there's a lot of it about. Useful, but fairly meaningless and facetious, rejoinder. Originally, perhaps, what you would say when someone remarked 'I've got the 'flu' (or some other medical complaint). Title of, and running gag in, a Spike Milligan series on BBC TV in 1982.

there's a sucker born every minute (or **there's one born every minute**). Meaning 'there are lots of fools waiting to be taken advantage of'. There is no evidence that P.T. Barnum, the American circus magnate (1810–91) ever used this expression – not least, it is said, because 'sucker' was not a common term in his day. He did, however, express the view that, 'The people like to be humbugged', which conveys the same idea. There was also a song of the period, 'There's a New Jay Born Every Day' (where 'jay' = 'gullible hick'). By whatever route, Barnum took the attribution.

there's gold in them thar hills. Meaning 'there are opportunities where indicated'. Presumably this phrase was established literally in US gold-mining by the end of the nineteenth century. It seems to have had a resurgence in the 1930s/40s, probably through use in Western films. Frank Marvin wrote and performed a song with the title in (I think) the 1930s. A Laurel and Hardy short called *Them Thar Hills* appeared in 1934. The melodrama *Gold in the Hills* by J. Frank Davis has been performed every season since 1936 by the Vicksburg Theatre Guild in Mississippi. *OED2*'s earliest citation is from 1941. According to the story, the Hays Office forbade Marlene Dietrich to utter the line after stuffing money down her cleavage in the film *Destry Rides Again* (US, 1939).

The phrase now has a jokey application to any enterprise which contains a hint of promise.

there's life in the old dog yet. This expression of wonder may be uttered at the unexpected possession of some power by someone or some thing thought to be 'past it' (especially when referring to the person's love life). It was used as the title of a painting (1838) – precisely 'The Life's in the Old Dog Yet' – by Sir Edwin Landseer, which shows a Scottish ghillie rescuing a deerhound which, unlike a stag and two other hunting dogs, has not just plunged to its death over a precipice.

there's no answer to that! See under MORECAMBE AND WISE SHOW.

there we are dear friends . . . See under COME TO CHARLIE.

there you go! Phrase of excuse, approbation or thanks, known in the US by 1844. Very common in Australia. In Britain c 1979, it was noticed as a fairly meaningless filler phrase used by Tony Blackburn, the disc jockey. A *Guardian* reader suggested that this might be his reaction to yet another disaffected listener switching off. An *Independent* Magazine profile (9 July 1994) noted that Blackburn was still punctuating his speech with the phrase in the form 'there yego'.

there you go again! In a TV debate with President Carter in 1980, the Republican challenger, Ronald Reagan, laughed off Carter's charge that he would dismantle federal health support for the elderly, saying: 'There you go again!' The phrase

stuck with the voters and became a
campaign refrain.

these are dynamite! The sort of thing
journalists think real people say, or which
people say because journalists expect it of
them. From the *Sun* (10 December 1984):
'Mr Little rushed to the Sun offices to study
the photographs and said: "These are
dynamite."' Andrew Neil, sometime editor
of the *Sunday Times*, quoted in the
Independent on Sunday (25 September 1994):
'Wait till you see the set and the titles we've
designed [for a TV current-affairs show] . . .
It's dynamite.'

these foolish things. Best known as the
title of a popular song ('These foolish
things/Remind me of you', lyrics by Eric
Maschwitz, 1936), picked up by Michael
Sadleir for a book called *These Foolish Things*
in 1937 and by Bertrand Tavernier as the
title of a film (1990) which included the
song on the soundtrack.

they all look the same in the dark. See
ALL WOMEN LOOK THE SAME IN THE DARK.

they call/called/are calling —. Whoever
'they' may be, they certainly do a lot of it
and are most helpful to journalists in search
of a tag. E.g. '[Of a mining disaster] . . . in
what they are calling the South African
Aberfan' (Martyn Lewis, ITN's *The Making
of '81*); 'Alfredo Astiz drank free
champagne in seat 9A of the executive suite
on a British Caledonian DC10 flight to Rio
yesterday. The man they call Captain
Death was being returned to his homeland
via Brazil' (*Daily Mail*, 12 June 1982); 'They
call it paradise. Now burnt-out cars litter
the roads, some the tombs of drivers who
could not beat the flames' (*The Times*, 19
February 1983); 'They called him [Bjorn
Borg] "The Iceberg"' (ITN report, 7
February 1989).

they came . . . Cliché of funeral
journalism. The chief thing is to start with
the word 'They'. From the opening of the
Observer report on the funeral of Jennie Lee
(27 November 1988): 'They scattered the
ashes of a proud Scots lassie yesterday on a
cold Welsh hillside . . .' But much better to
put 'They came . . .'. From *The Times* (11

April 1983): 'They came, 541 of them,
across half a world [to the Falklands] to
dedicate the war memorial on a treeless
hillside above Blue Beach, where British
forces first stepped ashore.'
    Also useful: **they buried their own** . . .

they don't like it up 'em. See under
DAD'S ARMY.

they don't make — like that any more.
From an *Independent* obituary (26 January
1989): '"They don't make them like that
any more" said Danny La Rue of Freddie
Carpenter, a director who was equally at
home with both the traditional and the
modern musical.' From the *Guardian* (30
January 1989): 'Paying the keenest
attention to the oil painting, when he
delivered his judgement it was one that
carried enormous authority. "They don't,"
he said, "make pigs like that any more."'
    Especially applied to songs in the form,
'They don't write songs like that any more!'
– to which the joke response is, 'Thank
goodness!'

**they laughed when I sat down at the
piano, but when I started to play . . . !** A
slogan for the US School of Music piano
tutor, from 1925. The copy underneath this
headline includes the following: 'As the last
notes of the Moonlight Sonata died away,
the room resounded with a sudden roar of
applause . . . Men shook my hand – wildly
congratulated me – pounded me on the
back in their enthusiasm! . . . And then I
explained [how] I saw an interesting ad for
the US School of Music . . .'
    This ad gave rise to various jokes: 'They
laughed when I sat down to play – someone
had taken away the stool/how did I know
the bathroom door was open/etc.' John
Caples, the copywriter, also came up with,
'They grinned when the waiter spoke to me
in French – but their laughter changed to
amazement at my reply' (presumably for
another client).
    In the film *Much Too Shy* (UK, 1942)
there is a song 'They Laughed When I Sat
Down at the Piano', inspired by the slogan.

they might be giants. A film (US, 1972)
was made from the play with the title *They
Might Be Giants* (1961) by James Goldman

about a man who thinks he is Sherlock Holmes. He recruits a female Dr Watson who says (in the film): 'You're just like Don Quixote, you think that everything is always something else.' 'Holmes' replies: 'He had a point – of course, he carried it a bit too far, that's all. He thought that every windmill was a giant . . . If we never looked at things and thought what they *might* be we'd still all be in the tall grass with the apes.' A US band took the name They Might Be Giants in *c* 1989.

See also TILT AT WINDMILLS.

they're playing our tune, darling. A phrase from romantic fiction when (presumably married and ageing) lovers hear a tune that makes them nostalgic. But I do not have any citations. All I can recall is a joke about the Queen saying it to Prince Philip when the National Anthem struck up. A musical *They're Playing Our Song* (by Marvin Hamlisch and Carole Bayer Sager) was presented in New York in 1979.

they're working well tonight. Comment on gags in terms of an audience's response to them. A stock phrase of 'Monsewer' Eddie Gray (1898–1978) of the British Crazy Gang.

Other Crazy Gang phrases included **aye, aye, taxi!** and **shut up, Cecil!** – both usually said by Jimmy Nervo – and SUCK IT AND SEE.

they shoot horses, don't they? The title of a novel (1935; film US, 1969) by Horace McCoy is apparently the source of this now quasi-proverbial expression.

thickens. See PLOT ~.

thin. See INSIDE EVERY FAT MAN . . .

thing. See JUST ONE OF THOSE ~S; REAL ~; ~, YOU KNOW, ER under NAY ~ THRICE AGAIN NAY!; THANK YOU, ~.

things ain't what they used to be. The title of the Frank Norman/Lionel Bart's musical *Fings Ain't Wot They Used T'be* (London, 1959) – which popularized an already existing catchphrase in a particular form – gave rise to one of the nicest juxtaposition jokes I have spotted. In an

edition of the *Liverpool Echo* of *c* 1960, an advertisement for the Royal Court Theatre announced:

THIS WEEK & NEXT
THEATRE CLOSED FOR
ALTERATIONS
Box Office Now Open for
Lionel Bart's Smash Hit Musical
'FINGS AIN'T WOT THEY
USED T'BE'

It should be remembered that a song by Mercer Ellington and Ted Persons, published in 1939, was called 'Things Ain't What They Used To Be'.

The thought is an old one. In Charles Dickens, *Sketches By Boz* (1836) – 'A Christmas Dinner': 'There are people who will tell you that Christmas is not to them what it used to be.'

things go better with Coke. See under PAUSE THAT REFRESHES.

things I've done for England, the. In Sir Alexander Korda's film *The Private Life of Henry VIII* (1933), Charles Laughton as the King is just about to get into bed with one of his many wives when, alluding to her ugliness, he sighs: 'The things I've done for England.' The screenplay was written by Lajos Biro and Arthur Wimperis.

This became a catchphrase, to be used ironically when confronted with any unpleasant task. In 1979, Prince Charles on a visit to Hong Kong sampled curried snake meat and, with a polite nod towards his forebear (however fictionalized), exclaimed, 'Boy, the things I do for England . . .'

think. See I DON'T ~!; YOU MIGHT ~ THAT . . .

thinking man's/person's/woman's —, the. As long ago as 1931, Pebeco toothpaste in the US was being promoted as 'The Toothpaste for Thinking People'. However, I think it was Frank Muir who set the more recent trend (now almost a cliché) when he talked of British broadcaster Joan Bakewell as 'the thinking man's crumpet'. That was in the 1960s. Much later, Chantal Cuer, a French-born broadcaster in Britain, said she had been described as 'the thinking man's croissant'.

And how about these for originality? 'Frank Delaney – the thinking man's Russell Harty (*Sunday Times*, 16 October 1983); 'Frank Delaney – the thinking man's Terry Wogan' (*Guardian*, 17 October 1983); 'the thinking woman's Terry Wogan, TV's Frank Delaney' (*Sunday Express*, 30 October 1983).

And still it goes on. Janet Suzman, the actress, tells me she has been described as 'the thinking man's Barbara Windsor'. From the *Independent* (28 January 1989): 'One member of the Government said: "[Kenneth Clarke's] the thinking man's lager lout."' From the *Observer* (29 January 1989): 'It was chaired by Nick Ross, the thinking woman's newspaper boy.' Also, from the *Observer* (13 September 1987): 'His performance as a trendy and hung-up LA painter in *Heartbreakers* made him the thinking woman's West Coast crumpet' – which brings us back more or less to where we started.

In February 1989, the American magazine *Spy* drew up a long list of examples of American variations on the theme: *Hobbies* magazine in 1977 had described Descartes as 'The thinking man's philosopher'; *Boating Magazine* (1984) described the Mansfield TDC portable toilet as 'the thinking man's head'; *Horizon* (1965) called Lake Geneva, 'the thinking man's lake', and, *Esquire* (1986) had called actor William Hurt, 'the thinking man's asshole'.

thinks . . . thanks to Horlicks. See under NIGHT STARVATION.

thin red line, the. A report by William Howard Russell in *The Times* (25 October 1854) described the first stage of the Battle of Balaclava in the Crimean War (the Charge of the Light Brigade followed a few hours later). Of the Russian charge repulsed by the British 93rd Highlanders, he wrote: 'The ground lies beneath their horses' feet; gathering speed at every stride, they dash on towards that thin red streak topped with a line of steel.' By the time he was writing *The British Expedition to the Crimea* (1877), Russell put: 'The Russians dashed on towards *that thin red line tipped with steel*' [his italics]. Thus was created the jingoistic Victorian phrase 'the thin red line',

standing for the supposed invincibility of British infantry tactics.

Compare Kipling's poem 'Tommy' from *Departmental Ditties* (1890) which goes: 'But it's "Thin red line of 'eroes" when the drums begin to roll.' In the 1939 version of the film *The Four Feathers*, the character played by C. Aubrey Smith is always reminiscing about it and draws the 'thin red line' in red wine on the dinner table. Someone asks him, 'Were they hungry?'

third man. A fielding position in cricket, but in the film *The Third Man* (UK, 1949) – about the black market in postwar Vienna – he is supposed to be one of three witnesses to a traffic accident which has taken the life of Harry Lime, a 'pusher', played by Orson Welles. It turns out that Lime himself is the Third Man and that he is very much alive. The film probably led to the use of 'Third Man', 'Fourth Man' and even 'Fifth Man' to describe those who were suspected of having tipped off the spies Burgess and Maclean to defect to Moscow in 1954. The 'Third Man' was later identified as Kim Philby, the 'Fourth Man' as Anthony Blunt.

thirsterooni. This occurs in Alfred Hitchcock's film *Psycho* (1960), in which a character, in need of a drink, says, 'I'm dying of thirsterooni.' More recently, a 'smackeroonie' has meant a kiss, though also a unit of money, usually a dollar (from Norman Mailer, *Miami and the Siege of Chicago*, 1968: 'Director of the most impressive funeral establishment . . . who certainly couldn't think much of you if, my goodness, you wouldn't spring ten thousand smackeroonies for a casket').

So, '-erooni' is an amusing suffix (as in 'thingerooni' meaning a 'thingumajig', a 'whatsit' or a DOOBRY) – what you call something when you cannot think what to call it or when the right word for something does not come into your mind. Adding the shorter suffix '-eroo' is also a recognized linguistic practice (e.g. 'flopperoo') and the *OED2* cites American discussions of the phenomenon in the 1940s and 1950s.

There may be some connection with Slim Gaillard (d 1991), the American jazz musician and singer, who, in the 1940s and 50s, created what he called 'Vouty' or 'voutarooni', a sort of hip nonsense language incorporating a number of Yiddishisms.

thirst knows no season. See PAUSE THAT REFRESHES.

thirteen years of Tory misrule. With the force of a slogan, this phrase was uttered in the run-up to the 1964 General Election, which Labour won. So it may be said to have had some effect. Also in the form **thirteen wasted years**. From the 1964 Labour Party manifesto: 'A New Britain . . . reversing the decline of thirteen wasted years.'

Compare Churchill's remark about 'four wasted years of Labour Government' (to Denis Kelly, in private conversation, 1949 – quoted in Martin Gilbert's *Never Despair*).

thirty-five years! See under BEYOND OUR KEN.

thirtysomething. The title of a US TV drama series (from 1987). There was nothing new about giving someone's age as 'twenty something' or 'thirty something', when you didn't know the exact figure, but the TV series about couples around that age helped popularize the usage. 'Eighties pop for the thirtysomethings' said an ad in *Barclaycard Magazine* (1989); 'Judy is a successful and attractive businesswoman toward the far end of her thirtysomething decade. Yet she feels frustrated, alone and angry about her failed relationships with men' (*Washington Post*, 13 March 1990).

Adaptable, of course: 'My generation, the twentysomethings, were fortunate enough to catch the golden age of American TV detectives' (*Guardian*, 3 May 1991).

this ad insults women. Usually attached to the offending sexist ad (in the UK) with a sticker, this was a slogan of the women's movement in the 1970s. I recall an Elliott shoe shop ad in 1979 which showed a pair of models wearing woollen thigh boots – upon which a graffitist had written 'This insults and degrades sheep'.

this great movement of ours. A British Labour Party phrase – or so it was noted in the early 1980s. Sometimes abbreviated to

'THIGMOU'. Compare from a speech by Harold Wilson in Huddersfield (May 1951): 'This Party of ours, this Movement of ours . . . is based on principles and ideals . . . This movement of ours is bigger than any individual or group of individuals.'

this has restored my faith in British justice. Cliché of journalistic reporting. What members of the public say, when prompted by journalists, after winning a court case.

this hurts me more than it hurts you. See HURTS ME . . .

this is a free country. (or **it's a . . .**) Partridge/*Slang* dates this as 'late C19' and calls it 'expressive of tolerance (or apathy, depending on points of view)'.

this is beautiful downtown Burbank. See under LAUGH-IN.

this is Cardew the Cad saying Cardew-do! See under HOW DO YOU DO?

this is Funf speaking! Spoken sideways into a glass tumbler on *ITMA*, this phrase was 'the embodiment of the nation's spy neurosis' (according to the producer, Francis Worsley). The first time Funf appeared was in the second edition of the show on 26 September 1939, just after the outbreak of the Second World War. Initially, he said, 'Dees ees Foonf, your favourite shpy!' Jack Train recalled that when Worsley was searching for a name for the spy, he overheard his six-year-old son, Roger, trying to count in German: '*Ein, zwei, drei, vier, funf*' – and that's where he always got stuck.

For a while it became a craze to start phone conversations with the words.

this *is* Henry Hall speaking and tonight is my guest night. What was the reason for the peculiar emphasis on 'is'? In 1934, the BBC Dance Orchestra had been playing while Henry Hall (1899–1989) was away in America and yet it was still announced as 'directed by Henry Hall'. A journalist wrote: 'Why do the BBC allow this to happen? How can Henry Hall possibly be conducting the orchestra when we know for a fact that at this moment he is on the high seas?' Hence, on his return, he said, 'Hello, everyone, this *is* Henry Hall speaking!' and it stayed with him for the rest of his long broadcasting career.

His sign-off was **here's to the next time!** – the title of his signature tune and, inevitably, of his autobiography (1956).

this is it! Phrase of agreement. Noted by Paul Beale in 1974 as occurring where a simple 'yes' or 'I agree' would do. Previously it may have been heard more at points in conversation when something significant had happened. Kenneth Tynan reviewing an idiomatic modern translation of *Medea* by Euripides (1948) noted Medea's reaction to Creon's notice of expulsion, 'This is *it*.'

The agreement version acquired catchphrase status through BBC Radio's satirical *Week Ending* show from about 1977 when two pub bores (played by David Jason and Bill Wallis) conversed on current topics. One would ritually say it, followed by **makes you think!**

this . . . is . . . London! A greeting that became familiar to American radio listeners to reports given by Edward R. Murrow from London during the Second World War. It was a natural borrowing from BBC announcers who had been saying **this is London calling** from the earliest days of station 2LO in the 1920s. One of them, Stuart Hibberd, entitled a book of his broadcasting diaries, *This Is London* (1950).

this is the city. See under DRAGNET.

this is/was war. Meaning 'this is very serious, and justifies the particular course adopted'. Wilson Goode, Mayor of Philadelphia, defending a police fire-bombing raid that went disastrously wrong: 'This was not child's play. This was war' (*Time*, 15 May 1985). Front page headline from the *Daily Express* (24 May 1985): 'Drug menace: now it's WAR'. After the Heysel football stadium disaster: 'Said a Belgian Red Cross rescue worker: "This is not sport. This is war."' (*Time*, 10 June 1985). Sign outside the Las Vegas Hilton promoting a big fight (February 1989): 'THIS TIME IT'S WAR. TYSON VS. BRUNO.'

Compare this earlier version from

President Nixon on 15 September 1972: 'We are all in it together. This is a war. We take a few shots and it will be over . . . I wouldn't want to be on the other side right now. Would you?' (*The White House Transcripts*, 1974).

this is where we came in. Meaning 'I am/you are beginning to repeat myself/yourself. This is where we should stop whatever it is we are doing'. Or 'we have been here (to this point) before, haven't we?' From the remark uttered in cinemas when continuous performances were the order of the day – from the 1920s to the 1970s. From 'Cato', *Guilty Men* (1940): 'When the news of the appointment [of Sir Samuel Hoare reappointed as Minister of Air in 1940] became known, an aged opponent of the administration rose from his seat, "This is where I came in," he said.'

— —, this is your life! Ralph Edwards hosted the original 1950s US TV series *This Is Your Life* in which a subject's life was told (*without* the warts and all) after he or she had been taken by surprise. The idea has since been taken up in many countries. Largely sentimental, the shows are notable for tearful reunions between the subject and long-lost relatives and friends. Edwards also hosted the first British edition when the BBC took up the idea in 1955. The first UK 'victim' to be hailed with the cry was Eamonn Andrews who went on to become the presenter of the long-running series with the BBC and then with Thames TV. He was still presenting it at his death in 1987, when Michael Aspel took over the role.

When surprised by Eamonn and his 'big Red Book', the victim heard him intone in his Irish drawl something like: 'Fred Pincushion, all-round-entertainer and mass-murderer, this is your loif!' (to which the victim all too rarely replied, 'Push off!').

this must be —. See IF IT'S —, THIS MUST BE —.

this one will run and run. Promotional cliché from *Private Eye*'s collection of phrases – this one (said of anything, but especially of a political dispute or a strike) was originally the sort of extract taken from critics' notices that theatrical managements liked to display outside their theatres to promote shows. Said originally to have derived from a review by Fergus Cashin of the *Sun*.

this play what I have wrote. See under *MORECAMBE AND WISE SHOW*.

this thing is bigger than both of us. 'This thing' = 'our love', of course. A whopping film cliché which I can hardly believe was ever uttered – at least, I am unable to give a citation. All I have examples of is the ironic use of the phrase. I am told that Milton Berle popularized it, satirically, in his American radio and TV shows in the US of the 1940s and 50s. In Britain, Frank Muir and Denis Norden did a similar job in their scripts for radio's *TAKE IT FROM HERE* (1947–58). For example, in this extract from their *Hamlet* with Hollywood subtitles: 'Oh, dear Ophelia, I have not art to reckon my groans but that I love thee best. ("DON'T FIGHT THIS THING, KID, IT'S BIGGER THAN BOTH OF US.")' In the 1976 remake of *King Kong*, with the giant ape brushing against the side of the house they are sheltering in, Jeff Bridges as Jack Prescott says to Jessica Lange as Dwan, 'He's bigger than both of us, know what I mean?'

this town ain't big enough for both/the two of us! In Western films, it might be said by the villain to the sherriff or to anyone else who is trying to bring him to book. The US/UK group Sparks had a hit with their recording of 'This Town Ain't Big Enough for Both of Us' in 1974.

this year, next year, now, never. Phrase from a children's counting-out game – like 'Tinker, tailor, soldier, sailor . . .' – which enables the player to find out when something is going to happen. In E.M. Forster, *A Room With a View* (1908), a young character is doing it with plum stones.
 This Year, Next Year was the title of a TV drama series (ITV, 1977) written by John Finch.

Thomas. See *DOUBTING ~*.

thought. See FOOD FOR ~; I ~ — UNTIL I DISCOVERED —; JUST WHEN YOU ~ IT WAS SAFE . . .

thousand. See CAST OF ~S; COOL HUNDRED; DEATH OF A ~ CUTS; FACE THAT LAUNCH'D A ~ SHIPS;

thousands cheered, (as). A natural enough phrase found in newspaper reports but sometimes echoic of the title *As Thousands Cheer*, a show with words and music by Irving Berlin (New York, 1933). From the *Daily Mail* (18 December 1993): 'When Maiden returned to Southampton in 1990, the triumph was enormous. A band played Tina Turner's "You're Simply The Best" as the girls sailed into the marina and thousands cheered and wept.' From the *Mail on Sunday* (27 February 1994): '. . . So when Paul O'Callaghan laid into an impersonation of Noel Edmonds's brain, thousands cheered.'

thou shalt have no other jeans before me. See under HE WHO LOVES ME . . .

three acres and a cow. See under TEN ACRES AND A MULE.

three most useless things in the world, the. Paul Beale's version in Partridge/*Slang* has the definition: 'The Pope's balls, a nun's cunt – and a vote of thanks.' He dates this 1950. In about 1971 I recall hearing (from a well-known comic actor) the British show biz version which is 'a nun's tits, the Pope's balls, and a rave review in the *Stage* [the trade paper]'.

thrice. See NAY, NAY – ~ AGAIN NAY!

thrilling days of yesteryear. See HI-YO, SILVER!

throat. See DEEP ~.

throw in one's chips. See CASH ONE'S CHIPS.

thumb in your bum. See WITH YOUR ~ . . .

thunder, to steal another's. Meaning 'to get in first and do whatever the other wanted to make a big impression with'. The

expression is said to derive from an incident involving the dramatist John Dennis (*d* 1734). He had invented a device for making the sound of thunder in plays and had used it in an unsuccessful one of his own at the Drury Lane Theatre, London.
Subsequently, at the same theatre, he saw a performance of *Macbeth* and noted that the thunder was being produced in his special way. He remarked: 'That is *my* thunder, by God; the villains will play my thunder, but not my play.'

Thunderer, the. Sobriquet of *The Times* newspaper. It was known as such from the 1830s onwards, because of its magisterial leading articles. The assistant editor, Edward Sterling (*d* 1847) said on one occasion: 'We thundered forth the other day in an article on the subject of social and political reform.'

thunderstorm. See DYING DUCK IN A ∼.

thus. See 'TWAS EVER ∼.

thus far shalt thou go and no further. Limit-setting phrase. Charles Stewart Parnell, the champion of Irish Home Rule, said in Cork in 1885: 'No man has a right to fix the boundary of the march of a nation; no man has a right to say to his country, Thus far shalt thou go and no further.' On the other hand, George Farquhar, the (Irish-born) playwright has this in *The Beaux' Stratagem* (III.ii; 1707): 'And thus far I am a captain, and no farther.' And then again, the Book of Job 38:11 has: 'Hitherto shalt thou come, but no further: and here shall thy proud waves be stayed.'

tich. See LITTLE ∼.

tickled. See HOW ∼ I AM.

tidy. See KEEP BRITAIN ∼.

tie. See OLD SCHOOL ∼.

tiger. See PUT A ∼ IN YOUR TANK.

tight. See PISSED AS A NEWT.

till death us do part. A phrase from the marriage service in the Prayer Book –

originally it was 'till death us depart' i.e. 'separate completely'. *Till Death Us Do Part* was the title of a BBC TV comedy series (1964–74), a sequel to which (1985) was called *In Sickness and In Health*. *Till Death* was remade in the US as *All In the Family*. Other films with titles from the marriage service include *For Better For Worse* (UK, 1954) and *To Have and To Hold* (UK, 1963).

till the cows come home. i.e. for a very long time. Recorded by 1610. Probably makes more sense when 'till the cows come home *unbidden*' is understood. One might say, 'We could end up waiting here till the cows come home' or, like Groucho Marx in *Duck Soup* (1933), say to a woman: 'I could dance with you till the cows come home. On second thoughts I'd rather dance with the cows till you come home.'

tilt at windmills, to. Meaning 'to try and overcome imaginary obstacles', from Don Quixote's belief in the novel (1605–15) by Cervantes that windmills were giants and needed to be fought. Compare THEY MIGHT BE GIANTS.

timber-r-r! A sawyer's traditional cry of warning during tree-felling, recorded in Canada by 1912. However, from the *New York Times* (30 March 1992): 'Loggers don't say "timmmmmmber", when a 200-foot Douglas fir comes crashing down . . . They never did, as far as anyone on the Olympic Peninsula [Washington State] can remember.'

time. See ANY ∼ . . . ; AT THIS MOMENT IN ∼; DOESN'T ∼ FLY WHEN . . . ; GOOD ∼ WAS HAD BY ALL; MANY, MANY ∼s under *ROUND THE HORNE*; ONCE UPON A ∼; ONLY ∼ WILL TELL.

Time And Relative Dimension In Space. See TARDIS.

'time for bed,' said Zebedee. Stock phrase from *Magic Roundabout*, the English version of a French series using stop-action puppets, on BBC TV 1965–77. The English commentary was written and spoken by Eric Thompson.

time has passed by —. Cliché of travel advertising and film travelogues. Memorably completed in the commentary to Muir and Norden's sketch 'Balham, Gateway to the South' (1949): 'Time has passed by this remote corner. So shall we.'

time is of the essence. Getting this thing done (or started) soon is of the utmost importance. Proverbial expression, not recorded before 1931.

time marches on. 'Time . . . Marches On' was a line used in – and to promote – the 'March of Time' news-documentary-dramas which ran on American radio for 14 years from 1931. The programmes were sponsored by *Time* magazine. I'm not sure to what extent the phrase existed before then as a way of saying, 'It's getting on, time is moving forward, time flies . . .' The phrase 'march of time' itself was known by 1833.

Times, The. See TOP PEOPLE TAKE ~.

time . . . the place . . . , the. The title of an itinerant British ITV audience debate series (from 1987) was *The Time, The Place*. It probably originated in the staccato narratives of 1940s/50s US (crime) fiction: 'The year, 1934; the place, Fresno, California . . .' In 1961, Bernard Braden was fronting a British TV show called *The Time, The Place and the Camera*. By *c* 1966, a British TV ad for Players Weights Tipped cigarettes was saying: 'The time . . . the pace [*sic*] . . . the cigarette.' A 1977 biography of Rita Hayworth by John Kobal was entitled *The Time, The Place and the Woman* (which would seem to link to COMETH THE HOUR, COMETH THE MAN).

time to re-tire. Slogan for Fisk Rubber Co. tyres, in the US from 1907. Burr Griffin did the original sketch for this long-running pun of an ad which showed a yawning youngster with candle, nightshirt – and tyre. The original slogan was, 'When it's time to re-tire, buy a Fisk'.

time to spare? go by air. Saying, perhaps dating from the days when air travel was subject to lengthier delays than it is now and suited the more leisurely traveller. Quoted in 1989.

TINA. See THERE IS NO ALTERNATIVE.

tin hat. See PUT THE ~ ON.

tinker's cuss/damn, not worth a. (or simply **a tinker's.**) The simplest explanation is that because tinkers swore so much, one of their cusses would not be worth very much. Or, because tinkers were not exactly oustanding figures, to be damned by one would not bother you. However, there was a thing called a tinker's 'dam' – a piece of bread used to plug a leak in a pot until solder had been poured in. This was not worth anything and was useless afterwards. Given the existence of the 'cuss' version, I think the expression must involve the idea of swearing and I would thus discount the second.

Emanuel Shinwell, the British Labour politician, said at an ETU Conference, Margate (7 May 1947): 'We know that you, the organised workers of the country, are our friends . . . As for the rest, they do not matter a tinker's curse.'

Tin Lizzie. Nickname of Henry Ford's Model T motor-car, the first mass-produced vehicle, inelegant but efficient and comparatively cheap. Fifteen million were produced between 1908 and discontinuation of the model in 1927. Ford is said to have encouraged jokes about them for the sake of publicity as they rattled around the world. 'Lizzie' may be a contraction of 'limousine' or be from the name applied to a domestic servant. The term 'Lady Lizzie' was used about the car in a 1913 advertisement. 'Tin Lizzie' was known by 1915, the 'tin' probably referring to the fact it was produced for the masses.

The Irish pop group Thin Lizzy (which, being Irish, pronounced itself 'Tin Lizzy') flourished 1973–83.

Tin Pan Alley. The name given, by 1908, to the area in Manhattan where most music publishers worked – because the noise of countless pianos being tinkled must have sounded like tin pans being bashed. A 'tin pan' was also (*c* 1900) the name given to a cheap tinny piano. In London, the equivalent area around Denmark Street, off the Charing Cross Road, was so known by 1934.

tin-pot dictator, a. 'Tin-pot' as a dismissive adjectival phrase referring to the cheap quality or noise of something has been around since the 1830s. The *Daily News* (23 March 1897) used the phrase 'tin-pot politicians'. The inevitable linkage to dictators probably has more to do with the repetition sound of the 't' sound.

tiny. See OUT OF YOUR ∼ CHINESE MIND.

tip of the iceberg, it is the. An indication that a greater and more significant amount of something remains hidden. Based on the well-known fact that only one-ninth of an iceberg projects above the water level. A relatively modern expression, recorded by 1969. From the *Independent* (16 July 1990): 'It will deepen the hole that the Government is in, because it makes it look as though Ridley's outburst was the tip of the iceberg. People are now aware it was not just a rash outburst by one Cabinet eccentric, but reflected deep prejudice within the Cabinet.'

tired. See SICK AND ∼.

tired and emotional, to be. Meaning 'drunk'. A pleasant euphemism, ideally suited to British newspapers which have to operate under libel laws effectively preventing any direct statement of a person's fondness for the bottle. The expression 't. and e.' (to which it is sometimes abbreviated) is said to have arisen when *Private Eye* printed a spoof Foreign Office memo suggesting it was a useful way of describing the antics of George Brown when he was Foreign Secretary (1966–8). An *Eye* cover showed him gesticulating while Harold Wilson explained to General de Gaulle: '*George est un peu fatigué, votre Majesté.*' Ironically, there was never any question that Brown *did* get drunk. Peter Paterson entitled his biography of Brown, *Tired and Emotional* (1993).

I am not convinced that *Private Eye* actually coined the phrase, though it undoubtedly popularized it. It has been suggested that a BBC spokesman said of Brown 'He was very tired and emotional' after the much-criticized appearance he made on TV on the night of President Kennedy's death in November 1963. In fact, it was ITV Brown appeared on and I cannot trace the remark, even if it was made.

tired, depressed, irritable?, are you. A seemingly standard ingredient in headache advertising, in both the UK and US by the 1960s, but hard to pin on a particular brand. 'Headache? **Tense, nervous headache?** Take Anadin' has been known in the UK. The question format is common in the US, too, as this graffito (1974) suggests: 'Are you nervous, tense? Try my 8–inch relaxer'. In MONTY PYTHON'S FLYING CIRCUS (28 December 1969), an undertaker says: 'Are you nervy, irritable, depressed, tired of life? Keep it up.'

tiswas, all of a. Meaning 'confused, in a state'. Known by 1960, this might be from an elaboration of 'tizz' or 'tizzy' and I suspect there is a hint of 'dizziness' trying to get in somewhere. But no one really knows. The acronym 'Today Is Saturday, Wear A Smile' seems not to have anything to do with the meaning of the word and to have been imposed later. The acronym-slogan was the apparent reason for the title *Tiswas* being given to a children's ITV show of the 1970s, famous for its bucket-of-water-throwing and general air of mayhem. Broadcast on Saturday mornings, its atmosphere was certainly noisy and confused.

tit. See I HAVEN'T BEEN SO HAPPY SINCE . . . ; MANNERS PLEASE, ∼ S FIRST; TELL ∼ TALE ∼ S.

titter ye not! See NAY, NAY ∼ THRICE AGAIN NAY!

tittle. See JOT AND ∼.

tit, tote and television. In the days when newspapers were still produced in Fleet Street, tabloid hacks would remind themselves that the chief preoccupations were encapsulated in this phrase (though I did not hear it myself until 1984).

An alternative recipe that I heard a year later is: 'Bosoms, QPR [Queen's Park Rangers football team] and "WHERE ARE THEY NOW?"'

In 1978, Derek Jameson, then editor-in-chief of Express Newspapers (though he denied saying it) was quoted as remarking of the launch of the *Daily Star*: 'It'll be all tits, bums, QPR and roll your own fags.'

TLC. See TENDER LOVING CARE.

toaster. See FEW VOUCHERS SHORT OF A POP-UP ~ .

to coin a phrase. Meaning to invent a phrase or to give it 'currency', and known by 1840. But, in the twentieth century, people have also started saying the whole phrase as an ironic way of excusing a cliché or banal statement they have just uttered.

tod. See ON ONE'S ~ .

today. See HERE ~ , GONE TOMORROW; I DIDN'T GET WHERE I AM ~ ; WHAT — THINKS ~ . . .

today is the first day of the rest of your life. Attributed to one Charles Dederich, founder of anti-heroin centres in the US, in *c* 1969, this may also have occurred in the form '*tomorrow* is the first etc' as a wall slogan.

'Today Is the First Day of the Rest of My Life' was apparently sung in a late 1960s musical *The Love Match* (by Maltby & Shire).

today —, tomorrow —. A foreign-language slogan occasionally impinges upon English speech. Such a construction capable of innumerable variations is 'today —, tomorrow the world!'

The concept can be glimpsed in embryo in the slogan for the National Socialist Press in Germany of the early 1930s: '*Heute Presse der Nationalsozialisten, Morgen Presse der Nation*' [Today the press of the Nazis, tomorrow the nation's press]. This reaches its final form in '*Heute gehört uns Deutschland – morgen die ganze Welt*' [Today Germany belongs to us – tomorrow the whole world]. Although John Colville in *The Fringes of Power* states that by 3 September 1939, Hitler 'had already . . . proclaimed that "Today Germany is ours; tomorrow the whole world" ', I have not found an example of Hitler actually saying it. However, in *Mein Kampf* (1925) he had

earlier said: 'If the German people, in their historic development, had possessed tribal unity like other nations, the German Reich today would be the master of the entire world.'

The phrase seems to have come from the chorus of a song in the Hitler Youth 'songbook'. It has the title '*Es zittern die morschen Knochen*' and was written by Hans Baumann in 1932:

> *Wir werden weiter marschieren*
> *Wenn alles in Scherben fällt*
> *Denn heute gehört uns Deutschland*
> *Und morgen die ganze Welt.*

Which may be roughly translated as:

> We shall keep marching on
> Even if everything breaks into fragments,
> For today Germany belongs to us
> And tomorrow the whole world.

Another version replaces the second line with '*Wenn Scheiße vom Himmel fällt*' [when shit from Heaven falls]. Sir David Hunt tells me he recalls hearing the song in 1933 or possibly 1934.

By the outbreak of the Second World War, the format was sufficiently well known, as John Osborne recalled in *A Better Class of Person* (1981), for an English school magazine to be declaring: 'Now soon it will be our turn to take a hand in the destinies of Empire. Today, scholars; tomorrow, the Empire.' In the 1941 British film *Forty-Ninth Parallel*, Eric Portman as a German U-boat commander gets to say, 'Today, Europe . . . tomorrow the whole world!'

So common is the construction now that a New York graffito (reported in 1974) stated: 'Today Hollywood, tomorrow the world', and one from El Salvador (March 1982) ran: '*Ayer Nicaragua, hoy El Salvador, mañana Guatemala!*' [Yesterday Nicaragua, today El Salvador, tomorrow Guatemala!] The *Guardian* (6 July 1982) carried an advertisement with the unwieldy headline: 'Self-managing Socialism: Today, France – Tomorrow, the World?'

A variation: from the black MP Paul Boateng's victory speech in the Brent South constituency (June 1987): 'Brent South today – Soweto tomorrow!' See also, for a 1932 example, LIFE BEGINS AT FORTY.

toil. See HORNY-HANDED SONS OF ~.

Tokyo Rose. See LORD HAW-HAW.

told. See I THINK WE SHOULD BE ~.

Tom and Jerry. (1) Characters in Pierce Egan, *Life in London; or, The Day and Night Scenes of Jerry Hawthorn, Esq., and his Elegant Friend Corinthian Tom* (1821) – riotous young men about town. (2) The cat (Tom) and mouse (Jerry) featuring in many short cartoon films (US, from 1937).

Tom, Dick and Harry. Any man – or body of men – taken from the common stock (indicated by the popularity of the name). Known by 1734, though more than a century previously, Shakespeare has 'Tom, Dick and Francis' mentioned in *Henry IV, Part 1*, II.iv.8 (1597).

Tommy. See FOR YOU, ~, THE WAR IS OVER; ROCK ON, ~!

tomorrow. See AND THE NEXT *TONIGHT* WILL BE ~ NIGHT; EAT, DRINK AND BE MERRY . . . ; HERE TODAY, GONE ~; TODAY —, ~ —; WHAT — THINKS TODAY . . .

tomorrow belongs to me/us. Has this ever been used as a political slogan, either as 'tomorrow belongs to me' or 'to us'? Harold Wilson in his final broadcast before the 1964 British General Election said, 'If the past belongs to the Tories, the future belongs to us – all of us.' At a Young Conservatives rally before the 1983 General Election, Margaret Thatcher asked, 'Could Labour have organized a rally like this? In the old days perhaps, but not now. For they are the Party of Yesterday, Tomorrow is ours.'

What one can say is that in the musical *Cabaret* (1968, filmed 1972), Fred Ebb (words) and John Kander (music) wrote a convincing pastiche of a Hitler Youth song:

The babe in his cradle is closing his eyes,
   the blossom embraces the bee,
But soon says a whisper, 'Arise, arise',
   Tomorrow belongs to me.

O Fatherland, Fatherland, show us the
   sign your children have waited to see,

The morning will come when the world
   is mine, Tomorrow belongs to me.

The idea seems definitely to have been current in Nazi Germany. A popular song, '*Jawohl, mein Herr*', featured in the 1943 episode of the German film chronicle *Heimat* (1984), includes the line, 'For from today, the world belongs to us.'

The nearest the slogan appears to have come to being used is by a right-wing youth organization, referred to in this report from the *Guardian* (30 October 1987): 'Contra leader Adolfo Calero . . . was entertained to dinner on Wednesday by Oxford University's Freedom Society, a clutch of hoorays . . . A coach-load of diners . . . got "hog-whimpering" drunk . . . and songs like "Tomorrow Belongs To Us" and "Miner, Cross that Picket Line" were sung on the return coach trip.'

The same paper, reporting a meeting held by the SDP leader, Dr David Owen, on 1 February 1988 noted: 'Down, sit down, he eventually gestured; his eyes saying Up, stay up. It reminded you of nothing so much as a Conservative Party conference in one of its most Tomorrow-belongs-to-us moods.'

It is perhaps an obvious slogan for a young people's political organization. I have a note of something once said by Saint-Simon: 'The future belongs to us. In order to do things one must be enthusiastic.'

tomorrow is another day. The last words of the film GONE WITH THE WIND (1939), spoken by Vivien Leigh as Scarlett O'Hara, are: 'Tara! Home! I'll go home, and I'll think of some way to get him back. After all, tomorrow is another day!' The last sentence is as it appears in Margaret Mitchell's novel, but the idea behind it is proverbial. In Rastell's *Calisto & Melebea* (c 1527) there occurs the line: 'Well, mother, to morrow is a new day.'

tongue. See CAT GOT YOUR ~?; OLD AS MY ~ . . .

Toni. See WHICH TWIN HAS THE ~?

tonight. See NOT ~, JOSEPHINE; THERE'LL BE DANCING IN THE STREETS ~.

Tonight. See AND THE NEXT ~. . . .

too clever by half. To say that someone is 'too clever by half' is to indicate that you think they are more clever than wise, and are overreaching themselves. As such, this is a fairly common idiom. However, the most notable political use of the phrase was by the 5th Marquess of Salisbury (1893–1972), a prominent Conservative, about another such, Iain Macleod. In a speech to the House of Lords in 1961, he said: 'The present Colonial Secretary has been too clever by half. I believe he is a very fine bridge player. It is not considered immoral, or even bad form to outwit one's opponents at bridge. It almost seems to me as if the Colonial Secretary, when he abandoned the sphere of bridge for the sphere of politics, brought his bridge technique with him.'

The remark seems to run in the family. The 3rd Marquess had anticipated him in a debate on the Irish Church Resolutions in the House of Commons on 30 March 1868, when he said of an amendment moved by Disraeli: 'I know that with a certain number of Gentlemen on this side of the House this Amendment is popular. I have heard it spoken of as being very clever. It is clever, Sir; it is too clever by half.'

Rodney Ackland's version of an Alexander Ostrovsky play was presented as *Too Clever by Half* at the Old Vic, London, in 1988. Previously, the Russian title had been translated as *The Diary of a Scoundrel* and *Even the Wise Can Err*, *Even a Wise Man Stumbles*, and *Enough Stupidity in Every Wise Man*.

Of Dr Jonathan Miller, the polymath, in the mid-1970s, it was said, 'He's too clever by three-quarters.'

toodeloo! Parting cry. Possibly connected with 'toot', as though one were to go 'toot, toot', like a horn, on leaving. Or perhaps it has something to do with 'toddling off' or 'tootling off'. Could 'I must tootle-o' have led to it?

A much better idea is that the word derives from the French *à tout à l'heure* ('see you soon').

too late! too late! the Captain cried, and shook his wooden leg. A fairly meaningless exclamation when some oportunity has been missed. T.A. Dyer noted (1994) that his father used to say (in the 1940s): ' "It's come too late!" the lady cried, as she waved her wooden leg – and passed out.' Mieder and Kingsbury's *A Dictionary of Wellerisms* (1994) gives two anonymous American citations of the form: ' "Aha!" she cried, as she waved her wooden leg and died' (1966) and ' "Hurrah!" as the old maid shouted waving her wooden leg' (1950).

Compare what Partridge/*Catch Phrases* calls originally a military catchphrase – 'Too late! too late!' spoken in a high falsetto, after the story of 'that luckless fellow who lost his manhood in a shark-infested sea very soon after he had summoned help'.

too little, too late. The American Professor Allan Nevins wrote in an article in *Current History* (May 1935): 'The former allies had blundered in the past by offering Germany too little and offering even that too late, until finally Nazi Germany had become a menace to all mankind.' That was where the phrase began. On 13 March 1940, the former Prime Minister David Lloyd George said in the House of Commons: 'It is the old trouble – too late. Too late with Czechoslovakia, too late with Poland, certainly too late with Finland. It is always too late, or too little, or both.'

From there the phrase passed into more general use, though usually political. From the *Notting Hill & Paddington Recorder* (25 January 1989): 'Junior Transport Minister, Peter Bottomley, came to West London last week to unveil plans for a £250m. relief road that will cut a swathe through the heart of the area . . . But Hammersmith and Fulham councillors are furious about the government consultation exercise which they claim is "too little too late".'

From the *Guardian* (30 January 1989): 'The Home Office is preparing a video to warn prisoners of the dangers [of AIDS] – but is it too little, too late?'

too many chiefs and not enough Indians. Phrase suggesting that in some confused situation there are too many leaders and not enough led, or that there are too many people giving orders and instructions but not enough people to carry them out. An alternative title of the film *Who Is Killing the Great Chefs of Europe?* (US/West Germany, 1978) was *Too Many Chefs* – which also neatly alludes to the proverb 'too many cooks spoil the broth'.

tooth. See FINE- ∼ COMB; LONG IN THE ∼.

top. See AND THAT'S THE ∼ OF THE NEWS . . . ; OVER THE ∼.

top hole! Excellent. Probably referring to holes or notches cut in a board to record the points scored in some games. The top hole represents the highest, best score. Known by 1899.

top people take *The Times*. In the mid-1950s, *The Times* was shedding circulation, the end of post-war newsprint rationing was in sight, and an era of renewed competition in Fleet Street was about to begin. In 1954, the paper's agency, the London Press Exchange, commissioned a survey to discover people's attitudes to 'The THUNDERER'. They chiefly found it dull, but the management was not going to change anything, least of all allow contributors to be identified by name. The paper would have to be promoted for what it was. A pilot campaign in provincial newspapers included one ad showing a top hat and pair of gloves with the slogan 'Men who make opinion read *The Times*'.

It was not the London Press Exchange but an outsider who finally encapsulated that superior view in a memorable way. G.H. Saxon Mills was one of the old school of advertising copywriters. But he was out of a job when he bumped into Stanley Morison of *The Times*. As a favour, Mills was asked to produce a brochure for visitors to the paper's offices. When finished, it contained a series of people who were supposed to read the paper – a barrister, a trade-union official and so on. Each was supported by the phrase, 'Top People take *The Times*'.

The idea was adopted for a more public promotional campaign and first appeared on posters during 1957, running into immediate criticism of its snob-appeal. But sales went up and, however toe-curling it may have been, the slogan won attention

for the paper and was allowed to run on into the early 1960s.

torch song, a. A love song (uually performed by a woman) which tells of unrequited love or an affair that has ended. Presumably, it comes from the expression 'to carry a torch for someone', meaning to express unreciprocated admiration or love – the torch representing the flame of love. American origin by 1927. The film *Torch Singer* was released in 1933 and was about an unwed mother who sang in nightclubs. *Torch Song Trilogy* was the title of a play by Harvey Fierstein (1982; film US, 1988).

Tory. See SALOON-BAR ∼; THIRTEEN YEARS OF ∼ MISRULE.

Tory Party at prayer, the. A description of the Church of England often attributed to Benjamin Disraeli. However, Robert Blake, the historian and author of *Disraeli* (1966) told the *Observer* (14 April 1985) that he could not say who had said it first, and that a correspondence in *The Times* some years before had failed to find an answer. Agnes Maude Royden, the social reformer and preacher, said in an address at the City Temple, London (1917): 'The Church should no longer be satisfied to represent only the Conservative Party at prayer' – but this sounds rather as though it is alluding to an already-established saying.

tosh. See under DON'T FORCE IT, PHOEBE.

tote. See TIT, ∼ AND TELEVISION.

Toto, I have a feeling we're not in Kansas any more! A line from the film *The Wizard of Oz* (1939) rather than from Frank L. Baum's original book, but one that has achieved catchphrase status. Judy Garland as Dorothy says it on arrival in the Land of Oz, concluding, 'We must be over the rainbow.' It is used when speakers want to express bewilderment at whatever new circumstances they find themselves in.

touch. See BARGE POLE, NOT TO ∼ . . .; NELSON ∼.

touch of hello folks and what about the workers, a. See under *BAND WAGGON*; WHAT ABOUT THE WORKERS?

touch of the —, a. See under DODGY!

touchpaper. See LIGHT THE BLUE ∼ . . . under *BAND WAGGON*.

touch someone/thing with a bargepole, not to. See BARGEPOLE.

tough. See WHEN THE GOING GETS ∼ . . .

tour. See COOK'S ∼; MAGICAL MYSTERY ∼ .

town. See THIS ∼ AIN'T BIG ENOUGH . . .

toy! toy! Theatrical good-luck wish, of obscure origin. Before the opening of his production of *Don Giovanni* at the English National Opera in 1985, Jonathan Miller explained that 'the cry is age-old, either from kissing or spitting, no one seems really sure'. See also BREAK A LEG!

trade. See AS WE SAY IN THE ∼; ROUGH OLD ∼ .

train(s). See AGE OF THE ∼ under WE'RE GETTING THERE; GRAVY ∼ . . .

train, put it on the. See under LET'S — AND SEE IF —.

transfer. See MANHATTAN ∼ .

trapeze. See DARING YOUNG MAN ON THE FLYING ∼ .

travel. See HAVE GUN WILL ∼ .

treacle. SOMEBODY PINCHED ME PUDDING.

tree(s). See BARK UP THE WRONG ∼; HELLO BIRDS, HELLO ∼ . . .

tree fell on him, a. Stock phrase from one of Spike Milligan's *Q* comedy series on BBC TV, in the early 1980s. For example: 'Q. Are you Jewish?' 'A. No, a tree fell on me.'

trendy. See LAST CHANCE ∼ .

trick. See HAT-∼; IT'S JUST A ∼ OF THE LIGHT under *ROUND THE HORNE*.

trick or treat? One of the least welcome imports to Britain from the US in recent years has been the Hallowe'en custom of children, suitably dressed up, knocking on the doors of complete strangers and demanding a 'trick or treat' – i.e. that the houseowners should hand over some small present (sweets, money) or have a trick played on them (a message written on the front door in shaving foam, for example). Fairly harmless in essence, the practice soon led to horror stories reaching the UK of children playing 'tricks' which did real damage and of their being given poisoned sweets as 'treats'.

The American origins of the custom seem somewhat obscure (*OED2* does not find the phrase before 1947). In the North of England, the traditional Mischief Night may have given rise to the same sort of demands, and may also have given rise to the jingle ending:

> If you haven't got a penny, a ha'penny will do,
> If you haven't got a ha'penny, your door's going through

– though, on the other hand, that appears to be a version of 'Christmas is coming'. In January 1989, a British ITV quiz show was launched called *Trick or Treat* which aimed to do one or the other to its contestants. *Trick or Treats* (US, 1992) was a low-budget horror picture.

tricky Dick(y). Nickname of Richard Milhous Nixon (1913–94), US President (1969–74), who resigned after the Watergate scandal. So dubbed at the start of his career by Helen Gahagan Douglas in 1950. During an election campaign in California he had hinted that she was a fellow traveller. Despite his many later achievements, the nickname was generally adopted to indicate Nixon's art of political manipulation and evasion.

trip. See CLUNK, CLICK, EVERY ∼ .

Trivial Pursuit. There had been a quiz game called 'Trivia' in the 1960s, but this was the title under which a hugely successful board game, using trivia questions, was launched from Canada in 1979. It reached its worldwide peak c 1985. Quite why it was given this name is a mystery, as describing something as a 'trivial pursuit' was hardly an established figure of speech.

trolley. See OFF ONE'S ~.

Trollope. See IN BED WITH ONE'S FAVOURITE ~.

troops. See THAT'S THE STUFF TO GIVE THE ~.

trouble at t'mill. A key phrase supposedly taken from English North Country dramas (especially set in the nineteenth century) but best known as a humorous allusion to the kind of line thought to be uttered in same. It might be used now by someone who is departing to sort out some problem but does not wish to spell it out what it is.

Allusively, the phrase was known by 1962. An actual example, though not as it happens from a North Country novel, can be found in *John Halifax, Gentlemen*, Chap. 26 (1856) by Dinah Maria Mulock: ' "Unless you will consent to let me go alone to Enderley!" She shook her head. "What, with those troubles at the mills?" '

troubles. See ELEPHANT IN YOUR . . .

trowel. See LAY IT ON WITH A ~.

truckin'. See KEEP ON ~.

true. See ALWAYS ~ TO YOU IN MY FASHION; STRANGE BUT ~.

true, O king! When I have made an obvious statement, perhaps even a pompous one, my wife has a way of saying to me, 'True, O King!' I wondered where she had picked up this habit until one day I happened to see an old film of Charles Laughton indulging in a public reading from the Bible, as he was latterly wont to do. He was telling the story of Nebuchadnezzar and the gentlemen who were cast into the burning fiery furnace (Daniel 3:24). 'Did not we cast three men bound into the midst of fire?'

Nebuchadnezzar asks. 'They answered and said unto the king, True, O king.'

The nearest Shakespeare gets is the ironical ' "True"? O God!' in *Much Ado About Nothing*, IV.i.68 (1598), though he has any number of near misses like 'true, my liege', 'too true, my lord' and 'true, noble prince'.

Just to show that my wife is not alone – Mrs H. Joan Langdale of Tunbridge Wells wrote to me in June 1988 to say, 'My father, a Classical Scholar and an Anglican priest, used to use my wife's quotation "True, O King!" and always added, "Live for ever." ' In the published *Diaries* of Kenneth Williams (entry for 5 January 1971), the comedian recounts being told by an Irishman that he was a bore on TV: 'I smiled acquiescence and said "How true, O King!" '

trumpet. See BLOW ONE'S OWN ~; MAN WITH THE GOLDEN . . .

trumpeter. See YOUR ~'S DEAD.

trust. See IN GOD WE ~.

truth. See ECONOMICAL WITH THE ~; ~, JUSTICE AND THE AMERICAN WAY under *SUPERMAN*; MOMENT OF ~ ; NOTHING BUT THE ~ under I SWEAR BY ALMIGHTY GOD . . .

try. See I'LL ~ ANYTHING ONCE.

try a little VC 10derness. See under BOAC TAKES GOOD CARE OF YOU.

try it – you'll like it! A slogan for Alka-Seltzer in the US in 1971 'was used by every comic, every mother, and certainly every waiter for the entire year of the campaign', according to the agency that wrote it. A year later, another line on the 'morning-after' theme of the agonies of overindulgence was **I can't believe I ate the whole thing.**

try to get some sleep now. See under LET'S GET OUTTA HERE!

T-shirt. See under BEEN THERE, DONE THAT . . .

TTFN. See under *ITMA*.

tuba mirum (spargens sonum). See MASS PHRASES.

tubes, to go down the. To be lost, finished, in trouble. An Americanism equivalent to the British 'to go down the drain', where tube = drain. First recorded in the US in the early 1960s.

Tuesday. See BLACK.

Tull. See JETHRO ~.

Tunbridge Wells. See DISGUSTED, ~.

tune. See under DO YOU KNOW . . . ?; TURN ON, ~ IN . . . ; THEY'RE PLAYING OUR ~.

tunnel. See LIGHT AT THE END OF THE ~.

turbulent priest. See BECKET . . .

tuppence coloured. See PENNY PLAIN . . .

turbulent priest. See under BECKET, TO DO A THOMAS A.

turn. See BUGGINS'S ~.

turned out nice again. See IT'S ~.

turning a tanker round, like. This phrase may be used to describe any slow, difficult task. 'Clive Leach, managing director, said that reversing the trend on [TV] advertising was rather like "turning a tanker round" ' (*Independent*, 24 May 1990). Similarly, in 1988, Dr Billy Graham was quoted as saying of the difficulty of converting China to Christianity: 'I think what Winston Churchill or somebody like that said is true: "You can't turn the Queen Mary on a dime." '

turning point, a. Meaning 'a key moment in a person's career, a crisis', this phrase seems to have arisen in religious writings. *OED2*'s earliest citation is from John Keble in 1836. On the other hand, Rev. Francis Kilvert, the English diarist (entry for 19 May 1873), found it as the title of a painting which impressed him at a Royal Academy exhibition: 'The beautiful face and eyes of the wife looking up to her husband's stern sullen countenance as she leans on his breast, beseeching him, pleading with him, oh so earnestly and imploringly, to give up drinking.' *The Turning Point* has been the title of two unrelated films (US 1952, 1977) though the latter is about ballet (so a pun of sorts).

turn on, tune in, drop out. 'Tune in to my values, reject those of your parents, turn on [drug] yourself; deal with your problems and those of society by running away from them' – this was the meaning of the hippie philosophy as encapsulated in a slogan by one of the movement's gurus, Dr Timothy Leary (*b* 1920). It was used as the title of a lecture by him in 1967, and the theme was explored further in his book *The Politics of Ecstasy*. I believe that more recently Leary has taken to attributing the origin of the phrase to Marshall McLuhan.

A joke variant of what was also known as 'the LSD motto', was: 'Turn on, tune in, drop dead'.

turn/roll over in one's grave, to. Meaning '[for a dead person] to demonstrate horror at what has just happened or been proposed by someone living'. Mencken has, 'It is enough to make — turn over in his grave' as an 'English saying, not recorded before the nineteenth century'. William Thackeray has: ' "Enough to make poor Mr Pendennis turn in his grave," said Mrs Wapshot' (*Pendennis*, Chap.16, 1848). In about 1976, one of the idiocies attributed to President Gerald Ford was: 'If Abraham Lincoln was alive today, he'd be turning in his grave'.

turns. See WHATEVER ~ YOU ON.

turn up for the book(s)!, what a. i.e. what an unexpected outcome, what a surprise! The 'books' here are those kept by bookies to maintain a record of bets placed on a race. Does the bookie have to turn up the corner of a page if a race has an unexpected outcome? No, the phrase merely means that something unexpected has 'turned up'.

tutti-frutti. Meaning 'all the fruits' in Italian, this phrase was first applied early in nineteenth-century America to ice cream containing pieces of various chopped-up fruits. Then it became the name of a proprietary brand of fruit-flavoured chewing gum. More recently, it has been immortalized as the title of a rock'n'roll number written and sung by Little Richard (from 1957). Alas, the lyrics are impenetrable and almost certainly have nothing to do with ice cream or chewing gum.

TV. See AS SEEN ON ~.

Twain, Mark. The pen-name of Samuel Langhorne Clemens (1835–1910), which comes from the cry 'mark twain' meaning 'two fathoms deep' used when taking soundings on the Mississippi steamboats.

'twas ever thus. An exclamation meaning almost the same as the more modern **so what's new?** and used nowadays as a self-conscious anachronism. It does not occur in Shakespeare or the Bible. In fact, the only examples I have turned up so far are: as the first line of 'Disaster' by C.S. Calverley (d 1884): ''Twas ever thus from childhood's hour!' (a parody of lines from Thomas Moore's 'The Fire Worshippers' in *Lalla Rookh* (1817): 'Oh! ever thus from childhood's hour!'); and, as the title, ''Twas Ever Thus' given to the parody of the same poem by Henry S. Leigh (1837–83). His version begins, 'I never rear'd a young gazelle.'

Twelfth. See GLORIOUS ~.

twelve good men and true. 'It is a maxim of English law that legal memory begins with the accession of Richard I in 1189 . . . with the establishment of royal courts, giving the same justice all over the country, the old diversity of local law was rapidly broken down, and a law common to the whole land and to all men soon took its place . . . The truth of [witnesses'] testimony [was] weighed not by the judge but by twelve "good men and true"' (Winston Churchill, *A History of the English-Speaking Peoples*, Vol.1). Probably there were twelve members of a jury because that was the number of Christ's disciples (or the tribes of Israel, or the signs of the zodiac). The overall phrase seems to have been established by the sixteenth century. 'Are

you good men and true' occurs on its own in Shakespeare's *Much Ado About Nothing*, III.iii.1 (1598). Dogberry puts the question, and, being a constable, would naturally use legal terminology.

twelve o'clock in London. See under FAMILY FAVOURITES.

twentieth century. See DRAGGED KICKING AND SCREAMING . . .

twenty-one. See FREE, WHITE AND ~.

Twenty Questions. See under ANIMAL, VEGETABLE AND/OR MINERAL.

twenty things you didn't know about —. A much-imitated journalistic format derived from a regular *Sun* feature of the 1980s (said to have been devised by Wendy Henry) in which trivia was listed about celebrities. From the *Independent* (24 April 1989): '20 Things You Didn't Know About Mrs T.'

twice a night, you're doing all right! See under ONCE A — . . .

twilight. See CELTIC ~.

twilight of empire, the. This phrase refers to Britain at any time after the death of Queen Victoria in 1901, but particularly when its colonies started moving towards independence. In Malcolm Muggeridge's diary (21 December 1947) he calls it a 'phrase which occurred to me long ago'. One suspects it is after 'twilight of the gods' (German '*Götterdämmerung*').

twilight zone, the. The phrase had existed in the early 1900s for an 'indistinct boundary area' (like NO MAN'S LAND) but undoubtedly *The Twilight Zone*, title of a US TV series about the supernatural (1959–65), reinforced it, e.g.: 'Several key officials charged with formulating foreign policy remain in a bureaucratic twilight zone one HUNDRED DAYS after Reagan's inauguration' (*Washington Post*, 26 April 1981).

twin. See WHICH ~ HAS THE TONI?

twins. See HEAVENLY ~; HELLO, ~!

Twinkletoes. See HELLO, IT'S ME, T. under
EDUCATING ARCHIE.

Twin Peaks. Title of a seriously weird TV
series (1990) directed by David Lynch (see
DAMN FINE CUP OF COFFEE . . .). The phrase
has a certain resonance. From the *Financial
Times* (1 February 1982): 'One of Mozart's
great masses is usually enough for a choir to
tackle in a single concert. But on Friday
John Eliot Gardiner and the Monteverdi
Choir and Orchestra paired the C minor
mass K427 with the Requiem K626,
traversing the twin peaks of Mozart's
church music in a single effort.' From *Today*
(26 April 1990): 'Undies that bring you out
on top . . . she warned that the 'twin peaks'
bust that accompanied the fuller figure of
the Fifties and Sixties is definitely out. Its
place will be taken by a more natural look
that completes the circle as we go back to
the future.' Tennyson wrote of 'Twin peaks
shadow'd with pine' in his poem 'Leonine
Elegiacs' (1830).

**twist slowly, slowly in the wind, (to
allow someone to).** From the *Guardian*
(28 January 1989): 'The foreign press
observed with admiration the way President
Bush stressed in words that he was not
ditching the beleaguered Mikhail
Gorbachev by playing his China card,
while making it clear he was doing exactly
that, and leaving the Soviet leader to twist a
little longer in the wind.'
Richard Nixon's henchmen may have
acted wrongly and, for much of the time,
spoken sleazily. Occasionally, however,
they minted political phrases that have
lingered on. John D. Ehrlichman (*b* 1925),
Nixon's Assistant for Domestic Affairs until
he was forced to resign over Watergate in
1973, came up with one saying that caught
people's imagination. In a telephone
conversation with John Dean (Counsel to
the President) on 7/8 March 1973 he was
speaking about Patrick Gray (Acting
Director of the FBI). Gray's nomination to
take over the FBI post had been withdrawn
by Nixon during Judiciary Committee
hearings – though Gray had not been told

of this. Ehrlichman said: 'I think we ought
to let him hang there. Let him twist slowly,
slowly in the wind.'

Twitcher. See JEMMY ~ .

two. See IT TAKES ~ TO TANGO.

**two countries separated by a common
language.** See under COUNTRIES . . .

two c(unt)s in a kitchen. (also **2CK**.)
British advertising expression for the type of
advert in which a female houseperson,
usually situated in a kitchen, reveals to her
female friend the magical properties of some
new product. Introduced to a wider
audience on the BBC TV *Washes Whiter*
series (April 1990).

2–4–6–8, who do we appreciate?/—!
This widely used chant was popularized on
the BBC radio GOON SHOW. In *c* 1954, for
example, members of the 'Wallace
Greenslade Fan Club' [he was one of the
show's announcers] had to cry: '2–4–6–8,
who do we appreciate? GREENSLADE!'
Compare, '2–4–6–8, gay is just as good as
straight, 3–5–7–9, lesbians are mighty fine'
– a chant of the Gay Liberation Front in the
1970s. Also '2–4–6–8, Motorway', the title
of a song recorded by the British Tom
Robinson Band in 1977.

twopence coloured. See PENNY PLAIN . . .

two-six, to do a. To do something speedily
and promptly. From British servicemen's
slang, especially in the RAF, and common
from the 1940s. As to why the numbers two
and six are mentioned, heaven knows,
though there could be an echo of 'do quick'
in it. Compare, however, 'one-two, one-
two', which a military person might bark
with same intention.

two-way family favourite. See under
FAMILY FAVOURITES.

TW3. See THAT WAS THE — THAT
WAS.

· U ·

UB40. The name of this British pop group (*fl.* 1980) derives from the number of the government form to be filled in by persons seeking *U*nemployment *B*enefit.

Ugandan. See DISCUSS ∼ AFFAIRS.

ugly. See SEX REARS ITS ∼ HEAD.

ullo, ullo, ullo. See under TAKE IT FROM HERE.

ultra. See NE PLUS ∼.

unacceptable face of —, the. In 1973, it was revealed that a former Tory Cabinet minister, Duncan Sandys, had been paid £130,000 in compensation for giving up his £50,000 a year consultancy with the Lonrho company. The money was to be paid, quite legally, into an account in the Cayman Islands to avoid British tax. This kind of activity did not seem appropriate when the Government was promoting a counter-inflation policy. Replying to a question from Jo Grimond MP in the House of Commons on 15 May, Edward Heath, the Prime Minister, created a format phrase which has since been used to describe almost anything. He said, 'It is the unpleasant and unacceptable face of capitalism, but one should not suggest that the whole of British industry consists of practices of this kind.' (In the text from which he spoke, it apparently had 'facet'.)

unaccustomed as I am to public speaking. On 26 July 1897, Winston Churchill made his first political speech at a Primrose League gathering near Bath: 'If it were pardonable in any speaker to begin with the well worn and time honoured apology, "Unaccustomed as I am to public speaking," it would be pardonable in my case, for the honour I am enjoying at this moment of addressing an audience of my fellow countrymen and women is the first honour of the kind I have ever received.'

It is somehow reassuring that even an orator of future greatness should have fallen back on the speechmaker's dreadful cliché to begin his first effort. From William Thackeray, *Pendennis*, Chap. 71 (1848–50): 'I'd like to read a speech of yours in the *Times* before I go – "Mr Pendennis said: Unaccustomed as I am to public speaking" – hey, sir?' In 1856, as Lord Dufferin explains in Letter VI of his *Letters from High Latitudes* (1857), he addressed a group of Icelanders in Latin: ' "Viri illustres," I began, "insolitis ut sum ad publicum loquendum." '

Opening a Red Cross bazaar at Oxford, Noël Coward once began: 'Desperately *accustomed* as I am to public speaking . . .'

uncle/UNCLE. See BOB'S YOUR ∼; MAN FROM ∼; I'M A MONKEY'S ∼.

Uncle Sam. The personification of the United States and known as such since 1813. It is no coincidence that Uncle Sam's initials are the same as those of the US. Flexner (1976) precisely locates the origin with Samuel Wilson, an inspecting superintendent at Troy on Hudson, New York, during the War of 1812. He was known as 'Uncle Sam' but the initials of his nickname were jokingly interpreted as standing for 'United States'. Uncle Sam did not appear visually – with his goatee beard, top hat and red, white and blue striped suit – until 1868. Compare JOHN BULL.

unconditional surrender. In almost every conflict a time arrives when one of the combatants decides that it will not be enough for the other side to stop fighting, there will have to be 'unconditional surrender':

(1) In the American Civil War, General Ulysses S. Grant sent a message to General Simon B. Buckner at Fort Donelson on

16 February 1862: 'No terms except an unconditional and immediate surrender can be accepted. I propose to move immediately upon your works.' (The capture of Fort Donelson was the first major Union victory.) One of Grant's nicknames became 'Unconditional Surrender', matching his initials, US.

(2) Prior to the Armistice in the First World War, the US General Pershing, in defiance of President Wilson, proposed to fight on until the Germans agreed to 'unconditional surrender'.

(3) In the 1926 General Strike, Winston Churchill, as Chancellor of the Exchequer, brought out an official government newspaper, the *British Gazette*, in which he denounced British working men as 'the enemy' and demanded 'unconditional surrender'.

(4) At the Casablanca conference of January 1943, President F.D. Roosevelt produced his terms for ending the Second World War, including the 'unconditional surrender' of Germany and Italy, a phrase he had used to his military advisers before leaving Washington and which was endorsed by Churchill (though the British would have preferred to exclude Italy). It was a controversial policy and later blamed for prolonging the war. According to Churchill's own account in Vol. 4 of *The Second World War*, Roosevelt admitted he had consciously been echoing U.S. Grant, though the phrase had been used even before Grant in both the US and UK.

under. See UP AND ∼; KEEP IT ∼ YOUR HAT.

underachiever and proud of it. See under *SIMPSONS, THE.*

under a gooseberry bush. See CABBAGE PATCH KIDS.

underbelly. See SOFT ∼.

underclothes. See ALL OVER THE PLACE LIKE . . .

underestimate. See NEVER ∼ THE POWER OF A WOMAN.

undersold. See NEVER KNOWINGLY . . .

under the sun, there is nothing new. Ecclesiastes 1:9 is, correctly, 'There is *no new thing* under the sun.' But Ecclesiastes finds almost everything 'under the sun'. Take, for example, **evil under the sun** – a phrase used as the title of Agatha Christie's thriller about murder in a holiday hotel (1941; film UK, 1982). Its origin is not explained in the text, though Hercule Poirot, the detective, remarks before any evil has been committed: 'The sun shines. The sea is blue . . . but there is evil everywhere under the sun.' Shortly afterwards, another character remarks: 'I was interested, M. Poirot, in something you said just now . . . It was almost a quotation from Ecclesiastes . . . "Yea, also the heart of the sons of men is full of evil, and madness is in their heart while they live."' But Ecclesiastes gets nearer than that: 'There is a sore evil which I have seen under the sun, namely, riches kept for the owners thereof to their hurt' (5:13) and: 'There is an evil which I have seen under the sun' (6:1, 10:1). Were it not for the clue about Ecclesiastes, one might be tempted to think that Christie had once more turned to an old English rhyme for one of her titles. In this one, the phrase appears exactly:

> For every evil under the sun,
> There is a remedy or there is none;
> If there be one, try and find it;
> If there be none, never mind it.

universal provider, the. See under PIN TO AN ELEPHANT.

universe. See AT ONE WITH THE ∼.

university of life. See under SCHOOL OF HARD KNOCKS.

unknown. See JOURNEY INTO THE ∼.

Unknown Soldier/Warrior, the. The 'Unknown Warrior' was buried in Westminster Abbey on Armistice Day 1920. On the tombstone, set into the floor of the Nave, is an inscription, written by Dean Ryle, concluding with the words: 'They buried him among the kings because he had done good toward God and toward his house.' This is based on 2 Chronicles 24:16 (concerning Jehoiada, a 130-year-old man): 'And they buried him in the city of David among the kings, because he had done good in Israel, both toward God, and toward his house.'

The idea of such a burial first came to a chaplain at the Front in 1916 after he had seen a grave in a back garden in Armentières, at the head of which was a rough wooden cross and the pencilled words: 'An unknown British Soldier'. The US 'Unknown Soldier' was buried on 11 November 1921 at Arlington National Cemetery and lies under the inscription: 'Here Rests in Honored Glory an American Soldier Known But to God'. Over the graves of most of the unknown dead, in Europe, had been put the simple inscription: 'A Soldier of the Great War Known unto God'.

unpleasantness. See LATE ~.

unpunished. See NO GOOD DEED GOES ~.

unturned. See LEAVE NO STONE ~.

unwashed. See GREAT ~.

unzipp a banana. Advertising slogan used by the Mather & Crowther agency in 1959 when it launched a joint promotion on behalf of the three main UK banana importers. Sometimes remembered as 'unzipp your banana', it underlies the sexual suggestiveness of the product, which no doubt explains some of its popular appeal and the humour surrounding it.

up. See ~ A BIT under BERNIE, THE BOLT!; SOMEONE ~ THERE LIKES ME.

up and down the country. See under SPIRIT OF —.

up and down the railway lines. Phrase from a monologue first recited by Jack Warner on the BBC radio programme *Monday Night at Eight* (late 1930s). It was about a wheel-tapper who won the pools and continued to refer to his old calling in a mixed Cockney and Mayfair drawl. Hence this phrase was pronounced distinctively as something like, 'Hup hand dahn the rawlaway lanes.'

up and running. See HIT THE GROUND RUNNING.

up and under. A rugby football term for a short, high kick which sends the ball high in the air enabling the kicker and his team-mates to run forward and regain possession of the ball. But to British TV viewers it was inseparably linked to the commentator Eddie Waring (1909–86). He broadcast commentaries, in his distinctive and highly imitable voice, for 20 years before he retired in 1981. Another of his expressions was **to take an early bath** – for a player being sent off the field early. This is the same as the American expression **to send someone to the showers**, in baseball or football, when a player is sent off early for disciplinary reasons.

up in Annie's room behind the clock, it's. (or . . . **behind the wallpaper**.) Explanation for when something disappears unaccountably. Partridge/*Slang* simply has 'Up in Annie's room' as a services' catchphrase from before the First World War, in reply to a query concerning someone's whereabouts. Partridge/*Catch Phrases* has 'Up in Annie's room behind the clock' as the civilian version of this.

uplands. See BROAD SUNLIT ~.

upstairs, downstairs. In the US, 'upstairs, downstairs' has become an expression for class and privilege differences, following on from *Upstairs, Downstairs*, the title of a British drama series from London Weekend Television (1970–75) about the lives of family and servants (i.e. 'above and below stairs') in a London house between 1900 and 1930. From *Newsweek* (4 January 1988): 'The upstairs-downstairs relationship between Jews and Arabs is conspicuous in Nazareth . . . the 20,000 Jews live in Upper Nazareth, where the schools are spacious and the streets are well maintained.'

Compare what I seem to recall were the names of two linked nightclubs (or discos) in New York City in the 1960s: 'Upstairs at the Downstairs' and 'Downstairs at the Upstairs'. And *Up the Down Staircase*, title of a film (US, 1967) about a teacher assigned to a school in a slum area.

up there, Cazaly! Roy Cazaly (1893–1963) was an Australian Rules footballer who played for the South Melbourne team from 1921 onwards and formed a 'ruck' combination with 'Skeeter' Fleiter and Mark Tandy, i.e. they were players who worked together but did not have fixed positions. According to the *Australian Dictionary of Biography*: 'Though only 5ft 11ins and twelve and a half stone, Cazaly was a brilliant high-mark; he daily practised leaping for a ball suspended from the roof of a shed at his home. He could mark and turn in mid-air, land and in a few strides send forward a long, accurate drop-kick or stab-pass. Fleiter's constant cry 'Up there, Cazaly!' was taken up by the crowds. It entered the Australian idiom, was used by infantry men in North Africa in World War II and became part of folklore.' The phrase was also incorporated in song.

up the wooden hill to Bedfordshire. Up the stairs to bed. Originally a nursery euphemism, this has become part of grown-up 'golf-club slang', as someone once termed it – i.e. a conversational cliché. Sir Hugh Casson and Joyce Grenfell included it in their *Nanny Says* (1972), together with 'Come on, up wooden hill, down sheet lane'. 'Up the Wooden Hill to Bedfordshire' was the title of the first song recorded by Vera Lynn, in 1936. The 'bed-fordshire' joke occurs in a synopsis of *Ali Baba and the Forty Thieves; or, Harlequin and the Magic Donkey* staged at the Alexandra Theatre, Liverpool, in 1868. Indeed, as so often, Jonathan Swift found it even earlier. In *Polite Conversation* (1738), the Colonel says, 'I'm going to the Land of Nod.' Neverout replies: 'Faith, I'm for *Bedfordshire*.' But then again, the poet Charles Cotton had used it in 1665.

up to a point Lord Copper. This phrase is employed when disagreeing with someone it is prudent not to differ with, or when simply disagreeing without being objectionable about it. It comes from Evelyn Waugh's novel about journalists, *Scoop* (1938): 'Mr Salter's side of the conversation was limited to expressions of assent. When Lord Copper [a newspaper proprietor] was right he said, "Definitely, Lord Copper"; when he was wrong, "Up to a point."' An example from the *Independent* (4 April 1990): 'We are told that [Norman Tebbit] was only trying to help . . . he was out to "stop Heseltine". Well, up to a point, Lord Whitelaw.'

up to my neck in muck and bullets. Phrase used by the British comedian Arthur Haynes (1914–66), in his tramp character in ITV shows of the 1960s. Sometimes remembered as 'mud and bullets'.

upturned faces. See SEA OF ∼.

up, up and away. See under SUPERMAN.

upwards. See ONWARDS AND ∼!

Urquhart. See SLIGGER ∼.

us. See IS HE ONE OF ∼?

use. See 'SNO ∼.

used car. See WOULD YOU BUY A ∼ . . .

useless. See THREE MOST ∼ THINGS IN THE WORLD; ∼ AS A CHOCOLATE KETTLE under AS BUSY AS . . .

usual. See BUSINESS AS ∼.

u-turn, to make a. The word 'u-turn' was probably first used in the US (by 1937) to describe the turn a motor car makes when the driver wishes to proceed in the opposite direction to the one he has been travelling in. The political use of the term to denote a reversal of policy was established in the US by 1961. In British politics, it was in use at the time of the Heath government (1970–74).

· V ·

vague. See DON'T BE ~ . . .

vale of tears, this. Phrase for life seen as composed of woe and sorrow. Known by 1554, though earlier as 'vale of troubles', 'vale of misery'. The Bible's 'Valley of Baca' (Psalm 84:6) is translated in the Revised Version as the 'Valley of Weeping'.

Valley Girl, a. An American pubescent teenage girl (aged 13 to 17) of a type first observed and indentified in California's San Fernando valley in the early 1980s. She is from a fairly well-to-do family, her passions are shopping, junk food, cosmetics, and speaking in a curious language – 'fer shurr', 'todally', **gag me with a spoon** [expression of disgust – 'you make me feel sick'], 'GRODY TO THE MAX'.

van. See under FOLLOW THAT TAXI!

vanities. See BONFIRE OF THE ~ .

varieties. See HEINZ 57 ~ .

vas you dere, Sharlie? ('Was you there, Charlie?') Hungarian-born Jack Pearl (*b* 1895) used to tell stories as 'Baron Munchausen' on American radio in the early 1930s. If his straight man, Charlie, expressed doubts on any aspect of the stories, Pearl would say, 'Vas you dere, Charlie?'

vegetable. See ANIMAL, ~ OR MINERAL.

velvet. See BLACK ~ ; BLUE ~ ; IRON FIST IN A ~ GLOVE; LITTLE GENTLEMAN IN BLACK ~ .

venture. See NOTHING ~ NOTHING WIN.

verse. See DEATHLESS PROSE.

very interesting . . . but stupid! See under *LAUGH-IN*.

very tasty . . . very sweet! The British radio comedy couple Kenway and Young (Nan Kenway and Douglas Young) used to say this, smacking their lips – in the 1930s/40s. E.g. Kenway: 'My nephew's getting on well in the Navy. He's a ship's carpenter. They say he's a very efficient chips.' Young: 'Fish and chips? I like them with a dollop of the old vinegar and a sprinkle of old salt. Goes down a treat I reckon. Very tasty, very sweet!'

Vestal Virgin(s). Members of the cult of the chaste Roman goddess Vesta, who presided over the fire in the domestic hearth. There were six of them. If they ceased to be virgins, they were buried alive, and if they managed to serve thirty years, they were allowed to marry. The term 'vestal virgin' may be now be applied to anyone of innocent, totally spotless behaviour.

V for victory. The 'V for Victory' slogan of the Second World War started as a piece of officially encouraged graffiti inscribed on walls in occupied Belgium by members of the anti-German 'freedom movement'. The Flemish word for freedom begins with a V – *Vrijheid* – and the French word for victory is, of course, *Victoire*. The idea came from Victor de Laveleye, the BBC's Belgian Programme Organizer, who, in a broadcast on 14 January 1941, suggested that listeners should adopt the letter 'V' as 'a symbol of their belief in the ultimate victory of the allies'. They were to go out and chalk it up wherever they could. From Belgium, the idea spread into the Netherlands and France and 'multitudes' of little Vs started appearing on walls in those countries. Winston Churchill spoke of the 'V' sign as a symbol of the 'the unconquerable will of the people of the occupied territories'.

The symbol was expressed in other ways, too. The opening three notes of

Beethoven's Fifth Symphony corresponded to the (. . . -) of the 'V' in Morse Code and, accordingly, the music was used in BBC broadcasts to occupied Europe. People gave the 'V for Victory' salute with parted middle index fingers – though Winston Churchill confused matters by presenting his fingers the wrong way round in a manner akin to the traditionally obscene gesture. Churchill's Private Secretary, John Colville, noted in his diary on 26 September 1941: 'The PM *will* give the v SIGN with two fingers in spite of the representations repeatedly made to him that this gesture has quite another significance'.

viator. See STA ∼.

vicar. See MORE TEA, ∼?

vicarage tea-party. See LIKE A ∼.

Vicar of Bray, a. Meaning 'a person who changes allegiance according to the WAY THE WIND BLOWS; a turncoat', after a vicar of Bray, Berkshire, in the sixteenth century who is supposed to have changed his religious affiliation from Roman Catholic to Protestant more than once during the reigns of Henry VIII to Elizabeth I. However, there was more than one vicar in this period. Whatever the case, by the time of Thomas Fuller's *Worthies* (1662) there was a proverb: 'The Vicar of Bray will be Vicar of Bray still.'

As for the song beginning 'In Good King Charles's Golden Days . . .', it was probably written at the beginning of the eighteenth century and describes a different (perhaps completely fictional) vicar of Bray who changed his religion to suit the different faiths of monarchs from Charles II to George I. Can there have been two such turncoat vicars – or was the song merely an updating of the circumstances of the actual first vicar?

vice anglais, le. Often thought to be the French term for the Englishman's predilection for homosexual over heterosexual behaviour. But originally it applied to the Englishman's supposed love of flagellation (derived in turn from his supposed enjoyment of corporal

punishment during his schooldays). *OED2* does not find the original use until 1942. On the other hand, Sir Richard Burton's 'Terminal Essay' in his translation of the *Arabian Nights* (1885), includes the observation on homosexuality, that: 'In our modern capitals, London, Berlin and Paris for instance, the Vice seems subject to periodical outbreaks. For many years, also, England sent her pederasts to Italy, and especially to Naples whence originated the term "*Il vizio Inglese*".'

vices. See ANCESTRAL ∼.

victim. See FASHION ∼.

Victorian values. In the General Election of 1983 and thereafter, the British Prime Minister Margaret Thatcher and some of her Cabinet ministers frequently commended the virtue of a return to Victorian values. The phrase appears to have been coined by Brian Walden in a TV interview with Mrs Thatcher on ITV's *Weekend World* on 17 January 1983. He suggested that she was trying to restore 'Victorian values'. She replied: 'Very much so. Those were the values when our country became great. But not only did our country become great internationally, also much advance was made in this country – through voluntary rather than state action.' Mrs Thatcher also said in an LBC radio interview on 15 April: 'I was brought up by a Victorian grandmother. We were taught to work jolly hard. We were taught to prove ourselves; we were taught self-reliance; we were taught to live within our income . . . You were taught that cleanliness is next to godliness. You were taught self-respect. You were taught always to give a hand to your neighbour. You were taught tremendous pride in your country. All of these things are Victorian values. They are also perennial values.' On 23 April, the *Daily Telegraph* quoted Dr Rhodes Boyson, the Minister for Schools, as saying: 'Good old-fashioned order, even Victorian order, is far superior to illiterate disorder and innumerate chaos in the classroom,' and Neil Kinnock, then Chief Opposition spokesman on education, as saying: 'Victorian Britain was a place where a few got rich and most got hell. The "Victorian values" that ruled were cruelty, misery, drudgery, squalor and ignorance.'

victory. See DIG FOR ∼.

Visible Panty Line. See VPL.

vital. See IT'S ABSOLUTELY ∼ . . .

voice(s). See ANCESTRAL ∼; HIS MASTER'S ∼; under OL' BLUE EYES.

Vorsprung durch Technik
[advancement through technology]. Slogan for Audi cars in the UK from 1982. The use of a German phrase (which few could understand) was apparently designed to bring home to British buyers that the Audi was, indeed, a German car (and hence a reliable, quality product). The phrase was the company's own exhortation to its workforce to be found written up over the factory gates in Germany.

In no sense can it be described as a catchphrase, as it did not catch on, but it certainly intrigued and tantalized and was noticed.

vote. See ONE MAN, ONE ∼.

vote early and vote often. A cynical political catchphrase of certain American origin. 'Josh Billings' (pseudonym of Henry Wheeler Shaw, the American humorist 1818–85) wrote that it was 'the Politishun's golden rule' in *Josh Billings' Wit and Humour* (1874), and seems merely to be recalling an adage. Indeed, earlier, William Porcher Miles had said in a speech to the House of Representatives (31 March 1858): ' "Vote early and vote often", the advice openly displayed on the election banners in one of our northern cities.' Another version is that the original jokester was John Van Buren, a New York lawyer (d 1866), who was the son of President Martin Van Buren.

vouchers. See FEW ∼ SHORT OF A POP–UP TOASTER.

vous pouvez cracher. See under *ITMA*.

vox populi. In British broadcasting of the 1950s/60s there was a vogue for what was known in the business as **vox pops** – namely, street interviews with passers-by presenting views on issues of the day which, with luck, were amusingly expressed and – for reasons of balance – effectively cancelled each other out. The abbreviation *Vox Pop* was also the title of an American radio show in the early 1940s.

In full, '*Vox populi*' [voice of the people] is of venerable origin. Alcuin wrote in a letter to the Emperor Charlemagne in AD 800: '*Nec audiendi sunt qui solent dicere, "Vox populi, vox Dei"; cum tumultuositas vulgi semper insaniae proxima sit*' [Nor should we listen to those who say, "The voice of the people is the voice of God", for the turbulence of the mob is always close to insanity].

'Fox populi' was a nickname given to Abraham Lincoln (presumably on account of his looks or his populism) by *Vanity Fair* magazine, London, in 1863. The same year, the US General W.T. Sherman wrote in a letter to his wife: 'Vox populi, vox humbug' – by which he meant 'the voice of the people is humbug'.

VPL. Initialese for 'Visible Panty Line', a delicate way of pointing out an unsightly feature of women's clothing when underwear shows through the outerwear. Known by the 1970s and presumably coined in the garment industry or among fashion journalists.

V sign. The obscene gesture so easily confused with Churchill's V FOR VICTORY sign may have come about as described by Anthony Sher in *Year of the King* (1985): 'The two-fingered sod-off sign comes from Agincourt. The French, certain of victory, had threatened to cut off the bow-fingers of all the English archers [this is attested for in a contemporary French account of the battle]. When the English were victorious, the archers held up their fingers in defiance'.

vulture. See CULTURE ∼.

· W ·

wage. See FAIR DAY'S ∼ .

wage freeze, a. The concept of 'freezing' wages – holding them at a stated level – was current in the US in the 1930s and 1940s. The term 'wage-freeze' itself had been formed by 1942 and also occurs in the film *To Catch a Thief* (US, 1955). It was later popularized in the UK by the Chancellor of the Exchequer, Selwyn Lloyd: 'Do you think the unions are going to respond to what amounts to a wage freeze in the public sector?' (radio broadcast, 25 July 1961). This was also termed (in the UK only) a **pay freeze** and a **pay pause**.

wagger pagger bagger, a. A wastepaper basket (sometimes just **wagger** or **wagger pagger**). From Act II of John Dighton's THE HAPPIEST DAYS OF YOUR LIFE (1948): 'If you don't mind, therefore, I shall deposit them in the wagger-pagger-bagger [*He drops the flowers into the wastepaper basket*].' This is an example of the (now rather dated) slang popular at the University of Oxford in the early years of the twentieth century. A whole range of words was transformed into different ones ending in 'agger'. The Prince of Wales (who studied at the university for a while) was the 'Pragger Wagger'. Jesus College was known as 'Jaggers'. And a curious working-class character who used to hang around Oxford and was known as 'the British Workman' came, inevitably, to be called the 'Bragger Wagger'.

The whole scheme is a variant upon the old English Public School custom of adding '-er' to everything: rugby becoming 'rugger', football becoming 'footer', and so on. Silly, but rather fun.

wait. See MAKE 'EM LAUGH . . .

waiting. See ACCIDENT ∼ TO HAPPEN.

wake up at the back there! See under TAKE IT FROM HERE.

wake up England! A reprimand delivered by the speaker to himself for not having spotted something fairly obvious. Also, according to Iona and Peter Opie, *The Lore and Language of Schoolchildren* (1959), a phrase used to greet a bearer of bad news. In origin it is a misquotation or, rather, a phrase that was not actually spoken. The future King George V made a speech at the Guildhall, London, on 5 December 1901, when Duke of York (but four days before he was created Prince of Wales). Returning from an Empire tour, he warned against taking the Empire for granted: 'To the distinguished representatives of the commercial interests of the Empire . . . I venture to allude to the impression which seemed generally to prevail among our brethren overseas, that the old country must wake up if she intends to maintain her old position of pre-eminence in her Colonial trade against foreign competitors.' This statement was encapsulated by the popular press in the phrase 'Wake up, England!' but George did not say precisely that himself.

wakey-wakey! *The Billy Cotton Band Show* ran on British radio and TV for over 20 years from the late 1940s. For one seven-year period it was broadcast on radio without a break for 52 weeks of the year. First would come a fanfare, then Billy Cotton's cry (without any 'rise and shine') would be followed by a brisk, noisy rendering of 'Somebody Stole My Gal'. The programme was first broadcast on Sunday 6 February 1949 at 10.30 a.m. Because of this unsocial hour, rehearsals had to begin at 8.45 – not the best time to enthuse a band which had just spent six days on the road. 'Oi, come on,' said Cotton, on one occasion, 'Wakey-wakey!' It worked, and eventually led to such a cheerful atmosphere that the producer said the show might as well start with it. Said Cotton (1899–1969): 'I thought of all those people lying in their beds and I remembered the sergeant who used to kick my bottom when I was a kid – and out came the catchword.' So it remained – even when the radio programme moved to its better-remembered spot at Sunday lunchtime.

walk. See HE CAN'T ∼ AND CHEW GUM . . . under HE CAN'T FART . . .

Walker, Johnnie. See BORN 1820 . . .

walkies! If proof were needed that life can begin at 70, it was provided by Barbara Woodhouse (1910–88). In 1980, after much badgering, she persuaded the BBC that she should present a programme called *Training Dogs the Woodhouse Way* (which involved training the owners, too). She instantly became a national figure of the eccentric kind the British like to have from time to time, and also found fame in the US. Her authoritative delivery of such commands as 'Walkies!' and 'Ssssit!' were widely imitated. However, by December 1981 she was a telling a newspaper that she was going to retreat a fraction from the public eye: 'It's just that I'm getting tired of people saying "Walkies!" to me wherever I go. Even in a village of 300 inhabitants in Queensland.'

The childish diminutive of 'walk' was not, of course, her coinage. It was in use by the 1930s.

walking. See LET YOUR FINGERS DO THE ∼.

walks. See GHOST ∼.

wall. See BACKS TO THE ∼; WEAKEST GO TO THE ∼.

wallpaper, behind the. See under UP IN ANNIE'S ROOM . . .

walls have ears. A security slogan in the Second World War, but the idea of inanimate objects being able to hear is a very old one. From W.S. Gilbert's *Rozenkrantz and Guildenstern* (1891): 'We know that walls have ears. I gave them tongues -/And they were eloquent with

promises.' In 1727, Jonathan Swift wrote: 'Walls have tongues, and hedges ears.' In Vitzentzos Kornaros's epic poem *Erotokritos* (c 1645) there is the following couplet (here translated from the Greek):

> For the halls of our masters have ears and
> hear,
> And the walls of the palace have eyes and
> watch.

Walter Mitty. The name of a fantasist who daydreams of achievements which are beyond him in real life (compare the character 'Billy Liar' in the 1959 novel of that name by Keith Waterhouse). It comes from the short story 'The Secret Life of Walter Mitty' (1939; film US, 1947) by James Thurber.

Walter Plinge. In British theatre, when an actor plays two parts, he traditionally uses this name rather than his own in one of them. It is said that the original Mr Plinge was a stage-struck pub landlord from near the Theatre Royal, Drury Lane, in the nineteenth century. Having his name so used was the nearest he ever came to being on the stage. From Laurence Olivier, *Confessions of an Actor* (1982): 'I took over the role of A.B. Raham in *Home and Beauty* [in 1969], in which for policy reasons . . . I put myself down in the programme as "Walter Plinge". (This is a professionally though not generally well-known *nom de theatre* used for various reasons, from uncertainty of final casting to merely wishing to even up the columns on a bill.)'

The US equivalent is 'George Spelvin'.

Wandering Hand Trouble. See WHT.

Wandering Jew, the. A legendary character, dating from medieval times, who was condemned to wander about the earth until Christ's second coming because he had urged Christ to move faster as he carried the cross to Calvary.

wanna. See I ∼ TELL YOU A STORY.

wanna buy a duck? Joe Penner (1904–41), a Hungarian-American, rocketed to fame on American radio in 1934 with rapid-fire one-liners and a number of catchphrases

including this one and **you naaasty man!**
He carried a real duck, called Goo Goo, in a
basket.

want. See IF YOU ~ ANYTHING . . . ; I ~ . . .

war. See ALL IS FAIR IN . . . ; COLD ~;
DADDY, WHAT DID YOU DO IN THE GREAT
~?; DAY ~ BROKE OUT; DON'T YOU KNOW
THERE'S A ~ ON; FIRST WORLD ~; FOR YOU,
TOMMY, THE ~ IS OVER; GO FORTH TO ~;
GOOD ~; HARD-FACED MEN WHO . . . ; LOSE A
BATTLE BUT NOT THE ~; MAKE LOVE, NOT
~; MORE EFFICIENT CONDUCT OF THE ~; NO
MORE ~; THERE AIN'T GONNA BE NO ~; THIS
IS ~; WORLD ~ TWO.

war between the states, the. This term
for the US Civil War (1861–65), like 'the
War Between the North and the South', did
not catch on until the conflict was well over
(1867 for 'between the States', popular with
Southerners, and possibly not until the
1890s for 'between North and South'). 'The
Civil War' was an earlier Northern name
for it (1861). Southerners had called it 'the
Revolution', 'the War of Independence',
'the Second War of Independence', or 'the
War of Secession'.
    Hence, the punning title of the novel
(1974) by Alison Lurie – *The War Between
the Tates*, a tale of family feuding.

war game. See under ARMY GAME.

warm. See WET AND ~.

warned, you have been. See under
FAMOUS LAST WORDS.

warrior. See HAPPY ~; UNKNOWN ~.

war's over, you know, the. Said to
someone who is being noticeably and
unnecessarily careful about wasting
food, electricity, etc. Current since the
Second World War and a natural
replacement for DON'T YOU KNOW THERE'S
A WAR ON?

war to end wars, the. Slogan of the First
World War (on the British and Allied
side), derived from *The War That Will End
War*, the title of a book (1914) by H.G.
Wells.

warts and all. This phrase about a portrait
or written description means 'including all
the details that someone might prefer to
have left out'. Traditionally, it is what
Oliver Cromwell is said to have instructed
Sir Peter Lely who was painting his portrait:
'Remark all these roughnesses, pimples,
warts, and everything as you see, otherwise
I will never pay a farthing for it.' It is now
thought more likely that Cromwell made
the remark to the miniaturist Samuel
Cooper (whom Lely copied). The anecdote
was first recorded in 1721.

wash. See IT'LL ALL COME OUT IN THE ~.

Washington. See under QUEEN ELIZABETH
SLEPT HERE.

was it good for you, too? What the
uncertain lover is supposed to say to his
sexual partner after intercourse. Indications
that the phrase had 'arrived' came when
Bob Chieger so entitled a book of
quotations about love and sex (1983).
Compare DID THE EARTH MOVE FOR YOU?

WASP. An acronym for 'White Anglo-
Saxon Protestant', denoting the dominant
middle- and upper-class ruling clique in the
US, which also happens to be descended
from early European immigrants. The
coinage has variously been ascribed to E.B.
Palmore (1962) and E. Digby Baltzell (1964).

—watch. The addition of this suffix to
signify any kind of regular attention to
something began in earnest in the UK
about 1985. It stemmed from
Neighbourhood Watch (sometimes Home
Watch) schemes, which had been started by
police in the UK a year or two before this –
schemes in which residents are encouraged
to 'police' their own and each other's
properties.
    The coinage originated in the US in the
early 1970s, but as early as 6 July 1975, the
Observer TV critic could write, 'Camden
Council employs a lone inspector to walk
the pavement on the lookout for citizens
allowing their dogs to foul it. In a sane
society he would command a department
called Shitwatch.' The comedian Les
Dawson had a BBC TV series entitled *The
Dawson Watch* by 1980.

In 1985 I noted the TV programme titles *Drugwatch*, *Nature Watch*, *Newswatch*, *Crimewatch UK*, *Firewatch*, not to mention a feature called 'Wincey's Animal Watch' on TV-am. In 1986 came *Birdwatch UK* and *Childwatch* (on TV). Since then I have become aware of *Railwatch* (BBC TV, 1989), *Weather Watch* (ITV, 1989), 'Longman Wordwatch', a scheme for readers to contribute to the *Longman Register of New Words*, and something called the Worldwatch Institute in Washington – which seems to be the ultimate in — watches.

watching. See BIG BROTHER IS ~ YOU.

watchman, what of the night? Not a street cry, but a quotation from the Bible. In Isaiah 21:11 the watchman replies, unhelpfully: 'The morning cometh, and also the night.' Used as the title of a Bernard Partridge cartoon in *Punch* (3 January 1900). Set to music several times, notably by Sir Arthur Sullivan.

watch the birdie! (also **watch the dicky bird!**) What photographers say to gain the attention of those they are photographing (especially children) and to make them look at the same point. I suppose originally they may have held a toy bird near the camera lens. A song 'Watch the Birdie' appeared in the film *Hellzapoppin'* (1942).

To obtain the semblance of a smile, the photographer says, 'Smile, please!' or 'Say "cheese!"' Cecil Beaton is reported to have encouraged (some of) his subjects to, 'Say "lesbian!"'

'Smile, please – watch the birdie!' was adopted as one of the many ITMA catchphrases.

watch the skies. The last words of the film *The Thing* (US, 1951) were: 'Watch everywhere, keep looking, watch the skies!' This phrase was subsequently used to promote the film *Close Encounters of the Third Kind* (1977) and, indeed, was its original title. Another slogan for the film was **we are not alone.**

watch this space. A light-hearted way of saying 'further details will follow'. I expect this probably came out of the US, though I

can't work out quite how. Perhaps it would be put on advertisement hoardings to await the arrival of a new poster? From there transferred to newspaper, even broadcasting, use – meaning 'pay attention to this slot'? The *OED2*'s earliest example is, however, taken from an advertisement in the *B.E.F. Times* [British Expeditionary Force] in 1917.

water. See COME HELL OR HIGH ~; DEAD IN THE ~; DON'T GO NEAR THE ~; HE'S FALLEN IN THE ~ under *GOON SHOW*; KING OVER THE ~; LEAVE IT IN THE ~ under LET'S — AND SEE IF —.

waterfront. See I COVER THE ~.

Watergate. The name for the scandal in US politics which led to the resignation of President Richard Nixon in 1974. It came from the Watergate apartment block in Washington DC where a bungled burglary by those seeking to re-elect the president led to a cover-up and then the scandal. Consequently, it has become standard practice to apply the suffix **—gate** to any political and Royal scandal in the US and UK. Among the scores there have been are: Koreagate, Lancegate, Billygate, Liffeygate, Westlandgate, Contragate, Irangate, Thatchergate and Squidgygate.)

For other Watergate phrases see: ALL THE PRESIDENT'S MEN; CUT OFF AT THE PASS; DEEP-SIX; DEEP THROAT; EXPLETIVE DELETED; I WOULD WALK OVER MY GRANDMOTHER; SMOKING GUN.

Waterloo, to meet one's. i.e. to meet one's ultimate challenge and fail, as Napoleon did at the Battle of Waterloo in 1815. An early use of the expression was by the American lawyer, Wendell Phillips, in the form, 'Every man meets his Waterloo at last' (at Brooklyn, 1 November 1859). He was referring to the failure of an attack by his fellow abolitionist, John Brown, on an arsenal in Virginia two weeks before.

On the other hand, earlier examples in the *OED2* show that, almost from the word go, a 'Waterloo' entered the language in this sense. Byron in 1816 called Armenian 'a Waterloo of an alphabet'. And John Aiton in his *Manual of Domestic Economy for Clergymen* (1842) wrote: 'If there must be a

Waterloo, let it be a conflict for all the minister's rights, so that he may never require to go to law in his lifetime again.'

Watford. See NORTH OF ∼.

Watson. See ELEMENTARY MY DEAR ∼.

waves. See WHAT ARE THE WILD ∼ SAYING?

wave your gladdies, possums! A stock phrase of 'Dame Edna Everage, the Housewife Superstar' from Australia. Barry Humphries (b 1934) has been playing this character since the 1950s. The somewhat phallic gladiolus-waving ritual in which he encouraged his audiences was certainly a feature of his stage show by the mid-1970s. Edna's use of the adjective **spooky!** in British TV shows of the 1980s was also noticeable.

way. See AND THAT'S THE ∼ IT IS; GREAT WHITE ∼; IT'S THE ∼ I TELL 'EM!; THAT'S THE ∼ THE COOKIE CRUMBLES; WE HAVE ∼S OF MAKING YOU TALK; WHAT A ∼ TO RUN A —.

Wayne's World. Title of a film (US, 1992; sequel 1994), based on a segment in the NBC TV show *Saturday Night Live* (from 1989), in which Mike Myers and Dana Carvey play Wayne and Garth, urban teenagers who are 'into' various aspects of pop culture, particularly HEAVY METAL, and run their own cable TV show from a basement den.

Catchwords and catchphrases are thick on the ground but the most notable creation has been the cry **Not!** tacked on to a statement and instantly negating its meaning. Hence, 'I believe you – NOT!' During the 1992 US presidential election, Democrats distributed lapel badges with the slogan 'Vote Republican. Not'. A Nike poster campaign had the slogan: 'Most excellent colours for Wimbledon. Not!' And so on. Mike Myers commented: ' "Not" was something my brother used to say to me, to torment me. And suddenly [George] Bush is saying it to torment the whole of the free world.' (Compare I DON'T THINK.)

Other catchphrases include: **Excellent!** and **Party on!** and the call/response **No way?!/Way!** The wail **We're not**

worthy, we're not worthy! goes up when the pair fall to their knees before such idols as Madonna, Alice Cooper and Aerosmith. Some of the phrases had earlier appeared in the films *Bill and Ted's Excellent Adventure* (1988) and *Bill and Ted's Bogus Journey* (1991), though quite what the connection is with *Wayne's World* is not clear, except that all the phrases may have originated in actual teenage slang.

See also IF YOU BUILD IT, HE WILL COME.

way the wind blows, the. Title of memoirs by Lord Home (1976), which his opening words explain. 'When I succeeded Mr Harold Macmillan as Prime Minister in 1963, an inquisitive journalist sought out our head-keeper and asked him, "What do you know about the Homes?" He was probably bamboozled by the reply: "Oh, the Home boys always seem to know which way the wind blows." Our game-keeper was not thinking of me as a political trimmer, but simply stating a fact of our family life; for my father was a countryman, and a naturalist, and on the right interpretation of wind or weather depended the action of the day.'

Compare *When the Wind Blows* (1982) by Raymond Briggs (about the results of a nuclear explosion); also the proverb, 'grass never grows *when* the wind blows' (known by 1836).

we. See ROYAL '∼'.

weaker vessel, the. A wife. From 1 Peter 3:7: 'Wives, be in subjection to your husbands . . . husbands, giving honour unto the wife, as unto the weaker vessel.' Hence, *The Weaker Vessel*, title of a book (1984) by Antonia Fraser about 'woman's lot in seventeenth-century England'.

weakest go to the wall, the. A proverbial expression established by the early sixteenth century. A play, possibly by John Webster, was entitled *Weakest Goeth to the Wall* (1600). For an unverified origin, see *The Book of Cloyne* (1993): 'Welcome to Cloyne Cathedral [in Ireland] . . . in the middle ages . . . there were no pews . . . [and] possibly the only seating in this part of the building would be around the walls for the benefit of the sick and infirm, hence the well known expression: "The weakest go to the wall".'

we appear to be considerably richer than you. See under LOADSAMONEY!

we are just good friends. Clichéd way of expressing to a newspaper (usually) that your relationship with another is not romantic. In James Joyce, *Ulysses* (1922), there occurs the original straightforward form: 'They would be just good friends like a big brother and sister without all that other.' The phrase probably established itself in the US during the 1930s, though in the film of Cole Porter's musical *Stock Stockings* (US 1957), the phrase is used several times as if not clichéd yet. From *Vivien: The Life of Vivien Leigh* by Alexander Walker (1987): 'At Cherbourg, Jack [Merivale – Vivien's lover as her marriage to Laurence Olivier was ending in 1960] experienced for the first time the bruising intrusiveness of the British Press who boarded the ship *en masse* to interrogate Vivien's handsome travelling companion. In self-defence, he fell back on the old "just good friends" cliché.'

Now only used as a consciously humorous evasion, especially when not true. A BBC sitcom current in 1984 was called *Just Good Friends* and several songs about that time also had the title.

we are not alone. See under WATCH THE SKIES.

we are not amused. The subject of whether Queen Victoria ever uttered this famous put-down was raised in the *Notebooks of a Spinster Lady* (1919) by Miss Caroline Holland: '[The Queen's] remarks can freeze as well as crystallize . . . there is a tale of the unfortunate equerry who ventured during dinner at Windsor to tell a story with a spice of scandal or impropriety in it. "We are not amused," said the Queen when he had finished.' Interviewed in 1978, Princess Alice, Countess of Athlone, said she had once asked her grandmother about the phrase and she had denied ever having said it.

we are the masters now. The boast of Sir Hartley Shawcross (later Lord Shawcross),

Attorney-General in Britain's first postwar Labour Government, in the House of Commons on 2 April 1946. What he actually said was: 'We are the masters at the moment.'

weary. See ART THOU ∼?

weasel. See POP GOES THE ∼.

weather. See LOVELY ∼ FOR DUCKS.

weathermen say/warn. British journalistic stand-bys. When snow and ice engulf us, 'There's more to come, say weathermen.' And when sun and heat smother us, 'Make the most of it, say weathermen.' By 1976.

we be doomed, we all be doomed! See under ROUND THE HORNE.

we bring you melodies from out of the sky/my brother and I. From the signature tune of the British entertainers Bob and Alf Pearson. Bob (*b* 1907) and Alf (*b* 1910) would sing comic songs at the piano and were popular on radio into the 1950s.

wedding begets/breeds/brings on another, going to one . . . A proverbial expression by 1634. From Jane Austen, *Northanger Abbey*, Chap. 15 (1818): 'Did you ever hear the old song, "Going to one wedding brings on another"?'

Also applied to funerals: 'One funeral makes many' (by 1894) – particularly if a lot of old people have to hang around in cold, damp churches and graveyards.

wedding cake. See BRIDEGROOM ON THE ∼.

Wednesday. See BLACK ∼; SEE YOU ∼.

week. See THAT WAS THE ∼ . . .

weekend. See SOMETHING FOR THE ∼ . . .

weekend starts here, the. Associated-Rediffusion TV's pop show *Ready, Steady, Go* was transmitted live on Friday evenings in the UK from 1963. The slogan for it was current by 1964. For some reason it stuck, and has been used by other programmes since.

week is a long time. See — IS A LONG TIME IN —.

weeks rather than months. Meaning 'sooner rather than later', e.g. 'Sir Simon Gourlay, President of the NFU, said the Government had to restore market confidence in "weeks rather than months", or farmers would go "needlessly out of business"' (*Independent*, 21 May 1990). This echoes the British Prime Minister Harold Wilson's use of the phrase at the Commonwealth Prime Ministers' Conference (January 1966): 'The cumulative effect of . . . sanctions [against Rhodesia] might well bring the rebellion to an end within a matter of weeks rather than months.'

we have lift-off. 'We have made a successful start'. From the announcement made by Mission Control at the start of American space flights (from the 1960s) – meaning that the rocket motors have successfully ignited and that the space vehicle is rising above the launch-pad.

we have met the enemy and he/they is/ are us. One's own faults are the cause of one's lack of success. The American cartoonist Walt Kelly's syndicated comic strip featured an opossum called Pogo. This phrase was used in a 1970 Pogo cartoon used on the 1971 Earth Day poster. Kelly had taken some time to get round to this formulation. In his introduction to *The Pogo Papers* (1953) he had earlier written: 'Resolve then, that on this very ground, with small flags waving and tinny blasts on tiny trumpets, we shall meet the enemy, and not only may he be ours, he may be us.'

we have ways (and means) of making you talk. The threat by evil inquisitor to victim appears to have come originally from 1930s Hollywood villains and was then handed on to Nazi characters from the 1940s onwards.

Douglass Dumbrille, as the evil Mohammed Khan, says, 'We have ways of making *men* talk' in the film *Lives of a Bengal Lancer* (US, 1935). He means by forcing

slivers of wood under the fingernails and setting fire to them . . . A typical 'film Nazi' use can be found in the film *Odette* (UK, 1950) in which the French Resistance worker (Anna Neagle) is threatened with unmentioned nastiness by one of her captors. Says he: 'We have ways and means of making you talk.' Then, after a little stoking of the fire with a poker, he urges her on with: 'We have ways and means of making a woman talk.'

Later, used in caricature, the phrase saw further action in TV programmes like *LAUGH-IN* (c 1968) – invariably pronounced with a German accent. Frank Muir presented a comedy series for London Weekend Television with the title *We Have Ways of Making You Laugh* (1968).

welcome. See HELLO, GOOD EVENING, AND ~.

well. See ALIVE AND ~ AND LIVING IN —; BOY DONE ~.

we'll all live till we die, unless dogs worry us, well. Kit Blease of Wallasey wrote (1994): 'This was used by my mother – a Yorkshire West Riding lady – usually after some minor disaster in the home.' Anne Gledhill of Mirfield, West Yorkshire, added: 'It was part of my background, too (born and brought up in Dewsbury in the West Riding).' Her version: 'We shall live till we dee – if t'dogs doesn't worry us' (the second part given an ironic twist).

G.L. Apperson in his *English Proverbs and Proverbial Phrases* (1929) has the basic expression, 'We shall live till we die' by 1600 and from Richard Jefferies, *Hedgerow* (1889), 'The old country proverb, "Ah, well, we shall live till we die if the pigs don't eat us, and then we shall go acorning."' From F.E. Taylor, *Lancashire Sayings* (1901), he has: 'We shan o live till we dee'n – iv th' dogs dunno wory us.'

well, Brian. A phrase associated with British TV sports interviews and post-game analysis – because the interviewer of verbally challenged players and managers on ITV football coverage (since 1967) has usually been Brian Moore. However, it may have caught on independently as a result of a sketch on *MONTY PYTHON'S FLYING CIRCUS*

(28 December 1969) when a very thick footballer replied either 'Good evening, Brian' or 'Well, Brian' to every question he was asked by a pretentious TV interviewer.

Compare, KNOW WHAT I MEAN, 'ARRY?

we'll get married just as soon as my divorce comes through. A cliché of seduction, probably more apparent in fiction (and parodies of same) than in real life. Registered in *Time* (14 December 1981).

well, he would, wouldn't he? 'Oscar Wilde said the Alps were objects of appallingly bad taste. He would, wouldn't he,' wrote Russell Harty (*Mr Harty's Grand Tour*, 1988). An innocuous enough phrase but one still used allusively because of the way it was spoken by Mandy Rice-Davies (*b* 1944) in 1963. A 'good time girl' and friend of Christine Keeler's, she was called as a witness when Stephen Ward, the ponce figure in the Profumo Affair [British Secretary of State for War John Profumo carried on with Keeler who was allegedly sharing her favours with the Soviet military attaché] was charged under the Sexual Offences Act.

During the preliminary Magistrates Court hearing on 28 June 1963, Rice-Davies was questioned about the men she had had sex with. When told by Ward's defence counsel that Lord Astor – one of the names on the list – had categorically denied any involvement with her, she replied, chirpily: 'Well, he would, wouldn't he?'

The court burst into laughter, the expression passed into the language, and is still resorted to because – as a good catchphrase ought to be – it is bright, useful in various circumstances, and tinged with innuendo.

well-known phrase or saying. See REARRANGE THE FOLLOWING . . .

we'll let you know. See DON'T CALL/RING US . . .

well, now then, sir, Miss Bankhead! Catchphrase from American radio in the 1930s. Thomas Millstead of Chicago wrote (1993): 'The phrase was used by the composer and orchestra leader Meredith Willson on actress Tallulah Bankhead's radio program *The Big Show* (mid to late 1940s). It was called "big" because it was a one and one-half hour variety show, very long for radio in those days. Mr Willson (who later wrote the famous Broadway show *The Music Man*) led the orchestra and also had many speaking opportunities. Miss Bankhead, of course, had an exceptionally deep voice. Thus Mr Willson's frequently addressing her as "sir".'

well to the right of Genghis Khan. See SOMEWHERE TO THE RIGHT OF GENGHIS KHAN.

we must export or die. See under EXPORTING IS FUN.

we must stamp out this evil in our midst. One-time cliché of British journalism. In June 1967, Chris Welch of *Melody Maker* wrote: 'We can expect a deluge of drivel about the new people [proponents of Flower Power, peace and love] any day now from the Sunday papers, with demands to "stamp out this evil in our midst".'

we name the guilty men. Cliché of journalism. From the *Observer* (16 April 1989): 'Like all the best Sunday journalists, I name the guilty men, and one guilty woman, if we include Mrs Shirley Williams.'

Guilty Men was the title of a tract 'which may rank as literature' (A.J.P. Taylor). It was written by Michael Foot, Frank Owen and Peter Howard using the pseudonym 'Cato'. Published in July 1940, it taunted the appeasers who had brought about the situation where Britain had had to go to war with Germany. The preface contains this anecdote: 'On a spring day in 1793 a crowd of angry men burst their way through the doors of the assembly room where the French Convention was in session. A discomforted figure addressed them from the rostrum. "What do the people desire?" he asked. "The Convention has only their welfare at heart." The leader of the angry crowd replied, "The people haven't come here to be given a lot of phrases. They demand a dozen guilty men."'

The phrase 'We *name* the guilty men' subsequently became a cliché of popular 'investigative' journalism. Equally popular was the similar, 'We name these *evil* men.'

The 'guilty men' taunt was one much used in the 1945 General Election by the Labour Party (and was referred to in a speech by Winston Churchill in the House of Commons, 7 May 1947).

we never closed. A slogan coined by Vivien Van Damm, proprietor of the Windmill Theatre, London – a venerable comedy and strip venue – which was the only West End showplace to remain open during the Blitz in the Second World War. An obvious variant: 'We never clothed.'

we never sleep. The slogan of Pinkerton's national detective agency which opened its first office in Chicago, 1850 (and which – through its open eye symbol *may* have given us the term PRIVATE EYE). Was there an echo of this in the line chosen to promote US Citibank's new 24–hour service in 1977: 'The Citi Never Sleeps' – apart, that is, from an allusion to the 1953 film title *The City That Never Sleeps*?

Nunquam dormio [I never sleep] has been used as the motto of various organizations and was (at some later stage) put under the original open-eye logo of the London *Observer* newspaper (founded 1791).

wept. See JESUS ∼!

we really move our tails for you. A slogan for Continental Airlines in the US, current 1975. In that year some of the airline's stewardesses threatened to sue over the 'bad taste' it had shown in selecting this slogan.

we're doomed! See under *DAD'S ARMY*; under *ROUND THE HORNE*.

we're gay and we're proud. See SAY IT LOUD.

we're getting there. A rather debatable slogan for British Rail, current 1985. In 1980, the organization had been promoted by the even more questionable **this is the age of the train**, which it undoubtedly wasn't (attracting the comments: 'Yes, it takes an age to catch one', 'Ours was 104' etc).

we're in. See MEREDITH, ∼!

we're just good friends. See WE ARE JUST GOOD FRIENDS.

we're not worthy! See *WAYNE'S WORLD*.

we're on a mission from God. Line spoken frequently by Dan Aykroyd as 'Elwood Blues' in *The Blues Brothers* (film US, 1980). The eponymous brothers justify their various activities with the suggestion that they are working on behalf of a Mother Superior who has been robbed.

we're with the Woolwich. A slogan for the Woolwich Equitable Building Society in the UK. In the late 1970s, there was a series of TV ads which posed the question 'Are you with the Woolwich?' More than most advertising lines, this one managed to work its way into jokes and sketches. Perhaps more correctly rendered as, 'No, I'm with the Woolwich' – in answer to such questions as, 'Are you with me?'

we shall not be moved. Shout/chant of defiance. According to Bartlett, it came originally from a 'Negro' spiritual (echoing more than one psalm): 'Just like a tree that's standing by the water/ We shall not be moved.' Later widely taken up as a song of the Civil Rights and labour movements, from the 1960s. In the UK, I fancy, only the simple slogan was chanted, not the whole spiritual.

we shall not see his like again. A cliché of obituaries, and alluding to Shakespeare, *Hamlet*, I.ii.187 (1600), where the Prince says of his late father:

A was a man, take him for all in all;
I shall not look upon his like again.

In *Joyce Grenfell Requests the Pleasure* (1976), the actress recalls being rung by the United Press for a comment on the death of Ruth Draper, the monologist: 'My diary records: "I said we should not see her like again. She was a genius." Without time to think, clichés take over and often, because that is why they have become clichés, they tell the truth.'

we shall overcome. This is the phrase from the song that became an American Civil Rights anthem of the early 1960s. It originated in pre-Civil War times, was adapted as a Baptist hymn called 'I'll Overcome Some Day' (c 1900) by C. Albert Hindley, and first became famous when sung by Black workers on a picket line in Charleston, South Carolina (1946). In the Spanish Civil War, there was a Republican chant '*venceremos!*' which means the same. Pete Seeger and others added verses including: 'Oh, deep in my heart, I know that I do believe/We shall overcome some day.'

Westchester. See under LET'S — AND SEE IF —.

Westward Ho! Name bestowed on a Devon seaside resort in the 1860s, replacing 'Northam Burrows', despite the misgivings of Charles Kingsley whose novel *Westward Ho!* had been published in 1855. Earlier, there had been a play *Westward Ho!* by Webster and Dekker (c 1600). *Westward Ha! or Around the World in 80 Clichés* was the title of a book (1948) by S.J. Perelman.

wet and warm. On being offered a drink, one might say, 'I don't mind what it is, as long as it's wet and warm.' Almost a conversational cliché. Mencken cites a 'Dutch proverb': 'Coffee has two virtues: it is wet and warm.' I am told that in Kenya, c 1950, there was a saying, 'Wet and warm like a honeymoon in Aden.'

we the people. These are the opening words of the Preamble to the 1787 Constitution of the United States: 'We the people of the United States . . . do ordain and establish this Constitution for the United States of America.'

wet your whistle?, would you like to. Would you like to have some liquid refreshment, have a drink? Known by 1611.

we've got a right one 'ere! See under *EDUCATING ARCHIE.*

we've soopped soom stooff tonight. See under RIGHT MONKEY!

we who are about to die . . . See *MORITURI.*

we wuz robbed! A notable reaction to sporting defeat came from the lips of Joe Jacobs (1896–1940), American manager of the boxer Max Schmeling. Believing his man to have been cheated of the heavyweight title in a fight against Jack Sharkey on 21 June 1932, Jacobs shouted his protest into a microphone – 'We wuz robbed!'

On another occasion, in October 1935, Jacobs left his sick bed to attend the World Series (ball game) for the one and only time. Having bet on the losers, he opined: **I should of stood in bed.**

whack. See 'AS 'E BIN IN, ~?

wharfies' picnic. See under AS BUSY AS . . .

what a beautiful day for —. See under HOW TICKLED I AM.

what about the workers? Usually written, 'Wot abaht . . .', this is the traditional proletarian heckler's cry during a political speech. It is almost a *Slogan* in its own right, but is now only used satirically. It occurs along with other rhetorical clichés during the 'Party Political Speech' (written by Max Schreiner) on the *Peter Sellers* comedy album *The Best of Sellers* (1958). Also in the 1950s, Harry Secombe as 'Neddie Seagoon' on the BBC radio GOON SHOW would sometimes exclaim (for no very good reason), 'Hello, folks, and what about the workers?!' Later, in the 1970s *MORECAMBE AND WISE SHOW*, Eric Morecambe incorporated it in a nonsense phrase of sexual innuendo when referring to 'a touch of hello-folks-and-what-about-the-workers!'

In 1984, in a TV programme to mark his hundredth birthday, Manny Shinwell, the veteran Labour MP, appeared to be claiming that he had been asking 'What about the workers?' – seriously – in 1904, but whether he meant literally or figuratively wasn't clear. He told John Mortimer in *Character Parts* (1986): 'I remember Bonar Law, future Prime Minister and Conservative Member of Parliament for the Gorbals, giving a speech in Glasgow, and it was all about Free Trade or something and they were applauding him! Unemployed men were applauding Bonar Law! So I shouted out, "What about the workers!" . . . I got my picture in the papers.'

See also BAND WAGGON.

what a carry on! See CARRY ON —.

what a difference a day makes! Almost proverbial, yet not listed in any proverb books. The phrase either expresses surprise at someone's rapid recovery from a mood which had laid them low, or expresses the old thought that time is a great healer. Did it begin in a song? 'What a Difference a Day Made' was a hit for Esther Phillips in 1975 (though adapted from a Mexican lyric in 1934).

what a gay day! See SHUT THAT DOOR!

what a name to go to bed with! Comment on an unusual name – but not intended as a proposition, despite the experience of Mrs D.M. Heigham of Aldershot, Hampshire (1994): 'It was New Year's Eve 1943. I was a Cypher Officer W.R.N.S. on watch at midnight. I was introduced to a man called Worthington Edridge. "Oh," I said, "What a name to go to bed with" (current remark at the time). He said, "Nobody asked you." I don't think you can beat that for a put down.'

Partridge/*Slang* has '. . . a *nice* name to go to bed with' – meaning 'an ugly name' – dating from 1887 and compares the French expression, '*un nom à coucher dehors*'.

what a performance! Phrase of the British comedian Sid Field (1904–50), spoken in 'sullen, flattened tones'. Used as the title of a play celebrating Field, written by William Humble and featuring David Suchet in the old routines (1994).

what are the wild waves saying? This is the title of a Victorian song with words by J.E. Carpenter and music by Stephen Glover:

What are the wild waves saying,
Sister, the whole day long:
That ever amid our playing,
I hear but their low, lone song?

The song is a duet between Paul and Florence Dombey and based on an incident in *Dombey and Son* (1848) by Charles Dickens. Nowhere in the novel does Dickens use the words, 'What are the *wild* waves saying?' though the book is fairly awash with the idea of a 'dark and unknown sea that rolls round all the world' (Chap. 1). The title of Chapter 16 is 'What the Waves were always saying'.

I treasure an advertisement for Igranic wireless coils, dating from the early 1920s, which plays upon the idea of radio waves and asks, 'What are the wild waves saying?'

what a revoltin' development this is! See under AND AWAY WE GO.

what are you doing after the show? A chat-up line, presumably of show business origin. *What Are You Doing After the Show?* was the title of a long-forgotten British ITV comedy show (1971). The previous year's Swedish film *Rötmånad* had been given the English title *What Are You Doing After the Orgy?*

what a way to run a —. A cartoon said to have appeared in the American *Collier's* magazine (though *Ballyhoo* in 1932 has also been suggested) shows two trains about to collide. An American signalman is looking out of his box and the caption is: 'Tch-tch-what a way to run a railroad!'

The Boston & Maine railroad picked up this line when it sought, 'a statement which would explain some of the problems of the railroad in times of inclement weather'. It took the 'stock railroad phrase', derived from the cartoon, and put it between each paragraph of the advertisement in the form, 'That's A ¡H**l of a Way to Run a Railroad!' Added at the foot of the ad was the line, 'But the railroad always runs.'

Thus the phrase came into the language as an exclamation concerning mis-management or chaos of any kind, in the form, 'What a way (or hell of a way) to run a railroad/railway.'

Echoes or developments of this construction occur in the title of G.F. Fiennes's *I Tried to Run a Railway* (1967) – he had worked for British Rail – and the Conservative Party 1968 poster: 'Higher unemployment . . . Higher unemployment

. . . Higher taxation . . . Higher prices . . . What a way to run a country!' And from the *Independent* Magazine (4 February 1989): 'The shop told me that it only had demonstration [satellite TV] dishes and suggested I call back in a fortnight. This is, surely, no way to run a revolution!'

what a world it is for woossit/worsted. Mrs F. Smith of Adel, Leeds, wrote (1994): 'I had a country-bred Grandmother and her sayings are now part of family lore. One, especially, was "What a world it is for woossit, and nobody knows how to knit" (and all are baffled by the word "woossit").' Vera Geddis of Eastleigh, Hampshire, misheard this last as 'What a world this is for *worsted*' and was reminded of a saying of her mother's: **what a world this is for worsted, fourteen balls of cotton for a penny!** She added: 'I cannot recall my mother ever explaining her saying – I am not certain whether the number of balls was fourteen or sixteen – but I assume that the point of it was that when tempted to bewail the state of the world, one cheered oneself up by changing it into a statement about the amazing cheapness of worsted.' Indeed, Wright's *English Dialect Dictionary* (c 1900) gives 'worset' as a form of 'worsted', so there seems to be more than the glimmer of an explanation here.

what becomes a legend most? A slogan for Blackglama mink in the US, current 1976. This was the headline from a series of advertisements showing mink coats being worn by dozens of 'legendary' figures, including the likes of Margot Fonteyn, Martha Graham, Rudolf Nureyev (all three together in one ad), Shirley Maclaine, Ethel Merman and Lillian Hellman.

what did Horace say? Harry Hemsley was a British entertainer who found fame as that contradiction in terms, a radio ventriloquist (though Edgar Bergen was to have great success on American radio with Charlie McCarthy and Peter Brough had *EDUCATING ARCHIE*). He first broadcast in 1923 and was still going in 1949. Hemsley conducted dialogues with his family – two girls, Winnie and Elsie, a boy, Johnny, and a baby, Horace, who spoke gibberish that

only Winnie could translate. Hence, 'what did Horace say?'

what did you do in the war, Daddy? See DADDY . . .

what does it matter what you do as long as you tear them up? See EYAYDON, YAUDEN . . .

what do you think of it so far? See under *MORECAMBE AND WISE SHOW*.

whatever else it will be, it will be well and truly – all your own. BBC TV's *All Your Own* in the 1950s was a showcase for young viewers who had some interesting hobby and could be seen to enjoy themselves doing it. Introduced by an avuncular Huw Wheldon, the programme would close with him looking forward to the next edition and intoning these words.

whatever happened to —? The conversational query occurs, for example, in Noël Coward's song 'I Wonder What Happened to Him?' (from *Sigh No More*, 1945) in the form, 'Whatever became of old Bagot . . . ?' But the film title *Whatever Happened to Baby Jane!* (1962) fixed the phrase in the way most usually employed by journalists. Like WHERE ARE THEY NOW? this became a standard formula for feature-writing on a slack day. In the early 1980s, the *Sunday Express* ran a weekly column, disinterring the stars of yesteryear, sometimes under the heading 'Where are they now . . . ?' but more usually, 'What ever happened to . . . ?' (See TIT, TOTE AND TELEVISION.)

Coty perfume was also advertised with the slogan 'Whatever Happened to Romance?' (quoted in 1984).

whatever turns you on. Latterly a jokey response to the announcement of some (slightly odd or, conceivably, sexy) enthusiasm. 'I like bathing in warm ass's milk' – 'Whatever turns you on, dear.' Originally, in the 1960s, it was part of an encouragement to pursue one's own enthusiasms, particularly with regard to the drugs which succeeded in 'turning you on' best: 'You should do whatever turns you on.'

what is a Beatle? See WHO ARE THE BEATLES?

what is a mum? See under WHITER THAN WHITE.

what is the difference between a chicken/duck? See under WHY IS A MOUSE WHEN IT SPINS?

what larks, Pip! An exclamatory phrase derived from the novel *Great Expectations* (1860–61) by Charles Dickens. It is a characteristic phrase of Joe Gargery, the blacksmith, who looks after his brother-in-law and apprentice, Pip, in the boy's youth. Chapter 13 has him saying 'calc'lated to lead to larks' and Chapter 57, 'And when you're well enough to go out for a ride – what larks!' The recent use of the phrase probably has more to do with the 1946 film of the book in which Bernard Miles played Joe. As he sees Pip off on a stage coach, he says, 'One day I'll come to see you in London and then, what larks, eh?' and similarly, after Pip's breakdown, 'You'll soon be well enough to go out again, and then – what larks!' Even here, the name Pip is not actually included in the phrase.

In *The Kenneth Williams Diaries* (1993) (entry for 30 August 1970), the actor writes: 'Tom played the piano and all the girls danced with us & I stuck me bum out and oh! what larks Pip!' Ned Sherrin dedicates his *Theatrical Anecdotes* (1991), 'For Judi [Dench] and Michael [Williams]: "What larks!"'

what me – in my state of health? See under *ITMA*.

what, me worry? Phrase of Alfred E. Newman, the cheerfully ignorant character in the US magazine *Mad* (founded 1952).

what price —? A format phrase, questioning the sacrifices and compromises that may have to be made in order to carry out any sort of mission. Known by 1893. From George Bernard Shaw, *Major Barbara* (1907): 'What prawce Selvytion nah?' The phrase was firmly established by *What Price Glory?* – the title of a play (1924; film US, 1952) about the stupidity of war, by Laurence Stallings and Maxwell Anderson.

What Price Hollywood? was the title of a film (US, 1932).

what's a nice girl like you doing in a joint/place like this? Cliché of conversation/chatting up, and now used only in a consciously arch way. It is listed among the 'naff pick-up lines' in *The Naff Sex Guide* (1984). I suspect it may have arisen in Hollywood Westerns of the 1930s. It was certainly established as a film cliché by the 1950s when Frank Muir and Denis Norden included this version in a TAKE IT FROM HERE parody: 'Thanks, Kitty. Say, why does a swell girl like you have to work in a saloon like this?' In the film *Kiss Me Stupid* (US, 1964) Ray Walston strokes Kim Novak's knee and whispers: 'What's a beautiful joint like this doing in a girl like you?' – thus 'reducing the age-old seducer's spiel, while telling the same old story' (as Walter Redfern comments in *Puns*, 1984). In 1973, *Private Eye* carried a cartoon of a male marijuana-smoker with a female, and the caption, 'What's a nice joint like you . . . ?'

what's bred in the bone. Meaning 'what's part of one's nature', this was the title of a novel (1985) by Robertson Davies, who cites 'what's bred in the bone will not out of the flesh' as an 'English proverb from the Latin, 1290'. The implication is that one's nature can't be repressed or cured.

what's it all about? 'What is the meaning of life?' T.S. Eliot's widow, Valerie, wrote a letter to *The Times* (7 February 1970) telling a tale that Eliot himself 'loved to recount'. A taxi-driver had said to the poet, 'You're T. S. Eliot . . . I've got an eye for a celebrity. Only the other evening I picked up Bertrand Russell . . . And I asked him, "What's it all about, guv?" – and, d'you know, he couldn't tell me!' The phrase gained additional resonance from its use in Bill Naughton's *Alfie*, the 1966 film script of his stage and radio play: 'It seems to me if they ain't got you one way then they've got you another. So what's it all about, that's what I keep asking myself, what's it all about?' Subsequently, the phrase 'What's it all about, Alfie?' was popularized by Burt Bacharach and Hal David's song of that title. This was not written for the film, which had a jazz score, with no songs, by

Sonny Rollins, but Cher recorded it and this version was added to the soundtrack for the American release of the picture. Cilla Black then recorded it in Britain and Dionne Warwick in the US.

When Michael Caine, who played Alfie in the film, published his autobiography in 1992, it was naturally entitled *What's It All About?*

what's new, pussycat? Of Warren Beatty, the film actor, Sheilah Graham wrote in *Scratch an Actor* (1969): 'He uses the telephone as a weapon of seduction. He curls up with it, cuddles it, whispers into it, "What's new, pussycat?" (He coined the phrase, and the picture was originally written for him.)'

The film with the title (and the Tom Jones song therefrom) came out in 1965. Perhaps Graham was right. Whatever the case, I would guess that the use of 'pussycat' to describe someone, particularly a woman, as 'attractive, amiable, submissive' (*OED2*) probably emanates from the US, if not precisely from Hollywood.

what's on the table, Mabel? See under HAVE A GO.

what's that got to do with the Prince of Wales? Meaning, 'what you have just said is irrelevant.' Told to me on an LBC radio phone-in, London, in June 1990, but otherwise untraced and unconfirmed. And which Prince of Wales is being talked about? Compare, however, 'What has that to do with Bacchus?' which Brewer finds in classical literature. Partridge/*Catch Phrases* has **what's that got to do with the price of eggs?** as being of American origin. Sir Joh Bjelke-Peterson, Premier of Queensland, was reported in *The Australian* (1 May 1985) as saying of something he thought was irrelevant, 'That's got nothing to do with the price of butter.'

what's the damage? Phrase used when asking how much the bill is (e.g. for drinks) or establishing who should pay it. *The Hallamshire Glossary* by the Rev. Joseph Hunter (*b* 1784) records that this was in common use in the Sheffield area between 1790 and 1810. In fact, the *OED2* has the word 'damage' = 'cost, expense' in 1755,

and in 1852 'What's the damage, as they say in Kentucky' appears in Harriet Beecher Stowe's *Uncle Tom's Cabin* (though not concerning drink). Presumably, the use derives from legal damages.

what's the recipe today, Jim? See under MORNING ALL!

what's up, doc? The characteristic inquiry of Bugs Bunny, the cartoon character, in the US film series which ran from 1937–63, addressed to Elmer Fudd, the doctor who devotes his life to attempting to destroy the rabbit. In full, the phrase is 'Er, what's up, Doc?' – followed by a carrot crunch. Its origins may lie in an old Texan expression introduced to the films by one of the animators, Tex Avery.

The voices of both Bugs and Elmer were done by Mel Blanc (1908–89) who, on emerging from a coma in 1983, inevitably put the question to his physician. The phrase was used as the title of a film starring Barbra Streisand and Ryan O'Neal (1972).

what the butler saw. 'What the Butler Saw' was the name given to a type of penny-in-the-slot machine introduced in Britain c 1880. It was a frisky development of the very old peep show. The female so observed was probably doing something fairly mild in corsets and, if this was an early version of soft porn, it wasn't exactly decadent.

The Museum of the Moving Image in London contains a Mutoscope as invented by Herman Casler in 1897 and links it to the arrival of 'What the Butler Saw', although there had been earlier machines through which pictures on cards were flipped to give an impression of movement. The museum notes that these penny-in-the-slot machines were in Britain for some 70 years, finally disappearing with the arrival of decimal coinage in 1971.

What the Butler Saw was used as the title of a comedy first performed at Wyndham's Theatre on 2 August 1905. An advertising postcard of the time shows a girl complaining to her parents, 'My dolly has been and broke itself!' which suggests that any butler in the piece was unlikely to have had his voyeuristic urge gratified. S.J. Perelman referred in one of his *New Yorker* pieces (reprinted 1978) to 'those penny-arcade tableaux called "What the Butler Saw Through the Keyhole"' which, presumably, indicates that the machines were known in the US.

The phrase was again used as a title by Joe Orton for his posthumously produced farce about goings-on in a psychiatric clinic (1969). In this piece, a butler definitely makes no appearance, though the characters do tend to wander about in their underpants, or less.

Other uses include acting as the title for an instrumental number recorded by Lord Rockingham's XI (in 1958) and for a song recorded by Squeeze in 1980. Very much earlier than both these, Florrie Forde, the music-hall star, recorded a song called 'What the Curate Saw', which is clearly an allusion.

An unlikely, though entertaining, suggestion about the phrase's origin concerns the spectacularly naughty 1884 judicial separation of Lord and Lady Colin Campbell, in which the case hinged on the evidence of a butler who claimed he saw goings-on through a keyhole. Piers Compton in his book *Victorian Vortex* (1977) describes how Lord Colin, son of the Duke of Argyll, accused his wife of adultery with any number of chaps ranging from members of the aristocracy to the chief of the Metropolitan Fire Brigade. At the trial, Lady C. countered that the husband had seduced her maid, and it was the maid, not the butler, who, in turn, testified that she had spied upon her Ladyship and the fire chief *in flagrante*.

'At that,' Compton informs us, 'the jury streamed out of the box and tramped to the Campbell residence in Cadogan Square, where they took turns in applying their judicial eyes to the keyhole, to see if the maid could have indeed witnessed such a *coup de théâtre* . . .'

From the *Observer* (20 May 1989): [Headline to book review] 'What the Butler Didn't See'.

what the dickens! Exclamation of incredulity. 'Dickens' has nothing to do with the novelist but is a euphemistic way of saying 'What the *devil*!' (and is perhaps a watered down version of 'devilkin', though that is not certain). Shakespeare has, 'I cannot tell what the dickens his name is' (*Merry Wives of Windsor*, III.ii.16; 1601).

what — thinks today, — will think tomorrow. Manchester was the original city nominated as the thought-setter for England as a whole when, in the nineteenth century, it was indeed a hub of industrial activity and innovation and the capital of free trade. It may date back to the 1840s. Quoting it in *English Journey* (1934), J.B. Priestley added: 'We still see some of the results . . . of what Manchester thought in what has been left to us, to mourn over, by the vast, greedy, slovenly, dirty process of industrialization for quick profits.'

On the other hand, *Notes and Queries* in 1908 discussed the phrase as, 'What Lancashire thinks (or says) today, England will think (or say) tomorrow' and also found 'What Birmingham says today, England will say tomorrow'.

what we've got here is failure to communicate. In the 1967 film *Cool Hand Luke*, Strother Martin (as a prison officer) says to Paul Newman (as a rebellious prisoner), 'What we've got here is failure to communicate. Some men you just can't reach.' The line was also used to promote the film.

what would you do, chums? See under BAND WAGGON.

what you see is what you get. See WYSIWYG.

wheel. See REINVENT THE ∼.

wheel has come/turned full circle, the. Now a cliché. Edmund the Bastard says: 'The wheel is come full circle' in Shakespeare's *King Lear*, V.iii.173 (1605). He is referring to the wheel of Fortune, being at that moment back down at the bottom where he was before it began to revolve. Chips Channon writes in his diary (13 October 1943): 'I turned on the wireless and heard the official announcement of Italy's declaration of war on Germany. So now the wheel has turned full circle.'

Full Circle was the title of Sir Anthony Eden's memoirs (1960).

whelk-stall. See COULDN'T RUN A ∼.

when. See <small>AND</small> ~ <small>DID YOU LAST</small> . . .

when are you going to finish off that dress? Cliché used in chatting up, flirting. Addressed to a woman with skimpy decolletage. Tom Jones can be heard so addressing a member of the audience on the LP *Tom Jones – Live at Caesar's Palace, Las Vegas* (1971).

when did you last see your father? See <small>AND WHEN</small> . . .

when did you stop beating your wife? An example of a leading question (because by attempting to start answering it you admit that you *did* once beat your wife). So, an example, too, of an unanswerable question?

when I'm dead and gone the game's finished. See under <small>HERE'S A FUNNY THING</small> . . .

when in Rome – do as the Romans do. This maxim suggests that one should adapt to prevalent customs. Its probable source is St Ambrose (*d* 397): '*Si fueris Romae, Romano vivito more;/Si fueris alibi, vivito sicut ibi*' [If you are at Rome, live in the Roman style; if you live elsewhere, live as they live elsewhere].

when it rains, it pours. See under <small>IT NEVER RAINS, BUT IT POURS.</small>

when it's night-time in Italy,/It's Wednesday over here. Title of a nonsense song written by the Americans James Kendis and Lew Brown in about 1923. It includes the nonsense riddles, 'Why does a fly? When does a bee?/How does a wasp sit down to have its tea?'

when I was in Patagonia . . . A regular participant in the BBC radio *Brains Trust* discussions of the 1940s was Commander A.B. Campbell. His stock phrase arose in an earlier version of the programme when it was still called *Any Questions* (in 1941). Donald McCullough, the chairman, said: 'Mr Edwards of Balham wants to know if the members of the Brains Trust agree with the practice of sending missionaries to foreign lands.' Prof. Joad and Julian Huxley

gave their answers and then Campbell began, 'When I was in Patagonia . . .'

In a book which used the phrase as its title, Campbell recalled: 'I got no further, for Joad burst into a roar of laughter and the other members of the session joined in. For some time the feature was held up while the hilarity spent itself. For the life of me I could not see the joke . . . Even today (1951), years after, I can raise a laugh if I am on a public platform and make an allusion to it.'

when one door closes another door closes. A cynical variant (which I first heard in 1969) of the old 'Irish proverb' (according to Mencken), 'God never shuts one door but He opens another.' Whether Irish or not, *CODP* has it as already proverbial by 1586. The cynical variant also comes – perhaps more usually – in the form **as one door closes, another door shuts.**

when people are starving in India . . . I am indebted to *The Complete Directory to Prime Time Network TV Shows* (1981) for the information that when a proposed US series called *B.A.D. Cats* crashed in 1980, Everett Chambers, its executive producer, said, 'We bought $40,000 worth of cars to smash up, and we never got a chance to smash them up. I think that's kind of immoral, $40,000 worth of cars to smash up when people are starving in India.'

I had always taken this to be a (British) nanny's expression, but the nearest I can find, recorded in *Nanny Says* by Sir Hugh Casson and Joyce Grenfell (1972) is, 'Think of all the poor starving children who'd be grateful for that nice plain bread and butter.'

Wasn't it also advised that it was polite to leave a little food on the side of the plate 'for the starving in India' if not for 'Mr Manners'?

Paul Beale in Partridge/*Catch Phrases*, commenting on the American 'Remember the starving Armenians' notes: 'The one used to exhort me as a child, late 1930s, to clear up my plate or to tackle something I found unpalatable was "think of all the poor starving children in China!"'

when the going gets tough, the tough get going. One of several axioms said to have come from the Boston-Irish political jungle or, more precisely, from President Kennedy's father, Joseph P. Kennedy (1888–1969). At this distance, it is impossible to say for sure whether this wealthy, ambitious businessman/ambassador/politician originated the expression, but he certainly instilled it in his sons.

Subsequently, it was used as a slogan for the film *The Jewel of the Nile* (1985) and a song with the title sung by Billy Ocean and the stars of the film was a No. 1 hit in 1986. The joke slogan **when the going gets tough, the tough go shopping** had appeared on T-shirts in the US by 1982.

when the — had to stop. Format phrase and journalistic cliché derived from *When the Kissing Had to Stop*, the title of a novel (1960) by Constantine Fitzgibbon about a Russian takeover of Britain, and adapted for TV in 1962. That title derives in turn from Robert Browning's poem 'A Toccata of Galuppi's' (1855): 'What of soul was left, I wonder,/When the kissing had to stop?'

In *Keep Taking the Tabloids* (1983), Fritz Spiegl noted these headline uses: 'When the Music had to Stop', 'WHEN THE TALKING HAD TO STOP'.

when the music stops. See under ARE YOU SITTING COMFORTABLY . . .

when the world was young. A wistful expression about 'long ago' and a time more innocent than the present. Also the English title of a song (1952) by Johnny Mercer, based on the French song 'Le Chevalier de Paris' or 'Ah! Les Pommiers Doux' (1950). The phrase may derive ultimately from a verse in the Apocrypha: 'For the world has lost his youth, and the times begin to wax old' (2 Esdras 14:10). Precisely as 'When the World Was Young', it is the title of a painting (1891) by Sir E.J. Poynter PRA which shows three young girls in a classical setting, relaxing by a pool. Compare the lines from 'Young and Old' in the *Water Babies* (1863) by Charles Kingsley:

When all the world is young, lad,
And all the trees are green
. . . Young blood must have its course, lad,
And every dog his day.

when you got it, flaunt it. Braniff Airline in the US used this headline over ads in *c* 1969 featuring celebrities such as Sonny Liston, Andy Warhol and Joe Namath. Probably the line was acquired from the 1967 Mel Brooks movie *The Producers* in which Zero Mostel as 'Max Bialystock' says to the owner of a large white limo: 'That's it, baby! When you got it, flaunt it! Flaunt it!' Later in the film he says, 'Take it when you can get it. Flaunt it! Flaunt it!'

The idea was obviously very much around at this time. In an episode of BBC radio's *Round the Horne* (15 May 1966), these lines occurred: 'The physique of a young Greek god and profile of classical perfection . . . Still, what I say is if you've got it, you may as well show it.'

when you hear the gong. From Radio Luxembourg in the 1950s and 60s (popular music service beamed at Britain): 'The time now – when you hear the gong – is six o'clock.' And they really did use a gong for the time signal.

where are they now? A popular journalistic formula when resurrecting people who have passed out of the headlines – compare WHATEVER HAPPENED TO —? The rhetorical question occurs rather differently in Wordsworth's ode 'Intimations of Immortality' (1807):

Whither is fled the visionary gleam?
Where is it now, the glory and the dream?

Where Are They Now? was the title of a radio play by Tom Stoppard in 1970.

—, where are you now? Usually employed as an ironical plea to someone who has long since departed because one finds that present circumstances are as bad as – or worse than – when the person was around. And so, one might have said during the Reagan Irangate scandal, 'Richard Nixon, where are you now?'

As such, it is a truncation of '. . . where are you now that your country needs you?' or an equivalent of **come back —, all is forgiven** which, once upon a time, might have been said about a warrior who had retired to his farm and fallen out of favour. The graffito 'Lee Harvey Oswald, where are you now that your country needs you?' appeared during the presidencies of both Lyndon Johnson and Richard Nixon.

where did you get that hat? A catchphrase of the 1890s originating in a comic song with the title (1888), variously attributed to J.J. Sullivan and J. Rolmaz. Hence, the cartoon in *Punch's Almanack for 1911* in which a professor is saying: 'I really think there must be something peculiar about my hat, for this morning some little boys enquired where I had purchased it, and do you know, Marion, for the life of me I could not remember.'

where did you learn to kiss like that? Bob Monkhouse noted in 1979: 'In my script-writing partnership with Denis Goodwin I must confess to the deliberate confecting of catchphrases. From our first major radio success, *Calling All Forces* [BBC, from 1950], came "Where did you learn to kiss like that?" But it was what we called a "vehicle phrase", not really constructed to catch on but to carry a fresh joke each week.'

where do we find such men? In 1984, on the fortieth anniversary of the D-Day landings, President Reagan visited Europe and made a speech in which he eulogized those who had taken part in the event. 'Where do we find such men?' he asked. On an earlier occasion he had said: 'Many years ago in one of the four wars in my lifetime, an admiral stood on the bridge of a carrier watching the planes take off and out into the darkness bent on a night combat mission and then found himself asking, with no one there to answer – just himself to hear his own voice – "Where do we find such men?"' But the very first time he had used the line he had made it clear where it came from. The story comes from James Michener's novel *Bridges at Toko-Ri*, later filmed (1954) with William Holden who asks: 'Where do we get such men?'

where do we go from here? A clichéd and pompous way of rounding off broadcasting discussions about the future of almost anything. Used as the title of a BBC TV inquiry in Scotland, 1968. 'Where Do We Go From Here?' was also the title of a

song of the 1940s, popular for a while in the Army. Alternatively, the question can be put to an individual (who has just been interviewed about his life and works) in the form, 'Well, where do you go from here?' A possible source was hinted at by Winston Churchill when, in a broadcast to the US from London on 8 August 1939, he said: 'And now it is holiday again, and where are we now? Or, as you sometimes ask in the United States – where do we go from here?'

In politics, as a theme for debates, it tends to be put even more pompously (though now, with luck, only jokingly) in the form **whither —— ?** (e.g. 'Whither Democracy?' 'Whither Europe?' 'Whither the Labour Party?'). A sketch from BBC TV *That Was the Week That Was* (1962–3 series) began: 'Question of the year, the future of our leader. How soon if ever will he be eased out of Admiralty House and into the Earldom of Bromley. After Macmillan – whither?' The first episode of MONTY PYTHON'S FLYING CIRCUS (1969) was subtitled 'Whither Canada?' The heading of a *Times* leader (14 January 1985) was 'WHITHER THE BBC?'

where have all the — gone? Format phrase based on the title of the song 'Where Have All the Flowers Gone' by Pete Seeger (1961). In *Keep Taking the Tabloids* (1983), Fritz Spiegl noted these headline uses: 'WHERE HAVE ALL THE GUITARS GONE', 'Where have all the Letters Gone'

where is it all leading us, I ask myself? See under MORNING ALL!

where it's at. See — IS THE NAME OF THE GAME.

where McGregor sits *is* the head o' the table. The fable has it that McGregor, who was head of the Scottish clan, was invited to an important function. At dinner, his host apologized for not placing him at the head of the table. To which McGregor responded, 'Where McGregor sits *is* the head o' the table.' There are various versions of this. In a letter from Lord Chesterfield to Lord Huntingdon (19 May 1756), Chesterfield quoted 'what the late Duke of Somerset [said] absurdly, when accidentally placed below himself one day at table, *the best place is wherever I sit*. A footnote to the 1923 publication of this letter states: 'The Highland Chief, The McNab, also said: "Where the McNab sits, there is the Head of the Table.'

whereof. See HE KNOWS ~ HE SPEAKS.

where's me shirt? See under HOW TICKLED I AM.

where that came from. See AND THERE'S MORE . . .

where's the beef? A classic example of an advertising slogan turning into a political catchphrase. The Wendy International hamburger chain promoted its wares in the US from 1984 with TV commercials, one of which showed three elderly women eyeing a small hamburger on a huge bun – a Wendy competitor's product. 'It certainly is a big bun,' asserted one. 'It's a very big fluffy bun,' the second agreed. But the third asked, 'Where's the beef?'

The line caught on hugely. Walter Mondale, running for the Democratic nomination, used it to question the substance of his rival Gary Hart's policies.

where the bodies are buried. See KNOW WHERE THE BODIES . . .

where the heart is. The title of the film *Where the Heart Is* (US, 1990), directed by John Boorman, comes from the proverb: **home is where the heart is**. Its first appearance may well have been in an 1870 play by J.J. McCloskey, but even then it was 'Home, *they say*, is where the heart is', so it was obviously an established saying by then. Mencken claims it as an 'American saying, author unidentified'.

. . . wherever you are. A tag usually referring to a dead person (i.e. either in heaven or hell). From the album *The Muppet Show* (1977) – when Zoot is about to prostitute his talents as a saxophonist by playing a number of which he disapproves, he says: 'Forgive me, Charlie Parker, wherever you are.' See also under HOW ABOUT THAT, THEN?

where've you been, who've you been with, what've you been doing, and why? From the British music-hall act of Old Mother Riley and her daughter in the 1930s/40s. Riley was played by Arthur Lucan and the daughter by his wife, Kitty McShane. Another of Riley's lines was 'Oh, did your hear that, **Mrs Girochie? SOS!** Me daughter's at it again!', though I have seen this presented as 'Mrs Ginocchi, SOS.'

where were you in '62? Title of a 1950s/60s nostalgia and trivia quiz that I presented on BBC Radio 2 (1983–85). As acknowledged, it was taken from the promotional slogan for the film *American Graffiti* (US, 1973).

where were you when the lights went out? The 1968 film *Where Were You When the Lights Went Out?* was inspired by the great New York blackout of 1965 when the electricity supply failed and – or so it was popularly believed – the birth rate shot up nine months later. The phrase echoes an old music-hall song and perhaps also the American nonsense rhyme 'Where was Moses when the light went out?/Down in the cellar eating sauerkraut.' This last appears to have developed from the 'almost proverbial' riddle (as the Opies call it in *The Lore and Language of Schoolchildren*, 1959):

Q. Where was Moses when the light went out?
A. In the dark.

The Opies find this in *The Riddler's Oracle*, c 1821. *Punch* in its *Almanack for 1873* (17 December 1872) has a 'comic chronology' in which AD 1220 marked the 'First asking of the question, "Where was Moses when the candle went out?"' Another response, current in the 1920s was: 'Running round the table with his shirt hanging out.'

which comes first, the music or the words? An interviewer's cliché question when faced with a lyricist, composer or songwriter. Having so designated it in my book *The Gift of the Gab* (1985), I found myself interviewing one of the breed on television and was dreadfully conscious of the error I could commit. And so I asked him, 'Which comes first, the words or the lyrics?'

Ah, well. When Sammy Cahn, the American lyricist who died in 1993, was posed the question, he would ritually answer: 'First comes the phone call.'

which twin has the Toni? An advertising headline that asks a question, a slogan that contains the brand name, and an idea that was dotty enough to be much copied. In the UK of the early 1950s, Toni home perms advertising featured pairs of identical twins (real ones) who also toured doing promotional work for the product. One twin had a Toni home perm, the other a more expensive perm – a footnote explained which was which in answer to the question.

During the 1970 British General Election, the Liberal Party produced a poster showing pictures of Harold Wilson and Edward Heath with the slogan, 'Which twin is the Tory?'

which would you rather, or go fishing?/which would you rather be, or a wasp? See under WHY IS A MOUSE WHEN IT SPINS?

whiff of grapeshot, a. A warning shot, a hint of force sufficient to impress. Thomas Carlyle uses the phrase as a chapter title and on two other occasions (one apparently quoting Napoleon) in his *History of the French Revolution* (1837). 'The whiff of grapeshot can, if needful, become a blast and tempest' refers to the ease with which Napoleon and the military dispersed the Paris insurrection of the Vendémiaire in 1795.

whimper. See NOT WITH A BANG BUT A ~.

whip. See FAIR CRACK OF THE ~.

Whippit Kwick. See under DON'T FORCE IT, PHOEBE.

Whispering Grass. Nickname given to Shaw Taylor (b 1924), British TV presenter of ITV's *Police Five* programmes since the 1960s. Asking the public to come forward with information to help solve crimes, Taylor reportedly attracted this nickname in the underworld. 'Whispering Grass' is

the title of a popular song (1940) and a 'grass' is underworld slang for an informer.

whispers. See CHINESE ~.

whistle. See BLOW THE ~ ON; under DO YOU KNOW . . . ?; IF YOU WANT ANYTHING, JUST ~; WOULD YOU LIKE TO WET YOUR ~.

whistles. See PUT THE BELLS AND ~ ON.

whistle stop, a. This was originally the name given to a place in the US too small to have scheduled train calling at it. If a passenger did want to alight, the conductor would signal to the engineer/driver and he would respond by pulling the whistle. As a political term for a short train visit to a place by a campaigning politician, it was introduced by Robert Taft (1948) in remarks about President Truman who had been criticizing Congress from the platform of a train in journeys about the country. A 'whistle-stop tour' might now be used of any series of quick visits, not necessarily by a politician or by train.

white. See FREE, ~ , AND TWENTY-ONE; GREAT ~ WAY.

white Christmas, a. The film *White Christmas* (US, 1954), inspired by Irving Berlin's '(I'm Dreaming of a) White Christmas' (1942) has combined with the classic song to ensure that the phrase and concept of a white Christmas (i.e. when it has snowed or is snowing) endures. An early use occurs in Charles Kingsley, *Two Years Ago* (1857): 'We shall have a white Christmas, I expect. Snow's coming.'

white coats. See MEN IN ~.

Whitehall. See FOGGY BOTTOM.

White House. See LOG CABIN TO ~.

Whitehouse, Mrs. See under MRS GRUNDY.

white man's burden. See KIPLING.

White man speak with forked tongue. Supposedly the way a Red Indian chief would pronounce on the duplicitous ways of the White man, in Western movies. Citations lacking.

White Rabbit, the. The name of a character in Lewis Carroll's *Alice In Wonderland* (1865) who is anxious because he fears he will be late for something, and thus applied to anyone similarly disposed. Compare DECISIONS DECISIONS!

The *White Rabbit* is the title of a book (1952) by Bruce Marshall about the exploits of Wing-Commander F.F.E. Yeo-Thomas, a British secret agent in the Second World War. The phrase was his nickname.

whiter than white. Meaning, 'absolutely pure', this phrase was in use by 1924 but was apparently later used as a slogan for Persil washing powder in the UK (quoted in 1976, but probably current a decade or two earlier). Later: 'TOWN THAT'S WHITER THAN WHITE' (*Guardian* headline, 19 March 1992).

Persil also popularized the theme of **someone's mother**, current in 1940 ('Aha . . . someone's mother isn't using Persil yet'), which it carried forward from posters and press ads to TV in the 1950s: 'What someone's mum really ought to know,/So someone's mum better get to know./That Persil washes whiter, whiter ~/**persil washes whiter**.' the theme **what is a mum?** featured in a series of persil tv ads from 1961.

whither. See WHERE DO WE GO FROM HERE?

Whittington, Dick. See STREETS PAVED WITH GOLD.

whoa, mama! See under SIMPSONS, THE.

who *are* the Beatles? At the height of Beatlemania in the '60s, when the newspapers were daily full of pieces about the FAB FOUR, a judge in the High Court is said to have lifted the flap of his wig quizzically and inquired of counsel, 'Who *are* the Beatles?' This has become the archetypal British judge's remark – often, of course, a question posed when the judge knows the answer, in order to further his reputation for fustiness and aloofness from the concerns of ordinary citizens. But did any judge actually ever pose the question?

I believe not. What I think happened was that an assumption was made, when the Beatles came along, that judges *would* ask the question – just as they had always done and still do. More recently, for example, in 1990, the year of the football World Cup, Mr Justice Harman actually asked, 'Who is Gazza? Isn't there an operetta called *La Gazza Ladra*?' Indeed, there is – but that has nothing to do with the footballer Paul 'Gazza' Gascoigne. A century before, in 1889, Mr Justice Stephen had asked, 'What is the Grand National?' (but *he* was eventually committed to a lunatic asylum, so perhaps that doesn't count). In *Geoffrey Madan's Notebooks* (edited by Gere and Sparrow, 1981), Lord Hewart (1870–1943) is credited with: 'Precedent compels me to ask: what is jazz?' Another query is reputedly, 'What is a G-string? Has it something to do with Bach?' In fiction, A.P. Herbert's Mr Justice Snubb asked 'What is a crossword?' An episode of the 'Flook' comic strip dating from 1963 had a judge asking: 'What does darling mean? What is a darling?' And, there may have been a cartoon by 'Vicky' just after the war which had a judge asking: 'What is a banana?' In the late 1940s a judge was supposed to have asked, 'What is oomph?' In the next issue of the *News of the World* there was a cartoon of a very curvaceous young woman saying, 'What is a judge?' (See also DARLING OF THE HALLS.)

I am encouraged to believe in the apocryphal nature of the Beatles query by a report in the *Guardian* on 10 December 1963 (when Beatlemania was rampant). A Queen's Counsel representing the Performing Right Society at a London tribunal in a case concerning copyright fees at pop concerts objected to a suggestion that tribunal members should attend such a concert in order to see and hear what it was like. Instead, they listened to a recording of a Beatles' concert. Another QC remarked to the court: 'You will only have to suffer two or three minutes.' The Guardian headline over its report of all this was: **what is a Beatle?** – which, as I say, appears to be a case of the old question being applied to a new phenomenon. But it does not appear to have been asked by an actual judge.

It should perhaps be allowed that when a judge asks a question like this, he often knows the answer and is merely asking so that things may be clarified for the jury.

who breaks a butterfly upon a wheel? Meaning 'who goes to great lengths to accomplish something trifling?' The expression comes from the 'Epistle to Dr Arbuthnot' (1735) by Alexander Pope. As 'Who Breaks a Butterfly on a Wheel', it was used as the headline to a leader in *The Times* (1 July 1967) when Mick Jagger, the pop singer, was given a three-month gaol term on drugs charges.

— who came in from the cold, the. A journalistic format derived from the title of John Le Carré's novel *The Spy Who Came In From the Cold* (1963), about a spy from the West getting even with his East German counterpart around the time of the erection of the Berlin Wall. From then on, any people or any thing, coming in from any kind of exposed position, or returning to favour, might be described as 'coming in from the cold'. From the *Financial Times* (21 March 1984): '[London Stock Exchange] Oils and leading Engineerings were well to the fore. Stores also joined in the recovery, while Life Insurances came in from the cold after a particularly depressing spell before and after abolition of Life Assurance premium relief.' On 22 June 1990, Douglas Hurd, British Foreign Secretary, speaking in Berlin, said: 'We should not forget the reason for which Checkpoint Charlie stood here for so many years but no one can be sorry that it is going. At long last we, we are bringing "Charlie" in from the cold.' In *Keep Taking the Tabloids* (1983), Fritz Spiegl noted these much earlier headline uses: 'Explorer comes in from cold', 'Stranger who flew in from the cold', 'Spy who came in from the Cold War', 'Dartmoor sheep come in from the cold', 'Quarter that came in from the cold'.

who dares wins. The British SAS (Special Air Service) regiment was founded by Col. David Stirling in 1950 although its origins lay in the Second World War. Its motto became famous after members of the crack regiment shot their way into the Iranian embassy in London, in May 1980, to end a siege (when wags suggested the motto should really be, 'Who dares use it [fire-power], wins'). A feature film about the supposed exploits of the SAS was made, using the motto as its title in 1982 and the *Daily Mirror* labelled its 'Win a Million' bingo promotion 'Who Dares Wins' in 1984.

The motto appears to have been borrowed from the Alvingham barony, created in 1929.

who do I have to fuck to get out of this — ? Presumably, from show biz. Having, as legend would have it, had to fuck to get cast in a show or picture, the speaker is wondering how the process can be reversed – because the show or film is having problems or turns out to be no good. Bob Chieger in *Was It Good For You, Too?* ascribes to 'Shirley Wood, talent coordinator for NBC's *The Tonight Show* in the 1960s', the quote: 'Who do you have to fuck to get *out* of show business?' The line 'Listen, who do I have to fuck to get *off* this picture?' occurs in Terry Southern's *Blue Movie* (1970). Steve Bach in *Final Cut* (1985) ascribes 'Who do I fuck to get off this picture?' simply to 'Anonymous Hollywood starlet (circa 1930)'.

who goes home? The cry that goes up in the House of Commons, echoed by policemen, when the House has finished a sitting and is about to close its doors. It dates from the days when, to protect themselves against robbers, MPs would form small groups for mutual protection on the way home. Chips Channon wrote in his diary (17 March 1937) on Stanley Baldwin's tribute to the late Austen Chamberlain: 'His closing sentence "Austen has at last gone home" made us all think of the attendant's call "Who goes home?"' On the same day, Harold Nicolson wrote in his diary: 'The Prime Minister makes an adequate oration but rather spoils it by introducing at the end a somewhat unsuccessful play on the phrase "Who Goes Home?"'

who he? Popularized by *Private Eye* in the 1980s, this editorial interjection after a little-known person's name shows some signs of catching on: 'This month, for instance, has been the time for remembering the 110th anniversary of the birth of Grigori Petrovsky. Who he?' – *New Statesman*, 26 February 1988. I suspect Richard Ingrams, when editor of the *Eye*, consciously borrowed the phrase from Harold Ross (1892–1951), editor of the *New Yorker*. James Thurber in *The Years with Ross* (1959), describes how Ross would customarily add this query to manuscripts on finding a name he did not know (sometimes betraying his ignorance). He said the only two names everyone knew were Houdini and Sherlock Holmes.

A book with the title *Who He? Goodman's Dictionary of the Unknown Famous* was published in 1984. The phrase echoes the Duke of Wellington's peremptory 'Who? Who?' on hearing the names of ministers in Lord Derby's new administration (1852).

who is to — what — is to —. Comparison format usually enabling one (if not both) of the people mentioned to be slighted. From the *Independent* (30 June 1990): '[Bobby] Charlton, who is to tact what Charlie Drake is to nuclear physics, found the Pontiff "smaller than I expected".'

whole new ball game, a. A state of affairs where new factors come into play. From American business jargon and established by the 1960s. 'Mr Gerry Fernback, chairman of ABTA's retail travel agents' council said last week: "For the first time British Airways is making the right noises. It's a whole new ball game now . . . it's in their interest and ours that cheap tickets are available to the public"' (*Observer*, 26 September 1983).

who loves ya, baby? Telly Savalas created a vogue for this phrase, as the lollipop-sucking New York police lieutenant in the TV series *Kojak* (1973–7). Inevitably, he also recorded a song with the title (1975).

whore. See HEAVENS, ELEVEN O'CLOCK . . .

who's for tennis? See under ANYONE FOR TENNIS?

whose — is it anyway? Format phrase derived from *Whose Life Is It Anyway?*, the title of a play (1978; film US, 1981) by Brian Clark. Later a BBC Radio/Channel 4 TV

improvisatory game was given the title *Whose Line Is It Anyway?* (by 1989). By 1993, the *Independent* Magazine was campaigning for the abolition of it as a headline cliché. Among a blizzard of examples, it cited: 'WHOSE QUEEN IS IT ANYWAY?' (London *Evening Standard*, 18 March 1993) and 'WHOSE WOMB IS IT ANYWAY?' (*Northern Echo*, 9 November 1992).

who shot J.R.? The hero/villain J.R. Ewing (played by Larry Hagman) of the top-rated US TV soap opera *Dallas* was shot in the cliffhanging last episode of the programme's 1979–80 season. For reasons not entirely clear, the question of who had inflicted this far from mortal wound caused a sensation in the US and UK. Consequently, the first episode of the next series attracted 53.3 per cent of the American viewing audience, the highest ever rating. All those who had posed the question, or who had even sported bumper-stickers declaring **I hate J.R.**, discovered that the guilty party was a jilted lover.

who was that lady I saw you with last night? A stock part of an American vaudeville routine in which the expected answer is, **that was no lady – that was my wife!** It seems generally agreed that the first comedians to perform this exchange were Joseph Weber (1867–1942) and Lew Fields (1867–1941). Bartlett (1992) dates this from 1887 and has the riposte as 'She ain't no lady; she's my wife.'

who you lookin' at? The yobbo or lout's challenge which caught on in the UK in the early 1990s. It was already being noted by a humorous columnist in *The Times* (8 August 1990): 'At the turn of the century, when civility was still the rule, people would introduce themselves to strangers with a cheery, "Who are you lookin' at, then?", to which the correct reply would be, "What's your problem?" One would then be invited by one's new acquaintance to "Come outside and say that".'

The phrase was used as the title of a short-lived ITV comedy series in 1993.

WHT. Social typing phrase, for identifying the type of man who has 'Wandering Hand Trouble' and is therefore a threat to women. Probably only British middle-class use. Known by the 1950s?

why. See AND ∼ NOT?

why are you telling me all this? See under ARCHERS, THE.

why is a mouse when it spins? A nonsense riddle to which the usual answer is, **because the higher, the fewer.** Remembered from the 1920s/30s. John Mack of Surbiton suggested (1987) that it originated in repartee between Jasper Maskelyne and Oswald Williams in magic shows at the St George's Hall in Langham Place, London, in about 1930. If not originated, he says, it was certainly much used by them.

Mrs Jean E. French of Finchampstead suggested that it might not be nonsensical if you substituted the word 'when' for 'why' in posing the riddle. From this I wondered whether it had anything to with 'Hickory, dickory, dock, the mouse ran up the clock, the clock struck one, the mouse fell down . . .'

A variation of the riddle (which doesn't help either) is:

Q. Why is a mouse when it's spinning its web?
A. Because the more the fewer the quicker.

Other phrases from nonsensical riddles:

Q. **How is a man when he's out?**
A. The sooner he does, the much.
Q. **What is the difference between a chicken/duck?**
A. One of its legs is both the same.
Q. **Which would you rather, or go fishing?** [or swimming/hunting?]
A. One rode a horse and the other rhododendron.

This last may not be a riddle at all and the answer may belong elsewhere. Partridge/Slang gives 'What shall we do, or go fishing' as a 'trick elaboration' of the straightforward 'What shall we do now?' (It is quoted in Dorothy L. Sayers, *The Nine Tailors,* 1934). And compare: **which would you rather be – or a wasp?**

why keep a cow when you can buy a bottle of milk? A common justification for not getting married. Hence, the comic confusion of the version: 'Why go out for a pint of milk when you've got an old cow at home?' Partridge/*Slang* also finds this 'cynical male gibe at marriage' in the forms **why buy a book when you can join a library?'** and **you don't have to buy a cow merely because you are fond of milk',** dating them from the late nineteenth century. He also suggests that the 'milk/cow' argument features in John Bunyan's *The Life and Death of Mr Badman* (1680), though this has not been verified and is probably not used in connection with marriage. G.L. Apperson in his *English Proverbs and Proverbial Phrases* (1929) also finds the simple expression 'Who would keep a cow when he may have a quart of milk for a penny?' by 1659.

why-y-y-y, Daddy? Stock phrase of Fanny Brice playing the part of 'Baby Snooks' on American radio from 1936.

why not the best? See JIMMY WHO?

wicked! See under CRUCIAL!

wickedest. See under BEAST 666.

Wicked Witch of the West, the. Name of a character in *The Wonderful Wizard of Oz* (1900) by L. Frank Baum. Allan Massie, writing on Margaret Thatcher (quoted in Michael Cockerell, *Live From Number 10,* 1989): 'It would not convert those for whom she is SHE WHO MUST BE OBEYED and the Wicked Witch of the West rolled into one.'

widow. See GRASS ∼.

width, feel the. See NEVER MIND THE QUALITY . . .

wife. See ALL THE WORLD AND HIS ∼; CAESAR'S ∼; ∼ IN EVERY PORT under GIRL IN EVERY PORT; MEET THE ∼ under 'AS 'E BIN IN, WHACK?; TAKE MY ∼ . . .; WHEN DID YOU STOP BEATING YOUR ∼?

Wigan Pier. An imaginary focus of jokes (compare the Swiss Navy), in this case, the creation of the music-hall comedian George

Formby Snr (1876–1921). Wigan, an industrial town in Lancashire, is not a seaside resort, but is one of those places dear to the British, the mere mention of whose name is sufficient to provoke laughter (compare Basingstoke, Scunthorpe, Chipping Sodbury, Neasden). A non-fiction book by George Orwell about 'unemployment and the proletarian life' was entitled *The Road To Wigan Pier* (1937). In the 1980s, a derelict warehouse alongside a basin of the Leeds-Liverpool canal, at Wigan, was renovated and given the name.

Wild Bill. The nickname of James Butler Hickock (1837–76), US frontiersman and marshal. His nickname probably arose during his wilder days when – in 1861 – he challenged a whole crowd to a fight. All the people scattered.

will, I. See I DO.

Willie. See JOHN ~, COME ON.

willies, to be given the. Meaning 'to be frightened, made nervous'. *OED2* suggests a US nineteenth-century origin. Another possible source is from 'wiffle woffle', meaning stomachache. Note also that in the ballet *Giselle* (Paris, 1841) there are things called *Wilis* – spirits of maidens who die before marriage.

— will never be the same again. Any change, however unremarkable, requires this journalistic cliché phrase. 'The Broadway musical would never be the same again' – TV promo, New York 1983. 'Life for George Bush will never be the same again' – Tim Ewart, ITN news, 20 January 1989 (the day of the president's inauguration).

will the real —, please stand up? In the American TV game *To Tell the Truth*, devised by Goodson-Todman Productions and shown from 1956–66, a panel had to decide which of three contestants, all claiming to be a certain person, was telling the truth. After the panellists had interrogated the challenger and the 'impostors', they had to declare which person they thought was the real one. MC Bud Collyer would then say: 'Will the

real — —, please stand up!' and he or she did so. The game was revived in the UK as *Tell the Truth* in the 1980s.

Ian Carmichael, the actor, entitled his autobiography *Will the Real Ian Carmichael . . .* (1979). In March 1984, Elizabeth Taylor, the actress, was quoted as saying: 'I'm still trying to find the real Elizabeth Taylor and make her stand up.'

win. See NOTHING VENTURE, NOTHING ~; WHO DARES ~S.

wind. See TWIST SLOWLY, SLOWLY IN THE ~; WAY THE ~ BLOWS.

wind and water. See LIKE THE BARBER'S CAT . . .

windmills. See TILT AT ~.

wind of change, a/the. Speaking to both Houses of the South African parliament on 3 February 1960, the British Prime Minister Harold Macmillan gave his hosts a message they cannot have wanted to hear: 'The most striking of all the impressions I have formed since I left London a month ago is of the strength of this African national consciousness. In different places it may take different forms, but it is happening everywhere. The wind of change is blowing through this continent. Whether we like it or not, this growth of national consciousness is a political fact.'

The phrase 'wind of change' – though not, of course, original – was contributed to the speechwriting team by the diplomat (later Sir) David Hunt. The *OED2* acknowledges that use of the phrase 'wind(s) of change' increased markedly after the speech. When Macmillan sought a title for one of his volumes of memoirs he plumped for the more common, plural, usage – *Winds of Change*.

In a similar windy metaphor Stanley Baldwin had said in 1934: 'There is a wind of nationalism and freedom round the world, and blowing as strongly in Asia as elsewhere.' President George Bush made 'a new breeze is blowing' the theme of his inauguration speech on 20 January 1989.

window of opportunity, a. (sometimes just **window**.) A period of limited duration which a task may be attempted. From the US space programme in the 1960s when a 'launch window' was the period of time during which a rocket had to be launched if it was to reach the correct orbit. Weather conditions and technical faults sometimes militated against the window being used. The figurative sense, in other fields of endeavour, was common by 1987.

wind(s) of heaven, the. This phrase might seem to suggest the movements and changes in our lives, as directed by heaven, but it may simply be poetic usage for 'winds' rather than religious. From George Eliot, *Silas Marner* (1861): 'Life . . . when it is spread over a various surface, and breathed on variously by the multitudinous currents from the winds of heaven to the thoughts of men.' Eliot is also quoted as having said in 1840: 'O how luxuriously joyous to have the wind of heaven blow on one after being stived in a human atmosphere.' *The Wind of Heaven* was a drama by Emlyn Williams, first performed in 1945.

winds of war, the. Phrase of uncertain origin (though compare WIND(S) OF HEAVEN). Used as the title of a US TV series (1983) based on the novel (1971) by Herman Wouk. Compare Winston Churchill's speech to the House of Commons, 3 September 1939: 'Outside, the storms of war may blow and the lands may be lashed with the fury of its gales, but in our own hearts this Sunday morning there is peace.'

wind-storm, fart in a. See under AS BUSY AS . . .

wing. See COMIN' IN ON A ~ AND A PRAYER.

wings of a dove, the. 'O for the wings of a dove' is the title of a song by Mendelssohn and derives from Psalm 55:6: 'And I said, Oh that I had wings like a dove! for then would I fly away, and be at rest.' A novel by Henry James had the title *The Wings of the Dove* (1902). It was adapted for the stage by Christopher Taylor (1966).

wink-wink. See under MONTY PYTHON'S FLYING CIRCUS.

winning isn't everything, it's the only thing. A sporting catchphrase or slogan (but also common in American business and politics). Various versions of this oft-repeated statement exist. Vince Lombardi, the football coach and general manager of the Green Bay Packers team from 1959 onwards, claimed *not* to have said it in this form but, rather, 'Winning is not everything – but making the effort to win is' (interview 1962). The first version of Lombardi's remarks to appear in print was in the form, 'Winning is not the most important thing, it's everything.' One Bill Veeck is reported to have said something similar. Henry 'Red' Sanders, a football coach at Vanderbilt University, *does* seem to have said it, however, c 1948, and was so quoted in *Sports Illustrated* (26 December 1955). John Wayne, playing a football coach, delivered the line in the 1953 film *Trouble Along the Way*.

Compare 'Winning in politics isn't everything; it's the only thing' – a slogan for the infamous 'Committee to Re-Elect the President' (Nixon) in 1972.

winter of discontent, a/the. Shakespeare's *Richard III* (1592) begins, famously, with Gloucester's punning and original metaphor:

> Now is the winter of our discontent
> Made glorious summer by this son of York;
> And all the clouds that lour'd upon our House
> In the deep bosom of the ocean buried

– even if the editor of the Arden edition does describe the entire image as 'almost proverbial'. The phrase 'winter of discontent' suffered the unpleasant fate of becoming a politicians' and journalists' cliché following the winter of 1978/9 when British life was disrupted by all kinds of industrial protests against the Labour government's attempts to keep down pay rises.

The first actual use I have found is in the *Sun* (30 April 1979). As part of a series on the issues in the forthcoming election, in the week before polling, the paper splashed across two pages the words: 'WINTER OF DISCONTENT. Lest we forget . . . the *Sun* recalls the long, cold months of industrial chaos that brought Britain to its knees.' (Sir) Larry Lamb, editor at the time, suggested in a Channel 4 TV programme *Benn Diaries II* (29 October 1989) that he had introduced the phrase 'in a small way' during the winter itself (it was imitated by others), then 'in a big way' during the election. James Callaghan, the Prime Minister who was destroyed by the phrase, seems to have claimed that he used it first (recalled in a TV programme, December 1991).

There is little new under the *Sun*, of course. J.B. Priestley, writing of earlier much harder times in *English Journey* (1934) ended his fourth chapter with: 'The delegates have seen one England, Mayfair in the season. Let them see another England next time, West Bromwich out of season. Out of all seasons except the winter of discontent.'

win this one for the Gipper. A slogan made very much his own by Ronald Reagan throughout his political career. It refers to George Gipp, a character he had played in *Knute Rockne – All-American* (1940). Gipp was a real-life football star who died young. At half-time in a 1928 Army game, Rockne, the team coach, recalled something Gipp had said to him: 'Rock, someday when things look real tough for Notre Dame, ask the boys to go out there and win one for me.' Reagan used the slogan countless times. One of the last was at a campaign rally for his would-be successor George Bush in San Diego, California on 7 November 1988. His peroration included these words: 'So, now we come to the end of this last campaign . . . And I hope that someday your children and grandchildren will tell of the time that a certain President came to town at the end of a long journey and asked their parents and grandparents to join him in setting America on the course to the new millenium . . . So, if I could ask you just one last time. Tomorrow, when mountains greet the dawn, would you go out there and win one for the Gipper? Thank you, and God bless you all.'

Interestingly, Richard Nixon included an allusion to the Reagan/Gipp phrase in his speech accepting the Republican nomination in 1968. Former President

Eisenhower was critically ill in hospital and Nixon said, 'There is nothing that would lift him more than for us to win in November. And I say, let us win this one for Ike.'

—wise. See THAT'S THE WAY COOKIE CRUMBLES.

wish. See I DON'T ~ TO KNOW THAT . . .

wish you were here! Although I have no citations for it in actual use, the cliché of holiday correspondence has been used as the title of songs (reaching the charts in 1953 and 1984) and of an ITV travel series (from 1973 onwards).

In the full form, '**Having a wonderful time**, wish you were here,' Partridge/*Catch Phrases* suggests a beginning in Edwardian times. But why not earlier, at any time since the introduction of the postcard in Britain, which was in 1870? To be sure, cards on which you wrote your own message did not come on the scene until 1894 and the heyday of the picture postcard was in Edwardian times. In the early days, perhaps the message was already printed on the card by the manufacturer? Nowadays, probably, the wording is only used in jest or ironically.

Having Wonderful Time, a play about a holiday hotel in the Catskills, by Arthur Kober (1937) became, in an exchange of phrases, the musical *Wish You Were Here* in 1952. *Wish You Were Here* was also used in 1987 as the title of a British film about sexual awakenings in a seaside resort.

wit and wisdom. An inevitable, alliterative conjunction – with a long pedigree. As long ago as 1297 the two words were put together in this combination. In Edgar Allan Poe's tale 'The Fall of the House of Usher' (1845), there is a poem including the line, 'To sing,/In voices of surpassing beauty,/The wit and wisdom of their king.' The earliest use, in the literary sense, of a collection of examples of the two things may be Sir Richard Burton's *Wit and Wisdom from West Africa* (1865). In the modern publishing sense, the first example may be *The Wit and Wisdom of Lloyd George* (1917), edited by D. Rider.

witch. See WICKED ∼ OF THE WEST.

with a little help from my/his/their friends. A suggestion as to how the world operates in terms of help from the 'old boy network', relatives, and old friends. But also hinting at how a person may 'get by' or 'cope' through use of drugs, alcohol and financial assistance. The phrase 'with a little help from my friends' (alluding specifically to drugs) was the title of a song written by Lennon and McCartney and included on the Beatles' *Sgt. Pepper's Lonely Hearts Club Band* album (1967).

with a name like Smuckers it must be good. A slogan for Smucker's preserves, from *c* 1960. Lois Wyse of Wyse Advertising, New York, recalled (1981): 'Slogans come and go but [this one] has become a part of the language. I wrote it for a company with an unusual name in answer to a challenge from Marc Wyse who said he didn't feel our Smucker advertising differed from the competition. The real job, however, was not thinking up the slogan but selling it to Paul Smucker. The then sales manager said, "If you run that line, Paul, we'll be out of business in six months"! But it's still in use after twenty years.'

with bells on. See under KNOBS ON, WITH.

with brass knobs on. See under KNOBS ON, WITH.

with friends like these who needs enemies? A phrase which may be used in desperation after one has been betrayed by a supporter – the earliest example to hand is of something Richard Crossman said of certain Labour MPs in 1969 – or ironically to others in difficulty. The *Daily Telegraph* used it as the headline over a picture spread of Richard Nixon's henchmen on 9 August 1974, but it is of much older provenance. Charlotte Brontë said it, in a letter, concerning the patronizing reviewer of one of her books. Partridge/*Slang* compares it to the proverb: 'With a Hungarian for a friend, who needs an enemy.' George Canning, the nineteenth-century British politician, wrote a verse ending: 'Save, save, Oh, save me from the candid friend.'

within. See ENEMY ∼.

with knobs on. See KNOBS ON, WITH.

with malice towards none. Phrase taken from Abraham Lincoln's Second Inaugural (1865), after the Civil War: 'With malice toward none; with charity for all; with firmness in the right . . . let us strive on to finish the work we are in.' Hence, the title of a book (1938) about the British by an American, Margaret Halsey.

with one bound/spring he/Jack was free. Said now of anyone who escapes miraculously from a tricky situation or tight corner. The phrase underlines the preposterousness of the adventures in which such lines can be 'spoken'. Author Barbara Newman, writing from Washington DC to the *Observer* (29 October 1989) said of TV correspondent and former Beirut hostage Charles Glass: 'His motivation is to keep alive the fiction that he miraculously escaped from his Hizbollah captors, offering a Ramboesque picture of himself amounting to "and with one spring Jack was free".'

At one time, I presumed that this construction came either from cartoon strips, subtitles to silent films, or from *Boy's Own Paper*-type serials of the early twentieth century where the hero would frequently escape from seemingly impossible situations, most usually after he had been condemned to them in a 'cliff-hanger' situation. Other suggestions were that the phrase might have originated with Jack Sheppard, the notorious eighteenth-century robber, who was always escaping from Newgate prison, or with Springheeled Jack, a legendary Superman-type hero (by 1840) who was supposed to have springs in the heels of his boots. But no citations were to hand.

Then I began to wonder if the origin wasn't more recent – from a comedy send-up of boy's adventure stories rather than the real thing? Well, almost. As E.S. Turner notes in *Boys Will Be Boys* (1948): 'There is a delightful story, attributed to more than one publishing house, of the serial writer who disappears in the middle of a story. As he shows no sign of turning up, it is decided to carry on without him.

Unfortunately he has left his hero bound to a stake, with lions circling him, and an avalanche about to fall for good measure (or some such situation). Relays of writers try to think of a way out, and give it up. Then at the eleventh hour the missing author returns. He takes the briefest look at the previous instalment and then, without a moment's hesitation, writes: "With one bound Jack was free."'

without hesitation, deviation or repetition. In the BBC Radio panel game *Just a Minute* (1967–), devised by Ian Messiter, and of which versions have been played in 57 countries, guests have to speak for one minute 'without hesitation, deviation or repetition'. From the *Independent* (6 September 1988): 'There is no protective, guiding commentary in Radio 1's new four-parter, in which youth speaks without hesitation, deviation or interruption about the things that really matter.' In 1982, an MP stood up in the House of Commons and said of a guillotine motion, that he thought all speeches on the Bill should be 'like those in that radio game "without deviation, repetition and . . . what was the other?' Prompts of: 'Hesitation!' from other MPs.

with respect. A somewhat weasel-like softening of a question or piece of point-making, most commonly in British TV political interviews. Sir Robin Day, the interviewer, entitled a selection of his greatest hits . . . *But With Respect* (1993) but it is more often than not the politicians themselves who use the phrase. Most notable was Denis Healey when in power as a Labour minister in the 1970s. The phrase is used in a joke told by Lord Geddes of Epsom (President of the TUC, 1954–5) in *Pass the Port* (1976). From 'things to be wary of' in *The Pillow Book of Eleanor Bron* (1985): 'People who start their sentences with the words "with respect", in order to sound less abrasive and to conceal, even from themselves, their own arrogance. Far from being respectful or deferential it signals contempt for an unworthy opponent and intellectual inferior. Politicians use it frequently, and deliberately, for this very reason.'

with your thumb in your bum and your mind in neutral. Idle, vacant, neutral. I first heard it from a military sort of person in 1960.

Wizard of the Dribble. A soubriquet applied to footballers who excel at this activity (kicking the ball forward very softly, so that it stays close to the boot). Hunter Davies commented in the *Independent* (10 April 1990): 'Anyone who's a regular follower of football will have noticed that dribbling has almost gone out of the game. The word itself sounds positively archaic. Yet, at one time, every team had at least one Wizard of the Dribble who would mesmerise the opposition. Where are they now?' According to *The Times* (31 January 1985), footballer Sir Stanley Matthews bore the title 'The "Wizard of Dribble"' for years.

wogs begin at Barnet. An ironic view of the North/South divide in Britain (Barnet being on the outer edge of north-west London), and clearly based on the old insular, foreigner-distrusting view that **wogs begin at Calais** (known by 1958). I first heard the Barnet version in 1964 (it was a motion for debate at the Oxford Union in the form 'When going North, the wogs begin at Barnet'). Compare NORTH OF WATFORD.

wolf from the door, to keep the. See KEEP THE WOLF . . .

woman. See BEHIND EVERY MAN . . . ; NEVER UNDERESTIMATE THE POWER OF A ~; PUT A ~ ON TOP . . .

woman in red, the. The 'woman/lady in red' was a phrase used to describe the mysterious girlfriend of the criminal John Dillinger ('PUBLIC ENEMY NO.1'), who alerted the FBI to his whereabouts and was herself the subject of a film (US, 1979) called *The Lady in Red*. The day after Dillinger was shot by the FBI in 1934, this graffiti verse appeared on a wall nearby:

> Stranger, stop and wish me well,
> Just say a prayer for my soul in Hell.
> I was a good fellow, most people said,
> Betrayed by a woman all dressed in red.

The Woman in Red has also been the title of two unrelated films (US, 1935 and 1984).

women. See ALL ∼ LOOK THE SAME IN THE DARK; UNDER HORSES SWEAT . . . ; THIS AD INSULTS ∼.

women and children first! Catchphrase used jokingly in a situation where people might appear to be behaving as though caught in a shipwreck (in a crowded bus or train perhaps). It originated in the incident involving HMS *Birkenhead*, one of the first ships to have a hull of iron, in 1852. She was taking 476 British soldiers to the eighth 'Kaffir War' in the Eastern Cape of South Africa when she ran aground 50 miles off the Cape of Good Hope. It was clear that the ship would go under but only three of the eight lifeboats could be used and these were rapidly filled with the 20 women and children on board. According to tradition, soldiers remained calm and did not even break ranks when the funnel and mast crashed down on to the deck, with the loss of 445 lives. Thus was born the tradition of 'women and children' first. In naval circles, this is still known as the Birkenhead Drill.

Somerset Maugham said he always chose to sail on French ships: 'Because there's none of that nonsense about women and children first!'

wonder. See NINE DAYS' ∼.

wonderful. See HAVING A ∼ TIME under WISH YOU WERE HERE!; YOUR POLICEMEN ARE ∼.

Wonderland. See ALICE IN ∼.

wood. See YOU CAN'T GET THE ∼ under *GOON SHOW*.

Woodbine. See AH, ∼ . . .

Woodbine Willy. Nickname of the Rev. Geoffrey Studdert Kennedy MC (*d* 1929), British poet and chaplain in the First World War – renowned for his courage and humility. Troops gave him this nickname because of his habit of walking through the trenches or casualty stations with a haversack full of Woodbine cigarettes. He chatted with the soldiers and always had

some 'fags' to offer the men in his care. As an ordained minister he was enrolled as a Forces' chaplain in 1916 and served until 1919.

wooden. See UP THE ∼ HILL TO BEDFORDSHIRE.

wooden horse have a hickory dick?, does a. See under IS THE POPE A CATHOLIC?

wooden leg. See under 'TOO LATE! TOO LATE!' . . .

woodpile. See NIGGER IN THE ∼.

woodshed. See SOMETHING NASTY IN THE ∼.

woofter. See under YER PLONKER!

wool. See PULL THE ∼ OVER . . .

woolly pully, a. A weekend driver in the UK, from their habit of wearing woollen pullovers. Partridge/*Slang* has the term applied simply to the pullover itself, from *c* 1960.

Woolwich. See WE'RE WITH THE ∼.

woopies. See under YUPPIE.

word(s). See AND NOW A ∼ FROM OUR SPONSOR; FAMOUS LAST ∼; GREEKS HAD A ∼ FOR IT; LORD OF ∼; MY ∼ IS MY BOND; PICTURE IS WORTH A THOUSAND ∼S; REARRANGE THE FOLLOWING ∼ . . . ; WHICH COMES FIRST . . .

work. See DIRTY ∼ AT THE CROSSROADS; EQUAL PAY FOR EQUAL ∼; FAIR DAY'S WAGES . . . ; GO TO ∼ ON AN EGG; NEVER ∼ WITH CHILDREN OR ANIMALS; ONLY FOOLS AND HORSES ∼.

workers. See BLACK-COATED ∼; WHAT ABOUT THE ∼?

working classes. See ON BEHALF OF THE ∼.

working well. See THEY'RE ∼ . . .

works wonders. See DOUBLE DIAMOND ∼.

world. See ALL THE ∼ LOVES A LOVER; under BEAST 666; FIRST ∼ WAR; JOIN THE ARMY AND SEE THE ∼; MONEY MAKES THE ∼ GO ROUND; THREE MOST USELESS THINGS IN THE ∼; WHAT A ∼ IT IS FOR WOOSSIT . . .; WHEN THE ∼ WAS YOUNG; ∼ WAR TWO; YOU GIVE US TWENTY MINUTES . . .

world owes one a living, to believe the. Walt Disney's film *The Grasshopper and the Ants* (1934), in the 'Silly Symphonies' series, was based on the Aesop fable 'Of the ant and the grasshopper' (as it is called in Caxton's first English translation, 1484), which tells of a grasshopper asking an ant for corn to eat in winter. The ant asks, 'What have you done all the summer past?' and the grasshopper can only answer, 'I have sung.' The moral is that you should provide yourself in the summer with what you need in winter.

Disney turns the grasshopper into a fiddler and gives him a song to sing – 'Oh! the world owes me a living.' This became quite well known and presumably helped John Llewellyn Rhys choose *The World Owes Me a Living* for his 1939 novel about a redundant RFC hero who tries to make a living with a flying circus (filmed 1944).

It is a little odd rendered in this form, because on the whole it is not something people say about themselves. More usually, another would say, pejoratively, 'The trouble with you is you think the world owes you a living.'

I have discovered the phrase used only once before Disney. In W.G. Sumner's *Earth Hunger* (1896), he writes: 'The men who start out with the notion that the world owes them a living generally find that the world pays its debt in the penitentiary or the poorhouse.' Sumner was an American author but I'm not totally certain that the phrase originated in the US.

world's favourite airline, the. See under BOAC TAKES GOOD CARE OF YOU.

world's greatest entertainer, the. A modest tag used, not unexpectedly, by Al Jolson (1886–1950).

world, the flesh and the Devil, the. From the Litany in the Prayer Book: 'From fornication, and all other deadly sins; and from all the deceits of the world, the flesh, and the devil, *Good Lord, deliver us.*' Title of films (UK, 1914 and US, 1959) and compare *Flesh and the Devil* (US, 1927).

world turned upside down, the. (1) A popular name for English inns (2) The title of an American tune played when the English surrendered at Yorktown (1781) (3) A figure of speech, as in Robert Burton's *The Anatomy of Melancholy* (1621–51): 'Women wear the breeches . . . in a word, the world turned upside downward' (4) The title of a well-known tract dating from the English Civil War concerning 'ridiculous fashions' (1646).

The origin for all these is possibly biblical: 'Behold, the Lord maketh the earth empty, and maketh it waste, and turneth it upside down' (Isaiah 24:1); 'These that have turned the world upside down are come hither also' (Acts 17:6). Compare the French expression *la vie à l'envers* [life upside down/the wrong way round], used as the title of a film (1964).

World War II/Two. After the FIRST WORLD WAR, what could be more natural than to have the **Second World War**? But, of course, it was not immediately recognized as such by all. At first, in 1939, some tried to refer to it as 'the war in Europe', but *Time* magazine was quick off the mark: 'World War II began last week at 5:20 am (Polish time) Friday, September 1, when a German bombing plane dropped a projectile on Puck, fishing village and air base in the armpit of the Hel Peninsula . . .' Soon after this, Duff Cooper published a book of his collected newspaper articles entitled *The Second World War*.

When it quite clearly *was* a world war, in 1942, President Roosevelt tried to find an alternative appellation. After rejecting 'Teutonic Plague' and 'Tyrants' War', he settled for 'The War of Survival'. But this did not catch on. Finally, in 1945, the US *Federal Register* announced that, with the approval of President Truman, the LATE UNPLEASANTNESS was to be known as 'World War II'. (In other less global conflicts, the name of a war depends on which side you are on: the Vietnam War is known to the Vietnamese as 'the American War'.)

In the Soviet Union, the Second World

War was known as *Velikaya Otechestvennaya Voyna* – **the Great Fatherland/Patriotic War.**

worried. See I'M ~ ABOUT JIM.

worry. See DON'T ~, BE HAPPY; WHAT ME, ~?

worse. See FATE ~ THAN DEATH.

worse than the Blitz. See IT WAS ~ . . .

worse things happen at sea. This consolatory phrase was first recorded in 1829 (Pierce Egan, *Boxiana*) in the form 'Worse accidents occur at sea!'

worsted. See under WHAT A WORLD IT IS FOR ~.

Worthington. See MRS ~.

worth one's salt, to be. To be of worth, of strong character and worth employing on any task or in any job. Neil Ewart in *Everyday Phrases* (1983) states that 'before money was introduced, soldiers and workers in ancient Roman times had their wages paid in salt'. One wonders whether they really liked this procedure. After all, what did they put the salt on if they did not have the money to buy food?

The *OED2* makes matters clearer when it states that a *salarium* was what was paid to soldiers *for the purchase of* salt. From *salarium* we get our word, 'salary'. If a man was not worth his salt, therefore, he was not worth his salary.

Brewer takes a middle course and says that a *salarium* was a salt ration which was later replaced by money but retained the same name.

wotalotigot! A slogan for Smarties chocolates, used in the UK from c 1958 to 1964. The slogan was found by the advertising agency's taping children playing with and chattering about the product.

At the end of the TV ads came the curious tag, **buy some for Lulu!**

wotcher, Tish!/wotcher, Tosh! See under DON'T FORCE IT, PHOEBE.

wot no — ? The most common graffito of the past 50 years in Britain – apart from KILROY WAS HERE (with which it was sometimes combined) – is the so-called figure of CHAD, 'Mr Chad' or 'The Chad'. In Britain at least, there is no doubt Chad made his first appearance in the early stages of the Second World War, accompanied by protests about shortages of the time, such as, 'Wot no cake?', 'Wot no char?', 'Wot no beer?'

The format was then used by Watneys London Ltd, the brewers, to promote their beer sometime in the 1940s or 50s. The slogan 'Wot no Watneys?' was shown written on a brick wall – or so everybody says. Possibly, however, they may be confusing this with the famous poster which showed graffiti on a brick wall declaring 'What we want is Watneys' or 'We want Watneys'? Alas, Watneys themselves have no copy of any of these adverts in their archives.

In 1933, at the end of Prohibition, Buster Keaton played in an American film farce with the title *What, No Beer?* As always, there's nothing new . . .

would. See WELL HE ~, WOULDN'T HE?

would the next challenger sign in please! See under IS IT BIGGER THAN A BREADBOX?

would you believe . . . ? Used when making some exaggerated suggestion. 'One of the cringe-phrases of the age . . . You couldn't go an hour without hearing someone say it in Los Angeles' – Derek Taylor, *It Was Twenty Years Ago Today* (1987). He attributes its popularity to the *Get Smart* TV show (1965–70), created by Buck Henry and Mel Brooks, and starring Don Adams. *The Complete Directory to Prime Time Network TV Shows* (1981) adds: 'Used whenever [a secret agent] of K.A.O.S. or someone on [Maxwell Smart's] own side didn't seem to accept one of his fabrications and he was trying to come up with a more acceptable alternative. That catch-phrase became very popular with young people in the late 1960s.'

Another of Don Adams's catchphrases in the show was **sorry about that!**

would you be more careful if it was you that got pregnant? Headline of a (British) Health Education Council poster showing a pregnant male (1970) and written by Jeremy Sinclair. The *Sun* commented that it 'made previous campaigns look like Mary Poppins'.

would you be shocked if I put on something more comfortable? A nudgingly provocative line, also rendered as, 'Do you mind if I put on something more comfortable?' and 'Excuse me while I slip into something more comfortable'. But the first is what Jean Harlow as Helen actually says to Ben Lyon as Monte in the US film *Hell's Angels* (1930). It is, of course, by way of a proposition and she duly exchanges her fur wrap for a dressing gown.

would you buy a used car from this man? Although attributed by some to Mort Sahl and by others to Lenny Bruce, and though the cartoonist Herblock had to deny that he was responsible for it (*Guardian*, 24 December 1975), this is just a joke and one is no more going to find an origin for it than for most such. The line dates from 1952 at least (before any of the above-named humorists really got going). My authority for this is Hugh Brogan, writing in *New Society* (4 November 1982): 'Nixon is a double-barrelled, treble-shotted twister, as my old history master would have remarked; and the fact has been a matter of universal knowledge since at least 1952, when, if I remember aright the joke, "Would you buy a second-hand car from this man?" began to circulate.'

It was a very effective slur, and by 1968 – when Nixon was running (successfully) for president, a poster was in circulation bearing a shifty-looking picture of him and the line.

One might use the phrase now about anybody one has doubts about. The *Encyclopedia of Graffiti* (1974) even finds: 'Governor Romney – would you buy a *new* car from this man?' In August 1984, John de Lorean said of himself – after being acquitted of drug-dealing – 'I have aged 600 years and my life as a hard-working industrialist is in tatters. Would you buy a used car from me?'

would you care for a Woodbine? See under BY GUM, SHE'S A HOT 'UN.

wrap. See IT'S A ~.

wrestle. See NEVER ~ WITH A CHIMNEY SWEEP.

wrinklies. See under YUPPIE.

writing on the wall, the. A hint, sign or portent, often doom-laden. The idea – though not the precise phrase – comes from the Bible (Daniel 5) where King Belshazzar is informed of the forthcoming destruction of the Babylonian Empire through the appearance of a man's hand writing on a wall.

I have often, in my role as graffiti-collector, been introduced as someone who saw 'the writing on the wall' – apparently an irresistible little joke. In a BBC broadcast to resistance workers in Europe (31 July 1941), 'Colonel Britton' (Douglas Ritchie) talked of the V FOR VICTORY sign which was being chalked up in occupied countries: 'All over Europe the V sign is seen by the Germans and to the Germans and the Quislings it is indeed the writing on the wall . . .'

wrong. See EATING PEOPLE IS ~; IF ANYTHING CAN GO ~, IT WILL; KING CAN DO NO ~; THAT'S RIGHT, YOU'RE ~.

wrote. See THIS PLAY WHAT I HAVE ~ under *MORECAMBE AND WISE SHOW*.

wu-hey! For his character of 'Alf Ippititimus', the British comedy performer Jack Douglas (*b* 1927) created what for me is one of the most compelling verbal and *visual* catchphrases of all. The bodily twitch that accompanies this phrase defies description. It was based on the nervous spasm of Eric Winstone, the bandleader, but arose when Douglas was appearing in a double-act with Joe Baker at a holiday camp. Baker managed to get himself locked out of the theatre and Douglas found himself alone on stage. 'My mind went completely blank and in sheer desperation I began twitching and falling about.' I recall seeing him in pantomime with Des O'Connor at Oxford in the mid-60s. The audience just waited for him to come on again and do his twitch.

WYSIWYG. 'What you see is what you get' – an acronym from computing, meant to suggest that what the operator sees on the computer screen is exactly how the material will appear when printed out (i.e. with correct typefaces, artwork, etc.). In use by 1982. Now an expression used to suggest that a person is not deceiving by appearances. President Bush said the full version on the first day of the Gulf War (16 January 1991) when asked how he was feeling.

· X ·

X marks the spot. From the use of the letter X or a cross to show the location of something (buried treasure perhaps) on a map. Mostly in fiction? The *OED2*'s earliest citation is in a letter from Maria Edgeworth (16 May 1813): 'The three crosses X mark the three places where we were let in.'

· Y ·

yabba-dabba-doo! Cry of delight from the US TV cartoon series *The Flintstones* (1960–66) which was a parody of suburban life set in the Stone Age and came from the Hanna-Barbera studios. Partridge/*Catch Phrases* has it popular with Australian surfers and British servicemen overseas in the early 1960s. It was used substantially in the promotion of the feature film *The Flintstones* (US, 1994) which used real actors in the cartoon roles. More than one critic of this film when advising audiences whether to go and see it, wrote, 'Yabba-dabba-don't!'

But surely the phrase must have predated *The Flintstones* – in jazz perhaps? The American novelty song 'Aba Daba Honeymoon' (telling of the love affair between a monkey and a chimpanzee) was published in 1914. And then there is the British expression '(to have the) screaming abdabs', meaning '(to be in) a state of extreme agitation, enraged frustration' and current by the 1940s.

yakkety-yak, to. To chatter non-stop. 'To ya(c)k' is American slang for 'to chatter' and was current by 1950. Made famous by the song 'Yakkety-Yak', written by Lieber and Stoller and recorded by the Coasters in 1958.

Yankee Clipper, the. Nickname of Joe DiMaggio, the leading US baseball player of the 1940s, after the type of US merchant ship built in the 1840s/50s (from *clip* meaning 'trim, shipshape', then 'fast-moving'). Earlier there had been a boxer known as the Baltimore Clipper.

yaroooo! When Billy Bunter, the famous fat boy created by Frank Richards, came to be recreated for BBC TV (1952–62), he was played memorably by Gerald Campion. The actor gave a memorably metallic ring to the phrase **I say you fellows!** and to this one.

Among the other pupils at Greyfriars School, the Indian boy, Hurree Jamset Ram (known as Inky), had a format phrase, **the —fulness is terrific!**, as in 'the rottenfulness is terrific' or as in this example from one of the original stories by Richards (in *The Magnet* No. 401, October 1915): ' "Are we not in a state of warfulness?" [asked Inky]. Bob Cherry chuckled: "The warfulness is terrific, as terrific as your variety of the English language, Inky." '

yeah. See YEH.

year. See DONKEY'S ~S; THIS ~, NEXT ~ . . .

Year of Living Dangerously, The. Title of a film (Australia, 1982) based on a novel by Christopher Koch. Much alluded to. From the *New York Times* (29 March 1992): 'Ross Perot is the untested wild man [in the Presidential election] . . . admirers say in this political year of living dangerously, anything is possible.' From Martin Amis, *London Fields* (prologue, 1989): 'Well, this was always destined to be the year of behaving strangely.' From the *Observer* (headline, 4 December 1994): 'Year of living cautiously'.

years. See FIRST — ~ ARE THE HARDEST; FOUR MORE ~ .

year zero. Term used *c* 1975 by the Khmer Rouge during their takeover of Cambodia – meaning that the past had been obliterated, nothing had come before. *Cambodia: Year Zero* is the title of a relevant book (1978) by François Ponchaud. The phrase has also been applied to other 'starting from scratch' positions: an Italian/West German film (1947) set in postwar Berlin was entitled *Germania, Anno Zero* [*Germany, Year Zero*]; a film (US, 1962) set in Los Angeles after a nuclear attack was called *Panic in Year Zero*.

yeh, yeh, yeh. 'Yeh' as a common corruption of 'yes' has been current (and derived from the US) since the 1920s. But whether spelt 'yeh-yeh-yeh', as in the published lyrics, or 'yeah-yeah-yeah' (which captures the Liverpudlian pronunciation better), this phrase became a hallmark of the Beatles after its use in their song 'She Loves You'. The record they made of the song was in the UK charts for 31 weeks from August 1963 and was for 14 years Britain's all-time best-selling 45 r.p.m. record.

Though most commonly associated with the Beatles, the phrase was not new. Some of the spadework in Britain had been done by the non-Liverpudlian singer Helen Shapiro who had a hit in September 1961 with 'Walking Back to Happiness' which included the refrain 'Whoop Bah Oh Yeah Yeah'. The Beatles had toured with Shapiro topping the bill before their own careers took off.

Following the Beatles' use, there was a French expression in the early 1960s – '*yé yé*' – to describe fashionable clothing.

yellow. See YOU'LL WONDER WHERE THE ~ WENT . . .

yellow peril, the. Phrase, first recorded in 1900, describing the supposed threat to White people or to the world generally from Asiatic peoples and especially the Chinese. On 4 September 1909, Winston Churchill said in a speech: 'It [the worst threat to Britain] is not in the Yellow Peril, or the Black Peril, or any danger in the wide circuit of colonial and foreign affairs. It is here in our midst.'

ye olde tea shoppe. The form 'ye olde' (pronounced 'yee oldee') has become the conventional way of evoking and reproducing the speech and writing of English earlier than, say, 1600. It is, however, based on a misconception that the letter 'þ' appearing on old manuscripts is the equivalent of the modern 'y'. In fact 'þ' – known to Old English and Icelandic philologists as the letter 'thorn' – is pronounced with a 'th' sound. Thus, even in Anglo-Saxon times – however peculiar some pronunciations might have been – 'þe' would have been pronounced like modern

'the'. 'Ye' did, of course, exist as the second person pronoun. The modern mispronunciation was recorded by 1925.

yer plonker! Abusive epithet ('you idiot!') popularized by Del Boy (David Jason) referring to his younger brother, Rodney, in the BBC TV comedy series *Only Fools and Horses* and current by 1986. In London dialect, 'plonker' = 'penis' (compare the epithets 'prick' and 'schmuck'). From the same series came the other abusive epithets **dipstick** (probably because rhyming with 'prick'), **noofter** and **woofter** (the last two rhyming with 'poofter' = homosexual). The term **lovely jubbly** for money, also used in the series, is derived from a post-Second World War advertisement for a soft drink called Jubbly.

yesterday. See I WASN'T BORN ~.

yesterday's men. This slogan had to be scrapped during the 1970 British General Election campaign. The Labour Party had issued a poster showing crudely-coloured models of Conservative politicians (Edward Heath, Iain Macleod, Lord Hailsham and others) and the additional line 'They failed before'. It was considered to be in poor taste. In fact, Labour lost the election to the men it had ridiculed as 'yesterday's' and the phrase continued to cause trouble. In 1971 it was used as the title of a BBC TV programme about how the defeated Labour leaders were faring in Opposition. This soured relations between the BBC and the Labour Party for a long while afterwards.

The phrase was an established idiom applied to any 'has-been' – a song with the title 'Yesterday Man' was a hit for Chris Andrews in the British charts (1965).

yesteryear, thrilling days of. See under HI–YO, SILVER.

ying-tong-iddle-i-po! See under GOON SHOW.

yo, dude! See under SIMPSONS, THE.

yonks. See under DONKEY'S YEARS.

yoo-hoo! See IT'S FOR ~.

Yorkshire Ripper, the. Nickname (after JACK THE RIPPER) applied to a murderer by a Yorkshire newspaper during the course of a prolonged police pursuit. As was eventually revealed, Peter Sutcliffe (*b* 1946) had murdered some 13 women in the North of England during the period 1975–80.

you ain't seen nothin' yet! President Ronald Reagan appropriated this catchphrase as a kind of slogan in his successful 1984 bid for re-election. He used it repeatedly during the campaign and, on 7 November, in his victory speech. Partridge/ *Catch Phrases* has a combined entry for 'you ain't seen nothin' yet' and **you ain't heard nothin' yet**, in which 'seen' is described as the commoner of the two versions. Both are said to date from the 1920s. One could add that Bachman-Turner Overdrive, the Canadian pop group, had a hit with a song called 'You Ain't Seen Nothin' Yet' in 1974.

As for 'heard', it seems that when Al Jolson exclaimed 'You ain't heard nothin' yet!' in the first full-length talking picture *The Jazz Singer* (1927), he wasn't just ad-libbing as is usually supposed. He was promoting the title of one of his songs. He had recorded 'You Ain't Heard Nothing Yet', written by Gus Kahn and Buddy de Sylva, in 1919, and had also used the words as a catchphrase in his act before making the film.

you and me. See THAT'S YOU AND ME.

you and yours. Phrase embracing a person's relatives and dependents, in use since 1300. A long-running BBC Radio programme *You and Yours* has dealt with family and personal matters since 1970.

you are Mr Lobby Lud and I claim . . . A circulation-raising stunt for British newspapers in the 1920s took the form of a challenge readers were encouraged to put to a man they were told would be in a certain place (usually a seaside resort) on a particular day. His description and a photograph were given in the paper and 'You are so-and-so and I claim my £10' (or whatever the prize was) became the formula. The reader had, of course, to be carrying a copy of that day's paper. The first

in the field was the *Westminster Gazette* in August 1927 and the correct challenge was: 'You are Mr Lobby Lud – I claim the *Westminster Gazette* prize' (which was initially £50, though if it was unclaimed it increased weekly). The name 'Lobby Lud' came from the *Gazette*'s telegraphic address – 'Lobby' because of the Westminster connection and 'Lud' from Ludgate Circus off Fleet Street. The stunt did nothing for the paper which closed the following year, but the idea was taken up by the *Daily News* and the *News Chronicle* and ran on for several years.

you are what you eat. This neat encapsulation of a sensible attitude to diet (known in the US by 1941) was used as the title of an 'alternative' American film that was first shown in Britain in 1969. The idea behind the phrase has been around for many a year, however. Compare: Brillat-Savarin in *La Physiologie du goût*: 'Tell me what you eat and I will tell you what you are' and L.A. Feuerbach: 'Man is what he eats [*Der Mensch ist, was er ißt*]' – in a review of Moleschott's *Lehre der Nahrungsmittel für das Volk* (1850). The German film chronicle *Heimat* (1984) included the version, '*Wie der Mensch ißt, so ist er* [As a man eats, so he is].'

you bet your sweet bippy! See under LAUGH-IN.

you can always look down and pick nothing up. Meaning 'try to better yourself rather than take the easy option'. Partridge/*Slang* has this as 'You can always stoop and pick up nothing!' and considers it mostly of Cockney use and a 'remark made by a friend after a "row" or by a parent concerning a child's intended husband (or wife)'.

you cannot be serious! By 1980, John McEnroe, the American tennis player and Wimbledon champion, had become celebrated for his 'Superbrat' behaviour towards umpires and linesmen – telling them 'You are the pits', and such like. 'You cannot be serious!' was elevated to catchphrase status through various show biz take-offs, including Roger Kitter's record, 'Chalk Dust – The Umpire Strikes Back' (UK, 1982).

you can run but you can't hide. In the wake of the hijacking of a TWA airliner to Beirut in the summer of 1985, President Reagan issued a number of warnings to international terrorists. In October, he said that America had, 'sent a message to terrorists everywhere. The message: "You can run, but you can't hide."'

He was alluding to an utterance of the boxer Joe Louis who said of an opponent in a World Heavyweight Championship fight in June 1946, 'He can run, but he can't hide.' The opponent was Billy Conn – who was a fast mover – and Louis won the fight on a knock-out.

I expect the saying probably pre-dates Louis, but it is very much associated with him.

you can't get the wood, you know. See under GOON SHOW.

you can't make an omelette without breaking eggs. You cannot achieve something worthwhile without hurting or offending somebody. Possibly based on a French proverb (and a saying that has been ascribed to Robespierre), but known in English by 1859. To the Nazi Hermann Goering in 1933 is attributed: 'If people say that here and there someone has been taken away and maltreated, then I can only reply: "You can't make an omelette without breaking eggs."'

you can't make a soufflé rise twice. See SOUFFLÉ RISE TWICE.

you can't see the join. See under MORECAMBE AND WISE SHOW.

you can't take it with you. The title of a play (1936; film US, 1938) by George S. Kaufman and Moss Hart, comes from the saying which suggests that there is no point in holding on to money as it will be no good to you when you are dead. An early appearance is in Captain Marryat's *Masterman Ready* (1841). An American version is 'You can't take your dough when you go.' Compare NO POCKETS IN SHROUDS, THERE ARE.

'You can always take one with you' was a slogan suggested by Winston Churchill when invasion by the Germans threatened in 1940.

you('d) better believe it! An emphatic 'yes'. Known in the US by 1865.

you dirty old man! An abusive term, usually coupled with some sexual accusation, and known by 1932. In the BBC TV comedy series *Steptoe and Son* (1964–73), the younger Steptoe (Harry H. Corbett) would shout it regularly at his father (Wilfred Brambell). See also DOM.

you dirty rat! Although impersonators of James Cagney (1899–1986) always have him saying 'You dirty rat!', it may be that he never said it like that himself. I am told, however, that in *Blonde Crazy* (1931) he calls someone a 'dirty, double-crossing rat' which amounts to much the same thing.

In Joan Wyndham's wartime diaries (*Love Lessons*, 1985) her entry for 1 October 1940 begins: 'Double bill at the Forum with Rupert. *Elizabeth and Essex*, and a gangster film where somebody actually *did* say "Stool on me would ya, ya doity rat!"' Note her surprise that the line was uttered at all. Although it was a strange double bill, I think she must have been watching a revival of *Taxi* (1931) which is about cabbies fighting off a Mob-controlled fleet. Cagney's exact words in that film are: 'Come out and take it, you dirty yellow-bellied rat, or I'll give it to you through the door.'

you dirty rotten swine you! See under GOON SHOW.

you don't hardly get those no more. See under I'LL BE A DIRTY BIRD!

you don't have to be Jewish . . . ('. . . to love Levy's Real Jewish Rye'.) Slogan current in the US in 1967. The point was reinforced by the words being set next to pictures of patently non-Jewish people (Indians, Chinese, Eskimos). There had been a show of Jewish humour with the title *You Don't Have to be Jewish* running on Broadway in 1965, which is probably where it all started.

Informal additions to the Levy bread posters were many. They included: '. . . to be offended by this ad/ . . . to be called one/ . . . to go to Columbia University, but it helps/ . . . to wear Levis/ . . . to be circumcised . . .'

you don't rewrite a hit. Meaning 'you don't tamper with what is already established as successful'. This show biz adage was quoted by Michael Grade in November 1987 when taking charge of the (rather unshow biz) Channel 4 on British TV.

you don't want to do that. See under LOADSAMONEY!

you give us 20 minutes, we'll give you the world. More than one all-news radio station in the US has used this slogan. I first came across it at KYW in Philadelphia in 1972. Ten years later, a TV satellite news channel was declaring: 'Give us *18* minutes. We'll give you the world.'

you have been warned. See under FAMOUS LAST WORDS.

you have either been listening to . . . See under BEYOND OUR KEN.

you *know* it makes sense. This was the endline to all British road safety advertisements from 1968 to 1970, but the phrase had been used with emphasis on BBC TV's *TW3* in 1963, so I expect it must have been used somewhere else before this.

you know what comes between me and my Calvins? – nothing. Brooke Shields, all of 15 years of age, said this in a Calvin Klein jeans ad in the US in 1980 and the line is remembered for its mild suggestiveness.

you'll be lucky . . . I say, you'll be lucky! See under RIGHT MONKEY!

you'll look a little lovelier each day (with fabulous Pink Camay). One of the catchiest slogans from the early days of British TV advertising, this one for Camay soap was around in *c* 1960. A year or two later, the BBC's *TW3* had a parody of it, concerning a Labour politician: 'You'll look a little lovelier each day/With fabulous Douglas Jay.'

you'll wonder where the yellow went when you brush your teeth with Pepsodent. Slogan for Pepsodent toothpaste, current in the 1950s. An appeal to vanity rather than health, but curiously memorable. From a David Frost/ Christopher Booker parody of political advertisements (BBC TV *That Was the Week That Was*, 1962–3 series): 'You'll wonder where the George Brown went/ When Harold forms his Government.'

you lucky people! The British comedian Tommy Trinder (1909–89) rode on a wave of publicity in the early 1940s. He even took space on advertising hoardings to declare, 'If it's laughter you're after, Trinder's the name. You lucky people!' The phrase (which came up first in concert-party work) was also used as the title of a film (UK, 1954).

you might think that; I couldn't possibly comment. Said to journalists by the fictitious British politician and Prime Minister, Francis Urquhart, in the political thrillers *House of Cards* and *To Play the King* by Michael Dobbs, adapted for television in 1990 and 1993, respectively, by Andrew Davies. The stock phrase, used repeatedly in the adaptations, was taken from the sort of comment politicians in government tend to make to inquisitive lobby journalists at Westminster. As a result of the serialization, actual politicians and the prime minister 'poached' the phrase and used it self-consciously all the more.

you must have seen a lot of changes in your time? Conversation-starter supposedly much used by members of the British Royal Family. Noted by the early 1980s.

you nasty man. See WANNA BUY A DUCK?

young. See BRIGHT ~ THINGS; NIGHT IS ~; WHEN THE WORLD WAS ~; YOU'RE ONLY ~ ONCE.

younger. See YOU KNOW YOU'RE GETTING OLDER . . .

young fogey, a. A man below the age of 40 who dresses and behaves as if he were prematurely middle aged. The species was fashionable in Britain from 1984 onwards although observed and commented on as early as 1909 (by the philosopher C.S. Peirce). Obviously, a play upon the phrase 'old fogey' (a Scots word from the 1780s) applied to a person displaying all the attitudes of old age.

young, gifted and —. From 'Young, Gifted and Black' the title of a hit song recorded by the Jamaican duo Bob and Marcia in 1970. The words were by Weldon J. Irvine and the music by Nina Simone. From *The Observer* (16 April 1989): 'They're young, gifted, and the hippest fun things since . . . CFC-free aerosols.' In June 1989, ITV was showing a comedy yarn about five young lads working on a Youth Training Scheme and called *Young, Gifted and Broke.*

young man! See under LOADSAMONEY!

youngster. See YOU'RE GOING OUT A ~ . . .

you 'orrible little man! Regimental Sergeant-Major Ronald Brittain (c 1899– 1981) was reputed to have one of the loudest voices in the British Army. As his obituary in *The Times* put it: 'With his stentorian voice and massive parade ground presence [he] came to epitomise the British Army sergeant. Though he himself denied ever saying it, he was associated with the celebrated parade ground expression "You 'orrible little man" – in some quarters, indeed, was reputed to have coined it . . . His **"wake up there!"** to the somnolent after a command had in his opinion been inadequately executed was legendary – doubtless the ancestor of all the Wake Up Theres which have succeeded it.'
        COMPARE WAKE UP AT THE BACK THERE! under TAKE IT FROM HERE.

you owe me a quarter's wages. See under YOUR BEER IS SOUR.

you play ball with me and I'll play ball with you. Coercive talk from headmasters, policemen, sergeant majors and similar. Recorded by 1944.

you press the button – we do the rest. Slogan for Kodak cameras, current 1890. 'It was literally edited out of a long piece of copy by George Eastman himself – one of the greatest advertising ideas' (Julian Lewis

Watkins, *The 100 Greatest Advertisements,* 1959).

your actual —. See under ROUND THE HORNE.

your beer is sour. Although it has taken the rise of the mass media to encourage the spread of catchphrases on a vast scale, it is quite clear that they did exist in the days of music-hall and vaudeville. Going back even further, it appears that Shakespeare was familiar with something akin to the phenomenon. In the First Quarto version of *Hamlet,* III.ii. (1603 – but not in the 1623 First Folio), the Prince's advice to the players ('Speak the speech, I pray you . . .') is extended to include: 'Let not your Clown speak/More than is set down . . . / And then you have some again, that keeps one suit/Of jests, as a man is known by one suit of/Apparel, and gentlemen quote his jests down/In their tables, before they come to the play, as thus:/**Cannot you stay till I eat my porridge?** and, **you owe me/A quarter's wages**: . . . /And, Your beer is sour.'

your best friends won't tell you. See EVEN YOUR BEST FRIENDS . . .

your cock's on the block. Unpleasant British business phrase (noticed in 1988), meaning, 'You're on the line, this is the testing moment. If you fail in this one, you'll be out of a job.'

your country needs you. The caption to Alfred Leete's famous First World War recruiting poster showing Field Marshal Lord Kitchener pointing at *you* is a brilliant example of a slogan that is inseparable from a visual. It first appeared on the cover of *London Opinion* on 5 September 1914 and was taken up for poster use the following week. Earlier, a more formal advertisement bearing the words 'Your King and Country need you' with the royal coat of arms had been used. The idea was widely imitated abroad. In the USA, James Montgomery Flagg's poster of a pointing Uncle Sam bore the legend 'I want *you* for the US army'. There was also a version by Howard Chandler Christy featuring a woman with a mildly come-hither look saying, 'I want you for the Navy'.

'Your country needs you' became a catchphrase used in telling a man he had been selected for a dangerous or disgusting task.

you're a hard man, McGee! See under SOMEBODY BAWL FOR BEULAH?

you're famous when they can spell your name in Karachi. This observation comes from American show biz and is quoted by Steve Aronson in *Hype* (1983).

you're going out a youngster – but you've got to come back a star! Not a cliché when new minted in the film *42nd Street* (1933). Warner Baxter as a theatrical producer says the line to Ruby Keeler as the chorus girl who takes over at short notice from an indisposed star.

you're never alone with a Strand. A slogan from a classic British ad for a brand of cigarettes from W.D. & H.O. Wills which caught the public imagination and yet failed to sell the product. Devised in 1960 by John May of the S.H. Benson agency, the campaign was to launch a new, cheap, filter cigarette called Strand. May decided to appeal to the youth market by associating the product not with sex or social ease but with 'the loneliness and rejection of youth'. 'The young Sinatra was the prototype of the man I had in mind,' says May. 'Loneliness had made him a millionaire. I didn't see why it shouldn't sell us some cigarettes.'

And so, a Sinatra clone was found in the 28-year-old actor, Terence Brook, who was also said to bear a resemblance to James Dean. He was shown mooching about lonely locations in raincoat and hat. In no time at all he had his own fan-club and the music from the TV ad – 'The Lonely Man Theme' – became a hit in its own right.

But the ads did not work. Viewers apparently revised the slogan in their own minds to mean, 'If you buy Strand, then you'll be alone.' However much the young may have wanted to identify with the figure, they did not want to buy him or his aura. Or perhaps it simply wasn't a very good cigarette? Either way, it hasn't been forgotten.

you're only as good as your last show. A British TV industry adage dating, I would say, from the 1960s. Sometimes adapted to fit other professions where past reputation counts for little. From *Jean Shrimpton: An Autobiography* (1990): 'Any photographer is only as good as his last photograph, and the results of every session must appear fresh and innovative.'

you're only young once. Modern proverbial expression, often employed to excuse an aspect of behaviour or taking part in an activity that would be frowned upon in anyone older. Recorded by 1941 in the US.

you're the greatest! See under AND AWA-A-AAY WE GO!

you're the kind of people who give me a bad name! See under HERE'S A FUNNY THING . . .

your friendly neighbourhood —. 'Usually ironic or facetious' notes *ODCIE* of this construction, and says it is derived from the slogan 'Your friendly neighbourhood policeman' in a police public-relations campaign of the 1960s. Myself, I would have suspected an American origin (compare SUPPORT YOUR LOCAL —) but *ODCIE* may well be right.

your future is in your hands. Slogan for the British Conservative Party in the 1950 General Election. The Conservatives were returned to power under Winston Churchill the following year. Churchill himself had used the idea in an address to Canadian troops aboard RMS *Queen Elizabeth* in January 1946: 'Our future is in our hands. Our lives are what we choose to make of them.' (See also under BATTLE OF BRITAIN.) The slogan led to an inevitably lavatorial joke, as in Keith Waterhouse, *Billy Liar* (1959): ' "No writing mucky words on the walls!" he called. I did not reply. Stamp began quoting, "Gentlemen, you have the future of England in your hands." '

your money or your life! The highwayman's/robber's challenge. In one of Jack Benny's most celebrated gags (playing on his legendary meanness), when the robber said this, Benny paused for a long time, and then replied, 'I'm thinking it over'. This was on American radio in the 1930s/40s.

'Your money *and* your life!' was an anti-smoking slogan in the UK in 1981.

your mother wouldn't like it. Ironic warning, used as the title of a rock music programme on London's Capital Radio, presented by Nicky Horne, from 1973. The phrase seems to have been very much around at the time. The slogan 'Mother wouldn't like it' was used in MG motor advertisements (by April 1972) and W.H. Auden is reported by Stephen Spender to have said 'Naughty! Naughty! Mother wouldn't like it!' to Philip Larkin, also in 1972. However, in Margaret Mitchell, *Gone With the Wind* (1936): 'There, [Scarlett] thought, I've said "nigger" and Mother wouldn't like that at all.'

your own, your very own. Old-time music hall from the Leeds City Varieties, *The Good Old Days* was a long-running BBC TV favourite from 1953–83. As its chairman, Leonard Sachs (1909–90) spoke in a florid way, presumably reproducing traditional music hall phrases. Before banging his gavel to bring on the next act, he would describe 'your own, your very own' artistes with alluring alliteration. At the end, the audience (all in period costume) would join in a sing-song: 'To conclude, we assemble the entire company, ladies and gentlemen – the entire company, the orchestra, but this time, ladies and gentlemen, **chiefly yourselves!**'

your policemen are wonderful. What visiting American stars are traditionally supposed to say to London interviewers. From the *Guardian* (4 June 1983): 'When Kristina Wayborn [an actress in a James Bond film] said that she loved British fish and chips it seemed a simple kindness to ask what she thought of our policemen. "They are so wonderful. They make you feel so secure," she replied in the BEST POSSIBLE TASTE.'

yours. See ONE DAY ALL THIS WILL BE ∼, MY SON.

yours to enjoy in the privacy of your own home. A traditional advertising line, probably ex-US? *Private Eye*, in 1964, ran a spoof advertisement for a part-work, including the lure: 'Now experience the First World War in the privacy of your own home.'

your trumpeter's dead. Rebuke to an egoist or to a person who will BLOW [HIS] OWN TRUMPET. G.L. Apperson in his *English Proverbs and Proverbial Phrases* (1929) finds the expression in use by 1729. From Baker's *Northamptonshire Glossary* (1854): 'Sometime it is said [again to an egotist], "your trumpeter's dead", i.e. no one sounds your praises, so you are compelled to extol yourself.'

you shouldn't be in the circus. See IF YOU CAN'T RIDE TWO HORSES AT ONCE . . .

you should use stronger elastic! Ted Ray (see RAY'S A LAUGH) was the first host of a BBC radio comedy show called *Calling All Forces* (1950 onwards). In the first show he had as a guest Freddie Mills, then world light heavyweight boxing champion. Mills – departing from his script – told of one punch he received when he momentarily lowered his boxing gloves: 'My trainer nearly fainted when he saw me drop 'em. I didn't mean to drop 'em.' Ted Ray immediately responded, 'You should use stronger elastic!'

Bob Monkhouse, the show's co-scriptwriter, soon engineered the return of this phrase, which really did catch on. Ray kept it in his stage act for many years.

you silly little man! See under BAND WAGGON.

you, too, can have a body like mine. 'Charles Atlas' was born Angelo Siciliano in Italy in 1894 and died in America in 1972. He won the title of 'The World's Most Perfectly Developed Man' in a 1922 contest sponsored by Bernarr Macfadden and his *Physical Culture* magazine. Then he started giving mail-order body-building lessons. A famous promotional strip cartoon showed 'How Joe's body brought him FAME instead of SHAME.' 'Hey! Quit kicking sand in our face,' Joe says to a bully on the beach. Then he takes a Charles Atlas course and ends up with a girl by his side who says, 'Oh, Joe! You are a real man after all!'

Like Joe, Atlas had himself been 'a skinny, timid weakling of only seven stone' (hence the expression **I was a seven stone weakling**). 'I didn't know what real health and strength were. I was afraid to fight – ashamed to be seen in a bathing costume.' But after watching a lion rippling its muscles at the zoo, he developed a method of pitting one muscle against another which he called 'Dynamic Tension'.

you've beaten the panel! See under IS IT BIGGER THAN A BREADBOX?

you've come a long way, baby. ('to get where you got to today'). Slogan for Virginia Slims cigarettes, in the US, from 1968. A slogan that rode on the feminist mood of the times in selling to women smokers. Indeed, the basic phrase has also been used on Women's Lib posters. One shows a woman giving a karate chop to a man's head. An article by Julie Baumgold with the title 'You've Come a Long Way, Baby' appeared in *New York* magazine on 9 June 1969. A song with the title followed in 1971. After the failure of the US Equal Rights Amendment in 1982, a T-shirt appeared bearing the words, 'I Haven't Come A Long Way'.

you've made an old man very happy. As though said by an old man to a woman for sexual favours granted, now a humorous way of expressing thanks about anything. Neatly inverted in the film *The Last Remake of Beau Geste* (1977). Terry-Thomas, as a prison governor, says to Ann-Margret, as a woman who has slept with him to secure an escape: 'Delighted you came, my dear, and I'd like you to know that you made a happy man feel very old.' From BBC radio's ROUND THE HORNE (29 May 1966): 'Thank you. You are so kind. You've made an old fiendish master mind very happy'; (4 June 1967): 'Thank you. You've made an old volcano very happy.'

In the film *It Happened One Night* (1934), the father of the runaway heiress gets to say to his daughter, 'You can make an old man happy' (by marrying the right man).

you've never had it so good. This is the phrase that will forever be linked with the name of Harold Macmillan (later 1st Earl of Stockton) (1894–1986). It was first used by him in a speech at Bedford on 20 July 1957. He took pains to use the phrase not boastfully but as a warning: 'Let's be frank about it. Most of our people have never had it so good. Go around the country, go to the industrial towns, go to the farms, and you'll see a state of prosperity such as we have never had in my lifetime – nor indeed ever in the history of this country. What is beginning to worry some of us is "Is it too good to be true?" or perhaps I should say "Is it too good to last?" For amidst all this prosperity, there is one problem that has troubled us, in one way or another, ever since the war. It is the problem of rising prices. Our constant concern is: Can prices be steadied while at the same time we maintain full employment in an expanding economy? Can we control inflation?'

Macmillan is said to have appropriated the phrase from Lord Robens (a former Labour minister who had rejected socialism and who had used the phrase in conversation with the Prime Minister not long before). However, as **you never had it so good**, it had been a slogan used by the Democrats in the 1952 US presidential election.

you want the best seats, we have them. Slogan for the Keith Prowse ticket agency in the UK, from 1925 until the company collapsed in 1991.

yowsir, yowsir, yowsir. The 1969 film THEY SHOOT HORSES DON'T THEY? (from Horace McCoy's 1935 novel – the title using what I presume to be an old Western expression for exhaustion) portrayed a dance marathon contest of the Depression years. Appropriately, it highlighted the cry 'yowsir, yowsir' (meaning 'yes, sir, yes, sir') originated in the 1930s by the orchestra leader and entertainer, Ben Bernie.

yumpie. See under YUPPIE.

yum, yum, pig's bum! A commonly known way of expressing that food is delicious. The actor Robin Bailey remembered it (in 1985) as a 'Black

Country' saying, in the form 'Our mam, pig's bum'.

yuppie. Meaning 'Young Urban Professional People/Person', this was one of a stream of acronyms created in the late 1970s and 1980s designed to identify select groups. This one lasted longest in the UK because it answered a need for an (eventually pejorative) term describing young, brash money-makers of the period. The term originated in the US, as in Piesman and Hartley's *The Yuppie Handbook* (1983), and may have been coined by syndicated columnist Bob Greene that same year. It featured prominently in reports of Senator Gary Hart's bid for the Democratic nomination in the 1984 presidential race. He and his supporters appeared to belong to the Yuppie tendency. The launch of the word was slightly confused by the similar-sounding **yumpie** ('Young Upwardly Mobile People'). Other similar coinages of the period, but less used, included: **dinkies** ('Dual Income No Kids'), **sitcoms** ('Single Income, Two Children, Outrageous Mortgage'), **woopies** ('Well Off Older People'), and the non-acronyms **wrinklies** (middle-aged person, aged 40–50) and **crinklies** (older person, 50–70), sometimes **crumblies** (said to date from the late 1970s).

· Z ·

Zebedee. See 'TIME FOR BED', SAID ~.

Zeppelin. See LED ~.

Zero. See HERO FROM ~; YEAR ~.

Zingari. See I ~.

zizz, to have a. To have a nap or sleep. From the cartoonist's way of showing that someone is sleeping – putting a wave of Z-Z-Z-Z-Z-Zs snoring away from the mouth. In use by 1941.

Zurich. See GNOMES OF ~.